Contemporary Marketing

Custom Edition for University of Arkansas-Fayetteville

16th Edition

Louis E. Boone | David L. Kurtz

CENGAGE
Learning·

Australia • Brazil • Japan • Korea • Mexico • Singapore • Spain • United Kingdom • United States

CENGAGE Learning

Contemporary Marketing: Custom Edition for University of Arkansas-Fayetteville, 16e

Contemporary Marketing, Update 2015, 16th Edition
Louis E. Boone | David L. Kurtz

Senior Manager, Student Engagement:

Linda deStefano

Janey Moeller

Manager, Student Engagement:

Julie Dierig

Marketing Manager:

Rachael Kloos

Manager, Production Editorial:

Kim Fry

Manager, Intellectual Property Project Manager:

Brian Methe

Senior Manager, Production and Manufacturing:

Donna M. Brown

Manager, Production:

Terri Daley

For product information and technology assistance, contact us at
Cengage Learning Customer & Sales Support, 1-800-354-9706

For permission to use material from this text or product,
submit all requests online at **cengage.com/permissions**
Further permissions questions can be emailed to
permissionrequest@cengage.com

This book contains select works from existing Cengage Learning resources and was produced by Cengage Learning Custom Solutions for collegiate use. As such, those adopting and/or contributing to this work are responsible for editorial content accuracy, continuity and completeness.

Compilation © 2014 Cengage Learning

ISBN-13: 978-1-305-01963-8
ISBN-10: 1-305-01963-6

WCN: 01-100-101

Cengage Learning
5191 Natorp Boulevard
Mason, Ohio 45040
USA

Cengage Learning is a leading provider of customized learning solutions with office locations around the globe, including Singapore, the United Kingdom, Australia, Mexico, Brazil, and Japan. Locate your local office at:
international.cengage.com/region.

Cengage Learning products are represented in Canada by Nelson Education, Ltd.
For your lifelong learning solutions, visit **www.cengage.com/custom.**
Visit our corporate website at **www.cengage.com.**

Brief Contents

Part 7: Pricing Decisions

PREFACE

Continuing a Legacy of Excellence—Boone & Kurtz ... In a Class by Itself!

PRODUCTS often begin their lives as something extraordinary, and as they grow, they continue to evolve. The most successful products in the marketplace are those that know their strengths and have branded and marketed those strengths to form a passionate, emotional connection with loyal users and relationships with new users every step of the way. Just like the very best brands in the business world, Boone & Kurtz, *Contemporary Marketing*, continues to evolve, both as a product and as a brand. This 2015 Update of *Contemporary Marketing* continues to develop and grow with new cases and examples, as well as a new emphasis on social media. As with every good brand, though, the patterns of innovation and excellence established at the beginning remain steadfast. The goals and standards of Boone & Kurtz, *Contemporary Marketing*, remain intact and focused on excellence, as always. I present to you a text and supplement package that will not only show you why we've been the standard-bearer for so long but also prove to you why Boone & Kurtz remains . . . in a class by itself!

PUTTING INSTRUCTORS IN A CLASS BY THEMSELVES

This new edition's supplement package is designed to propel the instructor into the classroom with all the materials needed to engage students and help them understand text concepts. All the major teaching materials have been combined into one resource—the Instructor's Manual. While this might not sound revolutionary, good brands know that the heart of the product is in its core strengths. In the same way, our Instructor's Manual combines all of the most important teaching materials in one place. The lecture outline walks step-by-step through chapter content. And for your convenience, we've included references to the tables, figures, and PowerPoint slides throughout the lecture notes. "Scripps Networks Interactive & Food Network," our continuing case, is highlighted in part videos, while chapter videos showcase a stellar group of companies from a variety of industries, including Zappos, GaGa SherBetter, Ski Butternut, and BoltBus.

We've heard your appreciation for our PowerPoint presentations and have once again tailored these to meet the needs of all instructors, offering two versions: our expanded collection and the basic collection. In addition, our certified test bank, which has been verified, gives instructors that extra edge needed to drive home key concepts, ignite critical thinking, and boost confidence and assurance when creating and issuing tests.

Finally, we've added a new online learning and teaching component to Boone & Kurtz, *Contemporary Marketing*. CourseMate provides unmatched learning tools for students and provides instructors with a valuable assessment data-tracking tool to record student progress and achievement. More information on CourseMate, the Engagement Tracker, and CengageNOW is included later in this Preface, or you can contact your Cengage representative for more information or a demo.

The evolution of a brand or product can be a powerful and compelling undertaking involving every aspect of the marketing process. Understanding this evolution can be a student's best help in understanding how marketing is conducted every day. Each chapter begins with "Evolution of a Brand," which discusses the evolution of the company or product that is the focus of the chapter's opening vignette. We've focused our efforts on showing how stellar brands evolve and what this evolution means in the grander scheme of marketing and product management.

HELPING STUDENTS STAND IN A CLASS BY THEMSELVES

An intriguing series of continuing videos—"Scripps Networks Interactive & Food Network"—provides insights into how Scripps Interactive & Food Network use various marketing techniques to connect advertisers and sponsors with their targeted customers and provide content via several channels, including TV and social media. As always, every chapter is loaded with up-to-the-minute marketing issues and examples to liven up classroom discussion and debate. Processes, strategies, and procedures are brought to life through videos highlighting real companies and employees, an innovative business model, and collaborative learning exercises. And to further enhance the student learning process, a number of text-specific quizzes, games, and videos are available within the CourseMate and CengageNOW platforms.

HOW BOONE & KURTZ'S *CONTEMPORARY MARKETING* EVOLVED INTO THE LEADING BRAND IN THE MARKET

For more than three decades, *Contemporary Marketing* has provided the latest in content and pedagogy. Our current editions have long been the model for our competitors' next editions. Consider Boone & Kurtz's proven record of providing instructors and students with pedagogical firsts:

- *Contemporary Marketing* was the first introductory marketing text written specifically for the student—rather than the instructor—featuring a conversational style that students readily understand and enjoy.

- *Contemporary Marketing* has always been based on marketing research, written the way instructors actually teach the course.

- *Contemporary Marketing* has always utilized extensive pedagogy—such as opening vignettes and boxed features—to breathe life into the exciting concepts and issues facing today's marketers.

- *Contemporary Marketing* was the first business text to offer end-of-chapter video cases as well as end-of-part continuing video cases filmed by professional producers who include text concepts in each video.

- *Contemporary Marketing* was the first to use multimedia technology to integrate all ancillary components—videos, overhead transparencies, and PowerPoint CD-ROMs for both instructors and students—enabling instructors to customize lively lecture presentations.

- *Contemporary Marketing* received the William Holmes McGuffey Award for Excellence and Longevity, a testament to its many contributions to the field of marketing.

SOCIAL MEDIA

In addition to a continuing commitment to focus on brand evolution, this new edition of *Contemporary Marketing* takes a hard look at an important new topic in the marketing world—social media. Although a relatively recent phenomenon, social media is shaping the way marketers and consumers connect through various channels. We have added a separate chapter on the topic in this edition, because we believe that social media has become an important component of marketing for all types of businesses. The new chapter offers a fascinating insight into how marketers can obtain consumer data quickly and shift their marketing strategies according to how consumers interact with each other and with the goods and services they purchase. In addition, opening vignettes, boxed features, cases, and text references throughout the book are dedicated to the discussion of how social media has provided both opportunities and challenges that have significant impact on the world of marketing.

Social media issues are prevalent today in every industry. Here is a sample look at social media, written in the style of an opening vignette:

WHERE ARE ALL THOSE AD DOLLARS GOING?

The nation's 100 biggest advertisers boosted their total U.S. ad spending in a recent year by 4.8 percent. But you wouldn't know spending was on the rise if you only looked at previous years' measured media.

Measured media is monitored by companies like Nielsen, which reports on things such as how many households watched the Super Bowl and the demographics of the viewers.

In a recent year, measured spending for the top 100 advertisers actually slipped slightly. A double-digit, measured-media gain for Internet display spending and a small increase in TV advertising did not make up for losses in newspapers, magazines, and radio.

So where's the money going? Into "unmeasured" channels—a vast pool that includes various digital plays (search marketing, online video, and some forms of social media), promotion, and direct marketing. The appeal is clear: Marketers are putting money into channels that directly connect them with targeted consumers. Note that the term "unmeasured" is not entirely accurate since many of the initiatives companies undertake, such as search optimization and click-throughs, can be accurately measured.

Let's take a look at how marketers can measure consumer-to-consumer dialogs about their goods or services. Marketers need the following questions answered: (1) On average, how many times do consumers share comments or information? (2) Given the choice of how to share with their friends, which channels do consumers prefer? (3) Which of these sharing channels drive the highest results for brands? (4) How

can marketers optimize program performance across the various media that can be tracked? In essence, are all channels created equal?

There are a number of ways in which consumers share a social referral program with their friends, including email, personal URL (PURL), Facebook, Twitter, Google+, and the statistics vary based on the marketing channel. Looking at a representative subset of customers, Extole, which is a leading social marketing company, has benchmarked sharing results to uncover volume of sharing, amplification, and conversion rates by channel.

Enabling a cross-channel approach to sharing in a social referral program drives the highest possible volume of shares, amplification, and conversions. Even with the explosion of online and social sharing, email is an incredibly powerful sharing channel, which sees the greatest volume of social referral program sharing and the highest conversion rate. Sharing via social channels (for example, Twitter and Facebook) sees the highest amplification and number of clicks per share but sees lower conversion rates. To launch an effective social referral program, marketers need to build a cross-channel approach to harness the power of traditional, as well as social, sharing between customer advocates and their friends and social communities.

Advertisers are reshaping the media pie. Publicis Groupe's ZenithOptimedia expects the Internet to surpass newspapers as the nation's second-largest advertising medium behind TV. By ZenithOptimedia's tally, the Internet was the fifth-largest ad medium until 2009, when it powered past magazines and radio into the overall No. 3 spot.

Sources: Bradley Johnson, "Top 100 Advertisers Boost Ad Spending But Not in Traditional Media," *Advertising Age,* accessed December 14, 2012, http://adage.com; Angela Bandlow, "Driving Measurable Results from Social Referral Programs," *Electronic Retailer Magazine,* accessed December 14, 2012, www.electronicretailermag.com; company website, "About Extole," http://extole.com, accessed December 14, 2012.

PEDAGOGY

The reason Gene Boone & David L. Kurtz came together to write the first edition of *Contemporary Marketing* was revolutionary. They wanted to write a book about marketing that wasn't an encyclopedia: a text students would find interesting, filled with appealing examples and pedagogy. As with every edition of *Contemporary Marketing,* the 2015 Update is packed with new pedagogical features to keep students interested and bring the text topics to life:

- **Assessment, Assessment, Assessment:** In every marketing department in the country, assessment and assurance of learning among students have become increasingly important. As a result, we've provided you with assessment checks after every main head in every chapter. In addition, the end-of-part video cases have been specifically designed to allow instructors to embed a signature assignment that can not only be used to assess the marketing competency and understanding of concepts by students but also has an associated rubric for assessing student communication ability, understanding of ethics, or application of technology that can then be used for a school's assurance of learning compliance.

- **Assurance of Learning Review:** Assurance of learning is further enhanced by end-of-chapter self-quizzes: in addition to ensuring that students are learning throughout the chapter, we've taken assessment one step further by incorporating self-quizzes called "Assurance of Learning Review" at the end of each chapter. These questions are designed to quickly assess whether students understand the basic concepts covered in the chapter.

- **Evolution of a Brand:** Products, brands, and people that evolve are the ones that succeed. The evolution of *Contemporary Marketing* is what has put Boone & Kurtz in a class by itself. Every chapter begins with a new opening vignette and "Evolution of a Brand" feature. This feature discusses the evolution of the company or product that is the focus of the chapter's opening vignette and what this evolution means in the larger picture of marketing strategy and product management. Companies profiled in opening vignettes include Tory Burch, Chipotle, Pinterest, Amazon, Apple, and Under Armour.

- **Career Readiness:** Schools realize it has become increasingly important to understand proper business etiquette when entering the business world, so more and more schools are adding business etiquette to their curriculums. Every chapter of *Contemporary Marketing* contains a new "Career Readiness" box, addressing all aspects of proper workplace behavior, including how to communicate effectively through email and social media; how to be a team player; how to negotiate with customers; and even how to avoid major distractions at work.

- **Marketing Success:** Highlighting what companies have done right in their marketing strategies, these features appear in each chapter and explore the key stages that companies went through to achieve marketing success. Companies discussed include The Weather Channel, Klout, Foursquare, H&M, Weight Watchers, and Audi.

CONTINUING TO BUILD THE BOONE & KURTZ BRAND

Because the business world moves at an unprecedented pace today, the Principles of Marketing course must race to keep up. Trends, strategies, and practices are constantly changing, though a few things remain the same—the need for excellence and the necessity to evolve and innovate.

You've come to trust *Contemporary Marketing* to cover every aspect of marketing with a critical but fair eye. Let's face it: there are best practices and those we'd never want to repeat. However, both provide learning opportunities, and we've always chosen to take a critical look at the way business is being done in the world and help students understand what they need to know in order to have a long and illustrious career in marketing. Keeping this in mind, here are just a few of the important trends and practices we've focused on for this edition:

- Overall changes from the previous edition include a social marketing theme, new end-of-chapter and continuing case videos, and all new opening vignettes, boxed features, and cases. Statistics for in-text examples throughout the book have been updated when new material was available. The Notes have also been moved from the back of the book to the end of each chapter.

- Chapter 1 includes the latest American Marketing Association (AMA) definition of marketing and covers the most cutting-edge marketing technologies in use today, including an increased emphasis on social marketing and sustainability. A fifth era of marketing—the social era—is introduced to the discussion. New examples have been added to Table 1.1.

- Chapter 2 has an updated Internet Exercise to reflect the split of Sara Lee company into two separate companies (Hillshire Brands).

- Chapter 3 has a strong focus on green marketing practices, including coverage of Chipotle's sustainability efforts and IBM's strong, ongoing commitment to corporate social responsibility.

- Chapter 4 is a new chapter and provides instructors and students with an overview of various social media platforms and topics and discusses how to prepare a marketing plan using social media concepts. Figure 4.1 has been revised.

- Chapter 5 has been thoroughly updated with an expanded discussion of online communities and social networks. Figure 5.2 has been updated. A new in-text example and photo have been added about a NJ company damaged by Superstorm Sandy.

- Chapter 7 has a new website link added to Internet Exercise #2.

- Chapter 8 has a revised Figure 8.1 to reflect recent data on top U.S. trading partners. The text discussion has been updated to reflect Croatia's entry into European Union in July 2013. Figure 8.2 updated as well.

- Chapters 9 and 10 switched places in the order of the Table of Contents.

- Chapter 9 has an updated Figure 9.1 updated to reflect U.S. state populations and Figure 9.4 was revised to reflect more accurate positioning of selected retailers.

- Chapter 10's section on government data has been updated using information from the 2010 Census. This chapter also includes an updated discussion of Internet-based methods of surveying participants, and coverage of interpretative research has been enhanced. A new website link has been added to Internet Exercise #2.

- Chapter 11 has added a new website links to Internet Exercises #1 and #3.

- Chapter 14 has updated the impact of natural disasters on the global supply chain.

- Chapter 15 has updated sections on pricing strategy, location and distribution strategy, and direct response retailing. The Bed Bath & Beyond photo is new to the chapter and replaced a Best Buy photo.

- Chapter 16 is now a combination of 2 chapters from the previous edition. The chapter includes new examples in the informative advertising, persuasive advertising, and reminder advertising sections. The text discussion on leaders in advertising expenditures has also been updated. A new web link has been added to Internet Exercise #1.

- Chapter 17 has an updated Figure 17.4 to reflect current data for Account Managers median pay and a new web link added to Internet Exercise #1.

- Chapter 19 has updated text discussions for HD TV & Kindle Fire pricing and lowest-priced car in U.S. Figure 19.2 has been updated to reflect current prices for gasoline component pricing. The text discussion has been updated about Comcast and its data usage cap, which has been eliminated.

- "Your Career in Marketing," which appeared as Appendix A in the previous edition, has been moved online. The feature is chock full of practical advice for the student who is looking at career options in the field of marketing and now ties in to the "Career Transitions" feature that is in Cengage Learning's CourseMate.

SCRIPPS NETWORKS INTERACTIVE & FOOD NETWORK CONTINUING VIDEO CASE

You've come to expect only the best from us in choosing our continuing video case concepts, and we do not disappoint with our focus on a fresh, timely topic: how Scripps Networks Interactive & Food Network use a strategic blend of media outlets to connect and market to consumers.

Written case segments at the end of each part of the text contain critical-thinking questions designed to stimulate discussion and interaction in the classroom setting. Answers to the questions are in the Instructor's Manual, as well as a complete video synopsis, a list of text concepts covered in the videos, and even more critical-thinking exercises.

END-OF-CHAPTER VIDEO CASES

In addition to a stellar, continuing video case, we've produced video cases for each and every chapter, designed to exceed your every expectation. Students need to know the basics about life in the real world of marketing and how businesses succeed and grow—but they don't need a bunch of talking heads putting them to sleep. So although we admit that you will indeed see a few talking heads, they're just there because they really do know what they're talking about, and they have something important for students to hear. But trust us … the videos included in this edition of *Contemporary Marketing* contain so much more!

A complete set of written cases accompanies these chapter videos and are located at the end of each chapter. The written segments contain discussion questions. As with the cases, answers to the discussion questions are in the Instructor's Manual, as well as a complete video synopsis, a list of text concepts covered in the videos, and even more critical-thinking exercises. The video cases are as follows:

Chapter 1: Geoffrey B. Small Is Big on Quality, Customers, Community

Chapter 2: Nederlander Producing Company Spotlights Customer Rewards

Chapter 3: Zappos Employees Do More Than Sell Shoes

Chapter 4: Zappos Connects with Customers

Chapter 5: Hubway: Boston's Online Bike-Sharing System

Chapter 6: Ski Butternut Offers Thrills—Not Spills

Chapter 7: Zappos Offers Insights to Other Businesses

Chapter 8: Nederlander Productions Hoof It Around the World

Chapter 9: Nederlander Targets Theatergoers Everywhere

Chapter 10: GaGa SherBetter Forecasts Hot Sales, Cold Flavors

Chapter 11: Pepe's Pizzeria Serves Success One Customer at a Time

Chapter 12: BoltBus Gives Bus Travel a Jump Start

Chapter 13: At Zappos, Passion Is Paramount

Chapter 14: Geoffrey B. Small Keeps Marketing Channels Tight

Chapter 15: GaGa SherBetter: Coming to a Market Near You?

THE *CONTEMPORARY MARKETING* RESOURCE PACKAGE

Since the first edition of this book was published, Boone & Kurtz has exceeded the expectations of instructors, and it quickly became the benchmark for other texts. With its precedent-setting learning materials, *Contemporary Marketing* has continued to improve on its signature package features—equipping students and instructors with the most comprehensive collection of learning tools, teaching materials, and innovative resources available. As expected, the 16th edition continues to serve as the industry benchmark by delivering the most extensive, technologically advanced, user-friendly package on the market.

FOR THE INSTRUCTOR

INSTRUCTOR'S MANUAL WITH MEDIA GUIDE AND COLLABORATIVE LEARNING EXERCISES

The 16th edition of *Contemporary Marketing* has a completely updated Instructor's Manual. This valuable tool integrates the various supplements and the text. A detailed lecture outline provides guidance about how to teach the chapter concepts. Collaborative learning exercises are included for each chapter, giving students a completely different way to apply chapter concepts to their own lives. References to the PowerPoint slides are included in the lecture outline. You'll also find answers to all of the end-of-chapter materials and various critical-thinking exercises. Full descriptions of all technology offerings can be found in the Media Guide along with complete video synopses and outlines. The Instructor's Manual is available on the Instructor's Resource CD-ROM or can be downloaded from the product support website.

CHAPTER VIDEO CASES AND SCRIPPS NETWORKS INTERACTIVE & FOOD NETWORK CONTINUING CASE ON DVD (ISBN: 978-1-133-60841-7)

End-of-chapter video cases for every chapter of the text focus on successful real companies' processes, strategies, and procedures. Real employees explain real marketing situations with which they have been faced, bringing key concepts from the chapter to life. The end-of-part videos focus on Scripps Networks Interactive & Food Network's marketing strategies and innovative approach to connecting with consumers through a variety of channels. The written and video cases are divided into seven sections and are tailored to be used at the end of each part of the text.

CERTIFIED TEST BANK POWERED BY COGNERO

Containing more than 3,800 questions, this Test Bank has been thoroughly verified to ensure accuracy—with each question and answer read and reviewed. The Test Bank includes true/false, multiple-choice, essay, and matching questions. Each question in the Test Bank is labeled with text objective, level of difficulty, and A-heads. Each question is also tagged to Interdisciplinary Learning Outcomes, Marketing Disciplinary Learning Outcomes, and Bloom's Taxonomy. The Test Bank can be downloaded from the product support website.

EXAMVIEW® TESTING SOFTWARE

Cengage Learning Testing Powered by Cognero is a flexible, online system that allows you to:

- author, edit, and manage test bank content from multiple Cengage Learning solutions
- create multiple test versions in an instant
- deliver tests from your LMS, your classroom or wherever you want

START RIGHT AWAY!

Cengage Learning Testing Powered by Cognero works on any operating system or browser.

- No special installs or downloads needed
- Create tests from school, home, the coffee shop—anywhere with Internet access

WHAT WILL YOU FIND?

- Simplicity at every step. A desktop-inspired interface features drop-down menus and familiar, intuitive tools that take you through content creation and management with ease.
- Full-featured test generator. Create ideal assessments with your choice of 15 question types (including true/false, multiple choice, opinion scale/likert, and essay). Multi-language support, an equation editor and unlimited metadata help ensure your tests are complete and compliant.
- Cross-compatible capability. Import and export content into other systems.

BASIC AND EXPANDED POWERPOINT PRESENTATIONS

After reviewing competitive offerings, we are convinced that our PowerPoint presentations are the best you'll find. We offer two separate collections. The Basic PowerPoint collection contains about 22 slides per chapter. The Expanded PowerPoint collection includes about 45 slides per chapter and provides a more complete overview of the chapter. The Expanded collection includes figures and tables from the chapter and Web links. The Basic and Expanded PowerPoint Presentations are available on the Instructor's Resource CD-ROM or can be downloaded from the product support website.

INSTRUCTOR'S RESOURCE CD (ISBN: 978-1-285-06933-3)

The Instructor's Resource CD-ROM includes electronic versions of all of the instructor supplements: Instructor's Manual with Media Guide and Collaborative Learning Exercises, Test Bank, and Basic and Expanded PowerPoint Presentations.

COURSEMATE

Interested in a simple way to complement your text and course content with study and practice materials? Cengage Learning's Marketing CourseMate brings course concepts to life with interactive learning, study, and exam preparation tools that support the printed textbook. Watch student comprehension soar as your class works with the printed textbook and CourseMate site. Marketing CourseMate goes beyond the book to deliver what you need! Marketing CourseMate includes an interactive e-book as well as interactive teaching and learning tools, including quizzes, flashcards, homework videos cases, simulations, and more. Engagement Tracker monitors student engagement in the course.

CENGAGENOW

Designed by instructors for instructors, this easy-to-use online resource saves you time with resources that mirror the way you teach. Easily prepare lectures, create assignments and quizzes, grade, and track student progress with CengageNOW™. This premium engagement tool also includes videos, Personalized Study Plans, and assignable visual learning outcome summaries. CengageNOW can be used on its own platform or integrated into most learning management systems, such as Blackboard and D2L.

KNOWNOW (IN COURSEMATE)

Discover the most current solution for the most convenient online news and classroom application. KnowNOW! brings news that's making a difference into your marketing course with online pages and applications.

CAREER TRANSITIONS (IN COURSEMATE)

A robust new component of the *Contemporary Marketing* student resources, Career Transitions is an online resource that will let students assess their skills and suggest appropriate careers, explore employment and internship opportunities locally and nationally, use assessment tools to help prepare a résumé, and practice their interviewing skills with a challenging job interview simulation.

CONTEMPORARY MARKETING, 16TH EDITION WEBSITE

Our text website is filled with a whole set of useful tools. Instructors will find all the key instructor resources in electronic format: Test Bank, PowerPoint collections, and Instructor's Manual with Media Guide and Collaborative Learning Exercises.

To access additional course materials and companion resources, please visit www.cengagebrain.com. At the CengageBrain.com home page, search for the ISBN of your title (from the back cover of your book) using the search box at the top of the page. This will take you to the product page where free companion resources can be found.

RESOURCE INTEGRATION GUIDE (RIG)

The RIG is written to provide the instructor with a clear and concise guide to all of the ancillaries that accompany the text as well as how best to use these items in teaching a Principles of Marketing course. Not only are all of the book's ancillaries organized clearly for you, but we also provide planning suggestions, lecture ideas, and help in creating assignments. This guide will help instructors prepare for teaching the course, execute teaching plans, and evaluate student performance. The RIG can be found on the text website.

CUSTOM SOLUTIONS FOR *CONTEMPORARY MARKETING*, 16TH EDITION

Cengage Learning Custom Solutions develops personalized solutions to meet your business education needs. Match your learning materials to your syllabus, and create the perfect learning solution. Consider the following when looking at your customization options for *Contemporary Marketing*, 16th edition:

- Remove chapters you do not cover, or rearrange their order, creating a streamlined and efficient text students will appreciate.

- Add your own material to cover new topics or information, saving you time and providing students with a fully integrated course resource.

Cengage Learning Custom Solutions offers the fastest and easiest way to create unique, customized learning materials delivered the way you want. Our custom solutions also include accessing on-demand cases from leading business case providers like **Harvard Business School Publishing, Ivey, Darden,** and **NACRA,** and building a tailored text online with our online custom publishing system, which allows you to incorporate your original materials. For more information about custom publishing options, contact your local Cengage Learning representative.

FOR THE STUDENT

COURSEMATE

The more your students study, the better the results. They can make the most of their study time by accessing everything they need to succeed in one place. They can read the textbook, take notes, review flashcards, watch videos, and take practice quizzes—online with CourseMate. Marketing CourseMate includes an interactive e-book allowing students to take notes, highlight, bookmark, search the text, and use in-context glossary definitions. The interactive teaching and learning tools include quizzes, flashcards, homework video cases, simulations, and more.

CENGAGENOW

CengageNOW is an easy-to-use online resource that helps your students study in less time to get the grade they want. This integrated system helps the student efficiently manage and complete homework assignments from the text. Students can take pretests to determine the areas that require more practice, and they are directed to review tutorials, homework video cases and simulations, demonstration exercises, videos, e-book content, and fun marketing games to help them learn the material. They also get feedback on posttests that check their comprehension afterward.

ACKNOWLEDGMENTS

Over the years, *Contemporary Marketing* has benefited from the suggestions of hundreds of marketing instructors. I am most appreciative of their efforts and thoughts. These people provided valuable feedback for the current revision:

Bruce Coscia
World College

Mark. A. Neckes
Johnson & Wales University

Paul M. Wellen
Roosevelt University

Dana Harris
Alabama A&M University

Nancy J. Thannert
Robert Morris University

Anurag Pant
Indiana University South Bend

Irene Woods Clampet
Three Rivers Community College

Curt J. Dommeyer
California State University at Northridge

Earlier reviewers and contributors include the following: Keith Absher, Kerri L. Acheson, Zafar U. Ahmed, Alicia T. Aldridge, M. Wayne Alexander, Bruce Allen, Linda Anglin, Allen Appell, Paul Arsenault, Dub Ashton, Amardeep Assar, Tom F. Badgett, Joe K. Ballenger, Wayne Bascom, Richard D. Becherer, Tom Becker, Richard F. Beltramini, Michael Bernacchi, Daniel W. Biddlecom, Robert Bielski, Carol C. Bienstock, Roger D. Blackwell, David Blanchette, Jocelyn C. Bojack, Barbara Brown, Reginald E. Brown, Michele D. Bunn, Marvin Burnett, Scott Burton, James Camerius, Les Carlson, John Carmichael, Jacob Chacko, Robert Collins, Elizabeth Cooper-Martin, Deborah L. Cowles, Howard B. Cox, James Coyle, John E. Crawford, Elizabeth Creyer, Geoff Crosslin, Michael R. Czinkota, Kathy Daruty, Grant Davis, Gilberto de los Santos, William Demkey, Carol W. DeMoranville, Fran DePaul, Gordon Di Paolo, John G. Doering, Jeffrey T. Doutt, Michael Drafke, Sid Dudley, John W. Earnest, Joanne Eckstein, Philip E. Egdorf, Larry T. Eiler, Michael Elliot, Amy Enders, Bob Farris, Lori Feldman, Sandra M. Ferriter, Dale Fodness, Gary T. Ford, Michael Fowler, John Frankel, Edward Friese, Sam Fullerton, Ralph M. Gaedeke, G. P. Gallo, Nimish Gandhi, Debbie Gaspard, Sheryl A. Gatto, Robert Georgen, Don Gibson, David W. Glascoff, Jeffrey L. Goldberg, Robert Googins, James Gould, Donald Granbois, John Grant, Arlene Green, Paul E. Green, William Green, Blaine Greenfield, Matthew Gross, Robert F. Gwinner, Raymond M. Haas, John H. Hallaq,

Cary Hawthorn, E. Paul Hayes, Hoyt Hayes, Joel Haynes, Betty Jean Hebel, Debbora Heflin-Bullock, John (Jack) J. Heinsius, Charlane Held, Sanford B. Helman, Nathan Himelstein, Robert D. Hisrich, Mabre Holder, Ray S. House, Andrew W. Honeycutt, George Housewright, Dr. H. Houston, Donald Howard, John Howe, Michael D. Hutt, Gregory P. Iwaniuk, Don L. James, James Jeck, Tom Jensen, Candida Johnson, David Johnson, Eugene M. Johnson, James C. Johnson, Harold H. Kassarjian, Bernard Katz, Stephen K. Keiser, Michelle Keller, J. Steven Kelly, Marcella Kelly, James H. Kennedy, Charles Keuthan, Maryon King, Stephen C. King, Randall S. Kingsbury, Gail H. Kirby, Donald L. Knight, Linda S. Koffel, Philip Kotler, Kathleen Krentler, Terrence Kroeten, Russell Laczniak, Martha Laham, L. Keith Larimore, Edwin Laube, Ken Lawrence, Francis J. Leary, Jr., Mary Lou Lockerby, Laddie Logan, James Lollar, Paul Londrigan, David L. Loudon, Kent Lundin, Dorothy Maass, Patricia Macro, James C. Makens, Lou Mansfield, Frank Markley, Tom Marshall, Warren Martin, Dennis C. Mathern, James McCormick, Carl McDaniel, Lee McGinnis, Michael McGinnis, James McHugh, Faye McIntyre, Robert M. McMillen, H. Lee Meadow, Norma Mendoza, Mohan Menon, William E. (Gene) Merkle, John D. Milewicz, Robert D. Miller, Laura M. Milner, Banwari Mittal, Anthony Miyazaki, Harry J. Moak, J. Dale Molander, John F. Monoky, James R. Moore, Jerry W. Moorman, Linda Morable, Thomas M. Moran, Diane Moretz, Eugene Moynihan, Margaret Myers, Susan Logan Nelson, Colin F. Neuhaus, Robert T. Newcomb, Steven Nichols, Jacqueline Z. Nicholson, Thomas S. O'Connor, Robert O'Keefe, Nita Paden, Sukgoo Pak, George Palz, Eric Panitz, Dennis D. Pappas, Constantine Petrides, Barbara Piasta, Dennis D. Pitta, Barbara Pletcher, Carolyn E. Predmore, Arthur E. Prell, George Prough, Warren Purdy, Bill Quain, Salim Qureshi, Rosemary Ramsey, Thomas Read, Thomas C. Reading, Joel Reedy, Gary Edward Reiman, Dominic Rella, Ken Ridgedell, Glen Riecken, Arnold M. Rieger, C. Richard Roberts, Patrick J. Robinson, William C. Rodgers, Fernando Rodriguez, William H. Ronald, Jack J. Rose, Bert Rosenbloom, Barbara Rosenthal, Carol Rowery, Lillian Roy, Ronald S. Rubin, Don Ryktarsyk, Arthur Saltzman, Rafael Santos, Elise T. Sautter, Duane Schecter, Buffie Schmidt, Dennis W. Schneider, Jonathan E. Schroeder, Larry J. Schuetz, Bruce Seaton, Howard Seigelman, Jack Seitz, Steven L. Shapiro, Farouk Shaaban, F. Kelly Shuptrine, Ricardo Singson, Norman Smothers, John Sondey, Carol S. Soroos, James Spiers, Miriam B. Stamps, William Staples, David Starr, Bob Stassen, David Steenstra, Bruce Stern, Robert Stevens, Kermit Swanson, G. Knude Swenson, Cathy Owens Swift, Clint B. Tankersley, Ruth Taylor, Sue Taylor, Donald L. Temple, Vern Terpstra, Ann Marie Thompson, Howard A. Thompson, Lars Thording, John E. Timmerman, Frank Titlow, Rex Toh, Dennis H. Tootelian, Fred Trawick, Pam Uhlenkamp, Richard Lee Utecht, Rajiv Vaidyanathan, Toni Valdez, Peter Vanderhagen, Dinoo T. Vanier, Sal Veas, Charles Vitaska, Cortez Walker, Roger Waller, Gayle D. Wasson, Mary M. Weber, Donald Weinrauch, Fred Weinthal, Susan B. Wessels, Vicki L. West, Elizabeth White, John J. Whithey, Debbora Whitson, David Wiley, William Wilkinson, James Williams, Robert J. Williams, Nicholas C. Williamson, Cecilia Wittmayer, Mary Wolfindarger, Joyce Wood, Van R. Wood, Julian Yudelson, and Robert J. Zimmer.

IN CONCLUSION

I would like to thank my associates, Ingrid Benson and Cate Rzasa. Their ability to meet tight deadlines is truly appreciated.

Let me conclude by mentioning that the new edition would never have become a reality without the superior efforts of the Cengage Learning editorial, production, and marketing teams. My editors—Michael Roche, Julie Klooster, Scott Dillon, and John Rich—my long-serving designer Stacy Shirley, and my marketing team—Gretchen Swann, Jonathan Monahan, and Robin LeFevre—all helped to produce another *Contemporary Marketing* winner.

Dave Kurtz

PART 1

Designing Customer-Oriented Marketing Strategies

Chapter 1

MARKETING:
The Art and Science of Satisfying Customers

1. Define *marketing*, explain how it creates utility, and describe its role in the global marketplace.
2. Contrast marketing activities during the five eras in the history of marketing.
3. Explain the importance of avoiding marketing myopia.
4. Describe the characteristics of not-for-profit marketing.
5. Identify and briefly explain each of the five types of nontraditional marketing.
6. Explain the shift from transaction-based marketing to relationship and social marketing.
7. Identify the universal functions of marketing.
8. Demonstrate the relationship between ethical business practices, social responsibility, sustainability, and marketplace success.

TORY BURCH MAKES HER BRAND ACCESSIBLE

When Tory Burch launched a line of ready-to-wear clothing and accessories, little did she know that a decade later she would be CEO of a global retail empire with an estimated $800 million in sales.

Burch believes the key to the company's success is the emotional connection she and her team develop with customers through various marketing channels—including digital and mobile.

A lack of money in the company's early years helped Burch think outside the box and motivate her to get creative about engaging customers via ongoing relationships and personal appearances. Shortly after opening her first store in New York City, Burch launched an e-commerce site that today generates more revenue than any of the company's more than 65 bricks-and-mortar locations.

Burch is one of only a few designers who maintain an ongoing dialogue with customers. She reaches out to customers via Twitter (@toryburch), personally tweeting and answering questions, discussing fashion trends, and inviting their feedback on a variety of topics.

The Tory Blog, run by a veteran fashion editor, is considered an industry leader in developing and communicating content about the company's brand. The company's chief marketing officer (CMO) says Burch wanted to tell her brand story in an editorial way—highlighting things that inspire and entertain her, be it an artist, an author, or even another fashion designer. The blog's unique strategy—rarely mentioning the CEO—has made it very successful.

Burch and her staff believe that "social shopping," or "F-commerce," as it's called, is the future of e-commerce and an important way to disseminate a brand across various customer demographics. For example, "F-commerce" (short for Facebook commerce) is typically used by a younger group of consumers who have not yet been exposed to Burch's line of fashion goods. The company's CMO says that fans of a brand on Facebook expect an exclusive benefit just for them, so the company is testing out various exclusive discounts for its F-commerce audience to drive excitement and sales of the company's brand to a new market segment. In the social shopping era, the company believes brands will continue to shift their strategies from focusing on competitors to connecting with their customers while strengthening brand identity.

Burch's success has prompted her to start the Tory Burch Foundation, which provides microloans to women entrepreneurs through a partnership with ACCION USA, a leading microlender. So far, the foundation has distributed more than 50 loans—about $500,000—to small business owners. Says Burch, "It's not charity; it's empowerment. It's an investment in our collective futures."[1]

EVOLUTION OF A

By exploring a variety of marketing channels, Tory Burch continues to expand her brand, making it accessible to a broader and wider audience of customers. The firm's CMO says that much of the company's success can be linked to an aggressive digital marketing strategy that includes Twitter, Facebook, the Tory Blog, a new smartphone app, and a thriving e-commerce site.

- Tory Burch manages the company's Twitter account, personally tweeting to more than 180,000 followers on a regular basis. How does this marketing strategy enhance customer connections and drive sales?
- The company has more than 300,000 Facebook fans. What other strategies can the company use to market its brand across other social media platforms and gain exposure to untapped consumer markets? How can the company use its relationship with its loyal customers to increase its brand recognition?

CHAPTER OVERVIEW

"I'll only drink Pepsi."

"I buy all my clothes at The Gap."

"I like to hang out with my friends at T.G.I. Friday's."

"I go to Detroit Red Wings games at Joe Louis Arena."

These words are music to a marketer's ears. They may echo the click of an online purchase, the ping of a cash register, the cheers of fans at a stadium. Customer loyalty is the watchword of 21st-century marketing. Individual consumers and business purchasers have so many goods and services from which to choose—and so many different ways to purchase them—that marketers must continually seek out new and better ways to attract and keep customers. When the world learned that Facebook had assigned two dozen engineers to improve the site's search engine, users and investors were abuzz. A more powerful search engine would mean significantly enhanced capability for Facebook users—and a direct assault on Google, the market leader in search engines and one of Facebook's chief rivals.[2]

The technology revolution continues to change the rules of marketing in the 21st century and will continue to do so in years beyond. The combined power of telecommunications and computer technology creates inexpensive global networks that transfer voice messages, text, graphics, and data within seconds. These sophisticated technologies create new types of products and demand new approaches to marketing existing products. Newspapers are learning this lesson the hard way, as circulation continues to decline around the country, victim in large part to the rising popularity of blogs and auction and job-posting sites. On the other hand, e-book readers like the Amazon Kindle, Barnes & Noble's Nook, and Apple's iPad are changing the way people read books.[3]

Communications technology also contributes to the globalization of today's marketplace, where businesses manufacture, buy, and sell across national borders. You can bid at eBay on a potential bargain or eat a Big Mac or drink Coca-Cola almost anywhere in the world, and your MP3 player was probably manufactured in China or South Korea. Both Mercedes-Benz and Hyundai SUVs are assembled in Alabama, while some Volkswagens are imported from Mexico. Finished products and components routinely cross international borders, but successful global marketing also requires knowledge to tailor products to regional tastes. A chain restaurant in the South might offer grits as an alternative to hash browns on its breakfast menu.

Rapidly changing business landscapes create new challenges for companies, whether they are giant multinational firms or small boutiques, profit-oriented or not-for-profit. Organizations must react quickly to shifts in consumer tastes, competitive offerings, and other market dynamics. Fortunately, information technologies give organizations fast new ways to interact and develop long-term relationships with their customers and suppliers. Such links have become a core element of marketing today.

Every company must serve customer needs—create customer satisfaction—to succeed. We call customer satisfaction an art because it requires imagination and creativity, and a science because it requires technical knowledge, skill, and experience. Marketing strategies are the tools that marketers use to identify and analyze customers' needs, then show that their company's goods and services can meet those needs. Tomorrow's market leaders will be companies that can make the most of these strategies to create satisfied customers.

This edition of *Contemporary Marketing* focuses

> ## "BRIEFLY SPEAKING"
>
> "A lot of companies have chosen to downsize, and maybe that was the right thing for them. We chose a different path. Our belief was that if we kept putting great products in front of customers, they would continue to open their wallets."
>
> —**Steve Jobs**
> *Co-founder, Apple Inc.*

on the strategies that allow companies to succeed in today's interactive marketplace. This chapter sets the stage for the entire text, examining the importance of creating satisfaction through customer relationships. Initial sections describe the historical development of marketing and its contributions to society. Later sections introduce the universal functions of marketing and the relationship between ethical business practices and marketplace success. Throughout the chapter—and the entire book—we discuss customer loyalty and the lifetime value of a customer.

WHAT IS MARKETING?

The production and marketing of goods and services—whether it's a new crop of organically grown vegetables or digital cable service—are the essence of business in any society. Like most business disciplines, marketing had its origins in economics. Later, marketing borrowed concepts from areas such as psychology and sociology to explain how people made purchase decisions. Mathematics, anthropology, and other disciplines also contributed to the evolution of marketing. These will be discussed in later chapters.

Economists contributed the concept of utility—the want-satisfying power of a good or service. Table 1.1 describes the four basic kinds of utility: form, time, place, and ownership.

Form utility is created when the company converts raw materials and component inputs into finished goods and services. Because of its appearance, gold can serve as a beautiful piece of jewelry, but because it also conducts electricity well and does not corrode, it has many applications in the manufacture of electronic devices like cell phones and global positioning satellite units. By combining glass, plastic, metals, circuit boards, and other components, Canon makes a digital camera and Sharp produces an LED television. With fabric and leather, Coach manufactures its high-fashion line of handbags. With a ship and the ocean, a captain and staff, food and entertainment, Royal Caribbean creates a cruise. Although the marketing function focuses on influencing consumer and audience preferences, the organization's production function creates form utility.

Define *marketing*, explain how it creates utility, and describe its role in the global marketplace. **1**

utility Want-satisfying power of a good or service.

TABLE 1.1 Four Types of Utility

Type	Description	Examples	Organizational Function Responsible
Form	Conversion of raw materials and components into finished goods and services	Dinner at Chili's; Samsung Galaxy phone; Levi jeans	Production*
Time	Availability of goods and services when consumers want them	Dental appointment; digital photographs; LensCrafters eyeglass guarantee; FedEx Overnight	Marketing
Place	Availability of goods and services at convenient locations	Technicians available at an auto repair facility; on-site day care; banks in grocery stores	Marketing
Ownership (possession)	Ability to transfer title to goods or services from marketer to buyer	Retail sales (in exchange for currency, credit, or debit card payment)	Marketing

*Marketing provides inputs related to consumer preferences, but creating form utility is the responsibility of the production function.

PepsiCo's special interactive vending machines that allow you to send a friend a beverage take the time and place utility of marketing to new heights.

Redbox takes advantage of time and place utility, positioning its kiosks for renting movies and games in high-traffic spots like supermarkets and drug stores around the country. Marketing creates time, place, and ownership utilities. *Time and place utility* occur when consumers find goods and services available when and where they want to purchase them. Vending machines and convenience stores focus on providing place utility for people buying newspapers, snacks, and soft drinks. PepsiCo's recently launched Social Vending System takes touch screen and wireless technology even further: a user can "send" a friend a Pepsi beverage simply by entering the recipient's name and cell phone number at a special vending machine. The user can include a text message or create a short video to accompany the gift. The recipient redeems the gift at any vending machine within the PepsiCo Social Vending network.[4]

The transfer of title to goods or services at the time of purchase creates *ownership utility*. Signing up for a Sandals tropical vacation or buying a TV creates ownership utility. All organizations must create utility to survive. Designing and marketing want-satisfying goods, services, and ideas are the foundation for the creation of utility. But where does the process start? In the toy industry, manufacturers try to come up with items that children will want to play with—creating utility. But that's not as simple as it sounds. At the Toy Fair held each February in New York, retailers pore through the booths of manufacturers and suppliers, looking for the next Webkinz toys or Lego building blocks—trends that turn into classics and generate millions in revenues over the years. Marketers also look for ways to revive flagging brands. The classic yo-yo might be making a high-tech comeback, as a line of precision-engineered models have emerged in limited editions, made of titanium and sporting price tags as lofty as $500.[5]

But how does an organization create a customer? Most take a three-step approach: identifying needs in the marketplace, finding out which needs the organization can profitably serve, and developing goods and services to convert potential buyers into customers. Marketing specialists are responsible for most of the activities necessary to create the customers the organization wants. These activities include the following:

- identifying customer needs;

- designing products that meet those needs;

- communicating information about those goods and services to prospective buyers;

- making the items available at times and places that meet customers' needs;

- pricing merchandise and services to reflect costs, competition, and customers' ability to buy; and

- providing the necessary service and follow-up to ensure customer satisfaction after the purchase.[6]

A DEFINITION OF MARKETING

The word *marketing* encompasses such a broad scope of activities and ideas that settling on one definition is often difficult. Ask three people to define marketing, and three different definitions are likely to follow. We are exposed to so much advertising and personal selling that most people link marketing only to those activities. But marketing begins long before a product hits the shelf. It involves analyzing customer needs, obtaining the information necessary to design and produce goods or services that match buyer expectations, satisfying customer preferences, and creating and maintaining relationships with customers and suppliers. Marketing activities apply to profit-oriented businesses such as Microsoft and Overstock.com as well as not-for-profit organizations such as the Juvenile Diabetes Research Foundation and the Red Cross. Even government-related agencies such as the U.S. Postal Service engage in marketing activities. Today's definition takes all these factors into account. **Marketing** is an organizational function and set of processes for creating, communicating, and delivering value to customers and for managing customer relationships in ways that benefit the organization and its stakeholders.[7]

The expanded concept of marketing activities permeates all functions in businesses and not-for-profit organizations. It assumes that organizations conduct their marketing efforts ethically and that these efforts serve the best interests of both society and the organization. The concept also identifies the marketing variables—product, price, promotion, and distribution—that combine to provide customer satisfaction. In addition, it assumes that the organization begins by identifying and analyzing who its potential customers are and what they need. At all points, the concept emphasizes creating and maintaining long-term relationships with customers and suppliers.

marketing An organizational function and set of processes for creating, communicating, and delivering value to customers and for managing customer relationships in ways that benefit the organization and its stakeholders.

TODAY'S GLOBAL MARKETPLACE

Several factors have forced marketers—and entire nations—to extend their economic views to events outside their own national borders. First, international agreements are negotiated to expand trade among nations. Second, the growth of electronic business and related computer technologies allows previously isolated countries to enter the marketplace for buyers and sellers around the globe. Third, the interdependence of the world's economies is a reality because no nation produces all of the raw materials and finished goods its citizens need or consumes all of its output without exporting some to other countries. Evidence of this interdependence is illustrated by the introduction of the euro as a common currency to facilitate trade among the nations of the European Union and the creation of trade agreements such as the North American Free Trade Agreement (NAFTA) and the World Trade Organization (WTO).

Rising oil prices affect the price that U.S. consumers pay for just about everything—not just gasoline at the pump. Dow Chemical raised the prices of its products up to 20 percent to adjust to its rising cost for energy. The largest U.S. chemical company, Dow, supplies companies in industries from agriculture to health care, all of whom were affected by the price hike. Airlines, too, responded to a near-doubling of the cost of jet fuel. Many carriers now charge customers for redeeming their reward miles, and nearly all impose fees of $20 or more for checked baggage on domestic flights.[8]

Ted Foxx/Alamy

UPS serves its global market by enabling customers in many countries to access the UPS website in their first language.

To remain competitive, companies must continually search for the most efficient manufacturing sites and most lucrative markets for their products. U.S. marketers now find tremendous opportunities serving customers not only in traditional industrialized nations but also in Latin America and emerging economies in central Europe, the Middle East, Asia, and Africa, where rising standards of living create increased customer demand for the latest products. Expanding operations beyond the U.S. market gives domestic companies access to more than 7 billion international customers. China is now the second-largest market in the world—only the United States is larger. And industry observers estimate that Chinese customers purchased 20 million cars in a recent year, so automakers worldwide are extending their operations to China.[9] In addition, companies based in these emerging economies are beginning to compete in the global market. China's exports to the United States, its leading trade partner, increased nearly 30 percent in a recent year. By contrast, overall imports into the United States rose less than 5 percent during the same period.[10] Interestingly, however, signs are mounting that China's increasing prosperity may be reducing its attractiveness as a low-cost labor source. Rising costs already are driving some U.S. manufacturers out of the country, according to the American Chamber of Commerce. Mexico has taken the lead as the lowest-cost country for outsourced production, with India and Vietnam second and third; China stands in sixth place.[11]

Service firms also play a major role in today's global marketplace. Telecommunications firms like South Africa's MTN, Luxembourg's Millicom International, and Egypt's Orascom Telecom Holding have carved out new global markets for their products by following the lead of Finnish firm Nokia, among the first high-tech firms to create durable and affordable cell phones specifically designed for emerging markets. The opportunities for such telecom innovators will continue to grow as long as electricity-reliant personal computers remain out of reach for millions in the developing world. The United States is also an attractive market for foreign competitors because of its size and the high standard of living American consumers enjoy. Companies such as Nissan, Sony, and Sun Life Financial of Canada operate production, distribution, service, and retail facilities in the United States. Foreign ownership of U.S. companies has increased also. Ben & Jerry's is a well-known firm with a foreign parent.

Although many global marketing strategies are almost identical to those used in domestic markets, more and more companies are tailoring their marketing efforts to the needs and preferences of consumers in foreign markets. It is often difficult to standardize a brand name on a global basis. The Japanese, for example, like the names of flowers or girls for their automobiles—names like Bluebonnet, Violet, and Gloria. Americans, on the other hand, prefer rugged outdoorsy names like Chevy Tahoe, Jeep Cherokee, and Dodge Challenger.

ASSESSMENT CHECK

1.1   Define *marketing,* and explain how it creates utility.

1.2   What three factors have forced marketers to embrace a global marketplace?

FIVE ERAS IN THE HISTORY OF MARKETING

2   Contrast marketing activities during the five eras in the history of marketing.

exchange process
Activity in which two or more parties give something of value to each other to satisfy perceived needs.

The essence of marketing includes managing customer relationships and the exchange process, in which two or more parties give something of value to each other to satisfy perceived needs. Often, people exchange money for tangible goods such as groceries, clothes, a car, or a house. In other situations, they exchange money for intangible services such as a haircut or a college education. Many exchanges involve a combination of goods and services, such as dinner in a restaurant—where dinner represents the good and the wait staff represents the service. People also make exchanges when they donate money or time to a charitable cause such as Habitat for Humanity. Managing customer relationships like these are the essence of successful marketing.

Although marketing has always been a part of business, its importance has varied greatly. Figure 1.1 identifies five eras in the history of marketing: (1) the production era, (2) the sales era, (3) the marketing era, (4) the relationship era, and (5) the social era.

ERA	Production	Sales	Marketing	Relationship	Social
PREVAILING ATTITUDE	"A good product will sell itself."	"Creative advertising and selling will overcome consumers' resistance and persuade them to buy."	"The consumer rules! Find a need and fill it."	"Long-term relationships with customers and other partners lead to success."	"Connecting to consumers via Internet and social media sites is an effective tool."
APPROXIMATE TIME PERIOD	Prior to 1920s	Prior to 1950s	Since 1950s	Since 1990s	Since 2000s

FIGURE 1.1
Five Eras of Marketing History

© Cengage Learning

THE PRODUCTION ERA

Before 1925, most firms—even those operating in highly developed economies in western Europe and North America—focused narrowly on production. Manufacturers stressed production of quality products and then looked for people to purchase them. The prevailing attitude of this era held that a high-quality product would sell itself. This **production orientation** dominated business philosophy for decades; business success often was defined solely in terms of production successes.

The production era reached its peak during the early part of the 20th century. Henry Ford's mass-production line exemplifies this orientation. Ford's slogan, "They [customers] can have any color they want, as long as it's black," reflected the prevalent attitude toward marketing. Production shortages and intense consumer demand ruled the day. It is easy to understand how production activities took precedence.

However, building a new product is no guarantee of success, and marketing history is cluttered with the bones of miserable product failures despite major innovations—more than 80 percent of new products fail. Inventing an outstanding new product is not enough because it must also fill a perceived marketplace need. Otherwise, even the best-engineered, highest-quality product will fail. Even Henry Ford's horseless carriage took a while to catch on. People were afraid of motor vehicles: they spat out exhaust, stirred up dust on dirt roads, got stuck in mud, and tied up horse traffic. Besides, at the speed of seven miles per hour, they caused all kinds of accidents and disruption. It took savvy marketing by some early salespeople—and eventually a widespread perceived need—to change people's minds about the product. Today, most of us could not imagine life without a car and have refined that need to preferences for certain types of vehicles, including SUVs, convertibles, trucks, and hybrids.

THE SALES ERA

As production techniques in the United States and Europe became more sophisticated, output grew from the 1920s into the early 1950s. As a result, manufacturers began to increase their emphasis on effective sales forces to find customers for their output. In this era, firms attempted to match their output to the potential number of customers who would want it. Companies with a **sales orientation** assume that customers will resist purchasing nonessential goods and services and that the task of personal selling and advertising is to persuade them to buy.

Although marketing departments began to emerge from the shadows of production and engineering during the sales era, they tended to remain in subordinate positions. Many chief marketing executives held the title of sales manager. But selling is only one component of marketing. As marketing scholar Theodore Levitt once pointed out, "Marketing is as different from selling as chemistry is from alchemy, astronomy from astrology, chess from checkers."

THE MARKETING ERA

Personal incomes and consumer demand for products dropped rapidly during the Great Depression of the 1930s, thrusting marketing into a more important role. Organizational survival dictated that

production orientation Business philosophy stressing efficiency in producing a quality product, with the attitude toward marketing that "a good product will sell itself."

"Customers don't always know what they want. The decline in coffee drinking was due to the fact that most of the coffee people bought was stale and they weren't enjoying it. Once they tasted ours and experienced what we call 'the third place,' a gathering place between home and work where they were treated with respect, they found we were filling a need they didn't know they had."

—Howard Schultz
Chairman and CEO, Starbucks

sales orientation Belief that consumers will resist purchasing nonessential goods and services, with the attitude toward marketing that only creative advertising and personal selling can overcome consumers' resistance and persuade them to buy.

seller's market A market in which there are more buyers for fewer goods and services.

buyer's market A market in which there are more goods and services than people willing to buy them.

consumer orientation Business philosophy incorporating the marketing concept that emphasizes first determining unmet consumer needs and then designing a system for satisfying them.

marketing concept Companywide consumer orientation with the objective of achieving long-run success.

relationship marketing Development and maintenance of long-term, cost-effective relationships with individual customers, suppliers, employees, and other partners for mutual benefit.

managers pay close attention to the markets for their goods and services. This trend ended with the outbreak of World War II, when rationing and shortages of consumer goods became commonplace. The war years, however, created only a pause in an emerging trend in business: a shift in the focus from products and sales to satisfying customer needs.

Emergence of the Marketing Concept

The marketing concept, a crucial change in management philosophy, can be linked to the shift from a seller's market—one in which there were more buyers for fewer goods and services—to a buyer's market—one in which there were more goods and services than people willing to buy them. When World War II ended, factories stopped manufacturing tanks and ships and started turning out consumer products again, an activity that had, for all practical purposes, stopped in early 1942.

The advent of a strong buyer's market created the need for consumer orientation by businesses. Companies had to market goods and services, not just produce and sell them. This realization has been identified as the emergence of the marketing concept. Marketing would no longer be regarded as a supplemental activity performed after completing the production process. Instead, the marketer played a leading role in product planning. *Marketing* and *selling* would no longer be synonymous terms.

Today's fully developed marketing concept is a *companywide consumer orientation* with the objective of achieving long-run success. All facets—and all levels, from top to bottom—of the organization must contribute first to assessing and then to satisfying customer wants and needs. From marketing manager to accountant to product designer, every employee plays a role in reaching potential customers. Even during tough economic times, when companies tend to emphasize cutting costs and boosting revenues, the marketing concept focuses on the objective of achieving long-run success instead of short-term profits. Because the firm's survival and growth are built into the marketing concept, companywide consumer orientation should lead to greater long-run profits.

Apple exemplifies the marketing concept in every aspect of its business. Its products are consistently stylish and cutting edge but without overwhelming users with every possible feature. "A defining quality of Apple has been design restraint," says one industry consultant. That hallmark restraint is a characteristic of Apple's late founder, Steve Jobs, and is reflected in the work of Apple's designers, managers, and engineers, whose contributions to the company's new products Jobs credited for the company's ability to constantly surprise the marketplace. The release of Apple's iPad 3, which represented an enhancement of a product designed to anticipate needs many consumers didn't even realize they had, motivated many people to wait in line for hours to purchase the new model. Within three days of its release, the company sold 3 million, which was considered the strongest launch yet of any iPad model.[12]

A strong market orientation—the extent to which a company adopts the marketing concept—generally improves market success and overall performance. It also has a positive effect on new-product development and the introduction of innovative products. Companies that implement market-driven strategies are better able to understand their customers' experiences, buying habits, and needs. They can, therefore, design products with advantages and levels of quality compatible with customer requirements.

THE RELATIONSHIP ERA

The fourth era in the history of marketing emerged during the 1990s and continues to grow in importance. Organizations now build on the marketing era's customer orientation by focusing on establishing and maintaining relationships with both customers and suppliers. Relationship marketing involves developing long-term, value-added relationships over time with customers and suppliers. Strategic alliances and partnerships among manufacturers, retailers,

Apple exemplifies the marketing concept, creating consistently stylish and cutting-edge products. When Apple releases a new product, people line up to purchase the new model.

and suppliers often benefit everyone. The Boeing 787 Dreamliner is the result of an international team of companies working on the technology, design, and construction of the planes. Boeing and more than 40 global suppliers, connected virtually at 135 sites around the world, worked together to complete the planes. Despite three years of production delays, the fuel-efficient aircraft was still in demand: at its launch, Boeing had orders for about 800 Dreamliners, and the 787 is now in service throughout the world.[13] The concept of relationship marketing, which is the current state of customer-driven marketing, is discussed in detail later in this chapter and in Chapter 11.

THE SOCIAL ERA

As the second decade of the new century gets underway, the social era of marketing is in full swing, thanks to consumers' accessibility to the Internet and the creation of social media sites such as Facebook and Twitter. Building on the relationship era, companies now routinely use the Web and social networking sites to connect to consumers as a way to market goods and services. On a personal level, see the "Career Readiness" feature for suggestions on creating and connecting to your own personal network, a key to success in marketing and in business generally.

CONVERTING NEEDS TO WANTS

Every consumer must acquire goods and services on a continuing basis to fill certain needs. Everyone must satisfy the fundamental needs for food, clothing, shelter, and transportation by purchasing items or, in some instances, temporarily using rented property and hired or leased transportation. By

CAREER READINESS

How to Be a Social Media Marketing Manager

Are you empathic, enthusiastic about connecting with others, well organized, and tech-savvy? If so, you might have the makings of a social media marketing manager, a dynamic new career that's springing up in companies that want to take creative control of their online communication with customers, suppliers, and potential new markets. Here are some ideas for handling the job successfully:

1. Make the most of any customer-service experience you've acquired; it will serve you well in figuring out how to reach people effectively with tools like Twitter, Facebook, LinkedIn, Pinterest, and YouTube.

2. Take a course to learn about video production. Online video offers marketers countless opportunities and can be quick and inexpensive to produce. Experience here could be invaluable.

3. Make sure you spend enough time listening to your customers. Listening is the most important communication skill, whether in person or online.

4. Connect with others in your industry. Share what you've learned and learn from the best practices of others in this young and growing field.

5. Keep your company's online presence unique, such as with a distinctive point of view and consistently creative and original content like contests, blogs, photos, audio, and of course video too.

Sources: Mikal E. Belicove, "The Daily Dose: Six Must-Have Attributes of Social Media Managers," *Entrepreneur*, http://www.entrepreneur.com/blog/224263, accessed August 24, 2012; Kent Lewis, "Why You Should Fire Your Social Media Manager," iMediaConnection.com, accessed October 26, 2012, http://blogs.imedia-connection.com; "Tips for Social Media Manager Training," Black Box Social Media. com, accessed October 26, 2012, http://blackboxsocialmedia.com.

focusing on the benefits resulting from these products, effective marketing converts needs to wants. A need for a pair of pants may be converted to a desire for jeans—and, further, a desire for jeans from Abercrombie & Fitch or Lucky Brand Jeans. The need for food may be converted to a desire for dinner at Pizzeria Uno or groceries from Publix. But if the need for transportation isn't converted to a desire for a Ford Focus or Mini Cooper, extra vehicles may sit unsold on a dealer's lot.

Consumers need to communicate. But converting that need to the desire for certain types of communication requires skill. It also requires listening to what consumers want. Consumers' demand for more cell phone and wireless services seems nearly unlimited, particularly with the surge in social networking sites—providing tremendous opportunities for companies. New products appear continually to feed that demand, such as increasingly popular broadband wireless services and the veritable flood of applications now available for smartphones, enabling consumers to use their phones in new ways—for example, to research health information, check for symptoms, and even count calories.[14]

ASSESSMENT CHECK

2.1 What is the major distinction between the production era and the sales era?

2.2 What is the marketing concept?

2.3 Describe the relationship era of marketing.

AVOIDING MARKETING MYOPIA

3 Explain the importance of avoiding marketing myopia.

marketing myopia
Management's failure to recognize the scope of its business.

The emergence of the marketing concept has not been devoid of setbacks. One troublesome problem led marketing scholar Theodore Levitt to coin the term marketing myopia. According to Levitt, marketing myopia is management's failure to recognize the scope of its business. Product-oriented rather than customer-oriented management endangers future growth. Levitt cites many service industries, such as dry cleaning and electric utilities, as examples of marketing myopia. But many firms have found innovative ways to reach new markets and develop long-term relationships.

For instance, for a long time, Apple has worked to develop greener and more sustainable manufacturing processes and products. Plans are underway for a 20-megawatt solar farm and a 5-megawatt fuel-cell farm—what some observers are calling the largest such company-owned facilities in the United States. In addition, the company recently won a patent for a simple, reliable process for recharging its products from solar energy sources.[15] Table 1.2 illustrates how firms in a number of industries have overcome myopic thinking by developing broader marketing-oriented business ideas that focus on consumer need satisfaction.

ASSESSMENT CHECK

3.1 What is marketing myopia?

3.2 Give an example of how a firm can avoid marketing myopia.

TABLE 1.2 Avoiding Marketing Myopia

Company	Myopic Description	Company Motto—Avoiding Myopia
Audi	Automobile	Truth in engineering
Club Med	Resort vacations	Where Happiness Means the World
MasterCard	Credit card company	There are some things money can't buy. For everything else, there's MasterCard.
Allegra	Antihistamine	Have it All
Goodyear	Tire manufacturer	The best tires in the world have Goodyear written all over them.
UPS	Express package	We ♥ logistics.

EXTENDING THE TRADITIONAL BOUNDARIES OF MARKETING

Today's organizations—both profit oriented and not-for-profit—recognize universal needs for marketing and its importance to their success. During a television commercial break, viewers might be exposed to an advertisement for a Kia Spectra, an appeal to help feed children in foreign countries, a message by a political candidate, and a commercial for McDonald's—all in the space of about two minutes. Two of these ads are paid for by firms attempting to achieve profitability and other objectives. The appeal for funds to feed children and the political ad are examples of communications by not-for-profit organizations and individuals.

MARKETING IN NOT-FOR-PROFIT ORGANIZATIONS

More than a quarter of all U.S. adults volunteer in one or more of the 1.5 million not-for-profit organizations across the country.[16] In total, these organizations generate hundreds of billions of dollars of revenues each year through contributions and from fund-raising activities. That makes not-for-profit organizations big business.

Not-for-profits operate in both public and private sectors. Federal, state, and local organizations pursue service objectives not keyed to profitability targets. The Federal Trade Commission oversees business activities; a state's department of motor vehicles issues car registrations and driver's licenses; a local school board is responsible for maintaining educational standards for its district. The private sector has an even greater array of not-for-profit organizations, including hospitals, libraries, the American Kennel Club, and the American Heart Association. Regardless of their size or location, all of these organizations need funds to operate. Adopting the marketing concept can make a great difference in their ability to meet their service objectives.

Conner Prairie in Fishers, Indiana, is an open-air re-creation of rural life in 1830s Indiana that features historic areas to explore, including a Lenape Indian camp, the Conner Homestead, a modern museum, and 800 acres of undeveloped land along with indoor play and learning areas for young children. Costumed staff host events that range from a festive wedding to the experience of slaves seeking freedom through the Underground Railroad. Thousands of families and school groups visit each year.[17]

Some not-for-profits form partnerships with business firms that promote the organization's cause or message. Target Stores funds a facility called Target House, which provides long-term housing for families with children treated at St. Jude Children's Research Hospital. The house has about 100 apartments, plus common areas where families can gather and children can play. Celebrities have also contributed to the house. Singer Amy Grant furnished a music room, the Jonas Brothers created a karaoke space for family fun, and Olympic gold-medalist Scott Hamilton donated an arts-and-crafts room. Other "friends" of the organization include Olympic snowboarder Shaun White and country singer-songwriter Brad Paisley. Sponsors like Yahoo! and Brooks Brothers also support the house.[18]

Generally, the alliances formed between not-for-profit organizations and commercial firms and their executives benefit both. The reality of operating with multimillion-dollar budgets requires not-for-profit organizations to maintain a focused business approach. Consider some current examples:

- Feeding America receives assistance from food manufacturers and grocery stores in distributing more than 3 billion pounds of food and grocery products to needy Americans. A few of the many businesses that support Feeding America include ConAgra Foods, General Mills, Kellogg Company, Nestle, PepsiCo, Procter & Gamble, and Walmart.[19]

- Corporate Angel Network works with the National Business Aviation Association to provide free

During October, the National Football League supports Breast Cancer Awareness month by permitting its players to wear pink gloves, headbands, or other pink items to show their support for the cause.

transportation for cancer patients traveling to and from their treatments using empty seats on corporate jets.

- Millions of dollars were raised through donations from individuals, companies, and charitable organizations for victims of recent Superstorm Sandy in New York, New Jersey, Connecticut, and the surrounding areas. Fundraising was led by the American Red Cross and the Salvation Army.[20]

The diversity of not-for-profit organizations suggests the presence of numerous organizational objectives other than profitability. In addition to their organizational goals, not-for-profit organizations differ from profit-seeking firms in several other ways.

CHARACTERISTICS OF NOT-FOR-PROFIT MARKETING

4 **Describe the characteristics of not-for-profit marketing.**

bottom line Reference to overall company profitability.

The most obvious distinction between not-for-profit organizations and for-profit firms is the financial **bottom line**, business jargon that refers to the overall profitability of an organization. For-profit organizations measure profitability, and their goal is to generate revenues above and beyond their costs to make money for all stakeholders involved, including employees, shareholders, and the organization itself. Not-for-profit organizations hope to generate as much revenue as possible to support their causes, whether it is feeding children, preserving wilderness areas, or helping single mothers find work. Historically, not-for-profits have had less exact goals and marketing objectives than for-profit firms, but in recent years, many of these groups have recognized that, to succeed, they must develop more cost-effective ways to provide services, and they must compete with other organizations for donors' dollars. Marketing can help them accomplish these tasks. Some groups are finding, for instance, that online social network sites, such as Facebook and Twitter, can bring them increased attention. But they are also using specialized networks devoted to social causes like YourCause.com, and easy payment systems like Piryx, to generate funds.[21]

Other distinctions exist between for-profit and not-for-profit organizations as well, each of which influences marketing activities. Like profit-seeking firms, not-for-profit organizations may market tangible goods or intangible services. Pink products have long been important in raising both funds for and recognition of National Breast Cancer Awareness month in October every year. During that month, the National Football League supports Susan G. Komen for the Cure by permitting its players to wear pink gloves, headbands, or other pink items to signal their support for the cause.[22] But profit-seeking businesses tend to focus their marketing on just one public—their customers. Not-for-profit organizations, however, often must market to multiple publics, which complicates decision making about the correct markets to target. Many deal with at least two major publics—their clients and their sponsors—and often many other publics as well. A college or university markets to prospective and current students, parents of students, major donors, alumni, faculty, staff, local businesses, and local government agencies.

A service user of a not-for-profit organization may have less control over the organization's destiny than customers of a profit-seeking firm. Not-for-profit organizations also often possess some degree of monopoly power in a given geographic area. An individual contributor might object to United Way's inclusion of a particular local agency, but that agency will receive a portion of any donor contribution.

NONTRADITIONAL MARKETING

5 **Identify and briefly explain each of the five types of nontraditional marketing.**

As marketing evolved into an organization-wide activity, its application has broadened far beyond its traditional boundaries of for-profit organizations that create and distribute tangible goods and intangible services. In many cases, broader appeals focus on causes, events, individuals, organizations, and places. Table 1.3 lists and describes five major categories of nontraditional marketing: person marketing, place marketing, cause marketing, event marketing, and organization marketing. These categories can overlap—promotion for an organization may also encompass a cause or a promotional campaign may focus on both an event and a place.

TABLE 1.3 Categories of Nontraditional Marketing

Type	Brief Description	Examples
Person marketing	Marketing efforts designed to cultivate the attention and preference of a target market toward a person	Athlete Aaron Rodgers, Green Bay Packers quarterback; celebrity Toby Keith, country singer
Place marketing	Marketing efforts designed to attract visitors to a particular area; improve consumer images of a city, state, or nation; and/or attract new business	California: "Find Yourself Here." Colorado: "Enter a Higher State." Illinois: "Right Here. Right Now."
Cause marketing	Identification and marketing of a social issue, cause, or idea to selected target markets	"Click it or ticket." "Refill, not landfill."
Event marketing	Marketing of sporting, cultural, and charitable activities to selected target markets	Rio 2016 Summer Olympics American Diabetes Association's Tour de Cure
Organization marketing	Marketing efforts of mutual-benefit organizations, service organizations, and government organizations that seek to influence others to accept their goals, receive their services, or contribute to them in some way	American Red Cross: "Together, we can save a life." March of Dimes: "Working together for stronger, healthier babies." St. Jude Children's Research Hospital: "Finding Cures. Saving Children."

© Cengage Learning

PERSON MARKETING

Person marketing involves efforts designed to cultivate the attention, interest, and preferences of a target market toward a celebrity or authority figure. Celebrities can be real people or fictional characters. Political candidates engage in person marketing as they promote their candidacy for office. Authors such as Suze Orman of *The Road to Wealth* use person marketing to promote their books. Rachael Ray uses person marketing to promote her *Every Day with Rachael Ray* magazine, where she appears on every cover.

An extension of person marketing is *celebrity endorsements,* in which well-known athletes, entertainers, and experts or authority figures promote products for companies or social causes for not-for-profit organizations. Actresses Halle Berry and Emma Stone are spokespersons for Revlon products, and Honda signed Jerry Seinfeld and Jay Leno to pitch the Acura. *Modern Family* actress Sofia Vergara dances her way through a Miami nightclub in pursuit of a Diet Pepsi, and Dennis Haysbert, who played President David Palmer in the popular TV series "24," represents Allstate.[23] But athletes are the big winners in the celebrity endorsement arena—soccer star David Beckham appears in a series of ads touting Burger King's revamped menu. Olympic speed skater Apolo Ohno is a celebrity spokesperson for Subway, and when Ohno recently completed the New York City Marathon, the sandwich chain donated $26,200—$1,000 per mile—to the Special Olympics. And NBA MVP LeBron James was recently named the highest paid basketball player on *Forbes'* list of the world's highest-paid athletes, ranking fourth overall with annual earnings of more than $50 million.[24]

PLACE MARKETING

Another category of nontraditional marketing is **place marketing**, which attempts to attract customers to particular areas. Cities, states, regions, and countries publicize their tourist attractions to lure vacation travelers. They also promote themselves as good locations for businesses. Place marketing has become more important in the world economy—not only for tourism but also to recruit business and workers. In an effort to revive a sagging Las Vegas economy, casino operator MGM built a multi-billion-dollar CityCenter complex that includes four 61-story hotel towers, high-end stores, and dozens of bars and restaurants—and, of course, a casino. However, the tourism enhancements haven't yet turned the economy around, despite a recent increase in gambling revenues.[25]

person marketing
Marketing efforts designed to cultivate the attention, interest, and preferences of a target market toward a person (perhaps a political candidate or celebrity).

place marketing
Marketing efforts to attract people and organizations to a particular geographic area.

© Dave G. Houser/Alamy

Spaceport America is an example of place marketing as it plans to attract people to New Mexico as one of the world's first public launch and landing sites for space vehicles.

Place marketing can be a showcase for ingenuity. Although commercial space travel remains a somewhat distant possibility, the New Mexico Spaceport Authority has already designed the world's first public launch and landing site for space vehicles. Spaceport America, home to Richard Branson's Virgin Galactic, is located next to the U.S. Army's White Sands Missile Range. Among its objectives, Spaceport America strives to encourage and inspire students in science and math, and partners with a science consortium to host an annual student launch. More than 800 students and teachers participated in a recent launch.[26]

Minnesota Tourism, a website that promotes the state's $11.3 billion travel and tourism industry, is backed by a strategic plan that details 16 separate programs and tactics to achieve its goals. They include traditional advertising, interactive marketing, partnership and group tour marketing, media relations, meetings and conventions, and the growth area of sports marketing, among others. Primary markets are the north central United States and Canada, Japan, the United Kingdom, Germany, Austria, Switzerland, and Scandinavia.[27]

In another area of the country, West Virginia has a hub for vacationers. For instance, the town of Davis is home to Timberline Four Season Resort which, as its name suggests, offers a wealth of outdoor activities year-round. During the summer, visitors can ride horses, mountain bike, or go whitewater rafting or hiking. In the winter, the resort boasts up to 200 inches of snow per year on its Herz Mountain. Timberline is sometimes overlooked by east coast skiers who routinely travel north and west; however, locals are convinced that their mountain, which recently upgraded the snowmaking capacity of its 37 slopes and trails, is about to be discovered.[28]

CAUSE MARKETING

A third category of nontraditional marketing, **cause marketing**, refers to the identification and marketing of a social issue, cause, or idea to selected target markets. Cause marketing covers a wide range of issues, including literacy, physical fitness, awareness of childhood obesity, environmental protection, elimination of birth defects, child-abuse prevention, and preventing drunk driving.

As mentioned earlier, an increasingly common marketing practice is for profit-seeking firms to link their products to social causes. Partnering with DoSomething.org, office supply giant Staples sponsors an annual school supply drive. In a recent drive, Staples donated more than $800,000 in school supplies for disadvantaged youth. To leverage the power of social networking, the company also set up a Facebook page to raise awareness among teens about DoSomething.org, which is dedicated to inspiring young people to recognize a need and take positive action.[29]

Surveys show strong support for cause-related marketing by both consumers and company employees. In a recent survey, 92 percent of consumers had a more positive image of companies that support important social causes, and four of five respondents said that they would change brands to support a cause if the price and quality of the two brands remained equal. Cause marketing can help build relationships with customers.

EVENT MARKETING

Event marketing refers to the marketing of sporting, cultural, and charitable activities to selected target markets. It also includes the sponsorship of such events by firms seeking to increase public awareness and bolster their images by linking themselves and their products to the events. Sports sponsorships have gained effectiveness in increasing brand recognition, enhancing image, boosting purchase volume, and increasing popularity with sports fans in demographic segments corresponding to sponsor business goals.

Some people might say that the premier sporting event is baseball's World Series. Others claim it's the Olympics or the World Cup. Still others might argue that it's the Super Bowl, which some consumers claim they watch only to see the debut of commercials. Those commercials are expensive,

cause marketing
Identification and marketing of a social issue, cause, or idea to selected target markets.

event marketing
Marketing of sporting, cultural, and charitable activities to selected target markets.

costing, on average, $3.5 million for 30 seconds of airtime. But in Super Bowl LXVI, for example, they reached a record 111.3 million viewers.[30] Companies now also feed their commercials to websites and make them available for downloading to personal computers, tablets, and smartphones. Experienced marketers caution that firms planning such a big expenditure should make it part of a larger marketing plan, not just a single shot at fame.

For those who prefer the international pageantry of the Olympics, marketers have plenty of plans. The promotion of upcoming Olympics—both summer and winter—begins years in advance. Before the end of each Olympics, hosts of the next games unveil their logo, and the marketing takes off from there. Corporate sponsors like Adidas try to target the next Olympic gold medal winners, draping them in clothing and gear with company logos. The 2012 Summer Olympics in London afforded opportunities for hundreds of firms to provide food and drink for hospitality events, frames and tents, jewelry, team uniforms, energy generation and temperature control systems, beds for the athletes' village, natural gas, cold and flu remedies, organic groceries, and computer and accounting services.[31]

Event marketing for the Olympics begins years in advance. Here is the logo for the 2016 Summer Games in Rio de Janeiro, Brazil.

Carr/MCT/Newscom

ORGANIZATION MARKETING

Organization marketing attempts to persuade people to accept the goals of, receive the services of, or contribute in some way to an organization. Organization marketing includes mutual-benefit organizations such as Service Employees International Union and the Republican and Democratic political parties; service and cultural organizations like DePaul University, Baylor College of Medicine, St. Louis's Barnes-Jewish Hospital, and Little Rock's Clinton Presidential Library; and government organizations such as the U.S. Coast Guard, the Newark Police Department, the Sacramento Fire Department, and the U.S. Postal Service. Colleges and universities use organizational marketing to help raise funds. The University of Texas leads all colleges and universities in the sale of licensed merchandise—the school receives more than $10 million a year from these sales.[32]

organization marketing Marketing by mutual-benefit organizations, service organizations, and government organizations intended to persuade others to accept their goals, receive their services, or contribute to them in some way.

transaction-based marketing Buyer and seller exchanges characterized by limited communications and little or no ongoing relationships between the parties.

⊕ ASSESSMENT CHECK

5.1   Identify the five major categories of nontraditional marketing.

5.2   Give an example of a way in which two or more of these categories might overlap.

FROM TRANSACTION-BASED MARKETING TO RELATIONSHIP MARKETING

As marketing progresses through the 21st century, a significant change is taking place in the way companies interact with customers. The traditional view of marketing as a simple exchange process, or **transaction-based marketing**, is being replaced by a different, longer-term approach that

Explain the shift from transaction-based marketing to relationship and social marketing.

6

emphasizes building relationships with one customer at a time. Traditional marketing strategies focused on attracting customers and closing deals. Today's marketers realize that, although it's important to attract new customers, it's even more important to establish and maintain a relationship with them so they become loyal repeat customers. These efforts must expand to include suppliers and employees as well. Over the long term, this relationship may be translated to the lifetime value of a customer—the revenues and intangible benefits that a customer brings to an organization over an average lifetime, minus the investment the firm has made to attract and keep the customer.

Marketers realize that consumers are becoming more and more sophisticated. They quickly recognize marketing messages and may turn away from them if the messages don't contain information that consumers want and need. So marketers need to develop new techniques to establish and build trusting relationships between companies and their customers. As defined earlier in this chapter, relationship marketing refers to the development, growth, and maintenance of long-term, cost-effective exchange relationships with individual customers, suppliers, employees, and other partners for mutual benefit. It broadens the scope of external marketing relationships to include suppliers, customers, and referral sources. In relationship marketing, the term *customer* takes on a new meaning. Employees serve customers within an organization as well as outside it; individual employees and their departments are customers of and suppliers to one another. They must apply the same high standards of customer satisfaction to intradepartmental relationships as they do to external customer relationships. Relationship marketing recognizes the critical importance of internal marketing to the success of external marketing plans. Programs that improve customer service inside a company also raise productivity and staff morale, resulting in better customer relationships outside the firm.

Relationship marketing gives a company new opportunities to gain a competitive edge by moving customers up a loyalty ladder—from new customers to regular purchasers, then to loyal supporters of the firm and its goods and services, and finally to advocates who not only buy its products but recommend them to others, as shown in Figure 1.2.

Relationship building begins early in marketing. It starts with determining what customers need and want, then developing high-quality products to meet those needs. It continues with excellent customer service during and after purchase. It also includes programs that encourage repeat purchases and foster customer loyalty.

Marketers may try to rebuild damaged relationships or rejuvenate unprofitable customers with these practices as well. Sometimes modifying a product or tailoring customer service to meet the needs of these customers can go a long way toward rebuilding a relationship.

FIGURE 1.2
Converting New Customers to Advocates

Advocate

Loyal Supporter

Regular Purchaser

New Customer

© Cengage Learning

mobile marketing
Marketing messages transmitted via wireless technology.

USING SOCIAL MARKETING TO BUILD RELATIONSHIPS

Today's technology allows people to transmit memos, reports, and drawings quickly and inexpensively over phone lines, cables, or wireless devices. People can subscribe to personalized news services that deliver article summaries on specified topics directly to their computers or smartphones. They can communicate via social media, email, voice mail, text messages, videoconferencing, and computer networks; pay bills using online banking services; and use online resources to get information about everything from theater events or restaurant reviews to a local Ford dealer's special sale.

CONVERTING NEW CUSTOMERS TO ADVOCATES

As an increasing number of Internet users in the United States use wireless devices such as smartphones or notebook computers to access the Web and check their email, the stage is set for mobile marketing—marketing messages transmitted via wireless technology.

Interactive media technologies combine computers and telecommunications resources to create software that users can control. Putting power into the hands of customers allows better communication, which can build relationships.

Interactive marketing refers to buyer–seller communications in which the customer controls the amount and type of information received from a marketer. This technique provides immediate access to key product information when the consumer wants it, and it is increasingly taking place on social media sites like Facebook, Twitter, and Pinterest. **Social marketing** is the use of online social media as a communications channel for marketing messages. Social media is now the top online activity. With 1 billion active users, it's estimated that if Facebook were a country, it would be the third most populous in the world, right after India.[33] And, as it celebrated six years in operation, Twitter announced that its 140 million active users post an average of 340 million tweets a day.[34] Over three-fourths of the *Fortune* 100 companies have joined Twitter, and more than 70 percent use Facebook.[35] The Weather Channel has used social media successfully to strengthen its marketing approach. See "Marketing Success" for more details.

Interactive marketing allows marketers and consumers to customize their communication. Customers may come to companies for information, creating opportunities for one-to-one marketing. They also can tell the company what they like or dislike about a product, and they can just as easily click the exit button and move on to another area. As interactive promotions grow in number and popularity, the challenge is to attract and hold consumer attention.

One small business making good use of social media is Hansen's Cakes in Beverly Hills, whose cake decorator Suzi Finer uses Facebook and Twitter several times a day to tell thousands of "friends" and "followers" what she's up to at work. Finer says her posts boosted sales 15 to 20 percent during the recent economic downturn. "People are still having birthday parties and weddings, and seeing these little bits about cakes on updates gets them excited about the possibilities."[36]

interactive marketing Buyer–seller communications in which the customer controls the amount and type of information received from a marketer through such channels as the Internet and virtual reality kiosks.

social marketing The use of online social media as a communications channel for marketing messages.

MARKETING SUCCESS

The Weather Channel

Background. The Weather Channel (WTC) began as a 24-hour television network delivering up-to-the-minute reporting about rain, sleet, snow, and sunshine.

The Challenge. As new electronic platforms emerged, WTC needed to find new ways to be relevant. How do you market the weather?

The Strategy. The Weather Channel (WTC) expanded its brand through marketing strategies that tap directly into the digital world. Now it operates a cable channel with original reality-show programming, a website highlighting conditions and forecasts for 100,000 locations worldwide plus educational and seasonal features, a radio network with 700 affiliates, a popular mobile app, and a Twitter partnership called Weather Channel Social.

Weather Channel Social offers real-time tweets and forecasts across mobile, broadcast, and Web platforms. Weather.com provides a local Social page with weather-related tweets plus other customer-created content. The iPhone app hosts interactive conversations by users—weather-related and social—while the TV channel integrates real-time tweets into live programming, and viewers can

participate. Cities with populations over 100,000 have 200 custom Twitter feeds offering local forecasts with three-hour updates.

The Outcome. "Adding Social to all of our platforms makes our storytelling more complete," says WTC's executive vice president of digital products. During the recent catastrophic Superstorm Sandy, the Weather Channel put its social strategies to good use. Anticipating many people would lose power, the Weather Channel streamed its live, round-the-clock storm coverage online so people could receive updates via mobile devices. The day before Hurricane Sandy devastated the East Coast, the Weather Channel's website, *weather.com,* recorded more than 300 million page views—almost 8 times the daily average.

Sources: Company website, www.weather.com, accessed November 5, 2012; Brian Stelter, "Weather Channel's Parent Company Is Renamed," *The New York Times,* accessed November 5, 2012, www.nytimes.com; Katie Leslie, "Sandy Gives Weather Channel a Chance to Shine," *Denver Post,* accessed November 5, 2012, www.denverpost.com; Christopher S. Stewart and Keach Hagey, "Sandy—The Social-Media Phenomenon," *The Wall Street Journal,* accessed November 5, 2012, http://online.wsj.com; Terri Schwartz, "Weather Channel Meteorologists Stress Severity of Hurricane Sandy," *Zap2It,* accessed November 5, 2012, http://blog.zap2it.com; Amir Efrati, "Today's Weather Channel Forecast: A Chance of Tweets," *The Wall Street Journal,* accessed November 5, 2012, http://blogs.wsj.com.

© Facebook © 2012/© Kodak Italia

Kodak's Facebook page in Italian allows Kodak to engage with the public through social media.

Social media also allow larger exchanges in which consumers communicate with one another using email or social networking sites. These electronic conversations can establish innovative relationships between users and the business, providing customized information based on users' interests and levels of understanding.

Eastman Kodak, the iconic pioneer in photography that recently filed for bankruptcy protection, uses social media extensively to engage with the public. It hosts a Facebook page for commercial users as well as numerous pages for consumers from North America and Latin America to Europe to the Middle East to Asia. Its My Kodak Moments Facebook app enables users to capture and organize their Facebook images attractively. Kodak also maintains Twitter and YouTube accounts along with several blogs, including A Thousand Words (where people can post their favorite photos), Plugged In (where Kodak employees share tips and hints), and Grow Your Biz (a place for business owners to share knowledge).[37]

By converting indifferent customers into loyal ones, companies generate repeat sales. The cost of maintaining existing customers is far below the cost of finding new ones, and these loyal customers are profitable. Some of the best repeat customers are those who are also willing to spread the word—create a buzz—about a product. *Buzz marketing* can be very effective in attracting new customers by bridging the gap between a company and its products. Companies as diverse as Microsoft and KFC have tapped customers to create a buzz about their products. Firms that make the most efficient use of buzz marketing warn that it is not a "one-way" approach to building customer relationships.

Buzz can be purely visual, too. "Visual buzz" can be thought of as the tangible expression of an issue or position. To help create jobs in communities with high unemployment throughout America, Starbucks recently partnered with a financial consortium to launch Create Jobs for USA. Under the program, donors who give $5 or more will receive a distinctive red-white-and-blue wristband adorned with the message "Indivisible" and available at Starbucks nationwide. The handmade wristbands are made in America from raw materials produced in America. Starbucks donated $5 million to seed the project.[38] Effective relationship marketing often relies heavily on information technologies such as computer databases that record customers' tastes, price preferences, and lifestyles. This technology helps companies become one-to-one marketers that gather customer-specific information and provide individually customized goods and services. The firms target their marketing programs to appropriate groups rather than relying on mass-marketing campaigns. Companies that study customer preferences and react accordingly gain distinct competitive advantages.

DEVELOPING PARTNERSHIPS AND STRATEGIC ALLIANCES

Relationship marketing does not apply just to individual consumers and employees. It also affects a wide range of other markets, including business-to-business relationships with the firm's suppliers and distributors as well as other types of corporate partnerships. In the past, companies often have viewed their suppliers as adversaries against whom they must fiercely negotiate prices, playing one off against the other. But this attitude has changed radically as both marketers and their suppliers discover the benefits of collaborative relationships.

The formation of strategic alliances—partnerships that create competitive advantages—is also on the rise. Alliances take many forms, including product development partnerships that involve shared costs for research and development and marketing, and vertical alliances in which one company provides a product or component to another firm, which then distributes or sells it under its own brand. Under Armour and Nike pay millions of dollars to outfit college football teams in exchange for the publicity gained from the teams' sometimes outlandish uniforms.[39]

strategic alliances
Partnerships in which two or more companies combine resources and capital to create competitive advantages in a new market.

ASSESSMENT CHECK

6.1 How does relationship marketing give companies a competitive edge?

6.2 Why are interactive and social marketing important tools for marketers?

6.3 What is a strategic alliance?

Not-for-profit organizations often use strategic alliances to raise awareness and funds for their causes. Recently, Dave & Buster's supported the Make-A-Wish Foundation by inviting customers to buy a Make-A-Wish star for a dollar. The restaurant chain augmented customers' donations with donations of cash and meal coupons for Make-A-Wish families of children with life-threatening health conditions.[40]

COSTS AND FUNCTIONS OF MARKETING

Firms must spend money to create time, place, and ownership utilities. Numerous attempts have been made to measure marketing costs in relation to overall product costs, and most estimates have ranged between 40 and 60 percent of total costs. On average, half of the costs involved in a product, such as a Subway sandwich, a pair of Gap jeans, or a financial planning lecture, can be traced directly to marketing. These costs are not associated with wheat, metal, or other raw materials, nor are they associated with baking, welding, or any of the other production functions necessary for creating form utility. What functions does marketing perform, and why are they important in creating customer satisfaction?

As Figure 1.3 reveals, marketing is responsible for the performance of eight universal functions: buying, selling, transporting, storing, standardizing and grading, financing, risk taking, and securing marketing information. Some functions are performed by manufacturers, others by retailers, and still others by marketing intermediaries called **wholesalers**.

Buying and selling represent **exchange functions**. Buying is important to marketing on several levels. Marketers must determine how and why consumers buy certain goods and services. To be successful, they must try to understand consumer behavior. In addition, retailers and other intermediaries must seek out products that will appeal to their customers. Marketers must also anticipate consumer preferences for purchases to be made several months later. Selling is the second half of the exchange process. It involves advertising, personal selling, and sales promotion in an attempt to match the firm's goods and services to consumer needs.

7 Identify the universal functions of marketing.

wholesalers
Intermediaries that operate between producers and resellers.

exchange functions
Buying and selling.

1. **Buying**
Ensuring that product offerings are available in sufficient quantities to meet customer demands

2. **Selling**
Using advertising, personal selling, and sales promotion to match products to customer needs

5. **Standardizing and Grading**
Ensuring that product offerings meet quality and quantity controls of size, weight, and other variables

6. **Financing**
Providing credit for channel members (wholesalers and retailers) and consumers

3. **Transporting**
Moving products from their point of production to locations convenient for purchasers

4. **Storing**
Warehousing products until needed for sale

7. **Risk Taking**
Dealing with uncertainty about future customer purchases

8. **Securing Marketing Information**
Collecting information about consumers, competitors, and channel members for use in making marketing decisions

FIGURE 1.3
Eight Universal Marketing Functions

© Cengage Learning

Transporting and storing are physical distribution functions. Transporting involves physically moving goods from the seller to the purchaser. Storing involves warehousing goods until they are needed for sale. Manufacturers, wholesalers, and retailers typically perform these functions.

The final four marketing functions—standardizing and grading, financing, risk taking, and securing marketing information—often are called facilitating functions because they help the marketer perform the exchange and physical distribution functions. Quality and quantity control standards and grades, frequently set by federal or state governments, reduce the need for purchasers to inspect each item. For example, if you request a certain size tire for your automobile, you expect to get it.

Financing is another marketing function because buyers often need access to funds to finance inventories prior to sales. Manufacturers often provide financing for their wholesale and retail customers. Some types of wholesalers perform similar functions for their markets. Finally, retailers frequently allow their customers to buy on credit with either store charge cards or major credit cards.

The seventh function, risk taking, is part of most ventures. Manufacturers create goods and services based on research and their belief that consumers need them. Wholesalers and retailers acquire inventory based on similar expectations of future consumer demand. Entrepreneurial risk takers accommodate these uncertainties about future consumer behavior when they market goods and services.

The final marketing function involves securing marketing information. Marketers gather information about potential customers: who they are, what they buy, where they buy, and how they buy. By collecting and analyzing marketing information, marketers can understand why consumers purchase some goods while passing others by. This information also helps determine what consumers want and need—and how to offer goods and services to satisfy them. So marketing is the direct connection between a firm and its customers, the link that helps build and maintain lasting relationships.

⊕ **ASSESSMENT CHECK**

7.1 Which two marketing functions represent exchange functions?

7.2 Which two functions represent physical distribution functions?

7.3 Which four functions are facilitating functions?

ETHICS AND SOCIAL RESPONSIBILITY: DOING WELL BY DOING GOOD

8 Demonstrate the relationship between ethical business practices, social responsibility, sustainability, and marketplace success.

ethics Moral standards of behavior expected by a society.

Ethics are moral standards of behavior expected by a society. Most companies do their best to abide by an ethical code of conduct, but sometimes organizations and their leaders fall short. Several years ago, the Houston-based energy giant Enron collapsed, taking with it the retirement savings of its employees and wiping out some investors. In another scandal, executives from Tyco were convicted of using millions of company dollars for their personal benefit. And chemical manufacturer Monsanto was convicted not only of polluting water sources and soil in a rural Alabama area for decades but of ignoring evidence its own scientists had gathered indicating the extent and severity of the pollution. New ethics issues surface regularly. See the "Solving an Ethical Controversy" feature for a discussion about New York City's recent ban on extra large, sugary drinks.

Most businesspeople follow ethical practices. More than half of all major corporations now offer ethics training to employees, and most corporate mission statements include pledges to protect the environment, contribute to communities, and improve workers' lives. This book encourages you to follow the highest ethical standards throughout your business and marketing career.

social responsibility Marketing philosophies, policies, procedures, and actions that have the enhancement of society's welfare as a primary objective.

Social responsibility includes marketing philosophies, policies, procedures, and actions whose primary objective is to enhance society and protect the environment through sustainable products and practices. Walmart, for instance, has made great strides in reducing its use of energy in its stores.

Social responsibility often takes the form of philanthropy, making gifts of money or time to humanitarian causes. Many firms, both large and small, include social responsibility programs as part of their overall mission. These programs often produce such benefits as improved customer relationships, increased employee loyalty, marketplace success, and improved financial performance.

SOLVING AN ETHICAL CONTROVERSY

Banning Sugary Drinks in NYC

In an effort to help reduce obesity rates among its residents, New York City tried to restrict the sale of extra-large sodas and other sugary drinks in at restaurants, street cars, stadiums, and movie theaters. The proposed ban would have begun in March of 2013. But one day before the ruling was set to be enforced, a New York Supreme Court judge ruled that the city could not impose the ban. Then, on June 30 of the same year, a New York appellate court rejected the ban, saying it was illegal.

Should cities be allowed to try to prevent consumers from buying extra-large, sugary drinks?

PRO

1. Obesity in this country, particularly among children, is out of control, and any means to make it difficult to purchase sugary drinks will help.

2. By limiting the size of sugary drinks, cities will help consumers reduce their sugar intake, which should help them lose weight.

CON

1. Government should not intervene in consumers' freedom of choice when it comes to what type and size of drinks they can purchase.

2. Limiting the size of drinks for sale could have an adverse affect on small businesses whose profit margins will suffer.

Summary:

NYC's ban on extra-large drinks would have taken effect in March of 2013. Even though Mayor Michael Bloomberg believed selling smaller-sized drinks would have helped reduce obesity rates and make people healthier in the long run, ultimately the courts didn't agree.

Sources: http://www.usatoday.com/story/news/2013/07/30/new-york-ban-on-larged-sized-sugary-drinks-rejected/2599429/?utm_source=feedburner&utm_medium=feed&utm_campaign=Feed%3A+UsatodaycomNation-TopStories+%28News+-+Nation+-+Top+Stories%29.

Sustainable products, those that can be produced, used, and disposed of with minimal impact on the environment, are another goal of socially responsible firms. Many such firms have added annual sustainability reports and a top-level executive position to develop and promote their sustainability efforts. One such executive is DuPont's chief sustainability officer, Linda Fisher, who joined the firm after working for the U.S. Environmental Protection Agency (EPA) for 12 years. Says Fisher about the challenges companies face in operating in environmentally responsible ways: "We believe the global companies that succeed in responding successfully and sustainably to 21st-century challenges will be those that master the art of collaboration. We are building alliances with customers, companies, governments, NGOs (non-governmental organizations), visionaries, thought leaders, and others around the world in an effort to address needs sustainably at the local level. We've adopted a new model that we call 'inclusive innovation'—solving problems by designing solutions in cooperation with those who will benefit directly from the product."[41]

What is the role of marketing in sustainability efforts? According to Fisher, DuPont's goals "address all stages of product development, from R&D efforts through marketing and sales. They also mark a turning point in our corporate thinking. Establishing goals that relied on our ability to

sustainable products
Products that can be produced, used, and disposed of with minimal impact on the environment.

help our customer do better for the environment and their consumers meant sustainability had to be embedded in the way we do business. Now the business of sustainability at DuPont was truly going to be business as usual."[42] Other sustainability and social responsibility officers agree that sustainability must permeate the firm's corporate strategy from the top down, so all areas in the firm can align their environmental goals in the same direction for the greatest effectiveness. As IBM notes in its A Smarter Planet website, "To be sustainable, organizations must embrace a new objective: optimize operations to minimize environmental impact and improve social outcomes in a manner that also maximizes performance."[43]

Firms stand to gain needed credibility from their efforts to protect the environment by reducing waste and pollution. Not only has the recent economic downturn made it important for them to cut waste and cost as never before, including the costs of damage to the environment, but consumers now are more aware of the real need for such drives—and ready to support them. Recent research by Accenture suggests that nearly two-thirds of respondents indicated willingness to pay a premium for goods or services that lower greenhouse gas emissions.[44]

Nokia recently won praise for its efforts to eliminate dangerous or polluting ingredients in its products. According to the company, 100 percent of the material used to manufacture Nokia cell phones is recyclable. What's more, Nokia offers a recycling program with about 6,000 drop-off centers in 100 countries.[45] To boost the economy and reduce the number of older, gas-guzzling cars on the road, the U.S. government recently offered a rebate of up to $4,500 (depending on various factors including the type of car) if a motorist traded in a working "clunker" for a more fuel-efficient car. The program was so successful at reducing the number of polluting cars on the road (the vehicles were disabled and then crushed or shredded so they could never be driven again) that it ran through most of its allocated $1 billion in funding in a little over a week. An additional $2 billion was added to keep the program running a few weeks longer. Some considered the program a success, but others say it should not have required consumers to buy another car, however fuel-efficient, or it should have mandated a big improvement in gas mileage for the new purchase.[46]

ASSESSMENT CHECK

8.1 Define *ethics*.

8.2 What is *social responsibility*?

8.3 What are *sustainable products*?

STRATEGIC IMPLICATIONS OF MARKETING IN THE 21ST CENTURY

Unprecedented opportunities have emerged out of electronic commerce and computer technologies in business today. These advances and innovations have allowed organizations to reach new markets, reduce selling and marketing costs, and enhance their relationships with customers and suppliers. Thanks to the Internet and social media tools, business has grown into a global market.

Both profit-seeking and not-for-profit organizations must broaden the scope of their activities to prevent myopic results in their enterprises. If they fail to do so, they lose out on promising opportunities.

Marketers must constantly look for ways to create loyal customers and build long-term relationships with those customers, often on a one-to-one basis. They must be able to anticipate customer needs and satisfy them with innovative goods and services. They must do this faster and better than the competition. And they must conduct their business according to the highest ethical and sustainability standards.

Get online now for additional learning tools to help you master your marketing knowledge—visit **WWW.CENGAGEBRAIN.COM** today!

REVIEW OF CHAPTER OBJECTIVES

1 Define *marketing*, explain how it creates utility, and describe its role in the global marketplace.

Marketing is an organizational function and a set of processes for creating, communicating, and delivering value to customers and for managing customer relationships in ways that benefit the organization and its stakeholders. Utility is the want-satisfying power of a good or service. Four basic kinds of utility exist: form, time, place, and ownership. Marketing creates time, place, and ownership utilities. Three factors have forced marketers to embrace a global marketplace: expanded international trade agreements, new technologies that have brought previously isolated nations to the marketplace, and greater interdependence of the world's economies.

2 Contrast marketing activities during the five eras in the history of marketing.

During the production era, businesspeople believed that quality products would sell themselves. The sales era emphasized convincing people to buy. The marketing concept emerged during the marketing era, in which there was a companywide focus on consumer orientation with the objective of achieving long-term success. The relationship era focuses on establishing and maintaining relationships between customers and suppliers. Relationship marketing involves long-term, value-added relationships. The social era encourages companies to use the Web and social media sites to connect to consumers as a way to market goods and services.

3 Explain the importance of avoiding marketing myopia.

Marketing myopia is management's failure to recognize a company's scope of business. It focuses marketers too narrowly on products and thus misses potential opportunities to satisfy customers. To avoid it, companies must broadly define their goals so that they focus on fulfilling consumer needs.

4 Describe the characteristics of not-for-profit marketing.

Not-for-profit organizations operate in both public and private sectors. The biggest distinction between not-for-profits and commercial firms is the bottom line—whether the firm is judged by its profitability levels. Not-for-profit organizations may market to multiple publics. A customer or service user of a not-for-profit organization may have less control over the organization's destiny than customers of a profit-seeking firm. In addition, resource contributors to not-for-profits may try to influence the organization's activities. Not-for-profits and for-profits may form alliances that effectively promote each other's causes and services.

5 Identify and briefly explain each of the five types of nontraditional marketing.

Person marketing focuses on efforts to cultivate the attention, interest, and preferences of a target market toward a celebrity or noted figure. Place marketing attempts to attract visitors and businesses to a particular destination. Cause marketing identifies and markets a social issue, cause, or idea. Event marketing promotes sporting, cultural, charitable, or political activities. Organization marketing attempts to influence others to accept an organization's goals or services and contribute to it in some way.

6 Explain the shift from transaction-based marketing to relationship and social marketing.

Relationship marketing represents a dramatic change in the way companies interact with customers. The focus on relationships gives a firm new opportunities to gain a competitive edge by moving customers up a loyalty ladder from new customers to regular purchasers and then to loyal supporters and advocates. Over the long term, this relationship may be translated to the lifetime value of a customer. Interactive technologies and social marketing (via Facebook, Twitter, and the like) allow marketers direct communication with customers, permit more meaningful exchanges, and put the customer in control. Organizations may form partnerships—called *strategic alliances*—to create a competitive advantage. These alliances may involve product development, raising awareness, and other activities.

7 Identify the universal functions of marketing.

Marketing is responsible for eight universal functions, divided into three categories: (1) exchange functions (buying and selling); (2) physical distribution (transporting and storing); and (3) facilitating functions (standardization and grading, financing, risk taking, and securing market information).

8 Demonstrate the relationship between ethical business practices, social responsibility, sustainability, and marketplace success.

Ethics are moral standards of behavior expected by a society. Companies that promote ethical behavior and social responsibility usually produce increased employee loyalty and a better public

image. This image often pays off in customer growth, because many buyers want to associate themselves with—and be customers of—such firms. Social responsibility includes marketing philosophies, policies, procedures, and actions whose primary objectives are the enhancement of society and the protection of the environment through sustainable products and practices. These actions also generally promote a firm's public image.

⊕ ASSESSMENT CHECK: ANSWERS

1.1 Define *marketing*, and explain how it creates utility. Marketing is an organizational function and a set of processes for creating, communicating, and delivering value to customers and for managing customer relationships in ways that benefit the organization and its stakeholders. It creates time, place, and ownership utilities.

1.2 What three factors have forced marketers to embrace a global marketplace? International agreements are negotiated to expand trade among nations. The growth of technology is bringing previously isolated countries into the marketplace. The interdependence of the world's economies is now a reality.

2.1 What is the major distinction between the production era and the sales era? During the production era, businesspeople believed that quality products would sell themselves. But during the sales era, emphasis was placed on selling—persuading people to buy.

2.2 What is the marketing concept? The marketing concept is a companywide consumer orientation with the objective of achieving long-term success.

2.3 Describe the relationship era of marketing. The relationship era focuses on building long-term, value-added relationships over time with customers and suppliers.

3.1 What is marketing myopia? Marketing myopia is management's failure to recognize the scope of a company's business.

3.2 Give an example of how a firm can avoid marketing myopia. A firm can find innovative ways to reach new markets with existing goods and services.

4.1 What is the most obvious distinction between a not-for-profit organization and a commercial organization? The biggest distinction between for-profit and not-for-profit organizations is the bottom line—whether an organization is judged by its profitability.

4.2 Why do for-profit and not-for-profit organizations sometimes form alliances? For-profits and not-for-profits may form alliances to promote each other's causes and offerings. For-profits may do so as part of their social responsibility efforts.

5.1 Identify the five major categories of nontraditional marketing. The five categories of nontraditional marketing are person, place, cause, event, and organization marketing.

5.2 Give an example of a way in which two or more of these categories might overlap. Overlap can occur in many ways. An organization might use a person to promote its cause or event. Two organizations might use one marketing effort to promote an event and a place; for example, Subway donating money to the Special Olympics in honor of one of its spokespersons, speed skater Apolo Ohno, who ran the New York Marathon.

6.1 How does relationship marketing give companies a competitive edge? Relationship marketing can move customers up a loyalty ladder, generating repeat sales and long-term relationships.

6.2 Why are interactive and social marketing important tools for marketers? Interactive marketing technologies create direct communication with customers, allow larger exchanges, and put the customer in control. Social marketing media (Facebook, Twitter, for example) let companies show customers they are listening and will respond quickly.

6.3 What is a strategic alliance? A strategic alliance is a partnership formed between two organizations to create a competitive advantage.

7.1 Which two marketing functions represent exchange functions? Buying and selling are exchange functions.

7.2 Which two functions represent physical distribution functions? Transporting and storing are physical distribution functions.

7.3 Which four functions are facilitating functions? The facilitating functions are standardization and grading, financing, risk taking, and securing market information.

8.1 Define *ethics*. Ethics are moral standards of behavior expected by a society.

8.2 What is *social responsibility*? Social responsibility involves marketing philosophies, policies, procedures, and actions whose primary objective is the enhancement of society.

8.3 What are *sustainable products*? Sustainable products are those that can be produced, used, and disposed of with minimal impact on the environment.

MARKETING TERMS YOU NEED TO KNOW

utility **5**

marketing **7**

exchange process **8**

production orientation **9**

sales orientation **9**

seller's market **10**

buyer's market **10**

consumer orientation **10**

marketing concept **10**

relationship marketing **10**

marketing myopia **12**

bottom line **14**

person marketing **15**

place marketing **15**

cause marketing **16**

event marketing **16**

organization marketing **17**

transaction-based
   marketing **17**

mobile marketing **18**

interactive marketing **19**

social marketing **19**

strategic alliances **20**

wholesalers **21**

exchange functions **21**

ethics **22**

social responsibility **22**

sustainable products **23**

ASSURANCE OF LEARNING REVIEW

1. Identify the four types of utility, and give an example of each.

2. What condition in the marketplace gave rise to the need for a consumer orientation by businesses after World War II?

3. Define *relationship marketing*, and describe how it fits into the marketing concept.

4. Why do not-for-profit organizations need to engage in marketing efforts?

5. Give an example of how the National Highway Traffic Safety Administration's "Click it or ticket" campaign could use one or more of the nontraditional marketing techniques to promote the cause in a state that is newly adopting it.

6. What might be some of the benefits of mobile marketing for firms that use it to reach out to consumers?

7. Describe the significance of the shift from transaction-based marketing to relationship marketing. When does relationship building begin?

8. How have social media like Twitter and Facebook changed marketing communications?

9. How do ethics and social responsibility help a firm achieve marketplace success?

10. What motivates firms to develop sustainable products?

PROJECTS AND TEAMWORK EXERCISES

1. Consider each of the following firms and describe how the firm's goods and services can create different types of utility. If necessary, go online to the company's website to learn more about it. You can do this alone or in a team.
   a. American Express, Visa, or MasterCard
   b. Flickr or other online digital photo service
   c. Club Med
   d. Amazon.com
   e. SuperValu supermarkets

2. With a classmate, choose a U.S.-based company whose products you think will do well in certain overseas markets. The company can be anything from a music group to a clothing retailer—anything that interests you. Suggestions include Papa John's Pizza, Zumba, StubHub, Lady Gaga, or Bass Pro Shops. Then write a plan for how you would target and communicate with overseas markets.

3. Choose a company that interests you from the following list or select one of your own. Research the company online, through business magazines, or through other sources to identify the scope of its business. Write a brief description of the company's current scope of business. Then describe strategies for avoiding marketing myopia, expanding the company's scope of business over the next ten years.
   a. FedEx

   b. Walt Disney World
   c. General Electric
   d. E*Trade
   e. Intel

4. With a classmate, choose one of the following not-for-profit organizations. Then come up with a for-profit firm with which you think your organization could form a strategic alliance. Create a presentation—an ad, a poster, or the like—illustrating and promoting the partnership.
   a. Humane Society
   b. The Water Project
   c. Habitat for Humanity
   d. National Multiple Sclerosis Society
   e. World Wildlife Fund

5. Research one of the following electronics companies, or another of your choosing, and study its efforts to improve the sustainability of its products, particularly their safe disposal. What does the company do well in this area? What could it do better?
   a. Toshiba
   b. Nintendo
   c. Microsoft
   d. Fujitsu
   e. Samsung

CRITICAL-THINKING EXERCISES

1. How does an organization create a customer?
2. How can marketers use interactive and social marketing to convert needs to wants and ultimately build long-term relationships with customers?
3. Why is utility such an important feature of marketing?
4. What benefits—monetary and nonmonetary—do social responsibility programs bring to a business?

5. Why is determining the lifetime value of a customer an important analysis for a company to make?
6. Why is it important for a firm to establish high ethical standards for sustainability? What role do you think marketers play in implementing these standards?

ETHICS EXERCISE

At a local coffee shop you run into a friend who works for a social media firm that competes with yours. After a brief conversation he remembers an errand he has to run, and he rushes off with a hasty good-bye. As you gather your things to leave a few minutes later, you realize your friend left a file folder on the chair; inside is a report about a client. Your company is very interested in doing some work for this client in the future.

1. Would you take a quick look inside the folder before you return it to your friend? Why or why not?
2. Would you share any information in the report with anyone in your office? Why or why not?
3. When you return the folder to your friend, would you mention the report and offer your own commentary on it? Why or why not?

INTERNET EXERCISES

1. **Marketing terminology.** Like many subjects, marketing appears to have a language of its own. Visit the website of the American Marketing Association. Click on "resource library" and then "dictionary." Define the following terms: A/B testing, dating, never-out list, and will-call.

   www.marketingpower.com

2. **Event marketing.** The Westminster Kennel Club runs the nation's largest dog show. Go to the event's website. Review the website and prepare a brief report relating what you learned to the material on event marketing in the chapter. Make sure to describe sponsor tie-ins and other joint marketing efforts.

   www.westminsterkennelclub.org

3. **Sustainability.** Johnson & Johnson engages in a major effort to incorporate sustainability into its wide-ranging business activities. Visit the website listed here and read about the firm's recent activities. How does Johnson & Johnson promote sustainability? What are some specific examples?

   www.jnj.com/connect/caring/environment-protection

Note: Internet Web addresses change frequently. If you don't find the exact site listed, you may need to access the organization's home page and search from there or use a search engine such as Google or Bing.

CASE 1.1
Oreos Turn 100 Years Young

Perhaps it's not entirely marketing expertise that has made Oreo reportedly the most popular cookie in the world. After all, it also tastes good, and it's fun to eat. But marketing has certainly helped the beloved chocolate wafer sandwich sail past competitors to celebrate its 100th birthday.

Successful early advertising pushed Oreos ahead of Hydrox, its nearest (and now defunct) rival. Wise strategizing led Oreo's producer to tailor the creme and wafers to different consumer tastes in China, Japan, Indonesia, and Argentina, and later to switch to a trans-fat-free formula. Innovative marketing led to partnerships with Burger King, Carl's Jr., and the Cheesecake Factory, all of which now promote their use of Oreos as ingredients in their dessert offerings. Oreos have gone digital, too. The cookie racked up the most Facebook "likes" ever in a single day and now has 28 million Facebook fans. So it's understandable that 70 million cookies are eaten globally every day, earning $2 billion a year for the Nabisco brand. But perhaps the most elaborate marketing plan of all is the year-long global birthday party.

Mondelez International (formerly Kraft Foods), which owns Nabisco, is celebrating with live events, prizes, promotions and public relations efforts around the world, plus a special ad campaign and online happenings, all tied to the theme, "Celebrate the kid inside." Fans can post photos, stories, and videos to a special Facebook gallery and qualify to be a "Birthday of the Day" celebrant on their own special day. "Flash" birthday parties in the United States culminated in a multinational celebration in New York. China hosted a fireworks display, a playground for all ages opened in Indonesia, and there were party games and cake in Dubai and piñatas in Venezuela. Fans in 200 countries watched these events in real time on Facebook, too. Television ads showcase adults and kids sharing Oreos and milk, print ads commemorate iconic moments of the last 100 years, and the company website features games and recipes. There's even a special birthday variety of the treat in stores around the world, with rainbow candy sprinkles.

QUESTIONS FOR CRITICAL THINKING

1. How do Oreo's birthday celebration activities meet the definition of marketing?

2. What accounts for Oreo's popularity on Facebook, and is Mondelez using this factor to the best marketing advantage?

Sources: Company website, www.mondelezinternational.com, accessed November 1, 2012; Nadia Arumugam, "Oreo Cookie Celebrates 100th Birthday with Sprinkles and World Domination," *Forbes,* accessed November 1, 2012, www.forbes.com; Brian Palmer, "The Unsinkable O," Slate.com, accessed November 1, 2012, www.slate.com; Rob Manker, "Oreo at 100," *The Chicago Tribune,* accessed November 1, 2012, http://articles.chicagotribune.com; news release, "Oreo Turns 100 Years Young," www.mondelezinternational.com, accessed November 1, 2012; Kim Peterson, "Oreo Turns 100," Money.com, accessed November 1, 2012, http://money.msn.com; Stuart Elliott, "The Oreo Turns 100 with a Nod to the Past," *The New York Times,* accessed November 1, 2012, www.nytimes.com.

VIDEO CASE 1.2
Geoffrey B. Small Is Big on Quality, Customers, Community

Geoffrey B. Small is a leading avant-garde fashion designer who wants you to think about your clothes—but not the style or color of the outfit you are wearing today, not what a great bargain it was, not the brand name or which celebrities wear the same design. He wants you to dig deeper than that, thinking about the quality and origin of fabrics you wear, their impact on the environment, and your own view of social responsibility as a consumer. Even if you can't afford his clothes (created in one or two of a kind, limited editions), you can take away his messages about quality, value, service to the customer and community, and the importance of activism.

Now based in Italy—with easy access to the Paris fashion shows—Small began his career selling jeans at the Gap in Boston. Today, he shrugs off the marketing tactics of the large, name-brand clothing designers and retail outlets, which he believes do little or nothing to create utility for the consumer, because they hide the true cost of the clothes they are selling. "Corporate advertising has made people unaware of what they're really spending their money on, and what things are really costing them," says Small. Cheap fabrics, poor construction, and lack of attention to detail all add up to low prices and nearly disposable garments—costing consumers more money in the long run. "We have to re-educate a lot of consumers because what they think is cheap is not cheap at all," asserts Small. "It's the most expensive."

Small's clothing designs provide form utility by creating the highest-quality garments. Although customers often have to wait months for these hand-made garments, Small believes this is an asset. "Fifty years ago, machine-made products were perfect, new and exciting," explains Small. That's no longer the case. "We don't care how long it takes," he insists. "We don't care what it costs. What we care about is that it's the very, very best it can possibly be," which is what his customers want. Consumers may view Small's clothes in motion at runway shows, at a select group of exclusive retail shops, or communicate with him directly. When they take ownership of a suit or coat, they have a highly individualized piece of clothing that some might call a work of art. "Customers are screaming for something personal and special," Small points out, "something that has a bond between one human being and another."

Small views his relationships with customers as critical to his success, referring to them as the "best and only financial backers" a designer should have. Since his clothes are made to last decades—25 to 30 years—he looks toward developing customer relationships that will survive just as long. "We're in a field where you normally do a lot of marketing," he observes. "I think it's more important to focus on great product, great service, value to the customer, and communicating with the customer honestly." That honest communication—about his products and his beliefs—has built Small a devoted following.

It would be easy for Small to hide in his design studio sketching clothes for a few high-end customers who want the novelty of something edgy and different to wear. Doing so could lead him into the quicksand of marketing myopia. But that's not Small's style. He looks for new ways to satisfy customers without compromising his ideals—in fact, he stitches his ideals right into the fabrics of his clothing. Small is a genuine activist for social causes as well as environmental sustainability, which has proved to be an effective tool for connecting with the people who appreciate his designs. Customers see his activism, and when they make a choice about where to spend their money, they choose his brand. "That's where we want to be positioned," says Small. "We want to do more than just supply clothes. We want to play a role in the community."

Looking forward, Small believes it is his company's responsibility to set an example for other businesses. "The biggest challenge now is not to compromise," he admits; "to focus on one piece at a time and make it the absolute best it can be."

QUESTIONS FOR CRITICAL THINKING

1. Why is the link between relationship marketing and social responsibility so important to Small's business success?

2. Geoffrey B. Small is an avant-garde designer and unconventional businessperson. What examples does he set, and what might marketers for large corporations learn from his views and practices?

Sources: "The Amazing Geoffrey B. Small Story," company website, accessed November 1, 2012, www.geoffreybsmall.net/gbsstory.htm; Geoffrey B. Small, "The Environment of Young Designers," *Not Just a Label*, accessed November 1, 2012, www.notjustalabel.com; Claire Ruhlin, "Recycle, Reconstruct, Redesign," *Community*, accessed November 1, 2012, http://communityathens.blogspot.com; Eugene Rabkin, "Review: Geoffrey B. Small, Fall/Winter 2012," *StyleZeitgeist*, accessed November 1, 2012, www.sz-mag.com.

NOTES

1. Company website, www.toryburch.com, accessed October 25, 2012; organization website, www.toryburchfoundation.org, accessed October 25, 2012; "CMO, Tory Burch, Talks International Expansion, F-Commerce & More," *The e-tail blog*, accessed October 25, 2012, http://www.theetailblog.com; CMO Network, "CMO Predictions for 2012—Part 2: Dell, Diageo, Saks, Tory Burch Double Down on Social Media," *Forbes*, accessed October 25, 2012, www.forbes.com; Zoe Geddes-Soltess, "How Tory Burch Achieved Social Media Success" (blog), http://www.radian6.com, accessed October 25, 2012; Meredith Lepore, "Tory Burch Has Secured a Place in Heaven Because She Helps Other Women," *The Grindstone*, accessed October 25, 2012, http://the grindstone.com; Lauren Indvik, "How Digital Marketing Fueled Fashion Label Tory Burch's Global Expansion," http://mashable.com, accessed October 25, 2012; "How Tory Burch Is Making Shopping More Social" (blog), http://blog.demandware.com, accessed October 25, 2012.

2. Tom Simonite, "Why Facebook's Search Engine Won't Be Anything Like Google's," *MIT Technology Review*, accessed October 25, 2012, www.technologyreview.com.

3. Simon Hill, "How to Pick the Right e-Reader," *Digital Trends*, accessed October 25, 2012, www.digitaltrends.com.

4. Dale Buss, "Pepsi's Next Innovation: Buy a Soda, Send a Gift, Play a Game, Charge Your Phone," *Brand Channel*, accessed October 25, 2012, www.brandchannel.com.

5. Company website, www.spindynamicsyoyo.com, accessed October 25, 2012.

6. Joseph P. Guiltinan and Gordon W. Paul, *Marketing Management*, 6th ed. (New York: McGraw-Hill), 1996, pp. 3–4.

7. American Marketing Association, "Resource Library," accessed October 25, 2012, www.marketingpower.com.

8. Company website, "Airline Fees," www.kayak.com, accessed October 25, 2012.

9. "Automobile Industry Introduction," Plunkett Research, Ltd., accessed October 26, 2012, www.plunkettresearch.com.

10. "China's Top Export Destinations, 2010," www.uschina.org, accessed October 26, 2012; "United States Imports," www.tradingeconomics.com, accessed October 26, 2012.

11. "2011 U.S. Manufacturing-Outsourcing Index," *Alixpartners.com*, www.alixpartners.com, accessed April 7, 2012.

12. Company website, "New iPad Tops Three Million," www.apple.com, accessed October 26, 2012.

13. Y Charts, "Pop Quiz: How Many Dreamliners Does Boeing Have to Deliver to Turn a Profit?" *Forbes*, accessed October 26, 2012, www.forbes.com.

14. Milt Freudenheim, "As Smartphones Become Health Aids, Ads May Follow," *The New York Times*, accessed October 26, 2012, www.nytimes.com.

15. Robert McMillan, "Apple Doubles Down on Maiden Solar Farm," *Wired*, accessed October 26, 2012, www.wired.com; Katie Fehrenbacher, "Apple Appears to Have Started Building Its Data Center Fuel Cell Project," *gigaom.com*, accessed October 26, 2012, http://gigaom.com; "Apple Wins Rights to Sixth Solar Panel Patent," *macnn.com*, accessed October 26, 2012, www.macnn.com.

16. Organization website, "Frequently Asked Questions," http://foundationcenter.org, accessed October 26, 2012; Bureau of Labor Statistics, "Volunteering in the United States, 2011," accessed October 26, 2012, www.bls.gov.

17. Organization website, www.connerprairie.org, accessed October 26, 2012.

18. Company website, "Target House Fact Sheet," www.stjude.org, accessed October 26, 2012.

19. Organization website, http://feedingamerica.org, accessed October 26, 2012.

20. Anais Strickland, "Update: Total Raised for Superstorm Sandy Relief Now Tops $92.3 Million," *The Chronicle of Philanthropy*, accessed November 18, 2012, http://philanthropy.com.

21. Hiba Haider, "Seven Creative Ways Nonprofits Can Use Social Media to Drive Donations," *hubspot.com*, accessed October 26, 2012, http://blog.hubspot.com; Organization website, www.piryx.com, accessed October 26, 2012; organization website, www.yourcause.com, accessed October 26, 2012.

22. Organization website, "NFL Supports Breast Cancer Awareness Month," www.nfl.com, accessed October 26, 2012.

23. Tim Nudd, "Jerry Seinfeld, Jay Leno to Pitch Acura's NSX on the Super Bowl," *Adweek*, accessed November 1, 2012, www.adweek.com; Tim Nudd, "Diet Pepsi Dances with Sofia Vergara," *Adweek*, accessed November 1, 2012, www.adweek.com.

24. Company website, www.subway.com, accessed November 1, 2012; Kurt Badenhausen, "Mayweather Tops List of the World's Highest-Paid Athletes," *Forbes*, accessed November 1, 2012, www.forbes.com; company website, "H&M Fashion Media Update—Fall 2012," www.hm.com, accessed November 1, 2012; Noreen O'Leary, "Burger King Turns to David Beckham in Campaign for New Menu," *Adweek*, accessed November 1, 2012, www.adweek.com.

25. Howard Stutz, "Nevada Gaming Revenues Top $1 Billion for July, Up Nearly 17 Percent," *Las Vegas Review-Journal*, accessed November 1, 2012, www.lvrj.com.

26. "Spaceport America Awards Three Contracts to Companies Located in New Mexico," press release, accessed November 1, 2012, www.spaceportamerica.com.

27. Organization website, http://industry.exploreminnesota.com, accessed November 1, 2012.

28. Company website, www.timberlineresort.com, accessed November 1, 2012.

29. Company website, www.staples.com, accessed November 1, 2012.

30. "Super Bowl TV Audience Reaches Record 111.3 Million," *Reuters*, accessed November 1, 2012, www.reuters.com; "Super Bowl Ads Cost an Average of $3.5M," *ESPN.com*, accessed November 1, 2012, http://espn.go.com.

31. Organization website, "London 2012 Olympic Games Partners," www.london2012.com, accessed November 1, 2012.

32. Patrick Beach, "Longhorns Top Sales of College Merchandise for Seventh Straight Year," *Austin American-Statesman*, accessed November 1, 2012, www.statesman.com.

33. Darrell Etherington, "Facebook Tops 1 Billion Monthly Active Users, CEO Mark Zuckerberg Shares a Personal Note," *Tech Crunch*, accessed November 1, 2012, www.techcrunch.com; "India's Population 2012," www.indiaonlinepages.com, accessed November 1, 2012.

34. Shea Bennett, "Twitter Now Has More Than 140 Million Active Users Sending 340 Million Tweets Every Day," Media Bistro, accessed November 1, 2012, www.mediabistro.com.

35. Sree Sreenivasan, "How the World's Biggest Companies Are Doing Social Media," *cnet.com*, accessed November 1, 2012, http://news.cnet.com.

36. Jefferson Graham, "Cake Decorator Finds Twitter a Tweet Recipe for Success," *USA Today*, accessed November 1, 2012, www.usatoday.com.

37. Associated Press, "Kodak's 3Q Loss Widens as Company Reorganizes," http://bigstory.ap.org, accessed November 1, 2012; company website, "Follow Us," www.kodak.com, accessed November 1, 2012; company website, http://growyourbiz.kodak.com, accessed November 1, 2012; company website, http://1000words.kodak.com, accessed November 1, 2012; company website, http://pluggedin.kodak.com, accessed November 1, 2012.

38. Organization website, www.createjobsforusa.org, accessed November 1, 2012; "Create Jobs for USA Program Launches in U.S. Starbucks Stores and Online," press release, http://news.starbucks.com, accessed November 1, 2012.

39. Dave Sheinin, "College Football Uniforms Are Getting More Outrageous, Thanks to Nike, Under Armour," *The Washington Post*, accessed November 1, 2012, www.washingtonpost.com.

40. Organization website, www.wish.org, accessed November 1, 2012.

41. "An Interview with Linda Fisher," *Globe-Net*, accessed November 1, 2012, www.globe-net.com.

42. Ibid.

43. Company website, "Sustainability on a Smarter Planet," www.ibm.com, accessed November 1, 2012.

44. Company website, www.accenture.com (news release), accessed November 1, 2012.

45. Company website, "Recycling," www.nokia.com, accessed November 1, 2012.

46. Kelsey Mays, "Cash for Clunkers, Two Years Later," *CarTalk.com*, http://blogs.cars.com, accessed November 1, 2012.

Stephen Lam/Reuters

Chapter 2

STRATEGIC
Planning in
Contemporary Marketing

NEW CEO PLANS YAHOO TURNAROUND

1 Distinguish between strategic planning and tactical planning.

2 Explain how marketing plans differ at various levels in an organization.

3 Identify the steps in the marketing planning process.

4 Describe successful planning tools and techniques, including Porter's Five Forces model, first and second mover strategies, SWOT analysis, and the strategic window.

5 Identify the basic elements of a marketing strategy.

6 Describe the environmental characteristics that influence strategic decisions.

7 Describe the methods for marketing planning, including business portfolio analysis and the BCG matrix.

Marissa Mayer, Yahoo's new CEO, has never shied away from hard work. The first female engineer hired at Google, she spent five years heading up search products and later directed the company's local, map, and location services. When the recent Yahoo CEO left, Mayer was approached by a job recruiter wanting to know if she was ready to take on yet another challenge: running Yahoo.

Yahoo went through four CEOs in five years before the company's board met with Mayer to discuss her interest in turning around Yahoo. Never one to run from a challenge, Mayer said yes to taking on the CEO position—at the same time telling the board she was pregnant. Two weeks after the birth of her son, Mayer returned to work to fine-tune her business strategies.

How will Mayer turn around the struggling Internet giant? One of her first initiatives called PB&J—process, bureaucracy, and jams—lays out a

plan of small changes to make Yahoo more productive. At her initial staff meeting, Mayer encouraged employees to suggest even more changes—a strategy Mayer believes will help shift the company's culture to empowering employees to become involved in the business process. In an email to employees, Mayer said she wanted to make Yahoo "the absolute best place to work."

Mayer continues to make changes and tweak the company's overall vision. She brought onboard several senior executives, including a new chief marketing officer, a new chief operating officer, and a new chief financial officer. Some executives came from Google, and some came from other top companies. Mayer also created a new position, executive vice president of people and development, who will be Yahoo's dealmaker, overseeing HR, business development, strategy, and mergers & acquisitions.

Mayer says that Yahoo will do more "acqui-hires" in the future—buying small companies not for their products but for their engineering talent. She also says the company will focus its efforts on reinventing its mobile strategy, which she believes is an important component for Yahoo's future success.

Mayer is the youngest CEO of a Fortune 500 company and recently joined Walmart's board of directors. She knows change is difficult, but she is committed to making Yahoo's turnaround a success. Her focused approach has both colleagues and competitors watching.[1]

EVOLUTION OF A BRAND

Yahoo's early success as a Web innovator has not sustained its ongoing business, as other companies such as Google and Facebook have taken over as the new Internet leaders. Yahoo's inability to execute a successful business plan has resulted in chaos, corporate bureaucracy, and an overall lack of direction. The revolving door in the CEO's office has left the company with little or no focus, which has had a negative impact on the company's bottom line, employee morale, and product innovation.

- Marissa Mayer's experience and success at Google should help reshape Yahoo's business strategies, exploit its technology, and provide a financial rebound. But change is never easy. How can Mayer use her Google experience to set the tone for both a financial and cultural shift at Yahoo?
- Mayer says one of the reasons Yahoo's mobile strategy has faltered is because the company's brands are "splintered," which has caused confusion among consumers. How can the company use its marketing channels to gather customer information and reinvigorate the Yahoo brand?

CHAPTER OVERVIEW

"More and more consumers are purchasing smaller, more fuel-efficient vehicles, such as the Ford Focus, Fusion, and Escape. The market for large trucks and SUVs is dwindling. Are fuel-efficient vehicles the wave of the future? Should we commit to building more of them and feature them prominently in our marketing?"

"We have fewer customers eating at our restaurant after 5 PM. Should we revamp our dinner menu? Lower our prices? Use special promotions? Update the dining-room décor?"

"Recent marketing research shows that we are not reaching our customer target—consumers in their early- to mid-20s. Should we consider another advertising agency?"

Marketers face strategic questions every day—planning strategy is a critical part of their job. The marketplace changes continually in response to changes in consumer tastes and expectations, technological developments, competitors' actions, economic trends, and political and legal events, as well as product innovations and pressures from suppliers and distributors. Although the causes of these changes often lie outside a marketer's control, effective planning can anticipate many of the changes.

When the price of gas and jet fuel soared recently, travelers opted to stay closer to home—taking "staycations" instead of booking vacations to exotic, faraway places. This represents an opportunity for places like Ocean City, Maryland, and Branson, Missouri. Local water parks and amusement parks,

nearby lakes, indoor playgrounds or gyms, and restaurants can market themselves as potential alternatives. Any destination that promotes itself to potential vacationers within a short drive could find itself adding up the profits.

This chapter provides an important foundation for analyzing all aspects of marketing by demonstrating the importance of gathering reliable information to create an effective plan. These activities provide a structure for a firm to use its unique strengths. Marketing planning identifies the markets a company can best serve as well as the most appropriate mix of approaches to satisfy the customers in those markets. While this chapter focuses on planning, we will examine in greater detail the task of marketing research and decision making in Chapter 8.

BRIEFLY SPEAKING

"How you gather, manage, and use information will determine whether you win or lose."

—**Bill Gates**
Founder and Chairman, Microsoft Corporation

MARKETING PLANNING: THE BASIS FOR STRATEGY AND TACTICS

Everyone plans. We plan which academic courses we want to take, which movie we want to see, and which outfit to wear to a party. We plan where we want to live and what career we want to pursue. Marketers plan as well. **Planning** is the process of anticipating future events and conditions and determining the best way to achieve organizational objectives. Of course, before marketing planning can even begin, an organization must define its objectives. Planning is a continuous process that includes identifying objectives and then determining the actions through which a firm can attain those objectives. The planning process creates a blueprint for marketers, executives, production staff, and everyone else in the organization to follow for achieving organizational objectives. It also defines checkpoints so that people within the organization can compare actual performance with expectations to indicate whether current activities are moving the organization toward its objectives.

Planning is important for both large and small companies. For years, Sir Richard Branson—founder of the airline Virgin Galactic—dreamed of launching a spaceship designed for commercial travel. The dream required complex design and engineering plans, including the launch of prototypes and rigorous rounds of safety testing. After one of the prototypes became the first privately owned, manned craft to reach space, the company's engineers in New Mexico went to work on a similar craft designed for commercial use, called SpaceShipTwo. Meanwhile, the idea of space travel has been marketed to wealthy clients, offering them the opportunity to pay $200,000 for a brief suborbital ride. Actor Ashton Kutcher recently became the 500th person to sign up for the historic trip. If the idea catches on, Branson and Virgin Galactic will have positioned themselves strategically to become the first—and possibly the only—firm to offer commercial space travel for the near future.[2]

Here on earth—and at the other end of the size spectrum—Shuttleworth, a small firm that manufactures conveyors, had to reevaluate its planning as its core business in electronics began to shrink. The company refocused its efforts on designing and building solar panel conveyors. Its new products have won acclaim, new customers, and a revitalized business.[3]

planning Process of anticipating future events and conditions and of determining the best way to achieve organizational objectives.

Richard Branson, shown here in a spacesuit costume to promote a contest, executed complex design and engineering plans to get Virgin Galactic into space.

© Peter Foley/EPA/Newscom

CAREER READINESS

Making a Good Impression at That First Real Job

Congratulations—you've won the job! Now how do you ensure you'll stand out at work for all the *right* reasons? Here are some tips:

- *Pay attention to the basics.* Every organization is different, so be sure to adopt your new employer's particular dress code and work ethic. Always be prompt, ask intelligent questions, avoid overly casual attire, do your Web surfing at home.

- *Remember names.* You'll meet a lot of new people in your first few weeks; make an effort to remember their names. Use mnemonics (memory tricks) if you need to, and if you forget a name, apologize and ask again.

- *Monitor your words and actions.* You never know who is connected or influential, especially when you're new, so be tactful, be circumspect, and avoid gossip.

- *Network with coworkers at all levels.* Meetings and team projects are good opportunities to meet helpful peers, invaluable support staff, and potential mentors. If opportunities like these don't readily come your way, volunteer.

- *Get involved outside work.* Participating in company outings, sports, and social responsibility efforts like community projects shows you're an enthusiastic member of the team.

Good luck!

Sources: Margaret Steen, "Eight Mistakes To Avoid in Your First 'Real' Job," Monster .com, accessed November 6, 2012, http://career-advice.monster.com; Randall S. Hansen and Katharine Hansen, "Quintessential Careers: Your First Days Working at a New Job: 20 Tips to Help You Make a Great Impression," Quintessential Careers.com, accessed November 6, 2012, www.quintcareers.com; "7 Tips for Department Meeting Rookies," Great Leadership, accessed November 6, 2012, www.greatleadershipbydan.com.

---

marketing planning
Implementing planning activities devoted to achieving marketing objectives.

Marketing planning—implementing planning activities devoted to achieving marketing objectives—establishes the basis for a marketing strategy. Product lines, pricing decisions, selection of appropriate distribution channels, and decisions relating to promotional campaigns all depend on plans formulated within the marketing organization. In today's boundaryless organizations, many planning activities take place over the Internet with *virtual conferences*—teleconferences with computer interfaces. These conferences represent a new way to build relationships among people who are in different geographic locations. Relationships like these are also important for new employees to help ensure their success. See the "Career Readiness" feature for some other tips about making a good impression in your first real job.

An important trend in marketing planning centers on relationship marketing, a firm's effort to develop long-term, cost-effective links with individual customers and suppliers for mutual benefit. Good relationships with customers can arm a firm with vital strategic weapons, and that's as true in business-to-business industries as anywhere else.

Many companies now include relationship-building goals and strategies in their plans. Relationship marketers typically maintain databases to track customer preferences. These marketers may also manipulate product spreadsheets to answer what-if questions related to prices and marketing performance. At Procter & Gamble, the inspiration for new or better products often comes from customers themselves. The company operates in more than 180 countries with 126,000 employees, many of whom serve as the eyes and ears of the firm. Some P&G marketers actually spend time in the homes of consumers, observing how they cook and eat meals, when they play, and where they shop. Other employees are trained simply to have conversations with friends and family about their lifestyles and the goods or services they use. All of this interaction helps build relationships, and the information helps develop products.[4]

STRATEGIC PLANNING VERSUS TACTICAL PLANNING

Distinguish between strategic planning and tactical planning. **1**

Planning often is classified on the basis of its scope or breadth. Some extremely broad plans focus on long-range organizational objectives that will significantly affect the firm for five or more years. Other more targeted plans cover the objectives of individual business units over shorter periods.

Strategic planning can be defined as the process of determining an organization's primary objectives and adopting courses of action that will achieve these objectives. This process includes, of course, allocation of necessary resources. The word *strategy* dates back to a Greek term meaning "the general's art." Strategic planning has a critical impact on a firm's destiny because it provides long-term direction for its decision makers.

Strategic planning is complemented by tactical planning, which guides the implementation of activities specified in the strategic plan. Unlike strategic plans, tactical plans typically address shorter-term actions that focus on current and near-future activities that a firm must complete to implement its larger strategies. Sometimes tactical planning requires swift decision making and actions. Disturbances on some recent commercial jet flights—one caused by a flight attendant and another by a pilot—resulted in public concern. Occurrences like these, while rare, give travelers concern about safety in an industry in which safety is paramount. Since those incidents, the airlines have had to work to regain the trust of their customers and the flying public in general.[5]

strategic planning
Process of determining an organization's primary objectives and adopting courses of action that will achieve these objectives.

tactical planning
Planning that guides the implementation of activities specified in the strategic plan.

> (+) **ASSESSMENT CHECK**
>
> 1.1 Define *planning*.
> 1.2 Give an example of strategic planning and tactical planning.

PLANNING AT DIFFERENT ORGANIZATIONAL LEVELS

Explain how marketing plans differ at various levels in an organization. **2**

Planning is a major responsibility for every manager, so managers at all organizational levels devote portions of their workdays to planning. Top management—the board of directors, chief executive officers (CEOs), chief operating officers (COOs), and functional vice presidents, such as chief marketing officers—spend greater proportions of their time planning than do middle-level and supervisory-level managers. Also, top managers usually focus their planning on long-range strategic issues. In contrast, middle-level managers—such as advertising executives, regional sales managers, and marketing research directors—tend to focus on operational planning, which includes creating and implementing tactical plans for their own business units. Supervisors often develop specific programs to meet goals in their areas of responsibility. Table 2.1 summarizes the types of planning undertaken at various organizational levels.

When it is most effective, the planning process includes input from a wide range of sources: employees, suppliers, and customers. Some marketing experts advocate developing a network of "influencers"—people who have influence over other people's opinions through authority, visibility, or expertise—to provide input and spread the word about company plans and products. According to a recent survey, more than half of respondents expected that companies would invest more resources in social media marketing in the coming year, indicating that this method of communicating with potential customers is gaining rapidly in popularity.[6]

> (+) **ASSESSMENT CHECK**
>
> 2.1 How do marketing plans vary at different levels of the organization?
> 2.2 Why is it important to get input from others when planning?

TABLE 2.1 Planning at Different Managerial Levels

Management Level	Type of Planning Emphasized at This Level	Examples
Top Management Board of directors Chief executive officer Chief operating officer Chief financial officer	Strategic planning	Organizationwide objectives; fundamental strategies; long-term plans; total budget
Middle Management General sales manager Team leader Director of marketing research	Tactical planning	Quarterly and semiannual plans; business unit budgets; divisional policies and procedures
Supervisory Management Regional sales manager Supervisor—telemarketing office	Operational planning	Daily and weekly plans; unit budgets; departmental rules and procedures

© Cengage Learning

STEPS IN THE MARKETING PLANNING PROCESS

3   Identify the steps in the marketing planning process.

mission Essential purpose that differentiates one company from others.

The marketing planning process begins at the corporate level with the definition of a firm's mission. It then determines its objectives, assesses its resources, and evaluates environmental risks and opportunities. Guided by this information, marketers within each business unit then formulate a marketing strategy, implement the strategy through operating plans, and gather feedback to monitor and adapt strategies when necessary. Figure 2.1 shows the basic steps in the process.

DEFINING THE ORGANIZATION'S MISSION AND OBJECTIVES

FIGURE 2.1
The Marketing Planning Process

The planning process begins with defining the firm's **mission**, the essential purpose that differentiates the company from others. The mission statement specifies the organization's overall goals and operational scope and provides general guidelines for future management actions. Adjustments in this statement reflect changing business environments and management philosophies.

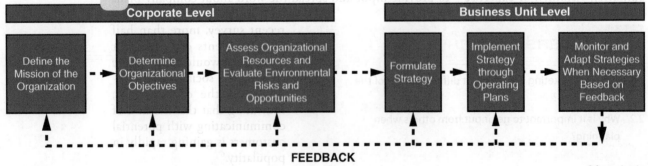

© Cengage Learning

Although management guru Peter Drucker cautioned that an effective mission statement should be brief enough "to fit on a T-shirt," organizations typically define themselves with slightly longer statements. But they often condense their mission statement into a catchy slogan such as these:

- Sephora: "The beauty authority."

- American Cancer Society: "The official sponsor of birthdays."

- Indiana Wesleyan University: "Change Your Life, Change Your World."

- Infiniti: "Inspired performance."

- IBM: "Welcome to the decade of smart."

An organization lays out its basic objectives, or goals, in its complete mission statement. These objectives guide development of supporting marketing objectives and plans. Soundly conceived objectives should state specific intentions, such as the following:

- Generate a 15 percent profit over the next 24 months.

- Add 25 new outlets within the next year.

- Improve five products within the next six months.

- Enter the Chinese market by the year 2015.

- Cut manufacturing costs by 10 percent.

- Reduce waste by 20 percent.

ASSESSING ORGANIZATIONAL RESOURCES AND EVALUATING ENVIRONMENTAL RISKS AND OPPORTUNITIES

The third step of the marketing planning process is to assess an organization's strengths, weaknesses, and available opportunities. Organizational resources include the capabilities of the firm's production, marketing, finance, technology, and employees. An organization's planners pinpoint its strengths and weaknesses. Strengths help them set objectives, develop plans for meeting those objectives, and take advantage of marketing opportunities.

Chapter 3 will discuss environmental factors that impact marketing opportunities. Environmental effects can emerge both from within the organization and from the external environment. For example, social media have transformed interpersonal communications as well as communications between companies and their customers.

FORMULATING, IMPLEMENTING, AND MONITORING A MARKETING STRATEGY

Once a firm's marketers figure out their company's best opportunities, they can develop a marketing plan designed to meet the overall objectives. A good marketing plan revolves around an efficient, flexible, and adaptable marketing strategy.

A **marketing strategy** is an overall, companywide program for selecting a particular target market and then satisfying consumers in that market through a careful blending of the elements of the marketing mix—product, distribution, promotion, and price—each of which is a component of the overall marketing strategy.

In the two final steps of the planning process, marketers put the marketing strategy into action; then, they monitor performance to ensure that objectives are achieved. Sometimes strategies need to be modified if the product's or company's actual performance is not in line with expected results. For years, Toronto-based Sun Life Financial, Canada's third-largest insurer, has sold life insurance and retirement-income to individuals and groups in the United States. But when the firm observed

marketing strategy
Overall, companywide program for selecting a particular target market and then satisfying consumers in that market through the marketing mix.

ASSESSMENT CHECK

3.1 Distinguish between an organization's mission and its objectives.

3.2 What is the importance of the final step in the marketing planning process?

that profit margins on individual policies had begun to decline, the company revisited its strategy and discontinued those sales, limiting their target market to groups. As Sun Life CEO Dean Connor put it, "We're changing course and setting a new vision."[7]

Sometimes a marketing strategy backfires. This can happen rapidly in the case of celebrity endorsements, as described in the "Solving an Ethical Controversy" feature.

SUCCESSFUL STRATEGIES: TOOLS AND TECHNIQUES

4 Describe successful planning tools and techniques, including Porter's Five Forces model, first and second mover strategies, SWOT analysis, and the strategic window.

We can identify a number of successful marketing planning tools and techniques. This section discusses four of them: Porter's Five Forces model, first and second mover strategies, SWOT analysis, and the strategic window. All planning strategies have the goal of creating a sustainable competitive advantage for a firm in which other companies simply cannot provide the same value to their customers that the firm does—no matter how hard they try.

SOLVING AN ETHICAL CONTROVERSY

How a Team Saves Face with Its Fans

Thousands of New England Patriots fans had purchased tight end Aaron Hernandez's jerseys during his three seasons with the team. Three years later, Hernandez was arraigned on murder charges and fans were stuck with team jerseys still emblazoned with his name. The jersey owners were left wondering what to do; they could keep the jerseys, sell them online, or throw them away. The Patriots Pro Shop came up with another solution—fans could trade the jerseys in for a different one.

According to the Patriot's Twitter post from the exchange, more than 1,200 Hernandez jerseys were returned in one day of the exchange.

Should team franchises disassociate themselves from a player facing criminal charges?

PRO 👍

1. Fans felt betrayed by Hernandez's actions and swapping his jersey for another player's would bolster their team spirit in a time of crises.

2. The Patriot's franchise keeps up their image by quickly denouncing Hernandez and making the jersey trade-ins free to fans.

CON 👎

1. If Hernandez is found not guilty, fans might be upset that the Patriots disassociated themselves from a player so quickly.

2. The Patriot's Pro Shop lost upwards of $250,000 when more than 2,500 jerseys were traded in over the two-day exchange.

Summary:

When New England Patriots tight end Aaron Hernandez was arraigned on murder charges, the franchise decided to disassociate themselves with the player and appease their fans in one move. Over a two-day period, the Patriots Pro Shop would exchange Hernandez jerseys for a different player's jersey for free.

Patriots' spokesman Stacey James said in a statement that he empathized with the parents of children who want to remain faithful to their team but wouldn't understand why they couldn't wear their Hernandez jerseys any longer.

Sources: http://www.cbssports.com/nfl/blog/eye-on-football/22660631/photos-aaron-hernandez-jersey-exchange-proves-popular-idea Accessed July 10, 2013
http://espn.go.com/boston/nfl/story/_/id/9454690/new-england-patriots-fans-line-trade-aaron-hernandez-jerseys Accessed July 10, 2013
http://mansfield-ma.patch.com/groups/business-news/p/how-many-hernandez-jerseys-were-exchanged-over-the-weekend_de830610 Accessed July 11, 2013

PORTER'S FIVE FORCES MODEL

A number of years ago, renowned business strategist Michael E. Porter identified five competitive forces that influence planning strategies in a model called **Porter's Five Forces**. Porter later updated his model to include the impact of the Internet on the strategies that businesses use. As illustrated in Figure 2.2, the five forces are potential new entrants, bargaining power of buyers, bargaining power of suppliers, threat of substitute products, and rivalry among competitors.

Potential new entrants sometimes are blocked by the cost or difficulty of entering a market. It is a lot more costly and complicated to begin building aircraft than it is to start up an Internet consulting business. The Internet has reduced the barriers to market entry in many industries. In fact, most businesses now view an Internet presence as a requirement for success. If customers have considerable bargaining power, they can greatly influence a firm's strategy. The Internet can increase a customer's buying power by providing information that might not otherwise be easily accessible such as alternate suppliers and price comparisons. Firms continue to compete to develop the most effective Internet marketing because they know that customers are savvy users of technology. Microsoft and Google, for example, operate competing online advertising exchanges—Microsoft's AppNexus and Google's DoubleClick—which allow ad sellers and buyers to negotiate in real time.[8]

The number of suppliers available to a manufacturer or retailer affects their bargaining power. If a seafood restaurant in the Midwest has only one supplier of Maine lobsters, that supplier has significant bargaining power. But seafood restaurants along the coast of Maine have many lobster suppliers, which gives their suppliers less bargaining power.

If customers have the opportunity to replace a company's products with goods or services from a competing firm or industry, the company's marketers may have to find a new market, change prices, or compete in other ways to maintain an advantage. McDonald's made what some considered a bold move when the firm announced the launch of its "McCafe," offering upgraded coffee drinks

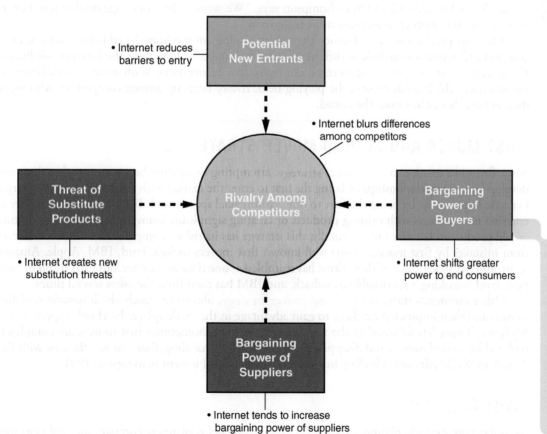

FIGURE 2.2
Porter's Five Forces Model

When McDonald's started offering high-end coffee drinks, they entered into direct competition with Starbucks and Dunkin' Donuts. The threat of a substitute product can create a need for a company's marketers to find new ways to compete.

© Richard B. Levine/Newscom

like lattes, cappuccinos, and mochas—in direct competition with Starbucks and Dunkin' Donuts. McCafe's beverage offerings later expanded with fruit smoothies, shakes, frappes, and frozen lemonade. As McDonald's CEO Don Thompson says, "We want to be a beverage destination. For us, growing markets with great margins is the place to be."[9]

The four previous forces influence the rivalry among competitors. In addition, issues such as cost and differentiation or lack of differentiation of products—along with the Internet—influence the strategies that companies use to stand out from their competitors. With increased availability of information, which tends to level the playing field, rivalry heats up among competitors who try to differentiate themselves from the crowd.

FIRST MOVER AND SECOND MOVER STRATEGIES

first mover strategy
Theory advocating that the company first to offer a product in a marketplace will be the long-term market winner.

Some firms like to adopt a first mover strategy, attempting to capture the greatest market share and develop long-term relationships by being the first to enter the market with a good or service, as Virgin Galactic hopes to do by being the first to offer commercial space travel. Being first may also refer to entering new markets with existing products or creating significant innovations that effectively turn an old product into a new one. Naturally, this strategy has its risks—companies that follow can learn from mistakes by first movers. Some well-known first movers include Ford, IBM, Apple, Amazon .com, and MySpace. Each of these firms has stumbled at one time or another, but each is still in business. Ford is making a remarkable comeback, and IBM has risen from the ashes several times.

second mover strategy Theory that advocates observing closely the innovations of first movers and then improving on them to gain advantage in the marketplace.

Other businesses thrive on a second mover strategy, observing closely the innovations of first movers and then improving on them to gain advantage in the marketplace. Facebook appeared after MySpace. Target has followed in the footsteps of Walmart. Sometimes first movers are completely replaced by second movers and disappear from the marketplace altogether—as was the case with Pan American World Airways, a leading international airline until it went bankrupt in 1991.

SWOT ANALYSIS

SWOT analysis
Review that helps planners compare internal organizational strengths and weaknesses with external opportunities and threats.

An important strategic planning tool, SWOT analysis helps planners compare internal organizational strengths and weaknesses with external opportunities and threats. (SWOT is an acronym for

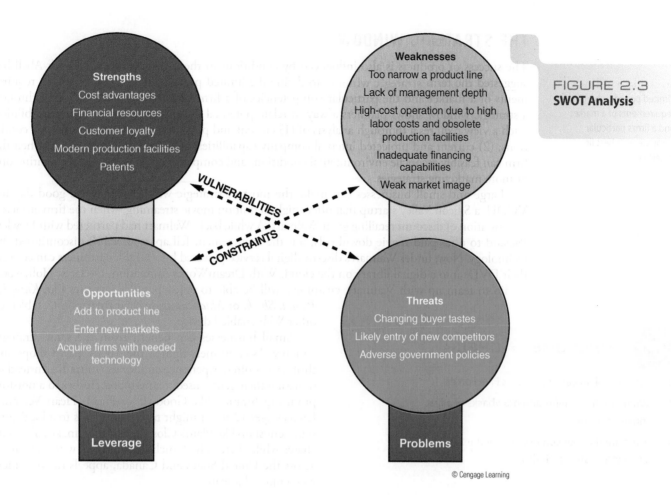

FIGURE 2.3
SWOT Analysis

© Cengage Learning

strengths, weaknesses, opportunities, and *threats.*) This form of analysis provides managers with a critical view of the organization's internal and external environments and helps them evaluate the firm's fulfillment of its basic mission.

A company's strengths reflect its core competencies—what it does well. Core competencies are capabilities that customers value and competitors find difficult to duplicate. As Figure 2.3 shows, matching an internal strength with an external opportunity produces a situation known as *leverage.* Marketers face a problem when environmental threats attack their organization's weaknesses. Planners anticipate constraints when internal weaknesses or limitations prevent their organization from taking advantage of opportunities. These internal weaknesses can create vulnerabilities for a company—environmental threats to its organizational strength. While the U.S. beverage maker Dr Pepper Snapple Group (DPSG) was under the umbrella of Britain's Cadbury, sales of its once popular drinks fizzled as distribution networks were neglected and marketers sometimes waited weeks or months for decisions from Cadbury headquarters. But once DPSG achieved a spin-off, it could concentrate on what it does best: making, distributing, and selling its more than 50 brands, which include Dr Pepper, Snapple, 7Up, RC Cola, Canada Dry, and others. Although soda consumption in the United States continues to decline, among the top five contenders, only Dr Pepper has seen growth. And DPSG recently unseated The Coca-Cola Company as the soft-drink vendor at Chicago's Soldier Field—a spot the Atlanta-based competitor had held for decades.[10]

Even if a company focuses on its core competencies, sometimes it needs to broaden its offerings to maintain a competitive edge. When marketing research revealed that parents were actually adding water to their children's juice drinks in order to reduce calories, DPSG came up with a new version of its Mott's apple juice, containing 40 percent less sugar but a full serving of juice. It's called Mott's for Tots. Another success has been Canada Dry Green Tea Ginger Ale, for consumers who are looking for the health benefits of green tea.[11]

THE STRATEGIC WINDOW

strategic window
Limited periods when key requirements of a market and a firm's particular competencies best fit together.

The success of products is also influenced by conditions in the market. Professor Derek Abell has suggested the term strategic window to define the limited periods during which the key requirements of a market and the particular competencies of a firm best fit together.[12] The view through a strategic window shows planners a way to relate potential opportunities to company capabilities. Such a view requires a thorough analysis of (1) current and projected external environmental conditions; (2) current and projected internal company capabilities; and (3) how, whether, and when the firm can feasibly reconcile environmental conditions and company capabilities by implementing one or more marketing strategies.

Large and small businesses can make the most of strategic windows. It was a good day for VUDU, a Silicon Valley startup that offers high-definition movie streaming, when the firm attracted the attention of discount retailing giant Walmart. A while back, Walmart had partnered with Hewlett Packard to offer paid movie downloads, but the arrangement fell apart after HP discontinued the technology. Now, under Walmart's disc-to-digital service powered by VUDU, customers can convert their DVDs into a digital library on the cloud. With DreamWorks Animation, the latest Hollywood studio to team up with Walmart, customers will be able to enjoy popular favorites like *Kung Fu Panda, Shrek,* or *Madagascar* on their smartphone, tablet, or other Web-enabled device.[13]

Small businesses can benefit from the same strategic window. As consumers tighten their belts, pawn shops and thrift stores often experience an increase in traffic. Instead of donating their gently used, name-brand clothes to a not-for-profit organization like Goodwill or Purple Heart Veterans, females ages 12 to 24 might take those items to a local consignment shop like Plato's Closet—and then make a few purchases while there. The franchise operation, with 300 stores across the United States and Canada, appeals to consumers who enjoy a bargain.[14]

⊕ ASSESSMENT CHECK

4.1   Briefly explain each of Porter's Five Forces.

4.2   What are the benefits and drawbacks of a first mover strategy?

4.3   What are the four components of the SWOT analysis? What is a strategic window?

Walmart and VUDU made the best of a strategic window recently when they partnered together. Now Walmart customers can convert their DVDs into a digital library using the VUDU service.

© Frances Roberts/Alamy

ELEMENTS OF A MARKETING STRATEGY

Success for a product in the marketplace—whether it is a tangible good, a service, a cause, a person, a place, or an organization—depends on an effective marketing strategy. It's one thing to develop a great product, but if customers don't get the message about it, the product will die. An effective marketing strategy reaches the right buyers at the right time, persuades them to try the product, and develops a strong relationship with them over time. The basic elements of a marketing strategy consist of (1) the target market and (2) the marketing mix variables of product, distribution, promotion, and price that combine to satisfy the needs of the target market. The outer circle in Figure 2.4 lists environmental characteristics that provide the framework within which marketing strategies are planned.

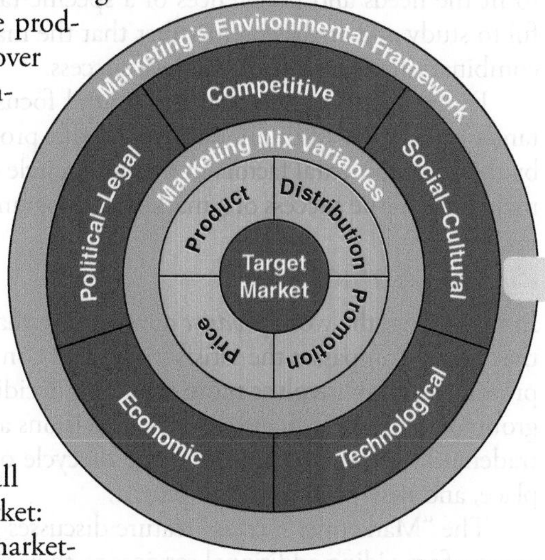

Identify the basic elements of a marketing strategy.

5

© Cengage Learning

FIGURE 2.4
Element of a Marketing Strategy and Its Environmental Framework

THE TARGET MARKET

A customer-driven organization begins its overall strategy with a detailed description of its target market: the group of people toward whom the firm aims its marketing efforts and ultimately its merchandise. Kohl's department stores serve a target market of consumers purchasing for themselves and their families. Other companies, such as Boeing, market most of their products to business buyers like Delta Airlines and government purchasers. Still other firms provide goods and services to retail and wholesale buyers. In every instance, however, marketers pinpoint their target markets as accurately as possible. Although the concept of dividing markets into specific segments is discussed in more detail in Chapter 9, it's important to understand the idea of targeting a market from the outset.

Although it may be hard to imagine the classic Oreo cookie as anything other than two discs of chocolate with a white cream filling, Kraft Foods (now called Mondelez International) reformulated the favorite to market it in China. The Chinese version consists of four layers of long, thin biscuits coated in chocolate, which marketers found was more appealing to consumers there. Since the cookie's makeover, Oreo sales in China have grown exponentially, and the Oreo's now the top-selling cookie in China. Says Lorna Davis, head of the company's biscuit division, "Any foreign company that comes to China and says 'There's 1½ billion people here, goody goody, and I only need 1 percent of that'…[is] going to get into trouble. You have to understand how the consumer operates at a really detailed level." The "remodeled" Oreo is now available in Australia and Canada, too.[15]

Diversity plays an ever-increasing role in targeting markets. According to the U.S. Census Bureau, the rapidly growing Hispanic population in the United States has surpassed African Americans as the largest minority group. The census reports more than 50 million Hispanics in America, or over 16 percent of the U.S. population.[16] With this phenomenal growth, marketers would be wise to pay attention to these and other markets—including women, seniors, and children of baby boomers—as they develop goods and services to offer consumers.

Targeting consumers in specific global markets also represents a challenge—and an opportunity. India is an enormous market that is culturally diverse within itself, containing 27 geographical states, numerous languages and religious practices, and a variety of lifestyles. Traditional Indian culture is infused with Western influences. And while nearly half of all Indian citizens earn less than $1 per day, a growing middle class boasts more than 50 million active users of social media. A recent Nielsen survey predicts that, soon, Indians will be more likely to access the Internet by their smartphone than their personal computer. Also, according to the survey, respondents want marketers to engage them with contests, sales and promotions, and tips on how to use their good or service.[17]

MARKETING MIX VARIABLES

After marketers select a target market, they direct their company's activities toward profitably satisfying that segment. Although they must manipulate thousands of variables to reach this goal, marketing decision making can be divided into four strategies: product, distribution, promotion, and pricing strategies. The total package forms the marketing mix—the blend of four strategic elements to fit the needs and preferences of a specific target market. While the fourfold classification is useful to study and analyze, remember that the marketing mix can—and should—be an ever-changing combination of variables to achieve success.

Figure 2.4 illustrates that the central focus of the marketing mix variables is the choice of the target market. In addition, decisions about product, distribution, promotion, and price are affected by the environmental factors in the outer circle of the figure. The environmental variables may play a major role in the success of a marketing program, and marketers must consider their probable effects.

Product Strategy

In marketing, the word *product* means more than a good, service, or idea. Product is a broad concept that also encompasses the satisfaction of all consumer needs in relation to a good, service, or idea. So product strategy involves more than just deciding what goods or services the firm should offer to a group of consumers. It also includes decisions about customer service, package design, brand names, trademarks, patents, warranties, the lifecycle of a product, positioning the product in the marketplace, and new-product development.

The "Marketing Success" feature discusses how retailers have brought back layaway programs as a way of providing additional services to their customers.

marketing mix
Blending of the four strategy elements—product, distribution, promotion, and pricing—to fit the needs and preferences of a specific target market.

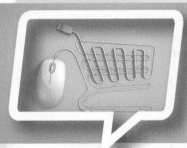

MARKETING SUCCESS

Layaway Programs Enjoy a Comeback

Background. In the past, retailers used layaway programs to offer customers the opportunity to put goods on hold and pay for them on a weekly basis, particularly during the holiday season. This strategy helped customers buy goods they thought could be out of stock as the holidays approached and pay for them in small cash deposits rather than use credit cards and often incur finance charges.

The Challenge. When the economy was booming several years ago, retailers did away with layaway programs because consumers had available credit to purchase goods outright, and the programs cost the retailers money that wasn't a good investment.

The Strategy. As the recession took hold, and consumers felt the pinch of less disposable income and higher credit card fees and interest rates, retailers found sales were lagging. To help increase the bottom line and attract more shoppers into their stores, retailers such as Walmart, Target, Kmart, and Toys "R" Us decided to bring back layaway programs.

The Outcome. Both retailers and consumers win with layaway programs. Retailers get shoppers to buy things they otherwise wouldn't buy, and the programs bring shoppers back in the store to pay off their layaway purchases on a weekly basis—perhaps encouraging them to buy more goods on their multiple visits. Consumers benefit from layaway programs because they are not incurring credit card debt with these retail purchases. In fact, competition among retailers has heated up for layaway purchases. Recently, Walmart started its holiday layaway program a month earlier than in previous years. Other retailers have waived layaway fees not only for holiday purchases but also for year-round purchases.

Sources: Brad Tuttle, "Why Stores and Shoppers Alike Are Embracing Layaway," *Time*, accessed November 6, 2012, http://business.time.com; Oliver St. John and Jayne O'Donnell, "Kmart Follows Toys R Us and Drops Layaway Fees," *USA Today*, accessed November 7, 2012, http://usatoday30.usatoday.com; Josh Sanburn, "The Latest Expansion of the Holiday Season: Layaway at Walmart Starts a Month Early This Year," *Time*, accessed November 7, 2012, http://business.time.com; Jay MacDonald, "Layaway Makes a Comeback," *Bankrate.com*, accessed November 7, 2012, www.bankrate.com.

Distribution Strategy

Marketers develop distribution strategies to ensure that consumers find their products in the proper quantities at the right times and places. Distribution decisions involve modes of transportation, warehousing, inventory control, order processing, and selection of marketing channels. Marketing channels are made up of institutions such as retailers and wholesalers—intermediaries that may be involved in a product's movement from producer to final consumer.

Technology continually opens new channels of distribution in many industries. The Internet has caused the biggest revolution in distribution since the mail-order catalog. Computer software and digital music files are obvious candidates, but everything from DVDs to motorcycles to houses can be found on the Web. E-readers like Amazon's Kindle and Barnes and Noble's Nook allow consumers to download and read books and periodicals that were once the domain of the printed page. Some publications, like *Bloomberg Businessweek* and *The Wall Street Journal*, offer both online and print content, with the online version sometimes free (although that is beginning to change). But other publications have abandoned print altogether or were established entirely online in the first place.

Promotion Strategy

Promotion is the communications link between sellers and buyers. Organizations use varied ways to send messages about their goods, services, and ideas. They may communicate messages directly through salespeople or indirectly through advertisements and promotions. Promotions often offer a product at a reduced price for a limited time, bundle two or more products together, or give away a premium (such as a toy) with purchase. National supermarket chains like Safeway periodically aim to stimulate sales by disseminating coupons that offer $5 or $10 off a large grocery purchase. Online sites for retailers like Lands End and Macy's frequently offer free shipping on orders. Eddie Bauer offered a "tax relief" discount of 15 percent at income-tax time. During a recent promotion to celebrate the release of the Dunkin' Donuts App, the company hosted a sweepstakes on Twitter, offering 20 lucky fans a chance to win a gift card for tweeting @DunkinDonuts with the hashtag #Dunkin App. The company has more than 160,000 Twitter followers.[18]

In developing a promotional strategy, marketers blend the various elements of promotion to communicate most effectively with their target market. Many companies use an approach called

As a promotion strategy to stimulate sales, Macy's offers free shipping on orders.

© NetPhotos/Alamy

integrated marketing communications (IMC) to coordinate all promotional activities so that the consumer receives a unified and consistent message. Consumers might receive newsletters, email updates, discount coupons, catalogs, invitations to company-sponsored events, and any number of other types of marketing communications about a product. Honda dealers mail maintenance and service reminders to their customers. Wendy's places discount coupons in local sales circulars. A political candidate may send volunteer workers through a neighborhood to invite voters to a local reception.

Pricing Strategy

Pricing strategy deals with the methods of setting profitable and justifiable prices. It is closely regulated and subject to considerable public scrutiny. One of the many factors that influence a marketer's pricing strategy is competition. The computer industry has become all too familiar with price cuts by both current competitors and new market entrants. After years of steady growth, the market has become saturated with low-cost computers, driving down profit margins even farther. A good pricing strategy should create value for customers, building and strengthening their relationship with a firm and its products. But sometimes conditions in the external marketing environment cause difficulties in pricing strategies. Political unrest overseas, the soaring price of fuel, or a freeze that destroys crops could all affect the price of goods and services. If the economy is booming, consumers generally have more confidence and are willing to shop more often and pay more for discretionary goods. But when the economy takes a downturn, consumers look for bargains—they want high quality at low prices. It is a challenge for marketers to strike the right balance in order to make enough profits to survive and grow. Currently, sales at luxury retailers like Saks and Abercrombie & Fitch are down. But sales at local dollar stores, cheaper supermarkets, and the larger discount retailers are much stronger—and are even luring shoppers away from traditional giants like Target and Walmart.[19]

ASSESSMENT CHECK

5.1 What are the two components of every marketing strategy?

5.2 Identify the four strategic elements of the marketing mix.

THE MARKETING ENVIRONMENT

6 Describe the environmental characteristics that influence strategic decisions.

Marketers do not make decisions about target markets and marketing mix variables in a vacuum. They must take into account the dynamic nature of the five dimensions of the marketing environment shown back in Figure 2.4: competitive, political–legal, economic, technological, and social–cultural factors. It's important to note that these five dimensions overlap, interact, and fluctuate.

Concerns about the natural environment have led to new and tighter regulations on air and water pollution, which affect the political–legal environment in which marketers operate. Efforts toward sustainability are now social–cultural factors as well because consumer awareness is turning into consumer preference. Automobile engineers, for instance, have turned public concerns and legal issues into opportunities by developing hybrid cars, autos that run on biodiesel, and electric vehicles. In fact, the race to bring to market the most fuel-efficient vehicles for the future has become extremely competitive.

Businesses are increasingly looking to foreign shores for new growth markets. Of course, these opportunities represent economic, political–legal, and social–cultural challenges as well. The U.S. Department of Commerce provides resources, including contact lists and matching services, for companies trying to enter the market in Romania. Its Gold Key Matching Service helps develop partnerships between U.S. firms and local firms in Romania. The export.gov website reports, "Romania offers significant opportunities to American businesses with products, services, or technologies that either meet growing private demand or contribute to the country's development priorities." For businesses, Romania's attractions include a well-educated workforce with over 50,000 IT specialists, an expanding economy, and access to the Black Sea and Asia.[20]

Technology continually changes the marketing environment. Marketers are now increasing efforts to get their messages to consumers via smartphone with free mobile apps. For example, Starbucks provides an app that lets customers pay for their coffee with their smartphone. Using the Marriott Mobile App, you can make a hotel reservation, browse city guides, or check your Marriott

Resale shops like Plato's Closet appeal to consumers' efforts to help the environment by recycling their gently used clothing.

Rewards account. In the mood for a pizza? Domino's recently launched an ordering app for both Android phones and iPhones. The company says pizza orders placed online or by mobile phone represent more than one-third of its business. To boost the already growing segment, the Ann Arbor, Michigan-based pizza maker offered free smartphones to eligible customers.[21]

In the competitive environment, some experts have coined the phrase *rule of three*, meaning that in any industry, the three strongest, most efficient companies dominate between 70 and 90 percent of the competitive market. Here are a few examples—all of which are household names:

Cereal manufacturers: General Mills, Kellogg's, Post

Running shoes: Nike, Fila USA, Reebok

Supermarkets: Walmart, Kroger, Supervalu

Pharmaceuticals: Merck, Pfizer, Bristol-Myers Squibb

While it may seem like an uphill battle for the remaining companies in any given industry, they can find a strategy for gaining competitive ground.

The social–cultural environment includes a variety of factors, including prevailing cultural norms. As the novelty of bidding for auction items on eBay has worn off for consumers who don't necessarily have the time or desire to wait several days or a week for auction results, eBay has begun to reshape itself. Fixed-price merchandise has become the new norm. The "Buy It Now" option—designed with smartphones in mind—now accounts for more than 60 percent of eBay purchases. The company expects mobile purchases to add revenues of nearly $5 billion per year.[22] This new trend also reflects economic factors, including how much consumers are willing and able to spend.

The entire marketing environment provides a framework for

ASSESSMENT CHECK

6.1 What are the five dimensions of the marketing environment?

6.2 How is concern over the natural environment affecting the other dimensions?

Domino's Pizza has Android and iPhone apps that let customers place orders for pizza. The company reports that online and mobile phone orders represent more than one-third of its business.

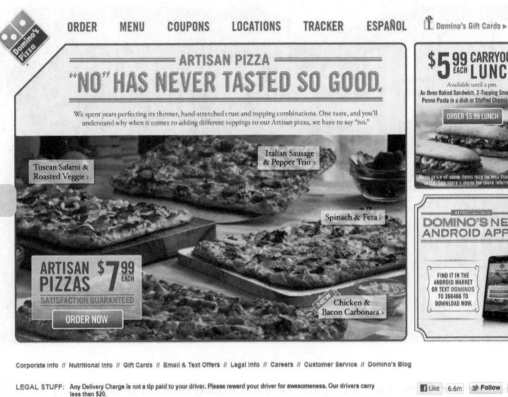

all marketing activity. Marketers consider environmental dimensions when they develop strategies for segmenting and targeting markets and when they study consumer and organizational buying behavior.

METHODS FOR MARKETING PLANNING

7 Describe the methods for marketing planning, including business portfolio analysis and the BCG matrix.

As growing numbers of companies have discovered the benefits of effective marketing planning, they have developed planning methods to assist in this important function. This section discusses two useful methods: the strategic business unit concept and the market share/market growth matrix.

BUSINESS PORTFOLIO ANALYSIS

Although a small company may offer only a few items to its customers, a larger organization frequently offers and markets many products to widely diverse markets. Bank of America offers a wide range of financial products to businesses and consumers. Kraft Foods stocks supermarket shelves with everything from macaroni and cheese to mayonnaise and offers everything from cookware to cutlery online. Top managers at these larger firms need a method for spotting product lines that deserve more investment as well as lines that aren't living up to expectations. So they conduct a portfolio analysis, in which they evaluate their company's products and divisions to determine the strongest and weakest. Similar to how securities analysts review their portfolios of stocks and bonds, deciding which to retain and which to discard, marketing planners must assess their products, the regions in which they operate, and other marketing mix variables. This is where the concept of an SBU comes in.

Strategic business units (SBUs) are key business units within diversified firms. Each SBU has its own managers, resources, objectives, and competitors. A division, product line, or single product may define the boundaries of an SBU. Each SBU pursues its own distinct mission and often develops its own plans independently of other units in the organization.

Strategic business units, also called categories, focus the attention of company managers so that they can respond effectively to changing consumer demand within limited markets. Companies may have to redefine their SBUs as market conditions dictate. IBM was once known as a manufacturer of high-quality clocks. Today, the firm markets everything from computer servers and systems, software, and Internet security to printing paper and toner. Its slogan, "Welcome to the Decade of Smart," conveys the firm's forward-thinking philosophy. The old IBM clocks have become valuable collectibles.[23]

The IBM clock was once sold as a product from one of IBM's strategic business units.

strategic business units (SBUs) Key business units within diversified firms.

THE BCG MATRIX

To evaluate each of their organization's strategic business units, marketers need some type of portfolio performance framework. A widely used framework was developed by the Boston Consulting Group (BCG). This market share/market growth matrix places SBUs in a four-quadrant chart that plots market share against market growth potential. Market share is the percentage of a market that a firm currently controls (or company sales divided by total market sales). The position of an SBU along the horizontal axis indicates its market share relative to those of competitors in the industry. Its position along the vertical axis indicates the annual growth rate of the market. After plotting all of a firm's business units, planners divide them according to the matrix's four quadrants. Figure 2.5 illustrates this matrix by labeling the four quadrants: stars, cash cows, question marks, and dogs. Firms in each quadrant require a unique marketing strategy.

Stars represent units with high market shares in high-growth markets. These products or businesses are high-growth market leaders. Although they generate considerable income, they need considerable inflows of cash to finance further growth. The Apple iPhone is the number-one-selling smartphone in the United States, but in order to maintain that position, Apple will have to continue offering new models to demanding and tech-savvy consumers.[24]

Cash cows command high market shares in low-growth markets. Marketers for such an SBU want to maintain this status for as long as possible. The business produces strong cash flows, but instead of investing heavily in the unit's own promotions and production capacity, the firm can use this cash to finance the growth of other SBUs with higher growth potentials. For instance, Microsoft uses the profits from sales of its Windows operating system to finance research and development for new Internet-based technologies.[25]

Question marks achieve low market shares in high-growth markets. Marketers must decide whether to continue supporting these products or businesses because question marks typically

Relative Market Share

	High	Low
High Industry Growth Rate	**Stars** Generate considerable income **Strategy:** Invest more funds for future growth	**Question Marks** Have potential to become stars or cash cows **Strategy:** Either invest more funds for growth or consider disinvesting
Low	**Cash Cows** Generate strong cash flow **Strategy:** Milk profits to finance growth of stars and question marks	**Dogs** Generate little profits **Strategy:** Consider withdrawing

FIGURE 2.5
BCG Market Share/ Market Growth Matrix

© Cengage Learning

require considerably more cash than they generate. If a question mark cannot become a star, the firm should pull out of the market and target other markets with greater potential.

U.S. Bancorp recently stopped making student loans, citing the high default rate on such loans and the bank's decision to expand its wholesale banking division. Industry observers also suggest that the federal government's stepped-up oversight of banks' loans to students played a role in U.S. Bancorp's decision.[26]

Dogs manage only low market shares in low-growth markets. SBUs in this category promise poor future prospects, and marketers should withdraw from these businesses or product lines as quickly as possible. In some cases, these products can be sold to other firms, where they are a better fit. Some firms build their entire business on other companies' dogs, purchasing recipes or manufacturing techniques. Blair Candy, an online candy retailer, specializes in hard-to-find favorites like Mallo Cups, Necco Wafers, and Zagnut candy bars.[27]

⊕ ASSESSMENT CHECK

7.1 What are SBUs?

7.2 Identify the four quadrants in the BCG matrix.

STRATEGIC IMPLICATIONS OF MARKETING IN THE 21ST CENTURY

Never before has planning been as important to marketers as the 21st century speeds ahead with technological advances. Marketers need to plan carefully, accurately, and quickly if their companies are to gain a competitive advantage in today's global marketplace. They need to define their organization's mission and understand the different methods for formulating a successful marketing strategy. They must consider a changing, diverse population and the boundaryless business environment created by the Internet. They must be able to evaluate when it's best to be first to get into a market and when it's best to wait. They need to recognize when they've got a star and when they've got a dog—when to hang on and when to let go. As daunting as this seems, planning can reduce the risk and worry of bringing new goods and services to the marketplace.

REVIEW OF CHAPTER OBJECTIVES

1 Distinguish between strategic planning and tactical planning.

Strategic planning is the process of identifying an organization's primary objectives and adopting courses of action toward these objectives. In other words, strategic planning focuses on the big picture of which industries are central to a firm's business. Tactical planning guides the implementation of the activities specified in the strategic plan. Once a strategy is set, operational managers devise methods (tactics) to achieve the larger goals.

2 Explain how marketing plans differ at various levels in an organization.

Top management spends more time engaged in strategic planning than middle- and supervisory-level managers, who tend to focus on narrower, tactical plans for their units. Supervisory managers are more likely to develop specific plans designed to meet the goals assigned to them, for example, streamlining production processes so that they operate more efficiently.

3 Identify the steps in the marketing planning process.

The basic steps in the marketing planning process are defining the organization's mission and objectives; assessing organizational resources and evaluating environmental risks and opportunities; and formulating, implementing, and monitoring the marketing strategy.

4 Describe successful planning tools and techniques, including Porter's Five Forces model, first and second mover strategies, SWOT analysis, and the strategic window.

Porter's Five Forces are identified as the five competitive factors that influence planning strategies: potential new entrants, bargaining power of buyers, bargaining power of suppliers, threat of substitute products, and rivalry among competitors. With a first mover strategy, a firm attempts to capture the greatest market share by being first to enter the market; with a second mover strategy, a firm observes the

innovations of first movers and then attempts to improve on them to gain advantage. SWOT analysis (strengths, weaknesses, opportunities, and threats) helps planners compare internal organizational strengths and weaknesses with external opportunities and threats. The strategic window identifies the limited periods during which the key requirements of a market and the competencies of a firm best fit together.

5 Identify the basic elements of a marketing strategy.

Development of a marketing strategy is a two-step process: (1) selecting a target market and (2) designing an effective marketing mix to satisfy the chosen target. The target market is the group of people toward whom a company decides to direct its marketing efforts. The marketing mix blends four strategy elements to fit the needs and preferences of a specific target market: product strategy, distribution strategy, promotion strategy, and pricing strategy.

6 Describe the environmental characteristics that influence strategic decisions.

The five dimensions of the marketing environment are competitive, political–legal, economic, technological, and social–cultural. Marketers must also address growing concern about the natural environment—including new regulations—and increasing cultural diversity in the global marketplace.

7 Describe the methods for marketing planning, including business portfolio analysis and the BCG matrix.

The business portfolio analysis evaluates a company's products and divisions, including strategic business units (SBUs). The SBU focuses the attention of company managers so that they can respond effectively to changing consumer demand within certain markets. The BCG matrix places SBUs in a four-quadrant chart that plots market share against market growth potential. The four quadrants are stars, cash cows, dogs, and question marks.

ASSESSMENT CHECK: ANSWERS

1.1 Define *planning*. Planning is the process of anticipating future events and conditions and of determining the best way to achieve organizational objectives.

1.2 Give an example of strategic planning and tactical planning. To survive in a challenging environment that includes soaring fuel costs, several airlines have decided to combine as part of their strategic planning. Tactical plans include cutting the number of flights and charging passengers extra for checked baggage.

2.1 How do marketing plans vary at different levels of the organization? Top managers usually focus their planning activities on long-range strategic issues. In contrast, middle-level managers focus on operational planning, which includes creating and implementing tactical plans for their own units. Supervisors develop specific programs to meet the goals in their areas of responsibility.

2.2 Why is it important to get input from others when planning? Input from a variety of sources—other employees, suppliers, or customers—helps ensure that many ideas are considered. Involving those people in planning can also turn them into advocates for the plan.

3.1 Distinguish between an organization's mission and its objectives. The firm's mission is the essential purpose that differentiates the company from others. Its objectives guide development of supporting marketing objectives and plans. Avon's mission is to be "the company for women." One of its objectives might be to convert all its packaging to recycled materials.

3.2 What is the importance of the final step in the marketing planning process? In the final step of the marketing planning process, managers monitor performance to ensure that objectives are achieved.

4.1 Briefly explain each of Porter's Five Forces. Porter's Five Forces are the threats of potential new entrants, which increases competition in a market; bargaining power of buyers, which can depress prices; bargaining power of suppliers, which can increase costs or reduce selection; threat of substitute products, which can lure customers to other products; and rivalry among competitors, which can bring about price wars or divert companies from their main goals.

4.2 What are the benefits and drawbacks of a first mover strategy? The benefits of a first mover strategy include capturing the greatest market share and developing long-term relationships with customers. Disadvantages include the possibility that companies that follow can learn from mistakes by first movers. Procter & Gamble has been a first mover with its line of Swiffer products.

4.3 What are the four components of the SWOT analysis? What is a strategic window? SWOT analysis helps planners compare internal organizational strengths and weaknesses with external opportunities and threats. SWOT is an acronym for *strengths*, *weaknesses*, *opportunities*, and *threats*. A strategic window defines the limited periods when key requirements of a market and a firm's particular competencies best fit together.

5.1 What are the two components of every marketing strategy? The basic elements of a marketing strategy are (1) the target market and (2) the marketing mix variables.

5.2 Identify the four strategic elements of the marketing mix. The marketing mix consists of product, distribution, promotion, and pricing strategies.

6.1 What are the five dimensions of the marketing environment? The five dimensions of the marketing environment are competitive, political–legal, economic, technological, and social–cultural factors.

6.2 How is concern over the natural environment affecting the other dimensions? Concerns over the natural environment have led to new and tighter regulations on pollution, which affect the political–legal environment in which marketers operate. Efforts toward sustainability are now social–cultural factors as well because consumer awareness is turning into consumer preference.

7.1 What are SBUs? Strategic business units (SBUs) are key business units within diversified firms. Each SBU has its own managers, resources, objectives, and competitors.

7.2 Identify the four quadrants in the BCG matrix. The BCG matrix labels SBUs stars, cash cows, question marks, and dogs. Stars are the products with high market shares in high-growth markets; cash cows command high market shares in low-growth markets; question marks achieve low market shares in high-growth markets; and dogs manage only low market shares in low-growth markets.

MARKETING TERMS YOU NEED TO KNOW

planning **35**

marketing planning **36**

strategic planning **37**

tactical planning **37**

mission **38**

marketing strategy **39**

Porter's Five Forces **41**

first mover strategy **42**

second mover strategy **42**

SWOT analysis **42**

strategic window **44**

marketing mix **46**

strategic business units (SBUs) **51**

ASSURANCE OF LEARNING REVIEW

1. State whether each of the following illustrates strategic or tactical planning:
   a. Global automakers begin setting up manufacturing plants in India.
   b. The merging of Play N Trade Video Games and Dimensions Games Corporation.
   c. The Washington Redskins trade multiple draft picks to draft Baylor QB Robert Griffin III.
   d. A regional airline looks for ways to expand to other areas of the country.

2. Imagine you had a chance to interview Google co-founders Larry Page and Sergey Brin. What questions might you ask each about strategic planning for individual divisions and for the firm overall?

3. What is the difference between a firm's mission and its objectives? Why is it important that both are conveyed clearly to employees and to customers?

4. Over which of Porter's Five Forces do consumers have the greatest influence? Over which do they have the least? How might these factors affect a firm's overall marketing strategy?

5. Why is it so important for a firm to identify its core competencies?

6. How might an understanding of diversity help formulate a firm's marketing strategy?

7. Suppose you have been hired as a marketer by an online retailer, like Bluefly or Amazon, to help develop a new marketing mix. State one thing you would do to improve the retailer's position through each of the four strategic elements: product, distribution, promotion, and pricing.

8. What is the *rule of three?* Suppose you worked for a small firm in a large industry—such as a small manufacturer of furniture. How might you actually use the rule of three to enhance your firm's position in the marketplace?

9. What is a *portfolio analysis?* What purpose does it serve for marketers?

10. How does the BCG matrix help marketers decide which products to offer? According to the matrix, which types of products are most desirable, and why?

PROJECTS AND TEAMWORK EXERCISES

1. Choose one of the following companies, or select another one whose goods and services are familiar to you. On your own or with a classmate, formulate a mission statement for that company. Then create a list of objectives that reflect your company's mission.
   a. Marathon Oil
   b. Scottrade
   c. Raytheon
   d. Verizon

2. Using a first mover strategy, Apple's iPod and iPhone have clearly established the lead in their markets. Research the products of another firm that produces either a digital music player or a smartphone to learn about its strategy. How has a second mover strategy benefited the firm? Has the second mover firm been able to catch Apple in sales?

3. When rivals Samsung and Sony each unveiled their new 3D TVs at a major electronics store, some consumers couldn't tell the difference between the two. But the firm's strategies were very different. Sony opted to use outside manufacturing firms to build its TVs, stating that the move would help cut costs and keep the company strong. But Samsung manufactures its own TVs, including its own computer chips. Since then, the two firms have experienced quite different outcomes.[28] With a classmate, research the two companies and their 3D TVs, evaluating their marketing strategy. Who is the target market for both of these TVs? How does product, distribution, promotion, and pricing fit into each firm's overall marketing strategy? In your opinion, how did the firms' strategies affect their respective outcomes?

4. Select one of the following industries and research which firms might fall into the top three in the industry, creating a rule of three:
   a. online securities trading
   b. upscale hotels
   c. electronics retailing
   d. auto manufacturing

5. On your own or with a classmate, research one of the following large corporations. Select several product lines and classify each in the BCG matrix.
   a. 3M
   b. Johnson & Johnson
   c. Condé Nast Publications
   d. General Electric (GE)

CRITICAL-THINKING EXERCISES

1. Suppose you are a marketer for a U.S. manufacturer of pet supplies. Two top executives have proposed expanding the company by opening retail stores and marketing pets on-site—puppies, kittens, rabbits, birds, fish, and the like. What are the potential benefits and drawbacks of making a move like this? How would you advise your company to proceed?

2. Netflix has made thousands of streaming videos available to its subscribers. How does this strategy demonstrate a strategic window for the company?

3. Choose one of the following products and describe how it may (or already has) become vulnerable to substitution. Then describe an overall strategy—with two or three tactics—for reducing this vulnerability.
   a. printed copies of periodicals or books
   b. television
   c. telephone landlines
   d. travel agencies

4. Research the website of one of the following retail firms to identify its target market. Then outline a strategy for expanding that target market.
   a. Quiznos
   b. Target
   c. Trader Joe's
   d. Nordstrom
   e. Dollar Tree

5. Research a company such as L.L. Bean or Mondelez International (formerly Kraft Foods) that has a number of different successful SBUs. What factors do you think make these units—and this company—successful from a marketing standpoint?

ETHICS EXERCISE

A recent news story reported a shocker from the Centers for Disease Control and Prevention (CDCP): bread is the number-one source of sodium in the average American diet. In fact, most people get twice as much sodium from bread and rolls as they do from a bag of salty snacks like chips or pretzels.[29] Imagine that you are a marketer for a baking company whose main product lines are bread and rolls. For years, your company has focused on "heart-healthy" as a key claim.

1. You have been assigned to create a new strategy and tactics for your firm's Facebook page. Would you continue to emphasize

the heart-healthy message? Would you refer to the CDCP study or ignore it?

2. As you review the Facebook site, you note that packaging for your company's bread uses the words "heart-healthy." Would you bring this to the attention of the marketing group responsible for product packaging? Or would you look for a way to obscure the package design online? Defend your answer.

INTERNET EXERCISES

1. **Business portfolio analysis.** Occasionally, companies sell parts of themselves to other firms. One stated motive for such divestitures is that the sold assets are a poor strategic fit for the rest of their business portfolios. One recent example is the sale of a controlling interest in NBC Universal by General Electric to cable giant Comcast. Using a major search engine, research the sale of NBC Universal. In the context of business portfolio analysis, why did GE decide to sell, and why did Comcast decide to buy, NBC Universal?

2. **Mission and objectives.** Visit the website of Hillshire Brands, whose slogan is "Go meat!". Define the firm's mission and objectives, and discuss how its brands and activities support both.
   www.hillshirebrands.com

3. **SWOT analysis.** Visit the website of an organization whose goods and services interest you—such as Columbia Sportswear, Major League Baseball, Travelocity, Apple, or Urban Outfitters. Based on your research, create a SWOT analysis for your firm. Outline your own ideas for increasing the firm's strengths and reducing its weaknesses.

Note: Internet Web addresses change frequently. If you don't find the exact site listed, you may need to access the organization's home page and search from there or use a search engine such as Google or Bing.

CASE 2.1
Hotels Market New Comforts Just for Millennials

Poised to become the largest consumer group in U.S. history, the Millennials (born between 1977 and 1994) wield spending power of about $200 billion a year. They differ from Baby Boomers (born 1946–1964) in many ways, including their preferences when staying at a hotel. Millennials feel "interesting is more important than comfort." They also lack brand loyalty for hotels, making competition for their business fierce.

Hotel chains are therefore hurrying to upgrade their facilities to attract these young guests in sneakers and baseball caps, who aren't completely at home in quiet lobbies that reek of Olde England. Chains like Hilton, Starwood, Marriott, and InterContinental have installed sleek and comfortable new lounges with stylish bars, plush furniture, areas for socializing, out-in-the-open power consoles for recharging electronics, and electronic concierge services. They've added state-of-the-art gyms, happy hours, free wine and tea tastings, yoga classes, designer shower heads, check-in kiosks to replace registration desks, and of course Wi-Fi access and high-speed Internet, which one observer described as "almost like air to Millennials."

While Baby Boomers enjoy the solitude of their rooms after a long day of business or sightseeing, Millennials like to visit several restaurants and bars during their travels, so some hotels are introducing multiple eateries and lounges, all designed with different themes to create variety and keep guests from spending their entertainment budgets elsewhere. New York's Plaza Hotel puts an iPad in every room that lets guests control light and temperature, skim the morning news, and place room-service orders. Starwood Hotels and Resorts Worldwide set up a 20-member team to monitor and respond to guests' complaints and suggestions—but not at a desk in the lobby. This team works solely online, constantly monitoring Twitter posts by their outspoken guests.

And, of course, hotels are increasing their own online presence, including on Facebook, Twitter, Google+, and YouTube, since the vast majority of travel arrangements are now made online. It's all part of the hotel industry's effort to woo a group whose travel spending rose 20 percent in one recent year. The business has come a long way from placing chocolates on the pillow at night.

QUESTIONS FOR CRITICAL THINKING

1. Hotel chains see Millennials as "critical" to their financial growth. What are some reasons why?

2. How should the hotel industry use social media to connect with younger travelers?

Sources: Erin Mulligan Nelson, "Millennials Want to Party with Your Brand But on Their Own Terms," *Advertising Age*, accessed November 6, 2012, www.adage.com; "Generation Y: More Emotional, Less Loyal," *MarketMetrix.com*, accessed November 6, 2012, www.marketmetrix.com; Janet Morrissey, "The Millennials Check In," *The New York Times*, accessed November 6, 2012, www.nytimes.com; Corey Eridon, "Why User-Generated Content Is More Important Than You Think," *Hubspot.com*, accessed November 6, 2012, http://blog.hubspot.com.

VIDEO CASE 2.2
Nederlander Producing Company Spotlights Customer Rewards

Three to five million people pass through the turnstiles of Nederlander Producing Company theaters each year in New York City. "Why can't they get something for that?" asks James L. Nederlander, president of the company. Nederlander, whose family founded and has run the Nederlander Producing Company for more than 100 years, touches on a central question for every business: How can we serve and reward our customers?

Serving customers, building a relationship with them, and achieving a competitive advantage while doing so requires strategic and tactical planning. Nederlander Producing Company is a third-generation family-owned company that owns and manages theaters as well as produces and promotes live shows across the United States and the United Kingdom. Nederlander presents such diverse acts as the Bolshoi Ballet, *The Lion King*, and Celine Dion. Strategic planning, which includes identifying Nederlander's primary objectives and figuring out how to attain them, is vital to the company's longevity. One of Nederlander's main objectives is to draw more people toward the performing arts—and keep them there.

Recently, the executive team at Nederlander came up with a new way to do exactly that: Audience Rewards. "When I buy Corn Flakes or a stick of gum, I get points," Nederlander observes. "So why can't our customers get points for buying a theater ticket?" The program functions much like a frequent-flyer plan for theatergoers. Consumers sign up online for free, get a membership number, and start earning points toward rewards, such as free theater tickets, seat upgrades, Broadway merchandise, and even a photo shoot at one of the red-carpet events. The idea is to motivate people to attend the theater more often and try different experiences. It's a tried-and-true tactic with several twists, implemented with digital marketing and the human resources to back it up.

You don't have to see a show in order to rack up points. You can enter online contests like "Predictions for Points," in which you predict the 26 Tony Award winners. You automatically get five points for any prediction, but you could win up to 100,000 points if you get them all right. You can answer Audience Rewards trivia questions throughout the year for points as well. And you can score points through Audience Reward partner companies, such as Starwood Hotels, Delta Airlines, US Airways, United Airlines, Amtrak, Best Buy, and Points.com.

Josh Lesnick, president and CEO of Audience Rewards, notes that large corporations have been eager to become partners in Audience Rewards because "we really bring forward a lifestyle product." For example, a couple who visits New York from Cincinnati may fly on Delta, stay at the Sheraton in Midtown, and buy tickets to see *Wicked*. Then there's the fact that the average annual household income for the Audience Rewards target market hovers around $200,000—and companies like Starwood and the major airlines want access to those consumers.

Audience Rewards doesn't just benefit theater enthusiasts—it also helps the show go on. Recently, Nederlander ran an Audience Rewards program for the Broadway show *Evita*, in which marketers sent out 5 million emails over 10 days, offering discounts on advance-purchase tickets as well as other perks. The push generated $1 million in pre-sales, allowing the theater producers to strategically reallocate some resources. On a broader scale, the program gives Nederlander and its partners a central platform across which to market different venues and performing arts genres, and opens the door to audience development—which circles back to that initial objective of attracting more theatergoers and keeping them in their seats.

As a first-mover strategy, Audience Rewards has already sealed the premier spot in the entertainment rewards arena. Nederlander has a century of connections to theater owners, producers, and presenters (not to mention its own string of theaters and productions) that would be tough for any competitor to break. "It would be hard for someone else to do an arts rewards program," explains Lesnick, "because you have to have the backing of theater companies, and they already back ours."

QUESTIONS FOR CRITICAL THINKING

1. How does the Audience Rewards program support Nederlander's overall strategic plan?

2. It might seem as though Nederlander's first-mover strategy has the entertainment rewards market locked up. But what strategies and tactics could a second-strategy mover use to gain access to theater customers?

Sources: "About Nederlander," www.nederlander.com, accessed November 6, 2012; "The Nederlander Organization Announces Audience Rewards, the First Patron Appreciation Program for Broadway," *PR Newswire*, http://iac.mediaroom.com, accessed November 6, 2012; "The Broadway League Names Audience Rewards the Official Patron Loyalty Program for Broadway," *PR Newswire*, www.prnewswire .com; "American Airlines Takes the Stage at the Nederlander Organization with New Partnership in New York City," *PR Newswire*, www.prnewswire.com, accessed November 6, 2012.

NOTES

1. Patricia Sellers, "Marissa Mayer: Ready to Rumble at Yahoo," *Fortune*, accessed November 2, 2012, http://postcards.blogs.fortune.cnn.com; Nicholas Carlson, "Here Is the Plan Marissa Mayer Just Announced to Yahoo Employees," *Business Insider*, accessed November 2, 2012, www.businessinsider.com; Jeff Bercovici, "No 'Giant Pivot' in Store for Yahoo, Says Marissa Mayer," *Forbes*, accessed November 2, 2012, www.forbes.com; Julianne Pepitone, "Yahoo Earnings 'Solid' for Marissa Mayer's First Quarter," *CNNMoney*, accessed November 2, 2012, http://money.cnn.com; Nicole Perlroth, "Yahoo's CEO, Marissa Mayer, Returns to Work with New COO," *The New York Times*, accessed November 2, 2012, www.nytimes.com.

2. Company website, "Our 500th Astronaut—Ashton Kutcher!" www.virgin.com/richard-branson/blog, accessed November 2, 2012; Christine Kearney, "Ashton Kutcher to Fly on Branson's First Spacecraft," *Reuters*, accessed November 2, 2012, www.reuters.com.

3. Company website, www.shuttleworth.com, accessed November 2, 2012.

4. Company website, www.pg.com, accessed November 2, 2012.

5. Texas News, "JetBlue Pilot in Disturbance Not Guilty Due to Insanity," *NBCDFW.com*, accessed November 2, 2012, www.nbcdfw.com; "Rant on American Airlines Flight Ends with Flight Attendant in Hospital," *ABC News*, accessed November 2, 2012, http://abcnews.go.com.

6. "Most Companies Increasing Social Media Marketing Investment," *Brafton.com*, accessed November 2, 2012, www.brafton.com.

7. Caroline Van Hasselt and Leslie Scism, "Sun Life Revamps Its U.S. Strategy," *The Wall Street Journal*, accessed November 2, 2012, http://online.wsj.com.

8. Zachary Rodgers, "Microsoft Retires AdECN, Migrates to AppNexus RTB Engine," *ClickZ.com*, accessed November 2, 2012, www.clickz.com.

9. Mark Brandau, "McDonald's McCafé: An Evolution," *Nation's Restaurant News*, accessed November 2, 2012, http://nrn.com.

10. Gregory Karp, "Soldier Field Drops Coke for Dr Pepper Snapple Group," *Chicago Tribune*, accessed November 2, 2012, www.chicagotribune.com; Karen Robinson-Jacobs, "Soft Drink Sales Fizzle Again, Dr Pepper Gains Ground," *Dallas News*, accessed November 2, 2012, www.dallasnews.com; Nanette Byrnes, "Why Dr Pepper Is in the Pink of Health," *Bloomberg Businessweek*, accessed November 2, 2012, www.businessweek.com.

11. Byrnes, "Why Dr Pepper Is in the Pink of Health."

12. Derek F. Abell, "Strategic Windows," *Journal of Marketing*, 42, no. 3 (July 1978), pp. 21–26, accessed November 2, 2012, http://www.jstor.org.

13. "DreamWorks Animation Joins Walmart's Disc-to-Digital Service," *Press Release*, accessed November 2, 2012, http://news.walmart.com; Kristin Jones, "Wal-Mart Adds DreamWorks Titles to Video Streaming," *MarketWatch*, accessed November 2, 2012, www.marketwatch.com.

14. Company website, www.platoscloset.com, accessed November 2, 2012.

15. Robert Smith, "Rethinking the Oreo for Chinese Consumers," *This American Life*, National Public Radio, accessed November 2, 2012, www.npr.org.

16. "U.S. Quick Facts from the U.S. Census Bureau," http://quickfacts.census.gov, accessed November 2, 2012.

17. "Connecting and Engaging with Digital Indian Consumers," *Nielsen Wire*, accessed November 2, 2012, http://blog.nielsen.com.

18. Company website, www.dunkindonuts.com, accessed November 2, 2012; Company website, www.eddiebauer.com, accessed November 2, 2012.

19. Brad Thomas, "Dollar Stores Take on Wal-Mart, and Are Starting to Win," *Forbes*, accessed November 2, 2012, www.forbes.com.

20. U.S. Department of Commerce, "Doing Business in Romania," http://export.gov, accessed November 2, 2012.

21. Amy Dusto, "Domino's Hits $1 Billion in Online Pizza Sales," *Internet Retailer*, accessed November 2, 2012, www.internetretailer.com; Company website, "Marriott Mobile Apps," www.marriott.com, accessed November 2, 2012; Scott Davis, "Getting Apps Right: How Domino's Is Beating the Odds," *Forbes*, accessed November 2, 2012, www.forbes.com; "Starbucks: Buy It, Own It, Love It," *Money*, accessed November 2, 2012, http://money.msn.com.

22. Alice Hines, "eBay's 'Buy It New' Rebranding Angers Devoted Used Goods Sellers," *Daily Finance*, accessed November 2, 2012, www.dailyfinance.com.

23. "1960s IBM Standard Issue Clock," *Hypebeast*, http://hypebeast.com, accessed November 2, 2012.

24. "Gartner Says Worldwide Smartphone Sales Declined 2.3 Percent in Second Quarter of 2012," *Press Release*, accessed November 2, 2012, www.gartner.com.

25. Christopher Davies, "Intel Profits Up But Microsoft's Windows OS Suffers," *Manufacturing Digital*, accessed November 2, 2012, www.manufacturingdigital.com.

26. "U.S. Bancorp Expands Wholesale Business and Quits Student Loans," *Forbes*, accessed November 2, 2012, www.forbes.com.

27. Company website, www.blaircandy.com, accessed November 2, 2012.

28. Tim Kelly, "Sony CEO to Lay Out Revival Strategy as Losses Pile Up," *Reuters*, November 2, 2012, www.reuters.com; Moon Ihlwan, "Sony and Samsung's Strategic Split," *Bloomberg Businessweek*, accessed November 2, 2012, www.businessweek.com; Reiji Murai and Hyunjoo Jin, "Sony to Sell LCD Venture Stake to Samsung for $940 Million," *Reuters*, accessed November 2, 2012, http://in.reuters.com.

29. Nanci Hellmich, "Bread Is a Big Source of Americans' Salt Intake, Too," *USA Today*, accessed November 2, 2012, www.usatoday.com.

Chapter 3

THE MARKETING
Environment, Ethics, and Social Responsibility

1   Identify the five components of the marketing environment.

2   Explain the types of competition marketers face and the steps necessary for developing a competitive strategy.

3   Describe how marketing activities are regulated and how marketers can influence the political–legal environment.

4   Outline the economic factors that affect marketing decisions and consumer buying power.

5   Discuss the impact of the technological environment on a firm's marketing activities.

6   Explain how the social–cultural environment influences marketing.

7   Describe the ethical issues in marketing.

8   Identify the four levels of the social responsibility pyramid.

Chipotle Mexican Grill has long relied on its use of fresh, natural, and sustainably grown meats and other ingredients as a marketing advantage and a positive way of "changing the way people think about and eat fast food." The chain's more than 1,200 fast-food outlets have grown from a single restaurant opened in 1993 and typically earn more than $2 billion a year, making the company a solid success.

Chipotle is looking for even more ways to do business responsibly. Among its latest initiatives is the Chipotle Cultivate Foundation, which was formed to support individuals and organizations dedicated to creating a more sustainable future, such as family farms and ranches and their communities. Breaking with its long practice of relying on radio, billboards, and digital advertising, Chipotle also recently produced an entertaining two-minute animated film called "Back to the Start," about a family farm that learns the benefits of sustainable farming.

Originally shown online and in movie theaters, the film features a soundtrack with Willie Nelson covering a Coldplay song and proved a fitting broadcast ad for the Grammy Awards, where its message and novelty made it a surprise hit. It even became one of the top 10 advertisements of the year in terms of Internet buzz, racking up more than 6 million views on YouTube and appearing on 10,000 movie screens as well. Chipotle is pouring proceeds from downloads of the song (more than 25,000) into its Cultivate Foundation, which is also funded by revenue from "Boorito," an annual Halloween event.

Cultivate is also the name of Chipotle's new annual food and music festival, featuring chefs from around the country, exhibits about how food is grown, and, of course, music. After drawing 17,000 attendees, the event is scheduled to expand in coming years, recently holding festivals in Chicago and Denver.

Chipotle has already donated millions of dollars to like-minded groups like Jamie Oliver's Food Revolution and the Nature Conservancy, emphasizing its commitment to sustainable farming and natural ingredients. The chain's customers can earn loyalty points, redeemable online, not for making extra purchases but for demonstrating their knowledge about how food is produced. And a recent effort to shift its marketing focus led the company to devise one-of-a-kind lunch bags made from its own recycled billboards, which would otherwise go to landfills. The bags were available for sale on Earth Day, accompanied by a free meal.[1]

EVOLUTION OF A  BRAND

With few exceptions, every enterprise faces competition. It's essential, then, for organizations to craft a strategy that sets them apart, so their message stands out in an often-crowded marketplace, and consumers can differentiate them from others offering similar goods or services. Chipotle Mexican Grill differentiates itself by articulating its mission as selling fresh, natural and sustainably grown food. Achieving that mission requires Chipotle to integrate ecofriendly practices into the company's operations—a task that can be costly and challenging.

For example, large-scale industrialized farming in the United States—often regarded as cost-saving for the consumer—has replaced many independent family farms.

However, some observers point out that many of the savings claimed by large commercial farms come at the expense of farm communities and the environment. By supporting the responsible use of America's resources, Chipotle continues in its quest to change how people think about fast food while also demonstrating corporate social responsibility.

- Chipotle has many competitors: both national chains and local eateries that serve Mexican-style dishes like burritos and tacos as well as any other destination where a consumer can grab a quick, affordable meal. However, Chipotle describes its offerings as "gourmet." How does this strategy help set it apart and give consumers a different meal option?
- Not all organizations are as dedicated to sustainability as Chipotle. How does its position on sustainability create a differentiator?

CHAPTER OVERVIEW

1 Identify the five components of the marketing environment.

Change is a fact of life for all people, including marketers. Adapting to change in an environment as complex and unpredictable as the world's energy usage is perhaps the supreme challenge. The airline industry was hit hard when the price of oil skyrocketed. In response, many airlines—including Delta and United—removed their less fuel-efficient aircraft from service and eliminated flights. Despite those moves, high energy costs continue to affect the bottom line—for airlines and the rest of the world. Delta recently announced plans to buy an oil refinery to help reduce its jet fuel costs.[2]

Although some change may be the result of sudden crises, more often it is the result of a gradual trend in lifestyle, income, population, and other factors. Consumers are increasingly interested in buying "green" products—goods that minimize their impact on the environment. Technology can trigger a sudden change in the marketplace: in one fell swoop, it appeared that Internet music downloads had replaced traditional CDs. And within mere months of offering its iPhone, Apple introduced the iPod Touch MP3 player, which borrowed touch-screen technology from the iPhone.

Marketers must anticipate and plan for change. They must set goals to meet the concerns of customers, employees, share-holders, and the general public. Industry competition, legal constraints, the impact of technology on product designs, and social concerns are some of the many important factors that shape the business environment. All potentially have an impact on a firm's goods and services. Although external forces frequently are outside the marketer's control, decision makers must still consider those influences together with the variables of the marketing mix in developing, and occasionally modifying, marketing plans and strategies that take these environmental factors into consideration.

This chapter begins by describing five forces in marketing's external environment: competitive, political–legal, economic, technological, and social–cultural. Figure 3.1 identifies them as the foundation for making decisions that involve the four marketing mix elements and the target market. These forces provide the frame of reference within which all marketing decisions are made. The second focus of this chapter is marketing ethics and social responsibility. That section describes the nature of marketers' responsibilities both to business and to society at large.

FIGURE 3.1
Elements of the Marketing Mix within an Environmental Framework

© Cengage Learning

ENVIRONMENTAL SCANNING AND ENVIRONMENTAL MANAGEMENT

Marketers constantly monitor crucial trends and developments in the business environment. Environmental scanning is the process of collecting information about the external marketing environment to identify and interpret potential trends. The goal of this process is to analyze the information and decide whether these trends represent significant opportunities or pose major threats to the company. The firm can then determine the best response to a particular environmental change.

In the United States, the Consumer Product Safety Commission (CPSC) is responsible for keeping unsafe products out of the marketplace. It recently issued a recall of American Girl Craft Pearly Beads & Ribbon Bracelets kits, citing high levels of lead in some of the beads. The CPSC also banned drop-side cribs after 150 babies died from injuries suffered when the cribs malfunctioned. The ban led to numerous recalls by crib manufacturers and retailers.[3]

Environmental scanning is a vital component of effective environmental management. Environmental management involves marketers' efforts to achieve organizational objectives by predicting and influencing the competitive, political–legal, economic, technological, and social–cultural environments. In the political–legal environment, managers who seek modifications of regulations, laws, or tariff restrictions may lobby legislators or contribute to the campaigns of sympathetic politicians. Consumer groups lobbying on behalf of credit card users persuaded Congress to create rules regarding credit cards—for example, barring banks from creating minimum interest rates, or "floors"; forbidding card issuers from arbitrarily picking dates with the highest prime rate to apply to interest rates; and prohibiting them from automatically enrolling cardholders in over-the-limit protection.[4]

For many domestic and international firms, competing with established industry leaders frequently involves strategic alliances—partnerships with other firms in which the partners combine resources and capital to create competitive advantages in a new market. Strategic alliances are especially common in international marketing, in which partnerships with local firms provide regional expertise for a company expanding its operations abroad. Members of such alliances share risks and profits. Alliances are considered essential in a country such as China where laws require foreign firms doing business there to work with local companies.

Through successful research and development efforts, firms may influence changes in their own technological environments. A research breakthrough may lead to reduced production costs or a technologically superior new product. While changes in the marketing environment may be beyond the control of individual marketers, managers continually seek to predict their impact on marketing decisions and to modify operations to meet changing market needs. Even modest environmental shifts can alter the results of those decisions.

environmental scanning Process of collecting information about the external marketing environment to identify and interpret potential trends.

environmental management Attainment of organizational objectives by predicting and influencing the competitive, political–legal, economic, technological, and social–cultural environments.

strategic alliance Partnership in which two or more companies combine resources and capital to create competitive advantages in a new market.

As an issue of safety, the Consumer Product Safety Commission recalled the American Girl Craft Pearly Beads & Ribbon Bracelets kits due to high levels of lead in some of the beads.

© AP Photo/U.S. Consumer Product Safety Commission

THE COMPETITIVE ENVIRONMENT

As organizations vie to satisfy customers, the interactive exchange creates the competitive environment. Marketing decisions by individual firms influence consumer responses in the marketplace. They also affect the marketing strategies of competitors. As a consequence, marketers must continually monitor their competitors' marketing activities: their products, distribution channels, prices, and promotional efforts.

Few organizations have monopoly positions as the sole supplier of a good or service in the marketplace. Utilities, such as natural gas, electricity, water, and cable TV service, have traditionally accepted considerable regulation from local authorities who controlled such marketing-related factors as rates, service levels, and geographic coverage. In exchange, the utilities gained exclusive rights to serve a particular group of consumers. But the deregulation movement of the past three decades has ended total monopoly protection for most utilities. Many shoppers can choose from alternative cable TV and Internet providers, cell phone and traditional telephone carriers, and even gas and electric utilities. Some firms, such as pharmaceutical giants Merck and Pfizer, have *temporary* monopolies provided by patents on new drugs. When the U.S. Food and Drug Administration (FDA) approves a new drug for lowering cholesterol or improving sleep, its manufacturer typically is granted exclusive rights to produce and market the product during the life of the patent. This gives the manufacturer a chance to recoup the millions spent on developing and launching the drug. Once the patent expires, all bets are off, and competitors can flood the market with generic versions of the drug.

But what about professional sports teams who are part of a league? Is it lawful for their league to operate as a monopoly without violating U.S. antitrust laws? Consider the experience of apparel manufacturer American Needle. For 20 years, the company had a contract to make team caps for the National Football League, but it lost the business after the league engaged Reebok as its exclusive provider. American Needle sued the NFL, saying its 32 teams had operated as a monopoly in terms of licensed providers. In a 9-0 ruling, the Supreme Court of the United States ruled that the NFL had violated antitrust laws.[5]

Rather than seeking sole dominance of a market, corporations increasingly prefer to share the pie with just a few rivals. Referred to by economists as an oligopoly, this structure of a limited number of sellers in an industry in which high start-up costs form barriers to keep out new competitors deters newcomers from breaking into markets while ensuring that corporations remain innovative. Commercial airplane manufacturers operate within an oligopolistic industry, currently dominated by Europe-based Airbus Industrie and U.S.-based Boeing. After earlier failures at building and marketing commercial airplanes, the Chinese government once again is attempting to enter this exclusive club. With increasing numbers of Chinese air travelers, the government founded the Commercial Aircraft Corporation of China to build fuel-efficient jets domestically, in the hope that China can "buy local" and reduce its dependence on aircraft made in the West. China's "Big Plane" project for the C919 is scheduled to debut its first test flight in the coming year.[6]

competitive environment Interactive process that occurs in the marketplace among marketers of directly competitive products, marketers of products that can be substituted for one another, and marketers competing for the consumer's purchasing power.

monopoly Market structure in which a single seller dominates trade in a good or service for which buyers can find no close substitutes.

antitrust Laws designed to prevent restraints on trade such as business monopolies.

oligopoly Market structure in which relatively few sellers compete and where high start-up costs form barriers to keep out new competitors.

TYPES OF COMPETITION

2   **Explain the types of competition marketers face and the steps necessary for developing a competitive strategy.**

Marketers face three types of competition. The most *direct* form occurs among marketers of similar products, as when a competitive gas station like Marathon opens across the street from a Shell retail outlet. The cell phone market provides consumers with such alternative suppliers as Verizon, AT&T, and T-Mobile.

Costco, which sells everything from home generators to birthday cakes, also takes direct aim at luxury retailers. The largest U.S. warehouse club operator, Costco offers diamond jewelry, billiard tables, and even Suzuki pianos.[7]

A second type of competition is *indirect*, involving products that are easily substituted. In the fast-food industry, pizza competes with chicken, hamburgers, and tacos. In entertainment, a movie could be substituted for a concert or a night at the bowling alley. Six Flags and Universal Studios amusement parks—traditional hot spots for family vacations—now compete with outdoor adventure trips. Many adults in the United States will decide not to make this year's vacation a tranquil week at the beach or a trip to Disney World. Instead, they'll choose to do something more adventurous—thrill-filled experiences like skydiving, whitewater rafting, or climbing Mount Rainier. So marketers have to find ways to attract consumers to their specific brand as well as to their type of product.

A change such as a price increase or an improvement in a product's attributes can also affect demand for substitute products. As the prices for one type of energy soar, consumers look for cheaper, and more environmentally friendly, alternatives. Growing consumer interest in energy efficiency has led shoppers to look for products that have earned the ENERGY STAR. Administered jointly by the U.S. Environmental Protection Agency and the Department of Energy, the program awards the ENERGY STAR credential to appliances, building materials, computers, new homes, tools, and more.[8]

Advances in technology can give rise to other substitute products. Wireless fidelity, or Wi-Fi, makes the Internet available via radio waves and can be accessed at any number of public "hot spots" in a variety of locations, including airports, coffee shops, hotels, and libraries. The number of registered hot spots continues to grow worldwide, with more than 1.3 million in existence.[9] While some hosts charge a fee, Wi-Fi increasingly is offered at no charge.

And as technology continues to advance, industry observers expect Wi-Fi eventually will be replaced as the wireless standard. The likely "next-generation" successor, LTE (an acronym for long-term evolution), offers enhanced capabilities for numerous applications and boasts a stronger, more secure signal and significantly greater range than does Wi-Fi. Verizon currently offers LTE in more than 400 markets; AT&T's LTE network spans 77 markets.[10]

The final type of competition occurs among all organizations that compete for consumers' purchases. Traditional economic analysis views competition as a battle among companies in the same

Wi-Fi in New York City's parks is offered at no charge.

© Richard Levine/Alamy

industry (direct competition) or among substitutable goods and services (indirect competition). But marketers know that *all* firms compete for a limited number of dollars that consumers can or will spend. In this broader sense, competition means that the purchase of a Honda Accord might compete with a Norwegian Cruise Line vacation.

Because the competitive environment often determines the success or failure of a product, marketers must continually assess competitors' marketing strategies. New products, updated features or technology, increased service, and lower prices are variations that marketers look for. When changes occur in the competition, marketers must decide how to respond.

DEVELOPING A COMPETITIVE STRATEGY

competitive strategy
Methods through which a firm deals with its competitive environment.

Marketers at every successful firm must develop an effective strategy for dealing with the competitive environment. One company may compete in a broad range of markets in many areas of the world. Another may specialize in particular market segments, such as those determined by customers' geographic location, age, or income characteristics. Determining a competitive strategy involves answering the following three questions:

1. Should we compete?
2. If so, in what markets should we compete?
3. How should we compete?

The answer to the first question depends on the firm's resources, objectives, and expected profit potential. A firm may decide not to pursue or continue operating a potentially successful venture that does not mesh with its resources, objectives, or profit expectations. The board of directors of Foster's Group voted to "demerge" the company's two divisions—a well-known Australian brewery and an international wine business—because of their different industry dynamics and business requirements. As independent businesses, Foster's and Treasure Wine Estates would be able to identify and implement cost savings.[11]

Answering the second question requires marketers to acknowledge their firm's limited resources—sales personnel, advertising budgets, product development capability, and the like. They must allocate these resources to the areas of greatest opportunity. Some companies gain access to new markets or new expertise through acquisitions or mergers. SAP, a leading provider of business management software, recently bought SuccessFactors, a leader in cloud-based human capital management solutions. The purchase enabled SAP to build its position in the cloud, strengthen its presence in the growing human capital management market, and gain a greater foothold in social media—an area where SuccessFactors excels.[12]

Answering the third question on the list requires marketers to make product, distribution, promotion, and pricing decisions that give the firm a competitive advantage in the marketplace. Firms can compete on a variety of bases, including product quality, price, and customer service. Family-owned Von Maur, is an upscale department store, opened in 1872 in Davenport, Iowa. It now has stores in eleven states across the Midwest and the South, thriving in a competitive retail marketplace on the basis of superlative customer service. Von Maur offers free shipping, free gift-wrapping service, and an interest-free charge account.[13]

TIME-BASED COMPETITION

time-based competition Strategy of developing and distributing goods and services more quickly than competitors.

With increased international competition and rapid changes in technology, a steadily growing number of firms use time as a strategic competitive weapon. Time-based competition is the strategy of developing and distributing goods and services more quickly than competitors. Although a video option on cell phones came late to the U.S. market, the new feature has been a big hit, attracting new customers to cell phone providers. The flexibility and responsiveness of time-based competitors enable them to improve product quality, reduce costs, and expand product offerings to satisfy new market segments and enhance customer satisfaction.

In rapidly changing markets, particularly those that involve technology, time-based competition is critical to a firm's success. The Transportation Security Administration (TSA) piloted the use of smartphone technology to move passengers through airports more quickly and to reduce the incidence of phony boarding passes. The innovation—the electronic boarding pass—is now in use on many airlines, including Alaska, Delta, and United. With its encrypted barcode, the boarding pass is transmitted directly to a passenger's cell phone or PDA. At check-in, the passenger simply presents the phone or PDA to a TSA officer, who uses a handheld scanner to validate the barcode.[14]

Time-based competition allowed for the creation of the electronic boarding pass to reduce the incidence of phony boarding passes.

AP Photo/Russel A. Daniels

⊕ ASSESSMENT CHECK

2.1 Distinguish between direct and indirect competition, and give an example of each.

2.2 What is time-based competition?

THE POLITICAL–LEGAL ENVIRONMENT

Before you play the game, learn the rules! You may find it hard to win a new game without first understanding the rules. Yet some businesspeople exhibit a lack of knowledge about marketing's **political–legal environment**—the laws and their interpretations that require firms to operate under competitive conditions and to protect consumer rights.

The existing U.S. legal framework was constructed piecemeal, often in response to issues that were important when individual laws were enacted. Businesspeople must be diligent to understand the legal system's relationship to their marketing decisions. Numerous laws and regulations affect those decisions, many of them vaguely stated and inconsistently enforced by a multitude of different authorities.

Federal, state, and local regulations affect marketing practices, as do the actions of independent regulatory agencies. These requirements and prohibitions touch on all aspects of marketing decision making: designing, labeling, packaging, distributing, advertising, and promoting goods and services. To cope with the vast, complex, and changing political–legal environment, many large firms maintain in-house legal departments; small firms often seek professional advice from outside attorneys. All marketers, however, should be aware of the major regulations that affect their activities.

political–legal environment
Component of the marketing environment consisting of laws and their interpretations that require firms to operate under competitive conditions and to protect consumer rights.

GOVERNMENT REGULATION

The history of U.S. government regulation can be divided into four phases. The first phase was the *antimonopoly period* of the late 19th and early 20th centuries. During this era, major laws, such as the Sherman Antitrust Act, Clayton Act, and Federal Trade Commission Act, were passed to maintain a competitive environment by reducing the trend toward increasing concentration of industry power in the hands of a small number of competitors. Laws enacted more than 100 years ago still affect business in the 21st century.

Describe how marketing activities are regulated and how marketers can influence the political–legal environment.

3

The Microsoft case is a good example of antitrust legislation at work. The U.S. Department of Justice was successful in proving Microsoft guilty of predatory practices designed to crush competition. By bundling its own Internet Explorer browser with its Windows operating system—which runs 90 percent of the world's personal computers—Microsoft grabbed the majority of the market from rival Netscape. It also bullied firms as large as America Online to drop Netscape Navigator in favor of its browser. Microsoft's supporters countered that consumers have clearly benefited from the integrated features in Windows and that its bundling decisions were simply efforts to offer customer satisfaction through added value.

The second phase, aimed at *protecting competitors*, emerged during the Great Depression era of the 1930s, when independent merchants felt the need for legal protection against competition from larger chain stores. Among the federal legislation enacted was the Robinson-Patman Act. The third regulatory phase focused on *consumer protection.* The objective of consumer protection underlies most laws, with good examples including the Sherman Act, Federal Trade Commission Act, and Federal Food and Drug Act. Additional laws have been enacted over the past 40 years. The fourth phase, *industry deregulation,* began in the late 1970s and continues to the present. During this phase, government has sought to increase competition in such industries as telecommunications, utilities, transportation, and financial services by discontinuing many regulations and permitting firms to expand their service offerings to new markets.

The newest regulatory frontier is *cyberspace.* Federal and state regulators are investigating ways to police the Internet and online services. The Federal Trade Commission (FTC), along with private organizations and other government agencies, has created a site, www.onguardonline.gov, where consumers can take quizzes designed to educate them about ID theft, spam (junk email), phishing (luring consumers to provide personal information), and online shopping scams. But cybercrime is spreading quickly. Attacks by malicious software that contain codes capable of stealing account logons, passwords, and other confidential data are on the rise. Numerous state laws as well as the federal Identity Theft Enforcement and Restitution Act enable victims of identity theft to seek restitution and make it easier for the government to prosecute phishing and those who threaten to steal or divulge information from a computer.[15]

Privacy and child protection issues are another important—but difficult—enforcement challenge. With the passage of the Children's Online Privacy Protection Act, Congress took the first step in regulating what children are exposed to on the Internet. The primary focus is a set of rules regarding how and when marketers need to get parental permission before obtaining marketing research information from children over the Web. Finally, the government's Do Not Call Registry, a list to which consumers can add their phone numbers, including cell phones, to avoid telemarketing calls, provides protection for consumers who do not want to be contacted by telemarketers. The law exempts callers representing not-for-profit organizations, companies with which the consumer has an existing relationship, and political candidates. Telemarketing firms must check the list quarterly, with fines of as much as $16,000 per occurrence. The government aggressively pursues offenders, resulting in settlements often totaling millions of dollars. A federal court recently ordered two telemarketers to pay $30 million in fines for making unlawful calls.[16]

Table 3.1 lists and briefly describes the major federal laws affecting marketing. Legislation covering specific marketing practices, such as product development, packaging, labeling, product warranties, and franchise agreements, is discussed in later chapters.

Marketers must also monitor state and local laws that affect their industries. Many states, for instance, allow hard liquor to be sold only in liquor stores while others prohibit the sale of alcoholic beverages on Sunday. California's stringent regulations for automobile emissions require special pollution control equipment on cars sold in the state.

GOVERNMENT REGULATORY AGENCIES

Federal, state, and local governments have established regulatory agencies to enforce laws. At the federal level, the FTC wields the broadest powers of any agency to influence marketing activities. The FTC enforces laws regulating unfair business practices and stops false and deceptive advertising. It regulates communication by wire, radio, and television. Other federal regulatory agencies include the Consumer Product Safety Commission, the Federal Power Commission, the Environmental Protection Agency (EPA), the Food and Drug Administration (FDA), and the National Highway

TABLE 3.1 Major Federal Laws Affecting Marketing

Date	Law	Description
A. LAWS MAINTAINING A COMPETITIVE ENVIRONMENT		
1890	Sherman Antitrust Act	Prohibits restraint of trade and monopolization; identifies a competitive marketing system as a national policy goal.
1914	Clayton Act	Strengthens the Sherman Act by restricting such practices as price discrimination, exclusive dealing, tying contracts, and interlocking boards of directors where the effect "may be to substantially lessen competition or tend to create a monopoly"; amended by the Celler-Kefauver Antimerger Act to prohibit major asset purchases that would decrease competition in an industry.
1914	Federal Trade Commission Act (FTC)	Prohibits unfair methods of competition; establishes the Federal Trade Commission, an administrative agency that investigates business practices and enforces the FTC Act.
1938	Wheeler-Lea Act	Amends the FTC Act to outlaw additional unfair practices; gives the FTC jurisdiction over false and misleading advertising.
1998	Digital Millennium Copyright Act	Protects intellectual property rights by prohibiting copying or downloading of digital files.
B. LAWS REGULATING COMPETITION		
1936	Robinson-Patman Act	Prohibits price discrimination in sales to wholesalers, retailers, or other producers; prohibits selling at unreasonably low prices to eliminate competition.
1993	North American Free Trade Agreement (NAFTA)	International trade agreement between Canada, Mexico, and the United States designed to facilitate trade by removing tariffs and other trade barriers among the three nations.
C. LAWS PROTECTING CONSUMERS		
1906	Federal Food and Drug Act	Prohibits adulteration and misbranding of food and drugs involved in interstate commerce; strengthened by the Food, Drug, and Cosmetic Act (1938) and the Kefauver-Harris Drug Amendment (1962).
1970	National Environmental Policy Act	Establishes the Environmental Protection Agency to deal with various types of pollution and organizations that create pollution.
1971	Public Health Cigarette Smoking Act	Prohibits tobacco advertising on radio and television.
1972	Consumer Product Safety Act	Created the Consumer Product Safety Commission, which has authority to specify safety standards for most products.
1998	Children's Online Privacy Protection Act	Empowers FTC to set rules regarding how and when marketers must obtain parental permission before asking children marketing research questions.
1998	Identity Theft and Assumption Deterrence Act	Makes it a federal crime to unlawfully use or transfer another person's identification with the intent to violate the law.
1999	Anti-cybersquatting Consumer Protection Act	Bans the bad-faith purchase of domain names that are identical or confusingly similar to existing registered trademarks.
2001	Electronic Signature Act	Gives electronic signatures the same legal weight as handwritten signatures.
2005	Real ID Act	Sets minimum standards for state driver's licenses and ID cards. To be phased in from 2010 through 2013.
2006	Consumer Telephone Records Act	Prohibits the sale of cell phone records.
2009	Fraud Enforcement and Recovery Act	Expands government's authority to investigate and prosecute mortgage fraud.
2009	Helping Families Save Their Homes Act	Helps homeowners avoid foreclosure and obtain affordable mortgages.
2009	Credit Card Accountability, Responsibility and Disclosure Act	Provides new rules governing credit card rate increases, fees, billing, and other practices.

TABLE 3.1 Major Federal Laws Affecting Marketing (*continued*)

Date	Law	Description
D. LAWS DEREGULATING SPECIFIC INDUSTRIES		
1978	Airline Deregulation Act	Grants considerable freedom to commercial airlines in setting fares and choosing new routes.
1980	Motor Carrier Act and Staggers Rail Act	Significantly deregulates trucking and railroad industries by permitting them to negotiate rates and services.
1996	Telecommunications Act	Significantly deregulates the telecommunications industry by removing barriers to competition in local and long-distance phone and cable and television markets.
2003	Amendments to the Telemarketing Sales Rule	Created the national Do Not Call Registry prohibiting telemarketing calls to registered telephone numbers. Restricted the number and duration of telemarketing calls generating dead air space with use of automatic dialers; cracked down on unauthorized billing; and required telemarketers to transmit their caller ID information.
2007	Do-Not-Call Improvement Act	Extends Telemarketing Sales Rule; allows registered numbers to remain on Do Not Call list permanently.
2007	Fee Extension Act	Extends Telemarketing Sales Rule; sets annual fees for telemarketers to access the Do Not Call Registry.

© Cengage Learning

Traffic Safety Administration (NHTSA). But regulatory agencies aren't always known for strict oversight. The NHTSA came under fire for not investigating hundreds of complaints from Lexus and Toyota drivers who reported sudden or unintended acceleration that, in some cases, resulted in injuries and even death. After initial resistance, Toyota was compelled to recall millions of Camrys, Corollas, Priuses, and other popular models, reconfiguring the gas pedal, installing brake override software, and making other fixes. After a lengthy investigation, the federal government fined Toyota nearly $49 million for its handling of the problems relating to vehicle safety and reliability. It appears that Toyota learned from that experience, however. When the automaker noticed a problem with faulty window switches in several of its models, it voluntarily issued a recall for more than 2.5 million cars before any incidents occurred.[17]

The FTC uses several procedures to enforce laws. It may issue a consent order through which a business accused of violations can agree to voluntary compliance without admitting guilt. If a business refuses to comply with an FTC request, the agency can issue a cease-and-desist order, which gives a final demand to stop an illegal practice. Firms often challenge cease-and-desist orders in court. The FTC can require advertisers to provide additional information about products in their advertisements, and it can force firms using deceptive advertising to correct earlier claims with new promotional messages. In some cases, the FTC can require a firm to give refunds to consumers misled by deceptive advertising.

The FTC and U.S. Department of Justice can stop mergers if they believe the proposed acquisition will reduce competition by making it harder for new companies to enter the field. In recent years, these agencies have taken a harder line on proposed mergers, especially in the computer, telecommunications, financial services, and health-care sectors.

Removing regulations also changes the competitive picture considerably. Following deregulation of the telecommunications and utilities industries, suppliers no longer have exclusive rights to operate within a territory. Natural gas utilities traditionally competed with electric companies to supply homeowners and businesses with energy needs. Because of deregulation, they now also compete with other gas companies. The restructuring of the electricity industry by state took hold immediately in the Northeast, ranging from Maine to Virginia and reaching through the Midwest in Ohio, Michigan, and Illinois. Indiana and Vermont abstained. Texas, Arizona, and Oregon also jumped on the bandwagon. But several states delayed deregulation activities, and California actually suspended them altogether. Restructuring caused major headaches for some utilities, leading to shortages and an inability to coordinate service with needs, nonmaintenance of power lines, and lack of funds for operating or decommissioning nuclear power plants. Thus, while deregulation may be designed to promote competition and provide better service and prices for consumers, it doesn't always work as planned.

The latest round of deregulation began with the passage of the Telecommunications Act of 1996 and its 2003 amendment, the Do Not Call law mentioned earlier. The Telecommunications Act removed barriers between local and long-distance phone companies and cable companies. It allowed the so-called Baby Bells—the regional Bell operating companies—to offer long-distance service; at the same time, long-distance companies offered local service. Satellite television providers such as Dish Network and DIRECTV and cable companies such as Comcast can offer phone service, while phone companies can get into the cable business. The change promises huge rewards for competitive winners. Consumers can shop around for the best deals and packages as more companies compete for their business by packaging services at reduced prices.

OTHER REGULATORY FORCES

Public and private consumer interest groups and self-regulatory organizations are also part of the legal environment. Consumer interest organizations have mushroomed since the late 1970s, and today hundreds of groups operate at national, state, and local levels. These organizations seek to protect consumers in as many areas as possible. Citing the need for a standardized credit scoring system, the three major credit-reporting agencies—Equifax, Experian, and TransUnion—collaborated to create VantageScore. But consumer groups and other industry observers have criticized the system for being inconsistent and of questionable value to consumers.[18] The Coalition for Fire-Safe Cigarettes worked state-by-state to pressure tobacco companies to produce cigarettes that will not smolder and start fires if left unattended. As a result of the Coalition's efforts, laws mandating fire-safe cigarettes have been passed in Canada, the District of Columbia, and all 50 states.[19]

Other groups attempt to advance the rights of minorities, senior citizens, and other causes. The power of these groups has also grown. AARP (formerly known as the American Association of Retired Persons) wields political and economic power, particularly as more and more people reach retirement age.[20]

Self-regulatory groups represent industries' attempts to set guidelines for responsible business conduct. The Council of Better Business Bureaus is a national organization devoted to consumer service and business self-regulation. The council's National Advertising Division (NAD) promotes truth and accuracy in advertising. It reviews and advocates voluntary resolution of advertising-related complaints between consumers and businesses. If NAD fails to resolve a complaint, an appeal can be made to the National Advertising Review Board, composed of advertisers, ad agency representatives, and public members. In addition, many individual trade associations set business guidelines and codes of conduct and encourage members' voluntary compliance.

The Direct Marketing Association (DMA) supports consumer rights through its Commitment to Consumer Choice. Under this principle, DMA's more than 3,600 member organizations are required to inform consumers of their right to modify or discontinue receiving solicitations.[21]

As mentioned earlier, regulating the online world poses a challenge. Favoring self-regulation as the best starting point, the FTC sponsored a privacy initiative for consumers, advertisers, online companies, and others as a way to develop voluntary industry privacy guidelines.

CONTROLLING THE POLITICAL–LEGAL ENVIRONMENT

Most marketers comply with laws and regulations. Doing so not only serves their customers but also avoids legal problems that could ultimately damage a firm's image and hurt profits. But smart marketers get ahead of the curve by providing products that will meet customers' future needs while also addressing government goals. Showing remarkable forward thinking, Toyota was one of the first automakers to commit to building hybrid cars. Its efforts were supported by a government tax break for purchasers of the first hybrids.

Consumer groups and political action committees within industries may try to influence the outcome of proposed legislation or

ASSESSMENT CHECK

3.1 Identify the four phases of U.S. government regulation of business. What is the newest frontier?

3.2 Which federal agency wields the broadest regulatory powers for influencing marketing activities?

change existing laws by engaging in political lobbying or boycotts. Lobbying groups frequently enlist the support of customers, employees, and suppliers to assist their efforts.

THE ECONOMIC ENVIRONMENT

4 Outline the economic factors that affect marketing decisions and consumer buying power.

The overall health of the economy influences how much consumers spend and what they buy. This relationship also works the other way: consumer buying plays an important role in the economy's health. In fact, consumer spending accounts for about 70 percent of the nation's total gross domestic product (GDP), the sum of all goods and services produced by a nation in a year. (Excluding what consumers pay for health care, that figure comes closer to 60 percent.)[22] Because marketing activities are directed toward satisfying consumer wants and needs, marketers must first understand how economic conditions influence the purchasing decisions consumers make.

Marketing's economic environment consists of factors that influence consumer buying power and marketing strategies. They include the stage of the business cycle, the global economic crisis, inflation and deflation, unemployment, income, and resource availability.

gross domestic product (GDP) Sum of all goods and services produced by a nation in a year.

economic environment Factors that influence consumer buying power and marketing strategies, including stage of the business cycle, inflation and deflation, unemployment, income, and resource availability.

business cycle Pattern of stages in the level of economic activity: prosperity, recession, depression, and recovery.

STAGES IN THE BUSINESS CYCLE

Historically, the economy has tended to follow a cyclical pattern consisting of four stages: prosperity, recession, depression, and recovery. Consumer buying differs in each stage of the business cycle, and marketers must adjust their strategies accordingly. In times of prosperity, consumer spending maintains a brisk pace, and buyers are willing to spend more for premium versions of well-known brands. Growth in services like banking and restaurants usually indicates a strong economy. When economists predict such conditions as low inflation and low unemployment, marketers respond by offering new products, increasing their promotional efforts, and expanding distribution. They might even raise prices to widen profit margins. But high prices for some items, such as energy, can affect businesses and consumers alike. Skyrocketing gasoline prices have led many consumers to seek other forms of transportation, including the electric bicycle which, in less than a decade, has grown to an $11 billion industry. Especially in China, India, and Europe, an electric bike enables many to postpone the more costly purchase of a car.[23]

During economic slowdowns, consumers focus on more basic, functional products that carry lower price tags. They limit travel, restaurant meals, and entertainment. They skip expensive vacations and cook their own meals. During a recession, marketers consider lowering prices and increasing promotions that include special offers to stimulate demand. They may also launch special value-priced products likely to appeal to cost-conscious buyers.

Skyrocketing gas prices have led consumers to seek other forms of transportation. In just a few years, the electric bicycle has grown to an $11 billion industry.

Imaginechina via AP Images

Consumer spending sinks to its lowest level during a depression. The last true depression in the United States occurred during the 1930s. Although a severe depression could occur again, most experts see it as a slim possibility. Through its monetary and fiscal policies, the federal government attempts to control extreme fluctuations in the business cycle that lead to depression.

In the recovery stage, the economy emerges from recession and consumer purchasing power increases. But while consumers have money to spend, caution often restrains their willingness to buy. A family might buy a new car if no-interest financing is available. A couple might decide to book a trip through a discount travel firm such as Expedia.com or Travelocity. Companies like these can make the most of an opportunity and develop loyal customers by offering superior service at lower prices. Recovery still remains a difficult stage for businesses just climbing out of a recession because they must earn profits while trying to gauge uncertain consumer demand. Many cope by holding down costs. Some trim payrolls and close branch offices. Others cut back on business travel budgets, substituting teleconferencing and videoconferencing.

Business cycles, like other aspects of the economy, are complex phenomena that, despite the efforts of government, businesspeople, and others to control them, sometimes have a life of their own. Unforeseen natural disasters, such as the recent spate of tornadoes and flooding across the United States; narrowly averted terrorist attacks, like the one attempted on a Detroit-bound jet on Christmas Day 2009; and the effects of war or peace all have an impact on business and the economy as a whole. The most effective marketers know how to recognize ways to serve their customers during the best (and worst) of times.

THE GLOBAL ECONOMIC CRISIS

Sometimes business cycles take a severe turn and affect consumers and businesses across the globe. That is the case with the recent recession, called the worst economic downturn since the Great Depression of the 1930s. Typically, nations' GDP rates grow—some modestly at 2 to 4 percentage points a year and some, such as India and China, near double digits. With the crisis, economists predicted that the world economy might shrink for the first time in 60 years.

A struggling economy generates its own downward spiral: fearing worse days ahead, consumers and businesses become cautious about spending money and, as they spend less, demand for many products also drops. Lessened demand forces employers to take extraordinary steps just to stay in business: institute a shortened workweek with reduced salaries or even slash the workforce. In the United States, layoffs resulted in double-digit unemployment during the recent recession.

Especially during a recession, marketers look to emphasize value in their offerings. Some slash prices or offer sales to help customers stretch their budget dollars. Automakers Ford and Hyundai recently assured new-car buyers that they would assist them with payments for a period of time if they lost their jobs or would take the cars back to avoid damaging consumers' credit. Retailers that emphasized affordable products, such as Walmart and McDonald's, saw their sales increase. With the severity of the recession, all marketers needed to reevaluate their strategies and concentrate on their most promising products. But it remains to be seen whether or how much consumers, now used to price reductions and special offers, will change their habits once they regain their economic footing in a recovery.

INFLATION AND DEFLATION

A major constraint on consumer spending, which can occur during any stage of the business cycle, is inflation—rising prices caused by some combination of excess demand and increases in the costs of raw materials, component parts, human resources, or other factors of production. Inflation devalues money by reducing the products it can buy through persistent price increases. These rising prices increase marketers' costs, such as expenditures for wages and raw materials, and the resulting higher prices may therefore negatively affect sales. U.S. inflation hit a heart-stopping high in 1979 of 13.3 percent. Recently, annual inflation hovered around 2.0 percent.[24]

> **BRIEFLY SPEAKING**
>
> "The Chinese use two brush strokes to write the word 'crisis.' One brush stroke stands for danger; the other for opportunity. In a crisis, be aware of the danger—but recognize the opportunity."
>
> —**John F. Kennedy**
> *35th President of the United States*

inflation Rising prices caused by some combination of excess consumer demand and increases in the costs of one or more factors of production.

If inflation is so bad, is its opposite, *deflation*, better? At first, it might seem so. Falling prices mean that products are more affordable. But deflation can be a long and damaging downward spiral, causing a freefall in business profits, lower returns on most investments, and widespread job layoffs. The last time the United States experienced significant deflation was in the Great Depression of the 1930s.

Unemployment

unemployment
Proportion of people in the economy actively seeking work that do not have jobs.

Unemployment is defined as the proportion of people in the economy who are actively seeking work but do not have jobs. Unemployment rises during recessions and declines in the recovery and prosperity stages of the business cycle. Like inflation, unemployment affects the way consumers behave. Unless unemployment insurance, personal savings, and union benefits effectively offset lost earnings, unemployed people have relatively little money to spend; they buy food, pay the rent or mortgage, and try to keep up with utility bills. After months of unemployment near 10 percent, joblessness recently declined nationally.[25] Not surprisingly, job cuts have a direct effect on consumer spending.

Income

discretionary income Money available to spend after buying necessities such as food, clothing, and housing.

Income is another important determinant of marketing's economic environment because it influences consumer buying power. By studying income statistics and trends, marketers can estimate market potential and plan to target specific market segments. A rise in income represents potential for increasing overall sales. Many marketers are particularly interested in **discretionary income**, the amount of money people have to spend after buying necessities such as food, clothing, and housing. Those whose industry involves the necessities seek to turn those needs into preferences for their goods and services. During the recent recession, American consumers experienced a drop in their net worth because their homes and stock investments lost value. At the same time, they spent less on nonessential items, and a greater proportion of their income went toward food, fuel, and other necessities.[26]

Changes in average earnings powerfully affect discretionary income. Historically, periods of major innovation have been accompanied by dramatic increases in living standards and rising incomes. Automobiles, televisions, telephones, and computers are just a few of the innovations that have changed consumers' lives—and standards of living. The Bureau of Economic Analysis, a division of the U.S. Department of Commerce, tracks personal income and discretionary income in the United States, then determines how much of that income is spent on personal consumption. Marketers can use these figures to plan their approaches to everything from product development to the promotion of their goods and services.

Not only does income affect how much money individuals donate to not-for-profit organizations, but it can also affect the amount of time they're willing to spend on charitable efforts. And some firms have also demonstrated their commitment not only to charities but also to conducting business in a responsible manner. Such activities often fall under the theme of corporate social responsibility (CSR). But charitable giving is not all there is to CSR, as the "Career Readiness" feature shows.

RESOURCE AVAILABILITY

Resources are not unlimited. Shortages, temporary or permanent, can result from several conditions, including political instability, high fuel costs, and the lack of raw materials, component parts, or labor. The global financial crisis, coupled with extreme weather conditions such as drought and typhoons, suggest the possibility of isolated worldwide food shortages.[27]

demarketing Process of reducing consumer demand for a good or service to a level that the firm can supply.

One reaction to a shortage is **demarketing**, the process of reducing consumer demand for a product to a level that the firm can reasonably supply. Oil companies publicize tips for consumers on how to cut gasoline consumption, and utility companies encourage homeowners to install more insulation to reduce heating costs. Volvo IT's mobile app, Commute Greener, encourages environmentally friendly commuting. Users can calculate the environmental impact of their trips to and from work or school, and can even form groups on Facebook to create friendly competition around

CAREER READINESS
Landing a Job in CSR

Are you eager to turn your passion for environmental causes or "green" technology into a career in corporate social responsibility? You can, if you keep some important ideas in mind.

- *Make sure you know what CSR really is.* While charitable giving still plays a big role in many companies' CSR efforts, and rightly so, it's not the whole story, as this chapter shows. Many CSR experts today feel "it's all about the environment," including problems like climate change and waste reduction.

- *Be ready to promote your CSR experience.* Don't have any? Volunteer or work a related internship to show your commitment to your field and gain a track record of real accomplishment. It's not enough to say you recycle at home.

- *Practice your persuasive skills.* Convincing other people within and outside your organization to change their behavior will be a big part of your daily responsibility.

- *Hone your leadership and communication skills.* These are critical in any field, but particularly in small departments like CSR that interact with other areas in a company like marketing, operations, legal, and human resources.

- *Cover the basics.* Perfect your résumé, network effectively, study the companies you're interested in, and prepare thoroughly for interviews.

Sources: "Landing a CSR Job," *WetFeet.com*, accessed October 22, 2012, www.wetfeet.com; C. B. Bhattacharya, "Corporate Social Responsibility: It's All About Marketing," *Forbes*, accessed October 22, 2012, www.forbes.com; James Epstein-Reeves, "How to Find a CSR Job in a Big Company," *Forbes*, October 22, 2012, www.forbes.com.

---

green commuting.[28] A shortage presents marketers with a unique set of challenges. They may have to allocate limited supplies, a sharply different activity from marketing's traditional objective of expanding sales volume. Shortages may require marketers to decide whether to spread limited supplies over all customers or limit purchases by some customers so that the firm can completely satisfy others.

Marketers have also devised ways to deal with increased demand for fixed amounts of resources. In its annual *Green Book*, the American Council for an Energy Efficient Economy (ACEEE) gives cars a "green score," rating vehicles on their manufacturers' use of scarce resources and attention to the environment in the production process. The recent winner? The ACEEE rated the electric battery-powered Mitsubishi i-MiEV at the top.[29]

THE INTERNATIONAL ECONOMIC ENVIRONMENT

In today's global economy, marketers must also monitor the economic environment of other nations. Just as in the United States, a recession in Europe or Japan changes consumer and business buying habits. Changes in foreign currency rates compared with the U.S. dollar also affect marketing decisions. Labor costs and other factors affect firms' decisions to shift manufacturing operations overseas, decisions that may result in cutbacks in U.S. jobs and boosts to other nations' workforces. Although U.S. workers worry about the number of jobs sent overseas, some manufacturing remains strong in the United States. While workers in Asia assemble computers, production of computer chips remains in the United States.

As China exports more and more goods to the world and to the United States in particular, some people voice concern over the widening trade gap. Only recently have broad economic reforms allowed China to play in the global marketplace. Some wonder if China's entry into world markets might help the West economically. However, with its gross domestic product still only a fraction of the U.S. GDP, economists say China cannot rescue the world economy—yet. But they point to China's expanding economy, fueled in part by a growing middle class with vast, untapped marketing potential.[30]

Politics in other countries affects the international economic environment as well. For instance, the recent turmoil in the Middle East and international restrictions on Iran could affect the oil industry.

The recent global recession has pushed some members of the European Union to the brink of bankruptcy, and the EU and the International Monetary Fund have provided financial bailouts for Greece, Ireland, and Portugal, with Greece recently receiving its second bailout in two years. The economies of two other EU members, Spain and Italy, are also faltering.[31]

ASSESSMENT CHECK

4.1   Identify and describe briefly the four stages of the business cycle.

4.2   Explain how inflation and income affect consumer buying decisions.

THE TECHNOLOGICAL ENVIRONMENT

5   Discuss the impact of the technological environment on a firm's marketing activities.

technological environment
Application to marketing of knowledge based on discoveries in science, inventions, and innovations.

The **technological environment** represents the application to marketing of knowledge based on discoveries in science, inventions, and innovations. Technology leads to new goods and services for consumers; it also improves existing products, offers better customer service, and often reduces prices through new, cost-efficient production and distribution methods. Technology can quickly make products obsolete—email, for example, quickly eroded both letter writing and the market for fax machines—but it can just as quickly open new marketing opportunities, sometimes in entirely new industries.

Pets have been wearing RFID—radio-frequency identification—transmitters for years, in case they got lost. Now RFID tags are used in many industries to locate everything from library books to laundry detergent. An RFID tag contains a computer chip with an antenna. A reader scans the tag and transmits the data from the tag to a computer. This innovation means that retailers, manufacturers, and others can locate and track inventory without opening packages. Guests on Disney Cruise Line ships wear wristbands with embedded RFID tags. The wristbands provide access to the ship's amenities and replace the need for a key card. To open their room, guests simply tap the door with the hand wearing the wristband. But the use of RFID to track the movement of humans is controversial because of the privacy implications.[32]

Technology can address social concerns. In response to pressure from the World Trade Organization and the U.S. government, automakers used technology to develop more fuel-efficient vehicles and reduce dangerous emissions. Increased use of ethanol made from corn was another solution, but researchers have stepped up efforts to develop biofuels to replace gasoline. One such fuel, cellulosic ethanol, comes from cellulose—grass clippings, wood chips, yard waste—anything organic, even old tires. The biofuel emits significantly less greenhouse gases than gasoline and, if spilled, is less damaging to the environment. Scientists believe advances in technology eventually will make the fuel cost-effective to produce. Meanwhile, several start-up companies are working to create fuel from another organic source: algae. Low-cost, fast-growing, and carbon neutral, algae shows promise as a source of alternative energy.[33]

Industry, government, colleges and universities, and other not-for-profit institutions all play roles in the development of new technology. Using technology developed by scientists at Argonne National Laboratory, the University of Chicago created a startup company called SmartSignal. The company's patented analytical software monitors machinery and diagnoses problems to head off equipment failures. GE Intelligent Platforms recently acquired SmartSignal, whose software supports a global clientele.[34]

Another major source of technology is the federal government, including the military. Air bags originated from Air Force ejection seats, digital computers were first designed to calculate artillery trajectories, and the microwave oven is a derivative of military radar systems. Even the Internet was first developed by the U.S. Department of Defense as a secure military communications system.

"BRIEFLY SPEAKING"

"Information technology and business are becoming inextricably interwoven. I don't think anybody can talk meaningfully about one without talking about the other."

—Bill Gates
Founder and Chairman, Microsoft Corporation

Although the United States has long been the world leader in research, competition from rivals in Europe, Japan, and other Asian countries is intense.

APPLYING TECHNOLOGY

Marketers monitor the technological environment for a number of reasons. Creative applications of new technologies not only give a firm a definite competitive edge but can also benefit society. Marketers who monitor new technology and successfully apply it may also enhance customer service.

VoIP—Voice over Internet Protocol—is an alternative to traditional telecommunications services provided by telephone companies. The telephone is not connected to a traditional phone jack but instead is connected to a personal computer with any type of broadband Internet connection. Special software transmits phone conversations over the Internet, rather than through telephone lines. A VoIP user dials the phone as usual. Recipients can receive calls made using VoIP through regular telephone connections, land or wireless. Moreover, you can call another person who has VoIP using a regular landline or cell phone. Globally, VoIP continues to attract growing numbers of users—both consumers and businesses—mainly because of the cost savings. The VoIP business is also growing worldwide, with hundreds of service providers in the United States alone. One of the largest, Skype, recently acquired by Microsoft, has more than 250 million monthly users.[35]

As convenient as the Internet, cell phones, and Wi-Fi are for businesspeople and consumers, the networks that facilitate these connections aren't yet compatible with each other. So engineers are working on a new standard that would enable these networks to connect with each other, paving the way for melded services such as video exchanges between a cell phone and a computer. Called the Internet Protocol Multimedia Subsystem (IMS), the new standard is attempting to create a common interface so that data can be carried across networks between different devices. The implications for various communications providers are enormous—not only will they find new ways to cooperate, but they will also find new ways to compete. Subsequent chapters discuss in more detail how companies apply technologies—such as databases, blogs, and interactive promotional techniques—to create a competitive advantage.

VoIP (Voice over Internet Protocol) A phone connection through a personal computer with any type of broadband Internet connection.

ASSESSMENT CHECK

5.1　What are some of the consumer benefits of technology?

5.2　Why must marketers monitor the technological environment?

THE SOCIAL–CULTURAL ENVIRONMENT

As a nation, the United States is becoming older, more affluent, and more culturally diverse. The birthrate is falling, and subculture populations are rising. People express concerns about the natural environment, buying ecologically friendly products that reduce pollution. They value their time with family and friends, cooking meals at home and exchanging vacation photos over the Internet. Marketers need to track these trends to be in tune with consumers' needs and desires. These aspects of consumer lifestyles help shape marketing's social–cultural environment—the relationship between marketing, society, and culture.

To remain competitive, marketers must be sensitive to society's demographic shifts and changing values. These variables affect consumers' reactions to different products and marketing practices. The baby boom generation—the 78 million Americans born between 1946 and 1964—represents a $2.1 trillion market. As boomers approach and enter retirement, marketers are scrambling to identify their needs and wants. With a longer life expectancy and the hope of more time and money to spend, baby boomers view retirement much differently than earlier generations did. Marketers already know that boomers feel young at heart and enjoy their leisure time, but they aren't playing cards and shuffleboard—they're becoming "social media mavens" who spend a significant portion of their free time

Explain how the social–cultural environment influences marketing.

6

social–cultural environment
Component of the marketing environment consisting of the relationship between the marketer, society, and culture.

surfing the Web and accessing sites like Facebook and LinkedIn on their smartphones.[36] Some even launch a second career, starting their own small business. And boomers have a whole new take on the concept of grandparenting. More than past generations, boomer grandparents get actively involved in their grandchildren's daily lives and are more inclined to spend money on them. An estimated 20 percent of all travel involves grandchildren with grandparents, with or without their parents along. As they age, boomers will need health-care goods and services and, should they live longer, they may need everything from physical therapy for a repaired knee to a motorized scooter to get around.

Another social–cultural consideration is the increasing importance of cultural diversity. The United States is a mixed society composed of various submarkets, each with its unique values, cultural characteristics, consumer preferences, and purchasing behaviors. In an effort to attract the millions of Hispanic viewers in the United States, satellite and cable TV companies now offer more Spanish-language programming. Spanish-language networks Univision and Telemundo, which once dominated the Hispanic TV market, now face competition from Comcast, Cablevision, Time Warner Cable, DISH Network, and DIRECTV. Traditional media companies are creating networks that target online financial advertising and investment news to Latin American audiences. Nearly 2,500 Hispanic media outlets operate in the United States, with over 200 of the sites online only.[37]

Marketers also need to learn about cultural and societal differences among countries abroad, particularly as business becomes more and more global. Marketing strategies that work in the United States often fail when used in other countries, and vice versa. In many cases, marketers must redesign packages and modify products and advertising messages to suit the tastes and preferences of different cultures. Chapter 8 explores the social–cultural aspects of global marketing.

CONSUMERISM

consumerism Social force within the environment that aids and protects the consumer by exerting legal, moral, and economic pressures on business and government.

Changing societal values have led to consumerism, defined as a social force within the environment that aids and protects the consumer by exerting legal, moral, and economic pressures on business and government. Today, everyone—marketers, industry, government, and the public—is acutely aware of the impact of consumerism on the nation's economy and general well-being.

Marketers see a rise in consumer activism. Americans use an estimated 102 billion plastic shopping bags a year—over 500 bags per consumer, most of which end up as solid waste in landfills, clog sewers, or litter waterways. Increasingly, however, retailers are helping to curb the use of plastic bags. Whole Foods discontinued the use of plastic shopping bags throughout its stores in the United States, Canada,

The importance of cultural diversity is a social–cultural consideration for marketers. There are more Spanish-language programs on TV today from satellite and cable TV companies.

© Agustin Salinas/El Universal de Mexico/Newscom

and the United Kingdom. They and other retailers, like CVS and Target, sell reasonably priced, reusable cloth alternatives. Whole Foods also offers a discount to shoppers for not using plastic bags.[38]

But firms cannot always adjust to meet the demands of consumer groups. The choice between pleasing all consumers and remaining profitable—thus surviving—defines one of the most difficult dilemmas facing business. This topic is discussed in the "Solving an Ethical Controversy" feature. Given these constraints, what do consumers have the right to expect from the companies from which they buy goods and services? The most frequently quoted answer to this question comes from a speech made by President John F. Kennedy more than 50 years ago. Although this list does not amount to a definitive statement, it offers good rules of thumb that explain basic consumer rights:

consumer rights List of legitimate consumer expectations suggested by President John F. Kennedy.

1. *The right to choose freely.* Consumers should be able to choose from among a range of goods and services.

2. *The right to be informed.* Consumers should be provided with enough education and product information to enable them to be responsible buyers.

3. *The right to be heard.* Consumers should be able to express their legitimate displeasure to appropriate parties—that is, sellers, consumer assistance groups, and city or state consumer affairs offices.

SOLVING AN ETHICAL CONTROVERSY

Was "Pink Slime" Coverage Fair or Foul?

Following a negative comment by a celebrity chef, U.S. media latched onto a story about boneless lean-beef trimmings, long a standard USDA-approved ingredient in 70 percent of the ground beef consumed in the United States. Dubbing the product "pink slime," reporters and talk-show hosts revealed that it is treated with ammonium hydroxide to kill bacteria, including *E. coli*. Its maker, Beef Products Inc., went on the defensive, backed by the beef industry. The company said the product is safe, nutritious, and 100% beef, but many communities insisted it be taken off school-lunch menus immediately. McDonald's and Burger King announced they had stopped using ammonia-treated beef, and Kroger, Safeway, and other grocery chains will stop carrying ground beef that includes it.

Did the media give Beef Products Inc. a fair shake?

PRO 👍

1. People have a right to know what they're eating and how safe it is. The media were doing their job.

2. Lean-beef trimmings are a low-cost ingredient that has allowed the beef industry to quietly increase its profits at consumers' expense.

CON 👎

1. The photo used by many media outlets to illustrate their relentless coverage was not a picture of boneless lean-beef trimmings. Much of the reporting was similarly misleading.

2. The media were simply looking for a sensational story to boost their ratings, whether it was fair or slanted.

Summary:

The American Meat Institute posted a YouTube video to educate consumers about beef products, and the USDA announced it would tell school districts which suppliers use the product known as "pink slime" so they could stop buying it if they want to. Beef Products Inc. suspended operations at three plants, affecting hundreds of employees.

Sources: Bryan Gruley and Elizabeth Campbell, "The Sliming of Pink Slime's Creator," *Bloomberg Businessweek*, accessed October 23, 2012, www.businessweek.com; Mickey Meece, "'Pink Slime' Controversy Takes a Toll on Beef Producers," *Forbes*, accessed October 23, 2012, www.forbes.com; "Behind the Slime: Pink Slime and Its Lessons for Marketers," *Pavone Food.com*, accessed October 23, 2012, www.pavonefood.com; "Pink Slime Myths," *Beef Is Beef.com*, accessed October 23, 2012, http://beefisbeef.com.

4. *The right to be safe.* Consumers should be assured that the goods and services they purchase are not injurious with normal use. Goods and services should be designed so that the average consumer can use them safely.

These rights have formed the conceptual framework of much of the legislation enacted during the first five decades of the consumer rights movement. However, the question of how best to guarantee them remains unanswered. Sometimes local, state, or federal authorities step in. New York was the first city in the United States to require fast-food and casual-dining restaurants to post calorie counts of the various items displayed on their menu—in an effort to address obesity, which has become a nationwide health problem. The federal government issued a similar mandate to restaurants with at least 20 locations. In response, many restaurants have revamped their menus to include more lower-calorie items.[39]

Consumers' right to safety encompasses a vast range of products, from automobiles to children's toys. Sometimes it seems as though safety recalls are reported in the media too regularly. You might even receive a letter in the mail from a manufacturer informing you of a recall for a part on your refrigerator or car. To streamline the exchange of information among federal agencies and to make it more convenient for consumers to learn about product recalls, the U.S. government has established the website www.Recalls.gov. This website consolidates recall information generated by the six federal agencies empowered to issue recalls, including the Consumer Product Safety Commission, the Food and Drug Administration, and others. The user-friendly site organizes information into broad categories: Boats, Consumer Products, Cosmetics, Environmental Products, Food, Medicine, and Motor Vehicles.[40]

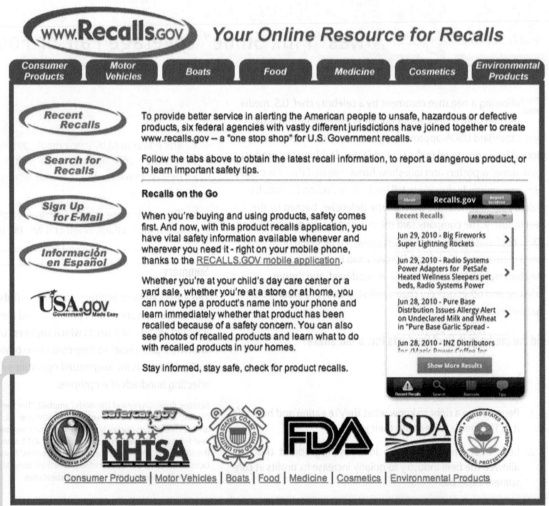

The U.S. government's mobile app for product recalls allows consumers to find information easily about product recalls from six federal agencies in one location.

Consumerism, along with the rest of the social–cultural environment for marketing decisions at home and abroad, is expanding in scope and importance. Today, no marketer can initiate a strategic decision without considering the society's norms, values, culture, and demographics. Understanding how these variables affect decisions is so important that some firms have created a new position—typically, manager of public policy research—to study the changing societal environment's future impact on their organizations.

ASSESSMENT CHECK

6.1 Define *consumerism*.

6.2 Identify the four consumer rights.

ETHICAL ISSUES IN MARKETING

The five environments described so far in this chapter do not completely capture the role that marketing plays in society and the resulting effects and responsibilities of marketing activities. Because marketing is closely connected with various public issues, it invites constant scrutiny. Moreover, because marketing acts as an interface between an organization and the society in which it operates, marketers often carry much of the responsibility for dealing with social issues that affect their firms.

Marketing operates outside the firm. It responds to that outside environment, and in turn is acted on by environmental influences. Relationships with employees, suppliers, the government, consumers, and society as a whole frame the social issues that marketers must address. The way that marketers deal with these social issues has a significant effect on their firm's eventual success. The diverse social issues that marketers face can be divided into two major categories: marketing ethics and social responsibility. While these two categories certainly overlap, this simple classification system provides a method for studying these issues.

Environmental influences have directed increased attention toward **marketing ethics**, defined as marketers' standards of conduct and moral values. Ethics concern matters of right and wrong: the responsibility of individuals and firms to do what is morally right. As Figure 3.2 shows, each element of the marketing mix raises its own set of ethical questions. Before any improvements to a firm's marketing program can be made, each element must be evaluated.

Creating an ethics program may be complicated and time consuming, but worthwhile. Some firms take their cue from the U.S. Federal Sentencing Guidelines for Organizations, which provides a framework for evaluating misconduct in business activities such as fraud or price fixing. After discovering that similar cases had been resolved differently by courts, the U.S. Sentencing Commission developed guidelines in 1991 that rely on what legislators call the "stick-and-carrot approach" to

Describe the ethical issues in marketing.

7

marketing ethics
Marketers' standards of conduct and moral values.

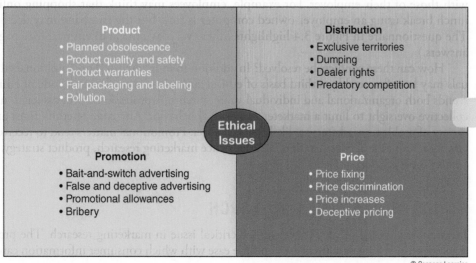

FIGURE 3.2
Ethical Questions in Marketing

© Cengage Learning

FIGURE 3.3
Ten Steps for Corporations to Improve Standards of Business Ethics

Source: From Ferrell/Fraedrich/Ferrell, *Business Ethics*, 9e. © 2013 Cengage Learning.

1. Appoint a senior-level ethics compliance officer.

2. Set up an ethics code capable of detecting and preventing misconduct.

3. Distribute a written code of ethics to employees, subsidiaries, and associated companies and require all business partners to abide by it.

4. Conduct regular ethics training programs to communicate standards and procedures.

5. Establish systems to monitor misconduct and report grievances.

6. Establish consistent punishment guidelines to enforce standards and codes.

7. Encourage an open-door policy, allowing employees to report cases of misconduct without fear of retaliation.

8. Prohibit employees with a track record of misconduct from holding positions with substantial discretionary authority.

9. Promote ethically aware and responsible managers.

10. Continually monitor effectiveness of all ethics-related programs.

corporate ethics: the financial penalties that the courts can impose for wrongdoing are the stick, while the existence of an effective ethics program can reduce the fines the courts can set, which serves as the carrot. Sentencing guidelines act as an incentive for corporations to implement effective ethics compliance programs—if they are hauled into court, the existence of such a program can help reduce penalties.

In some industries, organizations are required by law to maintain corporate-level positions responsible for ethics and legal compliance. Typically, ethics officers are responsible for creating and maintaining an ethical culture within the organization. They ensure that ethical protocols are established and enforced, and they serve as the chief source of information to all stakeholders inside and outside the organization regarding ethics. Figure 3.3 presents a step-by-step framework for building an effective program.

Because ethical behavior is so important to business conduct, some firms and universities have taken an unusual step. They invite convicted corporate criminals to speak to employees and students about their mistakes and the consequences of their actions.[41]

Ensuring ethical practices means promising customers and business partners not to sacrifice quality and fairness for profit. In exchange, organizations hope for increased customer loyalty toward their brands. Yet issues involving marketing ethics are not always clear-cut. The issue of cigarette advertising, for example, has divided the ranks of advertising executives. Is it right for advertisers to promote a product that, while legal, has known health hazards?

For years, charges of unethical conduct plagued the tobacco industry. In the largest civil settlement in U.S. history, tobacco manufacturers agreed to pay $206 billion to 46 states. Four other states—Florida, Minnesota, Mississippi, and Texas—had separate settlements totaling another $40 billion. The settlement freed tobacco companies from state claims for the cost of treating sick smokers. For their part, cigarette makers could no longer advertise on billboards or use cartoon characters in ads, nor could they sell nontobacco merchandise containing tobacco brands or logos. Initially, states used settlement monies to fund tobacco prevention programs, but in recent years nearly all states slashed program funding well below the level recommended by the Centers for Disease Control and Prevention. In a recent year, states collected nearly $26 billion from tobacco taxes and the tobacco settlement but spent less than 2 percent of that revenue on tobacco cessation programs.[42]

People develop standards of ethical behavior based on their own systems of values, which help them deal with ethical questions in their personal lives. However, the workplace may generate serious conflicts when individuals discover that their ethical beliefs are not necessarily in line with those of their employer. For example, employees may think that shopping online during a lunch break using an employer-owned computer is fine, but the company may decide otherwise. The questionnaire in Figure 3.4 highlights other everyday ethical dilemmas. (See page 94 for the answers.)

How can these conflicts be resolved? In addition to individual and organizational ethics, individuals may be influenced by a third basis of ethical authority—a professional code of ethics that transcends both organizational and individual value systems. A professional peer association can exercise collective oversight to limit a marketer's individual behavior. Any code of ethics must anticipate the variety of problems marketers are likely to encounter. Promotional matters tend to receive the greatest attention, but ethical considerations also influence marketing research, product strategy, distribution strategy, and pricing.

ETHICS IN MARKETING RESEARCH

Invasion of personal privacy has become a critical issue in marketing research. The proliferation of databases, the selling of address lists, and the ease with which consumer information can be gathered

---

Office Technology

1. Is it wrong to use company e-mail for personal reasons?
   ☐ Yes ☐ No

2. Is it wrong to use office equipment to help your children or spouse do schoolwork?
   ☐ Yes ☐ No

3. Is it wrong to play computer games on office equipment during the workday?
   ☐ Yes ☐ No

4. Is it wrong to use office equipment to do Internet shopping?
   ☐ Yes ☐ No

5. Is it unethical to blame an error you made on a technological glitch?
   ☐ Yes ☐ No

6. Is it unethical to visit pornographic Web sites using office equipment?
   ☐ Yes ☐ No

Gifts and Entertainment

7. What's the value at which a gift from a supplier or client becomes troubling?
   ☐ $25 ☐ $50 ☐ $100

8. Is a $50 gift to a boss unacceptable?
   ☐ Yes ☐ No

9. Is a $50 gift from the boss unacceptable?
   ☐ Yes ☐ No

10. Of gifts from suppliers: Is it OK to take a $200 pair of football tickets?
    ☐ Yes ☐ No

11. Is it OK to take a $120 pair of theater tickets?
    ☐ Yes ☐ No

12. Is it OK to take a $100 holiday food basket?
    ☐ Yes ☐ No

13. Is it OK to take a $25 gift certificate?
    ☐ Yes ☐ No

14. Can you accept a $75 prize won at a raffle at a supplier's conference?
    ☐ Yes ☐ No

Truth and Lies

15. Due to on-the-job pressure, have you ever abused or lied about sick days?
    ☐ Yes ☐ No

16. Due to on-the-job pressure, have you ever taken credit for someone else's work or idea?
    ☐ Yes ☐ No

*Ethics questionnaire answers are on page 94.

FIGURE 3.4

Test Your Workplace Ethics

Source: Ethics & Compliance Officer Association, Waltham, Massachusetts; Leadership Group, Wilmette, Illinois; survey sampled a cross-section of workers at large companies and nationwide; used with permission from Ethics & Compliance Officer Association.

through Internet technology have increased public concern. The issue of privacy will be explored in greater detail in Chapter 5. One marketing research tool particularly problematic is the promise of cash or gifts in return for marketing information that can then be sold to direct marketers. Consumers commonly disclose their personal information in return for an email newsletter or a favorite magazine.

Privacy issues have mushroomed with the growth of the Internet, with huge consequences to both consumers and marketers. A medical privacy breach of a database at Stanford Hospital in Palo Alto, California, resulted in information about 20,000 patients—including their names and diagnosis codes—being posted on a commercial website.[43] In another recent incident, hackers broke into a cloud-based software program used by NASDAQ's board of directors, enabling them to access the stock exchange's computer system.[44] Incidents like these point to the importance of using encryption programs to safeguard data.

Several agencies, including the FTC, offer assistance to Internet consumers. Consumers can go to http://ftc.gov/privacy for information. The Direct Marketing Association also provides services, such as the Mail, Telephone, and Email Preference Services, to help consumers get their names removed from marketers' targeted lists. Registration for the U.S. government's Do Not Call Registry is available at (888) 382–1222 and www.donotcall.gov. Unlistme.com and Junkbusters are free Web services that also help consumers remove their names from direct-mail and telemarketing lists.

"BRIEFLY SPEAKING"

"There is no such thing as a minor lapse of integrity."

—**Tom Peters**
*American writer on business management and co-author,
In Search of Excellence*

ETHICS IN PRODUCT STRATEGY

Product quality, planned obsolescence, brand similarity, and packaging all raise ethical issues. Feeling the competition, some marketers have tried packaging practices that might be considered misleading, deceptive, or unethical. Larger packages take up more shelf space, and consumers notice them. An odd-sized package makes price comparisons difficult. Bottles with concave bottoms give the impression that they contain more liquid than they actually do. Are these packaging practices justified in the name of competition, or are they deceptive? Growing regulatory mandates appear to be narrowing the range of discretion in this area.

How do you evaluate the quality of a product like a beverage? By flavor or by ingredients? Citing several studies, some consumer advocates say that the ingredients in soft drinks—mainly high sugar content—are linked to obesity in consumers, particularly children. Not surprisingly, the beverage industry disagrees, arguing that lack of exercise and a poor diet in general are greater contributors to weight gain than regular consumption of drinks.

ETHICS IN DISTRIBUTION

Two ethical issues influence a firm's decisions regarding distribution strategy:

1. What is the appropriate degree of control over the distribution channel?

2. Should a company distribute its products in marginally profitable outlets that have no alternative source of supply?

The question of channel control typically arises in relationships between manufacturers and franchise dealers. For example, should an automobile dealership, a gas station, or a fast-food outlet be forced to purchase parts, materials, and supplementary services from the parent organization?

The second question concerns marketers' responsibility to serve unsatisfied market segments even if the profit potential is slight. Should marketers build or rent retail stores in low-income areas, serve users of limited amounts of the firm's product, or continue to operate in a declining rural market? These problems are difficult to resolve because often they involve individuals rather than broad segments of the general public. An important first step is to ensure that the firm consistently enforces its channel policies.

ETHICS IN PROMOTION

Promotion raises many ethical questions because it is the most direct link between a firm and its customers. Personal selling has always been a target of criticism—and jokes about untrustworthiness. Used-car dealers, horse traders, and purveyors of quack remedies have been the targets of such barbs in the past. But promotion covers many areas, ranging from advertising to direct marketing, and it is vital for marketers to monitor their ethics in all marketing communications. Truth in advertising—representing accurately a product's benefits and drawbacks, warranties, price, and availability—is the bedrock of ethics in promotion.

Many organizations have modified how they advertise their products to children.

Jacquelyn Martin/AP Photo

Marketing to children has been under close scrutiny for many years because children have not yet developed the skills to receive marketing messages critically. They simply believe everything they see and hear. With childhood obesity a serious concern in America, Kellogg Company announced it would change how it advertises its breakfast cereals to children worldwide, focusing solely on products that meet nutrition guidelines. Other organizations like General Mills and Quaker Oats pledged to also emphasize healthy choices.[45] Yet, the Campaign for a Commercial-Free Childhood, a watchdog group, charged that some marketers are increasingly using the Web and social media to target children in promoting the least nutritious products.[46] The federal government recently suggested new nutritional standards for food advertising to children. Critics claim, however, that because the standards are guidelines and not regulations, they aren't enforceable.[47]

Promoting certain products to college students can raise ethical questions as well. College students are a prime market for firms that sell everything from electronics to beer. And although laws prohibit the sale of alcohol to anyone under 21, companies often advertise beer through popular items like hats, shirts, bar signs, and other collectibles. Critics have long claimed this practice supports underage drinking.

Another ethical issue involves paying universities for the use of their logo, team name, or mascot in advertising products and services to its students. Anheuser-Busch came under fire from colleges and universities across the nation for marketing Bud Light on campuses in "Fan Cans" specially designed in their school's colors. Citing concerns about alcohol use and trademark infringement, the schools contacted Anheuser-Busch to stop local distribution; some even threatened legal action. The Federal Trade Commission became involved, citing the promotion's appeal to underage drinking. Anheuser-Busch ended up discontinuing the promotion in many campus towns across the United States.[48]

ETHICS IN PRICING

Pricing is probably the most regulated aspect of a firm's marketing strategy. As a result, most unethical price behavior is also illegal. Some aspects of pricing, however, are still open to ethics abuses. For example, should some customers pay more for merchandise if distribution costs are higher in their areas? Do marketers have an obligation to warn vendors and customers of impending price, discount, or return policy changes?

Some credit card companies target consumers with poor credit ratings and offer them what industry observers call "subprime" or "fee-harvesting" credit cards. Under such an arrangement, the company lures consumers to sign up for the card, promising to improve their credit rating. The cardholder is then charged exorbitant annual fees, leaving them in worse financial shape than before.[49]

While consumers are almost always informed of credit card terms in their agreements, the print often is tiny and the language may be hard to understand. For instance, a credit card issuer might advertise the benefits of its premium card, but the fine print explains that the firm is allowed to substitute a different plan—with a higher interest rate—if the applicant doesn't qualify for the premium card.

The Credit Card Accountability, Responsibility and Disclosure Act, enacted in 2009, curbs abuses in the credit-card industry and ends many questionable practices of credit card companies regarding interest rates, billing cycles, finance charges, and more.[50]

All these concerns must be dealt with in developing a professional ethic for pricing products. The ethical issues involved in pricing for today's highly competitive and increasingly computerized markets are discussed in greater detail in Chapters 18 and 19.

 ASSESSMENT CHECK

7.1 Define *marketing ethics*.

7.2 Identify the five areas in which ethics can be a problem.

social responsibility
Marketing philosophies, policies, procedures, and actions that have the enhancement of society's welfare as a primary objective.

SOCIAL RESPONSIBILITY IN MARKETING

Companies can do business in such a way that everyone benefits—customers, the companies themselves, and society as a whole. While ethical business practices are vital to a firm's long-term survival and growth, social responsibility raises the bar even higher. In marketing, social responsibility involves accepting an obligation to give equal weight to profits, consumer satisfaction, and social well-being in evaluating a firm's performance. In addition to measuring sales, revenues, and profits, a firm must also consider ways in which it contributes to the overall well-being of its customers and society.

Identify the four levels of the social responsibility pyramid. 8

FIGURE 3.5
The Four Step Pyramid of Social Responsibility

Source: The Four Step Pyramid of Corporate Social Responsibility from *Business Horizons*, Vol. 34, 1991, page 92, Freeman & Liedtka, "Corp. Social Responsibility." Reprinted from *Business Horizons* © 1991 with permission from Elsevier.

Philanthropic
Be a good corporate citizen
▶ Contribute resources to the community; improve quality of life

Ethical
Be ethical
▶ Obligation to do what is right, just, and fair
▶ Avoid harm

Legal
Obey the law
▶ Law is society's codification of right and wrong
▶ Play by the rules of the game

Economic
Be profitable
▶ The foundation upon which all others rest

Social responsibility allows a wide range of opportunities for companies to shine. If companies are reluctant, government legislation can mandate socially responsible actions. Government may require firms to take socially responsible actions in matters of environmental policy, deceptive product claims, and other areas. Also, consumers, through their power to repeat or withhold purchases, may force marketers to provide honest and relevant information and fair prices. The four dimensions of social responsibility—economic, legal, ethical, and philanthropic—are shown in Figure 3.5. The first two dimensions have long been recognized, but ethical obligations and the need for marketers to be good corporate citizens have increased in importance in recent years. IBM is one company that is committed to being a good corporate citizen. The company has used this facet of corporate responsibility to its advantage in marketing the company's overall focus, as explained in the "Marketing Success" feature.

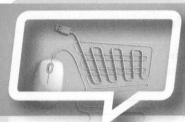

MARKETING SUCCESS

IBM's Corporate Social Responsibility Efforts

Background. IBM is a century-old U.S. firm with more than 430,000 employees operating in almost 170 countries. It holds itself to high standards of corporate social responsibility (CSR), in part because its operations support not only companies around the world but cities, communities, governments, and their infrastructures.

The Challenge. The company believes corporate citizenship "consists of far more than community service" and is constantly looking for ways to make a real difference to all levels of its huge network of stakeholders.

The Strategy. Many of IBM's CSR initiatives rely on sharing the expertise of its own employees. Most efforts are international in scope, like its Smarter Cities Challenge, which sends IBM experts to 100 cities worldwide to solve local problems in health, education,

transportation, and sustainability. The company's participation in Safer Internet Day allows IBMers around the world to help educate communities in dozens of countries from Finland to Romania about Internet safety for kids. IBM also lends employees to joint programs like the World Environment Center's Corporate Sustainability Council of Major Companies.

The Outcome. In addition to paid time they devote to CSR, each year IBM employees supply millions of hours as volunteers in an enormous variety of endeavors.

Sources: Company website, "Responsibility at IBM," accessed October 23, 2012, www.ibm.com; Organization website, "Safer Internet Day 2013," accessed October 23, 2012, www.saferinternet.org; Company press release, "IBM Names Worldwide Recipients of 2012 Smarter Cities Challenge Grants to Improve Urban Life," accessed October 23, 2012, www.justmeans.com; Company press release, "IBM Releases Free Internet Security Training Tools to Educate Students, Teachers and Parents on Digital Responsibility," accessed October 23, 2012, www.03.ibm.com.

The locus for socially responsible decisions in organizations has always been an important issue. But who should accept specific accountability for the social effects of marketing decisions? Responses include the district sales manager, the marketing vice president, the firm's CEO, and even the board of directors. Probably the most valid assessment holds that all marketers, regardless of their stations in the organization, remain accountable for the social aspects of their decisions.

MARKETING'S RESPONSIBILITIES

The concept of business's social responsibility has traditionally concerned managers' relationships with customers, employees, and stockholders. In general, managers traditionally have felt responsible for providing quality products at reasonable prices for customers, adequate wages and decent working environments for employees, and acceptable profits for stockholders. Only occasionally did the concept extend to relations with the government and rarely with the general public.

Today, corporate responsibility has expanded to cover the entire framework of society. A decision to temporarily delay the installation of a pollution-control device may satisfy the traditional sense of responsibility. Customers would continue to receive an uninterrupted supply of the plant's products, employees would not face layoffs, and stockholders would still receive reasonable returns on their investments. Contemporary business ethics, however, would not accept this choice as socially responsible.

Contemporary marketing decisions must consider their global effect. Some clothing manufacturers and retailers have come under fire for buying from foreign suppliers who force employees, including children, to work long hours in dangerous conditions or pay less than a living wage. In some cases, workers who attempted to form a union have been threatened, fired, or worse.[51]

Marketers must also consider the long-term effects of their decisions and the well-being of future generations. Manufacturing processes that damage the environment or that use up natural energy resources are easy targets for criticism.

Marketers can use several methods to help their companies behave in socially responsible ways. Chapter 1 discussed cause marketing as one channel through which firms can promote social causes and at the same time benefit by linking their people and products to worthy undertakings. Socially responsible marketing involves campaigns that encourage people to adopt socially beneficial behaviors such as safe driving, eating more nutritious food, or improving the working conditions of people half a world away. And organizations that sponsor socially responsible programs not only help society but also develop goodwill for an organization, which could help the bottom line in the long run.

One way entire communities can benefit is through socially responsible investing. Many local banks and credit unions are committed to investing in their communities. When consumers purchase certificates of deposit or open money market accounts, the bank or credit union can use the money to finance loans for affordable housing or for small businesses. The U.S. Treasury Department has certified more than 1,000 community development financial institutions that serve neighborhoods. These institutions serve an important purpose: to educate low-income borrowers.[52]

MARKETING AND ECOLOGY

Ecology—the relationship between organisms and their natural environments—has become a driving force in influencing how businesses operate. Many industry and government leaders rank the protection of the environment as the biggest challenge facing today's corporations. Environmental issues such as water pollution, waste disposal, acid rain, depletion of the ozone layer, and global warming affect everyone. They influence all areas of marketing decision making, including product planning and public relations, spanning such topics as planned obsolescence, pollution control, recycling waste materials, and resource conservation.

In creating new-product offerings that respond to consumer demands for convenience by offering extremely short-lived products such as disposable diapers, ballpoint pens, razors, and cameras, marketers occasionally find themselves accused of intentionally offering products with limited durability—in other words, of practicing planned obsolescence. In addition to convenience-oriented items, other products become obsolete when rapid changes in technology create superior alternatives. In the computer industry, changes take place so quickly that lawmakers in several states have

© Maurice Savage/Alamy

Manufacturers of printer cartridges provide postage-paid envelopes so consumers can mail back the empty cartridges for recycling.

green marketing
Production, promotion, and reclamation of environmentally sensitive products.

proposed legislation to force manufacturers to take back "e-waste"—used PCs and other technology products that contain toxic chemicals. For example, manufacturers of printer cartridges include a self-addressed, postage-paid pouch to mail empty cartridges back to the company for reuse.

Public concern about pollution of such natural resources as water and air affects some industries, such as pharmaceuticals or heavy-goods manufacturing, more than others. Still, the marketing system annually generates billions of tons of packaging materials such as glass, metal, paper, and plastics that add to the world's growing piles of trash and waste. Recycling such materials, as many manufacturers do, is another important aspect of ecology. Recycling can benefit society by saving natural resources and energy as well as by alleviating a major factor in environmental pollution—waste disposal.

Unwanted and outdated electronic waste is the latest trash to overrun landfills as technology advances motivate Americans to ditch their old electronics for newer models. Increasingly, consumers wonder how to dispose of their old computers, monitors, printers, TVs, phones, cameras, and other gadgets, especially since many of the older models contain lead and other hazardous materials requiring special handling. Best Buy, one of the nation's largest electronics retailer, sponsors a recycling program under which customers can drop off a wide variety of unwanted electronics products—even if they weren't bought at Best Buy.[53]

Many companies respond to consumers' growing concern about ecological issues through green marketing—production, promotion, and reclamation of environmentally sensitive products. In the green marketing revolution of the early 1990s, marketers were quick to tie their companies and products to ecological themes. Consumers have responded by purchasing more and more of these goods, providing profits and opportunities for growth to the companies that make and sell them. The Sustainability Consortium, an independent organization dedicated to driving sustainability in consumer goods, is working with companies including Dell, Samsung, Toshiba, and Walmart to create standards to help consumers make green choices in electronics.[54] The Motel 6 chain and Sofitel and Studio 6 brands—all part of the Accor North America portfolio—committed to a green rating

Fairmont Hotels & Resorts was recently named one of the top five eco-friendly hotel chains.

Courtesy of Fairmont Pittsburgh

program after Accor piloted it recently. Three of Marriott's brands—Courtyard, Residence Inn, and TownPlace Suites—have earned certification by the U.S. Green Building Council. And Fairmont Hotels & Resorts was recently named one of the top five eco-friendly hotel chains by a leading environmental organization.[55]

Major League Baseball was the first professional sports organization to partner with the Natural Resources Defense Council, an environmentalist group, to identify numerous ways to go green. Several ballparks, including Busch Stadium in St. Louis, Safeco Field in Seattle, and Kauffman Stadium in Kansas City, employ solar panels to reduce their energy costs. The Cleveland Indians lead the league in harnessing wind power, with a turbine atop Progressive Field. And on a recent Earth Day, fans at the Oakland A's game received a redwood seedling to plant to commemorate the holiday.[56]

ASSESSMENT CHECK

8.1 Identify the four levels of the social responsibility pyramid.

8.2 What are the benefits of green marketing?

STRATEGIC IMPLICATIONS OF MARKETING IN THE 21ST CENTURY

Marketing decisions that businesses make are influenced by changes in the competitive, political–legal, economic, technological, and social–cultural environments. Marketing ethics and social responsibility will continue to play important roles in business transactions in your hometown and around the globe.

As the Internet and the rapid changes in technology that it represents are fully absorbed into the competitive environment, competition is even more intense than before. Much of the competition results from innovations in technology and scientific discoveries. Business in the 21st century is propelled by information technologies but sustained by creative thinking and the willingness

of marketers to meet challenges. Marketers face new regulations as the political and legal environment responds to changes in the United States and abroad. As the population ages and the social–cultural environment evolves, marketers will seek to meet the demands for new goods and services for consumers, such as increased health-related merchandise. As always, they will try to anticipate and make the most of every opportunity afforded by the business cycle.

Ethics and social responsibility must underlie everything that marketers do in the 21st century—those who find ways to "do well by doing good" will succeed.

Get online now for additional learning tools to help you master your marketing knowledge—visit **WWW.CENGAGEBRAIN.COM** today!

REVIEW OF CHAPTER OBJECTIVES

1 Identify the five components of the marketing environment.

The five components of the marketing environment are (1) the *competitive environment*—the interactive process that occurs in the marketplace as competing organizations seek to satisfy markets; (2) the *political–legal environment*—the laws and interpretations of laws that require firms to operate under competitive conditions and to protect consumer rights; (3) the *economic environment*—environmental factors resulting from business fluctuations and variations in inflation rates and employment levels; (4) the *technological environment*—application to marketing of knowledge based on discoveries in science, inventions, and innovations; and (5) the *social–cultural environment*—the component of the marketing environment consisting of the relationship between the marketer and society and its culture.

2 Explain the types of competition marketers face and the steps necessary for developing a competitive strategy.

Three types of competition exist: (1) direct competition among marketers of similar products, (2) competition among goods or services that can be substituted for one another, and (3) competition among all organizations that vie for the consumer's purchasing power. To develop a competitive strategy, marketers must answer the following questions: (1) Should we compete? The answer depends on the firm's available resources and objectives as well as its expected profit potential. (2) If so, in what markets should we compete? This question requires marketers to make product, pricing, distribution, and promotional decisions that give their firm a competitive advantage. (3) How should we compete? This question requires marketers to make the technical decisions involved in setting a comprehensive marketing strategy.

3 Describe how marketing activities are regulated and how marketers can influence the political–legal environment.

Marketing activities are influenced by federal, state, and local laws that require firms to operate under competitive conditions and to protect consumer rights. Government regulatory agencies like the Federal Trade Commission enforce these laws and identify and correct unfair marketing practices. Public and private consumer interest groups and industry self-regulatory groups also affect marketing activities. Marketers may seek to influence public opinion and legislative actions through advertising, political action committees, and political lobbying.

4 Outline the economic factors that affect marketing decisions and consumer buying power.

The primary economic factors are (1) the stage in the business cycle, (2) inflation and deflation, (3) unemployment, (4) income, and (5) resource availability. All are vitally important to marketers because of their effects on consumers' willingness to buy and consumers' perceptions regarding changes in the marketing mix variables.

5 Discuss the impact of the technological environment on a firm's marketing activities.

The technological environment consists of application to marketing of knowledge based on discoveries in science, inventions, and innovations. This knowledge can provide marketing opportunities: it results in new products and improves existing ones and it is a frequent source of price reductions through new production methods or materials. Technological applications also pose a threat because they can make existing products obsolete overnight. The technological environment demands that marketers continually adapt to change because its scope of influence reaches into consumers' lifestyles, competitors' offerings, and industrial users' demands.

6 Explain how the social–cultural environment influences marketing.

The social–cultural environment is the relationship between marketing, society, and culture. To remain competitive, marketers must be sensitive to society's demographic shifts and changing values, which affect consumers' reactions to different products and marketing practices. Marketers must consider the increasing importance of cultural diversity, both in the United States and abroad. Changing societal values have led to consumerism, the social force within the environment designed to aid and protect the consumer by exerting legal, moral, and economic pressures on business. Consumer rights include the following: (1) the right to choose freely, (2) the right to be informed, (3) the right to be heard, and (4) the right to be safe.

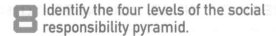

7 Describe the ethical issues in marketing.

Marketing ethics encompass the marketer's standards of conduct and moral values. Each element of the marketing mix raises its own set of ethical questions. Ethics in product strategy may involve quality and safety, packaging and labeling, and pollution. Ethics in distribution may involve territorial decisions. In promotion, ethical issues include honesty in advertising and promotion to children. Pricing may raise questions about price fixing and discrimination, increases deemed excessive, and deceptive pricing.

8 Identify the four levels of the social responsibility pyramid.

The four levels of social responsibility are: (1) *economic*—to be profitable, the foundation upon which the other three levels of the pyramid rest; (2) *legal*—to obey the law, society's codification of right and wrong; (3) *ethical*—to do what is right, just, and fair and to avoid wrongdoing; and (4) *philanthropic*—to be a good corporate citizen, contributing to the community and improving quality of life.

 ASSESSMENT CHECK: ANSWERS

1.1 Define *environmental scanning*. Environmental scanning is the process of collecting information about the external marketing environment to identify and interpret potential trends.

1.2 How does environmental scanning contribute to environmental management? Environmental scanning contributes to environmental management by providing current information about the five different environments so marketers can predict and influence changes.

2.1 Distinguish between direct and indirect competition, and give an example of each. Direct competition occurs among marketers of similar products, such as supermarkets or gas stations. Indirect competition involves products that are easily substituted. Fried chicken could compete with pizza or tacos. A baseball game could compete with a trip to a water park.

2.2 What is time-based competition? Time-based competition is the strategy of developing and distributing goods and services more quickly than competitors.

3.1 Identify the four phases of U.S. government regulation of business. What is the newest frontier? The four phases of government regulation of business are the antimonopoly period, protection of competitors, consumer protection, and industry regulation. The newest frontier is cyberspace.

3.2 Which federal agency wields the broadest regulatory powers for influencing marketing activities? The Federal Trade Commission has the broadest regulatory authority.

4.1 Identify and describe briefly the four stages of the business cycle. The four stages of the business cycle are prosperity, recession, depression, and recovery.

4.2 Explain how inflation and income affect consumer buying decisions. Inflation devalues money and therefore may restrict some purchasing, particularly goods and services

not considered necessary. Income also influences consumer buying power—the more discretionary income a household has, the more goods and services can be purchased.

5.1 What are some of the consumer benefits of technology? Technology can lead to new or improved goods and services, offer better customer service, and reduce prices. It can also address social concerns.

5.2 Why must marketers monitor the technological environment? Marketers need to monitor the technological environment to stay current with—and possibly ahead of—competitors. If they don't, they may wind up with obsolete offerings.

6.1 Define *consumerism*. Consumerism is a social force within the environment that aids and protects the buyer by exerting legal, moral, and economic pressures on business.

6.2 Identify the four consumer rights. The four consumer rights are the right to choose freely, the right to be informed, the right to be heard, and the right to be safe.

7.1 Define *marketing ethics*. Marketing ethics refers to the marketer's standards of conduct and moral values.

7.2 Identify the five areas in which ethics can be a problem. The five areas of ethical concern for marketers are marketing research, product strategy, distribution, promotion, and pricing.

8.1 Identify the four levels of the social responsibility pyramid. The four levels of social responsibility are economic, legal, ethical, and philanthropic.

8.2 What are the benefits of green marketing? Green marketing, which responds to consumers' growing concerns about ecological issues, offers consumers high-quality products without health risks or damage to the environment. Many industries, including appliances, consumer electronics, construction, hospitality, and more, are finding that incorporating green practices rejuvenates their business.

MARKETING TERMS YOU NEED TO KNOW

environmental scanning **63**

environmental management **63**

strategic alliance **63**

competitive environment **64**

monopoly **64**

antitrust **64**

oligopoly **64**

competitive strategy **66**

time-based competition **66**

political–legal
   environment **67**

gross domestic product
   (GDP) **72**

economic environment **72**

business cycle **72**

inflation **73**

unemployment **74**

discretionary income **74**

demarketing **74**

technological
   environment **76**

VoIP (Voice over Internet
   Protocol) **77**

social–cultural
   environment **77**

consumerism **78**

consumer rights **79**

marketing ethics **81**

social responsibility **85**

green marketing **88**

ASSURANCE OF LEARNING REVIEW

1. Why is environmental scanning an important activity for marketers?

2. What are the three different types of competition? Give an example of each.

3. What are the three questions marketers must ask before deciding on a competitive strategy?

4. What is the function of the Federal Trade Commission? The Food and Drug Administration?

5. Describe an industry or firm that you think might be able to weather an economic downturn and explain why.

6. Why do marketers monitor the technological environment?

7. How might marketers make the most of shifts in the social–cultural environment?

8. Describe the importance of consumer rights in today's marketing activities.

9. Why is it worthwhile for a firm to create an ethics program?

10. How can social responsibility benefit a firm as well as the society in which it operates?

PROJECTS AND TEAMWORK EXERCISES

1. With a classmate, choose two companies or brands that compete directly with each other. Select two of the following or choose your own. Then develop a competitive strategy for your firm while your partner develops a strategy for his or hers. Present the two strategies to the class. How are they similar? How are they different?
   a. Kmart and Target
   b. Verizon and T-Mobile
   c. Sea World and Universal Studios
   d. Visa and MasterCard
   e. Mazda and Hyundai
   f. Chili's and T.G.I. Friday's

2. Track your own consumer purchasing decisions as they relate to your income. Compare your decisions during the college year and the summer. Do you have a summer job that increases your income? How does that affect your decisions?

3. The U.S. Postal Service essentially enjoys a monopoly on the delivery of most mail. With a classmate, develop a strategy for

a business that would compete with the USPS in areas that firms—such as UPS and FedEx—do not already cover.

4. Choose one of the following products. Working in pairs or small groups, present arguments for and against having the United States impose certain regulations on the advertising of your product. (Note that some products already do have regulations—you can argue for or against them.)
   a. Smokeless tobacco
   b. Firearms
   c. State lottery
   d. Prescription medications

5. With a classmate, research a professional sports team that has threatened to move if locals don't approve subsidies to build a new stadium or arena. Do you think this is a savvy business move on the part of the team's owners? Or, is it an unethical move because area businesses will lose revenues if the team takes its business elsewhere?

CRITICAL-THINKING EXERCISES

1. Suppose you and a friend want to start a company that markets frozen fish dinners. What are some of the questions about the competitive environment you would like to have answered before you begin production? How will you determine whom your customers are likely to be? How will you reach them?

2. Emissions standards for motorcycles took effect in 2006 under rules adopted by the Environmental Protection Agency. There were no previous emissions controls for motorcycles at all, but even under the new laws, "dirt" bikes for off-road use will be exempt. The standards add about $75 to the average cost of a motorcycle according to the EPA, but $250 according to the Motorcycle Industry Council. Why do you think motorcycle makers did not adopt voluntary emissions standards? Should they have done so? Why or why not?

3. The social–cultural environment can have a strong influence on the decisions marketers must make. In recent years, animal rights groups have targeted the manufacture and sale of *foie gras,* a European food delicacy made from goose and duck liver. Activists cite the cruel treatment of these birds, while chefs and restaurant owners claim otherwise. Animal rights groups are pressuring restaurants to stop serving *foie gras.*

Others argue that consumers should be allowed a choice. What aspects of the social–cultural environment are affecting the marketing of *foie gras?* Which of the other components of the marketing environment may come into play, and how?

4. Nearly 400 million rebates—worth about $6 billion—are offered to U.S. consumers by marketers every year. But do consumers like them? Often rebates require more effort than a consumer is willing to make to receive the cash back. Critics of the promotional effort say that marketers know this and are banking on consumers not redeeming them, resulting in extra income for retailers and manufacturers. Do you think rebate programs are ethical? Why or why not?

5. The safe disposal of nuclear waste has been the topic of continuing public debate and an ongoing issue for marketers who work for nuclear power companies. This material is currently stored at 75 sites around the nation. To build a nuclear waste site, the U.S. Department of Energy must apply for and obtain a license. Supporters of such sites argue that they are important to building America's nuclear power capacity, while critics question their safety and usefulness. As a marketer, how would you approach this issue?

ETHICS EXERCISE

Some retail firms protect their inventory against theft by locking their premises after hours even though maintenance and other workers are inside the stores working all night. Employees have charged that they are forbidden to leave the premises during these hours and that during an emergency, such as illness or injury, precious time is lost waiting for a manager to arrive who is authorized to unlock the doors. Although workers could open an emergency exit, in some cases they claim that they will be fired for doing so.

Employers assert that managers with keys are on the premises (or minutes away) and that locking employees in ensures their own safety as well as cutting down on costly "shrinkage."

1. Under what circumstances, if any, do you think locking employees in at night is appropriate?

2. If you feel this practice is appropriate, what safeguards do you think should be put into effect? What responsibilities do employers and employees have in such circumstances?

INTERNET EXERCISES

1. **Economic environment.** The U.S. Census Bureau projects what the U.S. population will look like in the next 15 to 25 years. Visit the Census Bureau's website and compare its projections of the U.S. population to current figures. What will the U.S. population look like in the future? How is it different from the current population? List two or three products or industries you feel will benefit from future population trends.

   www.census.gov/population/projections/index.html

2. **Fair trade coffee.** Go to the website listed below to learn about so-called fair trade coffee. Prepare a brief report on the subject. How could a coffee manufacturer or retailer integrate fair trade products into its social responsibility efforts.

   www.globalexchange.org/campaigns/fairtrade/coffee

3. **Building a brand.** Visit the website for footwear maker Ugg to learn about its efforts at building its brand. How has Ugg answered each of the five questions listed in the chapter concerning the development of a competitive strategy?

   www.uggaustralia.com

Note: Internet Web addresses change frequently. If you don't find the exact site listed, you may need to access the organization's home page and search from there or use a search engine like Google or Bing.

ETHICS QUESTIONNAIRE ANSWERS

Questionnaire is on page 83.

1. 34% said personal email on company computers is wrong.

2. 37% said using office equipment for schoolwork is wrong.

3. 49% said playing computer games at work is wrong.

4. 54% said Internet shopping at work is wrong.

5. 61% said it's unethical to blame your error on technology.

6. 87% said it's unethical to visit pornographic sites at work.

7. 33% said $25 is the amount at which a gift from a supplier or client becomes troubling, while 33% said $50, and 33% said $100.

8. 35% said a $50 gift to the boss is unacceptable.

9. 12% said a $50 gift from the boss is unacceptable.

10. 70% said it's unacceptable to take $200 football tickets.

11. 70% said it's unacceptable to take $120 theater tickets.

12. 35% said it's unacceptable to take a $100 food basket.

13. 45% said it's unacceptable to take a $25 gift certificate.

14. 40% said it's unacceptable to take a $75 raffle prize.

15. 11% reported they lied about sick days.

16. 4% reported they have taken credit for the work or ideas of others.

CASE 3.1
Panera Cares® Community Cafés

You may have heard there's no such thing as a free lunch, but at four Panera Bread Co. restaurants in Illinois, Michigan, Missouri, and Oregon, there is.

After seeing how demoralizing it can be for a person waiting for a handout, Panera's co-founder and CEO Ron Shaich converted four stores into a separate nonprofit operation. The menu is the same as elsewhere in the popular salad and sandwich chain, but a donation box and the honor system replace the cash register in what Shaich calls "nonprofit community cafés of shared responsibility." These nonprofit Paneras do not charge for meals. Instead, customers get receipts with their orders that explain what the meal would have cost in a conventional Panera store.

About 60 percent of customers leave the suggested amount; 20 percent leave more; and the remainder pay less or nothing. Customers are requested to come no more than once a day to the pay-what-you-can cafés. Those who come in a few times a week to have a meal are asked to volunteer in the store, in keeping with posted signs reading, "We are not about a handout. We are about a hand up for those who really need it."

The pay-what-you-can cafés are breaking even and are on target to serve nearly a million meals in the coming year. The company recently announced that it will add a fifth Panera Cares® café in the near future.

QUESTIONS FOR CRITICAL THINKING

1. One critic called Panera's pay-what-you-can model "a marketing ploy." Do you agree? Why or why not?

2. Panera donates millions in cash and food each year but feels the cafés allow a direct connection to those in need. Why would that matter?

Sources: Organization website, http://paneracares.org, accessed October 23, 2012; Rahim Kanani, "How Restaurant Visionary Ron Shaich Is Tackling America's Hunger Crisis," *Forbes*, accessed October 23, 2012, www.forbes.com; Niala Boodhoo, "Panera Sandwich Chain Explores 'Pay What You Want' Concept," *NPR Chicago*, accessed October 23, 2012, www.npr.org/blogs/thesalt; Ron Ruggless, "Panera Cares Café opens in Chicago," *Nation's Restaurant News*, accessed October 23, 2012, http://nrn.com; Alexa Fee, "Panera to Open More 'Pay-What-You-Want' Stores," *The Daily Caller*, accessed October 23, 2012, www.dailycaller.com; Sylvia Rector, "Panera's Pay-What-You-Can Cafes Inspire Others," *USA Today*, accessed October 23, 2012, www.usatoday.com.

VIDEO CASE 3.2
Zappos Employees Do More Than Sell Shoes

It's hard to imagine not being able to buy a pair of shoes online. It's even harder to imagine not owning a pair of shoes at all. The founders and employees at Zappos are familiar with both situations. Co-founder and CEO Tony Hsieh got Zappos off the ground in 1999 when he and other investors realized that nowhere on the Internet could consumers find a real selection of shoes. You know how successful Zappos has become since then, despite subsequent competition—but you might not be aware of the company's efforts to give back to its community, including giving shoes away to children in need.

Zappos engages in social responsibility initiatives because "we feel that it's the right thing to do," explains Shannon Roy, the company's Happiness Hippie (her job title). The company develops relationships with charitable organizations that are similar to those it builds with customers and vendors, looking for ways that employees can interact directly with the community through these organizations. Some of the broad areas in which Zappos offers assistance are poverty and education, cancer research and care, and pets and nature. Specific efforts include partnerships with charitable organizations, such as Goodie Two Shoes, a foundation that provides new shoes and socks to children in crisis or need. Through its Goodie Two Shoes Giveaway each year, the organization teams up with Zappos and other firms to donate and distribute thousands of footwear products to children who need them. "It's giving back to the community," says Shannon Roy, who adds that Zappos employees feel driven to participate. "It's part of our being, part of our culture, it's very inherent in what Zappos is all about." Working at Zappos is "grander than the 9 to 5 job. It's doing something for the greater good."

It would be easy for an online retailer like Zappos to set up shop anywhere and ignore its surroundings. But that's not Zappos. Instead, the firm made a deal to renovate the vacant Las Vegas City Hall for $40 million, bringing about 2,000 employees to downtown Las Vegas—an area that could use an economic and social boost. CEO Tony Hsieh admits that originally he thought about building a "dream corporate campus," much like those of Apple, Google, and Nike. But when the Las Vegas opportunity came along, Hsieh and other Zappos managers thought: "Let's not be like the other companies. Let's not be insular and only care about our employees. We want to help contribute and help build a community and really integrate into a community around our campus." City officials predicted that the economic impact to the downtown area could top $336 million, bolstering real estate, health care, restaurants and hotels, retailers, and other businesses. "I think this is part of what our brand is about," observes Matt Burchard, senior director of marketing, photo, and video. "We've added a core tenet of what we stand for, and that's community."

Burchard notes that Zappos is committed to investing in things beyond its core business, like the infrastructure of downtown Las Vegas. Recently, The Downtown Project (founded by Hsieh and others) partnered with Venture for America to attract new college graduates for two-year stints to help startup businesses get off the ground in Las Vegas. In addition, The Downtown Project has bought up Las Vegas properties, such as an old Motel 6, a 7-Eleven building, and numerous condominiums for demolition or renovation. The idea is to revitalize the entire area—both economically and socially.

Zappos fulfills the four levels of the social responsibility pyramid: economic, legal, ethical, and philanthropic. The company is stable and profitable, giving it a solid platform from which to launch social responsibility initiatives. It operates with a strong legal and ethical base. Recently, when Zappos became the target of a cyber attack that gained access to its internal network (and the accounts of 24 million users), the firm acted fast, putting nearly every employee to work assisting in its response to the breach. Even though the breach did not reach complete credit card numbers or other critical data, the company notified its customers and reset all of their passwords. Zappos also warned customers to be on the lookout for phishing emails and other scams. Finally, Zappos is generous in its philanthropic efforts, donating money, shoes, and employee time to its various causes. "We don't overanalyze it," says Rob Siefker, director of the customer loyalty team. "We just know who we are and who we want to be. We act on that."

QUESTIONS FOR CRITICAL THINKING

1. Describe how the economic environment may influence Zappos' marketing efforts.

2. Explain how Zappos' move into downtown Las Vegas fulfills the four levels of the social responsibility pyramid.

Sources: Timothy Pratt, "What Happens in Brooklyn Moves to Vegas," *The New York Times*, accessed October 23, 2012, www.nytimes.com; Company website, www.zappos.com, accessed October 23, 2012; Goodie Two Shoes Foundation, www.goodietwoshoes.org, accessed October 23, 2012; Joe Schoenmann, "Zappos CEO Buys Motel, Strikes Deal to Bring Young Talent Downtown," *Las Vegas Sun*, accessed October 23, 2012, www.lasvegassun.com; Dave Toplikar, "Las Vegas City Council Approves Final Deal Bringing Zappos Downtown," *Las Vegas Sun*, accessed October 23, 2012; "100 Best Companies to Work For," *CNN Money*, accessed October 23, 2012, http://money.cnn.com; Andy Greenberg, "Zappos Says Hackers Accessed 24 Million Customers' Account Details," *Forbes*, accessed October 23, 2012, www.forbes.com.

NOTES

1. Organization website, www.cultivatefoundation.org, accessed October 22, 2012; "Chipotle Will Plant a Free Burrito in Your Lunch Bag to Celebrate Earth Day," *Reuters.com*, accessed October 22, 2012, www.reuters.com; Maureen Morrison, "Chipotle Bucks Fast-Food Convention While It Still Can," *Advertising Age*, accessed October 22, 2012; www.adage.com; "Chipotle Ad Upstages Some Grammy Performances," *Advertising Age*, accessed October 22, 2012, www.adage.com; Elizabeth Olson, "An Animated Ad with a Plot Line and a Moral," *The New York Times*, accessed October 22, 2012; www.nytimes.com; Company press release, "Chipotle Mexican Grill Creates 'Chipotle Cultivate Foundation,'" accessed October 22, 2012, http://ir.chipotle.com.

2. "Delta Air Lines: An Airline Buys an Oil Refinery," *The Economist*, accessed October 22, 2012, www.economist.com; "Delta's Oil Refinery Purchase: Should More Airlines Follow Suit?" *Yahoo! News*, accessed October 22, 2012, www.news.yahoo.com; Nancy Trejos, "Airlines Post Losses in Large Part Due to Rising Fuel Costs," *USA Today*, accessed October 22, 2012, http://travel.usatoday.com.

3. "Biggest Toy, Gear, and Clothing Recalls of 2011," *Parents*, accessed October 22, 2012, www.parents.com; U.S. Consumer Product Safety Commission, "EKSuccess Brands Recalls American Girl Crafts Jewelry Kit Due to Violation of Lead Paint Standard," *Press Release*, accessed October 22, 2012, www.cpsc.gov.

4. Connie Prater, "What the Credit Card Reform Law Means to You," *CreditCards.com*, accessed October 22, 2012, www.creditcards.com; Odysseas Papadimitriou, "What Does 2012 Have in Store for Your Wallet?" *U.S. News*, accessed October 22, 2012, http://money.usnews.com.

5. Mike Florio, "American Needle's Silver Lining Could Help NFL in Antitrust Case," *ProFootballTalk*, http://profootballtalk.nbcsports.com, accessed October 22, 2012; Ashby Jones, "American Needle: High Court Delivers 9-0 Shutout against NFL," *The Wall Street Journal*, http://blogs.wsj.com, accessed October 22, 2012.

6. "China's C919 Aircraft Draws Attention at Farnborough International Air Show 2012," *China TV News*, accessed October 22, 2012, http://English.cntv.cn; "China's Challenge for Air Supremacy," *CNN.com*, accessed October 22, 2012, www.cnn.com.

7. Company website, www.costco.com, accessed October 22, 2012.

8. ENERGY STAR website, www.energystar.gov, accessed October 22, 2012.

9. "Global Number of Public Hotspots from 2009 to 2015 (in millions)," *Statista*, accessed October 22, 2012, www.statista.com.

10. Company website, http://news.verizonwireless.com, accessed October 22, 2012; Company website, www.att.com, accessed October 22, 2012.

11. Company website, www.tweglobal.com, accessed October 22, 2012; Chris V. Nicholson, "Foster's to Separate Wine and Beer Businesses in May," *The New York Times*, accessed October 22, 2012, http://dealbook.nytimes.com.

12. Chris Kanaracus, "SAP Lays Out Cloud Strategy Post–SuccessFactors Deal," *PCWorld*, accessed October 22, 2012, www.pcworld.com; Bob Evans, "Success Factors' Lars Dalgaard: SAP Will Turbocharge Our Innovation," *Forbes*, accessed October 22, 2012, www.forbes.com; Ray Wang, "News Analysis: SAP Buys SuccessFactors for $3.4B Signals SAP's Commitment to Cloud, HCM, and Social," *SoftwareInsider*, accessed October 22, 2012, http://blog.softwareinsider.org.

13. Company website, www.vonmaur.com, accessed October 22, 2012.

14. Susan Stellin, "Yes! Download That Airline App," *The New York Times*, accessed October 22, 2012, www.nytimes.com.

15. Federal Trade Commission website, www.ftc.gov, accessed October 22, 2012.

16. Federal Trade Commission, "FTC Case Against Deceptive Robocallers Leads to Record $30 Million in Civil Penalties," *Press Release*, accessed October 22, 2012, www.ftc.gov.

17. Zach Bowman, "Toyota Recalls 2.5 Million Vehicles over Fire Risk," *Autoblog.com*, October 10, 2012, www.autoblog.com; "Toyota Accepts Huge Penalty, Raising Investigation Record Fine Total to Nearly $49 million," *The Weekly Driver*, accessed October 22, 2012, www.theweeklydriver.com.

18. Jeremy M. Simon, "VantageScore Turns 5: What It Is, and Why It Matters," *CreditCards.com*, www.creditcards.com, accessed October 22, 2012.

19. Organization website, www.nfpa.org, accessed October 22, 2012.

20. Organization website, www.aarp.org, accessed October 22, 2012.

21. Association website, www.the-dma.org, accessed October 22, 2012.

22. Ilan Kolet and Alex Kowalski, "Health Care Spurs Consumer Surge in U.S. GDP: Chart of the Day," *Bloomberg Businessweek*, accessed October 22, 2012, www.bloomberg.com.

23. Pike Research, "The Electric Bicycle Market in the United States Will More Than Triple by 2018," *Yahoo!Finance*, accessed October 22, 2012, http://finance.yahoo.com; J. David Goodman, "Electric Bikes Develop into a Global Industry," *Deccan Herald*, accessed October 22, 2012, www.deccanherald.com.

24. Bureau of Labor Statistics, "U.S. Annual Inflation Up to 2.0 Percent in September," *TradingEconomics.com*, October 16, 2012, www.tradingeconomics.com.

25. Bureau of Labor Statistics, "The Employment Situation—September 2012," *Press Release*, October 5, 2012, www.bls.gov.

26. Bureau of Economic Analysis, "Personal Income and Outlays, August 2012," accessed October 22, 2012, www.bea.gov.

27. World Hunger Education Service, "2012 World Hunger and Poverty Facts and Statistics," accessed October 22, 2012, www.worldhunger.org.

28. Organization website, www.commutegreener.com, accessed October 22, 2012; Leslie Guevarra, "Volvo's App for Greener Commutes Wins Sustainability Award," *GreenBiz.com*, accessed October 22, 2012, www.greenbiz.com.

29. Jim Gorzelany, "The Best 'Green' Cars for the Money," *Forbes.com*, accessed October 22, 2012, www.forbes.com; Organization website, "New Mitsubishi i-MiEV Unseats Honda Civic Natural Gas after 8 Consecutive Years at the Top," *Press Release*, accessed October 22, 2012, www.aceee.org.

30. Shaun Rein, "For U.S. Brands, There's No Middle in China's Middle Class," *Bloomberg Businessweek*, accessed October 22, 2012, www.businessweek.com.

31. Ian Traynor, "IMF and Europe in Dangerous Game of Brinkmanship over Failing Greek Bailout," *The Guardian*, accessed October 22, 2012, www.guardian.co.uk; Stephen Fidler, "Spanish Bailout Is No Fix for Italy's Woes," *The Wall Street Journal*, October 4, 2012, http://online.wsj.com.

32. "What Is Disney Doing with RFID at Its Theme Parks?" *Theme Park Tourist*, accessed October 22, 2012, www.themeparktourist.com; Jeff Heimbuch, "Disney World's RFID Program and You!" *Micechat.com*, accessed October 22, 2012, http://micechat.com.

33. Shlomo Sprung, "This Little Green Plant Could Be the Biofuel of the Future," *Business Insider*, accessed October 22, 2012, www.businessinsider.com; Sophie Bushwick, "Micro-Bubbles Cut Cost of Algae-Derived Biofuel," *Scientific American*, accessed October 22, 2012, www.scientificamerican.com.

34. Organization website, www.smartsignal.com, accessed October 22, 2012.

35. Nick Wingfield, "$8.5 Billion Deal for Calling Service Presents a Puzzle," *The New York Times*, accessed October 22, 2012, www.nytimes.com.

36. Erin Read Ruddick, "Social Media, Email and Top Online Activities of Baby Boomers and Beyond," *Social Media Today*, accessed October 22, 2012, www.socialmediatoday.com.

37. Manny Ruiz, "Top Trends in Hispanic Media," *PR Newswire*, accessed October 22, 2012, http://toolkit.prnewswire.com.

38. Kitt Doucette, "The Plastic Bag Wars," *Rolling Stone*, accessed October 22, 2012, www.rollingstone.com.

39. Stephanie Strom, "McDonald's Menu to Post Calorie Data," *The New York Times*, accessed October 23, 2012, www.nytimes.com.

40. Organization website, www.recalls.gov, accessed October 23, 2012.

41. Louis Lavelle, "Bernie Madoff: Lecturing MBAs on Ethics?" *Bloomberg Businessweek* (Business school blog), accessed October 23, 2012, www.businessweek.com.

42. Campaign for Tobacco-Free Kids, "New Report: States Slash Tobacco Prevention Funding by 36%, Spend Less than 2 Cents of Every Tobacco Dollar to Fight Tobacco Use," *Press Release*, accessed October 23, 2012, www.tobaccofreekids.org.

43. Kevin Sack, "Patient Data Posted Online in Major Breach of Privacy," *The New York Times*, www.nytimes.com, accessed October 23, 2012.

44. Jennifer LeClaire, "Hackers Spied on Board Directors after NASDAQ Breach," *Yahoo! News*, http://news.yahoo.com, accessed October 23, 2012.

45. John Ellett, "Quaker Oats New CMO Justin Lambeth Cooks Up Recipe for Growth," *Forbes*, accessed October 23, 2012, www.forbes.com; "General Mills Releases 2012 Global Responsibility Report," *Press Release*, accessed October 23, 2012, www.generalmills.com.

46. Kathy Crosett, "More Food Marketers to Reach Kids through Mobile Instead of TV," *Marketing Forecast*, accessed October 23, 2012, www.marketingforecast.com; Organization website, http://commercialfreechildhood.org, accessed October 23, 2012.

47. Bruce Horovitz, "Marketing to Kids Gets More Savvy with New Technologies," *USA Today*, accessed October 23, 2012, www.usatoday.com.

48. Jeannie Kever, "Bud Light Fan Can Promo Losing Its Fizz," *Houston Chronicle*, www.chron.com, accessed October 23, 2012; "Anheuser-Busch Pulls Some 'Fan Cans,'" *Associated Press*, www.msnbc.msn.com, accessed October 23, 2012.

49. Jessica Silver-Greenberg and Tara Siegel Bernard, "Lenders Again Dealing Credit to Risky Clients," *The New York Times*, accessed October 23, 2012, www.nytimes.com.

50. "How the Credit CARD Act Impacts Your Finances Today," *Forbes*, accessed October 23, 2012, www.forbes.com.

51. Organization website, www.laborrights.org, accessed October 23, 2012.

52. Organization website, www.cdfifund.gov, accessed October 23, 2012.

53. Martin Moylan, "Best Buy Toughens e-Recycling Rules," *Minnesota Public Radio*, accessed October 23, 2012, http://minnesota.publicradio.org; Company website, "Recycle FAQs," accessed October 23, 2012, www.bestbuy.com.

54. Organization website, http://sustainabilityconsortium.org, accessed October 23, 2012.

55. Leon Kaye, "Motel 6: Sustainability Means We'll No Longer Leave the Light on for You," *Triple Pundit*, accessed October 23, 2012, www.triplepundit.com; "Marriott LEED®'s the Way to Green Hotels," *Press Release*, accessed October 23, 2012, http://news.marriott.com; Marina Hanes, "How Eco-Friendly Are Fairmont Hotels & Resorts?" *1-800Recycling.com*, accessed October 23, 2012, http://1800recycling.com; Company website, www.accor-na.com, accessed October 23, 2012; Company website, www.fairmont.com/corporate-responsibility/environment, accessed October 23, 2012.

56. Mark Newman, "Earth Day Initiatives Becoming Commonplace," *MLB.com*, accessed October 23, 2012, http://mlb.mlb.com.

Chapter 5

E-BUSINESS:

Managing the Customer Experience

1 Describe the growth of Internet use worldwide.

2 Define *e-business* and *e-marketing*, and list the opportunities e-marketing presents.

3 Distinguish between a corporate website and a marketing website.

4 List the major forms of B2B e-marketing.

5 Explain business-to-consumer (B2C) e-marketing.

6 Identify online buyers and sellers.

7 Describe some of the challenges associated with online marketing and e-business.

8 Discuss how marketers use the communication function of the Web as part of their online marketing strategies.

9 Outline the steps involved in developing successful e-business websites, and identify methods for assessing website effectiveness.

PINTEREST SURGES AHEAD

Proving that a picture is worth a thousand words, about 70 percent of all Facebook activity revolves around uploading and sharing photos, and 10 percent of all the photos ever taken in the history of the world were snapped within the last 12 months. As cameras spread into more smart devices, and social media provide more opportunities to share the results, the online world is becoming increasingly visual.

So it's no surprise that Pinterest, the website where a community of users create bulletin board-like pages to "pin" and link photos of interest, is one of the fastest-growing online phenomena. Founded in late 2009 to little fanfare, the site took off like a rocket one year later. It now boasts 119 million visits per month, making it the third-most-popular social media site after Twitter and Facebook.

Unlike the youth-oriented Facebook and Twitter, however, Pinterest found its audience mostly among women aged 30 to 40, who use it to share photos and links to recipes and knitting patterns, blogs, child-care

tips, and favorite fashion items. Given that this demographic group controls purchasing decisions for many U.S. households, marketers for companies like Whole Foods, Nordstrom, Sony, and West Elm are looking for ways to capitalize. Whole Foods has discovered that consumer topics, rather than brand-related promotions, attract Pinterest users, so the site has become a great way to drive people to the company's recipe database. Happily for retailers, Pinterest has added a red "Pin It" button so members can link their boards to merchandisers' online catalogs with a single click. The new button is rapidly spreading to shopping sites, showing up next to similar buttons from Twitter and Facebook.

Given its link-sharing nature, Pinterest is a natural referral tool, and, in one recent month, it drove more referral traffic to third-party websites than even Twitter. To increase its utility and ease of use, the site added user profiles with prominent photos of the people each user most often "re-pins," so boards offer a visual snapshot of social influence for each member of the Pinterest community.

To make it even more effective for their goods and services, marketers will need to thoroughly master Pinterest's visual basis and community nature.[1]

EVOLUTION OF A BRAND

Pinterest tells its subscriber audience, "We want you to discover inspiration for just about anything." True to this declaration, Pinterest is a forum where subscribers can share photos of all the things that inspire them, from recipes to consumer goods. The site's simple grid structure has proved popular with its millions of users. Ben Silbermann, the site's founder, says, "We want to be this snapshot of what you're about and we wanted to represent that visually."

In a recent month, Pinterest sent more referral traffic—that arrives at a company's website from another source, such as a social media site—than Twitter. Companies recognize the tremendous potential of Pinterest to drive sales via marketing.

- In its preliminary research in setting up Pinterest pages, Sony found that people were already pinning Sony items, including ads, images of products, and photos taken with Sony cameras. Once the Sony Electronics Pinterest page was launched, traffic to Sony's online store increased 900 percent in a single month. What should Sony do to keep its mobile commerce strong?

- Before creating its Pinterest pages, Sony used other social platforms to announce the launch, including blog posts and tweets on Twitter. How do you think Sony should continue to use social media besides Pinterest, such as Twitter and Facebook, to promote its products?

CHAPTER OVERVIEW

e-business Conducting online transactions with customers by collecting and analyzing business information, carrying out the exchanges, and maintaining online relationships with customers.

During the past decade, marketing has become the cutting-edge tool for success on the Internet. Profit-seeking organizations are not the only benefactors of the Internet; organizations of all kinds are emphasizing marketing's role in achieving set goals. Colleges and universities, charities, museums, symphony orchestras, and hospitals now employ the marketing concept discussed in Chapter 1: providing customers the goods and services they want to buy when they want to buy them. Contemporary marketing continues to perform its function of bringing buyers and sellers together; it just does it faster and more efficiently than ever before. With just a few ticks of the clock and a few clicks of a mouse, the Internet revolutionizes every aspect of life. New terms have emerged, such as *shopping blog*, *RSS*, *VoIP*, and *XML*; and old words have new meanings never imagined a few years ago: *Web*, *Net*, *surfer* and *server*, *banner* and *browser*, *tweet* and *twitter*, *online* and *offline*.

Electronic business, or **e-business**, refers to conducting business via the Internet and has turned virtual reality into reality. With a computer and Internet access, a virtual marketplace is open 24/7 to provide almost anything anywhere to anyone, including clothes, food, entertainment, medicine, and information. You can pay your cell phone bill, make travel reservations, do research for a term paper, post a résumé at an employment bulletin board, or buy a used car—perhaps at a lower price than you could in person.

Internet marketers can reach individual consumers or target organizations worldwide through a vast array of computer and communications technologies. In just a few short years, hundreds of thousands of companies large and small have been connected to electronic marketing channels.

The size and scope of e-business is difficult to understate. For instance, in a recent year, an estimated 167 million online shoppers in the United States bought a total of $202 billion in goods. Although e-commerce was less than 6 percent of total retail sales, industry observers say online retail sales will continue to grow.[2]

E-business is much more than just buying and selling goods and services. Some surveys suggest that the Web is the number-one medium for new-product information, eclipsing catalogs, print ads, and trade shows. The Internet allows retailers and vendors to exchange vital information, improving the overall functioning of supply and distribution, lowering costs, and increasing profits. Moreover, an increasing number of Americans now get some of their news and information from *blogs* (online journals) rather than from traditional media such as television and newspapers. Consequently, a growing number of businesses use blogs to put human faces on their organizations and communicate directly with customers.

This chapter examines the current status and potential of e-business and online marketing. We begin by describing the growth of Internet use throughout the world. Next, we explore the scope of e-business and outline how marketers use the Internet to succeed, and then distinguish different types of Web business models. This discussion is followed by a review of the major types of B2B marketing online.

We then explore the types of goods and services most often traded in B2C marketing on the Internet, along with a profile of online buyers and sellers. We then describe some of the challenges associated with marketing on the Web, followed by a discussion of how marketers use the communication function of the Internet. We conclude the chapter by examining how to build an effective Web presence.

> **❝BRIEFLY SPEAKING❞**
>
> "In 6,000 years of storytelling, [people have] gone from depicting hunting on cave walls to depicting Shakespeare on Facebook walls."
>
> —**Joe Sabia**
> *Digital artist and consultant*

THE DIGITAL WORLD

In the past decade, the number of Internet users in the United States and worldwide has grown dramatically. Today, over 270 million people—more than 83 percent of the U.S. population—have access to the Internet at home, school, work, or public access sites. The number of Internet users worldwide totals almost 2.7 billion.[3] The map in Figure 5.1 shows the number of Internet users and Internet penetration for each of the world's continents and regions. *Internet penetration* is the percentage of a region's population who use the Internet.

Asia leads the world in the sheer number of users and the speed of growth in Internet use. Among individual countries with the highest number of Internet users, China ranks first, with almost one-quarter of the world's Internet users. The next three countries are the United States, India, and Japan.[4] China's Internet audience has grown by more than 2,000 percent since 2000; the United States' audience rose about 157 percent for the same period.[5] South Korea has the fastest Internet service in the world, followed by Japan, Hong Kong, The Netherlands, and Latvia. South Korea's Internet speed is three times faster than that in the United States, which recently ranked 13th in the world for Internet speed.[6]

What do people do online? Let's look at the two countries with the most Internet users—the United States and China. In the United States, Internet usage is mostly about communication, information, and purchases. Nearly all American users say they use email and use a search engine for information; almost 85 percent get news or look for maps or driving directions. About four-fifths search for health or medical news or check the weather. About three-quarters look for information about items they're interested in buying or go online just to pass the time or to have fun.[7] Among U.S. users under the age of 35, almost half in a recent survey said they check their Facebook pages when they wake up; over a quarter of those said that they check their Facebook pages on their mobile phones even before they get out of bed. The fastest-growing U.S. demographic group on Facebook is people 55 and over.[8] In China, where Internet users tend to be young (more than 80 percent are under 40) and low-wage earners, downloading and streaming music are the most popular activities, followed by using search engines, instant messaging, online gaming, videogaming, and other modes of social networking. After a relatively slow start, online purchase transactions in China have jumped recently, helped by the spread of local online payment systems.[9]

Describe the growth of Internet use worldwide.

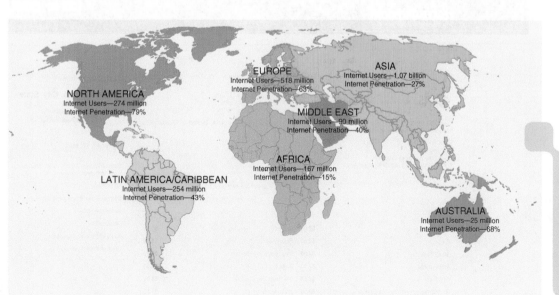

EUROPE
Internet Users—518 million
Internet Penetration—63%

ASIA
Internet Users—1.07 billion
Internet Penetration—27%

NORTH AMERICA
Internet Users—274 million
Internet Penetration—79%

MIDDLE EAST
Internet Users—90 million
Internet Penetration—40%

AFRICA
Internet Users—167 million
Internet Penetration—15%

LATIN AMERICA/CARIBBEAN
Internet Users—254 million
Internet Penetration—43%

AUSTRALIA
Internet Users—25 million
Internet Penetration—68%

FIGURE 5.1

Number of Internet Users and Internet Penetration Rate (by Region)

Source: Data from "Internet Usage Statistics," accessed November 12, 2012, www.internetworldstats.com.

So where is e-business going, and how can marketers capitalize on the digital links with consumers? In spite of the past success and future potential of the Internet, issues and concerns relating to e-business remain. Some highly touted e-business applications have proven less than successful, cost savings and profits have occasionally been elusive, and many privacy and security issues still linger. Nevertheless, the benefits and potential of e-business outweigh the concerns and problems.

E-BUSINESS AND E-MARKETING

2 Define *e-business* and *e-marketing*, and list the opportunities e-marketing presents.

Today, *e-business* describes the wide range of business activities taking place via Internet applications such as email and virtual shopping carts. E-business can be divided into the following five broad categories: (1) *e-tailing*, or virtual storefronts on websites; (2) business-to-business transactions; (3) electronic data interchanges (EDI), the business-to-business exchange of data; (4) email, instant messaging, blogs, podcasts, vlogs (video blogs), and other Web-enabled communication tools and their use as media for reaching prospective and existing customers; and (5) the gathering and use of demographic, product, and other information through Web contacts.

e-marketing Strategic process of creating, distributing, promoting, and pricing goods and services to a target market over the Internet or through digital tools.

The component of e-business of particular interest to marketers is *electronic marketing*, or **e-marketing**, the strategic process of creating, distributing, promoting, and pricing goods and services to a target market over the Internet or through such digital tools as smartphones. E-marketing is the means by which e-business is achieved. It encompasses such activities as the following:

- viewing your favorite band's latest videos on YouTube;

- ordering a meal from your favorite local takeout restaurant;

- researching digital cameras on CNET.com and then placing an order on Newegg.com; and

- accessing research site LexisNexis through your college's network, allowing you to work on a paper, and then checking apartment rentals online.

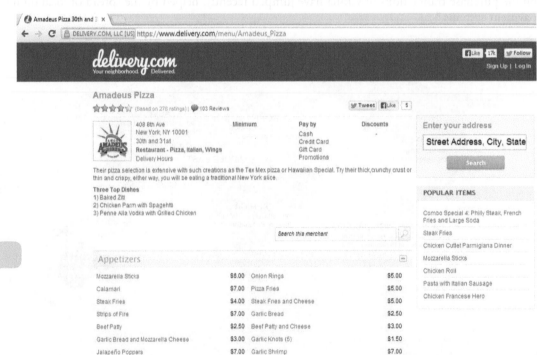

Ordering a meal from a takeout website like Delivery.com is an example of e-marketing.

Delivery.com

The application of these electronic tools to contemporary marketing has the potential to greatly reduce costs and increase customer satisfaction by increasing the speed and efficiency of marketing interactions. Just as e-business is a major function of the Internet, e-marketing is an integral component of e-business.

A closely related but somewhat narrower term than e-marketing is *online marketing*. While electronic marketing can encompass digital technologies ranging from DVDs to interactive store kiosks that do not involve computers, online marketing refers to marketing activities that connect buyers and sellers electronically through interactive computer systems.

OPPORTUNITIES OF E-MARKETING

E-marketing offers countless opportunities to reach consumers. This radical departure from traditional brick-and-mortar operations provides the following benefits to contemporary marketers (summarized in Table 5.1).

- *Global reach.* The Net eliminates the geographic protections and limitations of local business and gives smaller firms a wider audience. Independent filmmakers often have a difficult time forging relationships with traditional distributors who buy the rights to films and promote them as they see fit. As a result, independent films sometimes have a limited audience. But the Internet is allowing filmmakers to organize their own screenings, send messages to interested online communities, and sell DVDs directly through their websites.[10]

- *Personalization.* Road Runner Sports, which caters to running and walking enthusiasts, remembers customers' recent shoe purchases and alerts them when their favorite shoes are about to be discontinued. Its website also has a shoe-finder questionnaire to help customers find their perfect pair of shoes.[11]

- *Interactive marketing.* Using a concept called interactive marketing, McDonald's recently partnered with the social networking site Foursquare. The food giant gave one hundred $5 and $10 gift cards to randomly selected Foursquare users to attract them to local McDonald's restaurants. This move also caught the attention of the media, resulting in more than fifty articles on the special offer. Diners visited McDonald's outlets for a chance to collect a gift card, and 600,000 others chose to follow McDonald's via social media. The campaign resulted in a 33 percent increase in foot traffic in one day—and cost a mere $1,000. Rick Wion, McDonald's social media director, said, "I was able to go to some of our marketing people—some of whom had never heard of Foursquare—and say, 'Guess what. With this one little effort, we were able to get a 33 percent increase in foot traffic to the stores.'"[12]

interactive marketing Buyer–seller communications in which the customer controls the amount and type of information received from a marketer through such channels as the Internet and virtual reality kiosks.

TABLE 5.1 E-Marketing Capabilities

Capability	Description	Example
Global reach	The ability to reach anyone connected to the Internet anywhere in the world.	Independent filmmakers use the Internet to generate audiences and sales for their films.
Personalization	Creating products to meet customer specifications.	Lululemon Athletica has a website feature that allows buyers to mix and match items to complete outfits to suit their individual tastes.
Interactive marketing	Buyer–seller communications through such channels as the Internet and interactive kiosks.	Dell maintains an IdeaStorm site where users trade ideas, information, and product feedback.
Right-time marketing	The ability to provide a product at the exact time needed.	The United Airlines website lets customers make advance reservations, check in online, check flight status, and sign up for the carrier's rewards program.
Integrated marketing	Coordination of all promotional activities to produce a unified, customer-focused promotional message.	Sony uses the slogan "Make. Believe" in both online and offline promotions.

An effective online presence can improve the performance of traditional marketing operations. The cookware and kitchen supply retailer Williams-Sonoma advertises its in-store cooking classes on its website.

© David Paul Morris/Bloomberg via Getty Images

- *Right-time marketing.* Online retailers, such as BN.com and REI.com, can provide products when and where customers want them.

- *Integrated marketing.* The Internet enables the coordination of all promotional activities and communication to create a unified, customer-oriented promotional message.

In addition to the benefits listed here, an effective online presence can improve the performance of traditional marketing operations. Recent surveys of consumers found that, whether they purchase online or in person, well over half of shoppers do online product research before buying. In one recent survey, 70 percent of online shoppers said research would continue to be a critical factor in purchasing decisions over the next year, and a third use their mobile phones to scan QR or bar codes to search for information on a product or to compare prices.[13] The Internet is thus a powerful force in shaping consumer behavior, even if it is seldom the only avenue most consumers pursue in their search for product information. Meanwhile, with online sales growing by well over 10 percent each year while retail stores remain flat, brick-and-mortar stores are fighting back with options that online sellers can't deliver. Macy's department stores offer visitor services for travelers, including coat and package check and language assistance. The cookware and kitchen appliance dealer Williams-Sonoma offers in-store cooking classes and demonstrations; participants can get a 10 percent discount on in-store purchases on the day of the class.[14]

 ASSESSMENT CHECK

2.1 Define *e-marketing*.

2.2 Explain the difference between e-business and e-marketing.

2.3 What are the major benefits of e-marketing?

WEB BUSINESS MODELS

 Distinguish between a corporate website and a marketing website.

Virtually all businesses today have websites. They may offer general information, electronic shopping, and promotions such as games, contests, and online coupons. Type in the firm's Internet address, and the website's home page appears on your computer screen.

Two types of company websites exist. Many firms have established **corporate websites** to increase their visibility, promote their offerings, and provide information to interested parties. Rather than selling goods and services directly, these sites attempt to build customer goodwill and assist channel

© Sergio Morales Chavarra/La Nacion de Costa Rica/Newscom

Peets Coffee & Tea sells coffee, tea, and food items in its stores. On its website, the company sells everything from coffee beans to tea, coffee machines, and gift certificates.

members in their marketing efforts. For example, Burger King's website offers menus and nutrition information, a store locator, and videos and other types of promotions.[15] In addition to using the Web to communicate product information and build relationships with customers, many companies also use their corporate websites for a variety of other purposes, including disseminating financial information to investors; giving prospective employees the opportunity to apply online for jobs; and providing a communication channel for customers and other interested parties via email, blogs, and online forums.

Although marketing websites often include information about company history, products, locations, employment opportunities, and financial information, their goal is to increase purchases by visitors. For instance, the Peets Coffee & Tea website contains all of the information traditionally found on a corporate website, but it also includes an online store selling everything from coffee beans to tea, mugs, coffee machines, and electronic gift certificates.

Many marketing websites try to engage consumers in interactions that will move them closer to a demonstration, trial visit, purchase, or other marketing outcome. Some marketing websites, such as Sony.com, are quite complex. Visitors can compare the company's different models of digital cameras and other products, selecting five at a time for detailed feature comparisons as well as finding product registration and support, checking out weekly deals, signing up for news and promotions, and locating a Sony dealer.[16] But not all products lend themselves to sales on the Internet. Complex products or

corporate website Site designed to increase a firm's visibility, promote its offerings, and provide information to interested parties.

marketing website Site whose main purpose is to increase purchases by visitors.

 ASSESSMENT CHECK

3.1 Explain the difference between a corporate website and a marketing website.

3.2 Why would companies *not* sell products on their websites?

those requiring demonstration or trials may be better sold in person. And some companies have relationships with partners, such as dealers and franchisees, that sell their products. We discuss these relationships later in the chapter.

B2B E-MARKETING

4 List the major forms of B2B e-marketing.

business-to-business (B2B) e-marketing Use of the Internet for business transactions between organizations.

UPS's website is not designed to be flashy. Although it contains some graphics and a link to sign up for Webinars, its main purpose is not entertainment. Instead, it provides lots of practical information to help the firm's customers. The site enables customers to check rates, compare services, schedule package pickups and deliveries, track shipments, and order shipping supplies. This information is vital to UPS's customers, most of whom are businesses. Customers access the site thousands of times a day.

Business-to-business (B2B) e-marketing is the use of the Internet for business transactions between organizations. Although most people are familiar with such online firms as Amazon.com and eBay, the number of consumer transactions is dwarfed by their B2B counterparts. According to the U.S. Census Bureau, 91 percent of e-business activity consists of B2B transactions.[17]

In addition to generating sales revenue, B2B e-marketing also provides detailed product descriptions whenever needed. Payments and other information are exchanged on the Web, and B2B e-marketing can slash order-processing expenses. Business-to-business transactions, which typically involve more steps than consumer purchases, can be much more efficient on the Internet. Orders placed over the Internet usually contain fewer errors than handwritten ones, and when mistakes occur, the technology can locate them quickly. So the Internet is an attractive option for business buying and selling.

B2B e-marketing activity has become more varied in recent years. In addition to using the Web to conduct individual sales transactions and provide product information, companies use such tools as EDI, Web services, extranets, private exchanges, electronic exchanges, and e-procurement.

PROPRIETARY B2B TRANSACTIONS

One of the oldest applications of technology to business transactions is *electronic data interchange (EDI)*, computer-to-computer exchanges of price quotations, purchase orders, invoices, and other sales information between buyers and sellers. EDI requires compatible hardware and software systems to exchange data over a network. Use of EDI cuts paper flow, speeds the order cycle, and reduces errors. In addition, by receiving daily inventory status reports from vendors, companies can set production schedules to match demand.

Early EDI systems were limited due to the requirement that all parties had to use the same computer operating system. That changed with the introduction of *Web services*—Internet-based systems that allow parties to communicate electronically with one another regardless of the computer operating system they use. Web services rely on open-source XML (Extensible Markup Language, a formatting language) standards. EDI and Web services are discussed further in Chapter 11.

The Internet also offers an efficient way for businesses to collaborate with vendors, partners, and customers through *extranets*, secure networks used for e-marketing and accessible through the firm's website by external customers, suppliers, or other authorized users. Extranets go beyond ordering and fulfillment processes by giving selected outsiders access to internal information. Like other forms of e-marketing, extranets provide additional benefits such as enhanced relationships with business partners. *Intranets* are secure internal networks that help companies share information among employees, no matter how many or how widespread they are. The office-supply firm Staples has thousands of employees in 26 countries. In-store devices connect them to the company's intranet, The Hub, where they can exchange information and find job-related software. The Hub also carries customer-success stories and best practices from various Staples stores, as well as video updates on company news. Andrea Quinn, Staples's U.S. retail communications manager, says, "The Hub is one of our primary vehicles to talk to all store associates." The Hub recently has twice been named one of the ten best-designed intranets by the Nielsen Norman Group, a usability consulting agency.[18]

Security and access authorization remain critical issues, and most companies create virtual private networks that protect information traveling over public communications media. These networks control who uses a company's resources and what users can access. Also, they cost considerably less than leasing dedicated lines.

The next generation of extranets is the *private exchange*, a secure website where a company and its suppliers share all types of data related to e-marketing, from product design through order delivery. A private exchange is more collaborative than a typical extranet, so this type of arrangement is sometimes called *c-business*. The participants can use it to collaborate on product ideas, production scheduling, distribution, order tracking, and any other functions a business wants to include. For example, Walmart Stores has a private exchange it calls RetailLink. The system permits Walmart employees to access detailed sales and inventory information. Suppliers such as Procter & Gamble and Nestlé, in turn, can look up Walmart sales data and forecasts to manage their own inventory and logistics, helping them better meet the needs of the world's largest retailer and its millions of customers worldwide.

E-PROCUREMENT ON OPEN EXCHANGES

In the early stages of B2B transactions, marketers believed all types of products would be traded online. Entrepreneurs created electronic exchanges to bring buyers and sellers together in one electronic marketplace and cater to a specific industry's needs, but the performance of these sites was disappointing. Many suppliers weren't happy with the pressure to come in with the lowest bid each time, and buyers preferred to cultivate long-term relationships with their suppliers, even if those suppliers sometimes charged slightly more. Purchasing agents simply didn't see enough benefits from electronic exchanges to abandon suppliers they knew.

Evolving from electronic exchanges is e-procurement, Web-based systems that enable all types of organizations to improve the efficiency of their bidding and purchasing processes. Royal Dutch/ Shell Group, a group of energy companies with operations in 140 countries, purchases millions of dollars of parts, components, supplies, and services every day. Recently the firm decided to replace its network of more than 100 different purchasing systems with a streamlined new system to unify procurement and reduce costs. "E-procurement enables us to make radical changes to the way we buy, the speed at which we buy, the way we and our suppliers work together, and the way we can use information to manage our business in the connected economy," said the company's strategic sourcing advisor.[19]

E-procurement also benefits the public sector. The Scottish government recently awarded an £18.5 million ($30 million) contract to Amor Group, a Scottish IT services company. Amor Group now manages the government's eProcurement Scotland Service, or ePS. This online procurement service already has 50,000 registered users whose purchases are entirely electronic, from requisition to payment. The government has also asked Amor to improve service. The physical infrastructure servers will be decreased from 73 to 19. Amor says, "This represents a 75 percent reduction in the carbon footprint of the system which is equivalent to removing 200 vehicles from the road a year."[20] The state of Virginia maintains a website called eVay for its Web-based purchasing system. The site allows state and local agencies and government offices, as well as the state's colleges and universities, to invite bids, receive quotes, and place orders.[21]

e-procurement Use of the Internet by organizations to solicit bids and purchase goods and services from suppliers.

ASSESSMENT CHECK

4.1 What is B2B e-marketing? How large is it relative to consumer e-marketing?

4.2 Define *EDI* and *Web services*.

4.3 Briefly explain how e-procurement works.

B2C E-MARKETING

One area of e-business that consistently grabs news headlines is Internet shopping. Known as business-to-consumer (B2C) e-marketing, it is selling directly to consumers over the Internet. Driven by convenience and improved security for transmitting credit card numbers and other financial information, online retail sales—sometimes called *e-tailing*—have grown rapidly in recent years. During a recent holiday shopping period, Internet shopping sales hit a record $37.2 billion, marking a 15 percent increase from the previous year's holiday totals. Shopping on the Monday after Thanksgiving—known as "Cyber Monday"—recently totaled close to $2 billion.[22]

Explain business-to-consumer (B2C) e-marketing.

business-to-consumer (B2C) e-marketing Selling directly to consumers over the Internet.

With 140 million smartphones in the United States alone, mobile retail may be poised to take off, even though it currently makes up only about 1 percent of online sales. Over 91 percent of the top 100 brands now have mobile-commerce websites or applications that usually can be downloaded onto smartphones or tablet devices for free. Those brands include Disney, IBM, Sony, Coca-Cola, MTV, BMW, and GE. A recent survey predicts that although mobile commerce will account for only 7 percent of e-commerce by 2016, total sales will reach $31 billion—*ten times* the amount at the start of the decade.[23]

Most people think of the Web as a giant cybermall of retail stores selling millions of goods online. However, service providers are also important participants in e-marketing, including providers of financial services. Brick-and-mortar banks like PNC Financial and brokerage firms such as Charles Schwab have greatly expanded their online services. In addition, many new online service providers are rapidly attracting customers who want to do more of their own banking and investment trading at whatever time and day suits them. And where would individual buyers and sellers be without online classified ads?

ELECTRONIC STOREFRONTS

electronic storefronts
Company websites that sell products to customers.

Virtually all major retailers have staked their claims in cyberspace by setting up **electronic storefronts**, websites where they offer items for sale to consumers. Clothing retailer American Eagle sees e-retailing as a "significant growth opportunity" for all its brands and has been enjoying double-digit increases in electronic sales from year to year. The company's attractive website offers a store locator and wish list feature, gift card purchasing, a feedback link, and the opportunity to sign up for sales and other promotions. Clothing is organized by category—tops, bottoms, accessories, footwear, and so on—and the site has separate sections for sales and clearance items as well as for new arrivals and Web exclusives.[24]

electronic shopping cart File that holds items the online shopper has chosen to buy.

Generally, online retailers—such as Gap.com and LLBean.com—provide an online catalog where visitors click on items they want to buy. These items are placed in a file called an **electronic shopping cart** or *shopping bag*. When the shopper indicates that he or she wants to complete the transaction, the items in the electronic shopping cart are listed on the screen, along with the total amount due, so the customer can review the whole order and make changes before paying.

One factor having a significant influence on the growth of online shopping is the increased capability of smartphones, such as the iPhone and Android. But one report speculates that tablet devices such as the iPad may emerge as the next mobile shopping tool. Even though only 18 percent of online shoppers own tablets, many of them already have smartphones and computers—and they prefer to use their tablets for shopping. For one thing, tablets have larger screens than smartphones and are almost equally portable. Also, apps for tablet devices are far more versatile, permitting page flipping, scrolling, and other "real-world" conveniences. Retailers like tablet apps because they can emphasize features of their products rather than merely comparing prices. Ralph Lauren, Amazon, eBay, and other companies—both brick-and-mortar and Internet-based—have launched their own tablet apps.[25]

BENEFITS OF B2C E-MARKETING

Many consumers prefer shopping online to the time needed to drive to a store and select purchases. Why do consumers shop online? Three main reasons are most often cited in consumer surveys: competitive pricing, access and convenience, and personalized service.

Competitive Pricing

Many of the best deals on products, such as airfares and hotels, can be found on the Internet. Expedia .com is just one of several sites that offer packages with combinations of flight, hotel, and car rental, plus special sales and last-minute flight specials at attractive prices organized by city and date of travel.[26] Though most airlines now charge passengers for checked baggage, most offer reduced rates with branded credit cards.[27] The bookseller Barnes & Noble's website offers members discounts on a NOOK Color or NOOK Tablet, free express shipping on orders, and 40 percent off hardcover bestsellers.[28]

The Web is an ideal method for savvy shoppers to compare prices from dozens—even hundreds—of sellers. Online shoppers can compare features and prices at their leisure. Say, for instance, you're in the market for a new computer monitor. **Bots** aid consumers in comparison shopping. Bots—short for *robots*—are search programs that check hundreds of sites, gather and assemble information, and bring it back to the sender. For instance, at PriceGrabber.com, you can specify the type and size of monitor you're looking for, and the website displays a list of the highest-ranked monitors, along with the e-tailer offering the best price on each item and estimated shipping expenses. The website even ranks the e-marketers by customer experience and tells you whether a particular model is in stock.

bot (shopbot) Software program that allows online shoppers to compare the price of a particular product offered by several online retailers.

Access and Convenience

A second important factor in prompting online purchases is shopper convenience. Cybershoppers can order goods and services from around the world at any hour of the day or night. Most e-marketers allow customers to register their credit card and shipping information for quick use in making future purchases. Customers are required to select a user name and password for security. Later, when they place another order, registered customers are asked to type in their password. E-marketers typically send an email message confirming an order and the amount charged to the buyer's credit card. Another email is sent once the product is shipped, along with a tracking number, which the customer can use to follow the order through the delivery process. A new service provided by *Elle* magazine's British website is the ability to use online photos to conduct visual matches for desired shopping items. In other words, using a digital picture of what you want, say, a pair of shoes, you can locate similar items for sale online. After acquiring Like.com, Google is currently routing users from its Boutiques.com page to Google Product Search, which showcases everything from washing machines to clothing to watches. Shoppers can download Google Catalogs, an app for tablets that brings their favorite online catalogs together. Google Shopper, a smartphone app, allows subscribers to scan the cover art of books and electronic products such as DVDs or games to find those products—or simply

Google Product Search offers convenience to online shoppers. The website offers a wide range of products.

say the name of a product to find it. This app also allows subscribers to see nearby offers, find local stores, scan bar codes of products for more information, and check out online prices. Google Offers lists participating restaurants in the subscriber's local area.[29]

Personalized Service

Although online shopping transactions often operate with little or no human interaction, successful B2C e-marketing companies know how important personalization is to the quality of the shopping experience. Customer satisfaction is greatly influenced by the marketer's ability to offer service tailored to many customers. But each person expects a certain level of customer service. Consequently, most leading online retailers offer customized features on their websites.

The early years of e-business saw Web marketers casting their nets wide in an effort to land as many buyers as possible. Today, the emphasis has turned toward creating loyal customers likely to make repeat purchases. How does personalized marketing work online? Say you buy a book at Amazon.com and register with the site. The site welcomes you back for your next purchase by name. Using special software that analyzes your previous purchases, it also suggests several other books you might like. You even have the option of receiving periodic emails from Amazon.com informing you of new products. And the company now offers Amazon Prime, a membership program that provides expedited free shipping for a yearly fee. Many other leading e-marketers have adopted similar types of personalized marketing.

Some websites offer customized products to match individual consumer requirements. For instance, Nike offers online shoppers the opportunity to customize a running shoe, personalizing such features as the outsole, the amount of cushioning, and the width. The personalized shoe costs about $10 more than buying a product off store shelves. Some sites provide demonstrations and other product videos, and some, like Nordstrom, offer 3D (three-dimensional) product images and allow shopping by cost and by feature.

ASSESSMENT CHECK

5.1 What is B2C e-marketing?

5.2 Explain the difference between a shopping website and an informational website.

5.3 Discuss the benefits of B2C e-marketing.

ONLINE BUYERS AND SELLERS

6 Identify online buyers and sellers.

Recent research paints a picture of the characteristics of online users and buyers (see Figure 5.2). Women make up 63 percent of people who shop online. Male and female shoppers under age 45 spend more time online. The typical Internet user is likely to be between 18 and 64 years of age. More than half of all users make at least one purchase online each month, and more than six in ten research products online before buying them in a store. Half of all shoppers spend three quarters of total shopping time doing product research. Many online shoppers are loyal and buy mostly from a single site; Amazon and eBay are the most popular. A broader range of Internet users now purchase products online compared with a few years ago.[30]

Realizing that customers would have little or no opportunity to rely on many of the sense modes—smelling the freshness of direct-from-the-oven bread, touching the soft fabric of a new cashmere sweater, or squeezing fruit to assess its ripeness—early online sellers focused on offering products consumers were familiar with and tended

FIGURE 5.2
Characteristics of U.S. Internet Users

Source: Pew Research Center, "Demographics of Internet Users, Teens and Adults, August 2012," accessed November 12, 2012, www.pewinternet.org; Stine Thorhauge, "How People Spend Their Time Online [Infographic]," *Mindjumpers*, accessed November 13, 2012, www.mindjumpers.com.

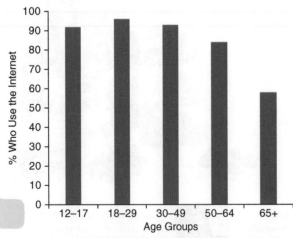

Average time online in a month (home and work): 32 hours
Average number of Web pages viewed per person in a month (home and work): 2,773

to buy frequently, such as books and music. Other popular early online offerings included computer hardware and software and airline tickets.

Event tickets, computers, and peripherals top the list of top products sold online. Sales of clothing and accessories have increased, with books showing a decline.[31]

Thanks to retailers' efforts, consumers' online shopping experiences have been steadily improving in quality and convenience. A recent survey indicated that 50 percent of Facebook users click through Facebook to visit the website of a retailer they already follow. Two-thirds of Twitter users have done the same. More than a quarter of Facebook users have used a retailer's Facebook link to buy goods or services. Large brands have had more success with Facebook links than smaller retailers, mainly due to problems with keeping inventory current. Also, people use social networking sites mainly for social networking. Revenue from shoppers who click through via social sites is $5.24 per click. Most of this traffic comes from "share" and "like" buttons on news-feed links, rather than Facebook ads. Email shoppers spend $3.18 per click.[32]

 ASSESSMENT CHECK

6.1 Who shops online? Are the characteristics of online shoppers changing?

6.2 What are some of the capabilities e-marketers might add to their websites in the future?

CHALLENGES IN E-BUSINESS AND E-MARKETING

For all their advantages, e-business and e-marketing face some problems and challenges. Some of the most significant include developing safe online payment systems, protecting consumer privacy, preventing fraud and scams, improving site design and customer service, and reducing potential channel conflicts and copyright disputes.

> 7 Describe some of the challenges associated with online marketing and e-business.

SAFETY OF ONLINE PAYMENT

In response to consumer concerns about the safety of sending credit card numbers over the Internet, companies have developed secure payment systems. Internet browsers, such as Microsoft Internet Explorer, contain sophisticated encryption systems to protect sensitive information. Encryption is the process of encoding data for security purposes. When such a system is active, users see a special icon that indicates they are at a protected website.

To further increase consumer security, most companies involved in e-business—including all major credit card companies—use Secure Sockets Layer (SSL) technology to encrypt information and provide authentication. SSL consists of a public key and a private key. The public key is used to encrypt information and the private key is used to decipher it. When a browser points to a domain with an SSL certificate, the technology authenticates the server and the visitor and establishes an encryption method and a unique session key. Both parties can then begin a secure session that guarantees message privacy and integrity. VeriSign is one of

encryption The process of encoding data for security purposes.

Secure Sockets Layer (SSL) Technology that secures a website by encrypting information and providing authentication.

© Jin Lee/Bloomberg via Getty Images

Square, a new mobile payment system, allows shoppers to make secure credit card purchases by swiping their card through a small device that plugs into a smartphone or tablet.

the leading providers of SSL technology used by more than 95 percent of *Fortune* 500 companies and 96 of the nation's 100 largest banks. Recently, Symantec acquired VeriSign's security arm.[33]

Many online shoppers are switching to payment services like Bill Me Later, Google Checkout, eBillme, and PayPal. Such services tend to speed checkout and make shopping more secure. They ensure that fewer merchants actually see the shopper's personal information and thus make it less vulnerable to hackers. These services benefit e-marketers, too, because they incur minimal marketing costs that then allow them to charge merchants lower transaction fees than credit card companies.[34] Square is the latest entry in the mobile payment services market; see the "Marketing Success" feature for the story.

PRIVACY ISSUES

electronic signatures
Electronic identification that allows legal contracts such as home mortgages and insurance policies to be executed online.

Marketing research indicates privacy as one of the top concerns of many Internet users. Recently, the European Commission adopted regulations that will require companies such as Google and Facebook to get specific consent to use consumers' personal data. The Federal Trade Commission has explored instituting a "Do Not Track" option, similar to the "Do Not Call" option to stop phone sales calls.[35]

More recently, **electronic signatures** have become a way to enter into legal contract policies online. With an e-signature, an individual obtains a form of electronic identification and installs it in his or her Web browser. Signing the contract involves looking up and verifying the buyer's identity with this software.

MARKETING SUCCESS

Square Spreads the Word

Background. Square, a new mobile payment system, allows shoppers to make credit card purchases by swiping a small white plastic device that plugs into a smartphone or tablet. Merchants using the system pay Square a 2.75 percent transaction fee.

The Challenge. With no mass-media marketing budget, Square needed to show businesses how easy it is to use the service and also create the same trust evoked by financial giants like Chase, Visa, and Citibank.

The Strategy. Square's co-founder and CEO Jack Dorsey knew Square should be "something that never gets in the way of our users doing what they want to do," which meant design and ease of use had to come first.

Outcome. By designing a simple and well-designed customer experience, the company attracted 1 million customers with little

more than word of mouth. Many users are small businesses, from cabbies to purveyors of handmade or luxury goods and services, who love its "transparency and simplicity." Square processes nearly $10 billion in payments per year and has attracted over $100 million in outside investments, including $25 million from Starbucks. Next it will add inventory data for its customers. If growth continues, analysts predict it will be acquired or go public: "Not a bad scenario."

Sources: Gerry Shih, "Burnished by Starbucks, Upstart Square Battles Payment Giants," *Reuters*, accessed November 13, 2012, http://www.reuters.com; Larry Magid, "Square and Starbucks Lead Transition to Mobile Payment," *Forbes*, accessed November 13, 2012, www.forbes.com; "The World's 50 Most Innovative Companies in Retail 2012," *Fast Company*, accessed November 13, 2012, www.fastcompany .com; Nick Bilton, "Disruptions: Design Sets the Tone at a New Start-Up," *The New York Times*, accessed November 13, 2012, http://bits.blogs.nytimes.com; Leena Rao, "Targeting Merchants, Square Debuts Register iPad App and Analytics: Now Processing $4B in Payments per Year," *TechCrunch.com*, accessed November 13, 2012, http://techcrunch.com.

Thanks to *cookies* and *spyware*—software used to automatically collect data from Internet browsers—online companies can track their customers' shopping and viewing habits. Amazon.com, for instance, has long employed sophisticated data collection systems to track customer preferences, and Google and other search engines gather users' search terms as a way to better target the ads that provide their revenue. The way companies use this technology has the potential both to make visits to the website more convenient and to invade computer users' privacy.

Most consumers want assurances that any information they provide won't be sold to others without their permission. In response to these concerns, online merchants take steps to protect consumer information. For example, many Internet companies have signed on with Internet privacy organizations such as TRUSTe. By displaying the TRUSTe logo on their websites, they indicate their promise to disclose how they collect personal data and what they do with the information. Prominently displaying a privacy policy is an effective way to build customers' trust.

Organizations, too, are concerned about the privacy of their data, and with good reason. Hackers recently launched a massive cyber-attack on Sony's PlayStation and Qriocity (music and video streaming) services, compromising over 77 million user accounts. The hackers were able to steal users' personal information, such as date of birth, email and home addresses, and log-in data. Sony later revealed that about 12 million credit card numbers were not encrypted and therefore accessible to the thieves. Sony took down the PlayStation network, restored service—and then had to shut the network down again when hackers were able to infiltrate the password-reset system. The company expects the hack to cost $178 million, not counting possible payouts in dozens of class-action lawsuits.[36]

To prevent intrusions, companies install combinations of hardware and software called *firewalls* to keep unauthorized Net users from tapping into private corporate data. A firewall is an electronic barrier between a company's internal network and the Internet that limits access into and out of the network. However, an impenetrable firewall is difficult to find. A determined and skilled hacker often can gain access, so it is important for firms to test their websites and networks for vulnerabilities and back up critical data in case an intruder breaches security measures.

FRAUD AND SCAMS

Fraud is another impediment to the growth of e-business and e-marketing. The FBI, the National White Collar Crime Center, and the Bureau of Justice Assistance have formed a partnership called the Internet Crime Complaint Center (IC3) to receive and refer criminal complaints about cyberfraud and other Internet crime.[37] CSO Security and Risk, the U.S. Secret Service, and other security organizations recently conducted a cybersecurity survey. The results suggest that although more attacks come from outside organizations, insider attacks are the most costly. Defenses against outside attacks and leaks are becoming more effective. According to the Insider Threat Center at Carnegie Mellon, it is a much more challenging problem to defend against insiders stealing classified information to which they have authorized access or against technically sophisticated users who want to disrupt operations.[38]

One growing type of Internet fraud is called phishing. It is a high-tech scam that uses email or pop-up messages that claim to be from familiar businesses or organizations such as banks, Internet service providers, or even government agencies. The message usually asks the reader to "update" or "validate" account information, often stating that some dire consequence will occur if the reader doesn't respond. The purpose of phishing is to get unsuspecting victims to disclose personal information such as credit card numbers, bank account numbers, Social Security numbers, or computer passwords. One recent phishing attack warns Facebook users that their accounts are about to be turned off because someone reported them. The users are then directed to a fake Facebook website that requests their personal information—then asks the user to make a payment on a credit card.[39] Phishing is also commonly used to distribute viruses and malicious spyware programs to computer users. In vishing, the voice equivalent of phishing, an email or VoIP phone call requests the user to make a phone call to a voice response system that asks for the caller's credit card number. Pindrop Security noted that, during the second half of a recent year, it observed over 1 million vishing attempts in which the vishers used real phone numbers in attempts to steal personal information from customers of 30 of the 50 largest U.S. banks.[40]

Payment fraud is another growing problem for many e-marketers. Orders are placed online and paid for using a credit card, and the retailer ships the merchandise. Then the cardholder asks

firewall Electronic barrier between a company's internal network and the Internet that limits access into and out of the network.

phishing High-tech scam that uses authentic-looking email or pop-up messages to get unsuspecting victims to reveal personal information.

vishing Scam that collects personal information through voice response systems; stands for *voice phishing*.

Companies like Staples that combine their store and catalog operations with e-business have been more successful than many "pure-play" dot-com retailers with little or no brick-and-mortar experience. Staples invites customers to reserve items online, and then pick up their purchases at the nearest store.

the credit card issuer for a chargeback to the e-tailer, claiming he or she never made the purchase or never received the merchandise. Some claims are legitimate, but many involve fraud. Because an online purchase doesn't require a customer's signature or credit card imprint, the merchant—not the card issuer—bears the liability in most fraud cases.

SITE DESIGN AND CUSTOMER SERVICE

For firms to attract—and keep—customers, e-marketers must meet buyers' expectations. For instance, customers want to find products easily and have questions answered quickly. However, websites are not always well designed and easy to use. Competition and customer expectations will also drive more sites to include three-dimensional product photos and video demonstrations, because industry experts estimate better site design can quadruple the number of shoppers who actually buy what they put in their shopping carts. Product reviews, shopping information, pop-up discount offers, and instant messaging for customer questions are other features that can help online retailers to close sales.[41]

Another challenge to successful e-business is merchandise delivery and returns. Retailers sometimes have trouble making deliveries to on-the-go consumers. And consumers don't want to wait for packages to be delivered. Also, if customers aren't satisfied with products, then they have to arrange for pickup or send packages back themselves. Retailers are addressing these issues. Most have systems on their websites that allow customers to track orders from placement to delivery. E-marketers have also worked hard on a process known as *reverse logistics.* Detailed directions on how to return merchandise, including preprinted shipping labels, are included in orders. Some, such as Nordstrom and Zappos.com, even pay the shipping cost for returns.

Many of the so-called "pure-play" dot-com retailers—those without traditional stores or catalogs—didn't survive for very long. They had no history of selling and satisfying customers. Because of expertise in all parts of retailing, companies that combine their store and catalog operations with e-business, such as REI, generally have been more successful than those with little or no retail experience. That's probably part of the reason why seven of the top ten online retailers—such as Walmart, Apple, and Staples—are companies that have traditional bricks-and-mortar stores. The three pure-play firms are Amazon, Dell, and Liberty Interactive Corp. (which owns HSN, Starz, and other cable TV channels), ranking first, fifth, and seventh, respectively. A recent study indicated that daily deals motivate almost half of shoppers to return to online retailers that offer them.[42]

The same lesson also applies to other service industries. To be successful at e-business, firms must establish and maintain competitive standards for customer service. When it began offering customers the opportunity to check flight schedules and purchase tickets online, Southwest Airlines worked hard to make sure its website had the same high service standards the airline is known for. Southwest.com has proved very popular and profitable for the airline.

CHANNEL CONFLICTS AND COPYRIGHT DISPUTES

Companies spend time and money nurturing relationships with their partners. But when a manufacturer uses the Internet to sell directly to customers, it can compete with its usual partners. Retailers often have their own websites, so they don't want their suppliers competing with them for sales. As e-business broadens its reach, producers must decide whether these relationships are more important than the potential of selling directly on the Web. Conflicts between producers, wholesalers, and retailers are called **channel conflicts**.

Mattel, well known for producing toys such as Barbie, Cabbage Patch dolls, and Matchbox cars, sells most of its products in toy stores and toy departments of other retailers such as Target and

channel conflicts
Conflicts among manufacturers, wholesalers, and retailers.

Walmart. The company wants an Internet presence, but it would cut the retailers out of this important source of revenue if it sold toys online to consumers. Mattel cannot afford to lose the goodwill and purchasing power of major retailers such as Toys "R" Us, so the company sells only specialty products online, including pricey American Girl dolls.

Another conflict arises in the area of copyright law, usually when a site hosts content to which someone else holds the rights. Over the last several years, Google has scanned more than a million books from libraries at Oxford and Harvard Universities and the New York Public Library to make them searchable online. The Authors Guild filed a copyright infringement suit to stop the project. The Guild and Google reached a settlement—which the presiding judge rejected when France and Germany opposed it. Publishers are still willing to settle with Google, but the Authors Guild and a coalition of photographers and illustrators have attempted to convert the original lawsuit into a class-action case. The outcome is still undecided.[43]

ASSESSMENT CHECK

7.1 What are the major challenges to growth in e-business and e-marketing?

7.2 Describe phishing and vishing.

7.3 Explain how e-marketing can create channel conflicts and copyright disputes.

MARKETING AND WEB COMMUNICATION

There are four main functions of the Internet: e-business, entertainment, information, and communication. Even though e-business is growing rapidly, communication still remains the most popular Web function. One survey estimates that about 90 *trillion* emails are sent per year. The volume of email today exceeds regular mail (sometimes called *snail mail*) by something like 81 to one.[44] Contemporary marketers also use the communication function of the Internet to advance their organizational objectives.

Companies have long used email to communicate with customers, suppliers, and other partners. Most companies have links on their websites that allow visitors to send email directly to the most appropriate person or division within the company. For instance, if you have a question concerning an online order from Williams-Sonoma, you can click on a link on the retailer's website and send an email to a customer service representative. Many online retailers have gone even further by offering their customers live help. Using a form of instant messaging, live help provides a real-time communication channel between customers and customer service representatives.

Firms also use email to inform customers about events such as new products and special promotions. While using email in this manner can be quite cost effective, companies have to be careful. A growing number of customers consider such emails to be spam, the popular name for junk email. A recent study found as much as 95 percent of all email is spam, up from 70 percent three years before the study.[45] It is no wonder many Internet users employ *spam filters* that automatically eliminate junk email from their in-boxes.

> Discuss how marketers use the communication function of the Web as part of their online marketing strategies.

> **spam** Popular name for junk email.

ONLINE COMMUNITIES AND SOCIAL NETWORKS

In addition to email, many firms use Internet forums, newsgroups, electronic bulletin boards, and social networks that appeal to people with common interests. All these sites take advantage of the communication power of the Internet. Members congregate online and exchange views and information on topics of interest. These communities may be organized for commercial or noncommercial purposes. JPMorgan Chase recently went to the Facebook community for input about which local charities should become recipients of $5 million in grants it planned to make. After collecting feedback, the bank was able to select 100 organizations from 31 states. Based on Facebook members' support, Chase plans to continue the community voting program.[46]

Online communities can take several forms, but all offer specific advantages to users and organizations alike. Online forums, for instance, are Internet discussion groups. Users log in and participate by sending comments and questions or receiving information from other forum members. Forums may operate as electronic bulletin boards, as libraries for storing information, or even as a type of classified ad directory. Firms often use forums to ask questions and exchange information with customers. Digg started as a community for technophiles, but its audience has since grown into millions of increasingly diverse users. Communities like these are built on trust. They thrive on shared information but can be undercut by false or misleading posts. See the "Solving an Ethical Controversy" feature for a discussion of fake customer reviews.

Newsgroups are noncommercial Internet versions of forums. Here, people post and read messages on specific topics. Tens of thousands of newsgroups are on the Internet, and the number continues to rise. **Electronic bulletin boards** are specialized online services that center on a specific topic or area of interest. For instance, mountain bikers might check online bulletin boards to find out about the latest equipment, new places to ride, or current weather conditions in popular biking locations. While newsgroups resemble two-way conversations, electronic bulletin boards are more like announcements.

Social networking sites have grown dramatically. Facebook currently claims to have over 800 million users—more than double the U.S. population—but that number may include individuals with multiple Facebook pages.[47] Twitter reportedly turned down an acquisition offer from Facebook. Growing astronomically, Twitter boasts 500 million registered users.[48]

electronic bulletin board Internet forum that allows users to post and read messages on a specific topic.

SOLVING AN ETHICAL CONTROVERSY

The Ethics of Fake Online Reviews

© Palto/Shutterstock.com

Some companies are offering product rebates for glowing online reviews posted by customers; others are hiring people to write essentially fake reviews, comments, and blogs about goods and services they haven't used, in hopes of not only increasing sales but also boosting their ranking in search engine results. Regulators are trying to crack down on "deceitful hyping." The FTC has expressed concern, and critics worry that customers making high-stakes decisions could be misled by the practice. But others defend it, saying it is little different from other marketing strategies.

Are paid online reviews a legitimate marketing strategy?

PRO 👍

1. One company that gave customers a rebate for posting Amazon reviews of its leather Kindle case only hinted that it would prefer a five-star score. Customers got the product they wanted for just shipping charges, sales increased, and no one was harmed.

2. Giving free items in exchange for a review merely provides an incentive for customers to voice their honest opinion for others' benefit, which many would not otherwise take time to do.

CON 👎

1. Fake reviews don't accurately represent the good or service and are simply unethical as a marketing strategy.

2. Misleading "customer" comments create an atmosphere of mistrust in the online community, and "if consumers don't trust the content, then there is no value for anyone," says a Yelp spokesperson.

Summary:

It's estimated that as many as 30 percent of online reviews may be fake. The FTC has prosecuted a few companies for fake reviews, and researchers are working on software algorithms that can help detect them, often with as much as 90 percent accuracy, compared to humans' scores of about 50 percent. All things considered, the old adage, "Let the buyer beware," still applies.

Sources: Max Nisen, "Fake Reviews Are Becoming an Even Bigger Problem for Businesses," *Business Insider*, accessed November 13, 2012, www.business insider.com; Brad Tuttle, "How Computer Geeks Aim to Put a Stop to Fake Online Reviews," *Time*, accessed November 13, 2012, http://moneyland .time.com; Armando Roggio, "Fake Reviews, A Despicable Practice?" *Practical Commerce.com*, accessed November 13, 2012, www.practicalcommerce.com.

Many observers believe marketers have quickly caught up to their customers in the savvy use of social networking communities, and that they will next become expert not only in exploiting their communication capabilities but also in tapping the huge and detailed databases they represent. Twitter recently began advertising to users. The service, called Promoted Tweets, places ads above lists of search results.[49] Twitter then expanded Promoted Tweets to mobile devices. Twitter released a blog post declaring that the new move is great for brands that want to increase the prominence and reach of their message to a particular type of mobile user. For example, mobile game and app sellers can now pinpoint Twitter users who are likely to purchase their products.[50]

To get the most from social networking communities, marketers may want to implement a mix of strategies, such as preparing their websites for social networking, carrying out email campaigns, and advertising on social networking sites.[51] Facebook boasts millions of business pages, including those of large companies such as Walmart, The Coca-Cola Company, Starbucks, The Walt Disney Company, JCPenney, Converse, and Pizza Hut, all of which have millions of Facebook fans. Mozilla has a Facebook page for its search engine Firefox, where its more than 12 million fans can download the latest version of Firefox and other Mozilla software, share links, and find help with support issues.[52]

Marketers can also step up to advertising on sites like Facebook, which offers a variety of ad-buying options. Thanks to the public information members share on their profiles, advertisers can precisely target their Facebook ads—especially now that Facebook has introduced Zip code targeting. This paves the way for local and small businesses to target Facebook members. Josh Constine of Inside Facebook says, "[Z]ip code targeting could make Facebook Ads significantly more valuable to local advertisers, which could draw in more local and small businesses and drive Facebook's revenues." Google AdWords recently followed suit.[53]

Many small companies have their own Facebook pages. When Mandie Miller left her job to become a stay-at-mom, she started baking cakes for fun. The response from friends was so enthusiastic that she started a business, Got What It Cakes. The company really took off when Miller's sister created a Facebook page for the business—orders went from 2 a week to more than 10, with Miller initially turning away more orders. Got What It Cakes has more than 7,000 Facebook fans.[54] Karen Gannon and her daughter Tia, of Hilton Head, South Carolina, once made their own Christmas tree decorations by hand, using pearlized shells and Swarovski crystals. Their family and friends so admired the decorations that the Gannons realized they could start their own business, which they called Sweet Palms. Tia persuaded her mother to set up a Facebook page for Sweet Palms instead of

Got What It Cakes of Charlotte, North Carolina, has its own Facebook page to connect with customers and build its fan base.

blog   Short for *Web log*—an online journal for an individual or organization.

wiki   Web page that anyone can edit.

podcast   Online audio or video file that can be downloaded to other digital devices.

a website. Sweet Palms updates its page regularly with new offerings, gift ideas, and information on where to buy its products. Tia says that most of their orders come from people who have visited the Sweet Palms Facebook page. She says, "People from all over the world have contacted us asking about the shells. Without Facebook, this would not be possible."[55]

Online communities are not limited to consumers. They also facilitate business-to-business marketing. Using the Internet to build communities helps companies find other organizations, including suppliers, distributors, and competitors, that may be interested in forming an alliance. Marketers wanting to expand internationally frequently seek advice from other members of their online community.

BLOGS AND PODCASTS

Another popular online communication method is the **blog**. Short for *Web log*, the term *blog* describes a Web page that is a publicly accessible journal for an individual or organization. Typically updated daily or even more frequently, these hybrid diary-guide sites are read regularly by almost 30 percent of American Internet users. Using *RSS (Really Simple Syndication)* software, readers continually are kept up-to-date on new material posted on their favorite blogs whenever they are online. Unlike email and instant messaging, blogs let readers post comments and ask questions aimed at the author, called a *blogger*. Some blogs also incorporate **wikis**. A wiki is a Web page anyone can edit so a reader can, in addition to asking questions or posting comments, actually make changes to the Web page. **Podcasts** are another emerging technology. Anyone from bloggers to traditional media sources can prepare an audio or video recording and then post it to a website from which it can be downloaded to any digital device that can play the file.

Given the growing interest in blogs and podcasts, it hasn't taken long for marketers to incorporate them into their e-business strategies. Of particular interest to marketers are blogs that focus on new-technology products, because they can prove effective at quickly forming public opinion. To try to reduce the damage from rumors and misinformation, some companies have decided to treat bloggers as members of the press and acknowledge their ability to spread news and influence. Other firms set up their own blogs. According to Nora Ganim Barnes, director of the Center for Marketing Research at the University of Massachusetts Dartmouth, blogging among top companies increased by 5 percent recently. One study shows that 50 percent of Inc. 500 companies have corporate blogs. It is significant that 71 percent also have corporate Facebook pages, 59 percent have Twitter accounts, and 44 percent say that Facebook is their most important social networking tool. Barnes says, "The adoption of social media by most industries on the … Inc. 500 list continues to grow and now includes Twitter, Facebook, Foursquare and LinkedIn…. This clearly demonstrates the growing importance of social media to this segment of the business world."[56]

Many companies allow, and even encourage, employees to start their own blogs, believing employee blogs can serve useful functions. With 400,000 employees in 170 countries, IBM was one of the earliest companies to encourage its employees to start blogs and engage in other types of social networking. The company claims that these blogs help to resolve differences among cultures and social divides and hopes that the blogs will foster "virtual societies" among its employees. Randy MacDonald, IBM's Senior Vice President of Human Resources, says, "Technology is the new watercooler."[57]

Some companies have strict policies about the content of employee blogs, and some employees have even been disciplined over what their employers thought was improper blogging. However, most companies today still have no official policies regarding employee blogs.

PROMOTIONS ON THE WEB

banner ad   Strip message placed in high-visibility areas of frequently visited websites.

pop-up ad   Separate window that pops up with an advertising message.

preroll video ad   Brief marketing message that appears before expected video content.

Rather than rely completely on their websites to attract buyers, companies frequently expand their reach in the marketplace by placing ads on sites their prospective customers are likely to visit. **Banner ads**, the most common form of Internet advertising, are typically small, strip messages placed in high-visibility areas of frequently visited websites. **Pop-up ads** are separate windows that pop up with an advertising message. The effectiveness of pop-up ads, however, is questionable. First, scam artists use pop-ups. Second, many Internet users simply hate pop-up ads—even those from legitimate companies. Consequently, most ISPs now offer software that blocks pop-up ads. Google and Microsoft also offer free pop-up ad-blocking software.

Preroll video ads, marketing messages that play before an online video, are becoming more popular. Although users have shown some resistance, YouTube is one of the few sites to let viewers opt out of watching. SpotXchange, which sells preroll video advertising, recently launched a new service called SkipIt that, for a small fee, allows viewers to opt out of viewing the ads.[58] **Widgets** are tiny interactive applications Internet users can copy and add to their social networking pages or their personal websites to play music, video, or slide shows. Marketers are adopting the use of widgets at a rapid rate.[59]

Another type of online advertising is **search marketing**. This is considered one of the most effective forms of Web-based advertising. Companies pay search engines fees to have their websites or ads pop up after a user enters certain words into the search engine, or to make sure their firm's listing appears toward the top of the search results. Google and other search engines include "Sponsored Links" on the right side of the search results page. A user who clicks on one of the sites listed under Sponsored Links is taken to that site, and the company pays the search engine a small fee. Google and Microsoft among others have made major investments in improving their search marketing services and capabilities.

widgets Tiny, interactive applications that Internet users can copy and add to their own pages to play music, video, or slide shows.

search marketing Paying search engines, such as Google, a fee to make sure the company's listing appears toward the top of the search results.

Another way companies use the Web to promote their products is through online coupons. For instance, customers can visit a company's website—for example, Aeropostale (www.aeropostale.com)—to learn about items on sale then print a discount coupon redeemable at participating retailers.

ASSESSMENT CHECK

8.1 What are online communities and social networks? Explain how online communities can help companies market their products and improve customer service.

8.2 What are blogs, wikis, and podcasts?

8.3 Explain the differences between a banner ad, a pop-up ad, a preroll video ad, a widget, and search marketing.

BUILDING AN EFFECTIVE WEB PRESENCE

An e-business website can serve many purposes. It can broaden customer bases, provide immediate access to current catalogs, accept and process orders, and offer personalized customer service. As technology becomes increasingly easy to use, anyone with Internet access can open an account and place a simple website on the Internet. How people or organizations use their sites to achieve their goals determines whether their sites will succeed. Figure 5.3 lists some key questions to consider in developing a website, and the "Career Readiness" feature introduces some ideas for making the best use of company websites where jobs are posted. Find out how to be the applicant who stands out in the crowd.

9 Outline the steps involved in developing successful e-business websites, and identify methods for assessing website effectiveness.

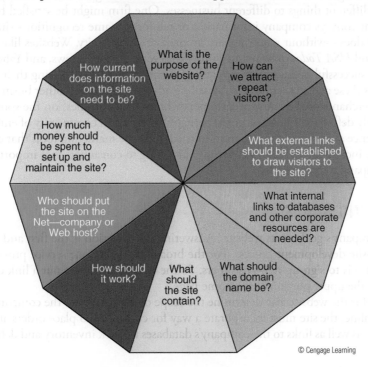

© Cengage Learning

FIGURE 5.3
Questions to Consider in Developing a Website

CAREER READINESS

Applying for Jobs Online

Firms like Starbucks and Procter & Gamble attract millions of online job applications a year, and they're forced to use screening software to eliminate thousands of applications that are never read. How can you make yours stand out in the crowd?

1. Be prepared to supply links to your blog or social networking account, especially if applying to a tech firm. Your "Web presence" says more about you than your résumé can.

2. Fill your résumé with key words applicable to the job, like "portfolio analysis" or "social media marketing expertise."

3. Recognize that an online application is a one-size-fits-all document that might not fit you. Avoid answering questions about your salary, for instance. Type "$100" and keep going.

4. Write "To be discussed" for the name of your current boss, especially if you are unemployed, and answer, "Available upon

strong mutual interest" to a request for references. Many advisors say these questions are premature until the interview.

5. If the application asks for a current job description, write "Please see résumé."

6. Finally, use your personal network to link your way to someone inside the firm where you're applying. A personal contact can still be the best way to land that all-important interview.

Sources: Susan Adams, "How to Make Them Respond When You Apply for a Job Online," *Forbes*, accessed November 13, 2012, www.forbes.com; Rachel Emma Silverman, "No More Résumés, Say Some Firms," *The Wall Street Journal*, accessed November 13, 2012, http://onlinewsj.com; Lauren Weber, "Your Résumé vs. Oblivion," *The Wall Street Journal*, accessed November 13, 2012, http://onlinewsj .com.

SUCCESSFUL SITE DEVELOPMENT

Most Web experts agree: "It is easier to build a bad website than a good one." When judging websites, success means different things to different businesses. One firm might be satisfied by maintaining a popular site that conveys company information or reinforces name recognition—just as a billboard or magazine ad does—without requiring any immediate sales activity. Websites like those of the *Los Angeles Times* and *USA Today* draw many visitors who want the latest news, and Yahoo!, Google, and ESPN.com are successful because they attract heavy traffic. Besides enhancing their brands, popular websites such as these add to their success by selling advertising space to other businesses.

Internet merchants need to attract customers who conduct business on the spot. Entrepreneurs are wise to clearly define their business goals, perhaps by creating a community of enthusiasts to build up sales in advance and to pay due attention to tried-and-true marketing tools that can complement Internet efforts, including television advertising. Listening to consumers is as important as talking to them via a company website or blog.

ESTABLISHING GOALS

What is the company's goal for its website? Answering this question is the first and most important step in the website development process. For the broadband telephone service provider Vonage, the primary objective is to sign up new customers. So the website designers put a link called "Sign Up" prominently in the upper portion of the home page.

Objectives for the website also determine the scope of the project. If the company's goal is to sell merchandise online, the site must incorporate a way for customers to place orders and ask questions about products, as well as links to the company's databases to track inventory and deliveries. The plan should include not only the appearance of the website but also the company's behind-the-scenes resources for making the website deliver on its promises.

Other key decisions include whether to create and maintain a site in-house or to contract with outside designers. Some companies prefer to retain control over content and design by producing their own sites. However, because acquiring the expertise to develop websites can be very time-consuming, hiring specialists may be more cost effective. Naming the website is another important early step in the planning process. A domain name should reflect the company and its products and be easy to remember. However, with millions of domain names already registered, the search for a unique, memorable, and easily spelled name can be difficult.

Websites like the one for Amazon are successful because they attract heavy traffic and offer shoppers a variety of products and deals as well as opportunities to join in discussions on a variety of topics via community forums.

IMPLEMENTATION AND INTEREST

Implementing the goals of the site is the next stage, and content is one of the most important factors in determining whether visitors return to a site. People obviously are more inclined to visit a site that provides material that interests them. Many e-business websites try to distinguish themselves by offering additional features. For example, Amazon's website lures traffic to the site with daily and hourly deals (called Lightning deals), a separate clothing store, garden supplies, music, movie, and book downloads, and various online community forums on a variety of topics. Many sites offer links to other sites that may interest visitors.

Standards for good content vary for every site, but available resources should be relevant to viewers; easy to access and understand; updated regularly; and written or displayed in a compelling, entertaining way. When the World Wide Web was a novelty, a page with a picture and a couple of paragraphs of text seemed entertaining. But such "brochureware" falls far short of meeting today's standards for interactivity, including the ability to accept customer data and orders, keep up-to-the-minute inventory records, and respond quickly to customer questions and complaints. Also, today's Internet users are less patient about figuring out how to make a site do what it promises. They won't wait ten minutes for a video clip to download or click through five different pages to complete a purchase. Revamping a site can help maintain interest and keep users on the site longer. Facebook recently rolled out a new design for its homepage that is more than just cosmetic. The changes are meant to improve site navigation and gather useful links and information in one part of the site.[60]

After making content decisions and designing the site, the next step is connecting to the Internet by placing the required computer files on a server. Companies can have their own dedicated Web servers or contract to place their websites on servers at Internet Service Providers (ISPs) or other host companies. Most small businesses lack the necessary expertise to set up and run their own servers; they are better off outsourcing to meet their hosting and maintenance needs. They also need to draw business to their site. This usually requires a listing with the major search engines, such as Google, Ask.com, and Bing.

> **"BRIEFLY SPEAKING"**
>
> "If you Google 'regret' and 'tattoo,' you will get 11.5 million hits."
>
> —**Kathryn Schulz**
> *Journalist*

PRICING AND MAINTENANCE

As with any technological investment, website costs are an important consideration. The highly variable cost of a website includes not only development expenses but also the cost of placing the site on a Web server, maintaining and updating it, and promoting it. A reasonably tech-savvy employee with off-the-shelf software can create a simple piece of brochureware for a few hundred dollars. A website that can handle e-business will cost at least $10,000. Creating it requires understanding how to link the website to the company's other information systems.

Although developing a commercial website with interactive features can cost tens of thousands of dollars, putting it online can cost as little as $30 a month for a spot on the server of a Web host such as Yahoo! and Web hosts such as Just Host deliver a huge audience.[61]

It's also important for a website to stay current. Visitors don't return to a site if they know that the information never changes or that claims about inventory or product selection are not relevant or current.[62] Consequently, updating design and content is another major expense. In addition, site maintenance should include running occasional searches to test that links to the company's website are still active.

ASSESSING SITE EFFECTIVENESS

How does a company gauge the return from investing in a website? Measuring the effectiveness of a website is tricky, and the appropriate process often depends on the purpose of the website. Figure 5.4 lists some measures of effectiveness. Profitability is relatively easy to measure in companies that generate revenues directly from online product orders, advertising, or subscription sales. Southwest Airlines generates more than 74 percent of its bookings online at Southwest.com. However, what's not clear is how many of those tickets Southwest would have sold through other channels if Southwest.com did not exist. Also, evidence exists that so-called Web-to-store shoppers—a group that favors the Internet primarily as a research tool and time-saving device for retail purchases made in stores—are a significant consumer niche.

Web-to-store shoppers Consumers who use the Internet as a tool when shopping at brick-and-mortar retailers.

For many companies, revenue is not a major website objective. Most company websites are classified as corporate websites, not shopping sites, meaning that firms use their sites to showcase their products and to offer information about their organizations. For such companies, online success is measured by increased brand awareness and brand loyalty, which presumably translates into greater profitability through offline transactions.

Some standards guide efforts to collect and analyze traditional consumer purchase data, such as how many Illinois residents purchased new Jeeps the previous year, watched *American Idol* on Fox, or tried Starbucks Blond Roast coffee. Still, the Internet presents several challenges for marketers. Although information sources are getting better, it is difficult to be sure how many people use the Internet, how often, and what they actually do online. Some Web pages display counters that measure the number of visits. However, the counters can't tell whether someone has spent time on the page or skipped over it on the way to another site, or whether that person is a first-time or repeat viewer.

click-through rate Percentage of people presented with a banner ad who click on it.

Advertisers typically measure the success of their ads in terms of click-through rates, meaning the percentage of people presented with a banner ad who click on it, thereby linking to a website or a pop-up page of information related to the ad. Recently, the average click-through rate has been declining to about 0.10 percent of those viewing an ad. This rate is much lower than the 1.38 to 3.42 percent response rate for direct-mail advertisements. Low click-through rates have made Web advertising less attractive than when it was new and people were clicking on just about anything online. Selling advertising has therefore become a less reliable source of e-business revenue.

conversion rate Percentage of visitors to a website who make a purchase.

engagement Amount of time users spend on sites.

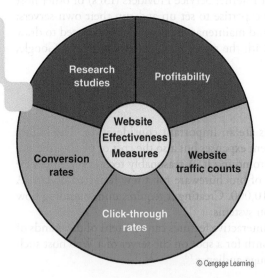

FIGURE 5.4
Measures of Website Effectiveness

© Cengage Learning

As e-business gains popularity, new models for measuring its effectiveness are being developed. A basic measurement is the conversion rate, the percentage of visitors to a website who make purchases. A conversion rate of 3 to 5 percent is average by today's standards. A company can use its advertising cost, site traffic, and conversion rate data to find out the cost to win each customer. E-business companies are trying to boost their conversion rates by ensuring their sites download quickly, are easy to use, and deliver on their promises. Many are turning to one of several firms that help companies improve the performance of their websites. Nielsen/Net Ratings developed a new way to rate websites that measures engagement, or how much time users spend on sites, rather than counting how many pages of a site they view. Google Analytics is a tool for tracking

⊕ **ASSESSMENT CHECK**

9.1 What are the basic questions a company should ask itself when planning a website?

9.2 How does the type of website affect measures of effectiveness?

9.3 Explain the difference between click-through rate, conversion rate, and engagement.

the number of visitors to a site, which pages they visit, where they come from, and whether they buy, among other statistics.[63]

Webtrends' Mobile Analytics offers similar measurements of consumer wireless activity. A recent version of its software, Webtrends Analytics 10, aims to integrate analytics from mobile, social, and Web channels. It can analyze marketing data from Facebook pages, iTunes Connect, and other media platforms. The company's CEO says, "Today marketers need to look across digital channels, including mobile and social, to get a holistic view of brand performance and customer engagement."[64]

STRATEGIC IMPLICATIONS OF MARKETING IN THE 21ST CENTURY

The future is bright for marketers who continue to take advantage of the tremendous potential of e-business and e-marketing. Online channels, such as podcasts, that seem cutting edge today will be eclipsed within the next decade by newer technologies, some of which haven't even been invented yet. First and foremost, e-business empowers consumers. For instance, already a significant percentage of car buyers show up at a dealership armed with information on dealer costs and option packages—information they obtained online. And the percentage of informed buyers is only going to increase. This trend isn't about being market led or customer focused; it is about consumer control. Some argue that the Internet represents the ultimate triumph of consumerism.

Since the end of World War II, there has been a fundamental shift in the retailing paradigm from Main Street to malls to superstores.

Each time the framework shifted, a new group of leaders emerged. The old leaders often missed the early warning signs because they were easy to ignore. When the first Walmart and Home Depot stores appeared, how many people really understood what impact these large retailers would have on the marketing environment? Similarly, marketers must understand the potential impact of the Web. Initially, some experts predicted the death of traditional retailing. This hasn't happened and probably will never happen. Rather, a marketing evolution for organizations has occurred, one that embraces Internet technologies as essential parts of their marketing strategies. E-business is fueled by information; marketers who effectively use the wealth of data available will survive—and thrive—in cyberspace.

Get online now for additional learning tools to help you master your marketing knowledge—visit **WWW.CENGAGEBRAIN.COM** today!

REVIEW OF CHAPTER OBJECTIVES

1 Describe the growth of Internet use worldwide.

The number of Internet users worldwide has reached almost 2.7 billion. Among individual countries with the highest number of Internet users, China is first with almost 514 million users, and the next three countries are the United States, India, and Japan.

2 Define *e-business* and *e-marketing*, and list the opportunities e-marketing presents.

E-business involves targeting customers by collecting and analyzing business information, conducting customer transactions, and maintaining online relationships with customers by means of computer networks such as the Internet. E-marketing is the strategic process of creating, distributing, promoting, and pricing goods and services to a target market over the Internet or through digital tools. The capabilities and benefits of e-business and e-marketing include the elimination of geographical boundaries, personalized marketing, interactive marketing, right-time marketing, and integrated marketing.

3 Distinguish between a corporate website and a marketing website.

Virtually all businesses have websites. Generally, these sites can be classified as either corporate websites or marketing websites. Corporate websites are designed to increase the firms' visibility, promote their offerings, and provide information to interested parties. Marketing websites are also designed to communicate information and build customer relationships, but the main purpose of marketing websites is to increase purchases by site visitors.

4 List the major forms of B2B e-marketing.

B2B e-marketing is the process of selling goods and services through online transactions. B2B e-marketing includes product information; ordering, invoicing, and payment processes; and customer service. In a B2B context, e-business uses Internet technology to conduct transactions between two organizations via electronic data interchange, Web services, extranets, private exchanges, electronic exchanges, and e-procurement.

5 Explain business-to-consumer (B2C) e-marketing.

Business-to-consumer (B2C) e-marketing is maturing. B2C uses the Internet to connect companies directly with consumers. E-tailing and electronic storefronts are the major forms of B2C online sales channels. B2C websites are either shopping sites or informational sites. Products can be purchased on shopping sites; informational sites provide product information along with links to sellers. Benefits of B2C e-marketing include competitive prices, increased access and convenience, and personalized service.

6 Identify online buyers and sellers.

Today's typical Internet user is from 18 to 64 years of age. Women now outnumber men online. During a recent year, the top products sold online included concert and theater tickets, computers and peripherals, clothes, electrical goods, movie tickets, and DVDs and music downloads.

7 Describe some of the challenges associated with online marketing and e-business.

One of the challenges to e-business is developing safe online payment methods. Most firms involved in e-business use Secure Sockets Layer technology to encrypt information and provide authentication. The growth of e-business has also been hampered by consumer security and privacy concerns and fraud. In addition, poor website design and service, unreliability of delivery and returns, and lack of retail expertise has limited e-business success. The Internet can also generate conflict among manufacturers, wholesalers, and retailers and present another avenue for copyright disputes.

8 Discuss how marketers use the communication function of the Web as part of their online marketing strategies.

Communication remains the most popular function of the Internet. Companies have long used email to communicate with customers, suppliers, and other partners. Online communities are groups of people who share common interests. Companies use online communities, such as forums and electronic bulletin boards, and social networking sites to communicate with and obtain feedback from customers and other partners. Blogs are online journals that have gained popularity in recent years. Wikis are Web pages anyone can edit, and podcasts are audio and video files that can be downloaded from the Web to any digital device. Web-based promotions include advertising on other websites using banner ads and pop-up ads, preroll video ads, widgets, and search marketing. Banner ads are strip messages placed in high-visibility areas of frequently visited websites. A pop-up ad is a separate window that pops up with an advertising message. Preroll video ads appear before a selected video, and widgets are interactive applications users can add to their pages to play music, video, and slide shows. Search marketing is an arrangement by which a firm pays a search engine such as Google a fee to make sure the firm's listing appears toward the top of the search results.

9 Outline the steps involved in developing successful e-business websites, and identify methods for assessing website effectiveness.

Businesses establish websites to expand their customer bases, increase buyer awareness of their products, improve consumer communications, and provide better service. Before designing a website, a company's decision makers must first determine what they want to achieve with the site.

Other important decisions include who should create, host, and manage the site; how to promote it; and how much funding to allocate. Successful websites contain informative, up-to-date, and visually appealing content. Sites should also download quickly and be easy to use. Finally, management must develop ways of assessing how well a site accomplishes its objectives. Common methods of measuring the effectiveness of websites include profitability, click-through rates, conversion rates, and engagement.

 ASSESSMENT CHECK: ANSWERS

1.1 How would you describe the growth of Internet use worldwide? Worldwide, the number of Internet users has reached almost 2.7 billion. Among individual countries with the highest number of Internet users, China is first with almost one quarter of the population online. The next three countries are the United States, India, and Japan. Growth in Asia has been rapid.

1.2 What do most U.S. consumers do online? Nearly all U.S. consumers say they use email; almost 85 percent get news, search for health or medical news, look for information about items they're interested in buying, or go online just to pass the time or to have fun.

2.1 Define e-marketing. E-marketing is the strategic process of creating, distributing, promoting, and pricing goods and services to a target market over the Internet.

2.2 Explain the difference between e-business and e-marketing. E-business involves a wide range of activities that take place via the Internet. It is divided into five broad categories: (1) e-tailing; (2) business-to-business transactions; (3) electronic data interchanges; (4) email, instant messaging, blogs, podcasts, and other Web-enabled communication; and (5) gathering and use of information through Web contacts. E-marketing transfers the traditional marketing functions of creating, distributing, promoting, and pricing goods and services to the Internet or through digital tools.

2.3 What are the major benefits of e-marketing? The major benefits of e-business include the elimination

of geographical boundaries, personalized marketing, interactive marketing, right-time marketing, and integrated marketing.

3.1 Explain the difference between a corporate website and a marketing website. A corporate website is designed to increase a firm's visibility, promote its offerings, and provide information for interested parties. A marketing website generally includes the same information found on a corporate website but is also designed to increase sales by site visitors.

3.2 Why would companies *not* sell products on their websites? Their products might not lend themselves to online sales, or the firms may have relationships with partners, such as dealers or franchisees, that sell their products instead.

4.1 What is B2B e-marketing? How large is it relative to consumer e-marketing? B2B e-marketing is the use of the Internet for business transactions between organizations. By some estimates, 91 percent of all e-marketing activity consists of B2B transactions.

4.2 Define *EDI* and *Web services*. An EDI is a computer-to-computer exchange of invoices, purchase orders, price quotations, and other sales information between buyers and sellers. All parties must use the same computer operating system. Web services consist of Internet-based systems that allow parties to communicate and exchange data regardless of the computer operating system they use.

4.3 Briefly explain how e-procurement works.
E-procurement systems are Web-based systems that enable all types of organizations to improve the efficiency of their bidding and purchasing processes.

5.1 What is B2C e-marketing? B2C e-marketing uses the Internet to connect companies directly with consumers either through shopping sites or through informational sites.

5.2 Explain the difference between a shopping website and an informational website. Consumers can purchase products on shopping sites, while informational sites provide product information along with links to sellers. However, consumers cannot actually purchase products on informational sites.

5.3 Discuss the benefits of B2C e-marketing. Benefits of B2C e-marketing include competitive prices, increased access and convenience, and personalized service.

6.1 Who shops online? Are the characteristics of online shoppers changing? The typical Internet user now is likely to be between 18 and 64 years of age and spend an average of 30 hours a month viewing more than 2,700 Web pages, including home and office Internet use. Men used to shop more frequently online than women did, but today women shoppers outnumber men.

6.2 What are some of the capabilities e-marketers might add to their websites in the future? E-marketers need to update their offerings at their websites at an increasing rate, speed the checkout process, add video segments to their online product catalogs, implement advanced and easy-to-use search and navigation technologies, and initiate network-type conversations with and among their customers.

7.1 What are the major challenges to growth in e-business and e-marketing? The major challenges include developing safe online payment, privacy concerns, and fraud and scams. In addition, poor site design and customer service, unreliability of delivery and returns, and lack of retail expertise have limited e-business success.

7.2 Describe phishing and vishing. Phishing is a scam that uses email or pop-up messages that claim to be from familiar banks, Internet service providers, or other organizations asking for personal information. The purpose of phishing is to get unsuspecting victims to disclose personal information such as credit card numbers. Vishing is the voice equivalent of phishing, and consists of a voice message or email telling the user to make a phone call designed to elicit credit card information.

7.3 Explain how e-marketing can create channel conflicts and copyright disputes. The Internet can generate conflict among manufacturers, wholesalers, and retailers—so-called channel conflicts. For instance, a channel conflict could be created when a manufacturer sells its products online and competes with its retail partners. Copyright disputes usually arise when a site hosts content to which someone else holds the rights.

8.1 What are online communities and social networks? Explain how online communities can help companies market their products and improve customer service. Online communities and social networks can take several forms and include Internet discussion groups and electronic bulletin boards, as well as networking sites such as Facebook and Twitter. Users log in and participate by sending comments and questions or receiving information from other forum members. Companies use online communities to ask questions and exchange information with customers.

8.2 What are blogs, wikis, and podcasts? A blog, short for *Web log*, is a Web page that serves as a publicly accessible journal for an individual or organization. A wiki is a Web page anyone can edit. A podcast is an audio or video file that can be downloaded from a website to a digital device. Companies use blogs, wikis, and podcasts as tools to build and maintain customer relationships.

8.3 Explain the differences between a banner ad, a pop-up ad, a preroll video ad, a widget, and search marketing. Banner ads are strip messages placed in high-visibility areas of frequently visited websites. A pop-up ad is a separate window that pops up with an advertising message. Preroll video ads are brief marketing messages that appear before expected video content. Widgets are tiny interactive applications Internet users can copy and add to their own pages to play music, video, or slide shows. Search marketing is an arrangement by which a firm pays a search engine—such as Google—a fee to make sure the firm's listing appears toward the top of the search results.

9.1 What are the basic questions a company should ask itself when planning a website? The first question deals with the purpose of the website. The second deals with whether the firm should develop the site itself or outsource it to a specialized firm. The third question is determining the name of the site.

9.2 How does the type of website affect measures of effectiveness? For a shopping site, profitability is an important measure of effectiveness, though profitability can be difficult to measure given the tendencies of Web-to-store shoppers. For company websites, online success is measured by increased brand awareness and loyalty, which presumably translate into greater profitability through offline transactions.

9.3 Explain the difference between click-through rate, conversion rate, and engagement. The click-through rate is the percentage of viewers who, when presented with a banner ad, click on it. The conversion rate is the percentage of visitors to a website who actually make purchases. Engagement measures how long a user spends on a site instead of how many pages he or she views.

MARKETING TERMS YOU NEED TO KNOW

e-business **136**	electronic storefronts **144**	vishing **149**	preroll video ad **154**
e-marketing **138**	electronic shopping cart **144**	channel conflicts **150**	widgets **155**
interactive marketing **139**	bot (shopbot) **145**	spam **151**	search marketing **155**
corporate website **141**	encryption **147**	electronic bulletin board **152**	Web-to-store shoppers **158**
marketing website **141**	Secure Sockets Layer (SSL) **147**	blog **154**	click-through rate **158**
business-to-business (B2B) e-marketing **142**	electronic signatures **148**	wiki **154**	conversion rate **158**
e-procurement **143**	firewall **149**	podcast **154**	engagement **158**
business-to-consumer (B2C) e-marketing **143**	phishing **149**	banner ad **154**	
		pop-up ad **154**	

ASSURANCE OF LEARNING REVIEW

1. List the five e-business categories.
2. Explain how a Web presence can improve the performance of traditional brick-and-mortar operations.
3. Describe the type and purpose of information found on a corporate website.
4. Which is larger, B2B or B2C e-marketing?
5. How is wireless access changing e-marketing?
6. List the reasons consumers give for why they shop online.
7. Describe how firms can alleviate some of the privacy concerns of online shoppers.
8. What is purchase fraud?
9. How can companies benefit from blogs and avoid their downsides?
10. Describe the issues that go into developing a successful website. How does the purpose of the website affect its implementation and cost?

PROJECTS AND TEAMWORK EXERCISES

1. In small teams, research the benefits of purchasing the following products online:
   a. tablet computers
   b. hotel rooms in Orlando
   c. movie tickets
   d. auto insurance
2. Assume your team is assigned to develop the website for a large online clothing retailer that also has traditional retail stores. Research the characteristics of Web users and online shoppers. What features would you want to incorporate into your website?
3. How can marketers use the concept of community to add value to their products? Give a real-world example of each type of community discussed in the chapter.
4. Working with a small group, assume your group designs e-business websites. Identify a local company that operates with little or no online presence. Outline a proposal that explains to the firm the benefits of either going online or significantly expanding its online presence. Sketch out what the firm's website should look like and the functions it should perform.
5. Working with a partner, identify and visit ten different e-business websites. These can be either B2C or B2B sites. Which of these sites, in your opinion, have the highest and lowest conversion rates? Explain your choices and suggest some ways in which the conversion rates of all ten sites could be improved.

CRITICAL-THINKING EXERCISES

1. Who are typical online buyers and sellers? What are some of the strategic implications of these facts to online marketers?

2. Some marketers argue that search marketing is a more effective means of using the Web to advertise than traditional pop-up or banner ads. Research the concept of search marketing. What are some of the benefits of using search marketing?

3. Assume you work for a U.S. company that markets its products throughout the world. Its current online presence outside the United States is limited. Outline some steps the company should take to expand its online presence internationally.

4. Visa offers a service called Verified by Visa. The purpose is to reduce Internet-related fraud (MasterCard and American Express have similar services). Research "Verified by Visa" and prepare a report summarizing the program and how it protects both buyers and sellers.

5. One factor that appears to impede growth in online sales is consumers' fear of receiving unsolicited email after a purchase is made. Given that fear, should companies continue to use email to communicate with customers? If so, how?

ETHICS EXERCISE

One of the lingering obstacles to e-business revolves around privacy concerns. Virtually all websites collect user data. Internet service providers, for example, can track where users go on the Web and store that information. Search engines keep detailed data on Internet searches by users. Those arguing that additional privacy laws and regulations are needed claim that users never know exactly what information is collected, nor when it is collected. Moreover, there is no means for determining whether websites follow their own privacy policies.

On the other hand, some say current laws and regulations are adequate because they make it illegal for firms to misrepresent their privacy policies or fail to disclose the type of information collected. Furthermore, there is no evidence that Internet companies are quietly passing on specific customer information to outside parties.

Aside from the strictly legal issues, Web privacy raises a number of ethical issues as well.

Assume your company collects and stores personal information about its online customers. The company's privacy policy allows the company to give limited amounts of that information to "selected" third parties.

1. Is this policy, in your opinion, appropriate and adequate? What ethical issues does your company's policy raise?

2. How would you change the privacy policy to reflect your ethical concerns?

3. From strictly an economic perspective, is the company's existing policy adequate and appropriate?

INTERNET EXERCISES

1. **Online shopping.** Assume you're in the market for a notebook computer. Visit at least two of the websites listed below and review shopping suggestions and model ratings. Next, list your top two models and, using a shopping site like Shopping .com (www.shopping.com), search for online retailers offering the best combination of price, user ratings, shipping, and other relevant criteria. Prepare a report summarizing your experience. What did this exercise teach you about the benefits and challenges of online retailing?

   www.pcmag.com

   www.notebookcomputers.com

   www.pcworld.com

   www.cnet.com

2. **Marketing uses of social networking.** Choose two online retailers and two manufacturers. Go to each website. Compare

and contrast how all four firms use social networking sites (such as Facebook and Twitter) to market their products. Which, in your opinion, uses social networking most effectively?

3. **Search marketing.** Visit the website listed below. Prepare a brief report outlining how to optimize the use of search marketing. Be sure to include a discussion on measuring the effectiveness of search marketing.

   www.toprankblog.com/2009/03/charting-search-engine-optimization

Note: Internet Web addresses change frequently. If you don't find the exact site listed, you may need to access the organization's home page and search from there or use a search engine such as Google or Bing.

CASE 5.1
Walgreens Embraces e-Commerce

With recent acquisitions of drugstore.com and beauty.com, Walgreens has put the business community on notice that the company is much more than a century-old, bricks-and-mortar retailer. The company believes consumers want choices, and it has implemented e-commerce and mobile strategies that will keep the brand in consumers' decision-making process.

Walgreens first stepped into e-commerce over a decade ago when it started walgreens.com, which recently ranked as one of the top retail sites on the Web with more than $890 million in sales. The company's new mobile shopping app allows consumers to track medication schedules, receive reminders, and order refills by scanning the barcode on prescription bottles with their smartphones. The company says more than 40 percent of Walgreens' online prescription refills come from mobile devices.

When consumers switched to digital cameras, many retailers got out of the one-hour photo-processing business—not Walgreens. With its QuickPrint function, the mobile app allows customers to take photos on their smartphones, find a local Walgreens, send images to the store for printing, and pick up the prints typically within an hour. The company believes the photo option provides additional revenues because so many pictures "live" on people's smartphones. Walgreens also recently announced agreements with several mobile photo-sharing companies to allow their subscribers to "print to Walgreens."

Walgreens learned that customers who are reached through multiple channels are three times as valuable to the company's bottom line as those customers reached through only one channel. With more than 8,000 stores in the U.S., and two-thirds of the population living within three miles of a store location, Walgreens believes its multi-faceted approach will continue to appeal to consumers of all ages.

QUESTIONS FOR CRITICAL THINKING

1. According to a recent Nielsen survey, there has been a significant increase in the number of consumers 65 years and older using smartphones. How can Walgreens take advantage of this demographic as the company expands its online retail presence?

2. Walgreens recently took a majority stake in Alliance Boots, a European pharmacy retailer, for more than $6 billion. What effects will this partnership have on the company's e-commerce strategies?

Sources: Michael Johnsen, "The 'What, Where and When' of e-Commerce," *Drug Store News*, accessed November 13, 2012, http://wwwdrugstorenews.com; Brian Quinton, "Walgreens Powers Multi-Touch Strategy with Mobile, Social and Ecommerce," *Chief Marketer*, accessed November 13, 2012, http://chiefmarketer.com; Andrew Stockwell, "Executive Q&Q with Sona Chawla, President, e-Commerce, Walgreens," *Forrester*, accessed November 13, 2012, http://blogs.forrester.com; Lauren Johnson, "Passbook Vaulted Walgreens App to No. 8 in Free App Store Day after Launch," *Mobile Commerce Daily*, accessed November 13, 2012, http://www.mobile commercedaily.com; Brian Dolan, "Walgreens App Adds Pill Reminders, Rx Transfer," *Mobile Health News*, accessed November 13, 2012, http://mobilehealthnews.com; Sarah Perez, "App Developers Can Now 'Print to Walgreens'; Company Outed as Aviary's Strategic Investor," *Tech Crunch*, accessed November 13, 2012, http://techcrunch .com; Mark Scott, "Walgreen to Take Stake in Alliance Boots for $6.7 Billion," *The New York Times*, accessed November 13, 2012, http://dealbook.nytimes.com.

VIDEO CASE 5.2
Hubway: Boston's Online Bike-Sharing System

If you've ever lived in a city, you know that getting around can be a challenge. Traffic jams, overflowing parking lots, crammed subway cars, drivers who plow through puddles that spray water on pedestrians—all of these may be enough to make you pack your bags and head for the suburbs. A company in Boston is trying to change that, using a fleet of bicycles and the Internet.

Hubway (sponsored by New Balance and operated by Alta Bicycle Share) is Boston's recently established bike-sharing system that features 60 stations, 600 bicycles, and an interactive component that allows urban consumers to borrow a bike at one location with the swipe of a credit card—and return it to another destination. On a Hubway bike, you can pedal to the gym or the grocery store; commute to work; or visit a friend across town. You can grab an available bike spur of the moment by swiping your credit card at one of the kiosk stations, giving you a 24-hour or three-day membership. Or you can sign up for an annual membership online; within a week, Hubway will mail you a station key with a printed code. The cost of membership includes unlimited rides that are less than 30 minutes, with additional fees for longer rides.

Hubway operates entirely in the realm of e-commerce, marketing to consumers and conducting transactions completely online. "There is no store or counter to get a key," says Hubway's Brogan Graham, who bears the title of Hype Master. "You put in your information online and we mail you a key." The touch screens at the bike stations are solar-powered, offering access 24 hours a day, 7 days a week, meaning that bike riders may rent a bike at any time without the assistance of another human being. General Manager Scott Mullen points to the efficiency of this operating system, as opposed to the "unwieldiness" of staffing each station with a Hubway representative, which he claims "would be a 1.0 solution to a 2.0 problem." Customer service does exist, however. If you cruise into a station with a flat tire or broken chain, you just hit the red "mechanic" button, which will secure the bike without letting someone else unwittingly take it out on the road. A Hubway mechanic will retrieve the bike and repair it. An app called Spot Cycle identifies the locations of different stations, including whether or not bikes are available at a specific station.

Hubway relies on the communication function of the Internet to provide current information to its customers. Consumers get station updates and marketing messages through social media sites, such as Facebook and Twitter; for example, if a station's Internet connection isn't working properly, Hubway will alert consumers via social media—including an estimated time for the station to go live. On its Facebook page, some Hubway members post suggestions for improvement (like which stations need more bikes on a regular basis) while others receive kudos for bicycling achievements (such as the first member to reach 250,000 rides). "We leverage the Internet," says Scott Mullen.

Hubway's typical customers tend to be those who are the most tech savvy about swiping credit cards at kiosks, using touch screens, and maximizing services via the company's website and social media accounts. But its marketers emphasize the fact that Hubway's system is easy to use. Most people need only to "use the system once to understand it because it is so intuitive," remarks Marketing Director Mary McLaughlin.

Whether we're talking about e-commerce or traditional commerce, the numbers don't lie. Hubway began with a goal of attracting 3,000 members and launching 100,000 rides during its first year of business. In fact, the company hit the 100,000-ride target in less than 11 weeks and topped 250,000 trips in 6 months. On one sample day, more than 2,500 station-to-station rides were recorded. By year's end, 3,700 members had signed on. With this kind of success, Hubway has already planned expansion into more Boston neighborhoods, as well as adjacent towns like Cambridge and Brookline—with the near-term goal of doubling the number of stations and increasing the number of bikes to 1,000. Riding is "cool and fun," says Brogan Graham. "It's a great way to explore a new city."

QUESTIONS FOR CRITICAL THINKING

1. What are the benefits of e-marketing for Hubway? What are the potential drawbacks?

2. Thus far, Hubway essentially engages in business-to-consumer (B2C) e-marketing. Cite two or three examples of ways in which Hubway might branch out into business-to-business (B2B) e-marketing.

Sources: Company website, www.thehubway.com, accessed November 13, 2012; Eric Moskowitz, "Hubway Bike-Sharing Program Is on a Roll," *Boston.com*, accessed November 13, 2012, http://articles.boston.com; Jonathan Simmons, "On Biking: Learning to Love Hubway," *Boston.com*, accessed November 13, 2012, http://articles.boston.com.

NOTES

1. Liz Gannes, "The Secret Behind Pinterest's Growth Was Marketing, Not Engineering, Says CEO Ben Silbermann," *All Things Digital*, accessed November 12, 2012, http://allthingsd.com; Debra Donston-Miller, "Pinterest's Success, by the Numbers," *Information Week*, accessed November 12, 2012, www.information.com; Gene Marks, "Drilling Down: What Small Businesses Should Know About Pinterest," *The New York Times*, accessed November 12, 2012, www.nytimes.com; Christine Lagorio, "Where Pinterest Will Go From Here," *Inc.*, accessed November 12, 2012, www.inc.com; Chas Edwards, "In Age of Pinterest, Instagram, Marketers Need an Image Strategy," *Advertising Age*, accessed November 12, 2012, http://adage.com; Eric Savitz, "Four Pinterest Marketing Tips," *Forbes*, accessed November 12, 2012, www.forbes.com; Janet Aronica, "Pinterest Sent More Referral Traffic than Google Referral, Twitter, and Stumbleupon, Slightly Edges Out Bing," *Shareaholic.com*, accessed November 12, 2012, http://blog .shareaholic.com.

2. Lauren Indvik, "U.S. Online Retail Sales to Reach $327 Billion by 2016 [STUDY]," *Mashable.com*, accessed November 12, 2012, http://mashable.com; Thomas Cornelius, "The Decade of Online to Offline Retail Commerce Disruption," *Daily Deal Media*, accessed November 25, 2012, www.dailydealmedia.com.

3. Internet World Stats, www.internetworldstats.com, accessed November 12, 2012.

4. "Top 20 Countries with the Highest Number of Internet Users," www.internetworldstats .com, accessed November 12, 2012.

5. Ibid.

6. "Which Country Has the Fastest Internet?" *Tales of Interest*, accessed November 12, 2012, www.talesofinterest.net.

7. "What Internet Users Do Online: Trend Data," *Pew Internet*, November 12, 2012, www.pewinternet.org.

8. "Facebook Statistics, Stats & Facts for 2011," *Digital Buzz*, accessed November 12, 2012, www.digitalbuzzblog.com; "It's a Social World: Social Networking Leads as Top Online Activity Globally, Accounting for 1 in Every 5 Online Minutes," press release, comScore.com, accessed November 12, 2012, www.comscore.com.

9. "China Internet Users by Numbers," *China Internet Watch*, accessed November 12, 2012, www.chinainternetwatch.com; China Internet Watch and Incitez, "China Internet Status Report 2010," *China Internet Watch*, accessed November 12, 2012, www.chinainternetwatch.com; CIW Team Staff, "China's B2C Market Exceeded 240 Billion Yuan in 2011," *China Internet Watch*, accessed November 12, 2012, www.chinainternetwatch.com.

10. Ibid.

11. Company website, www.roadrunnersports.com, accessed November 12, 2012.

12. Jennifer Van Grove, "McDonald's Foursquare Day Campaign Increased Checkins by 33%," *Mashable Business*, accessed November 12, 2012, http://mashable.com.

13. Power Reviews, "New Study Reveals Impact of Social Tools, Evolving Search Patterns and Mobile Technology on Consumer Shopping Behavior," *Marketwire*, accessed November 12, 2012, www.marketwire.com.

14. Company website, www1.macys.com, accessed November 12, 2012; Company website, www.williams-sonoma.com, accessed November 12, 2012.

15. Company website, www.burgerking.com, accessed November 12, 2012.

16. Company website, http://store.sony.com, accessed November 12, 2012.

17. U.S. Census Bureau E-Stats, "E-commerce 2010," accessed November 12, 2012, www.census.gov/econ/estats.

18. Jakob Nielsen, "10 Best Intranets of 2012," *Jakob Nielsen's Alertbox*, accessed November 12, 2012, www.useit.com; Kelly Kass, "Staples Intranet Is a Two-Time Winner—Here's Why," *HR Communication*, accessed November 12, 2012, www.hrcommunication.com.

19. "SAP Customer Success Story: Royal Dutch/Shell Group," www.sap.com, accessed November 12, 2012.

20. Antony Savvas, "Scottish Government Awards £18.5m E-Procurement Support Contract," *ComputerWorld UK*, accessed November 12, 2012, www.computerworlduk.com.

21. State website, www.eva.state.va.us, accessed November 12, 2012.

22. Greg Bensinger, "Online Sales Rose 30% on 'Cyber Monday,'" *The Wall Street Journal*, accessed November 28, 2012, http://online.wsj.com; Blake Ellis, "Cyber Monday Sales Reach New Record," *CNN Money*, accessed November 28, 2012, http://money.cnn.com.

23. Joshua Brustein, "Mobile Shopping Set to Spike, Says Forrester," *The New York Times*, accessed November 12, 2012, http://bits.blogs.nytimes.com; Sarah Perez, "Majority of Top Brands Now Have Mobile Apps," *TechCrunch*, accessed November 12, 2012, http://techcrunch.com; Barbara Thau, "5 Mobile Shopping Trends That Will Change the WayYou Buy," *DailyFinance*, accessed November 12, 2012, www.dailyfinance.com.

24. Company website, www.ae.com, accessed November 12, 2012.

25. Mark Walsh, "U.S. Tablet Users Double to 70 Million in 2012," *Online Media Daily*, accessed November 12, 2012, www.mediapost.com; Kristi Essick, "Online Shopping Tablet Style," *Cisco: The Network*, accessed November 12, 2012, http://newsroom.cisco.com.

26. S. J. Johnson, "Best Websites for Travel Deals and Online Travel Deal Tips," *Yahoo! Voices*, accessed November 12, 2012, http://voices.yahoo.com.

27. Ann Carrns, "Cards That Help Save on Airline Baggage Fees," *The New York Times*, accessed November 12, 2012, http://bucks.blogs.nytimes.com.

28. Company website, www.barnesandnoble.com, accessed November 12, 2012.

29. Leena Rao, "It's Official: Google Acquires Like.com," *TechCrunch*, accessed November 12, 2012, http://techcrunch.com; Company website, www.google.com/shopping, accessed November 12, 2012.

30. "30 Top Online-Shopping Trends," *TMCnet.com*, accessed November 12, 2012, www.tmcnet.com; U.S. Department of the Census, "Adult Computer and Adult Internet Users by Selected Characteristics, 2000 to 2010" and "Typical Daily Internet Activities of Adult Internet Users: 2011," www.census.gov, accessed November 2012; Mike Flacy, "Study: Average Person Spends Nearly Eight Hours a Month on Facebook," *Digital Trends*, accessed November 12, 2012, www.digitaltrends.com; E-Tailing Group, "The 2011 Social Shopping Study, Brief I: Consumer Research Dynamics, Mobile and User-Generated Content," *PowerReviews*, accessed November 12, 2012, www.powerreviews.com.

31. Marcia Kaplan, "Understanding the Shift to Online Shopping," *Practical eCommerce*, accessed November 12, 2012, www.practicalecommerce.com.

32. Peter Leech, "Is Shopping Really Happening on Facebook?" *Social Media Club*, accessed November 12, 2012, http://socialmediaclub.org; Erin Griffith, "Can Social Shopping Finally Take Off?" *Adweek*, accessed November 12, 2012, www.adweek.com.

33. Company website, www.symantec.com, accessed November 12, 2012.

34. U.S. Small Business Administration, "Online Payment Services," www.sba.gov, accessed November 12, 2012.

35. Katy Bachman, "Big Week in Washington for Online Privacy Issues," *Adweek*, accessed November 12, 2012, www.adweek.com.

36. Antone Gonsalves, "10 Biggest Security Breaches of 2011," *CRN*, accessed November 12, 2012, www.crn.com.

37. Government website, www.ic3.gov, accessed November 12, 2012.

38. "2011 CyberSecurity Watch Survey: Organizations Need More Skilled Cyber Professionals to Stay Secure," *Marketwire*, accessed November 12, 2012, www.marketwire.com.

39. David Jacoby, "Facebook Security Phishing Attack in the Wild," *Securelist*, accessed November 12, 2012, www.securelist.com.

40. Amanda Ciccatelli, "Pindrop Security Helps Victims Address Mounting Vishing Attacks," *TMCnet*, accessed November 12, 2012, www.tmcnet.com.

41. Mark Brohan, "Big Design Changes Drive Growth Online at Under Armour," *Internet Retailer*, accessed November 12, 2012, www.internetretailer.com.

42. "Top 500 List," *Internet Retailer*, accessed November 12, 2012, www.internetretailer.com; Zak Stambor, "Daily Deals Spur Repeat Business," *Internet Retailer*, accessed November 12, 2012, www.internetretailer.com.

43. Lance Whitney, "Google Asks Court to Ax Book-Scanning Suit from Authors Guild," *CNet News*, November 12, 2012, http://news.cnet.com.

44. Scott Beale, "Email vs. Snail Mail," *Laughing Squid*, accessed November 12, 2012, http://laughingsquid.com; Barry Shurtz, "Email Fun Fact: How Many Emails Are Sent Every Day," *Sendmail, Inc.*, accessed November 12, 2012, www.sendmail.com; Lucian Parfeni, "More than 95 Percent of All Email Is Spam," *Softpedia*, accessed November 12, 2012, http://news.softpedia.com.

45. Parfeni, "More than 95 Percent of All Email Is Spam."

46. Company website, www.facebook.com/chasecommunitygiving, accessed November 12, 2012.

47. "Facebook Marketing Statistics, Demographics, Reports, and New," *CheckFacebook.com*, accessed November 12, 2012, www.checkfacebook.com.

48. Joann Pan, "Will You Be Twitter's 500 Millionth User? [UPDATED]," *Mashable Social Media*, accessed November 12, 2012, http://mashable.com.

49. Julia Boorstin, "Twitter CEO Dick Costolo on the Business, IPOs, and Advertising," *CNBC.com*, accessed November 12, 2012, www.cnbc.com; Jessica E. Vascellaro, "Twitter to Start Rolling Out Advertising," *The Wall Street Journal*, accessed November 12, 2012, http://online.wsj.com.

50. Todd Wasserman, "Twitter Rolls Out Promoted Tweets for Mobile," *Mashable Social Media*, accessed November 12, 2012, http://mashable.com.

51. Justin James, "10 Things You Should Consider Before Launching a Social Media Marketing Campaign," *TechRepublic*, accessed November 12, 2012, www.techrepublic.com.

52. Company Facebook page, www.facebook.com/Mozilla, accessed November 12, 2012; Devon Glenn, "Which Social Networks Had the Most Fans in 2011? [Infographic]" *Social Times*, accessed November 12, 2012, www.socialtimes.com; Kim Woodbridge, "14 Creative Ways to Use Facebook Business Pages," *PCWorld*, accessed November 12, 2012, www.pcworld.com/businesscenter.

53. Jennifer Van Grove, "Facebook Advertisers Can Target Users by Zip Code," *Mashable Business*, accessed November 12, 2012, http://mashable.com; Helen Leggatt, "Zip Code Targeting Boosts Facebook Ad CTRs Two-Fold," *BizReport*, accessed November 12, 2012, www.bizreport.com; John Rampton, "Google AdWords Adds Zip Code Targeting, Location Insertion; Updates Location Targeting," *Search Engine Watch*, accessed November 12, 2012, http://searchenginewatch.com.

54. Eilene Zimmerman, "Small Retailers Open Up Storefronts on Facebook Pages," *The New York Times*, accessed November 20, 2012, www.nytimes.com.

55. Katy Finneran, "The Power of Facebook for Small Businesses," *FOXBusiness*, accessed November 12, 2012, http://smallbusiness.foxbusiness.com.

56. "Facebook Cited as Most Effective Social Networking Tool Among Inc. 500," *PRWeb*, press release, accessed November 12, 2012, www.prweb.com.

57. Susanne Gargiulo, "The Global Workforce: Challenge or Asset?" *CNN.com*, accessed November 12, 2012, http://edition.cnn.com.

58. Sam Thielman, "Want to Skip Those Veloster Pre-Roll Ads? What's It Worth to You?" *Adweek*, accessed November 12, 2012, www.adweek.com.

59. Michelle Megna, "Widgets Offer Viral Marketing and Affiliate Revenue," *ecommerce guide*, accessed November 12, 2012, www.ecommerce-guide.com.

60. Sarah Kessler, "Facebook Timeline Changed the Way We See Brand Pages: Here's How," *Mashable Business*, accessed November 12, 2012, http://mashable.com.

61. "2013 Best Web Hosting Comparisons and Reviews," *Top Ten Reviews*, accessed November 12, 2012, http://web-hosting-review.toptenreviews.com.

62. David Gitonga, "How to Keep Your Website Up to Date on a Small Budget," *TechRepublic*, accessed November 1, 2012, www.techrepublic.com.

63. Meghan Peters, "HOW TO: Get Started with Google Analytics," *Mashable Business*, accessed November 12, 2012, http://mashable.com.

64. Chelsi Nakano, "Webtrends Analytics 10: Analytics for Mobile, Social and Web," *CMS Wire*, accessed November 12, 2012, www.cmswire.com.

Scripps Networks Interactive & Food Network

© iStockphoto.com/amygdala_imagery / © Cengage Learning

PART 1
Designing Customer-Oriented Marketing Strategies

Cooking Up Social Media Strategies

Food, cooking, and social media seem like natural ingredients to stir together in the same stew pot. The portfolio of Scripps Networks Interactive—a leading developer of lifestyle content for media platforms—includes well-known television brands Food Network, Cooking Channel, HGTV, DIY Network, Travel Channel, and Great American Country (GAC). The food category of Food Network and Cooking Channel specifically brings consumers mouthwatering programming as well as online video, social media, and e-commerce opportunities.

With 2,000 employees based in Knoxville, Tennessee, Scripps generates about $2.1 billion in revenue each year on content viewed around the world. These numbers aren't chicken feed—they reflect an understanding of the target market and careful strategic planning. "We have an audience that knows us for ideas and inspirations around food and cooking," says Susie Fogelson, senior vice president, marketing, creative services, and public relations for Food Network and the Cooking Channel. Identifying this group of people helps Scripps and Food Network—one of its major brands—design content and develop a customer-driven marketing strategy to attract loyal viewers. "At Scripps we are constantly evolving and iterating how we deliver content," says Chris Powell, executive vice president of human resources. For Food Network, this involves three variables of the marketing mix: product strategy, distribution strategy, and promotion strategy, all designed to engage viewers who want to be inspired and educated about food.

By its very nature, social media lends itself to relationship building. Scripps marketers understand this and tailor the marketing strategy for Food Network and its other brands to use social media effectively. "Social media gives us a really great place to identify who our brand advocates and brand fans are and then message them" with relevant content, says Jonah Spegman, director of digital media and database marketing for Scripps. "Our brands are intrinsically social," he adds. Viewers love to talk about favorite dishes they've made themselves or enjoyed at restaurants—and they do it on Facebook, Twitter, Pinterest, YouTube, and Tumblr. When viewers are talking at these sites, Scripps and Food Network want to be there. "Wherever consumers are, we want to be," says Powell.

Despite what appears to be the obvious connection between culinary entertainment and social media, Scripps hasn't taken a first-mover strategy of adopting specific social-media sites or tools. Instead, the firm prefers a second-mover strategy. "You need to wait and adopt technology at the right time," observes Rich Ma, manager of digital marketing. "See what consumers are gravitating toward." For example, Facebook and Twitter are already considered well-established social media outlets, whereas Pinterest has soared during the last year. "It's important to be a market leader in those established places," says Ma. In addition, companies must learn how to leverage the technology, instead of jumping in without a plan.

Fogelson agrees with the importance of planning. "We have this enormous audience with this enormous demand to really feed the appetites of people who are looking for ideas and inspiration around cooking," she says. In order to serve this huge audience, Scripps and Food Network have begun to key in on what Fogelson refers to as the "tent poles"—the shows that have a certain focus (and target market) also have related shows and marketing wrapped around them. Such shows include *Food Network Star* and *Great Food Truck Race*. Marketers link these shows to the social sites to interact with fans, get feedback, create exchanges, and spark enthusiasm for other shows. In addition, marketers for all of Scripps' branded networks share the data they gather about social media marketing. If one network has success with Pinterest but not with Twitter, marketers will exchange the information. "All of the networks are experimenting and sharing the knowledge," says Jeffrey Kissinger, vice president of digital marketing and database marketing at Scripps. "Everyone is experimenting and trying, and we're always learning from each other." In addition, with competition for viewers an ongoing issue in the entertainment industry, Scripps and Food Network integrate this into their strategic planning. "The strategy going forward is to be as well known for entertainment in the digital and social space as we are for inspiring people to love food and cooking," says Fogelson.

Social media marketing brings with it a certain amount of social responsibility—and because of its global reach and interactive nature, it raises certain ethical issues, not the least of which is privacy. For example, Scripps and Food Network must ensure that any data they collect about consumers via interactive exchanges doesn't fall into unauthorized hands. But they respect the significance of their relationship with viewers and treat it like the gift of a good meal. "There's something special there, that you can have a relationship and communicate with your audience—and always be on," says Fogelson. "But that is a tremendous responsibility as much as it is an opportunity. So we're all asking a lot of questions about how to do it right."

QUESTIONS FOR CRITICAL THINKING

1. What steps could Scripps and Food Network take to avoid marketing myopia? Create a company motto for them reflecting your ideas.

2. Identify three trends in the social-cultural environment that you believe should be factors in strategic marketing planning for Scripps and Food Network.

3. How might Scripps and Food Network contribute to the highest level of the social responsibility pyramid—philanthropy?

4. What strategies might Scripps and Food Network use to become as well known for entertainment in digital and social media as they are for educating and inspiring people about food and cooking?

PART 2

Understanding Buyers and Markets

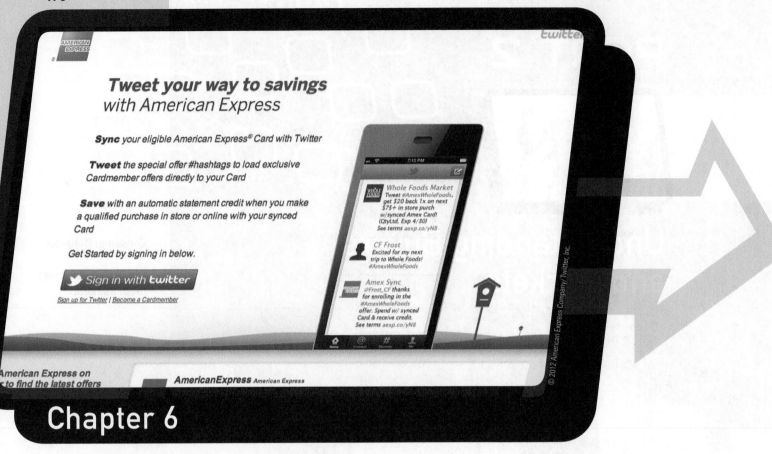

Chapter 6

CONSUMER

Behavior

1. Define *consumer behavior*, and describe the role it plays in marketing decisions.

2. Describe the interpersonal determinants of consumer behavior: cultural, social, and family influences.

3. Explain each of the personal determinants of consumer behavior: needs and motives, perceptions, attitudes, learning, and self-concept theory.

4. Distinguish between high-involvement and low-involvement purchase decisions.

5. Outline the steps in the consumer decision process.

6. Differentiate among routinized response behavior, limited problem solving, and extended problem solving by consumers.

AMERICAN EXPRESS IN SYNC WITH SOCIAL MEDIA

No newcomer to social media, American Express has been a presence on Twitter and Facebook since 2009, when it first got on board with the goal of providing additional customer service and merchant assistance through new digital avenues. With more than 2.7 million fans and 585,000 followers on those platforms (respectively) for its U.S. efforts alone, the credit card giant is now found on Foursquare, YouTube, LinkedIn, and Google+ as well. Customer service is still the aim. In fact, customer relationships drive the company's social media plan from top to bottom. "The community interests and feedback defined our strategy" for social media, says the company's senior vice president of digital partnerships.

AmEx recently added Twitter to the "Sync" program it started with Foursquare and Facebook several months ago. Now cardholders who tweet can get exclusive "couponless" deals at retailers like Whole Foods, Best Buy, H&M, Cheesecake Factory, Sports Authority, Ticketmaster, Zappos.com, and many others by simply including the appropriate hashtag (say, *#AmExWholeFoods*) in a tweet. It doesn't matter what else you say in the message; the hashtag qualifies you for a discount ranging from a $20 credit on your AmEx statement when you spend $75 or more at Whole Foods, to a $100 statement credit off $599 at Dell, to $5 for spending $5 at McDonald's.

And if you do happen to mention the deal in your tweet, AmEx will be just fine with that. In fact, the company hopes Twitter users will let their followers know about Sync offers to help spread the word. It already lists all the special offers on its own Twitter page and alerts its own Twitter followers when new deals open up. AmEx will even reach out to influential Twitterers if there's a specific Sync promotion it thinks they will like.

AmEx promises not to share any personal information about cardholders who sign up for the Sync program on Twitter, although it gives participating merchants general information about how consumers responded to the offer, what they spent on average, and who became a repeat customer within a specified time frame. "We are trying to bring more value to our card members," says an AmEx vice chairman about the program. "And we are also trying to help merchants with their digital marketing." Nine days after the Twitter launch of Sync promotions, 150,000 tweeters had scooped up more than $1.3 million in couponless savings.[1]

EVOLUTION OF A BRAND

With its Sync program, American Express seeks to offer cardholders a higher level of customer service and merchant assistance. At the same time, customer participation in Sync will give AmEx a greater understanding of its customers and—the company hopes—strengthen customer loyalty in the highly competitive credit-card industry. By leveraging the power of social media like Twitter and Foursquare, marketers at American Express learn more about their customers' likes and dislikes and strengthen their brand.

At the same time, the couponless deals have the potential to build business for participating merchants.

- Marketers at American Express know that there's more to shopping than a simple transaction; in most cases, it's about the shopper's total experience. How does that understanding relate to the study of consumer behavior?
- A host of national retailers have agreed to participate in the couponless offers American Express is promoting. Reportedly, it's AmEx and not the merchant who foots the bill for these deals. In your opinion, will the lure of these offers be sufficient to draw new cardholders to American Express?

171

CHAPTER OVERVIEW

Why do you call for Papa John's Pizza whenever you have a craving for extra cheese and pepperoni? Why does your roommate stock Jones soda in the fridge? Why does your best friend drive five miles out of the way for Caribou Coffee—when the local coffee shop is much closer? The answers to these questions aren't obvious, and they directly affect every aspect of marketing

> ## "BRIEFLY SPEAKING"
>
> "Know what your customers want most and what your company does best. Focus on where those two meet."
>
> —**Kevin Stirtz**
> *Web marketing consultant*

strategy, including the development of a product, the level at which it is priced, and the way it is promoted. Developing a marketing strategy requires an understanding of the process by which individual consumers buy goods and services for their own use and organizational buyers purchase business products for their organizations.

---

1 Define *consumer behavior,* and describe the role it plays in marketing decisions.

consumer behavior
Process through which buyers make purchase decisions.

A variety of influences affect both individuals buying items for themselves and personnel purchasing products for their firms. This chapter focuses on individual purchasing behavior, which applies to all of us as consumers. **Consumer behavior** is the process through which the ultimate buyer makes purchase decisions from toothbrushes to autos to vacations. Chapter 7 will shift the focus to business buying decisions.

The study of consumer behavior builds on an understanding of human behavior in general. In their efforts to understand why and how consumers make buying decisions, marketers borrow extensively from the sciences of psychology and sociology. The work of psychologist Kurt Lewin, for example, provides a useful classification scheme for influences on buying behavior. Lewin's proposition is

$$B = f(P, E)$$

This statement means that behavior (B) is a function (f) of the interactions of personal influences (P) and pressures exerted by outside environmental forces (E).

The statement usually is rewritten to apply to consumer behavior as follows:

$$B = f(I, P)$$

Consumer behavior (B) is a function (f) of the interactions of interpersonal influences (I)—such as culture, friends, classmates, coworkers, and relatives—and personal factors (P) such as attitudes, learning, and perception. In other words, inputs from others and an individual's psychological makeup affect his or her purchasing behavior. Before looking at how consumers make purchase decisions, we first consider how both interpersonal and personal factors affect consumers.

 ASSESSMENT CHECK

1.1   Why is the study of consumer behavior important to marketers?

1.2   Describe Kurt Lewin's proposition.

INTERPERSONAL DETERMINANTS OF CONSUMER BEHAVIOR

You don't live in a bubble—and you don't make purchase decisions there. You might not be aware of it, but every buying decision you make is influenced by a variety of external and internal factors. Consumers often decide to buy goods and services based on what they believe others expect of them. They may want to project positive images to peers or satisfy the expectations of family members. They may buy a certain book because someone they respect recommended it. Or they may make reservations at a particular restaurant based on a good review in the newspaper. They may buy a home in a neighborhood they think will impress their family and friends. Students may even choose which college or university to attend based on where their parents went, how the school is ranked for certain features, or on their friends' impression of the school. Marketers recognize three broad categories of interpersonal influences on consumer behavior: cultural, social, and family influences.

2 Describe the interpersonal determinants of consumer behavior: cultural, social, and family influences.

CULTURAL INFLUENCES

Culture can be defined as the values, beliefs, preferences, and tastes handed down from one generation to the next. Culture is the broadest environmental determinant of consumer behavior. Marketers need to understand their role in consumer decision making, both in the United States and abroad. They must also monitor trends in cultural values as well as recognize changes in these values. As attention to the environment becomes more prevalent in the United States and other cultures, marketers are responding to this change by offering products that either contain environmentally friendly components or are made with energy-saving processes. Utah homebuilder Garbett Homes now focuses its marketing messages on potential homebuyers' desire for energy-efficient features by positioning itself as Utah's "greenest" builder. The firm is constructing medium-sized, affordable solar- and thermal-powered homes called the Solaris Collection. All of these homes are built to the 100-percent ENERGY STAR specification, which decreases monthly energy bills for their owners.[2]

culture Values, beliefs, preferences, and tastes handed down from one generation to the next.

Marketing strategies and business practices that work in one country may be offensive or ineffective in another. Strategies may even have to be varied from one area of a country to another. Nowhere is that more true than the United States, where the population continues to diversify at a rapid rate. When you insert your bank card into an ATM, the first option on the screen often is what language you prefer for the transaction. Depending on where you live, you may choose between Spanish and English or French and English. The Las Vegas Convention and Visitors Authority recently advertised in Spanish, placing commercials completely in Spanish on English-language programs on A&E, Bravo, Fox Sports Net, and Logo. Marketers believe this is an effective strategy because the strength of the Las Vegas brand is so great, and the images are so striking, that not everyone watching has to understand every word being broadcast.

Having a real family dinner isn't impossible. You just need a little help.

"With our busy schedules, the only way we can share dinner as a family is if everyone pitches in. The youngest kids set the table, my daughter makes the salad and on Wednesday nights, the guys are in charge.

Everyone feels like dinner is something they own."

-Stacy McCallister

The McCallisters took the LET'S FIX DINNER CHALLENGE. See what happened and share your story at letsfixdinner.com

Stouffer's

© Société des Produits Nestlé S.A. Vevey, Switzerland/Stouffer's

In collaboration with the National Center on Addiction and Substance Abuse, Stouffer's "Let's Fix Dinner" marketing campaign emphasizes the core values of family and health as an important part of American culture.

Core Values in U.S. Culture

Some cultural values change over time, but basic core values do not. The work ethic and the desire to accumulate wealth are two core values in American society. Even though the typical family structure and family members' roles have shifted over the years, American culture still emphasizes the importance of family and home life. This value is strengthened during times of upheaval such as natural disasters—hurricanes, floods, wild-fires, or tornadoes. Other core values include the importance of education, individualism, freedom, youth, health, volunteerism, and efficiency. You can probably recognize yourself in some of these core values. Each of these values influences consumer behavior, including your own. Focusing on the core values of family and health, Stouffer's and The National Center on Addiction and Substance Abuse (CASA) at Columbia University launched a joint marketing campaign called "Let's Fix Dinner," which encouraged families to eat dinner together. Marketing messages emphasized the benefits of families dining together at home, including a CASA study that found children who eat five or more meals a week with their family are "more likely to think their parents are proud of them." The campaign featured Stouffer's prepared frozen meals and side dishes.[3]

Values that change over time also have their effects. As technology rapidly changes the way people exchange information, consumers adopt values that include communicating with anyone, anytime, anywhere in the world. The generation that includes older teens and young 20s is the most adept at learning and using rapidly changing communications technology, including smartphones. They regularly communicate via Facebook, Twitter, and other social media. Marketers are recognizing this, and in anticipation of more consumers adopting new communications technology, they are increasing their allocation of resources to reach consumers in this way. Starbucks customers can use a Starbucks app on their smartphone to pay for their purchases, reload their card, and even send a gift card to one of their phone or Facebook contacts.[4]

International Perspective on Cultural Influences

Cultural differences are particularly important for international marketers. Marketing strategies that prove successful in one country often cannot extend to other international markets because of cultural variations. Europe is a good example, with many different languages and a wide range of lifestyles and product preferences. Even though the continent is becoming a single economic unit as a result of the expansion of the European Union and the widespread use of the euro as currency, cultural divisions continue to define multiple markets.

For years, Domino's has been a known quantity in the United States, and now its business has gone global. Nearly half of its stores are outside the United States and soon, management predicts, overseas stores will outstrip U.S. ones. "We move very fast in international markets," says Domino's executive Peter Doyle. "When we see opportunities, we act on them."

What's behind this global success? In part, management says, it's fitting the product to local tastes. The Taiwanese like shrimp and peapods on their pizza; in England, tuna and sweet corn are favorites. And sometimes, a new ingredient just takes off. When Domino's arrived in Japan, the Japanese had no word for "pepperoni." Today, pepperoni is one of the most popular toppings in Japan.

While Domino's believes pizza is universal, in some countries, it's still an acquired taste. In China, for example, dairy hasn't always been part of the diet, and the concept of delivery cuisine is still new.[5]

AP Photo/Koji Sasahara

Domino's has been successful in the global market, even offering delivery in Japan, because it fits the product to local tastes.

Subcultures

Cultures are not homogeneous groups with universal values, even though core values tend to dominate. Each culture includes numerous subcultures—groups with their own distinct modes of behavior. Understanding the differences among subcultures can help marketers develop more effective marketing strategies.

subcultures Groups with their own distinct modes of behavior.

The United States, like many nations, is composed of significant subcultures that differ by ethnicity, nationality, age, rural versus urban location, religion, and geographic distribution. The southwestern lifestyle emphasizes casual dress, outdoor entertaining, and active recreation. Orthodox Jews purchase and consume only kosher foods. Younger consumers are quicker to use new technology than older consumers. Immigrants from various nations often seek out spices, vegetables, and meats that are considered tasty or popular in their homelands. Understanding these and other differences among subcultures contributes to successful marketing of goods and services.

America's population is aging. According to the U.S. Census Bureau, by the year 2050, the U.S. population will total about 439 million, up from over 313 million today. By the year 2030, nearly one in five residents will be age 65 or older.[6]

America's population is also becoming more diverse. The three largest and fastest-growing U.S. ethnic subcultures—Hispanics, African Americans, and Asians—are expected to become the majority. The Hispanic population, which constituted over 16 percent of the U.S. population in the last census, experienced a 43 percent increase in a decade. It is expected to rise to over 132 million by the year 2050. African Americans represented 12.6 percent of the U.S. population in the last census, up 15 percent from the previous decade. By the year 2050, the African American population is expected to reach 61 million, or 14.6 percent of the population, and Asians will account for 8 percent.[7] Figure 6.1 shows the current makeup of U.S. society by race.

Marketers need to be sensitive to these shifts in population and to the differences in shopping patterns and buying habits of the members of different subcultures. Businesses must develop marketing messages that consider the needs of these different types of consumers. For example, members of one subculture might be attracted to bargain offers while those of another might be offended by them. As important as differences in national origin may be, the differences in acculturation, or the degree to which newcomers have adapted to U.S. culture, plays a vital role in consumer behavior. Marketers should not assume that all Hispanics understand or speak Spanish—or the same dialect of Spanish. In addition, Asians come from a variety of countries, speak a wide range of languages, and eat different foods.

One thing that marketers must do is actually find where consumers of different subcultures live. The U.S. Census Bureau is now reporting that fewer Americans are relocating to different regions of the country, potentially making it easier to identify and develop relationships with groups of

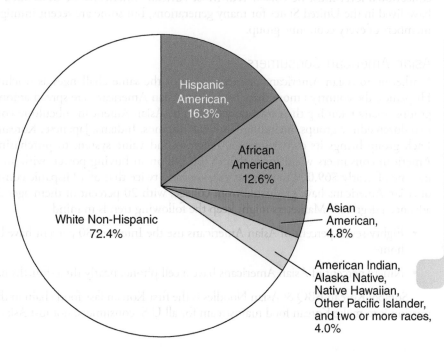

FIGURE 6.1
Ethnic and Racial Minorities as a Percentage of the Total U.S. Population

Note: Percentages do not total to 100 percent due to overlap of some racial and ethnic categories.

Source: Data from U.S. Census Bureau, "Overview of Race and Hispanic Origin: 2010," www.census.gov, accessed November 14, 2012

customers. Some of this trend has to do with a sluggish economy and weak housing market. "The mobility rate is lower than it has been in years," reports one demographer.[8]

Hispanic American Consumers

Marketers face several challenges in appealing to Hispanic consumers. The 52 million Hispanics in the United States are not a homogeneous group. They—or their parents and grandparents—come from a wide range of countries, each with its own culture. More than 32 million are from Mexico; more than 4.7 million are Puerto Rican, while about 1.9 million are Cuban. More than 1 million each are Guatemalan, Dominican, or Salvadoran. Colombia, Honduras, Ecuador, and Peru are also represented here in the United States.[9] Many distinct segments exist within the broad classification of Hispanic. More than three-fourths of the Hispanic population—and consumers—is distributed across California, Texas, Florida, New York, Illinois, Arizona, New Jersey, and Colorado.[10]

The increase in the Hispanic population is fueled by a sharp rise in births. Children make up nearly one-third of the population.[11] As this population begins to include the second, third, and fourth generation, the attitudes and values of these consumers are likely to shift toward those of their age group and region. Still, it is important for marketers to be aware of subtle cultural differences in preferences in goods and services as well as media. For example, a recent survey revealed that native-born Hispanics are more likely than Hispanics who are foreign-born to surf the Internet and to use cell phones. The survey also found that native-born Hispanics are more likely to use apps on their cell phone.[12] This information could have a huge impact on marketers who are trying to determine where and how to deliver their messages to this market. In addition, marketers should consider that Hispanics control more disposable income than any other minority group—currently more than $1 trillion.[13]

African American Consumers

The continuously growing African American market offers a tremendous opportunity for marketers who understand its buying patterns. The African American population stands at more than 42 million people, with their buying power set to top $1 trillion, roughly equal to that of Hispanics.[14] A couple of trends that marketers should consider include the following:

- More than half of African American consumers own a smartphone.

- Nearly 24 million African Americans are active Internet visitors, and more than three-fourths of them visit social media sites.[15]

Despite these trends, as with any other subculture, marketers must avoid approaching all African American consumers in the same way; demographic factors such as income, age, language, and educational level must be considered. Most African Americans are descended from families who have lived in the United States for many generations, but some are recent immigrants. And they are members of every economic group.

Asian American Consumers

Marketing to Asian Americans presents many of the same challenges as reaching Hispanics. Like Hispanics, the country's more than 14 million Asian Americans are spread among culturally diverse groups, many retaining their own languages. The Asian American subculture consists of more than two dozen ethnic groups, including Chinese, Filipinos, Indians, Japanese, Koreans, and Vietnamese. Each group brings its own language, religion, and value system to purchasing decisions. Asian American consumers wield more than $700 billion in buying power, with an average household income of nearly $69,000 in a recent year—nearly twice that of a Hispanic consumer. Fifty percent of Asian Americans have graduated from college, with 20 percent of them ages 25 or older holding advanced degrees.[16] Marketers might keep the following trends in mind:

- Eighty-seven percent of Asian Americans use the Internet; 80 percent have broadband access at home.

- Ninety percent of Asian Americans have a cell phone; nearly three-fourths have laptops.[17]

Sorabol Korean BBQ & Asian Noodles is the first Korean fast-food chain in the United States. Its mission is to make Korean food mainstream for all U.S. consumers, not just Asian Americans. While other restaurants are trying hard to add Asian items to their menus, Sorabol has actually "Americanized" its menu to appeal to a broader range of consumers while retaining a distinctly Asian foundation. Diners can order traditional *kabi* (barbequed short ribs) or *dak guyee* (barbequed chicken), stir-fried entrees or appetizers, or one of the many noodle dishes. In Korean culture, noodles are a symbol of long life and are served in a variety of ways. Noodles are a popular breakfast dish as well, because they are considered to be a healthy start to the day. Sorabol locates its restaurants in high-traffic retail locations, in financial districts, and on campuses. The restaurant chain seeks to offer an alternative to burgers and fries, making fast food "a pleasurable dining experience full of culture and flavor."[18]

© Fuse/Jupiterimages

SOCIAL INFLUENCES

As a consumer, you belong to a number of social groups. Your earliest group experience came from membership in a family. As you began to grow, you might have joined a group of friends in elementary school or in the neighborhood. Later, you might have played on a soccer team, sang in a chorus, or volunteered in the community. By the time you became an adult, you had already been a member of many social groups—as you are now.

With more than $700 billion in buying power, Asian American consumers are appealing to marketers.

Group membership influences an individual consumer's purchase decisions and behavior in both overt and subtle ways. Every group establishes certain norms of behavior. Norms are the values, attitudes, and behaviors a group deems appropriate for its members. Group members are expected to comply with these norms. Members of such diverse groups as the Harley Owners Group (H.O.G.), Volunteers of America, and the local swim club tend to adopt their organization's norms of behavior. Norms can even affect nonmembers. Individuals who aspire to membership in a group may adopt its standards of behavior and values.

Differences in group status and roles can also affect buying behavior. Status is the relative position of any individual member in a group; roles define behavior that members of a group expect of individuals who hold specific positions within that group. Some groups (such as the American Medical Association) define formal roles, and others (such as a book club among friends) impose informal expectations. Both types of groups supply each member with both status and roles; in doing so, they influence that person's activities—including his or her purchase behavior. Communities have regulations governing pet ownership—especially rules about cleaning up after pets. One company considers these rules an opportunity to create a competitive advantage for itself. Like other pet care businesses, DogSmith offers a full range of dog care services, from boarding to training to daily "park romps." But DogSmith goes the extra block—it also offers customers pet waste cleanup service for their yard.[19] Customers who have limited time for this necessary task of pet ownership—or who simply prefer to pay someone else to do it—appreciate the extra service.

People often make purchases designed to reflect their status within a particular group, particularly when the purchase is considered expensive by society. In the past few years, affluent consumers have spent money on home renovations and exotic trips. Loyal customers of Apple products are willing to pay top dollar for the latest gadgets, apps, and upgrades, not only because of their high quality, but because of the status they reflect.

As the economy fluctuates, affluent shoppers actually achieve status by joining warehouse clubs or shopping at discount stores and consignment shops. Searching for the best value becomes the new norm—and status symbol.[20] But these consumers are willing to spend more on fresh or organic produce, often found at upscale grocery markets. And they like to tout the health and environmental benefits of these foods. Over the past several years, as the economy has dipped and adjusted itself, a new norm has emerged for most U.S. consumers, regardless of their economic standing—restrained spending and an emphasis on value. In fact, a certain amount of frugality has become chic.

Regardless of a U.S. consumer's economic standing, restrained spending and an emphasis on value, found in warehouse clubs like this Costco, have become the norm in our economy.

© Katharine Andriotis/Alamy

The Asch Phenomenon

Groups influence people's purchase decisions more than they realize. Most people adhere in varying degrees to the general expectations of any group they consider important, often without conscious awareness. The surprising impact of groups and group norms on individual behavior has been called the Asch phenomenon, named after social psychologist S. E. Asch, who first documented characteristics of individual behavior. Through his research, Asch found that individuals conformed to majority rule, even if it went against their beliefs. The Asch phenomenon can be a big factor in many purchase decisions, from major choices such as buying a car to deciding whether to buy a pair of shoes on sale. One new company that promises to measure individuals' social media influence is called Klout; see the "Marketing Success" feature.

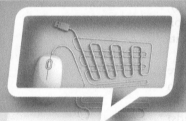

MARKETING SUCCESS

Klout Measures Your, Well, Clout

Background. The number of people posting, linking, and tweeting on a daily if not hourly basis offers marketers a potentially powerful new tool for leveraging word of mouth about their goods and services.

The Challenge. How do companies know who wields the most influence when it comes to product endorsements or recommendations? Is Bill Gates more credible than Kobe Bryant? How does Lady Gaga stack up against Justin Bieber? Marketers are searching for ways to identify and partner with the Web's most powerful individuals.

The Strategy. A San Francisco startup called Klout tracks what is in effect your "social credit score" by analyzing your online influence and the power of your network. The company tracks

retweets and Facebook "likes" to derive an influence score for what it says is more than 100 million people.

The Outcome. Nike, Disney, HP, and Audi are among Klout's first customers. The company, which has attracted $10 million in venture funding, puts these firms in touch with relevant influencers who have signed up with it, and then it's up to the marketers to offer deals they hope will persuade their influencers to generate the appropriate online buzz. By the way, Justin Bieber pulled a perfect 100, and Lady Gaga a 93.

Sources: Seth Stevenson, "What Your Klout Score Really Means," *Wired*, accessed November 15, 2012, www.wired.com; Dorie Clark, "Why You Should Care about Your Klout Score," *Forbes*, accessed November 15, 2012, www.forbes.com; Victor Hernandez, "Measuring Influence Online: A Q&A with Klout's CEO," *CNN*, accessed November 15, 2012, www.cnn.com; Tom Cheshire, "How Reputation-Ranking Site Klout Quantifies Your Influence," *Wired*, accessed November 15, 2012, www.wired.co.uk.

© iStockphoto.com/Marcello Bortolino

Reference Groups

Discussion of the Asch phenomenon raises the subject of reference groups—groups whose value structures and standards influence a person's behavior. Consumers usually try to coordinate their purchase behavior with their perceptions of the values of their reference groups. The extent of reference group influence varies widely among individuals. Strong influence by a group on a member's purchase requires two conditions:

1. The purchased product must be one that others can see and identify.

2. The purchased item must be conspicuous; it must stand out as something unusual, a brand or product that not everyone owns.

Reference group influence would significantly affect the decision to buy a luxury home in an upscale neighborhood but probably wouldn't have an impact on the decision to buy a loaf of bread, unless that loaf of bread was purchased at a gourmet bakery. Reference group influence can create what some marketers call "elastic consumers"—consumers who make decisions to save or splurge in the same economy. During a slow economy, a consumer might purchase generic brands at the supermarket but, because of reference group influence, spend those savings on designer jeans or a flat-screen TV. Banking on the fact that grandparents like to show off their grandchildren to friends—and are willing to spend the money to do so, even if they skimp on themselves—some retailers offer premium-priced apparel for babies and small children. At Portland-based Hanna Andersson, for example, one-piece sleepers for babies retail at $32; a cardigan sweater, $40. Keeping in mind that babies and toddlers outgrow clothing quickly, these tags translate to luxury prices.[21]

Children are especially vulnerable to the influence of reference groups. They often base their buying decisions on outside forces such as what they see on television and the Internet (including social networking sites) or the opinion of friends. Understanding this phenomenon, marketers sometimes take a step back so that older children, preteens, and teens can shop—even if they don't have their own money to spend. More retailers now welcome teens who browse but don't buy. These retailers know they are still developing loyal customers—the teens will return when they have their own or their parents' money.

In addition, marketers are recognizing the power of the Internet, including smartphones and social networking sites, as a tool for reaching children and teens—not just to market new or existing goods and services, but to learn more about reference groups and upcoming trends. Ninety-five percent of consumers ages 12 to 17 are online, visiting social networking sites, getting information, and forming opinions from these interactions. They download music, play games, and participate in interactive marketing online, but still prefer to shop at brick-and-mortar stores; less than 50 percent are making online purchases.[22]

Social Classes

W. Lloyd Warner's research identified six classes within the social structures of both small and large U.S. cities: the upper-upper, lower-upper, upper-middle, and lower-middle classes, followed by the working class and lower class. Class rankings are determined by occupation, income, education, family background, and residence location. Note that income is not always a primary factor; pipe fitters paid at union scale earn more than many college professors, but their purchase behavior may be quite different. Still, the ability to make certain purchases, such as a private jet or an ocean-view home, is an important factor in determining class.

Family characteristics, such as the occupations and incomes of one or both parents, have been the primary influences on social class. People in one social class may aspire to a higher class

reference groups
People or institutions whose opinions are valued and to whom a person looks for guidance in his or her own behavior, values, and conduct, such as a spouse, family, friends, or celebrities.

Even though a majority of 12- to 17-year-olds are online, visiting social sites, gathering information, and forming opinions, less than half of them are making online purchases. They prefer to do their shopping at brick-and-mortar stores.

© John Giustina/Iconica/Getty Images

and therefore exhibit buying behavior common to that class rather than to their own. Middle-class consumers often buy items they associate with the upper classes. Marketers of certain luxury goods appeal to these consumers. Coach, Tiffany, and Bloomingdale's—all traditionally associated with high-end luxury goods—now offer their items in price ranges and locations attractive to middle-class consumers. Saks Fifth Avenue, one of the nation's most well-known luxury retailers, recently unveiled a private-label collection of men's clothing priced less than some of its premier brands. The new collection features Italian wool suits for $1,000 and $135 dress shirts—but the retailer's marketers consider that a bargain when compared to the typical $8,000 price tag for its designer suits.[23]

Marketers use language in their marketing messages designed to appeal to certain social classes—or to those who aspire to them. Here are a few examples:

- Ocean Club, Bahamas: "50 years…oh the tales we could tell. Live the moment."

- Sagee Manor vacation homes: "The ultimate retreat in the Blue Ridge Mountains…priced for today's market, starting at $17.9 million."

- Dreams Resorts: "The Dreams Experience makes for an incredible vacation. The privileges of unlimited luxury make it even better."

- American Express Travel: "Extraordinary is being able to afford a trip that you just can't afford to miss."[24]

Opinion Leaders

opinion leaders
Trendsetters who purchase new products before others in a group and then influence others in their purchases.

In nearly every reference group, a few members act as **opinion leaders**. These trendsetters are likely to purchase new products before others in the group and then share their experiences and opinions via word of mouth. As others in the group decide whether to try the same products, they are influenced by the reports of opinion leaders. Generalized opinion leaders are rare; instead, individuals tend to act as opinion leaders for specific goods or services based on their knowledge of and interest in those products. Their interest motivates them to seek out information from mass media, manufacturers, and other sources and, in turn, transmit this information to associates through interpersonal communications. Opinion leaders are found within all segments of the population.

Information about goods and services may flow from the Internet, television, or other mass media to opinion leaders, and then from opinion leaders to others. Sometimes information flows directly from media sources to all consumers. In still other instances, a multistep flow carries information from mass media to opinion leaders and then on to other opinion leaders before dissemination to the general public.

Some opinion leaders influence purchases by others merely through their own actions. Oprah Winfrey is one such individual. Through her TV talk show, which ran for 25 seasons, she exerted influence on millions of viewers. Her on-air book club encouraged viewers to read. Through many on-air wellness programs, she motivated viewers to commit to a more healthful lifestyle through diet and exercise. Launching her "No Phone Zone" campaign, Winfrey urged viewers to sign an online pledge to refrain from texting or talking on their cell phones

Oprah Winfrey continues to influence people through her latest TV program, "Oprah's Next Chapter," as she shares enlightening conversations and locations around the world.

© EPA European Pressphoto Agency B.V./Alamy

while driving. Many celebrities, including Jerry Seinfeld and Nate Berkus, took the pledge. Winfrey continues to influence viewers' behavior with her latest TV program, "Oprah's Next Chapter."[25]

FAMILY INFLUENCES

Most people are members of at least two families during their lifetimes—the ones they are born into and those they eventually form later in life. The family group is perhaps the most important determinant of consumer behavior because of the close, continuing interactions among family members. Like other groups, each family typically has norms of expected behavior and different roles and status relationships for its members.

According to the U.S. Census Bureau, the structure of families has changed greatly over the last century. Today, only about half of all households are headed by married couples. Many couples are separated or divorced, so single heads of households are more common. In addition, there has been an increase in households headed by same-sex couples. Women are having fewer children, giving birth later in life, and spacing their children farther apart. More women are choosing to live alone, with or without children. And more senior citizens are living alone or without younger generations present in their homes. Still, to target a market for their goods and services, marketers find it useful to describe the role of each spouse in a household in terms of the following four categories:

1. Autonomic role is seen when the partners independently make equal numbers of decisions. Personal-care items would fall into the category of purchase decisions each would make for himself or herself.

2. Husband-dominant role occurs when the husband usually makes certain purchase decisions. Buying a generator or woodstove for the home is a typical example.

3. Wife-dominant role has the wife making certain buying decisions. Children's clothing is a typical wife-dominant purchase.

4. Syncratic role refers to joint decisions. The purchase of a house follows a syncratic pattern.

Numbers 2 and 3 on this list have changed dramatically over the years. The increasing occurrence of the two-income family means that women have a greater role in making large family purchases, such as homes, vacations, and automobiles. And studies show that women take the lead in choosing entertainment, such as movies and restaurants. Women now outspend men in the purchase of electronics. Conversely, as more highly educated women begin to out-earn their spouses, men are appearing more frequently at the grocery store because their wives are still at the office.[26] In addition, men are taking a more active role in child care. Both of these shifts in family life mean that marketers must consider both genders as potential consumers when creating their marketing messages. For example, although men still do most of the automobile buying in the United States, women tend to buy more energy-efficient models.[27]

Studies of family decision making have also shown that households with two wage earners are more likely than others to make joint purchasing decisions. Members of two-income households often do their shopping in the evening and on weekends because of the number of hours spent at the workplace. Shifting family roles have created new markets for a variety of products. Goods and services that save time, promote family togetherness, emphasize safety, or encourage health and fitness appeal to the family values and influences of today.

Children and Teenagers in Family Purchases

Children and teenagers represent a huge market—nearly 54 million strong—and they influence what their parents buy, from cereal to automobiles. These consumers are bombarded with messages from a variety of media. They are presented with a wide array of choices. Young people now wield $211 billion of their own spending

As teenagers influence their parents to make large purchases, they also influence the type of purchases their parents make, such as fuel-efficient cars that are cheaper to fill with gas.

© Lisa F. Young/Shutterstock.com

ASSESSMENT CHECK

2.1 List the interpersonal determinants of consumer behavior.

2.2 What is a subculture?

2.3 Describe the Asch phenomenon.

power.[28] They also have significant influence over the goods and services their families purchase. As teens obtain their driver's licenses, they put pressure on their families to purchase more vehicles. While parents tend to focus on safety features and cost, teens lean toward style and performance. But teens don't necessarily shy away from practicality—in fact, some studies show they want fuel-efficient cars that are environmentally friendly and cheaper to fill with gas.[29]

PERSONAL DETERMINANTS OF CONSUMER BEHAVIOR

3 Explain each of the personal determinants of consumer behavior: needs and motives, perceptions, attitudes, learning, and self-concept theory.

need Imbalance between a consumer's actual and desired states.

motive Inner state that directs a person toward the goal of satisfying a need.

Consumer behavior is affected by a number of internal, personal factors in addition to interpersonal ones. Each individual brings unique needs, motives, perceptions, attitudes, learned responses, and self-concepts to buying decisions. This section looks at how these factors influence consumer behavior.

NEEDS AND MOTIVES

Individual purchase behavior is driven by the motivation to fill a perceived need. A **need** is an imbalance between the consumer's actual and desired states. A person who recognizes or feels a significant or urgent need then seeks to correct the imbalance. Marketers attempt to arouse this sense of urgency by making a need "felt" and then influencing consumers' motivation to satisfy their needs by purchasing specific products.

Motives are inner states that direct a person toward the goal of satisfying a need. The individual takes action to reduce the state of tension and return to a condition of equilibrium.

Maslow's Hierarchy of Needs

Psychologist Abraham H. Maslow developed a theory that characterized needs and arranged them into a hierarchy. Maslow identified five levels of needs, beginning with physiological needs and progressing to the need for self-actualization. A person must at least partially satisfy lower-level needs, according to Maslow, before higher needs can affect behavior. In developed countries, where relatively large per-capita incomes allow most people to satisfy the basic needs on the hierarchy, higher-order needs may be more important to consumer behavior. Table 6.1 illustrates products and marketing themes designed to satisfy needs at each level.

Physiological Needs

Needs at the most basic level concern essential requirements for survival, such as food, water, shelter, and clothing. Pur promotes its water filtration system with the slogan, "Your water should be Pur." Its ads emphasize the need for clean water: "When you realize how often water touches your family's life, you discover just how important healthy, great-tasting water is."

Safety Needs

Second-level needs include financial or lifestyle security, protection from physical harm, and avoidance of the unexpected. To gratify these needs, consumers may buy life insurance, alarm systems, or retirement plans. In one of its ads Fidelity asks, "Will you be ready for the retirement you have in mind?" The answer to the question is, "Let Fidelity be your guide."

Social/Belongingness Needs

Satisfaction of physiological and safety needs leads a person to attend to third-level needs—the desire to be accepted by people and groups important to that individual. To satisfy this need, people may join organizations or programs to buy goods or services that make them feel part of a group. Chase offers its Blueprint program, "a new set of free features only for Chase customers."

TABLE 6.1 Marketing Strategies Based on Maslow's Hierarchy of Needs

Needs	Products	Marketing Themes
Physiological	Food, water, medicines, vitamins, exercise equipment and gym memberships, health care and cleaning products, sleep aids and mattresses, food for pets	Fresh Express salads: "Consistently, deliciously, fresh." GNC vitamins and supplements: "Live well." Colgate Total: "#1 recommended by dentists and hygienists." Purina pet food: "A difference you can see."
Safety	Health and life insurance, computer antivirus software, smoke and carbon monoxide detectors, antibacterial cleaners, business protection, auto safety features	Progressive Insurance: "Helping you save money. That's Progressive." Lysol household cleaners: "Disinfect to protect." Better Business Bureau: "Start with trust."
Belongingness	Cosmetics, food, entertainment, fashion, appliances and home furnishings, clubs and organizations, cars	Avon Walk for Breast Cancer: "In it to end it." Lowe's: "Let's build something together." Lee: "Get what fits." Payless shoes: "Save now. Feel good." Olay: "Love the skin you're in." Ford: "Drive one."
Esteem	Fashion, jewelry, gourmet foods, electronics, cosmetics, luxury cars, credit cards, investments, sports and hobbies, travel, spas	Rolex watches: "A crown for every achievement." Lincoln automobiles: "Travel well." L'Oréal Paris: "Because you're worth it." Visa Black Card: "The world awaits."
Self-actualization	Education, cultural events, sports and hobbies, motivational seminars, technology, travel, investments	University of Phoenix: "I'm a Phoenix." Tony Robbins: "Unleash the power within." Canyon Ranch: "The power of possibility."

© Cengage Learning

Esteem Needs

People have a universal desire for a sense of accomplishment and achievement. They also wish to gain the respect of others and even exceed others' performance once lower-order needs are satisfied. Pandora's jewelry ads encourage consumers to buy its pieces because "Life has its moments...make them unforgettable."

Self-Actualization Needs

At the top rung of Maslow's ladder of human needs is people's desire to realize their full potential and find fulfillment by expressing their unique talents and capabilities. Companies that run exotic adventure trips aim to satisfy consumers' needs for self-actualization. Not-for-profit organizations that invite paying volunteers to assist in such projects as archaeological digs or building homes for the needy appeal to these needs as well. Four Seasons resorts advertises one of its African locations by showing two of its guests riding elephants through the mist. "It's said they never forget," reads the tag line. "Neither will you."

Maslow believed that a satisfied need no longer has to be met. Once the physiological needs are met, the individual moves on to pursue satisfaction of higher-order needs. Consumers periodically are motivated by the need to relieve thirst and hunger, but their interests soon return to

Courtesy of The Advertising Archives

WEAR IT AND BLOOM
A rose is not just a rose. Stack our floral inspired RING UPON RING series with the beautifully hand-carved rose in black onyx, set in sterling silver.
be inspired at pandora.net

PANDORA
UNFORGETTABLE MOMENTS

People have a universal desire for a sense of accomplishment and achievement and wish to gain the respect of others. Pandora's jewelry ads encourage consumers to buy its pieces because "Life has its moments...make them unforgettable."

focus on satisfaction of safety, social, and other needs in the hierarchy. But people may not always progress through the hierarchy; they may fixate on a certain level. For example, consumers who live through an economic downturn may always be motivated to save money in order to avoid financial insecurity—a second-level need. Marketers who understand this can create opportunities for their firms by offering money-saving goods and services.

Critics have pointed out a variety of flaws in Maslow's reasoning. For example, some needs can be related to more than one level, and not every individual progresses through the needs hierarchy in the same order; some bypass social and esteem needs and are motivated by self-actualization needs. But the hierarchy of needs can offer an effective guideline for marketers who want to study consumer behavior.

PERCEPTIONS

perception Meaning that a person attributes to incoming stimuli gathered through the five senses.

Perception is the meaning that a person attributes to incoming stimuli gathered through the five senses—sight, hearing, touch, taste, and smell. Certainly a buyer's behavior is influenced by his or her perceptions of a good or service. Researchers now recognize that people's perceptions depend as much on what they want to perceive as on the actual stimuli. For this reason, Bloomingdale's and Target are perceived differently, as are Godiva chocolates and M&Ms. A person's perception of an object or event results from the interaction of two types of factors:

perceptual screens The mental filtering processes through which all inputs must pass.

1. *stimulus factors*—characteristics of the physical object such as size, color, weight, and shape

2. *individual factors*—unique characteristics of the individual, including not only sensory processes but also experiences with similar inputs and basic motivations and expectations.

Perceptual Screens

Creative marketers compete for the attention of consumers through the use of 3D billboards.

The average American consumer is constantly barraged with marketing messages. A typical supermarket now carries 30,000 different packages, each serving as a miniature billboard vying to attract consumers' attention. More than 6,000 commercials are aired on network TV each week. As marketers compete for attention—and dollars—they get more creative about where they place their messages. Consumers might find a carton of eggs stamped with the name of a television show, or takeout cartons emblazoned with the name of a major airline. Old-fashioned billboards—once thought to be obsolete—have made a comeback with 3D elements and large digital advertising screens.

The problem with many messages is they create clutter in the minds of consumers, causing them to ignore many promotional messages. People respond selectively to messages that break through their perceptual screens—the mental filtering processes through which all inputs must pass. Doubling the size of an ad, using certain colors or graphics, or developing unique packaging are some techniques that marketers use to elicit a positive response from consumers. For example, color is so suggestive that its use on product packaging and logos often is the result of a long and careful selection process. Red grabs the attention, and orange has been shown to stimulate appetite. Blue is associated with water—you'll find blue on cleaning products. Green connotes low-fat or healthful food products. The psychological concept of closure also helps marketers create messages that stand out. Closure is the human tendency to perceive a complete picture from an incomplete stimulus. Advertisements that allow consumers to do this often succeed in breaking through perceptual screens.

Marketers have become more and more creative in an effort to break through the barrier of clutter. Increasingly, for example, billboards incorporate one or more life-sized mannequins into the message. Emergency dispatchers frequently receive calls from worried motorists reporting what appears to be a dangerous situation. If the goal was to get people's attention, the billboards achieved their objective.[30]

Word of mouth is probably the oldest marketing technique in existence. It is also one of the most effective. If one satisfied customer tells a friend, relative, neighbor, or coworker about a positive experience with a product, that message quite often breaks through the listener's perceptual screen because trust between the two already exists.

On the other end of the scale lie newer, high-tech marketing tools. These include virtual reality (in which a consumer can test drive a car or tour a resort) and social media such as Facebook, Twitter, and LinkedIn. While investment in these new tools is increasingly rapidly, it is interesting to note that the old methods remain strong—with modification—as in the case of the billboard. Although some marketers predicted the certain demise of the traditional 30-second television commercial, that prediction has not come true.[31] Travel Michigan's "Pure Michigan" campaign includes a series of 30-second spots aired nationally in an effort to attract tourists. Each year's campaign features a different series of engaging Michigan scenes. According to a recent study, the latest campaign drew a record 3.2 million vacationers from outside the region, generating $1 billion in spending at Michigan businesses.[32]

The successful "Pure Michigan" campaign features traditional TV, radio, and magazine ads, along with billboards.

With selective perception at work screening competing messages, it is easy to see the importance of marketers' efforts in developing brand loyalty. Satisfied customers are less likely to seek information about competing products. Even when competitive advertising is forced on them, they are less apt than others to look beyond their perceptual filters at those appeals. Loyal customers simply tune out information that does not agree with their existing beliefs and expectations.

Subliminal Perception

More than 50 years ago, a New Jersey movie theater tried to boost concession sales by flashing the words "Eat Popcorn" and "Drink Coca-Cola" between frames of actress Kim Novak's image in the movie *Picnic*. The messages flashed on the screen every five seconds for a duration of one three-hundredth of a second each time. Researchers reported that these messages, though too short to be recognizable at the conscious level, resulted in a 58 percent increase in popcorn sales and an 18 percent increase in Coke sales. After the findings were published, advertising agencies and consumer protection groups became intensely interested in subliminal perception—the subconscious receipt of incoming information.

Subliminal advertising is aimed at the subconscious level of awareness to circumvent the audience's perceptual screens. The goal of the original research was to induce consumer purchases while keeping consumers unaware of the source of the motivation to buy. All later attempts to duplicate the test findings were unsuccessful. Although subliminal advertising is considered manipulative, it is exceedingly unlikely to induce purchasing except by people already inclined to buy. There are three reasons for this:

subliminal perception The subconscious receipt of incoming information.

1. Strong stimulus factors are required just to get a prospective customer's attention.

2. Only a very short message can be transmitted.

3. Individuals vary greatly in their thresholds of consciousness. Messages transmitted at the threshold of consciousness for one person will not be perceived at all by some people and will be all too apparent to others. The subliminally exposed message "Drink Coca-Cola" may go unseen by some viewers, while others may read it as "Drink Pepsi-Cola," "Drink Cocoa," or even "Drive Slowly."

Despite the findings about subliminal advertising, however, neuroscientists know that thoughts and emotions, including those a person may not be consciously aware of, play a vital role in decision making, and marketers are looking to find ways to elicit emotions that motivate people toward a purchase. Neuromarketing has already taken some concrete forms. Firms like Yahoo!, Hyundai, and Microsoft are using EEGs and MRIs—which measure brain activity—to study consumers' responses to certain stimuli associated with their products. Researchers at Frito-Lay used brain imaging to analyze the packaging for its potato chips. They discovered that, while shiny packages triggered activity in the area of the brain associated with guilt feelings, matte-beige packaging did not. This finding helped Frito-Lay choose the matte-finish packaging.[33]

Facial recognition technology offers yet another way of identifying and targeting specific consumers. See the "Solving an Ethical Controversy" feature for some of the issues it may raise.

ATTITUDES

Perception of incoming stimuli is greatly affected by attitudes. In fact, a consumer's decision to purchase an item is strongly based on his or her attitudes about the product, store, or salesperson.

SOLVING AN ETHICAL CONTROVERSY

Should Facial Recognition Technology Go Incognito?

It's already a commonplace marketing strategy to put cookies on users' computers that allow companies to identify their likes and dislikes in order to target online ads to these preferences. Now a parallel strategy is about to roll out that uses facial recognition technology to identify people as males or females in specific age brackets. The first users are expected to be bars, clubs, and restaurants that want to monitor the mix of customers, but other marketers see many opportunities. Facial recognition mechanisms at store entrances can help ensure customers see only digital and mobile ads that matter to them, for instance, but privacy advocates are concerned about potential misuse of the technology, such as lack of an opt-in or opt-out feature.

Is it acceptable for companies to use facial recognition technology without telling customers?

PRO 👍

1. Identifying customers lets markets pinpoint their ads, so people won't see advertising that doesn't relate to or interest them.

2. People who see messages about the right product at the right time are more likely to buy, benefitting everyone.

CON 👎

1. Facial recognition technology is yet another way for companies to amass personal data about people without their consent.

2. Unless there are industry standards, including an opt-out feature like Facebook had to add when its facial-recognition photo-tagging function angered users, companies will make up their own rules.

Summary:

Some casinos already use facial recognition for security purposes, but privacy advocates believe unchecked use of the technology could infringe on civil rights and give companies excess power. The worst outcome, say some, would link store cameras to social networks. So, instead of pitching ads based on a customer being, say, a woman between 20 and 40, a retailer could scan her online profile to mine her friends' network.

Sources: Tarun Wadhwa, "What Do Jell-O, Kraft, and Adidas Have in Common? They All Want to Know Your Face," *Forbes*, accessed November 15, 2012, www.forbes.com; Wendy Davis, "Consumers Union Urges Opt-In Consent for Facial Recognition Tech," *Media Post*, accessed November 15, 2012, www.mediapost.com; Shan Li and David Sarno, "Advertisers Start Using Facial Recognition to Tailor Pitches," *Los Angeles Times*, accessed November 15, 2012, http://articles.latimes.com.

Attitudes are a person's enduring favorable or unfavorable evaluations, emotions, or action tendencies toward some object or idea. As they form over time through individual experiences and group contacts, attitudes become highly resistant to change. New fees, a reduction in service hours, or a change in location can be difficult for customers to accept. Because favorable attitudes likely affect brand preferences, marketers are interested in determining consumer attitudes toward their offerings. Numerous attitude-scaling devices have been developed for this purpose.

attitudes Person's enduring favorable or unfavorable evaluations, emotions, or action tendencies toward some object or idea.

Attitude Components

An attitude has cognitive, affective, and behavioral components. The cognitive component refers to the individual's information and knowledge about an object or concept. The affective component deals with feelings or emotional reactions. The behavioral component involves tendencies to act in a certain manner. For example, in deciding whether to shop at a specific retailer for a laptop computer, a consumer might gather information about what the store offers from advertising, visits to the store, and input from family, friends, and coworkers—the cognitive component. The consumer might also receive affective input by listening to others about their shopping experiences at this store. Affective input might cause the consumer to make a judgment about people who shop at the store, and whether those people represent a group with which the consumer wants to be associated. Finally, the consumer might decide to buy his or her new laptop at that store—the behavioral component. All three components maintain a relatively stable and balanced relationship to one another. Together, they form an overall attitude about an object or idea.

Changing Consumer Attitudes

A favorable consumer attitude is vital to the success of a marketing effort. Marketers can approach this in one of two ways:

1. By attempting to produce consumer attitudes that will lead to the purchase of an existing product.
2. By evaluating existing consumer attitudes and creating or modifying products to appeal to these attitudes.

It's always easier to create and maintain a positive attitude toward a product than it is to change an unfavorable one to favorable. But if consumers view a product unfavorably, all is not lost. The seller might redesign the product, offer new or desired options, or enhance service. Sometimes an attitude isn't unfavorable, but consumers just don't feel a need for the product—they aren't motivated to make the purchase. So marketers must find a way to change shoppers' attitude to include the desire to buy. For example, although most consumers don't necessarily have a negative attitude toward sweet potatoes, they might not have a strong enough positive attitude to cause them to add sweet potatoes to their grocery list. In order to boost sales, marketers recently began to provide more information about sweet potatoes, including their high content of vitamins, antioxidants, and dietary fiber. This information addressed the cognitive component of consumers' attitude toward sweet potatoes, pushing it enough toward the positive that shoppers began to buy them more often.[34]

Modifying the Components of Attitude

Attitudes frequently change in response to inconsistencies among the three components. The most common inconsistencies result when new information changes the cognitive or affective components of an attitude. Marketers can modify attitudes by providing evidence of product benefits and by correcting misconceptions. Marketers may also change attitudes by engaging buyers in new behavior. Free samples might change attitudes by getting consumers to try a product.

Sometimes new technologies can encourage consumers to change their attitudes. Consumers who sign up to receive Internet coupons for goods and services might be more likely to try these products without knowing a lot about them. Personalized shopping alerts from firms such as Amazon. com might encourage consumers to purchase a new book or CD by making shoppers feel as though the retailer cares about their individual reading or listening preferences.

Good-looking cupcakes in a bakery window might influence a hungry person to stop in and buy a cupcake as a response to that cue.

learning Knowledge or skill acquired as a result of experience, which changes consumer behavior.

shaping The process of applying a series of rewards and reinforcements to permit more complex behavior to evolve.

LEARNING

Marketing is concerned as seriously with the process by which consumer decisions change over time as with the current status of those decisions. Learning, in a marketing context, refers to immediate or expected changes in consumer behavior as a result of experience. The learning process includes the component of drive, which is any strong stimulus that impels action. Fear, pride, greed, jealousy, hunger, thirst, comfort, and rivalry are examples of drives. Learning also relies on a cue—any object or signal in the environment that determines the nature of the consumer's response to a drive. Cues include a flashing neon sign in the window of a bakery (a cue for a hungry person) and a commercial for a get-rich-quick sales seminar (a cue for someone who wants more money). A response is the individual's reaction to a set of cues and drives. The hungry person might duck into the bakery to buy a pastry, while the person who wants more money might sign up for the seminar.

Reinforcement is the reduction in drive that results from a proper response. As a response becomes more rewarding, it creates a stronger bond between the drive and the purchase of the product, likely increasing future purchases by the consumer. Reinforcement is the rationale that underlies frequent-buyer programs that reward repeat purchasers for their loyalty. These programs may offer points for premiums or discounts, frequent-flyer miles, and the like. However, so many companies now offer these programs that marketers must find ways to differentiate them. And firms that don't offer the programs quickly learn that consumers will bypass their products and move on to those of competitors.

Customization is the latest trend toward attracting reward card users. Chase Sapphire card users can choose points or cash rewards, which never expire. In addition, they have access to live customer service representatives around the clock, personal concierge services, and premier travel services that include booking any flights with points they choose, without being subject to blackout dates.[35]

Applying Learning Theory to Marketing Decisions

Learning theory has some important implications for marketing strategists, particularly those involved with consumer packaged goods. Marketers must find a way to develop a desired outcome such as repeat purchase behavior gradually over time. Shaping is the process of applying a series of rewards and reinforcements to permit more complex behavior to evolve.

Both promotional strategy and the product itself play a role in the shaping process. Marketers want to motivate consumers to become regular buyers of certain merchandise. Their first step in getting consumers to try the product might be to offer a free-sample package that includes a substantial discount coupon for the next purchase. This example uses a cue as a shaping procedure. If the item performs well, the purchase response is reinforced and followed by another inducement—the coupon. The reason a sample works so well is that it allows the consumer to try the product at no risk. Supermarket shoppers have the opportunity to sample products on a regular basis—crackers, cheese, appetizers, salad dressings, cookies, and the like. A display is often set up near the aisle where the item is sold, staffed by a person who dispenses the sample along with a coupon for future purchase.

The second step is to entice the consumer to buy the item with little financial risk. The discount coupon enclosed with the free-sample prompts this action. Suppose the package that the consumer purchases has another, smaller discount coupon enclosed. Again, satisfactory product performance and the second coupon provide reinforcement.

The third step is to motivate the person to buy the item again at a moderate cost. A discount coupon accomplishes this objective, but this time the purchased package includes no additional coupon. The only reinforcement comes from satisfactory product performance.

The final test comes when the consumer decides whether to buy the item at its true price without a discount coupon. Satisfaction with product performance provides continuing reinforcement.

Repeat purchase behavior literally is shaped by effective application of learning theory within a marketing strategy context.

SELF-CONCEPT THEORY

Our **self-concept**—our multifaceted view of ourselves—plays an important role in our consumer behavior. Perhaps you see yourself as a creative person, someone who thinks outside the box. You pride yourself on keeping up with the latest trends—in fact, you like to think of yourself as a trendsetter, ahead of the wave. You might express this self-concept by wearing certain clothes, such as those offered by the Ed Hardy brand. Ed Hardy was created by designer Christian Audigier and tattoo artist Don Ed Hardy. The cooperation of these two creative people brought to market jeans, jackets, sweatshirts, sunglasses, hats, and other items bearing tattoo art. Fashion industry experts acknowledge that the Ed Hardy line established a new trend in "street fashion."[36] Perhaps your self-concept lets you see yourself as a genius multi-tasker, but if you find that you're often distracted at work, see the "Career Readiness" feature for some tips on regaining your focus.

© Kevan Brooks/AdMedia/Newscom

If you see yourself as a creative person keeping up with the latest trends, you might express this self-concept by purchasing clothes from the Ed Hardy line.

self-concept Person's multifaceted picture of himself or herself.

© iStockphoto.com/hh5800

CAREER READINESS

How to Avoid Major Distractions at Work

Phone calls, emails, and visitors are all part of every workday, but they can distract you from work. Here are some tips for getting your focus back.

1. Set a realistic schedule that prioritizes the week's tasks—including responding to emails—by deadline and importance. Now you have specific goals to focus on in orderly fashion. Update this schedule at the beginning or end of each week.

2. Check email just three times a day—morning, lunch, and close of business—and turn your email application off in between. If you can train yourself to check only twice a day, even better.

3. Don't hesitate to tell people you're busy or have a deadline. If you are polite, they'll understand. If they insist, invite them to walk with you while you grab lunch or head back to your office.

4. Let family members use the office number to reach you in an emergency, leaving you free to shut your personal phone off at work so personal calls don't interrupt you.

5. Leave Facebook, Twitter, LinkedIn, and the rest for off-hours. If your company doesn't already block these sites from employees' computers, you'll be grateful you can turn your smartphone off at work.

Sources: "How to Avoid the 5 Major Distractions at Work," Careerbright.com, accessed November 15, 2012, http://careerbright.com; Caroline Potter, "Work, Interrupted: Six Ways to Avoid Distractions," Monster.com, accessed November 15, 2012, http://career-advice.monster.com; Michael Pollick, "How Can I Avoid Distractions at Work?" *Wise Geek*, accessed November 15, 2012, www.wisegeek.com.

The concept of self emerges from an interaction of many of the influences—both personal and interpersonal—that affect buying behavior. A person's needs, motives, perceptions, attitudes, and learning lie at the core of his or her conception of self. In addition, family, social, and cultural influences affect self-concept.

A person's self-concept has four components: real self, self-image, looking-glass self, and ideal self. The real self is an objective view of the total person. The self-image, the way an individual views himself or herself, may distort the objective view. The looking-glass self, the way an individual thinks others see him or her, may also differ substantially from self-image because people often choose to project different images to others than their perceptions of their real selves. The ideal self serves as a personal set of objectives, because it is the image to which the individual aspires.

When making purchasing decisions, consumers will likely choose products that move them closer to their ideal self-images. For example, suppose your ideal self-image is one of a trendsetter, but you generally have a hard time wearing anything other than conventional clothes. You might buy an Ed Hardy cap or T-shirt in an effort to break out of the box and bring you closer to your ideal self-image. Social network media such as Facebook appeal to people's ideal self-image—users are often likely to post pictures and entries that paint themselves in a flattering light.

ASSESSMENT CHECK

3.1   Identify the personal determinants of consumer behavior.

3.2   What are the human needs categorized by Abraham Maslow?

3.3   How do perception and learning differ?

THE CONSUMER DECISION PROCESS

4   **Distinguish between high-involvement and low-involvement purchase decisions.**

high-involvement purchase decisions Purchases with high levels of potential social or economic consequences.

low-involvement purchase decisions Routine purchases that pose little risk to the consumer.

Although we might not be aware of it, as consumers, we complete a step-by-step process in making purchasing decisions. The time and effort devoted to a particular purchasing decision depend on how important it is.

Purchases with high levels of potential social or economic consequences are said to be **high-involvement purchase decisions**. Buying a car or deciding where to go to college are examples of high-involvement decisions. Routine purchases that pose little risk are **low-involvement purchase decisions**. Buying a loaf of bread or a pint of ice cream at the corner grocery store is a good example.

Consumers generally invest more time and effort in buying decisions for high-involvement products than in those for low-involvement products. A home buyer will visit a number of listings, compare asking prices, apply for a mortgage, have the selected house inspected, and even ask close friends or family members to visit the home before signing the final papers. Few buyers invest that much effort in choosing a brand of orange juice at the supermarket. Believe it or not, though, they will still go through the steps of the consumer decision process—but on a more compressed scale.

Figure 6.2 shows the six steps in the consumer decision process. First, the consumer recognizes a problem or unmet need, searches for appropriate goods or services, and evaluates the alternatives before making a purchase decision. The next step is the actual purchase. After buying the item, the consumer evaluates whether he or she made the right choice. Much of marketing involves steering consumers through the decision process in the direction of a specific product.

Consumers apply the decision process in solving problems and taking advantage of opportunities. Such decisions permit them to correct differences between their actual and desired states. Feedback from each decision serves as additional experience in helping guide subsequent decisions.

ASSESSMENT CHECK

4.1   Differentiate between high-involvement decisions and low-involvement decisions.

4.2   Categorize each of the following as a high- or low-involvement product: toothpaste, laptop, apartment, cup of coffee, and cell phone service.

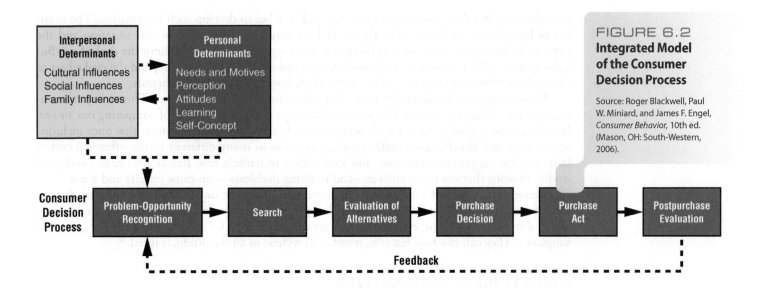

FIGURE 6.2
Integrated Model of the Consumer Decision Process

Source: Roger Blackwell, Paul W. Miniard, and James F. Engel, *Consumer Behavior*, 10th ed. (Mason, OH: South-Western, 2006).

PROBLEM OR OPPORTUNITY RECOGNITION

During the first stage in the decision process, the consumer becomes aware of a gap between the existing situation and a desired situation. You have experienced this yourself. Perhaps you open the refrigerator door and find a slice of cheese and a cup of yogurt. You are really hungry for a sandwich. By identifying the problem—not enough food in the refrigerator—you can resolve it with a trip to the grocery store. Sometimes the problem is more specific. You might have a full refrigerator, but no mustard or mayonnaise for sandwiches. This problem requires a solution as well.

Suppose you are unhappy with a particular purchase, say, a brand of cereal. The cereal might be too sweet or too crunchy. Or maybe you just want a change from the same old cereal every morning. This is the recognition of another type of problem or opportunity—the desire for change.

What if you just got a raise at work? You might decide to splurge on dinner at a restaurant. Or you might want to try a gourmet, prepared take-home dinner from the supermarket. Both dinners are more expensive than the groceries you have always bought, but now they are within financial reach. The marketer's main task during this phase of the decision-making process is to help prospective buyers identify and recognize potential problems or needs. This task may take the form of advertising, promotions, or personal sales assistance. A supermarket employee might suggest appetizers or desserts to accompany a gourmet take-home dinner.

SEARCH

During the second step in the decision process, a consumer gathers information about the attainment of a desired state. This search identifies different ways to solve the problem. A high-involvement purchase might mean conducting an extensive search for information, whereas a low-involvement purchase might require much less research.

The search may cover internal or external sources of information. An internal search is simply a mental review: Is there past experience with the product? Was it good or bad? An external search involves gathering information from all kinds of outside sources—for instance, family, friends, coworkers or classmates, advertisements or salespeople, online reviews, and consumer magazines. Because conducting an external search requires time and effort, it usually is done for high-involvement purchases.

The search identifies alternative brands or models for consideration and possible purchase. The collection of alternatives a consumer actually considers in making a purchase decision is known in marketing as the **evoked set**. In some cases, consumers already know which brands merit further

Outline the steps in the consumer decision process.

5

evoked set Number of alternatives a consumer actually considers in making a purchase decision.

consideration; in others, consumers make external searches to develop such information. The number of brands that are included in the evoked set may vary, depending on the situation and the person. An immediate need, such as filling a nearly empty gas tank, might limit the evoked set. But a driver with half a tank of gas, with more time to make a decision, might expand the evoked set to choose from a broader range of options that include lower prices or certain brands.

Consumers now choose among more alternative products than ever before. This variety can confuse and complicate the analysis that narrows the range of choices. Instead of comparing one or two brands, a consumer often faces a wide array of brands and sub-brands. Products that once included only regular and decaffeinated coffee now are available in many different forms—flavored coffee, latte, mocha, cappuccino, espresso, and iced coffee, to name a few. Researchers have conducted studies showing that too many choices—and resulting decisions—can cause anxiety and stress.[37]

Recognizing this, and wanting to help consumers find their way through the maze of choices, some firms have set up online sites where shoppers can compare products. The Biz Rate website allows shoppers to compare everything from air conditioners to GPS devices to barbecue grills and sunglasses. They can compare features, prices, and reviews of all the products listed.[38]

EVALUATION OF ALTERNATIVES

The third step in the consumer decision process is to evaluate the evoked set of options. Actually, it is difficult to completely separate the second and third steps because some evaluation takes place as the search progresses; consumers accept, distort, or reject information as they receive it. For example, knowing that you are looking for a new pair of boots, your roommate might tell you about this great online site for shoes she visited recently. But you don't particularly like her taste in shoes or boots, so you reject the information, even though the site might have a pair of boots that you would have bought.

The outcome of the evaluation stage is the choice of a brand or product within the evoked set, or possibly a decision to keep looking for alternatives. To complete this analysis, the consumer must develop a set of evaluative criteria to guide the selection. Evaluative criteria are the features a consumer considers in choosing among alternatives. These criteria can either be objective facts (a washing machine's energy rating) or subjective impressions (a favorable view of Free People clothing). Common criteria include price, brand name, and country of origin. Evaluative criteria can vary with the consumer's age, income level, social class, and culture; what's important to a senior citizen might not matter at all to a college student. When it comes to dining out, an affluent senior might look for a restaurant with an upscale atmosphere and high-quality food; a budget-conscious college student might choose a place that's inexpensive and fast to accommodate study hours or class.

Marketers attempt to influence the outcome of this stage in three ways. First, they try to educate consumers about attributes they view as important in evaluating a particular class of goods. They also identify which evaluative criteria are important to an individual and attempt to show why a specific brand fulfills those criteria. Finally, they try to induce a customer to expand the evoked set to include the marketed product.

PURCHASE DECISION AND PURCHASE ACT

The search and alternative evaluation stages of the decision process result in the purchase decision and the actual purchase. At this stage, the consumer has evaluated each alternative in the evoked set based on his or her personal set of evaluative criteria and narrowed the alternatives down to one.

The consumer then decides where—or from whom—to make the purchase. Sometimes this decision is part of the evaluation; perhaps one seller is offering a better price or better warranty than another. The purchase may be made online or in person at a retail store. The delivery options might also influence the decision of where to purchase an item. For example, a local electronics store might deliver your HDTV for free, whereas an online retailer might charge $50 for delivery.

POSTPURCHASE EVALUATION

The purchase act produces one of two results. The buyer feels either satisfaction at the removal of the discrepancy between the existing and desired states or dissatisfaction with the purchase. Consumers are generally satisfied if purchases meet—or exceed—their expectations.

evaluative criteria Features a consumer considers in choosing among alternatives.

Sometimes, however, consumers experience postpurchase anxiety called cognitive dissonance. This anxiety results from an imbalance among a person's knowledge, beliefs, and attitudes. You might experience some dissonance about your purchase of a TV if you can't figure out how to use it, if it doesn't have the features you thought it had, or if you see an ad the next week for the same model at a discount.

Dissonance is likely to increase (1) as the dollar value of a purchase increases, (2) when the rejected alternatives have desirable features that the chosen alternatives do not provide, and (3) when the purchase decision has a major effect on the buyer. In other words, dissonance is more likely with high-involvement purchases than with those that require low involvement. If you buy a diet soda and don't like the flavor, you can toss it and buy a different one. But if you have spent more than $1,000 on a TV and you aren't satisfied with it, you will most likely experience dissonance. You might try to reduce the dissonance by focusing on good reviews about your choice. Or you might show a friend all the neat features on your TV—without pointing out anything you find dissatisfactory.

Marketers can help buyers reduce cognitive dissonance by providing information that supports the chosen item. Automobile dealers recognize the possibility of "buyer's remorse" and often follow up purchases with letters or telephone calls from dealership personnel offering personal attention to any customer questions or potential problems. Advertisements that stress customer satisfaction also help reduce cognitive dissonance.

A final method of dealing with cognitive dissonance is to change products. The consumer may ultimately decide that one of the rejected alternatives would have been the best choice, and vow to purchase that item in the future. Marketers may capitalize on this with advertising campaigns that focus on the benefits of their products or with tag lines that say something like, "If you're unhappy with them, try us." But making a different choice isn't always an option, particularly if the item requires a large investment in time and money. If you decide you aren't happy with your TV, you could try selling it, perhaps on a website like eBay or Craigslist, before purchasing another one.

cognitive dissonance
Imbalance among knowledge, beliefs, and attitudes that occurs after an action or decision, such as a purchase.

ASSESSMENT CHECK

5.1 List the steps in the consumer decision process.

5.2 What is meant by the term *evoked set*?

5.3 What are evaluative criteria?

CLASSIFYING CONSUMER PROBLEM-SOLVING PROCESSES

As mentioned earlier, the consumer decision processes for different products requires varying amounts of problem-solving efforts. Marketers recognize three categories of problem-solving behavior: routinized response, limited problem solving, and extended problem solving. The classification of a particular purchase within this framework clearly influences the consumer decision process.

Differentiate among routinized response behavior, limited problem solving, and extended problem solving by consumers.

Routinized Response Behavior

Consumers make many purchases routinely by choosing a preferred brand or one of a limited group of acceptable brands. This type of rapid consumer problem solving is referred to as routinized response behavior. A routine purchase of the same brand of dog food or the renewal of a magazine subscription are examples. The consumer has already set evaluative criteria and identified available options. External search is limited in such cases, which characterize extremely low-involvement products.

Limited Problem Solving

Consider the situation in which the consumer previously set evaluative criteria for a particular kind of purchase but then encounters a new, unknown brand. The introduction of a new shampoo is an example of a limited problem-solving situation. The consumer knows the evaluative criteria for the product but has not applied these criteria to assess the new brand. Such situations demand moderate amounts of time and effort for external searches. Limited problem solving is affected by the number of evaluative criteria and brands, the extent of external search, and the process for determining preferences. Consumers making purchase decisions in this product category will likely feel involvement in the middle of the range.

ASSESSMENT CHECK

6.1 What is routinized response behavior?

6.2 What does limited problem solving require?

6.3 Give an example of an extended problem-solving situation.

Extended Problem Solving

Extended problem solving results when brands are difficult to categorize or evaluate. The first step is to compare one item with similar ones. The consumer needs to understand the product features before evaluating alternatives. Most extended problem-solving efforts involve lengthy external searches. High-involvement purchase decisions—cars, homes, and colleges—usually require extended problem solving.

© iStockphoto.com/Ferran Traite Soler

STRATEGIC IMPLICATIONS OF MARKETING IN THE 21ST CENTURY

Marketers who plan to succeed with today's consumers need to understand how their potential market behaves. Cultural influences play a big role in marketers' relationships with consumers, particularly as firms conduct business on a global scale but also as they try to reach diverse populations in the United States. In addition, family characteristics are changing—more women are in the workforce, more senior citizens are living alone—which forecasts a change in the way family units make purchasing decisions. One of the biggest shifts in family spending involves the amount of power that children and teens wield in the marketplace. These young consumers are more and more involved, in some cases

know more about certain products—such as electronics—than their parents do, and very often influence purchase decisions. This holds true even with high-involvement purchases such as autos and computers.

Marketers constantly work toward changing or modifying components of consumers' attitudes about their products to gain a favorable attitude and purchase decision. Finally, they refine their understanding of the consumer decision process and use their knowledge to design effective marketing strategies.

Get online now for additional learning tools to help you master your marketing knowledge—visit **WWW.CENGAGEBRAIN.COM** today!

REVIEW OF CHAPTER OBJECTIVES

1 Define *consumer behavior*, and describe the role it plays in marketing decisions.

Consumer behavior refers to the buyer behavior of individual consumers. Consumer behavior plays a huge role in marketing decisions, including what goods and services to offer, to whom, and where. If marketers can understand the factors that influence consumers, they can develop and offer the right products to those consumers.

2 Describe the interpersonal determinants of consumer behavior: cultural, social, and family influences.

Cultural influences, such as the general work ethic or the desire to accumulate wealth, come from society. Core values may vary from culture to culture. Group or social influences include social class, opinion leaders, and reference groups with which consumers may want to be affiliated. Family influences may come from spouses, parents, grandparents, or children.

3 Explain each of the personal determinants of consumer behavior: needs and motives, perceptions, attitudes, learning, and self-concept theory.

A need is an imbalance between a consumer's actual and desired states. A motive is the inner state that directs a person toward the goal of satisfying a need. Perception is the meaning that a person attributes to incoming stimuli gathered through the five senses. Attitudes are a person's enduring favorable or unfavorable evaluations, emotions, or action tendencies toward something. In self-concept theory, a person's view of himself or herself plays a role in purchasing behavior. In purchasing goods and services, people will likely choose products that move them closer to their ideal self-images.

4 Distinguish between high-involvement and low-involvement purchase decisions.

Purchases with high levels of potential social or economic consequences are called high-involvement purchase decisions. Examples include buying a new car or home. Routine purchases that pose little risk to the consumer are called low-involvement purchase decisions. Choosing a candy bar or a magazine are examples.

5 Outline the steps in the consumer decision process.

The consumer decision process consists of six steps: problem or opportunity recognition, search, alternative evaluation, purchase decision, purchase act, and postpurchase evaluation. The time involved in each stage of the decision process is determined by the nature of the individual purchases.

6 Differentiate among routinized response behavior, limited problem solving, and extended problem solving by consumers.

Routinized response behavior refers to repeat purchases made of the same brand or limited group of items. Limited problem solving occurs when a consumer previously set criteria for a purchase but then encounters a new brand or model. Extended problem solving results when brands are difficult to categorize or evaluate. High-involvement purchase decisions usually require extended problem solving.

ASSESSMENT CHECK: ANSWERS

1.1 Why is the study of consumer behavior important to marketers? If marketers can understand the behavior of consumers, they can offer the right products to consumers who want them.

1.2 Describe Kurt Lewin's proposition. Kurt Lewin proposed that behavior (*B*) is the function (*f*) of the interactions of personal influences (*P*) and pressures exerted by outside environmental forces (*E*). This research sheds light on how consumers make purchase decisions.

2.1 List the interpersonal determinants of consumer behavior. The interpersonal determinants of consumer behavior are cultural, social, and family influences.

2.2 What is a subculture? A subculture is a group within a culture that has its own distinct mode of behavior.

2.3 Describe the Asch phenomenon. The Asch phenomenon is the impact of groups and group norms on individual behavior.

3.1 Identify the personal determinants of consumer behavior. The personal determinants of consumer behavior are needs and motives, perceptions, attitudes, learning, and self-concept theory.

3.2 What are the human needs categorized by Abraham Maslow? The human needs categorized by Abraham Maslow are physiological, safety, social/belongingness, esteem, and self-actualization.

3.3 How do perception and learning differ? Perception is the meaning that a person attributes to incoming stimuli. Learning refers to immediate or expected changes in behavior as a result of experience.

4.1 Differentiate between high-involvement decisions and low-involvement decisions. High-involvement

decisions have high levels of potential social or economic consequences, such as selecting an Internet service provider. Low-involvement decisions pose little financial, social, or emotional risk to the buyer, such as a magazine or gallon of milk.

4.2 Categorize each of the following as a high- or low-involvement product: toothpaste, notebook computer, apartment, cup of coffee, cell phone service. High-involvement products are the notebook computer, apartment, and cell phone service. Low-involvement products are the toothpaste and cup of coffee.

5.1 List the steps in the consumer decision process. The steps in the consumer decision process are problem or opportunity recognition, search, alternative evaluation, purchase decision, purchase act, and postpurchase evaluation.

5.2 What is meant by the term *evoked set*? The evoked set is the number of alternatives a consumer actually considers in making a purchase decision.

5.3 What are evaluative criteria? Evaluative criteria are the features a consumer considers in choosing among alternatives.

6.1 What is routinized response behavior? Routinized response behavior is the repeated purchase of the same brand or limited group of products.

6.2 What does limited problem solving require? Limited problem solving requires a moderate amount of a consumer's time and effort.

6.3 Give an example of an extended problem-solving situation. An extended problem-solving situation might involve the purchase of a car or a college education.

MARKETING TERMS YOU NEED TO KNOW

ASSURANCE OF LEARNING REVIEW

1. What are core values? Describe what you think are three core values of American society. Do you consider these your core values as well?

2. Why is the concept of acculturation important to marketers who want to target such groups as Hispanic, Asian, or African American consumers?

3. Describe a purchase that a consumer might make that would reflect his or her status within a particular group. If that person's status increased, how might the purchase selection change?

4. What are the four role categories that describe each spouse in a household? Which role has changed the most in recent years, and why?

5. According to Maslow, what is the difference between needs and motives? How can marketers make use of these two concepts to lead consumers toward purchases?

6. What are the two factors that interact to create a person's perception of an object? How is this important for marketers?

7. What are the three reasons that subliminal perception is unlikely to result in a purchase? Despite these findings, what role is neuroscience now playing in the creation of marketing messages?

8. What are the components of attitude? Explain the two ways in which marketers can try to change consumer attitudes toward their products.

9. What is learning as it relates to marketing? Explain the four steps in the learning process and give examples as they relate to marketing.

10. For each of the following products, what steps might marketers take to transform them from a limited problem-solving situation for a consumer to a routinized response situation?
    a. gym membership
    b. magazine or newspaper subscription
    c. appointment at a hair salon
    d. office supplies
    e. oil change for a car

PROJECTS AND TEAMWORK EXERCISES

1. Choose a person whom you believe to be a true opinion leader. It might be a media celebrity, a political leader, a sports figure, or someone in another category entirely. Research ways in which the person has possibly shaped consumer attitudes toward various goods and services. Present your findings in class.

2. Consider your own participation in family purchases. How much influence did you have on your family's decisions as a child? As a teenager? Over what types of products did you have an influence—or not? Compare your answers with those of classmates.

3. One major trend in consumer spending that is likely to last for the next several years is a focus on value. Dollar stores and discount supermarkets have been profitable during the economic downtown, and their popularity shows no sign of abating.[39] While consumers search for bargains, manufacturers and retailers of luxury goods are struggling to change consumer attitudes toward their products. On your own or with a classmate, choose one of the following luxury brands (or select one of your own) and create an advertisement for the product

that seeks to change consumer attitudes about your product and show it would make a good purchase.
    a. Mercedes-Benz automobiles
    b. Louis Vuitton leather goods
    c. Tiffany jewelry
    d. Four Seasons Hotels and Resorts
    e. FlightOptions jet ownership

4. Consider a purchase decision involving one of the following types of products. Develop an evoked set of three alternatives for your purchase decision. Then create a list of evaluative criteria that you would use to choose among the alternatives. Research your alternatives in more detail—online, at a store, at a friend's apartment, and the like. Finally, make your purchase decision. Describe to the class how you made your decision—and why.

5. Choose a partner and select a low-involvement, routinized consumer product such as toothpaste, a jar of spaghetti sauce, laundry detergent, or kitchen trash bags. Create an ad you think could stimulate consumers to change their preferred brand to yours.

CRITICAL-THINKING EXERCISES

1. Describe a group to which you belong—it might be a team, a club, or your roommates. Outline the norms of the group, the major roles that different members play, and your own status within the group. Have you ever sought to change your status? Why or why not?

2. What are the two conditions that must exist for a consumer to be influenced by a reference group? Have you ever made a purchase based on reference group influence? If so, what was the purchase and how did you come to the decision to make it? If not, why not?

3. Marketers point out that the five levels in Maslow's hierarchy of needs are sometimes combined or even bypassed by consumers making purchase decisions. Explain how each of the following could fulfill more than one need:
   a. A download of "We Are the World: 25 for Haiti"
   b. A retirement investment account
   c. Philosophy body wash
   d. Dinner at a restaurant

4. What are some of the ways marketers can break through consumers' perceptual screens? If you were a marketer for a line of pet food for cats and dogs, what method might you use?

5. Suppose you are employed by a large electronics retailer, and a customer comes to you with cognitive dissonance over the purchase of an expensive computer system from your store the previous week. How would you work with the customer to help dispel that dissonance?

ETHICS EXERCISE

Marketers of online news content are struggling to change consumer attitudes about whether or not it is fair to charge for this content. While consumers are already willing to pay for movies, music, and games, they don't want to pay for news—whether it is from online versions of newspapers and magazines or online feeds of radio and talk shows. Yet these news formats are created by paid professionals, and can be expensive to produce. Increasingly, dailies in the United States have begun creating "pay walls" that require readers, after a while, to pay for a digital subscription.[40]

1. Express your own view. Is it ethical for marketers of online news content to begin charging consumers for their services? If so, under what circumstances? If not, why or why not?

2. Go online to research different news sources—those that are free (such as the headlines offered on Yahoo!) and those for which there is a charge (such as online magazine or newspaper subscriptions). Is there a difference in features or the extent of services offered?

3. Based on your research and your knowledge of consumer behavior, what steps do you think news marketers might take to change consumer attitudes about whether news should be offered for free?

INTERNET EXERCISES

1. **Marketing to children.** Advertising and other marketing efforts directed toward children have long been controversial. Visit the website of Children's Advertising Review Unit (CARU)—an organization created by the advertising industry to address issues associated with marketing to children. What is the purpose of CARU? What are the major issues regarding marketing to children? What have been some of its recent actions? Why have some prominent marketers, such as The Coca-Cola Company, decided to end advertising aimed at children? In your opinion, can industry self-regulation ever be an effective substitute for government regulation?

   www.caru.org

2. **Consumer decision making.** Assume you're in the market for both a new cell phone and cell phone provider. Follow the beginning stages in the consumer decision model described in the chapter—recognition of problem or opportunity, search, and evaluation of alternatives. Use the Internet to aid in your consumer decision process. Prepare a report summarizing your experience. Compare and contrast your experience with an actual consumer purchase decision you recently made.

3. **Marketing strategies and Maslow's Hierarchy of Needs.** Visit the websites listed here. Review the marketing strategies shown in each site. Which level of Maslow's Hierarchy of Needs does each site emphasize? Be prepared to defend your answers.
   www.michelinman.com
   www.starbucks.com
   http://shop.nordstrom.com
   www.hollandamerica.com
   www.unilever.com

Note: Internet Web addresses change frequently. If you don't find the exact site listed, you may need to access the organization's home page and search from there or use a search engine such as Google or Bing.

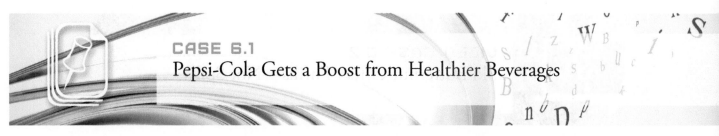

CASE 6.1
Pepsi-Cola Gets a Boost from Healthier Beverages

Pepsi recently dropped to third in the U.S. carbonated beverage market, behind Coke and Diet Coke. With declining sales and a flat share price, PepsiCo wants to engineer a change in its corporate fortunes in the North American beverage market.

In addition to trimming costs, the firm is adding $500 to $600 million to its beverage advertising and marketing budget. It has hired new Pepsi spokespeople, including actress Eva Longoria and rapper Nicki Minaj, and it introduced a mid-calorie Pepsi called Pepsi Next. But for several years U.S. consumers have been turning away from carbonated soft drinks and choosing healthier beverages including juices, teas, flavored water, and sports drinks. So PepsiCo wants to leverage that behavioral change by pumping up its Gatorade brand.

Gatorade was associated for years with male-dominated team sports at the youth level. Now PepsiCo will link it to a wider range of consumers, including women, and a broader spectrum of other athletic activities, including skateboarding, surfing, tennis, and dance, each represented by a professional athlete. The company recently introduced the G Series, a product extension that offers Gatorades for three phases of athletic activity, Prime, Perform, and Recover. Relying on marketing research revealing that high school and college athletes spend more on clothing and equipment than they do on nutrition products, PepsiCo is also unveiling a new Gatorade marketing campaign featuring prominent athletes like

Usain Bolt and Abby Wambach that stresses the importance of what you put *in* your body, as opposed to what you put *on* it.

Some Gatorade ads will carry a hashtag, to help PepsiCo monitor social media buzz in its new Gatorade Mission Control centers in the United States, the United Kingdom, and Latin America. The company will also send out a special sales and marketing team called G-Force, which includes many former college athletes, to foster marketing relationships with local retailers. "It's an aggressive, grass-roots effort," says Gatorade's president.

QUESTIONS FOR CRITICAL THINKING

1. How can PepsiCo capitalize on what it has learned about the buying behavior of young athletes?

2. Gatorade's president says, "We probably know more about who on Twitter is the most influential influencer of end user athletes than Twitter does, because we've made it our business to know that." What can social media tell PepsiCo about the market for Gatorade?

Sources: Natalie Zmuda, "Women Do the Heavy Lifting at Gatorade," *Advertising Age,* accessed November 15, 2012, http://adage.com; "PepsiCo Bubbles to $71 by Pumping Up Pepsi Next," *Forbes,* accessed November 15, 2012, www.forbes .com; "Q&A with Sarah Robb O'Hagan, Global CMO and North American President, Gatorade," *Marketing* magazine, accessed November 15, 2012, www.marketingmag .com; Pepsi Can Bubble Up to $71 But Needs Next Nooyi Thing," *Forbes,* accessed November 15, 2012, www.forbes.com; Natalie Zmuda, "Gatorade's New Selling Point: We're Necessary Performance Gear," *Advertising Age,* accessed November 15, 2012, http://adage.com.

VIDEO CASE 6.2
Ski Butternut Offers Thrills—Not Spills

"Ski Butternut is a true family mountain," says Matt Sawyer, director of marketing for the ski and snowboarding resort nestled in the Berkshire Mountains of western Massachusetts. Smaller than the peaks of Colorado or even the crags of the Green Mountains of Vermont and White Mountains of New Hampshire, Butternut is what Sawyer refers to as a "soft mountain"—one that beginners can enjoy while they grow comfortable on skis or snowboards. In fact, through extensive surveying and data collecting (as well as 50 years of experience), Ski Butternut has been able to identify exactly who its customers are—and what they want when they come to a mountain like Butternut.

A number of factors influence consumers' decision to try Butternut, ranging from interpersonal to personal determinants. The mountain's marketers, including Matt Sawyer and advertising consultant Ed Brooks, use various methods to tease out these factors in an effort to attract and keep customers. Cultural influences, such as the desire for quality recreation and leisure time, is one factor that drives people to a mountain resort; but there are plenty of such mountains scattered around New England and upstate New York. How does Ski Butternut compete? First, it focuses on families and the core value of spending time together. Matt Sawyer observes that Butternut's typical customers are families with young children, and "by capturing them early, we get to have them for a long time." Second, it reaches out to other subgroups, including senior citizens and those in the teen-to-25 age range. Senior citizens may want to perpetuate the image of themselves as physically active while enjoying membership in a group, while high school and college students want the thrills of challenging terrain. Other target groups for Ski Butternut include beginning skiers and those who race. Beginners aspire to be part of the skiing population, while racers aspire to reach achievement goals. Third, via social media, Ski Butternut engages customers and develops programs designed to keep them coming back for more.

Through more than 1,000 surveys across ski areas in the region as well as out west (and on its own mountain), Ski Butternut has amassed a comprehensive database that helps pinpoint who its customers are and what they want. "Ski Butternut believes in knowing as much as we can about our guests," explains Matt Sawyer. For example, Ski Butternut collects data during the equipment rental process. When a guest rents a pair of skis or a snowboard, that person provides standard information, such as name, address, and phone number. But the guest is also asked questions about age and ability to ski or snowboard, as well as the names of other winter resorts he or she has visited. The mountain compiles both individual and family profiles. In fact, says Sawyer, the average family skiing at Butternut has two children and one parent on the mountain (Ski Butternut offers day care for the youngest ski bunnies). All of this information helps Matt Sawyer, Ed Brooks, and others devise strategies designed to compete with other mountains in the region, such as beginner ski programs and three distinct racing programs—each targeted for a different level of interest in competition.

While the data show that first-time skiers generally keep their allegiance to the mountain on which they learn for about seven visits, Sawyer notes that the toughest group to capture is the teen-to-25 age range. A decade ago, this group (along with younger kids) was drifting off to other mountains that had more challenging terrain. So Ski Butternut built a terrain park—with a half pipe, jumps, and other obstacles—to lure them back. Sawyer points out with pride that Butternut is now the pre-eminent terrain park in the region covering southern New England and New York.

Another strategy for reaching this group is price discounts. Deciding where to spend recreation dollars falls in the high-involvement category for most of this group, with limited problem solving. So Ski Butternut decided to offer them an incentive—$20 off ticket prices on weekends and holidays (virtually unheard of in the industry). They marketed the offer mostly through social media—and the students "came in car loads," recalls Sawyer. With this group in mind, the company also recently updated its Web and mobile sites.

Looking for ways to draw consumers to the mountains for different reasons and at different times of the year, Ski Butternut also hosts weddings and banquets during the spring, summer, and fall. Thus, the ideal Butternut customers will get married on the mountain in the fall, honeymoon on the slopes during the winter, and return with their children for years after.

QUESTIONS FOR CRITICAL THINKING

1. Describe the social influences that might affect the decisions that consumers make about where to spend their winter recreation time and dollars.

2. The evaluation of alternatives is an important step in the buying decision for consumers who are considering whether to visit Butternut or some other mountain. What would be some of the evaluative criteria in this decision, and why?

Sources: Company website, www.skibutternut.com, accessed November 15, 2012; "New Website and Mobile Site for Ski Butternut," press release, accessed November 15, 2012, www.skibutternut.com; Kim Knox Beckius, "10 Tips for Snow Tubing at Ski Butternut in Massachusetts," *About.com*, accessed November 15, 2012, http://gonewenglandland.about.com.

NOTES

1. Erica Swallow, "How American Express Grows Its Massive Social Media Presence," *Mashable.com*, accessed November 14, 2012, http://mashable.com; Kunur Patel, "Twitter Users Grab $1.3 Million in AmEx Coupons for Burgers, Gear," *Advertising Age*, accessed November 14, 2012, http://adage.com; Tara Siegel Bernard, "American Express Incentives to Push Deals on Twitter," *The New York Times*, accessed November 14, 2012, http://bucks.blogs.nytimes.com.
2. Company website, www.garbetthomes.com, accessed November 14, 2012.
3. Company website, www.stouffers.com, accessed November 14, 2012.
4. Bethany Overland, "Starbucks Hopes New App Appeals to Smartphone Users," *TechFlash*, accessed November 14, 2012, www.techflash.com.
5. Company website, www.dominosbiz.com, accessed November 14, 2012; Annie Gasparro, "Domino's Has International Growth Spurt," *MarketWatch*, accessed November 14, 2012, www.marketwatch.com.
6. U.S. Population Clock Projection, www.census.gov, accessed November 14, 2012; U.S. Census Bureau, *The Next Four Decades*, "The Older Population in the United States: 2010 to 2050," accessed November 14, 2012, www.census.gov.
7. U.S. Census Bureau, "Hispanic Heritage Month 2012," press release, accessed November 14, 2012, www.census.gov; "African-Americans by the Numbers (from the U.S. Census Bureau)," *Info Please*, accessed November 14, 2012, www.infoplease.com; "Overview of Race and Hispanic Origin: 2010," accessed November 14, 2012, www.census.gov.
8. U.S. Department of Commerce, "Census Bureau Reports Mover Rate Reaches Record Low," accessed November 14, 2012, www.commerce.gov.
9. U.S. Census Bureau, "Hispanic Heritage Month 2012," press release, accessed November 14, 2012, www.census.gov; "2010 Census Shows Nation's Hispanic Population Grew Four Times Faster Than Total U.S. Population," accessed November 14, 2012, http://2010.census.gov.
10. U.S. Census Bureau, "2010 Census Shows Nation's Hispanic Population Grew Four Times Faster Than Total U.S. Population," accessed November 14, 2012, http://2010.census.gov.
11. Sudeep Reddy, "Latinos Fuel Growth in Decade," *The Wall Street Journal*, accessed November 14, 2012, http://online.wsj.com.
12. Frederic Lardinois, "Study: Hispanic Smartphone Owners Want Mobile Shopping Apps to Be Mobile," *Tech Crunch*, accessed November 14, 2012, http://techcrunch.com.
13. Shankar Pandiath, "Hispanic Affluence and Buying Power on the Rise," *TMCnet.com*, accessed November 14, 2012, www.tmcnet.com.
14. "Report: African-Americans Still Vital and Growing in U.S.," *Nielsen Wire*, accessed November 14, 2012, http://blog.nielsen.com; U.S. Census Bureau, "2010 Census Shows Black Population Has Highest Concentration in the South," press release, accessed November 14, 2012, http://2010.census.gov.
15. Ingrid Lunden, "Nielsen: Smartphones Used by 50.4% of U.S. Consumers, Android 48.5% of Them," *Tech Crunch*, accessed November 14, 2012, http://techcrunch.com; Social Media Mavens, "Nielsen: What's Hot List," *Black America Web*, accessed November 14, 2012, www.blackamericaweb.com.
16. "14 Important Statistics about Asian Americans," www.asian-nation.org, accessed November 14, 2012; Carolina Madrid, "Purchasing Power: Hispanics vs. Asian Americans," *Ameredian*, accessed November 14, 2012, www.ameredian.com.
17. "Asian-Americans and Technology," presentation by Lee Rainie, Director, Pew Internet Project, www.pewinternet.org, accessed November 14, 2012.
18. Restaurant website, www.sorabolrestaurants.com, accessed November 14, 2012.
19. Company website, www.dogsmith.com, accessed November 14, 2012.
20. Ann Zimmerman, "Frontier of Frugality," *The Wall Street Journal*, accessed November 15, 2012, http://online.wsj.com.
21. Company website, http://hannaandersson.com, accessed November 15, 2012.
22. Pew Internet, "Teens, Kindness and Cruelty on Social Network Sites," http://pewinternet.org, accessed November 15, 2012; "Teens Slowly Increase Online Shopping," *eMarketer*, accessed November 15, 2012, www.emarketer.com.
23. Adrianne Pasquarelli, "Private Labels Are Back in Fashion," *Crain's New York Business*, accessed November 15, 2012, www.crainsnewyork.com.
24. Company website, www.oceanclub.com, accessed November 15, 2012; company website, www.dreamresorts.com, accessed November 15, 2012; company website, http://travel.american express.com, accessed November 15, 2012; Christopher Quinn, "Owner Tries to Sell $17.9 Million Home Himself," *Atlanta Journal-Constitution*, accessed November 15, 2012, www.ajc.com.
25. Company website, www.oprah.com, accessed November 15, 2012.
26. "New Insights on Male Shoppers," *Progressive Grocer*, accessed November 15, 2012, www.progressivegrocer.com.
27. True Car, "Men Prefer Flashy or Brawny Vehicles; Women Prefer Import Brands and Smaller Vehicles According to TrueCar.com Study," press release, accessed November 15, 2012, http://blog.truecar.com.
28. Harris Interactive, "$211 Billion and So Much to Buy—American Youths, the New Big Spenders," press release, accessed November 15, 2012, www.harrisinteractive.com; U.S.Census Bureau, "Age and Sex Composition: 2010," accessed November 15, 2012, www.census.gov.
29. Kevin Davis, "Teens, Parents Face Special Issues When Buying Cars," *Crain's Chicago Business*, accessed November 15, 2012, www.chicagobusiness.com.
30. "Mannequin Installers," www.lvmannequins.com, accessed November 15, 2012.
31. "Brilliance of the 30-Second Spot," *Ad Contrarian*, accessed November 15, 2012, http://adcontrarian.com.
32. "Study: Pure Michigan Ads Attracted Record Number of Out-of-State Visitors," *Detroit News*, accessed November 15, 2012, www.detroitnews.com.
33. David Leibowitz, "Is Neuromarketing the Future of Advertising Research?" *ThreeMinds.com*, accessed November 15, 2012, www.threeminds.organic.com.
34. North Carolina Sweet Potatoes website, www.ncsweetpotatoes.com, accessed November 15, 2012.
35. Chase website, www.creditcards.chase.com, accessed November 15, 2012.
36. Company website, http://edhardyshop.com, accessed November 15, 2012.
37. "Rational and Irrational Buying Choices—The Paradox of Choice," *Imagemakers.com*, accessed November 15, 2012, http://blog.imagemakers-inc.com.
38. Biz Rate website, www.bizrate.com, accessed November 15, 2012.
39. Nin-Hai Tseng, "Why Dollar Stores Are Thriving, Even Post-Recession," *Fortune*, accessed November 15, 2012, http://finance.fortune.cnn.com.
40. Lauren Indvik, "20% of Newspapers Now Have Online Paywalls," *Mashable Business*, accessed November 15, 2012, http://mashable.com.

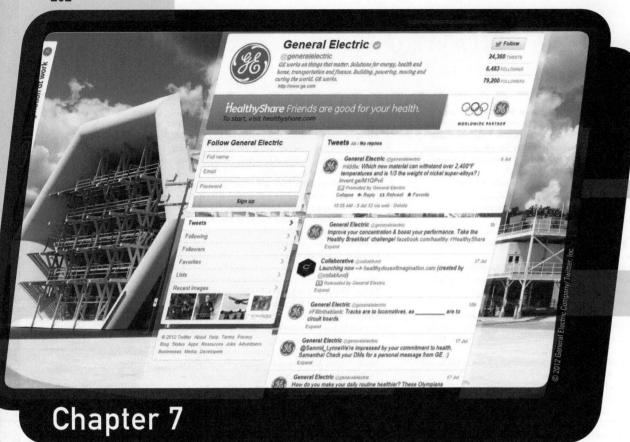

Chapter 7

BUSINESS-TO-
Business (B2B)
Marketing

1. Explain each of the components of the business-to-business (B2B) market.
2. Describe the major approaches to segmenting business-to-business (B2B) markets.
3. Identify the major characteristics of the business market and its demand.
4. Discuss the decision to make, buy, or lease.
5. Describe the major influences on business buying behavior.
6. Outline the steps in the organizational buying process.
7. Classify organizational buying situations.
8. Explain the buying center concept.
9. Discuss the challenges of, and strategies for, marketing to government, institutional, and international buyers.

SOCIAL MEDIA HELPS GE CONNECT

GE knows that about 90 percent of B2B buyers report using social media in their decision processes.

In fact, the company has developed an enviable reputation in its industry for its forward-thinking and successful use of social media and a growing list of mobile apps to find and generate new corporate business. GE's B2B marketing arm uses popular sites like LinkedIn, where it hosts several targeted groups, and Facebook, where its page has garnered more than 900,000 "likes," and almost 200,000 followers on Twitter. The company has been featured in a video on Apple's website as a prime example of how mobile apps for the iPad and iPhone can transform businesses, and it now has its own GE Mobile App store. With these digital and social media efforts, GE is building on the high standards it sets for the B2B customer experience in the industries in which it operates, which are as diverse as aviation, energy, media, health care technology, and financial services.

GE wants to deliver content it considers "micro-relevant," which means it reaches just the right customers rather than the biggest audience, and

with content that's specific to their needs. Its mobile apps allow restaurants to estimate the energy savings they can reap with more energy-efficient lighting, for instance, or let railroads monitor their tracks and gather diagnostics on their locomotives. Another app helps manage gas turbines and electric transformers, while still more offer business intelligence and presentations.

The company is so enthusiastic about using social media to reach its business-to-business (B2B) customers that it has even embraced the possibilities offered by Pinterest, the rapidly growing scrapbook-like website that's especially popular with

women ages 20 through 40. Some B2B marketers feel Pinterest has little to offer them, but GE is finding that its sample posts—selected inspirational words from Thomas Edison (the company's founder)—have drawn considerable Pinterest traffic. "We're experimenting," says the firm's executive director of global digital marketing, "and we're learning."

Despite the social media initiatives the company has already undertaken, GE believes it has only scratched the surface of mobile and social media marketing, especially for its B2B customers. Look for more to come.[1]

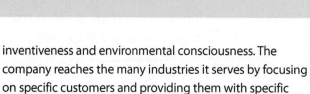

EVOLUTION OF A BRAND

When we think of social networking sites, we usually imagine ourselves posting status updates or photos to share with family and friends. But companies like GE recognize the potential for B2B outreach, given how many buyers rely on social media when making purchasing decisions. GE has wholeheartedly committed itself to social media, availing itself of social networking sites from Facebook and LinkedIn to Pinterest. Its Mobile App Store lists B2B applications, such as order tracking, order status, price, and availability. Its Ecomagination website features ideas that combine

inventiveness and environmental consciousness. The company reaches the many industries it serves by focusing on specific customers and providing them with specific content.

- Linda Boff, the company's executive director for global digital marketing, says, "We used the mantra 'business is social' increasingly at GE. Social is accessible no matter how big your company is." How does this type of marketing improve GE's B2B outreach?
- One possible future innovation in social networking is the mobile-friendly corporate website. How might such a website help GE reach its business customers even more directly?

CHAPTER OVERVIEW

business-to-business (B2B) marketing Organizational sales and purchases of goods and services to support production of other products, to facilitate daily company operations, or for resale.

We are all aware of the consumer marketplace. As consumers, we're involved in purchasing needed items almost every day. In addition, we can't help noticing the barrage of marketing messages aimed at us through a variety of media. But the business-to-business marketplace is, in fact, significantly larger. U.S. companies pay more than $300 billion each year just for office and maintenance supplies. Government agencies contribute to the business-to-business market even further; for example, the Department of Defense budget request for one recent year was more than $600 billion.[2] U.S. business-to-business commerce conducted over the Internet now totals over $3 trillion.[3]

Whether through face-to-face transactions, via telephone, or over the Internet, each day business marketers deal with complex purchasing decisions involving multiple decision makers. They range from simple reorders of previously purchased items to complex buys for which materials are imported from all over the world. They often involve the steady building of relationships between companies and customers as well as the ability to respond to changing circumstances in existing markets. Customer satisfaction and customer loyalty are major factors in the development of these long-term relationships.

This chapter discusses buying behavior in the business or organizational market. **Business-to-business (B2B) marketing** deals with organizational sales and purchases of goods and services to support production of other products, to facilitate daily company operations, or for resale. But you ask, "How do I go about distinguishing between consumer purchases and B2B transactions?" Actually, it's pretty simple. Just ask yourself two questions:

1. Who is buying the good or service?
2. Why is the purchase being made?

Consumer buying involves purchases made by individuals. We purchase items for our own use and enjoyment—and not for resale. By contrast, B2B purchases are made by businesses, government, and marketing intermediaries to be resold, combined with other items to create a finished product for resale, or used up in the day-to-day operations of the organization. So ask yourself the two questions—"Who is buying?" and "Why?"—and you have the answer.

NATURE OF THE BUSINESS MARKET

Firms usually sell fewer standardized products to organizational buyers than to ultimate consumers. Although you might purchase a cell phone for your personal use, a company generally has to purchase an entire communications system from a supplier such as AT&T, whose OneNet Service offers digital voice and Internet technology in a single business network.[4] Purchases like this require greater customization, more decision making, and usually more decision makers. So the buying and selling process becomes more complex, often involving teams and taking an average of 6 to 36 months to make decisions. Because of the complexity of the purchases, customer service is extremely important to B2B buyers. Advertising plays a much smaller role in the business market than in the consumer market, although advertisements placed in business magazines or trade publications are common. Business marketers advertise primarily to announce new products, to enhance their company image and presence, and to attract potential customers who would then deal directly with a salesperson. Personal selling plays a much bigger role in business markets than in consumer markets, distribution channels are shorter, customer relationships tend to last longer, and purchase decisions can involve multiple decision makers. Table 7.1 compares the marketing practices commonly used in both B2B and consumer marketing.

Like final consumers, an organization purchases products to fill needs. However, its primary need—meeting the demands of its own customers—is similar from firm to firm. A manufacturer buys raw materials, such as wood pulp, fabric, or grain, to create the company's product. A wholesaler or retailer buys the manufactured products—paper, clothing, or cereal—to resell. Mattel buys everything from plastic to paints to produce its toys; FAO Schwartz buys finished toys to sell to the public. And passenger airlines buy and lease aircraft from manufacturers such as Boeing and Airbus. Wilson Sporting Goods supplies the National Football League with its official game ball, "The Duke." Institutional purchasers such as government agencies and nonprofit organizations also buy products to meet the needs of their employees, whether it is global positioning system (GPS) mapping devices or meals ready to eat (MRE) for troops in the field.

Companies also buy services from other businesses. A firm may purchase legal and accounting services, office-cleaning services, call-center services, or recruiting services. Jan-Pro is a commercial cleaning service company that has been in business since 1991. The chain has more than 100 master franchise offices throughout the United States, Canada, and nine other countries, and more than 10,000 individual franchise operations in the United States alone.[5]

TABLE 7.1 Comparing Business-to-Business Marketing and Consumer Marketing

	Business-to-Business Marketing	Consumer Marketing
Product	Relatively technical in nature; exact form often variable; accompanying services very important	Standardized form; service important but less than for business products
Promotion	Emphasis on personal selling	Emphasis on advertising
Distribution	Relatively short, direct channels to market	Product passes through a number of intermediate links en route to consumer
Customer Relations	Relatively enduring and complex	Comparatively infrequent contact; relationship of relatively short duration
Decision-Making Process	Diverse group of organization members makes decision	Individual or household unit makes decision
Price	Competitive bidding for unique items; list prices for standard items	List prices

© Cengage Learning

Knoll Furniture sells office and home furniture to both the consumer and business markets.

Environmental, organizational, and interpersonal factors are among the many influences in B2B markets. Budget, cost, and profit considerations all play parts in business buying decisions. In addition, the business buying process typically involves complex interactions among many people. An organization's goals must also be considered in the B2B buying process. Later sections of the chapter will explore these topics in greater detail.

Some firms focus entirely on business markets. For instance, DuPont sells materials, such as polymers, coatings, and color technologies, to manufacturers that use them in a variety of products. Caterpillar makes construction and mining equipment, diesel and natural gas engines, and industrial gas turbines. SAP America provides collaborative business software that allows companies to work with customers and business partners using databases and other applications from every major software vendor. Other firms sell to both consumer and business markets. Knoll makes award-winning office furniture as well as stylish furniture for the home, and Intel's digital and wireless computer technology is found in business computing systems and personal computers. Note also that marketing strategies developed in consumer marketing often are appropriate for the business sector, too. Final consumers often are the end users of products sold into the business market and, as explained later in the chapter, can influence the buying decision.

The B2B market is diverse. Transactions can range from orders as small as a box of paper clips or copy machine toner for a home-based business to transactions as large as thousands of parts for an automobile manufacturer or massive turbine generators for an electric power plant. As mentioned earlier, businesses are also big purchasers of services such as telecommunications, computer consulting, and transportation services. See the "Solving an Ethical Controversy" feature for a discussion of one of the problems companies face in their increasing reliance on mobile phones.

Four major categories define the business market: (1) the commercial market, (2) trade industries, (3) government organizations, and (4) institutions.

COMPONENTS OF THE BUSINESS MARKET

1   Explain each of the components of the business-to-business (B2B) market.

commercial market Individuals and firms that acquire products to support, directly or indirectly, production of other goods and services.

trade industries Retailers or wholesalers that purchase products for resale to others.

resellers Marketing intermediaries that operate in the trade sector.

The commercial market is the largest segment of the business market. It includes all individuals and firms that acquire products to support, directly or indirectly, production of other goods and services. When Dell buys computer chips from Intel, Pepperidge Farm purchases wheat to mill into flour for an ingredient in its baked goods, and a plant supervisor orders light bulbs and cleaning supplies for a factory in Tennessee, these transactions take place in the commercial market. Some products aid in the production of other items (the computer chips). Others are physically used up in the production of a good or service (the wheat). Still others contribute to the firm's day-to-day operations (the maintenance supplies). The commercial market includes manufacturers, farmers, and other members of resource-producing industries; construction contractors; and providers of such services as transportation, public utilities, financing, insurance, and real-estate brokerage.

The second segment of the organizational market, trade industries, includes retailers and wholesalers, known as resellers, who operate in this sector. Most resale products, such as clothing, appliances, sports equipment, and automobile parts, are finished goods that buyers sell to final consumers. ACCO Brands supplies paper clips, ring binders, vinyl envelopes, sheet protectors, and fasteners to Office Depot.[6] In other cases, the buyers may complete some processing or repackaging before reselling the products. A retail meat market may purchase a side of beef and then cut individual pieces for its customers. Lumber dealers and carpet retailers may purchase in bulk and then provide quantities and sizes to meet customers' specifications. In addition to resale products, trade industries buy computers, display shelves, and other products needed to operate their

SOLVING AN ETHICAL CONTROVERSY

Making It Harder to Commit Mobile Crime

Phone spoofing is a strategy that allows callers to subvert caller ID by hiding behind someone else's number. Although the Federal Trade Commission (FTC) and Federal Communications Commission (FCC) both prohibit telemarketers from using phone spoofing services, which are inexpensive and legal, scammers are increasingly using them for illegal purposes. Criminals can perpetrate identify theft under cover of a legitimate business's phone number and gain access to mobile voice mailboxes, obtaining just enough personal information about the owner to enter the victim's online bank and credit card accounts and raid them for sensitive information. They can then call the bank to transfer cash or trigger the issuance of duplicate credit cards. Most major mobile carriers offer customers password protection for voice mail, but only Verizon Wireless requires it, making it more difficult for fraudsters to get in.

Should mobile phone carriers be required to make it harder for crooks to use phone spoofing?

PRO 👍

1. Privacy advocates find it "alarming that virtually anyone can get access to your payment and purchase information." Phone carriers can easily make this crime more difficult.

2. Businesses are especially at risk because banks often don't reimburse them for financial losses from online accounts. U.S. and European losses can total $1 billion a year.

CON 👎

1. Business and individual mobile users want ready access to their information. Mandating an extra step such as password verification reduces the convenience of the voice mail service for them.

2. Business owners should be savvy enough to use all available tools, such as the password option, to protect themselves from possible fraud.

Summary:

Both the FTC and the FCC are considering new and stronger rules against phone spoofing, and Congress passed the Truth in Caller ID Act recently. But businesses should be aware that any type of mobile communications is a growth area for spoofing.

Sources: Federal Communications Commission, "Caller ID and Spoofing," accessed November 15, 2012, www.fcc.gov; Sarah Wallace, "Investigation: Phone Spoofing," *WABC News*, accessed November 15, 2012, http://abclocal. go.com; Bryon Acohido, "Caller ID Spoofing Scams Aim for Bank Accounts," *USA Today*, accessed November 15, 2012, www.usatoday.com; Matt Richtel, "Who's on the Line? Increasingly, Caller ID Is Duped," *The New York Times*, accessed November 15, 2012, www.nytimes.com.

businesses. All of these goods—as well as maintenance items and specialized services such as scanner installation, newspaper inserts, and radio advertising—represent organizational purchases.

The government category of the business market includes domestic units of government—federal, state, and local—as well as foreign governments. This important market segment makes a wide variety of purchases, ranging from highways to military uniforms to Internet services. The primary motivation of government purchasing is to provide some form of public benefit, such as national defense or pollution control. But government agencies have also become creative when it comes to selling; local police departments and state and federal agencies sell unclaimed shipments, confiscated goods, and unclaimed items found in safe-deposit boxes on eBay. Lucky bidders might be able to buy a custom yacht for their business, a sausage grinder for their restaurant, or an auto transmission for their delivery truck through an Internet auction.[7]

Considered a reseller, Colorado-based Restaurant Source designs, sells, and installs food-service equipment for hotels, restaurants, and other institutions.

© Cultura Creative/Alamy

Institutions, both public and private, are the fourth component of the business market. This category includes a wide range of organizations, such as hospitals, churches, skilled care and rehabilitation centers, colleges and universities, museums, and not-for-profit agencies. Some institutions, like public higher education, must rigidly follow standardized purchasing procedures, but others have less formal buying practices. Business-to-business marketers often benefit by setting up separate divisions to sell to institutional buyers.

B2B MARKETS: THE INTERNET CONNECTION

Although consumers' use of Internet markets receives the bulk of public attention, about 91 percent of all Internet sales are B2B transactions.[8] Many business-to-business marketers have set up private portals that allow their customers to buy needed items. Service and customized pages are accessed through passwords provided by B2B marketers. Online auctions and virtual marketplaces offer other ways for buyers and vendors to connect with each other over the Internet. See the "Marketing Success" feature for the innovative way the online service Foursquare is connecting with new business customers.

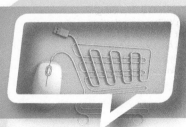

MARKETING SUCCESS

Foursquare Checks In with New Business Partners

Background. Foursquare, the free online service that helps users find out where friends are and what they're doing, has grown to include more than 25 million people worldwide. More than 1 million businesses have registered on its Merchant Platform, which allows them to offer custom deals and rewards, called "Specials," to Foursquare users who "check in" with the business.

The Challenge. Its developers have been looking for even more ways to expand the services Foursquare can offer to businesses, especially retailers that depend on foot traffic to drive sales volume. At the same time, it wants to improve users' experience of "exploring the real world" and let them tell friends even more about what they're doing.

The Strategy. Foursquare has partnered with third-party companies like MovieTickets.com, ESPN, and SongKick to launch

its new Events platform. This application provides users with information about events like movies, sporting events, and concerts that are taking place near them when they check in with local businesses.

The Outcome. Foursquare has high hopes for the new Events app and expects customers will share information about events the same way they now share news about Specials. The company is already working on developing partnerships with other third parties, like Zagat, the restaurant rating company.

Sources: Company website, www.foursquare.com/business, accessed November 15, 2012; Lauren Drell, "Everything You Need to Know about Foursquare's New Merchant Tools," *Mashable Business*, accessed November 15, 2012, http://mashable.com; Hess Thomas, "Foursquare: No Longer about Where You Are, But What You're Doing," *Forbes*, accessed November 15, 2012, www.forbes.com; Dylan Love and Steve Kovach, "How to Sign Your Business Up for Foursquare: A Step-by-Step Guide," *Business Insider*, accessed November 15, 2012, www.businessinsider.com.

© iStockphoto.com/Marcello Bortolino

During the early Internet boom, start-up companies rushed to connect buyers and sellers without considering basic marketing principles such as targeting their customers and making sure to fulfill their needs. As a result, many of these companies failed. But the companies that survived—and new firms that have learned lessons from others' mistakes—have established a much stronger marketing presence. For instance, they recognize that their business customers have a lot at stake and expect greater value and utility from the goods and services they purchase as well as streamlined marketing communications, such as email, blogs, and podcasts.[9] Another way for marketers to connect with each other online is through affiliate marketing. The Internet also opens up foreign markets to sellers. One such firm, which began as a cotton exchange called The Seam, survived the Internet boom and bust and is now bringing together global buyers of commodities like cotton, peanuts, and grain.[10]

DIFFERENCES IN FOREIGN BUSINESS MARKETS

When The Seam first moved into other countries, its marketers had to consider the fact that foreign business markets might differ due to variations in government regulations and cultural practices. Some business products need modifications to succeed in foreign markets. In Australia, Japan, and Great Britain, for instance, motorists drive on the left side of the road. American-made automobiles must be modified to accommodate such differences.

Business marketers must be willing to adapt to local customs and business practices when operating abroad. They should also research cultural preferences. Factors as deceptively simple as the time of a meeting and forms of address for associates can make a difference. A company even needs to consider what ink colors to use for documents because colors can have different meanings in different countries.

ASSESSMENT CHECK

1.1 Define *B2B marketing*.

1.2 What is the commercial market?

SEGMENTING B2B MARKETS

Business-to-business markets include wide varieties of customers, so marketers must identify the different market segments they serve. By applying market segmentation concepts to groups of business customers, a firm's marketers can develop a strategy that best suits a particular segment's needs. The overall process of segmenting business markets divides markets based on different criteria, usually organizational characteristics and product applications. Among the major ways to segment business markets are demographics (size), customer type, end-use application, and purchasing situation.

Describe the major approaches to segmenting business-to-business (B2B) markets.

SEGMENTATION BY DEMOGRAPHIC CHARACTERISTICS

As in consumer markets, demographic characteristics define useful segmentation criteria for business markets. For example, firms can be grouped by size, based on sales revenues or number of employees. Marketers may develop one strategy to reach *Fortune* 500 corporations with complex purchasing procedures and another strategy for small firms in which one or two people make the decisions. According to one study, many firms are actually increasing their outreach to small and midsize businesses. Overstock.com recently launched the Main Street Revolution, a partnership program with small and minority-owned businesses throughout the United States. The initiative enables those types of businesses to sell their products to consumers on Overstock.com and also to other businesses on O.biz, the company's B2B website. The company's CEO says the B2B website is designed to increase the visibility of small and minority-owned businesses that currently lack exposure to national markets. By joining the O.biz network, these small businesses can reduce their supply chain costs and open their products to a mass audience.[11]

SEGMENTATION BY CUSTOMER TYPE

Another useful segmentation approach groups prospects according to type of customer. Marketers can apply this concept in several ways. They can group customers by broad categories—manufacturer, service provider, government agency, not-for-profit organization, wholesaler, or retailer—and by industry. These groups may be further divided using other segmentation approaches discussed in this section.

customer-based segmentation Dividing a business-to-business market into homogeneous groups based on buyers' product specifications.

Customer-based segmentation is a related approach often used in the business-to-business marketplace. Organizational buyers tend to have much more precise—and complex—requirements for goods and services than ultimate consumers do. As a result, business products often fit narrower market segments than consumer products, which leads some firms to design business goods and services to meet detailed buyer specifications. Pasadena-based Tetra Tech provides a variety of environmental services, including technology development, design, engineering, and pollution remediation for organizations around the world. Because the company's customers include government agencies as well as private firms—and because customers' needs are different—Tetra Tech has 330 offices worldwide that offer a range of programs to suit each type of customer. For instance, the firm provides consulting services for utilities, helps communities clean up polluted water sources, and even conducts programs to clear public and private sites of unexploded military supplies.[12]

North American Industry Classification System (NAICS)

In the 1930s, the U.S. government set up a uniform system for subdividing the business marketplace into detailed segments. The Standard Industrial Classification (SIC) system standardized efforts to collect and report information on U.S. industrial activity.

SIC codes divided firms into broad industry categories: agriculture, forestry, and fishing; mining and construction; manufacturing; transportation, communication, electric, gas, and sanitary services; wholesale trade; retail trade; finance, insurance, and real-estate services; public administration; and nonclassifiable establishments. The system assigned each major category within these classifications its own two-digit number. Three-digit and four-digit numbers further subdivided each industry into smaller segments.

North American Industry Classification System (NAICS) Classification used by NAFTA countries to categorize the business marketplace into detailed market segments.

For roughly 70 years, B2B marketers used SIC codes as a tool for segmenting markets and identifying new customers. The system, however, became outdated with implementation of the North American Free Trade Agreement. Each NAFTA member—the United States, Canada, and Mexico—had its own system for measuring business activity. NAFTA required a joint classification system that would allow marketers to compare business sectors among the member nations. In effect, marketers required a segmentation tool they could use across borders. The North American Industry Classification System (NAICS) replaced the SIC and provides more detail than previously available. The NAICS created new service sectors to better reflect the economy of the 21st century. They include information; health care and social assistance; and professional, scientific, and technical services.

Table 7.2 demonstrates the NAICS system for wholesale home furnishings. The NAICS uses six digits, compared with the four digits used in the SIC. The first five digits are fixed among the members of NAFTA. The sixth digit can vary among U.S., Canadian, and Mexican data. In short, the sixth digit accounts for specific data needs of each nation.[13]

TABLE 7.2 NAICS Classification for Home Furnishing Merchant Wholesalers

42	Wholesale Trade
423	Merchant Wholesalers, Durable Goods
4232	Furniture and Home Furnishing Merchant Wholesalers
42322	Home Furnishing Merchant Wholesalers
423220	Home Furnishing Merchant Wholesalers in the U.S. Industry
Source: NAICS, U.S. Census Bureau, www.census.gov, accessed November 15, 2012.	

SEGMENTATION BY END-USE APPLICATION

A third basis for segmentation, end-use application segmentation, focuses on the precise way in which a business purchaser will use a product. For example, a printing equipment manufacturer may serve markets ranging from a local utility to a bicycle manufacturer to the U.S. Department of Defense. Each end use of the equipment may dictate unique specifications for performance, design, and price. Praxair, a supplier of industrial gases, for example, might segment its markets according to user. Steel and glass manufacturers might buy hydrogen and oxygen; food and beverage manufacturers need carbon dioxide. Praxair also sells krypton, a rare gas, to companies that produce lasers, lighting, and thermal windows. Many small and medium-sized companies also segment markets according to end-use application. Instead of competing in markets dominated by large firms, they concentrate on specific end-use market segments. The approximately two dozen companies that manufacture wooden baseball bats for Major League Baseball focus on specific end users who are very different from the youth and high-school players using aluminum bats.

> **end-use application segmentation** The division of a business-to-business market based on how industrial purchasers will use the product.

SEGMENTATION BY PURCHASE CATEGORIES

Firms have different structures for their purchasing functions, and B2B marketers must adapt their strategies according to those organizational buyer characteristics. Some companies designate centralized purchasing departments to serve the entire firm. Others allow each unit to handle its own buying. A supplier may deal with one purchasing agent or several decision makers at various levels. Each of these structures results in different buying behavior.

When the buying situation is important to marketers, they typically consider whether the customer has made previous purchases or this is the customer's first order, offering special rates or programs for valued clients. Verizon Wireless offers government customers cell phone discounts as either credits or reimbursements.[14]

Increasingly, businesses that have developed customer relationship management (CRM) systems—strategies and tools that reorient an entire organization to focus on satisfying customers—can segment customers in terms of the stage of the relationship between the business and the customer. A B2B company, for example, might develop different strategies for newly acquired customers than it would for existing customers to which it hopes to sell new products. Similarly, building loyalty among satisfied customers requires a different approach than developing programs to "save" at-risk customer relationships. CRM will be covered in more depth in Chapter 11.

> **customer relationship management (CRM)** Combination of strategies and tools that drives relationship programs, reorienting the entire organization to a concentrated focus on satisfying customers.

 ASSESSMENT CHECK

2.1 What are the four major ways marketers segment business markets?

2.2 What is the NAICS?

CHARACTERISTICS OF THE B2B MARKET

Businesses that serve both B2B and consumer markets must understand the needs of their customers. However, several characteristics distinguish the business market from the consumer market:

1. Geographic market concentration
2. The sizes and numbers of buyers
3. The purchase decision process
4. Buyer–seller relationships

The next sections consider how these traits influence business-to-business marketing.

> Identify the major characteristics of the business market and its demand. **3**

GEOGRAPHIC MARKET CONCENTRATION

The U.S. business market is more geographically concentrated than the consumer market. Manufacturers converge in certain regions of the country, making these areas prime targets for business marketers. For example, the Midwestern states that make up the East North Central region—Ohio, Indiana, Michigan, Illinois, and Wisconsin—lead the nation in manufacturing concentration. The South, the Southwest, and the West Coast have also gained strength in recent years.[15]

Certain industries locate in particular areas to be close to customers. Firms may locate sales offices and distribution centers in these areas to provide more attentive service. It makes sense that the Washington, DC, area is favored by companies that sell to the federal government.

In the automobile industry, suppliers of components and assemblies frequently build plants close to their customers. Volkswagen recently opened a supplier park near its Chattanooga assembly plant. The campus, which is expected to generate 2,000 jobs, allows suppliers to produce or assemble products close to the plant, reducing costs, controlling parts inventory, and increasing flexibility. The facility also includes the VW Training Academy, launched in partnership with Chattanooga State Community College. The academy combines classroom and lab instruction with hands-on training.[16] As Internet-based technology continues to improve, allowing companies to transact business even with distant suppliers, business markets may become less geographically concentrated. Much of government spending, for example, is now directed through the Internet.

SIZES AND NUMBERS OF BUYERS

In addition to geographic concentration, the business market features a limited number of buyers. Marketers can draw on a wealth of statistical information to estimate the sizes and characteristics of business markets. The federal government is the largest single source of such statistics. Every five years, it conducts both a Census of Manufacturers and a Census of Retailing and Wholesaling, which provide detailed information on business establishments, output, and employment. Many government units and trade organizations also operate websites that contain helpful information.

Many buyers in limited-buyer markets are large organizations. A few large buyers, such as McDonald's, Wendy's, and Burger King, dominate the fast-food industry. These chains have the power to name the price they will pay cattle farmers for meat and can dictate living conditions and standards of labor on ranches.

Trade associations and business publications provide additional information on the business market. Private firms like Dun & Bradstreet publish detailed reports on individual companies. These data are a useful starting point for analyzing a business market. Finding data in such a source requires an understanding of the NAICS, which identifies much of the available statistical information.

Having an enormous number of business customers with varying needs can pose quite a logistical challenge to a firm.

THE PURCHASE DECISION PROCESS

To market effectively to other organizations, businesses must understand the dynamics of the organizational purchase process. Suppliers who serve business-to-business markets must work with multiple buyers, especially when selling to larger customers. Decision makers at several levels may influence final orders, and the overall process is more formal and professional than the consumer purchasing process. Purchasers typically require a longer time frame because B2B involves more complex decisions. Suppliers must evaluate customer needs and develop proposals that meet technical requirements and specifications. Also, buyers need time to analyze competing proposals. Often, decisions require more than one round of bidding and negotiation, especially for complicated purchases.

BUYER–SELLER RELATIONSHIPS

An especially important characteristic of B2B marketing is the relationship between buyers and sellers. These relationships often are more complex than consumer relationships, and they require superior communication among the organizations' personnel. Satisfying one major customer may mean the difference of millions of dollars to a firm.

Relationship marketing involves developing long-term, value-added customer relationships. A primary goal of business-to-business relationships is to provide advantages that no other vendor can provide—lower price, quicker delivery, better quality and reliability, customized product features, more favorable financing terms, and so on. For the business marketer, providing these advantages means expanding the company's external relationships to include suppliers, distributors, and other organizational partners. CDW, for instance, relies on a variety of vendors to meet its own business, government, and education customers' technology needs with hardware, software, networking, and data storage. It has developed a CDW Supplier Diversity Program to increase and improve relationships with small-business suppliers owned by minorities, women, and veterans, and thus must manage its supplier as well as its customer relationships successfully.[17]

Close cooperation, whether through informal contacts or under terms specified in contractual partnerships and strategic alliances, enables companies to meet buyers' needs for quality products and customer service. This holds true both during and after the purchase process. Tetra Tech EC is a wholly owned subsidiary of Tetra Tech, mentioned earlier. Tetra Tech EC has instituted formal Client Service Quality and Shared Vision programs, designed to engage customers in continuous communication leading to customer satisfaction.

Relationships between for-profit and not-for-profit organizations are just as important as those between two commercial organizations. Walmart is a longtime corporate sponsor of Children's Miracle Network, an international organization that helps improve children's health and welfare by raising funds for state-of-the-art care, cutting-edge research, and education. In one recent year, Walmart raised and donated almost $28 million to 170 children's hospitals in the network.[18]

EVALUATING INTERNATIONAL BUSINESS MARKETS

Business purchasing patterns differ from one country to the next. Researching these markets poses a particular problem for B2B marketers. Of course, as explained earlier, the NAICS has corrected this problem in the NAFTA countries.

In a limited-buyer market like fast food, a few large buyers, such as McDonald's, Wendy's, and Burger King, are the major customers.

© AP Photo/Reed Saxon

In addition to assessing quantitative data such as the size of the potential market, companies must also carefully weigh its qualitative features. This process includes considering cultural values, work styles, and the best ways to enter overseas markets in general. The Coca-Cola Company, based in Atlanta, Georgia, has a presence in 90 markets worldwide. The company manages the sometimes volatile variations in culture and politics in Eurasia and Africa with a structure of six locally based business units in South Africa, Kenya, Turkey, Russia, India, and Dubai. A functional team in Istanbul manages finance, marketing, and strategy, working with each business unit to devise a strategic plan for that unit's market. For example, the business unit in Turkey developed a special marketing campaign for the Muslim holy month of Ramadan. The campaign proved so successful that the company expanded it to other Muslim countries where Coca-Cola has a presence. The president of Coca-Cola's Eurasia and Africa Group says, "This is not a bureaucratic approval-based system. Of course, there are approvals, but once the strategy and business plan are approved, local teams can execute."[19]

global sourcing
Purchasing goods and services from suppliers worldwide.

In today's international marketplace, companies often practice global sourcing, purchasing goods and services from suppliers worldwide. This practice can result in substantial cost savings, although product quality must be carefully monitored. India, Indonesia, and China are the world's top destinations for outsourcing. The Philippines, Singapore, Malaysia, Sri Lanka, Thailand, and Vietnam are also high on the list. South and Central American countries, such as Costa Rica, Mexico, Argentina, Chile, and Panama are also in the top 30.[20]

Global sourcing requires companies to adopt a new mindset; some must even reorganize their operations. Among other considerations, businesses sourcing from multiple multinational locations should streamline the purchase process and minimize price differences due to labor costs, tariffs, taxes, and currency fluctuations.

ASSESSMENT CHECK

3.1 Why is geographic segmentation important in the B2B market?

3.2 In what ways is the buyer–seller relationship important in B2B marketing?

3.3 What is global sourcing?

BUSINESS MARKET DEMAND

The previous section's discussion of business market characteristics demonstrated considerable differences between marketing techniques for consumer and business products. Demand characteristics also differ in these markets. In business markets, the major categories of demand include derived demand, volatile demand, joint demand, inelastic demand, and inventory adjustments. Figure 7.1 summarizes these different categories of business market demand.

derived demand
Demand for a resource that results from demand for the goods and services produced by that resource.

DERIVED DEMAND

Derived demand refers to the linkage between demand for a company's output and its purchases of resources, such as machinery, components, supplies, and raw materials. The demand for computer microprocessor chips is *derived* from the demand for personal computers. If more businesses and individuals buy new computers, the demand for chips increases; if fewer computers are sold, the demand for chips decreases. NewPage Corporation, an Ohio-based paper manufacturer, supplied paper for newspapers, magazines, and advertising brochures. But the advent of online news sources, the growth of online advertising, and rising prices for wood, pulp, and paper-making chemicals all combined to decrease the demand for paper. The company recently filed for bankruptcy, and its creditors have approved its reorganization plan.[21]

FIGURE 7.1
Categories of Business Market Demand

© Cengage Learning

Organizational buyers purchase two general categories of business products: capital items and expense items. Derived demand ultimately affects both. Capital items are long-lived business assets that must be depreciated over time. *Depreciation* is an accounting term that refers to charging a portion of a capital item's cost as a deduction against the company's annual revenue for purposes of determining its net income. Examples of capital items include major installations, such as new manufacturing plants, office buildings, and computer systems.

Expense items, in contrast, are items consumed within short time periods. Accountants charge the cost of such products against income in the year of purchase. Examples of expense items include the supplies necessary to operate the business, ranging from copy paper to machine lubricants.

VOLATILE DEMAND

Derived demand creates volatility in business market demand. Assume the sales volume for a gasoline retailer is increasing at an annual rate of 5 percent. Now suppose the demand for this gasoline brand slows to a 3 percent annual increase. This slowdown might persuade the firm to keep its current gasoline pumps and replace them only when market conditions improve. In this way, even modest shifts in consumer demand for a gasoline brand would greatly affect the pump manufacturer.

JOINT DEMAND

Another important influence on business market demand is **joint demand**, which results when the demand for one business product is related to the demand for another business product used in combination with the first item. Both lumber and concrete are required to build most homes. If the lumber supply falls, the drop in housing construction will most likely affect the demand for concrete. Another example is the joint demand for electrical power and large turbine engines. If consumers decide to conserve power, demand for new power plants drops, as does the demand for components and replacement parts for turbines.

joint demand Demand for a product that depends on the demand for another product used in combination with it.

INELASTIC DEMAND

Inelastic demand means that demand throughout an industry will not change significantly due to a price change. If the price of lumber drops, a construction firm will not necessarily buy more lumber from its suppliers unless another factor—such as lowered mortgage interest rates—causes more consumers to purchase new homes.

inelastic demand Demand that, throughout an industry, will not change significantly due to a price change.

INVENTORY ADJUSTMENTS

Adjustments in inventory and inventory policies can also affect business demand. Assume manufacturers in a particular industry consider a 60-day supply of raw materials as the optimal inventory level. Now suppose economic conditions or other factors induce these firms to increase their inventories to a 90-day supply. The change will bombard the raw-materials supplier with new orders.

Furthermore, **just-in-time (JIT)** inventory policies seek to boost efficiency by cutting inventories to absolute minimum levels and by requiring vendors to deliver inputs as the production process needs them. JIT allows companies to better predict which supplies they will require and the timing for when they will need them, markedly reducing their costs for production and storage. Widespread implementation of JIT has had a substantial impact on organizations' purchasing behavior. Firms that practice JIT tend to order from relatively few suppliers. In some cases, JIT may lead to **sole sourcing** for some items—that is, buying a firm's entire stock of a product from just one supplier. Electronic data interchange (EDI) and quick-response inventory policies have produced similar results in the trade industries. The latest inventory trend, **JIT II**, leads suppliers to place representatives at the customer's facility to work as part of an integrated, on-site customer–supplier team. Suppliers plan and order in consultation with the customer. This streamlining of the inventory process improves control of the flow of goods.

just-in-time (JIT)/ JIT II Inventory practices that seek to boost efficiency by cutting inventories to absolute minimum levels. With JIT II, suppliers' representatives work at the customer's facility.

sole sourcing Purchasing a firm's entire stock of an item from just one vendor.

ASSESSMENT CHECK

4.1   How does derived demand create volatile demand?

4.2   Give an example of joint demand.

4.3   How might JIT II strengthen marketing relationships?

Although inventory adjustments are critical in manufacturing processes, they are equally vital to wholesalers and retailers. Limited Brands, which owns Victoria's Secret and Bath & Body Works, recently upgraded its technology infrastructure and distribution centers. With a large variety of products, Victoria's Secret and Bath & Body Works benefited from improved inventory management, which sped up the process of keeping popular items in stock and removing those that didn't sell.[22]

THE MAKE, BUY, OR LEASE DECISION

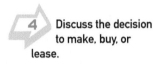

4 Discuss the decision to make, buy, or lease.

Before a company can decide what to buy, it should decide whether to buy at all. Organizational buyers must figure out the best way to acquire needed products. In fact, a firm considering the acquisition of a finished good, component part, or service has three basic options:

1. Make the good or provide the service in-house.

2. Purchase it from another organization.

3. Lease it from another organization.

If the company has the capability to do so, manufacturing the product itself may be the best route. It may save a great deal of money if its own manufacturing division does not incur costs for overhead that an outside vendor would otherwise charge.

On the other hand, most firms cannot make all the business goods they need. Often it would be too costly to maintain the necessary equipment, staff, and supplies. As a result, purchasing from an outside vendor is the most common choice. Xerox manufactures more than 50 different types of color printers to meet nearly any business need—from affordable color laser printers to high-performance ink-jet printers. Its wide array of products, coupled with its track record of a century of supplying businesses, has made it a leader in the B2B printer market.[23] Companies can also look outside their own plants for goods and services formerly produced in-house, a practice called *outsourcing*, which the next section will describe in more detail.

In some cases, however, a company may choose to lease inputs. This option spreads out costs compared with lump-sum costs for up-front purchases. The company pays for the use of equipment for a certain time period. A small business may lease a copier for a few years and make monthly payments. At the end of the lease term, the firm can buy the machine at a prearranged price or replace it with a different model under a new lease. This option can provide useful flexibility for a growing business, allowing it to easily upgrade as its needs change.

Companies can also lease sophisticated computer systems and heavy equipment. For example, some airlines prefer to lease airplanes rather than buy them outright because short-term leases allow them to adapt quickly to changes in passenger demand.

THE RISE OF OFFSHORING AND OUTSOURCING

Chances are, if you dial a call center for a firm like Dell, GE, American Express, or Nestlé, your call may be answered by someone in India. In recent years, a firestorm has been ignited by the movement of U.S. jobs to lower-cost overseas locations, a business practice referred to as offshoring. When Hugo Boss, the high-end clothing maker, announced it would close its Cleveland plant and lay off 400 workers, picketers including company employees, union organizers, and local community leaders braved freezing temperatures outside a local department store where Hugo Boss clothing was sold to draw attention to the loss of local jobs.[24] This relocation of business processes to a lower-cost location can involve production offshoring or services offshoring. China has emerged as the preferred destination for production offshoring, while India has emerged as the dominant player in services offshoring.

Some U.S.-based firms want to remain closer to home but take advantage of the benefits of locating some of their operations overseas. Mexico and Canada are attractive locations for these nearshoring operations. In today's highly competitive marketplace, firms look outside the United

offshoring Movement of high-wage jobs from one country to lower-cost overseas locations.

nearshoring Moving jobs to vendors in countries close to the business's home country.

States to improve efficiency and cut costs on just about everything, including customer service, human resources, accounting, information technology, manufacturing, and distribution. Outsourcing, using outside vendors to produce goods and services formerly produced in-house, is a trend that continues to rise. Businesses outsource for several reasons: (1) they need to reduce costs to remain competitive, (2) they need to improve the quality and speed of software maintenance and development, and (3) outsourcing has begun to offer greater value than ever before.

Outsourcing allows firms to concentrate their resources on their core business. It also allows access to specialized talent or expertise that does not exist within the firm. The most frequently outsourced business functions include information technology (IT) and human resources, along with other white-collar service jobs, such as accounting, drug research, technical research and development (R&D), and film animation. Although most outsourcing is done by North America–based companies, the practice is rapidly becoming commonplace in Asia, Europe, and Central America.

China has led the way in offshore manufacturing, making two-thirds of the world's copiers, microwaves, DVD players, and shoes, and virtually all of the world's toys. The size of its manufacturing workforce in the Guangdong province is estimated to rival that of the entire United States. In recent years, however, China's very success and the resulting rise of an increasingly wealthy middle class have pushed up its labor and management costs and may have helped shift many companies to suppliers in Vietnam and India, where such costs are still low.[25]

Outsourcing can be a smart strategy if a company chooses a vendor that can provide high-quality products and perhaps at a lower cost than could be achieved by the company itself. This priority allows the outsourcer to focus on its core competencies. Successful outsourcing requires companies to carefully oversee contracts and manage relationships. Some vendors now provide performance guarantees to assure their customers they will receive high-quality services that meet their needs.

> **outsourcing** Using outside vendors to provide goods and services formerly produced in-house.

PROBLEMS WITH OFFSHORING AND OUTSOURCING

Offshoring and outsourcing are not without their downsides. Many companies discover their cost savings are less than vendors sometimes promise. Also, companies that sign multiyear contracts may find their savings drop after a year or two. When proprietary technology is an issue, outsourcing raises security concerns. Similarly, if companies are protective of customer data and relationships they may think twice about entrusting functions such as customer service to outside sources.

In some cases, outsourcing and offshoring can reduce a company's ability to respond quickly to the marketplace, or they can slow efforts in bringing new products to market. Suppliers that fail to deliver goods promptly or provide required services can adversely affect a company's reputation with its customers.

Outsourcing and offshoring are controversial topics with unions, especially in the auto industry, as the percentage of component parts made in-house has steadily dropped. These practices can create conflicts between nonunion outside workers and in-house union employees, who fear job loss. Management initiatives to outsource jobs can lead to strikes and plant shutdowns. Even if they do not lead to disruption in the workplace, outsourcing and offshoring can have a negative impact on employee morale and loyalty.

 ASSESSMENT CHECK

5.1 Identify two potential benefits of outsourcing.

5.2 Identify two potential problems with outsourcing.

THE BUSINESS BUYING PROCESS

Suppose that MyMap Inc., a hypothetical manufacturer of GPS devices for automakers, decides to upgrade its manufacturing facility with $5 million in new automated assembly equipment. Before approaching equipment suppliers, the company must analyze its needs, determine goals the project should accomplish, develop technical specifications for the equipment, and set a budget. Once it receives vendors' proposals, it must evaluate them and select the best one. But what does *best* mean in this context? The lowest price or the best warranty and service contract? Who in the company is responsible for such decisions?

Describe the major influences on business buying behavior.

The business buying process is more complex than the consumer decision process. Business buying takes place within a formal organization's budget, cost, and profit considerations. Furthermore, B2B and institutional buying decisions usually involve many people with complex interactions among individuals and organizational goals. To understand organizational buying behavior, business marketers require knowledge of influences on the purchase decision process, the stages in the organizational buying model, types of business buying situations, and techniques for purchase decision analysis.

INFLUENCES ON PURCHASE DECISIONS

B2B buying decisions react to various influences, some external to the firm and others related to internal structure and personnel. In addition to product-specific factors like purchase price, installation, operating and maintenance costs, and vendor service, companies must consider broader environmental, organizational, and interpersonal influences.

Environmental Factors

Environmental conditions, such as economic, political, regulatory, competitive, and technological considerations, influence business buying decisions. MyMap may wish to defer purchases of the new equipment in times of slowing economic activity. During a recession, sales to auto companies might drop because households hesitate to spend money on a new car. The company would look at the derived demand for its products, possible changes in its sources of materials, employment trends, and similar factors before committing to such a large capital expenditure.

Environmental factors can also include natural disasters, such as the devastating earthquake and tsunami that struck Japan. Among the many industries affected was car manufacturing. The Toyota Prius is made only in Japan and was out of stock for several months, along with other models like the Camry. More recently, however, almost all the Japanese auto plants are back on line, some even ahead of schedule.[26]

Political, regulatory, and competitive factors also come into play in influencing purchase decisions. Passage of a privacy law that restricted GPS tracking would affect demand, as would competition from smartphones and other devices containing map features. Finally, technology plays a role in purchase decisions. When GPS systems were first introduced, many customers bought separate units to install in their cars. But as more new cars come factory-equipped with the units, the market for standalone boxes naturally decreases.

Organizational Factors

Successful business-to-business marketers understand their customers' organizational structures, policies, and purchasing systems. A company with a centralized procurement function operates differently from one that delegates purchasing decisions to divisional or geographic units. Trying to sell to the local store when head office merchandisers make all the decisions would clearly waste salespeople's time. Buying behavior also differs among firms. For example, centralized buying tends to emphasize long-term relationships, whereas decentralized buying focuses more on short-term results. Personal selling skills and user preferences carry more weight in decentralized purchasing situations than in centralized buying.

How many suppliers should a company patronize? Because purchasing operations spend more than half of each dollar their companies earn, consolidating vendor relationships can lead to large cost savings. However, a fine line separates maximizing buying power from relying too heavily on a few suppliers. Many companies engage in **multiple sourcing**—purchasing from several vendors. Spreading orders ensures against shortages if one vendor cannot deliver

Environmental factors include natural disasters, such as the earthquake that struck Japan, temporarily shutting down many industries, including car manufacturing. Most auto factories in the country are now back online, some ahead of schedule.

© Sam Yeh/AFP/Getty Images

on schedule. However, dealing with many sellers can be counterproductive and take too much time. Each company must set its own criteria for this decision.

multiple sourcing
Purchasing from several vendors.

Interpersonal Influences

Many people may influence B2B purchases, and considerable time may be spent obtaining the input and approval of various organization members. Both group and individual forces are at work here. When committees handle buying, they must spend time to gain majority or unanimous approval. Also, each individual buyer brings to the decision process individual preferences, experiences, and biases. See the "Career Readiness" feature for some tips on negotiating with these individual buyers.

Business marketers should know who in an organization will influence buying decisions for their products and should know each of their priorities. To choose a supplier for an industrial press, for example, a purchasing manager and representatives of the company's production, engineering, and quality control departments may be involved in deciding on a supplier. Each of these principals may have a different point of view that the vendor's marketers must understand.

To effectively address the concerns of all people involved in the buying decision, sales personnel must be well versed in the technical features of their products. They must also interact well with employees of the various departments involved in the purchase decision. Sales representatives for medical products—traditionally called "detailers"—frequently visit hospitals and doctors' offices to discuss the advantages of their products and leave samples with clinical staff.

> **"BRIEFLY SPEAKING"**
>
> "Think like a customer."
>
> —Paul Gillin
> *Author of* The New Influencers

The Role of Merchandisers and Category Advisors

Many large organizations attempt to make their purchases through systematic procedures employing professional buyers. In the trade industries, these buyers, often referred to as merchandisers, secure needed products at the best possible prices. Nordstrom has buyers for shoes and clothing that will ultimately be sold to consumers. Ford has buyers for components that will be incorporated

merchandisers Trade sector buyers who secure needed products at the best possible prices.

CAREER READINESS

How to Negotiate with Customers

In a business situation, there will be occasions when you'll need to rely on your negotiating skills to interact with customers. Here are some tried-and-true tips.

1. Do your homework first. Before you begin a negotiation, you should already have a good general idea what the customer's needs and wants are, and what other options they have for meeting these.

2. Listen. Now it pays to be a bit of a detective and simply listen while the other party tells you what you need to know in order to close the deal.

3. Read body language. Don't overlook the importance of what people are telling you with their gestures, position, and eye contact.

4. Agree in advance about what you are negotiating. Don't assume it's price. Customers may want to negotiate a better deal on service, an earlier delivery date, more add-on features, replacement parts, and the like.

5. Believe in the value of what you're selling.

6. Avoid the word "between." If you propose a range, you give the other party the ability to choose the lower price or later delivery date, giving up ground when you don't need to.

7. Don't commit anything to writing until the negotiation is over.

Sources: Ed Brodow, "Ten Tips for Negotiating in 2012," *Brodow.com*, accessed November 15, 2012, www.brodow.com; Mark Hunter, "6 Sales Negotiation Tips You MUST Know," *TheSalesHunter.com*, accessed November 15, 2012, http://thesaleshunter.com; Mike Hofman, "5 Things You Should Never Say While Negotiating," *Inc.*, accessed November 15, 2012, www.inc.com.

systems integration
Centralization of the procurement function within an internal division or as a service of an external supplier.

category advisor (category captain)
Trade industry vendor who develops a comprehensive procurement plan for a retail buyer.

into its cars and trucks. A firm's purchasing or merchandising unit devotes all of its time and effort in determining needs, locating and evaluating alternative suppliers, and making purchase decisions.

Purchase decisions for capital items vary significantly from those for expense items. Firms often buy expense items routinely with little delay. Capital items, however, involve major fund commitments and usually undergo considerable review.

One way a firm may attempt to streamline the buying process is through systems integration, or centralization of the procurement function. One company may designate a lead division to handle all purchasing. Another firm may choose to designate a major supplier as the systems integrator. This vendor then assumes responsibility for dealing with all of the suppliers for a project and for presenting the entire package to the buyer. In trade industries, this vendor is sometimes called a category advisor or category captain.

A business marketer may set up a sales organization to serve national accounts that deal solely with buyers at corporate headquarters. A separate field sales organization may serve buyers at regional production facilities.

Corporate buyers often use the Internet to identify sources of supplies. They view online catalogs and websites to compare vendors' offerings and obtain product information. Some use Internet exchanges to extend their supplier networks.

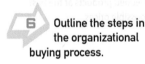

ASSESSMENT CHECK

6.1 Identify the three major factors that influence purchase decisions.

6.2 What are the advantages and disadvantages of multiple sourcing?

MODEL OF THE ORGANIZATIONAL BUYING PROCESS

6 Outline the steps in the organizational buying process.

An organizational buying situation takes place through a sequence of activities. Figure 7.2 illustrates an eight-stage model of an organizational buying process. Although not every buying situation requires all these steps, this figure provides a good overview of the whole process.

Stage 1: Anticipate or Recognize a Problem/Need/Opportunity and a General Solution

Both consumer and business purchase decisions begin when the recognition of problems, needs, or opportunities triggers the buying process. Perhaps a firm's computer system has become outdated or an account representative demonstrates a new service that could improve the company's performance. Companies may decide to hire an outside marketing specialist when their sales stagnate.

The problem may be as simple as needing to provide a good cup of coffee to a firm's employees. The founders of Vermont-based Keurig Incorporated, which supplies about 2.5 million individually brewed cups of coffee to U.S. homes and offices each day, started by asking themselves, "Why do we brew coffee a pot at a time when we drink it a cup at a time?"[27]

Stage 2: Determine the Characteristics and Quantity of a Needed Good or Service

The coffee problem described in stage 1 translated into a service opportunity for Keurig. The small firm was able to offer a coffee system that would brew one perfect cup of coffee at a time, according

FIGURE 7.2
Stages in the B2B Buying Process

Source: Based on Michael D. Hutt and Thomas W. Speh, *Business Marketing Management: B2B*, 11th ed. (Mason, OH: South-Western, 2013).

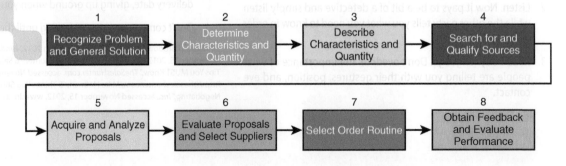

to the preferences of each employee. After finding success in the offices of many accounting, law, and medical practices, the company developed a single-cup brewer for home use. This model has a unique full-color touch screen that allows coffee lovers to readily customize each cup's temperature and strength. Recently, Keurig unveiled its Vue V1200 commercial brewer, intended for office use. Along with a touch screen and strength selection, the Vue V1200 also has radio frequency identification technology (RFID), which further ensures the quality of the final brew.[28]

Stage 3: Describe Characteristics and the Quantity of a Needed Good or Service

After determining the characteristics and quantity of needed products, B2B buyers must translate these ideas into detailed specifications. Customers told Keurig they wanted a foolproof, individual coffee maker. The Keurig system supplies a plastic K-Cup® or partially recyclable Vue pack™ individual portion pack, containing ground coffee that the coffee lover simply places in the proper coffee maker—no measuring of water or coffee is required. Out comes the perfect cup of coffee. Firms could easily base the quantity requirements of the Keurig system on the number of coffee-drinking employees they have or the amount of space they occupy.

Stage 4: Search for and Qualify Potential Sources

Both consumers and businesses search for good suppliers of desired products. The choice of a supplier may be relatively straightforward—because there was no other machine like it, its early adopters had no trouble selecting the Keurig coffee system. Other searches may involve more complex decision making. A company that wants to buy a group life or health insurance policy, for example, must weigh the varying provisions and programs of many different vendors.

Stage 5: Acquire and Analyze Proposals

The next step is to acquire and analyze suppliers' proposals, often submitted in writing. If the buyer is a government or public agency, this stage of the purchase process may involve competitive bidding. During this process, each marketer must develop its bid, including a price that will satisfy the criteria determined by the customer's problem, need, or opportunity. While competitive bidding is less common in the business sector, a company may follow the practice to purchase nonstandard materials, complex products, or products made to its own specifications.

Stage 6: Evaluate Proposals and Select Suppliers

Next in the buying process, buyers must compare vendors' proposals and choose the one that seems best suited to their needs. Proposals for sophisticated equipment, such as a large computer networking system, can include considerable differences among product offerings, and the final choice may involve trade-offs.

Price is not the only criterion for the selection of a vendor. Relationship factors such as communication and trust may also be important to the buyer. Other issues include reliability, delivery record, time from order to delivery, quality, and order accuracy. These are particularly important in the package delivery business. UPS recently announced that it is equipping its drivers worldwide with a new hand-held computer intended to speed uploading of package-tracking information and hence delivery to customers. This mobile device, called the Delivery Information Acquisition Device or DIAD V, is half the size and weight of the previous generation of package trackers. It also has a color camera for proof of delivery, is sturdier and can store more information. The DIAD V is the first to use Qualcomm's Gobi Radio Technology, which allows the device to switch instantly to another cellular carrier if the signal is lost. Dave Barnes, the chief information

The founders of Keurig Incorporated asked themselves, "Why do we brew coffee a pot at a time when we drink it a cup at a time?"

AP Photo/Kathy Willens

officer at UPS, says, "This computer accelerates the transfer of customer tracking data and makes it possible for UPS customers to track almost 16 million deliveries worldwide each day."[29]

Stage 7: Select an Order Routine

Once a supplier has been chosen, buyer and vendor must work out the best way to process future purchases. Ordering routines can vary considerably. Most orders will, however, include product descriptions, quantities, prices, delivery terms, and payment terms. Today, companies have a variety of options for submitting orders: written documents, phone calls, faxes, or electronic data interchange (EDI).

Stage 8: Obtain Feedback and Evaluate Performance

At the final stage, buyers measure vendors' performances. Sometimes this judgment may involve a formal evaluation of each supplier's product quality, delivery performance, prices, technical knowledge, and overall responsiveness to customer needs. At other times, vendors may be measured according to whether they have lowered the customer's costs or reduced its employees' workloads. In general, bigger firms are more likely to use formal evaluation procedures, while smaller companies lean toward informal evaluations. Regardless of the method used, buyers should tell vendors how they will be evaluated.

Sometimes firms rely on independent organizations to gather quality feedback and summarize results. J.D. Power and Associates conducts research and provides information to a variety of firms so they can improve the quality of their goods and services.

⊕ ASSESSMENT CHECK

7.1   Why does the organizational buying process contain more steps than the consumer buying process?

7.2   List the steps in the organizational buying process.

CLASSIFYING BUSINESS BUYING SITUATIONS

7 Classify organizational buying situations.

As discussed earlier, business buying behavior responds to many purchasing influences such as environmental, organizational, and interpersonal factors. This buying behavior also involves the degree of effort the purchase decision demands and the levels within the organization where it is made. Like consumer behavior, marketers can classify B2B buying situations into three general categories, ranging from least to most complex: (1) straight rebuying, (2) modified rebuying, and (3) new-task buying. Business buying situations may also involve reciprocity. The following sections look at each type of purchase.

Straight Rebuying

straight rebuy
Recurring purchase decision in which a customer repurchases a good or service that has performed satisfactorily in the past.

The simplest buying situation is a **straight rebuy**—a recurring purchase decision in which a customer reorders a product that has satisfied its needs in the past. The buyer already likes the product and terms of sale, so the purchase requires no new information. The buyer sees little reason to assess competing options and so follows a routine repurchase format. A straight rebuy is the business market equivalent of routinized response behavior in the consumer market. Purchases of low-cost items such as paper clips and pencils for an office are typical examples of straight rebuys. Reorders of coffee from Keurig would also be straight rebuys. Marketers who maintain good relationships with customers by providing high-quality products, superior service, and prompt delivery can go a long way toward ensuring straight rebuys.

Modified Rebuying

modified rebuy
Situation in which a purchaser is willing to reevaluate available options for repurchasing a good or service.

In a **modified rebuy**, a purchaser is willing to reevaluate available options. Buyers may see some advantage in looking at alternative offerings within their established purchasing guidelines. They might take this step if their current supplier has let a rebuy situation deteriorate because of poor service or delivery performance. Price, quality, and innovation differences can also provoke modified rebuys. Modified rebuys resemble limited problem solving in consumer markets.

B2B marketers want to induce current customers to make straight rebuys by responding to all of their needs. Competitors, on the other hand, try to lure those buyers away by raising issues that will persuade them to reconsider their decisions.

New-Task Buying

The most complex category of business buying is new-task buying—first-time or unique purchase situations that require considerable effort by the decision makers. For almost a decade and a half, the once-neglected Rolling Mill Hill site in Nashville, Tennessee, has been undergoing a dramatic renewal. Six historic former trolley barns, 80,000 square feet of space, have been transformed into offices and shops. Nearby, new, subsidized housing is being built from scratch. Former hospital buildings on the site have been turned into more housing. Plans for a hotel and other mixed-use buildings are under discussion. One of the companies involved in this transformation, Littlejohn Engineering Associates (LEA), designed the water, sewer, and storm water systems, as well as undertaking street design and other civil engineering, infrastructure, and inspection services. This one-time purchase of services required LEA to work closely with Nashville's Metropolitan Development & Housing Agency as well as private developers in rehabilitating a neglected site in the heart of the city into a vibrant, mixed-use community.[30] The consumer market equivalent of new-task buying is extended problem solving.

A new-task buy often requires a purchaser to carefully consider alternative offerings and vendors. A company entering a new field must seek suppliers of component parts that it has never before purchased. This new-task buying would require several stages, each yielding a decision of some sort. These decisions would include developing product requirements, searching out potential suppliers, and evaluating proposals. Information requirements and decision makers can complete the entire buying process, or they may change from stage to stage.

new-task buying
First-time or unique purchase situation that requires considerable effort by decision makers.

Reciprocity

Reciprocity—a practice of buying from suppliers who are also customers—is a controversial practice in a number of procurement situations. An office equipment manufacturer may favor a particular supplier of component parts if the supplier has recently made a major purchase of the manufacturer's products. Reciprocal arrangements traditionally have been common in industries featuring homogeneous products with similar prices, such as the chemical, paint, petroleum, rubber, and steel industries.

Reciprocity suggests close links among participants in the organizational marketplace. It can add to the complexity of B2B buying behavior for new suppliers trying to compete with preferred vendors. Although buyers and sellers enter into reciprocal agreements in the United States, both the Department of Justice and the Federal Trade Commission view them as attempts to reduce competition. Outside the United States, however, governments may take more favorable views of reciprocity. In Japan, close ties between suppliers and customers are common.

reciprocity Buying from suppliers who are also customers.

ANALYSIS TOOLS

Two tools that help professional buyers improve purchase decisions are value analysis and vendor analysis. Value analysis examines each component of a purchase in an attempt to either delete the item or replace it with a more cost-effective substitute. Airplane designers have long recognized the need to make planes as light as possible. Value analysis supports using composite materials like Kevlar in airplane construction because it weighs less than the metals it replaces. The resulting fuel savings are significant for buyers in this marketplace.

Vendor analysis carries out an ongoing evaluation of a supplier's performance in categories like price, EDI capability, back orders, delivery times, liability insurance, and attention to special requests. In some cases, vendor analysis is a formal process. Some buyers use a checklist to assess a vendor's performance. A checklist quickly highlights vendors and potential vendors that do not satisfy the purchaser's buying requirements.

value analysis
Systematic study of the components of a purchase to determine the most cost-effective approach.

vendor analysis
Assessment of supplier performance in categories such as price, back orders, timely delivery, and attention to special requests.

ASSESSMENT CHECK

7.3   What are the four classifications of business buying situations?

7.4   Differentiate between value analysis and vendor analysis.

THE BUYING CENTER CONCEPT

8 **Explain the buying center concept.**

buying center
Participants in an organizational buying decision.

The buying center concept provides a model for understanding B2B buying behavior. A company's **buying center** encompasses everyone involved in any aspect of its buying activity. A buying center may include the architect who designs a new research laboratory, the scientist who works in the facility, the purchasing manager who screens contractor proposals, the chief executive officer who makes the final decision, and the vice president of research who signs the formal contracts for the project. Buying center participants in any purchase seek to satisfy personal needs, such as participation or status, as well as organizational needs. A buying center is not part of a firm's formal organizational structure. It is an informal group whose composition and size vary among purchase situations and firms.

BUYING CENTER ROLES

user Individual or group that actually uses a business good or service.

Buying center participants play different roles in the purchasing decision process. **Users** are the people who will actually use the good or service. Their influence on the purchase decision may range from negligible to extremely important. Users sometimes initiate purchase actions by requesting products, and they may also help develop product specifications. Users often influence the purchase of office equipment.

gatekeeper Person who controls the information that all buying center members will review.

Gatekeepers control the information that all buying center members will review. They may exert this control by distributing printed product data or advertisements or by deciding which salespeople may speak to which individuals in the buying center. A purchasing agent might allow some salespeople to see the engineers responsible for developing specifications but deny others the same privilege. The office manager for a medical group may decide whether to accept and pass along sales literature from a pharmaceutical detailer or sales representative.

influencer Typically, technical staff who affect the buying decision by supplying information to guide evaluation of alternatives or by setting buying specifications.

Influencers affect the buying decision by supplying information to guide evaluation of alternatives or by setting buying specifications. Influencers typically are technical staff like engineers or quality-control specialists. Sometimes a buying organization hires outside consultants, such as architects, who influence its buying decisions.

decider Person who chooses a good or service, although another person may have the formal authority to complete the sale.

The **decider** chooses a good or service, although another person may have the formal authority to do so. The identity of the decider is the most difficult role for salespeople to pinpoint. A firm's buyer may have the formal authority to buy, but the firm's chief executive officer may actually make the buying decision. Alternatively, a decider might be a design engineer who develops specifications that only one vendor can meet.

buyer Person who has the formal authority to select a supplier and to implement the procedures for securing a good or service.

The **buyer** has the formal authority to select a supplier and to implement the procedures for securing the good or service. The buyer often surrenders this power to more influential members of the organization, though. The purchasing manager often fills the buyer's role and executes the details associated with a purchase order.

B2B marketers face the task of determining the specific role and the relative decision-making influence of each buying center participant. Salespeople can then tailor their presentations and information to the precise role an individual plays at each step of the purchase process. Business marketers have found their initial—and in many cases, most extensive—contacts with a firm's purchasing department often fail to reach the buying center participants who have the greatest influence, because these people may not work in that department at all.

Consider the selection of meeting and convention sites for trade or professional associations. The primary decision maker could be an association board or an executive committee, usually with input from the executive director or a meeting planner; these individuals might choose meeting locations, sometimes with input from members; finally, the association's annual meeting committee or program committee might make the meeting location selection. Because officers change periodically, centers of control may change frequently. As a result, destination marketers and hotel operators must constantly assess how an association makes its decisions on conference locations.

INTERNATIONAL BUYING CENTERS

Two distinct characteristics differentiate international buying centers from domestic ones. First, marketers may have trouble identifying members of foreign buying centers because of cultural differences in decision-making methods. Second, a buying center in a foreign company often includes more participants than U.S. companies involve. International buying centers employ from 1 to 50 people, with 15 to 20 participants commonplace in the United States. Global B2B marketers must recognize and accommodate this greater diversity of decision makers.

International buying centers can change in response to political and economic trends. Many European firms once maintained separate facilities in each European nation to avoid tariffs and customs delays. When the European Union lowered trade barriers between member nations, however, many companies closed distant branches and consolidated their buying centers. The Netherlands has been one of the beneficiaries of this trend.

ASSESSMENT CHECK

8.1 Identify the five roles of people in a buying center decision.

8.2 What are some of the problems that U.S. marketers face in dealing with international buying centers?

DEVELOPING EFFECTIVE BUSINESS-TO-BUSINESS MARKETING STRATEGIES

A business marketer must develop a marketing strategy based on a particular organization's buying behavior and on the buying situation. Clearly, many variables affect organizational purchasing decisions. This section examines three market segments whose decisions present unique challenges to B2B marketers: units of government, institutions, and international markets. Finally, it summarizes key differences between consumer and business marketing strategies.

Discuss the challenges of, and strategies for, marketing to government, institutional, and international buyers.

CHALLENGES OF GOVERNMENT MARKETS

Government agencies—federal, state, and local—together make up the largest customer group in the United States. Almost 90,000 government units buy a wide variety of products, including office supplies, furniture, concrete, vehicles, grease, military aircraft, fuel, and lumber, to name just a few.[31]

To compete effectively, business marketers must understand the unique challenges of selling to government units. One challenge results because government purchases typically involve dozens of interested parties who specify, evaluate, or use the purchased goods and services. These parties may or may not work within the government agency that officially handles a purchase.

Government purchases are also influenced by social goals, such as "Buy American" provisions and minority subcontracting programs. Government entities like the U.S. Postal Service strive to maintain diversity in their suppliers by making a special effort to purchase goods and services from small firms and companies owned by minorities and women. The Postal Service has developed a Supplier Diversity Corporate Plan to show its commitment to ensuring "a continued focus on—and improvement in—our relationships with small, minority-owned, and women-owned businesses."[32] The government also relies on its prime suppliers to subcontract to minority businesses.

Contractual guidelines create another important influence in selling to government markets. The government buys products under two basic types of contracts: fixed-price contracts, in which seller and buyer agree to a set price before finalizing the contract, and cost-reimbursement contracts, in which the government pays the vendor for allowable costs, including profits, incurred during performance of the contract. Each type of contract has advantages and disadvantages for B2B marketers. Although the fixed-price contract offers more profit potential than the alternative, it also carries greater risks from unforeseen expenses, price hikes, and changing political and economic conditions.

Government Purchasing Procedures

Many U.S. government purchases go through the General Services Administration (GSA), a central management agency involved in areas like procurement, property management, and information resources management. The GSA buys goods and services for its own use and for use by other government agencies. In its role as, essentially, the federal government's business manager, it purchases billions of dollars' worth of products. The Defense Logistics Agency (DLA) serves the same function for the Department of Defense.

By law, most federal purchases must be awarded on the basis of bids, or written sales proposals, from vendors. As part of this process, government buyers develop specifications—detailed descriptions of needed items—for prospective bidders. U.S. government purchases must comply with the Federal Acquisition Regulation (FAR), an approximately 30,000-page set of standards originally designed to cut red tape in government purchasing. FAR standards have been further complicated by numerous exceptions issued by various government agencies. Because they provide services to various federal government agencies like the Department of Energy, Environmental Protection Agency, and Department of Defense, large environmental engineering firms, such as MACTEC, Tetra Tech, and Weston Solutions, typically have procurement and contract specialists on staff. These specialists stay current with FAR standards and conduct internal quality-assurance and quality-control programs to make sure the standards are followed by their companies.

State and local government purchasing procedures resemble federal procedures. Most states and many large cities have created buying offices similar to the GSA. Detailed specifications and open bidding are common at this level as well. Many state purchasing regulations give preference to in-state bidders.

Government spending patterns may differ from those in private industry. Because the federal government's fiscal year runs from October 1 through September 30, many agencies spend much of their procurement budgets in the fourth quarter, from July 1 to September 30. They hoard their funds to cover unexpected expenditures, and if they encounter no such problems, they find themselves with money to spend in late summer. Companies understand this system and keep their eyes on government bulletins so that they can bid on the listed agency purchases, which often involve large amounts of money.

Online with the Federal Government

Like their colleagues in the private sector, government procurement professionals are streamlining purchasing procedures with new technology. Rather than paging through piles of paper catalogs and submitting typed purchase orders, government buyers now prefer online catalogs that help them compare competing product offerings. In fact, vendors find doing business with the government almost impossible unless they embrace electronic commerce.

Vendors can sell products to the federal government through three electronic options. Websites provide a convenient method of exchanging information for both parties. Government buyers locate and order products, paying with a federally issued credit card, and the vendors deliver the items within about a week. Another route is through government-sponsored electronic ordering systems, which help standardize the buying process. GSA Advantage allows federal employees to order more than 11 million goods and services directly over the Internet at the preferred government price and logs about 2,500 orders every day. "We were already operational while Amazon was still beta-testing its site," recalls the e-business director of GSA's Federal Supply Service.[33] The Phoenix Opportunity System, set up by the Department of Commerce, provides a similar service for minority-owned companies. The U.S. Treasury is increasing electronic check payments to speed up the settling of vendor invoices.

Despite these advances, many government agencies remain less sophisticated than private-sector businesses. The Pentagon, for instance, is still coping with procurement procedures that were developed over the past 50 years. However, it is introducing a streamlined approach to defense contracting that reduces the time necessary to develop specifications and select suppliers.

CHALLENGES OF INSTITUTIONAL MARKETS

Institutions constitute another important market. Institutional buyers include a wide variety of organizations, such as schools, hospitals, libraries, foundations, clinics, churches, and not-for-profit agencies.

Institutional markets are characterized by widely diverse buying practices. Some institutional purchasers behave like government purchasers because laws and political considerations determine their buying procedures. Many of these institutions, such as schools, may even be managed by government units.

Buying practices can differ between institutions of the same type. In a small hospital, the chief dietitian may approve all food purchases, while in a larger medical facility, food purchases may go through a committee consisting of the dietitian and a business manager, purchasing agent, and cook.

GSA Advantage is a program that allows federal employees to purchase goods and services directly via the Web at preferred government prices.

Other hospitals may belong to buying groups, perhaps health maintenance organizations or local hospital cooperatives. Still others may contract with outside firms to prepare and serve all meals.

Within a single institution, multiple buying influences may affect decisions. Many institutions, staffed by professionals such as physicians, nurses, researchers, and instructors, may also employ purchasing managers or even entire purchasing departments. Conflicts may arise among these decision makers. Professional employees may prefer to make their own purchase decisions and resent giving up control to the purchasing staff. This conflict can force a business marketer to cultivate both professionals and purchasers. A detailer for a pharmaceutical firm must convince physicians of the value to patients of a certain drug while simultaneously convincing the hospital's purchasing department that the firm offers competitive prices, good delivery schedules, and prompt service.

Group purchasing is an important factor in institutional markets because many organizations join cooperative associations to pool purchases for quantity discounts. Universities may join the Education and Institutional Purchasing Cooperative; hospitals may belong to regional associations; and chains of profit-oriented hospitals like HCA Healthcare can also negotiate quantity discounts. Central headquarters staff usually handles purchasing for all members of such a chain.

Diverse practices in institutional markets pose special challenges for B2B marketers. They must maintain flexibility in developing strategies for dealing with a range of customers, from large cooperative associations and chains to midsize purchasing departments and institutions to individuals. Buying centers can work with varying members, priorities, and levels of expertise. Discounts and effective distribution functions play important roles in obtaining—and keeping—institutions as customers.

CHALLENGES OF INTERNATIONAL MARKETS

To sell successfully in international markets, business marketers must consider buyers' attitudes and cultural patterns within areas where they operate. In Asian markets, a firm must maintain a local presence to sell products. Personal relationships are also important to business deals in

Buying practices can differ among institutions of the same type. In a small medical practice, a physician, in collaboration with office staff, approves purchases, while in a larger facility, such as a hospital, purchases may go through a committee or a separate purchasing group.

sjlocke/iStockphoto

Asia. Companies that want to expand globally often need to establish joint ventures with local partners. International marketers must also be poised to respond to shifts in cultural values.

Local industries, economic conditions, geographic characteristics, and legal restrictions must also be considered in international marketing. Many local industries in Spain specialize in food and wine; therefore, a maker of forklift trucks might market smaller vehicles to Spanish companies than to German firms, which require bigger, heavier trucks to serve the needs of that nation's large automobile industry.

remanufacturing
Efforts to restore older products to like-new condition.

Remanufacturing—efforts to restore worn-out products to like-new condition—can be an important marketing strategy in a nation that cannot afford to buy new products. Developing countries often purchase remanufactured factory machinery, which costs 35 to 60 percent less than new equipment.

Foreign governments represent another important business market. In many countries, government or state-owned companies dominate certain industries, such as construction and other infrastructure sales. Additional examples include airport and highway construction, telephone system equipment, and computer networking equipment. Sales to a foreign government can involve an array of regulations. Many governments, like that of the United States, limit foreign participation in their defense programs. Joint ventures and countertrade are common, as are local content laws, which mandate domestic production of a certain percentage of a business product's components.

⊕ ASSESSMENT CHECK

9.1   What are some influences on government purchases?

9.2   Why is group purchasing important in institutional purchases?

9.3   What special factors influence international buying decisions?

© iStockphoto.com/Ferran Traite Soler

STRATEGIC IMPLICATIONS OF MARKETING IN THE 21ST CENTURY

To develop marketing strategies for the B2B sector, marketers must first understand the buying practices that govern the segment they are targeting, whether it is the commercial market, trade industries, government, or institutions. Similarly, when selling to a specific organization, strategies must take into account the many factors that influence purchasing. B2B marketers must identify people who play the various roles in the buying decision and understand how these members interact with one another, other members of their own organizations, and outside vendors. Marketers must be careful to direct their marketing efforts to their organization, to broader environmental influences, and to individuals who operate within the constraints of the firm's buying center.

Get online now for additional learning tools to help you master your marketing knowledge—visit **WWW.CENGAGEBRAIN.COM** today!

REVIEW OF CHAPTER OBJECTIVES

1 Explain each of the components of the business-to-business (B2B) market.

The B2B market is divided into four segments: the commercial market, trade industries, governments, and institutions. The commercial market consists of individuals and firms that acquire products to be used, directly or indirectly, to produce other goods and services. Trade industries are organizations, such as retailers and wholesalers, that purchase for resale to others. The primary purpose of government purchasing at federal, state, and local levels is to provide some form of public benefit. The fourth segment, institutions, includes a diverse array of organizations, such as hospitals, schools, museums, and not-for-profit agencies.

2 Describe the major approaches to segmenting business-to-business (B2B) markets.

Business markets can be segmented by (1) demographics, (2) customer type, (3) end-use application, and (4) purchasing situation. The North American Industry Classification System (NAICS), instituted after the passage of NAFTA, further classifies types of customers by the use of six-digit codes.

3 Identify the major characteristics of the business market and its demand.

The major characteristics of the business market are geographic concentration, size and number of buyers, purchase decision procedures, and buyer–seller relationships. The major categories of demand are derived demand, volatile demand, joint demand, inelastic demand, and inventory adjustments.

4 Discuss the decision to make, buy, or lease.

Before a company can decide what to buy, it must decide whether to buy at all. A firm has three options: (1) make the good or service in-house, (2) purchase it from another organization, or (3) lease it from another organization. Companies may outsource goods or services formerly produced in-house to other companies either within their own home country or to firms in other nations. The shift of high-wage jobs from the home country to lower-wage locations is known as *offshoring*. If a company moves production to a country close to its own borders, it uses a *nearshoring* strategy. Each option has its benefits and drawbacks, including cost and quality control.

5 Describe the major influences on business buying behavior.

B2B buying behavior tends to be more complex than individual consumer behavior. More people and time are involved, and buyers often seek several alternative supply sources. The systematic nature of organizational buying is reflected in the use of purchasing managers to direct such efforts. Major organizational purchases may require elaborate and lengthy decision-making processes involving many people. Purchase decisions typically depend on combinations of such factors as price, service, certainty of supply, and product efficiency.

6 Outline the steps in the organizational buying process.

The organizational buying process consists of eight general stages: (1) anticipate or recognize a problem/need/opportunity and a general solution, (2) determine characteristics and quantity of needed good or service, (3) describe characteristics and quantity of needed good or service, (4) search for and qualify potential sources, (5) acquire and analyze proposals, (6) evaluate proposals and select supplier(s), (7) select an order routine, and (8) obtain feedback and evaluate performance.

7 Classify organizational buying situations.

Organizational buying situations differ. A straight rebuy is a recurring purchase decision in which a customer stays with an item that has performed satisfactorily. In a modified rebuy, a purchaser is willing to reevaluate available options. New-task buying refers to first-time or unique purchase situations that require considerable effort on the part of the decision makers. Reciprocity involves buying from suppliers who are also customers.

8 Explain the buying center concept.

The buying center includes everyone who is involved in some fashion in an organizational buying action. There are five buying center roles: users, gatekeepers, influencers, deciders, and buyers.

Discuss the challenges of, and strategies for, marketing to government, institutional, and international buyers.

A government purchase typically involves dozens of interested parties. Social goals and programs influence government purchases. Many U.S. government purchases involve complex contractual guidelines and often require detailed specifications and a bidding process. Institutional markets are challenging because of their diverse buying influences and practices. Group purchasing is an important factor because many institutions join cooperative associations to get quantity discounts. An institutional marketer must be flexible enough to develop strategies for dealing with a range of customers. Discounts and effective distribution play an important role. An effective international business marketer must be aware of foreign attitudes and cultural patterns. Other important factors include economic conditions, geographic characteristics, legal restrictions, and local industries.

⊕ ASSESSMENT CHECK: ANSWERS

1.1 Define B2B marketing. Business-to-business, or B2B, marketing deals with organizational purchases of goods and services to support production of other products, to facilitate daily company operations, or for resale.

1.2 What is the commercial market? The commercial market consists of individuals and firms that acquire products to be used, directly or indirectly, to produce other goods and services.

2.1 What are the four major ways marketers segment business markets? Business markets can be segmented by (1) demographics, (2) customer type, (3) end-use application, and (4) purchasing situation.

2.2 What is the NAICS? The North American Industry Classification System (NAICS) is a unified system for Mexico, Canada, and the United States to classify B2B market segments and ease trade.

3.1 Why is geographic segmentation important in the B2B market? Certain industries locate in particular areas to be close to customers. Firms may choose to locate sales offices and distribution centers in these areas to provide more attentive service. For example, the Washington, DC, area is favored by companies that sell to the federal government.

3.2 In what ways is the buyer–seller relationship important in B2B marketing? Buyer–seller relationships often are more complex than consumer relationships, and they require superior communication among the organizations' personnel. Satisfying one major customer could mean millions of dollars to a firm.

3.3 What is global sourcing? Global sourcing involves contracting to purchase goods and services from suppliers worldwide.

4.1 How does derived demand create volatile demand? Business demand often is derived from consumer demand. Even modest shifts in consumer demand can produce disproportionate—and volatile—shifts in business demand.

4.2 Give an example of joint demand. Both lumber and concrete are required to build most homes. If the lumber supply falls, the drop in housing construction will most likely affect the demand for concrete.

4.3 How might JIT II strengthen marketing relationships? Under JIT II, suppliers place representatives at the customer's facility to work as part of an integrated, on-site customer–supplier team. Suppliers plan and take orders in consultation with the customer. This streamlining of the inventory process improves control of the flow of goods.

5.1 Identify two potential benefits of outsourcing. Outsourcing allows firms to concentrate their resources on their core business. It also allows access to specialized talent or expertise that does not exist within the firm.

5.2 Identify two potential problems with outsourcing. Many companies discover that their cost savings are less than vendors sometimes promise. Also, companies that sign multiyear contracts may find that their savings drop after a year or two.

6.1 Identify the three major factors that influence purchase decisions. In addition to product-specific factors such as purchase price, installation, operating and maintenance costs, and vendor service, companies must consider broader environmental, organizational, and interpersonal influences.

6.2 What are the advantages and disadvantages of multiple sourcing? Spreading orders ensures against shortages if one vendor cannot deliver on schedule. However, dealing with many sellers can be counterproductive and take too much time.

7.1 Why does the organizational buying process contain more steps than the consumer buying process? The additional steps arise because business purchasing introduces new complexities that do not affect consumers.

7.2 List the steps in the organizational buying process. The steps in organizational buying are (1) anticipate or recognize a problem/need/opportunity and a general solution, (2) determine characteristics and quantity of a needed good or service, (3) describe characteristics and quantity of needed good or service, (4) search for and qualify potential sources, (5) acquire and analyze proposals, (6) evaluate proposals and select supplier(s), (7) select an order routine, and (8) obtain feedback and evaluate performance.

7.3 What are the four classifications of business buying situations? The four classifications of business buying are (1) straight rebuying, (2) modified rebuying, (3) new-task buying, and (4) reciprocity.

7.4 Differentiate between value analysis and vendor analysis. Value analysis examines each component of a purchase in an attempt either to delete the item or replace it with a more cost-effective substitute. Vendor analysis carries out an ongoing evaluation of a supplier's performance in categories such as price, EDI capability, backorders, delivery times, liability insurance, and attention to special requests.

8.1 Identify the five roles of people in a buying center decision. There are five buying center roles: users (those who use the product), gatekeepers (those who control the flow of information), influencers (those who provide technical information or specifications), deciders (those who

actually choose the product), and buyers (those who have the formal authority to purchase).

8.2 What are some of the problems that U.S. marketers face in dealing with international buying centers? International buying centers pose several problems. First, there may be cultural differences in decision-making methods. Second, a buying center in a foreign company typically includes more participants than is common in the United States. Third, international buying centers can change in response to political and economic conditions.

9.1 What are some influences on government purchases? Social goals and programs often influence government purchases.

9.2 Why is group purchasing important in institutional purchases? Group purchasing is an important factor because many institutions join cooperative associations to get quantity discounts.

9.3 What special factors influence international buying decisions? An effective international business marketer must be aware of foreign attitudes and cultural patterns. Other important factors include economic conditions, geographic characteristics, legal restrictions, and local industries.

MARKETING TERMS YOU NEED TO KNOW

business-to-business (B2B) marketing **204**
commercial market **206**
trade industries **206**
resellers **206**
customer-based segmentation **210**
North American Industry Classification System (NAICS) **210**
end-use application segmentation **211**

customer relationship management (CRM) **211**
global sourcing **214**
derived demand **214**
joint demand **215**
inelastic demand **215**
just-in-time (JIT)/just-in-time II (JIT II) **215**
sole sourcing **215**
offshoring **216**

nearshoring **216**
outsourcing **217**
multiple sourcing **219**
merchandisers **219**
systems integration **220**
category advisor (category captain) **220**
straight rebuy **222**
modified rebuy **222**
new-task buying **223**

reciprocity **223**
value analysis **223**
vendor analysis **223**
buying center **224**
user **224**
gatekeeper **224**
influencer **224**
decider **224**
buyer **224**
remanufacturing **228**

ASSURANCE OF LEARNING REVIEW

1. Which is the largest segment of the business market? What role does the Internet play in the B2B market? What role do resellers play in the B2B market?

2. How is customer-based segmentation beneficial to B2B marketers? Describe segmentation by purchasing situation.

3. How do the sizes and numbers of buyers affect B2B marketers? Why are buyer–seller relationships so important in B2B marketing?

4. Give an example of each type of demand.

5. For what reasons might a firm choose an option other than making a good or service in-house? Why is outsourcing on the rise? How is offshoring different from outsourcing?

6. What are some of the environmental factors that may influence buying decisions? Identify organizational factors that may influence buying decisions. Describe the role of the professional buyer.

7. Why are there more steps in the organizational buying process than in the consumer buying process? Explain why feedback between buyers and sellers is important to the marketing relationship.

8. Give an example of a straight rebuy and a modified rebuy. Why is new-task buying more complex than the first two buying situations?

9. What buying center participant is a marketer likely to encounter first? In the buying center, who has the formal authority to make a purchase?

10. Describe some of the factors that characterize U.S. government purchases. Why are institutional markets particularly challenging?

PROJECTS AND TEAMWORK EXERCISES

1. As a team or individually, choose a commercial product—such as computer chips, flour for baking, paint, or equipment—and research and analyze its foreign-market potential. Report your findings to the class.

2. In pairs, select a business product in one of two categories—capital or expense—and determine how derived demand will affect the sales of the product. Create a chart showing your findings.

3. Imagine you and your teammates are buyers for a firm such as Olive Garden, Dick's Sporting Goods, Marriott, or another company you like. Map out a logical buying process for a new-task purchase for your organization.

4. Form a team to conduct a hypothetical team selling effort for the packaging of products manufactured by a food company such as Kraft or General Mills. Have each team member cover a certain concern such as package design, delivery, and payment schedules. Present your marketing effort to the class.

5. Conduct research into the U.S. government's purchasing process. Select a federal agency or department such as the Environmental Protection Agency, the National Aeronautics and Space Administration (NASA), or the Department of Health and Human Services. What types of purchases does the agency make? What is the range of contract amounts? Who are the typical suppliers? What type of process is involved in buying?

CRITICAL-THINKING EXERCISES

1. Imagine you are a wholesaler for poultry products such as chicken and eggs, which are produced by a cooperative of small farmers. Describe what steps you would take to build relationships with both the producers—farmers—and retailers such as supermarkets.

2. Describe an industry that might be segmented by geographic concentration. Then identify some of the types of firms that might be involved in that industry. Keep in mind that these companies might be involved in other industries as well.

3. Imagine you are in charge of making the decision to lease or buy a fleet of trucks for the moving company for which you work. What factors would influence your decision and why?

4. Do you think online selling to the federal government benefits marketers? What might be some of the drawbacks to this type of selling?

ETHICS EXERCISE

Suppose you work for a well-known local restaurant, and a friend of yours is an account representative for a supplier of restaurant equipment. You know the restaurant owner is considering upgrading some of the kitchen equipment. Although you have no purchasing authority, your friend has asked you to arrange a meeting with the restaurant owner. You have heard unflattering rumors about this supplier's customer service.

1. Would you arrange the meeting between your friend and your boss?

2. Would you mention the customer service rumors either to your friend or your boss?

3. Would you try to influence the purchase decision in either direction?

INTERNET EXERCISES

1. **Marketing to airlines.** Boeing and Airbus are the two major manufacturers of commercial aircraft. Visit the websites of both firms. After you review the websites, prepare a report that compares and contrasts the marketing strategies employed by both firms.

   www.boeing.com/commercial

   www.airbus.com

2. **Marketing to small businesses.** According to some experts, there are important differences between marketing to large businesses and marketing to small businesses. Go to the websites listed here and review the material. Prepare a summary you can use in a class discussion on the topic.

   www.gianfagnamarketing.com/blog/2010/11/03/landing-the-big-one-10-tips-for-selling-to-large-companies

   http://webbiquity.com/marketing-strategy/business-to-business-for-small-business

   http://smallbiztrends.com/2007/02/five-mistakes-when-selling-to-small-business-owners.html

3. **Selling to the federal government.** The General Services Administration (GSA) purchases billions of dollars worth of goods and services for various federal agencies. Visit the GSA's website to learn more about selling to the federal government. What products does the GSA purchase? Who may sell products to the federal government? What are the requirements to become a federal government vendor?

   www.gsa.gov/portal/category/100000

Note: Internet Web addresses change frequently. If you don't find the exact site listed, you may need to access the organization's home page and search from there or use a search engine such as Google or Bing.

CASE 7.1
W.W. Grainger Goes Mobile

W.W. Grainger has such a good handle on who its 2 million business customers are that it recently redesigned its website to cater to two specific types: buyers in the field, using any of Grainger's 900,000 maintenance and repair products, and purchasing agents, placing orders for Grainger products from corporate headquarters. Customers who need a product right now in the field can enter their ZIP code to find out whether one of Grainger's 400 U.S. branches is nearby and has the required item. (The company has 600 branches worldwide.) If so, they can pick it up, often the same day. Purchasing agents take a longer view of their inventory, and they like Grainger's ability to recognize them online, tell them what they've ordered in the past, and help them check the status of their current orders.

Both types of customers benefit from Grainger's mobile apps. Field workers can request purchasing approval for needed items, while purchasing agents can approve the requests even if they're away from their desks, and without logging on to Grainger's website. Anyone ordering from the website can also use the handy *click to chat or click to call* buttons to directly connect with a Grainger customer service rep for help. In fact, the website alerts Grainger's staff when a customer is having a problem with an order, so a customer service employee can step in with a chat or call invitation to offer immediate help.

Grainger's successful development of its e-commerce division has enabled it to grow its online business more than twice as fast as its base operations, increasing it 17 percent in one recent year to reach more than $8 billion in annual revenues. According to the company's vice president of e-commerce, customers love to tell stories about how the company got them out of a bind with its huge inventory, convenient ordering process, and speedy response. Many of Grainger's customers are in government offices or schools; in heavy or light manufacturing operations; or in retail, wholesale, fleet maintenance, or asset management.

"We're doing our thinking around customer experience," the company's vice president of e-commerce says. "We're doing all we can to help our customers make the right decisions."

QUESTIONS FOR CRITICAL THINKING

1. Why is it important for W.W. Grainger to understand exactly who its B2B customers are?

2. In what other ways can Grainger provide a good customer experience via its website and mobile apps?

Sources: Company website, http://pressroom.grainger.com, accessed November 15, 2012; Paul Demery, "W.W. Grainger Budgets $40 Million for Online Growth," *Internet Retailer,* accessed November 15, 2012, www.internetretailer.com; "IRWD 2012: Listen. Create. Test. Repeat," *Internet Retailer,* accessed November 15, 2012, www.internetretailer .com; Sean Callahan, "Paul Miller," *BtoBonline.com,* accessed November 15, 2012, www.btobonline.com; "CMO Close-Up with Paul Miller, VP e-Commerce, W.W .Grainger," *BtoBonline.com,* accessed November 15, 2012, www.btobonline.com.

VIDEO CASE 7.2
Zappos Offers Insights to Other Businesses

How many firms throw open their doors to the business community, essentially offering access to trade secrets so other companies can learn and grow? Zappos does this—in fact, the online shoe retailer has created an entire division devoted to the effort, called Zappos Insights. Based on the company's core value of open and honest communication, Zappos conducts business-to-business marketing in an unusual way: giving away information for free. Zappos is well known among other businesses for two things it does extremely well: providing top-notch customer service and building a culture that spreads happiness.

Zappos' focus on customer service was born of necessity. When it started in the late 1990s, the company didn't have any money to market the novel idea of online shoe selling. So its founders sank everything they had into customer service, including the idea of free shipping both ways. As the company built its business and its reputation, it also created a culture in which people liked to work. "It's an environment where people are in service to each other," explains Robert Richman, product manager for Zappos Insights. Zappos' expertise in customer service has become a product itself, as Zappos Insights offers training to other firms in how to do what it does so well.

Access to the Zappos culture starts for free, with a tour of the company and information available to everyone online. From there, businesses can join Zappos Insights and pay for various levels of training, such as a two-day onsite boot camp at Zappos or a customized program conducted at an individual company's location. Membership benefits include training modules on leadership development, techniques for keeping team members engaged and empowered, and strategies for delivering Zappos' signature "WOW" service to customers. At a one-day seminar, a business owner or executive learns applications for such tenets as "culture drives success," "getting the culture right," "getting the right people on board," "creating a fun physical environment creates energy," and "communication is everything, and everything is communication." These aren't just taglines. They are organizational values that Zappos has proved to be successful.

Zappos segments its B2B customers by sifting through the data it has collected on companies that request the free portion of its program and determining what kind of business they do (customer type) as well as how they might use Zappos training to further their business (end-use application). In essence, explains Robert Richman,

it's about "offering a lot of free value and then seeing who wants to go deeper." In fact, Zappos Insights doesn't advertise or send direct email—for the most part, companies come to them. They may be as varied as Google, Eli Lilly, and Intuit—but they all want one thing: a culture driven by customer service. Why isn't Zappos worried about sharing its methods? "Culture can't be duplicated because it's based on people," says Richman. "So because of that, it's completely different when transferred from company to company."

The decision for an organization to pay for an in-depth membership to Zappos Insights requires consideration of certain factors, such as price (there are several levels) and availability (businesses can attend workshops and seminars at Zappos, or have Zappos come to them). The buying situation itself varies as well. As a client enters into a new relationship with Zappos Insights, it's a new-task purchase. Managers are involved not only in the purchase but probably in the experience itself. If a company continues its membership, adding services, upgrading, or renewing, it becomes a modified rebuy. Reciprocity also occurs, as some of Zappos' vendors are enrolled in the Zappos Insights program.

When you think about strategies for businesses marketing to each other, you might not necessarily consider the strategy of delivering happiness. But Zappos Insights places the concept of happiness in the business environment at the top of its list. The training programs offered by Zappos Insights "play into the larger vision of delivering happiness, because we are essentially training the people who are responsible for hundreds of thousands of other people," says Robert Richman. "We've seen the trickle effect." As Zappos trains companies to build places where employees like to work, all those employees deliver better experiences to their customers. "It's a rising tide that raises all boats," Richman muses. "If we create stronger cultures, everybody in business will have better relationships."

QUESTIONS FOR CRITICAL THINKING

1. Describe the buyer–seller relationship between Zappos Insights and its business clients.

2. How would you classify the business market demand for Zappos Insights training? Explain your answer.

Sources: Company website, www.zapposinsights.com, accessed November 15, 2012; Michael Kerr, "Zapped by Zappos: Lessons in How to Build a Workplace Culture That WOWS!" *Humor at Work,* accessed November 15, 2012, www.mikekerr.com; "Zendesk Joins Forces with Zappos Insights and Groupon to Launch Its First Ever Customer Service Hero Tour," *PR Newswire,* accessed November 15, 2012, www.prnewswire.com.

NOTES

1. Christina Austin, "How 8 Brands Became Masters of Social Media Content Publishing," *Business Insider*, accessed November 15, 2012, www.business.com; "GE: Reinventing Mobility," Apple, company website, accessed November 15, 2012, www.apple.com; Marc Brownstein, "It's Time to Bring B2B Marketers into the Social-Media World," *Advertising Age*, accessed November 15, 2012, http://adage.com; Jennifer Barron and Jesse Purewal, "B2B Marketers: Creating a Great Customer Experience," *MediaPost*, accessed November 15, 2012, www.mediapost.com; "Relevance Over Reach, Says GE Digital Chief," *Wordpress.com*, accessed November 15, 2012, http://brandleadership.wordpress.com; Kate Maddox, "GE's Boff Named 'BtoB's' Top Digital Marketer of the Year," *BtoBonline.com*, accessed November 15, 2012, www.btobonline.com; Sean Callahan, "Boff Details GE's Embrace of Social Media," *BtoBonline.com*, accessed November 15, 2012, www.btobonline.com; Brett Johnson, "GE and Caterpillar—B2B Mobile Is Serious Business," *Empower Network*, accessed November 15, 2012, www.empowernetwork.com; "Apple Recognizes GE as Mobile App Leader," company website, http://careers.geblogs.com, accessed November 15, 2012.

2. U.S. Department of Defense, "DOD Releases Fiscal 2013 Budget Proposal," press release, accessed November 15, 2012, www.defense.gov.

3. U.S. Census Bureau, "E-Stats," p. 2, accessed November 15, 2012, www.census.gov/estats.

4. "Bundled Offers: Simplify Billing and Save Money: AT&T OneNet Service," Company website, AT&T, accessed November 15, 2012, www.business.att.com.

5. Company website, www.jan-pro.com, accessed November 15, 2012.

6. Company website, www.acco.com, accessed November 15, 2012.

7. "Official Auction Government High End Assets Sale—April 22, 2012," *PRWeb*, accessed November 15, 2012, www.prweb.com.

8. U.S. Census Bureau, "E-Stats."

9. Nick Stamoulis, "How HubSpot Does B2B Internet Marketing Right," *Business 2 Community*, accessed November 15, 2012, www.business2community.com.

10. Company website, www.theseam.com, accessed November 15, 2012.

11. "Main Street Revolution," *Small Business Opportunities*, accessed November 15, 2012, www.sbomag.com; company website, accessed November 15, 2012, www.overstock.com.

12. Company website, www.tetratech.com, accessed November 15, 2012.

13. U.S. Census Bureau, "North American Industry Classification System (NAICS)," accessed November 15, 2012, www.census.gov/eos/www/naics.

14. Company website, http://business.verizonwireless.com, accessed November 15, 2012.

15. Joel Kotkin, "Manufacturing Stages a Comeback," *Forbes*, accessed November 15, 2012, www.forbes.com.

16. Mike Pare, "Volkswagen Eyes Expansion," *Times Free Press*, accessed November 15, 2012, www.timesfreepress.com; "Volkswagen Opens New $1 Billion Manufacturing Plant Today in Chattanooga,TN," *Area Development Online*, accessed November 15, 2012, www.areadevelopment.com; "Volkswagen Academy in Partnership with Chattanooga State," *Chattanooga State Community College*, accessed November 15, 2012, www.chattanoogastate.edu.

17. Company website, www.cdw.com, accessed November 15, 2012.

18. "Walmart and Sam's Club Raise $27.9 Million During Six-Week Campaign for Children's Miracle Network Hospitals," press release, accessed November 15, 2012, http://childrensmiraclenetworkhospitals.org.

19. William J. Holstein, "How Coca-Cola Manages 90 Emerging Markets," *strategy+business*, accessed November 15, 2012, www.strategy-business.com.

20. "Top Outsourcing Countries," *Sourcing Line*, accessed November 15, 2012, www.sourcingline.com.

21. Steven Church, "NewPage Settles with Creditors over Bankruptcy Plan," *Bloomberg*, accessed November 15, 2012, www.bloomberg.com.

22. Joel Schectman, "IT Investments Pay Off at Victoria's Secret, Bath & Body Works," *CIO Journal*, accessed November 15, 2012, http://mobile.blogs.wsj.com.

23. "Xerox at a Glance," Company website, www.xerox.com, accessed November 15, 2012.

24. Debbie Kline, "Hugo Boss Threatens to Move Overseas If Workers Refuse $4/Hr Pay Cut," *Jobs with Justice blog*, accessed November 15, 2012, www.jwjblog.org.

25. "Outsourcing and Offshoring Overview," *Plunkett Research Ltd.*, accessed November 15, 2012, www.plunkettresearch.com.

26. Nick Bunkley, "Toyota and Honda Bounce Back," *The New York Times*, accessed November 15, 2012, www.nytimes.com.

27. "The Keurig Story," Company website, www.keurig.com, accessed November 15, 2012.

28. Laura Carroll, "Big Names in Coffee Business Convene at Trade Show," *Las Vegas Business Press*, accessed November 15, 2012, www.lvbusinesspress.com; Christopher MacManus, "Drinking in the Vue: Keurig's K-Cup Successor," *CNET News*, accessed November 15, 2012, http://news.cnet.com.

29. "UPS Deploys Next High-Tech Mobile Computer to Drivers," company website, http://pressroom.ups.com, accessed November 15, 2012; Larry Dignan, "UPS Upgrades Driver Handhelds; Utilizes Gobi," *ZDNet*, accessed November 15, 2012, www.zdnet.com.

30. Bobby Allyn, "Reversing Years of Neglect on a Hill above Nashville," *The New York Times*, accessed November 15, 2012, www.nytimes.com; company website, accessed November 15, 2012, www.leainc.com.

31. Table 428. Number of Governmental Units by Type: 1962 to 2007, *The 2012 Statistical Abstract*, accessed November 15, 2012, www.census.gov.

32. Supplier Diversity Corporate Plan, *United States Postal Service*, accessed November 15, 2012, http://about.usps.com.

33. "GSA Advantage!" company website, www.gsaadvantage.com, accessed November 15, 20102.

PART 3

Target Market Selection

AP Photo/Sue Ogrocki

Chapter 9

MARKET
Segmentation, Targeting, and Positioning

1 Identify the essential components of a market.

2 Outline the role of market segmentation in developing a marketing strategy.

3 Describe the criteria necessary for effective segmentation.

4 Explain the geographic approach to segmenting consumer markets.

5 Discuss the demographic approach to segmenting consumer markets.

6 Outline the psychographic approach to segmenting consumer markets.

7 Describe product-related segmentation.

8 Identify the steps in the market segmentation process.

9 Discuss four basic strategies for reaching target markets.

10 Summarize the types of positioning strategies, and explain the reasons for positioning and repositioning products.

NIKE'S N7 SHOES: PERFECT FIT FOR NATIVE AMERICANS

Findings from research with more than 70 U.S. Native American tribes revealed that 90 percent of Native Americans have a wider foot than other people, and they have been unable to wear athletic shoes comfortably—until now. Working with the tribes, Nike has created a shoe for this specific group of consumers and, in doing so, has helped the Native American community take a strong stand against diabetes.

N7, named for the Iroquois philosophy that all decisions must be considered for their impact on the seventh-following generation, is a line of athletic wear that has all of Nike's significant design and marketing skills behind it. But these are shoes with a difference. In addition to taking into account the specific foot requirements of Native Americans, Nike has committed part of the proceeds from the N7 brand to the Nike's N7 Fund, which helps support sports and exercise programs for disease prevention in Native American communities. Fitness and nutrition are part of the first line of defense against diabetes, and, until recently, there were few such resources in Native American areas.

Among other activities, the N7 Fund awards cash grants to organizations like the Diabetes Prevention Program (DPP), an award-winning initiative that has helped half its pre-diabetic Native participants reduce their symptoms enough to no longer be pre-diabetic. DPP buys discounted N7 walking shoes from Nike for participants to use in their exercise programs, "a tangible way of telling people we believe in them," says the program manager of parent organization Community Wellness and Outreach (CWO).

More than 300 U.S. programs like DPP, and 75 more in Canada, participate in the Nike program, called Air Native. These programs decide on their own how best to incorporate N7 shoes, which boast Native American athletes as brand endorsers, including Major League Baseball's Jacoby Ellsbury and the long-distance runner Alvina Begay, both Navajos, and NFL quarterback Sam Bradford, a Cherokee. Nike says it hopes to "help native America and Aboriginal youth recognize their proud history and build on it for a triumphant future." The shoes themselves display this history, featuring colors with traditional Native meanings: turquoise for friendship, red for energy, white for life balance, and black for confidence.[1]

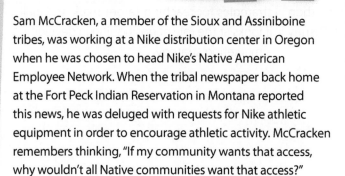

EVOLUTION OF A BRAND

Sam McCracken, a member of the Sioux and Assiniboine tribes, was working at a Nike distribution center in Oregon when he was chosen to head Nike's Native American Employee Network. When the tribal newspaper back home at the Fort Peck Indian Reservation in Montana reported this news, he was deluged with requests for Nike athletic equipment in order to encourage athletic activity. McCracken remembers thinking, "If my community wants that access, why wouldn't all Native communities want that access?"

Once Nike hired him as its manager of Native American business, McCracken became a man with a mission. He drew up the original business plan at Nike and has continued to build the Air Native program. He brought Bunky Echo-Hawk, a Pawnee/Yakima multimedia artist, on board to work with Nike's own designers on a distinctive N7 line. And he has emphasized that all the Native American brand endorsers are also ambassadors of the Native American community. The N7 line is popular not only with Native Americans but also with other shoppers who appreciate good design and good looks in athletic shoes and clothing.

- Market segmentation is an important element in developing a marketing strategy. How has Nike's strategy—developing a line of footwear to meet the needs of a very specific market—enabled it to market that line successfully?
- The Nike N7 page on Facebook has more than 27,000 followers. How has Nike used social media to market its N7 line?

CHAPTER OVERVIEW

Each of us is unique. We come from different backgrounds, live in different households, and have different interests and goals. You and your best friend may shop at different stores, listen to different music, play different sports, and take different courses in college. Suppose you like country music, but your best friend prefers rock. Marketers for all kinds of music-related products, ranging from digital songs to live concerts, want to capture your interest as well as that of your friends. Do you play an instrument or sing? Or are you a fan who goes to clubs and down-loads music? Marketers at Nike, for example, look at customers and potential customers to figure out what their characteristics are, whether they can identify certain subgroups, and how they can best offer products to meet their needs. Your interests and needs, your lifestyle and income, the town where you live, and your age all contribute to the likelihood that you will listen to and buy certain types of music—say, Lady Gaga or the score to *Rent*. All of these factors make up a market. A **market** is composed of people with sufficient purchasing power, authority, and willingness to buy. Marketers must use their expertise to understand the market for a good or service, whether it's a new athletic shoe for marathon runners or a vacation timeshare at Disney World.

Many markets include consumers with different lifestyles, backgrounds, and income levels. Nearly everyone buys toothpaste, but that does not mean every consumer has the same lifestyle, background, or income. So it is unusual for a single marketing mix strategy to attract all sectors of a market. By identifying, evaluating, and selecting a target market to pursue, such as consumers who prefer toothpaste made with all-natural ingredients or those who want an extra-whitening formula—marketers develop more efficient and effective marketing strategies. On the other hand, some products, such as luxury sports cars and fly-fishing supplies, are intended for a more specific market. In either case, the **target market** for a product is the specific segment of consumers most likely to purchase a particular item.

Marketing now takes place on a global basis more than ever, incorporating many target markets. To identify those markets, marketers must determine useful ways for segmenting different populations and communicating with them successfully. This chapter discusses useful ways to accomplish this objective, explaining the steps of the market segmentation process and surveying strategies for reaching target markets. Finally, it looks at the role of positioning in developing a marketing strategy.

market Group of people with sufficient purchasing power, authority, and willingness to buy.

target market Specific group of people a firm believes is most likely to buy its goods and services.

TYPES OF MARKETS

Products usually are classified as either consumer products or business products. Consumer products are bought by ultimate consumers for personal use—for example, cell phones, sports tickets, or fashion magazines. Business products are goods and services purchased for use either directly or indirectly in the production of other goods and services for resale. Most goods and services purchased by individual consumers, such as DVDs and restaurant meals, are considered consumer products. Rubber and raw cotton are examples of items generally purchased by manufacturers and therefore classified as business products. B. F. Goodrich buys rubber to manufacture tires; textile manufacturers such as Burlington Industries convert raw cotton into cloth.

However, in many cases, a single product can serve different uses. Tires purchased for the family car constitute consumer products, but tires purchased by Ford Motor Company to be mounted on its Ford Focus are business products because they become part of another product destined for resale. Or a product that was once a business product might be modified for consumer use, and vice versa. A line of professional cookware sold to restaurants—a business product—could be adapted by its manufacturer to become a line of cookware for home use—a consumer product. If you want to determine the classification of an item, just think about who is going to buy the product, who will use it, and how or why the product will be used. The bottle of mouthwash you buy at the supermarket is a consumer product, but if a big hotel chain purchases large quantities of the same mouthwash from a wholesaler, it becomes a business product.

ASSESSMENT CHECK

1.1 Define *target market*.

1.2 Distinguish between a consumer product and a business product.

> **Identify the essential components of a market.** `1`
>
> **consumer products**
> Products bought by ultimate consumers for personal use.
>
> **business products**
> Goods and services purchased for use either directly or indirectly in the production of other goods and services for resale.

THE ROLE OF MARKET SEGMENTATION

There are more than 7 billion people in the world today; of those, over 315 million live in the United States.[2] In today's business world, too many variables exist in consumer needs, preferences, and purchasing power to attract all consumers with a single marketing mix. That's not to say that firms must actually change products to meet the needs of different market segments—although they often do—but they must attempt to identify the factors that affect purchase decisions and then group consumers according to the presence or absence of these factors. Finally, they adjust marketing strategies to meet the needs of each group.

Consider motor vehicles. Unlike a century ago, when Henry Ford pronounced that customers could order any color of car they liked—as long as it was black—today there is a make, model, and color for every taste and budget. But auto manufacturers need to adjust their messages for different markets. And savvy marketers look toward markets that show growth, such as the U.S. Hispanic population—now the largest ethnic group in the country—and aging baby boomers, whose needs for goods and services are changing.

The division of the total market into smaller, relatively homogeneous groups is called market segmentation. Both profit-oriented and not-for-profit organizations practice market segmentation.

> **Outline the role of market segmentation in developing a marketing strategy.** `2`

ASSESSMENT CHECK

2.1 Define *market segmentation*.

2.2 Describe the role of market segmentation.

> **market segmentation**
> Division of the total market into smaller, relatively homogeneous groups.

CRITERIA FOR EFFECTIVE SEGMENTATION

3   Describe the criteria necessary for effective segmentation.

Segmentation doesn't automatically guarantee success in the marketing arena; instead, it is a tool for marketers to use. Its effectiveness depends on four basic requirements.

First, the market segment must present measurable purchasing power and size. With jobs, incomes, and decision-making power, female consumers represent a hefty amount of purchasing power, about $7 trillion, or over 60 percent of the nation's wealth.[3] Women control or influence the purchase of 85 percent of all consumer goods, including such items as stocks for investment, personal computers, and family vehicles.[4] With this information in mind, car manufacturers and dealers now market directly to women. In addition, websites like AskPatty.com offer advice to women on making car purchases—and certify "female-friendly" dealers and automotive centers that provide the kind of service that builds loyalty among female consumers.[5]

Second, marketers must find a way to promote and serve the market segment effectively. Because women now wield purchasing power in the technology market, marketers need to find different ways to appeal to them. Some companies have taken this advice to heart. T-Mobile and BlackBerry have created ads featuring working moms.

Third, marketers must then identify segments large enough to give them good profit potential. Because women significantly influence 80 to 90 percent of home purchases, homebuilders have turned their marketing efforts to them. The Nebraska-based Design Basics, the largest home-plan design company in the country, now focuses on designs aimed at women. Its guidelines include improving storage options, creating multipurpose rooms, and emphasizing the practicality of the back-door entry—with space for muddy boots and school backpacks, car keys, mail, and a cell-phone charger. The firm's Livability at a Glance division features color-coded layouts showing areas for entertaining (yellow), de-stressing (blue), storing (orange), and flexible living (green). To help women determine the kinds of spaces that best fit their family's lifestyle, the website offers a Livability at a Glance Lifestyle Quiz.[6]

Fourth, the firm must aim for segments that match its marketing capabilities. Targeting a large number of small markets can be an expensive, complex, and inefficient strategy, so smaller firms may decide to stick with a particular niche, or target market. But Harley-Davidson, once thought to be the exclusive domain of men, has experienced a surge in purchases by women, who are the fastest-growing segment of the motorcycle business and currently account for nearly one in four motorcyclists. So Harley-Davidson runs targeted ads in

Harley-Davidson hosts "garage parties" around the country, targeted specifically to women.

© Tim Boyle/Bloomberg via Getty Images

women's magazines and hosts annual "garage party" events throughout the United States, geared specifically to women and featuring demonstrations, social gatherings, and an "intimidation-free zone" where female riders can meet and network.[7]

SEGMENTING CONSUMER MARKETS

Market segmentation attempts to isolate the traits that distinguish a certain group of consumers from the overall market. An understanding of the group's characteristics—such as age, gender, geographic location, income, and buying patterns—plays a vital role in developing a successful marketing strategy. In most cases, marketers seek to pinpoint a number of factors affecting buying behavior in the target segment. Marketers in the travel industry consider employment trends, changes in income levels and buying patterns, age, lifestyle, and other factors when promoting their goods and services. To boost attendance at its theme parks, Disney World advertises to "empty nesters" and groups of friends instead of focusing entirely on families with young children. Marketers rarely identify totally homogeneous segments, in which all potential customers are alike; they almost always encounter some differences among members of a target group but must be careful to ensure their segments accurately reflect consumers.

In the next sections, we discuss the four common bases for segmenting consumer markets: geographic segmentation, demographic segmentation, psychographic segmentation, and product-related segmentation. These segmentation approaches offer important guidance for marketing strategies, provided they identify significant differences in buying behavior.

GEOGRAPHIC SEGMENTATION

Marketers have long practiced geographic segmentation—dividing an overall market into homogeneous groups based on their locations. Geographic location does not ensure all consumers in a location will make the same buying decisions, but this segmentation approach helps identify some general patterns.

The approximately 315 million people living in the United States are not scattered evenly across the country. For instance, many are concentrated in major metropolitan areas; New York is the largest U.S. city, with about 8.1 million residents, but the metropolitan area surrounding it includes 19 million people. Los Angeles ranks second, with 3.7 million, and a surrounding area of nearly 13 million.[8] Figure 9.1 shows populations of the ten largest cities in the United States and the ten states with the largest populations. California tops the list with almost 37.2 million residents. Wyoming is the least-populous state, with 563,000. In addition to total population, marketers need to look at the *fastest-growing* states to plan their strategies for the future. Texas gained the most in population since the 2010 Census, followed by California, Florida, Georgia, and North Carolina.[9]

A look at the worldwide population distribution illustrates why so many firms pursue customers around the globe. China has the most citizens, with more than 1.3 billion people. India is second with over 1.2 billion. The United States is third with over 315 million, and Indonesia is fourth with over 248 million. Japan is a distant tenth with over 127 million.[10] As in the United States, much of the world's population lives in urban environments. The two largest cities in the world are Shanghai, China, with 23.5 million and Mumbai, India, with 14.3 million. The two largest metropolitan areas are Tokyo, Japan, with 37.1 million and Jakarta, Indonesia, with over 26.1 million.[11]

Population size alone, however, may not be reason enough for a business to expand into a specific country. Businesses also need to look at a wide variety of economic variables. Some businesses may decide to combine their marketing efforts for countries that share similar population and product-use

Explain the geographic approach to segmenting consumer markets. 4

geographic segmentation Division of an overall market into homogeneous groups based on their locations.

FIGURE 9.1
The Ten Largest Cities and Ten Most Populous States in the United States

Sources: "States Ranked by Population," *Information You Can Trust*, accessed November 18, 2012, www.ipl.org; "Top 50 Cities in the U.S. by Population and Rank," *Info Please*, accessed November 18, 2012, www.infoplease.com.

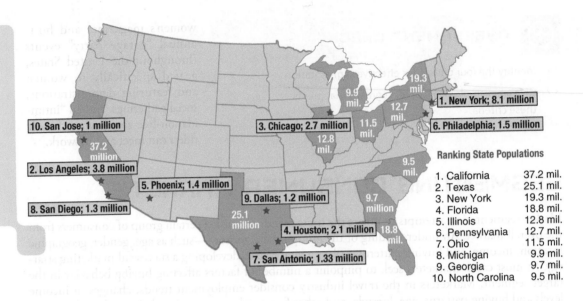

patterns instead of treating each country as an independent segment. This grouping is taking place with greater frequency throughout the European Union as the currency and trade laws of the member nations become more unified.

While population numbers indicate the overall size of a market, other geographic indicators like job growth give useful guidance to marketers, depending on the type of products they sell. Automobile manufacturers might segment geographic regions by household income, because it is an important factor in the purchase of a new car.

Geographic areas also vary in population migration patterns. Job transfer and retirement are two circumstances that cause people to move. Major natural disasters may affect population migration, as in the case of Hurricane Katrina, which devastated New Orleans. It's also important for marketers to observe who is moving where: people who leave the East Coast aren't necessarily jumping to the West Coast, and vice versa. New Yorkers tend to gravitate to the South or to Connecticut or New Jersey. Californians often move to other western states instead of coming farther east. The recession has caused other migration changes: while healthy economic times saw greater migration to the South and Southwest, when the recent recession hit, Florida and Nevada saw net losses. Overall, migration in the United States seems to have slowed down because many Americans have been unable to sell their homes and can't be sure they would find jobs even if they could relocate.[12]

The move from urban to suburban areas after World War II created a need to redefine the urban marketplace. This trend radically changed cities' traditional patterns of retailing and led to decline in many downtown shopping areas. Subsequently, traditional city boundaries become almost meaningless for marketing purposes. However, marketers now observe a trend toward the revitalization of some downtown urban areas.

In an effort to respond to these changes, the government now classifies urban data using the following categories:

- The category of **core based statistical area (CBSA)** refers collectively to metropolitan and micropolitan statistical areas. Each CBSA must contain at least one urban area with a population of 10,000 or more. Each metropolitan statistical area must have at least one urbanized area of 50,000 or more inhabitants. Each micropolitan statistical area must have at least one urban cluster with a population of at least 10,000 but less than 50,000. There are 366 metropolitan and 576 micropolitan statistical areas in the United States. Of the 366 metropolitan statistical areas, 178 are classified as large, meaning they contain more than 250,000 people.[13]

- A **metropolitan statistical area (MSA)** is a freestanding urban area with a population in the urban center of at least 50,000 and a total metropolitan statistical area population of 100,000 or more. Buyers in metropolitan statistical areas exhibit social and economic homogeneity and usually border on nonurbanized counties. Examples include Little Rock, Arkansas;

core based statistical area (CBSA) Collective term for metropolitan and micropolitan statistical areas.

metropolitan statistical area (MSA) Freestanding urban area with a population in the urban center of at least 50,000 and a total MSA population of 100,000 or more.

Kalamazoo–Battle Creek, Michigan; and Rochester, New York. Figure 9.2 identifies the ten largest metropolitan areas in the United States.

- A **micropolitan statistical area** has at least one town of 10,000 to 49,999 people—it can have several such towns—and proportionally few of its residents commuting outside the area. Recently, the government counted 576 such areas in the continental United States. Examples of micropolitan statistical areas include Corning, New York; Kalispell, Montana; Kahului-Wailuku, Hawaii; and Key West, Florida.

- The category of **consolidated metropolitan statistical area (CMSA)** includes the country's 25 or so urban giants, such as Detroit–Ann Arbor–Flint, Michigan; Los Angeles–Riverside–Orange County, California; and Philadelphia–Wilmington–Atlantic City. (Note that, in the third example, three states are involved: Pennsylvania, Delaware, and New Jersey.) A CMSA must include two or more primary metropolitan statistical areas, discussed next.

- A **primary metropolitan statistical area (PMSA)** is an urbanized county or set of counties with social and economic ties to nearby areas. PMSAs are identified within areas of 1-million-plus populations. Olympia, Washington, is part of the Seattle–Tacoma–Bremerton PMSA. Bridgeport, Connecticut, is part of the New York–northern New Jersey–Long Island PMSA, and Riverside–San Bernardino, California, is a PMSA within the Los Angeles–Riverside–Orange County PMSA.[14]

USING GEOGRAPHIC SEGMENTATION

Demand for some categories of goods and services can vary according to geographic region, and marketers must be aware of how these regions differ. Marketers of major brands are particularly interested in defining their **core regions**, the locations where they get 40 to 80 percent of their sales.

Residence location *within* a geographic area is an important segmentation variable. City dwellers often rely on public transportation and may get along fine without automobiles, whereas those who live in the suburbs or rural areas depend on their own cars and trucks. Also, those who live in the suburbs spend more on lawn and garden care products than city dwellers. Climate is another important segmentation factor; for example, at more than 41 quarts per person per year, consumers in the north central states eat the most ice cream in America. A recent survey found that, on average, Americans take in 300 milligrams of caffeine a day (approximately 10 ounces), including the consumption of coffee, tea, chocolate, and caffeinated energy drinks. Seattle tops the list in coffee consumption. Overall, 14 percent of American consumers are buying more hot coffee, and 10 percent are buying more iced tea. Marketers can use this information to determine where their products are most likely to be successful.[15]

Geographic segmentation provides useful distinctions when regional preferences or needs exist. A consumer may not want to invest in a snow blower or flood insurance but may *have* to because

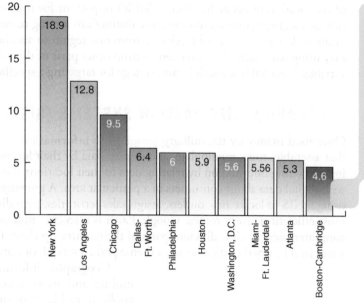

FIGURE 9.2
The Ten Largest Metropolitan Areas in the United States

Source: U.S. Census Bureau, *Statistical Abstract of the United States 2012*, Table 20: Large Metropolitan Statistical Areas—Population: 1990 to 2010, www.census.gov, accessed November 18, 2012.

micropolitan statistical area Area with at least one town of 10,000 to 49,999 people with proportionally few of its residents commuting to outside the area.

consolidated metropolitan statistical area (CMSA) Urban area that includes two or more PMSAs.

primary metropolitan statistical area (PMSA) Urbanized county or set of counties with social and economic ties to nearby areas.

core region Region from which most major brands get 40 to 80 percent of their sales.

of the location of his or her home. But it's important for marketers not to stop at geographic location as a segmentation method because distinctions among consumers also exist within a geographic location. Consider those who relocate from one region to another for work or family reasons. They may bring with them their preferences from other parts of the country. Using multiple segmentation variables is probably a much better strategy for targeting a specific market.

GEOGRAPHIC INFORMATION SYSTEMS (GISs)

geographic information systems (GISs) Software packages that assemble, store, manipulate, and display data by their location.

Once used mainly by the military, **geographic information systems (GISs)** are computer systems that assemble, store, manipulate, and display data by their location. GISs simplify the job of analyzing marketing information by relating data to their locations. The result is a geographic map overlaid with digital data about consumers in a particular area. A growing number of companies benefit from using a GIS to locate new outlets, assign sales territories, plan distribution centers, and map out the most efficient delivery routes. Google Earth is a recent application of GIS technology that allows computer users to view different parts of the country up close. Users simply type in an address and zoom into it, whether it's a house, a theme park, a school, or a store.

Geographic information systems are becoming more mobile and more social as people increasingly turn to applications like Foursquare and Facebook Places to locate restaurants, movies, and stores. Mark West is the owner of Monique's Chocolates, located in Palo Alto, California. To test the power of geographic networking, he started a "buy one, get one free" campaign. An advertisement in a local magazine cost him $350. Offering the same deal on Foursquare cost him nothing. The magazine ad brought in one new customer, but the Foursquare post brought in over 30—including some repeat customers.[16]

ASSESSMENT CHECK

4.1 Under what circumstances are marketers most likely to use geographic segmentation?

4.2 What are the five main categories for classifying urban data?

Monique's Chocolates tested the power of geographic networking by starting a "buy one, get one free" campaign.

Courtesy of Monique's Chocolates

DEMOGRAPHIC SEGMENTATION

The most common method of market segmentation—demographic segmentation—defines consumer groups according to demographic variables, such as gender, age, income, occupation, education, sexual orientation, household size, and stage in the family lifecycle. This approach is also called *socioeconomic segmentation*. Marketers review vast quantities of available data to complete a plan for demographic segmentation. One of the primary sources for demographic data in the United States is the Census Bureau. Marketers can obtain many of the Census Bureau's statistics online at www.census.gov.

The following discussion considers the most commonly used demographic variables. Keep in mind, however, that while demographic segmentation is helpful, it can also lead to stereotyping—a preconception about a group of people—which can alienate a potential market or cause marketers to miss a potential market altogether. The idea is to use segmentation as a starting point, not as an endpoint. Demographic segmentation can help marketers communicate effectively with their target markets, as described in the "Career Readiness" feature.

Discuss the demographic approach to segmenting consumer markets.

demographic segmentation Division of an overall market into homogeneous groups based on variables, such as gender, age, income, occupation, education, sexual orientation, household size, and stage in the family lifecycle; also called *socioeconomic segmentation*.

SEGMENTING BY GENDER

Gender is an obvious variable that helps define the markets for certain products, but segmenting by gender can be tricky. In some cases, the segmenting is obvious—lipstick for women, facial shaving products for men. However, in recent years, the lines have increasingly blurred. Some men wear earrings and use skin-care products, once both the province of women. Some of today's women purchase power tools and pickup trucks, once considered traditionally male purchases. So marketers of cars and trucks, power tools, jewelry, and skin-care products have had to change the way they segment their markets. Nivea, well known for its skin-care products for women and babies, created an entire line of men's skin-care products called Nivea for Men. Some companies successfully market the same—or similar—products to both men and women. Visa markets its small-business credit card services to firms owned by both men and women.

As purchasing power in many households has shifted toward women, marketers learned that female consumers who regularly use the Internet make most of the decisions about retail items. Based on this information, Yahoo! recently launched Shine, a site specifically for women. The site offers content in a variety of areas ranging from entertainment to finance and provides opportunities for advertisers to reach a targeted female audience. Kellogg's, Olay, and Purina are among the brands that advertise on the site.[17]

SEGMENTING BY AGE

Age is another variable marketers use to segment their markets. As with gender, age seems an easy distinction to make—baby food for babies, retirement communities for seniors. But the distinctions become blurred as consumers' roles and needs change, and as age distribution shifts and changes in each group take place. St. Joseph's baby aspirin is no longer marketed just to parents for their infants; now, it is also marketed to adults to help prevent heart disease.

School-Age Children

School-age children—and those even younger—exert considerable influence over family purchases, as marketers are keenly aware, particularly in the area of food. Children as young as 2 make choices about what they want to eat, play with, and wear. The food industry reportedly spends $10 billion each year marketing to children. Its advertisements for such products as breakfast cereals, snack foods, and beverages are designed to attract the attention of children under the age of 12—who in turn persuade their families to purchase them. With childhood obesity on the rise, nutritionists and pediatricians are concerned about the nutritional value of foods marketed to children. In fact, a recent study by the American Academy of Pediatrics revealed that the advertising of junk food plays a key role in childhood obesity.[18] See the "Solving an Ethical Controversy" feature for a discussion of the role of high-fructose corn syrup, a high-calorie ingredient whose use in a wide variety of foods concerns many.

SOLVING AN ETHICAL CONTROVERSY

Free to Choose High-Fructose Corn Syrup

High-fructose corn syrup is a common ingredient in many processed foods and drinks U.S. consumers buy and eat every day, from soda to baked goods and even yogurt. Made from corn kernels blended into a thick syrup, the ingredient is cheaper than sugar but high in calories with either little nutritional value or none (depending on whom you ask). It is blamed for a wide variety of health problems (including childhood obesity) and environmental impacts.

Should high-fructose corn syrup be banned from foods and soft drinks?

PRO 👍

1. Long-term consumption leads to high levels of body fat and cholesterol, which can contribute to obesity, diabetes, and heart disease.

2. High-fructose corn syrup requires the cultivation of corn as a monoculture, depleting the soil of nutrients while flooding soil and groundwater with pesticides.

CON 👎

1. High-fructose corn syrup helps baked, canned, and frozen goods look better and stay fresh and moist longer.

2. Even calories, in moderation, have their place in a balanced diet. Consumers should be able to make their own choices about what they eat.

Summary:

Given the wide use of the ingredient, a ban seems unlikely for now. As always, consumers should educate themselves in order to make wise decisions about what they buy and eat.

Sources: Jennifer K. Nelson, "Nutrition and Healthy Eating," *Mayoclinic.com*, accessed November 18, 2012, www.mayoclinic.com; Marin Gazzaniga, "Sickeningly Sweet: The Effects of High-Fructose Corn Syrup," *MSN Health Living,* accessed November 18, 2012, http://healthyliving.msn.com; Amanda Hermes, "The Pros & Cons of High Fructose Corn Syrup," *LiveStrong.com,* accessed November 18, 2012, www.livestrong.com; Nanci Heilmich, "Study: Kids Get More Added Sugar from Foods Than Drinks," *USA Today,* accessed November 18, 2012, http://yourlife.usatoday.com.

Tweens and Teens

Tweens—sometimes also called *preteens*—and teens are a rapidly growing market. This group is 71 million strong and packs a wallop when it comes to spending—some researchers estimate as much as $200 billion. But they also influence billions of dollars' worth of purchases made by their families. Although members of this group don't fall into a single category—they reflect the diversity of the U.S. population in general—the most popular purchases include candy and snacks, soft drinks, clothing, music, and electronics. If marketers could characterize this group with one word, it would likely be *interactive*. They grew up with the Internet, and they expect to be actively involved in their own entertainment. They might rather determine the outcome of a video game than watch to see who won a football game on TV. Even the TV shows they watch—like *American Idol*—provide opportunities for input. They are completely comfortable in a digital world, and many cannot imagine life without their smart phones and iPods. When they want to communicate with friends—or parents—they send text messages. They expect a vast array of choices in programming, media alternatives, and interactive experiences. The big challenge for marketers is keeping up with them—let alone staying a step ahead. Phone companies and car companies have increased their spending on advertising to older teens, while snacks, clothing, and video games claim the attention of the younger set.[19]

Some companies have expanded their product lines to include specific offerings to tweens and teens. LuLuLemon Athletica, which specializes in athletic wear for women, recently launched a website featuring Ivivva, a new line of athletic and dance clothing for girls.[20]

Generation X

The group born between 1968 and 1979, now generally in their early 30s to early 40s, are often referred to as *Generation X*. This group of an estimated 41 million faced some economic and career challenges as they began their adult lives and started families: housing costs were high and debt associated with college loans and credit cards was soaring. But their financial squeeze should ease as they enter their prime earning years. This group is very family oriented—not defining themselves by their careers as much as previous generations—well educated, and optimistic. Like their younger counterparts, Gen Xers are comfortable with the Internet; even if they make a purchase at a retail store, they are likely to have researched their choices online. But like their elders, they were raised on television—so the TV is still an important marketing tool.[21]

As this generation matures, they are growing more concerned about social issues and protecting the natural environment, both of which they view as affecting the well-being of their children. As a result, they are turning to goods and services that support certain causes. Singer-songwriter Jack Johnson, in his mid-30s, recorded an album using solar energy. He requires his concert promoters to recycle and launched an online social networking site, All At Once, where fans can support environmental not-for-profit organizations. Johnson, a member of Generation X, appeals both to his own age group and older teens.[22]

Baby Boomers

Baby boomers—those born between 1946 and 1964—are a popular segment to target because of their numbers and income levels. Approximately 78 million people were born during this period in the United States.[23] The values of this age group were influenced both by the Vietnam War era and the career-driven era that followed. They also came of age with early television and with TV commercials serving as a backdrop to most of their lives. They tried new breakfast cereals, ate TV dinners, and recall when cigarettes were advertised on television.

Some companies have expanded their product lines to include specific offerings to tweens and teens, such as LuLuLemon Athletica's Ivivva.

© ivivva athletica

Not surprisingly, baby boomers are a lucrative segment for many marketers. Baby boomers wield spending power estimated at $7 trillion, which is why businesses try to woo this group.[24] Different subgroups within this generation complicate segmentation and targeting strategies. Some boomers put off having children until their 40s, while others their age have already become grandparents. Boomers tend to value health and quality of life—a fact not lost on marketers for products like organic foods, financial investments, travel, and fitness. But boomers are also quick to embrace new technology, even as they age. According to a recent Pew Research Center study, baby boomers make up about 36 percent of Internet users. In addition, about 65 percent of all boomers maintain a Facebook page.[25]

The motorcycle industry has boomers clearly in its sights. As a group, baby boomers are significantly more physically active than their counterparts in previous generations. However, boomers are beginning to experience the wide range of health problems that typically come with age—arthritis, back pain, chronic joint and muscle issues, and more—making it difficult for them to continue to ride their two-wheelers. With baby boomers making up more than 40 percent of the motorcycling population, several manufacturers have introduced trikes—that is, three-wheeled motorcycles. The trikes even include luxury features, such as GPS navigation, cruise control, and stereo speakers.[26]

Seniors

As baby boomers age and Americans continue to live longer, the median age of the U.S. population has dramatically increased. Today, more than 40 million people are now over age 65. With discretionary income and rates of home ownership higher than those of other age groups, they also account for a major proportion of new-car sales and travel dollars spent. Many marketers have found that seniors are a group worth targeting. Although many seniors live on modest, fixed incomes, those who are well off financially have both time and money to spend on leisure activities and luxury items.

Other important characteristics of this group include the following:

- Families experienced economic hardship during this group's childhood.

- They built the suburbs.

- They value hard work.

- They like to associate with people who have similar views and backgrounds.

- They are concerned with personal safety.

- They spend money conservatively, but have reached a level of financial comfort where they like to indulge in some luxury.

- They are not likely to be the first to try new products.[27]

Understanding just a few of these characteristics helps marketers develop goods and services and create marketing messages that will reach this group. Road Scholar, a branch of Elderhostel, is a nonprofit organization that has been offering educational travel for seniors since 1975. Its "Adventures in Lifelong Learning" currently comprise 6,500 educational tours in every state and 150 countries. Instead of guides, the tours are run by instructors who are experts in their fields and by local educators. Lectures and field trips are included, and the Road Scholar Travel Assistance Plan, included in the cost of the programs, ensures that anyone with a medical emergency will be cared for. Participants pay tuition rather than fees, and the program is supported by donations.[28]

THE COHORT EFFECT: THE VIDEO GAME GENERATION

cohort effect Tendency of members of a generation to be influenced and bound together by events occurring during their key formative years—roughly ages 17 to 22.

Marketers can learn from a sociological concept called the cohort effect, the tendency of members of a generation with common characteristics—like an interest in sustainability—to be influenced and bound together by significant events occurring during their key formative years, roughly ages 17 to 22. These events help define the core values of the age group that eventually shape consumer preferences and behavior. For seniors, the events would be the Great Depression, World War II, and Korea because many were in this age bracket at that time. Later groups were influenced by the Cold

Elderhostel, Inc.

War, the civil rights movement, and the assassination of John F. Kennedy. For older baby boomers, it would be the Vietnam War and the women's movement.

The current cohort—generally consisting of those born during the late 1970s to the early 1990s—may be the most cohesive to date. Marketers have called this group by several names: *Generation Y,* the *Millennial Generation, Generation Next,* and *Echo Boomers.* Others called it the *9-11 Generation* because its members were in their formative years during the terrorist attacks of September 11, 2001.

But something else happened during this group's formative years to shape its preferences and behaviors: while they were coming of age, so too were video games. For this reason, we call this cohort the **Video Game Generation**.

The early versions of video games were developed during the 1950s and 1960s and were displayed on oscilloscopes, mainframe computers, and television screens. Atari and Magnavox were the first commercial entrants on the scene, with Atari introducing its Pong game, and Magnavox launching the Odyssey home video game system. During the late 1970s and 1980s, other competitors entered the market: Activision, Commodore, Electronic Arts, Nintendo, Sega, and more. As the technology improved, the games and systems became more sophisticated, with 3D, realistic graphics, laser disks, and handheld consoles. The industry has continued to evolve, with the introduction of PlayStation, the Nintendo DS, Microsoft's Xbox, and the Wii. Today, more consumers regularly play video games—at home, on their mobile phone, on the beach, anywhere—than go to the movies.

Members of the Video Game Generation are highly visual and are generally comfortable with all forms of technology. They gravitate to activities that provide constant entertainment and immediate gratification. They get their information from social media like Facebook and Twitter as opposed to traditional media, and they prefer instant messaging and texting to emails.

The significance of the cohort effect for marketers lies in understanding the general characteristics of the Video Game Generation as it responds to its life-defining events. The social and economic influences this generation experiences help form members' long-term beliefs and goals in life—and can have a lasting effect on their buying habits and the product choices they make.[29]

Video Game Generation A cohort whose preferences and behaviors were being shaped at the same time as video games.

SEGMENTING BY ETHNIC GROUP

According to the Census Bureau, America's racial and ethnic makeup is constantly changing. The three largest and fastest-growing racial/ethnic groups are Hispanics, African Americans, and Asian Americans. From a marketer's perspective, it is important to note that spending by these groups is rising at a faster pace than for U.S. households in general.

Hispanics and African Americans

Hispanics and African Americans are currently the largest racial/ethnic minority groups in the United States, with Hispanics surpassing African Americans at over 48 million, according to the most recent census data. In fact, the Census Bureau recently revealed that, although whites will still be a majority for some time to come, for the first time, there were more minority births than white births in the United States.[30] The Hispanic population is growing much faster than the African American population.[31] The population growth has created *majority-minority counties*—that is, places where more than half the population is a single racial or ethnic group other than non-Hispanic white. Majority-minority counties exist in several states.[32] Just as important for marketers, although U.S. Hispanics' disposable income is still significantly less than that of non-Hispanic whites, a recent study found that Hispanic buying power is rising at a rate nearly triple that of the national average. One estimate puts the buying power of the Hispanic community at $1 trillion.[33] See the "Marketing Success" feature to learn how Clorox is using a multi-pronged targeted approach to reach these consumers.

MARKETING SUCCESS

Clorox Targets Hispanic Consumers

Background. Clorox Company earns revenues of more than $5 billion a year from sales in over 100 countries. In the U.S. market, the buying power of the Hispanic market is expected to soon grow by about 50 percent, rising to $1.5 trillion.

The Challenge. Hispanic consumers are younger, on average, than the median market age. Heavy users of the Internet and mobile phones, they are influenced by technology and media. They make fewer shopping trips than non-Hispanics but spend more each time, and they often retain the strong family ties and Spanish language of their home cultures. Clorox needed to reach them in a carefully targeted way.

The Strategy. Clorox joined Vme, the Spanish-language network, in a marketing campaign to champion germ prevention, including flu shots, hand washing, and disinfection accomplished with Clorox cleaning products. The company also partnered with

Univision, a Spanish-language media company, to create networks among women using television, radio, and the Internet in the Sharing Among Friends program. It also joined a medical doctor to offer a Spanish website about health and health training and launched the Hispanic Nurses Network, a family resource that includes a Facebook page.

The Outcome. With these and other media efforts, Clorox is well positioned to reach the growing Hispanic market.

Sources: Tiffany Hsu, "Clorox Launches New Products, Campaign on Latino Cleaning Habits," *Los Angeles Times,* accessed November 18, 2012, http://articles. latimes.com; "Nielsen: Hispanic Consumers' Buying Power to Grow 50% by 2015," *Drug Store News,* accessed November 18, 2012, www.drugstorenews.com; Laurel Wentz, "Clorox Fraganzia Launch Targets U.S. Hispanic Consumers," *Advertising Age Hispanic,* accessed November 18, 2012, http://adage.com; Alaric Dearment, "Growing Hispanic Consumer Power Increases Need for Outreach from Retailers, Suppliers," *Drug Store News,* accessed November 18, 2012, www.drugstorenews. com; Allison Cerra, "Clorox, NAHN Introduce Hispanic Nurses Network," *Drug Store News,* accessed November 18, 2012, www.drugstorenews.com.

Many marketers have focused their efforts on the Hispanic population in the United States. Procter & Gamble, The Coca-Cola Company, and Walmart are among the largest advertisers to target this group of consumers. Still, many companies find it a challenge to reach Hispanic consumers and turn them into customers. Founded in 2001, Captura Group has performed marketing research enabling their clients to connect with Hispanic consumers. Based in San Diego, California, Captura provides marketing solutions in both English and Spanish. Among Captura Group's clients are PayPal, Allstate, Ford, and Pfizer.[34]

Like Hispanics, who originate from a variety of countries, the more than 40 million African Americans in the United States—who make up nearly 13 percent of the population—do not comprise a single category.[35] Instead, they represent broad diversity ranging from country of origin to income, age, education, and geographic location. Studies show that affluent African Americans are creating a significant impact on the consumer economy. The number of African American households earning $75,000 or more continues to grow. This group now has an estimated $1.038 trillion in buying power, an increase of 73 percent since 2000.[36] This growing segment represents an opportunity for advertisers, few of whom currently target African Americans in national campaigns. However, the bottled-water company Dasani (a division of The Coca-Cola Company) recently launched a Mother's Day campaign featuring Chilli of the Grammy-award-winning R&B group TLC and highlighting the advantages of health and hydration. Dasani's website featured fashions, health and beauty advice, and contests for spa vacations, all aimed at African American mothers. Yolanda White, Coca-Cola's assistant vice president for African American marketing, said, "Among African American consumers, African American moms are the gatekeepers to the household."[37]

Asian Americans

Although Asian Americans make up a smaller segment than either the African American or Hispanic populations, with more than 14 million in the United States, they were the fastest-growing segment of the population between 2000 and 2010. The Census Bureau estimates this group will grow to almost 19 million by the year 2020, more than 5 percent of the U.S. population.[38] Asian Americans are an attractive target for marketers because they also have the fastest-growing income.

The Asian American population is concentrated in fewer geographic areas than other ethnic markets. Half of Asians live in California, Texas, and New York. The population is diverse, however, because it represents numerous cultures, and its members speak a wide variety of languages, including Bengali, Cantonese, Hawaiian, Hindi, Hmong, Japanese, Korean, Laotian, Mandarin, Tamil, Telugu, Thai, Urdu, and Vietnamese. As a result, demographics differ widely by Asian group. For example, the median household income for Asian Indians in a recent year totaled nearly $91,000 while median income for Bangladeshi Americans during the same period was about $48,000.[39]

Native Americans

Another important minority group is Native Americans, whose current population numbers over 5 million, or 1.7 percent of the total U.S. population, including both American Indians and Alaska natives. In addition to tribes located in the continental United States, such as Cherokee, Apache, Navaho, Pueblo, and Iroquois, the Census Bureau includes Alaska native tribes like Aleut and Eskimo. The Native American population increased 26.7 percent between the 2000 and 2010 censuses, faster than the U.S. population in general, which grew 9.7 percent during the same period.[40]

In addition to population growth, Native American businesses are growing. In a recent year, almost 237,000 non-farm Native American firms operated in the United States, with $34.4 billion in receipts. Almost a third operated in the construction, maintenance and repair, retail, and services industries.[41] Reservation-based casinos and related gaming activities make up a multi-billion-dollar industry.

American Indian Business Leaders is "the only American Indian non-profit organization solely dedicated to empowering business students in the United States." This organization's goal is to increase the number of Native American and Native Alaskan businesspeople and entrepreneurs by providing business and leadership education opportunities. Among the diverse sponsors and supporters at its most recent national conference were the CIA, Toyota, Palo Alto Software, the Colorado Rapids soccer team, the Denver Nuggets basketball team, and the Rocky Mountain Indian Chamber of Commerce.[42] The National Center for American Indian Enterprise Development was founded

epa european pressphoto agency b.v./Alamy

in 1969 and has branches in Arizona, California, and the Northwest. This organization provides professional business and technical expertise to both tribes and individuals on and off the reservation. Among the ways it helps Native Americans manage, grow, and expand their business are marketing research and assistance, financial analysis, loan preparation, business plan development, and other services.[43]

People of Mixed Race

U.S. residents completing census forms now have the option of identifying themselves as belonging to more than one racial category. According to the Census Bureau, about 9 million U.S. residents classify themselves this way, and their numbers are growing.[44] Marketers need to be aware of this change. On one hand, it benefits marketers by making racial statistics more accurate; on the other hand, marketers may find it difficult to compare the new statistics with data from earlier censuses. In some cases, people of mixed race prefer to emphasize one part of their heritage over another; in other cases, they prefer not to make a choice. Recent estimates place about 45 percent of the U.S. mixed-race population under the age of 25, and these consumers are having their own families.[45] Forward-thinking marketers should keep tabs on this group, identifying their needs and preferences.

SEGMENTING BY FAMILY LIFECYCLE STAGES

family lifecycle Process of family formation and dissolution.

Still another form of demographic segmentation employs the stages of the family lifecycle—the process of family formation and dissolution. The underlying theme of this segmentation approach is that life stage, not age per se, is the primary determinant of many consumer purchases. As people move from one life stage to another, they become potential consumers for different types of goods and services.

An unmarried person setting up an apartment for the first time is likely a good prospect for inexpensive furniture and small home appliances. This consumer must probably budget carefully, ruling out expenditures on luxury items. Alternatively, a young single person still living at home will probably have more money to spend on products, such as a car, entertainment, and clothing. As couples marry, their consumer profiles change. Couples without children are frequent buyers of personalized gifts, power tools, furniture, and homes. Eating out and travel may also be part of their lifestyles.

The birth or adoption of a first child changes any consumer's profile considerably; parents must buy cribs, changing tables, baby clothes, baby food, car seats, and similar products. Parents usually spend less on the children who follow because they have already bought many essential items for the first child. Today, the average woman gives birth to fewer children than she did a century ago and usually waits until she is older to have them. Although the average age for American women to have their first child is 25, many women wait much longer, often into their 30s and even 40s. This means that, if they work outside the home, older women are likely more established financially with more money to spend. However, if a woman chooses to stay home after the birth of a child, income can drop dramatically.

Families typically spend the most during the years their children are growing—on everything including housing, food, clothing, braces, and college. Thus, they often look to obtain value wherever they can. Marketers can create satisfied and loyal customers among this group by giving them the best value possible.

Once children are on their own—or at least off to college—married couples enter the "empty nest" stage. Empty nesters may have the disposable incomes necessary to purchase premium products once college tuitions and mortgages are paid off. They may travel more, eat out more often, redecorate the house, or go back to school themselves. They may treat themselves to a new and more luxurious car or buy a vacation home. In later years, empty nesters may decide to sell their homes and become customers for retirement or assisted-living communities. They may require home-care services or more health care products as well. However, more older adults report they have not saved enough for retirement, which may include this type of care. People currently in this stage of life now say they would advise younger adults to address issues of a lifetime income, the cost of health care, and less reliance on Social Security benefits for income. Whether to meet expenses or for intellectual stimulation, many retired adults are returning to work at least part-time—as consultants in their field of expertise, starting their own businesses, or even working as Walmart greeters.[46]

One trend noted by researchers in the past decade is an increase in the number of grown children, or "boomerangs," who return home to live with their parents. A recent Pew Research Center study found that three out of ten young adults are boomerangs, some of them bringing along pets or families of their own.[47] Another trend is the growing number of grandparents who care for grandchildren on a regular basis—making them customers all over again for baby and child products, such as toys, food, and safety devices.[48]

SEGMENTING BY HOUSEHOLD TYPE

The first U.S. census in 1790 found an average household size of 5.8 people. Today, that number is below 3, due in part to a declining birth rate.[49] Sociologists attribute the decline to couples' reluctance to take on the added expense of a child.[50] The U.S. Department of Commerce cites several other reasons for the trend toward smaller households: lower fertility rates (including the decision to have fewer children or no children at all), young people's tendency to postpone marriage, the frequency of divorce, and the ability and desire of many people to live alone.

Today's U.S. households embody a wide range of diversity. They include households with a married couple and their children; households blended through divorce or loss of a spouse and remarriage; those headed by a single parent, same-sex parents, or grandparents; couples without children; groups of friends; and single-person households.

Couples without children may be young or old. If they are seniors, their children already may have grown and are living on their own. Some older couples choose to live together without marriage because they prefer to keep their finances separate, and because they could lose valuable health or pension benefits if they married. Younger couples without children are considered attractive to marketers, because they

Marketers have modified their messages and their products to meet the needs of single-person households, offering items like single-serving foods.

often have high levels of income to spend. These couples typically eat out often, take expensive vacations, and buy luxury cars.

Same-sex couples who share households—with or without children—are on the rise. More than 400,000 U.S. children are raised by same-sex couples. Even as the social debate over same-sex marriage and civil unions continues, marketers recognize these households as important customers. Walmart has introduced a line of wedding cards and commitment rings designed for same-sex couples. Companies like American Airlines, Campbell Soup, and General Motors also target gay and lesbian consumers.[51]

People live alone for a variety of reasons—sometimes by choice and sometimes by necessity, such as divorce or widowhood. In response, marketers have modified their messages and their products to meet the needs of single-person households. Food industry manufacturers are downsizing products, offering more single-serving foods, ranging from soup to macaroni and cheese.

<table>
<tr><td>

"BRIEFLY SPEAKING"

"Diversity: The art of thinking independently together."

—Malcolm S. Forbes
American publisher, Forbes magazine

</td></tr>
</table>

SEGMENTING BY INCOME AND EXPENDITURE PATTERNS

Part of the earlier definition of *market* described people with purchasing power. Not surprisingly, then, a common basis for segmenting the consumer market is income. Marketers often target geographic areas known for the high incomes of their residents. Or they might consider age or household type when determining potential buying power.

Engel's Laws

Engel's laws Three observations about the impact of household income on consumer spending behavior: as household income increases, a smaller percentage of expenditures goes for food; the percentage spent on housing, household operations, and clothing remains constant; and the percentage spent on other items (such as recreation and education) increases.

How do expenditure patterns vary with income? Over a century ago, Ernst Engel, a German statistician, published what became known as **Engel's laws**—three general statements based on his studies of the impact of household income changes on consumer spending behavior. According to Engel, as household income increases, the following will take place:

1. A smaller percentage of expenditures goes for food.

2. The percentage spent on housing, household operations, and clothing remains constant.

3. The percentage spent on other items (such as recreation and education) increases.

Are Engel's laws still valid? Recent studies say yes, with a few exceptions. Researchers note a steady decline in the percentage of total income spent on food, beverages, and tobacco as income increases. Although high-income families spend greater absolute amounts on food items, their purchases represent declining percentages of their total expenditures compared with food expenditures of low-income families.[52] In addition, the overall percentage of income spent on food has declined over the last century.[53] But as food prices become inflated, consumers change how they shop—they may spend the same to buy fewer items, spend more to buy the same items, or try to spend less and buy as many items as possible within the new budget. Marketers note that consumers are more selective, on the alert for bargains at the supermarket. One other recent finding splits the food dollar according to meals cooked and eaten at home versus meals eaten out at restaurants. Over the years, the proportion of food U.S. consumers ate away from home gradually increased, to nearly half their food dollar. However, with the belt-tightening that accompanies an economic downturn, the restaurant industry has seen a sustained dip in sales. Currently, U.S. consumers reportedly spend about 30 percent of their food dollar on meals eaten away from home.[54]

The second law remains partly accurate. However, the percentage of fixed expenditures for housing and household operations has increased over the past 30 years. And the percentage spent on clothing rises with increased income. Also, expenditures may vary from region to region. In general, residents of the Northeast and West spend more on housing than people who live in the Midwest and South.

The third law remains true, with the exception of medical and personal-care costs, which appear to decline as a percentage of increased income.

Engel's laws can help marketers target markets at all income levels. Regardless of the economic environment, consumers still buy luxury goods and services. One reason is some companies now offer their luxury products at different price levels. Mercedes-Benz has its lower-priced C-class models, while Tiffany sells a $125 sterling silver heart pendant with chain. Both of these firms continue to offer their higher-priced items but have broadened their market by serving other consumers.

DEMOGRAPHIC SEGMENTATION ABROAD

Marketers often face a difficult task in obtaining the data necessary for demographic segmentation abroad. Many countries do not have scheduled census programs. Germany skipped counting from 1970 to 1987, and France conducts a census about every seven years. By contrast, Japan and Canada conduct censuses every five years; however, the mid-decade assessments are not as complete as the end-of-decade counts.

Also, some foreign data include demographic divisions not found in the U.S. census. Canada collects information on religious affiliation, for instance. On the other hand, some of the standard segmentation data for U.S. markets are not available abroad. Many nations do not collect income data. Great Britain, Japan, Spain, France, and Italy are examples. Similarly, family lifecycle data are difficult to apply in global demographic segmentation efforts. Ireland acknowledges only three marital statuses—single, married, and widowed—while Latin American nations and Sweden count their unmarried cohabitants.

One source of global demographic information is the International Programs Center (IPC) at the U.S. Census Bureau. The IPC provides a searchable online database of population statistics for many countries on the Census Bureau's Web page. Another source is the United Nations, which sponsors national statistical offices that collect demographic data on a variety of countries.

In addition, private marketing research firms can supplement government data. Firms like Boston Consulting Group gather data on income of consumers around the world, focusing in particular on millionaire households. Although the global recession caused worldwide wealth to decline, the United States remains the country with the most millionaire households, with over 5.2 million, followed by Japan, China, the United Kingdom, and Germany. The country with the highest *density* of millionaire households is Singapore, followed by Switzerland, Qatar, Hong Kong, and Kuwait.[55]

ASSESSMENT CHECK

5.1 What is demographic segmentation?

5.2 What are the major categories of demographic segmentation?

PSYCHOGRAPHIC SEGMENTATION

Marketers have traditionally referred to geographic and demographic characteristics as the primary bases for dividing consumers into homogeneous market segments. Still, they have long recognized the need for fuller, more lifelike portraits of consumers in developing their marketing programs. As a result, psychographic segmentation can be a useful tool for gaining sharper insight into consumer purchasing behavior.

Outline the psychographic approach to segmenting consumer markets.

6

WHAT IS PSYCHOGRAPHIC SEGMENTATION?

Psychographic segmentation divides a population into groups with similar values and lifestyles. Lifestyle refers to a person's mode of living and describes how an individual operates on a daily basis. Consumers' lifestyles are composites of their individual psychological profiles, including their needs, motives, perceptions, and attitudes. A lifestyle also bears the mark of many other influences like family, job, social activities, and culture.

The most common method for developing psychographic profiles of a population is to conduct a large-scale survey asking consumers to agree or disagree with a collection of several hundred AIO statements. These AIO statements describe various activities, interests, and opinions. The resulting data allow researchers to develop lifestyle profiles. Marketers can then develop a separate marketing strategy that closely fits the psychographic makeup for each lifestyle segment.

psychographic segmentation Division of a population into groups having similar attitudes, values, and lifestyles.

AIO statements Items on lifestyle surveys that describe various activities, interests, and respondents' opinions.

Marketing researchers have conducted psychographic studies on hundreds of goods and services, such as beer and air travel. Hospitals and other health care providers use such studies to assess consumer behavior and attitudes toward health care in general, to learn the needs of consumers in particular marketplaces, and to determine how consumers perceive individual institutions. Many businesses turn to psychographic research to learn what consumers in various demographic and geographic segments want and need.

VALS™

Over a quarter-century ago, the research and consulting firm SRI International developed a psychographic segmentation system it called VALS, an acronym for *VAlues and LifeStyles*. Initially, VALS categorized consumers by their social values—how they felt about issues like legalization of marijuana or abortion, for example. Today, VALS is owned and managed by SRI Consulting Business Intelligence (SRIC-BI), an SRI spin-off that has revised the system to link it more closely with consumer buying behavior. The revised VALS system categorizes consumers by characteristics that correlate with purchase behavior. It is based on two key concepts: resources and self-motivation. VALS divides consumers into eight psychographic categories: innovators, thinkers, achievers, experiencers, believers, strivers, makers, and survivors. Figure 9.3 details the profiles for these categories and their relationships.

VALS Segmentation system that divides consumers into eight psychographic categories: innovators, thinkers, achievers, experiencers, believers, strivers, makers, and survivors.

The VALS framework in the figure displays differences in resources as vertical distances, and primary motivation is represented horizontally. The resource dimension measures income, education, self-confidence, health, eagerness to buy, and energy level. Primary motivations divide consumers into three groups: principle-motivated consumers who have a set of ideas and morals—principles—they live by; achievement-motivated consumers, influenced by symbols of success; and action-motivated consumers who seek physical activity, variety, and adventure.

SRIC-BI has created several specialized segmentation systems based on this approach. GeoVALS™, for instance, estimates the percentage of each VALS type in a U.S. residential zip code. Marketers can identify zip codes with the highest concentrations of the segment they want to reach, they can use the information to choose locations for retail outlets, and they can tailor marketing messages for a local audience. For example, a GeoVALS study can tell a marketer the percentage of consumers in Kettering, Ohio, who fall into each of the eight psychographic categories. Japan-VALS segments the Japanese marketplace with an emphasis on early adopters of new ideas and products. With a questionnaire of 49 items, marketers using Japan-VALS zero in on consumer needs, differentiate their brands, and develop more targeted tools and strategies.[56]

Other tools available include LifeMatrix, offered by the marketing research firm GfK Roper Consulting. LifeMatrix is a consumer segmentation system that crunches the numbers on hundreds of personal variables that include political views, religious affiliations, and social attitudes and comes up with ten psychographic categories reflecting today's lifestyles. Participants are asked to indicate how many hours each week they spend on certain activities, which helps shape the overall picture of their lives.[57]

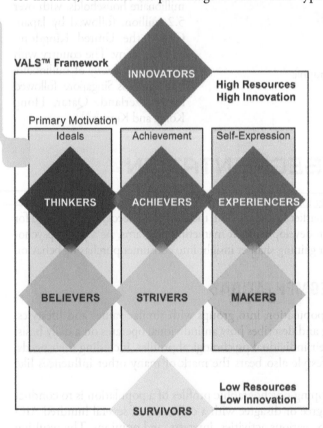

FIGURE 9.3
The VALS Framework

Source: SRI Consulting Business Intelligence (SRIC-BI); www.strategicbusinessinsights.com/vals accessed November 18, 2012.

VALS™ Framework

INNOVATORS

High Resources
High Innovation

Primary Motivation

Ideals　　Achievement　　Self-Expression

THINKERS　ACHIEVERS　EXPERIENCERS

BELIEVERS　STRIVERS　MAKERS

Low Resources
Low Innovation

SURVIVORS

PSYCHOGRAPHIC SEGMENTATION OF GLOBAL MARKETS

As Japan-VALS suggests, psychographic profiles can cross national boundaries. RoperASW, now part of the Germany-based GfK NOP, surveyed 7,000 people in 35 nations. From the data, Roper identified six psychographic consumer segments that exist in all 35 nations, although to varying degrees:

- *Strivers*, the largest segment, value professional and material goals more than the other groups. One-third of the Asian population and one-fourth of Russians are strivers. They are slightly more likely to be men than women.

- *Devouts* value duty and tradition. While this segment comprises 22 percent of all adults, they are most common in Africa, the Middle East, and developing Asia. They are least common in western Europe and developed Asian countries. Worldwide, they are more likely to be female.

- *Altruists* emphasize social issues and societal well-being. Comprising 18 percent of all adults, this group shows a median age of 44 and a slightly higher percentage of women.

- *Intimates* value family and personal relationships. They are divided almost equally between males and females. One American or European in four would be categorized as intimates, but only 7 percent of consumers in developing Asia fall into this category.

- *Fun seekers*, as you might guess from their name, focus on personal enjoyment and pleasurable experiences. They comprise 12 percent of the world's population, with a male–female ratio of 54 to 46. Many live in developed Asia.

- *Creatives*, the smallest segment, account for just 10 percent of the global population. This group seeks education, technology, and knowledge; their male–female ratio is roughly equal.

Roper researchers note that some principles and core beliefs—such as protecting the family—apply to more than one psychographic segment. In addition to Roper, GfK operates 115 companies in more than 100 countries, generating a wide range of marketing research. A recent venture involves a partnership of GfK's Mediamark Research & Intelligence, the Media Behavior Institute, and Nielsen to launch a U.S. cross-media research service of consumer activity that will help marketers identify when and where consumers are most receptive to marketers' messages.[58]

Altruists, who value social issues, comprise almost 18 percent of all adults, are typically in their mid-40s, and are divided almost equally between males and females.

Brand X Pictures/Jupiterimages

USING PSYCHOGRAPHIC SEGMENTATION

No one suggests that psychographic segmentation is an exact science, but it does help marketers quantify aspects of consumers' personalities and lifestyles to create goods and services for a target market. Psychographic profile systems such as those of Roper and SRIC-BI can paint useful pictures of the overall psychological motivations of consumers. These profiles produce much richer descriptions of potential target markets than other techniques can achieve. The enhanced detail aids in matching a company's image and product offerings with the types of consumers who use its products.

Identifying which psychographic segments are most prevalent in certain markets helps marketers plan and promote more effectively. Often, segments overlap; however, in a recent study of mobile phone users, consumer-research firm Experian Simmons discovered five distinct segments, which they named basic planners, mobile professionals, pragmatic adopters, social connectors, and mobirati. Mobile phones have become so prevalent that the user population is large enough to be studied—and segmented.[59]

Psychographic segmentation is a good supplement to segmentation by demographic or geographic variables. For example, marketers may have access to each consumer type's media preferences in network television, cable television, Internet use, radio format, magazines, and newspapers. Psychographic studies may then refine the picture of segment characteristics to give a more elaborate lifestyle profile of the consumers in the firm's target market. A psychographic study could help marketers of goods and services in Baltimore, Des Moines, or Seattle predict what kinds of products consumers in those cities would be drawn to and eliminate those that are not attractive.

⊕ ASSESSMENT CHECK

6.1　What is psychographic segmentation?

6.2　Name the eight psychographic categories of the U.S. VALS.

PRODUCT-RELATED SEGMENTATION

7 Describe product-related segmentation.

product-related segmentation Division of a population into homogeneous groups based on their relationships to a product.

Product-related segmentation involves dividing a consumer population into homogeneous groups based on their relationships to the product. This segmentation approach can take several forms:

1. segmenting based on the benefits people seek when they buy a product;

2. segmenting based on usage rates for a product; or

3. segmenting according to consumers' brand loyalty toward a product.

SEGMENTING BY BENEFITS SOUGHT

This approach focuses on attributes people seek and benefits they expect to receive from a good or service. It groups consumers into segments based on what they want a product to do for them. Consumers who drink Starbucks premium coffees are not just looking for a dose of caffeine. They are willing to pay extra to savor a pleasant experience, one that makes them feel pampered and appreciated. Women who work out at Curves want to look their best and feel healthy. Pet owners who feed their cats and dogs Science Diet believe they are giving their animals a great-tasting, healthful pet food. Case 9.1 at the end of this chapter outlines how cruise-ship companies offer cruises designed for very specific types of travelers.

Even if a business offers only one product line, however, marketers must remember to consider product benefits. Two people may buy the same product for very different reasons. A box of Arm & Hammer baking soda could end up being used as a refrigerator freshener, a toothpaste substitute, an antacid, or a deodorizer for a cat's litter box.

SEGMENTING BY USAGE RATES

Marketers may also segment a total market by grouping people according to the amounts of a product they buy and use. Markets can be divided into heavy-, moderate-, and light-user segments. The 80/20 principle holds that a big percentage of a product's revenues—maybe 80 percent—comes from a relatively small, loyal percentage of total customers, perhaps 20 percent. The 80/20 principle is sometimes referred to as *Praedo's law*. Although the percentages need not exactly equal these figures, the general principle holds true: relatively few heavy users of a product can account for the bulk of its consumption.

Depending on their goals, marketers may target heavy, moderate, or light users as well as nonusers. A company may attempt to lure heavy users of another product away from their regular brands to try a new brand. Nonusers and light users may be attractive prospects because other companies are ignoring them. Usage rates can also be linked to other segmentation methods such as demographic and psychographic segmentation.

SEGMENTING BY BRAND LOYALTY

A third product-related segmentation method groups consumers according to the strength of the brand loyalty they feel toward a product. A classic example of brand loyalty segmentation is the frequent-purchase program—it might be frequent flyer, frequent stay, or frequent purchase of books or gasoline. Other companies attempt to segment their market by developing brand loyalty over a period of time, through consumers' stages of life. Disney has a collection of toddler and children's shoes featuring their many animated characters. K-Swiss offers sneakers for infants and toddlers: tiny replicas of the famous tennis shoes for adults. Marketers for these companies are intent on creating brand loyalty for their shoes at the earliest stages of life.[60]

Companies spar for loyalty on just about every front. In recent years, fast-food chains like McDonald's and Burger King started offering breakfast menus. In order to win its own share of early-morning customers, Taco Bell recently joined with Cinnabon, Tropicana, Seattle's Best, and other brands to offer breakfast menu items. Among the new items on Taco Bell's menu are breakfast burritos with eggs and sausage, bacon, or steak; orange juice; and hot or iced coffee.[61]

USING MULTIPLE SEGMENTATION BASES

Segmentation can help marketers increase their accuracy in reaching the

© Hill's Pet Nutrition, Inc.

> ## BRIEFLY SPEAKING
>
> "You read a book from beginning to end. You run a business the opposite way. You start with the end, and then you do everything you must to reach it."
>
> **—Harold S. Geneen**
> *American businessman and former CEO of ITT*

Segmenting by benefits focuses on the attributes that people seek and the benefits they expect to receive from a good or service. This ad focuses on the healthy benefits of Science Diet Ideal Balance Grain Free dog food.

ASSESSMENT CHECK

7.1 List the three approaches to product-related segmentation.

7.2 What is the 80/20 principle?

right markets. Like other marketing tools, segmentation is probably best used in a flexible manner—for instance, combining geographic and demographic segmentation techniques or dovetailing product-related segmentation with segmentation by income and expenditure patterns. An important point to keep in mind is that segmentation is a tool to help marketers get to know their potential customers better and ultimately satisfy their needs with the appropriate goods and services.

THE MARKET SEGMENTATION PROCESS

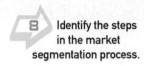

8 Identify the steps in the market segmentation process.

To this point, the chapter has discussed various bases on which companies segment markets. But how do marketers decide which segmentation base—or bases—to use? Firms may use a management-driven method, in which segments are predefined by managers based on their observation of the behavioral and demographic characteristics of likely users. Or they may use a market-driven method, in which segments are defined by asking customers for the attributes important to them. Then, marketers follow a four-stage process.

DEVELOP A RELEVANT PROFILE FOR EACH SEGMENT

After identifying promising segments, marketers should understand the customers in each one. This in-depth analysis of customers helps managers accurately match buyers' needs with the firm's marketing offers. The process must identify characteristics that both explain the similarities among customers within each segment and account for differences among segments.

The task at this stage is to develop a profile of the typical customer in each segment. Such a profile might include information about lifestyle patterns, attitudes toward product attributes and brands, product-use habits, geographic locations, and demographic characteristics.

FORECAST MARKET POTENTIAL

In the second stage, market segmentation and market opportunity analysis combine to produce a forecast of market potential within each segment. Market potential sets the upper limit on the demand competing firms can expect from a segment. Multiplying by market share determines a single firm's maximum sales potential. This step should define a preliminary go or no-go decision from management because the total sales potential in each segment must justify resources devoted to further analysis. For example, in deciding whether to market a new product to teens, electronics firms need to determine the demand for it and the disposable income of that group.

FORECAST PROBABLE MARKET SHARE

Once market potential has been estimated, a firm must forecast its probable market share. Competitors' positions in targeted segments must be analyzed, and a specific marketing strategy must be designed to reach these segments. These two activities may be performed simultaneously. Moreover, by settling on a marketing strategy and tactics, a firm determines the expected level of resources it must commit, that is, the costs it will incur to tap the potential demand in each segment.

Apple's iPod took the marketplace by storm, followed by the iPhone, and analysts believe these two products helped boost sales of the iMac computer as well. More recently, Apple's iPad3 was met with a flood of orders: 3 million were sold over the first weekend alone, about three times as many as during the launch of the original iPad.[62]

SELECT SPECIFIC MARKET SEGMENTS

The information, analysis, and forecasts accumulated throughout the entire market segmentation decision process allow management to assess the potential for achieving company goals and to justify committing resources in developing one or more segments. Demand forecasts, together with cost projections, determine the profits and the return on investment the company can expect from each segment. Marketing strategy and tactics must be designed to reinforce the firm's image, yet keep within its unique organizational capabilities.

At this point in the analysis, marketers weigh more than monetary costs and benefits; they also consider many difficult-to-measure but critical organizational and environmental factors. The firm may lack experienced personnel to launch a successful attack on an attractive market segment. Similarly, a firm with 60 percent of the market faces possible legal problems with the Federal Trade Commission if it increases its market concentration. This assessment of both financial and nonfinancial factors is a difficult but vital step in the decision process.

ASSESSMENT CHECK

8.1   Identify the four stages of market segmentation.

8.2   Why is forecasting important to market segmentation?

STRATEGIES FOR REACHING TARGET MARKETS

Marketers spend a lot of time and effort developing strategies that will best match their firm's product offerings to the needs of particular target markets. An appropriate match is vital to the firm's marketing success. Marketers have identified four basic strategies for achieving consumer satisfaction: undifferentiated marketing, differentiated marketing, concentrated marketing, and micromarketing. Social media is rapidly becoming a profitable means of reaching audiences in all these strategies; see the "Career Readiness" feature for some ways to do so successfully.

Discuss four basic strategies for reaching target markets.

CAREER READINESS

Reaching Target Markets with Social Media

Social media allows for more precise targeting of consumer and other markets than ever before. How can *you* make the most of it? Here are some tips.

1. Know your target market and its most important segments. How does your audience use your product, and what unsolved problems do they face?

2. Join the online communities where your target audience gathers, including Facebook, LinkedIn, Twitter, Google +, and/or Pinterest, and influential blogs.

3. Understand how these sites and their users differ from each other. All social media sites are not alike.

4. Start by spending some time listening, so you can learn about users' concerns, problems, and preferences. Learn and follow the social conventions of each community as well.

5. Start chiming in with helpful tips and advice that revolve around your market, not your product. Help users solve problems rather than pitching your product or service.

6. Find additional content that matters to your audience, and share it with them.

7. If you add additional tools, like widgets, make sure they're easy to use and require minimal effort.

8. Consider using audio and video. One-third of the U.S. population watches a video online every day.

Sources: Roxane Divol, David Edelman, and Hugo Sarrazin, "Demystifying Social Media," *McKinsey Quarterly*, accessed November 18, 2012, www.mckinseyquarterly.com; Anton Koekemoer, "Using Twitter, Facebook, and LinkedIn to Reach Your Target Audience," *Memeburn.com*, accessed November 18, 2012, http://memeburn.com; Phil Mershon, "5 Social Media Tips for Finding and Engaging Your Target Audience: New Research," *Social Media Examiner*, accessed November 18, 2012, www.socialmedia examiner.com; Jen Williams, "Reaching Your Target Market Through Social Media," *About Social Media*, accessed November 18, 2012, http://aboutsocialmedia.com.

UNDIFFERENTIATED MARKETING

A firm may produce only one product or product line and promote it to all customers with a single marketing mix; such a firm is said to practice undifferentiated marketing, sometimes called *mass marketing*. Undifferentiated marketing was much more common in the past than it is today.

While undifferentiated marketing is efficient from a production viewpoint, the strategy also brings inherent dangers. A firm that attempts to satisfy everyone in the market with one standard product may suffer if competitors offer specialized alternatives to smaller segments of the total market and better satisfy individual segments. In fact, firms that implement strategies of differentiated marketing, concentrated marketing, or micromarketing may capture enough small segments of the market to defeat another competitor's strategy of undifferentiated marketing. The golden arches of McDonald's have always stood for quick, inexpensive meals. Consumers could count on the same food and same dining experience at every McDonald's they visited. But McDonald's marketers are changing the firm's strategy somewhat in response to a trend that says consumers want a little luxury with their burger and fries and a more varied dining experience from restaurant to restaurant. Some stores feature a color scheme featuring earth tones. The company has also introduced new products, such as Chicken McBites and Fruit & Nut Oatmeal, and has extended operating hours at some stores.[63]

DIFFERENTIATED MARKETING

Firms that promote numerous products with differing marketing mixes designed to satisfy smaller segments are said to practice differentiated marketing. By providing increased satisfaction for each of many target markets, a company can produce more sales by following a differentiated marketing strategy than undifferentiated marketing would generate. Oscar Mayer, a marketer of a variety of meat products, practices differentiated marketing. It increased its sales by introducing Lunchables, aimed at children. The original Lunchables were so successful that Oscar Mayer introduced more choices in the line, including snack versions. In general, however, differentiated marketing also raises costs. Production costs usually rise because additional products and variations require shorter production runs and increased setup times. Inventory costs rise because more products require added storage space and increased efforts for record keeping. Promotional costs also rise because each segment demands a unique promotional mix.

Despite higher marketing costs, however, an organization may be forced to practice differentiated marketing to diversify and reach new customers. The travel industry now recognizes the need to target smaller groups of travelers with specialized interests. History buffs can attend special events at Colonial Williamsburg or at George Washington's estate, Mount Vernon.[64] The Sierra Club and other environmental organizations—in addition to commercial travel operators—offer hikes, kayaking expeditions, and bird-watching trips for outdoor enthusiasts.[65] Luxury travel company Tauck now offers a series of guided, all-inclusive trips called Tauck Bridges, designed with traveling families or grandparents and their grandchildren in mind.[66]

CONCENTRATED MARKETING

Rather than trying to market its products separately to several segments, a firm may opt for a concentrated marketing strategy. With concentrated marketing (also known as niche marketing), a firm focuses its efforts on profitably satisfying a single market segment. This approach can appeal to a small firm lacking the financial resources of its competitors and to a company offering highly specialized goods and services. American Express, a large firm with many financial products, recently introduced two new credit cards designed for very specific markets: The Knot, for engaged couples, and The Nest, for newlyweds.

Peanut Butter & Co. appeals to the world's peanut butter lovers with its proprietary brand of gourmet, natural peanut butter flavors including Smooth Operator, Crunch Time, and Dark Chocolate Dreams. Its Mighty Maple is intended for pancake fans, and The Bee's Knees can replace a humdrum jar of honey. Fans visiting the flagship store in New York City can sample favorites like "ants on a log" or grilled peanut butter, banana, honey, and bacon sandwiches; or they can shop for their favorite blends online.[67] But along with its benefits, concentrated marketing has its dangers. Because the strategy ties a firm's growth to a specific segment, sales can suffer if new competitors

Trekking the Ansel Adams Wilderness, California.
Photo: Andy Johnson.

© 2012 Sierra Club

appeal successfully to the same target. If another firm targets peanut butter lovers in the same manner, Peanut Butter & Co. may face a struggle. In addition, errors in forecasting market potential or customer buying habits can lead to severe problems, particularly if the firm has spent substantially on product development and promotion. If more people—children in particular—continue to develop peanut allergies, sales of Peanut Butter & Co.'s products may begin to decline. Anticipating this, the company could begin to diversify product offerings to include nonallergenic foods.

MICROMARKETING

The fourth targeting strategy, still more narrowly focused than concentrated marketing, is
micromarketing—targeting potential customers at a very basic level, such as by zip code, specific occupation, or lifestyle. Ultimately, micromarketing can even target individuals. A salesperson at your favorite clothing boutique may contact you when certain merchandise she thinks you might like arrives at the store. The Internet allows marketers to make micromarketing even more effective: by tracking specific demographic and personal information, marketers can send email directly to individual consumers most likely to buy their products.

When a shopper visits Amazon, the website will welcome the shopper by name and recommend products that shopper might be interested in buying, given previous purchases. Amazon also sends out emails recommending specific products similar to items shoppers have already purchased.

But micromarketing, like niche marketing, can become too much of a good thing if companies spend too much time, effort, and marketing dollars to unearth a market too small and specialized to be profitable. In addition, micromarketing may cause a company to lose sight of other, larger markets. So it's important for marketers to assess the situation and pursue the most profitable markets.

> **"BRIEFLY SPEAKING"**
>
> "Increasingly, the mass market is turning into a mass of niches."
>
> —**Chris Anderson**
> *Former editor in chief,* Wired *magazine, and author of* The Long Tail

micromarketing
Targeting potential customers at very narrow, basic levels, such as by zip code, specific occupation, or lifestyle—possibly even individuals themselves.

 ASSESSMENT CHECK

9.1 Explain the difference between undifferentiated and differentiated marketing strategies.

9.2 What are the benefits of concentrated marketing?

SELECTING AND EXECUTING A STRATEGY

Although most organizations adopt some form of differentiated marketing, no single choice suits all firms. Any of the alternatives may prove most effective in a particular situation. The basic determinants of a market-specific strategy are (1) company resources, (2) product homogeneity, (3) stage in the product life cycle, and (4) competitors' strategies.

A firm with limited resources may have to choose a concentrated marketing strategy. Small firms may be forced to select small target markets because of limitations in their sales force and advertising budgets. On the other hand, an undifferentiated marketing strategy suits a firm selling items perceived by consumers as relatively homogeneous. Marketers of grain, for example, sell standardized grades of generic products rather than individual brand names. Some petroleum companies implement undifferentiated marketing to distribute their gasoline to the mass market.

The firm's strategy may also change as its product progresses through the stages of the lifecycle. During the early stages, undifferentiated marketing might effectively support the company's effort to build initial demand for the item. In the later stages, however, competitive pressures may force modifications in products and in the development of marketing strategies aimed at segments of the total market.

The strategies of competitors also affect the choice of a segmentation approach. A firm may encounter obstacles to undifferentiated marketing if its competitors actively cultivate smaller segments. In such instances, competition usually forces each firm to adopt a differentiated marketing strategy.

positioning Placing a product at a certain point or location within a market in the minds of prospective buyers.

Having chosen a strategy for reaching their firm's target market, marketers must then decide how best to position the product. The concept of positioning seeks to put a product in a certain position, or place, in the minds of prospective buyers. Marketers use a positioning strategy to distinguish their firm's offerings from those of competitors and to create promotions that communicate the desired position. Restaurants that position themselves as "fast-casual" continue to outperform most other categories of restaurants. Top menu choices in this segment include Mexican, bakery café, pizzas, Asian, chicken, and hamburgers. Analysts believe fast-casual restaurants provide consumers with the chance to sit down to a dinner priced lower than what is offered at an upscale restaurant yet of higher quality than a fast-food restaurant. Fast-casual provides good value in the minds of many consumers. Many fast-casual restaurants currently are trying to upgrade their menu with new premium offerings, redesigning their interior to make it more inviting, and using Facebook and Twitter to attract even more customers.[68]

Restaurants that position themselves as "fast-casual," such as Panera Bread, continue to outperform most other categories of restaurants.

To achieve the goal of positioning, marketers follow a number of positioning strategies. Possible approaches include positioning a product according to the following categories:

1. *Attributes*—eBay, "Buy it. Sell it. Love it."

2. *Price/quality*—Omega watches, "We measure the 100th of a second that separates winning from taking part."

3. *Competitors*—Walmart, "Save money. Live better."

4. *Application*—Blue Cross Blue Shield health insurance, "Experience. Wellness. Everywhere."

5. *Product user*—Crane's stationery, "for the writer somewhere in each of us."

6. *Product class*—BMW, the "ultimate driving machine."

Whatever strategy they choose, marketers want to emphasize a product's unique advantages and differentiate it from competitors' options. A **positioning map** provides a valuable tool in helping managers position products by graphically illustrating consumers' perceptions of competing products within an industry. Marketers can create a competitive positioning map from information solicited from consumers or from their accumulated knowledge about a market. A positioning map might present two different characteristics—price and perceived quality—and show how consumers view a product and its major competitors based on these traits. The hypothetical positioning map in Figure 9.4 compares selected retailers based on possible perceptions of the prices and quality of their offerings.

Sometimes changes in the competitive environment force marketers to **reposition** a product—changing the position it holds in the minds of prospective buyers relative to the positions of competing products. Repositioning may even be necessary for already successful products or firms in order to gain greater market share. Encyclopaedia Britannica, published in multivolume print editions for 244 years, recently announced that it would only be available online. The company updates the online edition, which is far bigger than any print version, every twenty minutes.[69]

FIGURE 9.4
Hypothetical Positioning Map for Selected Retailers

High — Neiman Marcus / Macy's / Kohl's / Target / Walmart / Low — Dollar General. Price (vertical), Perceived Quality (horizontal, Low to High).

© Cengage Learning

positioning map Tool that helps marketers place products in a market by graphically illustrating consumers' perceptions of competing products within an industry.

repositioning Changing the position of a product within the minds of prospective buyers relative to the positions of competing products.

⊕ ASSESSMENT CHECK

10.1 What are the four determinants of a market-specific strategy?

10.2 What is the role of positioning in a marketing strategy?

STRATEGIC IMPLICATIONS OF MARKETING IN THE 21ST CENTURY

To remain competitive, today's marketers must accurately identify potential customers. They can use a variety of methods to accomplish this, including segmenting markets by gender and geographic location. The trick is to figure out the best combination of methods for segmentation to identify the most lucrative, long-lasting potential markets. Marketers must also remain flexible, responding to markets as they change—for instance, following a generation as it ages or reaching out to new generations by revamping or repositioning products.

The greatest competitive advantage will belong to firms that pinpoint and serve markets without segmenting them to the point at which they are too small or specialized to garner profits. Marketers who reach and communicate with the right customers have a greater chance of attracting and keeping those customers than marketers who search for the wrong buyers in the wrong place.

Get online now for additional learning tools to help you master your marketing knowledge—visit **WWW.CENGAGEBRAIN.COM** today!

REVIEW OF CHAPTER OBJECTIVES

1 Identify the essential components of a market.

A market consists of people and organizations with the necessary purchasing power, willingness, and authority to buy. Consumer products are purchased by the ultimate consumer for personal use. Business products are purchased for use directly or indirectly in the production of other goods and services. Certain products may fall into both categories.

2 Outline the role of market segmentation in developing a marketing strategy.

Market segmentation is the process of dividing a total market into several homogeneous groups. It is used in identifying a target market for a good or service. Segmentation is the key to deciding a marketing strategy.

3 Describe the criteria necessary for effective segmentation.

Effective segmentation depends on these four basic requirements: (1) the segment must have measurable purchasing power and size, (2) marketers can find a way to promote to and serve the market, (3) marketers must identify segments large enough for profit potential, and (4) the firm can target a number of segments that match its marketing capabilities.

4 Explain the geographic approach to segmenting consumer markets.

Geographic segmentation divides the overall market into homogeneous groups according to population locations.

5 Discuss the demographic approach to segmenting consumer markets.

Demographic segmentation classifies the market into groups based on characteristics such as age, gender, and income level.

6 Outline the psychographic approach to segmenting consumer markets.

Psychographic segmentation uses behavioral profiles developed from analyses of consumers' activities, opinions, interests, and lifestyles to identify market segments.

7 Describe product-related segmentation.

Product-related segmentation can take three basic forms: segmenting based on the benefits people seek when buying a product, segmenting based on usage rates for a product, and segmenting according to consumers' brand loyalty toward a product.

8 Identify the steps in the market segmentation process.

Market segmentation is the division of markets into relatively homogeneous groups. Segmentation follows a four-step sequence: (1) developing user profiles, (2) forecasting the overall market potential, (3) estimating market share, and (4) selecting specific market segments.

9 Discuss four basic strategies for reaching target markets.

Four strategies are (1) undifferentiated marketing—uses a single marketing mix; (2) differentiated marketing—produces numerous products, each with its own mix; (3) concentrated marketing—directs all the firm's marketing resources toward a small segment; and (4) micromarketing—targets potential customers at basic levels, such as zip code or occupation.

10 Summarize the types of positioning strategies, and explain the reasons for positioning and repositioning products.

Positioning strategies include positioning a good or service according to attributes, price/quality, competitors, application, product use, and product class. Positioning helps distinguish a firm's products from those of competitors and provides a basis for marketing communications. Repositioning a product—changing the position it holds in consumers' minds—may be necessary to gain greater market share.

ASSESSMENT CHECK: ANSWERS

1.1 Define *target market*. A target market is the specific segment of consumers most likely to purchase a particular product.

1.2 Distinguish between a consumer product and a business product. A consumer product is purchased by the ultimate buyer for personal use. A business product is purchased for use directly or indirectly in the production of other goods and services.

2.1 Define *market segmentation*. Market segmentation is the process of dividing a total market into several homogeneous groups.

2.2 Describe the role of market segmentation. The role of market segmentation is to identify the factors that affect purchase decisions and then group consumers according to the presence or absence of these factors.

3.1 Identify the four criteria for effective segmentation. The four criteria for effective segmentation are: (1) the market segment must present measurable purchasing power and size, (2) marketers must find a way to promote effectively and serve the market segment, (3) marketers must identify segments sufficiently large to give them good profit potential, and (4) the firm must aim for segments that match its marketing capabilities.

3.2 Give an example of a market segment that meets these criteria. Examples might include women, teenagers, Hispanics, empty nesters, and NASCAR enthusiasts.

4.1 Under what circumstances are marketers most likely to use geographic segmentation? Marketers usually use geographic segmentation when regional preferences exist and when demand for categories of goods and services varies according to geographic region.

4.2 What are the five main categories for classifying urban data? The five categories are core based statistical area (CBSA), metropolitan statistical area (MSA), micropolitan statistical area, consolidated metropolitan statistical area (CMSA), and primary metropolitan statistical area (PMSA).

5.1 What is demographic segmentation? Demographic segmentation defines consumer groups according to demographic variables such as gender, age, income, occupation, household, and family lifecycle.

5.2 What are the major categories of demographic segmentation? The major categories of demographic segmentation are gender, age, ethnic group, family lifecycle, household type, income, and expenditure patterns.

6.1 What is psychographic segmentation? Psychographic segmentation divides a population into groups with similar values and lifestyles.

6.2 Name the eight psychographic categories of the U.S. VALS. The eight categories are innovators, thinkers, achievers, experiencers, believers, strivers, makers, and survivors.

7.1 List the three approaches to product-related segmentation. The three approaches are segmenting by benefits sought, segmenting by usage rates, and segmenting by brand loyalty.

7.2 What is the 80/20 principle? The 80/20 principle states that a big percentage (80 percent) of a product's revenues comes from a relatively small number (20 percent) of loyal customers.

8.1 Identify the four stages of market segmentation. The four stages are developing user profiles, forecasting the overall market potential, estimating market share, and selecting specific market segments.

8.2 Why is forecasting important to market segmentation? Forecasting is important because it can define a preliminary go or no-go decision based on sales potential. It can help a firm avoid a disastrous move or point out opportunities.

9.1 Explain the difference between undifferentiated and differentiated marketing strategies. Undifferentiated marketing promotes a single product line to all customers with a single marketing mix. Differentiated marketing promotes numerous products with different marketing mixes designed to satisfy smaller segments.

9.2 What are the benefits of concentrated marketing? Concentrated marketing can allow a firm to focus on a single market segment, which is especially appealing to smaller firms and those that offer highly specialized goods and services.

10.1 What are the four determinants of a market-specific strategy? The four determinants are company resources, product homogeneity, stage in the product lifecycle, and competitors' strategies.

10.2 What is the role of positioning in a marketing strategy? Positioning places a product in a certain position in the minds of prospective buyers so marketers can create messages that distinguish their offerings from those of competitors.

MARKETING TERMS YOU NEED TO KNOW

market **272**
target market **272**
consumer products **273**
business products **273**
market segmentation **273**
geographic segmentation **275**
core based statistical area (CBSA) **276**
metropolitan statistical area (MSA) **276**

micropolitan statistical area **277**
consolidated metropolitan statistical area (CMSA) **277**
primary metropolitan statistical area (PMSA) **277**
core region **277**
geographic information systems (GISs) **278**
demographic segmentation **279**

cohort effect **282**
Video Game Generation **283**
family lifecycle **286**
Engel's laws **288**
psychographic segmentation **289**
AIO statements **289**
VALS **290**
product-related segmentation **292**

80/20 principle **293**
undifferentiated marketing **296**
differentiated marketing **296**
concentrated marketing (niche marketing) **296**
micromarketing **297**
positioning **298**
positioning map **299**
repositioning **299**

ASSURANCE OF LEARNING REVIEW

1. Classify each of the following as a business product or a consumer product:
   a. Detroit Tigers ticket
   b. bottle of body lotion
   c. fleet of delivery trucks
   d. bulk order of rice
   e. digital camera
   f. Carrie Underwood music CD

2. What are core regions? Why do marketers try to identify these regions?

3. What is the cohort effect? This chapter suggested that the rise of video games was sufficiently significant to have influenced and bound a generation together. Do you agree?

4. What is the fastest-growing racial/ethnic minority group in the United States? What types of things do marketers need to know about this group to market successfully to these consumers?

5. How is segmentation by family lifecycle and household type useful to marketers? Briefly describe your own family in these terms, identifying characteristics that might be helpful to marketers for a firm selling HDTVs.

6. What are AIO statements? How are they used by marketers?

7. Identify a branded product to which you are loyal, and explain why you are loyal to this item. What factors might cause your loyalty to change?

8. Choose another branded product. Create a relevant profile for the marketing segment this product serves.

9. What are the six categories generally used to position a product?

10. How does a positioning map work? What are its benefits?

PROJECTS AND TEAMWORK EXERCISES

1. On your own or with a partner, choose one of the following consumer products and think about how it could be used as a business product. Then create a business advertisement for your product.
   a. lawn care products
   b. microwave oven
   c. golf balls
   d. bottled water
   e. electric car
   f. vacuum cleaner

2. With a classmate, choose one of the following products you believe is generally targeted for either men or women and create an advertisement for the product aimed at the opposite gender.

   a. barbecue grill and accessories
   b. hunting or fishing supplies
   c. nail salon
   d. minivan
   e. online video game

3. Create a chart showing how your family's income and expenditure patterns have changed over the years as the family lifecycle changed. You don't need exact figures, just the general picture. If possible, ask other family members for additional information.

4. With a classmate, choose a product and come up with a slogan representing each of the six positioning approaches for the product.

5. On your own or with a classmate, select one of the following products. Visit the firm's website to see how the product is positioned, then create an advertisement showing how you think marketers could reposition the product to gain greater market share.

   a. Gatorade
   b. Dove soap
   c. Barilla pasta
   d. Fiskars scissors
   e. Hallmark cards

CRITICAL-THINKING EXERCISES

1. Create a profile of yourself as part of a market segment. Include the following:
   a. geographic location
   b. gender and age
   c. household type
   d. income and spending habits

2. Select one of the following products and explain how you would use segmentation by income and expenditure patterns to determine your targeted market.
   a. Busch Gardens theme parks
   b. Sony Cybershot digital camera
   c. Healthy Choice frozen entrées
   d. Kia Soul automobile

3. How do you think the Internet has affected differentiated marketing techniques?

4. Choose one of the following products and describe a marketing approach that segments the target market by benefits sought:
   a. Kryptonite bicycle lock
   b. A private college or university
   c. Pella windows and doors
   d. Coke Zero
   e. Edy's Grand Ice Cream

5. Visit the website of a large company, such as Kraft Foods, Sony, or Campbell Soup. Look for ways the firm practices differentiated marketing. How do you think this approach benefits the firm?

ETHICS EXERCISE

Marketers are making a new pitch to men—at the risk of political incorrectness. Marketers for firms such as Unilever and Wendy's were frustrated at their inability to reach young male consumers with their messages. After searching for clues about what this crowd likes, these firms created marketing campaigns designed to grab their attention—perhaps at the expense of other consumers. Some advertising is designed to appeal to "bad boy" attitudes, lowbrow humor, and sex.

1. What are some of the pitfalls of this kind of segmentation?

2. Do you think these ads will be successful in the long run? Why or why not?

3. Should marketers be concerned about offending one market segment when trying to reach another? Why or why not?

INTERNET EXERCISES

1. **Psychographic segmentation.** Visit the websites of Caterpillar, Hilton Hotels, and PepsiCo. How does each firm employ psychographic segmentation (such as the VALS approach) to the marketing of its products? Is there a relationship between the use of psychographic segmentation and the types of products sold by each firm?

   www.cat.com

   www.hilton.com

   www.pepsico.com

2. **Market segmentation.** Go to the website of Siemens. How does Siemens segment its markets, such as geographical, product related, demographic, or brand loyalty? Does the firm

   use more than one method of product segmentation? Why or why not?

   www.siemens.com/entry/cc/en

3. **Target market.** Visit the website of Philips. What strategy or strategies does the firm employ for reaching its target markets? Does it rely more on undifferentiated or differentiated marketing?

   www.usa.philips.com

Note: Internet Web addresses change frequently. If you don't find the exact site listed, you may need to access the organization's home page and search from there or use a search engine such as Google or Bing.

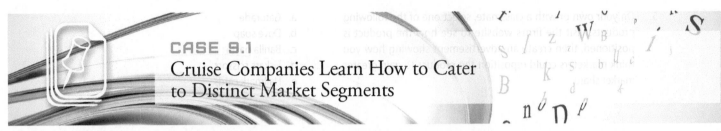

CASE 9.1
Cruise Companies Learn How to Cater to Distinct Market Segments

The typical cruise ship passenger may not actually exist. While the core target market for cruise vacations is 25 or older, with a passport and household income of at least $40,000 who is likely to have cruised at least once before, that description now covers more than 40 percent of the U.S. population. That's why cruise marketers no longer think in terms of an "average" customer. So many different specialty cruises are springing up to appeal to different market segments that almost anyone can find themselves in a target group.

What's your passion? Whether you like to cook, quilt, tango, snorkel, listen to jazz, play baseball, garden, watch movies, gaze at Impressionist art, explore investment strategies, hold a family reunion, or engage in a host of other pursuits, there's a themed cruise for you, with specific on-board and on-shore activities, workshops, and seminars hosted by skilled instructors. Even if you're attending a business meeting or conference rather than enjoying a vacation, you may well find yourself cruising for the occasion. Business managers find that meetings on cruise ships can save as much as a third of the cost of land-based gatherings, once all cost factors like meals, lodging, travel, and audio-visual equipment are taken into account. Besides, says the cofounder of a company that plans such events, cruising "excites people."

Passengers do fall into a number of traditional demographic categories that cruise marketers find useful. Analyzing factors like country of origin, language, economic status, and psychographics,

marketers have devised distinct market segments. "Explorers" are well-to-do repeat customers, a small group that's profitable but challenging to please. "Admirals" are older and loyal; they appreciate a traditional experience. "Marines" are young professionals on the lookout for a better experience each time; they're eager to parasail, surf, and rock climb. "Little Mermaids" are upper-middle-class families in search of a memorable vacation, while "Escapers" just want to get away from the daily grind without worries or complications. Finally, "Souvenirs" are in search of the best deal; price is their priority.

Marketers even have a term for those whose interest and income make them unlikely to become cruise customers. They are "Adrift."

QUESTIONS FOR CRITICAL THINKING

1. Is segmenting customers as "Explorers," "Admirals," and the like a useful marketing tool? Why or why not?

2. Which segments of the cruise market are most likely to be influenced by social media? Why?

Sources: Organization website, *Theme Cruise Finder,* www.themecruisefinder.com, accessed November 19, 2012; organization website, *Cruise Market Watch,* www .cruisemarketwatch.com, accessed November 19, 2012; "CLIA's 2011 Cruise Market Profile Study Reports Positive Customer Attitudes," *Cruising.org,* accessed November 19, 2012, www.cruising.org; "Specialty Cruises Ride Wave of Popularity with Landry & Kling," *MarketWatch,* accessed November 19, 2012, www.marketwatch.com; Anne Campbell, "Pursue Your Passions at Sea: Specialty Cruises," *USA Today,* accessed November 19, 2012, http://travel.usatoday.com.

VIDEO CASE 9.2
Nederlander Targets Theatergoers Everywhere

In order for marketers to send effective messages to customers, they need to know who those customers are—and what they want. Nederlander Producing Company has been in the theater business for a century, but its owners aren't looking backward. Instead they're focused forward, on the most advanced ways to identify and serve their audiences. "Everything we do along the food chain of the theater industry is about enhancing the customers' feeling when they experience a Broadway show," says Nick Scandalios, executive vice president of the Nederlander Organization. To do this, the company goes to great lengths to target exactly who those customers are.

Nederlander segments its audiences in a few ways: geographic, demographic, and psychographic. The company also engages in some product-related segmentation by building brand loyalty to its stable of theaters, productions, and concerts. Since Broadway is located in New York City, it's natural for Nederlander to market to consumers living within the tri-state area of New York, New Jersey, and Connecticut. But Nederlander also owns theaters and produces shows in Chicago, Los Angeles, Tucson, and Raleigh, among other cities—so the company markets to consumers living around those areas as well. Then there are the tourists who live elsewhere but travel to any of those cities—Nederlander makes sure to communicate with them too. Thus, the geographic range extends nationwide. "Nederlander was the first such company to develop a one-on-one digital interaction with all of the people who go to all of the Nederlander houses across the country, called Broadway Direct," says Scott Sanders, co-lead producer of the recent revival of the Broadway hit musical *Evita*. "There are over 2.5 million people on that list. It's a very valuable list, these are very targeted theatergoers."

Broadway Direct also helps Nederlander and its partners segment its audiences by demographics and psychographics. For example, by tapping the digital list, says Sanders, "we sold more than $500,000 to those customers, all at full price." These are consumers who can afford premium seats and performances and are willing to pay for them. They are people who enjoy the theater and make it part of their entertainment lifestyle. All of the data gathered by Broadway Direct creates user profiles that the company relies on for everything from deciding which shows to invest in or host, to which consumers will most likely attend each show. "The more we know about audience purchasing habits, the better we can become at serving them with the shows we think they'd find most interesting," notes Sean Free, vice president of sales and tracking at Nederlander.

The company doesn't stop with an initial communication blast to more than 2.5 million theatergoers. Instead, it follows up with what Free calls re-targeting, which further identifies audience members by their preferences. Each Broadway Direct newsletter contains opportunities for consumers to click on different options for content. "We put these people in specific buckets," explains Free. For example, as *Evita* approached its launch, Broadway Direct sent theatergoers an online newsletter containing feature articles, video, audio, a sweepstakes, and, of course, a "Buy Tickets" button. Consumers had a seven-day window in which to purchase tickets at a lower price, after which the price would go up. Those who clicked the button but didn't follow through with a purchase received a follow-up email from Broadway Direct a few days later, reminding them of the opportunity. Free estimates that the second email generated an additional 15 to 20 percent in sales.

Nederlander also carefully positions its offerings to differentiate itself not only from other theater productions but also from other types of entertainment on which consumers might spend their dollars. "We thought it was important to position *Evita* as an important event because it was the first time in 30 years the show had been on Broadway," notes Free. "So this was going to be a big deal." Nederlander and its partners treated it as such. When they landed Ricky Martin for the lead role of Che, they immediately contacted Martin's fan club and marketing team to launch a presale for Martin's fan base. These might not be regular theatergoers, but they wanted to see Martin on stage. Then Nederlander marketers followed up with a presale to its Audience Rewards customers, who are members of the company's loyalty program. "Loyalty is key for any venue or any show," acknowledges Free. "People want to come back to see shows and they should be rewarded for that." An excited audience crammed the theater in New York to see the premier of *Evita*. On opening night, Ricky Martin and the cast got a standing ovation.

QUESTIONS FOR CRITICAL THINKING

1. How does Nederlander achieve the three major criteria for effective market segmentation?

2. Where would you place *Evita's* audience members on the VALSTM framework? Explain your choice. How might Nederlander use this framework to identify audiences for future shows?

Sources: Company website, www.nederlander.com, accessed November 19, 2012; "Evita Broadway Premiere: A Star-Studded Opening Night for Ricky Martin," *International Business Times*, accessed November 19, 2012, www.ibtimes.com; "Ricky Martin Receives Standing Ovation at 'Evita' Broadway Opening Night," *Pink*, accessed November 19, 2012, www.pinkisthenewblog.com.

NOTES

1. Company website, Nike N7, http://nike7.com, accessed November 18, 2012; M. Jonas Greene, "Best of the West 2012: Nike N7 Footwear," *Cowboys & Indians*, accessed November 18, 2012, www.cowboysindians.com; Aaron Kr, "Nike N7 Zoom KD IV," accessed November 18, 2012, http://sneakernews.com; Terri Hansen, "Changing Diabetic Lives, One Pair of Nikes at a Time," *Indian Country Today*, accessed November 18, 2012, http://indiancountrytodaymedianetwork.com; Tesina Jackson, "Nike Releases New Nike Air Native N7 Shoes," *Cherokee Phoenix*, accessed November 18, 2012, www.cherokeephoenix.org.

2. U.S. Census Bureau, "U.S. & World Population Clock," www.census.gov, accessed November 18, 2012.

3. Ekaterina Walter, "The Top 30 Stats You Need to Know When Marketing to Women," *The Next Web*, accessed November 18, 2012, http://thenextweb.com.

4. Ibid.

5. Company website, www.askpatty.com, accessed November 18, 2012.

6. Company website, www.designbasics.com, accessed November 18, 2012; Mary Umberger, "Designing with Her Outlook," *Chicago Tribune*, accessed November 18, 2012, http://articles.chicagotribune.com.

7. Company website, www.harley-davidson.com, accessed November 18, 2012.

8. "Top 50 Cities in the U.S. by Population and Rank," *Infoplease.com*, accessed November 18, 2012, www.infoplease.com; G. Scott Thomas, "Population of New York City Area Reaches 19 Million," *The Business Journals*, accessed November 18, 2012, www.bizjournals.com.

9. U.S. Census Bureau, "Texas Gains the Most in Population Since the Census," accessed November 18, 2012, www.census.gov.

10. "Country Comparison: Population," *CIA World Factbook*, accessed November 18, 2012, www.cia.gov.

11. Liu Dong, "Shanghai Population Surges to 23.47 Million," *Global Times*, accessed November 18, 2102, www.globaltimes.cn; Wendell Cox, "World Urban Areas Population and Density: A 2012 Update," *New Geography*, accessed November 18, 2012, www.newgeography.com.

12. Jennifer Medina and Sabrina Tavernise, "Economy Alters How Americans Are Moving," *The New York Times*, accessed November 18, 2012, www.nytimes.com.

13. U.S. Census Bureau, "Metropolitan and Micropolitan Statistical Areas," accessed November 18, 2012, www.census.gov; "Census Estimates Show New Patterns of Growth Nationwide," press release, www.census.gov, accessed November 18, 2012.

14. U.S. Census Bureau, "Census 2010 Geographic Definitions," accessed November 18, 2012, www.census.gov.

15. "Ice Cream Consumption," *MakeIceCream.com*, accessed November 18, 2012, www.makeicecream.com; Patrick Hruby, "American Caffeine Addiction Races Full Speed Ahead," *Washington Times*, accessed November 18, 2012, www.washingtontimes.com; Christine Rankin, "U.S. Cities That Love Coffee!" *EzineArticles.com*, accessed November 18, 2012, http://ezinearticles.com; "Coffee, Tea Consumption Up," *Food Product Design*, accessed November 18, 2012, www.foodproductdesign.com.

16. Todd Wasserman, "5 Creative Location-Based Marketing Campaigns," *Mashable Social Media*, accessed November 18, 2012, http://mashable.com.

17. Shine website, "About Us," http://shine.yahoo.com, accessed November 18, 2012.

18. Amanda Gardner, "Doctors Urge Ban on Junk Food Ads During Kids' Shows," *US News and World Report*, accessed November 18, 2012, http://health.usnews.com.

19. Bea Fields, "Marketing to Gen Y: What You Can't Afford Not to Know," *Startup Nation*, accessed November 18, 2012, www.startupnation.com.

20. Company website, www.ivivva.com, accessed November 18, 2012; Kevin Woodward, "LuLuLemon Athletica Narrows Its Hunt for an e-Commerce Chief," *Internet Retailer*, accessed November 18, 2012, www.internetretailer.com; Bill Briggs, "LuLuLemon Athletica Kicks Off a U.S. e-Commerce Site for Girls," *Internet Retailer*, accessed November 18, 2012, www.internetretailer.com.

21. Martin Zwilling, "Gen-X Sets High Standards for Gen-Y Entrepreneurs," *Examiner.com*, accessed November 18, 2012, www.examiner.com; eMarketer, "Gen X Watches More TV, Online Video than Other Demo's," *BizReport*, accessed November 18, 2012, www.bizreport.com.

22. Jack Johnson website, www.jackjohnsonmusic.com, accessed November 18, 2012.

23. U.S. Census Bureau, "Selected Characteristics of Baby Boomers 42 to 60 Years Old in 2006," www.census.gov, accessed November 18, 2012.

24. "Don't Ignore Boomers—The Most Valuable Generation," *Nielsen Wire*, accessed November 18, 2012, http://blog.nielsen.com; Steve Olenski, "Advertisers Marketing to Baby Boomers Just Got an Additional Thirty Eight Million Prospects," *Business 2 Community*, accessed November 18, 2012, www.business2community.com.

25. Bill Ness, "Boomers: 26 Percent of the Population, 40 Percent of the Economy," *55Places.com*, accessed November 18, 2012, www.55places.com; Zak Stambor, "As Social Commerce Spreads, Half of American Adults Say They Use Social Networks," *Internet Retailer*, accessed November 18, 2012, www.internetretailer.com.

26. Theresa Campbell, "No Trikes Allowed on Main Street," *Daily Commercial*, accessed November 18, 2012, www.dailycommercial.com; Ken Freund, "Champion Trikes," *RoadRUNNER Motorcycle Touring & Travel*, accessed November 18, 2012, www.roadrunner.travel.

27. U.S. Census Bureau, "Resident Population by Sex and Age: 1980 to 2010," accessed November 18, 2012, www.census.gov; company website, "Marketing to Seniors," http://comingofage.com, accessed November 18, 2012.

28. Organization website, "Why Road Scholar?" www.roadscholar.org, accessed November 18, 2012.

29. Fields, "Marketing to Gen Y."

30. Daniel Dockterman, "Country of Origin Profiles," *Pew Hispanic Center*, accessed November 18, 2012, www.pewhispanic.org; Sabrina Tavernise, "Whites Account for Under Half of Births in U.S.," *The New York Times*, accessed May 17, 2012.

31. U.S. Census Bureau, "U.S. Population Projections, Table 4: Projections of the Population by Sex, Race, and Hispanic Origin for the United States: 2010 to 2051," accessed November 18, 2012, www.census.gov.

32. U.S. Census Bureau, "Overview of Race and Hispanic Origin: 2010," *2010 Census Briefs*, accessed November 18, 2012, www.census.gov.

33. U.S. Census Bureau, "Table 695: Money Income of Families—Number and Distribution by Race and Hispanic Origin: 2009," accessed November 18, 2012, www.census.gov; Rob Coven, "Dynamic Growth in Hispanic and Latino Purchasing Power in U.S.," *Spanish Language Domains*, accessed November 18, 2012, www.spanishlanguagedomains.com.

34. Company website, http://capturagroup.com, accessed November 18, 2012.

35. U.S. Census Bureau, "The Black Population: 2010," *2010 Census Briefs*, accessed November 18, 2012, www.census.gov.

36. Cable Advertising Bureau and Advertising Age, "In Plain Sight—The Black Consumer Opportunity," accessed November 18, 2012, http://brandedcontent.adage.com; "Report: The Power of the African-American Consumer," *Nielsen Wire*, accessed November 18, 2012, http://blog.nielsen.com.

37. Nadia Arumugam, "Why Minorities Reach for Bottled Water over Tap and How Marketers Persuade Them," *Forbes*, accessed November 18, 2012, www.forbes.com.

38. U.S. Census Bureau, "U.S. Population Projections, Table 4."

39. U.S. Census Bureau, "Profile America, Facts for Features: Asian/Pacific American Heritage Month: May 2012," accessed November 18, 2012, www.census.gov.

40. U.S. Census Bureau, "Profile America, Facts for Features: American Indian and Alaska Native Heritage Month: November 2012," accessed November 18, 2012, www.census.gov.

41. U.S. Census Bureau, "Profile America, Facts for Features: American Indian and Alaska Native Heritage Month"; U.S. Census Bureau, "Census Bureau Reports American Indian– and Alaska Native–Owned Businesses Generated $34 Billion in Receipts in 2007," press release, accessed November 18, 2012, www.census.gov.

42. Organization website, www.aibl.org, accessed November 18, 2012.

43. Organization website, www.ncaied.org, accessed November 18, 2012.

44. Nicholas A. Jones and Jungmiwha Bullock, "The Two or More Races Population," *2010 Census Briefs*, accessed November 18, 2012, www.census.gov.

45. U.S. Census Bureau, "Table 12: Resident Population Projections by Race, Hispanic Origin Status, and Age: 2010 and 2015," accessed November 18, 2012, www.census.gov.

46. Steven Greenhouse, "Working Late, by Choice or Not," *The New York Times*, accessed November 18, 2012, www.nytimes.com.

47. Kim Parker, "The Boomerang Generation: Feeling OK about Living with Mom and Dad," *Pew Research Center*, accessed November 18, 2012, www.pewsocialtrends.org.

48. Organization website, "Children Raised by Grandparents," *SeniorCare.net*, accessed November 18, 2012, www.seniorcare.net.

49. U.S. Census Bureau, "Average Household Size by Age," accessed November 18, 2012, http://factfinder2.census.gov.

50. Sabrina Tavernise, "Dip in Birth Rates Reflects Recession, Report Suggests," *The New York Times*, accessed November 18, 2012, www.nytimes.com.

51. Stuart Elliott, "Absolut Celebrates Its 30 Years of Marketing to Gay Consumers," *The New York Times*, accessed November 18, 2012, www.nytimes.com.

52. Aylin Kumcu and Phil Kaufman, "Food Spending Adjustments During Recessionary Times," *Amber Waves*, accessed November 18, 2012, www.ers.usda.gov.

53. U.S. Department of Agriculture, Food CPI and Expenditures: Table 7, www.ers.usda.gov, accessed May 18, 2012.

54. "Seven in Ten Americans Cooking More Instead of Going Out to Save Money," *Harris Interactive*, accessed November 18, 2012, www.harrisinteractive.com.

55. Boston Consulting Group, "Global Wealth 2012: The Battle to Regain Strength," press release, www.bcgperspectives.com, accessed November 18, 2012; Josh Sanburn, "Number of Millionaires in U.S. Decreases But Spikes Worldwide," *Time*, accessed November 18, 2012, http://business.time.com.

56. Company website, Japan-VALS™, www.strategicbusinessinsights.com, accessed November 18, 2012.

57. Company website, "LifeMatrix," www.gfkamerica.com, accessed November 18, 2012.

58. "GfK MRI, Nielsen Make Investments in Research Firm Media Behavior Institute," press release, accessed November 18, 2012, www.mediabehavior.com.

59. Helen Leggatt, "Experian Segments Mobile Users by Behavior/Attitudes," *BizReport*, accessed November 18, 2012, www.bizreport.com.

60. Company website, www.disneystore.com, accessed November 18, 2012; K-Swiss website, www.kswiss.com, accessed November 18, 2012.

61. Dale Buss, "Taco Bell Serves Breakfast, Pitching Fourth Meal as 'FirstMeal'," *Brand Channel*, accessed November 18, 2012, www.brandchannel.com.

62. M. G. Siegler, "Apple Quantifies Their iPad 'Record Weekend': 3 Million Sold in 3 Days," *TechCrunch*, accessed November 18, 2012, http://techcrunch.com.

63. Trefis Team, "McDonald's Makeover Is Paying Off as U.S. Growth Jumps," *Forbes*, accessed November 18, 2012, www.forbes.com.

64. Organization website, www.mountvernon.org, accessed November 18, 2012.

65. Organization website, www.sierraclub.org, accessed November 18, 2012.

66. Company website, www.tauck.com, accessed November 18, 2012.

67. Company website, http://ilovepeanutbutter.com, accessed November 18, 2012.

68. Tiffany Hsu, "Fast-Casual Restaurants Gobble Up Market Share," *Los Angeles Times*, accessed November 18, 2012, http://articles.latimes.com.

69. Judy Keen, "Encyclopaedia Britannica Turns a Page, Ends Print Edition," *USA Today*, accessed November 18, 2012, www.usatoday.com.

Chapter 10

MARKETING
Research and Sales Forecasting

1 Describe the development of the marketing research function and its major activities.

2 Explain the steps in the marketing research process.

3 Distinguish between primary and secondary data, and identify the sources of each type.

4 Explain the different sampling techniques used by marketing researchers.

5 Identify the methods by which marketing researchers collect primary data.

6 Explain the challenges of conducting marketing research in global markets.

7 Outline the most important uses of computer technology in marketing research.

8 Identify the major types of forecasting methods.

TARGET MASTERS BEHAVIORAL RESEARCH

Target stores feature a huge assortment of products, from food to electronics, and the company—with more than 1,700 U.S. locations—is acknowledged as one of the most savvy marketers around, thanks to its long practice of collecting information about its customers. Target assigns loyal buyers a unique identifier called a Guest ID number, which records demographic information like customers' age, income, marital status, credit cards carried, neighborhood, and even the distance they live from the store. The Guest ID program also tracks information supplied when customers pay with credit cards, use coupons, fill out surveys or rebate slips, call customer service, or visit Target's website. And, like most other major retailers, Target can buy additional market research information that delves even deeper into customers' personal history and buying habits. As one marketing research consultant said, "We're living through a golden age of behavioral research."

Target's marketing analysts devise ways of sifting all its market and customer data in order to predict purchases and develop more effective marketing programs. For instance, the company uses customer data to send customized coupon booklets featuring all the grocery items a customer purchased the preceding week. A former scientist for Amazon.com agrees that such data-crunching has risen to the top of many marketers' agendas: "Mathematicians are suddenly sexy," he says.

Shopping routines are particularly hard to break, which is one reason it is so important to a company like Target to find out which cues and rewards will encourage retail habits that lead to its doors. Target would also like to pinpoint customers who are shopping for very special non-routine occasions, such as the birth of a child, when it seems the one thing most people can count on is that all their habits will be disrupted and new ones will be formed.

Another way Target tries to anticipate what shoppers will buy is to test new merchandise. An especially effective way for its large stores to do this is to house specialty boutiques on their premises, such as the 25 Apple stores it is testing, or a separate program called The Shops at Target, which features store-within-a-store outlets of a rotating group of selected local retailers, stocked with hundreds of exclusive items at all price levels.

With all the information it collects, says Target, it may someday be sending you coupons for products before you know you want them.[1]

EVOLUTION OF A BRAND

While the principle "know your audience" applies in all walks of life, it's particularly true in the competitive retail sector, where businesses engage daily in an all-out battle to attract—and keep—customers. Understanding the customer mindset is a critical and ongoing task: What factors influence their buying preferences? How do they make purchase decisions? What's behind customer loyalty? With its tight focus on information gathering, Target is taking market research to new heights.

- Regular Target shoppers are assigned a "Guest ID." What would be the purpose of creating such an identifier and how would it aid Target marketers?
- Target also collects information about non-routine shopping occasions, like the birth of a child. Why would Target be interested in having such information? How do you suppose the retailer uses the data?

CHAPTER OVERVIEW

marketing research
Process of collecting and using information for marketing decision making.

Collecting and managing information about what customers need and want is a challenging task for any marketer. **Marketing research** is the process of collecting and using information for marketing decision making. Data comes from a variety of sources. Some results come from well-planned studies designed to elicit specific information. Other valuable information comes from sales force reports, accounting records, and published reports. Still other data emerges from controlled experiments and computer simulations. Thanks to new database technologies, some data companies collect are compiled for them by research specialists, and some are collected and compiled by in-house staff. Marketing research, by presenting pertinent information in a useful format, aids decision makers in analyzing data and in suggesting possible actions.

This chapter discusses the marketing research function. Marketers use research to understand their customers, target customer segments, and develop long-term customer relationships—all keys to profitability. Information collected through marketing research underlies much of the material on market segmentation discussed in the previous chapter. Clearly, the marketing research function is the primary source of information needed to make effective marketing decisions. The use of technology to mine data and gather business and competitive intelligence is also discussed, as is technology's vast impact on marketing research decision making and planning. This chapter also explains how marketing research techniques are used to make accurate sales forecasts, a critical component of marketing planning.

BRIEFLY SPEAKING

"Test fast, fail fast, adjust fast."

—**Tom Peters**
American writer on business management,
co-author, In Search of Excellence

THE MARKETING RESEARCH FUNCTION

1 Describe the development of the marketing research function and its major activities.

Before looking at how marketing research is conducted, we must first examine its historical development, the people and organizations it involves, and the activities it entails. Because an underlying purpose of research is to find out more about consumers, research is clearly central to effective customer satisfaction and customer relationship programs. Media technologies like the Internet and virtual reality are opening up new channels through which researchers can tap into consumer information.

DEVELOPMENT OF THE MARKETING RESEARCH FUNCTION

It has been more than 130 years since advertising pioneer N. W. Ayer conducted the first organized marketing research project in 1879. A second important milestone in the development of marketing research occurred 32 years later, when Charles C. Parlin organized the nation's first commercial research department at Curtis Publishing, publisher of *The Saturday Evening Post.*

Parlin got his start as a marketing researcher by counting soup cans in Philadelphia's garbage. Here is what happened. Parlin, an ad salesman, was trying to persuade the Campbell Soup Company to advertise in *The Saturday Evening Post*. Campbell Soup resisted, believing that the *Post* reached primarily working-class readers, who they thought preferred to make their own soup. Campbell Soup marketers were targeting higher-income people who could afford to pay for the convenience of soup in a can. To prove Campbell wrong, Parlin began counting soup cans in the garbage collected from different neighborhoods. His research revealed that working-class families bought more canned soup than wealthy households, who had servants to cook for them. Campbell Soup soon became a regular *Post* client. It is interesting to note that garbage remains a good source of information for marketing researchers even today. Prior to the cutbacks in food service, some airlines studied the leftovers from onboard meals to determine what to serve passengers.

Test kitchens inform marketers by allowing companies to introduce new products to a test market and avoid risking a real-world product launch that consumers might not like.

Most early research gathered little more than written testimonials from purchasers of firms' products. Research methods became more sophisticated during the 1930s as the development of statistical techniques led to refinements in sampling procedures and greater accuracy in research findings.

In recent years, advances in computer technology have significantly changed the complexion of marketing research. Besides accelerating the pace and broadening the base of data collection, computers have aided marketers in making informed decisions about problems and opportunities. Simulations, for example, allow marketers to evaluate alternatives by posing what-if questions. Marketing researchers at many consumer goods firms simulate product introductions through computer programs to determine whether to risk real-world product launches or even to subject products to test marketing.

WHO CONDUCTS MARKETING RESEARCH?

The size and organizational form of the marketing research function is usually tied to the structure of the company. Some firms organize research units to support different product lines, brands, or geographic areas. Others organize their research functions according to the types of research they need to perform, such as sales analysis, new-product development, advertising evaluation, or sales forecasting.

Many firms outsource their research needs and depend on independent marketing research firms. These independent organizations might specialize in handling just part of a larger study such as conducting consumer interviews. Firms can also contract out entire research studies.

Marketers usually decide whether to conduct a study internally or through an outside organization based on cost. Another major consideration is the reliability and accuracy of the information collected by an outside organization. Because collecting marketing data is what these outside organizations do full-time, the information they gather often is more thorough and accurate than that collected by less experienced in-house staff. Often an outside marketing research firm can provide technical assistance and expertise not available within the company's marketing unit. Interaction with outside suppliers also helps ensure that a researcher does not conduct a study only to validate a favorite viewpoint or preferred option.

Marketing research companies range in size from sole proprietorships to national and international firms such as Nielsen Company, Information Resources, and Arbitron. They can be classified as syndicated services, full-service suppliers, or limited-service suppliers depending on the types of services they offer to clients. Some full-service organizations are also willing to take on limited-service activities.

The coupons you might receive at self-service lanes in the grocery store have been specifically targeted to you in an effort to build and retain market share for certain products based on other purchases you've made.

© David Pearson/Alamy

syndicated service
Organization that provides standardized data on a periodic basis to its subscribers.

Syndicated Services

An organization that regularly provides a standardized set of data to all customers is called a syndicated service. Mediamark Research, for example, operates a syndicated product research service based on personal interviews with adults regarding their exposure to advertising media. Clients include advertisers, advertising agencies, magazines, newspapers, broadcasters, and cable TV networks.

Another syndicated service provider is J.D. Power and Associates, a global marketing information firm headquartered in California that specializes in surveying customer satisfaction, product quality, and buyer behavior. It serves clients in a wide range of industries, including automotive, financial services, health care, insurance, telecommunications, and travel and leisure.[2]

Full-Service Research Suppliers

full-service research supplier Marketing research organization that offers all aspects of the marketing research process.

An organization that contracts with clients to conduct complete marketing research projects is called a full-service research supplier. Brain Research, a Mexican marketing research firm, provides quantitative and qualitative research and various field studies, including face-to-face and telephone interviews, online interviews, multinational studies, B2B interviews, and even "mystery shopper" research to collect information about retail outlets. The company also studies public opinion and buyer behavior and evaluates Web pages and work environments. Its editing department reviews questionnaires before they are used, under strict supervision, by Brain Research's staff in interviews, focus groups, and other types of observation techniques, including video.[3] A full-service supplier becomes the client's marketing research arm, performing all of the steps in the marketing research process (discussed later in this chapter).

Limited-Service Research Suppliers

limited-service research supplier
Marketing research firm that specializes in a limited number of research activities, such as conducting field interviews or performing data processing.

A marketing research firm that specializes in a limited number of activities, such as performing data processing or conducting field interviews, is called a limited-service research supplier. Quick Test/Heakin, based in Jupiter, Florida, specializes in data collection in shopping malls. The company's employees conduct more than 2 million interviews a year.[4] The firm also prepares studies to help clients develop advertising strategies and to track awareness and interest. Syndicated services can also be considered a type of limited-service research supplier.

CUSTOMER SATISFACTION MEASUREMENT PROGRAMS

Firms often focus on tracking the satisfaction levels of current customers. Austin, Texas–based Bazaarvoice charges a monthly fee to clients and does everything from designing and managing a firm's customer feedback area on its website to moderating online discussion groups and analyzing comments.[5] Some marketers have also gained valuable insights by tracking the dissatisfaction that led customers to abandon certain products for those of competitors. Some customer defections are only partial; customers may remain somewhat satisfied with a business but not completely satisfied. Such attitudes could lead them to take their business elsewhere. Studying the underlying causes of customer defections, even partial defections, can be useful for identifying problem areas that need attention. The annual "Airline Quality Rating" survey scores specific carriers, and the airline industry in general, on such measures as on-time performance, baggage handling, diverted and

A national study recently reported that Hawaiian Airlines had the best on-time performance.

© Christopher Parypa/Shutterstock.com

cancelled flights, overbooking, and number of customer complaints. The national study, a joint effort by faculty at Purdue and Wichita State universities, recently reported that Hawaiian Airlines had the best on-time performance, while American Eagle captured the "most improved" designation.[6]

ASSESSMENT CHECK

1.1 Identify the different classifications of marketing research suppliers, and explain how they differ from one another.

1.2 What research methods can be used to measure customer satisfaction?

Some organizations conduct their own measurement programs through online polls and surveys. Kohl's shoppers find a URL on the bottom of their receipt. Accessing the URL brings up a customer satisfaction survey that offers respondents a chance to participate in a sweepstakes.[7]

THE MARKETING RESEARCH PROCESS

As discussed earlier, business executives rely on marketing research to provide the information they need to make effective decisions regarding their firm's current and future activities. The chances of making good decisions improve when the right information is provided at the right time during decision making. To achieve this goal, marketing researchers often follow the six-step process shown in Figure 10.1. In the initial stages, researchers define the problem, conduct exploratory research, and formulate a hypothesis to be tested. Next, they create a design for the research study and collect needed data. Finally, researchers interpret and present the research information. The following sections take a closer look at each step of the marketing research process.

Explain the steps in the marketing research process.

DEFINE THE PROBLEM

A popular anecdote advises that well-defined problems are half solved. A well-defined problem permits the researcher to focus on securing the exact information needed for the solution. Clearly defining the

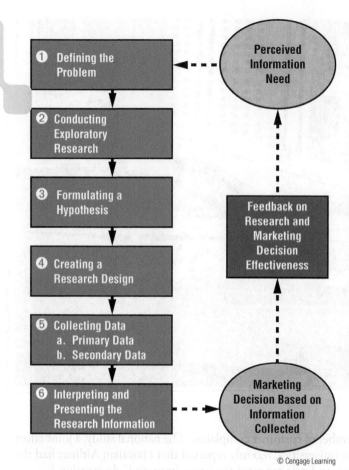

FIGURE 10.1
The Marketing Research Process

① Defining the Problem

② Conducting Exploratory Research

③ Formulating a Hypothesis

④ Creating a Research Design

⑤ Collecting Data
   a. Primary Data
   b. Secondary Data

⑥ Interpreting and Presenting the Research Information

Perceived Information Need

Feedback on Research and Marketing Decision Effectiveness

Marketing Decision Based on Information Collected

© Cengage Learning

question that the researcher needs to answer increases the speed and accuracy of the research process.

Researchers must carefully avoid confusing symptoms of a problem with the problem itself. A symptom merely alerts marketers that a problem exists. For example, suppose that a maker of frozen pizzas sees its market share drop from 8 to 5 percent in six months. The loss of market share is a symptom of a problem the company must solve. To define the problem, the firm must look for the underlying causes of its market share loss.

A logical starting point in identifying the problem might be to evaluate the firm's target market and marketing mix elements. Suppose, for example, a firm has recently changed its promotional strategies. Research might then seek to answer the question, "What must we do to improve the effectiveness of our marketing mix?" The firm's marketers might also look at possible environmental changes. Perhaps a new competitor entered the firm's market. Decision makers will need information to help answer the question, "What must we do to distinguish our company from the new competitor?"

When marketers at Target came up with what they called the "PFresh" concept—adding grocery departments in Target stores—the company first tested the concept for two years in two locations. After the company implemented PFresh at just 108 U.S. stores and saw sales rise over $4.5 million, it expanded more broadly. Today, more than two-thirds of Target stores have been reformatted with a grocery department—broadening the retailer's product categories and reducing its reliance on purchase of discretionary items.[8]

CONDUCT EXPLORATORY RESEARCH

exploratory research
Process of discussing a marketing problem with informed sources both within and outside the firm and examining information from secondary sources.

Once a firm has defined the question it wants to answer, researchers can begin exploratory research. Exploratory research seeks to discover the cause of a specific problem by discussing the problem with informed sources both within and outside the firm and by examining data from other information sources. Marketers at Chili's, part of the Dallas-based Brinker International family of restaurants, might talk with their customers, suppliers, and retailers. Executives at Brinker might also ask for input from the sales force or look for overall market clues. In addition, exploratory research can include evaluation of company records, such as sales and profit analyses, and available competitive data. Marketing researchers often refer to internal data collection as situation analysis. The term *informal investigation* is often used for exploratory interviews with informed people outside the researchers' firms.

Using Internal Data

sales analysis In-depth evaluation of a firm's sales.

Marketers can find valuable data in their firm's own internal records. Typical sources of internal data are sales records, financial statements, and marketing cost analyses. Marketers analyze sales performance records to gain an overall view of company efficiency and to find clues to potential problems. Prepared from company invoices or a computer database system, this sales analysis can provide important details to management. The study typically compares actual and expected sales based on a detailed sales forecast by territory, product, customer, and salesperson.

Once the sales quota—the level of expected sales to which actual results are compared—has been established, it is a simple process to compare actual results with expected performance. Randa Luggage is a global designer and licensed distributor of upscale luggage brands like Anne Klein, Perry Ellis, and Nautica. The New Jersey-based firm recently installed a centralized software system to track the comings and goings of the millions of items it distributes annually. Reports trigger restocking and inventory decisions and provide information for financial statements and reporting.[9]

Other possible breakdowns for sales analysis separate transactions by customer type, product, sales method (Internet, mail, telephone, or personal contact), type of order (cash or credit), and order size. Sales analysis is one of the least expensive and most important sources of marketing information available to a firm.

Accounting data, as summarized in the firm's financial statements, can be another good tool for identifying financial issues that influence marketing. Using ratio analysis, researchers can compare performance in current and previous years against industry benchmarks. These exercises may hint at possible problems, but only more detailed analysis would reveal specific causes of indicated variations.

A third source of internal information is *marketing cost analysis*—evaluation of expenses for tasks, such as selling, warehousing, advertising, and delivery, to determine the profitability of particular customers, territories, or product lines. Firms often examine the allocation of costs to products, customers, and territories. Marketing decision makers then evaluate the profitability of particular customers and territories on the basis of the sales produced and the costs incurred in generating those sales. Sometimes internal data can produce remarkably detailed customer profiles.

Like sales analysis and financial research, marketing cost analysis is most useful when it provides information linked to other forms of marketing research. A later section of this chapter will address how computer technologies can accomplish these linkages and move information among a firm's units.

FORMULATE A HYPOTHESIS

After defining the problem and conducting an exploratory investigation, the marketer needs to formulate a hypothesis—a tentative explanation for some specific event. A hypothesis is a statement about the relationship among variables that carries clear implications for testing this relationship. It sets the stage for more in-depth research by further clarifying what researchers need to test. For example, Olive Garden restaurants might want to see whether good customer service is related to its increased sales, so its marketers would conduct a survey of customers to test this hypothesis.

Not all studies test specific hypotheses, however, a carefully designed study can benefit from the rigor introduced by developing a hypothesis before beginning data collection and analysis.

hypothesis Tentative explanation for a specific event.

CREATE A RESEARCH DESIGN

To test hypotheses and find solutions to marketing problems, a marketer creates a research design, a master plan or model for conducting marketing research. In planning a research project, marketers must be sure the study will measure what they intend to measure. A second important research design consideration is the selection of respondents. Marketing researchers use sampling techniques (discussed later in the chapter) to determine which consumers to include in their studies.

Test kitchens and willing palates are indispensable in the fast-food business. At McDonald's test kitchen, "We guesstimate 1,800 new ideas a year we're exposed to," says the company's director of culinary innovation. After input from the business research and marketing teams about where the firm is looking to pick up business, the company's four chefs and suppliers' chefs get together for brainstorming. "When we're in that environment," says the culinary director, "I say, 'Look, we close the door, there are no bad ideas in this kitchen.'" About 30 ideas each year get a closer look, and about half of those are presented to the fast-food chain's management team. Between three and five are actually launched in a given year.[10]

research design Master plan for conducting market research.

secondary data
Previously published information.

primary data
Information collected for a specific investigation.

COLLECT DATA

Marketing researchers gather two kinds of data: secondary data and primary data. Secondary data is information from previously published or compiled sources. Census data is an example. Primary data refers to information collected for the first time specifically for a marketing research study. An example of primary data is statistics collected from a survey that asks current customers about their preferences for product improvements. Global research firm Ipsos collects primary data in 84 countries in the Americas, Asia, Europe, and the Middle East. The Paris-based firm conducts thousands of projects and focus groups and over 70 million interviews in a year and employs over 16,000 people—all under the corporate slogan "Nobody's unpredictable."[11]

Secondary data offer two important advantages: (1) such data are almost always less expensive to gather than primary data, and (2) researchers usually spend less time to locate and use secondary data. A research study that requires primary data may take three to four months to complete, while a researcher often can gather secondary data in a matter of days.

Secondary data have limitations that primary data do not. First, published information can quickly become obsolete. A marketer analyzing the population of various areas may discover that even the most recent census figures already are out of date because of rapid growth and changing demographics. Second, published data collected for an unrelated purpose may not be completely relevant to the marketer's specific needs. For example, census data do not reveal the brand preferences of consumers.

Although research to gather primary data can cost more and take longer, the results can provide richer, more detailed information than secondary data offer. The choice between secondary and primary data is tied to cost, applicability, and effectiveness. Many marketing research projects combine secondary and primary data to fully answer marketing questions. This chapter examines specific methods for collecting both secondary and primary data in later sections.

INTERPRET AND PRESENT RESEARCH DATA

The final step in the marketing research process is to interpret the findings and present them to decision makers in a format that allows managers to make effective judgments. Possible differences in interpretations of research results may occur between marketing researchers and their audiences due to differing backgrounds, levels of knowledge, and experience. Both oral and written reports should be presented in a manner designed to minimize such misinterpretations.

Marketing researchers and research users must cooperate at every stage in the research process. Too many studies go unused because management fears that the results are of little use, once they hear lengthy discussions of research limitations or unfamiliar terminology. Marketing researchers must remember to direct their reports toward management and not to other researchers. They should spell out their conclusions in clear and concise terms that can be put into action. Reports should confine technical details of the research methods to an appendix, if they are included at all. By presenting research results to all key executives at a single sitting, researchers can ensure that everyone will understand the findings. Decision makers can then quickly reach consensus on what the results mean and what actions need to be taken.

ASSESSMENT CHECK

2.1 What are the six steps in the marketing research process?

2.2 What is the goal of exploratory research?

MARKETING RESEARCH METHODS

Clearly, data collection is an integral part of the marketing research process. One of the most time-consuming parts of collecting data is determining what method the marketer should use to obtain the data. This section discusses the most commonly used methods by which marketing researchers find both secondary and primary data.

SECONDARY DATA COLLECTION

Secondary data come from many sources. The overwhelming quantity of secondary data available at little or no cost challenges researchers to select only data relevant to the problem or issue studied.

Secondary data consist of two types: internal and external data. Internal data, as discussed earlier, include sales records, product performance reviews, sales force activity reports, and marketing cost reports. External data come from a variety of sources, including government records, syndicated research services, and industry publications. Computerized databases provide access to vast amounts of data from both inside and outside an organization. The following sections on government data, private data, and online sources focus on databases and other external data sources available to marketing researchers.

Government Data

The federal government is the nation's most important source of marketing data. Census data provide the most frequently used government statistics. A census of population is conducted every ten years and is made available at no charge in local libraries, on computer disks, and via the Internet. Because of problems implementing a computerized system, the U.S. Census Bureau abandoned plans to go high-tech with handheld computers for 2010 data collection. Instead, it counted the country's more than 313 million residents by training workers to collect data with pen and paper from those who didn't respond to its mailed survey.[12] The Census Bureau also conducts a periodic census of housing, population, business, manufacturers, agriculture, minerals, and governments.

The 2010 U.S. Census

The U.S. Census of Population contains a wealth of valuable information for marketers. It breaks down the U.S. population of more than 313 million people by very small geographic areas, making it possible to determine population traits by city block or census tract in large cities. It also divides the populations of nonmetropolitan areas into census tracts, which are important for marketing analysis because they highlight small groups of about 1,500 to 8,000 people with similar traits. Census data, collected every ten years since 1790 as required by the U.S. Constitution and most recently completed in 2010, allow the government to allocate states' seats in the U.S. House of Representatives. Also at stake in 2010 were more than $400 billion of federal funds for hospitals, schools, senior centers, job training and public works projects, and emergency services. "If the community needs a firetruck, or training for EMTs, or they need a senior center, small communities are more aware now than ever before that the amount of [government] funds is based on the number of people in a community," said a state official in Alaska.[13]

The most recent census cost an estimated $14.7 billion. It featured a shortened version of the household questionnaire and was the first census to use handheld computing devices with GPS functions (to verify respondents' addresses). However, this census could be completed only

The most recent U.S. Census advertised to help make people aware of the ways the census information would be used to help their communities.

HELP OUR CHILDREN RECEIVE THEIR SHARE OF $400 BILLION

AP Photo/US Census Bureau

by mail and did not offer the option of responding via the Web (plans call for the 2020 Census to be conducted online).[14]

Marketers, such as local retailers and shopping center developers, can readily access census data to gather vital information about customers in an immediate neighborhood without spending time or money to conduct comprehensive surveys. Marketing researchers have found even more valuable resources in the government's computerized mapping database originally called the TIGER system, for Topographically Integrated Geographic Encoding and Referencing system. This system overlays topographic features, such as railroads, highways, and rivers, with census data like household income figures. Recently updated with an Oracle relational database, the new TIGER/Line Shapefiles are downloadable and cover all 50 states, the District of Columbia, and Puerto Rico.[15]

Marketers often get other information from the federal government, such as the following:

- *Monthly Catalog of United States Government Publications* and *Statistical Abstract of the United States*, published annually and available online as the *Catalog of U.S. Government Publications (CGP)*;

- *Survey of Current Business*, updated monthly by the Bureau of Economic Analysis; and

- *County and City Data Book*, typically published every three years and available online, providing data on all states, counties, and cities of more than 25,000 residents.

State and city governments serve as additional important sources of information on employment, production, and sales activities. In addition, university bureaus of business and economic research frequently collect and disseminate valuable information.

Private Data

Many private organizations provide information for marketing decision makers. A trade association may be an excellent source of data on activities in a particular industry. Thomson Gale's *Encyclopedia of Associations*, available in many libraries, can help marketers track down trade associations that may have pertinent data. Also, the advertising industry continuously collects data on audiences reached by various media.

Business and trade magazines also publish a wide range of valuable data. *Ulrich's Guide to International Periodicals*, another common library reference, can point researchers in the direction of trade publications that conduct and publish industry-specific research. General business magazines can also be good sources. *Sales & Marketing Management*, for instance, publishes an annual *Survey of Buying Power and Media Markets* that combines statistics for population, effective buying income (EBI), and retail sales into buying power indexes that indicate each geographic market's ability to buy.

Because few libraries carry specialized trade journals, the best way to gather data from them is either directly from the publishers or through online periodical databases, such as ProQuest Direct's ABI/Inform, available at many libraries. Most trade publications maintain Web home pages that allow archival searches. Larger libraries can often provide directories and other publications that can help researchers find secondary data. For instance, Guideline's *FindEx: The Directory of Market Research Reports, Studies, and Surveys* lists a tremendous variety of completed research studies available for purchase.

Several national firms offer information to businesses by subscription. GfK Roper is a global database service; GfK Roper Reports Worldwide provides continuing data on consumer attitudes, life stages, lifestyle, and buying behavior for more than 30 developed and developing countries. Wright Investors produces research reports and quality ratings on 31,000 companies from over 60 countries.

Electronic systems that scan UPC (Universal Product Code) bar codes speed purchase transactions and provide data used for inventory control, ordering, and delivery. Scanning technology is widely used by grocers and other retailers, and marketing research companies, such as Nielsen and Information Resources, store this data in commercially available databases. These scanner-based information services track consumer purchases of a wide variety of UPC-coded products.

Retailers can use this information to target customers with the right merchandise at the right time.

Techniques that rely on radio-frequency identification (RFID) technology (tags that use a tiny chip with identification information that can be read by a scanner using radio waves) are in growing use. American Apparel, a rapidly growing chain of U.S.-made clothing with 280 retail stores in the Americas, Asia, Australia, and Europe, tested RFID tags for stocking and inventory replenishment in its New York City store. The company found the tags reduced internal shrinkage by as much as 75 percent in some stores and enabled customers to find more items in the right size and color on the selling floor, increasing sales and freeing salespeople from restocking

Electronic systems that scan UPC bar codes speed purchase decisions and allow consumers to check a price before committing to the purchase.

© eStock Photo/Alamy

chores so they could spend more time helping shoppers. In addition, inventory counts that once occupied several salespeople for an entire day were more accurately handled by two people in a couple of hours. Based on its experience, American Apparel installed the RFID technology in all its stores.[16]

Nielsen SalesNet uses the Internet to deliver scanner data quickly to clients. Data are processed as soon as they are received from supermarkets and are then forwarded to marketing researchers so they can perform more in-depth analysis. At the same time, Nielsen representatives summarize the data in both graphic and spreadsheet form and post the data on the Internet for immediate access by clients.

Online Sources of Secondary Data

The tools of cyberspace sometimes simplify the hunt for secondary data. Hundreds of databases and other sources of information are available online. A well-designed, Internet-based marketing research project can cost less yet yield faster results than offline research.

The Internet has spurred the growth of research aggregators—companies that acquire, catalog, reformat, segment, and then resell premium research reports that have already been published. Aggregators put valuable data within reach of marketers who lack the time or the budget to commission custom research. Because Web technology makes their databases easy to search, aggregators like Datamonitor and eMarketer can compile detailed, specialized reports quickly and cost-effectively.[17] Social networking sites also yield valuable marketing information, such as secondary private data. Google Analytics, a business tool, measures online sales; tracks email, social media, and ad campaigns; and benchmarks key measures against competitors. Marketers use Google Analytics to collect information from sites mentioned on Twitter and other social-media sites. Facebook recently partnered with Nielsen Company to study the relationship between paid and unpaid advertising on brand awareness and engagement.[18] YouTube's YouTube Insight service gives its video-uploading account holders an array of statistics, graphs, and maps about the audiences they attract, far more specific than just the number of views it used to collect.[19]

However, marketers must carefully evaluate the validity of any information they find on the Internet. People without in-depth knowledge of a subject may post information. Similarly,

 ASSESSMENT CHECK

3.1 Distinguish between primary and secondary data.

3.2 What are the major methods of collecting secondary data?

3.3 What are the major methods of collecting primary data?

Web pages might contain information gathered using questionable research methods. The phrase *caveat emptor* ("let the buyer beware") should guide evaluation of secondary data on the Internet.

SAMPLING TECHNIQUES

4 Explain the different sampling techniques used by marketing researchers.

sampling Process of selecting survey respondents or research participants.

population (universe) Total group that researchers want to study.

probability sample Sample that gives every member of the population a chance of being selected.

simple random sample Basic type of probability sample in which every individual in the relevant universe has an equal opportunity of being selected.

stratified sample Probability sample constructed to represent randomly selected subsamples of different groups within the total sample; each subgroup is relatively homogeneous for a certain characteristic.

Before undertaking a study to gather primary data, researchers must first identify which participants to include in the study. Sampling is the process of selecting survey respondents or research participants. Sampling is important because, if a study fails to involve consumers who accurately reflect the target market, the research is likely to yield misleading conclusions.

The total group of people the researcher wants to study is called the population or universe. For a political campaign study, the population would be all eligible voters. For research about a new lipstick line, it might be all women in a certain age bracket. The sample is a representative group chosen from this population. Researchers rarely gather information from a study's total population, resulting in a census. Unless the total population is small, the costs of a census are simply too high. Sometimes limitations can reduce the size of the sample. Online surveys, for instance, often draw large but self-selected, rather than random, groups of respondents who don't usually represent the total population. Vague questions and surveys that are too long further reduce the number of respondents and can skew the results even further.

Samples can be classified as either probability samples or nonprobability samples. A probability sample is one that gives every member of the population a chance of being selected. Types of probability samples include simple random samples, stratified samples, and cluster samples.

In a simple random sample, every member of the relevant universe has an equal opportunity of selection. The draft lottery of the Vietnam era is an example. The days of the year were drawn and set into an array. The placement of a person's birthday in this list determined his likelihood of being called for service. In a stratified sample, randomly selected subsamples of different groups are represented in the total sample. Stratified samples provide efficient, representative groups that are relatively homogeneous for a certain characteristic for such studies as opinion polls in which groups of individuals share various divergent viewpoints. In a cluster sample, researchers select a sample of subgroups (or clusters) from which they draw respondents. Each cluster reflects the diversity of the whole population being sampled. This cost-efficient type of probability sample is widely used when the entire population cannot be listed or enumerated.

In contrast, a nonprobability sample relies on personal judgment somewhere in the selection process. In other words, researchers decide which particular groups to study. Types of nonprobability samples are convenience samples and quota samples. A convenience sample is a nonprobability sample selected from among readily available respondents; this sample often is called an *accidental sample* because those included just happen to be in the place where the study is being conducted. Mall intercept surveys and TV call-in opinion polls are good examples. Marketing researchers sometimes use convenience samples in exploratory research but not in definitive studies. A quota sample is a nonprobability sample divided to maintain the proportion of certain characteristics among different segments or groups seen in the population as a whole. In other words, each field worker is assigned a quota that specifies the number and characteristics of the people to contact. It differs from a stratified sample in which researchers select subsamples by some random process; in a quota sample, they handpick participants.

⊕ ASSESSMENT CHECK

4.1 What is sampling?

4.2 Explain the different types of probability samples.

4.3 Identify the types of nonprobability samples.

PRIMARY RESEARCH METHODS

5 Identify the methods by which marketing researchers collect primary data.

Marketers use a variety of methods for conducting primary research, as Figure 10.2 shows. The principal methods for collecting primary data are observation, surveys, and controlled experiments. The choice among these methods depends on the issues under study and the decisions that marketers need to make. In some cases, researchers may decide to combine techniques during the research process.

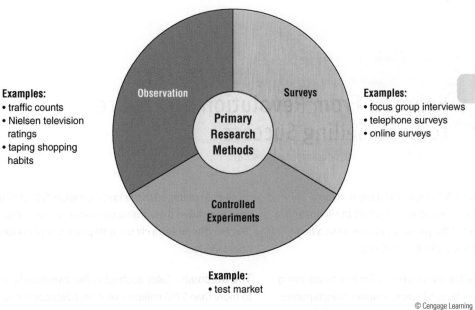

© Cengage Learning

FIGURE 10.2
Types of Primary Research

Observation Method

In observational studies, researchers view the overt actions of subjects being studied. Marketers trying to understand how consumers behave in certain situations find observation a useful technique. Observation tactics may be as simple as counting the number of cars passing by a potential site for a fast-food restaurant or checking the license plates at a shopping center near a state line to determine where shoppers live.

Technological advances provide increasingly sophisticated ways for observing consumer behavior. The television industry relies on data from people meters, electronic remote-control devices that record the TV viewing habits of individual household members to measure the popularity of TV shows. Traditional people meters require each viewer to press a button each time he or she turns on the TV, changes channels, or leaves the room.

Some observers expect that communications technology will also change the way consumers respond to advertising. Internet users are more willing than ever to use real money for purchases that arise during their social gaming and social networking sessions. For instance, in Diablo III, a video game from Blizzard Entertainment, players can sell items they discover while playing the game—or buy the loot they can't find while they play.[20]

Videotaping consumers in action is also gaining acceptance as a research technique. Cookware manufacturers may videotape consumers cooking in their own kitchens to evaluate how they use their pots and pans. A toothbrush manufacturer asked marketing research firm E-Lab to videotape consumers brushing their teeth and using mouthwash in its quest to develop products that would leave behind the sensation of cleanliness and freshness. Procter & Gamble used observations of customers doing their housecleaning to save its Febreze product from failure. See the "Marketing Success" feature for the story.

In an effort to understand what makes younger consumers tick, a trend-forecasting firm called Teenage Research Unlimited gathers the reflections of more than 30,000 teens in 40 markets across five continents. This primary data is used to create the firm's annual TRU Study report, a "living, breathing" document of teen insights.[21]

Interpretive Research

Another type of primary research is interpretive research, a method in which a researcher observes a customer or group of customers in their natural setting and interprets their behavior based on an understanding of the social and cultural characteristics of that setting. We discuss interpretive research in more detail later.

cluster sample
Probability sample in which researchers select a sample of subgroups (or clusters) from which they draw respondents; each cluster reflects the diversity of the whole population sampled.

nonprobability sample Sample that involves personal judgment somewhere in the selection process.

convenience sample Nonprobability sample selected from among readily available respondents.

quota sample Nonprobability sample divided to maintain the proportion of certain characteristics among different segments or groups seen in the population as a whole.

interpretive research Observational research method developed by social anthropologists in which customers are observed in their natural setting and their behavior is interpreted based on an understanding of social and cultural characteristics; also known as *ethnography*, or "going native."

MARKETING SUCCESS

Febreze: From Revolutionary Failure to Best-Selling Success

Background. After Procter & Gamble (P&G) spent millions creating an inexpensive but revolutionary product to eliminate household odors, it expected the product, Febreze, to be a huge success. But sales started low and fell from there.

The Challenge. P&G had begun marketing Febreze by assuming people would change their housecleaning routines to incorporate its use. It soon became apparent, however, that people didn't use it because they didn't recognize the odors that Febreze could eliminate from their homes. P&G needed to find a new marketing strategy or risk an expensive failure.

The Strategy. It took a little more research, including watching people use the product, for P&G to realize that it could market Febreze, reformulated with perfume, as a way for users to reward themselves with a fresh scent after completing their cleaning routine. A revamped marketing campaign delivered the reward message, rather than urging consumers to take what they perceived as an extra cleaning step to eliminate odors they didn't acknowledge.

The Outcome. Sales doubled within two months and soared to more than $200 million a year later. Febreze is now one of the best-selling products in the world. The spray and its many spinoff products account for more than $1 billion a year in P&G's sales.

Sources: Ellen Byron, "Febreze Joins P&G's $1 Billion Club," *The Wall Street Journal*, accessed November 20, 2012, http://onlinewsj.com; Peter Cohan, "Jurassic Park: How P&G Brought Febreze Back to Life," *Forbes*, accessed November 20, 2012, www.forbes.com; Dannielle Blumenthal, "Marketing Is More Important Than Innovation: Febreze," *Social Media Today*, accessed November 20, 2012, http://socialmediatoday.com; Charles Duhigg, "How Companies Learn Your Secrets," *The New York Times Magazine*, accessed November 20, 2012, www.nytimes.com.

SURVEY METHODS

Observation alone cannot supply all of the desired information. Researchers must ask questions to get information on attitudes, motives, and opinions. It is also difficult to get exact demographic information, such as income levels, from observation. To discover this information, researchers can use either interviews or questionnaires. South Bend, Indiana-based Press Ganey provides research on trends in the health care industry, relying on the data it gathers from the perspectives of millions of survey respondents.[22]

Due to the buying power of the teen market, it is important to capture the attitudes and opinions of this age group.

Telephone Interviews

Telephone interviews are a quick and inexpensive method for obtaining a small quantity of relatively impersonal information. Simple, clearly worded questions are easy for interviewers to pose over the phone and are effective at drawing appropriate responses. Telephone surveys have relatively high response rates, especially with repeated calls; calling a number once yields a response rate of 50 to 60 percent, but calling the same number five times raises the response rate to 85 percent. To maximize responses and save costs, some researchers use computerized dialing and digitally synthesized voices that interview respondents.

However, phone surveys have several drawbacks. Most important, many people refuse to take part in them. Their reasons include lack of time, the nuisance factor, negative associations of phone surveys with telemarketing, and poorly designed surveys or questions that are difficult to understand. The National Do Not Call Registry, which regulates telemarketing, allows calls made for research purposes.[23]

Many respondents hesitate to give personal characteristics about themselves over the telephone. Also, results may be biased by the omission of typical households in which adults are working during the day. Other households, particularly market segments such as single women and physicians, are likely to have unlisted numbers. While computerized random dialing can give access to unlisted numbers, it is restricted in several states.

The popularity of Caller ID systems to screen unwanted calls is another obstacle for telephone researchers. State laws on Caller ID vary. Some require vendors to offer a blocking service to callers who wish to evade the system. Marketers face other problems in obtaining responses from a representative sample of respondents using phone surveys: consumer perception of intrusion into their privacy and the number of consumers in the Do Not Call Registry.

Other obstacles restrict the usefulness of telephone surveys abroad. In areas where telephone ownership is rare, survey results will be highly biased. Telephone interviewing is also difficult in countries that lack directories or charge landline telephone customers on a per-minute basis, or where call volumes congest limited phone line capacity.

Personal Interviews

The best means for obtaining detailed information about consumers is usually the personal interview, because the interviewer can establish rapport with respondents and explain confusing or vague questions. In addition to contacting respondents at their homes or workplaces, marketing research firms can conduct interviews in rented space in shopping centers where they gain wide access to potential buyers of the merchandise they are studying. These locations sometimes feature private interviewing space, videotape equipment, and food preparation facilities for taste tests. As mentioned

© Dennis MacDonald/Alamy

The best means for obtaining detailed information about consumers is usually the personal interview.

earlier, interviews conducted in shopping centers typically are called mall intercepts. Downtown retail districts and airports provide other valuable locations for marketing researchers.

Focus Groups

Marketers also gather research information through the popular technique of focus group interviews. A focus group brings together 8 to 12 individuals in one location to discuss a subject of interest. Unlike other interview techniques that elicit information through a question-and-answer format, focus groups usually encourage a general discussion of a predetermined topic. Focus groups can provide quick and relatively inexpensive insight into consumer attitudes and motivations.

In a focus group, the leader, or moderator, typically begins by explaining the purpose of the meeting and suggesting an opening topic. The moderator's main purpose, however, is to stimulate interaction among group members to encourage their discussion of numerous points. The moderator may occasionally interject questions as catalysts to direct the group's discussion. The moderator's job is difficult, requiring preparation and group facilitation skills.

Focus group sessions often last one or two hours. Researchers usually record the discussion on tape, and observers frequently watch through a one-way mirror. Some research firms also allow clients to view focus groups in action through videoconferencing systems.

Focus groups are a particularly valuable tool for exploratory research, developing new-product ideas, and preliminary testing of alternative marketing strategies. They can also aid in the development of well-structured questionnaires for larger-scale research.

Focus groups have a few drawbacks. For instance, one argumentative participant can intimidate everyone else in the group, just as one person who won't open up in the discussion can hold others back. In addition, some group members may say what they think researchers want to hear, offer ideas and opinions for which they have no supporting evidence or experience, or assume everyone feels the same way they do.[24]

Researchers are finding ways to re-create the focus group environment over the Internet. With experienced moderators who have the technical skills to function fluently online, it is possible to gain valuable qualitative information at a fraction of the cost of running a traditional focus group session. Online focus groups can be both cost and time efficient, with immediate results in the form of chat transcripts. The convenience of online conversations tends to improve attendance as well, particularly among those who are otherwise difficult to include, such as professionals and people who travel frequently, and the problem of peer pressure is virtually eliminated. Some drawbacks include the lack of ability to see body language and nonverbal cues, the difficulty of testing any products in which taste or smell is relevant, and the potential for samples to be nonrepresentative, because they are limited to those who have Internet access and a certain comfort level with technology.

Mail and Fax Surveys

Although personal interviews can provide very detailed information, cost considerations usually prevent an organization from using personal interviews in a large-scale study. A mail survey can be a cost-effective alternative. Mail surveys can provide anonymity that may encourage respondents to give candid answers. They can also help marketers track consumer attitudes through ongoing research and sometimes provide demographic data that may be helpful in market segmentation.

Mail questionnaires do, however, have several limitations. First, response rates are typically much lower than for personal interviews. Second, because researchers must wait for respondents to complete and return questionnaires, mail surveys usually take a considerably longer time to conduct. Finally, unless they gather additional information from nonrespondents through other means, researchers must worry about possible bias in the results stemming from differences between respondents and nonrespondents.

The low response rates and long follow-up times associated with mail surveys have spurred interest in the alternative of faxing survey documents. In some cases, faxes may supplement mail surveys; in others, they may be the primary method for contacting respondents. Because millions of households do not have fax machines, securing a representative sample of respondents is a difficult undertaking in fax surveys of consumers. As a result, most of these surveys focus on business-related research studies.

The federal Junk Fax Prevention Act prohibits the sending by fax of "any material advertising the commercial availability or quality of any property, goods, or services which is transmitted to any person without that person's prior express invitation or permission, in writing or otherwise." Under the law, the first page of any fax solicitation must include information for the recipient about how to opt out of similar messages in the future.[25]

Online Surveys and Other Internet-Based Methods

The growing population of Internet users has spurred researchers to conduct online surveys. Using the Web, they are able to speed the survey process, increase sample sizes, ignore geographic boundaries, and dramatically reduce costs. While a standard research project can take up to eight weeks to complete, a thorough online project may take two weeks or less. Less intrusive than telephone surveys, online research allows participants to respond at their leisure. The novelty and ease of answering online may even encourage higher response rates. For some tips on creating surveys for mobile devices, see the "Career Readiness" feature.

Businesses and other organizations are increasingly including questionnaires on their Web pages to solicit information about consumer demographics, attitudes, and comments and suggestions for improving goods and services or improving marketing messages. Online polling is also increasingly popular. Worldwide, nearly one minute of every five that consumers spend online is spent on social networking sites, and this trend shows no sign of slowing down. Facebook has the largest number of unique users—more than 1 billion users worldwide and over 190 million in the United States alone.[26] While companies have struggled for ways to measure the impact of social media, more tools than ever exist for tracking which ones drive traffic to any particular site or sites and, thus, which would be the best sites for posting polls or questionnaires.

It took ten years, but Utah entrepreneur Dr. Bob Wagstaff hit paydirt with his invention, thanks to the power of social media. Despite thousands of dollars spent on infomercials, Wagstaff's creation, an oral hygiene tool called the Orabrush, barely attracted attention. National retailers like CVS and Walgreens declined to carry the tongue scraper, and toothbrush manufacturers weren't interested in buying the patent.

Then, Wagstaff presented his idea to a marketing class at Brigham Young University, where students conducted research. Most of them, however, advised Wagstaff that online was not the medium to pursue.

Luckily, one student disagreed. Jeffrey Harmon saw merit in using social media for an Orabrush introduction. He produced a funny YouTube video titled "Bad Breath Test." The video quickly went

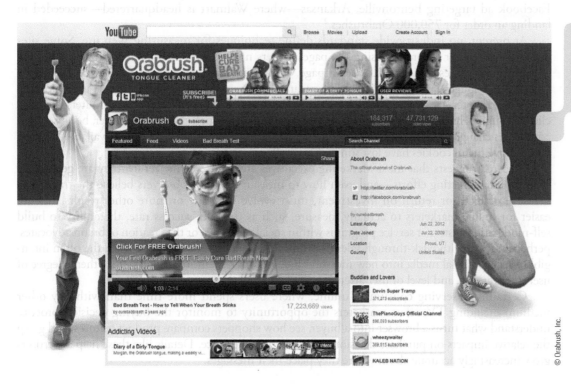

A funny YouTube video that went viral led to the popularity of a new product—Orabrush.

CAREER READINESS

Designing Surveys for Mobile Devices

Marketing surveys are increasingly migrating to mobile devices. But to earn a high response rate, such mobile questionnaires need to specifically reflect the electronic environment. Here are some tips for designing mobile surveys that get responses.

1. Design the survey with the mobile environment in mind. Consider the smart phone's smaller screen, for instance, and choose larger type and colors with good contrast.

2. Limit your use of images. Some email clients block them, and they slow down loading time on mobile devices.

3. Keep your survey short and simple. Try to reduce the amount of scrolling up and down respondents have to do for each question, and limit yourself to no more than 12 questions.

4. Offer an incentive. It doesn't have to be big, but incentives have been shown to draw 5 times as many responses.

5. Make sure you don't require the respondent to navigate away to a separate browser or interrupt the task he or she is doing.

6. Where possible, try to offer the choice to complete the survey on a computer. Completing a survey on a mobile device can take as much as 50 percent longer.

Sources: Andrew Grenville, "When Is Long and Slow More Satisfying? When It's Mobile Research," *Vision Critical University*, accessed November 20, 2012, http://vcu.visioncritical.com; Sherrie Mersdorf, "5 Best Practices for Designing Mobile Surveys," *Web Surveys Blog*, accessed November 20, 2012, http://survey.cvent.com; Jennifer Okula, "A KISS Is Not Enough: How to Launch Mobile Intercept Surveys," *iMedia Connection*, accessed November 20, 2012, http://blogs.imediaconnection.com.

viral and sold a million Orabrushes before a Walmart executive saw it and expressed interest. Before the all-important Walmart meeting, the Orabrush team produced yet another video. This one, a Facebook ad targeting Bentonville, Arkansas—where Walmart is headquartered—succeeded in landing an order for 750,000 Orabrushes.[27]

At present, no industrywide standards define techniques for measuring Web use. Some sites ask users to register before accessing the pages; others merely keep track of the number of "hits," or number of times a visitor accesses a page. Marketers have tried to place a value on a site's "stickiness"—longer-lasting site visits—as a means of measuring effectiveness. Others use "cookies," which, as Chapter 4 explained, are electronic identifiers deposited on viewers' computers, to track click-through behavior—the paths users take as they move through the site. However, because some consumers change their Internet service providers frequently and special software is available to detect and remove them, cookies have lost some of their effectiveness.

Research suggests that most marketing executives are unsure of the return they are getting for their online marketing efforts—and even how to measure it. Some observers believe the traditional measure of ROI, or return on investment, must evolve into one or more other results that are easier for online marketers to actually measure, such as the sales success rate, the ability to build self-moderating customer service programs within social networks, or the creation of brand advocates, perhaps tracked with click-through sales or promotional codes. Others look to turn the often intangible effects of social media into new measures like user time spent interacting with others, degree of user involvement, and level of user attention.[28]

Certainly observing consumers online, where users spend more time than with any other medium including TV, offers marketers the opportunity to monitor the buying decision process, understand what turns a browser into a buyer, see how shoppers compare product features, and grasp the relative impacts on purchase decisions of marketing and price. Details like these help advertisers grow increasingly accurate about where they place their messages.

Experimental Method

The third—and least-used—method for collecting primary data is the controlled experiment. A marketing research experiment is a scientific investigation in which a researcher controls or manipulates a test group (or groups) and compares the results with those of a control group that did not receive the experimental controls or manipulations.

The most common use of this method by marketers is test marketing, or introducing a new product in a specific area and then observing its degree of success. Up to this point, a product development team may have gathered feedback from focus groups. Other information may have come from shoppers' evaluations of competing products. Test marketing is the first stage at which the product performs in a real-life environment.

Procter & Gamble has used streaming ads on Facebook and MySpace to invite users to try free samples of new products or incentives.[29] Some firms omit test marketing and move directly from product development to full-scale production. These companies cite three problems with test marketing:

1. Test marketing is expensive. A firm can spend more than $1 million depending on the size of the test market city and the cost of buying media to advertise the product.

2. Competitors quickly learn about the new product. By studying the test market, competitors can develop alternative strategies.

3. Some products are not well suited to test marketing. Few firms test market long-lived, durable goods such as cars because of the major financial investments required for their development, the need to establish networks of dealers to distribute the products, and requirements for parts and servicing.

Companies that decide to skip the test-marketing process can choose several other options. A firm may simulate a test-marketing campaign through computer-modeling software. By plugging in data on similar products, it can develop a sales projection for a new product. Another firm may offer an item in just one region of the United States or in another country, adjusting promotions and advertising based on local results before going to other geographic regions. Another option may be to limit a product's introduction to only one retail chain to carefully control and evaluate promotions and results.

controlled experiment Scientific investigation in which a researcher manipulates a test group (or groups) and compares the results with those of a control group that did not receive the experimental controls or manipulations.

test marketing Marketing research technique that involves introducing a new product in a specific area and then measuring its degree of success.

⊕ ASSESSMENT CHECK

5.1 What are the principal methods for collecting primary data?

5.2 Identify the different types of survey methods.

CONDUCTING INTERNATIONAL MARKETING RESEARCH

As corporations expand globally, they need to correspondingly gather more knowledge about consumers in other countries. Although marketing researchers follow the same basic steps for international studies as for domestic ones, they often face some very different challenges.

U.S. organizations can tap many secondary resources as they research global markets. One major information source is the U.S. government, which offers a wealth of information through its dedicated website, Export.gov. Here, marketers can find marketing research, business leads, and other data on international trade and intellectual property protection drawn from sources across the U.S. government. The site's trove of international marketing research is organized by country (more than 130 nations) and by industry (more than 110 business sectors). Personalized counseling and customized research are available (the latter for a fee), as well as guidance on improving international business strategy, targeting markets overseas, evaluating international business partners, and increasing brand awareness around the world. U.S. trade show organizers can get help attracting foreign visitors.[30]

Explain the challenges of conducting marketing research in global markets.

When conducting international studies, companies must be prepared to deal with both language issues—communicating their message in the most effective way—and cultural issues, or capturing local citizens' interests while avoiding missteps that could unintentionally offend them. Companies also need to take a good look at a country's business environment, including political and economic conditions, trade regulations affecting research studies and data collection, and the potential for short- and long-term growth. Many marketers recommend tapping local researchers to investigate foreign markets.

Businesses may need to adjust their data collection methods for primary research in other countries, because some methods do not easily transfer across national frontiers. Face-to-face interviewing, for instance, remains the most common method for conducting primary research outside the United States.

While mail surveys are a common data collection method in developed countries, they are useless in many other nations because of low literacy rates, unreliable mail service, and a lack of address lists. Telephone interviews may also not be suitable in other countries, especially those where many people do not have phones. Focus groups can be difficult to arrange because of cultural and social factors. In Latin American countries, for example, highly educated consumers make up a sought-after and opinionated minority, but they have little time to devote to lengthy focus group discussions. Middle- to lower-income Latin Americans may not be accustomed to articulating their opinions about products and grow reticent in the presence of others, whereas in some countries where violence and kidnapping are common, affluent consumers are reluctant to attend meetings with strangers. To help with such difficulties, a growing number of international research firms offer experience in conducting global studies.

ASSESSMENT CHECK

6.1   What are some U.S. organizations that can serve as sources of international secondary marketing data?

6.2   What is the most common method of primary data collection outside the United States?

INTERPRETIVE RESEARCH

As mentioned earlier, interpretive research is a method that observes a customer or group of customers in their natural settings and then interprets their behavior based on an understanding of social and cultural characteristics of that setting.

Interpretive research has attracted considerable interest in recent years. Developed by social anthropologists as a method for explaining behavior that operates below the level of conscious thought, interpretive research can provide insights into consumer behavior and the ways in which consumers interact with brands.

ETHNOGRAPHIC STUDIES

In interpretive research, the researcher first spends an extensive amount of time studying the culture, and for that reason, the studies are often called *ethnographic* studies. The word *ethnographic* means that a researcher takes a cultural perspective of the population being studied. For that reason, interpretive research is often used to interpret consumer behavior within a foreign culture where language, ideals, values, and expectations are subject to different cultural influences. After experiencing a number of product failures in low-income markets in Latin America, Procter & Gamble began an "immersion research" program called "Living It," in which the company's managers and executives spent time with low-income families around the world, living in their homes to develop a better understanding of their needs and desires. P&G's subsequent sales suggest that the effort was worthwhile. Among the mistakes the firm corrected was a low sudsing detergent it introduced in Mexico, unaware that most of its customers there were manual laborers who associated suds with cleaning power.[31]

Interpretive research focuses on understanding the meaning of a product or the consumption experience in a consumer's life. Its methods capture consumers interacting with products in their environment—in other words, capturing what they actually do, not what they say they do. Typically, subjects are filmed in specific situations, such as socializing with friends in a bar for research into beverage consumption, or for extended periods of time for paid participants. Paid participants may be followed by a videographer who records their day-to-day movements and interactions, or they may film themselves. Some companies even pay consumers to wear mini video cameras attached to visors and linked to a sound recorder. These systems record consumer behavior while participants are shopping or doing chores.

Ethnographic studies capture consumers interacting with products in their environment.

© iStockphoto.com/Alex Potemkin

An iPhone application developed by Everyday Lives, a British research agency, allows ethnographic researchers to take photos, notes, and audio and video clips of subjects while conducting their studies. Users can organize the material by theme and send it to their email account to review it later. "We expect word of mouth to play a hugely important part in promoting the app," said Everyday Lives' founder.[32]

 ASSESSMENT CHECK

6.3 How is interpretive research typically conducted?

6.4 When should ethnographic research be employed?

COMPUTER TECHNOLOGY IN MARKETING RESEARCH

The ability to quickly gather and analyze business intelligence can create a substantial strategic advantage. Computer databases provide a wealth of data for marketing research, whether they are outside the company or designed specifically to gather important facts about its customers. Chapter 11 explores how companies use internal databases and customer relationship management technology. This section addresses important uses of computer technology related to marketing research: marketing information systems (MISs), marketing decision support systems (MDSSs), data mining, business intelligence, and competitive intelligence.

Outline the most important uses of computer technology in marketing research.

7

MARKETING INFORMATION SYSTEMS (MISs)

In the past, many marketing managers complained that their information problems resulted from too much rather than too little information. Reams of data were difficult to use and not always relevant. At times, information was almost impossible to find. Modern technological advances have made constraints like these obsolete.

A **marketing information system (MIS)** is a planned, computer-based system designed to provide decision makers with a continuous flow of information relevant to their areas of responsibility. A component of the organization's overall management information system, a marketing information system deals specifically with marketing data and issues.

A well-constructed MIS serves as a company's nerve center, continually monitoring the market environment—both inside and outside the organization—and providing instantaneous information. Marketers can store data for later use, classify and analyze that data, and retrieve it easily when needed.

marketing information system (MIS) Planned, computer-based system designed to provide managers with a continuous flow of information relevant to their specific decisions and areas of responsibility.

MARKETING DECISION SUPPORT SYSTEMS (MDSSs)

marketing decision support system (MDSS) Marketing information system component that links a decision maker with relevant databases and analysis tools.

A **marketing decision support system (MDSS)** consists of software that helps users quickly obtain and apply information in a way that supports marketing decisions. Taking MIS a step further, it allows managers to explore and connect such varying information as the state of the market, consumer behavior, sales forecasts, competitors' actions, and environmental changes. MDSSs consist of four main characteristics: they are interactive, investigative, flexible, and accessible. An MDSS can create simulations or models to illustrate the likely results of changes in marketing strategies or market conditions.

While an MIS provides raw data, an MDSS develops this data into information useful for decision making. For example, an MIS might provide a list of product sales from the previous day. A manager could use an MDSS to transform this raw data into graphs illustrating sales trends or reports estimating the impact of specific decisions, such as raising prices or expanding into new regions.

DATA MINING

data mining Process of searching through customer databases to detect patterns that guide marketing decision making.

Data mining is the process of searching through computerized data files to detect patterns. It focuses on identifying relationships not obvious to marketers—in a sense, answering questions that marketing researchers may not even have thought to ask. The data is stored in a huge database called a *data warehouse*. Software for the marketing decision support system often is associated with the data warehouse and is used to mine data. Once marketers identify patterns and connections, they use this intelligence to check the effectiveness of different strategy options.

Data mining is an efficient way to sort through huge amounts of data and to make sense of that data. It helps marketers create customer profiles, pinpoint reasons for customer loyalty or the lack thereof, analyze potential returns on changes in pricing or promotion, and forecast sales. Data mining offers considerable advantages in retailing, the hotel industry, banking, utilities, and many other areas, and holds the promise of providing answers to many specific strategic questions. Some are concerned, however, about the rapidly growing amount of personal data being gathered by companies like Facebook and Google, and the uses to which it may be put in the absence of any U.S. regulations governing such use. See the "Solving an Ethical Controversy" feature for a discussion.

But some uses of data mining remain controversial. Pharmacies in the United States are required by law to maintain records of doctors' prescriptions, and many sell those records to data-mining companies. After Vermont passed a law banning pharmaceutical firms from using the data to target physicians, the industry sued. Pharmaceutical companies called the law unconstitutional, claiming it hinders them from identifying their prospects. A ruling by the U.S. Supreme Court overturning Vermont's law has led other states to carefully consider how to word their own such legislation to resist a court challenge and still maintain consumer privacy.[33]

BUSINESS INTELLIGENCE

Business intelligence is the process of gathering information and analyzing it to improve business strategy, tactics, and daily operations. Using advanced software tools, marketers gather information from within and outside the organization. Business intelligence can thus tell the firm how its own sales operation is doing or how its top competitors are performing.

The key is not only gathering the information but also getting it into a form that employees can make sense of and use for decision making and strategizing. Software can help users collect, aggregate, and create reports with outside information available on the Web from such databases as, say, Dun & Bradstreet. SmartOrg, based in Menlo Park, California, is one firm that specializes in helping firms like Boeing and Hewlett-Packard identify and manage information. Boeing uses SmartOrg software in its decision making on aircraft like the 787 Dreamliner. The software also supported the creation of new businesses within Hewlett-Packard, many of them considered "disruptive innovations."[34]

SOLVING AN ETHICAL CONTROVERSY

Who Should Profit from Your Data?

Facebook makes over $3 billion in advertising a year by targeting ads based on information its users voluntarily post about themselves. Google makes more than 10 times as much with ads based on the contents of users' Gmail and Web searches. Other organizations use personal information gleaned online to turn people down for jobs, insurance coverage, or loans and credit, sometimes based on information about others with similar profiles, rather than on accurate data about the individuals themselves.

Should online companies be allowed to profit from using your personal data?

PRO

1. Privacy is a subjective concept; not everyone objects to the use of data they voluntarily provide, and those who do can leave it offline.

2. Knowing consumers' likes and dislikes lets companies efficiently target their marketing to present only the messages those users will welcome.

CON

1. No laws limit what online companies and data aggregators can do with the information they collect, so they do as they please without regard to individuals' privacy.

2. The possibilities for abuse and theft of the collected data are too great.

Summary:

Nearly 70 percent of respondents in a recent survey believed people have a right to know what an online company knows about them, and some advocate the passage of a corresponding law to that effect.

Sources: Seth Rosenblatt, "How to Protect Yourself Online in Three Easy Steps," *CNET News*, accessed November 20, 2012, http://news.cnet.com; Doug Walp, "Facebook Users Should Be Wary of Company's Data Mining," *The Daily Athenaeum*, accessed November 20, 2012, www.thedaonline.com; Lori Andrews, "Facebook Is Using You," *The New York Times*, accessed November 20, 2012, www.nytimes.com; "The Pros and Cons of Data Mining with Facebook Applications," *Connected Internet*, accessed November 20, 2012, www.connectedinternet.co.uk.

COMPETITIVE INTELLIGENCE

Competitive intelligence is a form of business intelligence that focuses on finding information about competitors using published sources, interviews, observations by salespeople and suppliers in the industry, government agencies, public filings such as patent applications, and other secondary sources, including the Internet. Its aim is to uncover the specific advantages a competitor has, such as new-product launches, innovative features in existing goods or services, or original marketing or promotional strategies. Even a competitor's advertising can provide clues. Marketers use competitive intelligence to make better decisions that strengthen their own competitive strategy in turn.

 ASSESSMENT CHECK

7.1 Distinguish between an MIS and an MDSS.

7.2 What is data mining?

7.3 Describe the process of collecting business and competitive intelligence.

SALES FORECASTING

8 Identify the major types of forecasting methods.

sales forecast Estimate of a firm's revenue for a specified future period.

qualitative forecasting Use of subjective techniques to forecast sales, such as the jury of executive opinion, Delphi technique, sales force composite, and surveys of buyer intentions.

quantitative forecasting Use of statistical forecasting techniques such as trend analysis and exponential smoothing.

A basic building block of any marketing plan is a **sales forecast**, an estimate of a firm's revenue for a specified future period. Sales forecasts play major roles in new-product decisions, production scheduling, financial planning, inventory planning and procurement, distribution, and human resources planning. An inaccurate forecast may lead to incorrect decisions in each of these areas. There are a number of software programs that offer companies sales forecasting applications to help automate the forecasting process. Table 10.1 outlines three of those programs.

Marketing research techniques are used to deliver effective sales forecasts. A sales forecast is also an important tool for marketing control, because it sets standards against which to measure actual performance. Without such standards, no comparisons can be made.

Planners rely on short-run, intermediate, and long-run sales forecasts. A short-run forecast usually covers a period of up to one year, an intermediate forecast covers one to five years, and a long-run forecast extends beyond five years. Although sales forecasters use an array of techniques to predict the future—ranging from computer simulations to studying trends identified by futurists—their methods fall into two broad categories: qualitative and quantitative forecasting.

Qualitative forecasting techniques rely on subjective data that reports opinions rather than exact historical data. **Quantitative forecasting** methods, by contrast, use statistical computations, such as trend extensions based on past data, computer simulations, and econometric models. As Table 10.2 shows, each method has benefits and limitations. Consequently, most organizations use a combination of both techniques.

QUALITATIVE FORECASTING TECHNIQUES

Planners apply qualitative forecasting methods when they want judgmental or subjective indicators. Qualitative forecasting techniques include the jury of executive opinion, Delphi technique, sales force composite, and survey of buyer intentions.

Jury of Executive Opinion

jury of executive opinion Qualitative sales forecasting method that assesses the sales expectations of various executives.

The technique called the **jury of executive opinion** combines and averages the outlooks of top executives from such areas as marketing, finance, and production. Top managers bring the following capabilities to the process: experience and knowledge about situations that influence sales, open-minded attitudes toward the future, and awareness of the bases for their judgments. This quick and inexpensive method generates good forecasts for sales and new-product development. It works best for short-run forecasting.

TABLE 10.1 A Sampling of Sales Forecasting Software Programs

Forecast Pro
- Input historical data, and then the software analyzes the data, selects the appropriate forecasting technique, and makes its statistical calculations.
- Adjust the information and save new changes.
- The software creates reports and graphs for presenting results.
- There are three editions available: Forecast Pro Unlimited, Forecast Pro TRAC, and Forecast Pro XE.

Right90
- Includes a four-step forecasting process: Capture, Vet, Analyze, Drive. Integrates with existing company IT applications.
- Available forecasting applications include: Right90 Sales Forecast Capture, Right90 Statistical Forecasting, Right90 Change Analytics, Right90 Trust Analytics.

SAS
- SAS/ETS Time Series Forecasting uses the following techniques: time series and econometric.
- SAS Forecast Server creates several forecasts quickly to allow a company to plan their future.

TABLE 10.2 Benefits and Limitations of Various Forecasting Techniques

Techniques	Benefits	Limitations
Qualitative Methods		
Jury of executive opinion	Opinions come from executives in many different departments; quick; inexpensive	Managers may lack background knowledge and experience to make meaningful predictions
Delphi technique	Group of experts may predict long-term events such as technological breakthroughs	Time-consuming; expensive
Sales force composite	Salespeople have expert customer, product, and competitor knowledge; quick; inexpensive	Inaccurate forecasts may result from low estimates of salespeople concerned about their influence on quotas
Survey of buyer intentions	Useful in predicting short-term and intermediate sales for firms that serve selected customers	Intentions to buy may not result in actual purchases; time-consuming; expensive
Quantitative Methods		
Test market	Provides realistic information on actual purchases rather than on intent to buy	Alerts competition to new-product plans; time-consuming; expensive
Trend analysis	Quick; inexpensive; effective with stable customer demand and environment	Assumes the future will continue the past; ignores environmental changes
Exponential smoothing	Same benefits as trend analysis, but emphasizes more recent data	Same limitations as trend analysis, but not as severe due to emphasis on recent data

© Cengage Learning

Delphi Technique

Like the jury of executive opinion, the Delphi technique solicits opinions from several people, but it also gathers input from experts outside the firm, such as academic researchers, rather than relying completely on company executives. It is most appropriately used to predict long-run issues, such as technological breakthroughs, that could affect future sales and the market potential for new products.

The Delphi technique works as follows: A firm selects a panel of experts and sends each a questionnaire relating to a future event. After combining and averaging the answers, the firm develops another questionnaire based on these results and sends it back to the same people. The process continues until it identifies a consensus. Although firms have successfully used Delphi to predict future technological breakthroughs, the method is both expensive and time-consuming.

Sales Force Composite

The sales force composite technique develops forecasts based on the belief that organization members closest to the marketplace—those with specialized product, customer, and competitive knowledge—offer the best insights concerning short-term future sales. It typically works from the bottom up. Management consolidates salespeople's estimates first at the district level, then at the regional level, and finally nationwide to obtain an aggregate forecast of sales that reflects all three levels.

The sales force composite approach has some weaknesses, however. Because salespeople recognize the role of their sales forecasts in determining sales quotas for their territories, they are likely to make conservative estimates. Moreover, their narrow perspectives from within their limited geographic territories may prevent them from considering the impact on sales of trends developing in other territories, forthcoming technological innovations, or the major changes in marketing strategies. Consequently, the sales force composite gives the best forecasts in combination with other techniques.

Delphi technique
Qualitative sales forecasting method that gathers and redistributes several rounds of anonymous forecasts until the participants reach a consensus.

sales force composite
Qualitative sales forecasting method based on the combined sales estimates of the firm's salespeople.

**survey of buyer
intentions** Qualitative
sales forecasting method that
samples opinions among
groups of present and potential
customers concerning their
purchasing plans.

trend analysis
Quantitative sales forecasting
method that estimates future
sales through statistical
analyses of historical sales
patterns.

**exponential
smoothing** Quantitative
forecasting technique that
assigns weights to historical
sales data, giving the greatest
weight to the most recent
data.

Survey of Buyer Intentions

A **survey of buyer intentions** gathers input through mail-in questionnaires, online feedback, telephone polls, and personal interviews to determine the purchasing intentions of a representative group of present and potential customers. This method suits firms that serve limited numbers of customers but often proves impractical for those with millions of customers. Also, buyer surveys gather useful information only when customers willingly reveal their buying intentions. Moreover, customer intentions do not necessarily translate into actual purchases. These surveys may help a firm predict short-run or intermediate sales, but they employ time-consuming and expensive methods.

QUANTITATIVE FORECASTING TECHNIQUES

Quantitative techniques attempt to eliminate the subjectiveness of the qualitative methods. They include such methods as test markets, trend analysis, and exponential smoothing.

Test Markets

One quantitative technique, the test market, frequently helps planners assess consumer responses to new-product offerings. The procedure typically begins by establishing one or more test markets to gauge consumer responses to a new product under actual marketplace conditions. These tests also permit experimenters to evaluate the effects of different prices, alternative promotional strategies, and other marketing mix variations by comparing results among different test markets.

The primary advantage of test markets is the realism they provide for the marketer. On the other hand, these expensive and time-consuming experiments may also communicate marketing plans to competitors before a firm introduces a product to the total market.

Trend Analysis

Trend analysis develops forecasts for future sales by analyzing the historical relationship between sales and time. It implicitly assumes the collective causes of past sales will continue to exert similar influences in the future. When historical data are available, planners can quickly and inexpensively complete trend analysis. Software programs can calculate the average annual increment of change for the available sales data. This average increment of change is then projected into the future to come up with the sales forecast. So if the sales of a firm have been growing $15.3 million on average per year, this amount of sales could be added to last year's sales total to arrive at next year's forecast.

Of course, trend analysis cannot be used if historical data are not available, as in new-product forecasting. Also, trend analysis makes the dangerous assumption that future events will continue in the same manner as the past. Any variations in the determinants of future sales will cause deviations from the forecast. In other words, this method gives reliable forecasts during periods of steady growth and stable demand. If conditions change, predictions based on trend analysis may become worthless. For this reason, forecasters have applied more sophisticated techniques and complex, new forecasting models to anticipate the effects of various possible changes in the future.

Exponential Smoothing

A more sophisticated method of trend analysis, the **exponential smoothing** technique, weighs each year's sales data, giving greater weight to results from the most recent years. Otherwise, the statistical approach used in trend analysis is applied here. For example, last year's sales might receive a 1.5 weight, while sales data from two years ago could get a 1.4 weighting. Exponential smoothing is considered the most commonly used quantitative forecasting technique.

ASSESSMENT CHECK

8.1 Describe the jury of executive opinion.

8.2 What is the Delphi technique?

8.3 How does the exponential smoothing technique forecast sales?

STRATEGIC IMPLICATIONS OF MARKETING IN THE 21ST CENTURY

Marketing research can help an organization develop effective marketing strategies. Most new products eventually fail to attract enough buyers to remain viable. Why? A major reason is the seller's failure to understand market needs.

Consider, for example, the hundreds of dot-com companies that went under. A characteristic shared by all of those failing businesses is that virtually none of them was founded on sound marketing research. Very few used marketing research techniques to evaluate sales potential, and even fewer studied consumer responses after the ventures were initiated. While research might not have prevented every dot-com meltdown, it may have helped a few of those businesses survive.

Marketing research ideally matches new products to potential customers. Marketers also conduct research to analyze sales of their own and competitors' products, gauge the performance of existing products, guide the development of promotional campaigns and product enhancements, and develop and refine products. All of these activities enable marketers to fine-tune their marketing strategies and reach customers more effectively and efficiently.

Marketing researchers have at their disposal a broad range of techniques with which to collect both quantitative and qualitative data on customers, their lifestyles, behaviors, attitudes, and perceptions. Vast amounts of data can be rapidly collected, accessed, interpreted, and applied to improve all aspects of business operations. Because of customer relationship management technology, that information is no longer generalized to profile groups of customers—it can be analyzed to help marketers understand every customer.

REVIEW OF CHAPTER OBJECTIVES

1 Describe the development of the marketing research function and its major activities.

Marketing research, or the collection and use of information in marketing decision making, began when Charles C. Parlin, an ad salesman, counted empty soup cans in Philadelphia's trash in an effort to persuade the Campbell Soup Company to advertise in *The Saturday Evening Post*. Today, the most common marketing research activities are (1) determining market potential, market share, and market characteristics and (2) conducting sales analyses and competitive product studies. Most large consumer goods companies now have internal marketing research departments. However, outside suppliers still remain vital to the research function. Some perform the complete research task, while others specialize in a limited area or provide specific data services.

2 Explain the steps in the marketing research process.

The marketing research process can be divided into six specific steps: (1) defining the problem, (2) conducting exploratory research, (3) formulating hypotheses, (4) creating a research design, (5) collecting data, and (6) interpreting and presenting the research information. A clearly defined problem focuses on the researcher's search for relevant decision-oriented information. Exploratory research refers to information gained outside the firm. Hypotheses, tentative explanations of specific events, allow researchers to set out specific research designs—that is, the series of decisions that, taken together, comprise master plans or models for conducting the investigations. The data collection phase of the marketing research process can involve either or both primary (original) and secondary (previously published) data. After the data are collected, researchers must interpret and present them in a way that is meaningful to management.

3 Distinguish between primary and secondary data, and identify the sources of each type.

Primary data can be collected by the firm's own researchers or by independent marketing research companies. Three principal methods of primary data collection are observation, survey, and experiment. Secondary data can be classified as either internal or external. Sources of internal data include sales records, product evaluation, sales force reports, and records of marketing costs. Sources of external data include the government and private sources such as business magazines. Both external and internal data can also be obtained from computer databases.

4 Explain the different sampling techniques used by marketing researchers.

Samples can be categorized as either probability samples or nonprobability samples. A probability sample is one in which every member of the population has a known chance of being selected. Probability samples include simple random samples, in which every item in the relevant universe has an equal opportunity to be selected; stratified samples, in which randomly selected subsamples of different groups are represented in the total sample; and cluster samples, in which geographic areas are selected from which respondents are drawn. A nonprobability sample is arbitrary and does not allow application of standard statistical tests. Nonprobability sampling techniques include convenience samples, in which readily available respondents are picked, and quota samples, divided so that different segments or groups are represented in the total sample.

5 Identify the methods by which marketing researchers collect primary data.

Observation data are gathered by observing consumers via devices like people meters or videotape. Survey data can be collected through telephone interviews, mail or fax surveys, personal interviews, focus groups, or a variety of online methods. Telephone interviews provide more than half of all primary marketing research data. They give the researcher a fast and inexpensive way to get small amounts of information but generally not detailed or personal information. Personal interviews are costly but allow researchers to get detailed information from respondents. Mail and fax surveys are a means of conducting national studies at a reasonable cost; their main disadvantage is potentially inadequate response rates. Focus groups elicit detailed, qualitative information that provides insight not only into behavior but also into consumer attitudes and perceptions. Online surveys can yield fast responses but face obstacles such as the adequacy of the probability sample. The experimental method creates verifiable statistical data through the use of test and control groups to reveal actual benefits from perceived benefits.

6 Explain the challenges of conducting marketing research in global markets.

Many resources are available to help U.S. organizations research global markets. Government resources include the Department of Commerce, state trade offices, small-business development centers, and foreign embassies. Private companies, such as marketing research firms and companies that distribute research from other sources, are another resource. Electronic networks offer online international trade forums, in which marketers can establish global contacts.

7 Outline the most important uses of computer technology in marketing research.

Important uses of computer technology in marketing research include (1) a marketing information system (MIS)—a planned, computer-based system designed to provide managers with a continuous flow of information relevant to their specific

decision-making needs and areas of responsibility; (2) a marketing decision support system (MDSS)—a marketing information system component that links a decision maker with relevant databases and analysis tools; (3) data mining—the process of searching through consumer information files or data warehouses to detect patterns that guide marketing decision making; (4) business intelligence—the process of gathering information and analyzing it to improve business strategy, tactics, and daily operations; and (5) competitive intelligence—the form of business intelligence that focuses on finding information about competitors using published sources, interviews, observations by salespeople and suppliers in the industry, government agencies, public filings like patent applications, and other secondary methods, including the Internet.

8 Identify the major types of forecasting methods.

There are two categories of forecasting methods. Qualitative methods are more subjective because they are based on opinions rather than exact historical data. They include the jury of executive opinion, the Delphi technique, the sales force composite, and the survey of buyer intentions. Quantitative methods include more factual and numerical measures, such as test markets, trend analysis, and exponential smoothing.

 ASSESSMENT CHECK: ANSWERS

1.1 Identify the different classifications of marketing research suppliers, and explain how they differ from one another. Marketing research suppliers can be classified as syndicated services, which regularly send standardized data sets to all customers; full-service suppliers, which contract to conduct complete marketing research projects; or limited-service suppliers, which specialize in selected activities.

1.2 What research methods can be used to measure customer satisfaction? Some companies look at feedback from existing customers, for instance, hiring marketing research firms to collect and analyze customer feedback at their websites. Other firms collect feedback about customer defections—why a customer no longer uses a product. Other organizations conduct research through online polls and surveys.

2.1 What are the six steps in the marketing research process? The marketing research process can be divided into six specific steps: (1) defining the problem, (2) conducting exploratory research, (3) formulating hypotheses, (4) creating a research design, (5) collecting

data, and (6) interpreting and presenting the research information.

2.2 What is the goal of exploratory research? Exploratory research seeks to discover the cause of a specific problem by discussing the problem with informed sources within and outside the firm and examining data from other information sources.

3.1 Distinguish between primary and secondary data. Primary data are original; secondary data have been previously published.

3.2 What are the major methods of collecting secondary data? Sources of internal data include sales records, product evaluations, sales force reports, and records of marketing costs.

3.3 What are the major methods of collecting primary data? Three principal methods of primary data collection are observation, survey, and experiment.

4.1 What is sampling? Sampling is the process of selecting representative survey respondents or research participants from the total universe of possible participants.

4.2 Explain the different types of probability samples. Types of probability samples include simple random samples, stratified samples, and cluster samples.

4.3 Identify the types of nonprobability samples. Nonprobability samples are convenience samples and quota samples.

5.1 What are the principal methods for collecting primary data? The principal methods for collecting primary data are observation, surveys, and controlled experiments.

5.2 Identify the different types of survey methods. Different survey methods may include telephone interviews, personal interviews, focus groups, mail surveys, fax surveys, and online or other Internet-based methods.

6.1 What are some U.S. organizations that can serve as sources of international secondary marketing data? The Departments of Commerce and State offer reports and guides to many countries. Other sources include state trade offices, small-business development centers, and U.S. embassies in various nations.

6.2 What is the most common method of primary data collection outside the United States? Face-to-face interviewing remains the most common method for conducting primary research outside the United States.

6.3 How is interpretive research typically conducted? Interpretive research observes a customer or group of customers in their natural setting and interprets their behavior based on social and cultural characteristics of that setting.

6.4 When should ethnographic research be employed? Ethnographic research is used to look at the consumer behavior of different groups of people.

7.1 Distinguish between an MIS and an MDSS. A marketing information system (MIS) is a planned, computer-based system designed to provide managers with a continuous flow of information relevant to their specific decision-making needs and areas of responsibility. A marketing decision support system (MDSS) is a marketing information system component that links a decision maker with relevant databases and analysis tools to help ask what-if questions.

7.2 What is data mining? Data mining is the process of searching through huge consumer information files or data warehouses to detect patterns that can help marketers ask the right questions and guide marketing decision making.

7.3 Describe the process of collecting business and competitive intelligence. Business intelligence is the process of gathering information and analyzing it to improve business strategy, tactics, and daily operations. Competitive intelligence focuses on finding information about competitors using published sources, interviews, observations by salespeople and suppliers in the industry, government agencies, public filings such as patent applications, and other secondary methods including the Internet.

8.1 Describe the jury of executive opinion. The jury of executive opinion combines and averages the outlooks of top executives from areas like marketing, finance, production, and purchasing.

8.2 What is the Delphi technique? The Delphi technique solicits opinions from several people but also includes input from experts outside the firm.

8.3 How does the exponential smoothing technique forecast sales? Exponential smoothing weighs each year's sales data, giving greater weight to results from the most recent years.

MARKETING TERMS YOU NEED TO KNOW

ASSURANCE OF LEARNING REVIEW

1. Outline the development and current status of the marketing research function.

2. What are the differences between full-service and limited-service research suppliers?

3. List and explain the steps in the marketing research process. Trace a hypothetical study through the stages in this process.

4. Distinguish between primary and secondary data. When should researchers collect each type of data?

5. What is sampling? Explain the differences between probability and nonprobability samples and identify the various types of each.

6. Distinguish among surveys, experiments, and observational methods of primary data collection. Cite examples of each method.

7. Define and give an example of each of the methods of gathering survey data. Under what circumstances should researchers choose a specific approach?

8. Describe the experimental method of collecting primary data and indicate when researchers should use it.

9. Describe business intelligence.

10. Contrast qualitative and quantitative sales forecasting methods.

PROJECTS AND TEAMWORK EXERCISES

1. Nielsen Company offers data collected by optical scanners from the United Kingdom, France, Germany, Belgium, the Netherlands, Austria, Italy, and Finland. This scanner data tracks sales of UPC-coded products in those nations. In small teams, imagine you are Nielsen clients in the United States. One team might be a retail chain, another an Internet company, and still another a videogame manufacturer. Discuss the types of marketing questions these data might help you answer. Share your list with other teams.

2. Sandwich maker Subway opened its first overseas store in 1984, in the Middle East. Today, it has over 38,000 stores in 100 countries. Discuss some of the challenges Subway might face in conducting marketing research in potential new international markets. What types of research would you recommend the company use in choosing new countries for expansion?

3. Working alone or with a partner, choose a new-product idea, or a variation on an existing product, that you think would appeal to your classmates, such as yogurt or an energy drink in a new flavor, and devise a test marketing plan for it. Determine where you will test your product and which variables you will assess, such as price and promotional activities. Be prepared to present your plan to the class and include a description of the information you hope your test market will provide.

4. Interpretive research offers marketing researchers many possibilities, including the opportunity to improve product features such as packaging for food or over-the-counter medication that is difficult for seniors or the disabled to open. List some other ways in which you think this observation method can help make existing product offerings more appealing or more useful to specific users. What kind of products would you choose, and how would you test them?

5. McDonald's conducts extensive marketing research for all its new products, including new menu items for its overseas stores. Because of cultural and other differences and preferences, the company cannot always extrapolate its results from one country to another. For instance, Croque McDo fried ham-and-cheese sandwiches are unlikely to be as popular in the United States as they are in France, which invented the *croque monsieur* sandwich on which the McDonald's product is based. Can you think of any other kinds of firms that share this limitation on global applications of their research? In contrast, what sorts of questions *could* multinational firms answer on a global basis? Why?

CRITICAL-THINKING EXERCISES

1. Some companies are broadening their markets by updating classic products to appeal to younger people's tastes and preferences. What primary and secondary marketing information would you want to have if you were planning to reinvigorate an established brand in each of the following categories? Where and how would you obtain the information?
   a. household cleaner
   b. moist packaged cat food
   c. spray starch
   d. electrical appliances

2. Marketers sometimes collect primary information by using so-called mystery shoppers who visit stores anonymously (as if they were customers) and note such critical factors as store appearance and ambiance, items in stock, and quality of service including waiting time and courtesy of employees. (The CEO of Staples has gone on mystery shopper trips and sometimes asked his mother to make similar trips.) Prepare a list of data you would want to obtain from a mystery shopper surveying a chain of gas stations in your area. Devise a format for gathering the information that combines your need to compile the data

electronically and the researcher's need to remain undetected while visiting the stores.

3. Select a sales forecasting method (or combination of methods) for each of the following information needs and explain your pick(s).
    a. prediction of next year's sales based on last year's figures
    b. prediction of next year's sales based on weighted data from the last five years
    c. expected sales categorized by district and by region

d. estimated product usage for the next year by typical consumers
e. probable consumer response to a new product

4. The Internet provides ready access to secondary information but is also a portal to an almost limitless store of primary information via social networking sites, message boards, chat rooms, email questionnaires, newsgroups, and website registration forms. What are some specific drawbacks of each of these methods for obtaining primary information from customers?

ETHICS EXERCISE

Consumer groups sometimes object to marketers' methods of collecting primary data from customers. They disagree with such means as product registration forms; certain types of games, contests, or product offers; and "cookies" and demographic questionnaires on company websites. Marketers believe these tools offer them an easy way to collect data. Most strictly control the use of such data and never link identifying information with consumers' financial or demographic profiles. However, the possibility of abuse or error always exists.

Research the code of ethics of the American Marketing Association (AMA). Especially note the guidelines for use of the Internet in marketing research.

1. Check the websites of a few large consumer products companies. How effectively do you think these sites are at informing visitors about the use of "cookies" on the sites? Do you think marketers could or should improve their protection of visitors' privacy? If so, how?

2. Do you think the AMA's code of ethics would be violated if marketers compiled a mailing list from information provided on warranty and product registration cards and then used the list to send customers new-product information? Why or why not? Does your opinion change if the company also sends list members special discount offers and private sale notices?

INTERNET EXERCISES

1. **Focus groups.** Visit the websites listed below. Each discusses the proper way to organize and conduct a focus group. After reviewing the material, prepare a brief report on the subject.

    www.businessweek.com/stories/2009-10-08/how-to-conduct-a-focus-group

    http://managementhelp.org/evaluatn/focusgrp.htm
    www.ehow.com/how_4393027_conduct-focus-group.html

2. **Marketing research firm services.** Nielsen is one of the world's largest marketing research firms. Go to the firm's U.S. website. Assume you run a small online retailer. What types of marketing research services could a firm like Nielsen provide to your company? What are some of the benefits?

    http://en-us.nielsen.com

3. **Data analysis.** The Census Bureau publishes the *Statistical Abstract of the United States* each year. Visit the website shown below. Collect the following data by state: per-capita income, percent of population living in urban areas, median age, percent of population with college degrees. Analyze the relationships between income and urban population, age, and education.

    www.census.gov/compendia/statab

Note: Internet Web addresses change frequently. If you don't find the exact site listed, you may need to access the organization's home page and search from there or use a search engine such as Google or Bing.

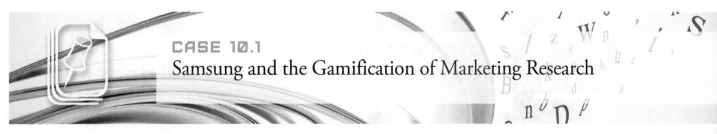

CASE 10.1
Samsung and the Gamification of Marketing Research

There's no stopping a good idea. As millions of avid fans enjoy online games like Farmville, businesses are responding with similar games on corporate websites, but their purpose isn't to amass virtual goods or defeat alien armies. Rather, these games are designed to build customer relationships, reward loyalty, and not incidentally, gather market research data.

Samsung Nation rewards users who post comments on the company's website, answer other users' questions, and link to Samsung.com from their Twitter accounts. Although a television set was offered as the top prize, players reaching higher levels in Samsung Nation enjoy only virtual rewards like colored badges and titles like "Connoisseur." They also spend more time on the company's site, share more product information, and let Samsung track their online behavior. The CEO of Badgeville, a start-up that designs corporate games like Samsung's, says his client companies "use gamification to measure and influence user behavior to meet their business goals." Increased site activity impresses potential customers; positive user comments can increase sales with lower marketing costs; and peer reviews are seen as highly trustworthy. For marketers, who also get to swell their customer databases, gamification is a win–win strategy.

Corporate games attract some unexpected demographic groups, like women in their late 30s who don't fit the typical gamer profile. That boosts companies' confidence that the data they're gathering accurately reflects their target segments. Sears, Groupon, the USA Network, Warner Brothers, and Verizon Wireless have adopted gaming techniques to draw more users to their websites and extend the time they spend there. Badgeville's CEO says some companies track hundreds of actions by millions of people.

Gamification is even growing within firms. The Big Four accounting firm Deloitte runs a game app called "Who, What, Where" on its internal social network Yammer. Employees are rewarded with status and virtual badges for sharing information with colleagues, nurturing client relationships, and completing training. Says one 25-year-old employee who values the program's visibility with upper management, success in the game "could be the difference between being known as an up-and-comer or not."

QUESTIONS FOR CRITICAL THINKING

1. Critics say marketing games manipulate customers into giving away an increasing amount of personal information without the real thrill of game playing. Do you agree? Why or why not?

2. Banks say they are cautious about adopting gamification techniques because of concerns about keeping the collected data secure. Are they right? Why or why not?

Sources: Erica Swallow, "How Three Businesses Scored Big with Gamification," *Entrepreneur*, accessed November 20, 2012, www.entrepreneur.com; David Rosenbaum, "The Games Businesses Play," *CFO*, accessed November 20, 2012, www.cfo.com; Natasha Singer, "You've Won a Badge (and Now We Know All About You)," *The New York Times*, accessed November 20, 2012, www.nytimes.com; Erica Swallow, "How Badgeville Is Gamifying the Internet," *Entrepreneur*, accessed November 20, 2012, www.entrepreneur.com; Becky Yerak, "Businesses Turn to Video Games to Generate Customer Loyalty," *Chicago Tribune*, accessed November 20, 2012, http://articles.chicagotribune.com.

It's a blazing hot day, and all you can think about is the cold, sweet sensation of ice cream on your tongue. Or maybe you prefer the tangy, icy taste of sherbet. GaGa SherBetter is both—or neither, depending on how your taste buds react to the tart flavor and smooth texture of this frozen confection. Less than a decade ago, Jim King decided to whip up a few batches of his grandmother GaGa's lemon sherbet to see if anyone outside his family liked it. He peddled the sherbet to grocery stores in Rhode Island before stopping at Munroe Dairy, where the owner fed it to his dog—who lapped up the lemon dessert. "I'll take 500 pints," said Munroe's owner. Although this wasn't the most scientific way to test a market, the purchase put King and his wife Michelle in business—and they've churned out thousands of pints ever since.

Despite the fact the product line has expanded from one flavor to seven (along with six novelty bar flavors), consumers still aren't quite sure what GaGa SherBetter is—which is a challenge for the Kings from a marketing standpoint. SherBetter is the Kings' own name for the product, meaning "sherbet but better." At only 160 calories and 4 grams of fat per serving, GaGa is lighter than ice cream, but it packs a creamy punch in the mouth. So they've positioned their product as the best of both: SherBetter. GaGa product cartons feature a tagline that spells it out: "Smooth as ice cream, fresh like sherbet."

Michelle King, now marketing director for the company, acknowledges, "We haven't had a very scientific approach to marketing research. We've called upon our own resources, our family and friends, and done a little bit of focus group research." They have conducted taste tests that confirm consumers' preference for GaGa over other products. At one taste test of nine frozen dessert products, Gaga ranked first or second with every participant.

The Kings also rely heavily on sampling at markets and events to get the word out among consumers and the products onto store shelves. Giving away the product "is the biggest way to increase sales," says CEO Jim King. If they are in a store, not only do people buy GaGa that day, they tend to return for more later on, trying new flavors like key lime or toasted coconut. The Kings track sales from these efforts to help forecast future potential sales and consumer preferences.

From the beginning, the Kings knew they couldn't compete with ice cream giants like Hood or Breyers. Sherbet accounts for only 4 percent of total ice cream sales, trimming the market even further. So they targeted the higher-end ice cream makers, such as Ben & Jerry's and Häagen-Dazs, but their product didn't fit there either. "The mistake we made was mis-marketing the product, trying to market it as something it's not, because we thought it would be more appealing to consumers," admits Michelle King. Finally, they hired a company to conduct some marketing research and received the advice they'd intuited all along: "Be true to ourselves."

The Kings would advise other young start-ups to conduct focus groups and other marketing research "right out of the gate" instead of waiting as they did. They continue to do the best they can with a tight budget, making the most of free marketing, such as sampling and social media. But they believe that all consumers need to do is try a spoonful of GaGa, and they'll become loyal followers. The dessert gets sweet reviews in the press and blogs, and it has made its way to some regional and national chains like Shaw's, Wegmans, and Whole Foods. As for the name, the Kings trademarked it long before Lady Gaga ever hit the stage. There's no research on what Jim's grandmother would have thought about that.

QUESTIONS FOR CRITICAL THINKING

1. How would you define the major problem faced by GaGa that a marketing research program could resolve? How has this problem affected the marketing of the company's products? How might marketing research help?

2. Identify the methods of collecting primary data, and give an example of how GaGa might implement each method.

Sources: Company website, http://gagagourmetsherbet.com, accessed November 20, 2012; "GaGa's Rainbow SherBetter," *On Second Scoop*, accessed November 20, 2012, www.onsecondscoop.com; Judi Atkins Bridges, "Summer Market Blackberries," *AL.com*, accessed November 20, 2012, http://blog.al.com; Curt Nickisch, "GaGa's for Lady Gaga? Coincidental Celebrity Lifts Local Brands," *NPR (Boston)*, accessed November 20, 2012, www.wbur.org.

NOTES

1. David Cooperstein, "How the Little Boston Shop Polka Dog Bakery Wound Up in Target," *Forbes*, accessed November 20, 2012, www.forbes.com; Charles Duhigg, "How Companies Learn Your Secrets," *The New York Times Magazine*, accessed November 20, 2012, www.nytimes.com; Jessica Wohl, "Target To Host Boutiques, and Apple, in Stores," *Reuters*, accessed November 20, 2012, www.reuters.com; Stephanie Clifford, "In a Test, Target Plans to Add an Apple 'Store' Inside 25 Stores," *The New York Times*, accessed November 20, 2012, www.nytimes.com.

2. Company website, www.jdpower.com, accessed November 20, 2012.

3. Company website, www.brain-research.com, accessed November 20, 2012.

4. Company website, www.quicktest.com, accessed November 20, 2012.

5. Company website, www.bazaarvoice.com, accessed November 20, 2012.

6. Molly McMillin, "Annual Quality Survey Shows Airline Performance Improved for 2011," *Wichita Eagle*, accessed November 20, 2012, www.kansas.com.

7. "Online Store Surveys," www.onlinestoresurveys.com, accessed November 20, 2012.

8. Elliot Zwiebach, "Target Executives Happy with PFresh Performance," *Supermarket News*, accessed November 20, 2012, http://supermarketnews.com.

9. Jim Utsler, "Carry-on Data," *IBM Systems* magazine, accessed November 20, 2012, www.ibmsystemsmag.com.

10. Company website, "Trends & Innovation: Chef Dan Coudreaut," www.mcdonalds.com, accessed November 20, 2012.

11. Company website, www.ipsos.com, accessed November 20, 2012.

12. U.S. POPClock Projection, www.census.gov, accessed November 20, 2012; John D. Sutter, "Bringing the Census into the Internet Age," *CNN*, accessed November 20, 2012, www.cnn.com.

13. U.S. POPClock Projection, www.census.gov, accessed November 20, 2012.

14. Haya El Nasser, "Census Chief: Online Survey Will Cut Cost of 2020 Headcount," *USA Today*, accessed November 20, 2012, http://content.usatoday.com; U.S. Census Bureau, "Data Protection and Privacy Policy," www.census.gov, accessed November 20, 2012; Sutter, "Bringing the Census into the Internet Age."

15. "2011 TIGER/Line® Shapefiles," www.census.gov, accessed November 20, 2012.

16. Claire Swedberg, "American Apparel Adopting RFID at Every Store," *RFID Journal*, accessed November 20, 2012, www.rfidjournal.com.

17. Company website, www.datamonitor.com, accessed November 20, 2012.

18. Company website, www.google.com, accessed November 20, 2012; "360i POV Nielsen Facebook Ad Effectiveness Study," *eBook Browse*, accessed November 20, 2012, http://ebookbrowse.com.

19. Company website, www.youtube.com, accessed November 20, 2012.

20. Ryan Matthew Pierson, "How Gamers Make Real Money from Video Games," *Lockergnome*, accessed November 20, 2012, www.lockergnome.com.

21. Company website, www.tru-insight.com, accessed November 20, 2012.

22. Company website, www.pressganey.com, accessed November 20, 2012.

23. National Do Not Call Registry website, www.donotcall.gov, accessed November 20, 2012.

24. Joanna L. Krotz, "Dos and Don'ts for Using Marketing Focus Groups," *Microsoft Business*, www.microsoft.com, accessed November 20, 2012.

25. "Fax Advertising," Federal Communications Commission, www.fcc.gov, accessed November 20, 2012.

26. Company website, "Key Facts," http://newsroom.fb.com, accessed November 20, 2012; Nick Clayton, "Social Networks Account for 20% of Time Spent Online," *The Wall Street Journal*, accessed November 20, 2012, http://blogs.wsj.com; David Murphy, "Singapore Delivers Highest Average Facebook Session Time. US: Fifth," *PC Magazine*, accessed November 20, 2012, www.pcmag.com.

27. Company website, "Case Study: How Social Media Landed Orabrush a Walmart Deal," http://sspr.com, accessed November 20, 2012.

28. Erica Swallow, "Measuring Social Media ROI: 3 Things to Consider," *Mashable*, accessed November 20, 2012, http://mashable.com.

29. Jim Edwards, "P&G to Lay off 1,600 after Discovering It's Free to Advertise on Facebook," *Business Insider*, accessed November 20, 2012, www.businessinsider.com.

30. Government website, http://export.gov, accessed November 20, 2012.

31. Company website, "Can P&G Win with $2-a-Day Consumers?" press release, http://news.pg.com, accessed November 20, 2012.

32. Marc Brenner, "Ethnography App Debuts on iTunes Store," *Research*, accessed November 20, 2012, www.research-live.com.

33. Ed Silverman, "State Grapples with the Infamous Data Mining Case," *Pharmalot.com*, accessed November 20, 2012, www.pharmalot.com; "Supreme Court Strikes Down Data Mining Law," *Pharmalot.com*, accessed November 20, 2012, www.pharmalot.com.

34. Company website, http://smartorg.com, accessed November 20, 2012.

PART 4

Product Decisions

Chapter 12

PRODUCT
and Service Strategies

1   Define *product*, and distinguish between goods and services and how they relate to the goods–services continuum.

2   Outline the importance of the service sector in today's marketplace.

3   List the classifications of consumer goods and services, and briefly describe each category.

4   Identify each of the types of business goods and services.

5   Discuss how quality is used by marketers as a product strategy.

6   Explain why firms develop lines of related products.

7   Describe the way marketers typically measure product mixes and make product mix decisions.

8   Explain the concept of the product lifecycle.

9   Discuss how a firm can extend a product's lifecycle, and explain why certain products may be deleted.

APPLE'S PRODUCTS SHINE

Apple has become one of the most successful and innovative companies in the world. It is no accident that the maker of the Mac, the iPhone, the iPod, and the iPad draws millions of people to its more than 400 stores every day, or that it generates more than $108 billion in sales each year. *Forbes* recently named Apple the most powerful brand in the world. What is the strategy behind the company's success? It relies on both products and customer service.

First, of course, Apple leads the industry in the design of sleek and highly functional products that are dependable and intuitively easy to use. Nearly all of its products have revolutionized or created and then dominated a market. The quality, features, and hi-tech appeal of Apple products ensures that more than 55 million U.S. homes own at least one; in fact, the average number owned is three, and one in four households plan to buy another Apple product in the next year. Though the most typical customers are young, college-educated males, the popularity of Apple devices cuts across all age groups, geographic areas, and even political parties, with Democrats and Republicans owning them in about equal numbers. The vice president of one marketing research firm says, "It's a fantastic business model—the more [Apple] products you own, the more likely you are to buy more."

Apple also introduces new devices, and new versions of existing products, at a dizzying rate. Innovation truly drives the firm, and it is not afraid to let new products take sales away from older ones. CEO Tim Cook says the company would rather let the iPad cannibalize sales of the Mac than lose those sales to a competing company.

Another big factor in Apple's continued success is the care with which it treats customers in its stores. Steve Jobs, the company's late founder, helped select

"Enriching lives" as Apple's retail vision, rather than focusing on selling per se. Staff in the stores don't earn commissions and are trained to create memorable customer experiences, even for visitors who don't buy anything. Building relationships, offering help and training, troubleshooting, and solving problems are stressed as part of the effort to touch customers at an emotional level and motivate them to become loyal to the Apple brand. That's why they recommend it to others.

With all this to offer, Apple can feel confident that its merchandise and customer service can command a premium price.[1]

EVOLUTION OF A

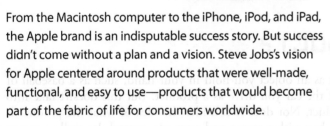

From the Macintosh computer to the iPhone, iPod, and iPad, the Apple brand is an indisputable success story. But success didn't come without a plan and a vision. Steve Jobs's vision for Apple centered around products that were well-made, functional, and easy to use—products that would become part of the fabric of life for consumers worldwide.

- As its retail vision, Apple marketers chose "Enriching lives." How does that simple statement inform the company's operations and how it relates with consumers?
- Quality is an important element in Apple's product strategy and a key differentiator for its product line. In your opinion, is quality always an important differentiator, or does it vary depending on the product type?

CHAPTER OVERVIEW

marketing mix Blending of the four strategy elements—product, distribution, promotion, and price—to fit the needs and preferences of a specific target market.

We've discussed how marketers conduct research to determine unfilled needs in their markets, how customers behave during the purchasing process, and how firms expand their horizons overseas. Now our attention shifts to a company's **marketing mix**, the blend of four elements of a marketing strategy—product, distribution, promotion, and price—to satisfy the target market. This chapter focuses on how companies like Apple select and develop the goods and services they offer, starting with planning which products to offer. The other variables of the marketing mix—distribution channels, promotional plans, and pricing decisions—must accommodate the product strategy selected.

Marketers develop strategies to promote both tangible goods and intangible services. Any such strategy begins with investigation, analysis, and selection of a particular target market, and it continues with the creation of a marketing mix designed to satisfy that segment. Tangible goods and intangible services both intend to satisfy consumer wants and needs, but the marketing efforts supporting them may be vastly different. Many firms sell both types of products, offering innovative goods and ongoing service to attract and retain customers for the long term. Doing so can be profitable, as you'll see in this chapter.

This chapter examines the similarities and differences in marketing goods and services. It then presents basic concepts—product classifications, development of product lines, and the product lifecycle—marketers apply in developing successful products. Finally, the chapter discusses product deletion and product mix decisions.

> **BRIEFLY SPEAKING**
>
> "What's a brand? A singular idea or concept that you own inside the mind of the prospect."
>
> —Al Ries
> *American marketer and author,*
> Positioning: The Battle for Your Mind

WHAT IS A PRODUCT?

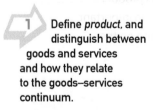

1 Define *product*, and distinguish between goods and services and how they relate to the goods–services continuum.

At first, you might think of a product as an object you hold in your hand, such as a baseball or a toothbrush. You might also think of the car you drive as a product. But this doesn't take into account the idea of a service as a product. Nor does it consider the idea of what the product is used for. So a television is more than a box with a screen and a remote control. It's really a means of providing entertainment—your favorite movies, news programs, or reality shows. Marketers acknowledge this broader conception of product; they realize that people buy *want satisfaction* rather than objects.

You might feel a need for a television to satisfy a want for entertainment. You might not know a lot about how the device itself works, but you understand the results. If you are entertained by watching TV, then your wants are satisfied. If, however, the television is working just fine, but you don't like the programming offered, you may need to satisfy your desire for entertainment by changing your service package to include premium channels. The service—and its offerings— is a product.

 ASSESSMENT CHECK

1.1 Define *product*.

1.2 Why is the understanding of want satisfaction so important to marketers?

Marketers think in terms of a product as a compilation of package design and labeling, brand name, price, availability, warranty, reputation, image, and customer service activities that add value for the customer. Consequently, a **product** is a bundle of physical, service, and symbolic attributes designed to satisfy a customer's wants and needs.

WHAT ARE GOODS AND SERVICES?

Services are intangible products. A general definition identifies **services** as intangible tasks that satisfy the needs of consumer and business users. But you can't hold a service in your hand the way you can **goods**—tangible products customers can see, hear, smell, taste, or touch. Most service providers cannot transport or store their products; customers simultaneously buy and consume these products, such as haircuts, car repairs, and visits to the dentist. One way to distinguish services from goods is the **goods–services continuum**, as shown in Figure 12.1.

This spectrum helps marketers visualize the differences and similarities between goods and services. A car is a pure good, but the dealer also offers repair and maintenance services or includes the services in the price of a lease. The car falls at the pure good extreme of the continuum, because the repair or maintenance services are an adjunct to the purchase. A dinner at an exclusive restaurant is a mix of goods and services. It combines the physical goods of gourmet food with the intangible services of an attentive wait staff, elegant surroundings, and perhaps a visit to your table by the chef or restaurant owner to make sure your meal is perfect. At the other extreme, a dentist provides pure service—cleaning teeth, filling cavities, taking X-rays. The dentist's office may also sell items like night guards, but it's the service that is primary in patients' minds.

You can begin to see the diversity of services. Services can be distinguished from goods in several ways:

1. *Services are intangible.* Services do not have physical features buyers can see, hear, smell, taste, or touch prior to purchase. Service firms essentially ask their customers to buy a promise—the haircut will be stylish, the insurance will cover injuries, the lawn will be mowed, and so on.

2. *Services are inseparable from the service providers.* Consumer perceptions of a service provider become their perceptions of the service itself. The name of a doctor, lawyer, or hair stylist is synonymous with the service they provide. A bad haircut can deter customers, while a good one will attract more to the salon. A house-cleaning service like Merry Maids depends on its workers to leave each house spotless, because its reputation is built on this service.

3. *Services are perishable.* Providers cannot maintain inventories of their services. A day spa can't stockpile facials or pedicures. A travel agent can't keep quantities of vacations on a shelf. For this reason, some service providers, such as airlines and hotels, may raise their prices during times of peak demand—during spring break from school, for example—and reduce them when demand declines.

4. *Companies cannot easily standardize services.* However, many firms are trying to change this. Most fast-food chains promise you'll get your meal within a certain number of minutes, and it

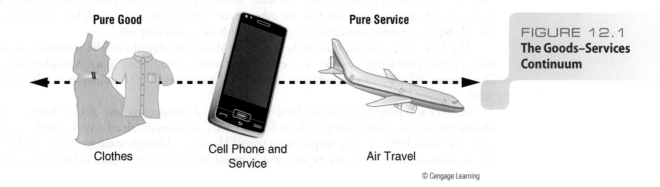

Pure Good   **Pure Service**

Clothes   Cell Phone and Service   Air Travel

© Cengage Learning

FIGURE 12.1
The Goods–Services Continuum

It isn't easy for companies to standardize services, but they do try. For example, a hotel chain might have the same amenities at each location, including a beautiful indoor pool.

will taste the way you expect it to. A hotel chain may have the same amenities at each location—a pool, fitness room, free breakfast, and HBO movies.

5. *Buyers often play important roles in the creation and distribution of services.* Service transactions frequently require interaction between buyer and seller at the production and distribution stages. When a traveler arrives at the airport to pick up a rental car, he or she may have a choice of vehicle and additional amenities, such as a GPS unit or car seat for a child. If the car is ready to go immediately, the customer will likely be satisfied. If the desired car is not available, not clean, or doesn't have a full tank of gas, the customer may not book with this company again.

6. *Service standards show wide variations.* New York City's posh Le Cirque and your local Pizza Hut are both restaurants. Depending on your expectations, both can be considered good restaurants. But the service standards at each vary greatly. At Le Cirque, you'll experience finely prepared cuisine served by a highly trained wait staff. At Pizza Hut, you may serve yourself fresh pizza from the buffet. If you receive your dinner from attentive wait staff at Le Cirque, you will be satisfied by the service standards. If the pizza at Pizza Hut is hot and fresh, and the buffet is replenished frequently, you will be satisfied by those standards as well.

Keep in mind that a product often blurs the distinction between services and goods. U-Haul is a service that rents trucks and moving vans, which are goods. LensCrafters provides eye examinations—services from optometrists—while also selling eyeglasses and contact lenses, which are goods.

⊕ ASSESSMENT CHECK

1.3   Describe the goods–services continuum.

1.4   List the six characteristics distinguishing goods from services.

IMPORTANCE OF THE SERVICE SECTOR

2   Outline the importance of the service sector in today's marketplace.

You would live a very different life without service firms to fill many needs. You could not place a phone call, log on to the Internet, flip a switch for electricity, or even take a college course if organizations did not provide such services. During an average day, you probably use many services without much thought, but these products play an integral role in your life.

The service sector makes a crucial contribution to the U.S. economy in terms of products and jobs. Yet, only three of *Fortune*'s top ten most admired companies are pure service firms—Google, FedEx, and Southwest Airlines. But the other seven firms in the top ten, all listed in Figure 12.2, provide highly regarded services in conjunction with the goods they sell.[2]

The U.S. service sector now makes up more than three-fourths of the economy, as the shift from a goods-producing economy to a service-producing economy continues. According to the U.S. Department of Labor, service industries are expected to account for 18 million new jobs by the year 2020.[3]

Services also play a crucial role in the international competitiveness of U.S. firms. While the United States runs a continuing trade deficit in goods, it has maintained a trade surplus in services every year since 1992, and the surplus is growing.[4] However, although some economists believe more precise measurements of service exports would reveal an even larger surplus, others worry about the effect of offshoring service jobs, such as customer service call centers to nations like India.

While some firms have found success with offshoring their call centers, others like Web retailers eBags and Hayneedle recently returned their call centers to the United States after determining they would save money and improve customer service efficiency by doing so.[5] Termed *backshoring,* this trend is growing and actually becoming a marketing tool for firms. "Foreign call centers feed into the perception that companies aren't interested in their customers," notes one marketing researcher. And some companies bringing their call centers back to the United States are taking another approach using home-based hourly workers, often managed by a private firm.[6]

An emerging trend, homeshoring enables firms to save on office space, furnishings, and supplies. In addition, most also save on health care and other benefits. JetBlue is one well-known firm to practice homeshoring; similarly, Miramar, Florida–based Arise Virtual Solutions supplies home-based employees to other companies, much the way an employment agency does.[7] Firms that practice homeshoring are experiencing another benefit: a reduction in the use of energy and other natural resources, which decreases these firms' impact on the environment. Because employees are not commuting to work every day, and because an office does not have to be heated, cooled, and supplied with electricity and water every day, firms not only experience reduced costs but also a drop in emissions. These companies can highlight their green practices in marketing messages to customers.

Observers cite several reasons for the growing importance of services, including consumer desire for speed and convenience and technological advances that allow firms to fulfill this demand. Services involving wireless communications, data backup and storage, and even meal preparation for busy families are on the rise. Grocery chain Trader Joe's is benefiting from this need for quick meals by offering partially cooked, fully cooked, and flash-frozen entrées that can be picked up and prepared in less time than meals made from scratch. Many traditional supermarkets offer prepared entrées and side dishes shoppers can buy at the store and heat quickly in the microwave at home. Consumers are also looking to advisors to help plan for a financially secure future and insurance to protect their homes and families.

Most service firms emphasize marketing as a significant activity for two reasons. First, the growth potential of service transactions represents a vast marketing opportunity. Second, the environment for services is changing. For instance, increased competition

FIGURE 12.2
World's Most Admired Companies

Source: "World's Most Admired Companies 2012," *Fortune,* accessed November 27, 2012, http://money.cnn.com.

1. Apple
2. Google
3. Amazon.com
4. The Coca-Cola Company
5. IBM
6. FedEx
7. Berkshire Hathaway
8. Starbucks
9. Procter&Gamble
10. Southwest Airlines

homeshoring Hiring workers to do jobs from their homes.

wavebreakmedia/Shutterstock.com

Homeshoring allows companies to save on office space, furnishings, and supplies as well as reducing their impact on the environment.

is forcing traditional service industries to differentiate themselves from their competitors. Providing superior service is one way to develop long-term customer relationships and compete more effectively. As we discussed earlier, relationship marketing is just one of the ways service firms can develop and solidify their customer relationships.

CLASSIFYING GOODS AND SERVICES FOR CONSUMER AND BUSINESS MARKETS

business-to-consumer (B2C) product Product destined for use by ultimate consumers.

business-to-business (B2B) product Product that contributes directly or indirectly to the output of other products for resale; also called industrial or organizational product.

A firm's choices for marketing a good or service depend largely on the offering itself and on the nature of the target market. Product strategies differ for consumer and business markets. **Business-to-consumer (B2C) products** are those destined for use by ultimate consumers, while **business-to-business (B2B) products** (also called *industrial* or *organizational products*) contribute directly or indirectly to the output of other products for resale. Marketers further subdivide these two major categories into more specific categories, as discussed in this section.

Some products fall into both categories. A case in point is prescription drugs. Traditionally, pharmaceutical companies marketed prescription drugs to doctors, who then made the purchase decision for their patients by writing the prescription. These medications would be classified as a business product. However, many drug companies now advertise their products in consumer-oriented media, including magazines, television, and the Internet. The ads suggest that consumers inquire about a certain drug when they go to their doctors. This direct-to-consumer advertising topped $2.4 billion in a recent year.[8]

TYPES OF CONSUMER PRODUCTS

unsought products Products marketed to consumers who may not yet recognize a need for them.

The most widely used product classification system focuses on the buyer's perception of a need for the product and his or her buying behavior. However, **unsought products** are marketed to consumers who may not yet recognize any need for them. Examples of unsought products are long-term-care insurance and funeral services.

However, relatively few products fall into the unsought category. Most consumers recognize their own needs for various types of consumer purchases and actively seek them, so the customer buying-behavior variations are key in distinguishing the various categories. The most common classification scheme for sought products divides consumer goods and services into three groups based on customers' buying behavior: convenience, shopping, and specialty. Figure 12.3 illustrates samples of these categories, together with the unsought classification.

Convenience Products

convenience products Goods and services consumers want to purchase frequently, immediately, and with minimal effort.

impulse goods and services Products purchased on the spur of the moment.

Convenience products refer to goods and services consumers want to purchase frequently, immediately, and with minimal effort. Milk, bread, and toothpaste are convenience products. Convenience services include 24-hour quick-stop stores, walk-in hair or nail salons, copy shops, and dry cleaners.

Marketers further subdivide the convenience category into impulse items, staples, or emergency items. **Impulse goods and services** are purchased on the spur of the moment—for example, a visit to a car wash or a pack of gum picked up at the supermarket register. Some marketers have even come up with ways to make impulse shopping on the Internet attractive. Last-minute shoppers can use ArtTownGifts.com's last-minute and emergency gifts service to choose and ship gifts quickly, even for same-day delivery. They can select balloon bouquets, flowers, fruit or wine baskets, and more. Emergency gifts don't come cheap—they range in price from about $40 to $215—but they fulfill an immediate need for goods and services. Shoppers can also sign up for the firm's reminder service, which sends them email reminders of loved ones' birthdays, anniversaries, and any other occasion that might require a gift.[9]

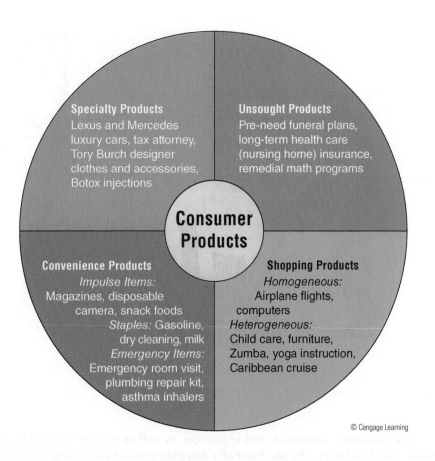

FIGURE 12.3
Classification of Consumer Products

Consumer Products

Specialty Products
Lexus and Mercedes luxury cars, tax attorney, Tory Burch designer clothes and accessories, Botox injections

Unsought Products
Pre-need funeral plans, long-term health care (nursing home) insurance, remedial math programs

Convenience Products
Impulse Items: Magazines, disposable camera, snack foods
Staples: Gasoline, dry cleaning, milk
Emergency Items: Emergency room visit, plumbing repair kit, asthma inhalers

Shopping Products
Homogeneous: Airplane flights, computers
Heterogeneous: Child care, furniture, Zumba, yoga instruction, Caribbean cruise

© Cengage Learning

Staples are convenience goods and services consumers constantly replenish to maintain a ready inventory: gasoline, shampoo, and dry cleaning are good examples. Marketers spend many hours and dollars creating messages for consumers about these products, partly because there are so many competitors.

Emergency goods and services are bought in response to unexpected and urgent needs. A snow blower purchased during a snowstorm and a visit to a hospital emergency room to treat a broken ankle are examples. Depending on your viewpoint, the products offered by ArtTownGifts.com's emergency service could also fall into this category.

Because consumers devote little effort to convenience product purchase decisions, marketers must strive to make these exchanges as simple as possible. Store location can boost a convenience product's visibility. Marketers compete vigorously for prime locations, which can make all the difference between a consumer choosing one gas station, vending machine, or dry cleaner over another.

In addition, location *within* a store can make the difference between success and failure of a product, which is why manufacturers fight so hard for the right spot on supermarket shelves. Typically, the largest grocery manufacturers, such as Kraft, Kellogg, and General Mills, get the most visible spots. But visibility to consumers sometimes comes at a price, often via a practice called *slotting allowances,* or *slotting fees*—money paid by producers to retailers to guarantee display of their merchandise. According to retailers, the purpose of slotting allowances is to cover their losses if products don't sell. But the Federal Trade Commission (FTC) investigated the practice of slotting allowances and found these fees vary greatly across product categories. In addition, a new trend regarding slotting allowances is emerging: growth in the private-label goods category has been so great over the past few years that retailers are willing to forfeit allowances they might receive so they can get into the manufacturing end themselves. This is particularly true of private-label organic and ethnic foods.

Shopping Products

In contrast to the purchase of convenience items, consumers buy shopping products only after comparing competing offerings on such characteristics as price, quality, style, and color. Shopping products typically cost more than convenience purchases. This category includes tangible items, such

staples Convenience goods and services consumers constantly replenish to maintain a ready inventory.

emergency goods and services Products bought in response to unexpected and urgent needs.

shopping products Products consumers purchase after comparing competing offerings.

Emergency goods and services are bought in response to urgent needs.

© Suzanne Tucker/Shutterstock.com

as clothing, furniture, electronics, and appliances, as well as services like child care, auto repairs, insurance, and hotel stays. The purchaser of a shopping product lacks complete information prior to the buying trip and gathers information during the buying process.

Several important features distinguish shopping products: physical attributes, service attributes, such as warranties and after-sale service terms, prices, styling, and places of purchase. A store's name and reputation have considerable influence on people's buying behavior. The personal selling efforts of salespeople also provide important promotional support.

Buyers and marketers treat some shopping products, such as refrigerators and washing machines, as relatively homogeneous products. To the consumer, one brand seems largely the same as another. Marketers may try to differentiate homogeneous products from competing products in several ways. They may emphasize price and value, or they may attempt to educate buyers about less obvious features that contribute to a product's quality, appeal, and uniqueness.

Other shopping products seem heterogeneous because of basic differences among them. Examples include furniture, physical-fitness training, vacations, and clothing. Differences in features often separate competing heterogeneous shopping products in the minds of consumers. Perceptions of style, color, and fit can all affect consumer choices.

Specialty Products

specialty products
Products with unique characteristics that cause buyers to prize those particular brands.

Specialty products offer unique characteristics that cause buyers to prize those particular brands. They typically carry high prices, and many represent well-known brands. Examples of specialty goods include Hermès scarves, Kate Spade handbags, Ritz-Carlton resorts, Tiffany jewelry, and Lexus automobiles. Specialty services include professional services, such as financial advice, legal counsel, and cosmetic surgery.

Purchasers of specialty goods and services know exactly what they want—and they are willing to pay accordingly. See the "Marketing Success" feature to find out how one consumer who knew what car she wanted was able to drive it free—for 24 hours. These buyers begin shopping with complete information, and they refuse to accept substitutes. Because consumers are willing to exert considerable effort to obtain specialty products, producers can promote them through relatively few retail locations. In fact, some firms intentionally limit the range of retailers carrying their products to add to their cachet. Both highly personalized service by sales associates and image advertising help

MARKETING SUCCESS

Audi Gets Social

Background. A woman in Washington, DC, was so sold on Audi's marketing campaign for its R8 model that she started a Twitter campaign using the hashtag #Want an R8. Audi took note of the woman's high Klout scores and sent a brand-new R8 to her home, lending her the car to drive for 24 hours.

The Challenge. "These kinds of opportunities are out there for marketers," said Audi's CMO. What Audi needed to do was figure out how to make the most of it.

The Strategy. Audi asked Twitter users whether they would like an R8 as well, and 75,000 people around the country said yes, so the company created a contest enabling four more people to drive an R8 for the day. It recently brought the promotion back for a second year, looking for creativity in the eight winning submissions, which can now include photos and videos, and adding a second prize option, a trip for two to an R8 One-Day Program at Infineon Raceway. Audi also put together a 30-second television spot (available on YouTube) to publicize the promotion.

The Outcome. "Why not merge the social and real world and make dreams come true?" asks Audi's CMO. Audi's inventive promotion may achieve even more. The company has more than 6 million "likes" on its Facebook page.

Sources: Company website, www.audiusa.com, accessed November 27, 2012; Ryan W. Neal, "Interview: Andy White, Creator of Audi's #WantAnR8 Campaign," *Magnet Labs*, accessed November 27, 2012, www.magnetmediafilms.com; Dale Buss, "Luxury Brands Still Lagging in American Auto-Sales Recovery," *Forbes*, accessed November 27, 2012, www.forbes.com; Jean Halliday, "Social Media, Audi Style," *Forbes*, accessed November 27, 2012, www.forbes.com; Dale Buss, "Audi's Brand Strength Is More than Sales," *Brand Channel*, accessed November 27, 2012, www.brandchannel.com.

marketers promote specialty items. Because these products are available in so few retail outlets, advertisements frequently list their locations or give toll-free telephone numbers that provide customers with this information.

In recent years, makers of some specialty products, such as Coach handbags and Donna Karan clothing, have broadened their market by selling some of their goods through company-owned discount outlets. The stores attract consumers who want to own specialty items but who cannot or do not wish to pay their regular prices. The goods offered, however, usually are last season's styles. Tiffany has taken a different approach—broadening its base within its own store. Shoppers who visit the store on Fifth Avenue in New York City can take the elevator to the second floor, where they may purchase a variety of items in sterling silver at prices significantly lower than those for gold and gemstone jewelry. A number of these items are also available in Tiffany's mail-order catalog.

CLASSIFYING CONSUMER SERVICES

Like tangible goods, services are also classified based on the convenience, shopping, and specialty products categories. But added insights can be gained by examining several factors unique to classifying services. Service firms may serve consumer markets, business markets, or both. A firm offering architectural services may design either residential or commercial buildings or both. A cleaning service may clean houses, offices, or both. In addition, services can be classified as equipment based or people based. A car wash is an equipment-based service, whereas a law office is people based. Marketers may ask themselves any of these five questions to help classify certain services:

1. What is the nature of the service?

2. What type of relationship does the service organization have with its customers?

List the classifications of consumer goods and services, and briefly describe each category.

3

Shoppers who visit the Tiffany & Company store in New York will notice a large variety of items at lower prices than those for gold and gemstone jewelry.

3. How much flexibility is there for customization and judgment on the part of the service provider?

4. Do demand and supply for the service fluctuate?

5. How is the service delivered?[10]

A person attempting to classify the activities of a boarding kennel would answer these questions in one way; a person evaluating a lawn-care service would come up with different answers. For example, customers would bring their pets to the kennel to receive service, while the lawn-care staff would travel to customers' homes to provide service. Workers at the kennel are likely to have closer interpersonal relationships with pet owners—and their pets—than lawn-care workers, who might not meet their customers at all. Someone assessing demand for the services of a ski resort or a food concession at the beach is likely to find fluctuations by season. And a dentist has flexibility in making decisions about a patient's care, whereas a delivery service must arrive with a package at the correct destination, on time.

APPLYING THE CONSUMER PRODUCTS CLASSIFICATION SYSTEM

The three-way classification system of convenience, shopping, and specialty goods and services helps guide marketers in developing a successful marketing strategy. Buyer behavior patterns differ for the three types of purchases. For example, classifying a new food item as a convenience product leads to insights about marketing needs in branding, promotion, pricing, and distribution decisions. Table 12.1 summarizes the impact of this classification system on the development of an effective marketing mix.

The classification system, however, also poses a few problems. The major obstacle to implementing this system results from the suggestion that all goods and services must fit within one of the three categories. Some fit neatly into one category, but others share characteristics of more than one category. How would you classify the purchase of a new automobile? Before classifying the expensive good, which is handled by only a few dealers in the area as a specialty product, consider other characteristics. New-car buyers often shop extensively among competing models and dealers before deciding on the best deal. And there is a wide range of models, features, and prices to consider. At one end of the spectrum is a basic car like a Nissan Versa or a Ford Fiesta that could be purchased for under $14,000.

TABLE 12.1 Marketing Impact of the Consumer Products Classification System

	Convenience Products	Shopping Products	Specialty Products
Consumer Factors			
Planning time involved in purchase	Very little	Considerable	Extensive
Purchase frequency	Frequent	Less frequent	Infrequent
Importance of convenient location	Critical	Important	Unimportant
Comparison of price and quality	Very little	Considerable	Very little
Marketing Mix Factors			
Price	Low	Relatively high	High
Importance of seller's image	Unimportant	Very Important	Important
Distribution channel length	Long	Relatively short	Short
Number of sales outlets	Many	Few	Very few
Promotion	Advertising and promotion by producer	Personal selling and advertising by producer and retailer	Personal selling and advertising by producer and retailer

© Cengage Learning

At the other end is what people are calling European supercars, such as the Lamborghini Murcielago, at $470,000, or the Aston Martin One-77, priced at $1.85 million. These cars are fast, powerful, and hard to find—which boosts their value.[11]

So it's a good idea to think of the categorization process in terms of a continuum representing degrees of effort expended by consumers. At one end of the continuum, they casually pick up convenience items; at the other end, they search extensively for specialty products. Shopping products fall between these extremes. In addition, car dealers may offer services, both during and after the sale, which play a big role in the purchase decision. On this continuum, the new car purchase might appear between the categories of shopping and specialty products but closer to specialty products.

A second problem with the classification system emerges because consumers differ in their buying patterns. One person may walk into a hair salon and request a haircut without an appointment, while another may check references and compare prices before selecting a stylist. But the first consumer's impulse purchase of a haircut does not make hair styling services a convenience item. Marketers classify goods and services by considering the purchase patterns of the majority of buyers.

ASSESSMENT CHECK

3.1 What are the three major classifications of consumer products?

3.2 Identify five factors marketers should consider in classifying consumer services.

TYPES OF BUSINESS PRODUCTS

Business buyers are professional customers. Their job duties require rational, cost-effective purchase decisions. For instance, General Mills applies much of the same purchase decision process to buying flour that Kellogg's does.

The classification system for business products emphasizes product uses rather than customer buying behavior. B2B products generally fall into one of six categories for product uses: installations, accessory equipment, component parts and materials, raw materials, supplies, and business services. Figure 12.4 illustrates the six types of business products.

4 Identify each of the types of business goods and services.

FIGURE 12.4
Classification of Business Products

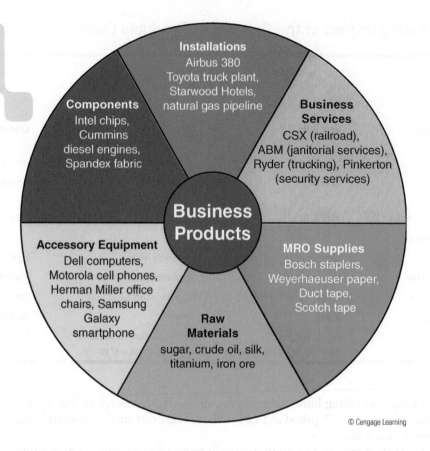

Installations
Airbus 380
Toyota truck plant,
Starwood Hotels,
natural gas pipeline

Components
Intel chips,
Cummins
diesel engines,
Spandex fabric

Business
Services
CSX (railroad),
ABM (janitorial services),
Ryder (trucking), Pinkerton
(security services)

**Business
Products**

Accessory Equipment
Dell computers,
Motorola cell phones,
Herman Miller office
chairs, Samsung
Galaxy
smartphone

MRO Supplies
Bosch staplers,
Weyerhaeuser paper,
Duct tape,
Scotch tape

Raw
Materials
sugar, crude oil, silk,
titanium, iron ore

© Cengage Learning

Installations

installations Major capital investments in the B2B market.

The specialty products of the business market are called installations. This classification includes major capital investments for new factories and heavy machinery and for telecommunications systems. Purchases of Boeing's 787 Dreamliner airplanes by Qantas and Kenya Airways are considered installations for those airlines.

Because installations last for long periods of time, and their purchases involve large sums of money, they represent major decisions for organizations. Negotiations often extend over several months and involve numerous decision makers. Vendors often provide technical expertise along with tangible goods. Representatives who sell custom-made equipment work closely with buying firms' engineers and production personnel to design the most satisfactory products possible.

Price typically does not dominate purchase decisions for installations, although a recent order for 230 Boeing 737s by the Indonesia-based carrier Lion Air totaled a record $22.4 billion.[12] A purchasing firm buys such a product for its efficiency and performance over its useful life. The firm also wants to minimize breakdowns. Downtime is expensive, because the firm must pay employees while they wait for repairs on a machine. In addition, customers may be lost during downtime; in this case, travelers might choose to fly with another airline. Installations are major investments often designed specifically for the purchasers. Training of the buyer's workforce to operate the equipment correctly, along with significant after-sale service, is usually also involved.

Lion Air recently bought an installation—a major capital investment—by purchasing 230 Boeing 737s for its fleet.

© ADEK BERRY/AFP/Getty Images/Newscom

As a result, marketers of these systems typically focus their promotional efforts on employing highly trained sales representatives, often with technical backgrounds. Advertising, if the firm uses it at all, emphasizes company reputation and directs potential buyers to contact local sales representatives.

Most installations are marketed directly from manufacturers to users. Even a one-time sale may require continuing contacts for regular product servicing. Some manufacturers prefer to lease extremely expensive installations to customers rather than sell the items outright, and they assign personnel directly to the lessees' sites to operate or maintain the equipment.

Accessory Equipment

Only a few decision makers may participate in a purchase of accessory equipment—capital items that typically cost less and last for shorter periods than installations. Although quality and service exert important influences on purchases of accessory equipment, price may significantly affect these decisions. Accessory equipment includes products, such as power tools, computers, smartphones, and cell phones. Although these products are considered capital investments, and buyers depreciate their costs over several years, their useful lives are generally much shorter than those of installations.

Marketing these products requires continuous representation and dealing with the widespread geographic dispersion of purchasers. To cope with these market characteristics, a wholesaler—often called an industrial distributor—might be used to contact potential customers in its own geographic area. Customers usually do not require technical assistance, and a manufacturer of accessory equipment can often distribute its products effectively through wholesalers. Advertising is an important component in the marketing mix for accessory equipment.

accessory equipment Capital items, such as desktop computers and printers, that typically cost less and last for shorter periods than installations.

industrial distributor Channel intermediary that takes title to goods it handles and then distributes these goods to retailers, other distributors, or business or B2B customers; also called a *wholesaler*.

Component Parts and Materials

Whereas business buyers use installations and accessory equipment in the process of producing their own final products, component parts and materials represent finished business products of one producer that become part of the final products of another producer. Some materials—for example, flour—undergo further processing before becoming part of finished products. Textiles, paper pulp, and chemicals are also examples of component parts and materials. Bose supplies its luxury sound systems to auto manufacturers like Audi, Infiniti, Cadillac, and Porsche. Marketers for the auto manufacturers believe that Bose systems are a good match between premium sound and their top-line vehicles, comparing the high performance of the Bose sound systems to the high performance of their cars.[13]

Purchasers of component parts and materials need regular, continuous supplies of uniform-quality products. They generally contract to purchase these items for set periods of time. Marketers commonly emphasize direct sales, and satisfied customers often become regular buyers. Wholesalers sometimes supply fill-in purchases and handle sales to smaller purchasers.

component parts and materials Finished business products of one producer that become part of the final products of another producer.

Raw Materials

Farm products, such as beef, cotton, eggs, milk, poultry, and soybeans, and natural resources like coal, copper, iron ore, and lumber, constitute raw materials. These products resemble component parts and materials since they become part of the buyers' final products. Cargill supplies many of the raw materials for finished food products—dry corn ingredients, flour, food starch, oils and shortenings, soy protein and sweeteners, and beef and pork. Food manufacturers then take and turn these materials into finished products, including cake and bread.[14]

See the "Solving an Ethical Controversy" feature to find out what happened when one cereal company discovered that consumers don't distinguish between "natural" and "organic" ingredients.

Most raw materials carry grades determined according to set criteria, assuring purchasers of the receipt of standardized products of uniform quality. As with component parts and materials, vendors commonly market raw materials directly to buying organizations. Wholesalers are increasingly involved in purchasing raw materials from foreign suppliers.

Price is seldom a deciding factor in a raw materials purchase since the costs are often set at central markets, determining virtually identical transactions among competing sellers. Purchasers buy raw materials from the firms they consider best able to deliver the required quantities and qualities.

raw materials Natural resources, such as farm products, coal, copper, or lumber that become part of a final product.

SOLVING AN ETHICAL CONTROVERSY

Natural vs. Organic: Who Is Responsible for Knowing the Difference?

Buyers of Kashi brand cereal were recently shocked to realize that the product, billed as "natural" by its maker, Kellogg Co., contained nonorganic soybeans, genetically modified as protection against a popular weed-killer. An organic grocer in Rhode Island took the cereal off the shelves, and the news quickly went viral, resulting in an online uproar, to which Kashi responded with a Facebook video. Kashi said it did not violate consumers' trust by labeling its product "natural," which it defines as minimally processed without artificial ingredients. The use of the term "organic," on the other hand, is federally regulated and excludes products with genetically engineered ingredients. Kashi did not call its cereal organic.

Are companies responsible for noting the difference between natural and organic in their products?

PRO

1. Consumers want wholesome products, and companies that want their business should be up-front about what is in their products.

2. Companies are taking advantage of consumers' confusion about the difference between "natural" and "organic."

CON

1. Consumers should educate themselves about what "organic" means under the law.

2. The Food and Drug Administration does not regulate the word "natural," so companies can define it as they wish.

Summary:

Kashi has promised that, by the end of 2013, all its cereal products will be certified to contain no genetically modified ingredients. Meanwhile, "natural" can mean whatever anyone wants it to.

Sources: Stephanie Armour, "Kellogg's Kashi Targeted as Web Food Fighting Escalates," *Bloomberg Businessweek*, accessed November 28, 2012, www.businessweek.com; Barry Silverstein, "Kashi GMO Flap Stirs Debate on 'Natural' and 'Organic,'" *Brand Channel*, accessed November 28, 2012, www.brandchannel.com; Elizabeth Weise, "Consumers Are Mad Because Kashi Products Aren't Organic or GM-Free," *Business Insider*, accessed November 28, 2012, http://articles.businessinsider.com; Emily Leaman, "Kashi Cereal Lovers Red-Faced over Company's 'Natural' Claims," *Philadelphia Magazine's Be Well Philly*, accessed November 28, 2012, http://blogs.phillymag.com.

Supplies

supplies Regular expenses a firm incurs in its daily operations.

MRO items Business supplies that include maintenance items, repair items, and operating supplies.

If installations represent the specialty products of the business market, operating supplies are its convenience products. **Supplies** constitute the regular expenses a firm incurs in its daily operations. These expenses do not become part of the buyer's final products.

Supplies are also called **MRO items** because they fall into three categories: (1) maintenance items, such as brooms, filters, and lightbulbs; (2) repair items, such as nuts and bolts used in repairing equipment; and (3) operating supplies, such as printer paper and cartridges, mouse batteries, and pens. Office Max sells all kinds of supplies to small, medium, and large businesses. Companies can purchase everything from paper and labels to filing cabinets, lighting, office furniture, computers, and copiers. The firm also offers printing and binding services, downloadable forms, and more.[15]

A purchasing manager regularly buys operating supplies as a routine job duty. Wholesalers often facilitate sales of supplies because of the low unit prices, the small order size, and the large number of potential buyers. Because supplies are relatively standardized, heavy price competition frequently keeps costs under control. However, a business buyer spends little time making decisions about these products. Exchanges of products involve simple telephone orders, Web or EDI orders, or regular purchases from a sales representative of a local wholesaler.

Business Services

The business services category includes the intangible products firms buy to facilitate their production and operating processes. Examples of business services are financial services, leasing and rental services that supply equipment and vehicles, insurance, security, legal advice, and consulting. As mentioned earlier, many service providers sell the same services to both consumers and organizational buyers—telephone, gas, and electricity, for example—although service firms may maintain separate marketing groups for the two customer segments.

Organizations also purchase many adjunct services that assist their operations but are not essentially a part of the final product. Cisco Systems offers its TelePresence meeting service to businesses seeking to link people in a single interactive conference. The service combines voice, data, and video on the same network, providing an interactive and collaborative experience for participants.[16]

Price may strongly influence purchase decisions for business services. The buying firm must decide whether to purchase a service or provide that service internally. This decision may depend on how frequently the firm needs the service and the specialized knowledge required to provide it. In the case of TelePresence, firms may decide the cost of the service is offset by savings in travel expenses for meeting participants. In addition, the service offers convenience.

Purchase decision processes vary considerably for different types of business services. A firm may purchase window-cleaning services through a routine and straightforward process similar to buying operating supplies. By contrast, a purchase decision for highly specialized environmental engineering advice requires complex analysis and perhaps lengthy negotiations similar to purchases of installations. This variability of the marketing mix for business services and other business products is outlined in Table 12.2.

business services
Intangible products firms buy to facilitate their production and operating processes.

Cisco Systems offers its TelePresence meeting service to businesses to link people from around the world in a single interactive conference.

TABLE 12.2 Marketing Impact of the Business Products Classification System

Factor	Installations	Accessory Equipment	Component Parts and Materials	Raw Materials	Supplies	Business Services
Organizational Factors						
Planning time	Extensive	Less extensive	Less extensive	Varies	Very little	Varies
Purchase frequency	Infrequent	More frequent	Frequent	Infrequent	Frequent	Varies
Comparison of price and quality	Quality very important	Quality and price important	Quality important	Quality important	Price important	Varies
Marketing Mix Factors						
Price	High	Relatively high	Low to high	Low to high	Low	Varies
Distribution channel length	Very short	Relatively short	Short	Short	Long	Varies
Promotion method	Personal selling by producer	Advertising	Personal selling	Personal selling	Advertising by producer	Varies

© Cengage Learning

 ASSESSMENT CHECK

4.1   What are the six main classifications of business products?

4.2   What are the three categories of supplies?

The purchase of the right business services can make a difference in a firm's competitiveness. The Regus Group provides businesses with facilities for meetings and conferences in 550 cities across 95 countries. The firm's more than 4,000 facilities are fully furnished and equipped with every electronic medium and amenity a business could possibly need and are staffed by trained support personnel. Regus serves large and small companies, including those relying on mobile and home-based workers. The firm's services allow businesses to customize their office and meeting needs while saving money during periods when office space is not necessary.[17]

QUALITY AS A PRODUCT STRATEGY

> **5** Discuss how quality is used by marketers as a product strategy.

No matter how a product is classified, nothing is more frustrating to a customer than having a new item break after just a few uses or having it not live up to expectations. The cell phone that hisses static at you unless you stand still or the seam that rips out of your new jacket aren't life-altering experiences, but they do leave an impression of poor quality that likely will lead you to make different purchases in the future. Then there's the issue of service quality—the department store that seems to have no salespeople, or the computer help line that leaves you on hold for 20 minutes.

total quality management (TQM) Continuous effort to improve products and work processes with the goal of achieving customer satisfaction and world-class performance.

Quality is a key component to a firm's success in a competitive marketplace. The efforts to create and market high-quality goods and services have been referred to as **total quality management (TQM)**. TQM expects all of a firm's employees to continually improve products and work processes with the goal of achieving customer satisfaction and world-class performance. This means engineers design products that work, marketers develop products people want, and salespeople deliver on their promises. Managers are responsible for communicating the goals of total quality management to all staff members and for encouraging workers to improve themselves and take pride in their work. Of course, achieving maximum quality is easier said than done, and the process is never complete. Many companies solicit reviews or feedback from customers to improve their goods and services.

WORLDWIDE QUALITY PROGRAMS

Although the movement began in the United States in the 1920s as an attempt to increase product quality by improving the manufacturing process, it was during the 1980s when the quality revolution picked up speed in U.S. corporations. The campaign to improve quality found the leaders at large manufacturing firms—such as Ford, Xerox, and Motorola—had lost market share to Japanese competitors. Smaller companies that supplied parts to large firms then began to recognize quality as a requirement for success. Today, commitment to quality has spread to service industries, not-for-profit organizations, government agencies, and educational institutions.

Congress established the Malcolm Baldrige National Quality Award to recognize excellence in quality management. Named after the late secretary of commerce Malcolm Baldrige, the award is the highest national recognition for quality a U.S. company can receive. The award works toward promoting quality awareness, recognizing quality achievements of U.S. companies, and publicizing successful quality strategies.

The quality movement is also strong in European countries. The European Union's ISO 9001:2008 standards define international, generic criteria for quality management and quality assurance. Originally developed by the International Organization for Standardization in Switzerland to ensure consistent quality among products manufactured and sold throughout the European Union (EU), the standards now include criteria for systems of management as well. Although most other ISO standards are specific to particular products or processes, ISO 9001 applies to any organization, regardless of the goods or services it produces. Many European companies require suppliers to achieve ISO certification, a rigorous process that takes several months to complete, as a condition of doing business with them. The U.S. member body of ISO is the National Institute of Standards and Technology (NIST).[18]

ISO 9001:2008
Standards developed by the International Organization for Standardization in Switzerland to ensure consistent quality management and quality assurance for goods and services throughout the European Union.

BENCHMARKING

Firms often rely on an important tool called benchmarking to set performance standards. The purpose of benchmarking is to achieve superior performance that results in a competitive advantage in the marketplace. A typical benchmarking process involves three main activities: identifying manufacturing or business processes that need improvement, comparing internal processes to those of industry leaders, and implementing changes for quality improvement. The practice of benchmarking has been around for a long time. Henry Ford is known to have developed his own version of the assembly line—an improvement to gain competitive advantage—by observing the way meat-packing plants processed their meat products.[19]

Benchmarking requires two types of analyses: internal and external. Before a company can compare itself with another, it must first analyze its own activities to determine strengths and weaknesses. This assessment establishes a baseline for comparison. External analysis involves gathering information about the benchmark partner to find out why the partner is perceived as the industry's best. A comparison of the results of the analysis provides an objective basis for making improvements. From time to time, firms of all sizes—particularly large firms—benchmark their operations and practices against their competitors and other players in their industry. Often, organizations follow a formal, complex program, but benchmarking can also take a simpler, more informal approach as well.

benchmarking Method of measuring quality by comparing performance against industry leaders.

BRIEFLY SPEAKING

"Your premium brand had better be delivering something special, or it's not going to get the business."

—**Warren Buffett**
American business magnate, investor, and philanthropist

QUALITY OF SERVICES

Everyone has a story about bad and good service—the waiter who forgot a dinner order, a car mechanic who offered a ride to and from the repair shop. As a consumer, your perception of the quality of the service you have purchased is usually determined during the service encounter—the point at which the customer and service provider interact. Employees, such as bank tellers, cashiers, and customer service representatives, have a powerful impact on their customers' decision to return or not. You might pass the word to your friends about the friendly staff at your local breakfast eatery, the slow cashiers at a local supermarket, or the huge scoops of ice cream you got at

service encounter
Point at which the customer and service provider interact.

Customers expect the items they purchase online to arrive in a timely manner.

Roel Smart/iStockphoto.com

service quality
Expected and perceived quality of a service offering.

the nearby ice cream stand. Those words form powerful marketing messages about the services you received.

Service quality refers to the expected and perceived quality of a service offering, and it has a huge effect on the competitiveness of a company. Online retailer Zappos.com (now part of Amazon) built its business on delivering exceptional customer service by, among other things, providing free shipping, maintaining a 365-day return policy, and paying rigorous attention to hiring only those whose passion for customer service matched the company's high standards. The decision to focus on customer service rather than on marketing enabled Zappos to grow to a billion-dollar company. In fact, in a recent consumer survey on customer service, respondents ranked Zappos number one.[20]

Unfortunately, poor service can cut into a firm's competitiveness. When server problems hit an Amazon data center recently, its cloud computing platform shut down. The outage also brought down several websites that rent cloud space from Amazon: Reddit, foursquare, and Quora. In all, the sites were out of commission, or at least partly disabled, for 11 hours. Although Amazon issued an apology and explanation, the outage underscored the unreliability of cloud computing.[21] Deserved or not, consumers often perceive such technology glitches as customer-service problems and, dissatisfied, they begin to seek alternatives.

Service quality is determined by five variables:

1. *Tangibles*, or physical evidence. A tidy office and clean uniforms are examples.

2. *Reliability*, or consistency of performance and dependability. "The right technology. Right away," asserts software solutions provider CDW.

3. *Responsiveness*, or the readiness to serve. "Citi never sleeps," say the ads for the banking giant.

4. *Assurances*, or the confidence communicated by the service provider. "Let your worries go," reassures Northwestern Mutual, an investment and insurance firm.

5. *Empathy*, which shows the service provider understands customers' needs and is ready to fulfill them. "Clear your mind. Relax your soul," says Hotel Nikko San Francisco.

A gap that exists between the level of service customers expect and the level they think they received can be favorable or unfavorable. If you get a larger steak than you expected, or your plane arrives ahead of schedule, the gap is favorable, and you are likely to try that service again. But if your steak is tiny, overcooked, and cold, or your plane is two hours late, the gap is unfavorable, and you may seek out another

ASSESSMENT CHECK

5.1 What is TQM?

5.2 What are the five variables of service quality?

CAREER READINESS

Email: Think Before You Send

Texting, Tweeting, and social networking are popular, but they haven't replaced email in business communication. It is true, however, that many people still make basic email errors that can backfire. Here's how to avoid some of them.

- Always use grammatically correct and concise language, avoid abbreviations and jargon, and watch your tone. Sarcasm and humor are easily misunderstood.

- Proofread everything.

- Never send an email whose presence on tomorrow's front page would embarrass you. If you're angry, wait an hour before writing anything, and think before sending. You never know who is storing your message.

- Make one point per email; many readers don't notice the second or third.

- Include an accurate subject line so your recipient can prioritize incoming messages.

- Be cautious about forwarding other people's emails, about blind copying others on your emails, and about hitting the infamous "Reply all" button.

- Never forward chain emails.

- Ask yourself whether your message is important enough to spend a stamp on it. If not, don't send it.

- Answer incoming email promptly and completely.

- Finally, remember the human touch. A phone call or quick visit to someone's office can be more effective than a long, complicated email.

Sources: Seth Godin, "Email Checklist," *Typepad.com*, accessed November 28, 2012, http://sethgodintypepad.com; "Email Etiquette," *Emailreplies.com*, accessed November 28, 2012, www.emailreplies.com; Alina Tugend, "What to Think About before You Hit 'Send,'" *The New York Times*, accessed November 28, 2012, www.nytimes.com; Emily Suess, "12 Tips for Writing More Effective Business Emails," *Small Business Bonfire*, accessed November 28, 2012, http://smallbusinessbonfire.com.

restaurant or decide to drive the next time. Emails are another way in which customers judge a company's service. See the "Career Readiness" feature for some tips about sending effective emails, both within and outside the company.

DEVELOPMENT OF PRODUCT LINES

Few firms today market only one product. A typical firm offers its customers a **product line**—that is, a series of related products. The motivations for marketing complete product lines rather than concentrating on a single product include the desire to grow, enhancing the company's position in the market, optimal use of company resources, and exploiting the product lifecycle. The following subsections examine each of the first three reasons. The final reason, exploiting the stages of the product lifecycle, is discussed in the section that focuses on strategic implications of the product lifecycle concept.

> **6** Explain why firms develop lines of related products.
>
> **product line** Series of related products offered by one company.

DESIRE TO GROW

A company limits its growth potential when it concentrates on a single product, even though the company may have started that way, as retailer L.L.Bean did with its single style of boots called Maine Hunting Shoes. Now, the company sells boots for men, women, and children, along with apparel, outdoor and travel gear, home furnishings, and even products for pets. The company, which has grown into a large mail-order and online retailer with a flagship store in Freeport, Maine, is a century old. It is unlikely the company would have grown to its current size if the successors of Leon Leonwood Bean had stuck to manufacturing and selling a single style of his original Maine Hunting Shoes.[22]

ENHANCING THE COMPANY'S MARKET POSITION

A company with a line of products often makes itself more important to both consumers and marketing intermediaries than a firm with only one product. A shopper who purchases a tent often buys related camping items. For instance, L.L.Bean now offers a wide range of products with which consumers can completely outfit themselves for outdoor activities or travel. They can purchase hiking boots, sleeping bags and tents, fishing gear, duffel bags, kayaks and canoes, bicycles, snowshoes and skis, as well as clothing for their adventures. In addition, the firm offers Outdoor Discovery Schools programs that teach customers the basics of kayaking, fly fishing, and other sports directly related to the products they purchase from the retailer. L.L.Bean also offers many of its products sized to fit children—from fleece vests to school backpacks.[23] If children grow up wearing L.L.Bean clothes and skiing on L.L.Bean skis, they are more likely to continue as customers when they become adults.

Servicing the variety of products a company sells can also enhance its position in the market. Bean's Outdoor Discovery Schools programs are a form of service, as are its policy to accept returns—no matter what. Schoolchildren who purchase the firm's backpacks can return them anytime for a new one—even if the child has simply outgrown the pack. Policies like this make consumers feel comfortable about purchasing many different products from L.L.Bean.

ASSESSMENT CHECK

6.1 List the four reasons for developing a product line.

6.2 Give an example of a product line with which you are familiar.

OPTIMAL USE OF COMPANY RESOURCES

By spreading the costs of its operations over a series of products, an organization may reduce the average production and marketing costs of each product. Hospitals have taken advantage of idle facilities by adding a variety of outreach services. Many now operate health and fitness centers that, besides generating profits themselves, also feed customers into other hospital services. For example, a blood pressure check at the fitness center might result in a referral to a physician.

THE PRODUCT MIX

7 Describe the way marketers typically measure product mixes and make product mix decisions.

product mix
Assortment of product lines and individual product offerings a company sells.

A company's **product mix** is its assortment of product lines and individual product offerings. The right blend of product lines and individual products allows a firm to maximize sales opportunities within the limitations of its resources. Marketers typically measure product mixes according to width, length, and depth.

PRODUCT MIX WIDTH

The *width* of a product mix refers to the number of product lines the firm offers. As Table 12.3 shows, Johnson & Johnson offers a broad line of retail consumer products in the U.S. market as well as business-to-business products to the medical community. Consumers can purchase over-the-counter medications, nutritional products, dental care products, and first-aid products, among others. Health-care professionals can obtain prescription drugs, medical and diagnostic devices, and wound treatments. LifeScan, one of the firm's subsidiaries, offers an entire suite of products designed to help diabetes patients manage their condition. DePuy, another subsidiary, manufactures orthopedic implants and joint replacement products. At the drugstore, consumers can pick up some of J&J's classic products, such as Motrin and Visine.[24]

PRODUCT MIX LENGTH

The *length* of a product mix refers to the number of different products a firm sells. Table 12.3 also identifies some of the hundreds of health-care products offered by Johnson & Johnson. Some of J&J's most recognizable brands are Band-Aid, Tylenol, and Listerine.

TABLE 12.3 Johnson & Johnson's Mix of Health-Care Products

Over-the-Counter Medicines	Nutritionals	Skin and Hair Care	Oral Care	Medical Devices and Diagnostics
Motrin pain reliever	Lactaid digestive aid	Aveeno lotions	Listerine oral rinse	Ethicon surgical instruments and systems
Tylenol pain reliever	Splenda artificial sweetener	Clean & Clear facial cleansers and toners	REACH dental floss	LifeScan diabetes management products
Benadryl antihistamine	Viactiv calcium supplement	Johnson's baby shampoo	Rembrandt whitening toothpaste	Orthopedic joint replacement products
Mylanta antacid	Benecol	Neutrogena soaps and shampoos	Listerine whitening strips	Veridex diagnostic tests

Source: Company website, www.jnj.com, accessed November 28, 2012.

PRODUCT MIX DEPTH

Depth refers to variations in each product the firm markets in its mix. Johnson & Johnson's Band-Aid brand bandages come in a variety of shapes and sizes, including Finger-Care Tough Strips, Comfort-Flex and Activ-Flex for elbows and knees, and Advance Healing Blister bandages.

PRODUCT MIX DECISIONS

Establishing and managing the product mix have become increasingly important marketing tasks. Adding depth, length, and width to the product mix requires careful thinking and planning; otherwise, a firm can end up with too many products, including some that don't sell well. To evaluate a firm's product mix, marketers look at the effectiveness of its depth, length, and width. Has the firm ignored a viable consumer segment? It may improve performance by increasing product line depth to offer a product variation that will attract the new segment. Can the firm achieve economies in its sales and distribution efforts by adding complementary product lines to the mix? If so, a wider product

Geox is expanding its product mix to include shoes and apparel for women, men, and children.

Alessia Pierdomenico/Bloomberg via Getty Images

mix may seem appropriate. Does the firm gain equal contributions from all items in its portfolio? If not, it may decide to lengthen or shorten the product mix to increase revenues. Geox is an Italian shoe manufacturer known for its patented breathable fabric that keeps feet cool and comfortable. With sales of more than $1 billion, Geox is expanding both ways—in width and length. The firm offers trendy shoe styles, including strappy sandals and retro-inspired bowling shoes. In addition, Geox has launched apparel and shoe lines for men and children, made of similar breathable fabrics that help keep consumers cool and dry.[25]

Another way to add to the mix is to purchase product lines from other companies. Or a firm can acquire entire companies through mergers or acquisitions. GE Healthcare's life sciences division recently acquired Massachusetts-based Xcellerex, a designer of innovative manufacturing technologies for the biopharmaceuticals industry. The acquisition enables GE Healthcare to expand its capability in manufacturing biopharmaceuticals—an area the global giant had targeted for growth.[26]

line extension
Development of individual offerings that appeal to different market segments while remaining closely related to the existing product line.

A firm should assess its current product mix for another important reason: to determine the feasibility of a line extension. A line extension adds individual offerings that appeal to different market segments while remaining closely related to the existing product line. To reinforce its "do it yourself" theme, Home Depot recently broadened its existing Martha Stewart Living product line to include craft furniture—tables, desks and storage units especially suited for pursuing craft hobbies—as well as an expanded line of holiday merchandise. Home Depot marketers say the additions will especially appeal to female shoppers, who comprise half their customers.[27]

The marketing environment also plays a role in a marketer's evaluation of a firm's product mix. In the case of Home Depot, the growing proportion of women do-it-yourselfers, the popularity of craftwork, and increased interest in Martha Stewart-branded merchandise all helped drive the retailer's decision to extend the product line.

Careful evaluation of a firm's current product mix can also help marketers make decisions about brand management and new-product introductions. Chapter 12 examines the importance of branding, brand management, and the development and introduction of new products.

ASSESSMENT CHECK

7.1 Define *product mix*.

7.2 How do marketers typically measure product mixes?

THE PRODUCT LIFECYCLE

8 Explain the concept of the product lifecycle.

product lifecycle
Progression of a product through introduction, growth, maturity, and decline stages.

Products, like people, pass through stages as they age. Successful products progress through four basic stages: introduction, growth, maturity, and decline. This progression, known as the product lifecycle, is shown in Figure 12.5.

The product lifecycle concept applies to products or product categories within an industry, not to individual brands. For instance, camera cell phones are moving rapidly from the introductory stage to

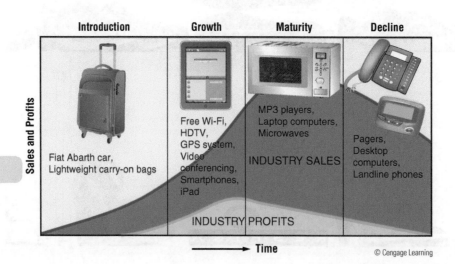

FIGURE 12.5
Stages in the Product Lifecycle

© Cengage Learning

the growth stage. Digital cameras are still in the growth stage but moving toward maturity. Film cameras have declined so much that it is difficult for consumers to purchase film for them. There is no set schedule or time frame for a particular stage of the lifecycle. CDs have been around for more than a quarter of a century but have been declining, in part due to the increase in digital music downloads.[28]

INTRODUCTORY STAGE

During the **introductory stage** of the product lifecycle, a firm works to stimulate demand for the new-market entry. Merchandise in this stage might bring new technology to a product category. Because the product is unknown to the public, promotional campaigns stress information about its features. Additional promotions try to induce distribution channel members to carry the product. In this phase, the public becomes acquainted with the item's merits and begins to accept it.

A product whose introductory stage has been successful is the GPS mapping device. Although global positioning systems have been around for a number of years, their introduction to the consumer market was recent. By promoting its practical applications and making the devices easy to use, marketers have seen GPS sales increase rapidly, moving the products quickly toward the growth stage. Garmin now holds more than 50 percent of the U.S. consumer market for GPS devices, followed by Magellan and TomTom.[29]

Technical problems and financial losses are common during the introductory stage as companies fine-tune product design and spend money on advertising. Many users remember early problems with the Internet—jammed portals, order fulfilling glitches, dot-coms that went bust. But DVD players and camera phones experienced few of these setbacks. Users of GPS devices reported some glitches but also conceded that some problems stem from learning how to operate the devices correctly.

introductory stage First stage of the product lifecycle, in which a firm works to stimulate sales of a new-market entry.

growth stage Second stage of the product lifecycle that begins when a firm starts to realize substantial profits from its investment in a product.

GROWTH STAGE

Sales volume rises rapidly during the growth stage as new customers make initial purchases and early buyers repurchase the product, such as camera phones and GPS devices. The **growth stage** usually begins when a firm starts to realize substantial profits from its investment. Word-of-mouth reports, mass advertising, and lowered prices all encourage hesitant buyers to make trial purchases of new products. In the case of big-screen TVs, low prices generally were not a factor—many cost several thousand dollars. "Big-screen" now refers to a TV that is about 60 inches. As sales volume rises, competitors enter the marketplace, creating new challenges for marketers. As plasma technology is gradually replaced by LCD and LED-LCD models, companies with competing technologies vied for dominance, the TVs themselves grew larger, and prices continued to range widely. Shoppers can purchase a 60-inch Sharp LED-LCD HDTV for about $1,200, a 46-inch Sony LED-LCD HDTV with 3D and Blu-ray for just under $1,000, or opt for the less-expensive 32-inch Sansui Signature LED-LCD model at less than $300.[30]

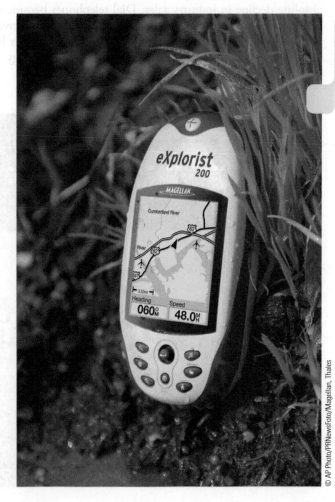

GPS mapping devices have had a successful introductory stage.

© AP Photo/PRNewsFoto/Magellan, Thales

MATURITY STAGE

Sales of a product category continue to grow during the early part of the **maturity stage**, but eventually reach a plateau as the backlog of potential customers dwindles. By this time, many competitors have entered the market, and the firm's profits begin to decline as competition intensifies.

At this stage in the product lifecycle, differences between competing products diminish as competitors discover the product and promotional characteristics most desired by customers. Available supplies exceed industry demand for the first time. Companies can increase their sales and market shares only at the expense of competitors, so the competitive environment becomes increasingly important. In the maturity stage, heavy promotional outlays emphasize any differences still separating competing products, and brand competition intensifies. Some firms try to differentiate their products by focusing on attributes like quality, reliability, and service. Others focus on redesign or other ways of extending the product lifecycle. Nike athletic shoes could be said to be in the maturity stage. With hundreds of athletic shoes on the market, it is difficult to differentiate competing products. But a Nike innovation has enabled the manufacture of shoes that weigh less than one ounce apiece yet are able to take the pounding of a professional athlete. The innovation is Flywire, a lightweight thread made of Vectran fibers. Flywire shoes are so simple and inexpensive to manufacture that Nike could be looking at a whole new lifecycle for its time-honored shoes. Nike has even applied Flywire technology to its newly designed uniforms for the National Football League. The lightweight thread is used in the uniform's collar and around the pads, sleeves, and torso, allowing for greater range of motion and a streamlined fit.[31]

DECLINE STAGE

In the **decline stage** of a product's life, innovations or shifts in consumer preferences bring about an absolute decline in industry sales. Dial telephones became touch-tone phones, which evolved into portable phones, which are now being replaced with conventional cell phones, which in turn are being replaced with camera phones. Thirty-five-millimeter home-movie film was replaced with videotape, which is now being replaced with DVD technology.

Nike athletic shoes could be in the maturity stage, but the new Nike Flywire innovation allows shoes that weigh less than one ounce to take the pounding of a professional athlete.

© Larry Busacca/Getty Images for Nike

Some manufacturers refuse to give up in the decline stage. Young consumers, accustomed to CDs and digital downloads, are beginning to turn their attention to vinyl records. They have discovered their parents' and grandparents' collections of LPs and have hauled old record turntables out of the attic. If curiosity led them to the discovery, the sound and graphics of a record seem to be holding their interest. Marketers in the music industry have taken notice, and some bands have begun to issue limited numbers of records along with CDs and MP3 formats. They don't expect vinyl to become the primary medium for music but are happy to resurrect a classic product for a new generation of listeners.[32] The next section of this chapter discusses more specific strategies for extending the lifecycle of a product.

It is important to remember that the traditional product lifecycle differs from fad cycles. Fashions and fads profoundly influence marketing strategies. Fashions are currently popular products that tend to follow recurring lifecycles. For example, bell-bottom pants popular in the 1960s and 1970s have returned as flares or boot-cut pants. In contrast, fads are products with abbreviated lifecycles. Most fads experience short-lived popularity and then quickly fade, although some maintain residual markets among certain segments. Webkinz (the stuffed animals that have their own online Webkinz World) are an example of a fad.

ASSESSMENT CHECK

8.1 Identify the four stages of the product lifecycle.

8.2 During which stage or stages are products likely to attract the most new customers?

EXTENDING THE PRODUCT LIFECYCLE

Marketers usually try to extend each stage of the lifecycles for their products as long as possible. Product lifecycles can stretch indefinitely as a result of decisions designed to increase the frequency of use by current customers; increase the number of users for the product; find new uses; or change package sizes, labels, or product quality.

9 Discuss how a firm can extend a product's lifecycle, and explain why certain products may be deleted.

INCREASING FREQUENCY OF USE

During the maturity stage, the sales curve for a product category reaches a maximum point if the competitors exhaust the supply of potential customers who previously had not made purchases. However, if current customers buy more frequently than they formerly did, total sales will rise, even though no new buyers enter the market.

For instance, consumers buy some products during certain seasons of the year. Marketers can boost purchase frequency by persuading these people to try the product year-round. For decades, most people used sunscreen only during warm and sunny seasons of the year. With greater warnings about the risks of sun damage and skin cancer, however, companies now advertise the benefits of using sunscreen year-round. In another change, Hershey now offers its famous Hershey's Kisses with personalized messages like "Congratulations," "It's a Boy," and "Happy Birthday" to celebrate personal events.

INCREASING THE NUMBER OF USERS

A second strategy for extending the product lifecycle seeks to increase the overall market size by attracting new customers who previously have not used the product. Marketers may find their products in different stages of the lifecycle in different countries. This difference can help firms extend product growth. Items that have reached the maturity stage in the United States may still be in the introductory stage somewhere else.

After years of operating exclusively in the United States and Canada, retail chain J. Crew recently announced it would open stores in Europe and Asia, with London and Hong Kong as its first new locations. While earlier, J. Crew's CEO had remarked that expanding overseas would distract the company from its North American operations, J. Crew now sees stores in Europe and Asia as an attractive way to grow sales.[33]

FINDING NEW USES

Finding new uses for a product is an excellent strategy for extending a product's lifecycle. New applications for mature products include oatmeal as a cholesterol reducer, antacids as a calcium supplement, and aspirin for promoting heart health.

Marketers sometimes conduct contests or surveys to identify new uses for their products. They may post the results or their own new ideas on their websites. Arm & Hammer's website lists a variety of alternative uses throughout the house for its baking soda. Consumers can use baking soda to clean crayon off walls, as an antacid to settle an upset stomach, and as an agent to balance the pH in swimming pool water. The firm has even developed products for using baking soda in household tasks, such as a plastic shaker container and an air filter that adheres to the inside of the refrigerator.[34]

CHANGING PACKAGE SIZES, LABELS, OR PRODUCT QUALITY

Many firms try to extend their product lifecycles by introducing physical changes in their offerings. Alternatively, new packaging and labels with updated images and slogans can help revitalize a product. General Mills found a way to remodel the packaging for its iconic Cheerios brand and create a more sustainable design. Previously, Cheerios sold at club stores like Costco and BJ's Wholesale came in an oversized box with two bags of cereal inside; for many homes, the box was cumbersome and didn't fit on a pantry shelf. In addition, the bags contained a considerable amount of head space because the cereal would settle during transit. However, a new technology developed at General Mills permits the Cheerios to settle while still on the production line, allowing more dense packing and a smaller box. For club shoppers, the new package actually consists of two smaller, detachable boxes—easier to store and serve. The new design also saves paperboard and even reduces the company's carbon footprint because more boxes can fit on a truck.[35]

Changes in packaging can lengthen a product's lifecycle. Food marketers have brought out small packages designed to appeal to one-person households and extra-large containers for customers who want to buy in bulk. Other firms offer their products in convenient packages for use away from home or at the office. The popularity of the Keurig single-cup brewing machine has skyrocketed, leading numerous coffee sellers to introduce "K-cup" portions of their brands. Starbucks was one such company that had inked a deal with Green Mountain Coffee Roasters—owners of the Keurig machine—to sell single-serve packs of Starbucks and Tazo coffees and teas. However, Starbucks recently announced it would introduce its own single-serve brewing machine, the Verismo, which will prepare espresso drinks as well as brewed coffee.[36]

New technology has allowed General Mills to pack cereal in smaller boxes for club shoppers, making the products easier to store.

© Terri Miller/E-Visual Communications, Inc.

PRODUCT DELETION DECISIONS

To avoid wasting resources promoting unpromising products, marketers must sometimes prune product lines and eliminate marginal products. Marketers typically face this decision during the late maturity and early decline stages of the product lifecycle. Periodic reviews of weak products should justify either eliminating or retaining them. After battling it out with Sony in the DVD player arena, Toshiba finally conceded defeat and announced it would stop making its HD DVD player. That left Sony the winner in the marketplace with its Blu-ray format.

A firm may continue to carry an unprofitable item to provide a complete line for its customers. For example, some grocery stores may lose money on bulky, low-unit-value items like salt, but they continue to carry these items to meet shopper demand.

Shortages of raw materials sometimes prompt companies to discontinue production and marketing of previously profitable items. A firm may even drop a profitable product that fails to fit into its existing line or doesn't fit the direction in which the firm wants to grow. Some of these "orphan brands" return to the market when other firms purchase and relaunch them. In the largest relaunch in hotel history, InterContinental Hotels Group recently completed a $1 billion relaunch of its Holiday Inn chain. Over a multi-year period, 3,300 Holiday Inns reemerged with a redesigned logo; upgraded lobbies and guest bathrooms; and new signage, landscaping, lighting, and bedding. All employees were retrained under the chain's new "Stay Real" program, which has reinvigorated the brand.[37]

ASSESSMENT CHECK

9.1 Describe the four strategies for extending a product's lifecycle.

9.2 Under what circumstances do firms decide to delete a product from their line?

© iStockphoto.com/Ferran Traite Soler

STRATEGIC IMPLICATIONS OF MARKETING IN THE 21ST CENTURY

Marketers who want their businesses to succeed continue to develop new goods and services to attract and satisfy customers. They engage in continuous improvement activities, focusing on quality and customer service. And they continually evaluate their company's mix of products.

Marketers everywhere are constantly developing new and better products that fit their firm's overall strategy. Technological

innovations are one area in which new products quickly replace old ones. Marketers are sometimes faced with the dilemma of lagging sales for formerly popular products. They must come up with ways to extend the lives of certain products to extend their firms' profitability and sometimes must recognize and delete those that no longer meet expectations.

Get online now for additional learning tools to help you master your marketing knowledge—visit **WWW.CENGAGEBRAIN.COM** today!

REVIEW OF CHAPTER OBJECTIVES

1 Define *product*, and distinguish between goods and services and how they relate to the goods–services continuum.

Marketers define a product as the bundle of physical, service, and symbolic attributes designed to satisfy customers' wants and needs. Goods are tangible products customers can see, hear, smell, taste, or touch. Services are intangible tasks that satisfy the needs of customers. Goods represent one end of a continuum, and services represent the other.

2 Outline the importance of the service sector in today's marketplace.

The service sector makes a crucial contribution to the U.S. economy in terms of products and jobs. The U.S. service sector now makes up more than three-fourths of the economy. Services have grown because of consumers' desire for speed, convenience, and technological advances.

3 List the classifications of consumer goods and services, and briefly describe each category.

Consumer products—goods and services—are classified as convenience products (frequently purchased items), shopping products (products purchased after comparison), and specialty products (those offering unique characteristics that consumers prize).

4 Identify each of the types of business goods and services.

Business products are classified as installations (major capital investments), accessory equipment (capital items that cost less and last for shorter periods than installations), component parts and materials (finished business products of one producer that become part of the final products of another producer), raw materials (natural resources, such as lumber, beef, or cotton), supplies (regular expenses a firm incurs in daily operations), and business services (the intangible products firms buy to facilitate their production and operating processes).

5 Discuss how quality is used by marketers as a product strategy.

Many companies use total quality management (TQM) in an effort to encourage all employees to participate in producing the best goods and services possible. Companies may also participate in ISO 9001:2008 certification or benchmarking to evaluate and improve quality. Consumers often evaluate service quality on the basis of tangibles, reliability, responsiveness, assurance, and empathy, so marketers of service firms strive to excel in all of these areas.

6 Explain why firms develop lines of related products.

Companies usually produce several related products rather than individual ones to achieve the objectives of growth, optimal use of company resources, and increased company importance in the market, and to make optimal use of the product lifecycle.

7 Describe the way marketers typically measure product mixes and make product mix decisions.

Marketers must decide the right width, length, and depth of product lines. Width is the number of product lines. Length is the number of products a company sells. Depth refers to the number of variations of a product available in a product line. Marketers evaluate the effectiveness of all three elements of the product mix. They may purchase product lines from other companies or extend the product line, if necessary. Firms may also acquire entire companies and their product lines through mergers and acquisitions.

8 Explain the concept of the product lifecycle.

The product lifecycle outlines the stages a product goes through, including introduction, growth, maturity, and decline. During the introductory stage, marketers work to stimulate demand for the new product. New customers make initial purchases and repurchases of the product in the growth stage. Sales continue to grow during the maturity stage but eventually level off. In the decline stage, sales are reduced due to innovations or a shift in consumer preferences.

Describe how a firm can extend a product's lifecycle, and explain why certain products may be deleted.

Marketers can extend the product lifecycle by increasing frequency of use or number of users; finding new uses for the product; or changing package size, label, or quality. If none of these is successful, or if the product no longer fits a firm's line, the firm may decide to delete it from its line.

ASSESSMENT CHECK: ANSWERS

1.1 Define the term *product*. A product is a bundle of physical, service, and symbolic attributes designed to satisfy a customer's wants and needs.

1.2 Why is the understanding of want satisfaction so important to marketers? The understanding of want satisfaction is important to marketers because it helps them understand why people purchase certain goods and services.

1.3 Describe the goods–services continuum. The goods–services continuum is a spectrum that helps marketers visualize the differences and similarities between goods and services.

1.4 List the six characteristics distinguishing services from goods. The six characteristics distinguishing services from goods are the following: (1) services are intangible, (2) services are inseparable from the service providers, (3) services are perishable, (4) companies cannot easily standardize services, (5) buyers often play important roles in the creation and distribution of services, and (6) service standards show wide variations.

2.1 Identify two reasons services are important to the U.S. economy and business environment. The service sector makes an important contribution to the economy in terms of products and jobs. Services also play a vital role in the international competitiveness of U.S. firms.

2.2 Why do service firms emphasize marketing? The growth of potential service transactions represents a vast marketing opportunity, and the environment for services is changing—so marketers need to find new ways to reach customers.

3.1 What are the three major classifications of consumer products? The three major classifications are convenience products, shopping products, and specialty products.

3.2 Identify five factors marketers should consider in classifying consumer services. Five factors are the following: (1) the nature of the service, (2) the relationship between the service organization and its customers,

(3) flexibility for customization, (4) fluctuation of supply and demand, and (5) the way the service is delivered.

4.1 What are the six main classifications of business products? The six main classifications of business products are the following: (1) installations, (2) accessory equipment, (3) component parts and materials, (4) raw materials, (5) supplies, and (6) business services.

4.2 What are the three categories of supplies? The three categories of supplies are maintenance items, repair items, and operating supplies.

5.1 What is TQM? TQM stands for total quality management, a process that expects all of a firm's employees to continually improve its products and work processes.

5.2 What are the five variables of service quality? The five variables of service quality are tangibles, reliability, responsiveness, assurances, and empathy.

6.1 List the four reasons for developing a product line. The four reasons firms want to develop product lines are the following: (1) a desire to grow, (2) enhancing the company's position in the market, (3) optimal use of company resources, and (4) exploiting the stages of the product lifecycle.

6.2 Give an example of a product line with which you are familiar. Product lines could include salad dressings, hybrid automobiles, sporting equipment, hotel chains, and so on.

7.1 Define *product mix*. The product mix is a company's assortment of product lines and individual product offerings.

7.2 How do marketers typically measure product mixes? The product mix is measured by width, length, and depth.

8.1 Identify the four stages of the product lifecycle. The four stages of the product lifecycle are introduction, growth, maturity, and decline.

8.2 During which stage or stages are products likely to attract the most new customers? Products usually attract the most new customers during the introductory and growth stages.

9.1 Describe the four strategies for extending a product's lifecycle. The four strategies are increasing frequency of use, increasing the number of users, finding new users, and changing packaging or quality.

9.2 Under what circumstances do firms decide to delete a product from their line? Firms may decide to delete a product if none of their strategies work, if raw materials become unavailable, or if the product no longer fits the existing or future product line.

MARKETING TERMS YOU NEED TO KNOW

marketing mix **380**	unsought products **384**	industrial distributor **391**	service encounter **395**
product **381**	convenience products **384**	component parts and materials **391**	service quality **396**
services **381**	impulse goods and services **384**	raw materials **391**	product line **397**
goods **381**	staples **385**	supplies **392**	product mix **398**
goods–services continuum **381**	emergency goods and services **385**	MRO items **392**	line extension **400**
homeshoring **383**	shopping products **385**	business services **393**	product lifecycle **400**
business-to-consumer (B2C) product **384**	specialty products **386**	total quality management (TQM) **394**	introductory stage **401**
business-to-business (B2B) product **384**	installations **390**	ISO 9001:2008 **395**	growth stage **401**
	accessory equipment **391**	benchmarking **395**	maturity stage **402**
			decline stage **402**

ASSURANCE OF LEARNING REVIEW

1. Choose one of the following products and explain how it blurs the distinction between goods and services.
   a. knee replacement surgery
   b. dinner at a popular restaurant
   c. purchase and installation of new roof
   d. live concert
   e. custom-made suit

2. What are the differences between consumer products and B2B products? Describe a product that could be used as both.

3. What are unsought products? Give an example of an unsought product, and explain how it might be marketed.

4. What important features distinguish shopping products from one another?

5. How do marketing for installations and accessory equipment differ?

6. How do firms use benchmarking?

7. Briefly describe how L.L.Bean achieved each of the objectives for developing a product line. Why do you think the firm has been successful?

8. What is a line extension? Describe how *one* of the following might create a line extension:
   a. Viva paper towels
   b. Kellogg's Frosted Flakes
   c. Starbucks Via coffee
   d. Gain laundry detergent

9. What steps do marketers take to make the introductory stage of the product lifecycle successful enough to reach the growth stage? What are some of the challenges they face?

10. Arm & Hammer extended the lifecycle of its baking soda by coming up with new uses for the product. Think of a product whose lifecycle you believe could be extended by finding new uses. Describe the product and your ideas for new uses.

PROJECTS AND TEAMWORK EXERCISES

1. On your own or with a classmate, choose one of the following goods (or choose one of your own). Visit the company's website to learn as much as you can about your product and the way it is marketed. Then create a marketing strategy for developing the services to support your product and make it stand out from others.
   a. Lucky Brand jeans
   b. Galaxy smartphone
   c. Sephora makeup
   d. HP laptop
   e. MINI Cooper car

2. On your own or with a classmate, create an advertisement for an unsought product, such as a remedial reading or math course, a warranty for a big-screen TV, a first-aid kit, or the like. How can your ad turn an unsought product into one actually desired by consumers?

3. Consider a customer service experience you have had in the last month or so. Was it positive or negative? Describe your experience to the class and then discuss how the firm might improve the quality of its customer service—even if it is already positive.

4. With a classmate, choose one of the following firms or another that interests you. Visit the firm's website and measure its product mix. Then create a chart like the one for Johnson & Johnson in Table 12.3 (on page 399), identifying the company's major product lines, along with a few specific examples.
   a. Champion athletic clothing
   b. Condé Nast magazines
   c. Wyndham Hotels
   d. Panasonic
   e. Volkswagen

5. With the same classmate, create a plan for further extending one of the firm's product lines. Describe the strategy you would recommend for extending the line as well as new products that might be included.

CRITICAL-THINKING EXERCISES

1. Draw a line representing the goods–services continuum. Then place each of the following along the continuum. Briefly explain your decision.
   a. Skype
   b. Teleflora.com
   c. Kohl's department stores
   d. Kia dealership
   e. Netflix

2. Make a list of all the convenience products you buy in a week. Does the list change from week to week based on need or your budget? What would it take to make you switch from one product to another?

3. Imagine your favorite restaurant. List as many installations, raw materials, and supplies as you can that you think the restaurant owner or manager must be responsible for purchasing.

4. Why is it important for even a small firm to develop a line of products?

5. Choose one of the following goods and services and describe your strategy for taking it to the next stage in its product lifecycle. For products in the maturity or decline stage, describe a strategy for extending their lifecycle.
   a. iPads (growth)
   b. MP3 players (maturity)
   c. Text messaging (growth)
   d. Landline phones (decline)
   e. Duct tape (maturity)

6. Describe a fad that has come and gone during your lifetime, such as Beanie Babies or Pokemon. Did you take part in the fad? Why or why not? How long did it last? Why do you think it faded?

ETHICS EXERCISE

The airline industry has suffered recent setbacks, such as the high cost of fuel, that have forced the major carriers to cut back on many of their services. Many airlines, like Delta and United, charge passengers a fee for checked baggage. Spirit Air announced it would also charge for carry-on bags. Most airlines charge for in-flight snacks or don't serve any at all. Airlines have reduced the number of flights they operate to certain destinations, packing planes full to overflowing, and recent restrictions on the use of frequent-flyer miles make it difficult to cash them in. Then there are the record-setting delays and lost-luggage claims. All of these factors add up to less-than-enjoyable flying experiences for most travelers, many of whom are opting to find other modes of transportation or just staying home.[38] Suppose you are a marketer for one of the major airlines. Your company is facing difficulty providing acceptable service to the passengers on its flights, but you need to find a way to emphasize the positive features of your airline's service.

1. Using the five variables of service quality as your guideline, what steps would you take—within your realm of control—to close the gap between the level of service passengers expect and the level they have been receiving?

INTERNET EXERCISES

1. **Product classification.** Visit the website of a company like Reckitt Benckiser, Colgate, or Unilever. Choose at least five different products and classify each as a convenience or shopping product. Explain your reasoning.

   www.rb.com
   www.colgate.com
   www.unilever.com

2. **ISO certification.** The International Organization for Standardization (ISO) is responsible for the development and implementation of product standards. Go to the ISO's website and answer the following questions:
   a. Who belongs to ISO and how is it administered?
   b. How are ISO standards developed?
   c. What are some of the advantages of ISO certification?
   www.iso.org

2. How might you attract business customers? Would you give them a level of service that is different from families and other consumers who are flying for pleasure?

3. **Product lifecycle.** Arm & Hammer baking soda was first sold more than 100 years ago. Visit the Arm & Hammer website. Review the history of the product and then prepare a brief report outlining how the makers of Arm & Hammer baking soda have been able to extend the product's lifecycle.
   www.armandhammer.com

Note: Internet Web addresses change frequently. If you don't find the exact site listed, you may need to access the organization's home page and search from there or use a search engine such as Google or Bing.

CASE 12.1
United and Continental Merge Their Services

When United and Continental Airlines merged to form the new United, the world's largest airline, thousands of systems unique to each carrier had to change. Getting it right would take "several years," according to the new company's CEO, "which I think is surprising to a lot of people."

Determining which airline's coffee service would prevail required months of meetings and taste tests, for example. Managers also had to determine whether to offer first and business class, whether to allow Jet Skis as baggage, which direction dog crates should face during loading, and in what order passengers should board. The two carriers had to merge their flight information services, which track speed, altitude, and arrival and departure times, and decide whether delayed planes should fly faster or arrive late. Both are costly, and United and Continental each had different algorithms for making that decision. Hundreds of employees worked on merging more than 400 in-flight operations manuals to 260 for Federal Aviation Administration approval.

Union negotiations related to the merger are still ongoing. United and Continental had two different seniority scales, and two different sets of uniforms for male and female employees. Yet to be determined are whether baggage handlers will wear steel-toed shoes, and how many different shirt and tie styles male employees will choose from. Pilots' unions signed a tentative agreement recently, but contracts with flight attendants and mechanics still need to be ironed out.

Then there were the two carriers' passenger information systems, with two different databases, websites, and loyalty programs. Although observers say the company's careful planning prevented a complete disaster when the integrated system recently went live, that aspect of the merger was not entirely problem free. Some United employees had too little experience dealing with the Continental system chosen for the merged carrier, and response time was slowed at the same time that call volume was rising. United has since hired 400 new customer service people and says service is back to normal. It's also promising a more user-friendly interface for its agents.

QUESTIONS FOR CRITICAL THINKING

1. The new United admits it may have hurt itself with customers by making too many passenger-service-related changes at once, like reducing the free baggage allowance at the same time it introduced the new passenger information system. Do you agree? Why or why not?

2. On the financial side, the merger is intended to boost revenue and shrink costs. What customer-service goals do you think the new United has? What customer goals should it have?

Sources: Jad Mouawad, "United Struggles Two Years after Merging with Continental," *The New York Times*, accessed December 7, 2012, www.nytimes.com; Christopher Elliott, "The Navigator: In United–Continental Airline Merger, a Chaotic Computer Switch," *The Washington Post*, accessed November 28, 2012, www.washingtonpost.com; Susan Carey, "Web of Air Routes: Merger Makeover," *The Wall Street Journal*, accessed November 28, 2012, http://online.wsj.com; Drake Bennett, "Making the World's Largest Airline Fly," *Bloomberg Businessweek*, accessed November 28, 2012, www.bloomberg.com; Andrew Bender, "How to Confuse and Alienate Customers with One Simple Email," *Forbes*, accessed November 28, 2012, www.forbes.com.

VIDEO CASE 12.2
BoltBus Gives Bus Travel a Jump Start

You see them rocketing down the interstate: black-and-orange buses slashed by a gray lightning bolt. This is not old-style bus travel, where you bought your ticket at a seedy terminal counter, then squeezed into a sweltering or freezing seat and wished your journey would end before it began. This is BoltBus, a division of Greyhound Lines and part of a new generation of bus companies that offer a surprising combination of cheap rates and upscale amenities.

BoltBus is a bundle of goods and services designed to meet the needs of travelers along the Northeastern corridor—and recently in the Pacific Northwest. "BoltBus is a bus company that meets the needs of the urban, educated, and adventurous type of customer," says Nicole Recker, senior marketing manager for the company. "We target college students, young professionals, and young families." The goods are the updated buses themselves—comfortable seating with extra legroom, along with power outlets and free Wi-Fi. The services include online ticket purchasing, confirmed reservations, express routes, and real-time status updates on Twitter. "It's more like an airline than it is like a traditional bus," observes David Hall, the company's general manager. "It's a reservation service, so when you buy a ticket you have a reservation on that bus."

Bus travel has been around for a long time. In fact, for a number of years, ridership experienced a steady decline. Customers were fed up with high prices (compared with train or air travel), inconvenient schedules, uncomfortable seating, and poor safety records. But in recent years the industry has changed dramatically. During the late 1990s, a different business model emerged: companies began selling tickets on the Internet instead of at ticket counters in terminals. Hall and his team observed that there might be an opportunity to jump start bus travel from a declining phase in the product life-cycle. Roughly 15 competitors already shared the Northeast market, many of whom had introduced online ticket sales. So BoltBus had to find ways to distinguish its brand from rivals. The average ticket price for a BoltBus trip is $20, which is a bargain in the Northeast. The combination of low prices and higher-end amenities has been a hit with travelers. In fact, BoltBus seats sell out so quickly that regular passengers know to book well in advance or they'll be riding another bus line. Travelers clearly appreciate the easily accessible power outlets and free Wi-Fi, in addition to the express-type service, which means the buses don't make many stops. Hall likes

to compare BoltBus to Southwest Airlines. "We wanted a brand that was affordable ... a fun, easy-to-use brand. We don't have a lot of rules and regulations."

BoltBus was launched in 2008 from its primary hub of New York City, running buses from there to Washington, DC, Philadelphia, and Boston. Other cities—including Baltimore and Newark—were added later. BoltBus hit the Pacific Northwest in 2012. Today, the company employs about 200 workers and operates 92 buses that carry more than 2 million passengers a year. "We try to stay lean and keep our costs down, which keeps ticket prices down," says Hall.

The marketing budget for BoltBus is lean too. The company relies heavily on word-of-mouth and social media. "We pride ourselves on offering customers the best possible rate they can get, which means we operate on a fixed budget when it comes to marketing," explains Nicole Recker, the company's senior marketing manager. "We don't take part in traditional marketing initiatives. We focus on local grass-roots efforts." Since many of the bus line's passengers are young and tech-savvy, Recker says that Twitter has given the company its biggest marketing boost. "The customers enjoy that real-time feedback. They can engage with us as a business." Passengers might Tweet about a delay while en route, receiving immediate responses and real-time updates from BoltBus about the status of the situation. BoltBus may Tweet to passengers about weather or road conditions that could affect the schedule. "This has proved to be extremely beneficial," says Recker. The company has found customer interactions via Twitter to be so effective that it has hired staff to monitor its Twitter account. Bus travel has taken to the highways again, and BoltBus is driving in the express lane.

QUESTIONS FOR CRITICAL THINKING

1. Where does BoltBus fall on the goods–services continuum? With this in mind, what strategies might BoltBus use to gain a competitive advantage over rival bus companies?

2. What steps could BoltBus marketers take to extend its product lifecycle?

Sources: Company website, www.boltbus.com, accessed November 28, 2012; Christine Whittemore, "Travel Marketing: What the Revitalized Bus Travel Industry Can Teach You about Reinventing Your Travel Brand," *5 to 9 Branding*, accessed November 28, 2012, http://5to9branding.com; Jennifer Sokolowsky, "BoltBus to Offer $1 Fares Between Seattle, Portland," *Puget Sound Business Journal*, accessed November 28, 2012, www.bizjournals.com.

NOTES

1. "The World's Most Potent Brands," *Forbes*, accessed November 27, 2012, www.forbes .com; company website, www.apple.com, accessed November 27, 2012; "The World's 50 Most Innovative Companies: 1. Apple," *Fast Company*, accessed November 27, 2012, www.fastcompany.com; Larry Dignan, "Five Not-So-Obvious Reasons Why Apple Won't Be Sony Redux," *ZDnet.com*, accessed November 27, 2012, www.zdnet .com; "Apple Retail Success," *MarketingApple.com*, accessed November 27, 2012, www.marketingapple.com; Carmine Gallo, "Enrich Lives: Reinvent Your Business the Apple Store Way," *Forbes*, accessed November 27, 2012, www.forbes.com; John Ashcroft, "What Can We Learn About Apple Corporate Strategy from the iPad 3," *JohnAshcroft.co.uk*, accessed November 27, 2012, www.johnashcroft.co.uk; Jodi Grainick, "Half of U.S. Homes Own Apple Products," *USA Today*, accessed November 27, 2012, www.usatoday.com.

2. "World's Most Admired Companies 2012," *CNNMoney.com*, accessed November 27, 2012, http://money.cnn.com.

3. U.S. Bureau of Labor Statistics, *Occupational Outlook Handbook*, "Overview of the 2010–20 Projections," accessed November 27, 2012, www.bls.gov.

4. Department of Commerce, "New Commerce Department Report Shows Record Services Trade Surplus That Continues to Grow," press release, accessed November 27, 2012, www.commerce.gov.

5. Stefany Moore, "Another E-Retailer Brings Its Call Center Back to the United States," *Internet Retailer*, accessed November 27, 2012, www.internetretailer.com.

6. Mandira Srivistava, "Cloud Call Center: Alpine Access Offering Home-Based Jobs," *TMCnet.com*, accessed November 27, 2012, http://cloud-call-center.tmcnet.com.

7. Kathryn Balch, "'Homeshoring' Brings Call Centers and Customers Closer," *Business News Daily*, accessed November 27, 2012, www.businessnewsdaily.com.

8. Bruce Japsen, "Drug Makers Dial Down TV Advertising," *The New York Times*, accessed November 27, 2012, http://prescriptions.blogs.nytimes.com.

9. Company website, www.arttowngifts.com, accessed November 27, 2012.

10. This concept was introduced in Christopher H. Lovelock, "Classifying Services to Gain Strategic Marketing Insights," *Journal of Marketing*, Summer 1983, p. 9.

11. Russ Heaps, "10 Cheapest Cars to Own and Operate in 2012," *Bankrate.com*, accessed November 28, 2012, www.bankrate.com; "Most Expensive Cars in the World: Top 10 List 2012–2013," *SuperCars.org*, accessed November 28, 2012, www.thesupercars.org; "The Most Expensive Cars 2012," *Forbes*, accessed November 28, 2012, www.forbes.com.

12. "Boeing Signs Record $22.4 Billion Order with Lion Air," *Reuters*, accessed November 28, 2012, www.reuters.com.

13. Company website, www.bose.com, accessed November 28, 2012.

14. Company website, www.cargill.com, accessed November 28, 2012.

15. Company website, www.officemax.com, accessed November 28, 2012.

16. Company website, www.cisco.com, accessed November 28, 2012.

17. Company website, www.regus.com, accessed November 28, 2012.

18. Organization website, "ISO 9001:2008," www.iso.org, accessed November 28, 2012; organization website, www.nist.gov, accessed November 28, 2012.

19. Public Broadcasting System, "Who Made America: Henry Ford," www.pbs.org, accessed November 28, 2012.

20. Marc Perton, "Survey: Zappos, Amazon Give Best Customer Services," *The Consumerist*, accessed November 28, 2012, http://consumerist.com.

21. Sharon Gaudin, "Amazon Gets 'Black Eye' from Cloud Outage," *Computerworld*, accessed November 28, 2012, www.computerworld.com.

22. Company website, www.llbean.com, accessed November 28, 2012.

23. Ibid.

24. Company website, www.lifescan.com, accessed November 28, 2012; company website, www.depuy.com, accessed November 28, 2012.

25. "GEOX SpA Sees FY 2012 Revenue Guidance at Bottom Part of Prior Range Conference Call," *Reuters*, accessed November 28, 2012, www.reuters.com.

26. "GE Healthcare Life Sciences Completes Acquisition of Xcellerex, Inc.," *Business Wire*, accessed November 28, 2012, www.businesswire.com.

27. "The Home Depot and Martha Stewart Living Omnimedia Extend and Expand Agreement for Popular Martha Stewart Living Product Line," *PR Newswire*, accessed November 28, 2012, www.prnewswire.com.

28. Piya Sinha-Roy, "U.S. Album Sales Slump, Digital Rises in First-Half 2012," *Reuters*, accessed November 28, 2012, www.reuters.com.

29. "GPS Buying Guide," *Consumer Reports*, accessed November 28, 2012, www.consumerreports.org.

30. Company website, www.bestbuy.com, accessed November 28, 2012.

31. "Nike and NFL Unveil New 2012 Uniforms with 32 NFL Athletes," *The Wall Street Journal*, accessed November 28, 2012, http://online.wsj.com.

32. Eric Felten, "It's Alive! Vinyl Makes a Comeback," *The Wall Street Journal*, accessed November 28, 2012, http://online.wsj.com.

33. Dana Mattioli, "J. Crew Suits Up for Overseas," *The Wall Street Journal*, accessed November 28, 2012, http://online.wsj.com.

34. Company website, www.armandhammer.com, accessed November 28, 2012.

35. Sheila Kley, "More Cereal, Less Package," *Taste of General Mills*, accessed November 28, 2012, www.blog.generalmills.com.

36. Julie Jargon, "Starbucks Unveils New Coffee Makers," *The Wall Street Journal*, accessed November 28, 2012, http://online.wsj.com.

37. Ed Watkins, "Holiday Inn Relaunch Drives Revenues, Satisfaction," *Lodging Hospitality*, accessed November 28, 2012, http://lhonline.com.

38. Aaron Smith, "Spirit Air to Charge up to $100 for Carry-on Bags," *CNN Money*, accessed November 28, 2012, http://money.cnn.com.

MAKE ATHLETES BETTER.

UNDER ARMOUR

CAREY PRICE

© Hand-out/Under Armour/Newscom

Chapter 13

DEVELOPING
and Managing Brand and Product Categories

1   Determine how to define a brand.

2   Identify the different types of brands.

3   Explain the strategic value of brand equity.

4   Explain the benefits of category and brand management.

5   Discuss how companies develop a strong identity for their product or brand.

6   Identify and briefly describe each of the new-product development strategies.

7   Describe the consumer adoption process.

8   List the stages in the new-product development process.

9   Explain the relationship between product safety and product liability.

UNDER ARMOUR SCORES

It might seem unlikely that a college athlete's efforts to overcome being "short and slow" could grow into a billion-dollar sports apparel company, but that's the story behind Under Armour, based in Baltimore. Founder Kevin Plank was a college football player who believed the sweat-collecting properties of cotton gear slowed him down on the field. Soon he was spending most of his spare time and meager savings on testing fabrics from tailors' shops to find a material that would carry moisture away from the body.

If he had been working in the apparel industry, Plank says, "I would have been too scared to do anything." But by being dogged and depending on his former teammates and their friends to test his sample shirts, Plank not only refined his product ideas, he also managed to start a successful word-of-mouth campaign that soon had him scrambling to fill orders from college teams.

Now the company is worth about $1.8 billion in annual sales and is expanding internationally, opening offices and expanding its retail

distribution around the world. Under Armour still makes its iconic moisture-wicking shirts, but it has added other athletic gear, including mouth guards, sports bras, basketball shoes, running shoes, and football cleats. It is the official uniform sponsor of a number of overseas teams, including the Tottenham Hotspurs in England, the Welsh Rugby Union, and soccer teams in Israel and Greece. Under Armour also recently launched its first major media marketing campaign in Europe, where its vice president of global marketing says, "It's time to tell our story…because we've built authenticity with our presence on the field." International sales make up about 10 percent of the company's business.

Under Armour sponsors some U.S. Olympic teams and has positioned itself as the go-to supplier for young athletes who can grow up with the company, unlike long-established brands like Nike that represent an older generation. Brandon Jennings, who plays for the NBA's Milwaukee Bucks, maintains a blog on the Under Armour website and engages younger customers via Twitter and Facebook as well.

The company's plans include even more growth and expansion. Its first-ever football cleat sold out online in two hours before moving into stores, and next up are innovative "coldblack" shirts, with a special fabric designed to reflect sunlight to keep wearers cool and dry. Plank sees many opportunities for the brand, and Under Armour is poised to take them.[1]

EVOLUTION OF A  BRAND

Under Armour recently announced that it would expand its business to Europe, launching a new TV and social media campaign in several European countries. Its most recent annual report stated, "We believe the future success of our brand depends on developing our business outside of North America." The company also has a presence in China.

Unlike other firms, Under Armour does all of its own campaigns and creative designs. Its employees' average age is 30, and many are ex-athletes. In one recent year, 26,000 prospective employees sent in their résumés, but just 215 landed spots in the firm.

- In the United States, Under Armour is associated with baseball and American-style football. How will the company need to adapt its approach to reach Europeans, for whom soccer is the most important sport?
- How do you think Under Armour's marketing to a youthful audience will serve the company in the future?

CHAPTER OVERVIEW

Brands play a huge role in our lives. We try certain brands for all kinds of reasons: on recommendations from friends, because we want to associate ourselves with the images certain brands convey, or because we remember colorful advertisements. We develop loyalty to certain brands and product lines for varying reasons as well—quality of a product, price, and habit are a few examples. This chapter examines the way companies make decisions about developing and managing the products and product lines they hope will become consumer necessities. Developing and marketing a product and product line and building a desired brand image are costly propositions. To protect its investment, a specialized marketer called a *category manager* must carefully nurture both existing and new products. The category manager is responsible for an entire product line.

This chapter focuses on two critical elements of product planning and strategy. First, it looks at how firms build and maintain identity and competitive advantage for their products through branding. Second, it focuses on the new-product planning and development process. Effective new-product planning and meeting the profit responsibility a category manager has for a product line require careful preparation. The needs and desires of consumers change constantly, and successful marketers manage to keep up with—or stay just ahead of—those changes.

> **"BRIEFLY SPEAKING"**
>
> "Our brand is a direct result of knowing how to market a brand and having the right people representing the brand."
>
> —**Greg Norman**
> *Successful entrepreneur and professional golfer*

MANAGING BRANDS FOR COMPETITIVE ADVANTAGE

1 Determine how to define a brand.

Think of the last time you went shopping for groceries. As you moved through the store, chances are your recognition of various brand names influenced many of your purchasing decisions. Perhaps you chose Colgate toothpaste over competitive offerings or loaded Heinz ketchup into your cart instead of the store brand. Walking through the snack food aisle, you might have reached for Orville Redenbacher popcorn or Lay's potato chips without much thought.

Marketers recognize the powerful influence products and product lines have on customer behavior, and they work to create strong identities for their products and protect them. Branding is the process of creating that identity. A **brand** is a name, term, sign, symbol, design, or some combination that identifies the products of one firm while differentiating these products from competitors' offerings. The tradition of excellence created by the Gucci Group is carried through in all the brands in its lineup—Gucci, Yves Saint Laurent, Stella McCartney, and Balenciaga, to name a few.

As you read this chapter, consider how many brands you are aware of, both those you are loyal to and those you have never tried or have sampled and abandoned. Table 13.1 shows some selected brands, brand names, and brand marks. Satisfied buyers respond to branding by making repeat purchases of the same product because they identify the item with the name of its producer. One buyer might derive satisfaction from an ice cream bar with the brand name Dove; another might derive the same satisfaction from one with the name Ben & Jerry's.

brand Name, term, sign, symbol, design, or some combination that identifies the products of one firm while differentiating them from those of the competition.

TABLE 13.1 Selected Brands, Brand Names, and Brand Marks

Brand type	Dr Pepper or A&W root beer
Private brand	Craftsman tools (Sears) or Trader Giotto's Italian pizza (Trader Joe's)
Family brand	RAID insect sprays or Progresso soups
Individual brand	Purex or Clorox
Brand name	Kleenex or Cheetos
Brand mark	Colonel Sanders for KFC or the gecko for Geico insurance

© Cengage Learning

BRAND LOYALTY

Brands achieve widely varying consumer familiarity and acceptance. A snowboarder might insist on a Burton snowboard, but the same consumer might show little loyalty to particular brands in another product category such as bath soap. Marketers measure brand loyalty in three stages: brand recognition, brand preference, and brand insistence.

Brand recognition is a company's first objective for newly introduced products. Marketers begin the promotion of new items by trying to make them familiar to the public. Advertising offers

brand recognition
Consumer awareness and identification of a brand.

SOLVING AN ETHICAL CONTROVERSY

Who Is Responsible for the Truth of Advertising Claims?

© Palto/Shutterstock.com

Some customers were shocked to find that Nutella, the chocolate-hazelnut spread from Europe that's becoming increasingly popular in the United States, was not an especially nutritious food, despite commercials showing a mother and children eating it in their kitchen, which these customers believe suggested Nutella might be part of a healthy breakfast for kids. A class-action suit against Ferrero USA Inc., which markets the spread in the United States, was settled in favor of consumers, who will be entitled to a token cash payment that could cost the company over $3 million if all the money is claimed.

Should consumers be responsible for correctly interpreting advertising claims?

PRO

1. Anyone reading the product label would know it contains 21 grams of sugar and 11 grams of fat per serving.

2. When has chocolate been a healthy breakfast food?

CON

1. Ferrero's marketing deliberately put the product in a wholesome setting, suggesting it has nutritional value.

2. The ads market Nutella as particularly suitable for kids' breakfasts, despite its high calorie content.

Summary:

Some consumers ridiculed the lawsuit, but Ferrero is also changing the product's labeling, withdrawing the commercials, producing new ones that the suit's plaintiffs will approve before filming, and altering its website. Nutella's caloric, fat, sodium, and sugar content will now appear on the front of the jar.

Sources: "Nutella Health Claims Net $3.05 Million Settlement in Class-Action Lawsuit," *CBS News*, accessed November 29, 2012, www.cbs.news.com; Caroline Scott-Thomas, "Ferrero Backs Away from Nutella Health Claims in $3M Class Action Settlement," *Food Navigator USA*, accessed November 29, 2012, www.foodnavigator-usa.com; Laurent Belsie, "Nutella Settles Lawsuit. You Can Get $20," *The Christian Science Monitor*, accessed November 29, 2012, www. csmonitor.com; Carly Rothman, "In Nutella Lawsuit over False Health Claims, a Two-Fold Lesson," *NJ.com*, accessed November 29, 2012, www.nj.com.

Coca-Cola, a familiar brand, drew on customers' recognition of its popular bottle shape when it introduced the PlantBottle, which is made partly from vegetable fiber. Coca-Cola's Dasani brand is shown here.

Designed to Make a Difference

1 unique redesigned plastic bottle

2 up to 30% made from plants

3 still 100% recyclable

© The Coca-Cola Company

plantbottle™

PlantBottle® packaging is made in part from renewable materials sourced from sugarcane production to bring you the pure, crisp taste of DASANI in a bottle designed with the planet in mind.

Now available nationwide.

©2011 The Coca-Cola Company PLANTBOTTLE, the PlantBottle Logo and DASANI are trademarks of The Coca-Cola Company

brand preference
Consumer choice of a product on the basis of a previous experience.

brand insistence
Consumer refusal of alternatives and extensive search for desired merchandise.

one effective way for increasing consumer awareness of a brand. Coca-Cola is a familiar brand worldwide, and it drew on customers' recognition of its familiar bottle shape when it introduced the PlantBottle, made from 30 percent plant fiber. Other tactics for creating brand recognition include offering free samples or discount coupons for purchases. Once consumers have used a product, seen it advertised, or noticed it in stores, it moves from the unknown to the known category, increasing the probability that some of those consumers will purchase it. Sometimes customers can misinterpret a marketing message, however, as happened to Nutella. See the "Solving an Ethical Controversy" feature to find out the result.

At the second level of brand loyalty, **brand preference**, buyers rely on previous experiences with the product when choosing it, if available, over competitors' products. You may prefer Steve Madden shoes or Juicy Couture clothes to other brands and buy their new lines as soon as they are offered. If so, those products have established brand preference.

Brand insistence, the ultimate stage in brand loyalty, leads consumers to refuse alternatives and to search extensively for the desired merchandise. A product at this stage has achieved a monopoly position with its consumers. Although many firms try to establish brand insistence with all consumers, few achieve this ambitious goal. Companies that offer specialty or luxury goods and services, such as Rolex watches or Lexus automobiles, are more likely to achieve this status than those offering mass-marketed goods and services.

 ASSESSMENT CHECK

1.1 What is a brand?

1.2 Differentiate among brand recognition, brand preference, and brand insistence.

TYPES OF BRANDS

2 Identify the different types of brands.

generic products
Products characterized by plain labels, no advertising, and the absence of brand names.

Brands are classified in many ways: private, manufacturer's or national, family, and individual brands. In making branding decisions, firms weigh the benefits and drawbacks of each type of brand. Some firms, however, sell their goods without any efforts at branding. These items are called **generic products**. They are characterized by plain labels, little or no advertising, and no brand names. Common categories of generic products include food and household staples. These no-name products were first sold in Europe at prices as much as 30 percent below those of branded products. This product strategy was introduced in the United States three decades ago. The market shares for generic products increase during economic downturns but subside when the economy improves. However, many consumers request generic substitutions for brand-name prescriptions at the pharmacy whenever they are available.

Manufacturers' Brands Versus Private Brands

Manufacturers' brands, also called *national brands*, define the image most people form when they think of a brand. A manufacturer's brand refers to a brand name owned by a manufacturer or other producer. Well-known manufacturers' brands include Hewlett-Packard, Sony, Pepsi-Cola, Dell, and French's. In contrast, many large wholesalers and retailers place their own brands on the merchandise they market. The brands offered by wholesalers and retailers usually are called private brands (or *private labels*). Although some manufacturers refuse to produce private-label goods, most regard such production as a way to reach additional market segments. Supervalu offers many private-label products in its retail grocery stores, including Equaline over-the-counter pharmaceuticals, Homelife household goods, and President's Choice foods.

The growth of private brands has paralleled that of chain stores in the United States. Manufacturers not only sell their well-known brands to stores but also put the store's own label on similar products. Such leading manufacturers as Westinghouse, Armstrong Rubber, and Heinz generate ever-increasing percentages of their total incomes by producing goods for sale under retailers' private labels. A recent survey found that private-label purchases make up almost 50 percent of in-store buying. Sixty-six percent of shoppers buy many private-label brands because they are less expensive. More than half of consumers surveyed said it would take a permanent price reduction of brand-name products—to the same price as the store brand—to persuade them to return to purchasing brand-name products.[2]

Consistent with its corporate goal to buy and sell green products, office supply retailer Office Depot launched Office Depot Green, a private-label line of environmentally sound products. The line includes recycled paper and paper products, ink and toner cartridges, compact fluorescent light bulbs, and other items that create minimal impact on the environment.[3]

manufacturer's brand Brand name owned by a manufacturer or other producer.

private brand Brand offered by a wholesaler or retailer.

Captive Brands

The nation's major discounters—such as Walmart, Target, and Kmart—have come up with a spinoff of the private-label idea. So-called captive brands are national brands sold exclusively by a retail chain. Captive brands typically provide better profit margins than private labels. Target's captive brands include housewares and apparel by Michael Graves and Mossimo Giannulli; Liz Lange maternity wear; furniture collections by Sean Conway; and moderately priced clothing by Zac Posen.[4]

captive brand National brand sold exclusively by a retail chain.

Family and Individual Brands

A family brand is a single brand name that identifies several related products. For example, All-Clad Metalcrafters markets a complete line of cookware under the All-Clad name, and Johnson & Johnson offers a line of baby powder, lotions, plastic pants, and baby shampoo under its name. All Pepperidge Farm products, including bread, rolls, and cookies, carry the Pepperidge Farm brand. Frito-Lay markets both chips and salsa under its Tostitos family brand.

Alternatively, a manufacturer may choose to market a product as an individual brand, which uniquely identifies the item itself, rather than promoting it under the name of the company or under an umbrella name covering similar items. Unilever, for example, markets Knorr, Bertolli, Lipton, and Slim-Fast food products; Pond's and Sunsilk beauty products; and Lifebuoy, Lux, and Dove soaps. PepsiCo's Quaker Oats unit markets Aunt Jemima breakfast products, Life and Cap'n Crunch cereals, and Rice-a-Roni side dishes along with Quaker oatmeal. Its Frito-Lay division makes Lays, Ruffles, and Doritos chips and Smartfood popcorn. The Pepsi-Cola brands include Mountain Dew, Sierra Mist, SoBe juices and teas, and Aquafina water. Individual brands cost more than family brands to market because the firm must develop a new promotional campaign to introduce each new product. Distinctive brands are extremely effective aids in implementing market segmentation strategies, however.

On the other hand, a promotional outlay for a family brand can benefit all items in the line. Family brands also help marketers introduce new products to both customers and retailers. Because supermarkets stock thousands of items, they hesitate to add new products unless they are confident they will be in demand.

family brand Single brand name that identifies several related products.

individual brand Single brand that uniquely identifies a product.

A family brand is a single brand name that identifies several related products. All-Clad markets a complete line of cookware under its name.

AP Images/Charles Krupa

Family brands should identify products of similar quality, or the firm risks harming its overall product image. If Rolls-Royce marketers were to place the Rolls name on a low-end car or a line of discounted clothing, they would severely tarnish the image of the luxury car line. Conversely, Lexus, Infiniti, and Porsche put their names on luxury sport-utility vehicles to capitalize on their reputations and to enhance the acceptance of the new models in a competitive market.

Individual brand names should, however, distinguish dissimilar products. Kimberly-Clark markets two different types of diapers for infants under its Huggies and Pull-Ups names. Procter & Gamble offers shaving products under its Gillette name; laundry detergent under Cheer, Tide, and other brands; and dishwasher detergent under Cascade.

ASSESSMENT CHECK

2.1   Identify the different types of brands.

2.2   How are generic products different from branded products?

BRAND EQUITY

3   Explain the strategic value of brand equity.

As individuals, we often like to say our strongest asset is our reputation. The same is true of organizations. A brand can go a long way toward making or breaking a company's reputation. A strong brand identity backed by superior quality offers important strategic advantages for a firm. First, it increases the likelihood that consumers will recognize the firm's product or product line when they make purchase decisions. Second, a strong brand identity can contribute to buyers' perceptions of product quality. Branding can also reinforce customer loyalty and repeat purchases. A consumer who tries a brand and likes it will probably look for that brand on future store visits. All of these benefits contribute to a valuable form of competitive advantage called *brand equity*.

brand equity Added value that a respected, well-known brand name gives to a product in the marketplace.

Brand equity refers to the added value a certain brand name gives to a product in the marketplace. Brands with high equity confer financial advantages on a firm because they often command comparatively large market shares and consumers may pay little attention to differences in prices. Studies have also linked brand equity to high profits and stock returns. Service companies are also aware of the value of brand equity.

In global operations, high brand equity often facilitates expansion into new markets. Currently, Apple, IBM, and Google are the most valuable—and most recognized—brands in the world.[5] Similarly, Disney's brand equity allows it to market its goods and services in Europe and Japan—and now, China. What makes a global brand powerful? According to Interbrand, which measures brand equity in dollar values, a strong brand has the power to increase a company's sales and earnings. A global brand generally is defined as one that sells at least 20 percent outside its home country.

Global advertising agency Young & Rubicam developed another brand equity system called the BrandAsset Valuator. Y&R's database of consumers' brand perceptions contains nearly 715,000 consumer interviews and information on 44,000 brands across 51 countries. According to Y&R, a firm builds brand equity sequentially on four dimensions of brand personality. These four dimensions are differentiation, relevance, esteem, and knowledge:

- *Differentiation* refers to a brand's ability to stand apart from competitors. Brands such as Porsche and Victoria's Secret stand out in consumers' minds as symbols of unique product characteristics.

- *Relevance* refers to the real and perceived appropriateness of a brand to a big consumer segment. A large number of consumers must feel a need for the benefits offered by the brand. Brands with high relevance include Microsoft and Hallmark.

- *Esteem* is a combination of perceived quality and consumer perceptions about a brand's growing or declining popularity. A rise in perceived quality or in public

Convery Flowers/Alamy

Most customers have knowledge, or awareness and understanding, of the Timberland brand.

opinion about a brand enhances a brand's esteem. But negative impressions reduce esteem. Brands with high esteem include General Mills and Honda.

- *Knowledge* refers to the extent of customers' awareness of the brand and understanding of what a good or service stands for. Knowledge implies that customers feel an intimate relationship with a brand. Examples include Jell-O and Timberland.[6]

ASSESSMENT CHECK

3.1 What is brand equity?

3.2 What are the four dimensions of brand personality?

THE ROLE OF CATEGORY AND BRAND MANAGEMENT

Because of the tangible and intangible value associated with strong brand equity, marketing organizations invest considerable resources and effort in developing and maintaining these dimensions of brand personality. Traditionally, companies assigned the task of managing a brand's marketing strategies to a brand manager. Today, because they sell about 80 percent of their products to national retail chains, major consumer goods companies have adopted a strategy called category management. In this strategy, a manufacturer's *category manager* maximizes sales for the retailer by overseeing an entire product line, often tracking sales history with data from the retail checkout point and aggregating it with sales data for the entire category (obtained from third-party vendors) and qualitative data, such as customer surveys.[7]

Unlike traditional product managers, category managers have profit responsibility for their product group and help the retailer's category buyer maximize sales for the whole category, not just the particular manufacturer's product. These managers are assisted by associates usually called *analysts*. Part of the shift to category management was initiated by large retailers, who realized they could benefit from the marketing muscle of large grocery and household goods producers such as SC Johnson and Procter & Gamble. As a result, producers began to focus their attention on in-store merchandising instead of mass-market advertising. Some manufacturers that are too small to dedicate a category manager to each retail chain assign a category manager to each major channel, such as convenience stores, drugstores, grocery stores, and so on.[8]

Explain the benefits of category and brand management. 4

brand manager
Marketer responsible for a single brand.

category management
Product management system in which a category manager—with profit and loss responsibility—oversees a product line.

Some of the steps companies follow in the category management process include defining the category based on the target market's needs, scoping out a consumer's decision process when shopping the category, identifying consumer groups and the store clusters with the greatest sales

ASSESSMENT CHECK

4.1 Define *brand manager*.

4.2 How does category management help retailers?

potential, creating a marketing strategy and performance goal for each cluster and using a scorecard to measure progress, defining and executing the tactics, and tracking progress.[9] Hershey's vending division offers category management services to its institutional customers, providing reduced inventory costs, improved warehouse efficiency, and increased sales.[10]

PRODUCT IDENTIFICATION

5 Discuss how companies develop a strong identity for their product or brand.

Organizations identify their products in the marketplace with brand names, symbols, and distinctive packaging. Almost every product distinguishable from another gives buyers some means of identifying it. Sunkist Growers, for instance, stamps its oranges with the name Sunkist. Iams stamps a paw print on all of its pet food packages. For well over a century, Prudential Financial has used the Rock of Gibraltar as its symbol.

Choosing how to identify a firm's output represents a major strategic decision for marketers. Produce growers have another option besides gummed paper stickers for identifying fruits and vegetables: dissolvable fruit stickers. Amron Experimental's Fruitwash Labels include the PLU (price look-up) code and eliminate sticky labels. Washing the fruit dissolves the label, which turns into an organic produce wash that eliminates wax, pesticides, dirt, and bacteria.[11]

BRAND NAMES AND BRAND MARKS

brand name Part of a brand, consisting of letters, numbers, or words, that can be spoken and that identifies and distinguishes a firm's offerings from those of its competitors.

brand mark Symbol or pictorial design that distinguishes a product.

A name plays a central role in establishing brand and product identity. The American Marketing Association defines a brand name as the part of a brand that can be spoken. It can consist of letters, numbers, or words and forms a name that identifies and distinguishes the firm's offerings from those of its competitors. Firms can also identify their brands by brand marks. A brand mark is a symbol or pictorial design that distinguishes a product, such as the Jolly Green Giant for Green Giant Vegetables.

Effective brand names are easy to pronounce, recognize, and remember. Short names, such as Nike, Ford, and Bounty, meet these requirements. Marketers try to overcome problems with easily mispronounced brand names by teaching consumers the correct pronunciations. For example, early advertisements for the Korean carmaker Hyundai explained that the name rhymes with *Sunday*. Sensitivity to clear communication doesn't end with the choice of brand name; marketers should also be aware of how well they get their point across in interpersonal communications.

A brand name should also give buyers the correct connotation of the product's image. Nissan's X-Terra connotes youth and extreme sports to promote the off-road SUV. Kodak's EasyShare tells consumers how simple printing digital pictures can be. ConAgra's Healthy Choice food line presents an alternative to fast foods that may be high in sodium or fat, and the iPod Nano uses a name that aptly suggests its tiny size. A brand name must also qualify for legal protection. The Lanham Act of 1946 states that registered trademarks must not contain words or phrases in general use, such as *automobile* or *suntan lotion*. These generic words actually describe particular types of products, and no company can claim exclusive rights to them.

Marketers feel increasingly hard-pressed to coin effective brand names, as multitudes of competitors rush to stake out names for their own products. Some companies register names before they have products to fit

Sometimes popular brands join forces to advertise their products. Nike and Apple combined their marketing efforts in a recent ad campaign for the Nike + iPod Sport Kit.

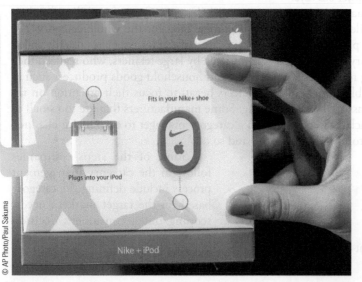

Fits in your Nike+ shoe

Plugs into your iPod

Nike + iPod

© AP Photo/Paul Sakuma

them to prevent competitors from using them. Some marketers use humor to connect with potential customers. Harley Davidson's Fat Boy series of motorcycles have become very successful because buyers liked the name.[12]

When a class of products becomes generally known by the original brand name of a specific offering, the brand name may become a descriptive generic name. If this occurs, the original owner loses exclusive claim to the brand name. The generic names nylon, aspirin, escalator, kerosene, and zipper started as brand names. Other generic names that were once brand names include cola, yo-yo, linoleum, and shredded wheat.

Marketers must distinguish between brand names that have become legally generic terms and those that seem generic only in many consumers' eyes. Consumers often adopt legal brand names as descriptive names. Jell-O, for instance, is a brand name owned exclusively by Kraft Foods, but many consumers casually apply it as a descriptive name for gelatin desserts. Similarly, many people use the term Kleenex to refer to any brand of facial tissues. English and Australian consumers use the brand name Hoover as a verb for vacuuming. One popular way to look something up on the Internet now is to "Google it." Xerox is such a well-known brand name that people frequently—though incorrectly—use it as a verb to mean photocopying. To protect its valuable trademark, Xerox Corporation has created advertisements explaining that Xerox is a brand name and registered trademark and should not be used as a verb.

TRADEMARKS

Businesses invest considerable resources in developing and promoting brands and brand identities. The high value of brand equity encourages firms to take steps in protecting the expenditures they invest in their brands.

A **trademark** is a brand for which the owner claims exclusive legal protection. A trademark should not be confused with a trade name, which identifies a company. The Coca-Cola Company is a trade name, but Coke is a trademark of the company's product. Some trade names duplicate companies' brand names.

Protecting Trademarks

Trademark protection confers the exclusive legal right to use a brand name, brand mark, and any slogan or product name abbreviation. It designates the origin or source of a good or service. Frequently, trademark protection is applied to words or phrases, such as *Bud* for Budweiser or *the Met* for the Metropolitan Opera in New York City. Robert Burck, better known as the Naked Cowboy—a New York street performer who plays guitar in Times Square wearing nothing but white cowboy boots, cowboy hat, and underpants—registered his likeness and the words "Naked Cowboy" as a trademark. Burck sued Mars, the makers of M&Ms, for trademark infringement after they erected a video billboard showing a blue M&M playing the guitar and clad only in white boots, hat, and underpants. The case was settled out of court, with Burck's lawyers arguing that Mars had infringed on his trademark rights. More recently, Burck sued CBS, whose soap opera *The Bold and the Beautiful* featured a character wearing only briefs and playing a guitar. CBS later uploaded the episode onto YouTube and labeled it "The Bold and the Beautiful—Naked Cowboy." Burck accused the network of harming his reputation, but he lost that lawsuit when the judge ruled that "even an unsophisticated viewer" would not mistake Burck for the character in the soap opera.[13]

Firms can also receive trademark protection for packaging elements and product features, such as shape, design, and typeface. U.S. law has fortified trademark protection in recent years. The Federal Trademark Dilution Act of 1995 gives a trademark holder the right to sue for trademark infringement even if other products using its brand are not particularly similar or easily confused in the minds of consumers. The infringing company does not even have to know it is diluting another's trademark. The act also gives a trademark holder the right to sue if another party imitates its trademark.

The Internet is the next battlefield for trademark infringement cases. Some companies are attempting to protect their trademarks by filing infringement cases against companies using similar Internet addresses or using unauthorized versions of the same name. Such was the case when a St. Louis–based technology firm called Bing! Information Design sued Microsoft for naming its search engine Bing. The design firm claimed that it had been using the "Bing!" name since before 2000,

trademark Brand for which the owner claims exclusive legal protection.

while Microsoft's use of the word "Bing" did not surface until mid-2009. The suit claimed that the duplication eroded the design firm's efforts to differentiate itself and caused confusion in the marketplace. The lawsuit was settled out of court.[14]

Trade Dress

trade dress Visual components that contribute to the overall look of a brand.

Visual cues used in branding create an overall look sometimes referred to as trade dress. These visual components may be related to color selections, sizes, package and label shapes, and similar factors. For example, the McDonald's golden arches, Merrill Lynch's bull, and the yellow of Shell's seashell are all part of these products' trade dress. Owens Corning has registered the color pink to distinguish its fiberglass insulation from that of its competition. A combination of visual cues can also constitute trade dress. Consider a Mexican food product that uses the colors of the Mexican flag: green, white, and red.

Trade dress disputes have led to numerous courtroom battles but no apparent consensus from the Supreme Court. Apple has sued Samsung, charging that the Korean industrial giant had infringed on Apple's trade dress, trademark, and design patents in manufacturing its Android smart phone. In an unusual twist, Samsung happens to be one of Apple's major parts suppliers. The courts recently awarded Apple more than $1 billion in damages, finding that Samsung had infringed on some of Apple's patents.[15]

DEVELOPING GLOBAL BRAND NAMES AND TRADEMARKS

Cultural and language variations make brand-name selection a difficult undertaking for international marketers; an excellent brand name or symbol in one country may prove disastrous in another. An advertising campaign for E-Z washing machines failed in the United Kingdom, because the British pronounce z as "zed." A firm marketing a product in multiple countries must also decide whether to use a single brand name for universal promotions or tailor names to individual countries. Most languages contain *o* and *k* sounds, so *okay* has become an international word. Most languages also have a short *a,* so Coca-Cola, Kodak, and Texaco are effective brands abroad.

In a recent dispute, two global companies recently squared off, with distiller Maker's Mark winning a judgment against Jose Cuervo International. As part of the manufacturing process of its Maker's Mark bourbon, the company seals the bottles by hand-dipping the tops in red wax, creating a free-form red seal. Makers of Jose Cuervo tequila had recently begun affixing a red wax seal on its bottles. The court agreed that the red wax seal was part of the Maker's Mark trademark and barred Jose Cuervo International from its further use.[16]

PACKAGING

A firm's product strategy must also address questions about packaging. Like its brand name, a product's package can powerfully influence buyers' purchase decisions.

Marketers apply increasingly scientific methods to their packaging decisions. Rather than experimenting with physical models or drawings, more and more package designers work on special computer graphics programs that create three-dimensional images of packages in thousands of colors, shapes, and typefaces. Another software program helps marketers design effective packaging by simulating the displays shoppers see when they walk down supermarket aisles.

The AT&T globe is part of the brand's trade dress.

© AP Photo/PRNewsFoto/AT&T Corporation

Companies conduct marketing research to evaluate current packages and to test alternative package designs. When Nestlé USA Prepared Foods recently wanted to update the packaging of its Lean Cuisine line of frozen entrees and dinners, the company conducted extensive market research. Lean Cuisine was first introduced more than 30 years ago as a line of healthful meals,

MARKETING SUCCESS

Packaging Variety Gives Heinz a Boost

Background. Flexible food pouches have been slower to catch on in the United States than in Europe, even though they are cheaper to manufacture than plastic bottles, have a modern look, and are easy to use. They also keep food exceptionally fresh.

The Challenge. While H. J. Heinz Co. hadn't redesigned its ketchup bottle since 1983, the company recognized that consumers today want smaller sizes, lower prices, and convenience but are unwilling to give up quality. Heinz wanted its iconic product to remain competitive, even in discount groceries where value is especially important.

The Strategy. Heinz introduced a flexible, 10-ounce ketchup pouch with pouring spout for half the price of the traditional 20-ounce bottle. There is also a food-service version of the pouch, whose unique "Dip and Squeeze" design holds three times as much ketchup as the original restaurant packets, so fewer are needed per order.

The Outcome. Heinz hopes the pouches' design and convenience will appeal especially to younger consumers, both in grocery stores and in food-service outlets. Heinz's vice president of global packaging innovation says, "We didn't meddle with the formula, we just changed the delivery mechanism." The food-service pouch has already sold more than 1 billion units, including to Wendy's and Chick-fil-A.

Sources: Elaine Watson, "Quote/Unquote: Heinz on Rocking the Boat…" *Food Navigator*, accessed November 29, 2012, www.foodnavigator-usa.com; Emily Bryson York, "More Foods Going to Pouch Packaging," *Chicago Tribune*, accessed November 29, 2012, http://articles.chicagotribune.com; Sarah Nassauer, "Old Ketchup Packet Heads for Trash," *The Wall Street Journal*, accessed November 29, 2012, http://onlinewsj.com.

but as the company's design manager put it, the brand is about bringing out the best by helping people to eat healthier every day. The company believed the old package design didn't reflect this attitude. Nestlé USA worked with a design firm to develop packaging that would reflect Lean Cuisine's "vibrant and optimistic personality." Another innovation was the packaging of some items in steam-in bags, which are increasingly popular in today's time-pressed world.[17] Heinz spent years testing new pouch-style packaging for its ketchup. See the "Marketing Success" feature for the story.

A package serves three major objectives: (1) protection against damage, spoilage, and pilferage; (2) assistance in marketing the product; and (3) cost effectiveness. Let's briefly consider each of these objectives.

Protection Against Damage, Spoilage, and Pilferage

The original objective of packaging was to offer physical protection for the merchandise. Products typically pass through several stages of handling between manufacturing and customer purchases, and a package must protect its contents from damage. Furthermore, packages of perishable products must protect the contents against spoilage in transit and in storage until purchased by the consumer. Fears of product tampering have forced many firms to improve package designs. Over-the-counter medicines are sold in tamper-resistant packages covered with warnings informing consumers not to purchase merchandise without protective seals intact. Many grocery items and light-sensitive products are packaged in tamper-resistant containers as well. Products in glass jars, such as spaghetti sauce and jams, often come with vacuum-depressed buttons in the lids that pop up the first time the lids are opened.

Even prescription medicine packaging can be revolutionized for the consumer's benefit, as Target found. Its ClearRx prescription dispensing system offers bottles with easy-to-read labels, in a shape designed to fit in the palm of the hand. An information card tucked into a sleeve on the back of the

Target's ClearRx prescription bottles offer easy-to-read labels in a shape designed to fit in the palm of the hand; an information card about the prescription tucked into a sleeve on the back of the bottle; and color-coded rings on the bottle's neck to help family members identify their medications at a glance.

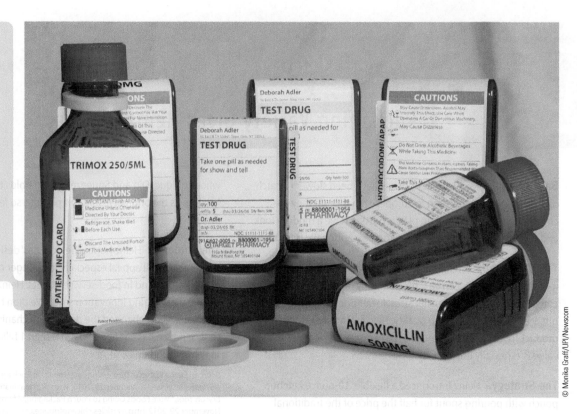

© Monika Graff/UPI/Newscom

bottle provides a brief summary of the medication's uses and side effects. For households where several people are taking medication, color-coded rings on the neck of the bottle help family members identify their medication at a glance.[18]

Many packages offer important safeguards against pilferage for retailers. Shoplifting and employee theft cost retailers several billion dollars each year. To limit this activity, many packages feature oversized cardboard backings too large to fit into a shoplifter's pocket or purse. Efficient packaging that protects against damage, spoilage, and theft is especially important for international marketers, which must contend with varying climatic conditions and the added time and stress involved in overseas shipping.

Assistance in Marketing the Product

The proliferation of new products, changes in consumer lifestyles and buying habits, and marketers' emphasis on targeting smaller market segments have increased the importance of packaging as a promotional tool. Many firms address consumer concerns about protecting the environment by designing packages made of biodegradable and recyclable materials. To demonstrate serious concern regarding environmental protection, Procter & Gamble, Coors, McDonald's, and other firms have created ads that describe their efforts in developing environmentally sound packaging.

In a grocery store where thousands of different items compete for notice, a product must capture the shopper's attention. Marketers combine colors, sizes, shapes, graphics, and typefaces to establish distinctive trade dress that sets their products apart from the products of competitors. Packaging can help establish a common identity for a group of items sold under the same brand name. Like the brand name, a package should evoke the product's image and communicate its value.

Some packages enhance convenience. Pump dispensers, for example, facilitate the use of products ranging from mustard to insect repellent. Squeezable bottles of honey and ketchup make those products easier to use and store. Packaging provides key benefits for convenience foods such as meals and soups packaged in microwavable containers, juice drinks in aseptic packages, and frozen entrées and vegetables packaged in single-serving portions.

Other firms increase consumer utility with packages designed for reuse. Empty jelly jars have long doubled as drinking glasses. Parents can buy bubble bath in animal-shaped plastic bottles suitable for bathtub play. Packaging is a major component in Avon's overall marketing strategy. The firm's decorative, reusable bottles have even become collectibles.

Cost-Effective Packaging

Although packaging must perform a number of functions for the producer, marketers, and consumers, it must do so at a reasonable cost. Sometimes changes in the packaging can make packages both cheaper and better for the environment. A redesign of the standard gallon milk jug has cut shipping costs and lessened its environmental impact. Kimberly-Clark is best known to consumers for its Kleenex, Scott, and Huggies brands, but its Kimberly-Clark Health Care and Kimberly-Clark Profession divisions make products for the medical field. Recently, those two divisions introduced new packaging for disposable medical gloves. Someone trying to take one glove out of a package often pulls out several that have to be discarded. The new SmartPULL packaging has a dual-opening tab for its paper cartons that greatly reduces wasted gloves.[19]

Labeling

Labels were once a separate element applied to a package; today, they are an integral part of a typical package. Labels perform both promotional and informational functions. A label carries an item's brand name or symbol, the name and address of the manufacturer or distributor, information about the product's composition and size, and recommended uses. The right label can play an important role in attracting consumer attention and encouraging purchases.

Consumer confusion and dissatisfaction over such descriptions as giant economy size, king size, and family size led to the passage of the Fair Packaging and Labeling Act in 1966. The act requires that a label offer adequate information concerning the package contents and that a package design facilitate value comparisons among competing products.

The Nutrition Labeling and Education Act of 1990 imposes a uniform format in which food manufacturers must disclose nutritional information about their products. In addition, the Food and Drug Administration (FDA) has mandated design standards for nutritional labels that provide clear guidelines to consumers about food products. The FDA has also tightened definitions for loosely used terms, such as *light, fat free, lean,* and *extra lean,* and it mandates that labels list the amounts of fat, sodium, dietary fiber, calcium, vitamins, and other components in typical servings. The latest ruling requires food manufacturers to include on nutritional labels the total amount of trans fats—hydrogenated oils that improve texture and freshness but contribute to high levels of cholesterol—in each product.

The Food Allergen Labeling and Consumer Protection Act requires that food labeling disclose all major food allergens in terms the average consumer can understand. According to the Food and Drug Administration, eight allergens account for most documented allergic reactions to food, and all must be identified. They are milk, eggs, peanuts, tree nuts (such as almonds, cashews, and walnuts), fish (like bass, cod, and flounder), shellfish (such as crab, lobster, and shrimp), soy, and wheat.[20]

Labeling requirements differ elsewhere in the world. In Canada, for example, labels must provide information in both English and French. The type and amount of information required on labels also vary among nations. International marketers must carefully design labels to conform to the regulations of each country in which they market their merchandise.

The universal product code (UPC) designation is another important aspect of a label or package. Introduced in 1974 as a method for cutting expenses in the supermarket industry, UPCs are numerical bar codes printed on packages. Optical scanner systems read these codes, and computer systems recognize items and print their prices on cash register receipts. Although UPC scanners are costly, they permit both considerable labor savings over manual pricing and improved inventory control. The universal product code is also a major asset for marketing research. However, many consumers feel frustrated when only a UPC is placed on a package without an additional price tag, because they do not always know how much an item costs if the price labels are missing from the shelf.

Radio-frequency identification (RFID) tags—electronic chips that carry encoded product identification—may replace some of the functions of UPC codes, such as price identification and inventory tracking. But consumer privacy concerns about the amount of information RFID tracking can accumulate may limit their use to aggregate packaging, such as pallets, rather than units sized for individual sale. When the FDA decided to require drug makers and marketers to place a scannable code on all drugs sold to U.S. hospitals at the level of patient unit doses, it chose UPC codes.

label Branding component that carries an item's brand name or symbol, the name and address of the manufacturer or distributor, information about the product, and recommended uses.

universal product code (UPC) Numerical bar code system used to record product and price information.

BRAND EXTENSIONS

brand extension
Strategy of attaching a popular brand name to a new product in an unrelated product category.

line extension
Development of individual offerings that appeal to different market segments while remaining closely related to the existing product line.

Some brands become so popular that marketers may decide to use them on unrelated products in pursuit of instant recognition for the new offerings. The strategy of attaching a popular brand name to a new product in an unrelated product category is known as **brand extension**. This practice should not be confused with **line extensions**, which refers to new sizes, styles, or related products. A brand extension, in contrast, carries over from one product nothing but the brand name. In establishing brand extensions, marketers hope to gain access to new customers and markets by building on the equity already established in their existing brands. This is the strategy behind Nautica's brand extension from fashion to furniture and bedding. Nintendo extended its participative Wii videogame line with Wii Fit Plus, an expansion on its popular Wii Fit fitness software.[21]

Targeting girls from preschool through the tween years, American Girl "celebrates girls and all they can be." Founded in 1986, American Girl introduced a set of historical characters—fictional 9-year-old heroines whose stories are set in America's past—and featured them in high-quality books, as 18-inch dolls, and in clothes, toys, and more. American Girl further extended its brand with the My American Girl line, dolls whose appearance can be customized with different hair and eye color and skin tone, plus such other features as braces, glasses, and earrings.

But the American Girl brand extends far beyond the dolls themselves. Girls can play on Innerstar University, American Girl's safe, online site offering games, activities, and networking. The firm publishes *American Girl* magazine, which encourages girls' creativity and affirms their self-esteem. American Girl retail stores in selected U.S. cities offer shopping, dining, party packages, special events like crafts workshops and cooking classes, and even salons where girls can have their dolls' hair cut and styled.[22]

BRAND LICENSING

brand licensing
Practice that expands a firm's exposure in the marketplace.

A growing number of firms authorize other companies to use their brand names. Even colleges license their logos and trademarks. Known as **brand licensing**, this practice expands a firm's exposure in the marketplace, much as a brand extension does. The brand name's owner also receives an extra source of income in the form of royalties from licensees, typically 8 to 12 percent of wholesale revenues.[23]

American Girl recently celebrated its 25th year in business. The company has extended its brand with the My American Girl line, dolls whose appearance can be customized with different hair, eye color, and skin tones, and with custom birthday celebrations at selected stores, complete with a signature American Girl cake.

Brand experts note several potential problems with licensing, however. Brand names do not transfer well to all products. The PetSmart PetsHotel was a winner, as was *American Idol* camp, but recent losers were Precious Moments coffins, Donald Trump steaks, and Girls Gone Wild apparel. If a licensee produces a poor-quality product or an item ethically incompatible with the original brand, the arrangement could damage the reputation of the brand. Consider the failure of two odd brand extensions: Burger King perfume and Colgate Kitchen Entrees.[24]

Harley Davidson has been selling motorcycles for over 100 years, basing its marketing campaigns on the association of its bikes with masculinity and the open road. Although some fans have gone so far as to get tattooed with the Harley Davidson name and logo, most are content with buying branded T-shirts, ornaments, and socks. Thinking that introducing more branded products would bring more sales, the company launched Harley Davidson after-shave, perfume, and even wine coolers. But those brand extensions were too much for even the most devoted fans.[25]

ASSESSMENT CHECK

5.1 Distinguish between a brand name and a trademark.

5.2 What are the three purposes of packaging?

5.3 Describe brand extension and brand licensing.

NEW-PRODUCT PLANNING

As its offerings enter the maturity and decline stages of the product lifecycle, a firm must add new items to continue to prosper. Regular additions of new products to the firm's line help protect it from product obsolescence.

New products are the lifeblood of any business, and survival depends on a steady flow of new entries. Some new products may implement major technological breakthroughs. Other new products simply extend existing product lines. In other words, a new product is one that either the company or the customer has not handled before.

Identify and briefly describe each of the new-product development strategies. **6**

PRODUCT DEVELOPMENT STRATEGIES

A firm's strategy for new-product development varies according to its existing product mix and the match between current offerings and the firm's overall marketing objectives. The current market positions of products also affect product development strategy. Figure 13.1 identifies four alternative development strategies as market penetration, market development, product development, and product diversification.

A **market penetration strategy** seeks to increase sales of existing products in existing markets. Firms can attempt to extend their penetration of markets in several ways. They may modify products, improve product quality, or promote new and different ways to use products. Packaged-goods marketers often pursue this strategy to boost market share for mature products in mature markets. Product positioning often plays a major role in such a strategy.

Product positioning refers to consumers' perceptions of a product's attributes, uses, quality, and advantages and disadvantages relative to competing brands. Marketers often conduct marketing research studies to analyze consumer preferences and to construct product positioning maps that plot their products' positions in relation to those of competitors' offerings.

Hyundai Motors has repositioned its Hyundai brand in the United States. Although the Hyundai entered the U.S. market as an inexpensive alternative to other cars, the company has ratcheted up the look and feel of its sedans to emphasize quality and safety as well as eco-friendliness. To attract buyers, Hyundai was one of the first brands to offer a 10-year, 100,000-mile warranty. Hyundai leads the industry in fuel economy and has frequently ranked first in customer loyalty.[26]

market penetration strategy Strategy that seeks to increase sales of existing products in existing markets.

product positioning Consumers' perceptions of a product's attributes, uses, quality, and advantages and disadvantages relative to competing brands.

	Old Product	**New Product**
Old Market	Market Penetration	Product Development
New Market	Market Development	Product Diversification

© Cengage Learning

FIGURE 13.1
Alternative Product Development Strategies

In addition to the original Calvin Klein scent for men, customers can choose flanker brands like Eternity and Obsession, both in men's and women's fragrances. Flanker brands are common in the fragrance industry.

market development strategy Strategy that concentrates on finding new markets for existing products.

product development Introduction of new products into identifiable or established markets.

ETERNITY
Calvin Klein
what begins here never ends

calvinkleinfragrances.com

Courtesy of The Advertising Archives

A **market development strategy** concentrates on finding new markets for existing products. Market segmentation, discussed in Chapter 9, provides useful support for such an effort. New Jersey–based supermarket chain Asian Food Markets once targeted chiefly Asian shoppers from China, Taiwan, Korea, and Japan to the Philippines, Southeast Asia, and India. Today, however, the family-owned enterprise has expanded its reach beyond Asian customers by offering a wide selection of fresh produce, meat and poultry, and fresh baked goods as well as Chinese-inspired dishes for takeout.[27]

The strategy of **product development** refers to the introduction of new products into identifiable or established markets. Responding to moviegoers' recently revived interest in the 3D format, Panasonic introduced the world's first 3D home entertainment system. The system includes a pair of special 3D eyewear as well as a Blu-ray player for watching movies at home in 3D format. Other manufacturers soon followed suit. However, the 3D glasses are expensive and dedicated—for example, Panasonic glasses won't work with a Samsung 3D system. Currently, the major 3D TV manufacturers are working to make the glasses compatible across systems.[28]

Firms may also choose to introduce new products into markets in which they have already established positions to try to increase overall market share. These new offerings are called *flanker brands*. The fragrance industry uses this strategy extensively when it develops scents related to their most popular products. The flanker scents are related in both their smell and their names. Calvin Klein has built a family of flanker brands around its original Calvin fragrance for men. The flanker brands include Eternity, Obsession, CK One, and Euphoria, all in men's and women's scents; and Beauty for women and CK Free for men. Recently, the company introduced "summer" versions of CK One and Eternity.[29]

product diversification strategy Developing entirely new products for new markets.

cannibalization Loss of sales of an existing product due to competition from a new product in the same line.

Finally, a **product diversification strategy** focuses on developing entirely new products for new markets. Some firms look for new target markets that complement their existing markets; others look in completely new directions. PepsiCo began diversifying its product lines beyond items that are "fun for you" to items that are "good for you," including juices, nuts, and oatmeal, several years ago. However, the company recently announced that, while it will continue to promote "good for you" items, it will also spend an additional $500 to $600 million on advertising and marketing of Pepsi's traditionally more profitable soft drinks and snacks, with a renewed emphasis on new-product development.[30]

In selecting a new-product strategy, marketers should keep in mind an additional potential problem: **cannibalization**. Any firm wants to avoid investing resources in a new-product introduction that will adversely affect sales of existing products. A product that takes sales from another offering in the same product line is said to cannibalize

⊕ **ASSESSMENT CHECK**

6.1   Distinguish between market penetration and market development strategies.

6.2   What is product development?

6.3   What is product diversification?

that line. A company can accept some loss of sales from existing products if the new offering will generate sufficient additional sales to warrant the investment in its development and market introduction.

THE CONSUMER ADOPTION PROCESS

In the **adoption process**, consumers go through a series of stages from first learning about the new product to trying it and deciding whether to purchase it regularly or reject it. These stages in the consumer adoption process can be classified as follows:

1. *Awareness.* Individuals first learn of the new product, but they lack full information about it.

2. *Interest.* Potential buyers begin to seek information about it.

3. *Evaluation.* They consider the likely benefits of the product.

4. *Trial.* They make trial purchases to determine its usefulness.

5. *Adoption/Rejection.* If the trial purchase produces satisfactory results, they decide to use the product regularly.

Marketers must understand the adoption process to move potential consumers to the adoption stage. Once marketers recognize a large number of consumers at the interest stage, they can take steps to stimulate sales by moving these buyers through the evaluation and trial stages. Burt's Bees, which offers natural skin-care, beauty, and personal-care products, recently introduced güd (pronounced "good"), a new line of natural products. Appealing to a younger generation, the products have names like Orange Petalooza, Pearanormal Activity, and Vanilla Flame. The company distributed 2.6 million scratch-and-sniff cards that direct you to a video on the company's Facebook page. As the video plays, it prompts you to scratch different parts of the card to sample different scents ranging from Burt's new Orange Petalooza Body Lotion to diesel fumes, cotton candy, a subway, flowers, and strawberries. The cards are also being distributed at selected college campuses. In-store promotions, print ads featuring the sniff card, and a $1 coupon for a güd purchase are among the other segments

Describe the consumer adoption process.

7

adoption process
Stages consumers go through in learning about a new product, trying it, and deciding whether to purchase it again.

Burt's Bees launched an all-out marketing campaign via various channels to introduce its new natural product line called güd.

© Güd, 2012

of the campaign, which also has a QR code on the back of the scratch-and-sniff card, a Twitter page, and its own website.[31]

ADOPTER CATEGORIES

consumer innovator
Someone who purchases a new product almost as soon as the product reaches the market.

First buyers of new products, the consumer innovators, are people who purchase new products almost as soon as these products reach the market. Later adopters wait for additional information and rely on the experiences of initial buyers before making trial purchases. Consumer innovators welcome innovations in each product area. Some computer users, for instance, rush to install new software immediately after each update becomes available.

A number of studies about the adoption of new products have identified five categories of purchasers based on relative times of adoption. These categories, shown in Figure 13.2, are consumer innovators, early adopters, early majority, late majority, and laggards.

diffusion process
Process by which new goods or services are accepted in the marketplace.

While the adoption process focuses on individuals and the steps they go through in making the ultimate decision of whether to become repeat purchasers of the new product or reject it as a failure to satisfy their needs, the diffusion process focuses on all members of a community or social system. The focus here is on the speed at which an innovative product is accepted or rejected by all members of the community.

Figure 13.2 shows the diffusion process as following a normal distribution from a small group of early purchasers *(innovators)* to the final group of consumers *(laggards)* to make trial purchases of the new product. A few people adopt at first, and then the number of adopters increases rapidly as the value of the product becomes apparent. The adoption rate finally diminishes as the number of potential consumers who have not adopted, or purchased, the product diminishes. Typically, innovators make up the first 2.5 percent of buyers who adopt the new product; laggards are the last 16 percent to do so. Figure 13.2 excludes those who never adopt the product.

IDENTIFYING EARLY ADOPTERS

It's no surprise that identifying consumers or organizations most likely to try a new product can be vital to a product's success. By reaching these buyers early in the product's development or introduction, marketers can treat these adopters as a test market, evaluating the product and discovering suggestions for modifications. Because early purchasers often act as opinion leaders from whom others seek advice, their attitudes toward new products quickly spread to others. Acceptance or rejection of the innovation by these purchasers can help forecast its expected success. New-car models are multiplying, for instance, and many are sporting a dizzying variety of options like ports

FIGURE 13.2
Categories of Adopters Based on Relative Times of Adoption

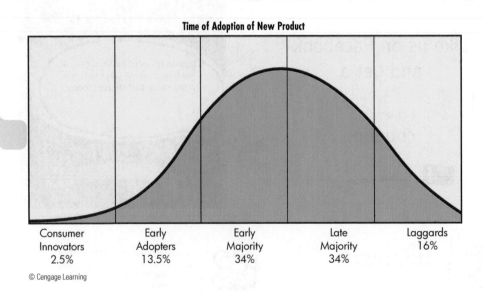

© Cengage Learning

to accommodate—and integrate—the driver's iPod, wireless phone, and laptop. Improved stability controls, collision warnings, and "smart engines" that save fuel are also available.

A large number of studies have established the general characteristics of first adopters. These pioneers tend to be younger, are better educated, and enjoy higher incomes than other consumers. They are more mobile than later adopters and change both their jobs and addresses more often. They also rely more heavily than later adopters on impersonal information sources; more hesitant buyers depend primarily on company-generated promotional information and word-of-mouth communications.

Rate of Adoption Determinants

Frisbees progressed from the product introduction stage to the market maturity stage in a period of six months. By contrast, the U.S. Department of Agriculture tried for 13 years to persuade corn farmers to use hybrid seed corn, an innovation capable of doubling crop yields. Five characteristics of a product innovation influence its adoption rate:

1. *Relative advantage.* An innovation that appears far superior to previous ideas offers a greater relative advantage—reflected in terms of lower price, physical improvements, or ease of use—and increases the product's adoption rate.

2. *Compatibility.* An innovation consistent with the values and experiences of potential adopters attracts new buyers at a relatively rapid rate. Consumers already comfortable with the miniaturization of communications technology may be attracted to smartphones, for instance, and the iPhone's 2- by 3-inch screen.

3. *Complexity.* The relative difficulty of understanding the innovation influences the speed of acceptance. In most cases, consumers move slowly in adopting new products they find difficult to understand or use. Farmers' cautious acceptance of hybrid seed corn illustrates how long an adoption can take.

4. *Possibility of trial use.* An initial free or discounted trial of a good or service means adopters can reduce their risk of financial loss when they try the product. A coupon for a free item or a free night's stay at a hotel can accelerate the rate of adoption.

5. *Observability.* If potential buyers can observe an innovation's superiority in a tangible form, the adoption rate increases. In-store demonstrations or even advertisements that focus on the superiority of a product can encourage buyers to adopt a product.

Marketers who want to accelerate the rate of adoption can manipulate these five characteristics at least to some extent. An informative promotional message about a new allergy drug could help consumers overcome their hesitation in adopting this complex product. Effective product design can emphasize an item's advantages over the competition. Everyone likes to receive something for free, so giving away small samples of a new product lets consumers try it at little or no risk. In-home demonstrations or trial home placements of items, such as furniture or rugs, can achieve similar results. Marketers must also make positive attempts to ensure the innovation's compatibility with adopters' value systems.

ORGANIZING FOR NEW-PRODUCT DEVELOPMENT

A firm needs to be organized in such a way that its personnel can stimulate and coordinate new-product development. Some companies contract with independent design firms to develop new products. Many assign product-innovation functions to one or more of the following entities: new-product committees, new-product departments, product managers, and venture teams.

New-Product Committees

The most common organizational arrangement for activities in developing a new product is to center these functions in a new-product committee. This group typically brings together experts in such areas as marketing, finance, manufacturing, engineering, and research. Committee members spend less time conceiving and developing their own new-product ideas than reviewing and approving new-product plans that arise elsewhere in the organization. The committee might review ideas from the engineering and design staff or perhaps from marketers and salespeople who are in constant contact with customers.

Because members of a new-product committee hold important jobs in the firm's functional areas, their support for any new-product plan likely foreshadows approval for further development. However, new-product committees in large companies tend to reach decisions slowly and maintain conservative views. Sometimes members compromise so they can return to their regular responsibilities.

New-Product Departments

Many companies establish separate, formally organized departments to generate and refine new-product ideas. The departmental structure overcomes the limitations of the new-product committee system and encourages innovation as a permanent full-time activity. The new-product department is responsible for all phases of a development project within the firm, including screening decisions, developing product specifications, and coordinating product testing. The head of the department wields substantial authority and typically reports to the chief executive officer, chief operating officer, or a top marketing executive.

Product Managers

product manager
Marketer responsible for an individual product or product line; also called a brand manager.

A **product manager** is another term for a brand manager, a function mentioned earlier in the chapter. This marketer supports the marketing strategies of an individual product or product line. Procter & Gamble, for instance, assigned its first product manager in 1927, when it made one person responsible for Camay soap.

Product managers set prices, develop advertising and sales promotion programs, and work with sales representatives in the field. In a company that markets multiple products, product managers fulfill key functions in the marketing department. They provide individual attention for each product and support and coordinate efforts of the firm's sales force, marketing research department, and advertising department. Product managers often lead new-product development programs, including creation of new-product ideas and recommendations for improving existing products.

However, most consumer-goods companies, such as Procter & Gamble and General Mills, have either modified the product manager structure or done away with it altogether in favor of a category management structure. Category managers have profit and loss responsibility, which is not characteristic of the product management system. This change has largely come about because of customer preference, but it can also benefit a manufacturer by avoiding duplication of some jobs and competition among the company's own brands and its managers.

Venture Teams

venture team Group of associates from different areas of an organization who work together in developing new products.

A **venture team** gathers a group of specialists from different areas of an organization to work together in developing new products. The venture team must meet criteria for return on investment, uniqueness of product, serving a well-defined need, compatibility of the product with existing technology, and strength of patent protection. Although the organization sets up the venture team as a temporary entity, its flexible life span may extend over a number of years. When purchases confirm the commercial potential of a new product, an existing division may take responsibility for that product, or it may serve as the nucleus of a new business unit or of an entirely new company. Some marketing organizations differentiate between venture teams and task forces. A new-product task force assembles an interdisciplinary group working on temporary assignment through their functional departments. Its basic activities center on coordinating and integrating the work of the firm's functional departments on a specific project. Check out the "Career Readiness" feature for some tips about working successfully in a group or team.

CAREER READINESS

How to Be a Team Player

Work groups and teams are more popular than ever. How can you turn your team assignment into a success for you and for your teammates?

- Cover the basics. That means being on time and prepared for meetings (virtual or face-to-face), completing your assigned tasks, communicating, and contributing actively to discussions.

- Help others in the group. Volunteer your assistance; perhaps you can help a team member catch up on his or her assignment or lend an extra effort to achieving a group goal.

- Be respectful of others. Listen to others' opinions with an open mind, accommodate their differences, and avoid criticizing.

- Play an active social role as appropriate for your organization. Go to lunch with team members or join company

extracurricular activities. You'll get to know team members in a different setting and might even make new connections across the organization that can help you and the team.

- Promote a positive team atmosphere. Some conflict is unavoidable, but don't be the source or the cause of it. Keep a positive attitude and avoid complainers and troublemakers.

- Be the person who gets things done. Your efforts won't go unnoticed.

Sources: "Tips to Succeeding as a Team Player," *Bayt International*, accessed November 29, 2012, www.bayt.com; "How to Be a Successful Team Player at Work," *eHow*, accessed November 29, 2012, www.ehow.com; "How to be a Team Player," *Doostang News*, accessed November 29, 2012, http://blog.doostang.com; Marty Brounstein, "Ten Qualities of an Effective Team Player," *Managing Teams for Dummies*, accessed November 29, 2012, www.dummies.com.

 ASSESSMENT CHECK

7.1 Who are consumer innovators?

7.2 What characteristics of a product innovation can influence its adoption rate?

Unlike a new-product committee, a venture team does not disband after every meeting. Team members accept project assignments as major responsibilities, and the team exercises the authority it needs to both plan and implement a course of action. To stimulate product innovation, the venture team typically communicates directly with top management but functions as an entity separate from the basic organization.

THE NEW-PRODUCT DEVELOPMENT PROCESS

Once a firm is organized for new-product development, it can establish procedures for moving new-product ideas to the marketplace. Developing a new product is often time-consuming, risky, and expensive. Usually, firms must generate dozens of new-product ideas to produce even one successful product. In fact, the failure rate of new products averages 80 percent. Products fail for a number of reasons, including inadequate market assessments, lack of market orientation, poor screening and project evaluation, product defects, and inadequate launch efforts. And these blunders cost a bundle: firms invest nearly half of the total resources devoted to product innovation on products that become commercial failures.

List the steps in the new-product development process. 8

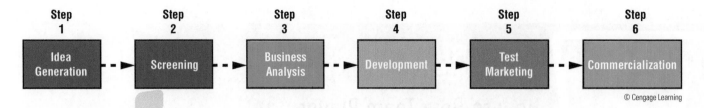

© Cengage Learning

FIGURE 13.3
Steps in the New-Product Development Process

A new product is more likely to become successful if the firm follows the six-step development process shown in Figure 13.3: (1) idea generation, (2) screening, (3) business analysis, (4) development, (5) test marketing, and (6) commercialization. Of course, each step requires decisions about whether to proceed further or abandon the project. And each step involves a greater financial investment.

Traditionally, most companies developed new products through phased development, which follows the six steps in an orderly sequence. Responsibility for each phase passes first from product planners to designers and engineers, then to manufacturers, and finally to marketers. The phased development method can work well for firms that dominate mature markets and can develop variations on existing products. But with rapid changes in technology and markets, many companies feel pressured to speed up the development process.

This time pressure has encouraged many firms to implement accelerated product development programs. These programs generally consist of teams with design, manufacturing, marketing, and sales personnel who carry out development projects from idea generation to commercialization. This method can reduce the time needed to develop products, because team members work on the six steps concurrently rather than in sequence.

Whether a firm pursues phased development or parallel product development, all phases can benefit from planning tools and scheduling methods, such as the program evaluation and review technique (PERT) and the critical path method (CPM). These techniques, originally developed by the U.S. Navy in connection with construction of the Polaris missile and submarine, map out the sequence of each step in a process and show the time allotments for each activity. Detailed PERT and CPM flowcharts help marketers coordinate all activities in the development and introduction of new products.

New-product development begins with ideas from many sources: suggestions from customers, the sales force, research and development specialists, competing products, suppliers, retailers, and independent inventors. Bose Corporation has built its brand by staying at the forefront of technology. Spending an estimated $100 million a year on research, the company leads the market for products using advanced technology: sound systems for businesses, cars, and consumer home use and the award-winning Wave radio and Wave and Acoustic wave music systems.[32] With the goal of winning 1 billion new customers over the next decade, the cosmetics and beauty company L'Oréal recently opened a global research center in Paris for the sole purpose of developing new hair-coloring, hair-care, and hair-styling products.[33] Similarly, ongoing research by scientists at lawn-care industry leader Scotts Miracle-Gro helps the company fine-tune its understanding of consumer needs as it develops products and incorporates environmentally responsible behavior throughout its operations.[34]

SCREENING

Screening separates ideas with commercial potential from those that cannot meet company objectives. Some organizations maintain checklists of development standards in determining whether a project should be abandoned or considered further. These checklists typically include factors like product uniqueness, availability of raw materials, and the proposed product's compatibility with current product offerings, existing facilities, and present capabilities. The screening stage may also allow for open discussions of new-product ideas among different parts of the organization.

BUSINESS ANALYSIS

A product idea that survives the initial screening must then pass thorough business analysis. This stage consists of assessing the new product's potential market, growth rate, and likely competitive strengths. Marketers must evaluate the compatibility of the proposed product with organizational resources.

Concept testing subjects the product idea to additional study prior to its actual development. This important aspect of a new product's business analysis represents a marketing research project that attempts to measure consumer attitudes and perceptions about the new-product idea. Focus groups and in-store polling can contribute effectively to concept testing. The Eclipse 500 Very Light Jet, a six-passenger airplane about the size of an SUV, weighs under 10,000 pounds and can fly faster and higher than other aircraft in its class. Before manufacturing the plane, Eclipse Aviation spent years testing its concept. During its research phase, the company sought input from small- and large-plane pilots as well as experts from both inside and outside the aviation industry.[35] The screening and business analysis stages generate extremely important information for new-product development because they (1) define the proposed product's target market and customers' needs and wants and (2) determine the product's financial and technical requirements. Firms willing to invest money and time during these stages tend to be more successful at generating viable ideas and creating successful products.

concept testing Method for subjecting a product idea to additional study before actual development by involving consumers through focus groups, surveys, in-store polling, and similar strategies.

DEVELOPMENT

Financial outlays increase substantially as a firm converts an idea into a visible product. The conversion process is the joint responsibility of the firm's development engineers, who turn the original concept into a product, and its marketers, who provide feedback on consumer reactions to the product design, package, color, and other physical features. Many firms implement computer-aided design and manufacturing (CAD/CAM) systems to streamline the development stage, and prototypes may go through numerous changes before the original mock-up becomes a final product. Southern California–based sports eyewear and apparel marketer Oakley uses a design approach called *sculptural physics,* which it views as the discipline of wrapping science with art. The company's ideas are born using CAD/CAM engineering and are given form as 3D prototypes. New products are evaluated and field-tested by the world's top athletes. Once finalized, they are released to the general public.

TEST MARKETING

As discussed in Chapter 10, many firms test market their new-product offerings to gauge consumer reaction. After a company develops a prototype, it may decide to test market it to measure consumer reactions under normal competitive conditions. Test marketing's purpose is to verify that the product will perform well in a real-life environment. If the product does well, the company can proceed to commercialization. If it flops, the company can fine-tune certain features and reintroduce it or pull the plug on the project altogether. Industries that rely heavily on test marketing are snack foods, automobiles, and movies. Of course, even if a product tests well and reaches the commercialization stage, it may still take a while to catch on with the general public.

COMMERCIALIZATION

When a new-product idea reaches the commercialization stage, it is ready for full-scale marketing. Commercialization of a major new product can expose the firm to substantial expenses. It must establish marketing strategies, fund outlays for production facilities, and acquaint the sales force, marketing intermediaries, and potential customers with the new product.

 ASSESSMENT CHECK

8.1 Where do ideas for new products come from?

8.2 What is concept testing?

8.3 What happens in the commercialization stage?

PRODUCT SAFETY AND LIABILITY

> **9** Explain the relationship between product safety and product liability.

> **product liability**
> Responsibility of manufacturers and marketers for injuries and damages caused by their products.

A product can fulfill its mission of satisfying consumer needs only if it ensures safe operation. Manufacturers must design their products to protect users from harm. Products that lead to injuries, either directly or indirectly, can have disastrous consequences for their makers. **Product liability** refers to the responsibility of manufacturers and marketers for injuries and damages caused by their products. Chapter 3 discussed some of the major consumer protection laws that affect product safety. These laws include the Flammable Fabrics Act of 1953, the Fair Packaging and Labeling Act of 1966, the Poison Prevention Packaging Act of 1970, and the Consumer Product Safety Act of 1972.

Federal and state legislation play a major role in regulating product safety. The Poison Prevention Packaging Act requires drug manufacturers to place their products in packaging that is child resistant yet accessible to all adults, even ones who have difficulty opening containers. The Consumer Product Safety Act created a powerful regulatory agency—the Consumer Product Safety Commission (CPSC). This agency has assumed jurisdiction over every consumer product category except food, automobiles, and a few other products already regulated by other agencies. The CPSC has the authority to ban products without court hearings, order recalls or redesigns of products, and inspect production facilities. It can charge managers of negligent companies with criminal offenses. The CPSC is especially watchful of products aimed at infants and young children.

The federal Food and Drug Administration must approve food, medications, and health-related devices like wheelchairs. The Food Allergen Labeling and Consumer Protection Act mentioned earlier increased the requirements for food labeling. The FDA can also take products off the market if concerns arise about the safety of these products.

The number of product liability lawsuits filed against manufacturers skyrocketed in recent years. Marketers' exposure to potential liability and litigation is also on the rise in many overseas markets. Many of these claims reach settlements out of court. The shoe company Skechers recently agreed to pay out $40 million to customers who sustained serious injury while wearing its Shape-Up shoes, Resistance Runners, Tone-ups, or Toners.[36]

The threat of lawsuit has led most companies to step up efforts to ensure product safety. Safety warnings appear prominently on the labels of such potentially hazardous products as cleaning fluids and drain cleaners to inform users of the dangers of these products, particularly to children. Changes in product design have reduced the hazards posed by such products as lawn mowers, hedge trimmers,

Volvo built a reputation for engineering safety features into its autos. Geely Holding Group, a private Chinese firm, bought the Sweden-based automaker and recently announced plans to build a Swedish-Chinese road safety research center near Beijing.

and toys. Product liability insurance has become an essential element for any new or existing product strategy. Premiums for this insurance have risen alarmingly, however, and insurers have almost entirely abandoned some kinds of coverage.

Regulatory activities and the increased number of liability claims have prompted companies to sponsor voluntary improvements in safety standards. Many companies, including Walmart and Mattel, have worked with the Consumer Product Safety Commission to improve their safety protocols. Walmart uses its Retailer Reporting Model to provide CPSC with detailed weekly reports about customer product safety complaints and concerns. Safety planning is now a vital element of product strategy, and many companies now publicize the safety planning and testing that go into the development of their products. Volvo, for example, is well known for the safety features it designs into its automobiles, and consumers recognize that fact when they decide to purchase a Volvo.

Due in part to companies' voluntary policing efforts, the tide may be turning on some liability lawsuits. In a huge decision for the medical device industry, the U.S. Supreme Court ruled that patients injured by medical devices could not sue the manufacturer. However, in another recent ruling, the Court said pharmaceutical companies could be sued in state court over their product's alleged defects, even if the Food and Drug Administration had approved use of the medication.[37]

ASSESSMENT CHECK

9.1 What is the role of the Consumer Product Safety Commission (CPSC)?

9.2 What safety issues come under the jurisdiction of the Food and Drug Administration (FDA)?

STRATEGIC IMPLICATIONS OF MARKETING IN THE 21ST CENTURY

Marketers who want to see their products reach the marketplace successfully have a number of options for developing them, branding them, and developing a strong brand identity among consumers and business customers. The key is to integrate all of the options so they are compatible with a firm's overall business and marketing strategy and, ultimately, the firm's mission. As marketers consider ideas for new products, they need to be careful not to send their companies in so many different directions as to

dilute the identities of their brands, making it nearly impossible to keep track of what their companies do well. Category management can help companies develop a consistent product mix with strong branding, while at the same time meeting the needs of customers. Looking for ways to extend a brand without diluting it or compromising brand equity is also an important marketing strategy. Finally, marketers must continue to work to produce high-quality products that are safe for all users.

Get online now for additional learning tools to help you master your marketing knowledge—visit **WWW.CENGAGEBRAIN.COM** today!

REVIEW OF CHAPTER OBJECTIVES

1 Determine how to define a brand.

Marketers recognize the powerful influence products and product lines have on customer behavior, and they work to create strong identities for their products and protect them. Branding is the process of creating that identity. A brand is a name, term, sign, symbol, design, or some combination that identifies the products of one firm while differentiating these products from competitors' offerings.

2 Identify the different types of brands.

A generic product is an item characterized by a plain label, no advertising, and no brand name. A manufacturer's brand is a brand name owned by a manufacturer or other producer. Private brands are brand names placed on products marketed by a wholesaler or retailer. A family brand is a brand name that identifies several related products. An individual brand is a unique brand name that identifies a specific offering within a firm's product line to avoid grouping it under a family brand.

3 Explain the strategic value of brand equity.

Brand equity provides a competitive advantage for a firm, because consumers are more likely to buy a product that carries a respected, well-known brand name. Brand equity also eases the path for global expansion.

4 Explain the benefits of category and brand management.

Category management is beneficial to a business because it gives direct responsibility for creating profitable product lines to category managers and their product group. Consumers respond to branding by making repeat purchases of favored goods and services. Therefore, good management of brands and categories of brands or product lines can result in a direct response from consumers, increasing profits and revenues for companies and creating consumer satisfaction. Brand and category managers can also enhance relationships with business customers such as retailers.

5 Discuss how companies develop a strong identity for their product or brand.

Effective brands communicate to a buyer an idea of the product's image. Trademarks, brand names, slogans, and brand icons create associations that satisfy the customer's expectation of the benefits that using or having those products will yield.

6 Identify and briefly describe each of the new-product development strategies.

The success of a new product can result from four product development strategies: (1) market penetration, in which a company seeks to increase sales of an existing product in an existing market; (2) market development, which concentrates on finding new markets for existing products; (3) product development, the introduction of new products into identifiable or established markets; and (4) product diversification, which focuses on developing entirely new products for new markets.

7 Describe the consumer adoption process.

In the adoption process, consumers go through a series of stages, from learning about the new product to trying it and deciding whether to purchase it again. The stages are called awareness, interest, evaluation, trial, and adoption/rejection.

8 List the stages in the new-product development process.

The stages in the six-step new-product development process are (1) idea generation, (2) screening, (3) business analysis, (4) development, (5) test marketing, and (6) commercialization. These steps can be performed sequentially or, in some cases, concurrently.

9 Explain the relationship between product safety and product liability.

Product safety refers to a manufacturer's goal of creating products that can be used safely and will protect consumers from harm. Product liability is the responsibility of marketers and manufacturers for injuries and damages caused by their products. Major consumer protection laws are in place to protect consumers from faulty products.

ASSESSMENT CHECK: ANSWERS

1.1 What is a brand? A brand is a name, term, sign, symbol, design, or some combination that identifies the products of one firm while differentiating these products from competitors' offerings.

1.2 Differentiate among brand recognition, brand preference, and brand insistence. Brand recognition is a company's first objective for newly introduced products and aims to make these items familiar to the public. Brand preference is buyers' reliance on previous experiences with the product when choosing it over competitors' products. Brand insistence leads consumers to refuse alternatives and to search extensively for the desired merchandise.

2.1 Identify the different types of brands. The different types of brands are manufacturer's (or national) brands, private brands, captive brands, family brands, and individual brands.

2.2 How are generic products different from branded products? Generic products are characterized by plain labels, little or no advertising, and no brand names.

3.1 What is brand equity? Brand equity refers to the added value a certain brand name gives to a product in the marketplace.

3.2 What are the four dimensions of brand personality? The four dimensions of brand personality are differentiation, relevance, esteem, and knowledge.

4.1 Define *brand manager*. A brand manager is the person at a company with the task of managing a brand's marketing strategies.

4.2 How does category management help retailers? Category management helps retailers by providing a person—a category manager—who oversees an entire product line and maximizes sales for that retailer. Category management teams the consumer goods producer's marketing expertise with the retailer's in-store merchandising efforts to track and identify new opportunities for growth.

5.1 Distinguish between a brand name and a trademark. A brand name is the part of the brand consisting of letters, numbers, or words that can be spoken and that forms a name distinguishing a firm's offerings from those of its competitors. A trademark is a brand for which the owner claims exclusive legal protection.

5.2 What are the three purposes of packaging? A package serves three major objectives: (1) protection against damage, spoilage, and pilferage; (2) assistance in marketing the product; and (3) cost effectiveness.

5.3 Describe brand extension and brand licensing. Brand extension is the strategy of attaching a popular brand name to a new product in an unrelated product category. Brand licensing is the strategy of authorizing other companies to use a brand name.

6.1 Distinguish between market penetration and market development strategies. In a market penetration strategy, a company seeks to increase sales of an existing product in an existing market. In a market development strategy, the company concentrates on finding new markets for existing products.

6.2 What is product development? Product development is the introduction of new products into identifiable or established markets.

6.3 What is product diversification? A product diversification strategy focuses on developing entirely new products for new markets.

7.1 Who are consumer innovators? Consumer innovators are the first buyers of new products—people who purchase new products almost as soon as these products reach the market.

7.2 What characteristics of a product innovation can influence its adoption rate? Five characteristics of a product innovation influence its adoption rate: relative advantage, compatibility, complexity, possibility of trial use, and observability.

8.1 Where do ideas for new products come from? New-product development begins with ideas from many sources: suggestions from customers; the sales force, or research and development specialists; suppliers, retailers, and independent inventors; and assessments of competing products.

8.2 What is concept testing? Concept testing subjects a product idea to additional study prior to its actual development.

8.3 What happens in the commercialization stage? When a new-product idea reaches the commercialization stage, it is ready for full-scale marketing.

9.1 What is the role of the Consumer Product Safety Commission (CPSC)? The Consumer Product Safety Commission is a powerful regulatory agency with jurisdiction over every consumer product category except food, automobiles, and a few other products already regulated by other agencies.

9.2 What safety issues come under the jurisdiction of the Food and Drug Administration (FDA)? The Food and Drug Administration must approve food, medications, and health-related devices like wheelchairs.

MARKETING TERMS YOU NEED TO KNOW

brand **416**

brand recognition **417**

brand preference **418**

brand insistence **418**

generic products **418**

manufacturer's brand **419**

private brand **419**

captive brand **419**

family brand **419**

individual brand **419**

brand equity **420**

brand manager **421**

category management **421**

brand name **422**

brand mark **422**

trademark **423**

trade dress **424**

label **427**

universal product code (UPC) **427**

brand extension **428**

line extension **428**

brand licensing **428**

market penetration strategy **429**

product positioning **429**

market development strategy **430**

product development **430**

product diversification strategy **430**

cannibalization **430**

adoption process **431**

consumer innovator **432**

diffusion process **432**

product manager **434**

venture team **434**

concept testing **437**

product liability **438**

ASSURANCE OF LEARNING REVIEW

1. What are the three stages marketers use to measure brand loyalty?

2. Identify and briefly describe the different types of brands.

3. Why is brand equity so important to companies?

4. What are the characteristics of an effective brand name?

5. What role does packaging play in helping create brand loyalty and brand equity?

6. What is category management, and what role does it play in the success of a product line?

7. Describe the different product development strategies.

8. What are the five stages of the consumer adoption process?

9. Describe the different ways companies can organize to develop new products.

10. List the six steps in the new-product development process.

PROJECTS AND TEAMWORK EXERCISES

1. Locate an advertisement for a product that illustrates an especially effective brand name, brand mark, packaging, and overall trade dress. Explain to the class why you think this product has a strong brand identity.

2. With a classmate, search a grocery store for a product you think could benefit from updated or new package design. Then sketch out a new package design for the product, identifying and explaining your changes as well as your reasons for the changes. Bring the old package and your new package design to class to share with your classmates.

3. What category of consumer adopter best describes you? Do you follow the same adoption pattern for all products? Or are you an early adopter for some and a laggard for others? Create a graph or chart showing your own consumer adoption patterns for different products.

4. Which product labels do you read? Over the next several days, keep a brief record of the labels you check while shopping. Do you read nutritional information when buying food products? Do you check care labels on clothes before you buy them? Do you read the directions or warnings on a product you haven't used before? Make notes about what influenced your decision to read or not read the product labels. Did you think they provided enough information, too little, or too much?

5. Some brands achieve customer loyalty by retaining an air of exclusivity and privilege, even though that often comes with high price tags. Louis Vuitton, the maker of luxury leather goods, is one such firm. What kind of brand loyalty is this, and how does Vuitton achieve it?

CRITICAL-THINKING EXERCISES

1. In this chapter, you learned that American Girl has expanded its products beyond the original American Girl dolls, intended for nine-year-old girls. Why has this strategy worked for the company? Identify another well-known product that appeals to a specific age group. Do you think a similar strategy would be successful? Why or why not?

2. General Mills and several other major food makers have begun producing organic foods. But they have deliberately kept their brand names off the packaging of these new products, thinking that the kind of customer who goes out of his or her way to buy organic products is unlikely to trust multinational brands. Other companies, however, such as Heinz, PepsiCo, and Tyson

Foods, are betting that their brand names will prove to be persuasive in the $25 billion organic foods market. Which strategy do you think is more likely to be successful? Why?

3. Recently, the mayor of New York City called for a ban on super-sized sugary drinks at delis, fast-food restaurants, and sports areas in the city. The mayor believes that obesity is a national epidemic and wants his city to take the lead in doing something about the problem. While some consumer groups are behind the proposed ban, other industry groups and companies are unhappy. Do you think the ban on super-sized drinks will help in the fight against obesity?

If you were a marketing manager for a fast-food restaurant chain, how would you handle the situation if the ban gets approved?

4. Brand names contribute enormously to consumers' perception of a brand. One writer has argued that alphanumeric brand names, such as the Toyota RAV4, Jaguar's X-Type sedan, the Xbox game console, and the GTI from Volkswagen, can translate more easily overseas than "real" names like Golf, Jetta, Escalade, and Eclipse. What other advantages and disadvantages can you think of for each type of brand name? Do you think one type is preferable to the other? Why?

ETHICS EXERCISE

As mentioned in the chapter, some analysts predict bar codes may soon be replaced by a wireless technology called *radio-frequency identification (RFID)*. RFID is a system of installing tags containing tiny computer chips on, say, supermarket items. These chips automatically radio the location of the item to a computer network where inventory data are stored, letting store managers know not only where the item is at all times but also when and where it was made and its color and size. Proponents believe RFID cuts costs and simplifies inventory tracking and reordering. It may also allow marketers to respond quickly to shifts in demand, avoid under- and overstocking, and reduce spoilage by automatically removing outdated perishables from the shelves. Privacy advocates, however, think the

chips provide too much product-preference information that might be identified with individual consumers. In the meantime, Walmart requires its major suppliers to use the new technology on products stocked by the giant retailer.

1. Do you think RFID poses a threat to consumer privacy? Why or why not?

2. Do you think the technology's possible benefits to marketers outweigh the potential privacy concerns? Are there also potential benefits to consumers? If so, what are they?

3. How can marketers reassure consumers about privacy concerns if RFID comes into widespread use?

INTERNET EXERCISES

1. **Ferrari brand.** Visit the Ferrari website. Review the material and prepare a report outlining how Ferrari—a company that produces products that only a handful of consumers can afford—has been able to build such a strong, recognizable brand.

   www.ferrari.com

2. **Trademark disputes.** Search an Internet news site, such as Google News and the U.S. Patent & Trademark Office, for recent trademark dispute cases. Select two of these cases and prepare a summary of each. Does the number of trademark dispute cases appear to be growing? If so, what is one possible explanation for this increase?

   http://news.google.com

   www.uspto.gov

3. **Brand equity.** Several sources compile lists each year of the world's most valuable brands. Two are *Bloomberg Businessweek* magazine and a consulting firm called Brand Finance. Visit both websites and review the most recent lists of the world's most valuable brands. How many firms are represented on both lists? Where are these firms located? What criteria do *Businessweek* and Brand Finance use in determining brand equity? Which brands have improved their values the most over the past couple of years?

   www.businessweek.com

   www.brandfinance.com

Note: Internet Web addresses change frequently. If you don't find the exact site listed, you may need to access the organization's home page and search from there or use a search engine such as Google or Bing.

CASE 13.1
Chobani Greek Yogurt Focuses on Tradition

When a Turkish immigrant converted an old food plant in upstate New York to create a kind of yogurt unlike anything many U.S. consumers had ever tasted, little did he dream his company would receive an Entrepreneurial Success of the Year award a few years later. Chobani, the company Hamdi Ulukaya founded with five employees in 2005, has become the number-one producer of Greek yogurt in the United States and is driving a dramatically rising trend.

Greek yogurt, with its thicker, creamier texture and slightly tart taste, now accounts for 35 percent of U.S. yogurt sales, and some observers believe there is no end in sight. Chobani and other brands of Greek yogurt have more protein and less sugar than products made by most U.S. firms, and consumers—especially women and upper-income shoppers—are snapping it up as fast as producers can manufacture it. Sales have reportedly more than doubled in each of the last three years, and the market has grown to a value of about $1.5 billion a year.

Chobani and Fage, one of its competitors, both have ambitious expansion plans, including enlarging their plants, which lie about an hour apart in New York State, where they have given a strong boost to the local economy. "We're literally building as we speak to keep up with demand," said Fage's director of U.S. marketing. With a third company building a new plant in the area, too, yogurt production in New York alone is increasing 40 to 60 percent each year,

creating what a dairy industry official calls a "once every two or three generations situation" for dairy farmers and yogurt producers alike. Chobani is also spending $250 million to open the largest plant of its kind in Idaho, in part to ease distribution of its products to western states. Meanwhile, mainstream yogurt makers like Dannon are introducing Greek-style yogurt products too.

Chobani has grown to employ 1,500 people and ships almost 2 million cases of yogurt across the United States every week. With "Nothing but good" as its corporate motto, the firm still pays individual attention to each batch. "We aimed at people who never liked yogurt," Ulukaya says, explaining that these consumers had never tasted Greek yogurt before, so they couldn't be blamed for not realizing how tasty it could be.

QUESTIONS FOR CRITICAL THINKING

1. What factors account for the rising popularity of Greek yogurt?

2. Do you think the sales trend will continue upward? Why or why not?

Sources: "The World's 50 Most Innovative Companies in 2012: Chobani," *Fast Company*, accessed November 29, 2012, www.fastcompany.com; Morgan Korn, "Greek Yogurt Takes America by Storm," *Yahoo Finance*, accessed November 29, 2012, http://finance.yahoo.com; Meghan Walsh, "Chobani Takes Gold in the Yogurt Aisle," *Bloomberg Businessweek*, accessed November 29, 2012, www.businessweek.com; J.D. Harrison, "Greek Yogurt Maker Chobani Takes Home 2012 SBA Entrepreneurship Award," *The Washington Post*, accessed November 29, 2012, www.washingtonpost.com; William Neuman, "Greek Yogurt a Boon for New York State," *The New York Times*, accessed November 29, 2012, www.nytimes.com.

VIDEO CASE 13.2
At Zappos, Passion Is Paramount

From its humble beginnings as the first online shoe store, Zappos has grown to nearly gargantuan proportions. Now wholly owned by Amazon, the online retailer carries most of the top footwear and apparel brands, along with handbags and luggage, and last but not least, home furnishings and beauty products. In other words, if Zappos were a brick-and-mortar store, you could live there.

"When Zappos first started out, it was all about the best selection of products," recalls Steve Hill, vice president of merchandising. In many respects that's still true—but as the company has expanded, it has adjusted the way it manages brands as well as entire categories of goods. A decade ago, Fred Mossler (former vice president of merchandising, recently promoted to the position of "no title") went to the annual World Shoe Accessories show in Las Vegas in hopes of luring a few brands to the site. He talked with more than 100 vendors there, but only three agreed to offer their products on Zappos. Today, the company carries 1,165 brands and counting. "We carry the top brands," says Hill.

The merchandising team, which includes lead buyers, buyers, assistant buyers, and merchandising assistants, scours the earth for the best brands in any product category—then meets with vendors and decides which will sell best at Zappos. Hill observes that Zappos buyers tend to select everything from a footwear brand line but are more likely to pick and choose specific items of apparel. Zappos buyers concentrate entirely on a single category of products. "Our buyers are aligned around lifestyles—so our hiking buyer will buy only hiking products and our running buyer will buy only running products." But specialization doesn't stop there. "Our buyers buy stuff that they're passionate about," explains Hill. "For example, our running buyers are running marathons and half-marathons and 5Ks." This makes them virtual experts in the category of goods they are buying for Zappos to sell online to consumers.

Zappos prefers to hire its buyers based on their passion for a specific activity or product category. "If we can hire them for their passion for the category, we can teach them all the skills of buying," says Hill. In fact, the buyers themselves have created categories at Zappos—based on their own interests. That's how Zappos began selling outdoor apparel and footwear, as well as designer fashions. The other avenue that Zappos takes for developing categories is through customer feedback—if enough customers request a new category or specific brand, Zappos will work hard to bring it to them.

Although Zappos remains focused on manufacturers' brands with names like Nike, Billabong, Guess, Lacoste, Steve Madden, and Mountain Hardwear, the retailer also has a few couture offerings, such as the family brands 10 Crosby by Derek Lam and Adidas by Stella McCartney. Recently, the company has been testing the waters with its own private label called The Cool People in footwear and apparel. It's not a huge chunk of business—instead filling niches not covered by Zappos' branded partners. One of the most successful private-label products for Zappos is a wide-calf boot for women—so much so that branded manufacturers have begun to create their own wide-calf boots.

While Zappos is the self-proclaimed merchant of happiness, managing the growing collection of brands is serious business. This doesn't mean Zappos employees don't have fun or enjoy what they are doing—it's quite the opposite. It's just that Zappos inspires its buyers with a sense of entrepreneurship within a large company. "We want buyers to feel like they're buying for their own boutique or storefront," explains Hill. "We call it the shopkeeper's mentality. We want them to feel if they don't buy the right stuff, they won't be able to keep the lights on. We are part of a much bigger company now, but we want everyone to feel like they're running their own business and in control of what they're doing."

Hill acknowledges that, despite the huge success of online retailing over the last decade, it still represents only about 8 to 9 percent of overall retailing in the United States. However, he and other marketing experts predict that number will grow to 30 percent in the next 10 years. This means that Zappos is poised to make huge gains if it continues to offer an expanding array of brands backed by superior customer service. Hill believes that his company's mix of products and services will keep shoppers coming back. "Once they find us," he says, "they'll stick with us and be loyal to us."

QUESTIONS FOR CRITICAL THINKING

1. Describe how Zappos is building brand equity along the four dimensions of brand personality.

2. What steps might Zappos take to build its private brands without endangering its relationship with the producers of manufacturing brands?

Sources: Company website, www.zappos.com, accessed November 29, 2012; Tricia Duryee, "Zappos Founder Focuses on Brand Loyalty for His Next Gig," *All Things Digital*, accessed November 29, 2012, http://allthingsd.com; "Show or Tell?" *Brand Story Online*, accessed November 29, 2012, www.brandstoryonline.com.

NOTES

1. Zacks Equity Research, "Under Armour Beats, Guides High," *Yahoo Finance*, accessed November 29, 2012, http://finance.yahoo.com; Trey Palmisano, "From Rags to Microfiber: Inside the Rapid Rise of Under Armour," *Sports Illustrated*, accessed November 29, 2012, http://sportsillustrated.cnn.com; Lorraine Mirabella, "Under Armour Poised for Greater Growth with New Products," *Baltimore Sun*, accessed November 29, 2012, http://articles.baltimoresun.com; Fred Dreier, "Under Armour Flexing Its Muscles Overseas," *Forbes*, accessed November 29, 2012, www.forbes .com; Candus Thompson, "Under Armour Bets on Bobsled to Fuel Global Growth," *Baltimore Sun*, accessed November 29, 2012, http://articles.baltimoresun.com; Mark J. Miller, "Under Armour: Wicky Business," *Brand Channel.com*, accessed November 29, 2012, www.brandchannel.com; "Under Armour's Kevin Plank: Creating the 'Biggest, Baddest Brand on the Planet,'" *Knowledge@* Wharton, accessed November 29, 2012, http://knowledge.wharton.upenn.edu.

2. Company website, "Accenture Study Finds Store Brands Thriving as U.S. Shoppers Prove Reluctant to Return to Old Buying Habits," accessed November 29, 2012, http://newsroom.accenture.com.

3. Company website, "Here's Your Guide to Buying Green," www.officedepot.com, accessed November 29, 2012.

4. Company website, http://pressroom.target.com, accessed November 29, 2012.

5. Georgina Prodhan, "Apple Still Dominates World's Top Brands: Study," *Reuters*, accessed November 29, 2012, www.reuters.com.

6. Company website, http://bavconsulting.com, accessed November 29, 2012.

7. Category Management Association website, "What Is Category Management?" www.cpgcatnet.org, accessed November 29, 2012.

8. Ibid.

9. Company website, www.igd.com, accessed November 29, 2012.

10. Company website, "Hershey's Convenience," www.hersheys.com, accessed November 29, 2012.

11. Company website, www.amronexperimental.com, accessed November 29, 2012; Audrey Quinn, "Dissolving Fruit Stickers," *Smart Planet*, accessed November 29, 2012, www.smartplanet.com.

12. Mariam Noronha, "Why You Should Not Be Afraid to Use Humor in Branding—3 Reasons Small Business Owners Can Use," *Noobpreneur.com*, accessed November 29, 2012, www.noobpreneur.com; company website, www.harley-davidson.com, accessed November 29, 2012.

13. Matthew Swyers, "Can a Shoe Color Really Be Trademarked?" *Inc.*, accessed November 29, 2012, www.inc.com; Jonathan Stempel, "Judge Strips Naked Cowboy of Claims vs. CBS," *Reuters*, accessed November 29, 2012, www.reuters.com.

14. The Simon Law Firm, "Trademark Infringement," company website, http://simonlawpc.com, accessed November 29, 2012.

15. Nick Wingfield, "Jury Awards $1 Billion to Apple in Samsung Patent Case," *The New York Times*, accessed November 29, 2012, www.nytimes.com.

16. Brett Barrouquere, "Maker's Mark Bourbon Wins Right to Dripping Wax Seal," *USA Today*, accessed November 29, 2012, http://usatoday30.usatoday.com.

17. Heidi Parsons, "Prepared and Packed," *Brand Packaging*, accessed November 29, 2012, www.brandpackaging.com.

18. Company website, "ClearRx/Pharmacy," http://sites.target.com, accessed November 29, 2012.

19. Jim Butschli, "Kimberly-Clark Uses Packaging to Reduce Product Waste," *Packaging World*, accessed November 29, 2012, www.packworld.com.

20. "Food Allergies: Understanding Food Labels," *Mayo Clinic* website, accessed November 29, 2012, www.mayoclinic.com.

21. Company website, http://wiifit.com, accessed November 29, 2012.
22. Monica Hesse, "For 25 Years, American Girls Have Been Defining Youths' Personalities," *Washington Post*, accessed November 29, 2012, www.washingtonpost.com.
23. "Licensing Royalty Rates," *Invention Statistics*, accessed November 29, 2012, www.inventionstatistics.com.
24. Lizzy Guterma, "The Good, the Bad & the Bizarre of Brand Extensions," *Brand Salsa*, accessed November 29, 2012, www.brandsalsa.com.
25. "Extension Failures: Harley Davidson Perfume," *Brand Failures*, accessed November 29, 2012, http://brandfailures.blogspot.com.
26. "Hyundai Ranks #1 in Brand Loyalty," *Corporate Eye*, accessed November 29, 2012, http://corporate-eye.com; Karl Greenberg, "ABC: Hyundai Coalesces Its *Marketing Plan*," Marketing Daily, accessed November 29, 2012, www.mediapost.com.
27. Company website, www.asianfoodmarkets.com, accessed November 29, 2012.
28. Company website, www.panasonic.com, accessed November 29, 2012; Joshua Condon, "Major 3D TV Manufacturers Look to Adopt Technology Standard," *Inc.*, accessed November 29, 2012, http://technology.inc.com.
29. Company website, www.calvinkleinfragrances.com, accessed November 29, 2012.
30. Geoff Colvin, "Indra Nooyi's Pepsi Challenge," *Fortune*, accessed November 29, 2012, http://management.fortune.cnn.com; Geoff Colvin, "Pepsi's CEO Faces Her Biggest Challenge," *Fortune*, accessed November 29, 2012, http://management.fortune.cnn.com; Adam Werbach, "Pepsi vs. Wall St.: Why Should a Soda Company Try to Be 'Good for You'?" *The Atlantic*, accessed November 29, 2012, www.theatlantic.com.
31. Company website, www.gudhappens.com, accessed November 29, 2012; Patricia Odell, "Burt's Bees Promotes New Products with Scratch-n-Sniff-Along Video," *Chief Marketer*, accessed November 29, 2012, http://chiefmarketer.com.
32. Company website, www.bose.com, accessed November 29, 2012.
33. Trefis Team, "L'Oréal Goes Global with Hair Research Center," *Forbes*, accessed November 29, 2012, www.forbes.com.
34. Company website, www.thescottsmiraclegrocompany.com, accessed November 29, 2012.
35. Company website, www.eclipseaerospace.net, accessed November 29, 2012.
36. Rene Lynch, "Skechers Lawsuit: How to Get Your Piece of the $40-Million Payout," *Los Angeles Times*, accessed November 29, 2012, www.latimes.com.
37. "Supreme Court Allows State Product Liability Lawsuits against Defective Medical Device Manufacturers," *BreakingLawsuitNews.com*, accessed November 29, 2012, www.breakinglawsuitnews.com; Jess Bravin, "High Court Eases Way to Liability Lawsuits," *The Wall Street Journal*, accessed November 29, 2012, http://online.wsj.com.

Scripps Networks Interactive & Food Network

PART 4
Product Decisions

The Line between Content and Commerce

When you're watching a cooking show, how do you define the product? Is it the show itself, the celebrity chef, the recipes demonstrated, or the sizzling pots and pans? In this case, the product is a little bit of everything—talent, entertainment, and food. It's a combination of goods and services bundled together in a single brand: Food Network. And while the selling of the brand is important, part of its value lies in its mission to entertain and inspire. "There's a line between where a brand is inspiring and when it becomes overtly commercial," points out Sergei Kuharsky, senior vice president and general manager of licensing and merchandising at Scripps Networks Interactive, which produces and markets Food Network. "Everyone walks that line."

Food Network's product mix serves up an array of popular shows that appeal to food-loving viewers. Cooking shows like *Barefoot Contessa, Giada At Home*, and *Paula's Best Dishes* demonstrate how to whip up delicious meals in various styles. Competition shows, such as *Food Network Star, Great Food Truck Race*, and *Chopped*, entertain viewers as they watch contestants cook off for bragging rights, cash, or a television contract. Celebrity shows like *Diners, Drive-ins, and Dives* and *Restaurant: Impossible* showcase famous chefs in various scenarios as they visit favorite eateries or try to help restaurant owners save their businesses. Each of these individual shows fits into the product line and overall product mix in a certain way—but all are designed to entertain and inspire.

Inspiration about food and cooking is integral to the Food Network brand—the challenge for marketers is to take this to the next level, from the TV screen to wherever consumers are in their daily lives. Social media has emerged as a major tool for Food Network marketers to converse with viewers on a regular basis. "Social media does so much for our brand," says Kate Gold, director of social media for the company. "It's really about being able to have a dialogue with our audience. It's being able to listen to them. It's the one platform where all day, every day, we're getting feedback." Several years ago, Scripps reorganized its social media marketing to reflect consumer categories: food, home, and travel. The shows offered by Food Network and the Cooking Channel fall into the first category. This reorganization helped marketers understand more clearly how consumers were behaving with social media and what those consumers wanted from the Food Network brand.

"We saw what was in the competitive market, and people not only wanted recipes, they wanted the tools to accompany them," observes Leora Schachter, vice president of digital strategy and planning for Scripps. So the company developed various apps to meet this need—and solidify the Food Network brand in consumers' minds. For example, the "Cupcakes" app stems from the popular shows *Cupcake Wars* and *Cupcake Champions*. The app provides additional content that consumers can use and enjoy—videos, recipes, and cooking or shopping tips. "In the Kitchen" is another popular Food Network app among consumers—listed as one of the top-five paid apps in the lifestyle category at Apple.

On a broader scale, Food Network's core social media platforms are Facebook, Twitter, and Pinterest. But the network is also active on Google+, Instagram, Foursquare, Tumblr, and GetGlue. Marketers use Foursquare to support location-based shows; for example, many viewers request a list of all the restaurants visited by host Guy Fieri in *Diners, Drive-ins, and Dives*. GetGlue is based on the same concept as Twitter but allows people to check in with a TV show instead of a location. Scripps and Food Network are selective about their choice of social media. "We're very careful about the new platforms that we expand into, based on audiences that are there, the actions that people are taking, and how our brand could fit in," explains Kate Gold. For example, Facebook is the ideal platform for Food Network to hold chats with celebrity chefs, while Twitter can give quick updates behind the scenes from a TV show.

Customer feedback is one of the most important factors in category and brand management. By its very nature, social media provides plenty of feedback to Food Network about its shows, celebrities, recipes, choice of restaurants to feature—the list is endless. Marketers also receive feedback on their choices about social media. This is true of Facebook posts and tweets, as well as the reviews of shows that viewers post on GetGlue. Apps are no exception. "When you're in an app store, you get direct feedback from your audience, which is unlike any other channel we have at Food Network," says Schachter. People rate and review an app immediately after using it, which means that Food Network can update and improve the app on a regular basis. "It's expensive," notes Schachter, "but worthwhile."

QUESTIONS FOR CRITICAL THINKING

1. How would you describe Food Network's product mix in terms of width, length, and depth?

2. Where would you place Food Network in the product lifecycle? What steps could marketers take to extend its lifecycle?

3. What sets Food Network brand apart from the brands of other networks? How has social media helped Food Network enhance its brand equity?

4. How might Food Network marketers use social media to speed the adoption rate of a new television show?

PART 5

Distribution Decisions

Chapter 14

MARKETING
Channels and Supply Chain Management

1 Describe the types of marketing channels and the roles they play in marketing strategy.

2 Outline the major channel strategy decisions.

3 Describe the concepts of channel management, conflict, and cooperation.

4 Identify and describe the different vertical marketing systems.

5 Explain the roles of logistics and supply chain management in an overall distribution strategy.

6 Identify the major components of a physical distribution system.

7 Compare the major modes of transportation.

8 Discuss the role of transportation intermediaries, combined transportation modes, and warehousing in improving physical distribution.

KIVA ROBOTS ADD TO DISTRIBUTION OPTIONS If you happen to be in an Amazon.com warehouse in the near future and spy some squat, square orange objects scurrying around the stacks, you're seeing the online retailer's Kiva robots at work. You might also see them at warehouses belonging to Staples, Crate and Barrel, Gap, Zappos, and Diapers.com (the latter two owned by Amazon), as well as at other prominent retailers' fulfillment centers.

Kiva Systems, founded in Boston in 2003, was recently purchased by Amazon, which will not only continue utilizing the battery-operated robots in its own warehouses but also blend them into the fulfillment services it offers other companies. "Kiva's technology is another way to improve productivity by bringing the products directly to employees to pick and stow," says Amazon's vice president of fulfillment.

Kiva has grown tremendously since its founding, hiring more employees every quarter and recording a 130 percent increase in sales in one recent year, for total revenues of more than $100 million. The company charges its clients $1 to $2 million for a robot "start-up kit"—outfitting a customer's entire warehouse with robots can cost 10 times as much and require six months of planning, testing, and training for human logistics managers. The payoff? Big savings at the warehouse, in both time and cost.

By locating the items in an order, moving around the warehouse to retrieve them, and stacking them on its surface to ferry them to employees, a Kiva robot can help fill three to four times as many orders as a worker acting alone who must walk the warehouse to retrieve items. Speedier order fulfillment makes customers happy, of course, because orders are shipped sooner than before, but employees are happy

too. At Crate and Barrel, for instance, 50 people and 50 robots pack up 2,000 orders a day, but the humans do much less physical labor, and there are no more noisy conveyor belts. Amazon says it will not eliminate any jobs at its own facilities as a result of its $775 million purchase of the company, which will remain based in Massachusetts.

The robots rely on sophisticated software that Kiva can customize for each of its clients, while a Wi-Fi network and floor grid of two-dimensional barcodes helps them navigate the space. They can even determine when they need to go recharge themselves.[1]

EVOLUTION OF A BRAND

After graduating from college with a degree in mechanical engineering, Mick Mountz joined the online grocery retailer Webvan. There he saw firsthand the consequences of an inefficient fulfillment system. Webvan failed because the warehouse workers couldn't select, pack, and ship all the orders in a timely and cost-effective fashion. While working at another job, Mountz suddenly hit on the idea of having the products come to the human warehouse workers, rather than the other way around. Why not have a warehouse run by robots?

Mountz left his job to found Kiva Systems. He asked some former classmates to help him build a prototype and

got investors to contribute $1.6 million in seed money. Then a mutual friend introduced him to Ajay Agarwal, a managing director at a major industrial firm who, over the next five years, invested $20 million in Kiva Systems.

At first, Mountz had a hard time persuading e-tailers to try using his robots. Then Staples agreed to try a small pilot program in one of its warehouses. Now Staples alone has 1,000 robots working at two warehouses. Other clients include The Gap, Saks Fifth Avenue, and Toys"R"Us.

- Human shoppers never see Kiva Systems robots, which to date are used only in warehouses. Do you think these robots might one day be used in retail stores? Why or why not?
- Why do you think companies were initially skeptical about the Kiva Systems robots?

CHAPTER OVERVIEW

distribution Movement of goods and services from producers to customers.

marketing (distribution) channel System of marketing institutions that enhances the physical flow of goods and services, along with ownership title, from producer to consumer or business user.

logistics Process of coordinating the flow of information, goods, and services among members of the distribution channel.

supply chain management Control of the activities of purchasing, processing, and delivery through which raw materials are transformed into products and made available to final consumers.

physical distribution Broad range of activities aimed at efficient movement of finished goods from the end of the production line to the consumer.

Distribution—moving goods and services from producers to customers—is the second marketing mix variable and an important marketing concern. Firms depend on distribution systems to be able to move their goods from one destination to another. A distribution strategy has two critical components: (1) marketing channels and (2) logistics and supply chain management.

A **marketing channel**—also called a **distribution channel**—is an organized system of marketing institutions and their interrelationships that enhances the physical flow and ownership of goods and services from producer to consumer or business user. The choice of marketing channels should support the firm's overall marketing strategy. In contrast, **logistics** refers to the process of coordinating the flow of information, goods, and services among members of the marketing channel. **Supply chain management** is the control of activities of purchasing, processing, and delivery through which raw materials are transformed into products and made available to final consumers. Efficient logistical systems support customer service, enhancing customer relationships—an important goal of any marketing strategy.

A key aspect of logistics is physical distribution, which covers a broad range of activities aimed at efficient movement of finished goods from the end of the production line to the consumer. Although some marketers use the terms *transportation and physical distribution* interchangeably, these terms do not carry the same meaning. **Physical distribution** extends beyond transportation to include such important decision areas as customer service, inventory control, materials handling, protective packaging, order processing, and warehousing.

Well-planned marketing channels and effective logistics and supply chain management provide ultimate users with convenient ways for obtaining the goods and services they desire. This chapter discusses the activities, decisions, and marketing intermediaries involved in managing marketing channels and logistics. Chapter 15 looks at other players in the marketing channel: retailers, direct marketers, and wholesalers.

THE ROLE OF MARKETING CHANNELS IN MARKETING STRATEGY

> **1** Describe the types of marketing channels and the roles they play in marketing strategy.

A firm's distribution channels play a key role in its overall marketing strategy because these channels provide the means by which the firm makes the goods and services available to ultimate users. Channels perform four important functions. First, they facilitate the exchange process by reducing the number of marketplace contacts necessary to make a sale. Suppose you've had a Nintendo Wii handheld game player in the past and been satisfied with it, so when you see an ad for the Nintendo Wii U, you are interested. You visit the Nintendo website, where you learn more about the Wii U and its unique features. You are particularly drawn to the games *Marvel Avengers: Battle for Earth* and *NBA 2K13*. But you want to see the game console in person, so you locate a dealer near enough for you to visit.[2] The dealer forms part of the channel that brings you—a potential buyer—and Nintendo—the seller—together to complete the exchange process. It's important to keep in mind that all channel members benefit when they work together; when they begin to disagree or—worse yet—compete directly with each other, everyone loses.

Distributors adjust for discrepancies in the market's assortment of goods and services via a process known as *sorting*, the second channel function. A single producer tends to maximize the quantity it makes of a limited line of goods, while a single buyer needs a limited quantity of a wide selection of merchandise. Sorting alleviates such discrepancies by channeling products to suit both the buyer's and the producer's needs.

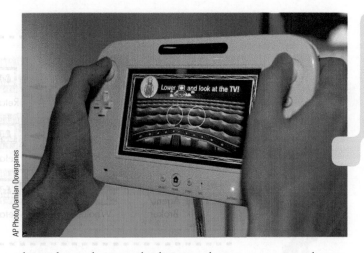

AP Photo/Damian Dovarganes

If you are interested in learning more about the Nintendo Wii U, you may want to see the game console in person by visiting a local dealer.

The third function of marketing channels involves standardizing exchange transactions by setting expectations for products, and it involves the transfer process itself. Channel members tend to standardize payment terms, delivery schedules, prices, and purchase lots, among other conditions. Standardization helps make transactions efficient and fair.

The final marketing channel function is to facilitate searches by both buyers and sellers. Buyers search for specific goods and services to fill their needs, while sellers attempt to learn what buyers want. Channels bring buyers and sellers together to complete the exchange process. Hundreds of distribution channels exist today, and no single channel best serves the needs of every company. Instead of searching for the best channel for all products, a marketing manager must analyze alternative channels in light of consumer needs to determine the most appropriate channel or channels for the firm's goods and services.

Marketers must remain flexible, because channels may change over time. Today's ideal channel may prove inappropriate in a few years, or the way a company uses that channel may have to change. Like many other companies, Procter & Gamble has used digital advertising for many years, taking advantage of digital's ability to home in on customers' needs. But finding the right combination of tactics—apps, tablets, mobile, social, and many others—is never easy. The world's largest advertiser, the company recently announced that it would shift its marketing focus even further to digital. Alex Tosolini, P&G's vice president of global e-business, says that the evolving nature of digital media prompted a change "from static marketing campaigns that we launch and adjust infrequently to real-time always-on brand building."[3]

The following sections examine the diverse types of channels available to marketers and the decisions marketers must make to develop an effective distribution strategy that supports their firm's marketing objectives.

66 BRIEFLY SPEAKING 99

"Confidence delivered"

—YRC Freight motto

TYPES OF MARKETING CHANNELS

The first step in selecting a marketing channel is determining which type of channel will best meet both the seller's objectives and the distribution needs of customers. Figure 14.1 depicts the major channels available to marketers of consumer and business goods and services.

Most channel options involve at least one marketing intermediary. A **marketing intermediary** (or **middleman**) is an organization that operates between producers and consumers or business users. Retailers and wholesalers are both marketing intermediaries. A retail store owned and operated by someone other than the manufacturer of the products it sells is one type of marketing intermediary. A **wholesaler** is an intermediary that takes title to the goods it handles and then distributes these goods to retailers, other distributors, or sometimes end consumers. Wholesalers are able to stockpile nonperishable goods, but perishables are another story. The specialty coffee market, once only 1 percent of the total, has increased to roughly 20 percent in only the last 25 years. The recent rise in the price of coffee and a worldwide increase in demand

marketing intermediary (middleman) Wholesaler or retailer that operates between producers and consumers or business users.

wholesaler Channel intermediary that takes title to the goods it handles and then distributes these goods to retailers, other distributors, or business or B2B customers.

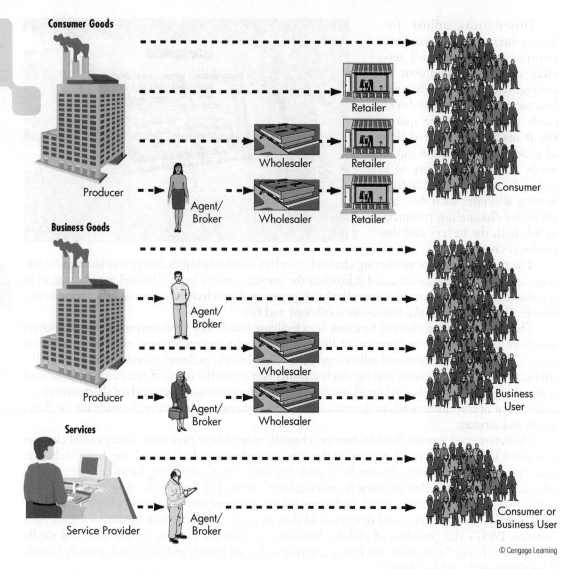

FIGURE 14.1
Alternative Marketing Channels

have made it more difficult for both wholesalers and independent specialty retailers to keep coffee affordable.[4]

A short marketing channel involves few intermediaries. By contrast, a long marketing channel involves several intermediaries working in succession to move goods from producers to consumers. Business products usually move through short channels due to geographic concentrations and comparatively fewer business purchasers. Service firms market primarily through short channels, because they sell intangible products and need to maintain personal relationships within their channels. Haircuts, manicures, and dental cleanings all operate through short channels. Not-for-profit organizations also tend to work with short, simple, and direct channels. Any marketing intermediaries in such channels usually act as agents, such as independent ticket agencies or fund-raising specialists.

Marketers must remain flexible, because channels change over time. Procter & Gamble, which once emphasized TV and print ads to sell its products, now relies more on digital media, including its recent contest "Take a Load Off" on the company's Facebook page.

DIRECT SELLING

The simplest and shortest marketing channel is a direct channel. A **direct channel** carries goods directly from a producer to the business purchaser or ultimate user. This channel forms part of **direct selling**, a marketing strategy in which a producer establishes direct sales contact with its product's final users. Direct selling is an important option for goods requiring extensive demonstrations in persuading customers to buy. The "Career Readiness" feature contains suggestions for closing a successful sale.

Direct selling plays a significant role in business-to-business marketing. Most major installations, accessory equipment, and even component parts and raw materials are sold through direct contacts between producing firms and final buyers. Many people in business enjoy successful sales careers. According to the *Occupational Outlook Handbook*, published by the U.S. Department of Labor, over 1.8 million people are employed as sales representatives in manufacturing and wholesaling industries.[5]

Direct selling is also important in consumer-goods markets. Direct sellers, such as Avon, Pampered Chef, and Tastefully Simple, sidestep competition in store aisles by developing networks of independent representatives who sell their products directly to consumers. Many of these companies practice a direct selling strategy called the *party plan*, originally popularized by Tupperware. The jewelry boutique company Stella & Dot is one such business. Launched by entrepreneur Jessica Herrin, Stella & Dot jewelry is sold at home-based parties, or "trunk shows," by independent sales representatives. The jewelry, which appeals to women of all ages, is accessible and affordable—and is often worn by TV celebrities. Stella & Dot recently approached $100 million in commissions.[6]

The Internet provides another direct selling channel for both B2B and B2C purchases. Consumers who want to sport designer handbags, but don't want to pay full price for them, can rent them from Bag Borrow or Steal, an e-commerce business. For those who like to change purses often but can't or won't pay the hundreds or thousands of dollars for Chanel's, Prada's, or Gucci's latest, Bag Borrow or Steal may be a real bargain. In addition to designer handbags, shoppers can find sunglasses and jewelry to complete their look.[7]

direct channel
Marketing channel that moves goods directly from a producer to the business purchaser or ultimate user.

direct selling Strategy designed to establish direct sales contact between producer and final user.

CAREER READINESS

How to Successfully Close a Sale

Closing a sale is often a challenge, but several steps can improve your success rate. Here are some basic strategies, and a few you might not have thought of.

- There's no substitute for preparation. Research your customer so you know what the company's needs are and what they've purchased before.

- Know the value of your product. It's not the same thing as the price.

- During the sales call, listen more than you speak. Some experienced salespeople say you should be talking only 20 percent of the time and listening the rest.

- Use your speaking time to ask about the challenges your customer faces, who all the decision makers are that you need to influence, and how you can help solve their problems.

- Assume objections are legitimate and address them as such. Your response to objections tells the prospect a lot about how you will treat him or her as a customer.

- Remain seated. Standing up, even if the prospect has done so, signals a change in the situation and can end negotiations before you're ready.

- Always carry a pen. More than one sale has been lost for want of a pen to sign it with.

- Don't forget to say thank you.

Sources: Paul Chenier, "7 Tips for Closing a Sale in One Call," *Ask Men*, accessed November 30, 2012, www.askmen.com; Barry Farber, "8 Steps to a Successful Sales Call," *Entrepreneur*, accessed November 30, 2012, www.entrepreneur.com; "12 Expert Tips for Closing That Sale," *Sold Lab*, accessed November 30, 2012, www.soldlab .com; Grant Cardone, "12 Commandments for Closing a Sale," *Entrepreneur*, accessed November 30, 2012, www.entrepreneur.com.

Direct mail can also be an important part of direct selling—or it can encourage a potential customer to contact an intermediary such as a retailer. Either way, it is a vital communication piece for many marketers.

CHANNELS USING MARKETING INTERMEDIARIES

Although direct channels allow simple and straightforward marketing, they are not practical in every case. Some products serve markets in different areas of the country or world, or have large numbers of potential end users. Other categories of goods rely heavily on repeat purchases. The producers of these goods may find more efficient, less expensive, and less time-consuming alternatives to direct channels by using marketing intermediaries. This section considers five channels that involve marketing intermediaries.

Producer to Wholesaler to Retailer to Consumer

The traditional channel for consumer goods proceeds from producer to wholesaler to retailer to user. This method carries goods between thousands of small producers with limited lines and local retailers. A firm with limited financial resources will rely on the services of a wholesaler that serves as an immediate source of funds and then markets to hundreds of retailers. On the other hand, a small retailer can draw on a wholesaler's specialized distribution skills. In addition, many manufacturers hire their own field representatives to service retail accounts with marketing information. Wholesalers may then handle the actual sales transactions.

Producer to Wholesaler to Business User

Similar characteristics in the organizational market often attract marketing intermediaries to operate between producers and business purchasers. The term *industrial distributor* commonly refers to intermediaries in the business market that take title to the goods.

Producer to Agent to Wholesaler to Retailer to Consumer

In markets served by many small companies, a unique intermediary—the agent—performs the basic function of bringing buyer and seller together. An agent may or may not take possession of the goods but never takes title. The agent merely represents a producer by seeking a market for its products or a wholesaler, which does take title to the goods, by locating a supply source.

Producer to Agent to Wholesaler to Business User

Like agents, brokers are independent intermediaries who may or may not take possession of goods but never take title to these goods. Agents and brokers also serve the business market when small producers attempt to market their offerings through large wholesalers. Such an intermediary, often called a **manufacturers' representative**, provides an independent sales force to contact wholesale buyers. A kitchen equipment manufacturer may have its own manufacturer's representatives to market its goods, for example.

manufacturers' representative Agent wholesaling intermediary that represents manufacturers of related but noncompeting products and receives a commission on each sale.

Producer to Agent to Business User

For products sold in small units, only merchant wholesalers can economically cover the markets. A merchant wholesaler is an independently owned wholesaler that takes title to the goods. By maintaining regional inventories, this wholesaler achieves transportation economies, stockpiling goods and making small shipments over short distances. For a product with large unit sales, however, and for which transportation accounts for a small percentage of the total cost, the producer-agent-business user channel is usually employed. The agent in effect becomes the producer's sales force, but bulk shipments of the product reduce the intermediary's inventory management function.

dual distribution Network that moves products to a firm's target market through more than one marketing channel.

DUAL DISTRIBUTION

Dual distribution refers to the movement of products through more than one channel to reach the firm's target market. Nordstrom, for instance, has a three-pronged distribution system, selling

Office Depot promotes eco-friendly practices by helping customers recycle their empty ink and toner cartridges and provides helpful information on their website.

through stores, catalogs, and the Internet. Marketers usually adopt a dual distribution strategy either to maximize their firm's coverage in the marketplace or to increase the cost-effectiveness of the firm's marketing effort. Nintendo and Netflix recently partnered to offer entertainment through more than one channel. Traditionally, customers order their favorite movies online and have the DVDs delivered to their mailboxes. Under the new agreement, Netflix subscribers with a $7.99 monthly subscription can stream movies and TV programs and view them on their Wii consoles at no extra cost.[8]

REVERSE CHANNELS

While the traditional concept of marketing channels involves the movement of goods and services from producer to consumer or business user, marketers should not ignore reverse channels— channels designed to return goods to their producers. Reverse channels have gained increased importance with rising prices for raw materials, increasing availability of recycling facilities, and passage of additional antipollution and conservation laws. Purchase a new set of tires, and you'll find a recycling charge for disposing of the old tires. The intent is to halt the growing litter problem of illegal tire dumps. Automotive and marine batteries contain potentially toxic materials, including 25 pounds of lead, plastic, and sulfuric acid. Yet 99 percent of the elements in a spent battery can be reclaimed, recycled, and reused in new batteries. Thirty-nine states now require consumers to turn in their old batteries when they purchase new ones. To help in this effort, the American Automobile Association (AAA) holds an annual AAA Great Battery Roundup in the United States and Canada, during which consumers can drop off their dead batteries.[9]

Some reverse channels move through the facilities of traditional marketing intermediaries. In states that require bottle deposits, retailers and local bottlers perform these functions in the soft-drink industry. For other products, manufacturers establish redemption centers, develop systems for rechanneling products for recycling, and create specialized organizations to handle disposal and

reverse channel
Channel designed to return goods to their producers.

ASSESSMENT CHECK

1.1   Distinguish between a marketing channel and logistics.

1.2   What are the different types of marketing channels?

1.3   What four functions do marketing channels perform?

recycling. Nike's Reuse-A-Shoe program collects people's cast-off athletic shoes and recycles virtually the entire shoe. This recycling effort is likely to help build customer loyalty and enhance the brand's reputation.[10]

Reverse channels also handle product recalls and repairs. An appliance manufacturer might send recall notices to the buyers of a washing machine. An auto manufacturer might send notices to car owners advising them of a potential problem and offering to repair the problem at no cost through local dealerships.

CHANNEL STRATEGY DECISIONS

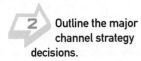

Outline the major channel strategy decisions.

Marketers face several strategic decisions in choosing channels and marketing intermediaries for their products. Selecting a specific channel is the most basic of these decisions. Marketers must also resolve questions about the level of distribution intensity, assess the desirability of vertical marketing systems, and evaluate the performance of current intermediaries.

SELECTION OF A MARKETING CHANNEL

Consider the following questions: What characteristics of a franchised dealer network make it the best channel option for a company? Why do operating supplies often go through both agents and merchant wholesalers before reaching their actual users? Why would a firm market a single product through multiple channels? Marketers must answer many such questions in choosing marketing channels.

A variety of factors affect the selection of a marketing channel. Some channel decisions are dictated by the marketplace in which the company operates. In other cases, the product itself may be a key variable in picking a marketing channel. Finally, the marketing organization could base its selection of channels on its size and competitive factors. Individual firms in a single industry may choose different channels as part of their overall strategy to gain a competitive edge. Book publishers, for instance, could sell books through bookstores, directly to consumers on their own websites, or through nontraditional outlets including specialty retailers, such as craft stores or home improvement stores.

Market Factors

Channel structure reflects a product's intended markets, for either consumers or business users. Business purchasers usually prefer to deal directly with manufacturers (except for routine supplies or small accessory items), but most consumers make their purchases from retailers. Marketers often sell products that serve both business users and consumers through more than one channel. Sometimes marketers must adapt to customers' preferences for ethical supply chain behavior. See the "Solving an Ethical Controversy" feature to learn how consumers brought about change in the cocoa industry.

Other market factors also affect channel choice, including the market's needs, its geographic location, and its average order size. To serve a concentrated market with a small number of buyers, a direct channel offers a feasible alternative. But in serving a geographically dispersed potential trade area in which customers purchase small amounts in individual transactions—the conditions that characterize the consumer goods market—distribution through marketing intermediaries makes sense.

Product Factors

Product characteristics also guide the choice of an optimal marketing channel strategy. Perishable goods, such as fresh fruit and vegetables, milk, and fruit juice, move through short channels. Trendy or seasonal fashions, such as swimsuits and skiwear, are also examples.

SOLVING AN ETHICAL CONTROVERSY

Hershey's Takes Responsibility for Its Supply Chain

A decade ago, when consumers learned of abusive conditions under which thousands of children were forced to work in Africa's cocoa industry, most major chocolate manufacturers bowed to public pressure. They promised to end human trafficking and child labor in West Africa, which produces more than 70 percent of the world's cocoa, and to buy sustainably produced ingredients. Hershey's, however, lagged behind other chocolate producers who made a commitment to ensure their products are made without child labor. Several human rights organizations recently banded together and besieged the Hershey's Facebook page, asking the company to "raise the bar" when it came to using suppliers who use child labor and inspiring more than 50,000 people to sign a petition on Change.org to get Hershey's to stop using suppliers who abused their young workers.

Should companies be responsible for the actions of their suppliers?

PRO 👍

1. Consumers want to know the products they're buying are not associated with abusive labor practices.

2. Multinational companies with small, unregulated suppliers that depend on their business have an opportunity to do good by insisting on fair labor practices.

CON 👎

1. Companies should not try to control what their suppliers in other cultures do or impose their own (or their customers') value systems on them.

2. Companies are responsible to their shareholders for finding the lowest-cost and most efficient production methods.

Summary:

As a result of several groups banding together to alert consumers about some of its suppliers' practices, Hershey's recently pledged $10 million over five years to educate West African farmers who supply cocoa for Hershey's products on improving their trade and combating child labor abuses.

Sources: Harry Stevens, "Child Labor Concerns across Hershey's Supply Chain Prove It Pays to Be Proactive," *Green Biz*, accessed November 30, 2012, www .greenbiz.com; Raise the Bar, "Why Hershey?" accessed November 30, 2012, www.raisethebarhershey.org; Mindy Lubber, "U.S. Companies Must Raise the Bar on Supply Chain Conditions," *Forbes*, accessed November 30, 2012, www .forbes.com; Julie Bort, "Group Used Facebook to Make Hershey Act on Child Slavery," *Business Insider*, accessed November 30, 2012, www.businessinsider .com; Alyce Lomax, "Hershey's Gets a Bit Safer for Africa's Exploited Kids," *Daily Finance*, accessed November 30, 2012, www.dailyfinance.com; Nick Malawskey, "Hershey Co. Invests $10 Million to Education Programs, CocoaLink in West Africa," *Penn Live*, accessed November 30, 2012, www.pennlive.com.

Vending machines represent another short channel. Typically, you can buy Skittles, SunChips, or a bottle of Dasani water from a vending machine. But how about cupcakes? The Los Angeles–based Sprinkles Cupcakes chain recently announced it would install machines to dispense cupcakes 24 hours a day at three of its stores in New York City.[11]

Complex products, such as custom-made installations and computer equipment, are often sold directly to ultimate buyers. In general, relatively standardized items that are also nonperishable pass through comparatively long channels. Products with low unit costs, such as cans of dog food, bars of soap, and packages of gum, typically travel through long channels. Perishable items—fresh flowers, meat, and produce—require much shorter channels.

Organizational and Competitive Factors

Companies with strong financial, management, and marketing resources feel less need for help from intermediaries. A large, financially strong manufacturer can hire its own sales force, warehouse its own

Instead of selling directly to customers, entrepreneurs Christine and Robert Hackett rely on big retail partners to get their products, Tiki Cat and Tiki Dog foods, into consumers' hands. On their website, Petropics, they list the partners selling their products at local retailers and online.

goods, and extend credit to retailers or consumers. But a small firm with fewer resources may do better with the aid of intermediaries. Christine and Robert Hackett founded Petropics, a small, Hawaii-based pet-food company that makes gourmet, whole-food dog and cat foods in Hawaiian-themed flavors, such as Lanai Luau for cats and Maui Luau for dogs. Petropics sells its products through local retailers and on the Web with big e-tail partners like Amazon, PawsChoice, and the Pet Center.[12]

A firm with a broad product line can usually market its products directly to retailers or business users, because its own sales force can offer a variety of products. High sales volume spreads selling costs over a large number of items, generating adequate returns from direct sales. Single-product firms often view direct selling as unaffordable.

The manufacturer's desire for control over marketing its products also influences channel selection. Some manufacturers sell their products only at their own stores. Manufacturers of specialty or luxury goods, such as scarves from Hermès and watches from Rolex, limit the number of retailers that can carry their products.

Businesses that explore new marketing channels must be careful to avoid upsetting their channel intermediaries. Conflicts frequently arose as companies began to establish an Internet presence in addition to traditional outlets. Today, firms look for new ways to handle both without damaging relationships. In an aggressive social media campaign, the athletic apparel and equipment manufacturer Under Armour recently unveiled a revamped website to showcase its new products, such as shoes, athletic bags, and hats. The site also has live chat and customer review apps. However, retail sales—most notably through Dick's Sporting Goods and The Sports Authority—still account for 26 percent of Under Armour sales. The new website also features a much more conspicuous brick-and-mortar store locater. John Rogers, Under Armour's vice president of global e-commerce, says, "The new store finder ensures consumers can find all stores near them to touch, feel, and try on Under Armour gear, but online we focus on telling the innovation and leadership product stories that create strong desire for our products across all distribution channels."[13]

Table 14.1 summarizes the factors that affect the selection of a marketing channel and examines the effect of each factor on the channel's overall length.

DETERMINING DISTRIBUTION INTENSITY

Another key channel strategy decision is the intensity of distribution. *Distribution intensity* refers to the number of intermediaries through which a manufacturer distributes its goods in a particular market.

TABLE 14.1 Factors Influencing Marketing Channel Strategies

	Characteristics of Short Channels	Characteristics of Long Channels
Market Factors	Business users	Consumers
	Geographically concentrated	Geographically dispersed
	Extensive technical knowledge and regular servicing required	Little technical knowledge and regular servicing not required
	Large orders	Small orders
Product Factors	Perishable	Durable
	Complex	Standardized
	Expensive	Inexpensive
Organizational Factors	Manufacturer has adequate resources to perform channel functions	Manufacturer lacks adequate resources to perform channel functions
	Broad product line	Limited product line
	Channel control important	Channel control not important
Competitive Factors	Manufacturer feels satisfied with marketing intermediaries' performance in promoting products	Manufacturer feels dissatisfied with marketing intermediaries' performance in promoting products

© Cengage Learning

Optimal distribution intensity should ensure adequate market coverage for a product. Adequate market coverage varies depending on the goals of the individual firm, the type of product, and the consumer segments in its target market. In general, however, distribution intensity varies along a continuum with three general categories: intensive distribution, selective distribution, and exclusive distribution.

Intensive Distribution

An **intensive distribution** strategy seeks to distribute a product through all available channels in a trade area. Because Dove practices intensive distribution for many of its products, you can pick up one of its chocolate bars or ice cream products just about anywhere—the supermarket, the convenience store, and even the drugstore. Usually, an intensive distribution strategy suits items with wide appeal across broad groups of consumers.

Selective Distribution

In another market coverage strategy, **selective distribution**, a firm chooses only a limited number of retailers in a market area to handle its line. Italian design firm Gucci sells its merchandise only through a limited number of select boutiques worldwide. By limiting the number of retailers, marketers can reduce total marketing costs while establishing strong working relationships within the channel. Moreover, selected retailers often agree to comply with the company's strict rules for advertising, pricing, and displaying its products. *Cooperative advertising*—in which the manufacturer pays a percentage of the retailer's advertising expenditures and the retailer prominently displays the firm's products—can

intensive distribution
Distribution of a product through all available channels.

selective distribution
Distribution of a product through a limited number of channels.

© Terri Miller/E-Visual Communications, Inc.

Dove uses intensive distribution for many of its products, which means you can pick up a Dove ice cream bar just about anywhere—the supermarket, the convenience store, or even the drugstore.

be used for mutual benefit, and marginal retailers can be avoided. Where service is important, the manufacturer usually provides training and assistance to the dealers it chooses.

Exclusive Distribution

exclusive distribution
Distribution of a product through a single wholesaler or retailer in a specific geographic region.

When a producer grants exclusive rights to a wholesaler or retailer to sell its products in a specific geographic region, it practices **exclusive distribution**. The automobile industry provides a good example of exclusive distribution. A city with a population of 60,000 probably has a single Jaguar dealer. Exclusive distribution agreements also govern marketing for some major appliance and apparel brands.

Marketers may sacrifice some market coverage by implementing a policy of exclusive distribution. However, they often develop and maintain an image of quality and prestige for the product. If it's harder to find a Free People silk dress, the item seems more valuable. In addition, exclusive distribution limits marketing costs because the firm deals with a smaller number of accounts. In exclusive distribution, producers and retailers cooperate closely in decisions concerning advertising and promotion, inventory carried by the retailers, and prices.

Legal Problems of Exclusive Distribution

Exclusive distribution presents potential legal problems in three main areas: exclusive dealing agreements, closed sales territories, and tying agreements. Although none of these practices is illegal per se, all may break the law if they reduce competition or tend to create monopolies.

As part of an exclusive distribution strategy, marketers may try to enforce an exclusive dealing agreement, which prohibits a marketing intermediary (a wholesaler or, more typically, a retailer) from handling competing products. Producers of high-priced shopping goods, specialty goods, and accessory equipment often require such agreements to ensure total concentration on their own product lines. Such contracts violate the Clayton Act only if the producer's or dealer's sales volumes represent a substantial percentage of total sales in the market area. While exclusive distribution is legal for companies first entering a market, such agreements violate the Clayton Act if used by firms with a sizable market share seeking to bar competitors from the market.

closed sales territory
Exclusive geographic selling region of a distributor.

Producers may also try to set up **closed sales territories** to restrict their distributors to certain geographic regions, reasoning that the distributors gain protection from rival dealers in their exclusive territories. Some beverage distributors have closed territories, as do distributors of plumbing fixtures.[14] But the downside of this practice is that the distributors sacrifice opportunities to open new facilities or market the manufacturers' products outside their assigned territories. The legality of a system of closed sales territories depends on whether the restriction decreases competition. If so, it violates the Federal Trade Commission Act and provisions of the Sherman and Clayton Acts.

tying agreement
Arrangement that requires a marketing intermediary to carry items other than those they want to sell.

The legality of closed sales territories also depends on whether the system imposes horizontal or vertical restrictions. Horizontal territorial restrictions result from agreements between retailers or wholesalers to avoid competition among sellers of products from the same producer. Such agreements consistently have been declared illegal. However, the U.S. Supreme Court has ruled that vertical territorial restrictions—those between producers and wholesalers or retailers—may meet legal criteria. The ruling gives no clear-cut answer, but such agreements likely satisfy the law in cases in which manufacturers occupy relatively small parts of their markets. In such instances, the restrictions may actually increase competition among competing brands; the wholesaler or retailer faces no competition from other dealers carrying the manufacturer's brand, so it can concentrate on effectively competing with other brands.

BRIEFLY SPEAKING

"You can do away with middlemen, but you can't do away with the functions they perform."

—American business saying

The third legal question of exclusive distribution involves **tying agreements**, which allow channel members to become exclusive dealers only if they also carry products other than those they want to sell. In the apparel industry, for example, an agreement might require a dealer to carry a comparatively unpopular line of clothing to get desirable, fast-moving items. Tying agreements violate the Sherman Act and the Clayton Act when they reduce competition or create monopolies that keep competitors out of major markets.

WHO SHOULD PERFORM CHANNEL FUNCTIONS?

A fundamental marketing principle governs channel decisions. A member of the channel must perform certain central marketing functions. Responsibilities of the different members may vary, however. Although independent wholesalers perform many functions for manufacturers, retailers, and other wholesaler clients, other channel members could fulfill these roles instead. A manufacturer might bypass its wholesalers by establishing regional warehouses, maintaining field sales forces, serving as sources of information for retail customers, or arranging details of financing. For years, auto manufacturers have operated credit units that offer new car financing; some have even established their own banks.

An independent intermediary earns a profit in exchange for providing services to manufacturers and retailers. This profit margin is low, however, ranging from 1 percent for food wholesalers to 5 percent for durable goods wholesalers. Manufacturers and retailers could retain these costs, or they could market directly and reduce retail prices—but only if they could perform the channel functions and match the efficiency of the independent intermediaries.

To grow profitably in a competitive environment, an intermediary must provide better service at lower costs than manufacturers or retailers can provide for themselves. In this case, consolidation of channel functions can represent a strategic opportunity for a company.

ASSESSMENT CHECK

2.1 Identify four major factors in selecting a marketing channel.

2.2 Describe the three general categories of distribution intensity.

CHANNEL MANAGEMENT AND LEADERSHIP

Distribution strategy does not end with the choice of a channel. Manufacturers must also focus on channel management by developing and maintaining relationships with the intermediaries in their marketing channels. Positive channel relationships encourage channel members to remember their partners' goods and market them. Manufacturers also must carefully manage the incentives offered to induce channel members to promote their products. This effort includes weighing decisions about pricing, promotion, and other support efforts the manufacturer performs.

Increasingly, marketers are managing channels in partnership with other channel members. Effective cooperation allows all channel members to achieve goals they could not achieve on their own. Keys to successful management of channel relationships include the development of high levels of coordination, commitment, and trust between channel members.

Not all channel members wield equal power in the distribution chain, however. The dominant member of a marketing channel is called the **channel captain**. This firm's power to control a channel may result from its control over some type of reward or punishment to other channel members such as granting an exclusive sales territory or taking away a dealership. Power might also result from contractual arrangements, specialized expert knowledge, or agreement among channel members about their mutual best interests.

In the grocery industry, food producers once were considered channel captains. Today, retail giants like Kroger, SuperValu, and Safeway face competition from all quarters: discounters like ALDI and Save-A-Lot, club stores like Costco and Sam's Club, and even dollar stores. And just as they do when shopping for clothes or other items, grocery shoppers use their smartphones or tablets to look for bargains either before or during their trips to the store. To survive in the competitive grocery industry, supermarket owners are diversifying their retail formats from traditional stores to include natural and organic and upscale specialty stores to satisfy a wider variety of customers, and to compete with such chains as Whole Foods Market and Trader Joe's.[15] But the pressure on

> Describe the concepts of channel management, conflict, and cooperation.
>
> **3**

> **channel captain**
> Dominant and controlling member of a marketing channel.

traditional chains is coming from another strategy: supercenters like Walmart and Target. Walmart is continuing its expansion in the grocery market; in fact, its grocery receipts now account for a whopping 55 percent of its U.S. sales.[16]

CHANNEL CONFLICT

Marketing channels work smoothly only when members cooperate in well-organized efforts to achieve maximum operating efficiencies. Yet channel members often perform as separate, independent, and even competing forces. Two types of conflict—horizontal and vertical—may hinder the normal functioning of a marketing channel.

Horizontal Conflict

Horizontal conflict sometimes results from disagreements among channel members at the same level, such as two or more wholesalers or retailers, or among marketing intermediaries of the same type, such as two competing discount stores or several retail florists. More often, horizontal conflict causes problems between different types of marketing intermediaries that handle similar products. For example, Hulu, Netflix, Streampix, and Amazon all offer streaming video service, allowing subscribers to view movies and, especially, TV shows on their televisions, computers, or mobile devices. The networking equipment maker Cisco predicts that by 2016, there will be 10 billion mobile devices, including sensors, tablets, and smartphones. The company also estimates that about three-quarters of Internet traffic will be streamed video. Although carriers are trying to slow down the rush of video use on mobile devices by charging higher prices for heavy data consumption, more and more people are buying and using smartphones that can carry videos, especially with smartphones costing only about $100 in some regions.[17]

Vertical Conflict

Vertical relationships may result in frequent and severe conflict. Channel members at different levels find many reasons for disputes, as when retailers develop private brands to compete with producers' brands or when producers establish their own retail stores or create mail-order operations that compete with retailers. Producers may annoy wholesalers and retailers when they attempt to bypass these intermediaries and sell directly to consumers. When booking plane flights and other travel arrangements online first became feasible, travelers dispensed with the services of travel agents and made their own arrangements. But it can sometimes take several hours to search airline websites to find the best combination of price and travel dates. In the wake of the recession, travelers have become much more cautious about spending money. And they have gotten much choosier about exactly what kind of vacation they want. Thus, travel agencies are experiencing a revival. Their job is also changing as they develop long-term, more advisory relationships with their clients.[18]

The Gray Market

gray goods Products manufactured abroad under license from a U.S. firm and then sold in the U.S. market in competition with that firm's own domestic output.

Another type of channel conflict results from activities in the so-called gray market. As U.S. manufacturers license their technology and brands abroad, they sometimes find themselves in competition in the U.S. market against versions of their own brands produced by overseas affiliates. These **gray goods**, goods produced for overseas markets often at reduced prices, enter U.S. channels through the actions of unauthorized foreign distributors. While licensing agreements usually prohibit foreign licensees from selling in the United States, no such rules inhibit their distributors. Other countries also have gray markets. For example, although Amazon is not yet licensed to sell its Kindle products in China, they are readily available on China's gray market.

Similarly, even before the iPad's official global release, enterprising individuals bought them up in the United States for resale at an inflated price in Hong Kong. A recent study indicated that half of iPad sales in China continue to be from the gray market.[19]

© Karel Gallas/Shutterstock.com

The vertical conflict that arose when consumers made their own travel arrangements online has been resolved as they rely more on travel advisors to help them plan the right vacation.

ACHIEVING CHANNEL COOPERATION

The basic antidote to channel conflict is effective cooperation among channel members. Cooperation is best achieved when all channel members regard themselves as equal components of the same organization. The channel captain is primarily responsible for providing the leadership necessary to achieve this kind of cooperation.

IMAX, Sony, and Discovery Communications formed a joint venture to create 3net, a 3D television channel. Distributed by Discovery, the new channel offers a broad programming mix that includes sports, entertainment, natural-history shows, and more.[20]

> ### ⊕ ASSESSMENT CHECK
>
> 3.1 What is a channel captain? What is its role in channel cooperation?
>
> 3.2 Identify and describe the three types of channel conflict.

VERTICAL MARKETING SYSTEMS

Efforts to reduce channel conflict and improve the effectiveness of distribution have led to the development of vertical marketing systems. A **vertical marketing system (VMS)** is a planned channel system designed to improve distribution efficiency and cost effectiveness by integrating various functions throughout the distribution chain.

A vertical marketing system can achieve this goal through either forward or backward integration. In **forward integration**, a firm attempts to control downstream distribution. For example, a manufacturer might set up a retail chain to sell its products. **Backward integration** occurs when a manufacturer attempts to gain greater control over inputs in its production process. A manufacturer might acquire the supplier of a raw material the manufacturer uses in the production of its products. Backward integration can also extend the control of retailers and wholesalers over producers that supply them.

vertical marketing system (VMS) Planned channel system designed to improve distribution efficiency and cost-effectiveness by integrating various functions throughout the distribution chain.

forward integration Process through which a firm attempts to control downstream distribution.

backward integration Process through which a manufacturer attempts to gain greater control over inputs in its production process, such as raw materials.

4 Identify and describe the different vertical marketing systems.

A VMS offers several benefits. First, it improves chances for controlling and coordinating the steps in the distribution or production process. It may lead to the development of economies of scale that ultimately saves money. A VMS may also let a manufacturer expand into profitable new businesses. However, a VMS also involves some costs. A manufacturer assumes increased risk when it takes control of an entire distribution chain. Manufacturers may also discover they lose some flexibility in responding to market changes.

Marketers have developed three categories of VMSs: corporate systems, administered systems, and contractual systems. These categories are outlined in the following sections.

CORPORATE AND ADMINISTERED SYSTEMS

corporate marketing system VMS in which a single owner operates the entire marketing channel.

administered marketing system VMS that achieves channel coordination when a dominant channel member exercises its power.

contractual marketing system VMS that coordinates channel activities through formal agreements among participants.

When a single owner runs an organization at each stage of the marketing channel, it operates a **corporate marketing system**. Phillips Auctioneers runs a corporate marketing system. An **administered marketing system** achieves channel coordination when a dominant channel member exercises its power. Even though Goodyear sells its tires through independently owned and operated dealerships, it controls the stock these dealerships carry. Another example of channel captains leading administered channels is McKesson, a health care technology company and pharmaceutical distributor.

CONTRACTUAL SYSTEMS

Instead of common ownership of intermediaries within a corporate VMS or the exercising of power within an administered system, a **contractual marketing system** coordinates distribution through formal agreements among channel members. In practice, three types of agreements set up these systems: wholesaler-sponsored voluntary chains, retail cooperatives, and franchises.

Wholesaler-Sponsored Voluntary Chain

Sometimes an independent wholesaler tries to preserve a market by strengthening its retail customers through a wholesaler-sponsored voluntary chain. The wholesaler adopts a formal agreement with its retailers to use a common name and standardized facilities and to purchase the wholesaler's goods. The wholesaler may even develop a line of private brands to be stocked by the retailers. This practice often helps smaller retailers compete with rival chains—and strengthens the wholesaler's position as well.

IGA (Independent Grocers Alliance) Food Stores is a good example of a voluntary chain. Other wholesaler-sponsored chains include Associated Druggists, Sentry Hardware, and Western Auto. Because a single advertisement promotes all the retailers in the trading area, a common store name and similar inventories allow the retailers to save on advertising costs.

Retail Cooperative

retail cooperative Group of retailers that establish a shared wholesaling operation to help them compete with chains.

In a second type of contractual VMS, a group of retailers establishes a shared wholesaling operation to help them compete with chains. This is known as a **retail cooperative**. The retailers purchase ownership shares in the wholesaling operation and agree to buy a minimum percentage of their inventories from this operation. The members typically adopt a common store name and develop common private brands. Ace Hardware is an example of a retail cooperative.

Franchise

franchise Contractual arrangement in which a wholesaler or retailer agrees to meet the operating requirements of a manufacturer or other franchiser.

A third type of contractual vertical marketing system is the **franchise**, in which a wholesaler or dealer (the franchisee) agrees to meet the operating requirements of a manufacturer or other franchiser. Franchising is a huge and growing industry—an estimated 3,000 U.S. companies distribute goods and services through systems of franchised dealers, and numerous firms also offer franchises in international markets. Nationwide, more than 825,000 retail outlets represent franchises.[21] Table 14.2 shows the 20 fastest-growing franchises in the United States, with Stratus Building Solutions, Subway, and CleanNet USA Inc. topping the list.

TABLE 14.2 The Top 20 Fastest-Growing Franchises

Rank	Company and Product
1	Stratus Building Solutions; commercial cleaning
2	Subway; submarine sandwiches and salads
3	CleanNet USA Inc.; commercial cleaning
4	Vanguard Cleaning Systems; commercial cleaning
5	H&R Block; tax preparation and electronic filing
6	Dunkin' Donuts; coffee, doughnuts, baked goods
7	Chester's; quick-service chicken restaurants
8	Liberty Tax Service; income-tax preparation
9	7-Eleven; convenience stores
10	Anytime Fitness; fitness centers
11	Jimmy John's Gourmet Sandwich Shops; gourmet sandwiches
12	CruiseOne; cruise and travel agency
13	Pizza Hut Inc.; pizza, pasta, wings
14	Jazzercise Inc.; dance fitness classes, apparel, and accessories
15	Papa John's Int'l. Inc.; pizza
16	System4; commercial cleaning
17	Kumon Math & Reading Centers; supplemental education
18	Sport Clips; men's sports-themed hair salon
19	Hampton Hotels; mid-priced hotels
20	Taco Bell Corp.; quick-service Mexican restaurant

Source: "2012 Fastest-Growing Franchise Rankings," *Entrepreneur*, accessed November 30, 2012, www.entrepreneur.com.

Franchise owners pay anywhere from several thousand to more than a million dollars to purchase and set up a franchise. Typically, they also pay a royalty on sales to the franchising company. In exchange for these initial and ongoing fees, the franchise owner receives the right to use the company's brand name as well as services like training, marketing, advertising, and volume discounts. Major franchise chains justify the steep price of entry because it allows new businesses to sell winning brands. But if the brand enters a slump or the corporation behind the franchise makes poor strategic decisions, franchisees are often hurt.

 ASSESSMENT CHECK

4.1 What are vertical marketing systems? Identify the major types.

4.2 Identify the three types of contractual marketing systems.

LOGISTICS AND SUPPLY CHAIN MANAGEMENT

Pier 1 imports its eclectic mix of items from vendors in more than 50 countries, most representing small companies. If high-demand items or seasonal products are late into its six North American distribution centers or are shipped in insufficient quantities, the company may miss opportunities to

5 Explain the roles of logistics and supply chain management in an overall distribution strategy.

supply chain Complete sequence of suppliers and activities that contribute to the creation and delivery of merchandise.

upstream management Controlling part of the supply chain that involves raw materials, inbound logistics, and warehouse and storage facilities.

downstream management Controlling part of the supply chain that involves finished product storage, outbound logistics, marketing and sales, and customer service.

deliver popular shopping choices to its more than 1,000 retail stores and could lose ground to such competitors as Pottery Barn and Crate & Barrel. The situation facing Pier 1 illustrates the importance of logistics. Careful coordination of Pier 1's supplier network, shipping processes, and inventory control is the key to its continuing success. In addition, the store's buyers develop relationships with suppliers in all participating countries.[22]

Effective logistics requires proper supply chain management, control of the activities of purchasing, processing, and delivery through which raw materials are transformed into products and made available to final consumers. The supply chain, also known as the *value chain*, is the complete sequence of suppliers and activities that contribute to the creation and delivery of goods and services. The supply chain begins with the raw material inputs for the manufacturing process of a product and then proceeds to the actual production activities. The final link in the supply chain is the movement of finished products through the marketing channel to customers. Each link of the chain benefits the consumers as raw materials move through manufacturing to distribution. The chain encompasses all activities that enhance the value of the finished goods, including design, quality manufacturing, customer service, and delivery. Customer satisfaction results directly from the perceived value of a purchase to its buyer. Read the "Marketing Success" feature to see how one restaurant chain manages its seafood supply chain.

To manage the supply chain, businesses must look for ways to maximize customer value in each activity they perform. Supply chain management takes place in two directions: upstream and downstream, as illustrated in Figure 14.2. Upstream management involves managing raw materials, inbound logistics, and warehouse and storage facilities. Downstream management involves managing finished product storage, outbound logistics, marketing and sales, and customer service.

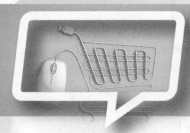

MARKETING SUCCESS

Red Lobsters "Seas" Food Differently

Background. Red Lobster, a division of Darden Restaurants, has been a popular seafood destination since 1968, serving reasonably priced fish and lobster dishes in almost 700 family-friendly locations in the United States and Canada.

The Challenge. As recession-weary families are eating out more cheaply or less often, Red Lobster must maintain its position as a desirable dining option, serving fresh and wholesome seafood at reasonable prices. Yet the world's supply of some ocean species is dwindling, and concerns about sustainability as well as food safety are more urgent than ever before.

The Strategy. Red Lobster has responded to the reduction of some ocean populations with menu changes that respect scarcity, and with initiatives that it hopes will improve sustainability. The company sources fish from only certified, sustainable farms, and

it requires suppliers to adhere to Best Aquaculture Practices set by the Global Aquaculture Alliance (parent company Darden was a cofounder). Darden also plans to establish the world's largest lobster farm in Malaysia, hoping to ensure a steady supply at low prices.

The Outcome. Red Lobster recently unveiled a new "Sea Food Differently" marketing campaign focusing on individuals in its supply chain and operations areas. The chain has reported a modest increase in sales.

Sources: "Red Lobster Unveils Most Comprehensive Menu Transformation in Brand History," *Market Watch*, accessed November 30, 2012, www.marketwatch.com; company website, www.redlobster.com, accessed November 30, 2012; Bret Thorn, "Darden Details Seafood Sustainability Efforts," *Nation's Restaurant News*, accessed November 30, 2012, http://nrn.com; Stuart Elliott, "Red Lobster Campaign to Showcase Some of Its Own Workers," *The New York Times*, accessed November 30, 2012, www.nytimes.com.

Companies choose a variety of methods for managing the supply chain. They can include high-tech systems like radio-frequency identification (discussed in the next section) and regular person-to-person meetings. The Arizona-based JDA Software Group helps other businesses track and manage their global supply chains. Using its proprietary software solutions, JDA helps its clients enhance customer service and improve inventory management.[23]

Logistics plays a major role in giving customers what they need when they need it, and thus is central in the supply chain. Another important component of this chain, *value-added service*, adds some improved or supplemental service that customers do not normally receive or expect. The following sections examine methods for streamlining and managing logistics and the supply chain as part of an overall distribution strategy.

> Careful coordination of Pier 1's supplier network, shipping process, and inventory control is the key to the company's continuing success.

RADIO-FREQUENCY IDENTIFICATION

One tool marketers use to help manage logistics is **radio-frequency identification (RFID)** technology. With RFID, a tiny chip with identification information that can be read by a radio-frequency scanner from a distance is placed on an item. These chips are already widely used in tollway pass transmitters, allowing drivers to zip through tollbooths without stopping or rolling down their windows to toss change into baskets.

They are also embedded in employee ID cards that workers use to open office doors without keys. But businesses like retail giant Walmart, manufacturer Procter & Gamble, credit card firms

radio-frequency identification (RFID) Technology that uses a tiny chip with identification information that can be read by a scanner using radio waves from a distance.

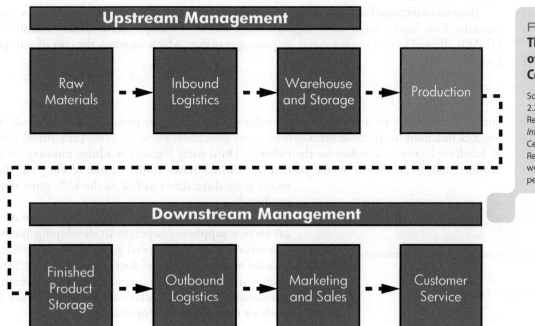

Upstream Management

Raw Materials → Inbound Logistics → Warehouse and Storage → Production

Downstream Management

Finished Product Storage → Outbound Logistics → Marketing and Sales → Customer Service

FIGURE 14.2
The Supply Chain of a Manufacturing Company

Source: Adapted from Figure 2.2, Ralph Stair and George Reynolds, *Principles of Information Systems*, 10th ed., Cengage Learning, © 2012. Reproduced by permission. www.cengage.com/permissions.

MasterCard and American Express, and German retailer Metro AG are eagerly putting this technology to wider use; they say it will speed deliveries, make consumer bar codes obsolete, and provide marketers with valuable information about consumer preferences. Walmart requires its biggest suppliers to attach RFID tags to pallets and cases of products like Coca-Cola and Dove soap, saying the technology vastly improves its ability to track inventory and keep the right amount of products in stock.

Several manufacturers have released an iPhone case with a built-in RFID reader, active RFID tags, and software that allows a user to alert friends, find people or things, or create a "virtual leash."[24]

ENTERPRISE RESOURCE PLANNING

enterprise resource planning (ERP) system Software system that consolidates data from among a firm's various business units.

Software is an important aspect of logistics management and the supply chain. An **enterprise resource planning (ERP) system** is an integrated software system that consolidates data from among the firm's units. Roughly two-thirds of ERP system users are manufacturers concerned with production issues, such as sequencing and scheduling. German software giant SAP offers systems that allow businesses to manage their customer relations. Recently, ERP suppliers have begun offering cloud-based technology, with its emphasis on subscription-based solutions.[25]

As valuable as it is, ERP and its related software aren't always perfect. For example, ERP failures were blamed for Hershey's inability to fulfill all of its candy orders during one Halloween period when a fall-off in sales was blamed on a combination of shipping delays, inability to fill orders, and partial shipments while candy accumulated in warehouses. The nation's major retailers were forced to shift their purchases to other candy vendors.

LOGISTICAL COST CONTROL

In addition to enhancing their products by providing value-added services to customers, many firms focus on logistics for another important reason: to cut costs. Distribution functions currently represent almost half of a typical firm's total marketing costs. To reduce logistical costs, businesses are reexamining each link of their supply chains to identify activities that do not add value for customers. By eliminating, reducing, or redesigning these activities, they can often cut costs and boost efficiency. As just described, new technologies like RFID can save businesses millions—or even billions—of dollars.

Because of increased security requirements in recent years, businesses involved in importing and exporting have faced a major rise in logistical costs. The U.S. Transportation Security Administration (TSA) is charged with screening cargo on passenger planes, which increases the cost of transporting goods even more.[26]

Third-Party Logistics

third-party (contract) logistics firm Company that specializes in handling logistics activities for other firms.

Some companies try to cut costs and offer value-added services by outsourcing some or all of their logistics functions to specialist firms. **Third-party (contract) logistics firms** (3PL firms) specialize in handling logistical activities for their clients. Third-party logistics is a huge industry, estimated at more than $126 billion in one year in the United States alone. In one recent year, the 3PL sector grew three times as fast as the U.S. gross domestic product.[27]

Through outsourcing alliances, producers and logistical service suppliers cooperate in developing innovative, customized systems that speed goods through carefully constructed manufacturing and distribution pipelines. Although many companies have long outsourced transportation and warehousing functions, today's alliance partners use similar methods to combine their operations.

ASSESSMENT CHECK

5.1 What is upstream management? What is downstream management?

5.2 Identify three methods for managing logistics.

PHYSICAL DISTRIBUTION

A firm's physical distribution system is an organized group of components linked according to a plan for achieving specific distribution objectives. It contains the following elements:

1. *customer service*—level of customer service the distribution activities support;

2. *transportation*—how the firm ships its products;

3. *inventory control*—quantity of inventory the firm maintains at each location;

4. *protective packaging and materials handling*—how the firm packages and efficiently handles goods in the factory, warehouse, and transport terminals;

5. *order processing*—how the firm handles orders; and

6. *warehousing*—the distribution system's location of stock and the number of warehouses the firm maintains.

Identify the major components of a physical distribution system. 6

All these components function in interrelated ways. Decisions made in one area affect efficiency in others. The physical distribution manager must balance each component so the system avoids stressing any single aspect to the detriment of overall functioning. A firm might decide to reduce transportation costs by shipping its products by less costly—but slow—water transportation. But slow deliveries would likely force the firm to maintain higher inventory levels, raising those costs. This mismatch between system elements often leads to increased production costs. So balancing the components is crucial.

The general shift from a manufacturing economy to a service economy in the United States has affected physical distribution in two key ways. First, customers require more flexible—yet reliable—transportation service. Second, the number of smaller shipments is growing much faster than the number of large shipments. Although traditional, high-volume shipments will continue to grow, they will represent a lower percentage of the transportation industry's revenues and volume.

THE PROBLEM OF SUBOPTIMIZATION

Logistics managers seek to establish a specified level of customer service while minimizing the costs of physically moving and storing goods. Marketers must first decide on their priorities for customer service and then figure out how to fulfill those goals by moving goods at the least cost. Meshing together all the physical distribution elements is a huge challenge that firms don't always meet.

Suboptimization results when the managers of individual physical distribution functions attempt to minimize costs, but the impact of one task leads to less than optimal results on the others. Imagine a hockey team composed of star players. Unfortunately, despite the individual talents of the players, the team fails to win a game. This is an example of suboptimization. The same thing can happen at a company when each logistics activity is judged by its own accomplishments instead of the way it contributes to the overall goals of the firm.

Suboptimization often happens when a firm introduces a new product that may not fit easily into its current physical distribution system.

Effective management of the physical distribution function requires some cost trade-offs. By accepting relatively high costs in some functional areas to cut costs in others, managers can minimize their firm's total physical distribution costs. Of course, any reduction in logistical costs should support progress toward the goal of maintaining customer service standards.

suboptimization
Condition that results when individual operations achieve their objectives but interfere with progress toward broader organizational goals.

CUSTOMER SERVICE STANDARDS

Customer service standards state the goals and define acceptable performance for the quality of service a firm expects to deliver to its customers. Internet retailers like RoadRunnerSports.com thrive because of their ability to ship within hours of receiving an order. Zappos.com has a 365-day return policy, which means a customer can return a purchase up to a year later for a full refund, as long as the merchandise has not been worn, is in the state it was received, and is in the original packaging.[28]

A pizza restaurant might set a standard to deliver customers' pizzas hot and fresh within 30 minutes. An auto repair shop may set a standard to complete all oil changes in a half hour. All are examples of customer service standards.

Designers of a physical distribution system begin by establishing acceptable levels of customer service. These designers then assemble physical distribution components in a way that will achieve this standard at the lowest possible total cost. This overall cost breaks down into five components: (1) transportation, (2) warehousing, (3) inventory control, (4) customer service/order processing, and (5) administrative costs.

TRANSPORTATION

The transportation industry was largely deregulated a number of years ago. Deregulation has been particularly important for motor carriers, railroads, and air carriers. Today, an estimated 15.5 million trucks are transporting goods throughout the United States; 2 million of these are tractor-trailers. It is estimated that more than 1.2 million trucking companies and nearly 3.5 million truck drivers operate in the country.[29] Railroads are enjoying a new boom: once hauling mostly commodities like corn and grain, they now transport cross-country the huge loads of goods coming from China through West Coast ports. Railroads can move a greater amount of freight for less fuel than trucks. In North America, more than 1.5 million rail cars carry freight on over 168,000 miles of track, with the industry generating almost $59 billion in annual revenues.[30]

Typically adding about 10 percent to the cost of a product, transportation and delivery expenses are the largest category of logistics-related costs for most firms. Also, for many items—particularly perishable ones like fresh fish or produce—transportation makes a central contribution to satisfactory customer service.

Many logistics managers have found that the key to controlling their shipping costs is careful management of relationships with shipping firms. Freight carriers use two basic rates: class and commodity rates. A class rate is a standard rate for a specific commodity moving between any pair of destinations. A carrier may charge a lower commodity rate, sometimes called a *special rate*, to a favored shipper as a reward for either regular business or a large shipment. Railroads and inland water carriers frequently reward customers in this way. In addition, the railroad and motor carrier industries sometimes supplement this rate structure with negotiated, or contract, rates. In other words, the two parties finalize the terms of rates, services, and other variables in a contract.

Classes of Carriers

common carriers
Businesses that provide transportation services as for-hire carriers to the general public.

Freight carriers are classified as common, contract, and private carriers. Common carriers, often considered the backbone of the transportation industry, provide transportation services as for-hire carriers to the general public. The government still regulates their rates and services, and they cannot conduct their operations without permission from the appropriate regulatory authority. Common carriers move freight via all modes of transport. FedEx is a major common carrier serving businesses and consumers. One way the firm remains competitive is by developing new methods for enhancing customer service. FedEx has a service called InSight, a free online service that essentially reverses the package-tracking process—instead of following a package from shipment to delivery, customers can go online to find out what will be delivered to them that day. One FedEx customer that has benefited greatly

FedEx serves businesses and consumers as a common carrier and offers customers a free online service called InSight to track deliveries.

AP Photo/Mark Lennihan

from this new service is Nashville–based Holtkamp Greenhouses, which ships perishable goods—begonias, miniature poinsettias, and other plants—to florists and nursery departments of such big-box stores as Home Depot, Lowe's, and Walmart. With InSight, the company can easily track the status of its shipments.[31]

Contract carriers are for-hire transporters that do not offer their services to the general public. Instead, they establish contracts with individual customers and operate exclusively for particular industries, such as the motor freight industry. These carriers operate under much looser regulations than common carriers.

Private carriers do not offer services for hire. These carriers provide transportation services solely for internally generated freight. As a result, they observe no rate or service regulations. The Interstate Commerce Commission (ICC), a federal regulatory agency, permits private carriers to operate as common or contract carriers as well. Many private carriers have taken advantage of this rule by operating their trucks fully loaded at all times.

ASSESSMENT CHECK

6.1 What are the six major elements of physical distribution?

6.2 What is suboptimization?

MAJOR TRANSPORTATION MODES

Logistics managers choose among five major transportation alternatives: railroads, motor carriers, water carriers, pipelines, and air freight. Each mode has its own unique characteristics. Logistics managers select the best options by matching these features to their specific transportation needs.

Railroads

Railroads continue to control the largest share of the freight business as measured by ton-miles. The term *ton-mile* indicates shipping activity required to move one ton of freight one mile. Rail shipments quickly rack up ton-miles because this mode provides the most efficient way for moving bulky commodities over long distances. Rail carriers generally transport huge quantities of coal, chemicals, grain, nonmetallic minerals, lumber and wood products, and automobiles. The railroads have improved their service standards through a number of innovative concepts, such as unit trains, run-through trains, **intermodal operations**, and double-stack container trains. Unit trains carry much of the coal, grain, and other high-volume commodities shipped. They run back and forth between single loading points (such as a mine) and single destinations (like a power plant) to deliver a commodity. Run-through trains bypass intermediate terminals to speed up schedules. They work like unit trains, but a run-through train may carry a variety of commodities.

In piggyback operations, one of the intermodal operations, highway trailers and containers ride on railroad flatcars, thus combining the long-haul capacity of the train with the door-to-door flexibility of the truck. A double-stack container train pulls special rail cars equipped with bathtub-shaped wells so they can carry two containers stacked on top of one another. By nearly doubling train capacity and slashing costs, this system offers enormous advantages to rail customers.

As mentioned earlier, the railroad industry is enjoying a resurgence—this also means it must build a better infrastructure to handle the increase in demand. Recently, the Association of American Railroads announced it would invest a record $13 billion on improvements to the U.S. freight rail system.[32]

Motor Carriers

The trucking industry is also an important factor in the freight industry—the American Trucking Association reports that trucks haul about 9 billion tons of freight each year, making deliveries to areas railroads simply can't reach.[33]

Trucking offers some important advantages over the other transportation modes, including relatively fast and consistent service for both large and small shipments. Motor carriers concentrate on shipping manufactured products, while railroads typically haul bulk shipments of raw materials.

contract carriers
For-hire transporters that do not offer their services to the general public.

private carriers
Transporters that provide service solely for internally generated freight.

Compare the major modes of transportation.

intermodal operations Combination of transport modes, such as rail and highway carriers (piggyback), air and highway carriers (birdyback), and water and air carriers (fishyback), to improve customer service and achieve cost advantages.

Motor carriers therefore receive greater revenue per ton shipped, because the cost for shipping raw materials is higher than shipping manufactured products.

Technology has also improved the efficiency of trucking. Many trucking firms now track their fleets via satellite communications systems. In-truck computer systems allow drivers and dispatchers to make last-minute changes in scheduling and delivery. The Internet is also adding new features to motor carrier services.

Even so, the trucking industry must adjust to changes in the marketing environment. Trucking firms report a shortage of long-haul drivers, causing delays in some deliveries and higher costs, along with the rising cost of fuel, to customers. Some firms offer drivers regional runs and dedicated routes for more predictable work hours, as well as better pay. They also recruit husband-and-wife teams for the long-haul routes, which is becoming a popular practice. Currently, long-haul trucking accounts for a full one-third of all the oil used in the United States. Recently, the government offered tax incentives for more fuel-efficient trucks and is encouraging the use of natural gas in long-haul trucking.[34]

Water Carriers

Two basic types of transport methods move products over water: inland or barge lines and oceangoing, deepwater ships. Barge lines efficiently transport bulky, low-unit-value commodities, such as grain, gravel, lumber, sand, and steel. A typical lower Mississippi River barge line may stretch more than a quarter mile across.

Large ships also operate on the Great Lakes, transporting materials like iron ore from Minnesota and harvested grain for market. These lake carrier ships range in size from roughly 400 feet to more than 1,000 feet in length.

Oceangoing supertankers from global companies like Maersk Line are the size of three football fields and almost double the capacity of other vessels. At full capacity, the ships can cut one-fifth of the cost of shipping a container across the Pacific Ocean. Shippers that transport goods via water carriers incur very low costs compared with the rates for other transportation modes. Standardized modular shipping containers maximize savings by limiting loading, unloading, and other handling.

Ships often carry large refrigerated containers called "reefers" for transporting everything from fresh produce to medical supplies. These containers, along with their nonrefrigerated counterparts, improve shipping efficiency because they can easily be removed from a ship and attached to trucks or trains. Although shipping by water has traditionally been less expensive than other modes of transportation, as explained earlier, costs for this mode have increased dramatically because of tightened security measures. Freight rates are based on the size of the vessel, the cost of fuel, and security requirements. Recently, container shipping has experienced an unprecedented downturn and has not had full employment since before the recent recession.[35]

DHL XML Services offers fully integrated Web service that provides clients with DHL's availability, shipping times, rates, shipment, and courier booking, as well as shipment tracking capability from over 140 countries. It also features in-house label printing and tracking. The company's totally customizable EDI Solutions provides for large-volume shipping and multi-site logistical operations.[36]

The expansion of the Panama Canal should be completed within the next several years. Once it is widened and deepened, the Panama Canal will allow larger-sized ships to pass through the all-water route from Asia to the U.S. Atlantic coast. The expansion doubles the amount of freight that can go through the canal and will have a significant impact on distribution. Ports in New York, New Jersey, Maryland, and Florida are racing to prepare for the arrival of the larger ships by investing in new infrastructure to allow the big ships to dock and unload their cargo.[37]

Pipelines

Although the pipeline industry ranks third after railroads and motor carriers in ton-miles transported, many people scarcely recognize its existence. More than 2.5 million miles of pipelines crisscross the United States in an extremely efficient network for transporting energy products—enough to circle the planet 100 times. The pipelines are operated by more than 3,000 large and small firms.[38] Oil pipelines carry two types of commodities: crude (unprocessed) oil and refined products, such as gasoline, jet fuel, and kerosene. In addition, one so-called slurry pipeline carries coal in suspension

AP Photo/Eckehard Schulz

DHL's XML Services and EDI Solutions offer customizable, fully integrated Web service for both large and small businesses.

after it has been ground up into a powder and mixed with water. The Black Mesa Pipeline, owned by Union Pacific, moves the coal mined by Peabody Coal from northern Arizona 290 miles south into southern Nevada. The planned Keystone Pipeline will move crude oil from Alberta, Canada, to the Gulf Coast.

Although pipelines offer low maintenance and dependable methods of transportation, a number of characteristics limit their applications. They have fewer locations than water carriers, and they can accommodate shipments of only a small number of products. Finally, pipelines represent a relatively slow method of transportation; liquids travel through this method at an average speed of only three to four miles per hour.

Air Freight

Although the air freight industry grew steadily for many years, recently that growth has dropped off—at least in certain market sectors like overnight delivery service. But firms are adapting. UPS recently revamped its services, now offering an expanded international express service called UPS Express Freight. The service provides guaranteed time-definite, overnight to three-day door-to-door delivery, including customs clearance, to large global metropolitan areas. UPS is also offering two less-expensive, nonguaranteed services: UPS Air Freight Direct and UPS Air Freight Consolidated. Both are available worldwide and provide package pickup, delivery, and customs clearance.[39]

Comparing the Five Modes of Transport

Table 14.3 compares the five transportation modes on several operating characteristics. Although all shippers judge reliability, speed, and cost in choosing the most appropriate transportation methods, they assign varying importance to specific criteria when shipping different goods. For example, while motor carriers rank highest in availability in different locations, shippers of petroleum products frequently choose the lowest-ranked alternative, pipelines, for their low cost. Examples of types of goods most often handled by the different modes of transport include:

- *railroads*—lumber, iron, steel, coal, automobiles, grain, and chemicals;
- *motor carriers*—clothing, furniture, fixtures, lumber, plastic, food, leather, and machinery;

TABLE 14.3 Comparison of Transport Modes

Mode	Speed	Dependability in Meeting Schedules	Frequency of Shipments	Availability in Different Locations	Flexibility in Handling	Cost
Rail	Average	Average	Low	Low	High	Average
Water	Very slow	Average	Very low	Limited	Very high	Very low
Truck	Fast	High	High	Very extensive	Average	High
Pipeline	Slow	High	High	Very limited	Very low	Low
Air	Very fast	High	Average	Average	Low	Very high

© Cengage Learning

ASSESSMENT CHECK

7.1 Identify the five major modes of transport.

7.2 Which mode of transport is currently experiencing a resurgence, and why?

- *water carriers*—fuel, oil, coal, chemicals, minerals, and petroleum products; automobiles and electronics from foreign manufacturers; and low-value products such as clothing and toys from foreign manufacturers;

- *pipelines*—oil, diesel fuel, jet fuel, kerosene, and natural gas; and

- *air freight*—flowers, medical testing kits, and gourmet food products sent directly to consumers.

FREIGHT FORWARDERS AND SUPPLEMENTAL CARRIERS

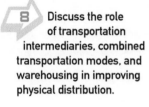

8 Discuss the role of transportation intermediaries, combined transportation modes, and warehousing in improving physical distribution.

Freight forwarders act as transportation intermediaries, consolidating shipments to gain lower rates for their customers. The transport rates on less-than-truckload (LTL) and less-than-carload (LCL) shipments often double the per-unit rates on truckload (TL) and carload (CL) shipments. Freight forwarders charge less than the highest rates but more than the lowest rates. They profit by consolidating shipments from multiple customers until they can ship at TL and CL rates. The customers gain two advantages from these services: lower costs on small shipments and faster delivery service than they could achieve with their own LTL and LCL shipments.

In addition to the transportation options reviewed so far, a logistics manager can ship products via a number of auxiliary, or supplemental, carriers that specialize in small shipments. These carriers include UPS, FedEx, and the U.S. Postal Service.

INTERMODAL COORDINATION

Transportation companies emphasize specific modes and serve certain kinds of customers, but they sometimes combine their services to give shippers the service and cost advantages of each. *Piggyback* service, mentioned in the section on rail transport, is the most widely used form of intermodal coordination. *Birdyback* service, another form of intermodal coordination, sends motor carriers to pick up a shipment locally and deliver that shipment to local destinations; an air carrier takes it between airports near those locations. *Fishyback* service sets up a similar intermodal coordination system between motor carriers and water carriers.

Intermodal transportation generally gives shippers faster service and lower rates than either mode could match individually because each method carries freight in its most efficient way. However, intermodal arrangements require close coordination between all transportation providers.

Recognizing this need, multimodal transportation companies have formed to offer combined activities within single operations. Piggyback service generally joins two separate companies: a railroad and a trucking company. A multimodal firm provides intermodal service through its own internal transportation resources. Shippers benefit because the single service assumes responsibility from origin to destination. This unification prevents disputes over which carrier delayed or damaged a shipment.

WAREHOUSING

Products flow through two types of warehouses: storage and distribution warehouses. A *storage ware-house* holds goods for moderate to long periods in an attempt to balance supply and demand for producers and purchasers. For example, controlled-atmosphere—also called *cold storage*—warehouses in Yakima and Wenatchee, Washington, serve nearby apple orchards. By contrast, a *distribution ware-house* assembles and redistributes goods, keeping them moving as much as possible. Many distribution warehouses or centers physically store goods for less than 24 hours before shipping them to customers.

Logistics managers have attempted to save on transportation costs by developing central distribution centers. A manufacturer might send a single, large, consolidated shipment to a break-bulk center—a central distribution center that breaks down large shipments into several smaller ones and delivers them to individual customers in the area. Many Internet retailers use break-bulk distribution centers.

Caterpillar Logistics Services is building a new parts distribution center in Spokane, Washington. The new facility will cover more than half a million square feet and employ up to 150 people. The new warehousing facility is intended to replace an existing 125,000-square-foot facility. The facility will be a convenient inbound receiving center close to suppliers and provide improved delivery of parts to Caterpillar dealers and customers.[40]

Automated Warehouse Technology

Logistics managers can cut distribution costs and improve customer service dramatically by automating their warehouse systems. Although automation technology represents an expensive investment, it can provide major labor savings for high-volume distributors like grocery chains. A computerized system might store orders, choose the correct number of cases, and move those cases in the desired sequence to loading docks. This kind of warehouse system reduces labor costs, worker injuries, pilferage, fires, and breakage.

Warehouse Locations

Every company must make a major logistics decision when it determines the number and locations of its storage facilities. Two categories of costs influence this choice: (1) warehousing and materials handling costs and (2) delivery costs from warehouses to customers. Large facilities offer economies of scale in facilities and materials handling systems; per-unit costs for these systems decrease as volume increases. Delivery costs, on the other hand, rise as the distance from warehouse to customer increases.

Clerkenwell_Images/iStockphoto

Products flow through two types of warehouses—storage and distribution warehouses. A storage warehouse holds goods for a moderate to long period of time while a distribution warehouse assembles and redistributes goods quickly.

Warehouse location also affects customer service. Businesses must place their storage and distribution facilities in locations from which they can meet customer demands for product availability and delivery times. They must also consider population and employment trends. For example, the rapid growth of metropolitan areas in the southern and western United States has caused some firms to open more distribution centers in these areas. Becton, Dickinson and Company, which manufactures medical devices, recently opened a new warehouse in Four Oaks, North Carolina. The warehouse ships 40 percent of the company's products to northern and southern destinations as well as to Europe. It employs 140 people, who use state-of-the-art technology to track their work via computer. When carrying large boxes from high shelves, the forklifts take advantage of gravity; the motion recharges their batteries. Skylights supply most of the building with light and can track the sun across the sky to provide light. Solar panels provide about one-fifth of the electricity supply, and the remainder of the roof is a "cool roof" that reflects sunlight. The facility became BD's first warehouse to earn gold certification from the LEED program.[41]

INVENTORY CONTROL SYSTEMS

Inventory control captures a large share of a logistics manager's attention, because companies need to maintain enough inventory to meet customer demand without incurring unneeded costs for carrying excess inventory. Some firms attempt to keep inventory levels under control by implementing just-in-time (JIT) production. Others, as discussed earlier in this chapter, are beginning to use RFID technology.

Retailers often shift the responsibility—and costs—for inventory from themselves back to individual manufacturers. Vendor-managed inventory (VMI) systems like this are based on the assumption that suppliers are in the best position to spot understocks or surpluses, cutting costs along the supply chain that can be translated into lower prices at the checkout. Datalliance provides VMI platform services in consumer and industrial applications. In the retail sector, it helps manufacturers that want to replenish supplies by sending them directly to retail stores rather than to distribution centers. Among its clients are Asics, Entertainment 1, and Elizabeth Arden.[42]

ORDER PROCESSING

Like inventory control, order processing directly affects the firm's ability to meet its customer service standards. A company may have to compensate for inefficiencies in its order-processing system by shipping products via costly transportation modes or by maintaining large inventories at many expensive field warehouses.

Order processing typically consists of four major activities: (1) conducting a credit check; (2) keeping a record of the sale, which involves tasks like crediting a sales representative's commission account; (3) making appropriate accounting entries; and (4) locating orders, shipping them, and adjusting inventory records. A stockout occurs when an order for an item is not available for shipment. A firm's order-processing system must advise affected customers of a stockout and offer a choice of alternative actions.

As in other areas of physical distribution, technological innovations improve efficiency in order processing. Many firms are streamlining their order-processing procedures by using email and the Internet. The outdoor-gear retailer REI, for example, pushes customers toward Web ordering—its least costly fulfillment channel—in its catalogs, store receipts, signs, mailers, and membership letters.

PROTECTIVE PACKAGING AND MATERIALS HANDLING

Logistics managers arrange and control activities for moving products within plants, warehouses, and transportation terminals, which together compose the materials handling system. Two important concepts influence many materials handling choices: unitizing and containerization.

Unitizing combines as many packages as possible into each load that moves within or outside a facility. Logistics managers prefer to handle materials on pallets (platforms, generally made of wood, on which goods are transported). Unitizing systems often lash materials in place with steel bands or shrink packaging. A shrink package surrounds a batch of materials with a sheet of plastic that shrinks

materials handling system Set of activities that move production inputs and other goods within factories, warehouses, and transportation terminals.

after heating, securely holding individual pieces together. Unitizing promotes efficient materials handling because each package requires minimal labor to move. Securing the materials together also minimizes damage and pilferage. American-Canadian Ridley Inc. manufactures animal feeds, which it sells to breeders and growers. At its Beloit, Kansas, plant, the company uses an efficient process in distributing its products as *unitized pallets*—that is, a pallet holding merchandise ready for storage and shipping to customers. To create these pallets, the company invested in a palletizing line that can handle 24 bags of feed per minute. The machine sprays a food-grade, water-soluble material called Lock n'Pop onto each bag, preventing spillage. The bags then enter a robotic palletizer. Instead of stretch wrap, the palletizer can be programmed with two types of adhesive spray for stacking the pallets. Dustin Varvil, Ridley's director of manufacturing, says, "We replaced 55 cents per pallet of stretch wrap with 5 cents of Lock n'Pop while eliminating a sizeable investment in new stretch equipment."[43]

Logistics managers extend the same concept through **containerization**—combining several unitized loads. A container of oil rig parts, for example, can be loaded in Topeka and trucked to Kansas City, where rail facilities place the shipment on a high-speed run-through train to New York City. There, the parts are loaded onto a ship headed to Saudi Arabia.

containerization
Process of combining several unitized loads into a single, well-protected load for shipment.

In addition to the benefits outlined for unitizing, containerization also markedly reduces the time required to load and unload ships. Containers limit in-transit damage to freight because individual packages pass through fewer handling systems en route to purchasers.

ASSESSMENT CHECK

8.1 What are the benefits of intermodal transportation?

8.2 Identify the two types of warehouses, and explain their function.

© iStockphoto.com/Ferran Traite Soler

STRATEGIC IMPLICATIONS OF MARKETING IN THE 21ST CENTURY

Several factors, including the e-business environment, security issues, and the cost of fuel, are driving changes in channel development, logistics, and supply chain management. As the Internet continues to revolutionize the ways manufacturers deliver goods to ultimate consumers, marketers must find ways to promote cooperation between existing dealer, retailer, and distributor networks while harnessing the power of the Web as a channel. This system demands not only delivery of goods and services faster and more efficiently than ever before, it also provides superior service to Web-based customers.

In addition, increased product proliferation—grocery stores typically stock almost 50,000 different items—demands logistics systems that can manage multiple brands delivered through multiple channels worldwide. Those channels must be finely tuned to identify and rapidly rectify problems like retail shortfalls or costly overstocks. The trend toward leaner retailing, in which the burden of merchandise tracking and inventory control is switching from retailers to manufacturers, means that, to be effective, logistics and supply chain systems must result in cost savings.

Get online now for additional learning tools to help you master your marketing knowledge—visit **WWW.CENGAGEBRAIN.COM** today!

REVIEW OF CHAPTER OBJECTIVES

1 Describe the types of marketing channels and the roles they play in marketing strategy.

Marketing (distribution) channels are the systems of marketing institutions that enhance the physical flow of goods and services, along with ownership title, from producer to consumer or business user. In other words, they help bridge the gap between producer or manufacturer and business customer or consumer. Types of channels include direct selling, selling through intermediaries, dual distribution, and reverse channels. Channels perform four functions: facilitating the exchange process, sorting, standardizing exchange processes, and facilitating searches by buyers and sellers.

2 Outline the major channel strategy decisions.

Decisions include selecting a marketing channel and determining distribution intensity. Selection of a marketing channel may be based on market factors, product factors, organizational factors, or competitive factors. Distribution may be intensive, selective, or exclusive.

3 Describe the concepts of channel management, conflict, and cooperation.

Manufacturers must practice channel management by developing and maintaining relationships with the intermediaries in their marketing channels. The channel captain is the dominant member of the channel. Horizontal and vertical conflict can arise when disagreement exists among channel members. Cooperation is best achieved when all channel members regard themselves as equal components of the same organization.

4 Identify and describe the different vertical marketing systems.

A vertical marketing system (VMS) is a planned channel system designed to improve distribution efficiency and cost-effectiveness by integrating various functions throughout the distribution chain. This coordination can be achieved by forward integration or backward integration. Options include a corporate marketing system, operated by a single owner; an administered marketing system, run by a dominant channel member; and contractual marketing systems, based on formal agreements among channel members.

5 Explain the roles of logistics and supply chain management in an overall distribution strategy.

Effective logistics requires proper supply chain management. The supply chain begins with raw materials, proceeds through actual production, and then continues with the movement of finished products through the marketing channel to customers. Supply chain management takes place in two directions: upstream and downstream. Tools that marketers use to streamline and manage logistics include radio-frequency identification (RFID), enterprise resource planning (ERP), and logistical cost control.

6 Identify the major components of a physical distribution system.

Physical distribution involves a broad range of activities concerned with efficient movement of finished goods from the end of the production line to the consumer. As a system, physical distribution consists of six elements: (1) customer service, (2) transportation, (3) inventory control, (4) materials handling and protective packaging, (5) order processing, and (6) warehousing. These elements are interrelated and must be balanced to create a smoothly functioning distribution system and to avoid suboptimization.

7 Compare the major modes of transportation.

The five major modes of transport are railroads, motor carriers, water freight, pipelines, and air freight. Railroads rank high on flexibility in handling products; average on speed, dependability in meeting schedules, and cost; and lower on frequency of shipments. Motor carriers are relatively high in cost but rank high on speed, dependability, shipment frequency, and availability in different locations. Water carriers balance their slow speed, low shipment frequency, and limited availability with lower costs. The special nature of pipelines makes them rank relatively low on availability, flexibility, and speed, but they are also lower in cost. Air transportation is high in cost but offers very fast and dependable delivery schedules.

8 Discuss the role of transportation intermediaries, combined transportation modes, and warehousing in improving physical distribution.

Transportation intermediaries facilitate movement of goods in a variety of ways, including piggyback, birdyback, and fishyback services—all forms of intermodal coordination. Methods like unitization and containerization facilitate intermodal transfers.

ASSESSMENT CHECK: ANSWERS

1.1 Distinguish between a marketing channel and logistics. A marketing channel is an organized system of marketing institutions and their interrelationships, designed to enhance the flow and ownership of goods and services from producer to user. Logistics is the actual process of coordinating the flow of information, goods, and services among members of the marketing channel.

1.2 What are the different types of marketing channels? The different types of marketing channels are direct selling, selling through intermediaries, dual distribution, and reverse channels.

1.3 What four functions do marketing channels perform? The four functions of marketing channels are (1) facilitating the exchange process by reducing the number of marketplace contacts necessary for a sale, (2) sorting, (3) standardizing exchange transactions, and (4) facilitating searches by buyers and sellers.

2.1 Identify four major factors in selecting a marketing channel. The four major factors in selecting a marketing channel are market, product, organizational, and competitive.

2.2 Describe the three general categories of distribution intensity. Intensive distribution seeks to distribute a product through all available channels in a trade area. Selective distribution chooses a limited number of retailers in a market area. Exclusive distribution grants exclusive rights to a wholesaler or retailer to sell a manufacturer's products.

3.1 What is a channel captain? What is its role in channel cooperation? A channel captain is the dominant member of the marketing channel. Its role in channel cooperation is to provide the necessary leadership.

3.2 Identify and describe the three types of channel conflict. Horizontal conflict results from disagreements among channel members at the same level. Vertical conflict occurs when channel members at different levels disagree. The gray market causes conflict because it involves competition in the U.S. market of brands produced by overseas affiliates.

4.1 What are vertical marketing systems? Identify the major types. Vertical marketing systems are planned channel systems designed to improve the effectiveness of

distribution, including efficiency and cost. The three major types are corporate, administered, and contractual.

4.2 Identify the three types of contractual marketing systems. The three types of contractual systems are wholesale-sponsored voluntary chains, retail cooperatives, and franchises.

5.1 What is upstream management? What is downstream management? Upstream management involves managing raw materials, inbound logistics, and warehouse and storage facilities. Downstream management involves managing finished product storage, outbound logistics, marketing and sales, and customer service.

5.2 Identify three methods for managing logistics. Methods for managing logistics include RFID technology, enterprise resource planning (ERP) systems, and logistical cost control.

6.1 What are the six major elements of physical distribution? The major elements of physical distribution are customer service, transportation, inventory control, materials handling and protective packaging, order processing, and warehousing.

6.2 What is suboptimization? Suboptimization occurs when managers of individual functions try to reduce costs but create less than optimal results.

7.1 Identify the five major modes of transport. The five major modes of transport are railroads, motor carriers, water carriers, pipelines, and air freight.

7.2 Which mode of transport is currently experiencing a resurgence, and why? Railroad transport is currently experiencing a resurgence because of the cost of fuel and its efficiency in transporting large amounts of freight while using less fuel.

8.1 What are the benefits of intermodal transportation? Intermodal transportation usually provides shippers faster service and lower rates than a single mode could offer.

8.2 Identify the two types of warehouses, and explain their function. The two types of warehouses are storage and distribution. Storage warehouses hold goods for moderate to long periods of time to balance supply and demand. Distribution warehouses assemble and redistribute goods as quickly as possible.

MARKETING TERMS YOU NEED TO KNOW

distribution **452**

marketing (distribution) channel **452**

logistics **452**

supply chain management **452**

physical distribution **452**

marketing intermediary (middleman) **453**

wholesaler **453**

direct channel **455**

direct selling **455**

manufacturers' representative **456**

dual distribution **456**

reverse channel **457**

intensive distribution **461**

selective distribution **461**

exclusive distribution **462**

closed sales territory **462**

tying agreement **462**

channel captain **463**

gray goods **464**

vertical marketing system (VMS) **465**

forward integration **465**

backward integration **465**

corporate marketing system **466**

administered marketing system **466**

contractual marketing system **466**

retail cooperative **466**

franchise **466**

supply chain **468**

upstream management **468**

downstream management **468**

radio-frequency identification (RFID) **469**

enterprise resource planning (ERP) system **470**

third-party (contract) logistics firm **470**

suboptimization **471**

common carriers **472**

contract carriers **473**

private carriers **473**

intermodal operations **473**

materials handling system **478**

containerization **479**

ASSURANCE OF LEARNING REVIEW

1. What is a marketing intermediary? What is the intermediary's role?

2. Explain why the following firms might choose a dual distribution strategy:
   a. Netflix
   b. Home Shopping Network
   c. Kohl's

3. Describe the three levels of distribution intensity. Give an example of a product in each level.

4. Compare and contrast the two types of channel conflict. Why is channel conflict damaging to all parties?

5. What are the benefits of owning a franchise? What are the drawbacks?

6. Why do firms choose to streamline their supply chains? Describe two or three ways a firm might go about streamlining its supply chain.

7. What are the five components associated with the cost of achieving customer service standards in a physical distribution system?

8. Which mode of transport would probably be most appropriate for the following goods?
   a. diesel fuel
   b. chain-link fencing
   c. locally grown blueberries
   d. automobiles made in South Korea
   e. T-shirts manufactured in Vietnam
   f. grain grown in Nebraska

9. Which two categories of costs influence the choice of how many storage facilities a firm might have and where they are located?

10. Describe the two concepts that influence materials handling choices. Give an example of a product that would be appropriate for each.

PROJECTS AND TEAMWORK EXERCISES

1. The traditional channel for consumer goods runs from producer to wholesaler to retailer to user. With a classmate, select a product from the following list (or choose one of your own) and create a chart that traces its distribution system. You may go online to the firm's website for additional information.
   a. kayak from the Orvis catalog or website
   b. tickets to a NFL game
   c. HD TV from Costco

2. On your own or with a classmate, identify, draw, and explain a reverse channel with which you are familiar. What purpose does this reverse channel serve for businesses? For the community? For consumers?

3. With a classmate, choose a product you think would sell best through a direct channel. Then create a brief sales presentation for your product and present it to the class. Ask for feedback.

4. With a classmate, choose a franchise that interests you. Visit the website of the company to learn more about how its goods and services are distributed. Create a chart outlining the firm's physical distribution system.

5. It takes a lot to move an elaborate stage show like Cirque du Soleil, Big Apple Circus, or a rock band from one location to another while it is on tour. With a classmate, choose a touring performance that interests you—a music group, a circus, a theater performance, or the like—and imagine you are in charge of logistics. Create a chart showing what modes of transportation you would select to move the performance, how you would warehouse certain items during downtime, and what methods you would use to control costs.

CRITICAL-THINKING EXERCISES

1. Imagine a vending machine that would charge more for hot drinks—coffee, tea, and cocoa—during cold weather. What is your opinion of a temperature-sensitive vending machine? Consumers who live in colder climates might pay more over a longer time period each year than consumers who live in warmer climates. Would your opinion change if alternatives were nearby, say, a convenience store or a vending machine that is not temperature-sensitive? Do you think such a machine would be successful? Why or why not?

2. Auto dealerships typically have exclusive distribution rights in their local markets. How might this affect the purchase choices consumers make? What problems might a dealership encounter with this type of distribution?

3. Choose one of the following firms and identify which marketing channel or channels you think would be best for its goods or services. Then explain the market factors, product factors, and organizational and competitive factors contributing to your selection.

   a. Pottery Barn
   b. Outback Steakhouse
   c. *Golf Digest* magazine
   d. LPGA
   e. The Gap

4. In their most basic form, RFID tags track the progress of products from warehouse to retail shelf to checkout counter. But they have great potential to provide marketers with more information about consumers' purchase patterns. In what ways might RFID technology be used to serve customers better? What problems might arise?

5. After a trip to India, where you were inspired by the craftsmanship of artisans who make jewelry and decorative artifacts, you decide to establish an import business focusing on their work. How would you determine distribution intensity for your business? What mode or modes of transportation would you use to get the goods to the United States? How and where would you warehouse the goods? Explain your answers.

ETHICS EXERCISE

As more and more firms do business globally, transporting goods from one part of the world to another, there has been a surge in piracy—criminals making off with cargo shipments of all kinds. A tractor-trailer loaded with electronics might be stolen from a truck stop; a warehouse with pallets of new clothing, video games, or other goods is susceptible to theft. Large, sophisticated cargo theft gangs have been identified by police in California, New Jersey, New York, and Texas and in cities such as Atlanta, Chicago, and Miami.

However, members of the supply chain can work together to close the net around would-be thieves, developing stronger relationships with each other and law enforcement.[44]

1. What steps might manufacturers take to achieve the kind of channel cooperation that could reduce or prevent cargo theft?

2. How might transportation firms use security measures to build trust with customers and strengthen their position in the marketplace?

INTERNET EXERCISES

1. **Channel conflicts.** Garmin produces a wide range of GPS devices for a variety of applications. Garmin uses several channels to sell its products, including its own Web store. Visit the Garmin USA website. How does Garmin avoid channel conflict? Explain your answer.

   www.garmin.com/us

2. **RFID developments.** Go to the website of the RFID Journal. Review the material and prepare a report outlining some of the more significant developments in RFID technology.

   www.rfidjournal.com

3. **Barge transportation statistics.** Visit the website of the American Waterways Operators. Click on "About the Industry" and answer the following questions:

   a. How many barges are in operation in the United States?

   b. What commodities are typically shipped by barge in the United States?

   c. Compared to railroads and trucks, why are barges a more economical way to ship certain types of commodities?

   www.americanwaterways.com

Note: Internet Web addresses change frequently. If you don't find the exact site listed, you may need to access the organization's home page and search from there or use a search engine such as Google or Bing.

CASE 14.1
Natural Disasters Disrupt the Global Supply Chain

Aside from tragic human losses and incalculable damage to property, manufacturers around the world were affected by two recent, unprecedented natural disasters. First came the magnitude 9.0 earthquake and tsunami that hit Japan, followed by deadly flooding in Thailand in the same year. While damage to Japan's automotive parts makers and Thailand's disk drive industry immediately affected customers like Honda and Apple, manufacturers as far away as Ohio and Denmark, making products from shoes to aircraft tires, also were hampered by supply chain disruptions.

Danish shoe manufacturer ECCO used scuba divers to retrieve specialized shoe molds from a flooded Thai factory to continue producing at other locations. Honda employees in Ohio grappled with temporarily reduced hours while awaiting parts from Thailand. Some key Honda suppliers in Japan had still not resumed shipments of components unobtainable anywhere else. Nissan, meanwhile, sent car parts normally intended for U.S. plants to Asia in order to continue production. Apple and Hewlett Packard predicted reduced future earnings, based on supply disruptions after hard-drive manufacturer Seagate suffered damage to its two Thai factories. And without hard drives, computer manufacturers had less need of computer chips, so Intel also predicted lower revenues.

In Japan alone the economic costs of the earthquake and tsunami were running at $210 billion before the year was over, and losses in Thailand reached an estimated $30 billion only weeks after the floods receded.

The two disasters' lingering (and sometimes cascading) effects led some companies to reconsider their reliance on lean, decentralized manufacturing methods, including just-in-time, all of which increase efficiency and reduce costs but may leave companies vulnerable to supply chain disruptions. Natural disasters are unavoidable, and even early warning offers limited advantages.

With the likelihood of more extreme weather to come, some companies have pulled back from lean methods and invested once again in redundancy—multiple suppliers, backup facilities, and stockpiles of critical parts. After all, in an insurance company's survey completed before the earthquake in Japan, 600 CFOs were asked what threat to their revenue drivers they most feared. The most common answer: supply chain disruptions.

QUESTIONS FOR CRITICAL THINKING

1. Do you think companies are wise to favor backup systems over lean manufacturing? Why or why not?

2. In what other ways could companies safeguard their supply chains, including transportation methods, against natural disasters?

Sources: Regina Cline, "One Year Later, Natural Disasters Still Rattling Supply Chains," *Bloomberg BNA*, accessed November 30, 2012, www.bna.com; Bill Powell, "The Global Supply Chain: So Very Fragile," *CNN Money*, accessed November 30, 2012, http://tech.fortune.cnn.com; Thomas Farole and Julia Oliver, "Shoe Molds and Scuba Divers: How Natural Disasters Affect Our Supply Chains," *World Bank Growth and Crisis Blog*, accessed November 30, 2012, http://blogs.worldbank.org; "Supply Chain News: Did Major Supply Chain Disruptions from Natural Disasters in 2011 Really Change Approach to Supply Chain Risk Management?" *Supply Chain Digest*, accessed November 30, 2012, www.scdigest.com.

VIDEO CASE 14.2
Geoffrey B. Small Keeps Marketing Channels Tight

Designer Geoffrey B. Small doesn't want you to buy his clothes. In fact, he might be disappointed if you were able to find them in a store at all. Small is an American designer who cut his teeth in the clothing industry by selling jeans at The Gap in Boston. Today, Small's overall marketing channel strategy is the opposite of The Gap's: the fewer pieces he sells, the more successful he becomes.

Small is blunt about the importance of exclusive distribution to the image of his goods and his relationships with retail partners as well as consumers. "We have one of the tightest distributions in the world-designer industry," says Small. "It's very difficult to find our collection. So it's very exclusive, and that's by choice, that's important for our customer. We're not for everybody, and we're not interested in being available to everybody." Small explains that the benefits of exclusive distribution outweigh the drawbacks. While it's true that his firm doesn't sell as many clothes as other clothing manufacturers (sometimes Small only makes four pieces of one design), he believes that reverse psychology works. "People want what they can't have," he observes. "Exclusivity is a fundamental part of our field," he comments. "If you're too available, nobody makes money." Small makes his profit by selling less—not more.

The flip side to the exclusivity coin is the mandate that a product represent the very best quality of its type in the world. Small is confident that his clothes meet the highest standards for fabric, tailoring, and workmanship. To achieve this goal, he headquarters his business in Italy right near his suppliers. "If you're trying to make the very best clothes in the world today in terms of materials, components, and accessories in collaborative work-partnerships, there's only one place in the world—and that's Italy." The designer deliberately keeps his supply chain very short. "We're in a region in Italy where we're very close to the best suppliers in the world, and we work with them," Small says.

Small partners with two fabric makers: one is the oldest woolen maker in the world, and the other is a multigenerational family company. Small is working with the second firm to develop what he hopes will be the world's best organic fiber, with the ultimate goal of making the world's best sustainable fabrics to be used in luxury fashion design. He is proud of the way these textile manufacturers complement the expertise his team brings to the design table. They bring "a level of artisanal excellence that is unique in the world," says Small. He also notes that the components of his garments reflect the highest concentration of handwork available that he's aware of.

Small also maintains a close relationship with his other channel partners, the retailers who carry his finished garments. Despite the extremely limited production runs of his clothing, Small's designs can be found in 10 countries. In addition to producing a handful of items to be sold across retailers (sometimes one jacket or pair of pants per country), Small works with his retail partners to come up with designs exclusively for the customers of a particular store. Because so few items are produced in any given year, Small says that visiting every store is difficult—but he does it. "The store is where the action is," he explains. He likes to meet with retail staff who, he believes, are the most connected to customers—yet are often underappreciated. Small believes that the retail staff holds key information about consumer needs and preferences. Small also likes to speak directly with customers on his retail visits, engaging in one-on-one communication with the people who buy his clothes.

You won't see a Geoffrey B. Small line at Target or even at Gap any time soon. Small doesn't want to sell you his clothes unless you share his outlook on fashion, appreciate his designs and fabrics, will happily pay top dollar for them, and know the right retailers. Although he wants to grow his business, he insists on doing it his own way: with the marketing channels as precise and tight as one of his hand-sewn stitches.

QUESTIONS FOR CRITICAL THINKING

1. Over the next 10 years, do you think Small's insistence on exclusivity will continue to benefit his business or begin to be detrimental? Why?

2. In your opinion, why does Small have such successful partnerships throughout his marketing channels?

Sources: "The Amazing Geoffrey B. Small Story," company website, www.geoffreybsmall.net/gbstory.htm, accessed November 30, 2012; Geoffrey B. Small, "The Environment of Young Designers," *Not Just a Label*, accessed November 30, 2012, www.notjustalabel.com; Claire Ruhlin, "Recycle, Reconstruct, Redesign," *Community*, accessed November 30, 2012, http://communityathens.blogspot.com; Eugene Rabkin, "Review: Geoffrey B. Small, Fall/Winter 2012," *Style Zeitgeist Magazine*, accessed November 30, 2012, www.sz-magazine.com.

NOTES

1. "The World's 50 Most Innovative Companies in 2012: Kiva Systems," *Fast Company*, accessed November 30, 2012, www.fastcompany.com; Spencer Ante, "Amazon Adds that Robotic Touch," *The Wall Street Journal*, accessed November 30, 2012, http://online.wsj.com; "Amazon Acquires Robot-Coordinated Order Fulfillment Company Kiva Systems for $775 Million in Cash," *TechCrunch.com*, accessed November 30, 2012, http://techcrunch.com; "Robots to the Rescue," *Alumni Bulletin*, Harvard Business School, accessed November 30, 2012, www.alumni.hbs.edu; Jennifer Alsever, "Robot Workers Take over Warehouses," *CNN Money*, accessed November 30, 2012, http://money.cnn.com; A. Selway Ryan, "Robots in Disguise," *Supply Chain Digital*, accessed November 30, 2012, www.supplychaindigital.com.

2. James Newton, "Ubisoft Announces Avengers Game for Wii U," *Nintendo Life*, accessed November 30, 2012, www.nintendolife.com; James Newton, "NBA 2K13 Confirmed for Wii U Launch Period," *Nintendo Life*, accessed November 30, 2012, www.nintendolife.com; Company website, http://e3.nintendo.com, accessed November 30, 2012.

3. Paula Bernstein, "The Right Fit: Social, Mobile, Display, Search, Video … How Marketers Are Choosing Their Digital Options," *Adweek*, accessed November 30, 2012, www.adweek.com.

4. Eric Markowitz, "Independent Coffee Shops Caught in Price Squeeze," *Inc.*, accessed November 30, 2012, www.inc.com; Susan J. Aluise, "Warning: Coffee Prices Are Headed Up," *Investor Place*, accessed November 30, 2012, www.investorplace.com.

5. "Sales Representatives, Wholesale and Manufacturing," *Occupational Outlook Handbook, 2012–2013*, Bureau of Labor Statistics, accessed November 30, 2012, www.bls.gov.

6. Company website, www.stelladot.com, accessed November 30, 2012; Marisa Meltzer, "At Stella & Dot, Hostesses with a Percentage," *The New York Times*, accessed November 30, 2012, www.nytimes.com.

7. Company website, www.bagborroworsteal.com, accessed November 30, 2012.

8. Don Reisinger, "Netflix Arrives on Nintendo 3DS," *CNET News*, accessed November 30, 2012, http://news.cnet.com.

9. "Great Battery Round-Up to Collect Used Car Batteries for Recycling," *Auto Car Battery*, accessed November 30, 2012, www.auto-car-battery.com.

10. Company website, www.nikereuseashoe.com, accessed November 30, 2012; company website, www.officedepot.com, accessed November 30, 2012.

11. Andy Newman, "Cupcake-Dispensing ATMs? What's Next?" *The New York Times*, accessed November 30, 2012, http://cityroom.blogs.nytimes.com.

12. Company website, http://petropics.com, accessed November 30, 2012; "Tiki Dog Food Reviews," *I Love Dogs*, accessed November 30, 2012, www.i-love-dogs.com; William Grimes, "Boeuf Bourguignon Again? Pet Foods Go Gourmet," *The New York Times*, accessed November 30, 2012, www.nytimes.com.

13. Mark Brohan, "A Conflicted Group: Top 500 Manufacturers Need to Address Channel Conflict and Speed Up Online Productivity," *Internet Retailer*, accessed November 30, 2012, www.internetretailer.com.

14. "The Changing World of Industrial Distribution," *B2B International*, accessed November 30, 2012, www.b2binternational.com.

15. "FMI Speaks: The State of the Food Retail Industry," *Food Marketing Institute*, accessed November 30, 2012, http://fmi.org.

16. Bruce Blythe, "Wal-Mart Bets on Grocery Sales for Growth," *The Packer*, accessed November 30, 2012, www.thepacker.com; "Walmart to Lower Its Grocery Prices by $1B," *Convenience Store News*, accessed November 30, 2012, www.csnews.com.

17. Tom Cheredar, "Comcast Launches 'Netflix-like' Streampix to Complement Expensive Cable Packages," *Venture Beat*, accessed November 30, 2012, http://venturebeat.com; "Daily Report: Netflix Transitions to TV Shows," *The New York Times*, accessed November 30, 2012, http://bits.blogs.nytimes.com; Quentin Hardy, "The Explosion of Mobile Video," *The New York Times*, accessed November 30, 2012, http://bits.blogs.nytimes.com.

18. Katia Hetter, "Travel Agents Know Something You Don't," *CNN*, accessed November 30, 2012, www.cnn.com; "Travel Agencies in the US Industry Market Research Report Now Available from IBISWorld," *PR Web*, accessed November 30, 2012, www.prweb.com; Daniel Bortz, "Why It Pays to Book with a Travel Agent," *U.S. News and World Report*, accessed November 30, 2012, http://money.usnews.com.

19. Darrell Etherington, "Big Shipment of Grey Market iPhones and iPads Busted at Hong Kong Border," *Tech Crunch*, accessed November 30, 2012, http://techcrunch.com; Michael Kan, "Half of iPads Sold in China from Gray Market," *Computerworld*,

accessed November 30, 2012, www.computerworld.com; Kevin Voigt, "iPad Hits Hong Kong—Before Global Release," *CNN.com*, accessed November 30, 2012, http://articles.cnn.com; Owen Fletcher, "Amazon Kindle Hits China's Grey Market," *MacWorld UK*, accessed November 30, 2012, www.macworld.co.uk.

20. Company website, www.3net.com, accessed November 30, 2012; "3net: A 3E Channel by Discovery, Sony, IMAX," *Adweek*, accessed November 30, 2012, www.adweek.com.

21. "Quick Franchise Facts, Franchising Industry Statistics," *A–Z Franchises*, accessed November 30, 2012, www.azfranchises.com.

22. Company website, "About Pier 1 Imports," www.pier1.com, accessed November 30, 2012.

23. Company website, www.jda.com, accessed November 30, 2012.

24. Claire Swedberg, "Treehouse Labs Unveils iPhone RFID System for Locating People and Things," *RFID Journal*, accessed November 30, 2012, www.rfidjournal.com.

25. Mark Smith, "SAP Spends Big on SuccessFactors for Cloud Computing and Talent Management," *Ventana Research*, accessed November 30, 2012, http://marksmith .ventanaresearch.com; Aaron Racardela, "Oracle Buys Taleo for $1.9 Billion," Bloomberg, accessed November 30, 2012, www.bloomberg.com; Tien Tzuo, "The End of ERP," Forbes, accessed November 30, 2012, www.forbes.com.

26. DC Velocity Staff, "U.S. Third-Party Logistics Sector Sees Solid Gains," *DC Velocity*, accessed November 30, 2012, www.dcvelocity.com.

27. DC Velocity Staff, "U.S. Third-Party Logistics Sector Sees Solid Gains"; Eric Snyder, "Logistics Industry Grows into Economic Giant," *Nashville Business Journal*, accessed November 30, 2012, www.bizjournals.com.

28. Company website, www.zappos.com, accessed November 30, 2012.

29. "Trucking Statistics," *Truck Info*, accessed November 30, 2012, www.truckinfo.net.

30. Organization website, "North American Freight Railroad Statistics," www.aar.org, accessed November 30, 2012.

31. FedEx Small Business Center, "Holtkamp Greenhouses," www.fedex.com, accessed November 30, 2012.

32. Christopher Mahoney, "AAR Announces Record Investment for 2012," *The Railroad Network*, accessed November 30, 2012, www.railroad.net; Association of American Railroads, "Railroad Infrastructure Investment," www.aar.org, accessed November 30, 2012.

33. Sean McNally, "ATA Truck Tonnage Index Fell 1.1% in April," *American Trucking Association*, accessed November 30, 2012, www.truckline.com.

34. Cyrus Sanati, "The Biggest Winners of Obama's Natural Gas Push," *Fortune*, accessed November 30, 2012, http://finance.fortune.cnn.com; "Truck Drivers Wanted—A Look at Husband and Wife Teams," *Drivers Wanted Headquarters*, accessed November 30, 2012, www.driverswantedhq.com.

35. Patrick Burnson, "Ocean Cargo Carriers Remain in Doldrums," *Logistics Management*, accessed November 30, 2012, www.logisticsmgmt.com.

36. Company website, www.dhl.com, accessed November 30, 2012.

37. Mark Thornton, "Panama Canal Expansion Could Bring Shift in Distribution Patterns," *RE Journals.com*, accessed November 30, 2012, www.rejournals.com; Robert Wright, "Panama Canal Upgrade Sparks US Ports Battle," *Financial Times*, accessed November 30, 2012, www.ft.com; Alex Leff, "Panama Canal Expansion a 'Game Changer,'" *The Tico Times*, accessed November 30, 2012, www.ticotimes.net.

38. U.S. Department of Transportation, Office of Pipeline Safety, "Pipeline Basics," PHMSA Stakeholder Communications, http://primis.phmsa.dot.gov, accessed November 30, 2012.

39. Company website, www.ups-scs.com, accessed November 30, 2012.

40. John Stucke, "West Plains Caterpillar Distribution Center on Track," *The Spokesman-Review*, accessed November 30, 2012, www.spokesman.com.

41. Colin Campbell, "Four Oaks Becomes a Hub," *Smithfield Herald*, accessed November 30, 2012, www.theherald-nc.com.

42. Company website, www.datalliance.com, accessed November 30, 2012; "Datalliance Expands Staff to Support Growth in VMI for Direct Store Replenishment," press release, *Reuters*, accessed November 30, 2012, www.reuters.com.

43. "Bags Shipped Trouble-Free without Stretch Wrap," Powder Bulk Solids, accessed November 30, 2012, www.powderbulksolids.com.

44. Inbound Logistics, "Preventing Cargo Theft," *Transport Security*, accessed November 30, 2012, www.transportsecurity.com.

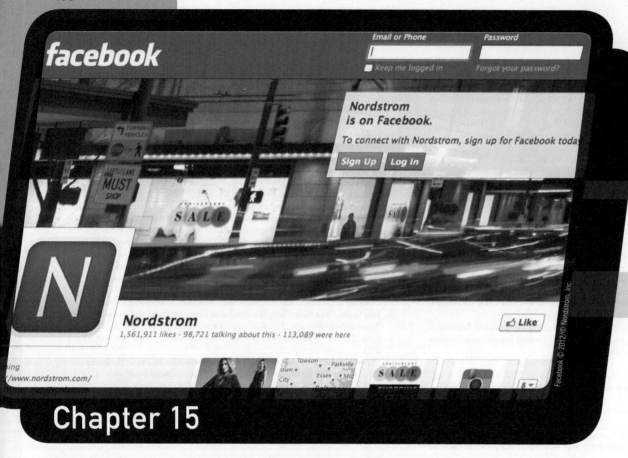

Chapter 15

RETAILERS,
Wholesalers, and Direct Marketers

1. Explain the wheel of retailing.
2. Discuss how retailers select target markets.
3. Show how the elements of the marketing mix apply to retailing strategy.
4. Explain the concepts of retail convergence and scrambled merchandising.
5. Identify the functions performed by wholesaling intermediaries.
6. Outline the major types of independent wholesaling intermediaries and the appropriate situations for using each.
7. Compare the basic types of direct marketing and nonstore retailing.
8. Describe how much the Internet has altered the wholesaling, retailing, and direct marketing environments.

What do you get when you pair the buzz of an Internet fashion startup with the deep pockets and brand recognition of a venerable fashion chain? For online menswear seller Bonobos and Seattle-based department store chain Nordstrom, the answer is increased sales.

Its recent $16.4 million purchase of Bonobos is just one of many ways Nordstrom is reaching into social media, mobile technology, and e-commerce, with promising results for the 112-year-old retailer. Looking for growth, and recognizing that it's unlikely to come from the company's 232 brick-and-mortar department stores and discount outlets, Nordstrom has also acquired or invested in the flash-site membership site HauteLook, the online shoe club Sole Society, and the kids' clothing e-tailer Peek. The president of its online division, Jamie Nordstrom, says calling a Facebook page a social media strategy is "a little shortsighted," so the company has taken an aggressive approach to moving online. It reconfigured its own website to create a seamless shopping experience and maintains a presence on trending sites like Instagram, Pinterest, and Polyvore, as well

as on social media venues like Facebook, Twitter, and YouTube.

Technology is also improving the in-store experience. Salespeople at Nordstrom's stores use iPads to help customers shop, make selections, and check inventory. Free Wi-Fi access for customers has been available at the stores for several years, and those who shop both online and in person can pick up their Internet purchases at the store. They won't waste a lot of time standing in line to pay, either. Thousands of iTouch devices, modified to function as point-of-sale units, have been distributed to Nordstrom's staff so they can offer "mobile checkout," bypassing the cash register to ring up sales from anywhere inside the company's stores.

Despite the recession, Nordstrom's online sales have grown 30 percent, rising to $10 billion for the first time, and the company plans to increase its investment in e-commerce to $140 million, the highest level yet. After Nordstrom purchased HauteLook for $180 million, the flash sale site's membership doubled to 7.5 million, and sales jumped 60 percent.

Its new partners are helping Nordstrom with more than improved sales. The company has adopted some of HauteLook's social media savvy to better personalize its customer emails, and executives from both HauteLook and Bonobos will be designing new mobile apps for Nordstrom.com. Now that it's notched improvements over past years in both the number of items sold and the average selling price, Nordstrom's aggressive hi-tech strategies seem to be paying off.[1]

EVOLUTION OF A  BRAND

In purchasing Bonobos and buying or investing in other online clothing retail sites, Nordstrom's became part of a trend in which traditional brick-and-mortar retailers are acquiring online rivals rather than trying to compete with them. Some big traditional retailers are also acquiring start-ups that specialize in social media applications.

More and more consumers use their smartphones or tablet devices while shopping in a store to compare prices and quality. Nordstrom's hasn't tried to buck this trend. Not only has it had free Wi-Fi access in its store for some time, but it has also equipped its staff with tablets that allow customers to pay for their purchases anywhere in the store.

This type of instant service fulfills two functions. It makes life easier for customers who don't want to wait at checkout counters, and it increases Nordstrom's profits by preventing customers from changing their minds or abandoning their purchases before getting to the head of the line. The company has also revamped its website to make online shopping easier.

- What might be some of the advantages of brick-and-mortar and e-tail stores joining forces? What could be some disadvantages?
- Think of a big-name traditional retailer in any field, not necessarily clothing. Now try to come up with some Web-only competitors with which it might align itself.

CHAPTER OVERVIEW

In exploring how today's retailing sector operates, this chapter introduces many examples that explain the combination of activities involved in selling goods to ultimate consumers. Then the chapter discusses the role of wholesalers and other intermediaries who deliver goods from the manufacturers into the hands of retailers or other intermediaries. Finally, the chapter looks at nonstore retailing. Direct marketing, a channel consisting of direct communication to consumers or business users, is a major form of nonstore retailing. It includes not just direct mail and telemarketing but also direct-response advertising, infomercials, and Internet marketing. The chapter concludes by looking at a less pervasive but growing aspect of nonstore retailing—automatic merchandising.

RETAILING

1 Explain the wheel of retailing.

retailing Activities involved in selling merchandise to ultimate consumers.

Retailers are the marketing intermediaries in direct contact with ultimate consumers. **Retailing** describes the activities involved in selling merchandise to these consumers. Retail outlets are contact points between channel members and ultimate consumers. In a very real sense, retailers represent the distribution channel to most consumers, because a typical shopper has little contact with manufacturers and virtually no contact with wholesaling intermediaries. Retailers determine locations, store hours, number of sales personnel, store layouts, merchandise selections, and return policies—factors that often influence consumers' images of the offerings more strongly than consumers' images of the products themselves. Both large and small retailers perform the major channel activities: creating time, place, and ownership utilities.

Retailers act as both customers and marketers in their channels. They sell products to ultimate consumers, and at the same time, they buy from wholesalers and manufacturers. Because of their critical location in the marketing channel, retailers often perform a vital feedback role. They

Retail outlets like Macy's are contact points between channel members and ultimate consumers.

© B. O'Kane/Alamy

obtain information from customers and transmit that information to manufacturers and other channel members.

EVOLUTION OF RETAILING

The development of retailing illustrates the marketing concept in operation. Early retailing in North America can be traced to the establishment of trading posts, such as the Hudson's Bay Company, and to pack peddlers who carried their wares to outlying settlements. The first type of retail institution, the general store, stocked a wide range of merchandise that met the needs of an isolated community or rural area. Supermarkets appeared in the early 1930s in response to consumers' desire for lower prices. In the 1950s and 1960s, discount stores delivered lower prices in exchange for reduced services. The emergence of convenience food stores in the 1960s satisfied consumer demand for fast service, convenient locations, and expanded hours of operation. The development of off-price retailers in the 1980s and 1990s reflected consumer demand for brand-name merchandise at prices considerably lower than those of traditional retailers. In recent years, Internet-enabled retailing has increased in influence and importance.

A key concept, known as the wheel of retailing, attempts to explain the patterns of change in retailing. According to the wheel of retailing, a new type of retailer gains a competitive foothold by offering customers lower prices than current outlets charge and maintains profits by reducing or eliminating services. Once established, however, the innovator begins to add more services, and its prices gradually rise. It then becomes vulnerable to new low-price retailers that enter with minimum services—and so the wheel turns. The retail graveyard is littered with the likes of Gottschalks, Sharper Image, Linens 'n Things, KB Toys, Circuit City, Harold's, and Levitz Furniture.

Many major developments in the history of retailing appear to fit the wheel's pattern. Early department stores, chain stores, supermarkets, discount stores, hypermarkets, and catalog retailers all emphasized limited service and low prices. Most of these retailers gradually increased their prices as they added services.

Some exceptions disrupt this pattern, however. Suburban shopping centers, convenience food stores, and vending machines never built their appeals around low prices. Still, the wheel pattern has been a good indicator enough times in the past to make it an accurate indicator of future retailing developments.

The wheel of retailing suggests that retailing is always changing. At a recent shareholders' meeting, Greg Wasson, the president and CEO of the drugstore chain Walgreens, outlined the company's new competitive strategy. Among the steps he announced were improving store design and making more products available; bringing together Walgreens' Take Care Health Systems and pharmacy departments; improving employee engagement with customers; combining retail stores with online service; and introducing a loyalty card program.[2]

wheel of retailing
Hypothesis that each new type of retailer gains a competitive foothold by offering lower prices than current suppliers charge, the result of reducing or eliminating services.

> **"BRIEFLY SPEAKING"**
>
> "No sale is really complete until the product is worn out, and the customer is satisfied."
>
> —**Leon Leonwood Bean**
> *Founder, L.L.Bean*

ASSESSMENT CHECK

1.1 What is retailing?

1.2 Explain the wheel-of-retailing concept.

RETAILING STRATEGY

Like manufacturers and wholesalers, a retailer develops a marketing strategy based on the firm's goals and strategic plans. The organization monitors environmental influences and assesses its own strengths and weaknesses in identifying marketing opportunities and constraints. A retailer bases its key decisions on two fundamental steps in the marketing strategy process:

1. selecting a target market; and

2. developing a retailing mix to satisfy the chosen market.

The retailing mix specifies merchandise strategy, customer service standards, pricing guidelines, target market analysis, promotion goals, location/distribution decisions, and store atmosphere

FIGURE 15.1
Components of Retail Strategy

© Cengage Learning

choices. The combination of these elements projects a desired retail image. Retail image communicates the store's identity to consumers. Kohl's, for instance, counts on its trendy, contemporary image to attract consumers. As Figure 15.1 points out, components of retailing strategy must work together to create a consistent image that appeals to the store's target market.

Offering high-quality local produce at low prices is the strategy of Sunflower Farmers Market. Launched a few years ago under the slogan "Serious food…silly prices," Sunflower targets consumers who look for quality but can't afford to pay boutique prices. In the face of an ongoing economic downturn, Sunflower emphasizes affordable organic produce, meats, and poultry. Sunflower recently merged with Sprouts Farmers Markets, and the combined company has more than 150 stores and nearly 11,000 employees. Operating under the Sprouts Farmers Market banner, the new organization expects to go public soon.[3] Whole Foods, in contrast, is an upscale retailer that has succeeded despite the recession. To learn how, see the story in the "Marketing Success" feature.

MARKETING SUCCESS

College Towns Keep Whole Foods Growing

Background. Although consumers are increasingly interested in Whole Foods' natural and organic products, grocery industry earnings remain flat as the recession lingers.

The Challenge. Whole Foods sought a way to grow, while maintaining its signature focus on healthy products and environmentally friendly practices rather than on price cutting.

The Strategy. The company takes a two-pronged approach to growth. First, it's opening stores in and around college towns, about two dozen a year, to tap a young, educated, environmentally aware, and affluent market segment. These locations also offer good real estate value, so even smaller stores can perform well. Second, it has fine-tuned its social media strategy to include not only its own website and blog but also Twitter, Facebook, Flickr, Foursquare, YouTube, and Pinterest (whose largely female

audience mirrors Whole Foods' own). The company maintains Facebook and Twitter accounts not just for each of its more than 300 stores but also for its specialty departments like wine and cheese, allowing finely targeted marketing appeals.

The Outcome. Whole Foods' stock is up nearly 40 percent as it continues to buy up small competitors and open new stores. Analysts say it is well on the way to becoming "the dominant force" in its upscale segment of the grocery market.

Sources: Jacqui MacKenzie, "Why I Follow Whole Foods," *Social Media Today*, accessed December 2, 2012, http://socialmediatoday.com; "What Makes Whole Foods Social Media Strategy a Difference Maker?" *Digital Spark Marketing*, accessed December 2, 2012, www.digitalsparkmarketing.com; Rebecca Coleman, "Social Media Marketing Case Study: Whole Foods," *Rebecca Coleman.com*, accessed December 2, 2012, www.rebeccacoleman.ca; Amanda Alix, "Whole Foods Market: A Steady Diet of Growth and Profit," *The Motley Fool*, accessed December 2, 2012, www.fool.com; "Whole Foods Market 2012," *Supermarket News*, accessed December 2, 2012, http://supermarketnews.com.

© iStockphoto.com/Marcello Bortolino

SELECTING A TARGET MARKET

A retailer starts to define its strategy by selecting a target market. Factors that influence the retailer's selection are the size and profit potential of the market and the level of competition for its business.

Retailers pore over demographic, geographic, and psychographic profiles to segment markets. In the end, most retailers identify their target markets in terms of certain demographics.

The importance of identifying and targeting the right market is dramatically illustrated by the erosion of department store retailing. While mall anchor stores struggle to attract customers, stand-alone store Target makes a memorable splash with edgy advertising that incorporates its signature red doughnut-shaped logo in imaginative ways. And although Target can be categorized as a discount retailer, it has differentiated itself from competitors like Walmart and Kmart by offering trendy, quality merchandise at low prices.[4]

Deep-discount chains, such as Deal$, Dollar General, Dollar Tree, Family Dollar Stores, and 99¢ Only, with their less glamorous locations and low-price merchandise displayed in narrow aisles, target lower-income bargain hunters. Attracted by cents-off basics like shampoo, cereal, and laundry detergent, customers typically pick up higher-margin goods—toys or chocolates—on their way to the checkout.

By creating stores with wide aisles and clean presentation and offering friendly service and high-end product lines, such as Laura Ashley paints, home improvement chain Lowe's competes with its archrival, Home Depot. Lowe's ambiance helps make the store more appealing to female shoppers, who do almost 44 percent of all do-it-yourself projects and account for half of all home improvement purchases.[5]

Discuss how retailers select target markets.

ASSESSMENT CHECK

2.1 How does a retailer develop a marketing strategy?

2.2 How do retailers select target markets?

After identifying a target market, a retailer must then develop marketing strategies to attract these chosen customers to its stores or website. The following sections discuss tactics for implementing different strategies.

MERCHANDISING STRATEGY

A retailer's merchandising strategy guides decisions regarding the items it will offer. A retailer must decide on general merchandise categories, product lines, specific items within lines, and the depth and width of its assortments. Shoe retailer DSW specializes in high-fashion, high-quality footwear.[6] The big-box electronics retailer Best Buy recently expanded its product offerings to include a full line of musical instruments. TakeLessons, which provides music and voice lessons in more than 2,800 cities, has joined with BestBuy to offer lessons in BestBuy stores.[7]

To develop a successful merchandise mix, a retailer must weigh several priorities. First, it must consider the preferences and needs of its previously defined target market, keeping in mind that the competitive environment influences these choices. The retailer must also consider the overall profitability of each product line and product category.

Show how the elements of the marketing mix apply to retailing strategy.

Category Management

As mentioned in Chapter 13, a popular merchandising strategy is *category management,* in which a category manager oversees an entire product line and is responsible for the profitability of the product group. Both vendors and retailers use this strategy. Category management seeks to improve the retailer's product category performance through more coordinated buying, merchandising, and pricing. Rather than focusing on the performance of individual brands, such as Flex shampoo or Kleenex tissue, category management evaluates performance according to each product category. Laundry detergent,

Lowe's has designed its stores and overall ambience to appeal to female shoppers, who do almost 44 percent of all do-it-yourself projects and make half of all home-improvement purchases.

© Jim R. Bounds/Bloomberg/Getty Images

skin-care products, and paper goods, for example, are each viewed as individual profit centers, and different category managers supervise each group. Those that underperform are at risk of being dropped from inventory, regardless of the strength of individual brands. To improve their profitability, for example, some department stores have narrowed their traditionally broad product categories to eliminate high-overhead, low-profit lines such as toys, appliances, and furniture.

The Battle for Shelf Space

As discussed in Chapter 14, large-scale retailers are increasingly taking on the role of channel captain within many distribution networks. Some have assumed traditional wholesaling functions, while others dictate product design and specifications to manufacturers. The result is a shift in power from the manufacturers of top-selling brands to the retailer who makes them available to customers.

Adding to the pressure is the increase in the number of new products and variations on existing products. To identify the varying items within a product line, retailers refer to a specific product offering as a **stock-keeping unit (SKU)**. Within the skin-care category, for example, each facial cream, body moisturizer, and sunscreen in a variety of sizes and formulations is a separate SKU. The proliferation of new SKUs has resulted in a fierce battle for space on store shelves.

stock-keeping unit (SKU) Offering within a product line, such as a specific size of liquid detergent.

Increasingly, major retailers like Target make demands in return for providing shelf space. They may, for example, seek pricing and promotional concessions from manufacturers as conditions for selling their products. Retailers like Walmart also require manufacturers to participate in their electronic data interchange (EDI) and quick-response systems. Manufacturers unable to comply may find themselves unable to penetrate this marketplace.

Slotting allowances are just one of the many nonrefundable fees grocery retailers receive from manufacturers to secure shelf space for new products. Manufacturers may pay a national retailer thousands of dollars to get their new product displayed on store shelves.[8] Other fees include failure fees that are imposed if a new product does not meet sales projections; annual renewal fees, a "pay to stay" inducement for retailers to continue carrying brands; trade allowances; discounts on high-volume purchases; and survey fees for research done by the retailers.

CUSTOMER SERVICE STRATEGY

Some stores build their retailing strategy around heightened customer services for shoppers. Gift wrapping, alterations, return privileges, bridal registries, consultants, interior design services, delivery and installation, and perhaps even electronic shopping via store websites are all examples of services that add value to the shopping experience. A retailer's customer service strategy must specify which services the firm will offer and whether it will charge customers for these services. Those decisions depend on several conditions: store size, type, and location; merchandise assortment; services offered by competitors; customer expectations; and financial resources.

The basic objective of all customer services focuses on attracting and retaining target customers, thus increasing sales and profits. Some services—such as convenient restrooms, lounges, and complimentary coffee—enhance shoppers' comfort. Other services are intended to attract customers by making shopping easier and faster than it would be without the services. Some retailers, for example, offer child-care services for customers.

Consumers can also get "virtual assistance" from companies like Virtuosity and CallWave, which manage phone calls by allowing users to switch between voice mail, email, and real-time cell and landline calls using voice commands. Virtuosity's Virtual Assistant software can answer, screen, and

Ace Hardware reassures customers with its familiar slogan, "The helpful place."

route calls much like a living, breathing administrative assistant. Similarly, CallWave's Voicemail-to-Text service screens mobile calls, converts voice mail to text, and helps users manage their time.[9]

A customer service strategy can also support efforts in building demand for a line of merchandise. For over 85 years, Ace Hardware stores have been a familiar sight, with more than 4,600 stores in cities and towns across the United States and around the world. Each store is independently owned; together, they form the largest cooperative in the hardware industry. The stores sell Ace's own private-label tools—over 12,000 kinds. The company refers to store personnel as the "Helpful Hardware Folks," in line with its familiar slogan, "The helpful place."

PRICING STRATEGY

Prices reflect a retailer's marketing objectives and policies. They also play a major role in consumer perceptions of a retailer. Consumers realize, for example, that when they enter a Hermès boutique, they will find such expensive merchandise as leather handbags priced at $3,275 and up, along with men's belts at $650 and up. In contrast, customers of Tuesday Morning or Big Lots expect totally different merchandise and prices.

Markups and Markdowns

The amount a retailer adds to a product's cost to set the final selling price is the **markup**. The amount of the markup typically results from two marketing decisions:

1. *Services performed by the retailer.* Other things being equal, stores that offer more services charge larger markups to cover their costs.

2. *Inventory turnover* rate. Other things being equal, stores with a higher turnover rate can cover their costs and earn a profit while charging a smaller markup.

A retailer's markup exerts an important influence on its image among present and potential customers. In addition, the markup affects the retailer's ability to attract shoppers. An excessive markup may drive away customers; an inadequate markup may not generate sufficient revenue to cover costs

markup Amount a retailer adds to the cost of a product to determine its selling price.

and return a profit. Retailers typically state markups as percentages of either the selling prices or the costs of the products.

Marketers determine markups based partly on their judgments of the amounts that consumers will pay for a given product. When buyers refuse to pay a product's stated price, however, or when improvements in other items or fashion changes reduce the appeal of current merchandise, a retailer must take a markdown. The amount by which a retailer reduces the original selling price—the discount typically advertised for a sale item—is the markdown. Markdowns are sometimes used to evaluate merchandisers. For example, a department store might base its evaluations of merchandise buyers partly on the average markdown percentages for the product lines for which they are responsible.

The formulas for calculating markups and markdowns are provided in the "Financial Analysis in Marketing" appendix at the end of this textbook.

LOCATION/DISTRIBUTION STRATEGY

Retail experts often cite location as a potential determining factor in the success or failure of a retail business. A retailer may locate at an isolated site, in a central business district, or in a planned shopping center. The location decision depends on many factors, including the type of merchandise, the retailer's financial resources, characteristics of the target market, and site availability.

In recent years, many localities have become saturated with stores. As a result, some retailers have reevaluated their location strategies. A chain may close individual stores that do not meet sales and profit goals. Other retailers have experimented with nontraditional location strategies. For instance, Starbucks is now found in some Macy's and Target stores as well as Barnes & Noble bookstores.

Locations in Planned Shopping Centers

Over the past several decades, retail trade has shifted away from traditional downtown retailing districts and toward suburban shopping centers. A planned shopping center is a group of retail stores designed, coordinated, and marketed to shoppers in a geographic trade area. Together, the stores provide a single convenient location for shoppers as well as free parking. They facilitate shopping by maintaining uniform hours of operation, including evening and weekend hours.

There are five main types of planned shopping centers. The smallest, the *neighborhood shopping center,* is likely to consist of a group of smaller stores, such as a drugstore, a dry cleaner, a card and gift shop, and perhaps a hair salon. This kind of center provides convenient shopping for 5,000 to 50,000 shoppers who live within a few minutes' commute. It contains 5 to 15 stores, and the product mix usually is confined to convenience items and some limited shopping goods.

A *community shopping center* serves 20,000 to 100,000 people in a trade area extending a few miles from its location. It contains anywhere from 10 to 30 retail stores, with a branch of a local department store or some other large store as the primary tenant. In addition to the stores found in a neighborhood center, a community center probably encompasses more stores featuring shopping goods, some professional offices, a branch bank, and perhaps a movie theater or supermarket.

Community shopping centers typically offer ample parking, and tenants often share some promotion costs. With the advent of stand-alone, big-box retailers, some community shopping centers have declined in popularity. Some department stores are also moving away from the strategy of locating in shopping centers and opting for freestanding stores.

A *regional shopping center* is a large facility with at least 300,000 square feet of shopping space. Its marketing appeal usually emphasizes major department stores with the power to draw customers, supplemented by as many as 200 smaller stores. A successful regional center needs a location within 30 minutes' driving time of at least 250,000 people. A regional center like Indianapolis's Fashion Mall at Keystone or a superregional center like Xanadu in New Jersey provides a wide assortment of convenience, shopping, and specialty goods, plus many personal service facilities. Some shopping centers are going green, working to reduce their carbon footprint with mandatory recycling programs, maximizing the use of natural light, and installing heat-reflecting roofing that reduces the need for air-conditioning.[10]

A *power cent*er, usually located near a regional or superregional mall, brings together several huge specialty stores, such as Sports Authority, Home Depot, and Bed Bath & Beyond, as stand-alone stores in a single trading area. Rising in popularity during the 1990s, power centers offered value because they underpriced department stores while providing a huge selection of specialty merchandise.

---

markdown Amount by which a retailer reduces the original selling price of a product.

planned shopping center Group of retail stores planned, coordinated, and marketed as a unit.

Heated competition from cost-cutter Walmart and inroads from more upscale discounters, such as Target and Kohl's, are currently hurting the drawing power of these centers.

A fifth type of planned center, the *lifestyle center,* is a retailing format offering a combination of shopping, movie theaters, stages for concerts and live entertainment, decorative fountains and park benches in greenways, and restaurants and bistros in an attractive outdoor environment. At around 300,000 to 1 million square feet, the centers are large, but they seek to offer the intimacy and easy access of neighborhood village retailing with a fashionable cachet. Convenience and pleasant ambiance are also part of the appeal. Here, shoppers find a mix of just the right upscale tenants—Williams-Sonoma, Banana Republic, Ann Taylor, Pottery Barn, and Restoration Hardware, for instance. Some lifestyle centers include office parks, townhouses, and condominiums. Customers visit such lifestyle centers as Santana Row in San Jose, California; Kierland Commons in Scottsdale, Arizona; Oak Brook Promenade in Oak Brook, Illinois; and St. John's Town Center in Jacksonville, Florida.[11]

To fill the empty spaces in malls and attract shoppers, malls are increasingly adding businesses that offer entertainment and experiences. Today, many shopping centers include restaurants, movie-theater complexes, indoor playgrounds, art galleries, arcade games, bowling alleys, and more. The upscale NorthPark Center in Dallas exhibits works by artists like Andy Warhol and Roy Lichtenstein and acts as a venue for the Dallas International Film Festival. The plans for the American Dream Meadowlands in northern New Jersey include a skydive simulator, complete amusement and water parks, and an indoor ski/snowboard slope.[12]

PROMOTIONAL STRATEGY

To establish store images that entice more shoppers, retailers use a variety of promotional techniques. Through its promotional strategy, a retailer seeks to communicate to consumers information about its stores—locations, merchandise selections, hours of operation, and prices. If merchandise selection changes frequently to follow fashion trends, advertising is typically used to promote current styles effectively. In addition, promotions help retailers attract shoppers and build customer loyalty.

Innovative promotions can have interesting results. General Electric recently put one of its latest-model refrigerators on a flatbed truck, hooked it up to a generator, and sent it around the country with a chef and a refrigerator engineer. A film crew recorded the trip in reality-show style, following the two men on a 2,000-mile journey to Texas to reach a wildlife biologist in the field

Lifestyle centers, such as Navy Pier in Chicago, offer a combination of shopping, movie theaters, restaurants, carnival rides, and other forms of entertainment.

© Rob Wilson/Shutterstock.com

and cook a meal for him. During the trip, which took a week, the chef picked up supplies along the way from local farmers and fishermen, carefully storing them in the refrigerator. The film was turned into a Web series, "Freshpedition," and was promoted through a TV commercial as well as the company's Facebook and Twitter accounts.[13]

National retail chains often purchase advertising space in newspapers, on radio, and on television. Other retailers promote their goods over the Internet or use wireless technology to send marketing messages to customers' cell phones. Consumers are increasingly using their smartphones and tablet devices to surf the Web. Analytics firm Flurry provides clients with details on how mobile phone and tablet users engage with apps and recently launched Ad Analytics, which measures data on how smartphone and tablet users interact with advertisements *within* apps.[14]

Retailers also try to combine advertising with in-store merchandising techniques that influence buyer behavior at the point of purchase. As part of Whole Foods Market's goal of "satisfying and delighting our customers," stores reach out to engage their communities by offering in-store education on food, free samples, and lively social media content.[15]

A friendly, well-trained, and knowledgeable salesperson plays a vital role in conveying the store's image to consumers and in persuading shoppers to buy. To serve as a source of information, a salesperson must possess extensive knowledge regarding credit policies, discounts, special sales, delivery terms, layaways, and returns. To increase store sales, the salesperson must persuade customers that the store sells what those customers need. To this end, salespeople should receive training in selling up and suggestion selling.

By *selling up,* salespeople try to persuade customers to buy higher-priced items than originally intended. For example, an automobile salesperson might persuade a customer to buy a more expensive model than the car the buyer had initially considered. Of course, the practice of selling up must always respect the constraints of a customer's real needs. If a salesperson sells customers something they really do not need, the potential for repeat sales dramatically diminishes.

Another technique, *suggestion selling,* seeks to broaden a customer's original purchase by adding related items, special promotional products, or holiday or seasonal merchandise. Here, too, the salesperson tries to help a customer recognize true needs rather than unwanted merchandise. Beauty advisors in upscale department stores are masters of suggestion selling. Smartphones can become beauty advisors, too. Recently, IMAN Cosmetics, which specializes in cosmetics for women of color, introduced an application called "Find Your Shade." IMAN has added QR codes to all of its products, online advertising, promotional materials, and some in-store items, including signs. When a customer scans the code, it directs her to her skin color, along with advice on selecting the right products for her coloring.[16]

Just as knowledgeable and helpful sales personnel can both boost sales and set retailers apart from competitors, poor service influences customers' attitudes toward a retailer. Increasing customer complaints about unfriendly, inattentive, and uninformed salespeople have prompted many retailers

From anywhere in the world, a shopper can launch the IMAN Cosmetics "Find Your Shade" app to find just the right makeup for her skin tone.

AP Photo/PRNewsFoto/IMAN Cosmetics

to intensify their attention to training and motivating salespeople. Older training methods are giving way to online learning in many firms.

STORE ATMOSPHERICS

While store location, merchandise selection, customer service, pricing, and promotional activities all contribute to a store's consumer awareness, stores also project their personalities through atmospherics—physical characteristics and amenities that attract customers and satisfy their shopping needs. Atmospherics include both a store's exterior and interior décor.

A store's exterior appearance, including architectural design, window displays, signs, and entryways, helps identify the retailer and attract its target market shoppers. The Saks Fifth Avenue script logo on a storefront and McDonald's golden arches are exterior elements that readily identify these retailers. Other retailers design eye-catching exterior elements aimed at getting customers' attention. Colorful, lifelike recreations of jungle animals flank the theatrically lit entrances of the popular Rainforest Cafés, and the tropical motif carries over to the interiors, decorated with wall-sized aquariums. Sometimes the design can be too good to be true; as fake electronics continue to flood global markets, counterfeiters have even managed to open fake Apple stores in China. See the "Solving an Ethical Controversy" feature to read more.

atmospherics
Combination of physical characteristics and amenities that contribute to a store's image.

SOLVING AN ETHICAL CONTROVERSY

Who Should Control the Spread of Fake Stores and Counterfeit Products?

New York City police who stopped an unlicensed street vendor hawking an iPhone for $150 were surprised at the defense he offered: the phone was just a fake. It came from a nearby store, where officers confiscated thousands of others. A U.S. blogger made worldwide headlines after posting pictures of a fully staffed, authentic-looking Apple store in China that also proved a fake, like all the products inside. The store was so authentic that the Chinese staff members really believed they were working for Apple. The global proliferation of counterfeit electronics continues unabated, especially in Asia, with counterfeit products cobbled together from fake or stolen parts.

Should governments step in to stop the flood of fakes?

PRO 👍

1. All governments should respect intellectual property rights so multinational companies can safely bring jobs and investment dollars to their countries.

2. Governments should protect their citizens from fake products that perform poorly, if at all.

CON 👎

1. In some cultures, such as China's, innovation is difficult, intellectual property is not protected, and functioning fakes are accepted.

2. Governments should not restrict what companies manufacture, and consumers should look out for themselves.

Summary:

Wide-scale government action abroad seems unlikely, especially in Asia, where sophisticated fakes—like replaceable-battery iPhones—are often preferred by consumers, because the products are less expensive than the real thing.

Sources: Abe Sauer, "How Western Brands Get Shanghaied on China's Shanzhai Express," *Brand Channel*, accessed December 2, 2012, www.brandchannel.com; Panos Mourdoukoutas, "Why China Imitates Western Brands," *Forbes*, accessed December 2, 2012, www.forbes.com; "Fake Apple Store: Update with Video," *WordPress.com*, accessed December 2, 2012, http://birdabroad.wordpress.com; Nick Bilton, "Fake Apple Stores Get Fake News Video," *The New York Times*, accessed December 2, 2012, http://bits.blogs.nytimes.com; "Are You Listening, Steve Jobs?" *WordPress.com*, accessed December 2, 2012, http://birdabroad.wordpress.com; Michael Wilson, "An iPhone That's Cheaper, But Fake," *The New York Times*, accessed December 2, 2012, www.nytimes.com; Louis Bedigian, "Apple's Worst Nightmare Comes from an Unlikely Source," *Forbes*, accessed December 2, 2012, www.forbes.com.

© Palto/Shutterstock.com

Whole Foods Markets have long been known for their shopper-friendly design.

Justin Sullivan/Getty Images

The interior décor of a store should also complement the retailer's image, respond to customers' interests, and, most importantly, induce shoppers to buy. Interior atmospheric elements include store layout, merchandise presentation, lighting, color, sounds, scents, and cleanliness. By strategically positioning the sections where aroma or fragrance is key—the flower shop, the bakery, and the deli where table-ready fried chicken or pizza is sold—supermarkets can boost impulse sales. Some hotels even use hidden devices to waft a fragrance throughout their lobbies.[17]

When designing the interior and exterior of a store, marketers must remember that many people shop for reasons other than just purchasing needed products. Other common reasons for shopping include escaping the routine of daily life, avoiding weather extremes, fulfilling fantasies, and socializing with family and friends. Retailers expand beyond interior design to create welcoming and entertaining environments that draw shoppers. Some retailers offer a "store within a store" to sell selected merchandise in a more intimate setting—for example, the British clothing chain AllSaints within Bloomingdale's and Cos Bar beauty-product stores within Target stores.[18]

ASSESSMENT CHECK

3.1   What is an SKU?

3.2   What are the two components of a markup?

3.3   What are store atmospherics?

TYPES OF RETAILERS

Because new types of retailers continue to evolve in response to changes in consumer demand, a universal classification system for retailers has yet to be devised. Certain differences do, however, define several categories of retailers: (1) forms of ownership, (2) shopping effort expended by customers, (3) services provided to customers, (4) product lines, and (5) location of retail transactions.

As Figure 15.2 points out, most retailing operations fit in several different categories. A 7-Eleven outlet may be classified as a convenience store (category 2) with self-service (category 3) and a relatively broad product line (category 4). It is both a store-type retailer (category 5) and a member of a chain (category 1).

FIGURE 15.2
Bases for Categorizing Retailers

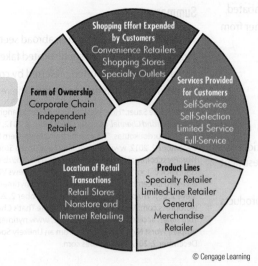

Shopping Effort Expended by Customers
Convenience Retailers
Shopping Stores
Specialty Outlets

Services Provided for Customers
Self-Service
Self-Selection
Limited Service
Full-Service

Form of Ownership
Corporate Chain
Independent Retailer

Location of Retail Transactions
Retail Stores
Nonstore and Internet Retailing

Product Lines
Specialty Retailer
Limited-Line Retailer
General Merchandise Retailer

© Cengage Learning

CLASSIFICATION OF RETAILERS BY FORM OF OWNERSHIP

Perhaps the easiest method for categorizing retailers is by ownership structure, distinguishing between chain stores and independent retailers. In addition, independent retailers may join wholesaler-sponsored voluntary chains, band together to form retail cooperatives, or enter into franchise agreements with manufacturers, wholesalers, or service provider organizations. Each type of ownership has its own unique advantages and strategies.

Chain Stores

Chain stores are groups of retail outlets that operate under central ownership and management and handle the same product lines. Chains have an advantage over independent retailers in economies of scale. Volume purchases allow chains to pay lower prices than their independent rivals must pay. Because a chain may have hundreds of retail stores, it can afford extensive advertising, sales training, and computerized systems for merchandise ordering, inventory management, forecasting, and accounting. Also, the large sales volume and wide geographic reach of a chain may enable it to advertise in a variety of media.

Independent Retailers

As the second-largest industry in the United States by number of establishments as well as number of employees, the retailing structure supports a large number of small stores, many medium-size stores, and a small number of large stores. It generated about $4.7 trillion in retail sales in a recent year. Of the total U.S. gross domestic product, perhaps two-thirds is retail consumption.[19]

Independent retailers compete with chains in a number of ways. The traditional advantage of independent stores is friendly, personalized service. Cooperatives offer another strategy for independents. For instance, cooperatives like Sunkist and Valu-Rite Pharmacies help independents compete by providing volume buying power as well as advertising and marketing programs.

CLASSIFICATION BY SHOPPING EFFORT

Another classification system is based on the reasons consumers shop at particular retail outlets. This approach categorizes stores as convenience, shopping, or specialty retailers.

Convenience retailers focus their marketing appeals on accessible locations, extended store hours, rapid checkout service, and adequate parking facilities. Local food stores, gasoline stations, and dry cleaners fit this category. Pennsylvania-based Wawa convenience stores offer customers a variety of items, including gasoline and private-labeled breakfast treats, deli sandwiches, ready-to-eat salads, and seasonal fresh fruit. The company recently announced an expansion into central Florida.

Shopping stores typically include furniture stores (like Ethan Allen), appliance retailers, clothing outlets, and sporting goods stores. Consumers usually compare prices, assortments, and quality levels at competing outlets before making purchase decisions. Consequently, managers of shopping stores attempt to differentiate their outlets through advertising, in-store displays, well-trained and knowledgeable salespeople, and appropriate merchandise assortments.

Specialty retailers combine carefully defined product lines, services, and reputations in attempts to persuade consumers to expend considerable effort to shop at their stores. Examples include Bergdorf Goodman, Neiman Marcus, Nordstrom, and Dillard's.

CLASSIFICATION BY SERVICES PROVIDED

Another category differentiates retailers by the services they provide to customers. This classification system consists of three retail types: self-service, self-selection, or full-service retailers.

The ampm mini-mart is classified as a self-service store, while Safeway and Kroger grocery stores are examples of self-selection stores. Both categories sell convenience products people can purchase frequently with little assistance. In the clothing industry, the catalog retailer Lands' End is a self-selection store. Full-service retailers like Macy's focus on fashion-oriented merchandise, backed by a complete array of customer services.

CLASSIFICATION BY PRODUCT LINES

Product lines also define a set of retail categories and the marketing strategies appropriate for firms within those categories. Grouping retailers by product lines produces three major categories: specialty stores, limited-line retailers, and general-merchandise retailers.

convenience retailer Store that appeals to customers by having an accessible location, long hours, rapid checkout, and adequate parking.

specialty retailer Store that combines carefully defined product lines, services, and reputation to persuade shoppers to spend considerable shopping effort there.

Specialty Stores

A *specialty store* typically handles only part of a single product line. However, it stocks this portion in considerable depth or variety. Specialty stores include a wide range of retail outlets, including fish markets, grocery stores, men's and women's shoe stores, and bakeries. Although some specialty stores are chain outlets, most are independent, small-scale operations. They represent perhaps the greatest concentration of independent retailers who develop expertise in one product area and provide narrow lines of products for their local markets.

Specialty stores should not be confused with specialty products. Specialty stores typically carry convenience and shopping goods. The label *specialty* reflects the practice of handling a specific, narrow line of merchandise. For example, Lady Foot Locker is a specialty store that offers a wide selection of name-brand athletic footwear, apparel, and accessories made specifically for women. Gloria Jean's Coffees sells whole-bean coffees, beverages, and gifts.[20]

Limited-Line Retailers

limited-line store
Retailer that offers a large assortment within a single product line or within a few related product lines.

Customers find a large assortment of products within one product line or a few related lines in a limited-line store. This type of retail operation typically develops in areas with a large enough population to sufficiently support it. Examples of limited-line stores are IKEA (home furnishings and housewares) and Rubensteins of New Orleans (men's clothing). These retailers cater to the needs of people who want to select from complete lines in purchasing particular products.

category killer Store offering huge selections and low prices in single product lines.

A unique type of limited-line retailer is known as a category killer. These stores offer huge selections and low prices in single product lines. Stores within this category, such as Best Buy, Bed Bath & Beyond, and Home Depot, are among the most successful retailers in the nation. Category killers at first took business away from general merchandise discounters, which were not able to compete in selection or price. Recently, however, expanded merchandise and aggressive cost cutting by warehouse clubs and Walmart have turned the tables. Competition from Internet companies that can offer unlimited selection and speedy delivery has also taken customers away. While they still remain a powerful force in retailing, especially for local businesses, category killers are not invulnerable.

General Merchandise Retailers

general merchandise retailer Store that carries a wide variety of product lines, stocking all of them in some depth.

General merchandise retailers, carrying a wide variety of product lines stocked in some depth, distinguish themselves from limited-line and specialty retailers by the large number of product lines they carry. Target stores are examples of general merchandise retailers. The general store described earlier in this chapter was an early form of a general merchandise retailer. This category includes variety stores, department stores, and mass merchandisers, such as discount houses, off-price retailers, and hypermarkets.

Variety Stores

A retail outlet that offers an extensive range and assortment of low-price merchandise is called a *variety store*. Less popular today than they once were, many of these stores have evolved into or given way to other types of retailers like discount stores. In recent years, many pharmacies have become drugstore–variety store combinations. Walgreens, for example, has more than 8,000 drugstores nationwide and filled more than 780 million prescriptions during a recent year.[21] The nation's variety stores now account for less than 1 percent of all retail sales. However, variety stores remain popular in other parts of the world. Many retail outlets in Spain and Mexico are family-owned variety stores.

Considered a category killer, Bed Bath & Beyond offers huge selections and low prices.

James Houck/Alamy

Department Stores

In essence, a **department store** is a series of limited-line and specialty stores under one roof. By definition, this large retailer handles a variety of merchandise, including men's, women's, and children's clothing and accessories; household linens and dry goods; home furnishings; and furniture. It is a one-stop shopping destination for almost all personal and household products.

Department stores like Bloomingdale's built their reputations by offering wide varieties of services, such as charge accounts, delivery, gift wrapping, and liberal return privileges. As a result, they incur relatively high operating costs, averaging about 45 to 60 percent of sales.

Department stores have faced intense competition over the past several years. Relatively high operating costs have left them vulnerable to retailing innovations, such as discount stores, Internet retailers, and hypermarkets. In addition, department stores' original locations in downtown business districts have suffered from problems associated with limited parking, traffic congestion, and population migration to the suburbs.

Department stores have fought back in a variety of ways. Many have closed certain sections, such as electronics, in which high costs kept them from competing with discount houses and category killers. They have added bargain outlets, expanded parking facilities, and opened major branches in regional shopping centers. Marketers have attempted to revitalize downtown retailing in many cities by modernizing their stores, expanding store hours, making special efforts to attract the tourist and convention trade, and serving the needs of urban residents. Over the years, U.S. department stores have also undergone massive consolidation, with only a handful of companies owning many department-store chains that were once freestanding.[22]

Mass Merchandisers

Mass merchandising has made major inroads into department store sales by emphasizing lower prices for well-known brand-name products, high product turnover, and limited services. A **mass merchandiser** often stocks a wider line of items than a department store but usually without the same depth of assortment within each line. Discount houses, off-price retailers, hypermarkets, and catalog retailers are all examples of mass merchandisers. Examples include Sears and Fred Meyer stores on the West Coast.

Discount Houses

A **discount house** charges low prices and offers fewer services. Early discount stores sold mostly appliances. Today, they offer soft goods, drugs, food, gasoline, and furniture.

By eliminating many of the "free" services provided by traditional retailers, these operations can keep their markups 10 to 25 percent below those of their competitors. Some of the early discounters have since added services, stocked well-known name brands, and boosted their prices. In fact, many now resemble department stores.

A discount format gaining strength is the *warehouse club*. Costco, BJ's, and Sam's Club are the largest warehouse clubs in the United States. These no-frills, cash-and-carry outlets offer consumers access to name-brand products at deeply discounted prices. Selection at warehouse clubs includes gourmet popcorn, fax machines, peanut butter, luggage, and sunglasses sold in vast, warehouse-like settings. Attracting business away from almost every retailing segment, warehouse clubs now even offer fresh food and gasoline. Customers must be members to shop at warehouse clubs.

Off-Price Retailers

Another version of a discount house is an *off-price retailer*. This kind of store stocks only designer labels or well-known brand-name clothing at prices equal to or below regular wholesale prices and then passes the cost savings along to buyers. While many off-price retailers are located in outlets in downtown areas or in freestanding buildings, a growing number are concentrating in *outlet malls*—shopping centers that house only off-price retailers.

Inventory at off-price stores changes frequently as buyers take advantage of special price offers from manufacturers selling excess merchandise. Off-price retailers, such as Loehmann's, Marshalls, Ross, Stein Mart, and T.J. Maxx, also keep their prices below those of traditional retailers by offering fewer services. Off-price retailing has been well received by today's shoppers. France-based retailer Vente-privée.com sells high-fashion overstock merchandise through invitation-only clearance sales conducted solely on the Web.[23]

department store
Large store that handles a variety of merchandise, including clothing, household goods, appliances, and furniture.

mass merchandiser
Store that stocks a wider line of goods than a department store, usually without the same depth of assortment within each line.

discount house Store that charges low prices but may not offer services such as credit.

Off-price retailers like T.J. Maxx keep their prices below those of traditional retailers by offering fewer services.

© iStockphoto.com/Lee Walters

hypermarket Giant one-stop shopping facility offering wide selections of grocery items and general merchandise at discount prices, typically filling up 200,000 or more square feet of selling space.

supercenter Large store, usually smaller than a hypermarket, that combines groceries with discount store merchandise.

retail convergence Situation in which similar merchandise is available from multiple retail outlets, resulting in the blurring of distinctions between types of retailers and merchandise offered.

Hypermarkets and Supercenters

Another innovation in discount retailing is the creation of hypermarkets—giant, one-stop shopping facilities that offer wide selections of grocery and general merchandise products at discount prices. Store size determines the major difference between hypermarkets and supercenters. Hypermarkets typically fill up 200,000 or more square feet of selling space, about a third larger than most supercenters. Michigan-based Meijer stores offer a vast array of items in dozens of departments, including housewares, groceries, apparel, drugs, hardware, electronics, and photo finishing in more than 190 stores in five states.[24]

Showroom and Warehouse Retailers

These retailers send direct mail to their customers and sell the advertised goods from showrooms that display samples. Backroom warehouses fill orders for the displayed products. Low prices are important to catalog store customers. To keep prices low, these retailers offer few services; store most inventory in inexpensive warehouse space; limit shoplifting losses; and handle long-lived products such as luggage, small appliances, gift items, sporting equipment, toys, and jewelry.

CLASSIFICATION OF RETAIL TRANSACTIONS BY LOCATION

Although most retail transactions occur in stores, nonstore retailing serves as an important marketing channel for many products. In addition, both consumer and business-to-business marketers rely on nonstore retailing to generate orders or requests for more information that may result in future orders.

Direct marketing is a broad concept that includes direct mail, direct selling, direct-response retailing, telemarketing, Internet retailing, and automatic merchandising. The last sections of this chapter consider each type of nonstore retailing.

RETAIL CONVERGENCE AND SCRAMBLED MERCHANDISING

4 Explain the concepts of retail convergence and scrambled merchandising.

Many traditional differences no longer distinguish familiar types of retailers, rendering any set of classifications less useful. Retail convergence, whereby similar merchandise is available from multiple retail outlets distinguished by price more than any other factor, is blurring distinctions between types of retailers and the merchandise mix they offer. A few years ago, a customer looking for a fashionable

© iStockphoto.com/hh5800

CAREER READINESS

Tips on Knowing Your Competition

A classic article in the *Harvard Business Review* claimed that railroads would have continued to grow if they had correctly identified their competition as everyone in the transportation business. How can you thoroughly analyze your competitors to avoid making a similar mistake?

- Define "competition" to include any and everything that might take your customers away. Anticipate market entries from existing and new directions. Movie theaters compete with all forms of live and recorded entertainment, for instance, not just other theater chains.

- Become your competitors' customer. Buy and try the product, visit the store and the website, talk to other customers in person or online. What are your competitors doing well? Where are they weak?

- Go to trade shows and conferences, and let competitors' reps tell you all about their new products, goals, and selling strategies.

- Investigate competitors' company websites, Facebook and Twitter pages, and blogs. Sign up for their marketing messages, including newsletters and mobile ads. How effectively are they reaching their customers—and yours?

- On a search engine, type in "Link:" followed by the full URL of your competitors' website, to see which sites are sending Web traffic to your rivals. Will they do the same for you?

Sources: "Analyze the Competition to Keep Your Edge," *All Business*, accessed December 2, 2012, www.allbusiness.com; Rhonda Abrams, "7 Tips for Analyzing the Business Competition," *USA Today*, accessed December 2, 2012, http://usatoday30.usatoday.com; Isabel Isidro, "How to Beat the Competition," *PowerHomeBiz.com*, accessed December 2, 2012, www.powerhomebiz.com.

---

coffeemaker might have headed straight for Williams-Sonoma or Starbucks. Today, one is just as likely to pick that product up at Target or Sam's Club, where that customer can also check out new spring fashions and stock up on paper goods. The Gap is no longer pitted only against American Eagle Outfitters or L.L.Bean but against designer-label brands at department stores and Kohl's, too. Grocery stores compete with Walmart Supercenter, Sam's Club, and Costco. Walmart has beefed up its already robust product mix to include VUDU broadband streaming services for the consumer electronics products it sells alongside the apparel, housewares, fine jewelry, and more.[25] All these examples highlight how important it is to know your competition. See the "Career Readiness" feature for some tips on how to stay ahead of your competitors.

Scrambled merchandising—in which a retailer combines dissimilar product lines in an attempt to boost sales volume—has also muddied the waters. Drugstores not only fill prescriptions but sell cameras, cards, housewares, magazines, and even small appliances. In addition, Walgreens, CVS, Target, and other stores have discovered another consumer need: in-store health clinics that diagnose and treat minor illnesses and injuries quickly and affordably.[26]

scrambled merchandising Retailing practice of combining dissimilar product lines to boost sales volume.

 ASSESSMENT CHECK

4.1 How do we classify retailers by form of ownership?

4.2 Categorize retailers by shopping effort and by services provided.

4.3 List several ways to classify retailers by product line.

WHOLESALING INTERMEDIARIES

Recall from Chapter 14 that several distribution channels involve marketing intermediaries called **wholesalers**. These firms take title to the goods they handle and sell those products primarily to retailers or to other wholesalers or business users. They sell to ultimate consumers only in insignificant

wholesaler Channel intermediary that takes title to goods it handles and then distributes those goods to retailers, other distributors, or B2B customers.

wholesaling intermediary
Comprehensive term that describes wholesalers as well as agents and brokers.

quantities, if at all. Wholesaling intermediaries, a broader category, include not only wholesalers but also agents and brokers who perform important wholesaling activities without taking title to the goods.

FUNCTIONS OF WHOLESALING INTERMEDIARIES

5 Identify the functions performed by wholesaling intermediaries.

As specialists in certain marketing functions, as opposed to production or manufacturing functions, wholesaling intermediaries can perform these functions more efficiently than producers or consumers. The importance of these activities results from the utility they create, the services they provide, and the cost reductions they allow.

Creating Utility

Wholesaling intermediaries create three types of utility for consumers. They enhance time utility by making products available for sale when consumers want to purchase them. They create place utility by helping deliver goods and services for purchase at convenient locations. They create ownership (or possession) utility when a smooth exchange of title to the products from producers or intermediaries to final purchasers is complete. Possession utility can also result from transactions in which actual title does not pass to purchasers, as in rental car services.

Providing Services

Table 15.1 lists a number of services provided by wholesaling intermediaries. The list clearly indicates the marketing utilities—time, place, and possession utility—that wholesaling intermediaries create or

TABLE 15.1 Wholesaling Services for Customers and Producer-Suppliers

Service	Beneficiaries of Service	
	Customers	**Producer-Suppliers**
Buying	Yes	No
Anticipates customer demands and applies knowledge of alternative sources of supply; acts as purchasing agent for customers.		
Selling	No	Yes
Provides a sales force to call on customers, creating a low-cost method for servicing smaller retailers and business users.		
Storing	Yes	Yes
Maintains warehouse facilities at lower costs than most individual producers or retailers could achieve. Reduces risk and cost of maintaining inventory for producers.		
Transporting	Yes	Yes
Customers receive prompt delivery in response to their demands, reducing their inventory investments. Wholesalers also break bulk by purchasing in economical carload or truckload lots, then reselling in smaller quantities, thereby reducing overall transportation costs.		
Providing Marketing Information	Yes	Yes
Offers important marketing research input for producers through regular contacts with retail and business buyers. Provides customers with information about new products, technical information about product lines, reports on competitors' activities and industry trends, and advisory information concerning pricing changes, legal changes, and so forth.		
Financing	Yes	Yes
Grants credit that might be unavailable for purchases directly from manufacturers. Provides financing assistance to producers by purchasing products in advance of sale by promptly paying bills.		
Risk Taking	Yes	Yes
Evaluates credit risks of numerous, distant retail customers and small-business users. Extends credit to customers that qualify. By transporting and stocking products in inventory, the wholesaler assumes risk of spoilage, theft, or obsolescence.		

© Cengage Learning

enhance. These services also reflect the basic marketing functions of buying, selling, storing, transporting, providing marketing information, financing, and risk taking.

Of course, many types of wholesaling intermediaries provide varying services, and not all of them perform every service listed in the table. Producer-suppliers rely on wholesaling intermediaries for distribution and selection of firms that offer the desired combinations of services. In general, however, the critical marketing functions listed in the table form the basis for any evaluation of a marketing intermediary's efficiency. The risk-taking function affects each service of the intermediary.

California-based Ingram Micro is a leading technology distributor with business clients in about 150 countries and vendors all over the world. Ranking number 81 in the *Fortune* 500, it offers a wide range of information technology services for order management and fulfillment, contract manufacturing and warehousing, transportation management, and credit and collection management, as well as distributing and marketing information technology products to businesses worldwide.[27]

FIGURE 15.3
Transaction Economies through Wholesaling Intermediaries

20 Contacts

9 Contacts

© Cengage Learning

Lowering Costs by Limiting Contacts

When an intermediary represents numerous producers, it often cuts the costs of buying and selling. The transaction economies are illustrated in Figure 15.3, which shows five manufacturers marketing their outputs to four different retail outlets. Without an intermediary, these exchanges require a total of 20 transactions. Adding a wholesaling intermediary reduces the number of transactions to nine.

United Stationers is a wholesale distributor of business products ranging from paper clips to technology equipment and office furniture. It serves discount chains, independent stores, and Internet resellers. Although big-box retailers buy in bulk directly from manufacturers, they can order low-volume specialty goods faster and more efficiently from United Stationers. By ordering online, mom-and-pop stores have access to about 100,000 items from more than 1,000 manufacturers, delivered either to the store or directly to customers overnight. A one-stop warehousing, logistics, and distribution network, United Stationers has a product mix that even includes industrial products and janitorial and breakroom supplies.[28]

ASSESSMENT CHECK

5.1 What is a wholesaler? How does it differ from a wholesaling intermediary?

5.2 How do wholesaling intermediaries help sellers lower costs?

TYPES OF WHOLESALING INTERMEDIARIES

Various types of wholesaling intermediaries operate in different distribution channels. Some provide wide ranges of services or handle broad lines of goods, while others specialize in individual services, goods, or industries. Figure 15.4 classifies wholesaling intermediaries by two characteristics: ownership and title flows—whether title passes from manufacturer or wholesaling intermediary. The three basic ownership structures are as follows: (1) manufacturer-owned facilities, (2) independent wholesaling intermediaries, and (3) retailer-owned cooperatives and buying offices. The two types of

Outline the major types of independent wholesaling intermediaries and the appropriate situations for using each.

6

FIGURE 15.4
Major Types of Wholesaling Intermediaries

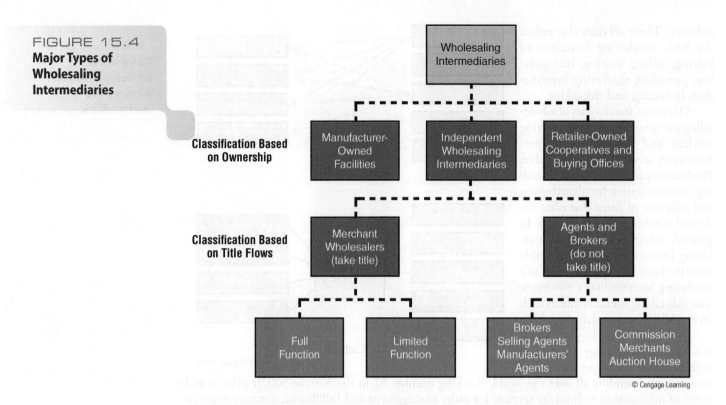

© Cengage Learning

independent wholesaling intermediaries are merchant wholesalers, which take title of the goods, and agents and brokers, which do not.

Several reasons lead manufacturers to distribute their goods directly through company-owned facilities. Some perishable goods need rigid control of distribution to avoid spoilage; other goods require complex installation or servicing. Some goods need aggressive promotion. Goods with high unit values allow profitable sales by manufacturers directly to ultimate purchasers. Manufacturer-owned facilities include sales branches, sales offices, trade fairs, and merchandise marts.

A *sales branch* carries inventory and processes orders for customers from available stock. Branches provide a storage function like independent wholesalers and serve as offices for sales representatives in their territories. They are prevalent in marketing channels for chemicals, commercial machinery and equipment, and petroleum products.

A *sales office,* in contrast, does not carry inventory, but it does serve as a regional office for a manufacturer's sales personnel. Locations close to the firm's customers help limit selling costs and support effective customer service. For example, numerous sales offices in the Detroit area serve the domestic automobile industry.

A *trade fair* (or trade exhibition) is a periodic show at which manufacturers in a particular industry display their wares for visiting retail and wholesale buyers. The world's largest consumer technology trade show, and the largest trade show of any kind in America, the annual International Consumer Electronics Show (CES), takes place in January in Las Vegas. In a recent year, CES attracted more than 156,000 industry professionals from over 150 countries and featured over 3,300 exhibitors.[29]

A *merchandise mart* provides space for permanent showrooms and exhibits, which manufacturers rent to market their goods. One of the world's largest merchandise marts is Chicago's Merchandise Mart, a 4.2-million-square-foot complex with its own zip code that hosts more than 30 seasonal buying markets each year.

Independent Wholesaling Intermediaries

Many wholesaling intermediaries are independently owned. These firms fall into two major categories: merchant wholesalers, and agents and brokers.

The International Consumer Electronics Show (CES) in Las Vegas is the world's largest consumer technology trade show.

Merchant Wholesalers

A **merchant wholesaler** takes title to the goods it handles. Merchant wholesalers account for roughly 60 percent of all sales at the wholesale level. Further classifications divide these wholesalers into full-function or limited-function wholesalers, as indicated in Figure 15.4.

A full-function merchant wholesaler provides a complete array of services for retailers and business purchasers. Such a wholesaler stores merchandise in a convenient location, allowing customers to make purchases on short notice and minimizing inventory requirements. The firm typically maintains a sales force that calls on retailers, makes deliveries, and extends credit to qualified buyers. Full-function wholesalers are common in the drug, grocery, and hardware industries. In the business-goods market, full-function merchant wholesalers—often called *industrial distributors*—sell machinery, inexpensive accessory equipment, and supplies.

A **rack jobber** is a full-function merchant wholesaler that markets specialized lines of merchandise to retailers. A rack jobber supplies the racks, stocks the merchandise, prices the goods, and makes regular visits to refill shelves. Sometimes rack jobbers are the exclusive supplier of a retailer—as in the case of Anderson Merchandisers, a rack jobber in the entertainment sector, which grew by being the supplier to Walmart stores' consumer electronics departments.[30]

Limited-function merchant wholesalers fit into four categories: cash-and-carry wholesalers, truck wholesalers, drop shippers, and mail-order wholesalers. Limited-function wholesalers serve the food, coal, lumber, cosmetics, jewelry, sporting goods, and general merchandise industries.

A *cash-and-carry* wholesaler performs most wholesaling functions, except for financing and delivery. Although feasible for small stores, this kind of wholesaling generally is unworkable for large-scale grocery stores. Today, cash-and-carry operations typically function as departments within regular full-service wholesale operations. Cash-and-carry wholesalers are commonplace outside the United States, such as in the United Kingdom.

A **truck wholesaler** (or **truck jobber**) markets perishable food items like bread, tobacco, potato chips, candy, and dairy products. Truck wholesalers make regular deliveries to retailers, perform sales and collection functions, and promote product lines. Regional wholesale distributor S. Abraham & Sons delivers brand-name groceries, health and beauty aids, and other merchandise to convenience, drug, and grocery stores in the Midwest.[31]

A **drop shipper**, such as Tampa's ONEinc., accepts orders from customers and forwards these orders to producers, which then ship the desired products directly to customers. Although drop shippers

merchant wholesaler Independently owned wholesaling intermediary that takes title to the goods it handles; also known as an industrial distributor in the business goods market.

rack jobber Full-function merchant wholesaler that markets specialized lines of merchandise to retail stores.

truck wholesaler (truck jobber) Limited-function merchant wholesaler that markets perishable food items.

drop shipper Limited-function merchant wholesaler that accepts orders from customers and forwards those orders to producers, which then ship directly to the customers who placed the orders.

TABLE 15.2 Comparison of the Types of Merchant Wholesalers and Their Services

Service	Full-Function	Cash-and-Carry	Limited-Function Wholesaler		
			Truck	Drop Shipper	Mail-Order
Anticipates customer needs	Yes	Yes	Yes	No	Yes
Carries inventory	Yes	Yes	Yes	No	Yes
Delivers	Yes	No	Yes	No	No
Provides marketing information	Yes	Rarely	Yes	Yes	No
Provides credit	Yes	No	No	Yes	Sometimes
Assumes ownership risk by taking title	Yes	Yes	Yes	Yes	Yes

© Cengage Learning

take title to goods, they never physically handle or even see the merchandise. These intermediaries often operate in industries selling bulky goods, such as coal and lumber, which customers buy in large lots.

mail-order wholesaler
Limited-function merchant wholesaler that distributes catalogs instead of sending sales personnel to contact customers.

A **mail-order wholesaler** is a limited-function merchant wholesaler that distributes physical or online catalogs as opposed to sending sales representatives to contact retail, business, and institutional customers. Customers then make purchases by mail, by phone, or online. Such a wholesaler often serves relatively small customers in outlying areas. Mail-order operations mainly exist in the hardware, cosmetics, jewelry, sporting goods, and specialty food lines as well as in general merchandise. Some popular mail-order products are pharmaceuticals, roasted bean coffee, Christmas trees and wreaths, and popcorn.

Table 15.2 compares the various types of merchant wholesalers and the services they provide. Full-function merchant wholesalers and truck wholesalers rank as relatively high-cost intermediaries because of the number of services they perform, while cash-and-carry wholesalers, drop shippers, and mail-order wholesalers provide fewer services and set lower prices because they incur lower operating costs.

Agents and Brokers

A second group of independent wholesaling intermediaries, agents and brokers, may or may not take possession of the goods they handle, but they never take title. They normally perform fewer services than merchant wholesalers, working mainly to bring together buyers and sellers. Agents and brokers fall into five categories: commission merchants, auction houses, brokers, selling agents, and manufacturers' representatives (reps).

commission merchant Agent wholesaling intermediary that takes possession of goods shipped to a central market for sale, acts as the producer's agent, and collects an agreed-upon fee at the time of the sale.

Commission merchants, which predominate in the markets for agricultural products, take possession when producers ship goods like grain, produce, and livestock to central markets for sale. Commission merchants act as producers' agents and receive agreed-upon fees when they make sales. Because customers inspect the products and prices fluctuate, commission merchants receive considerable latitude in marketing decisions. The owners of the goods may specify minimum prices, but

Auction house eBay offers a wide variety of products in all price ranges.

Hocus Focus Studio/iStockphoto.com

the commission merchants sell these goods at the best possible prices. The commission merchants then deduct their fees from the sales' proceeds.

An *auction house* gathers buyers and sellers in one location and allows potential buyers to inspect merchandise before submitting competing purchase offers. Auction house commissions typically reflect specified percentages of the sales prices of the auctioned items. Auctions are common in the distribution of tobacco, used cars, artwork, livestock, furs, and fruit. The Internet has led to a new type of auction house that connects customers and sellers in the online world. A well-known example is eBay, which auctions a wide variety of products in all price ranges.

Brokers work mainly to bring together buyers and sellers. A broker represents either the buyer or the seller—but not both—in a given transaction, and the broker receives a fee from the client when the transaction is completed. Intermediaries that specialize in arranging buying and selling transactions between domestic producers and foreign buyers are called *export brokers.* Brokers operate in industries characterized by large numbers of small suppliers and purchasers, such as real estate, frozen foods, and used machinery. Because they provide one-time services for sellers or buyers, they cannot serve as effective channels for manufacturers seeking regular, continuing service. A firm that seeks to develop a more permanent channel might choose instead to use a selling agent or manufacturer's agent.

A **selling agent** typically exerts full authority over pricing decisions and promotional outlays, and it often provides financial assistance for the manufacturer. Selling agents act as independent marketing departments, because they can assume responsibility for the total marketing programs of client firms' product lines. Selling agents mainly operate in the coal, lumber, and textiles industries. For a small, weakly financed, production-oriented firm, such an intermediary might prove the ideal marketing channel.

While a manufacturer may deal with only one selling agent, a firm that hires **manufacturers' representatives** often delegates marketing tasks to many of these agents. Such an independent salesperson may work for a number of firms that produce related, noncompeting products. Manufacturers' reps are paid on a commission basis, such as 6 percent of sales. Unlike selling agents, who may contract for exclusive rights to market a product, manufacturers' agents operate in specific territories. They may develop new sales territories or represent relatively small firms and those firms with unrelated lines.

Modern Supply Company, based in Knoxville, Tennessee, supplies kitchen and bath lighting, appliances, and cabinets, as well as consulting services for home remodeling or building, in eastern Tennessee and western Virginia. Recently named Wholesaler of the Year by *Supply House Times,* the company suffered during the recent recession. Modern Supply revamped some of its internal practices and launched a new presence on Twitter and Facebook—Modern's Millie, a lively cartoon character. The company's goal for Millie is a balance of 80 percent information and 20 percent selling. Modern's Millie already has over a thousand followers on Twitter and has won the company an award for innovative marketing.[32]

The importance of selling agents in many markets has declined because manufacturers want better control of their marketing programs than these intermediaries allow. In contrast, the volume of sales by manufacturers' agents has more than doubled and now accounts for 37 percent of all sales by agents and brokers. Table 15.3 compares the major types of agents and brokers on the basis of the services they perform.

broker Agent wholesaling intermediary that does not take title to or possession of goods in the course of its primary function, which is to bring together buyers and sellers.

selling agent Agent wholesaling intermediary for the entire marketing program of a firm's product line.

manufacturers' representative Agent wholesaling intermediary that represents manufacturers of related but noncompeting products and receives a commission on each sale.

(+) ASSESSMENT CHECK

6.1 What is the difference between a merchant wholesaler and a rack jobber?

6.2 Differentiate between agents and brokers.

TABLE 15.3 Services Provided by Agents and Brokers

Service	Commission Merchant	Auction House	Broker	Manufacturers' Agent	Selling Agent
Anticipates customer needs	Yes	Sometimes	Sometimes	Yes	Yes
Carries inventory	Yes	Yes	No	No	No
Delivers	Yes	No	No	Sometimes	No
Provides marketing information	Yes	Yes	Yes	Yes	Yes
Provides credit	Sometimes	No	No	No	Sometimes
Assumes ownership risk by taking title	No	No	No	No	No

© Cengage Learning

RETAILER-OWNED COOPERATIVES AND BUYING OFFICES

Retailers may assume numerous wholesaling functions in an attempt to reduce costs or provide special services. Independent retailers sometimes band together to form buying groups that can achieve cost savings through quantity purchases. Other groups of retailers establish retailer-owned wholesale facilities by forming cooperative chains. Large chain retailers often establish centralized buying offices to negotiate large-scale purchases directly with manufacturers.

DIRECT MARKETING AND OTHER NONSTORE RETAILING

7 **Compare the basic types of direct marketing and nonstore retailing.**

direct marketing
Direct communications, other than personal sales contacts, between buyer and seller, designed to generate sales, information requests, or store or website visits.

Although most retail transactions occur in stores, nonstore retailing is an important marketing channel for many products. Both consumer and business-to-business marketers rely on nonstore retailing to generate leads or requests for more information that may result in future orders.

Direct marketing is a broad concept that includes direct mail, direct selling, direct-response retailing, telemarketing, Internet retailing, and automatic merchandising. Direct and interactive marketing expenditures amount to hundreds of billions of dollars in yearly purchases. The last sections of this chapter consider each type of nonstore retailing.

DIRECT MAIL

Direct mail is a major component of direct marketing. It comes in many forms: sales letters, postcards, brochures, booklets, catalogs, house organs (periodicals published by organizations to cover internal issues), and DVDs. Both not-for-profit and profit-seeking organizations make extensive use of this distribution channel.

Direct mail offers several advantages, such as the ability to select a narrow target market, achieve intensive coverage, send messages quickly, choose from various formats, provide complete information, and personalize each mailing piece. Response rates are measurable and higher than other types of advertising. In addition, direct mailings stand alone and do not compete for attention with magazine articles and television programs. On the other hand, the per-reader cost of direct mail is high, effectiveness depends on the quality of the mailing list, and some consumers object to direct mail, considering it "junk mail."

Direct-mail marketing relies heavily on database technology in managing lists of names and in segmenting these lists according to the objectives of the campaign. Recipients get targeted materials, often personalized with their names within the ad's content.

Catalogs are a popular form of direct mail, with more than 20,000 different consumer specialty mail-order catalog companies—and thousands more for business-to-business sales—whose catalogs find their way to almost every mailbox in the United States. In a typical year, about 20 million mail-order catalogs are mailed; about half of all American consumers buy from catalogs.[33] Catalog marketing continues to grow at a faster rate than brick-and-mortar retailers. Catalogs can be a company's only or primary sales method. Pajamagram, Fetch Dog, Popcorn Factory, and Improvements are well-known examples. Brick-and-mortar retailers such as Crate & Barrel, Coldwater Creek, Land of Nod, and Orvis also distribute catalogs.

Environmental concerns and new technologies are changing catalog marketing. More than 22 million American consumers have registered with Catalog Choice to have their names removed from catalog mailing lists. Most cite a desire to save natural resources for their decision to stop receiving a blizzard of paper catalogs by mail.[34] By moving a catalog online, a merchant can update content easily and quickly, providing consumers with the latest information and prices. Online technology also allows marketers to use video and other techniques to display their merchandise. For example, Nordstrom's online shoe store catalog allows browsers to zoom in and out and view a shoe from different angles and in different colors.

DIRECT SELLING

Through direct selling, manufacturers completely bypass retailers and wholesalers. Instead, they set up their own channels to sell their products directly to consumers. Amway, Avon, Pampered Chef, and Tupperware are all direct sellers. This channel was discussed in detail in Chapter 14.

DIRECT-RESPONSE RETAILING

Customers of a direct-response retailer can order merchandise by mail or telephone, by visiting a mail-order desk in a retail store, or by computer or fax machine. The retailer then ships the merchandise to the customer's home or to a local retail store for pickup.

Many direct-response retailers rely on direct mail, such as catalogs, to create telephone and mail-order sales and to promote in-store purchases of products featured in the catalogs. Some firms, such as Lillian Vernon, make almost all their sales through catalog orders. Mail-order sales have grown at about twice the rate of retail store sales in recent years.

Direct-response retailers are increasingly reaching buyers through the Internet and through unique catalogs that serve special market niches. Many catalogs sell specialty products, such as kitchenware for the professional cook, art supplies, or supplies for the home renovator.

Direct-response retailing also includes home shopping, which runs promotions on cable television networks to sell merchandise through telephone orders. One form of home shopping, the *infomercial,* has existed for years. Infomercials can be short—one to two minutes—or run up to 30 minutes. Both have demonstrated success at generating revenues. Collette Liantonia is known as the "Queen of Infomercials," having produced more than 2,000 of them over 30 years. Among them are pitches for the George Foreman Grill, the Perfect Pasta Pot, and Pajama Jeans.[35]

 ASSESSMENT CHECK

7.1 What is direct marketing?

7.2 What is direct mail?

> **BRIEFLY SPEAKING**
>
> "People shop and learn in a whole new way compared to just a few years ago, so marketers need to adapt or risk extinction."
>
> —Brian Halligan
> *Coauthor of* Inbound Marketing *and CEO, Hubspot*

TELEMARKETING

Telemarketing refers to direct marketing conducted entirely by telephone. It is the most frequently used form of direct marketing. It provides marketers with a high return on their expenditures, an immediate response, and the opportunity for personalized two-way conversations. Telemarketing is discussed in further detail in Chapter 17.

> **8** Describe how much the Internet has altered the wholesaling, retailing, and direct marketing environments.

INTERNET RETAILING

Internet-based retailers sell directly to customers via virtual storefronts on the Web. They usually maintain little or no inventory, ordering directly from vendors to fill customer orders received via their websites. In recent years, conventional retailers have anxiously watched the rise—and then the demise—of many poorly planned, financed, and marketed Internet-based retailers. During the dot-com bust, 130 e-tailers failed. Even early successes like Ezshop, an online home furnishings retailer, eventually ran aground. Traditional retailers, using the Web to support brick-and-mortar stores—the so-called *brick-and-click retailers*—have had much better staying power. The Gap, Best Buy, and Lands' End, for example, succeeded in extending their success to the Web. Office Max offers thousands of office-supply products on its website, which also offers email alerts, favorite-item lists, and a customer loyalty program. Chapter 5 discussed Internet retailing and other forms of e-business in more detail.

AUTOMATIC MERCHANDISING

The world's first vending machines dispensed holy water for 5-drachma coins in Egyptian temples around 215 B.C. This retailing method has grown rapidly ever since; today, nearly 30,000 vending machine operators sell about $7 billion in convenience goods annually in the United States alone.[36]

Although U.S. vending machines primarily sell items like snacks, soft drinks, or lottery tickets, Japanese consumers use automatic merchandising for everything, including fresh sushi and new underwear. Recently, U.S. marketers have begun to realize the potential of this underused marketing tool. Several vending-machine companies, such as the California-based Fresh Healthy Vending and Vend Natural, with offices on both coasts, work with schools to replace traditional vending-machine offerings with fresh, healthy snacks.[37] The three major soft-drink companies recently agreed to remove sweetened drinks, such as soda and iced tea from vending machines in elementary and high schools nationwide. The calorie-laden drinks will be replaced by bottled water, low-fat milk, and 100 percent fruit juice or sports drinks. The ability to accept credit cards has enabled vending machines to sell high-end items, such as iPods, headphones, and Sony PlayStation games. Technological advances like touch screens, animation, and digital imagery make the buying experience fun—and even allow customers to read the back of the package before they buy.[38]

ASSESSMENT CHECK

8.1   Describe Internet-based retailers.

8.2   Explain how the Internet has enhanced retailers' functions.

STRATEGIC IMPLICATIONS OF MARKETING IN THE 21ST CENTURY

© iStockphoto.com/Ferran Traite Soler

As the Internet revolution steadily becomes a way of life—both for consumers and for the businesses marketing goods and services to them—technology will continue to transform the ways in which retailers, wholesalers, and direct marketers connect with customers.

In the retail sector, the unstoppable march toward lower prices has forced retailers from Neiman Marcus to dollar stores to reevaluate everything, including their logistics and supply networks and their profit margins. Many have used the power of the Internet to strengthen such factors as store image, the merchandising mix, customer service, and the development of long-term relationships with customers.

Although manufacturers first anticipated that Internet technology would enable them to bypass such intermediaries as wholesalers

and agents, bringing them closer to the customer, the reality is quite different. Successful wholesalers have established themselves as essential links in the supply, distribution, and customer service network. By leveraging technology, they have carved out new roles, providing such expert services as warehousing and fulfillment to multiple retail clients.

The Internet has empowered direct marketers by facilitating ever more sophisticated database segmentation. Traditional catalog and direct-mail marketers have integrated Internet sites, Web advertising, and emailing programs into a cohesive targeting, distribution, and repeat-buying strategy.

Get online now for additional learning tools to help you master your marketing knowledge—visit **WWW.CENGAGEBRAIN.COM** today!

REVIEW OF CHAPTER OBJECTIVES

1 Explain the wheel of retailing.

The wheel of retailing is the hypothesis that each new type of retailer gains a competitive foothold by offering lower prices than current suppliers and maintains profits by reducing or eliminating services. Once established, the innovator begins to add more services. Its prices gradually rise, making it vulnerable to new low-price retailers. This turns the wheel again.

2 Discuss how retailers select target markets.

A retailer starts to define its strategy by selecting a target market. The target market dictates, among other things, the product mix, pricing strategy, and location strategy. Retailers deal with consumer behavior at the most complicated level, and a clear understanding of the target market is critical. Strategies for selecting target markets include merchandising, customer services, pricing, location/distribution, and promotional strategies.

3 Show how the elements of the marketing mix apply to retailing strategy.

A retailer must first identify a target market and then develop a product strategy. Next, it must establish a customer service strategy. Retail pricing strategy involves decisions on markups and markdowns. Location is often the determining factor in a retailer's success or failure. A retailer's promotional strategy and store atmosphere play important roles in establishing a store's image.

4 Explain the concepts of retail convergence and scrambled merchandising.

Retail convergence is the coming together of shoppers, goods, and prices, resulting in the blurring of distinctions among types of retailers and the merchandise mix they offer. Similar selections are available from multiple sources and are differentiated mainly by price. Scrambled merchandising refers to retailers' practice of carrying dissimilar product lines in an attempt to generate additional sales volume. Retail convergence and scrambled merchandising have made it increasingly difficult to classify retailers.

5 Identify the functions performed by wholesaling intermediaries.

The functions of wholesaling intermediaries include creating utility, providing services, and lowering costs by limiting contacts.

6 Outline the major types of independent wholesaling intermediaries and the appropriate situations for using each.

Independent wholesaling intermediaries can be divided into two categories: merchant wholesalers, and agents and brokers. The two major types of merchant wholesalers are full-function merchant wholesalers, such as rack jobbers, and limited-function merchant wholesalers, including cash-and-carry wholesalers, truck wholesalers, drop shippers, and mail-order wholesalers. Full-function wholesalers are common in the drug, grocery, and hardware industries.

The food, coal, lumber, cosmetics, jewelry, sporting goods, and general-merchandise industries sometimes use limited-function wholesalers. Agents and brokers do not take title to the products they sell; this category includes commission merchants, auction houses, brokers, selling agents, and manufacturers' reps. Companies seeking to develop new sales territories, firms with unrelated lines, and smaller firms use manufacturers' reps. Commission merchants are common in the marketing of agricultural products. Auction houses are used to sell tobacco, used cars, livestock, furs, and fruit. Brokers are prevalent in the real estate, frozen foods, and used machinery industries.

7 Compare the basic types of direct marketing and nonstore retailing.

Direct marketing is a distribution channel consisting of direct communication to a consumer or business recipient. It generates orders and sales leads that may result in future orders. Because direct marketing responds to fragmented media markets and audiences, growth of customized products, and shrinking network broadcast audiences, marketers consider it an important part of their planning efforts. Although most U.S. retail sales take place in stores, such nonstore retailing activities as direct mail, direct selling, direct-response retailing, telemarketing, Internet retailing, and automatic merchandising are important in marketing many types of goods and services.

Describe how much the Internet has altered the wholesaling, retailing, and direct marketing environments.

The Internet has affected every aspect of marketing, including how supply networks operate and how relationships are formed with customers. Successful wholesalers have carved out a niche as a source of expertise offering faster, more efficient, Web-enabled distribution and fulfillment. The Internet has allowed retailers to enhance their merchandising mix and their customer service by, among other things, giving them access to much broader selections of goods. Direct marketers have merged their traditional catalog or direct-mail programs with an Internet interface that allows for faster, more efficient, and more frequent contact with customers and prospects.

ASSESSMENT CHECK: ANSWERS

1.1 What is retailing? Retailing refers to the activities involved in selling merchandise to ultimate consumers.

1.2 Explain the wheel-of-retailing concept. The wheel of retailing is the hypothesis that each new type of retailer gains a competitive foothold by offering lower prices than current suppliers and maintains profits by reducing or eliminating services.

2.1 How does a retailer develop a marketing strategy? A retailer develops a marketing strategy that is based on its goals and strategic plans.

2.2 How do retailers select target markets? Strategies for selecting target markets include merchandising, customer services, pricing, location/distribution, and promotional strategies.

3.1 What is an SKU? An SKU, or stock-keeping unit, is a specific product offering within a product line.

3.2 What are the two components of a markup? A markup consists of the product's cost and an amount added by the retailer to determine its selling price.

3.3 What are store atmospherics? Store atmospherics are the physical characteristics and amenities that attract customers and satisfy their shopping needs.

4.1 How do we classify retailers by form of ownership? There are two types of retailers by form of ownership: chain stores and independent retailers.

4.2 Categorize retailers by shopping effort and by services provided. Convenience retailers and specialty retailers are classified by shopping effort; self-service, self-selection, and full-service describe retailers in terms of services provided.

4.3 List several ways to classify retailers by product line. Retailers classified by product line include specialty stores, limited-line retailers, and general merchandise retailers. General merchandise retailers include variety stores, department stores, and mass merchandisers.

5.1 What is a wholesaler? How does it differ from a wholesaling intermediary? A wholesaler is a channel intermediary that takes title to goods it handles and then distributes these goods to retailers, other distributors, or B2B customers. A wholesaling intermediary can be a wholesaler, an agent, or a broker and can perform wholesaling activities without taking title to the goods.

5.2 How do wholesaling intermediaries help sellers lower costs? Wholesaling intermediaries reduce the number of transactions between manufacturers and retail outlets, thus lowering distribution costs.

6.1 What is the difference between a merchant wholesaler and a rack jobber? A merchant wholesaler takes title to the goods it handles. A rack jobber is a full-function merchant wholesaler that markets specialized lines of merchandise to retailers.

6.2 Differentiate between agents and brokers. Agents and brokers may or may not take possession of the goods they handle, but they never take title. Brokers work mainly to bring together buyers and sellers. A selling agent typically exerts full authority over pricing decisions and promotional outlays and often provides financial assistance for the manufacturer.

7.1 What is direct marketing? Direct marketing is a distribution channel consisting of direct communication to a consumer or business recipient. It generates orders and sales leads that may result in future orders.

7.2 What is direct mail? Direct mail is a form of direct marketing that includes sales letters, postcards, brochures, booklets, catalogs, house organs, and DVDs.

8.1 Describe Internet-based retailers. Internet-based retailers sell directly to customers via virtual storefronts on the Web. They usually maintain little or no inventory, ordering directly from vendors to fill customers' orders.

8.2 Explain how the Internet has enhanced retailers' functions. The Internet has allowed retailers to enhance their merchandising mix and their customer service by, among other things, giving them access to much broader selections of goods. Direct marketers have merged their traditional catalog or direct-mail programs with an Internet interface that allows for faster, more efficient, and more frequent contact with customers and prospects.

MARKETING TERMS YOU NEED TO KNOW

retailing **490**
wheel of retailing **491**
stock-keeping unit (SKU) **494**
markup **495**
markdown **496**
planned shopping center **496**
atmospherics **499**
convenience retailer **501**
specialty retailer **501**

limited-line store **502**
category killer **502**
general merchandise
   retailer **502**
department store **503**
mass merchandiser **503**
discount house **503**
hypermarket **504**
supercenter **504**

retail convergence **504**
scrambled merchandising **505**
wholesaler **505**
wholesaling intermediary **506**
merchant wholesaler **509**
rack jobber **509**
truck wholesaler
  (truck jobber) **509**
drop shipper **509**

mail-order wholesaler **510**
commission merchant **510**
broker **511**
selling agent **511**
manufacturers'
  representative **511**
direct marketing **512**

ASSURANCE OF LEARNING REVIEW

1. Find some examples of retailers that demonstrate the concept of the wheel of retailing. Explain the stages they have gone through and which stage they are in currently.

2. How do retailers identify target markets? Explain the major strategies by which retailers reach their target markets.

3. Explain the importance of a retailer's location to its strategy.

4. What is *retail convergence?*

5. Define *scrambled merchandising*. Why has this practice become so common in retailing?

6. What is a wholesaling intermediary? Describe the activities it performs.

7. Distinguish among the different types of manufacturer-owned wholesaling intermediaries. What conditions might suit each one?

8. Differentiate between direct selling and direct-response retailing. Cite examples of both.

9. In what ways has the Internet changed direct-response retailing?

10. Define *automatic merchandising*, and explain its role in U.S. retailing today and in the future.

PROJECTS AND TEAMWORK EXERCISES

1. Research and then classify each of the following retailers:
   a. Home Depot
   b. H&M
   c. hhgregg
   d. Dillard's
   e. Gymboree

2. Visit a local Walmart store and observe product placement, shelf placement, inventory levels on shelves, traffic patterns, customer service, and checkout efficiency. Discuss what makes Walmart the world's most successful retailer.

3. Target has become known for trendy clothes and stylish housewares, all readily available in spacious stores at reasonable prices. Visit a local Target store or the company's website and compare its product selection to that of your local hardware store or a department store. Make a list of each store's advantages and disadvantages, including convenience, location, selection, service, and general prices. Do any of their product lines overlap? How are they different from each other?

4. Match each industry with the most appropriate type of wholesaling intermediary.

    ___hardware   a. drop shipper
    ___perishable foods b. truck wholesaler
    ___lumber   c. auction house
    ___wheat   d. full-function merchant wholesaler
    ___used cars   e. commission merchant

5. In teams, develop a retailing strategy for an Internet retailer. Identify a target market and then suggest a mix of merchandise, promotion, service, and pricing strategies that would help a retailer reach that market via the Internet. What issues must Internet retailers address that do not affect traditional store retailers?

6. With a classmate, visit two or three retail stores that compete with each other in your area and compare their customer service strategies. (You might want to visit each store more than once to avoid making a snap judgment.) Select at least five criteria and use them to assess each store. How do you think each store sees its customer service strategy as fitting into its overall retailing strategy? Present your findings in detail to the class.

7. Visit a department store and compare at least two departments' pricing strategies based on the number of markdowns

you find and the size of the discount. What, if anything, can you conclude about the success of each department's retailing strategy?

8. Think of a large purchase you make on a nonroutine basis, such as a new winter coat or expensive clothing for a special occasion. Where will you shop for such items? Will you travel out of your way? Will you go to the nearest shopping center? Will you look on the Internet? Once you have made your decision, describe any strategies used by the retailer that led you to

this decision. What might make you change your mind about where to shop for this item?

9. Outlet malls are a growing segment of the retail market. Visit a local outlet mall or research one on the Internet. What types of stores are located there? How do the product selection and price compare with typical stores?

10. Torrid is a national chain of about 150 stores that feature clothing for plus-size women. Recommend an appropriate retailing strategy for this type of retailer.

CRITICAL-THINKING EXERCISES

1. The retail chain Anthropologie sells a unique mix of women's clothing and home furnishings. Since its founding in 1992, Anthropologie has opened stores across the United States, in Canada, and in Great Britain. The retailer aims to create a shopping "experience" where its customers—independent-minded, college-educated female professionals between ages 30 and 45—can find their own look. No two Anthropologie stores are exactly alike, and the chain does not use advertising. Visit the website at www.anthropologie.com. How does it differentiate itself from its competitors?

2. Several major retailers have begun to test the extreme markdown strategy that lies behind popular dollar stores such as Dollar General and Family Dollar Stores. Kroger, A&P, Walmart, and others have opened sections in selected stores that feature items from snacks to beauty supplies, all priced at $1. Is this experiment simply a test of pricing strategy? What else might motivate these retailers to offer such deep discounts?

3. When Tower Records filed for bankruptcy, it was only one symptom of the general decline of the retail music store. Industry watchers blame everything, including music downloading programs and changes in consumers' tastes. Most, however, feel that music stores will somehow remain viable. What are some changes these retailers could make in their merchandising, customer service, pricing, location, and other strategies to try to reinvent their business?

4. McDonald's has traditionally relied on a cookie-cutter approach to its restaurant design. One store looked essentially like every other—until recently. The chain has decided to loosen its corporate design mandate to fit within special markets and to update its image with customers. Research McDonald's makeover efforts. What types of changes has the company made and where? How have changes in atmospherics helped the chain with customers? Have the changes you researched modified your perception of McDonald's at all? If so, how?

ETHICS EXERCISE

As the largest company in the world, with more than two million employees worldwide and more than $440 billion in sales in a recent year, Walmart has become big and powerful enough to influence the U.S. economy. It is responsible for 10 percent of total U.S. imports from China and about 12 percent of U.S. productivity gains since the late 1990s. Some observers believe Walmart is also responsible for the low U.S. inflation rates of recent years. However, its unbeatable buying power and efficiency have sometimes forced local stores to close when Walmart opens a new store in their area.

1. Some economists fear what might happen to the U.S. economy if Walmart has a bad year. (So far, it has had more than four

decades of nonstop growth.) Should a single retailer have that much influence on the economy? Why or why not?

2. Walmart is selective about what it sells—refusing, for instance, to carry music or computer games with mature ratings, magazines with content it considers too adult, or, in some of its stores, handguns. Because of its sheer size, these decisions can influence American culture. Do you think this is a positive or negative effect of the growth of this retailer? Why?

INTERNET EXERCISES

1. **Shopping center trends.** Visit the website below. Click on "development" and then "trends." Review the material, and then prepare a brief report on some of the major trends in shopping center development.

   http://retailtrafficmag.com/

2. **Online retailing strategy.** Visit Kohl's website. Using the material in this chapter on retailing strategy, answer the following questions:

   a. How does the design and layout of Kohl's online store appeal to the retailer's target market?

   b. In your opinion, what is the main strategic objective of Kohl's online store? Is it to generate revenue independent of its brick-and-mortar stores? Or is the online store's main purpose to support so-called Web-to-store shoppers (shoppers who

   use the Web mainly to obtain product information and prices but make actual purchases at brick-and-mortar stores)?

   www.kohls.com

3. **Wholesaling industry.** Visit the website of the *Statistical Abstract of the United States* (published by the Census Bureau). Click on "wholesale and retail trade." Review the data and prepare a brief report identifying five major facts about the U.S. wholesaling industry.

   www.census.gov/compendia/statab

   Note: Internet Web addresses change frequently. If you don't find the exact site listed, you may need to access the organization's home page and search from there or use a search engine such as Google or Bing.

CASE 15.1

Costco Plays Catch-Up in Online Sales

Costco, the $99 billion warehouse-style chain, is the third-largest retailer in the United States. With low prices, low employee turnover, and steady growth, the company would seem to be an all-around success. It even boasts above-average survey scores on the quality of the shopping experience and customer service in its more than 600 stores worldwide.

But Costco is playing catch-up online, a sector that's growing faster than in-store retailing and where nimble competitors like Walmart hope to gain most of their future expansion. A rarity in store retailing because it has been profitable since day one, Costco has big plans for boosting its e-commerce business, but it has also missed some opportunities.

Costco.com takes in about $2 billion a year with a broad assortment of products that are not always found in the stores. These range from electronics and lawn furniture to caskets and pricey diamond jewelry (delivered by Brink's). The convenience of free shipping and assembly are usually included. Most of Costco's online customers are a bit more affluent than customers of the warehouse stores, and their average purchases tend to be bigger too.

But despite being a brick-and-mortar presence in eight countries abroad, Costco currently limits its online operations to the United States and Canada. Critics have also found flaws in the company's online marketing efforts. Customers are not always aware of the product variety online, nor do they realize that the special offers

outlined in the company's emails, which go to about 12 million registered customers, promote products unique to the website. Another problem is that products on the website don't readily turn up in shoppers' search engine results because of the way the website's pages are named, a condition Costco hopes to improve via the technical process of search engine optimization. The website also isn't as user-friendly as it could be, say critics, with "rookie mistakes" like visual clutter and poorly labeled photographs. One search engine consultant said the company's online division is "undoubtedly leaving some sales on the table."

QUESTIONS FOR CRITICAL THINKING

1. How can Costco.com better inform its online customers of the product variety available and the real value of its special offers?

2. What priority do you think Costco should put on expanding its online business abroad? Is this more or less important than improving sales from the existing e-commerce operations in the United States and Canada? Explain your reasoning.

Sources: Company profile, http://phx.corporate-ir.net, accessed December 2, 2012; Melissa Allison, "Costco Makes Plans for Boosting Its Online Sales," *The Seattle Times*, accessed December 2, 2012, http://seattletimes.nwsource.com; Brad Tuttle, "Survey: Costco Given Retail Crown for Best Shopping Experience," *Time*, accessed December 2, 2012, http://moneyland.time.com.

VIDEO CASE 15.2
GaGa SherBetter:
Coming to a Market Near You?

Everyone likes ice cream—or sherbet. But suppose you could have the best of both, in one cup or cone? And what if you could buy your favorite treat at your local market? Jim King, founder and CEO of GaGa, is doing his best to see that your frozen dessert wishes come true. Nearly 10 years ago, King—a former TV news anchor—began experimenting with his grandmother GaGa's recipe for lemon sherbet. He made a few batches and peddled them to retailers in his home state of Rhode Island before stopping in at Munroe Dairy, a home-delivery dairy farm. The owner ordered 500 pints on the spot—and GaGa was in business. Suddenly, King and his wife Michelle had to figure out how to make and store a large batch of the "Sherbetter"—Jim's name for the product, which he described as "sherbet but better." Eventually, Jim purchased a batch freezer for $2,800 at an IRS auction.

Once the Munroe Dairy order was filled, the Kings had to decide where and how to sell their product—directly to consumers, via wholesalers, or to retailers. Early on, they tried selling through an ice cream company. "We sold zero," recalls Michelle. Consumers would have to pay about $100 for a six-pint order instead of $4.99 for a pint at the grocery market, because the cost of shipping was astronomical—the SherBetter had to be shipped overnight in a heavy box with dry ice. The television shopping networks HSN and QVC also invited the Kings to sell their product on television; as a former news anchor, Jim would be a natural on camera. But the Kings declined—again because of the high cost of shipping directly to consumers.

Jim also researched the possibility of becoming a retailer himself—opening his scoop shop. But he quickly realized that the business model just wouldn't work for his company. Successful scoop shops must be located near a beach, lake, or other recreational area, and have no other direct competitors nearby. Furthermore, in the New England area, ice cream shops are mostly seasonal. Jim also determined that the projected expense of purchasing and maintaining a building and property was too high for GaGa. In addition, ice cream shops generally offer a wide variety of products, including ice cream, sherbet, frozen yogurt, diabetic-friendly and dairy-free frozen desserts, smoothies, shakes, and more. GaGa just had SherBetter—albeit in a growing array of flavors.

So the Kings decided that retailers would be the best outlet for their product. "Basically, we're a marketing agency," Jim comments. Jim works with a broker who arranges for Jim and Michelle to meet with retailers and demonstrate GaGa SherBetter at their stores, giving out free samples and promoting the product. If the retailers and their customers like the product, it is added to the grocery shelves.

The smaller or specialty markets like Whole Foods generally stock GaGa, because the Kings can't afford the huge slotting allowances charged by larger supermarkets. Jim explains that a slotting fee in the frozen section of a large supermarket chain could run as much as $35,000 to $40,000 just to place one product on the shelf at 600 to 800 stores. Jim notes that Whole Foods, which doesn't require a slotting allowance, may initially ask for free products to see if they will sell. "That's affordable," acknowledges Jim. "We can make that back pretty quickly." Not only is the cost of putting a product on the shelves of a large supermarket chain prohibitive, those customers aren't necessarily the consumers who would buy GaGa anyway. "Because we are a super-premium product and perceived as expensive, we don't sell well" in those stores, Michelle points out. "People who go into a market like that are looking for a deal." So they've decided to target the specialty markets, because that's where their true customers shop.

Looking to the future, Jim believes that ultimately GaGa could become an umbrella brand for a wider range of products, by building out the current line of SherBetter products and eventually adding new categories. He also wants to make a second stab at the wholesale food service channel since the first attempt didn't work out. He tried to make a push into food wholesaler Sysco but was unsuccessful—largely because the price of GaGa was double that of Sysco's price for super-premium ice cream. "Restaurants are more concerned about price," says Jim. He's now searching for a wholesale outlet connected with a nationwide restaurant chain that would agree to put GaGa dessert on the menu.

For now, Jim remains focused on the job at hand—getting GaGa into the stores. "We've got this great name," he remarks. "We've got this great product."

QUESTIONS FOR CRITICAL THINKING

1. Experience has taught the Kings that smaller, specialty markets are the strongest retail outlets for their GaGa SherBetter. Under what conditions might they begin to make a successful move into the larger supermarket chains?

2. How might the right wholesaler ultimately create marketing utility for GaGa?

Sources: Company website, http://gagagourmetsherbet.com, accessed December 2, 2012; "GaGa's Rainbow SherBetter," *On Second Scoop*, accessed December 2, 2012, www.onsecondscoop.com; Judi Atkins Bridges, "Summer Market Blackberries," *AL.com*, accessed December 2, 2012, http://blog.al.com; Curt Nickisch, "GaGa's for Lady Gaga? Coincidental Celebrity Lifts Local Brands," NPR (Boston), accessed December 2, 2012, www.wbur.org.

NOTES

1. Bill Siwicki, "Thanksgiving Weekend Mobile Sales Up 110% at HauteLook," *Internet Retailer*, accessed December 2, 2012, www.internetretailer.com; David Hatch, "Nordstrom in Fashion with Social Media, Mobile Tech," *U.S. News & World Report*, accessed December 2, 2012, http://money.usnews.com; Evelyn M. Rusli, "Stores Go Online to Find a Perfect Fit," *The New York Times*, accessed December 2, 2012, http://dealbook.nytimes.com; Kelly Clay, "Nordstrom Sees Sales Boost from Mobile POS Devices," Forbes, accessed December 2, 2012, www.forbes.com; Lydia Dishman, "Nordstrom Bolsters Its Smart-Shopping Cred with Flash Seller HauteLook," *CBS News*, accessed December 2, 2012, www.cbsnews.com; "Complete List of Nordstrom Locations," *AggData*, accessed December 2, 2012, www.aggdata.com.

2. Michael Johnsen, "Walgreens Outlines Five Key Strategies to Change the Pharmacy Retail Industry," *Drug Store News*, accessed December 2, 2012, http://drugstorenews.com.

3. Company website, www.sprouts.com, accessed December 2, 2012; company website, "Sprouts and Sunflower Are Joining Forces," www.1farmersmarket.com, accessed December 2, 2012; Soma Biswas, Michael Ballaban, and Ian Thomas, "Sprouts Farmers Markets to Go Public in 1H13, *Financial Times*, accessed December 2, 2012, www.ft.com.

4. Jessica Wohl, "Target Raises Profit Forecast; Shares Inch Up," *Reuters*, accessed December 2, 2012, www.reuters.com.

5. "Women's Roles in Home Improvement," *ABC News*, accessed December 2, 2012, http://abcnews.go.com.

6. Company website, www.dswinc.com, accessed December 2, 2012.

7. "TakeLessons Raises $6 Million Venture Round Led by Crosslink Capital," *Business Wire*, accessed December 2, 2012, www.businesswire.com.

8. "Business Idea Center: Specialty Foods," *Entrepreneur*, accessed December 2, 2012, www.entrepreneur.com.

9. Company website, www.callwave.com, accessed December 2, 2012.

10. Company website, www.lapalmera.com, accessed December 2, 2012.

11. Elaine Misonzhnik, "Lifestyle Centers Launch a Comeback," *Retail Traffic*, accessed December 2, 2012, http://retailtrafficmag.com.

12. Joe Yogerst, "America's Most Visited Shopping Malls," *Travel + Leisure*, accessed December 2, 2012, www.travelandleisure.com.

13. Andrew Adam Newman, "A Web Series for G.E. Tests a Refrigerator and Freshness," *The New York Times*, accessed December 2, 2012, www.nytimes.com.

14. Mark Walsh, "Flurry to Debut Mobile Ad Analytics Tool," *Online Media Daily*, accessed December 2, 2012, www.mediapost.com.

15. William L. McComb, "Clicks and Mortar: Why In-Store Experience Matters (Now More than Ever)," *Forbes*, accessed December 2, 2012, www.forbes.com.

16. "IMAN Cosmetics Launches Digital Beauty Advisor," press release, *PR Newswire*, accessed December 2, 2012, www.prnewswire.com.

17. Gus Lubin, "15 Ways Supermarkets Trick You into Spending More Money," *Business Insider*, accessed December 2, 2012, www.businessinsider.com; "The Secret Weapon Luxe Hotels Use to Lure Guests In," *Forbes*, accessed December 2, 2012, www.forbes.com.

18. Adrianne Pasquarelli, "Department Stores Fill Their Floors with Shop-in-Shops," *Crain's New York Business*, accessed December 2, 2012, www.crainsnewyork.com.

19. Barbara Farfan, "Retail Industry Information: Overview of Facts, Research, Data & Trivia 2011," *About.com*, accessed December 2, 2012, http://retailindustry.about.com.

20. Company website, www.gloriajeans.com, accessed December 2, 2012.

21. Company website, http://news.walgreens.com, accessed December 2, 2012.

22. Sarah Shannon, "Deloitte Sees EU Clothing Retailers Merging," *Bloomberg*, accessed December 2, 2012, www.bloomberg.com.

23. Company website, http://sale.vente-privee.com, accessed December 2, 2012.

24. Company website, www.meijer.com, accessed December 2, 2012.

25. Mark Hachman, "Walmart, Vudu to Rip Your DVDs to the Cloud," *PC Magazine*, accessed December 2, 2012, www.pcmag.com.

26. Fiona Soltes, "Milk, Bread … and a Doctor Visit," Stores, accessed December 2, 2012, www.stores.org.

27. Company website, "Ingram Micro Fact Sheet," http://phx.corporate-ir.net, accessed December 2, 2012.

28. Company website, www.unitedstationers.com, accessed December 2, 2012.

29. "World's Largest Technology Tradeshow Sees 22 Percent Growth in Exhibitors and 13 Percent Growth in International Attendance," press release, www.cesweb.org, accessed December 2, 2012; Gary Shapiro, "Want Innovation? Go to a Tradeshow," Forbes, accessed December 2, 2012, www.forbes.com.

30. "Merchandising Services Companies," *Product Profitability*, accessed December 2, 2012, www.productprofitability.com.

31. Company website, www.sasinc.com, accessed December 2, 2012.

32. John McNally, "2011 Wholesaler of the Year: Modern Supply," *Supply House Times*, accessed December 2, 2012, www.supplyht.com.

33. American Catalog Mailers Association, "Catalog Industry Fact Sheet," accessed December 2, 2012, www.catalogmailers.org.

34. Catalog Choice, www.catalogchoice.org, accessed December 2, 2012; Todd Woody, "Catalog Choice and Its Junk Mail-Zapping App Acquired by TrustedID," *Forbes*, accessed December 2, 2012, www.forbes.com.

35. Lesley Kennedy, "Collette Liantonio, Queen of Infomercials," *MORE* Magazine, accessed December 2, 2012, www.more.com.

36. "Vending Machine Operators in the U.S.: Market Research Report," *IBIS World*, accessed December 2, 2012, www.ibisworld.com.

37. Barri Bronston, "New Orleans Area Schools Test Healthy Snack Vending Machines," *New Orleans Times*-Picayune, accessed December 2, 2012, www.nola.com; Winnie Hu, "Schools Dangle Carrot Snacks, But It's a Tough Sale," *The New York Times*, accessed December 2, 2012, www.nytimes.com.

38. Bruce Horovitz, "Vending World Tries New Tech to Court Gen Y," *USA Today*, accessed December 2, 2012, http://usatoday30.usatoday.com.

Scripps Networks Interactive & Food Network

Pushing Content into New Channels

"We're a content-first company," notes Sergei Kuharsky, senior vice president and general manager of licensing and merchandising for Scripps Networks Interactive. How do you build a distribution (or marketing) channel system for content featuring a product that customers can't actually see, smell, hear, touch, or taste? Food Network, one of the branded networks owned by Scripps Networks Interactive, creates and produces the content (concept, script, and other programming details) for an array of television shows focused on food and cooking. Television is the first distribution channel that comes to mind—but the company's website and magazine are also two important channels for getting the content out to consumers. Then there are all the social and digital options: Facebook, Twitter, Pinterest, GetGlue, and more. Finally, there is the retailer who agrees to stock its shelves with Food Network's branded kitchen supplies.

Scripps and Food Network marketers partner to handle the logistics of delivering Food Network's products—ranging from programming to frying pans. By coordinating the flow of marketing information, goods, programming content, and services to members of the overall marketing channel, marketers extend Food Network's reach. Food Network's huge cache of original recipes is a good example. Viewers love to try recipes they see on Food Network's various cooking shows, whether it's Bobby Flay's *Barbecue Addiction* or Melissa D'Arabian's *Ten Dollar Dinners*. Marketers had to determine the best way to get those recipes into the kitchens of viewers by facilitating searches. So they posted the recipes on the Food Network website, making it easy for consumers to locate and use. Then they pushed the recipes out farther by creating digital and print cookbooks (often in partnership with Food Network stars like Paula Deen or Cat Cora). The cookbooks have been extremely popular; during one recent year, 10 Food Network cookbooks hit the *New York Times* best seller list.

When Food Network decided to create a line of kitchen and cooking supplies—cookware, dinnerware, table linens, and more—marketers considered the options and settled on an exclusive distribution partnership with Kohl's. Kuharsky notes that while ubiquity—being everywhere—can be a very good thing because it eliminates barriers to consumers, it also poses challenges. "With it, you lose control, and then you risk quality," he explains. So Food Network remains selective in its choice of distribution channels. Today, Kohl's sells more than 1,100 Food Network items at its retail stores and online. And since food is, after all, about the senses, Food Network has partnered with about 2,200 sports arenas across the country to offer everything from sizzling burgers to crispy fries at exclusive concessions. Sports fans can belly up to the Food Network stand and enjoy their favorite arena snacks while

cheering their teams. Kuharsky summarizes the company's overall distribution strategy this way: "You look at all the different consumer touch points and what the challenges are. You want the ones that give you the best opportunity to present the brand and deepen your relationship."

Managing all of the interactive digital channels for delivering content as well as marketing messages is a vital job for Scripps and Food Network marketers. "I think our strongest channel right now is probably the Food Network website, for its reach," observes Tanya Edwards, digital programming director. One reason for this is that people engage online while they are watching the television shows, giving Food Network a prime opportunity to hold onto viewers' attention after a show is over. For example, at the end of *Restaurant: Impossible*, viewers see a prompt to the Food Network website, where they learn more about the featured restaurant. They might catch an interview with the owners or updates on the restaurant's success.

Edwards notes that Food Network has enjoyed great success with its apps, especially those that focus on recipes and cooking tips, such as "In the Kitchen." The app delivers content right to consumers wherever they are, whether it's the grocery store, farmers' market, or kitchen. This also helps build brand loyalty. "People trust our brand as someone who will help them get dinner, create a great dessert, or bake cupcakes to take to a party," Edwards says.

Because social media is by definition interactive, it creates some unique challenges as part of the overall marketing channel system. For example, it's unclear how to monetize a social media presence. But social media is still one of the best ways to capture valuable data as people talk about the brand. In the end, says Kuharsky, it's all about "looking for all those fun touch points that food goes where we go, and trying to be people's best friend in food."

QUESTIONS FOR CRITICAL THINKING

1. Food Network adopts a dual distribution strategy. In your opinion, what are the benefits of this?

2. Scripps and Food Network appear to have achieved channel cooperation. However, describe a scenario in which channel conflict might arise.

3. How does social media marketing support Food Network's distribution strategy?

4. Do you think Kohl's is the best choice of retail outlet for Food Network's products? Why or why not?

PART 6

Promotional Decisions

523

© Joselito Briones/the Agency Collection/Jupiterimages / Miroslav Georgijevic/iStockphoto.com

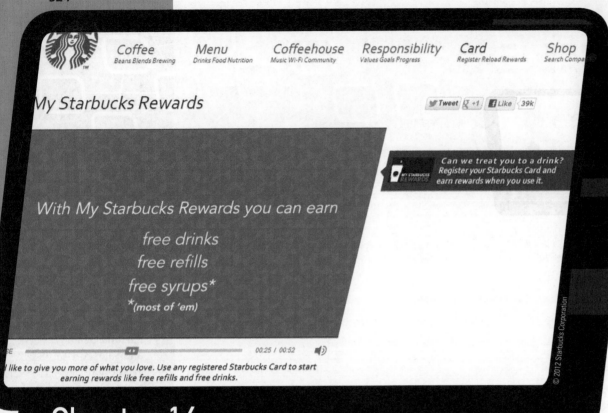

With My Starbucks Rewards you can earn

free drinks
free refills
free syrups*
*(most of 'em)

Can we treat you to a drink?
Register your Starbucks Card and
earn rewards when you use it.

...like to give you more of what you love. Use any registered Starbucks Card to start earning rewards like free refills and free drinks.

© 2012 Starbucks Corporation

Chapter 16

INTEGRATED

Marketing Communications, Advertising, and Public Relations

8 Explain the roles of public relations, publicity, cross-promotion, and ethics in an organization's promotional strategy.

9 Discuss the factors that influence the effectiveness of a promotional mix and how marketers measure effectiveness.

1 Define integrated marketing communications and explain how it relates to the development of an optimal promotional mix.

2 Describe the communication process and how it relates to the AIDA concept.

3 Identify the elements of the promotional mix.

4 Name the three major advertising objectives and the two basic categories of advertising.

5 Identify the major advertising strategies and the process of creating an advertisement.

6 Describe the major types of advertising appeals, and discuss their uses.

7 List and compare the major advertising media.

STARBUCKS
BREWS
SUCCESSFUL
MEDIA STRATEGY

Starbucks doesn't only serve great coffee drinks in the comfortable cafés it calls the "third place" between home and office. It also engages customers with an integrated marketing message that builds loyalty and keeps customers coming back. In fact, the company was recently ranked number one in a study of "most socially engaged companies" by an advertising research firm.

Starbucks' marketing approach is multilayered, reaches across various platforms, and continues to evolve. The company knows its customers appreciate marketing messages that recognize how they want to be perceived by others in their everyday lives as well as in their social networks. Its media efforts thus consistently appeal to, and let customers express, their "idealized self." For instance, Starbucks' Web page invites visitors to post their unique product preferences and share their own personal Starbucks experiences. A recent television ad highlights this focus on individuals by featuring a Starbucks drink created for a single individual. The ad begins with a seedling coffee plant labeled "Sue" yielding beans that cycle all the way through production, quality control, and shipping bearing her name until they become an iconic cup of Starbucks coffee with "Sue" written on it.

Starbucks supports one-to-one marketing communications with its mobile marketing strategy, which offers purchase and special-occasion incentives through its loyalty program as well as a store finder, nutrition information about menu items, the ability to check My Starbucks Rewards balances and reload payment cards, and tap-and-pay capability for smartphones. The loyalty program has quickly grown to nearly 5 million members, and 25 percent of all purchases are now paid via the card instead of cash. Starbucks invites customers to sign up for informative emails about its products, and text messages are consistent with its strategy too. The company hopes recipients will share these messages with friends—something that takes only a click to do.

Starbucks' media strategy is also visible in its cafés. Its Starbucks Digital network provides unique news and entertainment content delivered on its free in-store Wi-Fi service. Free access to subscription content from *The Wall Street Journal* and *The New York Times* is available, along with *USA Today, The Economist,* and *ESPN Insider.* And when it's time for customers to collect rewards benefits, Starbucks quickly loads rewards on members' loyalty cards and mobile devices.[1]

EVOLUTION OF A BRAND

From the opening of its first store in Seattle's Pike Place Market in 1971, Starbucks has known success—in large part because of its uncanny ability to identify and understand its audience and develop its products with that audience in mind. Since then, Starbucks marketers have promoted their iconic brand using every medium available to them, building lasting relationships with their customers.

- How does Starbucks use social media to keep its marketing strategies fresh and relevant?
- Rewards programs have become a popular means of building customer loyalty. Yet, according to some industry experts, many such programs are failing. What steps can Starbucks take to ensure that its loyalty program remains successful?

CHAPTER OVERVIEW

promotion
Communication link between buyers and sellers; the function of informing, persuading, and influencing a consumer's purchase decision.

marketing communications
Messages that deal with buyer–seller relationships.

integrated marketing communications (IMC) Coordination of all promotional activities to produce a unified, customer-focused promotional message.

Two of the four components of the marketing mix—product and distribution strategies—were discussed in previous chapters. The two chapters in Part 6 analyze the third marketing mix variable—promotion. **Promotion** is the function of informing, persuading, and influencing the consumer's purchase decision.

This chapter introduces the concept of integrated marketing communications. It describes the elements of a promotional mix and discusses the factors that influence its effectiveness. Chapter 17 completes this part of the book by focusing on two other elements of the promotional mix: personal selling and sales promotion.

Throughout *Contemporary Marketing*, special emphasis has been given to showing how technology is changing the way marketers approach *communication,* the transmission of a message from a sender to a receiver. Consumers receive **marketing communications**—messages that deal with buyer–seller relationships—from a variety of media, including television, radio, magazines, direct mail, the Internet, and smartphones. Marketers can broadcast an ad on the Web to mass markets or design a customized appeal targeted to a small market segment. Each message the customer receives from any source represents the brand, company, or organization. A company must coordinate the

messages for maximum total impact and to reduce the likelihood that the consumer will completely tune them out.

To prevent this loss of attention, marketers turn to **integrated marketing communications (IMC)**, which coordinates all promotional activities—media advertising, direct mail, personal selling, sales promotion, public relations, and sponsorships—to produce a unified, customer-focused promotional message, as shown in Figure 16.1. IMC is a broader concept than marketing communications and promotional strategy. It uses database technology to refine the marketer's understanding of the target audience, segment this audience, and select the best type of media for each segment.

IMC involves not only the marketer but all other organizational units that interact with the consumer. Marketing managers set the goals and objectives of the firm's promotional strategy in accordance with overall organizational objectives and marketing goals. Based on these objectives, elements of the promotional strategy are formulated into an integrated communications plan, which becomes a central part of the firm's total marketing strategy. The feedback mechanism, including marketing research and field reports, identifies any deviations from the plan and suggests improvements.

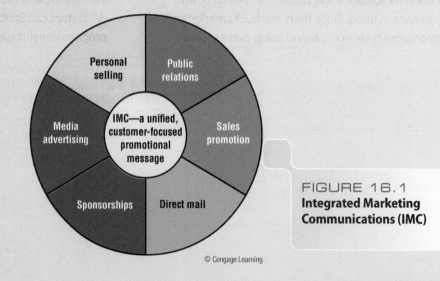

© Cengage Learning

FIGURE 16.1
Integrated Marketing Communications (IMC)

INTEGRATED MARKETING COMMUNICATIONS

Stop and think for a moment about all the marketing messages you receive in a day. Click on the TV for the news, and you see commercials. Listen to the car radio on the way to work or school, and you can sing along with the jingles. You get catalogs and coupons in the mail. You may find promotional flyers under your car's windshield wiper when it sits in a parking lot. Online, you see banner and pop-up ads and marketing-related emails. Marketers know you receive many types of communication. They compete for your attention, so they look for ways to reach you in a coordinated manner through integrated marketing communications.

Successful marketers use the marketing concept and relationship marketing to develop customer-oriented marketing programs. The customer is at the heart of integrated marketing communications. An IMC strategy begins not with the organization's goods and services but with consumer wants or needs, and then works in reverse to the product, brand, or organization. It sends receiver-focused (rather than product-focused) messages.

Instead of separating the parts of the promotional mix and viewing them as isolated components, IMC looks at these elements from the consumer's viewpoint: as information about the brand, company, or organization. Although messages come from different sources—sales presentations, word of mouth, TV, radio, newspapers, billboards, direct mail, coupons, public relations, social media—consumers may perceive all of them as "advertising" or a "sales pitch." IMC broadens promotion to include all the ways a customer has contact with an organization, adding to traditional media and direct mail with such sources as package design, store displays, sales literature, and online and interactive media. Unless the organization takes an integrated approach to present a unified, consistent message, it may send conflicting information that confuses consumers.

Today's business environment is characterized by many diverse markets and media creating both opportunities and challenges. The success of any IMC program depends on identifying the members of an audience and understanding what they want. Without accurate, current information about existing and potential customers and their purchase histories, needs, and wants, marketers may send the wrong message. But they cannot succeed simply by improving the quality of the messages or by sending more of them. IMC must not only deliver messages to intended audiences but also gather responses from them. Databases and interactive marketing are important IMC tools that help marketers collect information from customers and then segment markets according to demographics and preferences. Marketers can then design specialized communications programs to meet the needs of each segment.

Young male consumers can be hard to pin down. That's why the U.S. Navy became a sponsor of the ESPN X Games, a favorite of extreme sports fans—usually boys 13 to 17 years of age. By signing on for the highest level of sponsorship rights, the Navy enjoys a variety of perks, including on-site signage and activation and integrated media exposure across ESPN's TV, digital, print, and radio platforms.[2]

The increase in media options provides more ways to give consumers product information; however, it can also create information overload. Marketers have to spread available dollars across fragmented media markets and a wider range of promotional activities to achieve their communication goals. Mass media like TV ads, while still useful, are no longer the mainstay of marketing campaigns. In 1960, a marketer could reach about 90 percent of U.S. consumers by advertising on the three major TV networks—CBS, NBC, and ABC. Today, even though overall TV viewing is at an all-time high, consumers spend considerably fewer viewing hours watching these stations. Instead, they turn to such cable channels as ESPN, FOX, CNN, TNT, the History Channel, Disney, and the Food Network for their viewing enjoyment.[3] So to reach targeted groups of consumers, organizations must turn to niche marketing—advertising in special-interest magazines, buying time on cable

Define integrated marketing communications and explain how it relates to the development of an optimal promotional mix. **1**

The U.S. Navy uses the ESPN X Games to reach potential recruits.

© Doug Pensinger/Getty Images

TV channels, reaching out through telecommunications media like smartphones and the Web, and sponsoring events and activities. Without an IMC program, marketers often encounter problems within their own organizations, because separate departments have authority and responsibility for planning and implementing specific promotional mix elements.

The coordination of an IMC program often produces a competitive advantage based on synergy and interdependence among the various elements of the promotional mix. With an IMC strategy, marketers can create a unified personality for the product or brand by choosing the right elements from the promotional mix to send the message. At the same time, they can develop more narrowly focused plans to reach specific market segments and choose the best form of communication to send a particular message to a specific target audience. IMC provides a more effective way to reach and serve target markets than less-coordinated strategies. See how global retailer H&M accomplished this strategy by reading the "Marketing Success" feature.

MARKETING SUCCESS

H&M Integrates Its David Beckham Campaign

Background. H&M, the Swedish fashion retailer operating in 43 countries, collaborated with international soccer star and veteran brand spokesman David Beckham on a new line of men's bodywear.

The Challenge. The company wanted to ensure the success of the Beckham line in North America and integrated all of its related marketing communications.

The Strategy. H&M took the bold step of airing an ad during the Super Bowl, a hip, black-and-white 30-second spot featuring Beckham modeling the new collection. It also took out national and local print ads and out-of-home advertising, including a giant billboard in midtown Manhattan with a body-length image of Beckham wearing trunks. The image was hand-painted over a two-week period leading up to the Super Bowl, and the process was captured in a time-lapse video uploaded to YouTube. H&M also bought numerous search ads, uploaded the Super Bowl ad to its home page, inserted poster-sized images from the ad in free New

York City newspapers, and gave away booklet ads and Beckham shopping bags in its stores. Beckham appeared as a fashion mannequin on the company's website, and the campaign was featured on the company's Facebook and Twitter pages.

The Outcome. By using a variety of marketing media, H&M's Beckham campaign has generated an increasing volume of online buzz and created more opportunities to engage with consumers. Despite a challenging economy, the retailer recently announced an increase in profits and market share and attributed the favorable results to its new collections being received favorably by consumers around the world.

Sources: Company website, http://dbcollaboration.hm.com, accessed December 3, 2012; Michael Stothard, "H&M Reports Jump in Pre-Tax Profits," *Financial Times*, accessed December 3, 2012, www.ft.com; Vic Drabicky, "3 Steps to Better Marketing Through David Beckham's Abs," *Marketing Land*, accessed December 3, 2012, http://marketingland.com; "Beckham Is Effectively Integrated," *Retail Communication*, accessed December 3, 2012, http://retailcommunication.wordpress.com; Megan Conniff, "H&M: Lessons Learned from David Beckham's Super Bowl Ad," *Retail's Big Blog*, accessed December 3, 2012, http://blog.nrf.com.

© iStockphoto.com/Marcello Bortolino

IMPORTANCE OF TEAMWORK

IMC requires a big-picture view of promotional planning, a total strategy that includes all marketing activities, not just promotion. Successful implementation of IMC requires that everyone involved in every aspect of promotion function as a team, presenting a consistent, coordinated effort at every point of customer contact. This saves time and money, avoids duplication of effort, and increases effectiveness. In other words, the result is greater than the sum of its parts.

Teamwork involves both in-house resources and outside vendors. A firm gains nothing from a terrific advertisement featuring a great product, an informational website, and a toll-free number if unhelpful salespeople frustrate customers when they answer the phones. The company must train its representatives to send a single positive message to consumers and to solicit information for the firm's customer database.

IMC also challenges the traditional role of the outside advertising agency. A single agency may no longer fulfill all of a client's communications requirements, such as traditional advertising and sales promotion, interactive marketing, database development, direct marketing, and public relations. To best serve client needs, agencies must often partner with other firms to get the job done.

Networking, another form of teamwork, is an important skill for building a career. The "Career Readiness" feature provides networking tips.

ROLE OF DATABASES IN EFFECTIVE IMC PROGRAMS

The Internet empowers marketers to gather more information faster and to organize it more easily than ever before. By sharing this detailed knowledge appropriately among all relevant parties, a company can lay the foundation for a successful IMC program.

The move from mass marketing to a customer-specific marketing strategy—a characteristic of online marketing—requires not only a means of identifying and communicating with the firm's target market but also information regarding important characteristics of each prospective

© iStockphoto.com/hh5800

CAREER READINESS

Tips for Career Networking

You may already have a wide network of friends, but what about your professional network? Here are ideas for building and maintaining a network for your career and future job searches.

- Keep in mind that most job openings are filled by word of mouth, not by advertising, and that people like to deal with those they know or who are recommended to them.

- Start with friends, family, neighbors, current and former colleagues, teachers, former bosses, and anyone you would use as a reference. Ask them for other recommendations to add to your network.

- Don't wait until you're looking for a job to contact your network. Keep in touch on a regular basis by passing along articles and

information of interest so your contacts are fresh, people remember you, and your communication is a two-way street.

- When you're ready to look for a job, don't ask for one; ask for advice instead, which avoids putting your contacts on the spot but still opens the door. Be specific so your contacts will know how to respond.

- Follow up, thank people for helping you, let them know the result, and stay in touch.

Sources: Randall S. Hansen, "Networking Your Way to a New Job," *Quintessential Careers*, accessed December 3, 2012, www.quintcareers.com; Alison Doyle, "Job Search and Career Networking Tips," *About.com*, accessed December 3, 2012, http://jobsearch.about.com; "Job Networking Tips," *HelpGuide.org*, accessed December 3, 2012, www.helpguide.org.

customer. As discussed in Chapter 11, organizations can compile different kinds of data into complete databases with customer information, including names, addresses, demographics, lifestyle considerations, brand preferences, and buying behavior. This information provides critical guidance in designing an effective IMC strategy that achieves organizational goals and finds new opportunities for increased sales and profits. This increased ability to acquire huge amounts of data poses a new challenge: how to sift through it efficiently so it becomes useful information. Newer technology allows researchers to do exactly that—work with millions of sets of data to make very specific analyses.

Direct sampling is another method frequently used to quickly obtain customer opinions regarding a particular firm's goods and services. If you've ever received a free sample of laundry detergent, air freshener, breakfast cereal, or even a new magazine in your mailbox, you've been the recipient of direct sampling.

THE COMMUNICATION PROCESS

2 Describe the communication process and how it relates to the AIDA concept.

When you have a conversation with someone, do you wonder whether the person understood your message? Do you worry that you might not have heard the person correctly? Marketers have the same concerns: when they send a message to an intended audience or market, they want to make sure it gets through clearly and persuasively. That is why the communication process is so important to marketing. The top portion of Table 16.1 shows a general model of the communication process and its application to promotional strategy.

The **sender** acts as the source in the communication system as he or she seeks to convey a **message** (a communication of information, advice, or a request) to a receiver. An effective message accomplishes three tasks:

1. It gains the receiver's attention.

2. It achieves understanding by both receiver and sender.

3. It stimulates the receiver's needs and suggests an appropriate method of satisfying them.

Table 16.1 also provides several examples of promotional messages. Although the types of promotion may vary from a highly personalized sales presentation to such nonpersonal promotions as television advertising and dollar-off coupons, each goes through every stage in the communications process.

The three tasks just listed are related to the **AIDA concept** (**a**ttention, **i**nterest, **d**esire, **a**ction), the steps consumers take in reaching a purchase decision. First, the promotional message must gain the potential consumer's attention. It then seeks to arouse interest in the good or service. At the next stage, it stimulates desire by convincing the would-be buyer of the product's ability to satisfy his or her needs. Finally, the sales presentation, advertisement, or sales promotion technique attempts to produce action in the form of a purchase or a more favorable attitude that may lead to future purchases.

sender Source of the message communicated to the receiver.

message Communication of information, advice, or a request by the sender to the receiver.

AIDA concept Steps through which an individual reaches a purchase decision: attention, interest, desire, and action.

The message begins with *encoding*—that is, translating it into understandable terms and transmitting it through a communications channel. *Decoding* is the receiver's interpretation of the message. The receiver's response, known as *feedback*, completes the system. Throughout the process, *noise* (in such forms as ineffective promotional appeals, inappropriate advertising media, or poor radio or television reception) can interfere with the transmission of the message and reduce its effectiveness.

The marketer is the message sender in Table 16.1. He or she encodes the message in the form of sales presentations, advertising, displays, or publicity releases. The *channel* for delivering the message may be a salesperson, a PR outlet, a website, or an advertising medium. Decoding is often the toughest step in marketing communications, because consumers do not always interpret messages the same

TABLE 16.1 Relating Promotion to the Communication Process

Type of Promotion	Sender	Encoding by Sender	Channel	Decoding by Receiver	Response	Feedback
Personal selling	SAP system	Sales presentation on new applications of system	SAP sales representative	Office manager and employees discuss sales presentation and those of competing suppliers.	Customer places order for SAP system.	Customer asks about a second system for a subsidiary company.
Dollar-off coupon (sales promotion)	SC Johnson	Coupon for Pledge Duster Plus	Coupon insert in Sunday newspaper	Newspaper reader sees coupon for Pledge Duster Plus.	Product is purchased by consumer using coupon.	SC Johnson researchers see increase in market share.
Television advertising	Capital One	Advertisement featuring "What's in Your Wallet" slogan	Network television ads during program with high percentages of viewers 20–40 years old	Adults 20–40 see an ad and decide to try out the card.	Customer applies for Capital One card.	Customer makes purchases with Capital One card.

© Cengage Learning

way as senders do. Since receivers usually decode messages according to their own frame of reference or experience, a sender must carefully encode a message to match the target's frame of reference. Consumers today are bombarded daily by thousands of messages through many media channels. This barrage can create confusion as noise in the channel increases. Because the typical person will choose to process only a few messages, ignored messages are wasted communications expenditures.

The AIDA concept is also vital to online marketers. It is not enough to say a website has effective content or high response rates. Marketers must know just how many "eyeballs" are looking at the site, how often they come to view a message, and what they are examining. Most important, they must find out what consumers do besides just look. The bottom line: if no one responds to a website, it might as well not exist. Experts advise attracting users' attention by including people in advertisements and other communications in addition to new content and formats.

For the Olympic Games in London, NBC offered some creative advertising packages, segmenting the sponsorships in certain areas like financial services into several categories, such as retail banking, wealth management, and self-directed investing. NBC also used the vast Olympics audience as a platform for touting its fall lineup and testing the popularity of live video streaming by showing every event live in some format. Before the games, NBC sold more than $900 million in advertising, including $50 million in digital sales.[4]

Feedback lets marketers evaluate the effectiveness of the message and tailor their responses accordingly. It may take the form of attitude change, a purchase, or a nonpurchase. In some instances, marketers use promotion to create favorable attitudes toward their goods or services in the hope of future purchases. Other promotional communications aim to directly stimulate consumer purchases. Marketers using infomercials that urge the viewer to call a toll-free number to place orders for their products can easily measure success by counting the number of calls they receive that result in orders.

Even a nonpurchase is feedback. Failure to purchase may result from ineffective communication: do receivers believe the message? Do they even remember it? And do they associate it with the correct firm? Receivers may remember it correctly, but the message may have failed to persuade them to buy. Marketers must be keenly aware of why messages fail.

Noise represents interference at some stage in the communication process. It may result from disruptions like transmissions of competing promotional messages over the same communications channel, misinterpretation of a sales presentation or advertising message, receipt of the promotional message by the wrong person, or random events like people conversing or leaving the room during a television commercial. Noise can also result from distractions within an advertising message itself. Buzzwords and jargon can create a linguistic jungle for consumers who are just trying to find out more about a product. In a recent survey of about 1,200 adults, AARP found more than half were

BMW used the London Summer Olympics in its advertising as a way to create favorable attitudes toward their cars in the hope of future purchases.

confused by the language of the investment industry, often saving too little or making costly mistakes, because they didn't understand terms like *basis point* and *expense ratio.* "We learned that jargon is one of the key reasons for investor hesitation and missteps, and so off-putting for some, that it discourages investing altogether."[5]

Noise can be especially problematic in international communications. One problem is that there may be too many competing messages. Italian television channels broadcast all advertisements during a single half-hour slot each night. Or technology may be poor, and language translations inaccurate. Nonverbal cues like body language and tone of voice are important to the communication process, and cultural differences may lead to noise and misunderstandings. For example, in the United States, the round "O" sign made with the thumb and index finger means "okay." But in Mediterranean countries, the same gesture means "zero" or "the worst." A Tunisian interprets this sign as "I'll kill you," and to the Japanese, it means "money." It's easy to see how misunderstandings could arise from a single gesture.

 ASSESSMENT CHECK

2.1   Identify the four steps of the AIDA concept.

2.2   What is noise?

ELEMENTS OF THE PROMOTIONAL MIX

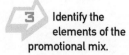 Identify the elements of the promotional mix.

promotional mix
Subset of the marketing mix in which marketers attempt to achieve the optimal blending of the elements of personal and nonpersonal selling to achieve promotional objectives.

Like the marketing mix, the promotional mix requires a carefully designed blend of variables to satisfy the needs of a company's customers and achieve organizational objectives. The **promotional mix** works like a subset of the marketing mix, with its product, distribution, promotion, and pricing elements. With the promotional mix, the marketers attempt to create an optimal blend of various elements to achieve promotional objectives. The components of the promotional mix are personal selling and nonpersonal selling, including advertising, sales promotion, direct marketing, public relations, and guerrilla marketing.

Personal selling, advertising, and sales promotion usually account for the bulk of a firm's promotional expenditures. However, direct marketing, guerrilla marketing, sponsorships, and public relations also contribute to integrated marketing communications. These activities will be discussed later in the chapter.

PERSONAL SELLING

Personal selling, the oldest form of promotion, dates back to the beginning of trading and commerce. Traders vastly expanded markets and product varieties as they led horses and camels along the Silk Road from China to Europe from 300 BCE to 1600 CE, conducting personal selling at both ends. Personal selling may be defined as a seller's promotional presentation conducted person-to-person with the buyer. It may take place face-to-face, over the telephone, through videoconferencing, or by computer links between buyer and seller.

Today, nearly 15 million people in the United States have careers in sales and related occupations. They may sell real estate, insurance, and financial investments or tractors, automobiles, and vacuum cleaners; they may work in retail or wholesaling; they may be regional managers or in the field. In other words, the range of jobs, as well as the products they represent, is huge.[6]

personal selling
Interpersonal influence process involving a seller's promotional presentation conducted on a person-to-person basis with the buyer.

NONPERSONAL SELLING

Nonpersonal selling includes advertising, product placement, sales promotion, direct marketing, public relations, and guerrilla marketing. Advertising and sales promotion are usually regarded as the most important forms of nonpersonal selling. About one-third of marketing dollars spent on nonpersonal selling activities are allocated for media advertising; the other two-thirds fund trade and consumer sales promotions.

nonpersonal selling
Promotion that includes advertising, product placement, sales promotion, direct marketing, public relations, and guerrilla marketing—all conducted without being face-to-face with the buyer.

ADVERTISING

Advertising is any paid, nonpersonal communication through various media about a business firm, not-for-profit organization, product, or idea by a sponsor identified in a message intended to inform, persuade, or remind members of a particular audience. It is a major promotional mix component for thousands of organizations—total ad spending in the United States rose to more than $158 billion in a recent year despite a sluggish economy, and online ad spending was estimated at $39 billion.[7] Mass consumption and geographically dispersed markets make advertising particularly appropriate for marketing goods and services aimed at large audiences likely to respond to the same promotional messages.

Advertising primarily involves the mass media, such as newspapers, television, radio, magazines, movie screens, and billboards, but it also includes electronic and computerized forms of promotion like Web commercials, streaming videos, and TV monitors at supermarkets. The rich potential of the Internet as an advertising channel to reach millions of people—one at a time—has attracted the attention of companies large and small, local and international. As consumers become increasingly savvy— and tune out messages that don't interest them—marketers are finding new ways to grab their attention.

advertising Paid, nonpersonal communication through various media about a business firm, not-for-profit organization, product, or idea by a sponsor identified in a message intended to inform or persuade members of a particular audience.

PRODUCT PLACEMENT

Product placement is a form of nonpersonal selling in which the marketer pays a fee to display his or her product prominently in a film or TV show. The practice gained attention more than two decades ago in the movie *E.T.: The Extra-Terrestrial* when Elliott, the boy who befriends E.T., lays out a trail of Reese's Pieces candy for the extraterrestrial to follow, to draw the alien from his hiding place. Product sales for Reese's Pieces went through the roof (interestingly, this was not the moviemaker's first choice of candy: Mars turned down the opportunity to have its M&Ms appear in the film). Today, hundreds of products appear in movies and on television shows, and the fees charged for these placements have soared. Brands as diverse as Fruity Pebbles, Quiznos, and Manolo Blahnik shoes can be seen on Showtime's TV series *Nurse Jackie,* and Sony products were featured prominently in *Skyfall,* a recent James Bond movie. Brands even pay celebrities to post about them on Twitter.[8]

product placement
Form of promotion in which a marketer pays a motion picture or television program owner a fee to display a product prominently in the film or show.

SALES PROMOTION

Sales promotion consists of marketing activities other than personal selling, advertising, guerrilla marketing, and public relations that stimulate consumer purchasing and dealer

sales promotion
Marketing activities other than personal selling, advertising, guerrilla marketing, and public relations that stimulate consumer purchasing and dealer effectiveness.

effectiveness. This broad category includes displays, trade shows, coupons, contests, samples, premiums, product demonstrations, and various one-time selling efforts. Sales promotion provides a short-term incentive, usually in combination with other forms of promotion, to emphasize, assist, supplement, or otherwise support the objectives of the promotional program. Restaurants, including those serving fast food, often place certain items on the menu at a lower price "for a limited time only." Advertisements may contain coupons for free or discounted items for a specified period of time. Or companies may conduct sweepstakes for prizes, such as new cars or vacations, which may even be completely unrelated to the products the companies are selling.

Sales promotion geared to marketing intermediaries is called trade promotion. Companies spend about as much on trade promotion as on advertising and consumer-oriented sales promotion combined. Trade promotion strategies include offering free merchandise, buyback allowances, and merchandise allowances, along with sales contests to encourage wholesalers and retailers to sell more of certain items or product lines.

trade promotion Sales promotion that appeals to marketing intermediaries rather than to consumers.

DIRECT MARKETING

direct marketing Direct communications, other than personal sales contacts, between buyer and seller, designed to generate sales, information requests, or store or website visits.

Another element in a firm's integrated promotional mix is direct marketing, the use of direct communication to a consumer or business recipient designed to generate a response in the form of an order, a request for further information (lead generation), or a visit to a place of business to purchase specific goods or services (traffic generation). While many people equate direct marketing with direct mail, this important promotional category also includes telemarketing, direct-response advertising and infomercials on television, direct-response print advertising, and electronic media.

PUBLIC RELATIONS

public relations Firm's communications and relationships with its various publics.

Public relations refers to a firm's communications and relationships with its various publics. These publics include customers, suppliers, stockholders, employees, the government, and the general public. Public relations programs can conduct either formal or informal contacts. The critical point is that every organization, whether or not it has a formally organized program, must be concerned about its public relations.

Publicity is the marketing-oriented aspect of public relations. It can be defined as nonpersonal stimulation of demand for a good, service, person, cause, or organization through unpaid placement of significant news about it in a published medium or through a favorable presentation of it on the radio or television. Compared with personal selling, advertising, and sales promotion, expenditures for public relations are usually low in most firms. Because companies do not pay for publicity, they have less control over whether the press or electronic media publish good or bad news. But this often means consumers find this type of news source more believable than company-disseminated information. Of course, bad publicity can damage a company's reputation and diminish brand equity. Organizations that enjoy good publicity generally try to make the most of it. Those who have suffered from bad publicity try to turn the situation around.

GUERRILLA MARKETING

guerrilla marketing Unconventional, innovative, and low-cost marketing techniques designed to get consumers' attention in unusual ways.

Guerrilla marketing—using unconventional, innovative, and low-cost techniques to attract consumers' attention—is a relatively new approach typically used when an organization doesn't have the funds for a full marketing program. Firms that can't afford the huge costs of print and broadcasting often look for an innovative, low-cost way to reach their market. But some large companies, such as PepsiCo and Toyota, engage in guerrilla marketing as well.

As mentioned in Chapter 11, *buzz marketing* can be part of guerrilla marketing. This type of marketing works well to reach college students and other young adults. Marketing firms may hire students to mingle among their own classmates and friends, creating buzz about a product. Often called *campus ambassadors,* they may wear logo-bearing T-shirts or caps, leave Post-it notes with marketing messages around campus, and chat about the good or service with friends during class breaks or over meals.

Viral marketing, also mentioned in Chapter 11, is another form of guerrilla marketing that has rapidly caught on with large and small firms. When shoe retailer Steve Madden recently partnered with Zappos.com to create an online contest called "Steve Madden's SOLE SEARCH powered by Zappos," they received nearly 4,000 entries of original shoe designs from consumers. The contest generated almost 38,000 votes and nearly a million views.[9]

The results of guerrilla marketing can be funny and outrageous—even offensive to some people. But they almost always get consumers' attention. Some guerrilla marketers stencil their company and product names anywhere graffiti might appear. Street artists are hired to plaster company and product logos on blank walls or billboards.

ADVANTAGES AND DISADVANTAGES OF TYPES OF PROMOTION

As Table 16.2 indicates, each type of promotion has both advantages and shortcomings. Although personal selling entails a relatively high per-contact cost, it involves less wasted effort than nonpersonal forms of promotion like advertising. Personal selling often provides more flexible promotion than the other forms because the salesperson can tailor the sales message to meet the unique needs—or objections—of each potential customer.

The major advantages of advertising come from its ability to create instant awareness of a good, service, or idea; build brand equity; and deliver the marketer's message to mass audiences for a relatively low cost per contact. Major disadvantages include the difficulty of measuring advertising effectiveness and high media costs. Sales promotions, by contrast, can be more accurately monitored and measured than advertising, produce immediate consumer responses, and provide short-term sales increases. Direct marketing gives potential customers an action-oriented choice, permits

TABLE 16.2 Promotional Mix Elements: A Comparison

	Personal Selling	Advertising	Sales Promotion	Direct Marketing	Public Relations	Guerrilla Marketing
Advantages	Permits measurement of effectiveness	Reaches a large group of potential consumers for a relatively low price per exposure	Produces an immediate consumer response	Generates an immediate response	Creates a positive attitude toward a product or company	Is low cost
	Elicits an immediate response	Allows strict control over the final message	Attracts attention and creates product awareness	Covers a wide audience with targeted advertising	Enhances credibility of a product or company	Attracts attention because it is innovative
	Tailors the message to fit the customer	Can be adapted to either mass audiences or specific audience segments	Allows easy measurement of results	Allows complete, customized, personal message		Is less cluttered with competitors trying the same thing
			Provides short-term sales increases	Produces measurable results		
Disadvantages	Relies almost exclusively on the ability of the salesperson	Does not permit totally accurate measurement of results	Is nonpersonal in nature	Suffers from image problem	May not permit accurate measurement of effect on sales	May not reach as many people
	Involves high cost per contact	Usually cannot close sales	Is difficult to differentiate from competitors' efforts	Involves a high cost per reader	Involves much effort directed toward non-marketing-oriented goals	If the tactics are too outrageous, they may offend some people
				Depends on quality and accuracy of mailing lists		
				May annoy consumers		

© Cengage Learning

segmentation and customization of communications, and produces measurable results. Public relations efforts like publicity frequently offer greater credibility than other promotional techniques. For marketers with limited funds, guerrilla marketing can be innovative and effective at a low cost, as long as the tactics are not too outrageous, but it is more difficult to reach people. Marketers must determine the appropriate blend of these promotional mix elements to effectively market their goods and services.

SPONSORSHIPS

Commercial sponsorship of an event or activity involves personal selling, advertising, sales promotion, and public relations in achieving specific promotional goals. Sponsorships have become a multibillion-dollar business.

sponsorship
Relationship in which an organization provides funds or in-kind resources to an event or activity in exchange for a direct association with that event or activity.

Sponsorship consists of an organization providing money or in-kind resources in exchange for a direct association with an event or activity. The sponsor purchases access to the activity's audience and the image associated with the activity. Sponsorships typically involve advertising, direct mail and sales promotion, publicity in the form of media coverage of the event, and personal selling at the event itself. They also involve relationship marketing, bringing together the event, its participants, sponsoring firms, and channel members and major customers. Marketers underwrite varying levels of sponsorships depending on types of events and the amount their company wants to spend.

Commercial sponsorship is not a new concept. It dates back to ancient Rome, where aristocrats sponsored gladiator competitions and chariot races featuring teams supported financially by competing businesses. During the 1880s, some local baseball teams in the United States were sponsored by streetcar companies.

Today's sponsorships are most prevalent in sports—golf, soccer, NASCAR, the Olympics, the World Cup, the Super Bowl, NCAA basketball, and more. Companies may also sponsor reading and child-care programs, concerts, art exhibits, humanitarian programs like the Special Olympics, and even hospital units.

The escalating costs of traditional advertising make commercial sponsorships a cost-effective alternative. Except for really large events, which often have multiple sponsors, most sponsorships are less costly than an advertising campaign that employs television, print, and other media. In addition, sponsors often gain the benefit of media coverage anyway, because associated events are covered as news. And in the case of naming rights of venues like sports arenas—such as Lucas Oil Stadium (Indianapolis), Tropicana Field (Tampa), and Staples Center (Los Angeles)—the name serves as a perpetual advertisement. Cities are even considering sponsorship for mass-transit systems, naming station stops after sponsoring firms. Apple has first right of refusal if the Chicago Transit Authority decides to sell naming rights to the North/Clybourn Red Line transit station, recently refurbished with Apple's investment of nearly $4 million.[10]

While marketers have considerable control over the quantity and quality of market coverage when they advertise, sponsors have little control of sponsored events beyond matching the audiences to profiles of their own target markets. Instead, event organizers control the coverage, which typically focuses on the event, not the sponsor. By contrast, a traditional advertisement allows a marketer to create an individual message containing an introduction, a theme, and a conclusion.

⊕ **ASSESSMENT CHECK**

3.1 Differentiate between personal and nonpersonal selling.

3.2 What are the six major categories of nonpersonal selling?

3.3 How is sponsorship different from advertising?

4   Name the three major advertising objectives and the two basic categories of advertising.

ADVERTISING

Advertising in the 21st century is closely linked to integrated marketing communications (IMC) in many respects. While IMC involves a message dealing with buyer–seller relationships, advertising seeks to inform or persuade members of a particular audience. Marketers use advertising to reach target markets with messages designed to appeal to business firms, not-for-profit organizations, or ultimate consumers.

The United States is home to many of the world's leading advertisers. Procter & Gamble, Comcast, and L'Oreal top a recent list, with P&G spending close to $3 billion in advertising.[11] Advertising varies among industries as well as companies. Retail, automotive, local services, and telecom services make up the top four categories, each spending more than $8 billion on advertising in a recent year.[12]

TYPES OF ADVERTISING

Advertisements fall into two broad categories: product and institutional. **Product advertising** is nonpersonal selling of a particular good or service. This is the type of advertising the average person usually thinks of when talking about most promotional activities.

Institutional advertising, in contrast, promotes a concept, an idea, a philosophy, or the goodwill of an industry, company, organization, person, geographic location, or government agency. This term has a broader meaning than *corporate advertising* that is typically limited to advertising sponsored by a specific profit-seeking firm. Institutional advertising is often closely related to the public relations function.

OBJECTIVES OF ADVERTISING

Marketers use advertising messages to accomplish three primary objectives: to inform, to persuade, and to remind. These objectives may be used individually or, more typically, in conjunction with each other. For example, an ad for a not-for-profit agency may inform the public of the existence of the organization and at the same time persuade the audience to make a donation, join the organization, or attend a function.

Informative advertising develops initial demand for a good, service, organization, person, place, idea, or cause. The success of a new market entry often depends simply on announcing its availability or explaining its benefits, as in the case of Activia, the yogurt whose TV commercials often feature screen star Jamie Lee Curtis.

Persuasive advertising works to increase demand for an existing good, service, organization, person, place, idea, or cause. Persuasive advertising is typically used during the growth stage and the early part of the maturity stage of the product lifecycle.

Reminder advertising strives to reinforce previous promotional activity by keeping the name of a good, service, organization, person, place, idea, or cause before the public. It is common in the latter part of the maturity stage and throughout the decline stage of the product lifecycle. In the competitive beer market, the Dos Equis brand languished until a recent campaign introduced The Most Interesting Man in the World—a Dos Equis drinker whose personal résumé is as entertaining as it is astonishing. With his signature signoff, "Stay thirsty, my friends," the campaign has caused Dos Equis sales to soar.[13]

Figure 16.2 illustrates the relationship between advertising objectives and the stages of the product lifecycle. Informative advertising tends to work best during the early stages, while reminder advertising is effective later on. Persuasive advertising, if done well, can be effective through the entire lifecycle.

Traditionally, marketers stated their advertising objectives as direct sales goals. A more

product advertising Nonpersonal selling of a particular good or service.

institutional advertising Promotion of a concept, an idea, a philosophy, or the goodwill of an industry, company, organization, person, geographic location, or government agency.

informative advertising Promotion that seeks to develop initial demand for a good, service, organization, person, place, idea, or cause.

persuasive advertising Promotion that attempts to increase demand for an existing good, service, organization, person, place, idea, or cause.

reminder advertising Advertising that reinforces previous promotional activity by keeping the name of a good, service, organization, person, place, idea, or cause before the public.

© Dos Equis

The Most Interesting Man in the World campaign—with the signature signoff, "Stay thirsty, my friends"—revitalized sales of the Dos Equis brand.

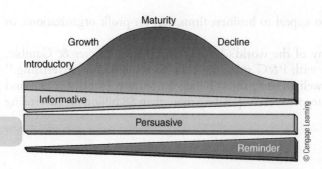

FIGURE 16.2
Advertising Objectives in Relation to Stage in the Product Lifecycle

⊕ **ASSESSMENT CHECK**

4.1   What are the goals of institutional advertising?

4.2   At what stage in the product lifecycle are informative ads used?

current and realistic standard, however, views advertising as a way to achieve communications objectives—including informing, persuading, and reminding potential customers of the product. Advertising attempts to condition consumers to adopt favorable viewpoints toward a promotional message. The goal of an ad is to improve the likelihood that a customer will buy a particular good or service. In this sense, advertising illustrates the close relationship between marketing communications and promotional strategy.

To get the best value for a firm's advertising investment, marketers must first determine a firm's advertising objectives. Effective advertising can enhance consumer perceptions of quality in a good or service, leading to increased customer loyalty, repeat purchases, and protection against price wars. In addition, perceptions of superiority pay off in the firm's ability to raise prices without losing market share.

ADVERTISING STRATEGIES

5 Identify the major advertising strategies and the process of creating an advertisement.

If the primary function of marketing is to bring buyers and sellers together, then advertising is the means to an end. Effective advertising strategies accomplish at least one of three tasks: informing, persuading, or reminding consumers. The secret to choosing the best strategy is developing a message that best positions a firm's product in the audience's mind. Among the advertising strategies available for use by 21st-century marketers are comparative advertising and celebrity advertising, as well as decisions about global and interactive ads. Channel-oriented decisions, such as retail and cooperative advertising, can also be devised.

Marketers often combine several of these advertising strategies to ensure the advertisement accomplishes set objectives. As markets become more segmented, the need for personalized advertising increases.

COMPARATIVE ADVERTISING

comparative advertising Advertising strategy that emphasizes messages with direct or indirect promotional comparisons between competing brands.

Firms whose products are not the leaders in their markets often favor comparative advertising, a promotional strategy that emphasizes advertising messages with direct or indirect comparisons to dominant brands in the industry. By contrast, advertising by market leaders seldom acknowledges that competing products even exist, and when they do, they do not point out any benefits of the competing brands.

Wireless telecommunications carriers have been battling it out in media advertising, promoting their calling plans and inviting comparison to competitors. Some offer "in" calling, free text messaging, no roaming charges, or extended hours at reduced rates.

Comparative advertising was once frowned upon, but the Federal Trade Commission now encourages it, believing such ads keep marketers competitive and consumers better informed about their choices. Scotts and Pennington recently took their battle to the airwaves, comparing their respective brands of grass seed—each claiming their brand was superior.[14]

Generally speaking, when competition through advertising exists, prices tend to go down because people can shop around. This benefit has proved increasingly true for online consumers, who now use shopping bots to help find the best prices on goods and services.

CELEBRITY TESTIMONIALS

A popular technique for increasing advertising readership and improving effectiveness involves the use of celebrity spokespeople. This type of advertising is also popular in foreign countries. In Japan, a majority of ads use celebrities, including both local and international stars. Ads using Olympic athletes, such as speed skater Apolo Ohno, are also popular. The most decorated U.S. athlete in Winter Olympic history, Ohno scored endorsement deals from several advertisers.

Both the number of celebrity ads and the dollars spent on them have risen in recent years. Professional athletes like NBA star LeBron James are among the highest-paid product endorsers. In a recent year, James reportedly earned $40 million from endorsement deals with such firms as The Coca-Cola Company, McDonald's, Nike, and State Farm. And with the exception of Nike, none of the others have anything to do with basketball.[15]

One advantage of associations with big-name personalities is improved product recognition in a promotional environment filled with hundreds of competing 15- and 30-second commercials. Advertisers use the term *clutter* to describe this situation. As e-marketing continues to soar, one inevitable result has been the increase in advertising clutter as companies rush to market their goods and services online.

A celebrity testimonial generally succeeds when the celebrity is a credible source of information for the product. The most effective testimonial ads link the celebrity and the advertised good or service. Studies of consumer behavior show that celebrities improve the product's believability, product recall, and brand recognition. However, celebrity endorsements can also go awry. A personality who endorses too many products may create marketplace confusion. Customers may remember the celebrity but not the product or brand; worse, they might connect the celebrity to a competing brand. Another problem arises if a celebrity isn't credible. When Chrysler engaged Jennifer Lopez to promote its Fiat 500, the campaign fell flat. Viewers were unconvinced that someone with a reputation for luxurious tastes would drive such a modest car.[16]

Some advertisers try to avoid problems with celebrity endorsers by using cartoon characters as endorsers. The GEICO gecko, the cocky reptile with a Cockney accent, has appeared in GEICO ads for years.[17] Some advertisers may actually prefer cartoon characters because the characters never say anything negative about the product, they do exactly what the marketers want them to do, and they cannot get involved in scandals.

RETAIL ADVERTISING

Most consumers are confronted daily with **retail advertising**, which includes all advertising by retail stores that sell goods or services directly to the consuming public. While this activity accounts for a sizable portion of total annual advertising expenditures, retail advertising varies widely in its effectiveness. One study showed that consumers often respond with suspicion to retail price advertisements.

The evidence against vacuum cleaners with bags keeps piling up.

Because bags clog, bag cleaners lose suction... ...leaving this behind in your home.

The Dyson has no bag, so it's the only cleaner to maintain 100% suction, 100% of the time.

dyson

Courtesy of The Advertising Archives

Comparative advertising, as shown in this Dyson ad, keeps marketers competitive and consumers informed of the choices they have in brands.

retail advertising
Advertising by stores that sell goods or services directly to the consuming public.

An advertiser once quipped that the two most powerful words to use in an ad are "New" and "Free"—and these terms often are capitalized on in retail ads. Although "Free" may be featured only in discussions of customer services, the next best term—"Sale"—is often the centerpiece of retail promotions. And "New" typically describes new-product lines. However, many retail stores continue to view advertising as a secondary activity, although that is changing. Local independent retailers rarely use advertising agencies, probably because of the expense involved. Instead, store managers may be responsible for advertising in addition to their other duties. Management can begin to correct this problem by assigning one person sole responsibility and authority for developing an effective retail advertising program.

cooperative advertising Strategy in which a retailer shares advertising costs with a manufacturer or wholesaler.

A retailer often shares advertising costs with a manufacturer or wholesaler in a technique called **cooperative advertising**. For example, an apparel marketer may pay a percentage of the cost of a retail store's newspaper advertisement featuring its product lines. Cooperative advertising campaigns originated to take advantage of the media's practice of offering lower rates to local advertisers than to national ones. Later, cooperative advertising became part of programs to improve dealer relations. The retailer likes the chance to secure advertising that it might not be able to afford otherwise. Cooperative advertising can strengthen vertical links in the marketing channel, as when a manufacturer and retailer coordinate their resources. It can also involve firms at the same level of the supply chain. In a horizontal arrangement, a group of retailers—for example, all the Ford dealers in a state—might pool their resources.

INTERACTIVE ADVERTISING

interactive advertising Two-way promotional messages transmitted through communication channels that induce message recipients to participate actively in the promotional effort.

Because marketers realize that two-way communications are more effective in achieving promotional objectives, they are interested in interactive media. **Interactive advertising** involves two-way promotional messages transmitted through communication channels that induce message recipients to participate actively in the promotional effort. Achieving this involvement is the difficult task facing contemporary marketers. Although interactive advertising has become nearly synonymous with e-marketing and the Web, it also includes other formats like kiosks in shopping malls and text messages on cell phones. Multimedia technology, the Internet, and commercial online services are changing the nature of advertising from a one-way, passive communication technique to more effective, two-way marketing communications. Interactive advertising creates dialogue between marketers and individual shoppers, providing more materials at the user's request. The advertiser's challenge is to gain and hold consumer interest in an environment where these individuals control what they want to see.

Successful interactive advertising adds value by offering the viewer more than just product-related information. A website can do more than display an ad to promote a brand; it can create a company store, provide customer service, and offer additional content. And many marketers, at companies both large and small, hope such ads will soon be so finely targeted that they can cut through increasing advertising clutter and reach only consumers ready to hear their messages. And, despite an economic downturn driving only modest gains in ad spending overall, online advertising continues to climb and is predicted to outpace TV ad spending within the next several years.[18]

CREATING AN ADVERTISEMENT

With millions of dollars at stake, marketers must create effective, memorable ads that increase sales and enhance their organization's image. Research helps them by pinpointing the three goals an ad needs to accomplish: educating consumers about product features, enhancing brand loyalty, or improving consumer perception of the brand. These objectives should guide the design of the ad. Marketers can also discover what appeals to consumers and can test ads with potential buyers before committing funds for a campaign.

Marketers sometimes face specific challenges as they develop advertising objectives for services. They must find a creative way to fill out the intangible images of most services and successfully convey the benefits consumers receive. With the words "Like a good neighbor, State Farm is there," State Farm demonstrates how advertising can make the intangible nature of its services—insurance—tangible to consumers.

TRANSLATING ADVERTISING OBJECTIVES INTO ADVERTISING PLANS

Once a company defines its objectives for an advertising campaign, it can develop its advertising plan. Marketing research helps managers make strategic decisions that guide choices in technical areas, such as budgeting, copywriting, scheduling, and media selection. Posttests, discussed in greater detail later in the chapter, measure the effectiveness of advertising and form the basis for feedback concerning possible adjustments. The elements of advertising planning are shown in Figure 16.3. Experienced marketers know the importance of following even the most basic steps in the process, such as market analysis.

As Chapter 9 explained, positioning involves developing a marketing strategy that aims to achieve a desired position in a prospective buyer's mind. Marketers use a positioning strategy that distinguishes their good or service from those of competitors. Effective advertising then communicates the desired position by emphasizing certain product characteristics, such as performance attributes, price/quality, competitors' shortcomings, applications, user needs, and product classes.

ADVERTISING MESSAGES

The strategy for creating a message starts with the benefits a product offers and moves to the creative concept phase, in which marketers strive to bring an appropriate message to consumers using both visual and verbal components. Marketers work to create an ad with meaningful, believable, and distinctive appeals—one that stands out from the clutter and is more likely to escape "zapping" by the television remote control or clicking by a mouse.

Ads usually are created not individually, but as part of specific campaigns. An **advertising campaign** is a series of different but related ads that use a single theme and appear in different media within a specified time period. Retail chain Target's "Hello … Good Buy" ads featuring the Beatles' music is one example. Different products flash across the screen in the spots, but all have the catchy song playing in the background while the familiar red bull's-eye logo appears. In developing a creative strategy, advertisers must decide how to communicate their marketing message. They must balance message characteristics—for example, the tone of the appeal, the information provided, and the conclusion to which it leads the consumer— with the side of the story the ad tells, and its emphasis on verbal or visual primary elements.

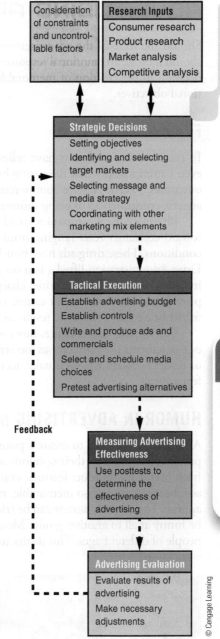

FIGURE 16.3
Elements of the Advertising Planning Process

Consideration of constraints and uncontrollable factors

Research Inputs
Consumer research
Product research
Market analysis
Competitive analysis

Strategic Decisions
Setting objectives
Identifying and selecting target markets
Selecting message and media strategy
Coordinating with other marketing mix elements

Tactical Execution
Establish advertising budget
Establish controls
Write and produce ads and commercials
Select and schedule media choices
Pretest advertising alternatives

Feedback

Measuring Advertising Effectiveness
Use posttests to determine the effectiveness of advertising

Advertising Evaluation
Evaluate results of advertising
Make necessary adjustments

© Cengage Learning

⊕ ASSESSMENT CHECK

5.1 What is comparative advertising?

5.2 What makes for a successful celebrity testimonial?

5.3 What is an advertising campaign?

5.4 What are an advertisement's three main goals?

advertising campaign Series of different but related ads that use a single theme and appear in different media within a specified time period.

ADVERTISING APPEALS

6   Describe the major types of advertising appeals, and discuss their uses.

Should the tone of the advertisement focus on a practical appeal such as price or gas mileage, or should it evoke an emotional response by appealing to, say, fear, humor, or sex? This is another critical decision in the creation of memorable ads that possess the strengths needed to accomplish promotional objectives.

FEAR APPEALS

In recent years, marketers have relied increasingly on fear appeals. Ads for insurance, autos, and even batteries imply that the wrong buying decision could lead to property loss, injury, or other bad outcomes. Recent Allstate commercials feature "Mayhem," a wild-eyed character who describes the adverse consequences of being uninsured.[19]

Pharmaceutical companies spend several billion dollars a year on advertising, much of it directed toward consumer fears ranging from hair loss to allergic attacks to heart attacks and other serious conditions. These drug ads have flourished in print, online, and broadcast media since the Food and Drug Administration lifted a ban on such advertising on TV. Although drug firms insist the ads are informative to consumers, critics charge that a high percentage of them use fear appeals and very few provide enough detail about causes and risk factors for medical conditions or lifestyle changes that might bring about the same results as the drug.

Fear appeals can backfire, however. Viewers are likely to practice selective perception and tune out statements they perceive as too strong or not credible. Some consumer researchers believe viewer or reader backlash will eventually occur due to the amount of prescription drug advertising based on fear appeals.

HUMOR IN ADVERTISING MESSAGES

A humorous ad seeks to create a positive mood related to a firm's goods or services, but advertising professionals differ in their opinions of the ads' effectiveness. Some believe humor distracts attention from brand and product features; consumers remember the humor but not the product. Humorous ads, because they are so memorable, may lose their effectiveness sooner than ads with other kinds of appeals. In addition, humor can be tricky because what one group of consumers finds funny may not be funny at all to another group. Men and women sometimes have a different sense of humor, as do people of different ages. This distinction may become even greater across cultures.

Humorous ads seek to create a positive mood related to a firm's goods or services. These hamster characters provide humor in this Kia TV commercial.

ADS BASED ON SEX

Ads with sex-based appeals immediately attract attention. Advertisements for Victoria's Secret lingerie and clothing are designed this way. While many people accept these and other ads, they do not appeal to everyone. And marketers using sex-based appeals know they walk a fine line between what is acceptable to the consumers they want to reach and what is not.

DEVELOPING AND PREPARING ADS

The final step in the advertising process—the development and preparation of an advertisement—should flow logically from the promotional theme selected. This process should create an ad that becomes a complementary part of the marketing mix with a carefully determined role in the total marketing strategy. Preparation of an advertisement should emphasize features, such as its creativity, its continuity with past advertisements, and possibly its association with other company products.

What immediate tasks should an advertisement accomplish? Regardless of the chosen target, an ad should (1) gain attention and interest, (2) inform or persuade, and (3) eventually lead to a purchase or other desired action. It should gain attention in a productive way; that is, it should instill some recall of the good or service. Otherwise, it will not drive a purchase.

Gaining attention and generating interest—cutting through the clutter—can be formidable tasks. Stimulating buying action is often difficult because an advertisement cannot actually close a sale. Nevertheless, if an ad gains attention and informs or persuades, it probably represents a worthwhile investment of marketing resources. Too many advertisers fail to tell consumers how to buy the product. Creative design should eliminate this shortcoming.

Figure 16.4 shows the four major elements of a print advertisement: headline, illustration, body copy, and signature. *Headlines* and *illustrations* (photographs, drawings, or other artwork) should work together to generate interest and attention. *Body copy* informs, persuades, and stimulates buying action. The *signature,* which may include the company name, address, phone number, Web address, slogan, trademark, or simply a product photo, names the sponsoring organization. An ad may also have one or more subheadings that either link the main headline to the body copy or subdivide sections of the body copy.

After advertisers conceive an idea for an ad that gains attention, informs and persuades, and stimulates purchases, their next step involves refining the thought sketch into a rough layout. Continued refinements of the rough layout eventually produce the final version of the advertisement design ready to be executed, printed, or recorded.

The creation of each advertisement in a campaign requires an evolutionary process that begins with an idea and ultimately results in a finished ad ready for distribution through print or electronic media. The idea itself must first be converted into a thought sketch—a tangible summary of the intended message. Advances in technology allow advertisers to create novel, eye-catching advertisements. Innovative computer software packages allow artists to merge multiple images to create a single image with a natural, seamless appearance.

FIGURE 16.4
Elements of a Typical Ad

Courtesy of the Advertising Archives

CREATING INTERACTIVE ADS

Web surfers want engaging, lively content that takes advantage of the medium's capabilities and goes beyond what they find elsewhere. The Web's major advantages enable advertisers to provide that, offering speed, information, two-way communications, self-directed entertainment, and personal choice. Web ads are also vibrant in their visual appeal, and some believe they will not experience the swings in spending that traditional ad media do.

Web ads have grown from information-based home pages to innovative, interactive channels for transmitting messages to cyber audiences, including banners, pop-ups, keyword ads, advertorials, and interstitials. *Advergames* are either online games created by marketers to promote their products to targeted audiences in an interactive way or ads or product placements inserted into online video games. Automakers use these product placements to reach younger audiences—those who may not watch their TV commercials as often. Recently, Coke Zero launched an advergame known as "The Battle for Everything," to support the movie *Battleship*. Gamers compare their scores with friends on Facebook and Twitter and can enter a sweepstakes online for valuable prizes.[20]

Banner advertisements on a Web page that link to an advertiser's site are the most common type of advertising on the Internet. They can be free of charge or cost thousands of dollars per month, depending on the amount of hits the site receives. Online advertisers often describe their Internet ads in terms of "richness," referring to the degree to which such technologies as streaming video, 3D animation, JavaScript, video layers, and interactive capabilities are implemented in the banners.

Banners have evolved into a more target-specific technique for Internet advertising with the advent of *missiles:* messages that appear on the screen at exactly the right moment. When a customer visits the site of Company A's competitor, a missile can be programmed to appear on the customer's monitor, allowing the customer to click on a direct link to Company A's site. However, many people feel the use of such missiles is a questionable practice.

Keyword ads are an outcropping of banner ads. Used in search engines, keyword ads appear on the results page of a search and are specific to the searched term. Advertisers pay search engines to target their ads and display the banners only when users search for relevant keywords, allowing marketers to target specific audiences. For example, if a user searched for the term "digital camera," keyword ads might appear for electronic boutiques or camera shops that sell digital cameras and film.

Then there are *pop-ups*—little advertising windows appearing in front of the top window of a user's computer screen—and *pop-unders* that appear under the top window. Many users complain

Coke Zero launched an advergame, "The Battle for Everything," to support the movie *Battleship*.

that interstitials, like pop-ups and missiles, are intrusive and unwanted. Interstitials are more likely to contain large graphics and streaming presentations than banner ads and therefore are more difficult to ignore than typical banner ads. But despite complaints, some studies show that users are more likely to click interstitials than banners.

Perhaps the most intrusive form of online advertising is *adware,* which allows ads to be shown on users' screens via software downloaded to their computers without their consent or through trickery. Such software can be difficult to remove, and some industry experts believe marketers should avoid dealing with Internet marketing firms that promote the use of adware.

Revenues for *social network advertising* on sites like Facebook and LinkedIn are skyrocketing. In a recent year, firms worldwide spent an estimated $12 billion on this type of advertising, and industry observers predict continued double-digit growth. However, the very nature of the advertising makes it difficult to evaluate and measure its effectiveness. For example, if a virtual bottle of Coca-Cola appears on Facebook or LinkedIn, how likely is it that consumers will actually purchase Coke the next time they want something to drink?[21]

ASSESSMENT CHECK

6.1 What are some common emotional appeals used in advertising?

6.2 What are the main types of interactive ads?

MEDIA SELECTION AND SCHEDULING

One of the most important decisions in developing an advertising strategy is the selection of appropriate media to carry a firm's message to its audience. The media selected must be capable of accomplishing the communications objectives of informing, persuading, and reminding potential customers of the good, service, person, or idea advertised.

Research identifies the ad's target market to determine its size and characteristics. Advertisers then match the target characteristics with the media best able to reach that particular audience. The objective of media selection is to achieve adequate media coverage without advertising beyond the identifiable limits of the potential market. Finally, cost comparisons between alternatives should determine the best possible media purchase.

List and compare the major advertising media.

7

TELEVISION

Television—network and cable combined—still accounts for 40 cents of every advertising dollar spent in the world.[22] The attractiveness of television advertising is that marketers can reach local and national markets. Whereas most newspaper advertising revenues come from local advertisers, the greatest share of television advertising revenues comes from organizations that advertise nationally. A newer trend in television advertising is virtual ads—banner-type logos and brief messages superimposed onto television coverage of sporting events so they seem to be a part of the arena's signage but cannot be seen by anyone attending the game. Then there are streaming headlines run by some news stations and paid for by corporate sponsors whose names and logos appear within the news stream.

Other trends in TV advertising include the abbreviated spot—a 15- or 30-second ad that costs less to make and buy

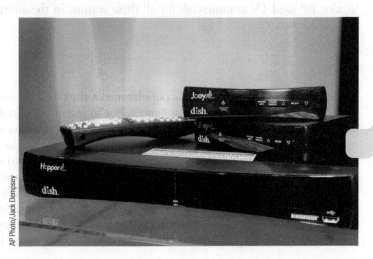

Dish Network began installing an "ad eraser" feature in its DVRs to allow viewers to skip the TV commercials.

AP Photo/Jack Dempsey

and is too quick for most viewers to zap with their remote control—and single-advertiser shows. These advertisements work well when viewers are watching live, but as more consumers record programs with DVRs, many fast-forward past even the briefest commercials. In fact, Dish Network recently began installing an "ad eraser" feature in its DVRs that enables viewers to skip over commercial content altogether.[23]

Websites that aggregate TV programming have become top video destinations on the Internet, where viewers can watch complete, high-resolution episodes of current TV programs on their computer, smartphone, or other wireless device. The sites are free and require no additional wires or boxes for access. Instead, viewers see brief ads in order to watch their favorite programming. Under Hulu's Hulu Plus feature, viewers can pay a monthly fee to watch a complete season of TV shows. Clicker offers 40,000 movies, over a million episodes from 12,000 TV shows, and 90,000 music videos from 20,000 artists.[24]

In the past decade, cable television's share of ad spending and revenues has grown tremendously. Satellite television has contributed to increased cable penetration; almost three-fourths of all Americans now have cable installed in their homes. In response to declining ratings and soaring costs, network television companies like NBC, CBS, ABC, and FOX are refocusing their advertising strategies with a heavy emphasis on moving onto the Internet and social media sites to capture younger audiences.

Because cable audiences have grown, programming has improved, and ratings risen, advertisers have earmarked more of their advertising budgets for this medium. Cable advertising offers marketers access to more narrowly defined target audiences than other broadcast media can provide—a characteristic referred to as *narrowcasting*. The great variety of special-interest channels devoted to subjects like cooking, golf, history, home and garden, health, fitness, and various shopping channels attract specialized audiences and permit niche marketing.

Television advertising offers the advantages of mass coverage, powerful impact on viewers, repetition of messages, flexibility, and prestige. Its disadvantages include loss of control of the promotional message to the telecaster, which can influence its impact; high costs; and some viewer distrust. Compared with other media, television can suffer from lack of selectivity because specific TV programs may not reach consumers in a precisely defined target market without a significant degree of wasted coverage. However, the growing specialization of cable TV channels can help resolve the problem. Finally, some types of products are banned from television advertising. Tobacco goods, such as cigarettes, cigars, and smokeless tobacco, fall into this category.

With the high cost of television advertising, some companies seek cheaper alternatives, such as print ads, online blogs, and Facebook, for launch campaigns. To launch Goodies, a subscription, mail-order sampling program featuring gourmet foods and other food products, Walmart turned to e-commerce. The Goodies campaign included both online and offline ads. By measuring consumer interest in the various items in the Goodies program, Walmart marketers will determine which, if any, products are offered "à la carte."[25]

Television commercials can promote more than a firm's products; they can highlight the organization's efforts to address a crisis, repair a corporate reputation, and attempt to solidify customer loyalty. BP used TV commercials for all these reasons in the aftermath of a massive oil spill in the Gulf of Mexico.

RADIO

Radio advertising has always been a popular media choice for up-to-the-minute newscasts and targeting advertising messages to local audiences. But in recent years, radio has become one of the fastest-growing media alternatives. As more and more people find they have less and less time, radio provides immediate information and entertainment at work, at play, and in the car. In addition, as e-business continues to grow globally, more people are traveling abroad to seek out new markets. For these travelers, radio stations, including those aired over the Internet, are a means of staying in touch with home—wherever that may be. Marketers frequently use radio advertising to reach local audiences. But in recent years, it plays an increasingly important role as a national—and even global—listening favorite. Thousands of online listeners use the Internet to tune in to radio stations from almost every city—an easy-listening station in London, a top 40 Hong Kong broadcaster, or a chat show from

Toronto. Other listeners equip their vehicles with satellite radio to maintain contact with hometown or destination stations during long trips.

Satellite radio offers much higher-quality digital signals than regular radio stations, with many more channels mostly free of Federal Communications Commission oversight as well as commercials. XM Radio, the first such service to be licensed, began airing commercials on a few of its nearly 200 music, sports, and talk channels. Both XM and its competitor, Sirius, charged an annual subscription fee. When the two merged, they initially agreed to offer à la carte pricing, under which subscribers could select the programming they preferred.

Advertisers like radio for its ability to reach people while they drive because they are a captive audience. Other benefits include low cost, flexibility, and mobility. Stations can adapt to local preferences by changing format, such as going from country and western to an all-news or sports station. The variety of stations allows advertisers to easily target audiences and tailor their messages to those listeners.

Disadvantages to radio advertising include highly segmented audiences (reaching most people in a market may require ads placed on multiple stations), the temporary nature of messages (unlike print, radio and TV ads are instantaneous and must be rebroadcast to reach consumers a second time), and a minimum of research information compared with television.

While most radio listening is often done in cars or with headset-equipped portables, technology has given birth to Internet radio. Webcast radio allows customers to widen their listening times and choices through their computers. With an estimated weekly audience of nearly 80 million people, online radio listenership continues to grow.[26]

NEWSPAPERS

Newspaper advertising continues to dominate local markets and is estimated to account for slightly more than $19 billion of annual advertising expenditures.[27] In addition to retail advertisements, classified advertising is an important part of newspaper revenues. Although some predict the decline of newspaper audiences, when online readers are included in circulation figures, newspapers are as popular as ever. Most newspapers have their own websites, which attract growing numbers of visitors—113 million unique visits in a recent year and, on average, 25 million daily. Although newspaper advertising as a whole has decreased, activity on newspaper websites creates new opportunities for marketers.[28]

Newspapers' primary advantages start with flexibility, because advertising can vary from one locality to the next. Newspapers also allow intensive coverage for ads. Readers sometimes keep the printed advertising message, unlike television or radio advertising messages, and can refer back to newspaper ads. Newspaper advertising does have some disadvantages: hasty reading and relatively poor reproduction quality, although that is changing as technology improves. The high quality of ads in *USA Today* is an example of the strides in newspaper ad quality made possible by new technologies.

Newspapers have also begun to struggle to "get through the noise" of other advertisers. To retain big advertisers like trendy designers and national retailers, some have launched their own annual or semiannual fashion magazines, taking advantage of their finely tuned distribution capabilities.

MAGAZINES

Advertisers divide magazines into two broad categories: consumer magazines and business magazines. These categories are also subdivided into monthly and weekly publications. The top magazine by circulation is *AARP The Magazine*.[29] The primary advantages of magazine advertising include the ability to reach precise target markets, quality reproduction, long life, and the prestige associated with some magazines (such as *National Geographic*). The primary disadvantage is that magazines lack the flexibility of newspaper, radio, and TV.

Media buyers study circulation numbers and demographic information for various publications before choosing optimal placement opportunities and negotiating rates. The same advertising categories have claimed the title for big spenders for several years running. Automotive, retail, and movies and media advertising have held their first, second, and third places, respectively, each year and continue to show strong growth. Advertisers can reach their target markets by advertising in the appropriate magazines.

DIRECT MAIL

As discussed in Chapter 15, direct-mail advertising includes sales letters, postcards, leaflets, folders, booklets, catalogs, and house organs—periodicals published by organizations to cover internal issues. Its advantages come from direct mail's ability to segment large numbers of prospective customers into narrow market niches, speed, flexibility, detailed information, and personalization. Disadvantages of direct mail include high cost per reader, reliance on the quality of mailing lists, and some consumers' resistance to it.

The advantages of direct mail explain its widespread use. Data are available on previous purchase patterns and preferred payment methods as well as household characteristics, such as number of children or seniors. Direct mail accounts for more than $50 billion of advertising spending annually.[30] The downside to direct mail is clutter, otherwise known as *junk mail*. So much advertising material is stuffed into people's mailboxes every day that the task of grabbing consumers' attention and evoking some interest can be daunting to direct-mail advertisers.

OUTDOOR ADVERTISING

Outdoor advertising, sometimes called *out-of-home advertising*, is one of the oldest and simplest media businesses. Advertisers in the United States spend about $6.3 billion annually on outdoor advertising.[31] Traditional outdoor advertising takes the form of billboards, painted displays such as those that appear on the walls of buildings, and electronic displays. Transit advertising includes ads placed inside and outside buses, subway trains, commuter trains, and stations. Some firms place ads on the roofs of taxicabs, on bus shelters and benches, on entertainment and sporting event turnstiles, in public restrooms, and even on parking meters. A section of highway might be cleaned up by a local real estate company or restaurant, with a nearby sign indicating the firm's contribution. All of these are forms of outdoor advertising.

Outdoor advertising quickly communicates simple ideas. It also offers repeated exposure to a message and strong promotion for locally available products. Outdoor advertising is particularly effective along metropolitan streets and in other high-traffic areas. But like every other type of ad, outdoor advertising produces clutter. It also suffers from the brevity of exposure to its messages by passing motorists. Driver concerns about rush-hour safety and limited time also combine to limit the length of exposure to outdoor messages. As a result, most of these ads use striking, simple illustrations, short selling points, and humor to attract people interested in products, such as beverages, vacations, local entertainment, and lodging.

Another problem relates to public concerns over aesthetics. Legislation regulates the placement of outdoor advertising near interstate highways. Also, local ordinances in many cities regulate the size and placement of outdoor messages. Hawaii prohibits them altogether.

New technologies are helping revive outdoor advertising, livening up the billboards themselves with animation, large sculptures, and laser images. Digital message signboards display winning lottery numbers or timely messages like weather and traffic reports. Of the 450,000 billboards in the United States, more than 2,000 are digitized, and their numbers are growing. While safety advocates express concern that such billboards constitute a driving hazard, studies are under way to confirm that the high-tech signage poses no risk.[32]

New uses may help revive outdoor advertising. The city of Minneapolis recently began using digital billboards to warn motorists about snow emergencies.[33]

INTERACTIVE MEDIA

Interactive media—especially the Internet and social media sites—are growing up. Keyword ads dominate online advertising. In a recent year, Google's ad revenues totaled nearly $38 billion, and a growing number of firms are increasing their interactive advertising budgets.[34]

As video and broadcast capabilities expand, advertising comes to cell phones in interesting ways. Mobile advertising revenues in the United States recently hit an estimated $4 billion and are expected to continue their explosive growth. Through an emerging technology known as *augmented reality*, virtual imaging can be incorporated into real-time video on a mobile phone, creating an exciting new experience for cell phone users.[35]

A digital billboard in Colorado alerts drivers to road closures due to weather.

AP Photo/David Zalubowski

OTHER ADVERTISING MEDIA

As consumers filter out appeals from traditional and Internet ads, marketers need new ways to catch their attention. One such device is Total Immersion's D'Fusion system, consisting of a kiosk, Web cameras, and software that can recognize, track, and render images on the screen. At the kiosk, customers can see themselves on a screen through the webcam while holding up a two-dimensional brochure of an advertiser's product. The system transforms the picture into a three-dimensional image of the consumer with the product. Marketers believe this type of system increases an advertiser's engagement with the consumer in a new way.[36]

Ads also appear on T-shirts, on store flooring, in printed programs of live theater productions, and as previews on movie DVDs. Directory advertising includes the Yellow Pages and numerous business directories. Some firms pay to have their advertising messages placed on hot-air balloons, blimps, banners behind airplanes, and scoreboards at sporting events. Some advertisers pay to have their logos and company messages placed on autos by firms like Adz in Motion and Autowrapped. Motorists are chosen based on their driving habits, routes, occupations, and living and working locations and are paid a monthly fee for the use of the outside of their vehicles as advertising space.[37]

MEDIA SCHEDULING

Once advertisers have selected the media that best matches their advertising objectives and promotional budget, attention shifts to media scheduling—setting the timing and sequence for a series of advertisements. A variety of factors influence this decision—sales patterns, repurchase cycles, and competitors' activities are the most important variables.

Seasonal sales patterns are common in many industries. An airline might reduce advertising during peak travel periods and boost its media schedule during low travel months. Repurchase cycles may also play a role in media scheduling—products with shorter repurchase cycles will more likely require consistent media schedules throughout the year. Competitors' activities are still other influences on media scheduling. A small firm may avoid advertising during periods of heavy advertising by its rivals.

media scheduling
Setting the timing and sequence for a series of advertisements.

Recently, marketers have questioned the effectiveness of reach and frequency to measure ad success online. The theory behind frequency is that the average advertising viewer needs a minimum of three exposures to a message to understand it and connect it to a specific brand. For Web surfers, the "wear-out" is much quicker—hence, the greater importance of building customer relationships through advertisements.

A media schedule is typically created as follows. Suppose an auto manufacturer wants to advertise a new model designed primarily to appeal to professional consumers in their 40s. The model would be introduced in November with a direct-mail piece offering test drives. Outdoor, newspaper, and magazine advertising would support the direct-mail campaign but also follow through the winter and into the spring and summer. Early television commercials might air during a holiday television special in mid-December, and then one or more expensively produced, highly creative spots would be first aired during the Super Bowl in late January. Another television commercial—along with new print ads—might be scheduled for fall clearance sales as the manufacturer gets ready to introduce next year's models. This example illustrates how marketers might plan their advertising year for just one product.

⊕ ASSESSMENT CHECK

7.1　What types of products are banned from advertising on television?

7.2　What are some advantages radio offers to advertisers? What about newspapers?

7.3　Define *media scheduling,* and identify the most important factors influencing the scheduling decision.

PUBLIC RELATIONS

8　Explain the roles of public relations, publicity, cross-promotion, and ethics in an organization's promotional strategy.

Earlier, we defined public relations as the firm's communications and relationships with its various publics, including customers, employees, stockholders, suppliers, government agencies, and the society in which it operates. Organizational public relations efforts date back to 1889, when George Westinghouse hired two people to publicize the advantages of alternating-current electricity and refute arguments originally championed by Thomas Edison for direct-current systems.

Public relations is an efficient, indirect communications channel through which a firm can promote products, although it serves broader objectives than those of other components of promotional strategy. It is concerned with the prestige and image of all parts of the organization. Today, public relations plays a larger role than ever within the promotional mix, and it may emphasize more marketing-oriented information. In addition to its traditional activities, such as surveying public attitudes and creating a good corporate image, PR also supports advertising in promoting the organization's goods and services.

Although there are about 64,000 public relations managers in the United States, nearly 320,000 people actually work in the public relations field for both profit-centered and not-for-profit organizations.[38] Public relations is in a period of major growth as a result of increased public pressure on industries regarding corporate ethical conduct and environmental and international issues. International expenditures on public relations are growing more rapidly than those for advertising and sales promotion. Many top executives are becoming more involved in public relations as well. The public expects top managers to take greater responsibility for company actions than they have accepted in the past. Those who refuse are widely criticized.

The PR department is the link between the firm and the media. It provides press releases and holds news conferences to announce new products, the formation of strategic alliances, management changes, financial results, or similar developments. The PR department may also issue its own publications, including newsletters, brochures, and reports.

MARKETING AND NONMARKETING PUBLIC RELATIONS

nonmarketing public relations Organizational messages about general management issues.

Nonmarketing public relations refers to a company's messages about general management issues. When a company makes a decision that affects any of its publics, input from PR specialists can help smooth its dealings with those publics. A firm that decides to close a plant would need advice on dealing with the local community, while an employer dealing with a long strike might try to achieve a favorable attitude from the public. Either of these situations might be considered a crisis, as would a massive product recall. Companies that have a plan of action and can effectively handle a crisis by generating positive public relations generally can survive these types of crises.

In contrast, **marketing public relations (MPR)** refers to focused PR activities that directly support marketing goals. MPR involves an organization's relationships with consumers or other groups about marketing concerns and can be either proactive or reactive.

With proactive MPR, the marketer takes the initiative and seeks out opportunities for promoting the firm's products, often including distribution of press releases and feature articles. For example, companies send press releases about new products to newspapers; television stations; and relevant consumer, business, and trade publications. It is a powerful marketing tool because it adds news coverage that reinforces direct promotion activities.

Reactive MPR responds to an external situation that has potential negative consequences for an organization. When Honda discovered a glitch in the assembly of the driveshaft in certain recent Civic sedans and coupes, it issued a voluntary recall. Although the automaker had received no reports of accidents related to the matter, it took steps to notify owners and made arrangements for free checkups and replacements.[39]

marketing public relations (MPR)
Focused public relations activities that directly support marketing goals.

The Honda Civic recall website provides information to consumers about the voluntary driveshaft recall.

PUBLICITY

The aspect of public relations most directly related to promoting a firm's products is *publicity*, the nonpersonal stimulation of demand for a good, service, place, idea, person, or organization by unpaid placement of significant news regarding the product in a print or broadcast medium. It has been said that if advertising is the hammer, publicity is the nail. It creates credibility for the advertising to follow. Firms generate publicity by creating special events, holding press conferences, and preparing news releases and media kits. Many businesses, like Starbucks and Sam's Club, built their brands with virtually no advertising.

While publicity generates minimal costs compared with other forms of promotion, it does not deliver its message entirely for free. Publicity-related expenses include the costs of employing staff assigned to create and submit publicity releases, printing and mailing costs, and related expenses.

Firms often pursue publicity to promote their images or viewpoints. Other publicity efforts involve organizational activities, such as plant expansions, mergers and acquisitions, management changes, and research breakthroughs. A significant amount of publicity, however, provides information about goods and services, particularly new products.

Because many consumers consider news stories to be more credible than advertisements as sources of information, publicity releases are often sent to media editors for possible inclusion in news stories. The media audiences perceive the news as coming from the communications media, not the sponsors. The information in a publicity release about a new good or service can provide valuable assistance for a television, newspaper, or magazine writer, leading to eventual broadcast or publication.

However, not all publicity is positive for a firm. Because companies cannot control the news that surrounds their decisions and actions, negative publicity can create a poor image in consumers' minds. Air travel, once regarded as an exciting adventure, has now become more of a chore. As the airline industry struggles to survive increased costs, many carriers have cut flights, raised fares, and added many fees. The result has been bad publicity.

CROSS-PROMOTION

cross-promotion
Promotional technique in which marketing partners share the cost of a promotional campaign that meets their mutual needs.

In recent years, marketers have begun to combine their promotional efforts for related products using a technique called **cross-promotion**, in which marketing partners share the cost of a promotional campaign that meets their mutual needs—an important benefit in an environment of rising media costs. Relationship marketing strategies like comarketing and cobranding, discussed in Chapter 11, are forms of cross-promotion. Marketers realize these joint efforts between established brands provide greater benefits in return for both organizations; investments of time and money on such promotions will become increasingly important to many partners' growth prospects.

ETHICS AND PROMOTIONAL STRATEGIES

Chapter 3 introduced the topic of marketing ethics and noted that promotion is the element in the marketing mix that raises the most ethical questions. People actively debate the question of whether marketing communications contribute to better lives. The final section of this chapter takes a closer look at ethical concerns in advertising and public relations.

Even though ads promoting alcohol or targeting children are technically legal, these types of promotions raise ethical issues. In the case of advertising aimed at children, when it comes to influencing parents' purchase decisions, nothing beats influencing kids. By promoting goods and services directly to children, firms can sell not only to them but to the rest of the household, too. However, as the feature "Solving an Ethical Controversy" points out, many question the ethics of promoting directly to children. Their argument: at a time when kids need to learn how to consume healthy food, they are inundated with promotional messages teaching the opposite.

Another issue is the insertion of product messages in media programs without full disclosure of the marketing relationship to audiences. To woo younger consumers, especially teens and those in their 20s, advertisers attempt to make these messages appear as different from advertisements as possible; they design ads that seem more like entertainment.

SOLVING AN ETHICAL CONTROVERSY

Fast-Food Advertising to Children

The U.S. Centers for Disease Control and Prevention reports that one child in six is overweight or obese, triple the number 30 years ago. Many blame the increased role of fast food and the heavy influence of colorful advertising aimed at susceptible children. The American Academy of Pediatrics' 65,000 member doctors recently called for a ban of fast-food advertising during children's TV programs.

Should fast-food advertising to children be banned?

PRO 👍

1. Research shows children familiar with many fast-food ads are twice as likely to be obese as their peers.

2. One study reported that banning fast-food ads could decrease obesity, which invites serious health problems in adulthood, by 17 percent.

CON 👎

1. Parents buy fast food for their children; banning ads on kids' programs won't affect their purchases.

2. Banning advertising comes too close to censorship.

Summary:

Disney announced new nutritional standards for all products advertised on its TV channels, websites, and radio stations, banning candy, sugared cereal, and fast food. Foods sold in Disney theme parks will contain 25 percent less sodium. McDonald's rejected shareholder calls for menu changes aimed at curbing childhood obesity but announced that new kids' advertising will feature messages about physical activity and nutrition.

Sources: Brooks Barnes, "Promoting Nutrition, Disney to Restrict Junk-Food Ads," *The New York Times*, accessed December 3, 2012, www.nytimes.com; Doug Tynan, "Whose Responsibility Is Childhood Obesity?" *KevinMD.com*, accessed December 3, 2012, www.kevinmd.com; Anthony Gucciardi, "McDonald's Rejects Anti-Obesity Campaign, 'Proud' of 'Responsible' Menu," *Natural Society*, accessed December 3, 2012, http://naturalsociety.com; Mark Brandau, "McDonald's CEO Skinner Takes on Critics at Final Shareholder Meeting," *Nation's Restaurant News*, accessed December 3, 2012, http://nrn.com; Emily Bryson York, "McDonald's to Kids: Eat Fruit, Drink Milk, Visit Arches," *Chicago Tribune*, accessed December 3, 2012, http://articles.chicagotribune.com; "Familiarity with Television Fast-Food Ads Linked to Obesity," American Academy of Pediatrics, accessed December 3, 2012, www.aap.org; Emma Gray, "Do Fast Food Ads Make Kids Fat?" *That's Fit*, accessed December 3, 2012, www.thatsfit.com.

In online ads, it is often difficult to separate advertising from editorial content, because many sites resemble magazine and newspaper ads or television infomercials. Another ethical issue surrounding online advertising is the use of *cookies*, small text files automatically downloaded to a user's computer whenever a site is visited. Each time the user returns to that site, the site's server accesses the cookie and gathers information: What site was visited last? How long did the user stay? What was the next site visited? Marketers claim this device helps them determine consumer preferences and argue that cookies are stored in the user's PC, not the company's website. The problem is that cookies can and do collect personal information without the user's knowledge.

Puffery and Deception

Puffery refers to exaggerated claims of a product's superiority or the use of subjective or vague statements that may not be literally true. A company might advertise the "most advanced system" or claim that its product is "most effective" in accomplishing its purpose.

Exaggeration in ads is not new. Consumers seem to accept advertisers' tendencies to stretch the truth in their efforts to distinguish their products and get consumers to buy them. This inclination may provide one reason that advertising does not encourage purchase behavior as successfully as sales promotions do. A tendency toward puffery does raise ethical questions, though: Where is the line between claims that attract attention and those that provide implied guarantees? To what degree do advertisers deliberately make misleading statements?

The Uniform Commercial Code standardizes sales and business practices throughout the United States. It makes a distinction between puffery and any specific or quantifiable statement about product quality or performance that constitutes an "express warranty," which obligates the company to stand behind its claim. Boasts of product superiority and vague claims are puffery, not warranties. They are considered so self-praising or exaggerated that the average consumer would not rely on them to make a buying decision. A quantifiable statement, on the other hand, implies a certain level of performance.

ASSESSMENT CHECK

8.1 Distinguish between marketing public relations and nonmarketing public relations.

8.2 What is publicity?

8.3 What are the advantages of cross-promotion?

ETHICS IN PUBLIC RELATIONS

Several public relations issues open organizations to criticism. Various PR firms perform services for the tobacco industry; publicity campaigns defend unsafe products. Also, marketers must weigh ethics before they respond to negative publicity. For example, do firms admit to problems or product deficiencies, or do they try to cover them up? It should be noted that PR practitioners violate the Public Relations Society of America's Code of Professional Standards if they promote products or causes widely known to be harmful to others.

PROMOTIONAL MIX EFFECTIVENESS

9 Discuss the factors that influence the effectiveness of a promotional mix and how marketers measure effectiveness.

Because quantitative measures are not available to determine the effectiveness of each component of a promotional mix in a given market segment, developing an effective promotional mix is one of a marketer's most difficult tasks. Several factors influence the effectiveness of a promotional mix.

NATURE OF THE MARKET

The marketer's target audience has a major impact on the choice of a promotion method. When a market includes a limited number of buyers, personal selling may prove a highly effective technique. However, markets characterized by large numbers of potential customers scattered over sizable geographic areas may make the cost of contact by salespeople prohibitive. In such instances, extensive use of advertising often makes sense. The type of customer also affects the promotional mix. Personal selling works better in high-priced, high-involvement purchases—for instance, a target market made up of business purchasers or wholesale buyers—than in a target market consisting of ultimate consumers. Similarly, pharmaceuticals firms use large sales forces to sell prescription drugs directly to physicians and hospitals, but they also advertise to promote over-the-counter and prescription drugs for the consumer market. So the drug firm must switch its promotional strategy from personal selling to consumer advertising based on the market it is targeting.

NATURE OF THE PRODUCT

The product itself is an important factor in determining promotional mix effectiveness. Highly standardized products with minimal servicing requirements usually depend less on personal selling than custom products with technically complex features or requirements for frequent maintenance. Marketers of consumer products are more likely to rely heavily on advertising than business products. For example, soft drinks lend themselves more readily to advertising than large pieces of business machinery.

Promotional mixes vary within each product category. In the B2B market, for example, installations typically rely more heavily on personal selling than marketing of operating supplies. In contrast, the promotional mix for a convenience product is likely to involve more emphasis on manufacturer advertising and less on personal selling.

STAGE IN THE PRODUCT LIFECYCLE

The promotional mix must also be tailored to a product's stage in the product lifecycle. In the introductory stage, both nonpersonal and personal selling are used to acquaint marketing intermediaries and final consumers with the merits of the new product. Heavy emphasis on personal selling helps inform the marketplace of the merits of the new good or service.

Salespeople contact marketing intermediaries to secure interest in and commitment to handling the newly introduced item. Trade shows are frequently used to inform and educate prospective dealers and ultimate consumers about its merits over current competitive offerings. Advertising and sales promotion are also used during this stage to create awareness, answer questions, and stimulate initial purchases.

As the product moves into the growth and maturity stages, advertising gains relative importance in persuading consumers to make purchases. Marketers continue to direct personal selling efforts at marketing intermediaries in an attempt to expand distribution. As more competitors enter the marketplace, advertising begins to stress product differences to persuade consumers to purchase the firm's brand. In the maturity and early decline stages, firms frequently reduce advertising and sales promotion expenditures as market saturation is reached and newer items with their own competitive strengths begin to enter the market.

PRICE

The price of an item is the fourth factor that affects the choice of a promotional mix. Advertising dominates the promotional mixes for low-unit-value products due to the high per-contact costs in personal selling. Advertising permits a low promotional expenditure per sales unit because it reaches mass audiences. For low-value consumer goods, such as chewing gum, soft drinks, and snack foods, advertising is the most feasible means of promotion. On the other hand, consumers of high-priced items like luxury cars expect lots of well-presented information from qualified salespeople. High-tech direct marketing promotions, such as video presentations on a tablet or smartphone, fancy brochures, and personal selling by informed, professional salespeople, appeal to these potential customers.

FUNDS AVAILABLE FOR PROMOTION

Budget size can present a stumbling block to implementing promotional strategy. For example, the cost of a single 30-second slot during a recent Super Bowl telecast was $3.5 million.[40] While millions of viewers may see the commercial, making the cost per contact relatively low, such an expenditure exceeds the entire promotional budgets of thousands of firms, a dilemma that at least partially explains how guerrilla marketing got its start. And if a company wants to hire a celebrity to promote its goods and services, the fee can run into millions of dollars a year.

Traditional methods used for creating a promotional budget include the percentage-of-sales and fixed-sum-per-unit methods, along with techniques for meeting the competition and achieving task objectives.

The *percentage-of-sales method* is perhaps the most common way of establishing promotional budgets. The percentage can be based on sales either from some past period (such as the previous year) or forecasted for a future period (the current year). While this plan is appealingly simple, it does not effectively support the achievement of basic promotional objectives. Arbitrary percentage allocations can't provide needed flexibility. In addition, sales should depend on promotional allocation rather than vice versa.

The *fixed-sum-per-unit method* allocates a predetermined amount to each sales or production unit. This amount can also reflect either historical or forecasted figures. Producers of high-value consumer durable goods, such as automobiles, often use this budgeting method.

The *meeting competition method* simply matches competitors' outlays, either in absolute amounts or relative to the firm's market shares. But this method doesn't help marketers gain a competitive edge. A budget appropriate for one company may not be appropriate for another.

The *task-objective method* develops a promotional budget based on a sound evaluation of the firm's promotional objectives. The method has two steps:

1. Define realistic and quantifiable communication goals for the promotional mix (for example, "Achieve a 25 percent increase in brand awareness"). Such objectives become an integral part of the promotional plan.

2. Determine the amount and type of promotional activity required for each objective. Combined, these units become the firm's promotional budget.

A crucial assumption underlies the task-objective approach: marketers can measure the productivity of each promotional dollar. That assumption explains why the objectives must be carefully chosen, quantified, and accomplished through promotional efforts. Generally, budgeters should avoid such general marketing objectives as "Achieve a 5 percent increase in sales." A sale is a culmination of the effects of all elements of the marketing mix. A more appropriate promotional objective might be "Achieve an 8 percent response rate from a targeted direct-mail advertisement."

Promotional budgeting always requires difficult decisions. Still, recent research studies and the emergence of computer-based models make it a more manageable task.

EVALUATING PROMOTIONAL EFFECTIVENESS

Evaluating the effectiveness of a promotion today is a far different exercise in marketing research than it was even a few decades ago. For years, marketers depended on store audits conducted by large organizations like ACNielsen. Other research groups conducted warehouse withdrawal surveys of shipments to retail customers. These studies were designed to determine whether sales had risen as a direct result of a particular promotional campaign. During the 1980s, scanners and automated checkout lanes completely changed marketing research. For the first time, retailers and manufacturers had a tool to obtain sales data quickly and efficiently. The problem was that the collected data were used for little else other than determining how much of which product was bought at what price and at what time.

With the advent of the Internet and the proliferation of social media sites, marketing research has entered another evolutionary period. Now marketers can delve into each customer's purchase behavior, lifestyle, preferences, opinions, and buying habits. All this information can be obtained in a matter of seconds.

Most marketers would prefer to use a *direct sales results test* to measure the effectiveness of promotion. Such an approach would reveal the specific impact on sales revenues for each dollar of promotional spending. This type of technique has always eluded marketers, however, because of their inability to control other variables operating in the marketplace. A firm may receive $20 million in additional sales orders following a new $1.5 million advertising campaign, but the market success may really have resulted from the products receiving more intensive distribution, as more stores decide to carry them, or price increases for competing products rather than from the advertising outlays.

Marketers often encounter difficulty isolating the effects of promotion from those of other market elements and outside environmental variables. *Indirect evaluation* helps researchers concentrate on quantifiable indicators of effectiveness, such as recall and readership. The basic problem with indirect measurement is the difficulty in relating these variables to sales.

Marketers need to ask the right questions and understand what they are measuring. Promotion to build sales volume produces measurable results in the form of short-term returns, but brand-building efforts to generate or enhance consumers' perceptions of value in a product, brand, or organization cannot be measured over the short term.

MEASURING ADVERTISING EFFECTIVENESS

Although promotional prices vary widely, advertisers typically pay a fee based on the cost to deliver the message to viewers, listeners, or readers—the so-called *cost per thousand impressions (CPM)*.

Billboards are the cheapest way to spend advertising dollars, with television and some newspapers the most expensive. But while price is an important factor in media selection, it is by no means the only one—or all ads would appear on billboards.

Because promotion represents such a major expenditure for many firms, they need to determine whether their campaigns accomplish appropriate promotional objectives. Companies want their advertising agencies and in-house marketers to demonstrate how promotional programs contribute to increased sales and profits. Marketers are well aware of the number of advertising messages and sales promotions consumers encounter daily, and they know these people practice selective perception and simply screen out many messages.

By measuring promotional effectiveness, organizations can evaluate different strategies, prevent mistakes before spending money on specific programs, and improve their promotional programs. As the earlier discussion of promotional planning explained, any evaluation program starts with objectives and goals; otherwise, marketers have no yardstick against which to measure effectiveness. However, determining whether an advertising message has achieved its intended objective is one of the most difficult undertakings in marketing. Sales promotions and direct marketing are somewhat easier to evaluate, because they evoke measurable consumer responses. Like advertising, public relations is also difficult to assess on purely objective terms.

MEDIA AND MESSAGE RESEARCH

Measures to evaluate the effectiveness of advertising, although difficult and costly, are essential parts of any marketing plan. Without an assessment strategy, marketers will not know whether their advertising achieves the objectives of the marketing plan or whether the dollars in the advertising budget are well spent. To answer these questions, marketers can conduct two types of research. **Media research** assesses how well a particular medium delivers the advertiser's message, where and when to place the advertisement, and the size of the audience. Buyers of broadcast time base their purchases on estimated Nielsen rating points, and the networks have to make good if ratings do not reach promised levels. Buyers of print advertising space pay fees based on circulation. Circulation figures are independently certified by specialized research firms.

The other major category, **message research**, tests consumer reactions to an advertisement's creative message. Pretesting and posttesting, the two methods for performing message research, are discussed in the following sections.

As the role of marketing expands in many organizations, marketers are employing increasingly sophisticated techniques to measure marketing effectiveness not only throughout the company but through the entire marketing channel. As more firms also conduct multichannel promotional efforts, keeping track of the data is a challenge. However, when they do so, they can better track which channels are most effective.

Pretesting

To assess an advertisement's likely effectiveness before it actually appears in the chosen medium, marketers often conduct **pretesting**. The obvious advantage of this technique is the opportunity to evaluate ads when they are being developed. Marketers can conduct a number of different pretests, beginning during the concept phase in the campaign's earliest stages, when they have only rough copy of the ad, and continuing until the ad layout and design are almost completed.

Pretesting uses several evaluation methods. For example, focus groups can discuss their reactions to mock-ups of ads using different themes, headlines, or illustrations. To screen potential radio and television advertisements, marketers often recruit consumers to sit in a studio and indicate their preferences by pressing two buttons, one for a positive reaction to the commercial and the other for a negative reaction. Sometimes proposed ad copy is printed on a postcard that also offers a free product; the number of cards returned represents an indication of the copy's effectiveness. In a *blind product test*, people are asked to select unidentified products on the basis of available advertising copy.

Mechanical and electronic devices offer yet another method of assessing how people read advertising copy. One mechanical test uses a hidden camera to photograph eye movements of readers. The results help advertisers determine headline placement and copy length. Another mechanical approach measures the galvanic skin response—changes in the electrical resistance of the skin produced by emotional reactions.

media research
Advertising research that assesses how well a particular medium delivers an advertiser's message, where and when to place the advertisement, and the size of the audience.

message research
Advertising research that tests consumer reactions to an advertisement's creative message.

pretesting Research that evaluates an ad during its development stage.

Posttesting

Posttesting assesses advertising copy after it has appeared in the appropriate medium. Pretesting generally is a more desirable measurement method than posttesting because it can save the cost of placing ineffective ads. However, posttesting can help in planning future advertisements and adjusting current advertising programs.

In one of the most popular posttests, the *Starch Readership Report* interviews people who have read selected magazines to determine whether they observed various ads in them. A copy of the magazine is used as an interviewing aid, and each interviewer starts at a different point in the magazine. For larger ads, respondents are also asked about specifics, such as headlines and copy. All such *readership tests,* also called recognition tests, assume that future sales are related to advertising readership.

Unaided recall tests are another method of posttesting the effectiveness of advertisements. Respondents do not see copies of the magazine after their initial reading but are asked to recall the ads from memory. Podcasts are a popular medium for advertisers because posttests reveal that unaided recall among respondents is high. *Inquiry tests* are another popular form of posttest. Advertisements sometimes offer gifts— generally product samples—to people who respond to them. The number of inquiries relative to the advertisement's cost forms a measure of its effectiveness.

Split runs allow advertisers to test two or more ads at the same time. Although advertisers traditionally place different versions in newspapers and magazines, split runs on cable television systems frequently test the effectiveness of TV ads. With this method, advertisers divide the cable TV audience or a publication's subscribers in two; half view advertisement A and the other half view advertisement B. The relative effectiveness of the alternatives is then determined through inquiries or recall and recognition tests.

Regardless of the exact method marketers choose, pretesting and posttesting are expensive efforts that must be used as effectively as possible.

MEASURING PUBLIC RELATIONS EFFECTIVENESS

Organizations must measure PR results based on their objectives both for the PR program as a whole and for specific activities. In the next step, marketers must decide what they want to measure. This choice includes determining whether the message was heard by the target audience and whether it had the desired influence on public opinion.

The simplest and least costly level of assessment measures outputs of the PR program: whether the target audience received, paid attention to, understood, and retained the messages directed to them. To make this judgment, the staff could count the number of media placements and gauge the extent of media coverage. They could count attendees at any press conference, evaluate the quality of brochures and other materials, and pursue similar activities. Formal techniques include tracking publicity placements, analyzing how favorably their contents portrayed the company, and conducting public-opinion polls.

To analyze PR effectiveness more deeply, firms conduct focus groups, interviews with opinion leaders, and more detailed and extensive opinion polls. The highest level of effectiveness measurement looks at outcomes: did the program change people's opinions, attitudes, and behavior? PR professionals measure outcomes through before-and-after polls and more advanced techniques, such as psychographic analysis (discussed in Chapter 9).

EVALUATING INTERACTIVE MEDIA

Marketers have used various methods to measure the effectiveness of Web communication: *hits* (user requests for a file), *impressions* (the number of times a viewer sees an ad), and *click-throughs* (when the user clicks the ad to get more information). *View-through* rates measure responses over time. However, all of these measures can be misleading: it takes more than "eyeballs" to measure the effectiveness of online media. What matters is not how many times a website is visited but how well the communication elicits the desired behavior.

Traditional numbers that work for other media forms are not necessarily relevant indicators of effectiveness for a website. For one thing, the Web combines both advertising and direct marketing. Web pages effectively integrate advertising and other content, such as demonstrations, coupons, product information, and interactive features, which may often prove to be the page's main—and most effective—feature. For another consideration, consumers generally choose the advertisements they want to see on the Internet, whereas traditional broadcast or print media automatically expose consumers to ads.

Two major techniques for setting Internet advertising rates are cost per impression and cost per response. *Cost per impression* is a measurement technique that relates the cost of an ad to every thousand people who view it. In other words, anyone who sees the page containing the banner or other form of ad creates one impression. This measure assumes the site's primary purpose is to display the advertising message. *Cost per response* (or *click-throughs*) is a direct marketing technique that relates the cost of an ad to the number of people who click it. However, not everyone who clicks on an ad makes a purchase. So marketers measure the *conversion rate*—the percentage of website visitors who actually make a purchase. All three rating techniques have merit. Site publishers point out that click-through rates are influenced by the creativity of the ad's message. Advertisers, on the other hand, point out that the Web ad has value to those who click it for additional information.

Internet marketers price ad banners based on cost per thousand (CPM). Websites that sell advertising typically guarantee a certain number of impressions—the number of times an ad banner is downloaded and presumably seen by visitors. Marketers then set a rate based on that guarantee times the CPM rate.

Marketers can measure performance by incorporating some form of direct response into their promotions. This technique also helps them compare different promotions for effectiveness and rely on facts rather than opinions.

ASSESSMENT CHECK

9.1 What five factors affect the choice of a promotional mix?

9.2 Why is the choice of a mix a difficult task for marketers?

9.3 What is the most common way of establishing a promotional budget?

9.4 What is the direct sales results test? Why is it difficult to administer?

STRATEGIC IMPLICATIONS OF MARKETING IN THE 21ST CENTURY

With the incredible proliferation of promotional messages in the media, today's marketers—consumers themselves—must find new ways to reach customers without overloading them with unnecessary or unwanted communications. Integrating marketing communications into an overall consumer-focused strategy that meets a company's promotional and business objectives has become more and more critical in a busy global marketplace.

It is difficult to overstate the impact of the Internet and social media on the promotional mix of 21st-century marketers. As greater portions of corporate ad budgets continue to migrate to the Web, marketers must be increasingly aware of the benefits and pitfalls of Internet advertising. But they should not forget the benefits of other types of advertising as well. Promotion industry experts agree that e-business and social media broaden marketers' job tasks, though many promotional objectives still remain the same.

Get online now for additional learning tools to help you master your
marketing knowledge—visit **WWW.CENGAGEBRAIN.COM** today!

REVIEW OF CHAPTER OBJECTIVES

1 Define integrated marketing communications and explain how it relates to the development of an optimal promotional mix.

Integrated marketing communications (IMC) refers to the coordination of all promotional activities to produce a unified, customer-focused promotional message. Developing an optimal promotional mix involves selecting the personal and nonpersonal selling strategies that will work best to deliver the overall marketing message as defined by IMC.

2 Describe the communication process and how it relates to the AIDA concept.

In the communication process, a message is encoded and transmitted through a communications channel; then it is decoded, or interpreted by the receiver; finally, the receiver provides feedback, which completes the system. The AIDA concept (attention, interest, desire, action) explains the steps through which a person reaches a purchase decision after being exposed to a promotional message. The marketer sends the promotional message, and the consumer receives and responds to it via the communication process.

3 Identify the elements of the promotional mix.

The elements of the promotional mix are personal selling and nonpersonal selling (advertising, product placement, sales promotion, direct marketing, and public relations). Guerrilla marketing is frequently used by marketers with limited funds and firms attempting to attract attention for new-product offerings with innovative promotional approaches. Sponsorship occurs when an organization pays money or in-kind resources to an event or activity in exchange for a direct association with that event or activity.

4 Name the three major advertising objectives and the two basic categories of advertising.

The three major objectives of advertising are to inform, persuade, and remind. The two major categories of advertising are product advertising and institutional advertising. Product advertising involves the nonpersonal selling of a good or service. Institutional advertising is the nonpersonal promotion of a concept, idea, or philosophy of a company or organization.

5 Identify the major advertising strategies and the process of creating an advertisement.

The major strategies are comparative advertising, which makes extensive use of messages with direct comparisons between competing brands; celebrity, which uses famous spokespeople to boost an advertising message; retail, which includes all advertising by retail stores selling products directly to consumers; and interactive, which encourages two-way communication via the Internet, social media sites, or kiosks.

An advertisement evolves from pinpointing goals, such as educating consumers, enhancing brand loyalty, or improving a product's image. From those goals, marketers move to the next stages: creating a plan, developing a message, developing and preparing the ad, and selecting the appropriate medium (or media).

6 Describe the major types of advertising appeals, and discuss their uses.

Advertisements often appeal to consumers' emotions, and these appeals to fear, humor, or sex can be effective. However, marketers need to recognize that fear appeals can backfire; people's sense of humor can differ according to sex, age, and other factors; and use of sexual imagery must not overstep the bounds of taste.

7 List and compare the major advertising media.

The major media include broadcast (TV and radio), newspapers and magazines, direct mail, outdoor, and interactive. Each medium has benefits and drawbacks. Newspapers are flexible and dominate local markets. Magazines can target niche markets. Interactive media foster two-way communication. Outdoor advertising in a high-traffic location reaches many people every day; television and radio reach even more. Direct mail allows effective segmentation. Once advertisers select the media that best matches their advertising objectives and promotional budgets, their attention shifts to setting the time and sequence for a series of ads.

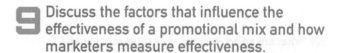

8 Explain the roles of public relations, publicity, cross-promotion, and ethics in an organization's promotional strategy.

Public relations consists of the firm's communications and relationships with its various publics, including customers, employees, stockholders, suppliers, government, and the society in which it operates. Publicity is the dissemination of newsworthy information about a product or organization. This information activity is frequently used in new-product introductions. Although publicity is welcomed by firms, negative publicity is easily created when a company enters a gray ethical area with the use of its promotional efforts. Cross-promotion, illustrated by tie-ins between popular movies and fast-food restaurants, permits marketing partners to share the cost of a promotional campaign that meets their mutual needs. Marketers should be careful to construct ethically sound promotional campaigns, avoiding such practices as puffery and deceit. In addition, negative publicity may occur as a result of some action a firm takes—or fails to take—such as a product recall.

9 Discuss the factors that influence the effectiveness of a promotional mix and how marketers measure effectiveness.

Marketers face the challenge of determining the best mix of components for an overall promotional strategy. Several factors influence the effectiveness of the promotional mix: (1) the nature of the market, (2) the nature of the product, (3) the stage in the product lifecycle, (4) price, and (5) the funds available for promotion.

Marketers may choose among several methods for determining promotional budgets, including percentage-of-sales, fixed-sum-per-unit, meeting competition, or task-objective, which is considered the most flexible and most effective. Today, marketers use either direct sales results tests or indirect evaluation to measure effectiveness. Both methods have their benefits and drawbacks because of the difficulty of controlling variables.

The effectiveness of advertising can be measured by pretesting and posttesting. Pretesting assesses an ad's effectiveness before it is actually used. Posttesting assesses an ad's effectiveness after it has been used. Commonly used posttests include readership tests, unaided recall tests, inquiry tests, and split runs.

 ASSESSMENT CHECK: ANSWERS

1.1 Define _promotion_. Promotion is the function of informing, persuading, and influencing the consumer's purchase decision.

1.2 What is the difference between marketing communications and integrated marketing communications (IMC)? Marketing communications are messages that deal with buyer–seller relationships, from a variety of media. IMC coordinates all promotional activities to produce a unified, customer-focused promotional message.

2.1 Identify the four steps of the AIDA concept. The four steps of the AIDA concept are attention, interest, desire, and action.

2.2 What is noise? Noise represents interference at some stage in the communication process.

3.1 Differentiate between personal and nonpersonal selling. Personal selling is promotion conducted person-to-person between a seller and a buyer. It may take place face-to-face, over the telephone, through videoconferencing, or by computer links between buyer and seller. Nonpersonal selling is promotion conducted without being face-to-face with the buyer.

3.2 What are the six major categories of nonpersonal selling? The six categories of nonpersonal selling are

advertising, product placement, sales promotion, direct marketing, public relations, and guerrilla marketing.

3.3 How is sponsorship different from advertising? Although sponsorship generates brand awareness, the sponsor has little control over the message or even the coverage, unlike advertising.

4.1 What are the goals of institutional advertising? Institutional advertising promotes a concept, an idea, a philosophy, or the goodwill of an industry, company, organization, person, geographic location, or government agency.

4.2 At what stage in the product lifecycle are informative ads used? Informative ads are common in the introductory stage of the product lifecycle.

5.1 What is comparative advertising? Comparative advertising makes extensive use of messages with direct comparisons between competing brands.

5.2 What makes a successful celebrity testimonial? Successful celebrity ads feature figures who are credible sources of information for the promoted product.

5.3 What is an advertising campaign? An advertising campaign is a series of different but related ads that use a single theme and appear in different media within a specified time period.

5.4 What are an advertisement's three main goals? Advertising's three main goals are to educate consumers about product features, enhance brand loyalty, and improve consumer perception of the brand.

6.1 What are some common emotional appeals used in advertising? Advertisers often focus on making emotional appeals to fear, humor, or sex.

6.2 What are the main types of interactive ads? Interactive ads include Internet banners, pop-ups, keyword ads, advertorials, advergames, and interstitials.

7.1 What types of products are banned from advertising on television? Tobacco goods like cigarettes, cigars, and smokeless tobacco are banned from television advertising.

7.2 What are some advantages radio offers to advertisers? What about newspapers? Radio ads allow marketers to target a captive audience and offer low cost, flexibility, and mobility. Newspaper ads are flexible and provide nearly complete coverage of the market. Readers can also refer back to newspaper ads.

7.3 Define *media scheduling,* **and identify the most important factors influencing the scheduling decision.** Media scheduling sets the timing and sequence for a series of advertisements. Sales patterns, repurchase cycles, and competitors' activities are the most important variables in the scheduling decision.

8.1 Distinguish between marketing public relations and nonmarketing public relations. Marketing public relations refers to focused public relations activities that directly support marketing goals. Nonmarketing public

relations refers to a company's messages about general issues.

8.2 What is publicity? Publicity is nonpersonal stimulation of demand for a good, service, place, idea, person, or organization by unpaid placement of significant news regarding the subject in a print or broadcast medium.

8.3 What are the advantages of cross-promotion? Cross-promotion divides the cost of a promotional campaign that meets the mutual needs of marketing partners and provides greater benefits for both in return.

9.1 What five factors affect the choice of a promotional mix? The five factors are (1) nature of the market, (2) nature of the product, (3) stage in the product lifecycle, (4) price, and (5) funds available for promotion.

9.2 Why is the choice of a mix a difficult task for marketers? Developing an effective promotional mix is difficult, because marketers lack quantitative measures to determine the effectiveness of each component of a promotional mix in a given market segment.

9.3 What is the most common way of establishing a promotional budget? The most common method of establishing a promotional budget is the percentage-of-sales method.

9.4 What is the direct sales results test? Why is it difficult to administer? The direct sales results test reveals the specific impact on sales revenues for each dollar of promotional spending. Administering this test is difficult because marketers cannot control other variables operating in the marketplace.

MARKETING TERMS YOU NEED TO KNOW

promotion **526**

marketing communications **526**

integrated marketing communications (IMC) **526**

sender **530**

message **530**

AIDA concept **530**

promotional mix **532**

personal selling **533**

nonpersonal selling **533**

advertising **533**

product placement **533**

sales promotion **533**

trade promotion **534**

direct marketing **534**

public relations **534**

guerrilla marketing **534**

sponsorship **536**

product advertising **537**

institutional advertising **537**

informative advertising **537**

persuasive advertising **537**

reminder advertising **537**

comparative advertising **538**

retail advertising **539**

cooperative advertising **540**

interactive advertising **540**

advertising campaign **541**

media scheduling **549**

nonmarketing public relations **550**

marketing public relations (MPR) **551**

cross-promotion **552**

media research **557**

message research **557**

pretesting **557**

posttesting **558**

split runs **558**

ASSURANCE OF LEARNING REVIEW

1. What is the role of integrated marketing communications (IMC) in a firm's overall marketing strategy? When executed well, what are its benefits?

2. Differentiate between advertising and product placement. Which do you think is more effective, and why?

3. Why is sponsorship such an important part of a firm's IMC?

4. For each of the following goods and services, indicate which direct marketing channel or channels you think would be best:
   a. Pittsburgh Pirates tickets
   b. denim jacket
   c. custom-made bracelet
   d. lawn-care service
   e. magazine subscription

5. How does the nature of the market for a firm's goods or services affect the choice of a promotion method?

6. What are the three primary objectives of advertising? Give an example of when each one might be used.

7. Identify the different types of emotional appeals in advertising. What are the benefits and pitfalls of each?

8. Compare and contrast interactive ads and traditional ads.

9. Identify and describe the different advertising media. Which are on the rise? Which are facing possible decline?

10. Describe how marketers assess promotional effectiveness.

PROJECTS AND TEAMWORK EXERCISES

1. On your own or with a classmate, select a print advertisement that catches your attention and analyze it according to the AIDA concept (attention, interest, desire, action). Identify features of the ad that catch your attention, pique your interest, make you desire the product, and spur you toward a purchase. Present your findings to the class.

2. Watch a television show and see how many products you can find placed within the show. Present your findings to the class.

3. With a classmate, choose a good or service you think could benefit from guerrilla marketing. Imagine you have a limited

promotional budget, and come up with a plan for a guerrilla approach. Outline several ideas, and explain how you plan to carry them out. Present your plan to the class.

4. Cut out a print ad and place it on a poster board. With a marker, identify all the elements of the ad. Then identify what you believe is the ad's objective. Next, identify the strategy used. If the ad has an interactive component, note that as well.

CRITICAL-THINKING EXERCISES

1. What are some benefits and drawbacks of using celebrity testimonials in advertising? Identify an ad that uses a celebrity's endorsement effectively, and explain why.

2. Identify a corporate sponsorship for a cause or program in your area, or find a local company that sponsors a local charity or other organization. What does the sponsor gain from its actions? Be specific. What does the sponsored organization receive? Is this sponsorship good for your community? Explain.

3. Select two different advertisers' TV or print ads for the same product category (cars or soft drinks, for instance) and decide what emotion each appeals to. Which ad is more effective, and why?

4. Think back to publicity you have heard recently about a company or its products. If it was good publicity, how was it generated, and what media were used? If it was bad publicity, where did you learn about it, and how did the firm try to control or neutralize it?

ETHICS EXERCISE

Pop-up ads, those unsolicited messages that sometimes pop onto your computer screen and block the site or information you're looking for until you close or respond to them, are inexpensive to produce and cost nearly nothing to send. But they are so annoying to some computer users that dozens of special programs have been written to block them from appearing on the screen during Internet use.

1. Do you think that, because they are unsolicited, pop-up ads are also disruptive? Are they an invasion of privacy? Explain your reasoning.

2. Do you consider the use of pop-up ads to be unethical? Why or why not?

INTERNET EXERCISES

1. **Super Bowl advertising.** Visit the websites listed here. How many different organizations ran ads during the most recent Super Bowl? Which organizations have run the most ads in Super Bowls? During the most recent Super Bowl, which ads were the highest rated? The lowest rated? How much has the cost of a 30-second Super Bowl ad changed since the first game was played?

   www.superbowl-commercials.org

   www.cbsnews.com/8334-31751_162-57372039-10391697/top-2012-super-bowl-ad-campaigns-with-the-most-online-views/

2. **Not-for-profit advertising.** Review the material in the chapter on creating an advertisement and then go to the website listed here. It outlines the basic steps involved in creating an advertisement for a not-for-profit organization. Review the material and prepare a brief report comparing and contrasting the process of creating an advertisement for a for-profit and a not-for-profit organization.

   http://marketing.about.com/cs/nonprofitmrktg/a/8stepnonprofit.htm

3. **Public relations.** Visit the websites of at least three large, multinational corporations. Examples include Siemens, DuPont, and ExxonMobil. Review the material on the websites and prepare a brief report outlining how each firm includes public relations as part of its promotional strategy.

   www.siemens.com

   www.dupont.com

   www.exxonmobil.com

Note: Internet Web addresses change frequently. If you don't find the exact site listed, you may need to access the organization's home page and search from there or use a search engine such as Google or Bing.

CASE 16.1
The Richards Group: A Unique Advertising Agency

The popular image of an advertising agency is of a vibrantly creative place without much corporate structure, where copywriters, artists, and executives enjoy free rein, an anything-goes culture, and freedom to come and go at will. That picture usually doesn't include a list of rules employees must follow, such as punching a time clock, logging work time in precise 15-minute intervals, paying a fine for tardiness, getting closed out of meetings if late, and going home at precisely 6 PM. But those are some of the strictly enforced practices at The Richards Group, a successful independent 36-year-old Dallas agency recently named one of Advertising Age's Best Places to Work.

If the rules sound repressive, Stan Richards, the company's 78-year-old founder, will admit they aren't for everybody. One of his former writers says, "The genius of the place is completely counter-intuitive." But that genius has produced a steady stream of memorable campaigns for clients like Chick-fil-A, Motel 6, and Corona beer, and it has kept more than two dozen creative group heads on board with Richards for an average tenure of 17 years.

Life at the agency isn't all about the rules, either. Richards learned early in his advertising design education at New York's Pratt Institute that creativity can come from any source, but that expressing it requires meticulous hard work and tolerates few shortcuts. Since founding the agency, he has relaxed a few rules, however, like the dress code, and he no longer personally approves every piece of work, although he still encourages face time with colleagues and clients over emails. And there are perks—though fancy titles aren't among them. In fact, there are no titles; instead, every employee is expected to be "a leader in every situation." Those who have the longest tenure get the best parking spots and the desks nearest the windows, but any of Richards' 650 employees can take the company's private plane to client meetings. And after 20 years with the company, they can take their families on a free trip anywhere in the world, even as far away as the Galapagos Islands.

QUESTIONS FOR CRITICAL THINKING

1. Stan Richards believes that "the way you treat your people is exactly how they treat clients." Do you agree or disagree? Explain your reasoning.

2. Evaluate Richards's belief that creativity requires hard work. Do you think this is true? Does it apply only to marketing and advertising? Why or why not?

Sources: Burt Helm, "Stan Richards's Unique Management Style," *Inc.*, accessed December 3, 2012, www.inc.com; "Richards Group Is No. 37 on *Ad Age's* Best Places to Work List," *Advertising Age*, accessed December 3, 2012, http://adage.com; Lauren Lawley Head, "Minority Business Leader Award Winners Make Their Own Luck," *Dallas Business Journal*, accessed December 3, 2012, www.bizjournals.com.

VIDEO CASE 16.2
Pepe's Pizzeria Delivers Every Day

If you're a pizza lover, you'd say that a sizzling hot, fresh pizza sells itself. If you happen to live in southern New England—and be a pizza lover—you'd probably say that everyone knows about Pepe's Pizzeria. But Ken Berry, CEO of Pepe's, understands the importance of spreading the word about his company's pizza, even though it's practically got a cult following. Founded by Frank Pepe in New Haven, Connecticut, pizzeria employees still hand-toss every single pizza. "Our pizza really has a heritage," observes Berry. "It goes back 87 years, virtually unchanged during those 87 years." He notes that the company has added refrigerators and air-conditioning, but that's about all. When diners visit the restaurant, they enjoy the sights, sounds, smells, and flavors of this heritage. "It's a way for people to step back in time," Berry says. The pizza dough is still made fresh daily, and the ingredients come from many of the same sources they did decades ago.

Pepe's has built a loyal following through the years. "People have adopted Pepe's as their own through generations," notes Berry. This word-of-mouth advertising is impossible to buy or replicate, and it helps strengthen the brand. But it also represents a challenge, in that these loyal customers arrive at the restaurant with high expectations. If they bring friends or family, they expect those guests to be served a top-notch meal, much as if they were entertaining in their own home. "If you don't deliver on your promise, they'll let you know right away," warns Berry.

When Pepe's co-owners decided to expand from its initial location several years ago, their strategy included replicating every aspect of the Pepe's dining experience—right down to the furniture and uniforms of the wait staff. They wanted customers to walk into the new location in Fairfield, Connecticut, and feel right at home. They didn't anticipate a backlash—a small core of regular New Haven customers who objected to the expansion of their beloved Pepe's. These customers staged a protest outside the new restaurant as it opened to the public. But publicity surrounding the opening of a new Pepe's swelled beyond the protestors—and 200 people showed up to wait in line for their own piece of Pepe's pie. If anything, the buzz surrounding the protest likely attracted more customers to the new location.

Pepe's approach to advertising is pretty straightforward. The pizza sells itself—one bite, and pizza lovers are hooked. So the main objective is to make consumers aware of the restaurant, which now has several locations in the tri-state area surrounding New York City. As the Fairfield restaurant neared its opening date, Pepe's alerted current customers with a simple message printed on top of each pizza box (coincidentally, many of Pepe's regular New Haven diners actually lived in Fairfield). The company also published press releases and advertised the grand opening of the new restaurant. Billboards along the interstate highway proved to be effective with travelers, as did some direct-mail efforts. Pepe's recently ventured into social media with a Facebook page and Twitter account, which Berry refers to as "the new word of mouth." Pepe's posts photos, blurbs about menu items, and relives a few proud moments on Facebook. Customers comment about their favorite pizza flavors (such as spinach and gorgonzola), and share experiences (like driving 50 miles each way for a Pepe's pizza). Berry notes that Pepe's presence in social media keeps the relationships with customers going.

Educating consumers about Pepe's is the second advertising objective. With such a tasty product, what better way to attract new customers than to let them discover that the proof really is in the pie? Now when Pepe's launches a new restaurant, they give away free pizza for about a week before the grand opening. That's right: free pizza, for a week. Ken Berry explains that this promotion serves three purposes: It trains the new employees, tests the new ovens, and introduces Pepe's pizza to new customers. The giveaway generates plenty of good buzz about Pepe's pizzas and makes an important statement to the public: Pepe's is so confident about the quality of its food that they're willing to give it away for a week—certain that consumers will become regular customers.

Pepe's also enjoys positive public relations surrounding its charitable giving. The company website has a tab allowing customers to request donations for their particular charities, and the restaurant conducts regular "Good Neighbors Nights," from which it donates 15 percent of its proceeds to a designated not-for-profit group. All of these efforts roll together into cohesive marketing communications with one major goal. "Our challenge is to build our brand and protect it," says Berry, "and to make sure we deliver every day."

QUESTIONS FOR CRITICAL THINKING

1. Describe how the Pepe's pizza giveaway promotion relates to each step in the AIDA concept.

2. How might Pepe's use guerilla marketing to promote its brand among college students?

Sources: Company website, www.pepespizzeria.com, accessed December 3, 2012; company Facebook page, www.facebook.com/FrankPepes, accessed December 3, 2012.

NOTES

1. Company website, www.starbucks.com, accessed December 3, 2012; Joseph Ruiz, "6 Reasons Starbucks Marketing Communications Strategy Is So Effective," *Strategic Marketing Solutions*, accessed December 3, 2012, www.strategicdriven.com; Alice G. Walton, "Starbucks' Power Over Us Is Bigger than Coffee: It's Personal," *Forbes*, accessed December 3, 2012, www.forbes.com; Rahim Kanani, "Chief Digital Officer for Starbucks on Technology, Change and Community," *Forbes*, accessed December 3, 2012, www.forbes.com; "Starbucks Rates Number 1 in Study of Most Socially Engaged Companies by Research Firm PhaseOne," *PhaseOne*, accessed December 3, 2012, www.phaseone.net; Alan Chung, "Commentary: Loyalty Marketing Drives Sales and Brand Affinity," *QSRweb.com*, accessed December 3, 2012, www.qsrweb.com; Phillip Britt, "Starbucks Announces Loyalty Program Changes," *Loyalty 360*, accessed December 3, 2012, http://loyalty360.org.

2. Tripp Mickle, "X Games Puts Three Sponsors into the Action," *Sports Business Daily*, accessed December 3, 2012, www.sportsbusinessdaily.com.

3. Sara Bibel, "TV Ratings Broadcast Top 25: 'America's Got Talent' Tops Week 38 Viewing," *TV by the Numbers*, accessed December 3, 2012, http://tvbythenumbers.zap2it.com; Sara Bibel, "ESPN Number One in Cable Primetime Adults 18–49 & Primetime Total Viewers for Week Ending November 25, 2012," *TV by the Numbers*, accessed December 3, 2012, http://tvbythenumbers.zap2it.com.

4. David Bauder, "NBC to Live Stream Events at London Olympics," *Christian Science Monitor*, accessed December 3, 2012, www.csmonitor.com; "Inside NBC's London Olympics Sales Pitch," *Advertising Age*, accessed December 3, 2012, http://adage.com.

5. "AARP Financial Inc. Survey Finds: When It Comes to Financial Jargon, Americans Are Befuddled," *PR Newswire*, accessed December 3, 2012, www.prnewswire.com.

6. Bureau of Labor Statistics, "Employment Projections: 2010–20," press release, accessed December 3, 2012, www.bls.gov.

7. "US Online Advertising to Surpass Print in 2012," *eMarketer*, www.emarketer.com, accessed December 3, 2012; George Assimakopoulos, "The Outlook for Online Ad Spending Is GOOD!" *Penton Marketing Services*, accessed December 3, 2012, www.pentonmarketingservices.com.

8. "Product Placement in Pictures: Skyfall," *Brands & Films*, accessed December 3, 2012, http://brandsandfilms.com; "Product Placement Deals on Twitter," *Product Placement*, accessed December 3, 2012, http://productplacement.biz.

9. "Steve Madden and Zappos.com Pick the Winner," *Brickfish*, accessed December 3, 2012, www.brickfish.com.

10 Marcus Gilmer, "CTA Finally Has a Good Idea with Station Naming-Rights Pitch," *AV Club*, accessed December 3, 2012, www.avclub.com; Joseph Askins, "Riding the Red Line: North/Clybourn," *Yo Chicago*, accessed December 3, 2012, www.yochicago.com.

11. "Kantar Media Reports U.S. Advertising Expenditures Increased 0.9 Percent in the Second Quarter of 2012," press release, accessed December 3, 2012, http://kantarmediana.com.

12. Ibid.

13. E. J. Schultz, "How This Man Made Dos Equis a Most Interesting Marketing Story," *Creativity Online*, accessed December 3, 2012, http://creativity-online.com.

14. Gillian Mohney, "Turf-Grass War Heats Up Airwaves," *ABC News*, accessed December 3, 2012, http://abcnews.go.com; Jack Neff, "Turf War Sprouts in Grass-Seed Advertising," *Advertising Age*, accessed December 3, 2012, http://adage.com.

15. Kurt Badenhausen, "Mayweather Tops List of the World's Highest Paid Athletes," *Forbes*, accessed December 3, 2012, www.forbes.com.

16. Samantha Ettus, "Jennifer Lopez and Angelina Jolie: When Paired with Brands, Can You Spot the Fake?" *Forbes*, accessed December 3, 2012, www.forbes.com.

17. Company website, www.geico.com, accessed December 3, 2012.

18. Ryan Lawler, "Survey Says: Online Video Is Catching Up to TV in Ad Effectiveness," *Tech Crunch*, accessed December 3, 2012, http://techcrunch.com; Robert Hof, "Online Ad Spend to Overtake TV by 2016," *Forbes*, accessed December 3, 2012, www.forbes.com.

19. Steve Johnson, "Behind the Scenes with Allstate's Mayhem Man," *Chicago Tribune*, accessed December 3, 2012, http://articles.chicagotribune.com.

20. Anna Sanina, "Coke Zero Has Unveiled the Battle for Everything Game," *Popsop* (online brand magazine), accessed December 3, 2012, www.popsop.com.

21. Miranda Miller, "Social Media Revenue Forecast to Hit $16.9 Billion in 2012," *Search Engine Watch*, accessed December 3, 2012, http://searchenginewatch.com.

22. "U.S. Ad Spend Reported Up in '11, Forecast to Grow 2.2% in '12," *Marketing Charts*, accessed December 3, 2012, www.marketingcharts.com.

23. Brian Stelter, "A DVR Ad Eraser Causes Tremors at TV Upfronts," *The New York Times*, accessed December 3, 2012, www.nytimes.com.

24. Company website, www.clicker.com, accessed December 3, 2012.

25. Jack Neff, "Walmart.com to Launch Subscription-Sampling Program," *Advertising Age*, accessed December 3, 2012, http://adage.com.

26. "Online Radio: Weekly Audience Jumps More Than 30%, Boosted by Smart Phones," *Media Buyer Planner*, accessed December 3, 2012, www.mediabuyerplanner.com.

27. "U.S. Ad Spend Reported Up in '11, Forecast to Grow 2.2% in '12."

28. Paul Gillin, "Traffic to Newspaper Websites Continues to Surge," *Newspaper Death Watch*, accessed December 3, 2012, http://newspaperdeathwatch.com; Jeremy W. Peters, "Newspaper Circulation Figures Show Some Digital Growth," *The New York Times*, accessed December 3, 2012, http://mediadecoder.blogs.nytimes.com.

29. "Top Media Outlets: Newspapers, Blogs, Consumer Magazines, Websites & Social Networks," *Burrelles Luce*, accessed December 3, 2012, www.burrellesluce.com.

30. Ryan Joe, "North American Advertising Spend to Increase in 2012," *Direct Marketing News*, accessed December 3, 2012, www.dmnews.com.

31. Association website, www.oaaa.org, accessed December 3, 2012.

32. Matt Richtel, "Digital Billboards, Diversions Drivers Can't Escape," *The New York Times*, accessed December 3, 2012, www.nytimes.com.

33. "Electronic Signs to Warn Motorists of Snow Emergencies," *CBS Minnesota*, accessed December 3, 2012, http://Minnesota.cbslocal.com.

34. John C. Abell, "Who Buys All Those Google Ads? An Infographic Breakdown," *Wired*, accessed December 3, 2012, www.wired.com.

35. "Twitter Tops Facebook in US Mobile Advertising Revenue," *eMarketer*, accessed December 3, 2012, www.emarketer.com.

36. Dusan Belic, "Total Immersion's D'Fusion Studio 3.2 Allows Developers to Create a 'New Breed' of AR Apps and Games," *IntoMobile*, accessed December 3, 2012, www.intomobile.com.

37. Company website, www.autowrapped.com, accessed December 3, 2012.

38. Organization website, http://media.prsa.org, accessed December 3, 2012; Bureau of Labor Statistics, "Public Relations Managers and Specialists," *Occupational Outlook Handbook*, accessed December 3, 2012, www.bls.gov.

39. Suzanne Kane, "2012 Honda Civic: Recall Alert," *Washington Post*, accessed December 3, 2012, www.washingtonpost.com.

40. Chris Smith, "Super Bowl Ad Rates Can Double Within Ten Years," *Forbes*, accessed December 3, 2012, www.forbes.com.

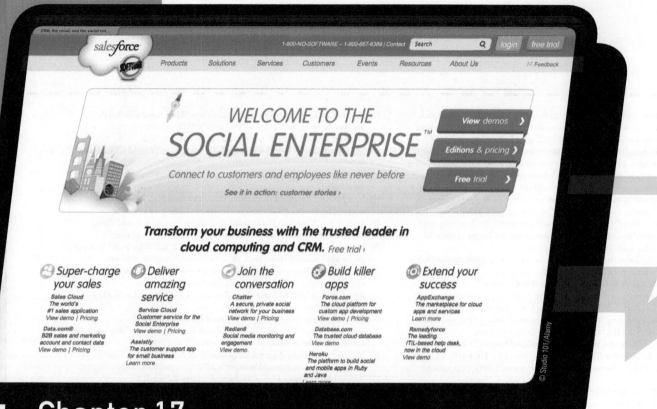

Chapter 17

PERSONAL SELLING

and Sales Promotion

1 Describe the role of today's salesperson.
2 Describe the four sales channels.
3 Describe the major trends in personal selling.
4 Identify and briefly describe the three basic sales tasks.
5 Outline the seven steps in the sales process.
6 Identify the seven basic functions of a sales manager.
7 Explain the role of ethical behavior in personal selling.
8 Describe the role of sales promotion in the promotional mix, and identify the different types of sales promotions.

One of the most influential recent trends in marketing is the use of social media like Facebook, Twitter, LinkedIn, and Google+ to reach customers, develop relationships with them, and shape their brand preferences and buying habits. Having a presence on these sites is such a given that "Facebook has become the new corporate home page," says one hi-tech CEO. Many companies need help today integrating all those social and mobile platforms with their own customer relationship management (CRM) systems, so they know, for instance, what Facebook users are saying about their goods and services and can quickly react. That's where Salesforce.com comes in. More than 100,000 companies already rely on this cloud-computing pioneer to help them tap into social media in an effective and efficient way that yields useful information.

Salesforce, a company based in San Francisco with more than 6,000 employees worldwide, initially focused on providing cloud-computing services for sales operations and information management. Now it

is ramping up its investment in what it calls the Salesforce Marketing Cloud so it can extend its services to chief marketing officers, leading a trend that's expected to make corporate marketing departments the biggest information technology spenders in many organizations.

With recent acquisitions of Buddy Media, Radian6, and GoInstant, Salesforce has invested more than $1 billion in leading companies in the analysis, management, and sharing of social media and Web information. These acquisitions put Salesforce in a strong position to offer CMOs new integrated marketing services that allow them to track and act on the "crucial insights about themselves" that social media users volunteer online. According to Radian6's

CEO, Salesforce's strategy confirms that social media has evolved to become "the central core" of most corporate marketing operations.

Salesforce operates a social network of its own, called Chatter, which serves its own clients exclusively but will now (thanks to the Radian6 acquisition) also allow them to see customers' posts on Facebook, Twitter, blogs, and more data in real time. Salesforce believes it's on track to develop a billion-dollar business with the new suite of services available on its Marketing Cloud. It is so confident it can help its clients excel at multichannel CRM, in fact, that "CRM" is the symbol the company uses for its NYSE stock listing.[1]

EVOLUTION OF A

Industry observers predict that digital marketing will replace traditional marketing as the engine of business growth in the near future. Salesforce's acquisitions of Radian6, Buddy Media, and GoInstant reflect the firm's plans to strengthen its social marketing and Web presence across various media. As companies learn how to use the various kinds of social media to market their goods and services, Salesforce's newly unified platform can make that process easier.

- What sorts of problems will traditional marketers face as they adapt to the new world of digital marketing?

- How can Salesforce's Marketing Cloud help its clients identify their customers' needs and meet those needs?

CHAPTER OVERVIEW

The Salesforce.com story illustrates how important it is for marketers to not simply sell products but to understand their customers and connect with them through product innovations that make life easier. In exploring personal selling strategies, this chapter gives special attention to the relationship-building opportunities that the selling situation presents.

Personal selling is the process of a seller's person-to-person promotional presentation to a buyer. The sales process is essentially interpersonal, and it is basic to any enterprise. Accounting, engineering, human resource management, production, and other organizational activities produce no benefits unless a seller matches the needs of a client or customer. The nearly 15 million people employed in sales occupations in the United States testify to the importance of selling.[2] Personal selling is much more costly and time consuming than other types of promotion because of its direct contact with customers. This makes personal selling the single largest marketing expense in many firms.

Personal selling is a primary component of a firm's promotional mix when one or more of several well-defined factors are present:

1. customers are geographically concentrated;

2. individual orders account for large amounts of revenue;

3. the firm markets goods and services that are expensive, technically complex, or require special handling;

4. trade-ins are involved;

5. products move through short channels; or

6. the firm markets to relatively few potential customers.

For example, personal selling is an important component of the promotional mix for a car dealer, although both dealers and manufacturers also rely heavily on advertising. Because cars and trucks are expensive, customers usually like to go to a dealership to compare models or discuss a purchase, and trade-ins are often involved. So, a dealer's salespeople provide valuable assistance to the customer.

Table 17.1 summarizes the factors that influence the importance of personal selling in the overall promotional mix based on four variables: consumer, product, price, and marketing channels. This chapter also explores *sales promotion*, which includes all marketing activities—other than personal selling, advertising, and publicity—that enhance promotional effectiveness.

TABLE 17.1 Factors Affecting the Importance of Personal Selling in the Promotional Mix

Variable	Conditions That Favor Personal Selling	Conditions That Favor Advertising
Consumer	Geographically concentrated	Geographically dispersed
	Relatively low numbers	Relatively high numbers
Product	Expensive	Inexpensive
	Technically complex	Simple to understand
	Custom made	Standardized
	Special handling requirements	No special handling requirements
	Transactions frequently involve trade-ins	Transactions seldom involve trade-ins
Price	Relatively high	Relatively low
Channels	Relatively short	Relatively long

THE EVOLUTION OF PERSONAL SELLING

Selling has been a standard business activity for thousands of years. As long ago as 2000 BCE, the Code of Hammurabi protected the rights of the Babylonian salesman, who was referred to as a *peddler*. Throughout U.S. history, selling has been a major factor in economic growth. Even during the 1700s, Yankee peddlers took their carts full of goods from village to village and farm to farm, helping expand trade among the colonies. Today, professional salespeople are problem solvers who focus on satisfying the needs of customers before, during, and after sales are made. Armed with knowledge about their firm's goods or services, those of competitors, and their customers' business needs, salespeople pursue a common goal of creating mutually beneficial long-term relationships with customers.

Personal selling is a vital, vibrant, dynamic process. As domestic and foreign competition increases the emphasis on productivity, personal selling is taking on a more prominent role in the marketing mix. Salespeople must communicate the advantages of their firms' goods and services over those of competitors. They must be able to do the following:

- Focus on a customer's situation and needs and create solutions that meet those needs.

- Follow through and stay in touch before, during, and after a sale.

- Know the industry and have a firm grasp not only of their own firm's capabilities but also of their competitors' abilities.

- Work hard to exceed their customers' expectations.

Relationship marketing affects all aspects of an organization's marketing function, including personal selling. This means marketers in both internal and external relationships must develop different sales skills. Instead of working alone, many salespeople now operate in sales teams. The customer-focused firm wants its salespeople to form long-lasting relationships with buyers by providing high levels of customer service rather than going for quick sales. Even the way salespeople perform their jobs is constantly changing. Growing numbers of companies have integrated communications and computer technologies into the sales routine. These trends are covered in more detail later in the chapter.

Personal selling is an attractive career choice for today's college students. According to the Bureau of Labor Statistics, jobs in sales and related fields are expected to grow by about 12.5 percent over the next decade.[3] Company executives usually recognize a good salesperson as a hard worker who can solve problems, communicate clearly, and be consistent. In fact, many firms are headed by executives who began their careers in sales.

Describe the role of today's salesperson.

⊕ ASSESSMENT CHECK

1.1 What is personal selling?

1.2 What is the main focus of today's salespeople?

THE FOUR SALES CHANNELS

Personal selling occurs through several types of communication channels: over-the-counter selling, including online selling; field selling; telemarketing; and inside selling. Each of these channels includes business-to-business and direct-to-customer selling. Although telemarketing and online selling are lower-cost alternatives, their lack of personal interaction with existing or prospective customers often makes them less effective than personalized, one-to-one field selling and over-the-counter channels. In fact, many organizations use a number of different channels.

Describe the four sales channels.

OVER-THE-COUNTER SELLING

over-the-counter selling Personal selling conducted in retail and some wholesale locations in which customers come to the seller's place of business.

The most frequently used sales channel, over-the-counter selling, typically describes selling in retail and some wholesale locations. Most over-the-counter sales are direct-to-customer, although business customers are frequently served by wholesalers with over-the-counter sales reps. Customers typically visit the seller's location on their own initiative to purchase desired items. Some visit their favorite stores because they enjoy shopping. Others respond to many kinds of appeals, including direct mail; personal letters of invitation from store personnel; and advertisements for sales, special events, and new-product introductions.

Marketers are getting increasingly creative in their approach to over-the-counter selling. Recently, Macy's shifted its marketing focus from attracting new customers to retaining and cultivating their existing customer base. According to the company, customer loyalty is key, and it has put the customer at the center of its decisions. To retain and grow its customer base, Macy's believes it has to personalize the in-store and online shopping experiences for its customers. The retail chain launched "MyMacy's"—a strategy to tailor merchandise in each store to the wants and likes of the local consumer. This new approach to selling has helped the company double its earnings over the last several years.[4]

Enterprise Rent-A-Car, the world's largest car-rental company, recently formed a partnership with Kansas-based Career Athletes, a firm that matches former student-athletes with career opportunities in the business world. Enterprise has over 7,700 locations, annual revenues of over $15 billion, and more than 74,000 employees. The company already has a record of hiring former college athletes. The new recruits will learn to work with profit and loss statements as well as marketing and customer-service skills. The vice president of talent acquisition at Enterprise says, "Partnering with Career Athletes allows Enterprise to connect with its nationwide network of athletic departments and student athletes, and we look forward to a very productive partnership."[5]

Clothing retailers have begun to enhance the shopping experience by expanding the capabilities of the fitting room. Ann Taylor has redesigned its fitting rooms to look like walk-in closets, complete with chandeliers. Old Navy has moved its fitting rooms from the back of the store to the center and also has "quick change" areas for its targeted customers—young mothers pressed for time. Macy's has been adding communal waiting areas for children, boyfriends, or husbands who accompany

Ann Taylor's new fitting rooms resemble a shopper's dream of an ideal walk-in closet, complete with chandelier.

shoppers. Located near the fitting rooms, the waiting areas have flat-screen TVs showing cartoons or sports as well as comfortable sofas.[6]

Regardless of a retailer's innovation, a few things remain the same in selling. For example, customers never like hearing salespeople say the following:

- "That's not my department."
- "If it's not out (on the rack or shelf), we don't have it."
- "I don't know" or "I'm new."
- "I'm closing" or "I'm on a break."
- "The computer is down."

Although these quotes may seem humorous, they also ring true. You've probably heard them, and you may have said them yourself if you've worked in a retail environment. But each statement conveys the message that the salesperson is not willing or able to serve the customer—exactly the opposite of what every marketer wants to convey.

FIELD SELLING

Field selling involves making sales calls on prospective and existing customers at their businesses or homes. Some situations involve considerable creative effort, such as the sale of major computer installations. Often, the salesperson must first convince customers that they need the good or service and then that they need the particular brand the salesperson is selling. Field sales of large industrial installations, such as Airbus's A380 double-deck airliner, often require considerable technical expertise.

Largely because it involves travel, field selling is considerably more expensive than other selling options. Rising prices of fuel, airfares, car rentals, and hotel rates have forced up the cost of business trips. Needing to find ways to trim costs while increasing productivity, some firms have replaced certain travel with conference calls, while others require salespeople to stay in less expensive hotels and spend less on meals. Some firms have simply shortened the time allowed for trips.

In fairly routine field selling situations, such as calling on established customers in industries like food, textiles, or wholesaling, the salesperson basically acts as an order taker who processes regular customers' orders. But more complex situations may involve weeks of preparation, formal presentations, and many hours of postsales call work. Field selling is a lifestyle that many people enjoy; they also cite some of the negatives, such as travel delays and impact on family life.

Some firms view field selling as a market in itself and have developed goods and services designed to help salespeople do their jobs. Panasonic manufactures the Toughbook series— lines of laptop computers and tablet devices loaded with Microsoft Office software and designed with field sales reps in mind. Each Toughbook

field selling Sales presentations made at prospective customers' locations on a face-to-face basis.

Panasonic manufactures a family of Toughpad tablet devices as well as Toughbook laptop computers with field sales reps in mind.

product has a magnesium alloy case—significantly stronger than the plastic cases of standard computers—and is built for rugged handling. The toughest Toughbooks can withstand a six-foot drop and are rain-, dust-, and vibration-resistant.[7]

Taking their cue from the successes of businesses like Avon, Pampered Chef, and Tupperware, many smaller businesses now rely on field selling in customers' homes. Often called **network marketing**, this type of personal selling relies on lists of family members and friends of the salesperson or "party host," who organizes a gathering of potential customers for an in-home demonstration of products. For several years, Vault Denim has bought the previous season's designer jeans from manufacturers. Its consultants then sell the jeans at home parties for about half the retail price.[8]

network marketing
Personal selling that relies on lists of family members and friends of a salesperson, who organizes gatherings of potential customers for an in-home presentation of selected products.

TELEMARKETING

telemarketing
Promotional presentation involving the use of the telephone on an outbound basis by salespeople or on an inbound basis by customers who initiate calls to obtain information and place orders.

outbound telemarketing Sales method in which sales personnel place phone calls to prospects and try to conclude the sale over the phone.

Telemarketing is a channel in which the selling process is conducted by phone and serves two general purposes—sales and service—and two general markets—business-to-business and direct-to-customer. Both inbound and outbound telemarketing are forms of direct marketing.

Outbound telemarketing involves sales personnel who rely on the telephone to contact potential buyers, reducing the substantial costs of personal visits to customers' homes or businesses. Technologies like predictive dialers, autodialing, and random-digit dialing increase chances that telemarketers will reach people at home. *Predictive dialers* weed out busy signals and answering machines, nearly doubling the number of calls made per hour. *Autodialing* allows telemarketers to dial numbers continually; when a customer answers the phone, the call is automatically routed to a sales representative. However, the Telephone Consumer Protection Act of 1991 prohibits the use of autodialers to contact (or leave messages on) telephone devices such as answering machines.[9] *Random-digit dialing* allows telemarketers to reach unlisted numbers and block Caller ID.

A major drawback of telemarketing is that most consumers dislike the practice, and more than 209 million have signed up for the national Do Not Call Registry.[10] If an unauthorized telemarketer does call any of these numbers, the marketer is subject to a fine of up to $16,000.[11] Organizations exempt from the fine include not-for-profits, political candidates, companies that have obtained the customer's permission, marketing researchers, and firms that have an existing business relationship with the customer.

Why do some firms still use telemarketing? The average call cost is low, and companies point to a significant rate of success. In a recent year, total incremental sales from telemarketing exceeded $2 trillion. According to the Direct Marketing Association, about 1.3 million people work in telemarketing jobs that support 7.9 million other jobs, for a total of 9.2 million jobs in the United States.[12]

At home parties, Vault Denim consultants sell last year's jeans at about half the retail price.

Inbound telemarketing typically involves a toll-free number that customers can call to obtain information, make reservations, and purchase goods and services. When a customer calls a toll-free number, the caller can be identified and routed to the representatives with whom he or she has done business before, creating a human touch not possible before. This form of selling provides maximum convenience for customers who initiate the sales process. Many large catalog merchants, such as Pottery Barn, L.L. Bean, Lands' End, and Performance Bike, keep their inbound telemarketing lines open 24 hours a day, seven days a week.

Some firms are taking dramatic steps to incorporate inbound telemarketing into their overall marketing strategy. JetBlue Airways, for example, keeps operating costs low by employing 1,800 customer support agents who work from home.[13]

Kristian sekulic/iStockphoto.com

Some firms use telemarketing, because the average call cost is low and companies point to a significant rate of success.

inbound telemarketing Sales method in which prospects call a seller to obtain information, make reservations, and purchase goods and services.

INSIDE SELLING

The role of many of today's telemarketers is a combination of field selling techniques applied through inbound and outbound telemarketing channels with a strong customer orientation, called inside selling. Inside sales reps perform two primary jobs: they turn opportunities into actual sales, and they support technicians and purchasers with current solutions. Inside sales reps do far more than read a canned script to unwilling prospects. Their role goes beyond taking orders to solving problems, providing customer service, and selling. A successful inside sales force relies on close working relationships with field representatives to solidify customer relationships.

The six-member inside sales force—the Client Experience Team—of the NBA's Detroit Pistons supports the team's marketing efforts, such as special events for season ticket holders, including backstage tours, tipoff parties, and privileges like getting into games 30 minutes early. Season-ticket holders are also issued the official Pistons On-Court Jacket, which comes with an embedded microchip, to get 20 percent off at concessions and 30 percent off merchandise. Pistons sales reps use online chat, telephone, and email to stay connected.[14]

inside selling Selling by phone, mail, and electronic commerce.

INTEGRATING THE VARIOUS SELLING CHANNELS

Figure 17.1 illustrates how firms are likely to blend alternative sales channels, from over-the-counter selling and field selling to telemarketing and inside selling, to create a successful cost-effective sales organization. Existing customers whose business problems require complex solutions are likely best served by the traditional field sales force. Other current customers who need answers but not the same attention as the first group can be served by inside sales reps who contact them as needed. Over-the-counter sales reps serve existing customers by supplying information and advice and completing sales transactions. Telemarketers may be used to strengthen communication with customers or to reestablish relationships with customers that may have lapsed over a few months.

ASSESSMENT CHECK

2.1 What is over-the-counter selling?

2.2 What is field selling?

2.3 Distinguish between outbound and inbound telemarketing.

BRIEFLY SPEAKING

"The way to get started is to quit talking and begin doing."

—Walt Disney
American entertainment pioneer and founder of The Walt Disney Company

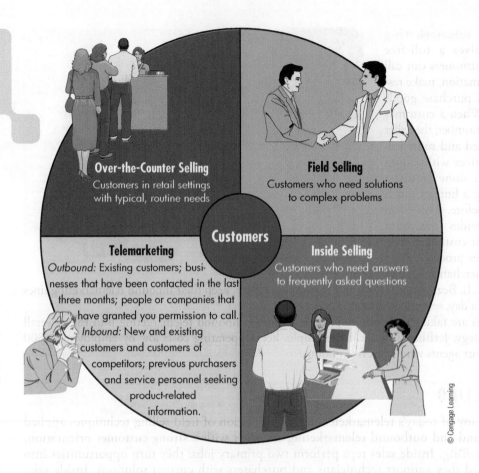

Over-the-Counter Selling
Customers in retail settings with typical, routine needs

Field Selling
Customers who need solutions to complex problems

Customers

Telemarketing
Outbound: Existing customers; businesses that have been contacted in the last three months; people or companies that have granted you permission to call.
Inbound: New and existing customers and customers of competitors; previous purchasers and service personnel seeking product-related information.

Inside Selling
Customers who need answers to frequently asked questions

© Cengage Learning

TRENDS IN PERSONAL SELLING

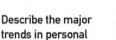

3 Describe the major trends in personal selling.

In today's complex marketing environment, effective personal selling requires different strategies from those used by salespeople in the past. As pointed out in the discussion of *buying centers* in Chapter 7, rather than selling one-on-one, in B2B settings it is now customary to sell to teams of corporate representatives who participate in the client firm's decision-making process. In business-to-business sales situations involving technical products, customers expect salespeople to answer technical questions—or bring along someone who can. They also want representatives who understand technical jargon and can communicate using sophisticated technological tools. Patience is also a requirement because the B2B sales cycle, from initial contact to closing, may take months or even years. To address all of these concerns, companies rely on three major personal selling approaches: relationship selling, consultative selling, and team selling. Regardless of the approach, however, experts agree on a few basic guidelines for conducting successful personal selling.

RELATIONSHIP SELLING

relationship selling
Regular contacts between sales representatives and customers over an extended period to establish a sustained buyer–seller relationship.

Most firms now emphasize **relationship selling**, a technique for building a mutually beneficial partnership with a customer through regular contacts over an extended period. Such buyer–seller bonds become increasingly important as companies cut back on the number of suppliers and look for companies that provide high levels of customer service and satisfaction. Salespeople must also find ways to distinguish themselves and their products from competitors. To create strong, long-lasting relationships with customers, salespeople must meet buyers' expectations. Table 17.2 summarizes the results of several surveys that indicate what buyers expect of professional salespeople.

The success of tomorrow's marketers depends on the relationships they build today in both the business-to-consumer and business-to-business markets. Sovereign Bank, located

TABLE 17.2 What Buyers Expect from Salespeople

Buyers prefer to do business with salespeople who:

- Orchestrate events and bring whatever resources are necessary to satisfy the customer
- Provide counseling to the customer based on in-depth knowledge of the product, the market, and the customer's needs
- Solve problems proficiently to ensure satisfactory customer service over extended time periods
- Demonstrate high ethical standards and communicate honestly at all times
- Willingly advocate the customer's cause within the selling organization
- Create imaginative arrangements to meet buyers' needs
- Arrive well prepared for sales calls

© Cengage Learning

throughout the Northeast, knew that first impressions are particularly important in relationship selling. To allow its staff to spend more time with customers, the bank automated many sales processes and implemented sales effectiveness tools to help it become more customer focused.[15]

Relationship selling is equally important in business-to-business sales, if not more so. Firms may invest millions of dollars in goods and services from a single firm, so creating relationships is vital. Barnett, a leading national distributor of plumbing, heating and air conditioning, electrical, and hardware products, uses barcode technology to keep its contractors' trucks well stocked with all sorts of supplies—just in case they are needed on a job. After a contractor finishes at a site, he or she uses a scanner to record the parts used in the job. The parts are automatically reordered at the end of the day, and Barnett replenishes the inventory.[16]

CONSULTATIVE SELLING

Field representatives and inside sales reps require sales methods that satisfy today's cost–conscious, knowledgeable buyers. One such method, consultative selling, involves meeting customer needs by listening to customers, understanding—and caring about—their problems, paying attention to details, and following through after the sale. It works hand in hand with relationship selling in building customer loyalty. Richardson, a sales consulting firm based in Philadelphia, recently trained sales staff at Fireman's Fund Insurance in consultative selling techniques. Earlier, Fireman's had adopted a new customer-focused sales strategy, and the sales force needed to sharpen its skills to align better with the new strategy. During the training, participants learned how to prepare for sales meetings, position the company's products to meet needs, close deals, and build relationships, and they received coaching and feedback. As a result of the training, the sales representatives were able to adapt to the new strategy and win business.[17] One important aspect of consultative selling is being prepared for a sales call, including dressing professionally.

Online companies have instituted consultative selling models to create long-term customers. Particularly for complicated, high-priced products that require installation or specialized service, Web sellers must quickly communicate the benefits and features of their products. They accomplish this through consultative selling.

Cross-selling—offering multiple goods or services to the same customer—is another technique that capitalizes on a firm's strengths. It costs a bank five times as much to acquire a new customer as to cross-sell to an existing one. Moreover, research shows that the more a customer buys from an institution, the less likely that person is to leave. So, a customer who opens a checking account at a local bank may follow with a safe-deposit box, retirement savings account, and a mortgage loan. Wells Fargo relies on cross-selling to promote its broad array of banking products and services. See the "Marketing Success" feature to learn more.

consultative selling
Meeting customer needs by listening to them, understanding their problems, paying attention to details, and following through after the sale.

cross-selling Selling multiple, often unrelated, goods and services to the same customer based on knowledge of that customer's needs.

MARKETING SUCCESS

Wells Fargo's Successful Cross-Selling Strategies

Background. Wells Fargo, which recently acquired Wachovia Corp., is the nation's fourth-largest bank and, like its competitors, is seeking increased revenue even as low interest rates have made loans a less profitable business.

The Challenge. The company, which provides retail banking, retirement, and wealth management services among others, wants to be the "the premier provider of financial services in every one of our markets."

The Strategy. Wells Fargo has elevated the sales strategy of cross-selling to an art. Its representatives are encouraged to suggest new products and packages of time- and money-saving services to existing customers, pitching a broad array of offerings while keeping a customer-centric approach. They use information about customers' financial situations to understand their other

financial needs. Wells Fargo is then able to offer personalized suggestions to increase the number of checking accounts, credit cards, debit cards, home equity loans, savings and retirement accounts, and online banking services its customers use.

The Outcome. The company's sales per household have continued to increase over the last decade, while its customer service ratings remain high. The average U.S. household uses about 16 banking products from various financial institutions. Wells Fargo sells each customer an average of 5.9. Other banks are beginning to emulate Wells Fargo's cross-selling strategy.

Sources: Company website, www.wellsfargo.com, accessed December 4, 2012; Andrew Dunn, "1 Year in, Change Visible at Wells Fargo," *Charlotte Observer*, accessed December 4, 2012, www.charlotteobserver.com; Rick Rothacker, "Wells Fargo's Carroll Eyes Cross-Selling by Brokers," *Reuters*, accessed December 4, 2012, www.reuters.com; Halah Tourhalai, "The Art of the Cross-Sell," *Forbes*, accessed December 4, 2012, www.forbes.com.

team selling Selling situation in which several sales associates or other members of the organization are employed to help the lead sales representative reach all those who influence the purchase decision.

TEAM SELLING

Another development in the evolution of personal selling is **team selling**, in which a salesperson joins with specialists from other functional areas of the firm to complete the selling process. Teams can be formal and ongoing or created for a specific, short-term selling situation. Although some salespeople have hesitated to embrace the idea of team selling, preferring to work alone, a growing number believe team selling brings better results. Customers often prefer the team approach, which makes them feel well served. Consider a restaurant meal. If the host, servers, wine steward, chef, and kitchen crew are all working well together as a team, your experience at the restaurant is likely to be positive. But if the service stops and starts, your order is recorded wrong, the food is cold, the silverware is dirty, and the staff seems grouchy, you probably won't eat at that restaurant again. In fact, you may not even finish the meal.

Another advantage of team selling is the formation of relationships between companies rather than between individuals. In sales situations that call for detailed knowledge of new, complex, and ever-changing technologies, team selling offers a distinct competitive edge in meeting customers' needs. In most computer software B2B departments, a third of the sales force is made up of technically trained, nonmarketing experts like engineers or programmers. A salesperson continues to play the lead role in most sales situations, but technical experts bring added value to the sales process. Some companies establish permanent sales-and-tech teams that conduct all sales presentations together; others have a pool of engineers or other professionals who are on call for different client visits.

Some resourceful entrepreneurs are building a virtual sales team—a network of strategic partners, suppliers, and others qualified and willing to recommend a firm's goods or services. Michelle Marciniak and Susan Walvius, both former college basketball coaches, came up with a new use for the moisture-wicking fabric that workout clothes are made of—bedsheets. Together they founded Sheex, which makes bedsheets that are cool to the touch and transfer body heat away from the sleeper. Rather than a traditional sales force, a virtual sales force of "sleep ambassadors" promotes Sheex bedsheets. Athletes, such as NFL wide receiver Steve Smith, golfer Diana D'Alessio, and snowboarder Steve Fisher, post discount codes via Twitter or other social media. They receive commissions based on sales of Sheex. "It's kind of a virtual sales team of athletes," Susan Walvius says.[18]

virtual sales team
Network of strategic partners, suppliers, and others who recommend a firm's goods or services.

ASSESSMENT CHECK

3.1 Identify the three major personal selling approaches.

3.2 Distinguish between relationship selling and consultative selling.

SALES TASKS

Today's salesperson is more concerned with establishing long-term buyer–seller relationships and helping customers select the correct products for meeting their needs than with simply selling whatever is available. Where repeat purchases are common, the salesperson must be certain that the buyer's purchases are in his or her best interest; otherwise, no future relationship will be possible. The seller's interests are tied to the buyer's in a mutually beneficial relationship.

Although all sales activities help the customer in some manner, they are not all alike. Three basic sales tasks can be identified: (1) order processing, (2) creative selling, and (3) missionary sales. Most of today's salespeople are not limited to performing tasks in a single category. Instead, they often perform all three tasks to some extent. A sales engineer for a computer firm may do 50 percent missionary sales, 45 percent creative selling, and 5 percent order processing. Most sales positions are classified on the basis of the primary selling task performed.

Then there's the philosophy that *everyone* in the organization, regardless of what his or her job description is, should be engaged in selling. Southwest Airlines believes delivering great customer service is paramount for every employee, from the reservations agent to the baggage handler to the flight attendant. All Southwest employees are trained to put the customer's needs first, and the airline relies heavily on technology to coordinate the effort.[19]

4 Identify and briefly describe the three basic sales tasks.

ORDER PROCESSING

Order processing, which can involve both field selling and telemarketing, is most often typified by selling at the wholesale and retail levels. For instance, a Snapple route salesperson who performs this task must take the following steps:

1. *Identify customer needs.* The route salesperson determines that a store has only seven cases of Snapple left in stock when it normally carries an inventory of 50.

2. *Point out the need to the customer.* The route salesperson informs the store manager of the inventory situation.

3. *Complete (write up) the order.* The store manager acknowledges the need for more of the product. The driver unloads 43 cases of Snapple, and the manager signs the delivery slip.

Order processing is part of most selling positions. It becomes the primary task in situations in which needs can be readily identified and are acknowledged by the customer. Even in such instances,

order processing
Selling, mostly at the wholesale and retail levels, that involves identifying customer needs, pointing them out to customers, and completing orders.

however, salespeople whose primary responsibility involves order processing will devote some time persuading their wholesale or retail customers to carry more complete inventories of their firms' merchandise or handle additional product lines. They are also likely to try to motivate purchasers to feature some of their firms' products, increase the amount of shelf space devoted to these items, and improve product location in the stores.

Technology now streamlines order-processing tasks. Interactive store kiosks at brick-and-mortar retailers, such as Macy's and Adidas, provide a touch screen that lets customers browse a store's catalog, compare brands and product features, and even place their order—all from a single user-friendly device, eliminating endless cruising of store aisles.[20]

CREATIVE SELLING

When a considerable amount of decision making is involved in purchasing a good or service, an effective salesperson uses creative selling techniques to solicit an order. In contrast to the order-processing task, which deals mainly with maintaining existing business, creative selling is generally used to develop new business either by adding new customers or introducing new goods and services. New products or upgrades to more expensive items often require creative selling. The salesperson must first identify the customer's problems and needs and then propose a solution in the form of the item offered. When attempting to expand an existing business relationship, creative selling techniques are used in over-the-counter selling, field selling, inside selling, and telemarketing.

Creative selling can generate "buzz" for a product. Digital marketing agency Rockfish, based in Rogers, Arkansas, developed a creative campaign for BUNN, which manufactures high-quality commercial coffee- and tea-making equipment. BUNN recently launched a line of commercial-quality machines for the home. Rockfish merged BUNN's two at-home websites, initiated a social-media campaign with online interactive videos, search-engine marketing, social media placement, and holiday-themed advertising, all of which resulted in a dramatic increase in website visits and sales.[21]

MISSIONARY SELLING

Missionary selling is an indirect approach to sales. Salespeople sell the firm's goodwill and educate their customers, often providing technical or operational assistance. A cosmetics company salesperson may call on retailers to demonstrate how a new product is used or check on special promotions and overall product movement, while a wholesaler takes orders and delivers merchandise. For years, large pharmaceutical companies operated the most aggressive missionary selling, courting doctors (the indirect customers) by providing lavish restaurant meals, educational seminars, and other incentives in the hope of persuading them to prescribe a particular brand to patients. Although the doctor is clearly the decision maker, the transaction is not complete until the patient hands the prescription over to a pharmacist, and, traditionally, pharmaceutical companies measured success in terms of number of prescriptions for their drugs. But recent changes in the industry code of conduct now prohibit missionary salespeople—called detailers—from offering any incentives of value to their customers. Instead, the Pharmaceutical Research and Manufacturers of America decreed that meetings with doctors must focus exclusively on education, not freebies. Some pharmaceutical companies are now asking their sales forces to change their focus to becoming resources for doctors in treating patients and providing practical support.[22]

Some missionary sales may offer sales incentives, such as trips, gas cards, free product upgrades, and other inducements. Missionary sales may involve both field selling and telemarketing. Many aspects of team selling can also be seen as missionary sales, as when technical support salespeople help design, install, and maintain equipment; when they train customers' employees; and when they provide information or operational assistance.

ASSESSMENT CHECK

4.1 What are the three major tasks performed by salespeople?

4.2 What are the three steps of order processing?

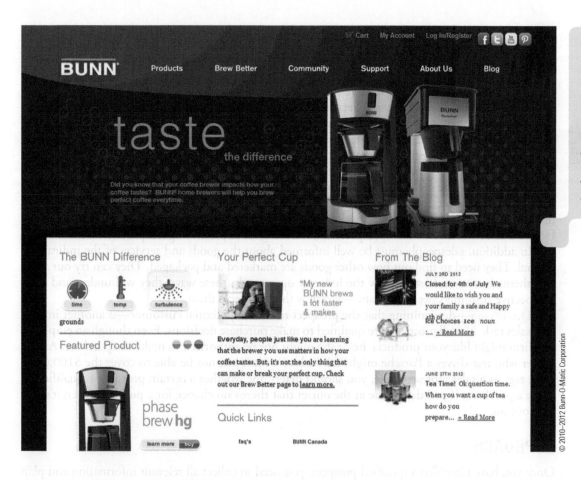

When BUNN wanted to create excitement around its new at-home coffee-brewing machines, it launched an online campaign that featured interactive videos and social media, such as Facebook, Twitter, Pinterest, and YouTube.

THE SALES PROCESS

If you have worked in a retail store, or if you've sold magazine subscriptions or candy to raise money for your school or sports team, you will recognize many of the activities involved in the following list of steps in the sales process. Personal selling encompasses the following sequence of activities: (1) prospecting and qualifying, (2) approach, (3) presentation, (4) demonstration, (5) handling objections, (6) closing, and (7) follow-up.

As Figure 17.2 indicates, these steps follow the AIDA concept (attention, interest, desire, action). Once a sales prospect has been qualified, an attempt is made to secure his or her attention. The presentation and demonstration steps are designed to generate interest and desire. Successful handling of buyer objections should arouse further desire. Action occurs at the close of the sale.

Salespeople modify the steps in this process to match their customers' buying processes. A neighbor who eagerly looks forward to the local symphony orchestra's new concert season each year needs no presentation except for details about scheduled performances and perhaps whether any famous musicians will be on the bill. But the same neighbor would expect a demonstration from an auto dealer when looking for a new car or might appreciate a presentation of dinner specials by the server prior to ordering a meal at a restaurant.

Outline the seven steps in the sales process. **5**

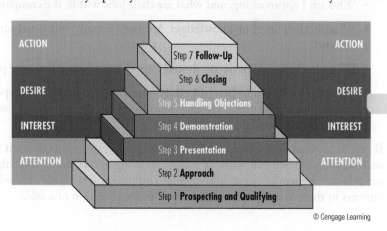

FIGURE 17.2
The AIDA Concept and the Personal Selling Process

© Cengage Learning

PROSPECTING AND QUALIFYING

prospecting Personal selling function of identifying potential customers.

Prospecting—the process of identifying potential customers—may involve hours, days, or weeks of effort, but it is a necessary step. Leads about prospects come from many sources: the Internet, computerized databases, trade show exhibits, previous customers, friends and neighbors, other vendors, nonsales employees in the firm, suppliers, and social and professional contacts. Although a firm may emphasize personal selling as the primary component of its overall promotional strategy, direct mail and advertising campaigns are also effective in identifying prospective customers.

Before salespeople begin their prospecting effort, they must be clear about what their firm is selling and create a "brand story," that is, define their product in terms of what it can do for a customer. Because customers are generally looking for solutions to problems or ways to make their lives better or businesses more successful, this focus on the customer is critical. Once they develop a brand story, the sales team must be consistent about telling it at every possible point of contact, whether in a face-to-face conversation with a prospect, in advertising, or in promoting the product to the media.[23]

In addition, salespeople must be well informed about the goods and services of the industry in general. They need to find out how other goods are marketed and packaged. They can try out a service themselves to understand how the industry operates. In these ways, they will understand what prospective customers need and want—and how they can serve them.

qualifying Determining a prospect's needs, income, and purchase authority as a potential customer.

Qualifying—determining that the prospect really is a potential customer—is another important sales task. Not all prospects are qualified to make purchase decisions. Even though an employee in a firm might like your products, he or she might not be authorized to make the purchase. A consumer who test-drives a Porsche might fall in love with it but not be able to cover the $100,000+ price tag. As a sales representative, you should determine whether a certain prospect is qualified to make a purchase. If you determine at the outset that there's no chance for a purchase, then it's best to move on.

APPROACH

approach Salesperson's initial contact with a prospective customer.

Once you have identified a qualified prospect, you need to collect all relevant information and plan an approach—your initial contact with the prospective customer. If your firm already has a business relationship with the customer or has permission to contact the person, you may use telemarketing. But before you do so, gather as much information as you can.

precall planning Use of information collected during the prospecting and qualifying stages of the sales process and during previous contacts with the prospect to tailor the approach and presentation to match the customer's needs.

Information gathering makes precall planning possible. As mentioned earlier, educate yourself about the industry in general, as well as goods and services offered by competitors. Read any marketing research available. Go to trade shows—you can learn a lot about many companies and their products at one location, usually in one day. Learn as much as you can about the firm you plan to approach: browse the company's website; find online news articles and press releases about the company; and talk with other people in the industry. Know its product offerings well. Identify ways you can help the firm do better. Without invading an individual customer's privacy, see if you have anything in common—perhaps you grew up in the same state, or you both like to play tennis. All of this planning will help you make an effective approach.

As you plan your approach, try to answer the following questions:

- Who am I approaching, and what are their jobs within the company?

- What is their level of knowledge? Are they already informed about the idea I am going to present?

- What do they want or need? Should I speak in technical terms or provide general information?

- What do they need to hear? Do they need to know more about specific products or how those products can serve them? Do they need to know how the product works? Do they need to know about cost and availability?

If you are a retail salesperson, you can ask a shopper questions to learn more about his or her needs and preferences. Say you work at a large sporting goods store. You might ask a young male shopper whether he works out at home, what equipment he already has, what his fitness goals are. The answers to these questions should lead you in the direction of a sale.

PRESENTATION

In a **presentation**, you convey your marketing message to the potential customer. You describe the product's major features, point out its strengths, and cite other customers' successes with the product. One popular form of presentation is a "features-benefits" framework, wherein you talk about the good or service in terms meaningful to the buyer. If you work for a car dealership, you might point out safety features like side airbags and built-in car seats to a young couple.

Your presentation should be well organized, clear, and concise. If appropriate, use visual sales support materials, such as a chart, a brochure, a DVD, or even streaming video from your laptop. If this is your first presentation to a potential customer, it will likely be more detailed than a routine call to give an existing customer some updates. Regardless of the situation, though, be attuned to your audience's response so you can modify your presentation—even on the spur of the moment—to meet their needs.

Many presentations now use computer-based multimedia, which can offer everything from interactivity to current pricing information. Companies like SlideShare and the cloud-based Brainshark, which enable users to share their presentations online, also offer video capabilities. Users can embed video into their presentations along with traditional PowerPoint slides and other images. Brainshark's app SlideShark has multiuser functionality.[24]

However, technology must be used efficiently to be effective. For example, a company's website can be an excellent selling tool if it is easy for salespeople to present and buyers to use. A salesperson can actually use the site during a presentation by showing a potential customer how to use it to learn about and purchase products.

In a **cold calling** situation, the approach and presentation often take place at the same time. Cold calling means phoning or visiting the customer without a prior appointment and making a sales pitch on the spot. Cold calling requires nerve, skill, and creativity, but salespeople who are successful at it still point to the importance of preparation. See the "Career Readiness" feature for some tips on making cold calling work for you. During economic downturns, the ability to make cold calls becomes even more essential, as Tom Wood discovered recently. Wood is the president and CEO of

presentation Personal selling function of describing a product's major features and relating them to a customer's problems or needs.

cold calling Contacting a prospect without a prior appointment.

CAREER READINESS

Making a Successful Cold Call

Cold calling might be one of selling's biggest challenges. Here's how to tackle it with confidence.

- Think of the cold call as a conversation, not a sales call. Introduce yourself and ask an attention-getting question whose answer leads to an advantage of your good or service.

- Follow up with leading questions that let the customer acknowledge the benefits of purchasing from you. This helps forestall objections later.

- If you reach voice mail, leave a very brief but intriguing message that piques the prospect's interest without giving any selling information away.

- If you have to get past a gatekeeper, try just asking politely for help reaching the decision maker. Most people want to see themselves as helpful. Always thank the gatekeeper for putting your call through.

- You may need to make an average of 50 calls to log one sale, but be sure you sound fresh and confident each time. Frequently changing your opening statement will help you achieve this, as well as letting you find the opening that works best.

- If you're calling to make an appointment, sell the appointment, not the product.

- If all else fails, ask the prospect whom else you might call.

Sources: Chris Joseph, "Sales Techniques for Cold Calls in Marketing," *eHow.com*, accessed December 4, 2012, www.ehow.com; Carl Ruenheck, "Warming Up Those Necessary Cold Calls," *Business Know How*, accessed December 4, 2012, www.businessknowhow.com; Sean McPheat, "Tips on Cold Calling," *MTD Sales Training*, accessed December 4, 2012, www.mtdsalestraining.com; "9 Tips for Successful Cold Calling," *WAHM.com*, accessed December 4, 2012, www.wahm.com; Geoffrey James, "How to Make a Successful Cold Call," *Inc.*, accessed December 4, 2012, www.inc.com.

Floor Coverings International (FCI) in Norcross, Georgia. FCI struggled financially during the recent recession, with some of its franchisees going out of business altogether. Although FCI had continued its Web ads and local direct mail, Wood decided that the company had to do more to help the remaining franchisees find new potential customers. The company's Fast Start program turned its corporate employees loose to teach franchise owners the tried-and-true methods: knocking on doors, cold calling, and networking. Fast Start also showed the franchisees how to develop relationships with other companies, such as real estate agents, restoration and remodeling companies, and home inspectors, which could be sources of future leads. Wood says, "We were going out and finding customers before they even needed flooring. It was a culture shift ... but that's just what it took to survive." FCI's franchisees have increased, and sales went up 17 percent in one recent year and 31 percent in the next.[25]

DEMONSTRATION

demonstration Stage in the personal selling process in which the customer has the opportunity to try out or otherwise see how a good or service works before purchase.

One of the most important advantages of personal selling is the opportunity to demonstrate a product. During a **demonstration**, the buyer gets a chance to try the product or at least see how it works. A demonstration might involve a test drive of the latest hybrid car or an in-store cooking class using pots and pans that are for sale.

Many firms use new technologies to make their demonstrations more outstanding than those of their competitors. Multimedia interactive demonstrations are now common. Visitors to the Black & Decker website can click on video demonstrations of such products as the Matrix Quick Connect System or launch the Clean Lawn Calculator to gauge the environmental impact of mowing, trimming, and blowing their lawns every week.[26] The key to an outstanding demonstration—one that gains the customer's attention, keeps his or her interest, is convincing, and stays in the customer's memory—is planning. But planning should also include time and space for free exchanges of information. During your demonstration, you should be prepared to stop and answer questions, demonstrate a certain feature again, or let the customer try the product firsthand.

HANDLING OBJECTIONS

objection Expression of sales resistance by the prospect.

closing Stage of the personal selling process in which the salesperson asks the customer to make a purchase decision.

Potential customers often have legitimate questions and concerns about a good or service they are considering. **Objections** are expressions of resistance by the prospect, and it is reasonable to expect them. Objections might appear in the form of stalling or indecisiveness. "Let me call you back," your prospect might say, or "I just don't know about this." Or your buyer might focus on something negative like high price.

You can answer objections without being aggressive or rude. Use an objection as an opportunity to reassure your buyer about price, features, durability, availability, and the like. If the objection involves price, you might be able to suggest a less-expensive model or a payment plan. If the objection involves a comparison to competitive products, point out the obvious—and not so obvious—benefits of your own. If the objection involves a question about availability, a few clicks on your laptop should show how many items are in stock and when they can be shipped.

Giving the customer the opportunity to try a product is an important advantage of personal selling.

CLOSING

The moment of truth in selling is the **closing**—the point at which the salesperson asks the prospect for an order. If your presentation has been effective and you have handled all objections, a closing would be the natural conclusion to the meeting. But you may still find it difficult to close the sale. Closing does not have to be thought of in terms of a "hard sell." Instead, you can ask your customer, "Would you like to give this a try?" or, "Do I have your approval to proceed?"

Other methods of closing include the following:

1. Addressing the prospect's major concern about a purchase and then offering a convincing argument. *"If I can show you how the new heating system will reduce your energy costs by 25 percent, would you be willing to let us install it?"*

2. Posing choices for the prospect in which either alternative represents a sale. *"Would you prefer the pink sweater or the green one?"*

3. Advising the buyer that a product is about to be discontinued or will go up in price soon (but be completely honest about this—you don't want a customer to learn later that this was not true).

4. Remaining silent so the buyer can make a decision on his or her own.

5. Offering an extra inducement designed to motivate a favorable buyer response, such as a quantity discount, an extended service contract, or a low-interest payment plan.

Even if the meeting or phone call ends without a sale, the effort is not over. You can use a written note or an email to keep communication open, letting the buyer know you are ready and waiting to be of service.

FOLLOW-UP

The word *close* can be misleading because the point at which the prospect accepts the seller's offer is where much of the real work of selling begins. In today's competitive environment, the most successful salespeople make sure that today's customers will also be tomorrow's.

It is not enough to close the sale and move on. Relationship selling involves reinforcing the purchase decision and ensuring the company delivers the highest-quality merchandise. As a salesperson, you must also ensure that customer service needs are met and that satisfaction results from all of a customer's dealings with your company. Otherwise, some other company may get the next order.

These postsale activities, which often determine whether a person will become a repeat customer, constitute the sales **follow-up**. Sales experts believe in a wide array of follow-up techniques, ranging from information folders to holiday cards to online greetings. Some suggest phone calls at regular intervals. Others prefer automatic email reminders when it is time to renew or reorder. At the very least, however, you should contact customers to find out if they are satisfied with their purchases. This step allows you to psychologically reinforce the customer's original decision to buy. It also gives you an opportunity to correct any problems and ensure the next sale. Follow-up helps strengthen the bond you are trying to build with customers in relationship selling. You have probably experienced follow-up as a customer—if your auto dealership called to see if you were satisfied with recent service or if your doctor's office phoned to find out if you were feeling better.

follow-up Postsale activities that often determine whether an individual who has made a recent purchase will become a repeat customer.

> ⊕ **ASSESSMENT CHECK**
>
> 5.1 Identify the seven steps of the sales process.
>
> 5.2 Why is follow-up important to the sales effort?

MANAGING THE SALES EFFORT

The overall direction and control of the personal selling effort are in the hands of a firm's sales managers. In a typical geographic sales structure, a district or divisional sales manager might report to a regional or zone manager. This manager in turn reports to a national sales manager or vice president of sales.

Currently, there are about 342,100 sales managers in the United States.[27] The sales manager's job requires a unique blend of administrative and sales skills, depending on the specific level in the sales hierarchy. Sales skills are particularly important for first-level sales managers, because they are

 Identify the seven basic functions of a sales manager. 6

involved daily in the continuing process of training and directly leading the sales force. But as people rise in the sales management hierarchy, they require more managerial skills and fewer sales skills to perform well. Candace Plourd recently became the inside sales manager for Jupiter Systems, which makes digital display walls and networked PCs. Her earlier career was in sales, working for Digital Equipment and Compaq. At both companies, she worked in channel sales as well as with end users, managing major accounts like CVS, American Express, and John Deere. At both companies, she gained experience in delivering exceptional service to high-profile customers. In her role as inside sales manager for Jupiter Systems, she works with the company's regional sales managers and will be involved in activities related to customer satisfaction.[28]

Sales force management links individual salespeople to general management. The sales manager performs seven basic managerial functions: (1) recruitment and selection, (2) training, (3) organization, (4) supervision, (5) motivation, (6) compensation, and (7) evaluation and control. Sales managers perform these tasks in a demanding and complex environment. They must manage an increasingly diverse sales force. Women account for slightly more than half of U.S. professional salespeople, and their numbers are growing at a faster rate than that for men. As the workforce composition continues to change, an even more diverse blend of people will be needed to fill a growing number of sales positions.[29]

RECRUITMENT AND SELECTION

Recruiting and selecting successful salespeople are among the sales manager's greatest challenges. After all, these workers will collectively determine just how successful the sales manager is. New salespeople—like you—might come from colleges and universities, trade and business schools, the military, other companies, and even the firm's current nonsales staff. A successful sales career offers satisfaction in all of the following five areas a person generally considers when deciding on a profession:

1. *Opportunity for advancement.* Studies have shown that successful sales representatives advance rapidly in most companies.

2. *Potential for high earnings.* Salespeople have the opportunity to earn a very comfortable living.

3. *Personal satisfaction.* A salesperson derives satisfaction from achieving success in a competitive environment and helping customers satisfy their wants and needs.

4. *Job security.* Selling provides a high degree of job security because there is always a need for good salespeople.

5. *Independence and variety.* Salespeople often work independently, calling on customers in their territory. They have the freedom to make important decisions about meeting their customers' needs and frequently report that no two workdays are the same.

Careful selection of salespeople is important for two reasons. First, a company invests a substantial amount of time and money in the selection process. Second, hiring mistakes can damage relationships with customers and overall performance and are costly to correct.

During an interview, recruiters look for enthusiasm, organizational skills, sociability, and other traits.

Abel Mitja Varela/iStockphoto.com

Most large firms use a specific seven-step process in selecting sales personnel: application screening, initial interview, in-depth interview, testing, reference checks, physical examination, and hiring decision. An application screening is typically followed by an initial interview. If the applicant looks promising, an in-depth interview takes place. During the interview, a sales manager looks for the person's enthusiasm, organizational skills, ambition, persuasiveness, ability to follow instructions, and sociability.

Next, the company may administer aptitude, interest, and knowledge tests. One popular testing approach is the assessment center. This technique uses situational exercises, group discussions, and various job simulations, allowing the sales manager to measure a candidate's skills, knowledge, and ability. Assessment centers enable managers to see what potential salespeople can do rather than what they say they can do. Before hiring a candidate, the firm checks references, reviews company policies, and may request a physical examination.

TRAINING

To shape new sales recruits into an efficient sales organization, managers must conduct an effective training program. The principal methods used in sales training are on-the-job training, individual instruction, in-house classes, and external seminars.

Popular training techniques include instructional videos or DVDs, lectures, role-playing exercises, and interactive computer programs. Simulations can help salespeople improve their selling techniques. Many firms supplement their training by enrolling salespeople in executive development programs at local colleges and by hiring specialists to teach customized training programs. In other instances, sales reps attend courses and workshops developed by outside companies. Best Buy recently received some negative press for training its salespeople to push extended warranties on customers, which many felt caused customer service to suffer. See the "Solving an Ethical Controversy" feature for opposing views on this strategy.

SOLVING AN ETHICAL CONTROVERSY

When the Sale Doesn't Benefit the Customer

Although reputable sources like *Consumer Reports* say most product failures occur late in a product's life, making extended warranties a poor value, selling such "protection" is so profitable that many companies push it anyway, at prices that run to 20 percent of the item's purchase price or more. Best Buy is one retailer that aggressively pitches warranties for electronics on the grounds that products break, customers handle them clumsily, or the plans are cheap and save time and money. Some critics insist such plans are scams.

Is it appropriate for companies to sell extended warranties that might not be in the customer's best interest?

PRO 👍

1. Some customers want the "peace of mind" of knowing they can repair or replace an item in a few years at no extra charge.

2. Buyers will make up their own minds about what is a good value.

CON 👎

1. Most product failures occur so early that repair is still covered under the manufacturer's own short-term warranty.

2. Some extended warranties are so overpriced that it's cheaper to buy a replacement item.

Summary:

For consumers, there doesn't seem to be a clear-cut answer about whether to spend the extra money to buy extended warranties. In the meantime, many retailers continue to provide their salespeople with incentives to sell extended warranties because of the revenue the warranties generate for the company.

Sources: "How to Beware of Extended Warranty Scams," *eHow.com,* accessed December 4, 2012, www.ehow.com; Damon Darlin, "Don't Worry, Be Happy: The Warranty Psychology," *The New York Times,* accessed December 4, 2012, www .nytimes.com; Marianne Goldstein, "Are Extended Warranties Worth the Money?" *CBS News,* accessed December 4, 2012, www.cbsnews.com; Jim Henry, "Buyer Beware: Common Scams Related to Extended Warranties," *Forbes,* accessed December 4, 2012, www.forbes.com; Rick Aristotle Munarriz, "Best Buy's Turnaround Plan Sends Retailer in the Wrong Direction," *The Motley Fool,* accessed December 4, 2012, www.dailyfinance.com; Rafi Mohammed, "Consumer Reports Is Wrong about Extended Warranties," *Harvard Business Review* Blog Network, accessed December 4, 2012, http://blogs.hbr.org; Larry Downes, "The People vs. Best Buy Round Two," *Forbes,* accessed December 4, 2012, www.forbes.com.

Although sales meetings are often packed with a variety of topics, they can be an excellent vehicle for sales training. New York–based Santinelli International, the manufacturer of lens edging equipment to the optical industry, uses its national sales meeting as a platform for training. The practical advice and give-and-take in such sessions motivates colleagues to reassess their own skills and try new techniques.[30]

Ongoing sales training is important for all salespeople, even veterans. Sales managers often conduct this type of training informally, traveling with field reps and then offering sales-related advice. Like sales meetings, classes and workshops are other ways to reinforce training. Mentoring is also a key tool in training new salespeople.

ORGANIZATION

Sales managers are responsible for the organization of the field sales force. General organizational alignments—usually made by top marketing management—may be based on geography, products, types of customers, or some combination of these factors. Figure 17.3 presents a streamlined organizational chart illustrating each of these alignments.

A product sales organization is likely to have a specialized sales force for each major category of the firm's products. This approach is common among B2B companies that market large numbers of highly technical, complex products sold through different marketing channels.

Firms that market similar products throughout large territories often use geographic specialization. Multinational corporations may have different sales divisions on different continents and in different countries. A geographic organization may also be combined with one of the other organizational methods.

However, many companies are moving away from using territorial sales reps as they adopt customer-focused sales forces. For example, a single territory that contains two major customers might be redefined so that the same sales rep covers both customers. Customer-oriented organizations use different sales force strategies for each major type of customer served. Some firms assign separate sales forces for their consumer and organizational customers. Others have sales forces for specific industries, such as financial services, educational, and automotive. Sales forces can also be organized by customer size, with a separate sales force assigned to large, medium, and small accounts.

national accounts organization
Promotional effort in which a dedicated sales team is assigned to a firm's major customers to provide sales and service needs.

Many firms using a customer-oriented structure adopt a national accounts organization. This format strengthens a firm's relationship with its largest customers by assigning senior sales personnel or sales teams to major accounts. Organizing by national accounts helps sales representatives develop cooperation among departments to meet special needs of the firm's most important customers. An example of national account selling is the relationship of Walmart and its major vendors. SC Johnson, Unilever, H. J. Heinz, Johnson & Johnson, Kimberly-Clark, Nestlé, Hormel, and Colgate Palmolive are just some of the companies that have sales offices near Walmart's headquarters in Bentonville, Arkansas.

As companies expand their market coverage across national borders, they could use a variant of national account sales teams. These global account teams may be staffed by local sales representatives

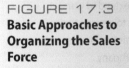

FIGURE 17.3
Basic Approaches to Organizing the Sales Force

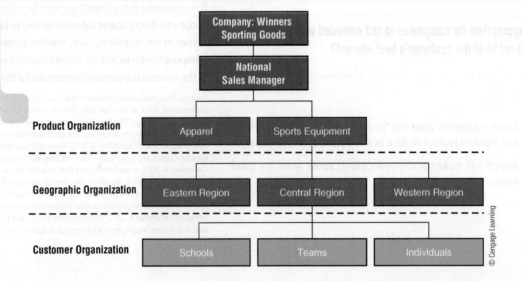

© Cengage Learning

in the countries in which a company is operating. In other instances, the firm selects highly trained sales executives from its domestic operations. In either case, specialized training is critical to the success of a company's global sales force.

The individual sales manager also must organize the sales territories within his or her area of responsibility. Factors like sales potential, strengths and weaknesses of available personnel, and workloads are considered in territory allocation decisions.

SUPERVISION

Sales managers have differing opinions about the supervision of a sales force. Individuals and situations vary, so it is impossible to write a recipe for the exact amount of supervision needed in all cases. However, a concept known as span of control helps provide some general guidelines. Span of control refers to the number of sales representatives who report to first-level sales managers. The optimal span of control is affected by such factors as complexity of work activities, ability of the individual sales manager, degree of interdependence among individual salespeople, and the extent of training each salesperson receives. A 6-to-1 ratio has been suggested as the optimal span of control for first-level sales managers supervising technical or industrial salespeople. In contrast, a 10-to-1 ratio is recommended if sales representatives are calling on wholesale and retail accounts.

span of control
Number of representatives who report to first-level sales managers.

MOTIVATION

What motivates salespeople to perform their best? The sales manager is responsible for finding the answer to this question. The sales process involves problem solving, which sometimes includes frustration—particularly when a sale is delayed or falls through. Information sharing, recognition, bonuses, incentives, and benefits can all be used to help defray frustration and motivate a sales staff. Developing an enthusiastic sales staff who are happy at their jobs is the goal of the sales manager. Motivation is an important part of a company's success.

Creating a positive, motivating environment doesn't necessarily mean instituting complex or expensive incentive programs. Monetary reward—cash—is often considered king. But sometimes simple recognition—a thank-you, a dinner, a year-end award—can go a long way. It is important for the sales manager to figure out what types of incentives will be most effective with his or her particular group of employees. Some firms go all out, dangling luxury items like computers, digital cameras, or trips in front of the sales force as rewards. A Caribbean cruise, a trip to Disney World, or a weekend in Las Vegas could be the carrot that works, particularly if family members are included. Some firms purchase gift cards from retailers, such as L.L.Bean or Lowe's, to distribute to sales staff who perform well.

But not all incentive programs are effective at motivating employees. A program with targets set too high, that isn't publicized, or that allows only certain sales personnel to participate, can actually backfire. So it is important for sales management to plan carefully for an incentive program to succeed.

Sales managers can also gain insight into the subject of motivation by studying the various theories of motivation developed over the years. One theory that has been applied effectively to sales force motivation is expectancy theory, which states that motivation depends on the expectations an individual has of his or her ability to perform the job and on how performance relates to attaining rewards the individual values.

expectancy theory
Theory that motivation depends on an individual's expectations of his or her ability to perform a job and how that performance relates to attaining a desired reward.

Sales managers can apply the expectancy theory of motivation by following a five-step process:

1. Let each salesperson know in detail what is expected in terms of selling goals, service standards, and other areas of performance. Rather than setting goals just once a year, many firms do so on a semiannual, quarterly, or even monthly basis.

2. Make the work valuable by assessing the needs, values, and abilities of each salesperson and then assigning appropriate tasks.

3. Make the work achievable. As leaders, sales managers must inspire self-confidence in their salespeople and offer training and coaching to reassure them.

4. Provide immediate and specific feedback, guiding those who need improvement and giving positive feedback to those who do well.

5. Offer rewards each salesperson values, whether it is an incentive as described previously, opportunity for advancement, or a bonus.

COMPENSATION

Money is an important part of any person's job, and the salesperson is no exception. So deciding how best to compensate the sales force can be a critical factor in motivation. Sales compensation can be based on a commission, a straight salary, or a combination of both. Bonuses based on end-of-year results are another popular form of compensation. The increasing popularity of team selling has also forced companies to set up reward programs to recognize performance of business units and teams. Today, about 25 percent of firms reward business-unit performance.

A **commission** is a payment tied directly to the sales or profits a salesperson achieves. A salesperson might receive a 5 percent commission on all sales up to a specified quota and a 7 percent commission on sales beyond that point. This approach to sales compensation is increasingly popular. But while commissions reinforce selling incentives, they may cause some sales force members to overlook nonselling activities like completing sales reports, delivering promotion materials, and servicing existing accounts. In addition, salespeople who operate entirely on commission may become too aggressive in their approach to potential customers, which could backfire.

A **salary** is a fixed payment made periodically to an employee. A firm that bases compensation on salaries rather than commissions might pay a salesperson a set amount every week, twice a month, or once a month. A company must balance benefits and disadvantages in paying predetermined salaries to compensate managers and sales personnel. A straight salary plan gives management more control over how sales personnel allocate their efforts, but it may reduce the incentive to find new markets and land new accounts.

Many firms find it's best to develop compensation programs that combine features of both salary and commission plans. A new salesperson often receives a base salary while in training, even if he or she moves to full commission later on. If the salesperson does a lot of driving as part of the job, he or she may receive a vehicle. If the person works from home, there might be an allowance toward setting up an office there.

Total compensation packages vary according to industry, with the finance, insurance, and real estate industries coming out on top, followed closely by general services. They also vary according to years of experience in sales. Figure 17.4 reflects the findings of a recent pay survey of *account managers*—another name for a salesperson responsible for one or more customers, or *accounts*. The data show how account managers' median base pay, bonus, and commissions vary by years of experience.

commission Incentive compensation directly related to the sales or profits achieved by a salesperson.

salary Fixed compensation payment made periodically to an employee.

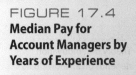

FIGURE 17.4
Median Pay for Account Managers by Years of Experience

Source: Data from Account Manager Sales Salary, *PayScale*, accessed December 4, 2012, www.payscale.com.

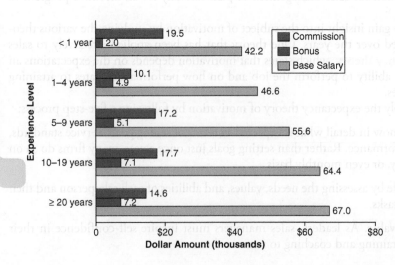

EVALUATION AND CONTROL

Perhaps the most difficult tasks required of sales managers are evaluation and control. Sales managers are responsible for setting standards and choosing the best methods for measuring sales performance. Sales volume, profitability, and changes in market share are the usual means of evaluating sales effectiveness. They typically involve the use of **sales quotas**—specified sales or profit targets that the firm expects salespeople to achieve. A particular sales representative might be expected to generate sales of $2.25 million in his or her territory during a given year. In many cases, the quota is tied to the compensation system. Technology has greatly improved the ability of sales managers to monitor the effectiveness of their sales staffs. Databases help sales managers to quickly divide revenues by salesperson, account, and geographic area.

In today's marketing environment, other measures, such as customer satisfaction, profit contribution, share of product-category sales, and customer retention, also come into play. This is the result of three factors:

1. A long-term orientation that results from emphasis on building customer relationships.

2. The fact that evaluations based on sales volume alone may lead to overselling and inventory problems that may damage customer relationships.

3. The need to encourage sales representatives to develop new accounts, provide customer service, and emphasize new products. Sales quotas tend to put focus on short-term selling goals rather than long-term relationships.

The sales manager must follow a formal system that includes a consistent series of decisions. This way, the manager can make fair and accurate evaluations. The system helps the sales manager answer three general questions:

1. *Where does each salesperson's performance rank relative to predetermined standards?* This comparison takes into consideration any uncontrollable variables on sales performance, such as a natural disaster or unforeseen change in the industry. Each adjusted rank is stated as a percentage of the standard.

2. *What are the salesperson's strong points?* The manager might list areas of the salesperson's performance in which he or she has performed above the standard. Or strong points could be placed in such categories as technical ability, processes, and end results.

3. *What are the salesperson's weak points?* No one likes to hear criticism, but when it is offered constructively, it can be motivation to improve performance. The manager and employee should establish specific objectives for improvement and set a timetable for judging the employee's improvement.

In completing the evaluation summary, the sales manager follows a set procedure so all employees are treated equally:

- Each aspect of sales performance for which a standard exists should be measured separately. This helps prevent the so-called halo effect, in which the rating given on one factor influences those on other performance variables.

- Each salesperson should be judged on the basis of actual sales performance rather than potential ability. This is why rankings are important in the evaluation.

- Sales managers must judge each salesperson on the basis of sales performance for the entire period under consideration, rather than for a few particular incidents.

- The evaluation should be reviewed by a third party, such as the manager's boss or a human resources manager, for completeness and objectivity.

Once the evaluation is complete, both manager and salesperson should focus on positive action—whether it is a drive toward new goals or correcting a negative situation. An evaluation should be motivation for improved performance.

sales quota Level of expected sales for a territory, product, customer, or salesperson against which actual results are compared.

⊕ ASSESSMENT CHECK

6.1 What are the seven basic functions performed by a sales manager?

6.2 Define *span of control*.

6.3 What are the three main questions a sales manager must address as part of a salesperson's evaluation?

ETHICAL ISSUES IN SALES

7 Explain the role of ethical behavior in personal selling.

Promotional activities can raise ethical questions, and personal selling is no exception. A difficult economy or highly competitive environment may tempt some salespeople—particularly those new to the business—to behave in ways they might later regret. They might use the company car for a family trip. They might give personal or expensive gifts to customers. They might try to sell a product they know is not right for a particular customer's needs. But today's experienced, highly professional salespeople know long-term success requires a strong code of ethics. They also know a single breach of ethics could have a devastating effect on their careers.

Sales managers and top executives can do a lot to foster a corporate culture that encourages honesty and ethical behavior. Here are some characteristics of such a culture:

- *Employees understand what is expected of them.* A written code of ethics—which should be reviewed by all employees—in addition to ethics training helps educate employees in how to conduct ethical business.

- *Open communication.* Employees who feel comfortable talking with their supervisors are more apt to ask questions if they are uncertain about situations or decisions and to report any violations they come across.

- *Managers lead by example.* Workers naturally emulate the ethical behavior of managers. A sales manager who is honest with customers, doesn't accept inappropriate gifts, and leaves the company car at home during vacation is likely to be imitated by his or her sales staff.

Regardless of corporate culture, every salesperson is responsible for his or her own behavior and relationship with customers. If, as a new salesperson, you find yourself uncertain about a decision, ask yourself the questions that follow. The answers should help you make the ethical choice.

ASSESSMENT CHECK

7.1 Why is it important for salespeople to maintain ethical behavior?

7.2 What are the characteristics of companies that foster corporate cultures that encourage ethical behavior?

1. Does my decision affect anyone other than myself and the bottom line?

2. Is my success based on making the sale or creating a loyal customer?

3. Is my dealings with a customer in their best interest and not exploiting their trust?

4. What price will I pay for this decision?

SALES PROMOTION

8 Describe the role of sales promotion in the promotional mix, and identify the different types of sales promotions.

sales promotion
Marketing activities other than personal selling, advertising, and publicity that enhance consumer purchasing and dealer effectiveness.

Sales promotion includes marketing activities other than personal selling, advertising, and publicity designed to enhance consumer purchasing and dealer effectiveness. In the United States, companies have been giving away trinkets and premiums for more than 100 years.

Sales promotion techniques were originally intended as short-term incentives aimed at producing an immediate response: a purchase. Today, however, marketers recognize sales promotion as an integral part of the overall marketing plan, and the focus has shifted from short-term goals to long-term objectives of building brand equity and maintaining continuing purchases. A frequent-flyer program enables a new airline to build a base of loyal customers. A frequent-stay program allows a hotel chain to attract regular guests.

Both retailers and manufacturers use sales promotions to offer consumers extra incentives to buy. These promotions are likely to stress price advantages, giveaways, or special offerings. The general objectives of sales promotion are to speed up the sales process and increase sales volume. Promotions can also help build loyalty. Through a consumer promotion, a marketer encourages consumers to try the product, use more of it, and buy it again. The firm also hopes to foster sales of related items and increase impulse purchases. Holiday specials are one type of sales promotion. On

Retailers often use sales promotions to offer consumers extra incentives to buy, especially around the holidays.

the day after Christmas in one recent year, Target offered 50 percent off on women's and children's clothing as well as on holiday decorations. The store also had extended hours, opening at 7:00 am and closing at 11:00 pm.[31]

Today, consumers have many more choices among products than in the past, and, for this reason, many marketers create special programs to build loyalty among their customers. However, with loyalty programs no longer unique, marketing and sales professionals work to build loyalty among their customers by managing customer relationships and regularly evaluating those relationships to determine how they can enhance them.[32]

Because sales promotion is so important to a marketing effort, an entire promotion industry exists to offer expert assistance in its use and to design unique promotions, just as the entire advertising industry offers similar services for advertisers. These companies, like advertising agencies, provide other firms with assistance in promoting their goods and services. Figure 17.5 shows current spending by companies for different types of promotions, many of which are conducted by these firms.

Sales promotions often produce their best results when combined with other marketing activities. Ads

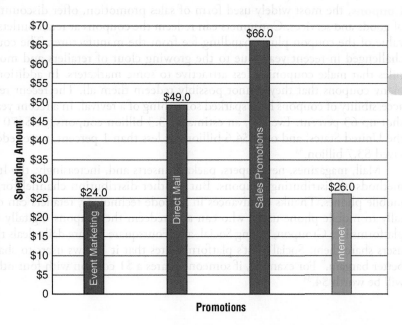

Promotions

Spending Amount: Event Marketing $24.0, Direct Mail $49.0, Sales Promotions $66.0, Internet $26.0

FIGURE 17.5
Current Spending by Companies for Different Types of Promotions (in billions)

Source: Data from ZenithOptimedia, "Advertising Expenditure Forecasts: Major Media and Marketing Services," *Advertising Age Data Center*, www.adage.com, accessed December 4, 2012.

create awareness, while sales promotions lead to trial or purchase. After a presentation, a salesperson may offer a potential customer a discount coupon for the good or service. Promotions encourage immediate action because they impose limited time frames. Discount coupons and rebates usually have expiration dates. In addition, sales promotions produce measurable results, making it relatively easy for marketers to evaluate their effectiveness. If more people buy shoes during a buy-one-pair-get-one-free promotion at a shoe store, its owners know the promotion was successful.

It is important to understand what sales promotions can and cannot do. They can encourage interest in both new and mature products, help introduce new products, encourage trial and repeat purchases, increase usage rates, neutralize competition, and reinforce advertising and personal selling efforts. On the other hand, sales promotions cannot overcome poor brand images, product deficiencies, or poor training for salespeople. While sales promotions increase volume in the short term, they may not lead to sales and profit growth in the long run.

Sales promotion techniques may serve all members of a marketing channel. In addition, manufacturers may use trade promotion methods to promote their products to resellers. Promotions are usually employed selectively. Sales promotion techniques include the following consumer-oriented promotions: coupons, refunds, samples, bonus packs, premiums, contests, sweepstakes, and specialty advertising. Trade-oriented promotions include trade allowances, point-of-purchase advertising, trade shows, dealer incentives, contests, and training programs.

CONSUMER-ORIENTED SALES PROMOTIONS

In the promotion industry, marketers use all types of sales promotions, including games, contests, sweepstakes, and coupons to persuade new and existing customers to try their products. Consumer-oriented sales promotions encourage repurchases by rewarding current users, boosting sales of complementary products, and increasing impulse purchases. These promotions also attract consumer attention in the midst of advertising clutter.

It's important for marketers to use sales promotions selectively; if they are overused, consumers begin to expect price discounts at all times, which ultimately diminishes brand equity. The following sections describe the various forms of consumer-oriented sales promotions.

Coupons and Refunds

coupon Sales promotion technique that offers a discount on the purchase price of goods or services.

Coupons, the most widely used form of sales promotion, offer discounts on the purchase price of goods and services. Consumers can redeem the coupons at retail outlets, which receive the face value of the coupon plus a handling fee from the manufacturer. The coupon industry has been challenged in recent years due to the growing clout of retailers and more complex accounting rules that make couponing less attractive to some marketers. In addition, consumers receive so many coupons that they cannot possibly redeem them all. The recent recession and the mobile accessibility of coupons have sparked something of a revival. In a recent year, coupon redemptions shot up 63 percent. Even so, an estimated 3.3 billion coupons, or $470 billion, were offered in the United States, and only $4.6 billion, or less than 1 percent, were redeemed. Still, consumers saved $3.7 billion.[33]

Mail, magazines, newspapers, package inserts and, increasingly, the Internet are the standard methods of distributing coupons. But another distribution channel for coupons has emerged: mobile phones. Thanks to advances in barcode technology, retailers can distribute coupons digitally to mobile phone users, who can also redeem the coupons digitally when they shop. Social platforms like Groupon, Living Social, and Foursquare feature daily deals that often improve when users share them. SocialTwist's platform states that it "allows users to share in order to receive a better bargain." For example, if someone shares a $1 coupon with four other people, that coupon will be worth $4.[34]

Refunds, or rebates, offer cash back to consumers who send in proof of purchasing one or more products. Refunds help packaged-goods companies increase purchase rates, promote multiple purchases, and reward product users. Although many consumers find the refund forms too bothersome to complete, plenty still do.

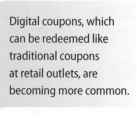

© Tyler Olson/Shutterstock.com

Samples, Bonus Packs, and Premiums

Marketers are increasingly adopting the "try it, you'll like it" approach as an effective means of getting consumers to try and then purchase their goods and services. **Sampling** refers to the free distribution of a product in an attempt to obtain future sales. Samples may be distributed door-to-door, by mail, online, via demonstrations in stores or at events, or by including them in packages with other products.

Sampling produces a higher response rate than most other promotions. In supermarkets, an estimated 70 million consumers receive samples of some kind each quarter, with one-third making a product purchase during the same shopping trip. In a recent year, total annual spending on this sales promotion technique topped $2.2 billion.[35]

With sampling, marketers can target potential customers and be certain the product reaches them. Sampling provides an especially useful way to promote new or unusual products, because it gives the consumer a direct product experience.

A major disadvantage of traditional sampling is the high cost involved. Not only must the marketer give away small quantities of a product that might otherwise have generated revenues through regular sales, but the market is also in effect closed for the time it takes consumers to use up the samples. In addition, the marketer may encounter problems in distributing the samples. Hellman's marketers once annoyed consumers instead of pleasing them when the firm distributed sample packets of Italian and French salad dressing in home-delivered copies of *The New York Times*. Many of the packets burst when the papers hit the driveways.

A recent sampling method is an alternative to the traditional trial sizes that companies send through the mail. A company called Young America, together with Citi Prepaid Services, is formulating a prepaid card. At stores, consumers can redeem the card for almost any type of full-size product, including foods, beverages, laundry detergent, or even light bulbs. This new method "not only reduces shipping costs and packaging waste, but it also significantly increases the ability to build brand awareness," said the CEO of Young America.[36]

A **bonus pack** is a specially packaged item that gives the purchaser a larger quantity at the regular price. For instance, Quaker recently offered two free extra bars in every box of its Chewy Granola Bars. **Premiums** are items given free or at reduced cost with purchases of other products. For example, Clairol recently offered its Natural Instincts Hair Color with a premium of a 12-ounce bottle of Pantene shampoo. Premiums have proven effective in motivating consumers to try new products or different brands. A premium should have some relationship with the product or brand it accompanies, though. For example, a home improvement center might offer free measuring tapes to its customers.

Contests and Sweepstakes

Firms often sponsor contests and sweepstakes to introduce new goods and services and attract additional customers. **Contests** require entrants to complete a task, such as solving a puzzle or answering questions in a trivia quiz, and they may also require proofs of purchase. **Sweepstakes,**

refund Cash given back to consumers who send in proof of purchase for one or more products.

sampling Free distribution of a product in an attempt to obtain future sales; process of selecting survey respondents or research participants.

bonus pack Specially packaged item that gives the purchaser a larger quantity at the regular price.

premium Item given free or at a reduced cost with purchases of other products.

contest Sales promotion technique that requires entrants to complete a task, such as solving a puzzle or answering questions on a quiz, for a chance to win a prize.

sweepstakes Sales promotion technique in which prize winners are selected by chance.

on the other hand, choose winners by chance, so no product purchase is necessary. They are more popular with consumers than contests because they do not take as much effort for consumers to enter. Marketers like them, too, because they are inexpensive to run, and the number of winners is predetermined. With some contests, the sponsors cannot predict the number of people who will correctly complete the puzzles or gather the right number of symbols from scratch-off cards.

Marketers are increasingly turning to the Internet for contests and sweepstakes because of its relatively low cost and ability to provide data immediately. Interactivity is also a key part of the online experience: as consumers become more engaged in the contest or sweepstakes event, they also build a relationship with the firm's products. Friendly Planet Travel, which conducts group tours around the world, recently held a sweepstakes as part of its "Win the World" Facebook sweepstakes. The prize was a free, all-inclusive week-long vacation in Ireland. Contestants entered a contact on Friendly Planet's Facebook page. If a contestant shared the page with a Facebook friend, his or her name was entered again for another chance at winning.[37] Given the number of recent court rulings and legal restrictions, the use of contests requires careful administration. A firm contemplating this promotional technique might consider the services of online promotion specialists like WebStakes or NetStakes.

Specialty Advertising

The origin of specialty advertising has been traced to the Middle Ages, when artisans gave wooden pegs bearing their names to prospects, who drove them into the walls at home to serve as convenient hangers for armor. Corporations began putting their names on a variety of products in the late 1800s, as newspapers and print shops explored new methods to earn additional revenues from their expensive printing presses. Today, just about everyone owns a cap or T-shirt with the name or logo of a company, organization, or product displayed on it.

specialty advertising
Sales promotion technique that places the advertiser's name, address, and advertising message on useful articles that are then distributed to target consumers.

Specialty advertising is a sales promotion technique that places the advertiser's name, address, and advertising message on useful articles that are then distributed to target consumers. Wearable products are the most popular, accounting for nearly a third of specialty advertising sales. Pens, mugs, glassware, and calendars are other popular forms.

Advertising specialties help reinforce previous or future advertising and sales messages. Consumers like these giveaways, which generate stronger responses to direct mail, resulting in three times the dollar volume of sales compared with direct mail alone. Companies use this form of promotion to highlight store openings and new products, motivate salespeople, increase visits to trade show booths, and remind customers about their products.

TRADE-ORIENTED PROMOTIONS

trade promotion Sales promotion that appeals to marketing intermediaries rather than consumers.

Sales promotion techniques can also contribute effectively to campaigns aimed at retailers and wholesalers. Trade promotion is sales promotion that appeals to marketing intermediaries rather than final consumers. Marketers use trade promotions in push strategies by encouraging resellers to stock new products, continue to carry existing ones, and promote both effectively to consumers. The typical firm spends about half of its promotional budget on trade promotion—as much money as it spends on advertising and consumer-oriented sales promotions combined. Successful trade promotions offer financial incentives. They require careful timing and attention to costs and are easy to implement by retailers. These promotions should bring quick results and improve retail sales.

Trade Allowances

trade allowance
Financial incentive offered to wholesalers and retailers that purchase or promote specific products.

Among the most common trade promotion methods are trade allowances—special financial incentives offered to wholesalers and retailers that purchase or promote specific products. These offers take various forms. A buying allowance gives retailers a discount on goods. They include off-invoice allowances through which retailers deduct specified amounts from their invoices or receive free goods, such as one free case for every 10 ordered. When a manufacturer offers a promotional allowance, it agrees to pay the reseller a certain amount to cover the costs of special promotional displays or extensive advertising that features the manufacturer's product. The goal is to increase sales to consumers by encouraging resellers to promote their products effectively.

Point-of-Purchase Advertising

A display or other promotion located near the site of the actual buying decision is known as **point-of-purchase (POP) advertising**. This method of sales promotion capitalizes on the fact that nearly two-thirds of shoppers make their purchase decisions as they walk through a store, so it encourages retailers to improve on-site merchandising. Product suppliers assist the retailer by creating special displays designed to stimulate sales of the promoted item.

Freestanding POP promotions often appear at the ends of shopping aisles. On a typical trip to the supermarket, you might see a POP display for Disney videos, Coppertone sunscreen, or Duracell batteries. Warehouse-style retailers, such as Home Depot and Sam's Club, along with Staples and Kmart, all use POP advertising displays frequently. Electronic kiosks, which allow consumers to place orders for items not available in the store, have begun to transform the POP display industry, as creators of these displays look for ways to involve consumers more actively as well as entertain them.

point-of-purchase (POP) advertising Display or other promotion placed near the site of the actual buying decision.

Trade Shows

To influence resellers and other members of the distribution channel, many marketers participate in **trade shows**. These shows are often organized by industry trade associations; frequently, they are part of these associations' annual meetings or conventions. Vendors who serve the industries display and demonstrate their products for attendees. Industries that hold trade shows include manufacturers of sporting goods, medical equipment, electronics, automobiles, clothing, and home furnishings. Service industries include hair styling, health care, travel, and restaurant franchises.

trade show Product exhibition organized by industry trade associations to showcase goods and services.

Because of the expense involved in trade shows, a company must assess the value of these shows on several criteria, such as direct sales, any increase in product awareness, image building, and any contribution to the firm's marketing communications efforts. Trade shows give especially effective opportunities to introduce new products and generate sales leads. Some types of shows reach ultimate consumers as well as channel members. Home, recreation, and automobile shows, for instance, allow businesses to display and demonstrate home improvement, recreation, and other consumer products.

Dealer Incentives, Contests, and Training Programs

Manufacturers run dealer incentive programs and contests to reward retailers and their salespeople who increase sales and, more generally, to promote specific products. These channel members receive incentives for performing promotion-related tasks and can win contests by reaching sales goals. Manufacturers may offer major prizes to resellers like trips to exotic places. **Push money**—which retailers commonly refer to as *spiffs*—is another incentive that gives retail salespeople cash rewards for every unit of a product they sell. This benefit increases the likelihood that the salesperson will try to persuade a customer to buy the product rather than a competing brand.

push money Cash reward paid to retail salespeople for every unit of a product they sell.

For more expensive and highly complex products, manufacturers often provide specialized training for retail salespeople. This background helps sales personnel explain features, competitive advantages, and other information to consumers. Training can be provided in several ways: a manufacturer's sales representative can conduct training sessions during regular sales calls, or the firm can distribute sales literature and DVDs.

 ASSESSMENT CHECK

8.1 Define *sales promotion*.

8.2 Identify at least four types of consumer-oriented sales promotions.

8.3 Identify at least three types of trade-oriented sales promotions.

STRATEGIC IMPLICATIONS OF MARKETING IN THE 21ST CENTURY

Today's salespeople are a new breed. Richly nourished in a tradition of sales, their roles are strengthened even further through technology. However, as many companies are discovering, nothing can replace the power of personal selling in generating sales and building strong, loyal customer relationships.

Salespeople today are a critical link in developing relationships between the customer and the company. They communicate customer needs and wants to coworkers in various units within an organization, enabling a cooperative, companywide effort in improving product offerings and better satisfying individuals within the target market. For salespeople, the greatest benefit of electronic technologies is the ability to share knowledge when it is needed with those who need to know, including customers, suppliers, and employees.

Because buyers are now more sophisticated, demanding more rapid and lower-cost transactions, salespeople must be quick and creative as they find solutions to their customers' problems. Product lifecycles are accelerating, and customers who demand more are likely to switch from one product to another. Recognizing the long-term impact of keeping satisfied buyers—those who make repeat and cross-purchases and provide referrals—versus dissatisfied buyers, organizations are increasingly training their sales forces to provide superior customer service and rewarding them for increasing satisfaction levels.

The traditional skills of a salesperson included persuasion, selling ability, and product knowledge. But today's sales professionals are also likely to possess strong communication and problem-solving skills. Earlier generations of sales personnel tended to be self-driven; today's sales professional is more likely to be a team player as well as a customer advocate who serves his or her buyers by solving problems.

The modern professional salesperson is greatly assisted by the judicious use of both consumer- and trade-oriented sales promotions. Sales promotion is often overlooked in discussions of high-profile advertising; the typical firm allocates more promotional dollars for sales promotion than for advertising. The proven effectiveness of sales promotion makes it a widely used promotional mix component for most marketers.

Get online now for additional learning tools to help you master your marketing knowledge—visit WWW.CENGAGEBRAIN.COM today!

REVIEW OF CHAPTER OBJECTIVES

1 Describe the role of today's salesperson.

Today's salesperson seeks to form long-lasting relationships with customers by providing high levels of customer service rather than going for the quick sale. Firms have begun to integrate their computer and communications technologies into the sales function, so people involved in personal selling have an expanded role.

2 Describe the four sales channels.

Over-the-counter (retail) selling takes place in a retail location and usually involves providing product information and completing a sale. Field selling involves making personal sales calls on customers. Under certain circumstances, telemarketing is used to provide product information and answer questions from customers who call. Inside selling relies on phone, mail, and e-marketing to provide sales and product services for customers on a continuing basis.

3 Describe the major trends in personal selling.

Companies are turning to relationship selling, consultative selling, and team selling. Relationship selling occurs when a salesperson builds a mutually beneficial relationship with a customer on a regular basis over an extended period. Consultative selling involves meeting customer needs by listening to customers, understanding and caring about their problems, paying attention to the details, and following through after the sale. Team selling occurs when the salesperson joins with specialists from other functional areas of the firm to complete the selling process.

4 Identify and briefly describe the three basic sales tasks.

Order processing is the routine handling of an order. It characterizes a sales setting in which the need is made known and is acknowledged by the customer. Creative selling is persuasion aimed at making the prospect see the value of the good or service presented. Missionary selling is indirect selling, such as making goodwill calls and providing technical or operational assistance.

5 Outline the seven steps in the sales process.

The basic steps in the sales process are prospecting and qualifying, approach, presentation, demonstration, handling objections, closing, and follow-up.

6 Identify the seven basic functions of a sales manager.

A sales manager links the sales force to other aspects of the internal and external environments. The manager's functions are recruitment and selection, training, organization, supervision, motivation, compensation, and evaluation and control.

7 Explain the role of ethical behavior in personal selling.

Ethical behavior is vital to building positive, long-term relationships with customers. Although some people believe ethical problems are inevitable, employers can do much to foster a corporate culture that encourages honesty and ethical behavior. In addition, each salesperson is responsible for his or her own behavior and relationship with customers.

8 Describe the role of sales promotion in the promotional mix, and identify the different types of sales promotions.

Sales promotion includes activities other than personal selling, advertising, and publicity designed to enhance consumer purchasing and dealer effectiveness. Sales promotion is an integral part of the overall marketing plan, intended to increase sales and build brand equity. Promotions often produce their best results when combined with other marketing activities. Consumer-oriented sales promotions include coupons, refunds, samples, bonus packs, premiums, contests and sweepstakes, and specialty advertising. Trade-oriented promotions include trade allowances, point-of-purchase (POP) advertising, trade shows, dealer incentives, contests, and training programs.

ASSESSMENT CHECK: ANSWERS

1.1 What is personal selling? Personal selling is the process of a seller's person-to-person promotional presentation to a buyer.

1.2 What is the main focus of today's salespeople? The main focus of today's salespeople is to build long-lasting relationships with customers.

2.1 What is over-the-counter selling? Over-the-counter selling describes selling in retail and some wholesale locations. Most of these transactions take place directly with customers.

2.2 What is field selling? Field selling involves making sales calls on prospective and existing customers at their businesses or homes.

2.3 Distinguish between outbound and inbound telemarketing. Outbound telemarketing takes place when a salesperson phones customers; inbound telemarketing takes place when customers call the selling firm.

3.1 Identify the three major personal selling approaches. The three major personal selling approaches are relationship selling, consultative selling, and team selling.

3.2 Distinguish between relationship selling and consultative selling. Relationship selling is a technique for building a mutually beneficial partnership with a customer. Consultative selling involves meeting customers' needs by listening to, understanding, and paying attention to their problems, then following up after a sale.

4.1 What are the three major tasks performed by salespeople? The three major tasks are order processing, creative selling, and team selling.

4.2 What are the three steps of order processing? The three steps of order processing are identifying customer needs, pointing out the need to the customer, and completing the order.

5.1 Identify the seven steps of the sales process. The seven steps of the sales process are prospecting and qualifying, approach, presentation, demonstration, handling objections, closing, and follow-up.

5.2 Why is follow-up important to the sales effort? Follow-up allows the salesperson to reinforce the customer's

purchase decision, strengthen the bond, and correct any problems.

6.1 What are the seven basic functions performed by a sales manager? The seven basic functions of a sales manager are recruitment and selection, training, organization, supervision, motivation, compensation, and evaluation and control.

6.2 Define *span of control*. Span of control refers to the number of sales representatives who report to first-level sales managers.

6.3 What are the three main questions a sales manager must address as part of a salesperson's evaluation? The three main questions a sales manager must address are the following: Where does each salesperson's performance rank relative to predetermined standards? What are the salesperson's strong points? What are the salesperson's weak points?

7.1 Why is it important for salespeople to maintain ethical behavior? Salespeople need to maintain ethical behavior, because it is vital to their firm's relationships with customers, and because they represent their company. A breach of ethics could also be detrimental to an individual's career.

7.2 What are the characteristics of companies that foster corporate cultures that encourage ethical behavior? Characteristics of corporations fostering ethical behavior include the following: employees who understand what is expected of them, open communication, and managers who lead by example.

8.1 Define *sales promotion*. Sales promotion includes marketing activities other than personal selling, advertising, and publicity designed to enhance consumer purchasing and dealer effectiveness.

8.2 Identify at least four types of consumer-oriented sales promotions. Consumer-oriented sales promotions include coupons, refunds, samples, bonus packs, premiums, contests, sweepstakes, and specialty advertising.

8.3 Identify at least three types of trade-oriented sales promotions. Trade-oriented sales promotions include trade allowances, POP advertising, trade shows, dealer incentives, contests, and training programs.

MARKETING TERMS YOU NEED TO KNOW

personal selling **570**	virtual sales team **579**	objection **584**	sampling **595**
over-the-counter selling **572**	order processing **579**	closing **584**	bonus pack **595**
field selling **573**	creative selling **580**	follow-up **585**	premium **595**
network marketing **574**	missionary selling **580**	national accounts	contest **595**
telemarketing **574**	sales incentives **580**	organization **588**	sweepstakes **595**
outbound telemarketing **574**	prospecting **582**	span of control **589**	specialty advertising **596**
inbound telemarketing **575**	qualifying **582**	expectancy theory **589**	trade promotion **596**
inside selling **575**	approach **582**	commission **590**	trade allowance **596**
relationship selling **576**	precall planning **582**	salary **590**	point-of-purchase (POP)
consultative selling **577**	presentation **583**	sales quota **591**	advertising **597**
cross-selling **577**	cold calling **583**	sales promotion **592**	trade show **597**
team selling **578**	demonstration **584**	coupon **594**	push money **597**
		refund **595**	

ASSURANCE OF LEARNING REVIEW

1. How does each of the following factors affect the decision to emphasize personal selling or advertising and sales promotion?
   a. geographic market concentration
   b. length of marketing channels
   c. degree of product technical complexity

2. Which of the four sales channels is each of the following sales-people most likely to use?
   a. salesperson in a Macy's store
   b. RE/MAX real estate agent
   c. route driver for Keebler snack foods (sells and delivers to local food retailers)
   d. technical support for HP

3. What is team selling? Describe a situation in which you think it would be effective.

4. Why is it important for a salesperson to understand order processing—regardless of the type of selling he or she is engaged in?

5. What is the role of a sales incentive?

6. Suppose you are hired as a salesperson for a firm that offers prep courses for standardized tests. Where might you find some leads?

7. What is expectancy theory? How do sales managers use it?

8. What is the role of sales promotion in the marketing effort?

9. What are the benefits of sampling? What are the drawbacks?

10. What is trade promotion? What are its objectives?

PROJECTS AND TEAMWORK EXERCISES

1. Cross-selling can be an effective way for a firm to expand. Locate an advertisement for a firm you believe could benefit from cross-selling. List ways it could offer multiple goods or services to the same customer. Then create a new ad illustrating the multiple offerings.

2. With a partner, choose one of the following sales situations. Then take turns coming up with creative ways to close the deal, with one of you playing the customer and the other playing the salesperson. Present your closing scenarios to the class.
   a. You are a sales associate at a car dealership, and a potential customer has just test-driven one of your newest models. You have handled all the customer's objections and settled on a price. You don't want the customer to leave without agreeing to purchase the car.

   b. You operate a lawn-care business and have visited several homeowners in a new development. Three of them have already agreed to give your service a try. You are meeting with the fourth and want to close that sale, too.

3. As sales representatives for a cooperative of organic farmers, you and your team are about to make a sales presentation to a national supermarket chain. List the most important messages you wish to relate and then role-play the sales presentation.

4. On your own or with a classmate, go online and research a firm like General Mills, Ford, or Burger King to find out what kinds of consumer-oriented promotions the company is conducting for its various brands or individual products. Which promotions seem the most appealing to you as a consumer? Why? Present your findings to the class.

5. With a classmate, design a specialty advertising item for one of the following companies or its products, or choose one of your own. Present your design sketches to the class.
   a. SeaWorld or Busch Gardens
   b. Dunkin' Donuts
   c. Verizon Wireless
   d. Equal Exchange coffee
   e. Apple iPad

CRITICAL-THINKING EXERCISES

1. Since the implementation of the national Do Not Call Registry, some Americans have noticed an increase in door-to-door selling as well as emails containing sales messages. As a marketer, do you think this type of selling is effective? Why or why not?

2. Green Mountain Coffee Roasters is well known for its specialty coffees, available in many retail outlets like supermarkets and convenience stores. But visit a medical office or a car dealership, and you might find it there as well—in one-cup dispensers, ready for individuals to brew while waiting. This requires personal selling to office managers, doctors, and the like. What role does relationship selling play in this situation? What kind of training might Green Mountain sales reps receive?

3. Assume that a friend asks you to solicit donations for a local charity (you pick the charity). Outline your approach and presentation as a salesperson would.

4. Why is the recruitment and selection stage of the hiring process one of a sales manager's greatest challenges?

5. Food manufacturers often set up tables in supermarkets and offer free samples to shoppers, along with coupons for the promoted items. Sometimes restaurants offer free coffee or drink refills. What other products might lend themselves to sampling? Make a list. Pick one of the items and come up with a sampling plan for it. Where and when would you sample? To whom would you offer samples?

ETHICS EXERCISE

You have been hired by a discount sporting-goods retailer in an over-the-counter sales position. You have completed a training course that includes learning about the products, assisting customers, and cross-selling. You have made several good friends in the training course and sometimes get together after work to go running, play golf, or have dinner. You've noticed that one of your friends has really taken the training course to heart and has adopted a very aggressive attitude toward customers in the store, pushing them to buy just about anything, whether they need it or not.

1. Do you agree with your friend's actions? Why or why not?

2. Should you discuss the situation with your friend? Should you discuss it with your supervisor? Explain your response.

INTERNET EXERCISES

1. **Sales careers.** Visit the three websites listed here and review the material on careers in sales. Make a list of five interesting facts about sales careers. Did this exercise make you more or less interested in a sales career? Explain your answer.
   www.collegegrad.com/careers/marke.shtml
   http://money.usnews.com/careers/best-jobs/sales-manager
   www.bls.gov/oco/ocos020.htm

2. **Compensation systems.** Go to the websites listed below and review the material on compensation systems. Prepare a report outlining the major issues associated with designing a sales compensation system.
   www.evancarmichael.com/Sales/414/Compensation-systems-in-sales-organizations.html
   www.inc.com/guides/sales-compensation-plan.html
   www.davekahle.com/compfeature.html

3. **CES.** The Consumer Electronics Show (CES) is one of the largest trade shows in the world. Visit the CES website and answer the following questions:
   a. When and where is the CES held?
   b. How many attended the most recent CES? How many firms and organizations had exhibits?
   c. What were the major new products introduced at the most recent CES?
   www.cesweb.org

Note: Internet Web addresses change frequently. If you don't find the exact site listed, you may need to access the organization's home page and search from there or use a search engine such as Google or Bing.

CASE 17.1
Selling a Tennis Star's Image

Since becoming a national tennis star at an early age, Serbian player Novak Djokovic has transformed himself as a way to achieve even higher goals. He recently changed his diet and fitness routine, as well as his serve, in order to become one of the top-seeded male players in the world. He also changed his publicist.

Djokovic's eye is not only on continuing to win the world's top tennis tournaments, such as the U.S. Open and Wimbledon. Only 25 years of age, he also hopes to become one of sports' top personalities, with profitable product endorsements like those enjoyed by his on-court rivals Rafael Nadal and Roger Federer. Djokovic may be closing in on that ambitious goal; he recently placed 9th on the list of "Power 100" sports figures compiled by CSE, an Atlanta-based sports and marketing firm. Nadal and Federer were ranked 5th and 6th respectively, while Eli Manning, the year's Super Bowl–winning quarterback, placed 15th.

But despite a string of victories that followed the best start of his career, appearances on *The Tonight Show* and other talk shows, and a new five-year endorsement contract with a Japanese apparel maker, Djokovic, whose chief marketing strategist is his uncle, has until recently been better known abroad than in the United States. The young athlete's quirky personality (he specializes in comic imitations of fellow tennis pros) has won him U.S. fans, and those who are aware of his name have positive associations with it. Winning will

continue to be an important step forward, in his professional career and for his name recognition, and he recently won 57 of 59 matches as well as 9 tournaments in the space of a few months. But Djokovic may still have a way to go before he reaches his ultimate goal—a possible second career in Hollywood.

If he doesn't continue to advance his off-court goals, however, there could be one other marketing avenue open to him. "What he has done to get in shape," says former tennis great Jimmy Connors, "he should bottle that and sell it."

QUESTIONS FOR CRITICAL THINKING

1. Explore the Internet to find out the extent of Djokovic's online presence. How do you think he might improve it to promote himself?

2. What else can Djokovic and his marketing team do to increase his name recognition in the United States?

Sources: Randy Walker, "Novak Djokovic Tops Roger Federer for ATP World Tour Finals Title and 2012 Bragging Rights," *World Tennis,* accessed December 4, 2012, www.worldtennismagazine; Venessa Wong, "Drew Brees Tops the Power 100 in 2012," *Bloomberg Businessweek,* accessed December 4, 2012, www.businessweek.com; Greg Bishop, "Next Makeover for a New No. 1 Is in Marketing," *The New York Times,* accessed December 4, 2012, www.nytimes.com; "Novak Djokovic Signs Up as Uniqlo Global Brand Ambassador," *Business and Leadership,* accessed December 4, 2012, www.businessandleadership.com; Bob Simon, "Novak Djokovic: From War to Wimbledon," *CBS News,* accessed December 4, 2012, www.cbsnews.com.

VIDEO CASE 17.2
Hubway Rolls Out Partners and Promotions

Commuting by subway, bus, train, or car can be expensive and inconvenient for workers trying to navigate around a city or its suburbs. Burning all that fossil fuel (or battery power) isn't the greenest way to travel, either. While it's true that these modes of transportation sometimes are the most time-efficient (and the safest way to move during bad weather), there's another method to consider for short hops and busy city streets: bicycle riding. Hubway is a bike-sharing system based in New England that was conceived by its founders as a regional network tying together Boston, Cambridge, Brookline, and the surrounding communities. Hubway serves a greater purpose than just renting bikes to consumers. "It's not just about bikes," observes general manager Scott Mullen. "This is just another piece of the transit puzzle." The Hubway system harbors the flexibility to fill gaps left open by public transit. For example, suppose you catch a subway that deposits you four blocks from your workplace. Instead of walking, if you're a Hubway member, you can swipe your card at a designated bike station, grab a bike, and ride straight to your job.

Launching and running a bike-share system requires partners (Alta Bicycle Share and New Balance are Hubway's main partners). It also requires support from corporate members. Brogan Graham, who holds the official title of hypemaster at Hubway, is responsible for corporate sales—convincing other companies to create corporate accounts through which their employees may join the Hubway system. Corporations have the option to join at several levels, depending on whether they want to contribute 100 percent of their employees' memberships or a certain percentage. Once a company signs up, a Hubway representative visits the firm to talk with workers about bike sharing, encourage participation, and point out the benefits of commuting via bicycle as a physical fitness and green initiative. As a motivator, Hubway provides the business customer with a tally of rides, calories burned, and CO2 saved. Hubway representatives also work with other business partners, such as retailers who are willing to offer Hubway members bike helmets at low cost. For example, instead of paying $50 or $75 for a bike helmet, Hubway members may pick one up for $7.99 at locations ranging from participating CVS pharmacies to City Sports to several hospital gift shops. "Marketing is partnerships, communication, working together as a team," notes Graham.

Hubway has conducted several consumer-oriented promotions since its launch. At its initial roll-out, marketers recruited students to dress as Minute Men and colonial soldiers, and sent them out as the Revolutionary Riders to proclaim the coming of Hubway. After the first year of operation, Graham and his team calculated the top several men and women Hubway riders (by number of rides), dubbed them the Gold Club, and went to their homes and workplaces to present them with gold T-shirts. Other media picked up on these riders and featured them in articles and online postings. Some promotions involve short-term discounts, such as the recent "Get Hubway for the Holidays." Halfway through one December, Hubway slashed the cost of an annual membership to $60 ($25 savings)—a price good until the end of that month. As Hubway approached the kick-off of its second year in operation, members were invited to grab a bike and ride to the Boston Public Library for the festivities where, upon check-in, their use of the bike for the day would be free. The first 100 riders also received a free burrito from Boloco Burritos. New members could join at the event for a reduced membership price. Hubway spread the news about the event via Twitter and Facebook—and people came in droves.

Social media is an important part of the Hubway promotional mix. Hubway uses social media to spread the word about promotions like the Boston Public Library event, sending targeted messages to consumers, who then become virtual ambassadors for the brand. Graham notes that a single tweet may reach 4,000 people, who not only respond to Hubway, but also strike up conversations with each other about their riding experiences, including attending special events. Without a big advertising budget, explains marketing director Mary McLaughlin, Hubway relies on this type of grassroots marketing. "The one-to-one model is the best way to spread the word," says McLaughlin.

QUESTIONS FOR CRITICAL THINKING

1. Describe how Hubway can use relationship selling to build partnerships with retailers and corporations.

2. How might Hubway create sales promotions using specialty advertising?

Sources: Company website, www.thehubway.com, accessed December 4, 2012; Eric Moskowitz, "Hubway Bike-Sharing Program Is on a Roll," *Boston.com*, accessed December 4, 2012, http://articles.boston.com; Jonathan Simmons, "On Biking: Learning to Love Hubway," *Boston.com*, accessed December 4, 2012, http://articles.boston.com.

NOTES

1. Liz Gannes, "Salesforce to Acquire 'Co-Browsing' Start-Up GoInstant for $76M in Cash," *All Things Digital*, accessed December 4, 2012, http://allthingsd.com; Drew Fitzgerald and Kristin Jones, "Update: Salesforce to Buy Buddy Media for $689M, Revises View," *The Wall Street Journal*, accessed December 4, 2012, http://online.wsj.com; Larry Dignan, "Salesforce Doubles Down on Social with Buddy Media, Following CMO Spending," *ZDnet.com*, accessed December 4, 2012, www.zdnet.com; Tim Peterson, "Salesforce Buys Buddy Media for $689 Million," *Adweek*, accessed December 4, 2012, www.adweek.com; "With Buddy Media Deal, Salesforce Targets CMOs," *Advertising Age*, accessed December 4, 2012, http://adage.com; Peter Kafka, "Sales Set to Snap Up Facebook Friend Buddy Media for More Than $800 Million," *All Things Digital*, accessed December 4, 2012, http://allthingsd.com; Ian Schafer, "Will Salesforce's Acquisition of Buddy Media Make Social CRM Real?" *Advertising Age*, accessed December 4, 2012, http://adage.com; Lisa Arthur, "Five Years from Now, CMOs Will Spend More on IT Than CIOs Do," *Forbes*, accessed December 4, 2012, www.forbes.com; David A. Kaplan, "Salesforce's Happy Workforce," *Fortune*, accessed December 4, 2012, http://tech.fortune.cnn.com.

2. U.S. Bureau of Labor Statistics, Employment Projections, Table 1.1, www.bls.gov, accessed December 4, 2012.

3. Ibid.

4. "Macy's Multi-Pronged Strategy for an Informed Customer Loyalty Program," *Merchandising Matters*, accessed December 4, 2012, www.merchandisingmatters.com; Alex Palmer, "Macy's Transformation," *Direct Marketing News*, accessed December 4, 2012, www.dmnews.com; Jennifer Schonberger, "A Change in Business Strategy Proves Profitable for Macy's," *Kiplinger's Personal Finance*, accessed December 4, 2012, www.kiplinger.com.

5. "Enterprise Rent-A-Car Looks to Hire Student-Athletes, Partners with Career Athletes," press release, *PR Web*, accessed December 4, 2012, www.prweb.com; company website, www.enterpriseholdings.com, accessed December 4, 2012.

6. Elizabeth Holmes and Ray A. Smith, "Why Are Fitting Rooms So Awful?" *The Wall Street Journal*, accessed December 4, 2012, http://online.wsj.com.

7. Hayley Tsukayama, "Panasonic Expands 'Toughbook' Line to Tablets," *Washington Post*, accessed December 4, 2012, www.washingtonpost.com.

8. Melissa Stern, "Ozarks Company Launches Jean Parties with Big Bargains," *Ozarks First*, accessed December 4, 2012, http://ozarksfirst.com.

9. Federal Communications Commission, "Unwanted Telephone Marketing Calls," www.fcc.gov, accessed December 4, 2012.

10. Jeff Rossen and Sandra Thomas, "Rossen Reports: Telemarketers Ignore Do Not Call List," *Today*, accessed December 4, 2012, http://today.msnbc.msn.com.

11. Lesley Fair, "Ringing in the New Year," Bureau of Consumer Protection, *Business Center Blog*, accessed December 4, 2012, http://business.ftc.gov.

12. Direct Marketing Association "What Is the Direct Marketing Association: Overview," www.the-dma.org, accessed December 4, 2012.

13. Blue Tales, "A Day in the Life: Customer Support," *JetBlue Blog*, accessed December 4, 2012, http://blog.jetblue.com.

14. Company website, www.nba.com, accessed December 4, 2012.

15. "Salesnet CRM Case Study—Sovereign Bank," *Salesnet*, accessed December 4, 2012, www.salesnet.com.

16. Kelly Faloon, "Vendor-Managed Truck Replenishment," *Plumbing & Mechanical* magazine, accessed December 4, 2012, www.pmmag.com.

17. "Fireman's Fund Insurance Company," *Richardson*, accessed December 4, 2012, www.richardson.com.

18. Michelle Juergen, "A Hot Business Idea—Between the Sheets," *Entrepreneur*, accessed December 4, 2012, www.entrepreneur.com.

19. Company website, www.southwest.com, accessed December 4, 2012.

20. Hadley Malcolm, "Touch-Screens Create Online Shopping Experiences at Stores," *USA Today*, accessed December 4, 2012, http://usatoday30.usatoday.com.

21. Rockfish Interactive, "BUNN Ecommerce," http://rockfishinteractive.com, accessed December 4, 2012.

22. Jonathan D. Rockoff, "Drug Reps Soften Their Sales Pitches," *The Wall Street Journal*, accessed December 4, 2012, http://online.wsj.com.

23. Ibid.

24. Kelly Liyakasa, "Brainshark Releases SlideShark Team Edition," *CRM* magazine, accessed December 4, 2012, www.destinationcrm.com.

25. Diana Ransom, "An Old-Fashioned Approach to Finding Customers," *Entrepreneur*, accessed December 4, 2012, www.entrepreneur.com.

26. Company website, www.blackanddecker.com, accessed December 4, 2012; Clean Lawn Calculator, http://cleanairlawncare.com, accessed December 4, 2012.

27. U.S. Bureau of Labor Statistics, "Sales Managers," *Occupational Outlook Handbook, 2012–2013*, accessed December 4, 2012, www.bls.gov.

28. "Jupiter Systems Hires New Head of Engineering, Expands Sales and Field Support," *Reuters*, accessed December 4, 2012, www.reuters.com.

29. U.S. Department of Labor, Women's Bureau, "20 Leading Occupations of Employed Women: 2010 Annual Average," accessed December 4, 2012, www.dol.gov; U.S. Bureau of Labor Statistics, "Overview of the 2010–20 Projections," *Occupational Outlook Handbook, 2012–2013*, accessed December 4, 2012, www.bls.gov.

30. Company website, http://santinelli.com, accessed December 4, 2012; "Santinelli Holds Annual National Sales Meeting in San Francisco," press release, www.santinelli.com, accessed December 4, 2012.

31. David Kaplan, "Mighty Monday Looms for Retailers," *Houston Chronicle*, accessed December 4, 2012, www.chron.com.

32. "CRM Best Practices," *CRM Trends*, accessed December 4, 2012, www.crmtrends.com.

33. "The Coupon Comeback," *Coupons.org*, accessed December 4, 2012, http://coupons.org.

34. Jeff Hudson, "What's Next for Digital Coupons?" *Mashable*, accessed December 4, 2012, http://mashable.com.

35. Patricia Odell, PROMO: "Steady Growth," *Chief Marketer*, accessed December 4, 2012, www.chiefmarketer.com.

36. Brad Hanna, "CPG Marketing Trends: New Alternative Sampling Method for Full-Size Products," *CPG Marketing Trends*, accessed December 4, 2012, www.cpgtrends.com.

37. "Get 'A Taste of Ireland' with Friendly Planet's Facebook Sweepstakes Giveaway," *Enhanced Online News*, accessed December 4, 2012, http://eon.businesswire.com.

Scripps Networks Interactive & Food Network

Generating Buzz

Scripps Networks Interactive's brands—Food Network, Cooking Channel, HGTV, DIY Network, Travel Channel, and Great American Country (GAC)—are founded on lifestyles that promote exploration, imagination, and passion within the confines of everyday life as well as the broad spectrum of adventure and global influence. The company's marketing communications strategy is a natural extension of this kind of lifestyle programming. "It's talking to people about the right things at the right times, in the right places," says Jonah Spegman, director of digital media and database marketing for Scripps Networks Interactive.

Marketers at Scripps engage in integrated marketing communications (IMC) not only within each branded television network but also across most of its programming. "A lot of our networks play in the same spaces; women age 25 to 54 is a common target audience across most of our networks," notes Spegman. Many of Scripps' cross-promotional efforts have a lot of touchpoints for the same audiences; it's a natural fit. For example, a single commercial might involve HGTV speaking to the Food Network audience about an upcoming *Design Star* episode that features celebrity chef Paula Deen.

While traditional TV advertising conjures up the 30-second spot with a catchy jingle, advertising at Food Network is much more complex and interactive. Because the audience is so connected to the content of its shows, advertisers actually look to Scripps for ideas and resources that they can use. "Advertisers are very sophisticated now," observes Traci Topham, senior vice president of interactive ad sales marketing at Scripps. Advertisers approach Scripps looking to integrate with the Scripps social media space. Topham and others develop ideas that their advertising clients may run on the Food Network website or across their own mobile platforms. For example, food manufacturer Kraft might develop recipes with Food Network that consumers can access from their mobile devices.

"We're programming and selling advertising to all the screens," Topham continues. Recipes from a single episode of *Chopped* or *Iron Chef* may be driven to an advertiser's website or Food Network's site, where consumers can access them to try on their own. Non-food advertisers participate as well. If Lexus wants to advertise its RX Hybrid on an episode of *Restaurant: Impossible,* Food Network may integrate the car into the show by having host Robert Irvine drive it—then stream that footage online at the Food Network site where Lexus ads are being shown.

Sponsors and other advertisers also want to tie Food Network talent to their own Facebook pages with celebrity testimonials. Some even develop recipes in conjunction with Food Network to post on their Facebook pages. Scripps and Food Network marketers don't see this as a competitive threat; instead they view it as co-marketing. "We try to do a 360," explains Sergei Kuharsky, senior vice president and general manager of licensing and merchandising. Food Network joins marketing assets with its partners—such as retailer Kohl's—in order to gain greater exposure and interaction with consumers. "Generally, in marketing you want that kind of crescendo," Kuharsky advises. He points out that one of the great advantages of being a media brand with a daily dialogue with an audience is that when the conversation focuses on a topic—such as a television show episode, a particular restaurant, or a competition—something positive happens.

Sales promotions are an important part of the Food Network promotional mix. "Promotions always have the opportunity to generate buzz and excitement around a show," says Rich Ma, manager of digital marketing for Food Network. "People love to win stuff." Ma explains that an effective sales promotion must go beyond a simple giveaway. Food Network's promotional goal is to engage viewers, so marketers tie their promotions to the TV experience. During the series *Great Food Truck Race,* Food Network marketers created an interactive promotion that allowed viewers to nominate their own local food trucks at the Food Network website, then vote for the "best" food truck in the country. The contest generated buzz for the show as well as for local food truck businesses. "That's the nature of social," says Ma. "When you have something that's hot, people start talking about it and you can add fuel to the fire by contributing to that conversation." It's also free advertising—for the network and the local businesses.

Social media is still very much in the growth stage of the product lifecycle, which means that corresponding promotional efforts are as well. Susie Fogelson, senior vice president for marketing, creative services, and public relations at Food Network, acknowledges that she has "far more questions than answers" about the most effective ways to leverage social media in an integrated marketing communications strategy. In fact, she encourages marketers to ask the most basic questions. "It's being willing to learn, explore, and be a little outside your comfort zone," Fogelson says.

QUESTIONS FOR CRITICAL THINKING

1. If you were a Food Network marketer, how would you state the network's overall marketing message?

2. Describe the types of advertising appeals that you think would be most effective with Food Network viewers.

3. In what ways do Food Network and its advertisers benefit from cross-promotion?

4. How might Food Network marketers use sales promotion techniques to build loyalty among viewers?

PART 7

Pricing Decisions

Chapter 18

PRICING
Concepts

1   Outline the legal constraints on pricing.

2   Identify the major categories of pricing objectives.

3   Explain price elasticity and its determinants.

4   List the practical problems involved in applying price theory concepts to actual pricing decisions.

5   Explain the major cost-plus approaches to price setting.

6   List the chief advantages and shortcomings of using breakeven analysis in pricing decisions.

7   Explain the use of yield management in pricing decisions.

8   Identify the major pricing challenges facing online and international marketers.

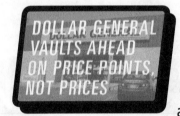

DOLLAR GENERAL VAULTS AHEAD ON PRICE POINTS, NOT PRICES

Dollar General, the Tennessee–based chain of discount retailers, recently opened its 10,052nd U.S. store and announced quarterly earnings that reached a new high, rising 20 percent to over $4 billion. Like other "extreme value" stores, such as Dollar Tree and Family Dollar, the fast-growing chain is drawing many more customers than before, and these shoppers are spending more per visit than in the past. Not only are low-income families shopping at Dollar General, which recently undertook a large-scale investment and remodeling in many of its stores; middle-class shoppers hit by job losses or budget worries are now stopping in as well.

How does Dollar General earn so much with such low prices on brand names like Kimberly Clark, Procter & Gamble, Kellogg, Nabisco, and General Mills? The answer is that the company doesn't really offer low prices; by selling products in smaller sizes than other discount chains like Walmart, it actually offers low price *points*, which yield higher profit margins. In other words, although the items in the store carry nominally low prices,

their smaller sizes mean customers are paying more per ounce than they would pay for the same item at Walmart. But because they have low purchasing power at any given time, Dollar General shoppers can afford to buy only small amounts at a time and must also shop more frequently. Dollar General caters to their buying habits and financial constraints.

Dollar General calls itself "the nation's largest small-box discount retailer." The company expects sales to continue to increase, rising by as much as 8 to 9 percent over the coming year as it opens another 625 new stores. It has remodeled about 575 existing locations, spending $600 to $650 million in store openings and capital improvements. Most Dollar General outlets stock between 10,000 and 12,000 different items.

The chain's success, based on low-priced items and the convenience of so many locations, is beginning to encroach on the market segment that has traditionally been a stronghold of chains like Walmart, Target, and Costco. Dollar General is also taking share from grocery stores and drug chains. With locations in 40 states and 11 distribution centers, Dollar General believes it could profitably operate as many as 20,000 stores nationwide.[1]

EVOLUTION OF A BRAND

Extreme-value stores like Dollar General are encroaching on a target market that Walmart, Kmart, Target, Costco, and other "big box" stores long believed was firmly in their grasp. Extreme-value stores like Dollar General have long been common in poorer regions of the country. Struggling U.S. families have increasingly turned to them during a weak economy.

- How does Dollar General's policy of carrying smaller sizes of major brand-name products appeal to its target audience? How might a "big box" store attempt to regain the customers it has lost to the extreme-value stores?

- Visit Dollar General's website (www2.dollargeneral.com) and enter your zip code to see the specials for the store nearest you. Choose one item—a bag of potato chips, for example, and note the price—and size—of the package. Now visit the website of a "big box" store like Costco and find the same product. What is the difference in the size of the package? In the price? Which store will give you a better buy for the product you chose? Why?

CHAPTER OVERVIEW

price Exchange value of a good or service.

One of the first questions shoppers ask is, "How much does it cost?" Marketers understand the critical role price plays in the consumer's decision-making process. For products as varied as lipstick and perfume, automobiles and gasoline, and doughnuts and coffee, marketers must develop strategies that price products to achieve their firms' objectives.

As a starting point for examining pricing strategies, consider the meaning of the term *price*. A **price** is the exchange value of a good or service; in other words, it represents whatever that product can be exchanged for in the marketplace. Price does not necessarily denote money. In earlier times, the price of an acre of land might have been 20 bushels of wheat, three head of cattle, or one boat. Even though the barter process continues to be used in some transactions, in the 21st century, price typically refers to the amount of funds required to purchase a product. Prices are both dynamic and difficult to set; they shift

in response to a number of variables. A higher-than-average price can convey an image of prestige, while a lower-than-average price may connote good value, as the trend toward consumers' purchases of private-label store brands shows. In other instances, though, a price much lower than average may be interpreted as an indicator of inferior quality, and a higher price—like the increasing price of gasoline—may reflect both high demand and scarce supply. And pricing can also be used to modify consumer behavior.

This chapter discusses the process of determining a profitable but justifiable (or fair) price. The focus is on management of the pricing function, including pricing strategies, price–quality relationships, and pricing in various sectors of the economy. The chapter also looks at the effects of environmental conditions on price determination, including legal constraints, competitive pressures, and changes in global and online markets.

PRICING AND THE LAW

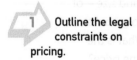

1 Outline the legal constraints on pricing.

Pricing decisions are influenced by a variety of legal constraints imposed by federal, state, and local governments. Included in the price of products are not only the costs of the raw materials, processing and packaging, and profit for the business, but also various taxes. For instance, excise taxes are levied on a variety of products, including real estate transfers, alcoholic beverages, and motor fuels. Sales taxes can be charged on clothing, furniture, restaurant meals, and many other purchases.

In the global marketplace, prices are directly affected by special types of taxes called *tariffs*. These taxes—levied on the sale of imported goods and services—often make it possible for firms to protect their local markets while still setting prices on domestically produced goods well above world market levels. The average tariff on fruits and vegetables around the world is more than 50 percent, although it varies considerably from country to country. The United States levies tariffs of 10 to 20 percent on fruit and vegetable imports from European Union (EU) countries, although these two trading partners have expressed interest in eliminating tariffs on all agricultural trade. Under the North American Free Trade Agreement (NAFTA), in transactions with the United States' largest trading partners in the produce market—Mexico and Canada—tariffs for both imports and exports are zero.[2] In other instances, tariffs are levied to prevent foreign producers from engaging in a practice described in Chapter 8: *dumping* foreign-produced products in international markets at prices lower than those set in their domestic market.

The United States is not the only country that imposes tariffs to protect domestic suppliers. These tariffs raise the prices overseas consumers must pay to purchase U.S. goods. Recently, China imposed tariffs of up to 22 percent on imported large cars and SUVs from the United States. Then a trade skirmish erupted when the United States charged Chinese manufacturers with illegally dumping inexpensive solar panels on the American market. The U.S. Department of Commerce imposed high tariffs on Chinese imports to protect American manufacturers.[3]

Not every "regulatory" price increase is a tax, however. Rate increases to cover costly government regulations imposed on the telecommunications industry have been appearing on Internet and cell phone bills as "regulatory cost recovery fees" or similarly named costs. But these charges are not taxes, because the companies keep all the income from the fees and apply only some of it to complying with the regulations. In essence, such "recovery fees" are a source of additional revenues in an industry so price sensitive that any announced price increase is likely to send some customers fleeing to competitors.

Many people looking for a ticket to a high-demand sporting or concert event have encountered an expensive, often illegal, form of pricing called *ticket scalping*. Scalpers camp out in ticket lines—or hire someone else to stand in line—to purchase tickets they expect to resell at a higher price. Although some cities and states have enacted laws prohibiting the practice, it continues to occur in many locations.

But the ticket reselling market is both highly fragmented and susceptible to fraud and distorted pricing. In response, buyers and sellers are finding that the Internet is helping create a market in which both buyers and sellers can compare prices and seat locations. Web firms like StubHub.com and TicketsNow.com, the latter owned by Ticketmaster, are ticket clearinghouses for this secondary market. These firms have signed deals with several professional sports teams that allow season ticket holders to sell unwanted tickets and buyers to purchase them with a guarantee. NHL and NBA fans have saved up to 30 percent by buying playoff tickets from StubHub at the last minute.[4]

Pricing is also regulated by the general constraints of U.S. antitrust legislation, as outlined in Chapter 3. The following sections review some of the most important pricing laws for contemporary marketers.

China, rapidly becoming the world's largest market for cars, taxes imported auto parts and finished vehicles at high rates, raising the price of imported cars there.

AP Photo/Imaginechina via AP Images

ROBINSON-PATMAN ACT

Robinson-Patman Act Federal legislation prohibiting price discrimination not based on a cost differential; also prohibits selling at an unreasonably low price to eliminate competition.

The **Robinson-Patman Act** (1936) typifies Depression-era legislation. Known as the Anti-A&P Act, it was inspired by price competition triggered by the rise of grocery store chains; it is said that the original draft was suggested by the U.S. Wholesale Grocers Association. Enacted in the midst of the Great Depression, when legislators viewed chain stores as a threat to employment in the traditional retail sector, this law was primarily intended to save jobs.

The Robinson-Patman Act was an amendment to the Clayton Act, enacted 22 years earlier, which had applied only to price discrimination between geographic areas, injuring local sellers. Broader in scope, Robinson-Patman prohibits price discrimination in sales to wholesalers, retailers, and other producers. It rules that differences in price must reflect cost differentials and prohibits selling at unreasonably low prices to drive competitors out of business. Supporters justified the amendment by arguing that the rapidly expanding chain stores of that era might be able to attract substantial discounts from suppliers anxious to secure their business, while small, independent stores would continue to pay regular prices.

Price discrimination, in which some customers pay more than others for the same product, dates back to the very beginnings of trade and commerce. Today, however, technology has added to the frequency and complexity of price discrimination as well as the strategies marketers adopt to get around it. For example, marketers may encourage repeat business by inviting purchasers to become "preferred customers," entitling them to average discounts of 10 percent. As long as companies can demonstrate that their price discounts and promotional allowances do not restrict competition, they avoid penalties under the Robinson-Patman Act. Direct-mail marketers frequently send out catalogs of identical goods but with differing prices for different catalogs. Zip code areas that traditionally consist of high spenders get the higher-price catalogs, while price-sensitive zip code customers receive catalogs with lower prices. Firms accused of price discrimination often argue that they set price differentials to meet competitors' prices and that cost differences justify variations in prices. When a firm asserts it maintains price differentials as good-faith methods of competing with rivals, a logical question arises: What constitutes good-faith pricing behavior? The answer depends on the particular situation.

A defense based on cost differentials works only if the price differences do not exceed the cost differences resulting from selling to various classes of buyers. Marketers must then be prepared to justify the cost differences. Many authorities consider this provision one of the most confusing areas in the Robinson-Patman Act. Courts handle most charges brought under the act as individual cases. Therefore, domestic marketers must continually evaluate their pricing actions to avoid potential Robinson-Patman violations.

UNFAIR-TRADE LAWS

unfair-trade laws State laws requiring sellers to maintain minimum prices for comparable merchandise.

Most states supplement federal legislation with their own **unfair-trade laws**, which require sellers to maintain minimum prices for comparable merchandise. Enacted in the 1930s, these laws were intended to protect small specialty shops, such as dairy stores, from so-called *loss-leader* pricing tactics in which chain stores might sell certain products below cost to attract customers. Typical state laws set retail price floors at cost plus some modest markup. Although most unfair-trade laws have remained on the books for decades, marketers had all but forgotten them until recently, when several lawsuits were brought against different warehouse clubs over their practice of loss-leader gasoline pricing. Most were found to violate no laws.

FAIR-TRADE LAWS

fair-trade laws Statutes enacted in most states that once permitted manufacturers to stipulate a minimum retail price for their product.

The concept of fair trade has affected pricing decisions for decades. **Fair-trade laws** allow manufacturers to stipulate minimum retail prices for their products and to require dealers to sign contracts agreeing to abide by these prices.

Fair-trade laws assert that a product's image, determined in part by its price, is a property right of the manufacturer. Therefore, the manufacturer should have the authority to protect its asset by requiring retailers to maintain a minimum price. Exclusivity is one method manufacturers use to achieve this. By severely restricting the number of retail outlets that carry their upscale clothing and accessories, designers can exert more control over their prices and avoid discounting, which might adversely affect their image.

Like the Robinson-Patman Act, fair-trade legislation has its roots in the Depression era. In 1931, California became the first state to enact fair-trade legislation. Most other states soon followed; only Missouri, the District of Columbia, Vermont, and Texas failed to adopt such laws. A U.S. Supreme Court decision invalidated fair-trade contracts in interstate commerce, and Congress responded by passing the Miller-Tydings Resale Price Maintenance Act (1937). This law exempted interstate fair-trade contracts from compliance with antitrust requirements, thus freeing states to keep these laws on their books if they so desired.

 ASSESSMENT CHECK

1.1 What was the purpose of the Robinson-Patman Act?

1.2 What laws require sellers to maintain minimum prices for comparable merchandise?

1.3 What laws allow manufacturers to set minimum retail prices for their products?

Over the years, fair-trade laws declined in importance as discounters emerged and price competition gained strength as a marketing strategy component. These laws became invalid with the passage of the Consumer Goods Pricing Act (1975), which halted all interstate enforcement of resale price maintenance provisions, an objective long sought by consumer groups.

PRICING OBJECTIVES AND THE MARKETING MIX

The extent to which any or all of the factors of production—natural resources, capital, human resources, and entrepreneurship—are employed depends on the prices those factors command. A firm's prices and the resulting purchases by its customers determine the company's revenue, influencing the profits it earns. Overall organizational objectives and more specific marketing objectives guide the development of pricing objectives, which in turn lead to the development and implementation of more specific pricing policies and procedures.

A firm might, for instance, set an overall goal of becoming the dominant producer in its domestic market. It might then develop a marketing objective of achieving maximum sales penetration in each region, followed by a related pricing objective of setting prices at levels that maximize sales. These objectives might lead to the adoption of a low-price policy implemented by offering substantial price discounts to channel members. One start-up company's pricing strategy to signal the prestige value of its scented housecleaning products was so successful the company was snapped up by a larger firm. See the "Marketing Success" feature for the story.

Price affects and is affected by the other elements of the marketing mix. Product decisions, promotional plans, and distribution choices all affect the price of a good or service. For example, products distributed through complex channels involving several intermediaries must be priced high enough to cover the markups needed to compensate wholesalers and retailers for services they provide. Basic so-called fighting brands are intended to capture market share from higher-priced, options-laden competitors by offering relatively low prices. Those cheaper products are intended to entice customers to give up some options in return for a cost savings.

Pricing objectives vary from firm to firm, and they can be classified into four major groups: (1) profitability objectives, (2) volume objectives, (3) meeting competition objectives, and (4) prestige objectives. Not-for-profit organizations as well as for-profit companies must consider objectives of one kind or another when developing pricing strategies. Table 18.1 outlines the pricing objectives marketers rely on to meet their overall goals.

2 Identify the major categories of pricing objectives.

MARKETING SUCCESS

The Pricey Smell of Success

Background. Caldrea and Mrs. Meyer's Clean Day are the two brands of Caldrea Company, a maker of upscale, environmentally friendly household cleaning products founded more than a decade ago in Minneapolis, Minnesota.

The Challenge. Caldrea's founder, Monica Nassif, wanted to create beautifully scented household cleaning and laundry products, priced higher than average, that shoppers would treat as a small indulgence.

The Strategy. "Caring for our homes should be just as luxurious as caring for our bodies," Nassif decided. She developed her company's biodegradable products in aromatherapy scents derived from essential oils and cosmetic-grade plant derivatives. The varieties, which are not tested on animals, include citrus mint, basil blue sage, lavender pine, and lemon verbena. Mrs. Meyer's products help homeowners care for surfaces ranging from wood to stainless, while Caldrea products, the more expensive of the two brands, are packaged attractively enough

to display on bathroom and kitchen countertops. Their high-end pricing confers such status that they are often purchased as gifts. And the company also makes a private-label line for Williams-Sonoma.

The Outcome. Caldrea and Mrs. Meyer's products are mostly sold at high-end retailers like Whole Foods and the Container Store, but recently introduced an "essentials" line of products at Target. Their luxury appeal and reliable performance command prices at least 30 percent higher than ordinary brands. The company's rapid success led to its purchase by SC Johnson, and Nassif believes partnering with SC Johnson will help the company rapidly expand its sales opportunities.

Sources: Anne Marie Chaker, "The Pampered Countertop," *The Wall Street Journal,* accessed December 5, 2012, http://online.wsj.com; Monica Nassif, "5 Steps to Creating a Powerful Attraction Marketing Plan for 2010," *Ladies Who Launch,* accessed December 5, 2012, www.ladieswholaunch.com; "Spring Cleaning . . . Holiday Cleaning," *The Nibble,* accessed December 5, 2012, www.thenibble.com; Thomas Lee, "Mr. Muscle Marrying Mrs. Meyer," *Minneapolis Star Tribune,* accessed December 5, 2012, www.startribune.com.

TABLE 18.1 Pricing Objectives

Objective	Purpose	Example
Profitability objectives	Profit maximization	Samsung's initially high price for the Blu-ray disc player
	Target return	
Volume objectives	Sales maximization	Delta's low fares in new markets
	Market share	
Meeting competition objectives	Value pricing	Target's lower prices on private house brands
Prestige objectives	Lifestyle	High-priced luxury autos such as Bentley
	Image	
Not-for-profit objectives	Profit maximization	Reduced or zero tolls for high-occupancy vehicles to encourage carpooling
	Cost recovery	
	Market incentives	
	Market suppression	

PROFITABILITY OBJECTIVES

Marketers at for-profit firms must set prices with profits in mind. Even not-for-profit organizations realize the importance of setting prices high enough to cover expenses and provide a financial cushion to cover unforeseen needs and expenses. As the Russian proverb says, "There are two fools in every market: one asks too little, one asks too much." For consumers to pay prices either above or below what they consider the going rate, they must be convinced they are receiving fair value for their money.

Economic theory is based on two major assumptions. It assumes, first, that firms will behave rationally and, second, that this rational behavior will result in an effort to maximize gains and minimize losses. Some marketers estimate profits by looking at historical sales data; others use elaborate calculations based on predicted future sales. It has been said that setting prices is an art, not a science. The talent lies in a marketer's ability to strike a balance between desired profits and the customer's perception of a product's value.

Marketers should evaluate and adjust prices continually to accommodate changes in the environment. The technological environment, for example, forces Internet marketers to respond quickly to competitors' pricing strategies. Search capabilities performed by shopping bots (described in Chapter 5) allow customers to compare prices locally, nationally, and globally in a matter of seconds.

Intense price competition, sometimes conducted even when it means forgoing profits altogether or reducing services, often results when rivals battle for leadership positions. For some years, passenger airlines cut costs to compete on pricing. Computer technology allowed them to automate many services and put passengers in charge of others, such as making reservations online and checking in at electronic kiosks. Now, thanks to increased industry concentration and the high price of jet fuel, airlines struggle to cover their costs. As a result, passengers now pay sharply higher fares and find amenities, such as in-flight meals, have all but disappeared. Recently, some airlines have increased the number of seats reserved for frequent fliers—or passengers who are willing to pay extra. For an average fee of $50 for a round trip, passengers can get the more desirable seats next to windows, on an aisle, or with more legroom. For families, this fee could add up to hundreds of dollars more so that parents and children can sit together.[5]

Profits are a function of revenue and expenses:

$$\text{Profits} = \text{Revenue} - \text{Expenses}$$

Revenue is determined by the product's selling price and number of units sold:

$$\text{Total revenue} = \text{Price} \times \text{Quantity sold}$$

Therefore, a profit-maximizing price rises to the point at which further increases will cause disproportionate decreases in the number of units sold. A 10 percent price increase that results in only an 8 percent cut in volume will add to the firm's revenue. However, a 10 percent price hike that results in an 11 percent sales decline will reduce revenue.

Economists refer to this approach as *marginal analysis*. They identify *profit maximization* as the point at which the addition to total revenue is just balanced by the increase in total cost. Marketers must resolve a basic problem of how to achieve this delicate balance when they set prices. Relatively few firms actually hit this elusive target. A significantly larger number prefer to direct their effort toward more realistic goals.

Consequently, marketers commonly set *target-return objectives*—short-run or long-run goals usually stated as percentages of sales or investment. The practice has become particularly popular among large firms in which other pressures

BRIEFLY SPEAKING

"The bitterness of poor quality is remembered long after the sweetness of low price has faded from memory."

—**Aldo Gucci**
Co-owner of Gucci, an elite Italian fashion-design house

marginal analysis Method of analyzing the relationship among costs, sales price, and increased sales volume.

profit maximization Point at which the additional revenue gained by increasing the price of a product equals the increase in total costs.

target-return objective Short-run or long-run pricing objectives of achieving a specified return on either sales or investment.

Industry consolidation and fuel prices have contributed to some airlines charging additional fees to passengers who wish to sit in a window seat.

interfere with profit-maximization objectives. In addition to resolving pricing questions, target-return objectives offer several benefits for marketers. For example, these objectives serve as tools for evaluating performance; they also satisfy desires to generate "fair" profits as judged by management, stockholders, and the public.

VOLUME OBJECTIVES

Some economists and business executives argue that pricing behavior actually seeks to maximize sales within a given profit constraint. In other words, they set a minimum acceptable profit level and then seek to maximize sales (subject to this profit constraint) in the belief that the increased sales are more important in the long-run, competitive picture than immediate high profits. As a result, companies should continue to expand sales as long as their total profits do not drop below the minimum return acceptable to management.

Sales maximization can also result from nonprice factors, such as service and quality. Stacy's Greenhouses of York, South Carolina, charges higher prices for some of its plants than for others. According to the company's president, knowing what customers value is important in setting a price, so the company tailors its prices according to the segment of the market it wants to reach. For example, in today's economy, experienced gardeners value longer life spans in the plants they buy and therefore are willing to pay more for them.[6]

market-share objective Volume-related pricing objective with the goal of controlling a portion of the market for a firm's product.

Another volume-related pricing objective is the market-share objective—the goal of controlling a specified minimum share of the market for a firm's good or service. Procter & Gamble experienced poor sales growth in some markets when it increased prices on some products to cover its costs. Recently, the company announced it would roll back those price increases in the hope of winning back some of the market share it lost.[7]

The PIMS Studies

Profit Impact of Market Strategies (PIMS) project Research that discovered a strong positive relationship between a firm's market share and product quality and its return on investment.

Market-share objectives may prove critical to the achievement of other organizational objectives. High sales, for example, often mean more profits. The Profit Impact of Market Strategies (PIMS) project, an extensive and now classic study conducted by the Marketing Science Institute, analyzed more than 2,000 firms and revealed that two of the most important factors influencing profitability were product quality and market share. Companies, such as the outdoor gear maker REI, introduced their loyalty programs as a means of retaining customers and protecting their market share. However, a recent Gallup survey indicated that only a small percentage of a company's customer base actively participates in loyalty programs—and that customers who are fully involved with a loyalty program tend to spend more money. One managing consultant at Gallup says the way companies can create more value is by fully engaging customers by building an emotional connection with their brand or product.[8]

The relationship between market share and profitability is evident in PIMS data that reveal an average 32 percent return on investment (ROI) for firms with market shares above 40 percent. In contrast, average ROI decreases to 24 percent for firms whose market shares are between 20 and 40 percent. Firms with a minor market share (less than 10 percent) generate average pretax investment returns of under 10 percent.[9]

The relationship also applies to a firm's individual brands. PIMS researchers compared the top four brands in each market segment they studied. Their data revealed the leading brand typically generates after-tax ROI of 18 percent, considerably higher than the second-ranked brand. Weaker brands, on average, fail to earn adequate returns.

Marketers have developed an underlying explanation of the positive relationship between profitability and market share. Firms with large shares accumulate greater operating experience and lower overall costs relative to competitors with smaller market shares. Accordingly, effective segmentation strategies might focus on obtaining larger shares of smaller markets and on avoiding smaller shares of larger ones. A firm might achieve higher financial returns by becoming a major competitor in several smaller market segments than by remaining a relatively minor player in a larger market.

Meeting Competition Objectives

A third set of pricing objectives seeks simply to meet competitors' prices. In many lines of business, firms set their own prices to match those of established industry price leaders. Price is a pivotal factor in the ongoing competition between long-distance telephone services and wireless carriers. In addition to unlimited calls to the United States and Canada for $2.99 a month, Skype, the Internet calling company now owned by Microsoft, allows unlimited calls to overseas landline phones in 40 other countries for $13.99 a month. The countries include most of Europe as well as Australia, New Zealand, China, Japan, Korea, Malaysia, and Taiwan.[10]

Pricing objectives tied directly to meeting prices charged by major competitors deemphasize the price element of the marketing mix and focus more strongly on nonprice variables. Pricing is a highly visible component of a firm's marketing mix and an easy and effective tool for obtaining a differential advantage over competitors. It is, however, a tool other firms can easily duplicate through price reductions of their own. Because price changes directly affect overall profitability in an industry, many firms attempt to promote stable prices by meeting competitors' prices and competing for market share by focusing on product strategies, promotional decisions, and distribution—the nonprice elements of the marketing mix.

Value Pricing

When discounts become normal elements of a competitive marketplace, other marketing mix elements gain importance in purchase decisions. In such instances, overall product value—not just price—determines product choice. In recent years, a new strategy, value pricing, has emerged that emphasizes the benefits a product provides in comparison to the price and quality levels of competing offerings. This strategy typically works best for relatively low-priced goods and services. Kroger, a major player in the grocery industry, offers product discounts, marked by yellow tags, in its more than 2,400 stores in 31 states. Reduced-price products include meat, produce, and health and beauty aids. Seniors receive a regular 10 percent discount on store-brand products, including cereal, bread, and skin-care products.[11]

value pricing Pricing strategy that emphasizes benefits derived from a product in comparison to the price and quality levels of competing offerings.

Value-priced products generally cost less than premium brands, but marketers point out that value does not necessarily mean *inexpensive*. The challenge for those who compete on value is to convince customers that low-priced brands offer quality comparable to that of a higher-priced product. An increasing number of alternative products and private-label brands has resulted in a more competitive marketplace in recent years. Trader Joe's—a rapidly growing grocery chain that began in the Los Angeles area and has since expanded throughout the West, Midwest, and Mid-Atlantic states—stands out from other specialty food stores with its cedar plank walls, nautical décor, and a captain

(the store manager), first mate (the assistant manager), and the other employees (known as crew members) all attired in colorful Hawaiian shirts. The chain uses value pricing for the over 2,000 upscale food products it develops or imports. It sells wines, cheeses, meats, fish, and other unique gourmet items at everyday close-out prices, mostly under its own brand names. If the high quality doesn't persuade customers at its 340-plus stores to buy, they can also note that Trader Joe's tuna are caught without environmentally dangerous nets, its dried apricots contain no sulfur preservatives, and its peanut butter is organic.[12]

Kroger offers thousands of product discounts, marked by yellow tags, in its more than 2,400 stores.

Value pricing is perhaps best seen in the personal computer (PC) industry. In the past few years, PC prices collapsed, reducing the effectiveness of traditional pricing strategies intended to meet competition. However, in a recent quarter, PC sales weakened; one manufacturer experienced a 10 percent decline from the same quarter in the previous year. Floods in Thailand, where some components are made, were one factor. Worldwide PC sales were

© ZUMA Wire Service/Alamy

Trader Joe's uses value pricing to sell upscale food products.

expected to rise as economic recovery strengthened, but prices for hard drives and memory have recently increased. Apple's Macintosh computers and iPad tablets use a different type of memory, for which prices are falling, so Apple may have a competitive edge.[13]

PRESTIGE OBJECTIVES

The final category of pricing objectives, unrelated to either profitability or sales volume, is prestige objectives. Prestige pricing establishes a relatively high price to develop and maintain an image of quality and exclusiveness that appeals to status-conscious consumers. Such objectives reflect marketers' recognition of the role of price in creating an overall image of the firm and its product offerings.

Prestige objectives affect the price tags of such products as David Yurman jewelry, Tag Heuer watches, Baccarat crystal, and Lenox china. When a perfume marketer sets a price of $400 or more per ounce, this choice reflects an emphasis on image far more than the cost of ingredients. Analyses have shown that ingredients account for less than 5 percent of a perfume's cost. Thus, advertisements for Clive Christian's No. 1 that promote the fragrance as the "the world's most expensive perfume" use price to promote product prestige. Diamond jewelry also uses prestige pricing to convey an image of quality and timelessness.

In the business world, private jet ownership imparts an image of prestige, power, and high price tags—too high for most business travelers to consider. Most owners are worth $10 million or more, according to one industry researcher, and include those who see private ownership, enabling them to visit three cities in a day as a business need, not a luxury. Recognizing that cost is the primary factor that makes jet ownership prohibitive, companies like NetJets have created an alternative: fractional ownership. Corporate boards of directors pressed to cut costs in a weak economy are much more willing to pay for a share in a jet than to purchase a whole new aircraft.[14]

PRICING OBJECTIVES OF NOT-FOR-PROFIT ORGANIZATIONS

Pricing is also a key element of the marketing mix for not-for-profit organizations. Pricing strategy can help these groups achieve a variety of organizational goals:

1. *Profit maximization.* While not-for-profit organizations by definition do not cite profitability as a primary goal, numerous instances exist in which they try to maximize their returns on single events or a series of events. A $1,000-a-plate political fund-raiser is a classic example.

2. *Cost recovery.* Some not-for-profit organizations attempt to recover only the actual cost of operating the unit. Mass transit, toll roads and bridges, and most private colleges and universities are common examples. In Brooklyn, New York, the Atlantic Avenue subway station now carries the sponsored name Barclays Center. London-based Barclays Bank will pay the Metropolitan Transportation Authority, which operates the New York City subway system, $4 million over 20 years.[15]

3. *Market incentives.* Other not-for-profit groups follow a lower-than-average pricing policy or offer a free service to encourage increased usage of the good or service. *Smithsonian* magazine sponsors

Prestige objectives help market exclusive products like fractional ownership of private jets.

Museum Day Live!—free admission on a specific day to more than 1,400 museums around the country in an effort to educate the general public about art, science, and historical events.[16]

4. *Market suppression.* Price can also discourage consumption. High prices help accomplish social objectives independent of the costs of providing goods or services. Illustrations include tobacco and alcohol taxes—the so-called sin taxes—parking fines, tolls, and gasoline excise taxes. Recently, the Illinois state legislature voted to nearly double the tax on cigarettes and other tobacco-related products. The revenue the new tax generates will go to state-funded programs.[17]

METHODS FOR DETERMINING PRICES

Marketers determine prices in two basic ways: by applying the theoretical concepts of supply and demand and by completing cost-oriented analyses. During the first part of the 20th century, most discussions of price determination emphasized the classical concepts of supply and demand. During the last half of the century, however, the emphasis began to shift to a cost-oriented approach. Hindsight reveals certain flaws in both concepts.

After a harsh winter devastated Florida's orange crop, Tropicana shrank its half-gallon orange-juice containers by 5 ounces and charged the same price rather than raise the price for a full half-gallon container.

Jfmdesign/iStockphoto.com

customary prices
Traditional prices that customers expect to pay for certain goods and services.

Treatments of this subject often overlook another concept of price determination—one based on the impact of custom and tradition. Customary prices are retail prices consumers expect as a result of tradition and social habit. Candy makers have attempted to maintain traditional price levels by greatly reducing overall product size. Similar practices have prevailed in the marketing of soft drinks, chips, mayonnaise, soap, and ice cream as manufacturers attempt to balance consumer expectations of customary prices with the realities of rising costs. Sometimes customary prices hide a real price increase, however, when the quantity of the product has been imperceptibly reduced. After a freeze in Florida one recent winter that devastated the orange crop, Tropicana and Florida's Natural shrank their half-gallon orange-juice containers by 5 ounces rather than raise the price for a full half gallon. Tropicana commented that research showed consumers are willing to pay the same price even for a little less juice. Kraft Foods' macaroni and cheese comes with two different noodle shapes, spiral and elbow. The spiral kind contains 5.5 ounces of pasta, while the elbow kind has 7.25 ounces—but both come in the same size box and sell for the same price. The company says that the manufacturing process for spiral pasta is more complicated and that it manufactures more elbow pasta.[18]

The changing price of U.S. gasoline presents another example of supply and demand. When average prices for a gallon of gas rise substantially, frustrated drivers begin demanding to know who, if anyone, is cashing in on the price spike. Even though the United States is the world's largest refiner of gasoline, strong demand leads to an increase in oil imports. Higher gas prices have effects on other consumer costs as well. The U.S. Department of Energy counts 57 different major uses of petroleum in addition to gasoline, in products ranging from cosmetics to chewing gum. The rising costs of raw materials and energy have caused many tire manufacturers to charge more for their tires. China mines almost 95 percent of rare-earth metals, which are used in energy-efficient light bulbs and electric cars. The country has recently begun taking steps to reduce the high levels of pollution caused by the mining and processing of rare earths—steps that have driven up the price of these important metals.[19]

With fuel costs at record highs, hybrid cars are in greater demand than ever before, and some dealers have had months-long waiting lists even at premium prices. Toyota recently unveiled a new model of its fuel-efficient Prius plug-in hybrid, which promises an average of 45 miles per gallon. Unlike other hybrids, the Prius plug-in gives drivers the choice of running on electricity alone or hybrid without draining the battery.[20]

Drivers face yet another high cost—that of traveling on the nation's bridges and roads. Their situation is complicated in the East and Northeast by the different prices set for drivers from different E-Z Pass states, which many drivers feel is unfair. See the "Solving an Ethical Controversy" feature to find out more.

ASSESSMENT CHECK

2.4   What goals does pricing strategy help a not-for-profit organization achieve?

2.5   What are the two basic ways in which marketers determine prices?

demand   Schedule of the amounts of a firm's product that consumers will purchase at different prices during a specified time period.

supply   Schedule of the amounts of a good or service that firms will offer for sale at different prices during a specified time period.

PRICE DETERMINATION IN ECONOMIC THEORY

Microeconomics suggests a way of determining prices that assumes a profit-maximization objective. This technique attempts to derive correct equilibrium prices in the marketplace by comparing supply and demand. It also requires more complete analysis than actual business firms typically conduct.

SOLVING AN ETHICAL CONTROVERSY

Differential Pricing for Highway Tolls

Some drivers are paying more to use bridges and highways in the 14 states served by the association of 24 toll agencies called E-Z Pass. The agencies set their own prices and policies, while E-Z Pass distributes transponders (more than 22 million to date) that let drivers zip through toll booths by paying electronically. Most member agencies have little-known discount plans that depend on where drivers bought their E-Z Pass. Those who bought in West Virginia, Rhode Island, New York, New Hampshire, and several other states pay lower tolls in those states than other pass holders.

Should E-Z Pass agencies charge out-of-state drivers higher tolls?

PRO 👍

1. Out-of-state drivers who travel on toll roads in New York and New Jersey should help defray the $900 million deficit faced by the region's Metropolitan Transportation Authority.

2. Differential pricing exists in many other markets, including household products.

CON 👎

1. Higher tolls take advantage of some drivers.

2. Usually only the cash price is posted, so drivers don't even know they're paying more than others when they use the E-Z Pass.

Summary:

Differential toll charges are the biggest complaint the AAA hears from its members across the country. West Virginia claims its four discount plans are too complicated to post at tollbooths. How many motorists will scour E-Z Pass members' websites to find out how to pay less?

Sources: Organizational website, E-Z Pass Group, www.ezpassiag.com, accessed December 5, 2012; "Discounts on E-Z Pass Tolls Vary by State," *Charleston Daily Mail*, accessed December 5, 2012, www.dailymail.com; David Segal, "Trouble at the Tollbooth," *The New York Times*, accessed December 5, 2012, www.nytimes.com; Jeff Plungis, "New York, New Jersey Overcharge Some Motorists, AAA Says," *Bloomberg News*, accessed December 5, 2012, www.bloomberg.com; "CBS2 Investigates: Living Through an E-Z Pass Nightmare," *CBS News*, accessed December 5, 2012, http://newyork.cbslocal.com.

Demand refers to a schedule of the amounts of a firm's product that consumers will purchase at different prices during a specified time period. **Supply** refers to a schedule of the amounts of a good or service that will be offered for sale at different prices during a specified period. These schedules may vary for different types of market structures. Businesses operate and set prices in four types of market structures: pure competition, monopolistic competition, oligopoly, and monopoly.

Pure competition is a market structure with so many buyers and sellers that no single participant can significantly influence price. Pure competition presupposes other market conditions as well: homogeneous products and ease of entry for sellers due to low start-up costs. The agricultural sector exhibits many characteristics of a purely competitive market, making it the closest actual example. Still, many U.S. ranchers have switched their beef herds to an all-grass diet in an attempt to differentiate their product from those raised in feedlots.

Monopolistic competition typifies most retailing and features large numbers of buyers and sellers. These diverse parties exchange heterogeneous, relatively well-differentiated products, giving marketers some control over prices.

Relatively few sellers compete in an **oligopoly**. Pricing decisions by each seller are likely to affect the market, but no single seller controls it. High start-up costs form significant barriers to entry for new competitors. Each firm's demand curve in an oligopolistic market displays a

pure competition
Market structure characterized by homogeneous products in which there are so many buyers and sellers that none has a significant influence on price.

monopolistic competition Market structure involving a heterogeneous product and product differentiation among competing suppliers, allowing the marketer some degree of control over prices.

TABLE 18.2 Distinguishing Features of the Four Market Structures

Characteristics	Type of Market Structure			
	Pure Competition	Monopolistic Competition	Oligopoly	Monopoly
Number of competitors	Many	Few to many	Few	No direct competitors
Ease of entry into industry by new firms	Easy	Somewhat difficult	Difficult	Regulated by government
Similarity of goods or services offered by competing firms	Similar	Different	Can be either similar or different	No directly competing goods or services
Control over prices by individual firms	None	Some	Some	Considerable
Demand curves facing individual firms	Totally elastic	Can be either elastic or inelastic	Kinked; inelastic below kink; more elastic above	Can be either elastic or inelastic
Examples	Indiana soybean farm	Best Buy stores	Verizon Wireless	Waste Management

© Cengage Learning

oligopoly Market structure in which relatively few sellers compete and where high start-up costs form barriers to keep out new competitors.

unique kink at the current market price. Because of the impact of a single competitor on total industry sales, competitors usually quickly match any attempt by one firm to generate additional sales by reducing prices. Price cutting in such industries is likely to reduce total industry revenues. Oligopolies operate in the petroleum refining, automobile, tobacco, and airline industries.

Airline mergers, rising fuel prices, and a slow economy have led U.S. airlines to not only raise prices but also cut capacity, limiting flights to major cities and eliminating service to small and mid-size airports. The president of Cambridge Aviation Research says, "The airlines are shrinking and putting a premium on their core network. The bottom states have suffered most and have not kept up with the growth in the most robust airports in the country."[21]

monopoly Market structure in which a single seller dominates trade in a good or service for which buyers can find no close substitutes.

A **monopoly** is a market structure in which only one seller of a product exists and for which there are no close substitutes. Antitrust legislation has nearly eliminated all but temporary monopolies, such as those created through patent protection. Regulated industries constitute another form of monopoly. The government allows regulated monopolies in markets in which competition would lead to an uneconomical duplication of services. In return for such a license, the government reserves the right to regulate the monopoly's rate of return.

variable cost Cost that changes with the level of production (such as labor and raw materials costs).

The four types of market structures are compared in Table 18.2 on the following bases: number of competitors, ease of entry into the industry by new firms, similarity of competing products, degree of control over price by individual firms, and the elasticity or inelasticity of the demand curve facing the individual firm. Elasticity—the degree of consumer responsiveness to changes in price—is discussed in more detail in a later section.

fixed cost Cost that remains stable at any production level within a certain range (such as a lease payment or insurance cost).

COST AND REVENUE CURVES

Marketers must set a price for a product that generates sufficient revenue to cover the costs of producing and marketing it. A product's total cost is composed of total variable costs and total fixed costs. Variable costs, such as raw materials and labor costs, change with the level of production, and fixed costs, such as lease payments or insurance costs, remain stable at any production level within a certain range. Average total costs are calculated by dividing the sum of the variable and fixed costs by the number of units produced. Finally, marginal cost is the change in total cost that results from producing an additional unit of output.

average total cost Cost calculated by dividing the sum of the variable and fixed costs by the number of units produced.

marginal cost Change in total cost that results from producing an additional unit of output.

The demand side of the pricing equation focuses on revenue curves. Average revenue is calculated by dividing total revenue by the quantity associated with these revenues. Average revenue

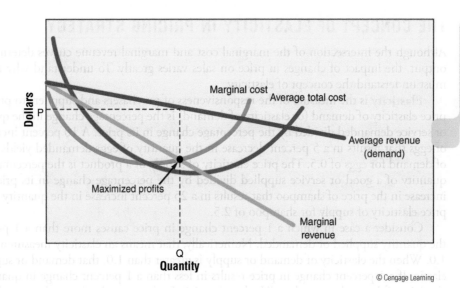

FIGURE 18.1
**Determining
Price by Relating
Marginal Revenue to
Marginal Cost**

is actually the demand curve facing the firm. Marginal revenue is the change in total revenue that results from selling an additional unit of output. Figure 18.1 shows the relationships of various cost and revenue measures; the firm maximizes its profits when marginal costs equal marginal revenues.

Table 18.3 illustrates why the intersection of the marginal cost and marginal revenue curves is the logical point at which to maximize revenue for the organization. Although the firm can earn a profit at several different prices, the price at which it earns maximum profits is $22. At a price of $24, $66 in profits is earned—$4 less than the $70 profit at the $22 price. If a price of $20 is set to attract additional sales, the marginal costs of the extra sales ($7) are greater than the marginal revenues received ($6), and total profits decline.

ASSESSMENT CHECK

2.6 What are the four types of market structures?

2.7 Identify the two types of costs that make up a product's total cost.

TABLE 18.3 Price Determination Using Marginal Analysis

Price	Number Sold	Total Revenue	Marginal Revenue	Total Costs	Marginal Costs	Profits (Total Revenue Minus Total Costs)
—	—	—	—	—	—	$(50)
$34	1	$34	$34	$57	$7	(23)
32	2	64	30	62	5	2
30	3	90	26	66	4	24
28	4	112	22	69	3	43
26	5	130	18	73	4	57
24	6	144	14	78	5	66
22	7	154	10	84	6	70
20	8	160	6	91	7	69
18	9	162	2	100	9	62
16	10	160	(2)	101	11	50

© Cengage Learning

3 Explain price elasticity and its determinants.

elasticity Measure of responsiveness of purchasers and suppliers to a change in price.

THE CONCEPT OF ELASTICITY IN PRICING STRATEGY

Although the intersection of the marginal cost and marginal revenue curves determines the level of output, the impact of changes in price on sales varies greatly. To understand why it fluctuates, one must understand the concept of elasticity.

Elasticity is the measure of the responsiveness of purchasers and suppliers to price changes. The price elasticity of demand (or elasticity of demand) is the percentage change in the quantity of a good or service demanded divided by the percentage change in its price. A 10 percent increase in the price of eggs that results in a 5 percent decrease in the quantity of eggs demanded yields a price elasticity of demand for eggs of 0.5. The price elasticity of supply of a product is the percentage change in the quantity of a good or service supplied divided by the percentage change in its price. A 10 percent increase in the price of shampoo that results in a 25 percent increase in the quantity supplied yields a price elasticity of supply for shampoo of 2.5.

Consider a case in which a 1 percent change in price causes more than a 1 percent change in the quantity supplied or demanded. Numerically, that means an elasticity measurement greater than 1.0. When the elasticity of demand or supply is greater than 1.0, that demand or supply is said to be elastic. If a 1 percent change in price results in less than a 1 percent change in quantity, a product's elasticity of demand or supply will be less than 1.0. In that case, the demand or supply is called *inelastic.* For example, the demand for cigarettes is relatively inelastic; research studies have shown that a 10 percent increase in cigarette prices results in only a 4 percent sales decline.

In some countries whose economies are in shambles, price levels bear little resemblance to the laws of elasticity or supply and demand. Prices in Zimbabwe once rose at unheard-of rates, the result of hyperinflation that rose to more than 7,600 percent in a *month*—estimated to be as high as 12.5 million percent a year. More recently, however, changes in the country's monetary policies, including the abandonment of its local currency, began to bring prices down and it appeared that inflation in Zimbabwe may continue to drop.[22]

Determinants of Elasticity

Why is the elasticity of supply or demand high for some products and low for others? What determines demand elasticity? One major factor influencing the elasticity of demand is the availability of substitutes or complements. If consumers can easily find close substitutes for a good or service, the product's demand tends to be elastic. A product's role as a complement to the use of another product

A 10 percent increase in the price of eggs that results in a 5 percent decrease in the quantity of eggs demanded yields a price elasticity of demand for eggs of 0.5.

© Feng Yu/Shutterstock.com

also affects its degree of price elasticity. For example, the relatively inelastic demand for motor oil reflects its role as a complement to a more important product, gasoline. High prices for gasoline, in turn, are fueling a search for alternative fuels.[23]

As increasing numbers of buyers and sellers complete their business transactions online, the elasticity of a product's demand is drastically affected. Take major discounters and other price-competitive stores, for example. Small businesses and individual do-it-yourselfers shop Lowe's for tools, such as wheelbarrows; parents look for birthday gifts at Walmart; and homeowners go to Home Depot for new refrigerators or stoves. Today, however, the Internet lets consumers contact many more providers directly, often giving them better selections and prices for their efforts with service sites, such as Shopzilla.com for consumer goods and electronics, Net-à-Porter.com for high-fashion clothing, Kayak.com for travel bargains, and Shoebuy.com for shoes from dozens of different manufacturers. The increased options available to shoppers combine to create a market characterized by demand elasticity.

Elasticity of demand also depends on whether a product is perceived as a necessity or a luxury. The Four Seasons chain of luxury hotels and resorts enjoys a strong reputation for service, comfort, and exclusiveness and is a favorite among affluent individual travelers and business professionals.

Elasticity also depends on the portion of a person's budget spent on a good or service. For example, people no longer really need matches; they can easily find good substitutes. Nonetheless, the demand for matches remains very inelastic, because people spend so little on them that they hardly notice a price change. In contrast, the demand for housing or transportation is not totally inelastic, even though they are necessities, because both consume large parts of a consumer's budget.

Elasticity of demand also responds to consumers' time perspectives. Demand often shows less elasticity in the short run than in the long run. Consider the demand for home air conditioning. In the short run, people pay rising energy prices, because they find it difficult to cut back on the quantities they use. Accustomed to living with specific temperature settings and dressing in certain ways, they prefer to pay more during a few months of the year than to explore other possibilities. Over the long term, though, they may consider insulating their homes and planting shade trees to reduce cooling costs.

Elasticity and Revenue

The elasticity of demand exerts an important influence on variations in total revenue as a result of changes in the price of a good or service. Assume, for example, that Atlanta's Metropolitan Atlanta Rapid Transit Authority (MARTA) officials are considering alternative methods of raising more money for their budget. One possible method for increasing revenues would be to change rail pass fares for commuters. But should MARTA raise or lower the price of a pass? The correct answer depends on the elasticity of demand for transit rides. A 10 percent decrease in fares should attract more riders, but unless it stimulates more than a 10 percent increase in riders, total revenue will fall. A 10 percent increase in fares will bring in more money per rider, but if more than 10 percent of the riders stop using the system, total revenue will fall. A price cut will increase revenue only for a product with elastic demand, and a price increase will raise revenue only for a product with inelastic demand. MARTA officials seem to believe the demand for rapid rail transit is inelastic; they raise fares when they need more operating funds.

ASSESSMENT CHECK

3.1 What are the determinants of elasticity?

3.2 What is the usual relationship between elasticity and revenue?

PRACTICAL PROBLEMS OF PRICE THEORY

Marketers may thoroughly understand price theory concepts but still encounter difficulty applying them in practice. What practical limitations interfere with setting prices? First, many firms do not attempt to maximize profits. Economic analysis is subject to the same limitations as the assumptions on which it is based—for example, the proposition that all firms attempt to maximize profits. Second, it is difficult to estimate demand curves. Modern accounting procedures provide managers with a clear understanding of cost structures, so managers can readily comprehend the supply side of the pricing equation. But they find it difficult to estimate demand at various price levels. Demand curves must be based on marketing research estimates that may be less exact than cost figures. Although the demand element can be identified, it is often difficult to measure in real-world settings.

4 List the practical problems involved in applying price theory concepts to actual pricing decisions.

ASSESSMENT CHECK

4.1 List the three reasons why it is difficult to put price theory into practice.

PRICE DETERMINATION IN PRACTICE

5 **Explain the major cost-plus approaches to price setting.**

cost-plus pricing
Practice of adding a percentage of specified dollar amount—or markup—to the base cost of a product to cover unassigned costs and to provide a profit.

The practical limitations inherent in price theory have forced practitioners to turn to other techniques. Cost-plus pricing, the most popular method, uses a base-cost figure per unit and adds a markup to cover unassigned costs and to provide a profit. The only real difference among the multitude of cost-plus techniques is the relative sophistication of the costing procedures employed. For example, a local apparel shop may set prices by adding a 45 percent markup to the invoice price charged by the supplier. The markup is expected to cover all other expenses and permit the owner to earn a reasonable return on the sale of clothes. Car dealerships often rely on a markup when they set their prices; see the "Career Readiness" feature for some tips on using pricing savvy when buying a car.

In contrast to this rather simple pricing mechanism, a large manufacturer may employ a complex pricing formula requiring several calculations. However, this method merely adds a more complicated procedure to the simpler, traditional method for calculating costs. In the end, someone must still make a decision about the markup. The apparel shop and the large manufacturer may figure costs differently, but they are remarkably similar in completing the markup side of the equation.

Cost-plus pricing often works well for a business that keeps its costs low, allowing it to set its prices lower than those of competitors and still make a profit. Walmart keeps costs low by buying most of its inventory directly from manufacturers, using a supply chain that slashes inventory costs by quickly replenishing inventory as items are sold and relying on other intermediaries only in special instances such as localized items. This strategy has played a major role in the discounter's becoming the world's largest retailer.

CAREER READINESS

Getting the Best Price on Your Auto Purchase

Making a big purchase like a car is good practice for other major decisions you may make in your career. Here's how to get the most for your money.

- Don't fall in love with a car until you own it. It's a mistake to buy a car you can't afford just because you decide you have to have it.

- Do your homework before you visit a dealership. Research the safety, fuel economy, and reliability of the car or cars you're considering, and test-drive well ahead of purchasing.

- Know exactly what you can afford. Find the dealer's invoice price for the car online, and be prepared to visit more than one dealer to shop for the best price.

- Make an offer close to the invoice price, and let the dealer know you plan to shop around.

- Check out financing options on your own. Even if you decide on dealer financing, you'll want to be sure it's really cheaper than the rate at a bank or credit union.

- If you have a car to trade in, find out its true value at an auto-pricing website.

- If you can, pay cash. It reduces the dealer's administrative costs and the savings should pass on to you.

Sources: Miriam Caldwell, "How to Buy Your First Car," *About.com,* accessed December 5, 2012, http://moneyfor20s.about.com; "Car Buying Advice," *Consumer Reports,* accessed December 5, 2012, www.consumerreports.org; "Buying Your First Car? A Guide to Successfully Closing the Deal," *NYE Automotive Group,* accessed December 5, 2012, http://nyeauto.com; Phil M. Fowler, "How to Get the Best Price on a New Car," *eHow,* accessed December 5, 2012, www.ehow.com.

ALTERNATIVE PRICING PROCEDURES

The two most common cost-oriented pricing procedures are the full-cost method and the incremental-cost method. **Full-cost pricing** uses all relevant variable costs in setting a product's price. In addition, it allocates fixed costs that cannot be directly attributed to the production of the specific priced item. Under the full-cost method, if job order 515 in a printing plant amounts to 0.000127 percent of the plant's total output, then 0.000127 percent of the firm's overhead expenses are charged to that job. This approach allows the marketer to recover all costs plus the amount added as a profit margin.

The full-cost approach has two basic deficiencies. First, no consideration of competition or demand exists for the item; perhaps no one wants to pay the price the firm has calculated. Second, any method for allocating overhead (fixed expenses) is arbitrary and may be unrealistic—in manufacturing, overhead allocations are often tied to direct labor hours; in retailing, the square footage of each profit center is sometimes the factor used in computations. Regardless of the technique employed, it is difficult to show a cause–effect relationship between the allocated cost and most products.

One way to overcome the arbitrary allocation of fixed expenses is with **incremental-cost pricing**, which attempts to use only costs directly attributable to a specific output in setting prices. Consider a very small-scale manufacturer with the following income statement:

Sales (10,000 at $10)		$ 100,000
Expenses:		
Variable	$50,000	
Fixed	40,000	90,000
Net profit		$ 10,000

Suppose the firm is offered a contract for an additional 5,000 units. Because the peak season is over, these items can be produced at the same average variable cost. Assume the labor force would otherwise be working on maintenance projects. How low should the firm price its product to get the contract?

Under the full-cost approach, the lowest price would be $9 per unit. This figure is obtained by dividing the $90,000 in expenses by an output of 10,000 units. The incremental approach, on the other hand, could permit any price above $5, which would significantly increase the possibility of securing the additional contract. This price would be composed of the $5 variable cost associated with each unit of production plus a $0.10-per-unit contribution to fixed expenses and overhead. With a $5.10 proposed price, the income statement now looks like this:

Sales (10,000 at $10; 5,000 at $5.10)		$ 125,500
Expenses:		
Variable	$75,000	
Fixed	40,000	$115,000
Net profit		$ 10,500

Profits thus increase under the incremental approach.

Admittedly, the illustration is based on two assumptions: (1) the ability to isolate markets such that selling at the lower price will not affect the price received in other markets and (2) the absence of legal restrictions on the firm. The example, however, does illustrate that profits can sometimes be enhanced by using the incremental approach.

full-cost pricing Pricing method that uses all relevant variable costs in setting a product's price and allocates those fixed costs not directly attributed to the production of the priced item.

incremental-cost pricing Pricing method that attempts to use only costs directly attributable to a specific output in setting prices.

 ASSESSMENT CHECK

5.1 What is full-cost pricing?

5.2 What is incremental-cost pricing?

BREAKEVEN ANALYSIS

breakeven analysis
Pricing technique used to determine the number of products that must be sold at a specified price to generate enough revenue to cover total cost.

Breakeven analysis is a means of determining the number of goods or services that must be sold at a given price to generate sufficient revenue to cover total costs. Figure 18.2 graphically depicts this process. The total cost curve includes both fixed and variable segments, and total fixed cost is represented by a horizontal line. Average variable cost is assumed to be constant per unit as it was in the example for incremental pricing.

The breakeven point is the point at which total revenue equals total cost. In the example in Figure 18.2, a selling price of $10 and an average variable cost of $5 result in a per-unit contribution to fixed cost of $5. The breakeven point in terms of units is found by using the following formula, in which the per-unit contribution equals the product's price less the variable cost per unit:

$$\text{Breakeven point (in units)} = \frac{\text{Total fixed cost}}{\text{Per-unit contribution to fixed cost}}$$

$$\text{Breakeven point (in units)} = \frac{\$40{,}000}{\$5} = 8{,}000 \text{ units}$$

The breakeven point in dollars is found with the following formula:

$$\text{Breakeven point (in dollars)} = \frac{\text{Total fixed cost}}{1 - \text{Variable cost per unit price}}$$

$$\text{Breakeven point (in dollars)} = \frac{\$40{,}000}{1 - (\$5/\$10)} = \frac{\$40{,}000}{0.5} = \$80{,}000$$

Sometimes breakeven is reached by reducing costs. Several years after declaring bankruptcy and being bailed out by the U.S. government, General Motors is once again the world's biggest auto manufacturer. It regained that status by reducing costs and shutting some factories.[24]

Once the breakeven point has been reached, sufficient revenues will have been obtained from sales to cover all fixed costs. Any additional sales will generate per-unit profits equal to the difference between the product's selling price and the variable cost of each unit. As Figure 18.2 reveals, sales of 8,001 units (1 unit above the breakeven point) will produce net profits of $5 ($10 sales price less per-unit variable cost of $5). Once all fixed costs have been covered, the per-unit contribution will become the per-unit profit.

Target Returns

Although breakeven analysis indicates the sales level at which the firm will incur neither profits nor losses, most marketers include a targeted profit in their analyses. In some instances, management sets a desired dollar return when considering a proposed new product or other marketing strategy. A retailer may set a desired profit of $250,000 in considering whether to expand to a second location. In other instances, the target return may be expressed in percentages, such as a 15 percent return on sales. These target returns can be calculated as follows:

FIGURE 18.2
Breakeven Chart

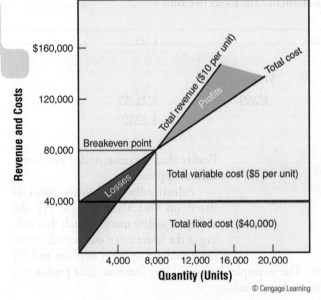

© Cengage Learning

$$\text{Breakeven point (including specific dollar target return)} = \frac{\text{Total fixed cost} + \text{Profit objective}}{\text{Per-unit contribution}}$$

$$\text{Breakeven point (in units)} = \frac{\$40,000 + \$15,000}{\$5} = 11,000 \text{ units}$$

If the target return is expressed as a percentage of sales, it can be included in the breakeven formula as a variable cost. Suppose the marketer in the preceding example seeks a 10 percent return on sales. The desired return is $1 for each product sold (the $10 per-unit selling price multiplied by the 10 percent return on sales). In this case, the basic breakeven formula will remain unchanged, although the variable cost per unit will be increased to reflect the target return, and the per-unit contribution to fixed cost will be reduced to $4. As a result, the breakeven point will increase from 8,000 to 10,000 units:

$$\text{Breakeven point} = \frac{\$40,000}{\$4} = 10,000 \text{ units}$$

 ASSESSMENT CHECK

6.1 What is the formula for finding the breakeven point in units and in dollars?

6.2 What adjustments to the basic breakeven calculation must be made to include target returns?

Evaluation of Breakeven Analysis

Breakeven analysis is an effective tool for marketers in assessing the sales required for covering costs and achieving specified profit levels. It is easily understood by both marketing and nonmarketing executives and may help them decide whether required sales levels for a certain price are realistic goals. However, it has its shortcomings.

First, the model assumes costs can be divided into fixed and variable categories. Some costs, such as salaries and advertising outlays, may be either fixed or variable depending on the particular situation. In addition, the model assumes per-unit variable costs do not change at different levels of operation. However, these may vary because of quantity discounts, more efficient use of the workforce, or other economies resulting from increased levels of production and sales. Finally, the basic breakeven model does not consider demand. It is a cost-based model and does not directly address the crucial question of whether consumers will purchase the product at the specified price and in the quantities required for breaking even or generating profits. The marketer's challenge is to modify the breakeven analysis and the other cost-oriented pricing approaches to incorporate demand analysis. Pricing must be examined from the buyer's perspective. Such decisions cannot be made by only considering cost factors.

 ASSESSMENT CHECK

6.3 What are the advantages of breakeven analysis?

6.4 What are the disadvantages of breakeven analysis?

THE MODIFIED BREAKEVEN CONCEPT

Traditional economic theory considers both costs and demand in determining an equilibrium price. The dual elements of supply and demand are balanced at the point of equilibrium. In actual practice, however, most pricing approaches are largely cost oriented. Because purely cost-oriented approaches to pricing violate the marketing concept, modifications that add demand analysis to the pricing decision are required.

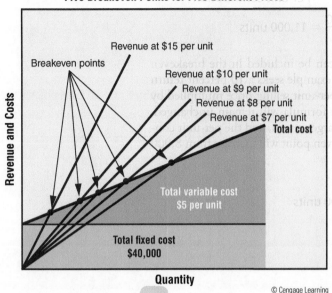

(a)
Five Breakeven Points for Five Different Prices

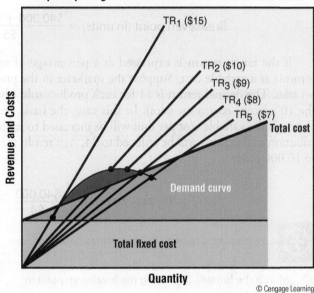

(b)
Superimposing a Demand Curve on the Breakeven Chart

© Cengage Learning

FIGURE 18.3
Modified Breakeven Chart: Parts A and B

modified breakeven analysis Pricing technique used to evaluate consumer demand by comparing the number of products that must be sold at a variety of prices to cover total cost with estimates of expected sales at the various prices.

Consumer research on such issues as degree of price elasticity, consumer price expectations, existence and size of specific market segments, and buyer perceptions of strengths and weaknesses of substitute products is necessary for developing sales estimates at different prices. Because much of the resulting data involves perceptions, attitudes, and future expectations of present and potential customers, such estimates are likely to be less precise than cost estimates. The breakeven analysis method illustrated in Figure 18.2 assumes a constant $10 retail price, regardless of quantity. But what happens at different retail prices? As Figure 18.3 shows, a more sophisticated approach, **modified breakeven analysis**, combines the traditional breakeven analysis model with an evaluation of consumer demand.

Table 18.4 summarizes both the cost and revenue aspects of a number of alternative retail prices. The $5 per-unit variable cost and the $40,000 total fixed cost are based on the costs used in the basic breakeven model. The expected unit sales for each specified retail price are obtained from marketing research. The table contains the information necessary for calculating the breakeven point for each of the five retail price alternatives. These points are shown in Figure 18.3(a).

The data shown in the first two columns of Table 18.4 represent a demand schedule that indicates the number of units consumers are expected to purchase at each of a series of retail prices. As Figure 18.3(b) shows, these data can be superimposed onto a breakeven chart to identify the range of feasible prices for the marketer to charge.

TABLE 18.4 Revenue and Cost Data for Modified Breakeven Analysis

	Revenues		Costs				
Price	Quantity Demanded	Total Revenue	Total Fixed Cost	Total Variable Cost	Total Cost	Breakeven Point (Number of Sales Required to Break Even)	Total Profit (or Loss)
$15	2,500	$37,500	$40,000	$12,500	$52,000	4,000	$(15,000)
10	10,000	100,000	40,000	50,000	90,000	8,000	10,000
9	13,000	117,000	40,000	65,000	105,000	10,000	12,000
8	14,000	112,000	40,000	70,000	110,000	13,334	2,000
7	15,000	105,000	40,000	75,000	115,000	20,000	(10,000)

© Cengage Learning

Figure 18.3 reveals that the range of profitable prices exists from a low of approximately $8 (TR4) to a high of $10 (TR2), with a price of $9 (TR3) generating the greatest projected profits. Changing the retail price produces a new breakeven point. At a relatively high $15 retail price (TR1), the breakeven point is 4,000 units; at a $10 retail price, it is 8,000 units; and at the lowest price considered, $7 (TR5), it is 20,000 units.

The contribution of modified breakeven analysis is that it forces the marketer to consider whether the consumer is likely to purchase the number of units required for achieving breakeven at a given price. It demonstrates that a large number of units sold does not necessarily produce added profits, because—other things being equal—lower prices are necessary for stimulating additional sales. Consequently, it is important to consider both costs and consumer demand in determining the most appropriate price.

 ASSESSMENT CHECK

6.5 What is modified breakeven analysis?

YIELD MANAGEMENT

When most of a firm's costs are fixed over a wide range of outputs, the primary determinant of profitability will be the amount of revenue generated by sales. **Yield management** strategies allow marketers to vary prices based on such factors as demand, even though the cost of providing those goods or services remains the same. OpenTable, based in San Francisco, matches empty tables at restaurants in its network with diners and provides reservation and guest-management software to its restaurant clients. The company has more than 26,000 restaurants on its customer list and has reserved tables for more than 385 million diners in the United States, Canada, Germany, Japan, Mexico, and the United Kingdom.[25]

Similar yield management strategies typify the marketing of such goods and services as the following:

- *sports teams*—the San Francisco Giants charge more for weekend games, and the Colorado Rockies raise ticket prices based on the crowd-pleasing power of visiting teams

- *lodging*—lower prices in the off-season and higher prices during peak-season periods; low-priced weekend rates (except in locations such as Las Vegas, New Orleans, and Charleston, with high weekend tourist visits)

- *auto rental*—lower prices on weekends when business demand is low and higher prices during the week when business demand is higher

- *airfares*—lower prices on nonrefundable tickets with travel restrictions such as advance purchase and Saturday-night stay requirements and penalties for flight changes and higher prices on refundable tickets that can be changed without penalty.

 **ASSESSMENT CHECK**

7.1 Explain the goal of yield management.

Explain the use of yield management in pricing decisions. 7

yield management
Pricing strategy that allows marketers to vary prices based on such factors as demand, even though the cost of providing those goods or services remains the same.

GLOBAL ISSUES IN PRICE DETERMINATION

It is equally important for a firm engaging in global marketing to use a pricing strategy that reflects its overall marketing strategy. Prices must support the company's broader goals, including product development, advertising and sales, customer support, competitive plans, and financial objectives.

Identify the major pricing challenges facing online and international marketers. 8

In general, firms can use five pricing objectives to set prices in global marketing. Four of them are the same pricing objectives we discussed earlier in the chapter: profitability, volume, meeting competition, and prestige. In addition, international marketers work to achieve a fifth objective: price stability.

In the global arena, marketers may choose profitability objectives if their company is a price leader that tends to establish international prices. Profitability objectives also make sense if a firm is a low-cost supplier that can make a good profit on sales.

Volume objectives become especially important on the global stage. Ralph Lauren was the official outfitter of the U.S. Olympic and Paralympic teams at the 2012 London games. The spectacularly choreographed opening and closing ceremonies provide a runway as large as any clothing designer could desire. Replicas of the Lauren U.S. Team apparel line were sold at Ralph Lauren retail stores, at the designer's website, and through U.S. Olympic and Team USA shops.[26]

Increased competition in Europe has spurred firms to work toward the third pricing objective of meeting competitors' prices. The widespread adoption of the euro, the currency of the European Union, became a driving force in price convergence. Now more than 320 million people in 23 European countries use it. The European Commission believed that the adoption of a single currency would promote stability, low inflation, low interest rates, and increased price transparency, all of which help facilitate international trade. However, the recent recession led to a weakening of the euro and financial crisis in heavily indebted Greece and Spain, among other countries. The EU countries agreed to recapitalize failing banks, but with unemployment in the euro zone still very high, the crisis has yet to be resolved.[27]

Prestige is a valid pricing objective in international marketing when products are associated with intangible benefits, such as high quality, exclusiveness, or attractive design. The greater a product's perceived benefits, the higher its price can be. Marketers must be aware, however, that cultural perceptions of quality can differ from one country to the next. Sometimes items that command prestige prices in the United States are considered run-of-the-mill in other nations; sometimes products that are anything but prestigious in America seem exotic to overseas consumers. American patrons, for instance, view McDonald's restaurants as affordable fast-food eateries, but in China, they are seen as fashionable and relatively expensive.

The fifth pricing objective, price stability, is desirable in international markets, although it is difficult to achieve. Wars, terrorism, economic downturns, changing governments and political parties, and shifting trade policies can alter prices. The U.S. convenience-store giant 7-Eleven, usually associated with American suburbia, faces fierce competition at home and abroad, as well as a backlash among consumers against its growing dominance in some urban areas. Rather than put local stores out of business, the chain has launched a Business Conversion Program to convert existing stores into franchises for $25,000. (Normally, franchise fees for new 7-Elevens range from $200,000 to $400,000.) The company also offers its franchisees access to its proprietary Retail Information System, which tracks sales data for stocking purposes. The chain hopes to win over 134 conversions in New York City alone over the next several years but has met some resistance from residents, who prize their often quirky local stores and their contribution to neighborhood flavor.[28]

Price stability can be especially important for producers of commodities—goods and services that have easily accessible substitutes that other nations can supply quickly. Countries that export international commodities, such as wood, chemicals, and agricultural crops, suffer economically when their prices fluctuate. A nation such as Nicaragua, which exports sugarcane, can find that its balance of payments changes drastically when the international price for sugar shifts. This makes it vulnerable to stiff price competition from other sugarcane producers. In contrast, countries that export value-oriented products, rather than commodities, tend to enjoy more stable prices. Prices of electronic equipment and automobiles tend to fluctuate far less than prices of crops such as sugarcane and bananas.

 ASSESSMENT CHECK

8.1 What are five pricing objectives in global and online marketing?

8.2 Why is price stability difficult to achieve in online and global marketing?

STRATEGIC IMPLICATIONS OF MARKETING IN THE 21ST CENTURY

This chapter has focused on traditional pricing concepts and methods—principles critical to all marketing strategies, especially in e-business. Consumers can now compare prices quickly, heightening the already intense competitive pricing environment. The Web allows for prices to be negotiated on the spot, and nearly anything can be auctioned. For products as varied as sports tickets and automobiles, the Web allows consumers to name their price.

While Internet shopping has not resulted in massive price cutting, it has increased the options available to consumers. Online price comparison engines, known as *shopping bots,* promise to help consumers find the lowest price for any good or service. Reverse auctions offered by sites like Priceline.com, which allow

customers to submit the highest price they are willing to pay for airline tickets, could conceivably be extended to other types of goods and are already gaining in popularity in business-to-business purchasing.

Electronic delivery of music, books, and other goods and services will only lead to further price reductions. E-business has smoothed out the friction of time, which kept pricing relatively static. The current obsession with time and the ability to measure it will change the perceptions and pricing of tangible goods. A growing number of products are not made until they are ordered, and increasingly, their prices are no longer fixed; instead, prices can shift up and down in response to changing market conditions.

Get online now for additional learning tools to help you master your marketing knowledge—visit **WWW.CENGAGEBRAIN.COM** today!

REVIEW OF CHAPTER OBJECTIVES

1 Outline the legal constraints on pricing.

A variety of laws affect pricing decisions. Antitrust legislation provides a general set of constraints. The Robinson-Patman Act amended the Clayton Act to prohibit price discrimination in sales to other producers, wholesalers, or retailers not based on a cost differential. This law does not cover export markets or sales to the ultimate consumer. At the state level, unfair-trade laws require sellers to maintain minimum prices for comparable merchandise. These laws have been less frequently enforced in recent years. Fair-trade laws were one legal barrier to competition that was removed in the face of growing price competition. These laws permitted manufacturers to set minimum retail prices for products and require their dealers to sign contracts agreeing to abide by such prices. The Consumer Goods Pricing Act banned interstate use of fair-trade laws.

2 Identify the major categories of pricing objectives.

Pricing objectives are the natural consequence of overall organizational goals and more specific marketing goals. They can be classified into four major groups: (1) profitability objectives, including profit maximization and target returns; (2) volume objectives, including sales maximization and market share; (3) meeting competition objectives; and (4) prestige objectives.

3 Explain price elasticity and its determinants.

Elasticity is an important element in price determination. The degree of consumer responsiveness to price changes is affected by such factors as (1) availability of substitute or complementary goods, (2) the classification of a good or service as a luxury or a necessity, (3) the portion of a consumer's budget spent on an item, and (4) the time perspective.

4 List the practical problems involved in applying price theory concepts to actual pricing decisions.

Three problems complicate applying price theory in actual practice. First, many firms do not attempt to maximize profits,

a basic assumption of price theory. Second, it is difficult to estimate demand curves accurately. Finally, inadequate training of managers and poor communication between economists and practitioners make it difficult to apply price theory in the real world.

5 Explain the major cost-plus approaches to price setting.

Cost-plus pricing uses a base-cost figure per unit and adds a markup to cover unassigned costs and to provide a profit. It is the most commonly used method of setting prices today. There are two primary cost-oriented pricing procedures. Full-cost pricing uses all relevant variable costs in setting a product's price and allocates those fixed costs that cannot be directly attributed to the production of the priced item. Incremental-cost pricing attempts to use only those costs directly attributable to a specific output in setting prices to overcome the arbitrary allocation of fixed expenses. The basic limitation of cost-oriented pricing is that it does not adequately account for product demand.

6 List the chief advantages and shortcomings of using breakeven analysis in pricing decisions.

Breakeven analysis is a means of determining the number of goods or services that must be sold at a given price to generate revenue sufficient for covering total costs. It is easily understood by marketers and may help them decide whether required sales levels for a certain price are realistic goals. Its shortcomings are as follows. First, the model assumes cost can be divided into fixed and variable categories and ignores the problems of arbitrarily making some allocations. Second, it assumes that per-unit variable costs do not change at different levels of operation, ignoring the possibility of quantity discounts, more efficient use of the workforce, and other possible economies. Third, the basic breakeven model does not consider demand. It is a cost-based model and fails to directly address the crucial question of whether consumers will actually purchase the product at the specified price and in the quantities required for breaking even or generating profits. The modified breakeven concept combines traditional breakeven analysis with an evaluation of consumer demand.

It directly addresses the key question of whether consumers will actually purchase the product at different prices and in what quantities.

 7 Explain the use of yield management in pricing decisions.

Yield management pricing strategies are designed to maximize revenues in situations in which costs are fixed, such as airfares, auto rentals, and theater tickets.

 **8 Identify the major pricing challenges facing online and international marketers.**

In general, firms can choose from among five pricing objectives to set prices in global marketing. Four of these objectives are the same pricing objectives discussed earlier: profitability, volume, meeting competition, and prestige. The fifth objective is price stability, which is difficult to achieve because wars, border conflicts, terrorism, economic trends, changing governments and political parties, and shifting trade policies can alter prices. The same types of changes can alter pricing in online marketing.

⊕ ASSESSMENT CHECK: ANSWERS

1.1 What was the purpose of the Robinson-Patman Act? The Robinson-Patman Act amended the Clayton Act to prohibit price discrimination in sales to other producers, wholesalers, or retailers that are not based on a cost differential.

1.2 What laws require sellers to maintain minimum prices for comparable merchandise? At the state level, unfair-trade laws require sellers to maintain minimum prices for comparable merchandise.

1.3 What laws allow manufacturers to set minimum retail prices for their products? Fair-trade laws permitted manufacturers to set minimum retail prices for products and require their dealers to sign contracts agreeing to abide by such prices.

2.1 What are target-return objectives? Target-return objectives are short-run or long-run goals usually stated as percentages of sales or investment.

2.2 What is value pricing? Value pricing emphasizes the benefits a product provides in comparison to the price and quality levels of competing offerings.

2.3 How do prestige objectives affect a seller's pricing strategy? Prestige pricing establishes a relatively high price to develop and maintain an image of quality that appeals to status-conscious customers. The seller uses price to create an overall image of the firm.

2.4 What goals does pricing strategy help a not-for-profit organization achieve? Pricing strategy helps not-for-profit organizations achieve a variety of goals: profit maximization, cost recovery, market incentives, and market suppression.

2.5 What are the two basic ways in which marketers determine prices? Marketers determine prices by applying

the theoretical concepts of supply and demand and by completing cost-oriented analysis.

2.6 What are the four types of market structures? The four types of market structures are pure competition, monopolistic competition, oligopoly, and monopoly.

2.7 Identify the two types of costs that make up a product's total cost. A product's total cost is composed of total variable costs and total fixed costs.

3.1 What are the determinants of elasticity? The degree of consumer responsiveness to price changes—elasticity—is affected by such factors as (1) availability of substitute or complementary goods, (2) the classification of a good or service as a luxury or a necessity, (3) the portion of a consumer's budget spent on an item, and (4) the time perspective.

3.2 What is the usual relationship between elasticity and revenue? A price cut increases revenue only for a product with elastic demand. A price increase raises revenue only for a product with inelastic demand.

4.1 List the three reasons that it is difficult to put price theory into practice. A basic assumption of price theory is all firms attempt to maximize profits. This does not always happen in practice. A second reason is demand curves can be extremely difficult to estimate. Finally, there is poor communication between economists and practitioners, making it difficult to apply price theory in the real world.

5.1 What is full-cost pricing? Full-cost pricing uses all relevant variable costs in setting a product's price.

5.2 What is incremental-cost pricing? Incremental-cost pricing attempts to use only costs directly attributable to a specific output in setting prices to overcome the arbitrary allocation of fixed expenses.

6.1 What is the formula for finding the breakeven point, in units and in dollars? Breakeven point in units = Total fixed cost/Per-unit contribution to fixed cost. Breakeven point in dollars = Total fixed cost/(1 − Variable cost per unit price).

6.2 What adjustments to the basic breakeven calculation must be made to include target returns? Breakeven point (including specific dollar target return) = (Total fixed cost + Profit objective)/Per-unit contribution.

6.3 What are the advantages of breakeven analysis? Breakeven analysis is easily understood by managers and may help them decide whether required sales levels for a certain price are realistic goals.

6.4 What are the disadvantages of breakeven analysis? First, the model assumes cost can be divided into fixed and variable categories and ignores the problems of arbitrarily making some allocations. Second, it assumes that per-unit variable costs do not change at different levels of operation, ignoring the possibility of quantity discounts, more efficient use of the workforce, and other possible economies. Third, the basic breakeven model does not consider demand.

6.5 What is modified breakeven analysis? The modified breakeven concept combines traditional breakeven analysis with an evaluation of consumer demand. It directly addresses the key question of whether consumers will actually purchase the product at different prices and in what quantities.

7.1 Explain the goal of yield management. Yield management pricing strategies are designed to maximize revenues in situations in which costs are fixed, such as airfares, auto rentals, and theater tickets.

8.1 What are five pricing objectives in global and online marketing? Five pricing objectives in global and online marketing are profitability, volume, meeting competition, prestige, and price stability.

8.2 Why is price stability difficult to achieve in online and global marketing? Price stability is difficult to achieve because wars, border conflicts, terrorism, economic trends, changing governments and political parties, and shifting trade policies can alter prices.

MARKETING TERMS YOU NEED TO KNOW

price **610**
Robinson-Patman Act **612**
unfair-trade laws **612**
fair-trade laws **612**
marginal analysis **615**
profit maximization **615**
target-return objective **615**
market-share objective **616**

Profit Impact of Market Strategies (PIMS) project **616**
value pricing **617**
customary prices **620**
demand **620**
supply **620**
pure competition **621**

monopolistic competition **621**
oligopoly **622**
monopoly **622**
variable cost **622**
fixed cost **622**
average total cost **622**
marginal cost **622**

elasticity **624**
cost-plus pricing **626**
full-cost pricing **627**
incremental-cost pricing **627**
breakeven analysis **628**
modified breakeven analysis **630**
yield management **631**

ASSURANCE OF LEARNING REVIEW

1. Distinguish between fair-trade and unfair-trade laws. As a consumer, would you support either fair-trade or unfair-trade laws? Would your answer change if you were the owner of a small store?

2. Give an example of each of the major categories of pricing objectives.

3. What are the major price implications of the PIMS studies? Suggest possible explanations for the relationships the PIMS studies reveal.

4. Identify each factor influencing elasticity and give a specific example of how it affects the degree of elasticity in a good or service.

5. What are the practical problems in applying price theory concepts to actual pricing decisions?

6. Explain the advantages and drawbacks of using incremental-cost pricing rather than full-cost pricing.

7. How can locating the breakeven point assist in price determination?

8. Explain the advantage of modified breakeven analysis over the basic breakeven formula.

9. Explain how the use of yield management can result in greater revenue than other pricing strategies.

10. How do pricing objectives for a global firm differ from those used generally?

PROJECTS AND TEAMWORK EXERCISES

1. In small teams, categorize each of the following as a specific type of pricing objective. Suggest a company or product likely to use each pricing objective. Compare your findings.
   a. 7 percent increase in profits over the previous year
   b. prices no more than 8 percent higher than prices quoted by independent dealers
   c. 5 percent increase in market share
   d. 15 percent return on investment (before taxes)
   e. setting the highest prices in the product category to maintain favorable brand image

2. How are the following prices determined and what do they have in common?
   a. admission to a local museum
   b. college tuition
   c. local sales tax rate
   d. printing of business cards
   e. lawn mowers

3. WebTech Development of Nashville, Tennessee, is considering the possible introduction of a new product proposed by its research and development staff. The firm's marketing director estimates the product can be marketed at a price of $70. Total fixed cost is $278,000, and average variable cost is calculated at $48.
   a. What is the breakeven point in units for the proposed product?
   b. The firm's CEO has suggested a target profit return of $214,000 for the proposed product. How many units must be sold to both break even and achieve this target return?

4. Research the price schedule at your local movie theater multiplex. Which pricing strategy accounts for any price differentials you discover? Why don't matinee prices constitute price discrimination against those who don't qualify for the discounts?

5. How do cell phone companies make money by charging a flat rate per month for a set number of minutes, such as $35 for 300 minutes? Can you think of a more profitable plan? Would it appeal to consumers?

CRITICAL-THINKING EXERCISES

1. Prices at amusement parks might rise if operators such as Disney and Universal Studios add new rides. The parks also have to deal with high fuel prices. List as many things as you can think of that such parks offer patrons in return for their money. Which of these do you think are directly reflected in the price of admission?

2. Recording artists earn only about 9 percent in royalties per CD, using a royalty base of retail price less 25 percent for packaging costs. The rest goes to the producer and to cover recording costs, promotion, copies given away to radio stations and reviewers, and other costs such as videos. What do you think happens to the artist's royalties when a CD is marked down to sell faster? Consider two cases: (a) the marked-down CD sells more copies; and (b) it sells the same number of copies as before.

3. Some finance experts advise consumers not to worry about rising gasoline prices, the cost of which can easily be covered by forgoing one takeout meal a month, but to worry about how high energy prices will affect the rest of the economy. For example, each dollar-a-barrel price increase is equivalent to a $20 million-a-day "tax" on the economy. Explain what this means.

4. Ajax Motor Company recently announced that it will rely less on high-volume strategies such as discounts and rebates to improve its profitability. Another strategy it will employ is to sell fewer cars to rental fleets, which eventually return the cars to Ajax for sale at low auction prices. How do these types of sales affect Ajax's profitability?

ETHICS EXERCISE

You work for a major restaurant in your town. The manager is facing cost pressures from rising food prices and says she needs to raise revenues. She decides to reduce the size of the meal portions and use cheaper cuts of meat and fish in some entrées while holding the menu prices constant. She tells you and other staff members not to mention the changes to customers and to deflect any questions or complaints you hear. The descriptions in the menu will not be changed, she says, "because the printing costs would be too high."

1. You know the restaurant advertises the quality of its ingredients in the local media. But the menu changes are not advertised, and it bothers you. What course of action would you take?

2. A customer mentions that the beef in the dish he ordered is "tough and dry" and the order seems smaller than before. What would you do?

INTERNET EXERCISES

1. **Price competition.** Using a popular travel site, look up airfares for each of the following pairs of cities:

    New York to Los Angeles
    Atlanta to Detroit
    Jacksonville, Florida, to Dallas
    Chicago to Omaha
    Denver to Albuquerque

    Do some fares appear higher (on a per-mile basis) than others? Do these differences reflect how many airlines provide nonstop service between each pair of cities? What about the impact on fares of so-called discount airlines (such as JetBlue)?

    www.expedia.com
    www.kayak.com

2. **Yield management.** Say you'd like to visit Walt Disney World. Visit the website to price week-long stays at various times of the year. Be sure to choose similar hotels. Which weeks are the most and least expensive? Do the days of arrival and departure make any difference? Prepare a summary of your findings and bring it to class so you can participate in a discussion on yield management.

    http://disneyworld.disney.go.com/vacation-packages

3. **Airbus and Boeing subsidies.** The United States and European Union have had a long-running dispute over allegations of improper government subsidies to commercial aircraft manufacturers (the U.S. about Airbus and the EU about Boeing). Government subsidies may give the manufacturer a price advantage over its competition. Both sides have filed complaints with the World Trade Organization. Go to the website of the WTO and write a report outlining the trade dispute and its current status.

    www.wto.org

Note: Internet Web addresses change frequently. If you don't find the exact site listed, you may need to access the organization's home page and search from there or use a search engine such as Google or Bing.

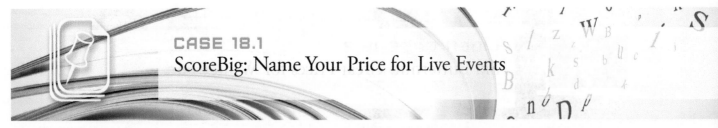

CASE 18.1
ScoreBig: Name Your Price for Live Events

If you've ever tried to get tickets for a game, show, or concert that ended up being sold out, you may be surprised to find that 20 to 40 percent of seats for many such events actually go unsold. High prices keep many otherwise-willing people away from arenas and concert halls, although the live-event business earns $22 billion a year in the United States. The recessionary economy is having an impact on sales, causing even headline acts to cancel performances when tickets priced at hundreds of dollars don't sell.

Now, however, you can bid on hundreds of thousands of those unsold seats through a fast-growing, Los Angeles–based start-up called ScoreBig, which lets consumers make an offer for the event of their choice in much the same way that PriceLine.com auctions hotel rooms and airline tickets.

ScoreBig operates a website through which visitors can bid on upcoming events, and a daily auction on its mobile app for the iPhone, called ScoreBig Daily, for those who don't need to plan ahead and who live in Los Angeles, San Francisco, or New York. In both channels, the company lists events with excess inventories of seats and invites customers to bid for the chance to pay at least 10 percent less and sometimes as much as 60 percent less than the original price, often within a seating area of their choice. The company provides a ballpark price for bidders. If the bid is accepted, a confirming email is sent immediately and the customer prints out the ticket. The average savings is 42 percent, and because

ScoreBig deals directly with event promoters, there are no fees or handling charges.

ScoreBig Daily, the iPhone app, will soon be available on other wireless platforms. It offers tickets for about six performances a day and stores customers' event preferences, whether for sports, music, theater, comedy, or family events. It will offer the same deal to friends if the bidder shares a purchase via social media and will even save nearby seats for friends.

QUESTIONS FOR CRITICAL THINKING

1. Critics say event promoters are to blame for the high number of unsold tickets, because they have continued to raise ticket prices to compensate for unsold seats until they rise out of range for most audiences. Yet promoters feel discounts damage their brands. Can you suggest possible answers to this pricing strategy problem?

2. Is auctioning the best way to eliminate unsold seats? Why or why not?

Sources: Company website, www.scorebig.com, accessed December 5, 2012; Alex Pham, "Start-Up Tries Reverse Scalping to Sell Concert and Sports Tickets," *Los Angeles Times*, accessed December 5, 2012, http://articles.latimes.com; Chris Smith, "ScoreBig Helps New Yorkers See Live Sports Events at a Major Discount," *Forbes*, accessed December 5, 2012, www.forbes.com; Joshua Brustein, "Are You Free Tonight? Bargains to Get You Out," *The New York Times*, accessed December 5, 2012, www.nytimes.com; Tricia Duryee, "ScoreBig Uses Priceline's Model to Name Your Own Price for Live Events," *All Things Digital*, accessed December 5, 2012, http://allthingsd.com; Jason Parker, "ScoreBig on Tickets to Sporting Events and Shows," *CNET.com*, accessed December 5, 2012, http://reviews.cnet.com.

VIDEO CASE 18.2
Ski Butternut: Great Prices for Winter Fun

You might not be a skier or live anywhere near a mountain. Perhaps your idea of fun leans more toward sun, sand, and waves. But as a marketer, you can appreciate the seasonal nature of a small ski resort like Ski Butternut that's tucked away in the Berkshire Mountains of western Massachusetts. How do marketers approach pricing objectives and set prices for a recreational experience that is vulnerable to the whims of weather, climate, overall economic shifts, and the cost of everything from electricity to labor—not to mention the changing incomes and lifestyles of consumers? Ski Butternut has been in business for 50 years, which means that its owners have solved at least some of the pricing puzzle. Matt Sawyer, director of marketing at Ski Butternut, puts it this way: "Our customers are looking for a great value. They're willing to be loyal if we treat them correctly."

Ski Butternut takes both sides of this equation—great value and loyal customers—into consideration for its pricing objectives. Sawyer readily points out that, while Ski Butternut is a for-profit company, the mountain doesn't realize a profit every winter. "Weather plays a huge role," he says. "You don't know whether you're going to be profitable until the end of February." Running a ski resort involves huge up-front costs and a lot of uncertainty. Target-return objectives for the ski school or holiday periods may melt with an early thaw. Ski Butternut managers must try to project a typical operating budget and find ways to carve out profits as their expert customers carve turns on the slopes.

Plenty of ski resorts dot the New England landscape, which puts Ski Butternut in competition for consumers' recreation dollars. So Ski Butternut offers value to customers, hoping to capture market share and increase the volume of skiers on its slopes. The mountain offers value pricing to everyone, with special attention to first-time skiers, families, and season pass-holders. In order to boost the number of skiers who hit the mountain during the week (reducing gridlock on the slopes during weekends), Ski Butternut sets its Monday-Friday lift ticket price at $25. Unlike other mountains, Ski Butternut doesn't offer special deals, such as a "half-price Tuesday" or "ladies' Wednesday." Sawyer believes that customers prefer this straightforward approach to pricing. "It's easy to understand, it's predictable," he explains.

To attract more skiers and snowboarders to the mountain, Ski Butternut offers first-timers a learn-to-ski package for $75, which includes a lift ticket, lesson, and rental equipment (if purchased separately, these three items would total $135). The offer is good every day, all season—no blackout periods for weekends or holidays. "We want people to come when they can," explains Sawyer. For the second visit, skiers can purchase a $100 package ($35 off). "This price point allows people to get exposed to the sport," notes Sawyer. The mountain also offers midweek ski-and-stay packages for $45 per person/per night—a great deal especially when compared to some of the larger, more glamorous resorts.

Kids and families are a special focus for Ski Butternut, which has created several special programs for them. For example, fifth graders ski free Sunday through Friday when accompanied by a paying adult (children who have never skied before get a free first-timers' package). Ski Butternut targets this group, because it's the optimum age to get started, experience success, and continue with a lifetime of skiing or snowboarding. Since New England is home to a number of colleges and universities, Ski Butternut offers a $20 discount to college students, giving them a reason to get outside and ski—and become loyal Butternut customers.

Sawyer points to season pass-holders as one of Ski Butternut's most important customer segments. With a $275 price tag and a break-even point of only five visits, a Ski Butternut season pass represents huge savings to regular skiers. In return, those skiers spend dollars on food, lessons, and other mountain services. And once they've spent the money for the pass, they tend to ski at least 10 to 15 times during a season. "That's great because they are the strongest word-of-mouth advertising we're going to find," acknowledges Sawyer.

Finally, Ski Butternut boosts its volume by offering special rates to groups under its "You Serve, You Save" program, along with Boy Scouts and preregistered ski clubs. Members of the military, police officers, firefighters, and EMT professionals (and their families) receive discounted packages when they make advance reservations. "We want to give them an incentive and say thank you," explains Sawyer.

QUESTIONS FOR CRITICAL THINKING

1. Ski Butternut avoids pricing to meet the competition. Instead, it focuses on the value that it creates for customers. In your opinion, why is this a successful strategy?

2. What factors might determine demand elasticity for Ski Butternut's offerings?

Sources: Company website, www.skibutternut.com, accessed December 5, 2012; "New Website and Mobile Site for Ski Butternut," press release, www.skibutternut.com, accessed December 5, 2012.

NOTES

1. Company website, www2.dollargeneral.com, accessed December 5, 2012; Brad Thomas, "Dollar Stores Take on Wal-Mart, and Are Starting to Win," *Forbes*, accessed December 5, 2012, www.forbes.com; Abram Brown, "Pocket Change Adds Up to Record Q4 Sales for Dollar General," *Forbes*, accessed December 5, 2012, www.forbes.com; Rocco Huang, "Extreme Value Stores," *Market Playground.com*, accessed December 5, 2012, http://marketplayground.com.

2. "Zero Tariffs on U.S.-EU Agricultural Trade," *Fresh Plaza*, accessed December 5, 2102, www.freshplaza.com.

3. Don Lee, "Tariff Escalates U.S.-China Trade Tensions," *Los Angeles Times*, accessed December 5, 2012, http://articles.latimes.com; Todd Woody, "U.S. Solar Industry Booming Despite China Trade War," *Forbes*, accessed December 5, 2012, www.forbes.com.

4. "StubHub Finds Savvy Fans Save 30 Percent Making Last Minute Plans," *Business Wire*, accessed December 5, 2012, www.businesswire.com.

5. Tim Hume, "Fliers Stung by Charges for Window and Aisle Seats," *CNN Travel*, accessed December 5, 2012, www.cnn.com.

6. Richard Jones, "Plant Sales: Quality over Quantity," *Greenhouse Grower*, accessed December 5, 2012, www.greenhousegrower.com.

7. Trefis Team, "P&G Cuts Prices to Save Market Share amid Weaker Outlook," *Trefis*, accessed December 5, 2012, www.trefis.com.

8. Bryant Orr, "Making Loyalty Programs Work," *Gallup Business Journal*, accessed December 5, 2012, http://businessjournal.gallup.com.

9. Robert D. Buzzell, Bradley T. Gale, and Ralph G. M. Sultan, "Market Share—A Key to Profitability," *Harvard Business Review*, accessed December 5, 2012, http://hbr.org.

10. Company website, www.skype.com, accessed December 5, 2012.

11. Company website, www.kroger.com, accessed December 5, 2012; "Operations," corporate website, www.thekrogerco.com, accessed December 5, 2012.

12. Company website, http://traderjoes.com, accessed December 5, 2012; Glenn Llopis, "Why Trader Joe's Stands Out from All the Rest in the Grocery Business," *Forbes*, accessed December 5, 2012, www.forbes.com.

13. Agam Shah, "Hard Drive Supply Issues Weigh on Dell's Q4 Earnings," *PC World*, accessed December 5, 2012, www.pcworld.com; Brian Caulfield, "Advantage Apple: Hard Drive Shortage and Rising Memory Prices Hit PC Costs," *Forbes*, accessed December 5, 2012, www.forbes.com.

14. Company website, www.netjets.com, accessed December 5, 2012; Thomas Black and Noah Buhayar, "Buffett Pounces in Private-Jet Slump with $9.6 Billion," *Bloomberg Businessweek*, accessed December 5, 2012, www.businessweek.com.

15. Michael Cooper, "Your Ad Here, on a Fire Truck? Broke Cities Sell Naming Rights," *The New York Times*, accessed December 5, 2012, www.nytimes.com.

16. Organization website, "Museum Day Live! 2012," www.smithsonianmag.com, accessed December 5, 2012.

17. Rick Pearson and Ray Long, "Lawmakers OK $1-a-Pack Cigarette Tax Hike," *Chicago Tribune*, accessed December 5, 2012, http://articles.chicagotribune.com.

18. Amy Leap, "Less for Your Money," *Mail Tribune*, accessed December 5, 2012, www.mailtribune.com.

19. "Raw Material Costs Rise, So Do Bridgestone Prices," *Modern Tire Dealer*, accessed December 5, 2012, www.moderntiredealer.com; Keith Bradsher, "China Consolidates Grip on Rare Earth," *The New York Times*, accessed December 5, 2012, www.nytimes.com.

20. Aaron Cole, "2012 Prius Plug-in: The 'Current' Generation of Hybrid," *Aurora Sentinel*, accessed December 5, 2012, www.aurorasentinel.com.

21. Jad Mouawad, "Air Service Cutbacks Hit Hardest Where Recession Did," *The New York Times*, accessed December 5, 2012, www.nytimes.com.

22. Anders Kelto, "After a Free Fall, Zimbabwe Finds a Bit of Stability," WBUR and NPR, accessed December 5, 2012, www.wbur.org; Tawanda Musarurwa, "Zimbabwe: Inflation Declines Marginally," *Zimbabwe Herald*, accessed December 5, 2012, www.herald.co.zw.

23. David Baugher, "Lack of Infrastructure, Slow Consumer Acceptance Complicate Quest for Alternative Fuels," *St. Louis Beacon*, accessed December 5, 2012, www.stlbeacon.org.

24. Tim Higgins and Chris Reiter, "GM Says Opel Turnaround Plan May Take a 'Couple' of Months," *Bloomberg News*, accessed December 5, 2012, www.bloomberg.com.

25. Company website, "About OpenTable," www.opentable.com, accessed December 5, 2012.

26. "Heather Mitts, Ryan Lochte, Bryan Clay Anchor Ralph Lauren 2012 Olympic Roster," *Big Lead*, accessed December 5, 2012, http://thebiglead.com; Jillian Eugenios, "Sneak a Peek at Team USA's Official Olympic Outfits," *Today*, accessed December 5, 2012, http://todayinlondonblog.today.com.

27. "Member States," organization website, http://eurunion.org, accessed December 5, 2012; Matt Rosenberg, "Euro Countries," *About.com Geography*, accessed December 5, 2012, http://geography.about.com; Nelson D. Schwartz, "Whatever Greek Voters Decide, the Euro Looks Likely to Suffer," *The New York Times*, accessed December 5, 2012, www.nytimes.com; Edward I. Altman, "The Fate of the Euro Hinges on Italy. Italy's Looking Iffy," *Forbes*, accessed December 5, 2012, www.forbes.com; David Jolly, "Unemployment in Euro Zone Hits Record High," *The New York Times*, accessed December 5, 2012, www.nytimes.com.

28. Will Staley, "The Big Gulp: How 7-Eleven Plans to Put the Bodega Out of Business," *New York* magazine, accessed December 5, 2012, http://nymag.com.

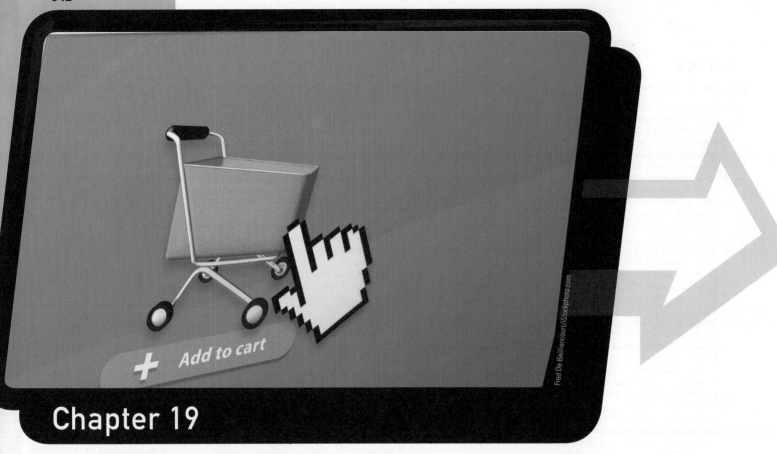

642

Chapter 19

PRICING
Strategies

1 Compare the alternative pricing strategies, and explain when each strategy is most appropriate.

2 Describe how prices are quoted.

3 Identify the various pricing policy decisions marketers must make.

4 Relate price to consumer perceptions of quality.

5 Contrast competitive bidding and negotiated prices.

6 Explain the importance of transfer pricing.

7 Compare the three alternative global pricing strategies.

8 Relate the concepts of cannibalization, bundle pricing, and bots to online pricing strategies.

DISCOUNTS REDUCE NUMBER OF ABANDONED E-CARTS

The volume of online shopping continues to grow, reaching more than $37 billion in one recent holiday season, up 15 percent from the year before. But another statistic, equally revealing and often overlooked, is the number of online shoppers who abandon their electronic shopping carts, purchasing nothing before moving on.

That number ranges between 65 and 89 percent of e-shoppers (the exact figure depends on who is measuring and when). Some customers simply change their minds about the purchase, while others are distracted or interrupted. A few of these may return on their own to complete their transaction. Still others balk at shipping costs on their way to the checkout page, while some aren't really shopping in the first place—they're comparing prices and may move on to buy the item elsewhere.

Marketers are increasingly aware of the large number of abandoned carts and the huge dollar value of the purchases being left on the table,

but surprisingly few are doing anything about it. Industry analysts and marketing researchers urge action, however, saying that an immediate email, at the very least, can be cost effective and extremely influential in bringing customers back to close the sale. Multiple emails and even a phone call have increased sales in some cases. Yet it's believed that only about half of online retailers currently send even one reminder, and the number could be as low as 15 percent. Those that do include giants like Lands' End, Best Buy, Home Depot, and Zappos.

Some smaller online retailers hesitate because they don't have the technology to follow up, or because they fear customers are simply waiting to be offered a better deal. Shoppers say they are positively influenced by such offers, but some retailers fear that by using them, they may be training their customers to resist paying full price or to "game" any system in order to receive more or increasingly generous enticements to buy.

Systems can be set up to prevent abuse of discount offers, of course (such as discount codes that can be used only once), and retailers can first simply ask whether the customer had difficulty checking out and offer help. But some observers believe that shaving the price, one way or the other, is the best means of pushing the growing queue of abandoned carts through the checkout line. Online retailers will have to decide whether it's worth offering a small discount to close the sale.[1]

EVOLUTION OF A BRAND

Successfully closing a sale is a challenge for all marketers, whether bricks-and-mortar or online retailers. Some companies like Lands' End know how to handle "unfinished" transactions, but a surprising number of e-retailers don't have pricing strategies in place for dealing with abandoned shopping carts—an omission that adds up to billions of dollars each year.

• Have you ever abandoned a shopping cart at an online store? Did the e-retailer follow up? If so, how soon? What incentives—if any—did the e-retailer offer to persuade you to come back? Did the follow-up convince you to return to the website and complete your purchase? Why or why not?

• Imagine that you are an e-retailer and that you are trying to come up with a creative solution to the abandoned-shopping-cart problem. You'd like to offer an incentive to entice shoppers to return and complete their purchases. What are some ways to bring shoppers back—without letting them game the system?

CHAPTER OVERVIEW

Setting prices is neither a one-time decision nor a standard routine. As illustrated by the strategies undertaken by Lands' End, Home Depot, and others, pricing is just one aspect of the overall marketing effort. Pricing is a dynamic function of the marketing mix. While about half of all companies change prices once a year or less frequently, one in ten does so every month. Online companies may adjust prices more often, depending on what they are selling. Some firms negotiate prices on the spot, as in the case of a car dealership or an antique shop.

Companies translate pricing objectives into pricing decisions in two major steps. First, someone takes responsibility for making pricing decisions and administering the resulting pricing structure. Second, someone sets the overall pricing structure—that is, basic prices and appropriate discounts for channel members, quantity purchases, and geographic and promotional considerations.

The decision to make price adjustments is directly related to demand. Most businesses slowly change the amounts they charge customers, even when they clearly recognize strong demand. Instead of raising prices, they may scale down customer service or add fees. They may also wait to raise prices until they see what their competitors do.

Few businesses want the distinction of being the first to charge higher prices. Because many firms base their prices on manufacturing costs rather than consumer demand, they may wait for increases in their own costs before responding with price changes. These increases generally emerge more slowly than changes in consumer demand. Finally, because many business executives believe steady prices help preserve long-term relationships with customers, they are reluctant to raise prices even when strong demand probably justifies the change.

Chapter 18 introduced the concept of price and its role in the economic system and marketing strategy. This chapter examines various pricing strategies and price structures, such as reductions from list prices and geographic considerations. It then looks at the primary pricing policies, including psychological pricing, price flexibility, product-line pricing, and promotional pricing, as well as price–quality relationships. Competitive and negotiated prices are discussed, and one section focuses entirely on transfer pricing. Finally, the chapter concludes by describing important factors in pricing goods and services for online and global markets.

PRICING STRATEGIES

> 1 Compare the alternative pricing strategies, and explain when each strategy is most appropriate.

The specific strategies firms use to price goods and services grow out of the marketing strategies they formulate to accomplish overall organizational objectives. One firm's marketers may price their products to attract customers across a wide range; another group of marketers may set prices to appeal to a small segment of a larger market; still another group may simply try to match competitors' price tags. In general, firms can choose from three pricing strategies: skimming, penetration, and competitive pricing. The following sections look at these choices in more detail.

SKIMMING PRICING STRATEGY

Derived from the expression "skimming the cream," **skimming pricing strategies** are also known as **market-plus pricing**. They involve intentionally setting a relatively high price compared with the prices of competing products. Although some firms continue to use a skimming strategy throughout most stages of the product lifecycle, it is more commonly used as a market-entry price for distinctive goods or services with little or no initial competition. When the supply begins to exceed demand, or when competition catches up, the initial high price is dropped.

Such was the case with high-definition televisions (HDTVs), whose average price was $19,000, including installation, when they were first introduced. The resulting sticker shock kept them out of the range of most household budgets. But a decade later, price cuts have brought these LCD models into the reach of mainstream consumers. At Buy.com, shoppers can pick up a Philips 19-inch flat-panel LCD model for about $112. On the higher end, they can purchase a Samsung 55-inch flat-panel LCD model at Amazon.com for about $930.[2]

A company may practice a skimming strategy in setting a market-entry price when it introduces a distinctive good or service with little or no competition. Or it may use this strategy to market higher-end goods. Amazon's Kindle e-reader was first launched in 2007 and was priced at $400. When Barnes & Noble released its first Nook the following year, both were priced at $259, in contrast to Sony's Reader Touch Edition, which sold for $299.99. Since then, the prices for e-readers have steadily decreased, with the Nook selling for $99 and the Kindle Fire for $159.[3]

In some cases, a firm may maintain a skimming strategy throughout most stages of a product's lifecycle. The jewelry category is a good example. Although discounters, such as Costco and Home Shopping Network (HSN), offer heavier gold pieces for a few hundred dollars, firms like Tiffany and Cartier command prices 10 times that amount just for their brand names. Exclusivity justifies the pricing—and the price, once set, rarely falls.

Sometimes maintaining a high price through the product's lifecycle works, but sometimes it does not. High prices can drive away otherwise loyal customers. Baseball fans may shift from attending major league games to minor league games—if available—because of ticket, parking, and food prices. Amusement park visitors may shy away from high admission prices and head to the beach instead. If an industry or firm has been known to cut prices at certain points in the past, consumers—and retailers—will expect it. If the price cut doesn't come, consumers must decide whether to pay the higher tab or try a competitor's products.

Significant price changes in the retail gasoline and airline industries occur in the form of a **step out**, in which one firm raises prices and then waits to see if others follow suit. If competitors fail to respond by increasing their prices, the company making the step out usually reduces prices to the original level. Although airlines are prohibited by law from collectively setting prices, they can follow each other's example.

Despite the risk of backlash, a skimming strategy does offer benefits. It allows a manufacturer to quickly recover its research and development (R&D) costs. Pharmaceutical companies, fiercely protective of their patents on new drugs, justify high prices because of astronomical R&D costs: an average of 16 cents of every sales dollar, compared with 8 cents for computer makers and 4 cents in the aerospace industry. To protect their brand names from competition from lower-cost generics, drug makers frequently make small changes

Andrea Renault/Bloomberg via Getty Images

skimming pricing strategy Pricing strategy involving the use of a high price relative to competitive offerings.

market-plus pricing Intentionally setting a relatively high price compared with the prices of competing products; also known as *skimming pricing*.

step out Pricing practice in which one firm raises prices and then waits to see if others follow suit.

Amazon applied a skimming strategy when it first launched the Kindle e-reader. When Barnes & Noble released the Nook the following year, their prices were identical.

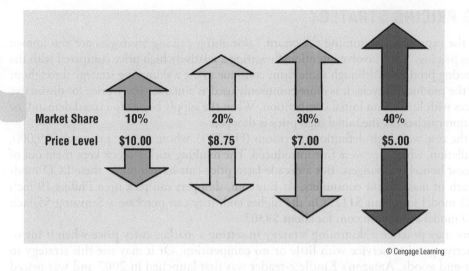

FIGURE 19.1
Price Reductions to Increase Market Share

to their products—such as combining the original product with a complementary prescription drug that treats different aspects of the ailment.

A skimming strategy also permits marketers to control demand in the introductory stages of a product's lifecycle and then adjust productive capacity to match changing demand. A low initial price for a new product could lead to fulfillment problems and loss of shopper goodwill if demand outstrips the firm's production capacity. The result will likely be consumer and retailer complaints and possibly permanent damage to the product's image. Excess demand occasionally leads to quality issues, as the firm strives to satisfy consumer desires for the product with inadequate production facilities.

During the late growth and early maturity stages of its lifecycle, a product's price typically falls for two reasons: (1) the pressure of competition and (2) the desire to expand its market. Figure 19.1 shows that 10 percent of the market may buy Product X at $10.00, and another 20 percent could be added to its customer base at a price of $8.75. Successive price declines may expand the firm's market size and meet challenges posed by new competitors.

A skimming strategy has one major chief disadvantage: it attracts competition. Potential competitors see innovative firms reaping large financial returns and may decide to enter the market. This new supply may force the price of the original product even lower than its eventual level under a sequential skimming procedure. However, if patent protection or some unique proprietary ability allows a firm to exclude competitors from its market, it may extend a skimming strategy.

PENETRATION PRICING STRATEGY

penetration pricing strategy Pricing strategy involving the use of a relatively low entry price compared with competitive offerings, based on the theory that this initial low price will help secure market acceptance.

A **penetration pricing strategy** sets a low price as a major marketing weapon. Marketers often price products noticeably lower than competing offerings when they enter new markets characterized by dozens of competing brands. Once the product achieves some degree of recognition through consumer trial purchases stimulated by its low price, marketers may increase the price to the level of competing products. Marketers of consumer products, such as dish soap, often use this strategy. A penetration pricing strategy may also extend over several stages of the product lifecycle as the firm seeks to maintain a reputation as a low-price competitor.

A penetration pricing strategy is sometimes called *market-minus pricing* when it implements the premise that a lower-than-market price will attract buyers and move a brand from an unknown newcomer to at least the brand-recognition stage or even the brand-preference stage. Because many firms begin penetration pricing with the intention of increasing prices in the future, success depends on generating many trial purchases. Penetration pricing is common among credit card firms, which typically offer low or zero interest rates for a specified introductory period, then raise the rates. If competitors view the new product as a threat, marketers attempting to use a penetration strategy often discover that rivals will simply match their prices.

T. Carter/Photri Images/Alamy

Because the market already contains so many competing brands, dish-soap marketers often use a penetration pricing strategy when they enter the market, pricing products noticeably lower than the competition.

Retailers may use penetration pricing to lure shoppers to new stores. Strategies might take such forms as zero interest charges for credit purchases at a new furniture store, two-for-one offers for dinner at a new restaurant, or an extremely low price on a single product purchase for first-time customers to get them to come in and shop.

Penetration pricing works best for goods or services characterized by highly elastic demand. Large numbers of highly price-sensitive consumers pay close attention to this type of appeal. The strategy also suits situations in which large-scale operations and long production runs result in low production and marketing costs. Finally, penetration pricing may be appropriate in market situations in which introduction of a new product will likely attract strong competitors. Such a strategy may allow a new product to reach the mass market quickly and capture a large share prior to entry by competitors.

Some auto manufacturers have been using penetration pricing for some new models to attract customers who might not otherwise consider purchasing a vehicle during a given year or who might be looking at a more expensive competitor. India's Tata Motors launched the world's cheapest car: the Nano, which carries a price tag of $2,600 in India. Tata hopes to eventually sell a less stripped-down version of the Nano in Western Europe and the United States but has not set a date—or a price. Currently, the lowest-priced car in the United States is the Nissan Versa, with a sticker price of $12,880.[4]

Everyday Low Pricing

Closely related to penetration pricing is **everyday low pricing (EDLP)**, a strategy devoted to continuous low prices as opposed to relying on short-term price-cutting tactics like cents-off coupons, rebates, and special sales. EDLP can take two forms. In the first, retailers such as Walmart and Lowe's compete by consistently offering consumers low prices on a broad range of items. Through its EDLP policy, Lowe's pledges to not only match any price the consumer sees elsewhere but to also take off an additional percentage in some cases. Walmart states that it achieves EDLP by negotiating better prices from suppliers and by cutting its own costs. In addition, Walmart holds suppliers to a strict four-day delivery window. Goods that arrive at the regional distribution center before or after the window are assessed a 3 percent penalty.[5] Chili's Grill & Bar is another company that has had success with everyday pricing, as well as two-tier pricing for steaks. See the "Marketing Success" feature to learn how.

everyday low pricing (EDLP) Pricing strategy of continuously offering low prices rather than relying on such short-term price cuts as cents-off coupons, rebates, and special sales.

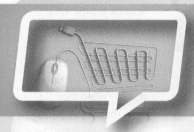

MARKETING SUCCESS

Chili's Serves Everyday Value

Background. Chili's Grill & Bar is a chain of about 1,600 casual-dining restaurants owned by Brinker International, based in Dallas.

The Challenge. Chili's needed to improve its profit margins, as a lingering recession and slow recovery led diners to eat out less often and order fewer drinks and desserts, which are typically high-margin items. Prices for many ingredients were also rising, including staples like beef, cooking oil, and dairy products.

The Strategy. In addition to large-scale cost-cutting and kitchen remodeling efforts, Chili's also made profitable menu changes, extending its successful "everyday value" $20 Dinner for Two and Lunch Combo. The company also upgraded ingredients in popular dishes like fajitas and salads. Perhaps the most successful strategy,

however, was offering steak at two price levels, a 6-ounce sirloin, competitively priced in the Dinner for Two, and a 10-ounce sirloin for less price-sensitive diners. A 12-ounce rib eye is also available.

The Outcome. Chili's is serving three times the number of steaks as before, as guests "trade up" to a better value and higher lunch check. "Our top-line growth is a result of the changes we have made providing everyday value, enhancing our menu and upgrading our atmosphere," said the company's president and CEO.

Sources: Ben Fox, "Brinker Profit Rises 18%," *Market Watch*, accessed December 6, 2012, www.marketwatch.com; Ron Ruggless, "Chili's Steak Deals Boost Brinker's 3Q Sales," *Nation's Restaurant News*, accessed December 6, 2012, http://nrn.com; Ron Ruggless, "Brinker Expands Value Strategy at Chili's," *Nation's Restaurant News*, accessed December 6, 2012, http://nrn.com.

© iStockphoto.com/Marcello Bortolino

The second form of the EDLP pricing strategy involves its use by the manufacturer in dealing with channel members. Manufacturers may seek to set stable wholesale prices that undercut offers competitors make to retailers, offers that typically rise and fall with the latest trade promotion deals. Many marketers reduce list prices on a number of products while simultaneously reducing promotion allowances to retailers. While reductions in allowances mean retailers may not fund such in-store promotions as shelf merchandising and end-aisle displays, the manufacturers hope stable low prices will stimulate sales instead.

Some retailers oppose EDLP strategies. Many grocery stores, for instance, operate on "high–low" strategies that set profitable regular prices to offset losses of frequent specials and promotions. Other

Lowe's employs everyday low pricing, a strategy devoted to continuous low prices instead of special sales and other short-term pricing tactics.

AP Photo/Paul Sakuma

retailers believe EDLP will ultimately benefit both sellers and buyers. Supporters of EDLP in the grocery industry point out that it already succeeds at two of the biggest competitors: Walmart and warehouse clubs like Costco or Sam's Club.

One popular pricing myth is that a low price is a sure sell. Low prices are an easy means of distinguishing the offerings of one marketer from other sellers, but such moves are easy to counter by competitors. Unless overall demand is price elastic, overall price cuts will mean less revenue for all firms in the industry. In addition, low prices may generate an image of questionable quality.

COMPETITIVE PRICING STRATEGY

Although many organizations rely heavily on price as a competitive weapon, even more implement competitive pricing strategies. These organizations try to reduce the emphasis on price competition by matching other firms' prices and concentrating their own marketing efforts on the product, distribution, and promotion elements of the marketing mix. As pointed out earlier, while price offers a dramatic means of achieving competitive advantage, it is also the easiest marketing variable for competitors to match. In fact, in industries with relatively homogeneous products, competitors must match each other's price reductions to maintain market share and remain competitive.

Retailers like Home Depot and Lowe's both use price-matching strategies, assuring consumers that they will meet—and beat—competitors' prices. Grocery chains, such as Kroger's and Stop & Shop, may compete with seasonal items: soft drinks and hot dogs in the summer, hot chocolate and turkeys in the winter. As soon as one store lowers the price of an item, the rest follow suit.

Another form of competitive pricing is setting an opening price point within a category. Retailers often achieve this by pricing a quality private-label product below the competition. Grocery giants Publix and Kroger have begun actively advertising their private-label goods, most of which are priced below those of manufacturers' brands. In a tough economy, more consumers are giving private-label products a try, and many say the quality is comparable to that of national brands.[6]

Prices can really drop when companies continually match each other's prices, as evident in the airline and computer industries. But competitive pricing can be tricky; a price reduction affects not only the first company but also the entire industry as other firms match the reduction. Unless lower prices can attract new customers and expand the overall market enough to offset the loss of per-unit revenue, the price cut will leave all competitors with less revenue. Research shows that nearly two-thirds of all firms set prices using competitive pricing as their primary pricing strategy.

Once competitors are routinely matching each other on price, marketers must turn away from price as a marketing strategy, emphasizing other variables to develop areas of distinctive competence and attract customers. That might mean offering personalized services, such as gift wrapping, or a sales associate who knows the type of clothing or books you like.

 ASSESSMENT CHECK

1.1 What are the three major pricing strategies?

1.2 What is EDLP?

> **competitive pricing strategy** Pricing strategy designed to deemphasize price as a competitive variable by pricing a good or service at the level of comparable offerings.

> **opening price point** An opening price below that of the competition, usually on a high-quality, private-label item.

❝❝BRIEFLY SPEAKING❞❞

"Pricing is actually a pretty simple and straightforward thing. Customers will not pay literally a penny more than the true value of the product."

—**Ron Johnson**
CEO, JC Penney

PRICE QUOTATIONS

The choice of the best method for quoting prices depends on many industry conditions, including competitive trends, cost structures, and traditional practices, along with the policies of individual firms. This section examines the reasoning and methodology behind price quotation practices.

Most price structures are built around list prices—the rates normally quoted to potential buyers. Marketers usually determine list prices by one or a combination of the methods discussed in Chapter 18. The sticker price on a new automobile is a good example: it shows the list price for the basic model and then adds the prices of the options. The sticker price for a new Mazda Miata sports convertible is $23,720. But you can add such features as cruise control, a trip computer, and full power accessories—all at additional cost. Most car manufacturers bundle features into packages for one price. So if you order the Convenience Package on the Miata, you'll automatically get those features, among other add-ons.[7]

The price of oil is equally important to consumers—particularly those who drive cars—because it directly affects the list price of gasoline. Disruptions like hurricanes and wars affect the price of oil, and ultimately the price that drivers pay at the pump. Prices may also fluctuate seasonally, as demand

 Describe how prices are quoted.

> **list price** Established price normally quoted to potential buyers.

FIGURE 19.2
Components of Retail Gasoline Prices

Source: Data from U.S. Energy Information Administration, "Gasoline and Diesel Fuel Update," accessed December 10, 2012, http://eia.gov.

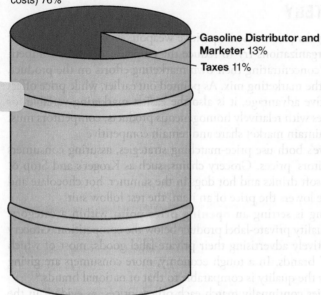

Who gets the money from retail gas sales?

Oil Wholesaler (includes crude oil price and refinery costs) 76%

Gasoline Distributor and Marketer 13%

Taxes 11%

Note: Percentages are rounded to nearest percent.

market price Price a consumer or marketing intermediary actually pays for a product after subtracting any discounts, allowances, or rebates from the list price.

cash discount Price reduction offered to a consumer, business user, or marketing intermediary in return for prompt payment of a bill.

for gasoline rises and falls. Figure 19.2 illustrates where the money from a gallon of gas goes on its journey from the oil field to your gas tank.

REDUCTIONS FROM LIST PRICE

The amount a consumer pays for a product—its **market price**—may or may not equal the list price. Discounts and allowances sometimes reduce list prices. A list price often defines a starting point from which discounts set a lower market price. Marketers offer discounts in several classifications: cash, trade, and quantity discounts.

Cash Discounts

Consumers, industrial purchasers, or channel members sometimes receive reductions in price in exchange for prompt payment of bills; these price cuts are known as **cash discounts**. Discount terms usually specify exact time periods, such as 2/10, net 30. This notation means the customer must pay within 30 days, but payment within 10 days entitles the customer to subtract 2 percent from the amount due. Consumers may receive a cash discount for immediate payment, say, paying with cash instead of a credit card at the gas pump or paying the full cash amount up front for elective health-care services like orthodontia. Cash discounts represent a traditional pricing practice in many industries. They fulfill legal requirements provided that all customers can take the same reductions on the same terms.

In recent years, sellers have increasingly attempted to improve their own liquidity positions, reduce their bad-debt losses, and cut collection expenses by moving to a form of *negative cash discount*. Confronted with purchasers who may defer paying their bills as long as possible, another notice has begun to appear on customer statements:

Past-due accounts may be turned over to collection agencies.

Trade Discounts

trade discount Payment to a channel member or buyer for performing marketing functions; also known as a *functional discount*.

Payments to channel members for performing marketing functions are known as **trade discounts**, or functional discounts. Services performed by various channel members and the related costs were discussed in Chapters 14 and 15. A manufacturer's list price must incorporate the costs incurred by channel members in performing required marketing functions and expected profit margins for each member.

Trade discounts initially reflected the operating expenses of each category, but they have become more or less customary practices in some industries. The Robinson-Patman Act allows trade discounts as long as all buyers in the same category, such as all wholesalers or all retailers, receive the same discounts.

Figure 19.3 shows how a chain of trade discounts works. In the first instance, the trade discount is "40 percent, 10 percent off list price" for wholesalers. In other words, the 40 percent discount on the

$40 product is the trade discount the retailer receives to cover operating expenses and earn a profit. The wholesaler receives 10 percent of the $24 price to retailers to cover expenses and earn a profit. The manufacturer receives $21.60 from the whole-saler for each order.

In Figure 19.3's second example, the manufacturer and retailer decide to bypass the wholesaler. The producer offers a trade discount of 45 percent to the retailer. In this instance, the retailer receives $18 for each

"40 PERCENT, 10 PERCENT OFF" TRADE DISCOUNT			
List Price	− Retail Trade Discount	− Wholesale Trade Discount	= Manufacturer Proceeds
$40	$16 ($40 x 40%)	$2.40 ($24 x 10%)	= $21.60 ($40 − $16 − $2.40)

"45 PERCENT" TRADE DISCOUNT		
List Price	− Retail Trade Discount	= Manufacturer Proceeds
$40	$18 ($40 x 45%)	= $22 ($40 − $18)

© Cengage Learning

FIGURE 19.3
Chain of Trade Discounts

product sold at its list price, and the manufacturer receives the remaining $22. Either the retailer or the manufacturer must assume responsibility for the services previously performed by the wholesaler, or they can share these duties between them.

Quantity Discounts

Price reductions granted for large-volume purchases are known as **quantity discounts**. Sellers justify these discounts on the grounds that large orders reduce selling expenses and may shift some costs for storage, transportation, and financing to buyers. The law allows quantity discounts provided they are applied on the same basis to all customers.

Quantity discounts may specify either cumulative or noncumulative terms. **Cumulative quantity discounts** reduce prices in amounts determined by purchases over stated time periods. Annual purchases of at least $25,000 might entitle a buyer to a 3 percent rebate, and purchases exceeding $50,000 would increase the refund to 5 percent. These reductions are really patronage discounts because they tend to bind customers to a single supply source.

Noncumulative quantity discounts provide onetime reductions in the list price. For example, a firm might offer the following discount schedule for a product priced at $1,000 per unit:

1 unit	List: $1,000
2–5 units	List less 10 percent
6–10 units	List less 20 percent
More than 10 units	List less 25 percent

Many businesses have come to expect quantity discounts from suppliers. Online photo supply retailer Shutterfly offers volume discounts for photo books and discounts of up to 50 percent on prepaid orders.[8] Marketers typically favor combinations of cash, trade, and quantity discounts. See's Candies offers a quantity discount for a minimum purchase of $655, plus continued savings throughout the year.[9]

Allowances

Allowances resemble discounts by specifying deductions from list price. The major categories of allowances are trade-ins and promotional allowances. **Trade-ins** are often used in sales of durable goods, such as automobiles. The new product's basic list price remains unchanged, but the seller accepts less money from the customer along with a used product—usually the same kind of product as the buyer purchases.

Promotional allowances reduce prices as part of an attempt to integrate promotional strategies within distribution channels. Manufacturers often return part of the prices buyers pay in the form of advertising and sales-support allowances for channel members. Automobile manufacturers frequently offer allowances to retail dealers to induce them to lower prices and stimulate sales. In an effort to

quantity discount Price reduction granted for a large-volume purchase.

cumulative quantity discount Price discount determined by amounts of purchases over stated time periods.

noncumulative quantity discount Price reduction granted on a one-time-only basis.

allowance Specified deduction from list price, including a trade-in or promotional allowance.

trade-in Credit allowance given for a used item when a customer purchases a new item.

promotional allowance Promotional incentive in which the manufacturer agrees to pay the reseller a certain amount to cover the costs of special promotional displays or extensive advertising.

alert consumers to the difference between a car's sticker price and the price the dealer actually pays to the manufacturer, *Consumer Reports* sells car and truck buyers a breakdown on dealers' wholesale costs. The information reveals undisclosed dealer profits, such as manufacturers' incentives, rebates from the dealer-invoice price, and "holdbacks"—amounts refunded to the dealer after sales are completed.[10] Dealers dislike the move to reveal their markups, arguing that no other retail sector is forced to give consumers details of their promotional allowances.

minimum advertised pricing (MAP) Fees paid to retailers who agree not to advertise products below set prices.

Minimum advertised pricing (MAP) occurs when a manufacturer pays a retailer to not advertise a product below a certain price. Recently, the U.S. Supreme Court ruled that retailers are required to stick to their MAPs on items. However, some electronics manufacturers have announced that they are imposing unilateral pricing policies (UPPs) that set the same prices for some types of TVs no matter where they are sold. Some manufacturers plan to monitor retailers' compliance. Some manufacturers have warned retailers that, if they sell an item in the UPP program for less than the minimum advertised price, the manufacturer will remove their authorization and stop supplying products.[11]

Rebates

rebate Refund of a portion of the purchase price, usually granted by the product's manufacturer.

In still another way to reduce prices, marketers may offer a rebate—a refund of a portion of the purchase price. Rebates appear everywhere—on appliances, electronics, and auto promotions—by manufacturers eager to get consumers to try their merchandise or move products during periods of slow sales. The contact-lens manufacturer ACUVUE offers rebates to current and new customers who buy boxes of the company's disposable contact lenses.

Rebates can have their problems. Many consumers complain about the paperwork they have to fill out to get a rebate, particularly on larger items like computers and kitchen appliances. Some say they fill out the paperwork only to be denied the claim on a technicality. Others report never receiving the rebate—or even a response—at all. The Better Business Bureau notes that the number of complaints filed relating to rebates has grown significantly in the past few years. Some state legislators have moved to require companies to fulfill rebate requests within a certain period of time while also requiring consumers to file their requests promptly. Yet companies argue that many consumers never even apply for their legitimate rebates.[12]

GEOGRAPHIC CONSIDERATIONS

In industries dominated by catalog and online marketers, geographic considerations weigh heavily on the firm's ability to deliver orders in a cost-effective manner at the right time and place. In other instances, geographic factors affect the marketer's ability to receive additional inventory quickly in response to demand fluctuations. And although geographic considerations strongly influence prices when costs include shipping heavy, bulky, low-unit-value products, they can also affect lightweight, lower-cost products.

Buyers and sellers can handle transportation expenses in several ways: (1) the buyer pays all transportation charges, (2) the seller pays all transportation charges, or (3) the buyer and the seller share the charges. This decision has major effects on a firm's efforts to expand its geographic coverage to distant markets. How can marketers compete with local suppliers in distant markets who are able to avoid the considerable shipping costs that their firms must pay? Sellers can implement several alternatives for handling transportation costs in their pricing policies.

FOB (free on board) plant (FOB origin) Price quotation that does not include shipping charges.

Rebates refund a portion of the purchase price for items like disposable contact lenses. Marketers offer rebates as a way to reduce the price paid by customers.

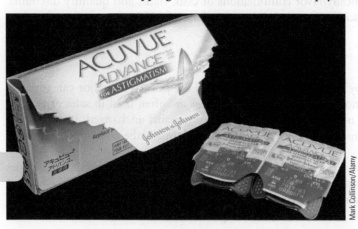

FOB Pricing

FOB (free on board) plant, or FOB origin, prices include no shipping charges. The buyer must pay all freight charges to transport the product from the manufacturer's loading dock. The seller only pays to load the merchandise aboard the carrier selected by the buyer. Legal title and responsibility pass to the buyer after the seller's employees load the purchase and get a receipt from the representative of the common carrier. Firms like Walmart often handle freight charges over the entire supply chain. Because Walmart sources so many products from China, "FOB China" is now becoming common.

Many marketing intermediaries sell only on FOB plant terms to downstream channel members. These distributors believe their customers have more clout than they do in negotiating with carriers. They prefer to assign transportation costs to the channel members in the best positions to secure the most cost-effective shipping terms.

Sellers may also quote prices as **FOB origin-freight allowed**, or **freight absorbed**. These terms permit buyers to subtract transportation expenses from their bills. The amount such a seller receives for its product varies with the freight charged against the invoice. This alternative is popular among firms with high fixed costs, because it helps them expand their markets by quoting the same prices regardless of shipping expenses.

Uniform-Delivered Pricing

When a firm quotes the same price, including transportation expenses, to all buyers, it adopts a **uniform-delivered pricing** policy. This method of handling transportation expenses is the exact opposite of FOB origin pricing. The uniform-delivered system resembles the pricing structure for mail service, so it is sometimes called **postage-stamp pricing**. The price quote includes a transportation charge averaged over all of the firm's customers, meaning that distant customers actually pay a smaller share of shipping costs while nearby customers pay what is known as *phantom freight*—the amount by which the average transportation charge exceeds the actual cost of shipping.

Zone Pricing

Zone pricing modifies a uniform-delivered pricing system by dividing the overall market into different zones and establishing a single price within each zone. This pricing structure incorporates average transportation costs for shipments within each zone as part of the delivered price of goods sold there; by narrowing distances, it greatly reduces but does not completely eliminate phantom freight. The primary advantage of zone pricing comes from its simplified administration that helps a seller compete in distant markets. The U.S. Postal Service's parcel rates depend on this system of pricing.

Zone pricing helps explain why gasoline can cost more in one suburb than in a neighborhood just two or three miles down the road. One way in which gasoline marketers boost profits is by mapping out areas based on formulas that factor in location, affluence, or simply what the local market will bear. Dealers are then charged different wholesale prices, which are reflected in the prices paid at the pump by customers. Some dealers argue that zone pricing should be prohibited. When drivers shop around for cheaper gas in other zones, stations in high-price zones are unable to compete.

Basing-Point Pricing

In **basing-point pricing**, the price of a product includes the list price at the factory plus freight charges from the basing-point city nearest the buyer. The basing point specifies a location from which freight charges are calculated—not necessarily the point from which the goods are actually shipped. In either case, the actual shipping point does not affect the price quotation. Such a system seeks to equalize competition between distant marketers because all competitors quote identical transportation rates. Few buyers would accept a basing-point system today, however.

For many years, the best-known basing-point system was the Pittsburgh-plus pricing structure common in the steel industry. Steel buyers paid freight charges from Pittsburgh regardless of where the steel was produced. As the industry matured, manufacturing centers emerged in Chicago; Gary, Indiana; Cleveland; and Birmingham. Still, Pittsburgh remained the basing point for steel pricing, forcing a buyer in Atlanta who purchased steel from a Birmingham mill to pay phantom freight from Pittsburgh.

FOB origin-freight allowed (freight absorbed) Price quotation system that allows the buyer to deduct shipping expenses from the cost of purchases.

uniform-delivered pricing Pricing system for handling transportation costs under which all buyers are quoted the same price, including transportation expenses. Sometimes known as *postage-stamp pricing*.

postage-stamp pricing System for handling transportation costs under which all buyers are quoted the same price, including transportation expenses; also known as *uniform-delivered price*.

zone pricing Pricing system for handling transportation costs under which the market is divided into geographic regions and a different price is set in each region.

basing-point pricing System used in some industries during the early 20th century in which the buyer paid the factory price plus freight charges from the basing-point city nearest the buyer.

⊕ **ASSESSMENT CHECK**

2.1 What are the three major types of discounts?

2.2 Identify the four alternatives for handling transportation costs in pricing policies.

PRICING POLICIES

3   Identify the various pricing policy decisions marketers must make.

pricing policy General guideline that reflects marketing objectives and influences specific pricing decisions.

Pricing policies contribute important information to buyers as they assess the firm's total image. A coherent policy provides an overall framework and consistency that guide day-to-day pricing decisions. Formally, a pricing policy is a general guideline that reflects marketing objectives and influences specific pricing decisions.

Decisions concerning price structure generally tend to focus on technical, detailed questions, but decisions concerning pricing policies cover broader issues. Price-structure decisions take the firm's pricing policy as a given, from which they specify applicable discounts. Pricing policies have important strategic effects, particularly in guiding competitive efforts. They form the basis for more practical price-structure decisions.

Firms implement variations of four basic types of pricing policies: psychological pricing, price flexibility, product-line pricing, and promotional pricing. Specific policies deal effectively with various competitive situations; the final choice depends on the environment within which marketers must make their pricing decisions. Regardless of the strategy selected, however, marketers sometimes must raise prices. Although it is never easy to deliver this decision to customers, if it is accomplished with honesty and tact, customers are likely to remain loyal.

PSYCHOLOGICAL PRICING

psychological pricing Pricing policy based on the belief that certain prices or price ranges make a good or service more appealing than others to buyers.

odd pricing Pricing policy based on the belief that a price ending with an odd number just under a round number is more appealing, for instance, $9.97 rather than $10.

unit pricing Pricing policy in which prices are stated in terms of a recognized unit of measurement or a standard numerical count.

Psychological pricing applies the belief that certain prices or price ranges make products more appealing than others to buyers. No research offers a consistent foundation for such thinking, however, and studies often report mixed findings. Nevertheless, marketers practice several forms of psychological pricing. Prestige pricing, discussed in Chapter 18, sets a relatively high price to convey an image of quality and exclusiveness. Two more psychological pricing techniques are odd pricing and unit pricing.

In odd pricing, marketers set prices at odd numbers just under round numbers. Many people assume that a price of $9.95 appeals more strongly to consumers than $10.00, supposedly because buyers interpret it as $9.00 plus change. Odd pricing originated as a way to force clerks to make change, thus serving as a cash-control device, and it remains a common feature of contemporary price quotations.

Some producers and retailers practice odd pricing but avoid prices ending in 5, 9, or 0. These marketers believe customers view price tags of $5.95, $5.99, or $6.00 as regular retail prices, but they think of an amount like $5.97 as a discount price. Walmart, for example, avoids using 9s as ending prices for their merchandise.

Unit pricing states prices in terms of some recognized unit of measurement (such as grams and liters) or a standard numerical count. Unit pricing began to be widely used during the late 1960s to make price comparisons more convenient following complaints by consumer advocates about the difficulty of comparing the true prices of products packaged in different sizes. These advocates thought posting prices in terms of standard units would help shoppers make better-informed purchases. However, unit pricing has not improved consumers' shopping habits as much as supporters originally envisioned. Instead, research shows standard price quotes most often affect purchases only by relatively well-educated consumers with high earnings.

PRICE FLEXIBILITY

price flexibility Pricing policy permitting variable prices for goods and services.

Marketing executives must also set company policies that determine whether their firm will permit price flexibility—that is, whether or not to set one price that applies to every buyer or to permit variable prices for different customers. Generally, one-price policies suit mass-marketing programs, whereas variable pricing is more likely to be applied in marketing programs based on individual bargaining. In a large department store, customers do not expect to haggle over prices with retail salespeople. Instead, they expect to pay the amounts shown on the price tags. Usually, customers pay less only when the retailer replaces regular prices with sale prices or offers discounts on damaged merchandise. Variable pricing usually applies to larger purchases, such as automobiles, real estate, and hotel room rates. While variable pricing adds some flexibility to selling situations, it may conflict with provisions of the Robinson-Patman Act. It may also lead to retaliatory pricing by competitors, and it may stir complaints among customers who find they paid higher prices than necessary.

Some Internet service providers have set usage caps on their customers and require subscribers who download the most content to pay the most. To help subscribers gauge how many gigabytes they're using, Comcast has made a free online usage meter available in many areas in the United States. Recently the company introduced usage-based pricing, eliminating the monthly cap for its Internet subscribers and billing them for the amount of data they use. Despite Comcast's move, some consumer advocates have asked Congress to investigate the monthly limits, because they could discourage online video and other high-bandwidth applications.[13]

PRODUCT-LINE PRICING

Because most firms market multiple product lines, an effective pricing strategy must consider the relationships among all of these items instead of viewing each in isolation. **Product-line pricing** is the practice of setting a limited number of prices for a selection of merchandise. For example, one well-known clothier might offer three lines of men's suits: one priced at $350, a second at $595, and the most expensive at $1,095. These price points help the retailer define important product characteristics that differentiate the three product lines and help the customer decide on whether to trade up or down.

Retailers practice extensive product-line pricing. In earlier days, five-and-dime variety stores exemplified this technique. It remains popular, however, because it offers advantages to both retailers and customers. Shoppers can choose desired price ranges and then concentrate on other product variables, such as colors, styles, and materials. Retailers can purchase and offer specific lines in limited price categories instead of more general assortments with dozens of different prices.

Sunglasses have become a hot fashion item in recent years, and prices for designer glasses have jumped from an average of $250 per pair to as much as $900 for Thornhill Aviators at Bergdorf Goodman in New York. While sales of other luxury goods have softened, sunglass sales are getting long looks from retailers. Younger consumers—teens and young women—seem to be snapping up designer shades most often. Bvlgari, Dolce & Gabbana, Prada, Stella McCartney, and Versace all offer high-end glasses carried by luxury retailers. Those who want their shades studded with diamonds can grab a pair from Gold & Wood's Temptation collection, which features a jeweled nose bridge and earpieces. A pair of Gold & Wood's Prestige collection, with 253 diamonds, retailed at $55,000.[14]

A potential problem with product-line pricing is that once marketers decide on a limited number of prices to use as their price lines, they may have difficulty making price changes on individual items. Rising costs, therefore, force sellers to either change the entire price-line structure, which results in confusion, or cut costs through production adjustments. The second option opens the firm to customer complaints that its merchandise is not what it used to be.

PROMOTIONAL PRICING

promotional pricing
Pricing policy in which a lower-than-normal price is used as a temporary ingredient in a firm's marketing strategy.

In **promotional pricing**, a lower-than-normal price is used as a temporary ingredient in a firm's marketing strategy. Some promotional pricing arrangements form part of recurrent marketing initiatives, such as a shoe store's annual "buy one pair, get the second pair for one cent" sale. Another example is "7 CDs for 1 cent." This artificially low price attracts customers who must then agree to purchase a set number of CDs at regular prices within a specified time limit. Another firm may introduce a promotional model or brand with a special price to begin competing in a new market. The nation's wireless providers signed up millions of customers with the promise of unlimited data access, but three of the four biggest carriers now face such capacity constraints that, instead of rationing bandwidth via price, they're reducing access speed to levels that users find frustrating. Read the "Solving an Ethical Controversy" feature for the pros and cons of this strategy.

Managing promotional pricing efforts requires marketing skill. Customers may get hooked on sales and other promotional pricing events. If they know their favorite department store has a one-day sale every month, they will likely wait to make their purchases on that day. Car shoppers have been offered so many price incentives that it is becoming harder and harder for manufacturers and

SOLVING AN ETHICAL CONTROVERSY

Limiting "Unlimited" Data Plans

A mong wireless providers, only Sprint still offers new subscribers unlimited data plans, while Verizon, AT&T, and T-Mobile have all resorted to "throttling" the top 5 percent of unlimited data users in their areas. Unlimited plans were inaugurated when iPhones were new and fewer customers engaged heavily in video streaming and gaming activities. Now, struggling to upgrade their capacity to handle surging use, carriers are drastically slowing data speeds (or throttling) to near dial-up levels for the heaviest users, to maintain service to all without raising prices. Throttled customers are fuming, and some have gone to court.

Should wireless providers raise prices for unlimited data plans?

PRO

1. Users would be better served by the option to pay more for a better experience.

2. It's only fair for the heaviest users to pay more for what they get.

CON 👎

1. Customers contracted for usable access at a set price and should not have to pay more for faster download speed.

2. Higher prices merely punish customers when providers should be encouraging them to use more wireless service.

Summary:

Congress is expected to open more bandwidth to wireless providers, but it will take much time and money. It's likely that Sprint may have to join the other wireless providers and adopt the throttling strategy before more bandwidth is available.

Sources: David Murphy, "AT&T Drops Plans to Appeal, Pays Throttled Data Plan User $935 Settlement," *PC* magazine, accessed December 6, 2012, www.pcmag.com; Robert Hahn and Peter Passell, "Why Mobile Data Plan 'Throttling' Is Actually a Good Thing," *U.S. News & World Report*, accessed December 6, 2012, www.usnews.com; Hayley Tsukayama, "AT&T Clarifies Throttling on Data Plans," *The Washington Post*, accessed December 6, 2012, www.washingtonpost.com; Todd Wasserman, "It's Official: AT&T Will Throttle Your Unlimited Data Plan," *Mashable,* accessed December 6, 2012, http://mashable.com; Brian X. Chen, "Is Data Throttling a Necessary Evil for Cellphone Carriers," *The New York Times*, accessed December 6, 2012, http://bits.blogs.nytimes.com; "AT&T Puts Limit on 'Unlimited Data' Plans, Surprising Customers," *Fox News,* accessed December 6, 2012, www.foxnews.com.

dealers to take them away—or to come up with new ones. As part of the Coastal Uncorked festival in Myrtle Beach, South Carolina, several restaurants teamed up to offer promotional pricing on fixed-price dinners of three or more courses to attract new customers.[15]

In an effort to preserve customer traffic despite a tough economy, fast-food restaurants are trying a variety of promotions designed to attract business.

Loss Leaders and Leader Pricing

Retailers rely most heavily on promotional pricing. In one type of technique, stores offer loss leaders: goods priced below cost to attract customers who, the retailer hopes, will also buy regularly priced merchandise. Loss leaders can form part of an effective marketing program, but states with unfair-trade laws limit the practice. The milk at your grocery store is likely a loss leader, as is fruit in season. Around Thanksgiving, many grocers offer the traditional turkey as a loss leader in the hope that customers will buy the trimmings there as well.[16]

Retailers frequently use a variant of loss-leader pricing called leader pricing. To avoid violating minimum-markup regulations and earn some return on promotional sales, they offer so-called leader merchandise at prices slightly above cost. Among the most frequent practitioners of this combination pricing/promotion strategy are supermarkets and mass merchandisers, such as Walmart, Target, and Kmart. Retailers sometimes treat private-label products, such as Sam's Choice colas at Walmart stores, as leader merchandise because the store brands cost, on average, about 27 percent less than those of comparable national brands. While store brand items generate lower per-unit revenues than national brands, higher sales volume will probably offset some of the difference as will related sales of high-margin products such as toiletries and cosmetics.

Digital cameras are a good example. Although a digital point-and-shoot camera once ranged from $400 to $600, today, for the same money, shoppers can get a more technologically advanced digital SLR camera. Meanwhile, prices on the point-and-shoot models have dropped. Many of the cameras in Canon's PowerShot series—formerly priced in the hundreds of dollars—are now available for $200 or less.[17]

But marketers should anticipate two potential pitfalls when making a promotional pricing decision:

1. Some buyers are not attracted by promotional pricing.

2. By maintaining an artificially low price for a period of time, marketers may lead customers to expect it as a customary feature of the product. That is the situation currently faced by U.S. car manufacturers: sales of their models lag when they do not offer price incentives.

> **loss leader** Product offered to consumers at less than cost to attract them to stores in the hope that they will buy other merchandise at regular prices.

> **leader pricing** Variant of loss-leader pricing in which marketers offer prices slightly above cost to avoid violating minimum-markup regulations and earn a minimal return on promotional sales.

 ASSESSMENT CHECK

3.1 Define *pricing policy*.

3.2 Describe the two types of psychological pricing other than prestige pricing.

3.3 What is promotional pricing?

PRICE–QUALITY RELATIONSHIPS

One of the most thoroughly researched aspects of pricing is its relationship to consumer perceptions of product quality. In the absence of other cues, price is an important indicator of a product's quality to prospective purchasers. Many buyers interpret high prices as signals of high-quality products. Prestige is also often associated with high prices. However, distance in time can also be a factor in people's assessment. In a recent study, participants were told that a new e-reader was not very expensive ($120) or was somewhat expensive ($250). They were also told that it would be available in either a few days or several months. For those who were told that the e-reader would be available in a few months, price didn't seem to be much of a factor in their assessment of the reader's value. However, those who were told that the reader would be out in a few days and would be inexpensive thought it was a better buy than if it was available in a few days but would be expensive.[18]

> **Relate price to consumer perceptions of quality.** **4**

A new type of prestige surrounds ecofriendly products. Many consumers are willing to pay more for green goods and services—those made with environmentally friendly materials and processes. These purchases make consumers feel good about themselves and convey status to others.

Despite the appeal of prestige, nearly every consumer loves a good deal. Marketers work hard to convince consumers they are offering high-quality products at the lowest possible price. Motels were once considered both cheap and outdated. The Motel 6 chain, for example, was so named because, when it opened in 1962, a room cost $6 a night, plus tax. Today, a night at Motel 6 is still low priced—about $45 plus tax—and the chain is renovating its properties to convey a chic yet efficient look, with pedestal beds, 32-inch flat-screen TVs, granite countertops, wood-look laminate floors, and other amenities.[19]

ASSESSMENT CHECK

4.1 Describe the price–quality connection.

4.2 What are price limits?

Probably the best statement of the price–quality connection is the idea of price limits. Consumers define certain limits within which their product-quality perceptions vary directly with price. A potential buyer regards a price below the lower limit as too cheap, and a price above the higher limit seems too expensive. This perception holds true for both national brands and private-label products.

COMPETITIVE BIDDING AND NEGOTIATED PRICES

5 Contrast competitive bidding and negotiated prices.

competitive bidding
Inviting potential suppliers to quote prices on proposed purchases or contracts.

Many government and organizational procurement departments do not pay set prices for their purchases, particularly for large purchases. Instead, they determine the lowest prices available for items that meet specifications through **competitive bidding**. This process consists of inviting potential suppliers to quote prices on proposed purchases or contracts. Detailed specifications describe the good or service the government agency or business organization wishes to acquire. One of the most important procurement tasks is to develop accurate descriptions of products the organization seeks to buy. This process generally requires the assistance of the firm's technical personnel, such as engineers, designers, and chemists.

In competing for students, colleges and universities differentiate themselves on many dimensions, including price. In order to keep operating costs down, institutions routinely invite competitive bids in many areas of operation, including building maintenance and janitorial services, landscaping, and food service. With costs soaring for everything related to academic life, schools look for ways to economize without diminishing their appeal in the eyes of prospective students and their parents.

A select group of state troopers test potential police cars every year to determine the best model—and price—for their organization. Although Ford's Crown Victoria Police Interceptor was on top for many years, it was increasingly challenged by the Dodge Charger and the Chevy Caprice. Recently, Ford introduced two new Interceptors, one a conventional four-door sedan based on the Taurus, the other an SUV.[20]

In some cases, business and government purchasers negotiate contracts with favored suppliers instead of inviting competitive bids from all interested parties. The terms of such a contract emerge

Goods made with environmentally friendly materials and processes have a new prestige. Many consumers are willing to pay more for these eco-friendly products.

through offers and counteroffers between the buyer and the seller. When only one supplier offers a desired product, or when projects require extensive research and development, buyers and sellers often set purchase terms through negotiated contracts. In addition, some state and local governments permit their agencies to skip the formal bid process and negotiate product purchases under certain dollar limits—say, $500 or $1,000. This policy seeks to eliminate economic waste that would result from obtaining and processing bids for relatively minor purchases. In contrast, the city of Glendale, Arizona, requires that any services totaling $50,000 or more be subject to competitive bidding. However, with rising prices for most services, it is easy for proposals to exceed that ceiling.[21]

NEGOTIATING PRICES ONLINE

Many people see the Internet as one big auction site. Whether it's toys, furniture, or automobiles, an online auction site seems to be waiting to serve every person's needs—buyer and seller alike. Auctions are the purest form of negotiated pricing.

Ticket sales are an online auction favorite. Consumers can bid on tickets for all sorts of events: Broadway shows, professional sports, and rock concerts. Razor Gator and Ticket Liquidator are two such online ticket sellers. Razor Gator specializes in finding tickets to sold-out events and providing a "VIP experience." Ticket Liquidator offers low prices on tickets for thousands of events daily.[22]

Online auctions also take place at sites like eBay and uBid.com, where consumers can snap up items as varied as diamond-and-gold cuff links and an entire—deserted—Italian village. Recently, eBay reported that more than half of its transactions concern fixed-price products, and income from its Marketplace website has been overtaken by PayPal, which eBay owns and has 117 million active accounts around the world. Home Depot recently began accepting PayPal; the pilot project spread to 2,000 stores in only two months. Fifteen new retail partners have joined this service, which translates to almost 17,000 stores. A PayPal customer swipes the PayPal card or keys in his or her mobile phone number and PIN.[23]

ASSESSMENT CHECK

5.1 What is competitive bidding?

5.2 Describe the benefits of an auction—to the buyer and the seller.

Auctions are considered the purest form of negotiating prices and can occur in many places, including on the Internet. In addition to eBay, uBid. com is one of the most popular online auction sites.

THE TRANSFER PRICING DILEMMA

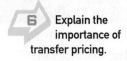

6 Explain the importance of transfer pricing.

transfer price Cost assessed when a product is moved from one profit center within a firm to another.

profit center Any part of an organization to which revenue and controllable costs can be assigned.

A pricing problem peculiar to large-scale enterprises is the determination of an internal transfer price—the price for moving goods between profit centers, which are any part of the organization to which revenue and controllable costs can be assigned, such as a department. As companies expand, they tend to decentralize management and set up profit centers as a control device in the newly decentralized operation.

In a large company, profit centers might secure many needed resources from sellers within their own organization. The pricing problem thus poses several questions: What rate should profit center A (maintenance department) charge profit center B (production department) for the cleaning compound used on B's floors? Should the price be the same as it would be if A did the work for an outside party? Should B receive a discount? The answers to these questions depend on the philosophy of the firm involved.

Transfer pricing can be complicated, especially for multinational organizations. The government closely monitors transfer pricing practices because these exchanges offer easy ways for companies to avoid paying taxes on profits. For example, Congress passed a bill outlawing federal contractors from hiring workers through offshore "shell"—nonexistent—companies and thus avoiding having to pay Social Security and Medicare taxes.

Figure 19.4 shows how this type of pricing manipulation might work. Suppose a South Korean manufacturer of DVD players sells its machines to its Irish subsidiary for distribution to dealers throughout the United Kingdom. Although each unit costs $25 to build, the manufacturer charges the distributor $75. In turn, the distributor sells the DVD players to retailers for $125 each. This arrangement gives the South Korean manufacturer a $50 profit on each machine, on which it pays taxes only in South Korea. Meanwhile, the Irish distributor writes off $50 for advertising and shipping costs, leaving it with no profits—and no tax liability.

ASSESSMENT CHECK

6.1 Define *transfer price*.

6.2 What is a profit center?

GLOBAL CONSIDERATIONS AND ONLINE PRICING

7 Compare the three alternative global pricing strategies.

Throughout this course, we have seen the impact of the Internet on every component of the marketing mix. This chapter has touched on the outer edges of the Internet's influence on pricing practices. Remember: every online marketer is inherently a global marketer that must understand the wide variety of internal and external conditions affecting global pricing strategies. Internal influences include the firm's goals and marketing strategies; the costs of developing, producing, and marketing its output; the nature of the products; and the firm's competitive strengths.

External influences include general conditions in international markets, especially those in the firm's target markets; regulatory limitations; trade restrictions; competitors' actions; economic events; and the global status of the industry.

TRADITIONAL GLOBAL PRICING STRATEGIES

In general, a company can implement one of three export pricing strategies: a standard worldwide price, dual pricing, or market-differentiated pricing. Exporters often set standard worldwide prices,

FIGURE 19.4
Transfer Pricing to Escape Taxation

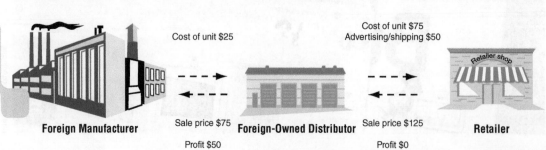

Cost of unit $25

Cost of unit $75
Advertising/shipping $50

Foreign Manufacturer

Sale price $75
Profit $50

Foreign-Owned Distributor

Sale price $125
Profit $0

Retailer

© Cengage Learning

regardless of their target markets. This strategy can succeed if foreign marketing costs remain low enough that they do not affect overall costs or if their prices reflect average unit costs. A company that implements a standard pricing program must monitor the international marketplace carefully, however, to make sure domestic competitors do not undercut its prices.

The dual pricing strategy distinguishes prices for domestic and export sales. Some exporters practice cost-plus pricing to establish dual prices that fully allocate their true domestic and foreign costs to product sales in those markets. These prices ensure an exporter makes a profit on any product it sells, but final prices may exceed those of competitors. Other companies opt for flexible cost-plus pricing schemes that allow marketers to grant discounts or change prices according to shifts in the competitive environment or fluctuations in the international exchange rate.

The third strategy, market-differentiated pricing, makes even more flexible arrangements to set prices according to local marketplace conditions. The dynamic global marketplace often requires frequent price changes by exporters who choose this approach. Effective market-differentiated pricing depends on access to quick, accurate market information.

ASSESSMENT CHECK

7.1 What are the three traditional global pricing strategies?

7.2 Which is the most flexible global pricing strategy?

CHARACTERISTICS OF ONLINE PRICING

To deal with the influences of the Internet on pricing policies and practices, marketers are applying old strategies in new ways, and companies are updating operations to compete with electronic technologies. Some firms offer online specials that do not appear in their stores or mail-order catalogs. These may take such forms as limited-time discounts, free shipping offers, or coupons that are good only online.

> Relate the concepts of cannibalization, bundle pricing, and bots to online pricing strategies.

The Cannibalization Dilemma

By pricing the same products differently online, companies run the risk of cannibalization. The new twist on an old tactic is companies' self-inflicting price cuts by creating competition among their own products. During the first decade of e-business, marketers debated whether it was worth taking the risk of alienating customers and channel members by offering lower prices for their products online—then an unproven retail outlet. But today, marketers are more savvy about integrating marketing channels, including online sites and affiliated stores—different stores owned by the same company. The trend is moving toward standardizing pricing across channels. Comparison shopping can still pay off, however. See the "Career Readiness" feature for some tips on using mobile apps to compare prices.

> **cannibalization** Loss of sales of an existing product due to competition from a new product in the same line.

Walmart was one of the first brick-and-mortar retailers to introduce a "Site to Store" feature to its website so shoppers could choose how and where they want to make purchases, all at the same price. Recently, the company announced a "Pay with Cash" offer for online orders. Customers order online, pay cash at a local Walmart store for the goods, and the order is then shipped to their homes. Or, if a customer chooses "Site to Store" after paying for the order, he or she will receive a text or email when the order is ready to pick up.

Retailers are adopting this convenience feature in increasing numbers: the Container Store's "GoShop! Click & Pickup" and Lowe's "20-Minute Pick Up In Store—Free" services are two such examples. As consumers become *multichannel shoppers,* shopping their preferred retailers both online and off, they are embracing this feature and expect the retailer to recognize them as regular shoppers, regardless of the channel they choose. Research shows that multichannel shoppers are more profitable than those who stick to one channel.[24]

Use of Shopbots

A second characteristic of online pricing is the use of search programs called bots or shopbots—derived from the word *robots*—that act as comparison shopping agents. Bots search the Web for a specific product and print a list of sites offering the best prices. In online selling, bots force marketers to keep prices low. However, marketing researchers report that the majority of online shoppers check out several sites before buying, and price is not the only variable they consider when making a

> **bot (shopbot)** Software program that allows online shoppers to compare prices of a particular product offered by several online retailers.

CAREER READINESS

Using Smartphone Apps for Comparison Shopping

Some shoppers like visiting brick-and-mortar stores to check prices before they buy. If that isn't you, here are some tips for using your smartphone to do some savvy comparison shopping.

- Price Check is Amazon's free iPhone and Android app for instantly checking online and in-store prices. It can compare based on pictures of the product or verbal input of its name and will show you customer reviews as well.

- ShopSavvy scans product barcodes to show you the best online and in-store prices on the iPhone or Android. You can also use it for one-tap purchases at Walmart, Target, and Best Buy.

- Goodzer lists all the stores in your area that carry the product you're looking for, complete with maps and directions. The app is only for the iPhone as of now, but you can access the website with any smartphone.

- Pic2shop is a barcode reader with tens of millions of items in its database and works with the iPhone, Android phone, and Windows Phone 8.

- RedLaser reads barcodes to check prices and customer reviews on eBay and Half.com and can provide in-stock reports at local stores.

- Still can't make up your mind? Check Decide.com's iPhone app or website to get price predictions. They'll help you decide whether to buy now or wait for a sale.

Sources: Katherine Murray, "Five Free Comparison-Shopping Smartphone Apps," *Tech Republic,* accessed December 6, 2012, www.technrepublic.com; Melanie Pinola, "The 9 Best Mobile Shopping Apps," *About.com,* accessed December 6, 2012, http://mobileoffice.about.com; Michael Estrin, "Shopping Around Too Tiring? Use Smartphone," *Fox Business,* accessed December 6, 2012, www.foxbusiness.com; "Pic2shop," *Windows 8 Apps,* accessed December 6, 2012, www.windows8apps.com.

Walmart recently announced a "Pay with Cash" option for online orders.

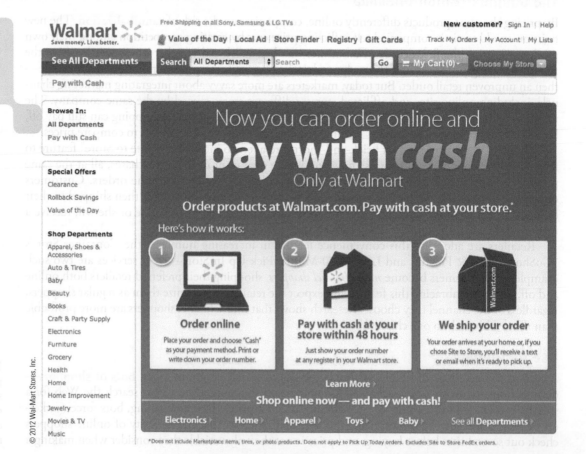

purchase decision. Service quality and support information are powerful motivators in the decision process. Also, while price is an important factor with products like books and DVDs, it is not as important with complex or highly differentiated products, such as real estate or investment banking. Brand image and customer service may outweigh price in these purchase decisions.

BUNDLE PRICING

As marketers have watched e-business weaken their control over prices, they have modified their use of the price variable in the marketing mix. Whenever possible, they have moved to an approach called **bundle pricing**, in which customers acquire a host of goods and services in addition to the tangible products they purchase.

Nowhere is bundle pricing more prevalent than in the telecommunications industry. Consumers are bombarded daily by advertisements for all kinds of Internet, cell phone, and cable TV packages. Verizon offers three fiber-optic service bundles that include HD TV, Internet, and digital voice services. Signing up for enhanced plans also provides access to thousands of Wi-Fi hot spots in the United States—a plus for sales representatives whose work takes them on the road.[25]

But sometimes consumers resist the practice of bundling, claiming they are forced to pay for services they don't want in order to receive the ones they do. This is particularly the case with cable television. Cable companies insist they have spent billions of dollars to expand their networks and technology and would be left with unused capacity if they sold only a few channels at a time to each customer. Consumer advocates argue that customers are not only forced to pay for unwanted services but also wind up paying inflated prices. The solution seems to be à la carte pricing—allowing consumers to pick and choose the shows or channels they want. Although in the past some industry observers believed that bundling kept prices low, today, the market shows signs of change. Time Warner Cable recently introduced TV Essentials, a low-cost package that doesn't include sports channels, which are becoming increasingly expensive.[26]

bundle pricing
Offering two or more complementary products and selling them for a single price.

 ASSESSMENT CHECK

8.1 What is cannibalization?

8.2 What is bundle pricing?

STRATEGIC IMPLICATIONS OF MARKETING IN THE 21ST CENTURY

Price has historically been the marketing variable least likely to be used as a source of competitive advantage. However, using price as part of a marketing program designed to meet a firm's overall organizational objectives can be a powerful strategy.

Technology has forever changed the marketplace, which affects the pricing function. Traditional geographic boundaries that allowed some businesses to operate have been broken by the Internet as well as mass merchandisers who offer a larger selection and lower prices. A customer in Wyoming might want to purchase a hand-carved walking cane from Kenya or an ornamental fan from Kyoto. Not a problem—the Web connects buyers and sellers around the globe. Similarly, the cost of shipping an overnight

FedEx package from New York to California is no more than shipping it to a nearby city.

Not only is it possible to escape the boundaries of time and space on the Internet, but price is no longer a constant in the marketing process. With the increasing number of auction sites and search technologies like bots, customers now have more power to control the prices of goods and services. Consumers can find the lowest prices on the market, and they can also negotiate prices for many of the products they buy. To succeed, marketers will continue to offer value—fair prices for quality goods and services—and superior customer service. Those traditions will always be in style.

REVIEW OF CHAPTER OBJECTIVES

1 Compare the alternative pricing strategies, and explain when each strategy is most appropriate.

The alternative pricing strategies are skimming pricing strategy, penetration pricing strategy, and competitive pricing strategy. Skimming pricing is commonly used as a market-entry price for distinctive products with little or no initial competition. Penetration pricing is used when a wide array of competing brands exists. Everyday low pricing (EDLP), a variant of penetration pricing, is used by discounters attempting to hold the line on prices without having to rely heavily on coupons, rebates, and other price concessions. Competitive pricing is employed when marketers wish to concentrate their competitive efforts on marketing variables other than price.

2 Describe how prices are quoted.

Methods for quoting prices depend on such factors as cost structures, traditional practices in a particular industry, and policies of individual firms. Price quotes can involve list prices, market prices, cash discounts, trade discounts, quantity discounts, and allowances like trade-ins, promotional allowances, and rebates. Shipping costs often figure heavily into the pricing of goods. A number of alternatives for dealing with these costs exist: FOB plant pricing, in which the price includes no shipping charges; FOB origin-freight allowed, or freight absorbed, which allows the buyer to deduct transportation expenses from the bill; uniform-delivered price, in which the same price, including shipping expenses, is charged to all buyers; and zone pricing, in which a set price exists within each region.

3 Identify the various pricing policy decisions marketers must make.

A pricing policy is a general guideline based on pricing objectives and is intended for use in specific pricing decisions. Pricing policies include psychological pricing, unit pricing, price flexibility, product-line pricing, and promotional pricing.

4 Relate price to consumer perceptions of quality.

The relationship between price and consumer perceptions of quality has been the subject of considerable research. In the absence of other cues, price is an important influence on how the consumer perceives the product's quality. A well-known and accepted concept is that of price limits—limits within which the perception of product quality varies directly with price. The concept of price limits suggests that extremely low prices may be considered too cheap, thus indicating inferior quality, and prices set above an expected limit are seen as too expensive.

5 Contrast competitive bidding and negotiated prices.

Competitive bidding and negotiated prices are pricing techniques used primarily in the B2B sector and in government and organizational markets. Sometimes prices are negotiated through competitive bidding, in which several buyers quote prices on the same service or good. Buyer specifications describe the item the government or B2B firm wishes to acquire. Negotiated contracts are another possibility in many procurement situations. The terms of the contract are set through negotiations between buyer and seller.

6 Explain the importance of transfer pricing.

A phenomenon in large corporations is transfer pricing, in which a company sets prices for transferring goods or services from one company profit center to another. The term *profit center* refers to any part of the organization to which revenue and controllable costs can be assigned. In large companies whose profit centers acquire resources from other parts of the firm, the prices charged by one profit center to another will directly affect both the cost and profitability of the output of both profit centers.

7 Compare the three alternative global pricing strategies.

Companies can choose from three export pricing strategies: a standard worldwide price, dual pricing, or market-differentiated pricing. A standard worldwide price may be possible if foreign marketing costs are so low that they do not affect overall costs or if the price is based on an average unit cost. The dual pricing approach establishes separate price strategies for domestic and exported products. Some exporters use cost-plus pricing methods to establish dual prices that fully allocate their true domestic and foreign costs to their product; others choose flexible cost-plus pricing. Market-differentiated pricing is the most flexible export pricing strategy, because it allows firms to price their products according to marketplace conditions. It requires easy access to quick, accurate market information.

 Relate the concepts of cannibalization, bundle pricing, and bots to online pricing strategies.

To deal with the influences of the Internet on pricing policies and practices, marketers are applying old strategies in new ways, and companies are updating operations to compete with electronic technologies. Cannibalization secures additional sales through lower prices that take sales away from the marketer's other products. Bots, also known as shopbots, act as comparison-shopping agents. Bundle pricing involves offering two or more complementary products and selling them for a single price.

ASSESSMENT CHECK: ANSWERS

1.1 What are the three major pricing strategies? The three major pricing strategies are skimming, penetration, and competitive.

1.2 What is EDLP? EDLP stands for "everyday low pricing." It is a variation of penetration pricing often used by discounters.

2.1 What are the three major types of discounts? The three major types of discounts are cash discounts, trade discounts, and quantity discounts.

2.2 Identify the four alternatives for handling transportation costs in pricing policies. The four alternatives for handling transportation costs are FOB pricing, uniform-delivered pricing, zone pricing, and basing-point pricing.

3.1 Define *pricing policy*. A pricing policy is a general guideline that reflects marketing objectives and influences specific pricing decisions.

3.2 Describe the two types of psychological pricing other than prestige pricing. The two additional types of psychological pricing are odd pricing, in which marketers set prices at odd numbers just under round numbers; and unit pricing, which states prices in terms of a recognized unit of measurement.

3.3 What is promotional pricing? Promotional pricing is a lower-than-normal price for a set period of time.

4.1 Describe the price–quality connection. Price is an important indicator of a product's quality. However, many marketers now work hard to convince consumers they are offering high-quality products at the lowest possible price.

4.2 What are price limits? Price limits indicate certain boundaries within which consumers' product-quality perceptions vary directly with price. A price set lower than

expected seems too cheap, and one set above the expected limit is seen as too expensive.

5.1 What is competitive bidding? Competitive bidding consists of inviting potential suppliers to quote prices on proposed purchases or contracts.

5.2 Describe the benefits of an auction—to the buyer and the seller. An auction can provide buyers with opportunities to buy goods and services at very low prices. It can also offer sellers an opportunity to sell to a wider audience (online), perhaps at a higher price than otherwise would be possible, if an item is particularly popular.

6.1 Define *transfer price*. A transfer price is the price for moving goods between profit centers.

6.2 What is a profit center? A profit center is any part of the organization to which revenue and controllable costs can be assigned.

7.1 What are the three traditional global pricing strategies? The three global pricing strategies are standard worldwide pricing, dual pricing, and market-differentiated pricing.

7.2 Which is the most flexible global pricing strategy? The most flexible global pricing strategy is market-differentiated pricing, which allows firms to set prices according to actual conditions.

8.1 What is cannibalization? Cannibalization involves a company losing sales of an existing product by introducing a new product in the same selling channel.

8.2 What is bundle pricing? Bundle pricing involves combining a number of goods or services together and offering them at a set price.

MARKETING TERMS YOU NEED TO KNOW

skimming pricing strategy **645**

market-plus pricing **645**

step out **645**

penetration pricing strategy **646**

everyday low pricing (EDLP) **647**

competitive pricing strategy **649**

opening price point **649**

list price **649**

market price **650**

cash discount **650**

trade discount **650**

quantity discount **651**

cumulative quantity discount **651**

noncumulative quantity discount **651**

allowance **651**

trade-in **651**

promotional allowance **651**

minimum advertised pricing (MAP) **652**

rebate **652**

FOB (free on board) plant (FOB origin) **652**

FOB origin-freight allowed (freight absorbed) **653**

uniform-delivered pricing **653**

postage-stamp pricing **653**

zone pricing **653**

basing-point pricing **653**

pricing policy **654**

psychological pricing **654**

odd pricing **654**

unit pricing **654**

price flexibility **654**

product-line pricing **655**

promotional pricing **656**

loss leader **657**

leader pricing **657**

competitive bidding **658**

transfer price **660**

profit center **660**

cannibalization **661**

bot (shopbot) **661**

bundle pricing **663**

ASSURANCE OF LEARNING REVIEW

1. What is the difference between a skimming price strategy and a penetration pricing strategy? Under which circumstances is each most likely to be used?

2. Why is competitive pricing risky for marketers?

3. What is the difference between a list price and a market price?

4. What are allowances? How do they work?

5. Describe the three ways buyers and sellers handle transportation expenses.

6. How is product-line pricing helpful to both retailers and their customers?

7. What is the difference between loss leader and leader pricing? Give an example of when retailers would use each of these pricing strategies.

8. What is the difference between a competitive bid and a negotiated price?

9. Describe briefly the three traditional global pricing strategies. Give an example of a firm or product that would be likely to adopt one of the three approaches, and explain why.

10. Although cannibalization generally forces price cuts, in what ways can it actually benefit a firm?

PROJECTS AND TEAMWORK EXERCISES

1. With a classmate, create two advertisements for the same product. One advertisement should feature a high price; the other advertisement should feature a low price. Present your advertisements to your classmates. Record their perceptions of the price–quality relationship. Which price do most of them seem to prefer?

2. Figure out how much it will cost to buy and own one of the following new cars from a dealership, or select another model. What is the list price? What price could you negotiate?
   a. Ford Escape hybrid
   b. Lexus RX 350
   c. Hyundai Santa Fe
   d. Scion tC

3. Assume that a product sells for $100 per ton and that Pittsburgh is the basing-point city for calculating transportation charges. Shipping from Pittsburgh to a potential customer in Cincinnati costs $10 per ton. The actual shipping costs of suppliers in three other cities are $8 per ton for Supplier A, $11 per ton for Supplier B, and $10 per ton for Supplier C. Using this information, answer the following questions:

   a. What delivered price would a salesperson for Supplier A quote to the Cincinnati customer?
   b. What delivered price would a salesperson for Supplier B quote to the Cincinnati customer?
   c. What delivered price would a salesperson for Supplier C quote to the Cincinnati customer?
   d. How much would each supplier net (after subtracting actual shipping costs) per ton on the sale?

4. On your own or with a classmate, visit a local supermarket to find examples of promotional pricing and loss leaders. Note instances of both. Does the promotional pricing make you more likely to purchase a product? Does knowing the store uses loss-leader pricing of bananas make you more inclined to buy them? Present your findings and opinions to the class.

5. Decide on a trip you'd really like to take. Then go online to several of the travel sites—Travelocity, Priceline.com, or others—and compare prices for your trip, including airfare, hotels, car rental, and so forth. Does bundling the different components give you a price break? Note any coupons or promotions for restaurants and attractions as well. Decide which trip is the best deal, and explain why.

CRITICAL-THINKING EXERCISES

1. When Chinese automakers recently began exporting cars, rather than focusing on developed nations in the West, they are shipping autos to emerging markets in countries like Algeria, Russia, Chile, and South Africa. In these markets, even used vehicles from multinational manufacturers are relatively scarce—and relatively expensive. The Chinese automakers, whose priority is keeping costs down rather than design or even safety, applied a penetration-pricing strategy. A woman in Santiago, Chile, who bought a new Chery S21 explained, "The price factor is fairly decisive. I paid $5,500 new and full. Toyota with similar features costs around $12,000." Why do you think Chinese automakers chose that pricing strategy? Do you think it was successful? As Chinese regulators pressure these manufacturers to make their cars safer, do you think they will be able to keep their prices low compared with those of the international automakers? Why or why not?[27]

2. As a consumer, would you rather shop at a store that features a sale once a month or a store that practices everyday low pricing (EDLP)? Why?

3. Under Staples' Easy Rebates program, customers can submit most of their rebate applications online for products purchased over the Internet, through the catalog, and in Staples stores. Customers may also submit several rebates at once and receive emails about the status of their rebates at every stage.[28] Staples claims the rebates are processed much faster than those of other companies. Do you think the Easy Rebates program will increase the number of rebates customers actually submit? Why or why not? Do you think other firms will follow with similar programs?

4. Go online to a shopping site you use regularly and note the prices for different types of products. Does this firm use psychological pricing? Product line pricing? Note any pricing strategies you can identify. Do any of these strategies make you prefer the site over a competitor's site?

5. Why is competitive bidding an important factor in major purchase decisions such as vehicles for a police force, the construction of a bridge, or the manufacture of military uniforms?

ETHICS EXERCISE

The law allows companies in a variety of industries to add what many refer to as "hidden" charges to customers' bills. Phone bills, airline tickets, and hotel receipts often contain charges that are difficult to identify. A visitor who stays in a hotel might be hit with a "hospitality fee," a "resort fee," or an "automatic gratuity," to name just a few. These charges are not taxes, and although they are itemized, it is difficult for the average traveler to make sense of them. Most people either don't check their bills thoroughly or are in a hurry to check out and don't bother to dispute the charges, which may be

only a few dollars. But these charges add up over the course of hundreds or thousands of visitors each year, and hotels are pocketing them—legitimately.[29]

1. Do you think adding hidden charges to hotel visitors' bills is a smart marketing strategy? Why or why not?

2. Visit the website of a hotel chain with which you are familiar to learn if it gives any information about additional surcharges. If consumers were informed about the charges ahead of time, would you feel differently about them? Why or why not?

INTERNET EXERCISES

1. **Price competition.** Using several online ticket sellers, look up prices for an event you would like to attend. Are the prices comparable? What other fees are included in the price-per-ticket? Are discounts offered for purchasing multiple tickets? Is there a loyalty program for consumers who frequent a specific ticket seller?
www.ticketmaster.com
www.stubhub.com
www.livenation.com

2. **Pricing strategies.** Say you'd like to go on a Caribbean cruise. Visit the Royal Caribbean website to price cruises at various times of the year—for example, summer vacation, spring break week, and Thanksgiving week. Which cruises are the most and least expensive? Prepare a summary of your findings and bring it to class so you can participate in a discussion on pricing strategies.
www.royalcaribbean.com/findacruise

3. **Bundle pricing.** Using online websites for several insurance companies, look up pricing for bundling several different types of insurance policies—for example, auto and renter's insurance. Is there an advantage to buying two or more different policies with the same company? What are some of the disadvantages to consumers for bundling insurance coverage with one company? What are some of the other factors that impact the cost of bundling insurance policies?
www.progressive.com
www.geico.com
www.esurance.com

Note: Internet Web addresses change frequently. If you don't find the exact site listed, you may need to access the organization's home page and search from there or use a search engine such as Google or Bing.

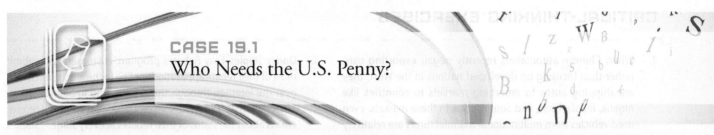

CASE 19.1
Who Needs the U.S. Penny?

Does an object that costs more to make than it's worth have any value in today's economy? If the object is the U.S. penny, a growing consensus says "no."

Canada will soon stop producing its penny, following the lead of Australia, New Zealand, Brazil, Norway, Switzerland, Finland, and Britain, which all dropped their lowest-valued coins from circulation with no ill effects. And Canada's penny wasn't as big of a drain on the country's treasury as the U.S. penny. It cost only 1.6 cents to make, whereas the U.S. penny—a copper plate covered by a 99 percent zinc core—cost taxpayers 2.4 cents each. In one recent year, the U.S. Treasury spent $60 million minting pennies, more than double the cost in 1982, all for coins that have no real purchasing power.

Canada's government will ask citizens to bring unwanted pennies to banks to be melted down or donated to charities. Canadians who want to continue using the pennies still in circulation are free to do so. They will have fewer opportunities than before, however, since cash sales will be rounded to the nearest five cents.

The zinc industry wants to keep supplying raw material to the U.S. government, of course, but as the cost of zinc keeps rising, some people feel it's time to follow Canada's example and simply eliminate the penny, saving the government the cost of manufacturing it and diverting the metal to some other, better use.

Other people worry that, if all prices are rounded up to the nearest nickel, rather than down, those most affected will be the poor. Others feel that rounded prices will acquire what economists call "stickiness" and resist further increases (which would have to be at least 5 cents) for a few years, thus helping all consumers. "A 99-cent price might go down to 95 cents rather than up to $1 to avoid crossing that higher price threshold," says a senior economist at the Federal Reserve.

QUESTIONS FOR CRITICAL THINKING

1. What do you think would happen to retail prices if the United States withdrew the penny from circulation? Why?

2. Some observers suggest eliminating the nickel as well, since each one costs more than 11 cents to make and distribute. Do you agree, and why or why not? What would be the effect of such a decision on prices?

Sources: Neal Conan, "The Problems with Pennies," National Public Radio interview, accessed December 6, 2012, www.npr.org; Daniel Akst, "Whaddya Zinc? Let's Kill the Penny," *Newsday,* accessed December 6, 2012, www.newsday.com; Jeff Somer, "Penny Wise, or 2.4 Cents Foolish?" *The New York Times,* accessed December 6, 2012, www.nytimes.com; Matthew Yglesias, "No Pennies for Your Thoughts," *Slate,* accessed December 6, 2012, www.slate.com; Robert Whalpes, "It's Time to Eliminate the Penny," *CNN Opinion,* accessed December 6, 2012, http://articles.cnn.com.

VIDEO CASE 19.2
BoltBus: Ride for the Right Price

It's hard to find a real bargain these days, but BoltBus is the real deal. Those black-and-orange buses you see trundling past you on the highway or along a city street could be your ticket to ride—for $1. BoltBus, owned by Greyhound Lines, operates 92 buses along the Northeastern corridor and in the Pacific Northwest, moving more than 2 million passengers each year. The company's primary customers are those in the 18- to 34-year-old range—college students, recent grads, young professionals, and young families. These riders tend to be budget-minded, and BoltBus caters to them. Pricing is a major component of the bus line's marketing strategy.

When BoltBus launched its line in the Northeast, at least 15 other competitors were already operating in the region. In addition, travelers could opt for planes or trains, or drive their own cars. So the bus line had to offer a brand that sold tickets online, at a very competitive cost. "Pricing is really crucial because it's such a competitive environment," says William Koen, a business analyst for BoltBus. With so many other options available to consumers, BoltBus opted for penetration pricing—including its now-famous $1 ticket—relying on the buzz generated by travelers who nabbed the golden ticket as well as those who began to ride the bus line for its average $20 fare. Typically, BoltBus will sell one $1 ticket per route, selling the remainder of seats for around $20. Whoever gets the $1 ticket often posts their lucky draw on Facebook or Twitter—and the news goes viral. "The $1 ticket is meant to be fun," explains Nicole Recker, senior marketing manager, and the strategy seems to work. Everyone hopes to be the $1 ticket holder, but no one minds paying the regular fare, which is significantly lower than those of competing bus lines.

BoltBus does have to monitor its costs, particularly those of fuel and labor. When these two factors have risen, the company has increased prices in small increments to keep up, with the goal of maintaining both value and profitability. The company also continuously monitors the competition to make sure its service is priced less than its rivals while meeting its costs. BoltBus takes into account the price of gasoline, tolls, and parking for those consumers who choose to drive—and tries to offer a cheaper, more convenient service. "Generally in New York City you'll pay more in parking per day than for a one-way ticket on our buses, so having that value for our customers has driven our explosive growth," notes Koen. "It's opening up an entire new market for the bus industry."

BoltBus also takes demand into consideration when setting prices. Using historical data, marketers see how many people its buses have carried along a certain route on any given day or time period. Then they tweak certain variables—such as the frequency of runs—to maximize revenue and profitability without cutting value to customers. For example, ridership tends to increase during the weekends and holiday periods, so BoltBus offers more runs during those high-volume periods, while cutting runs during the midweek when the buses aren't filled. During low-demand periods (such as Wednesdays), BoltBus may offer a lower price in order to attract more volume; conversely, during high-demand periods (such as Friday evenings), ticket prices are a bit higher. This type of pricing to demand is similar to the strategy of hotels and airlines; consumers pay more to fly or stay in a hotel during popular vacation weeks. Since seats generally sell out during these high-volume periods, BoltBus doesn't need to discount the ticket price. But an empty seat represents a loss of revenue to the company, so a discounted sale is better than no sale—which is why BoltBus offers lower prices during quieter times of the week or year. "It's a high-volume business model," explains general manager David Hall. "We keep the price low and the volume high."

BoltBus' pricing policy is attractive to consumers. Prices are straightforward and easy to understand; consumers know what to expect, and what they are getting for their dollar. "Transparency has been key to our success," says Recker. "It's done a lot to enhance our brand." BoltBus charges no hidden or additional fees and doesn't jack up its prices without warning. "We're very honest with our customer," says Recker.

QUESTIONS FOR CRITICAL THINKING

1. How does BoltBus use a combination of penetration pricing and everyday low pricing (EDLP) to achieve its objectives?

2. BoltBus is well-known for its $1 ticket sales promotion. Though it has been successful thus far, could it ever backfire? If so, how?

Sources: Company website, www.boltbus.com, accessed December 6, 2012; Christine Whittemore, "Travel Marketing: What the Revitalized Bus Travel Industry Can Teach You about Reinventing Your Travel Brand," *5 to 9 Branding*, accessed December 6, 2012, http://5to9branding.com; Jennifer Sokolowsky, "BoltBus to Offer $1 Fares from Seattle, Portland," *Puget Sound Business Journal*, accessed December 6, 2012, wwwbizjournals.com.

NOTES

1. Brad Tuttle, "The Passive-Aggressive Way to Haggle Online: Abandon Your Shopping Cart," *Time*, accessed December 6, 2012, http://business.time.com; "U.S. Online Holiday Shopping Season Reaches Record $37.2 Billion for November-December Period, Up 15 Percent vs. Year Ago," *ComScore*, accessed December 6, 2012, www.comscore.com; Beth Pinsker Gladstone, "Abandon Online Shopping Cart, Reap Discount?" *Reuters.com*, accessed December 6, 2012, www.reuters.com; Eric Savitz, "Online Retailers: Fixing Shopping Cart Abandonment," *Forbes*, accessed December 6, 2012, www.forbes.com; Megan Ouellet, "Shopping Cart Abandonment Practices of the Internet Retailer 1000 Companies," *Listrak*, accessed December 6, 2012, www.listrak.com; Kern Lewis, "Abandoned Online Shopping Carts: How to Close Those Deals," *Forbes*, accessed December 6, 2012, www.forbes.com.

2. Company website, www.buy.com, accessed December 6, 2012; company website, www.amazon.com, accessed December 6, 2012.

3. Pete Pachal, "Amazon Drops Price of 7-Inch Kindle Fire to $159," *Mashable*, accessed December 6, 2012, http://mashable.com; Kyle Wagner, "The History of Amazon's Kindle So Far," *Gizmodo*, accessed December 6, 2012, http://gizmodo.com; Harry McCracken, "Your First Look at Nook: The *Technologizer* Review," *Technologizer*, accessed December 6, 2012, http://technologizer.com.

4. "CEO Defends Tata Nano, World's Cheapest Car," *USA Today*, accessed December 6, 2012, http://content.usatoday.com; Anita Lienert, "2013 Nissan Versa Sedan Clings to Cheapest Car in America Title," *Edmunds*, accessed December 6, 2012, www.edmunds.com.

5. Trefis Team, "Lowe's Still Worth $34 though Trails Home Depot's Recovery," *Forbes*, accessed December 6, 2012, www.forbes.com; H. Butler, "Macquarie Forecasts 'Benign' Peak Season," *JOC Sailings*, accessed December 6, 2012, www.jocsailings.com.

6. Matthew Boyle, "Why Grocers Are Boosting Private Labels," *Bloomberg Businessweek*, accessed December 6, 2012, www.businessweek.com.

7. "2013 Mazda Miata Prices," *Motor Trend*, accessed December 6, 2012, www.motortrend.com.

8. Company website, www.shutterfly.com, accessed December 6, 2012.

9. Company website, http://qd.sees.com, accessed December 6, 2012.

10. Organization website, www.consumerreports.org, accessed December 6, 2012.

11. Carl Laron, "New TV Pricing Policies a Tough Sell for Customers," *Consumer Search*, accessed December 6, 2012, www.consumersearch.com.

12. Jill Cataldo, "Super-Couponing Tips: When Rebates Go Awry," *Lehigh Valley Live*, accessed December 6, 2012, www.lehighvalleylive.com; "Advice on Rebates and Refunds," *Better Business Bureau*, accessed December 6, 2012, http://memphis.bbb.org.

13. "Comcast Trying Out Usage Pricing, Dropping Caps," *Reuters*, accessed December 6, 2012, www.reuters.com; Stacey Higginbotham, "Which ISPs Are Capping Your Broadband, and Why?" *Gigaom.com*, accessed December 6, 2012, http://gigaom.com;

Wendy Davis, "Senate Urged to Probe Data Caps," *Online Media Daily*, accessed December 6, 2012, www.mediapost.com.

14. Company website, www.bergdorfgoodman.com, accessed December 6, 2012; company website, www.sunglasshut.com, accessed December 6, 2012; company website, www.gold-and-wood.com, accessed December 6, 2012; "Gold and Wood Releases $55,000 Diamond Eyeglasses," *Optical Vision Site*, accessed December 6, 2012, http://opticalvisionresources.com.

15. "Restaurant Week 2012: Outstanding Meals for Just $20.12," *Coastal Uncorked*, accessed December 6, 2012, www.coastaluncorked.com.

16. Matthew Yglesias, "Why Does Turkey Get Cheaper Around Thanksgiving?" *Slate*, accessed December 6, 2012, www.slate.com.

17. Company website, www.bestbuy.com, accessed December 6, 2012.

18. Art Markman, "Price, Quality, and Value: How Do Shoppers Use Price to Judge Quality and Value?" *Psychology Today*, accessed December 6, 2012, www.psychologytoday.com.

19. Company website, www.motel6.com, accessed December 6, 2012.

20. Huw Evans, "2013 Ford Police Interceptor Test Drive—Video," *AutoGuide.com*, accessed December 6, 2012, www.autoguide.com; Chris Paukert, "2012 Chevrolet Caprice PPV: Anything But a Trivial Pursuit," *Autoblog*, accessed December 6, 2012, www.autoblog.com.

21. "Court Says Glendale Did Not Violate Bidding Process," *Peoria Times*, accessed December 6, 2012, www.peoriatimes.com.

22. Company website, www.razorgator.com, accessed December 6, 2012; company website, www.ticketliquidator.com, accessed December 6, 2012.

23. "Number of PayPal's Total Active Registered User Accounts from 1st Quarter 2010 to 3rd Quarter 2012," *Statista*, accessed December 6, 2012, www.statista.com; company website, www.ubid.com, accessed December 6, 2012; Marilyn Alva, "EBay Goes Brick-and-Mortar, Tags Future to Mobile Too," *Investor's Business Daily*, accessed December 6, 2012, http://news.investors.com.

24. "Walmart Announces 'Pay with Cash' for Online Purchases," press release, *PR Newswire*, accessed December 6, 2012, www.bizjournals.com; company website, www.containerstore.com, accessed December 6, 2012; company website, www.lowes.com, accessed December 6, 2012.

25. Company website, www22.verizon.com, accessed December 6, 2012.

26. David Lieberman, "Time Warner Cable to Offer Low-Cost Service Plan, without ESPN," *Deadline.com*, accessed December 6, 2012, www.deadline.com.

27. Keith Bradsher, "Chinese Cars Make Valuable Gains in Emerging Markets," *The New York Times*, accessed December 6, 2012, www.nytimes.com.

28. Company website, www.stapleseasyrebates.com, accessed December 6, 2012.

29. Dan Gillmor, "The High Price of Hidden Charges," *The Guardian*, accessed December 6, 2012, www.guardian.co.uk; Jessica Dickler, "Hotels Piling On Hidden Fees," *CNN Money*, accessed December 6, 2012, http://money.cnn.com.

Scripps Networks Interactive & Food Network

Good, Better, Best

How do you put a price on the experience of serving friends or family the best dinner you ever cooked? Its value is far greater than the cost of ingredients or the amount of time you spent making the meal. Instead, its value lies in your original inspiration, your goal of producing a great meal, and all the care you blended into your creation—not to mention the enjoyment of your diners. Food Network marketers face this same question when considering pricing objectives for everything from advertising to branded cookware sold by retailer Kohl's.

Although Food Network does sell time to advertisers and charge cable and digital distributors for content, the network's ultimate customer is the consumer. "For us, the primary relationship is with the consumer," explains Chris Powell, executive vice president for human resources at Scripps. Food Network delivers relevant content to viewers, creating value for them that allows the network to charge advertising and distribution rates. Advertisers and distributors then have access to those consumers through a variety of outlets—whether it's placing their products in specific episodes or tweeting about an upcoming show premier. Lexus marketers may consider paying a higher price to place a new model in *Restaurant: Impossible* for the privilege of having its luxury auto featured on a popular show as a worthwhile investment. Distributors may agree to rates that meet Food Network's profitability objectives.

Food Network also designs and sells tangible goods—kitchen utensils, cookware, dinnerware, table linens, and more. Creating a pricing strategy for these products involves integrating the target audience for its television shows with its choice of retailer: Kohl's. Since Food Network products are sold exclusively by Kohl's, marketers can zoom in on a target market for its pricing decisions. Using a competitive pricing strategy, Food Network positions its kitchen goods along the "good, better, best" continuum. "We try to anchor ourselves at the high end of better," observes Sergei Kuharsky, senior vice president and general manager for licensing and merchandising. "We want to be quality first, but we want to be accessible as well." If Food Network priced its kitchen goods too high, fans would view them as unaffordable—undermining sales and potentially doing damage to the lifestyle image of the network. Gabe Gordon, vice president of research for Food Network, agrees with this assessment, particularly during economically difficult times. "If you're overtly leaning toward luxury, you turn a lot of people off," he points out.

When developing its kitchen products, Food Network partners with a team of culinary experts who help design, test, and review everything from frying pans to baking dishes. If these items survive hard use in the test kitchens for four to eight weeks, they'll likely perform well in consumers' homes. Quality combined with the right price creates value for consumers. Kohl's sets the actual retail prices for these items, with

product-line pricing—but the price–quality relationship is important to Food Network. "We look at our products as professionally inspired but priced for the home cook, and we want them to be as good if not better for the money than anything else out there," says Kuharsky.

Although consumers don't pay for Food Network programming (except through cable or other media subscriptions), the network takes into consideration pricing issues as it creates the line-up of shows. "I do think our programming is very aspirational," comments Gordon. "We give you the tools to make things your own." When the economy shifted downward several years ago, Food Network marketers noticed that daytime viewers responded well to shows that offered special deals or featured less-expensive menus and recipes. "When times change and money is tight, people will look for ways to cut corners in a less painful way," explains Gordon. In addition, people tend to entertain at home more—instead of dining out—so they gravitate toward shows that provide low-cost but fun or attractive ideas for social gatherings. These programs "help people live a better food life," Gordon continues. Here, price limits go to work in the minds of consumers. They establish a budget for groceries or entertaining, then shop within those limits. But they want to create the tastiest meal or trendiest party those boundaries will allow—and Food Network is there to help.

Price limits also apply to wealthier viewers who might be able to afford to buy more expensive ingredients or cookware but choose not to. If they see a certain dish featured on one of the cooking shows, they might snub it as too exotic for their family's tastes, or simply too complicated or lengthy to make at home. "Surprisingly, you end up turning off more of the upscale people in the audience," warns Gordon. In the end, everyone must eat to live—but Food Network aspires to bring out the inner cook in all of us, upscale or not. "Food is how people express themselves," says Gordon.

QUESTIONS FOR CRITICAL THINKING

1. In your opinion, should Food Network try to attain prestige objectives through pricing? Why or why not?

2. How would you classify the market structure for Food Network's offerings (both content and tangible goods)? Explain.

3. How might Food Network and Kohl's use product-line pricing to expand their partnered offerings?

4. Describe the price–quality relationship of Food Network's programming and its Kohl's cookware products.

Developing an Effective
MARKETING PLAN

OVERVIEW

> *"What are our mission and goals?"*
> *"Who are our customers?"*
> *"What types of products do we offer?"*
> *"How can we provide superior customer service?"*

These are some of the questions addressed by a marketing plan—a detailed **description of the resources and actions needed to achieve stated marketing objectives.** Chapter 2 discussed **strategic planning**—the process of anticipating events and market conditions and deciding how a firm can best achieve its organizational objectives. Marketing planning encompasses all the activities devoted to achieving marketing objectives, establishing a basis for designing a marketing strategy. This appendix deals in depth with the formal marketing plan, which is part of an organization's overall business plan. At the end of this appendix, you'll see what an actual marketing plan looks like. Each plan component for a hypothetical firm called Blue Sky Clothing is presented.

marketing plan
Detailed description of the resources and actions needed to achieve stated marketing objectives.

strategic planning
Process of anticipating events and market conditions and deciding how a firm can best achieve its organizational objectives.

COMPONENTS OF A BUSINESS PLAN

A company's **business plan** is one of its most important documents. The business plan puts in writing what all of the company's objectives are, how they will be met, how the business will obtain financing, and how much money the company expects to earn over a specified time period. Although business plans vary in length and format, most contain at least some form of the following components:

business plan
Formal document that outlines what a company's objectives are, how they will be met, how the business will obtain financing, and how much money the company expects to earn.

- An *executive summary* briefly answers the *who, what, when, where, how,* and *why* questions for the plan. Although the summary appears early in the plan, it typically is written last, after the firm's executives have worked out the details of all the other sections.

- A *competitive analysis* section focuses on the environment in which the marketing plan is to be implemented. Although this section is more closely associated with the comprehensive business plan, factors specifically influencing marketing are likely to be included here.

- The *mission statement* summarizes the organization's purpose, vision, and overall goals. This statement provides the foundation on which further planning is based.

- The overall business plan includes a series of *component* plans that present goals and strategies for each functional area of the enterprise. They typically include the following:

  o The *marketing plan*, which describes strategies for informing potential customers about the goods and services offered by the firm as well as strategies for developing long-term relationships. At the end of this appendix, a sample marketing plan for Blue Sky Clothing is presented.

o The *financing plan*, which presents a realistic approach for securing needed funds and managing debt and cash flows.

o The *production plan*, which describes how the organization will develop its products in the most efficient, cost-effective manner possible.

o The *facilities plan*, which describes the physical environment and equipment required to implement the production plan.

o The *human resources plan*, which estimates the firm's employment needs and the skills necessary to achieve organizational goals, including a comparison of current employees with the needs of the firm, and which establishes processes for securing adequately trained personnel if a gap exists between current employee skills and future needs.

This basic format encompasses the planning process used by nearly every successful organization. Whether a company operates in the manufacturing, wholesaling, retailing, or service sector—or a combination—the components described here are likely to appear in its overall business plan. Regardless of the size or longevity of a company, a business plan is an essential tool for a firm's owners because it helps them focus on the key elements of their business. Even small firms just starting out need a business plan to obtain financing. Figure A.1 shows the outline of a business plan for Blue Sky Clothing.

FIGURE A.1
Outline of a Business Plan

The Blue Sky Clothing Business Plan

I. Executive Summary
  • Who, What, When, Where, How, and Why

II. Table of Contents

III. Introduction
  • Mission Statement
  • Concept and Company
  • Management Team
  • Product

IV. Marketing Strategy
  • Demographics
  • Trends
  • Market Penetration
  • Potential Sales Revenue

V. Financing the Business
  • Cash Flow Analysis
  • Pro Forma Balance Sheet
  • Income Statement

VI. Facilities Plan
  • Physical Environment
  • Equipment

VII. Human Resources Plan
  • Employment Needs and Skills
  • Current Employees

VIII. Résumés of Principals

CREATING A MARKETING PLAN

Keep in mind that a marketing plan should be created in conjunction with the other elements of a firm's business plan. In addition, a marketing plan often draws from the business plan, restating the executive summary, competitive analysis, and mission statement to give its readers an overall view of the firm. The marketing plan is needed for a variety of reasons:

• To obtain financing, because banks and most private investors require a detailed business plan—including a marketing plan component—before they will even consider a loan application or a venture capital investment

• To provide direction for the firm's overall business and marketing strategies

• To support the development of long- and short-term organizational objectives

• To guide employees in achieving these objectives

• To serve as a standard against which the firm's progress can be measured and evaluated

In addition, the marketing plan is where a firm puts into writing its commitment to its customers and to building long-lasting relationships. After creating and implementing the plan, marketers must reevaluate it periodically to gauge its success in moving the organization toward its goals. If changes are needed, they should be made as soon as possible.

FORMULATING AN OVERALL MARKETING STRATEGY

Before writing a marketing plan, a firm's marketers formulate an overall marketing strategy. A firm may use a number of tools in marketing planning, including business portfolio analysis and the BCG matrix. Its executives may conduct a SWOT analysis, take advantage of a strategic window, study Porter's Five Forces model as it relates to their business, or consider adopting a first or second mover strategy, all of which are described in Chapter 2.

In addition to the planning strategies discussed in Chapter 2, marketers are also likely to use spreadsheet analysis, which lays out a grid of columns and rows that organize numerical information in a standardized, easily understood format. Spreadsheet analysis helps planners answer various "what if" questions related to the firm's financing and operations. The most popular spreadsheet software is Microsoft Excel. A spreadsheet analysis helps planners anticipate marketing performance given specified sets of circumstances. For example, a spreadsheet might project the outcomes of various pricing decisions for a new product, as shown in Figure A.2.

Once general planning strategies are determined, marketers begin to flesh out the details of the marketing strategy. The elements of a marketing strategy include identifying the target market, studying the marketing environment, and creating a marketing mix. When marketers have identified the target market, they can develop the optimal marketing mix to reach their potential customers:

- *Product strategy.* Which goods and services should the company offer to meet its customers' needs?

- *Distribution strategy.* Through which channel(s) and physical facilities will the firm distribute its products?

- *Promotional strategy.* What mix of advertising, sales promotion, and personal selling activities will the firm use to reach its customers initially and then develop long-term relationships?

- *Pricing strategy.* At what level should the company set its prices?

spreadsheet analysis Grid that organizes numerical information in a standardized, easily understood format.

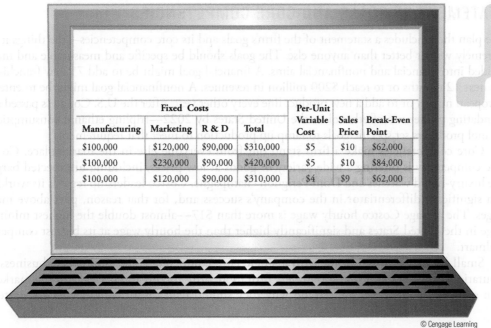

FIGURE A.2
How Spreadsheet Analysis Works

	Fixed Costs			Per-Unit Variable Cost	Sales Price	Break-Even Point
Manufacturing	Marketing	R & D	Total			
$100,000	$120,000	$90,000	$310,000	$5	$10	$62,000
$100,000	$230,000	$90,000	$420,000	$5	$10	$84,000
$100,000	$120,000	$90,000	$310,000	$4	$9	$62,000

© Cengage Learning

THE EXECUTIVE SUMMARY, COMPETITIVE ANALYSIS, AND MISSION STATEMENT

Because these three elements of the business plan often reappear in the marketing plan, it is useful to describe them here. Recall that the executive summary answers the *who, what, when, where, how,* and *why* questions for the business. In the early days of Google, the executive summary of the company's business plan included references to its strategic planning process for its search services, which involved "developing the perfect search engine … [one that] understands exactly what you mean and gives you back exactly what you want."[1] The summary also answered such questions as who was involved (key people and organizations), what length of time the plan represented, and how the goals would be met.

The competitive analysis focuses on the environment in which the marketing plan is to be implemented. Trenton, New Jersey–based TerraCycle manufactures a wide variety of products, all made from recycled materials. Believing the green movement will eventually hold sway in consumer products, TerraCycle's business goal is to become the leading ecofriendly organic brand in each of the product categories in which it competes. It doesn't attempt to overpower the category leader; instead, it aims to beat other ecofriendly competitors. For example, TerraCycle wants its window cleaner to outsell green competitors Mrs. Meyers and Seventh Generation, but it is less concerned about beating Windex, the category leader. Today, many of TerraCycle's ecofriendly products are available at major retailers like Target and Walmart.[2]

The mission statement puts into words an organization's overall purpose and reason for being. According to Nintendo's corporate mission, the company is "strongly committed to producing and marketing the best products and support services available." Not only does Nintendo strive to manufacture the highest-quality video products, but it also attempts "to treat every customer with attention, consideration and respect." Nintendo is similarly committed to its employees and believes in treating them "with the same consideration and respect that we, as a company, show our customers."[3]

DESCRIPTION OF THE COMPANY

Near the beginning of the marketing plan—typically following the executive summary and before the mission statement—a description of the company is included. The company description may include a brief history or background of the firm, the types of products it offers or plans to introduce, and recent successes or achievements—in short, it consists of a few paragraphs containing the kind of information often found on the home page of a company's website.

STATEMENT OF GOALS AND CORE COMPETENCIES

The plan then includes a statement of the firm's goals and its core competencies—the things it does extremely well or better than anyone else. The goals should be specific and measurable and may be divided into financial and nonfinancial aims. A financial goal might be to add 75 new franchises in the next 12 months or to reach $200 million in revenues. A nonfinancial goal might be to enter the European market or to add a new product line every other year. After the U.S. Congress passed a law mandating greater use of ethanol in the United States by 2022—tripling ethanol consumption—ethanol producers set specific goals to ramp up production to meet that requirement.[4]

Core competencies make a firm stand out from everyone else in the marketplace. Costco's core competency is offering a wide variety of goods at low prices, including unexpected bargains like luxury-brand watches and Dom Perignon champagne. Costco leadership regards its workforce as a significant differentiator in the company's success and, for that reason, pays above-market wages. The average Costco hourly wage is more than $17—almost double the highest minimum wage in the United States and significantly higher than the hourly wage at its biggest competitor, Walmart.[5]

Small businesses often begin with a single core competency and build their business and reputation on it. It is important for a new firm to identify its core competency in the marketing plan so investors or banks understand why they should lend the firm money to get started or to grow to the next stage. As a college student, David Kim found he enjoyed tutoring children. When he discovered a real demand for skilled tutoring, he decided to launch a tutoring business, which he named C2 Education. Because C2's core competency is helping students to excel, employees are hired and trained according to rigorous standards. Today, C2 Education serves students from elementary through high school, operating in 110 locations in the United States and Canada.[6]

OUTLINE OF THE MARKETING ENVIRONMENT (SITUATION ANALYSIS)

Every successful marketing plan considers the marketing environment—the competitive, economic, political–legal, technological, and social–cultural factors that affect the way a firm formulates and implements its marketing strategy. Marketing plans may address these issues in different ways, but the goal is to present information that describes the company's position or situation within the marketing environment. J. Crew, for instance, has a well-known brand name and a CEO with an impressive track record, Mickey Drexler, who previously headed The Gap. The retail environment for stores like J. Crew is highly competitive. Merchandise that doesn't appeal to enough customers ends up on a clearance rack and hurts the bottom line. According to Drexler, the key to J. Crew's success is that it sells merchandise that "cannot be sold anywhere else." Drexler pushes his buyers to "out-product" their competitors.[7] A marketing plan for J. Crew would include an evaluation of competing stores, such as The Gap and Urban Outfitters; any technological advances that would affect such factors as merchandise distribution or inventory; social–cultural issues such as fashion preferences and spending habits of customers; and economic issues affecting a pricing strategy.

One such method for outlining the marketing environment in the marketing plan is to include a SWOT analysis, described in Chapter 2. SWOT analysis identifies the firm's strengths, weaknesses, opportunities, and threats within the marketing environment. A SWOT analysis for J. Crew might include strengths such as its corporate leadership, brand name, and upscale target market. Weaknesses might include the risks inherent in the business of correctly spotting fashion trends. A major opportunity lies in the fact that J. Crew can expand almost anywhere. For example, after J. Crew acquired Madewell, a retailer that sells hip, casual clothes to an upscale audience, it expanded the chain to 39 U.S. cities and launched an e-commerce site. Threats for J. Crew could include competition from other trendy stores, sudden changes in customer preferences, and financial crises that affect spending.[8] A SWOT analysis can be presented in chart format so that it is easy to read as part of the marketing plan. The sample marketing plan in this appendix includes a SWOT analysis for Blue Sky Clothing.

THE TARGET MARKET AND MARKETING MIX

The marketing plan identifies the target market for the firm's products. The Cute Overload website (www.cuteoverload.com) contains photos and videos of animals that visitors can share and about which they can post comments. But the site also offers a page-a-day desk calendar of the same name featuring images of puppies, kittens, birds, and chipmunks with humorous captions. Cute Overload targets women ages 18 to 34 who need a laugh and a brief escape from the real world. The calendars are also offered for sale on Amazon.com, and the retailer's inventory recently sold out in one day, which astonished the developer.[9] Weight Watchers has long regarded women as its primary target market and, in fact, females currently make up 90 percent of its clientele. However, as the company saw increasing interest from men, marketers for Weight Watchers began to tap into that segment, launching a men-only website and a $10 million advertising campaign directed solely at men.[10]

The marketing plan also discusses the marketing mix the firm has selected for its products. Hollywood studios are known for implementing lavish strategies for promoting their films. Not only did Paramount Pictures and Nickelodeon Movies use traditional means to launch their recent movie, *Rango,* but they also partnered with other organizations to promote the movie. Social gaming company Zynga integrated *Rango* references and the movie trailer into its popular FrontierVille game on Facebook. FrontierVille players could embark on three different quests to find the elusive Rango somewhere on the frontier, enlist their Facebook friends to help by "sending" them water buckets, and, conceivably, win a *Rango* statue. With an estimated 15 million-plus Facebook users playing FrontierVille daily, *Rango* received great exposure.[11]

BUDGET, SCHEDULE, AND MONITORING

Every marketing plan requires a budget, a time schedule for implementation, and a system for monitoring the plan's success or failure. At age 21, entrepreneur Joe Cirulli of Gainesville, Florida, made a to-do list of ten life goals, which included "Own a health club" and "Make it respected in the community." By age 33, Cirulli had achieved all ten of his life goals, including the opening of his Gainesville Health & Fitness Center. As Cirulli's business grew, however, he discovered a larger mission: to make Gainesville the healthiest community in America. Today, Gainesville is the first and only city to win the Gold Well City award from the Wellness Council of America, and Cirulli's fitness center is widely regarded as one of the best in the industry. Whether or not he realized it at the time, Cirulli's life and business plan at age 21 had the makings of a marketing plan, with goals and budgets, setting a timeline, and measuring progress—a formula for business success.[12]

Most long-range marketing plans encompass a two- to five-year period, although companies that do business in industries like auto manufacturing, pharmaceuticals, or lumber may extend their marketing plans further into the future, because it typically takes longer to develop these products. However, marketers in most industries will have difficulty making estimates and predictions beyond five years because of the many uncertainties in the marketplace. Firms also may opt to develop short-term plans to cover marketing activities for a single year.

The marketing plan, whether it is long term or short term, predicts how long it will take to achieve the goals set out by the plan. A goal may be opening a certain number of new stores, increasing market share, or achieving an expansion of the product line. Finally, the marketing program is monitored and evaluated for its performance. Monthly, quarterly, and annual sales targets are usually tracked; the efficiency with which certain tasks are completed is determined; customer satisfaction is measured; and so forth. All of these factors contribute to the overall review of the program.

At some point, a firm may implement an *exit strategy*, a plan for the firm to leave the market. A common way for a large company to do this is to sell off a business unit. A number of these strategies have been implemented recently. Dover Corporation is a diversified global manufacturer of equipment and components for the communication, energy, and printing industries. In keeping with the company's long-term growth strategy, it recently sold a business unit, Heil Trailer International, a Tennessee-based manufacturer of specialty transportation trailers and equipment. With the transaction, Dover exited the transportation trailer business. The move is expected to help improve Dover's financial performance.[13]

Another example of an exit strategy involves pharmaceutical giant Pfizer. Founded in 1849, over time, the company expanded its operations beyond its core business—the development and manufacture of prescription medications—to include nutrition and animal health. To return the focus to its core business of developing new drugs, Pfizer recently sold its infant nutrition business to Nestlé.[14]

SAMPLE MARKETING PLAN

The following pages contain an annotated sample marketing plan for Blue Sky Clothing. At some point in your career, you will likely be involved in writing—or at least contributing to—a marketing plan. And you'll certainly read many marketing plans throughout your business career. Keep in mind that the plan for Blue Sky is a single example; no one format is used by all companies. Also, the Blue Sky plan has been somewhat condensed to make it easier to annotate and illustrate the most vital features. The important point to remember is that the marketing plan is a document designed to present concise, cohesive information about a company's marketing objectives to managers, lending institutions, and others involved in creating and carrying out the firm's overall business strategy.

Five-Year Marketing Plan
Blue Sky Clothing, Inc.

Table of Contents

EXECUTIVE SUMMARY

This five-year marketing plan for Blue Sky Clothing has been created by its two founders to secure additional funding for growth and to inform employees of the company's current status and direction. Although Blue Sky was launched only three years ago, the firm has experienced greater-than-anticipated demand for its products, and research has shown that the target market of sports-minded consumers and sports retailers would like to buy more casual clothing than Blue Sky currently offers. As a result, Blue Sky wants to extend its current product line as well as add new product lines. In addition, the firm plans to explore opportunities for online sales. The marketing environment has been very receptive to the firm's high-quality goods—casual clothing in trendy colors with logos and slogans that reflect the interests of outdoor enthusiasts around the country. Over the next five years, Blue Sky can increase its distribution, offer new products, and win new customers.

COMPANY DESCRIPTION

Blue Sky Clothing was founded three years ago by entrepreneurs Lucy Neuman and Nick Russell. Neuman has an undergraduate degree in marketing and worked for several years in the retail clothing industry. Russell operated an adventure business called Go West!, which arranges group trips to locations in Wyoming, Montana, and Idaho, before selling the enterprise to a partner. Neuman and Russell, who have been friends since college, decided to develop and market a line of clothing with a unique—yet universal—appeal to outdoor enthusiasts.

Blue Sky Clothing reflects Neuman's and Russell's passion for the outdoors. The company's original cotton T-shirts, baseball caps, and fleece jackets and vests bear logos of different sports, such as kayaking, mountain climbing, bicycling, skating, surfing, and horseback riding. But every item shows off the company's slogan: "Go Play Outside." Blue Sky sells clothing for both men and women, in the hottest colors with the coolest names—sunrise pink, sunset red, twilight purple, desert rose, cactus green, ocean blue, mountaintop white, and river rock gray.

Blue Sky attire is currently carried by small retail stores that specialize in outdoor clothing and gear. Most of these stores are concentrated in northern New England, California, the Northwest, and the South. The high quality, trendy colors, and unique message of the clothing have gained Blue Sky a following among consumers between ages 25 and 45. Sales have tripled in the last year alone, and Blue Sky is currently working to expand its manufacturing capabilities.

Blue Sky is also committed to giving back to the community by contributing to local conservation programs. Ultimately, the company would like to develop and fund its own environmental programs. This plan will outline how Blue Sky intends to introduce new products, expand its distribution, enter new markets, and give back to the community.

BLUE SKY'S MISSION AND GOALS

Blue Sky's mission is to be a leading producer and marketer of personalized, casual clothing for consumers who love the outdoors. Blue Sky wants to inspire people to get outdoors more often and enjoy family and friends while doing so. In addition, Blue Sky strives to design programs for preserving the natural environment.

The executive summary outlines the *who, what, where, when, how,* and *why* of the marketing plan. Blue Sky is only three years old and is successful enough that it now needs a formal marketing plan to obtain additional financing from a bank or private investors for expansion and the launch of new products.

The company description summarizes the history of Blue Sky—how it was founded and by whom, what its products are, and why they are unique. It begins to "sell" the reader on the growth possibilities for Blue Sky.

It is important to state a firm's mission and goals, including financial and nonfinancial goals. Blue Sky's goals include growth and profits for the company as well as the ability to contribute to society through conservation programs.

During the next five years, Blue Sky seeks to achieve the following financial and nonfinancial goals:

Financial goals

1. Obtain financing to expand manufacturing capabilities, increase distribution, and introduce two new product lines

2. Increase revenues by at least 50 percent each year

3. Donate at least $25,000 a year to conservation organizations

Nonfinancial goals

4. Introduce two new product lines—customized logo clothing and lightweight luggage

5. Enter new geographic markets, including Southwest and Mid-Atlantic regions

6. Develop a successful Internet site, while maintaining strong relationships with retailers

7. Develop its own conservation program aimed at helping communities raise money to purchase open space

CORE COMPETENCIES

Blue Sky seeks to use its core competencies to achieve a sustainable competitive advantage, in which competitors cannot provide the same value to consumers that Blue Sky does. Already Blue Sky has developed core competencies in (1) offering a high-quality, branded product whose image is recognizable among consumers; (2) creating a sense of community among consumers who purchase the products; and (3) developing a reputation among retailers as a reliable manufacturer, delivering their orders on schedule. The firm intends to build on these competencies through marketing efforts that increase the number of products offered as well as distribution outlets.

By forming strong relationships with consumers, retailers, and suppliers of fabric and other goods and services, Blue Sky believes it can create a sustainable competitive advantage over its rivals. No other clothing company can say to its customers with as much conviction, "Go Play Outside"!

SITUATION ANALYSIS

The marketing environment for Blue Sky represents overwhelming opportunities. It also contains some challenges the firm believes it can meet successfully. Figure A illustrates a SWOT analysis of the company conducted by its marketers to highlight Blue Sky's strengths, weaknesses, opportunities, and threats.

The SWOT analysis presents a thumbnail sketch of the company's position in the marketplace. In just three years, Blue Sky has built some impressive strengths while looking forward to new opportunities. Its dedicated founders, the growing number of brand-loyal customers, and sound financial management place the company in a good position to grow. However, as Blue Sky considers expansion of its product line and entry into new markets, the firm will have to guard against marketing myopia (the failure to recognize the scope of its business) and quality slippages. As the company finalizes plans for new products and expanded Internet sales, its management will also have to guard against competitors who attempt to duplicate the products. However, building strong relationships with consumers, retailers, and suppliers should help thwart competitors.

This section reminds employees and those outside the company (such as potential lenders) exactly what Blue Sky does so well and how it plans to achieve a sustainable competitive advantage over rivals. Note here and throughout the plan: Blue Sky focuses on relationships.

The situation analysis provides an outline of the marketing environment. A SWOT analysis helps marketers and others identify clearly a firm's strengths, weaknesses, opportunities, and threats. Again, relationships are a focus. Blue Sky has also conducted research on the outdoor clothing market, competitors, and consumers to determine how best to attract and keep customers.

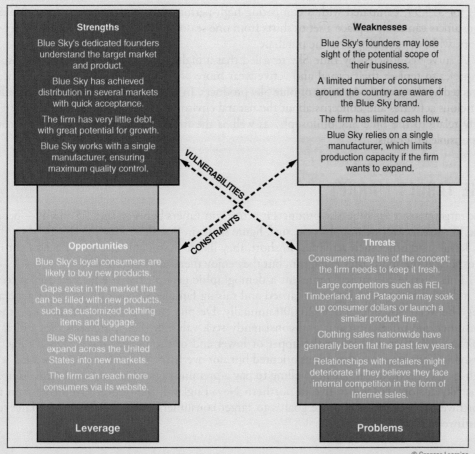

FIGURE A
SWOT Analysis for Blue Sky Clothing, Inc.

© Cengage Learning

COMPETITORS IN THE OUTDOOR CLOTHING MARKET

The outdoor retail sales industry sells about $5 billion worth of goods annually, ranging from clothing to equipment. The outdoor apparel market has many entries. L.L.Bean, Dick's Sporting Goods, REI, Timberland, Bass Pro Shops, Cabela's, The North Face, and Patagonia are among the most recognizable companies offering these products. Smaller competitors like Title Nine, which offers athletic clothing for women, and Ragged Mountain, which sells fleece clothing for skiers and hikers, also capture some of the market. The outlook for the industry in general—and Blue Sky in particular—is positive for several reasons. First, consumers are participating in and investing in recreational activities near their homes. Second, consumers are looking for ways to enjoy their leisure time with friends and family without overspending. Third, consumers tend to be advancing in their careers and are able to spend more.

While all of the companies listed earlier can be considered competitors, most of them sell performance apparel in high-tech manufactured fabrics. With the exception of the fleece vests and jackets, Blue Sky's clothing is made strictly of the highest-quality cotton, so it may be worn both on the hiking trail and around town. Finally, Blue Sky products are offered at moderate prices, making them affordable in multiple quantities. For instance, a Blue Sky T-shirt sells for $15.99, compared with a competing high-performance T-shirt that sells for $29.99. Consumers can easily replace a set of shirts from one season to the next, picking up the newest colors, without agonizing over the purchase.

A survey conducted by Blue Sky revealed that a high percentage of responding consumers prefer to replace their casual and active wear more often than other clothing, so they are attracted by the moderate pricing of Blue Sky products. In addition, as the trend toward health-conscious activities and concerns about the natural environment continue, consumers increasingly relate to the Blue Sky philosophy as well as the firm's future contributions to socially responsible programs.

THE TARGET MARKET

> Blue Sky has identified its customers as active people between ages 25 and 45. However, that doesn't mean someone who is older or prefers to read about the outdoors isn't a potential customer as well. By pinpointing where existing customers live, Blue Sky can plan for growth into new outlets.

The target market for Blue Sky products is active consumers between ages 25 and 45—people who like to hike, rock climb, bicycle, surf, figure skate, in-line skate, ride horses, snowboard or ski, kayak, and other such activities. In short, they like to "Go Play Outside." They might not be experts at the sports they engage in, but they enjoy themselves outdoors.

These active consumers represent a demographic group of well-educated and successful individuals; they are single or married and raising families. Household incomes generally range between $60,000 and $120,000 annually. Despite their comfortable incomes, these consumers are price conscious and consistently seek value in their purchases. Regardless of their age (whether they fall at the upper or lower end of the target range), they lead active lifestyles. They are somewhat status oriented but not overly so. They like to be associated with high-quality products but are not willing to pay a premium price for a certain brand. Current Blue Sky customers tend to live in northern New England, the South, California, and the Northwest. However, one future goal is to target consumers in the Mid-Atlantic states and Southwest as well.

THE MARKETING MIX

> The strongest part of the marketing mix for Blue Sky involves sales promotions, public relations, and nontraditional marketing strategies, such as attending outdoor events and organizing activities like day hikes and bike rides.

The following discussion outlines some of the details of the proposed marketing mix for Blue Sky products.

Product Strategy

Blue Sky currently offers a line of high-quality outdoor apparel items, including cotton T-shirts, caps, and fleece vests and jackets. All bear the company logo and slogan, "Go Play Outside." The firm has researched the most popular colors for its items and given them names that consumers enjoy—sunset red, sunrise pink, cactus green, desert rose, and river rock gray, among others. Over the next five years, Blue Sky plans to expand the product line to include customized clothing items. Customers may select a logo that represents their sport, say, rock climbing. Then they can add a slogan to match the logo, such as "Get Over It." A cap with a bicyclist might bear the slogan, "Take a Ride." At the beginning, there would be ten new logos and five new slogans; more would be added later. Eventually, some slogans and logos would be retired, and new ones introduced. This strategy will keep the concept fresh and prevent it from becoming diluted with too many variations.

The second way in which Blue Sky plans to expand its product line is to offer lightweight luggage—two sizes of duffel bags, two sizes of tote bags, and a daypack. These items would also come in trendy and basic colors, with a choice of logos and slogans. In addition, every product would bear the Blue Sky logo.

Distribution Strategy

Currently, Blue Sky is marketed through regional and local specialty shops scattered along the California coast, into the Northwest, across the South, and in northern New England. So far, Blue Sky has not been distributed through national sporting goods and apparel chains. Climate and season tend to dictate the sales at specialty shops, which sell more T-shirts and caps during warm weather and more fleece vests and jackets during colder months. Blue Sky obtains much of its information about overall industry trends in different geographic areas and at different types of retail outlets from its trade organization, Outdoor Industry Association.

Over the next three years, Blue Sky seeks to expand distribution to retail specialty shops throughout the nation, focusing next on the Southwest and Mid-Atlantic regions. The firm has not yet determined whether it would be beneficial to sell through a major national chain, as these outlets could be considered competitors.

In addition, Blue Sky plans to expand online sales by offering the customized product line via the Internet only, thus distinguishing between Internet offerings and specialty shop offerings. Eventually, the firm may be able to place Internet kiosks at some of the more profitable store outlets so consumers could order customized products from the stores. Regardless of its expansion plans, Blue Sky fully intends to monitor and maintain strong relationships with distribution channel members.

Promotion Strategy

Blue Sky communicates with consumers and retailers about its products in a variety of ways. Information about Blue Sky—the company as well as its products—is available via the Internet, through direct mailings, and in person. The firm's promotional efforts also seek to differentiate its products from those of its competitors.

The company relies on personal contact with retailers to establish the products in their stores. This contact, whether in person or by phone, helps convey the Blue Sky message, demonstrate the products' unique qualities, and build relationships. Blue Sky sales representatives visit each store two or three times a year and offer in-store training on the features of the products for new retailers or for those who want a refresher session. As distribution expands, Blue Sky will adjust to meet greater demand by increasing sales staff to make sure its stores are visited more frequently.

Sales promotions and public relations currently make up the bulk of Blue Sky's promotional strategy. Blue Sky staff works with retailers to offer short-term sales promotions tied to events and contests. In addition, Nick Russell is currently working with several trip outfitters to offer Blue Sky items on a promotional basis. Because Blue Sky also engages in cause marketing through its contribution to environmental programs, good public relations have followed.

Nontraditional marketing methods that require little cash and a lot of creativity also lend themselves perfectly to Blue Sky. Because Blue Sky is a small, flexible organization, the firm can easily implement ideas, such as distributing free water, stickers, and discount coupons at outdoor sporting events. During the next year, the company plans to engage in the following marketing efforts:

- Create a Blue Sky Tour, in which several employees take turns driving around the country to campgrounds to distribute promotional items, such as Blue Sky stickers and discount coupons.

- Attend canoe and kayak races, bicycling events, and rock climbing competitions with our Blue Sky truck to distribute free water, stickers, and discount coupons for Blue Sky shirts or hats.

- Organize Blue Sky hikes departing from participating retailers.

- Hold a Blue Sky design contest, selecting a winning slogan and logo to be added to the customized line.

An actual plan will
include more specific
financial details, which
will be folded into the
overall business plan. For
more information, see
Appendix B, "Financial
Analysis in Marketing." In
addition, Blue Sky states
that at this stage, it does
not have plans to exit the
market by merging with
another firm or making a
public stock offering.

Pricing Strategy

As discussed earlier in this plan, Blue Sky products are priced with the competition in mind. The firm is not concerned with setting high prices to signal luxury or prestige, nor is it attempting to achieve the goals of offsetting low prices by selling large quantities of products. Instead, value pricing is practiced so customers feel comfortable purchasing new clothing to replace the old, even if it is just because they like the new colors. The pricing strategy also makes Blue Sky products good gifts—for birthdays, graduations, or "just because." The customized clothing will sell for $2 to $4 more than the regular Blue Sky logo clothing. The luggage will be priced competitively, offering a good value against its competition.

BUDGET, SCHEDULE, AND MONITORING

Though its history is short, Blue Sky has enjoyed a steady increase in sales since its introduction three years ago. Figure B shows these three years, plus projected sales for the next three years, including the introduction of the two new product lines. Additional financial data are included in the overall business plan for the company.

The timeline for expansion of outlets and introduction of the two new product lines is shown in Figure C. The implementation of each of these tasks will be monitored closely and evaluated for its performance.

FIGURE B
**Annual Sales for
Blue Sky Clothing:
2013–2017**

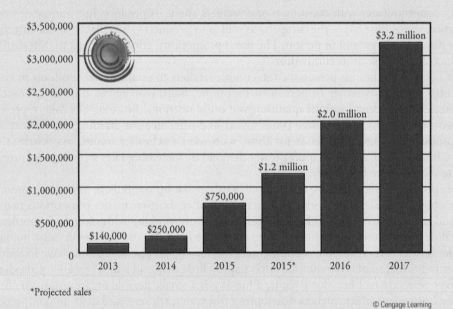

© Cengage Learning

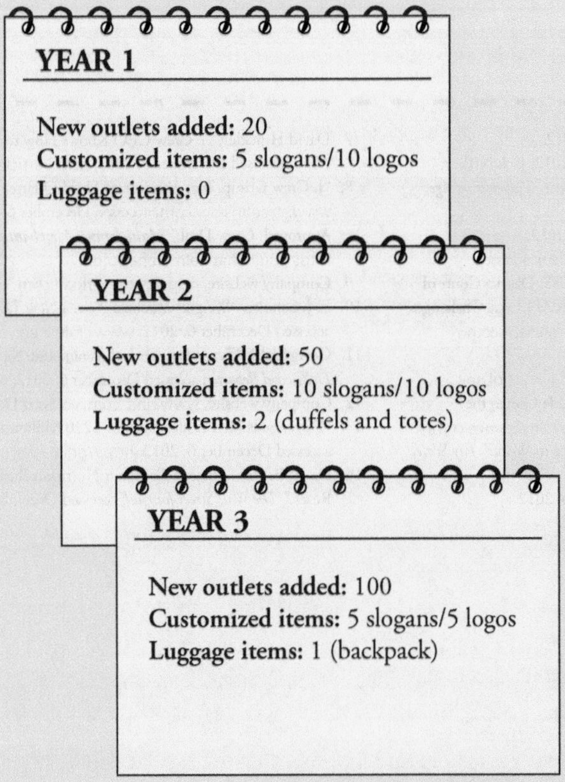

FIGURE C
**Timeline for First
Three Years of
Marketing Plan**

YEAR 1

New outlets added: 20
Customized items: 5 slogans/10 logos
Luggage items: 0

YEAR 2

New outlets added: 50
Customized items: 10 slogans/10 logos
Luggage items: 2 (duffels and totes)

YEAR 3

New outlets added: 100
Customized items: 5 slogans/5 logos
Luggage items: 1 (backpack)

© Cengage Learning

Blue Sky anticipates continuing operations into the foreseeable future, with no plans to exit this market. Instead, as discussed throughout this plan, the firm plans to increase its presence in the market. At present, there are no plans to merge with another company or to make a public stock offering.

NOTES

1. Company website, www.google.com, accessed December 6, 2012.
2. Company website, www.terracycle.net, accessed December 6, 2012; Jack Neff, "TerraCycle: Building a Small Empire on a Foundation of Compost," *Advertising Age*, accessed December 6, 2012, http://adage.
3. Company website, www.nintendo.com, accessed December 6, 2012.
4. "Meeting the RFS2 Requires Market Access for Ethanol," *Illinois Corn*, accessed December 6, 2012, www.ilcorn.org; National Biodiesel Board, "U.S. District Court of Appeals for the District of Columbia 'Unanimously Denies' NPRA/API Legal Challenges to RFS2," press release, *Iowa Soybean Association* website, www.iasoybeans.com, accessed December 6, 2012.
5. U.S. Department of Labor, "Minimum Wage Laws in the States," www.dol.gov, accessed December 6, 2012; Ashley Lutz, "The Formula That Made Costco the Anti-Walmart," *Daily Finance*, accessed December 6, 2012, www.dailyfinance.com; Lydia Dishman, "Target vs. Walmart: Which One Is a Better Place to Work?" *Pay Scale*, accessed December 6, 2012, http://blogs.payscale.com.
6. Company website, http://c2educate.com, accessed December 6, 2012.
7. David Hinckley, "J. Crew CEO Knows How to Tailor a Comeback," *New York Daily News*, accessed December 6, 2012, http://articles.nydailynews.com.
8. "J. Crew Group, Inc. Announces Third Quarter Fiscal 2012 Results," press release, www.streetinsider.com, accessed December 6, 2012; Jim Tierney, "Shareholders Approve J. Crew Deal," *Multichannel Merchant*, accessed December 6, 2012, http://multichannelmerchant.com.
9. Company website, http://cuteoverload.com, accessed December 6, 2012.
10. E. J. Schultz, "Weight Watchers Picks a New Target: Men," *Crain's New York Business*, accessed December 6, 2012, www.crainsnewyork.com.
11. Georg Szalai, "Zynga Partners with Paramount/Nickelodeon Movies on 'Rango' Promotion," *Hollywood Reporter*, accessed December 6, 2012, www.hollywoodreporter.com.
12. Company website, www.ghfc.com, accessed December 6, 2012.
13. "Dover Sells Heil Trailer Unit for $220 Million in Proceeds," *The Wall Street Journal*, accessed December 6, 2012, http://online.wsj.com.
14. David Benoit, "Pfizer Sells Infant Nutrition Business for $11.9 Billion—Analysts React," *The Wall Street Journal*, accessed December 6, 2012, http://blogs.wsj.com.

Financial Analysis
IN MARKETING

A number of basic concepts from accounting and finance offer invaluable tools to marketers. Understanding the contributions made by these concepts can improve the quality of marketing decisions. In addition, marketers often must be able to explain and defend their decisions in financial terms. These accounting and financial tools can be used to supply quantitative data to justify decisions made by marketing managers. In this appendix, we describe the major accounting and finance concepts that have marketing implications and explain how they help managers make informed marketing decisions.

FINANCIAL STATEMENTS

All companies prepare a set of financial statements on a regular basis. Two of the most important financial statements are the income statement and balance sheet. The analogy of a movie is often used to describe an *income statement*, because it presents a financial record of a company's revenues, expenses, and profits over a period of time, such as a month, quarter, or year. By contrast, the *balance sheet* is a snapshot of what a company owns (called *assets*) and what it owes (called *liabilities*) at a point in time, such as at the end of the month, quarter, or year. The difference between assets and liabilities is referred to as *owner's, partners', or shareholders' equity*—the amount of funds the firm's owners have invested in its formation and continued operations. Of the two financial statements, the income statement contains more marketing-related information.

A sample income statement for Worthy Composites is shown in Figure B.1. Headquartered in a Boston suburb, Worthy Composites is a B2B producer and marketer. The firm designs and manufactures a variety of composite components for manufacturers of consumer, industrial, and government products. Total sales revenues for 2015 amounted to $675.0 million. Total expenses, including taxes, for the year were $583.1 million. The year 2015 proved profitable for Worthy Composites—the firm reported a profit, referred to as net income, of $91.9 million. While total revenue is a fairly straightforward number, several of the expenses shown on the income statement require additional explanation.

For any company that makes its own products (a manufacturer) or simply markets one or more items produced by others (an importer, retailer, or wholesaler), the largest single expense usually is a category called *cost of goods sold*. This reflects the cost, to the firm, of the goods it markets to its customers. In the case of Worthy Composites, the cost of goods sold represents the cost of components and raw materials as well as the cost of designing and manufacturing the composite panels the firm produces and markets to its business customers.

The income statement illustrates how cost of goods sold is calculated. The calculation uses the value of the firm's inventory at the beginning of 2015. Inventory is the value of raw materials, partially completed products, and finished products held by the firm at the end of some time period, say, the end of the year. The cost of materials Worthy Composites purchased during the year and the direct cost of manufacturing the finished products are then added to the beginning inventory figure. The result is the cost of goods the firm has available for sale during the year. Once the firm's accountants subtract the value of inventory held by the firm at the end of 2015, they know the cost of goods sold. By simply subtracting cost of goods sold from total sales revenues generated during the year, they determine that Worthy achieved gross profits of $270 million in 2015.

Worthy Composites, Inc.
2893 Fitzgerald Parkway
Southampton, MA 02349

WCI

INCOME STATEMENT
For the Year Ended December 31, 2015
(in $ millions)

Sales	675.0
Cost of Goods Sold	405.0
Gross Income	270.0
Selling, Administrative, and General Expenses	82.1
Research and Development Expenses	25.4
Operating Income	162.5
Depreciation	18.6
Net Interest Expense	2.5
Before-tax Income	141.4
Provision for Income Taxes	49.5
Net Income	91.9

Cost of Goods Sold Calculation

Beginning Inventory		158.0
plus	Raw Materials Purchased	200.7
plus	Direct Manufacturing Expenses	226.3
Total Cost of Goods		585.0
minus	Ending Inventory	(180.0)
Cost of Goods Sold		405.0

© Cengage Learning

Operating expenses are another significant cost for most firms. This broad category includes such marketing outlays as sales compensation and expenses, advertising and other promotions, and the expenses involved in implementing marketing plans. Accountants typically combine these financial outlays into a single category with the label *Selling, Administrative, and General Expenses.* Other expense items included in the operating expenses section of the income statement are administrative salaries, utilities, and insurance.

Another significant expense for Worthy Composites is research and development (R&D). This category includes the cost of developing new products and modifying existing ones. Firms like pharmaceuticals, biotechnology, and computer companies spend significant amounts of money each year on R&D. Subtracting selling, administrative, and general expenses and R&D expenses from the gross profit equals the firm's operating income. For 2015, Worthy had operating income of $162.5 million.

Depreciation represents the systematic reduction over time in the value of certain company assets, such as production machinery or office furniture. Depreciation is an unusual expense, because it does not involve an actual cash expense. However, it does reflect the reality that equipment owned by the company is physically wearing out over time from use and/or from technological obsolescence. Also, charging a portion of the total cost of these long-lived items to each of the years in which they are used results in a more accurate determination of the total costs involved in the firm's operation each year.

Net interest expense is the difference between what a firm paid in interest on various loans and what it collected in interest on investments it might have made during the time period involved. Subtracting depreciation and net interest expense from the firm's operating profit reveals the firm's taxable income. Worthy had depreciation of $18.6 million and a net interest expense of $2.5 million for the year, so its 2015 taxable income was $141.4 million.

Profit-seeking firms pay taxes calculated as a percentage of their taxable income to the federal government as well as state income taxes in most states. Worthy paid $49.5 million in taxes in 2015. Subtracting taxes from taxable income gives us the firm's *net income*, $91.9 million.

PERFORMANCE RATIOS

Managers often compute a variety of financial ratios to assess the performance of their firm. These ratios are calculated using data found on both the income statement and the balance sheet. Ratios are then compared with industry standards and with data from previous years. Several ratios are of particular interest to marketers.

A number of commonly used financial ratios focus on *profitability measures*. They are used to assess the firm's ability to generate revenues in excess of expenses and earn an adequate rate of return. Profitability measures include gross profit margin, net profit margin, and return on investment (or sales).

Gross Profit Margin

The gross profit margin equals the firm's gross profit divided by its sales revenues. In 2015, Worthy had a gross profit margin of

$$\frac{\text{Gross profit}}{\text{Sales}} = \frac{\$270.0 \text{ million}}{\$675.0 \text{ million}} = 40\%$$

The gross profit margin is the percentage of each sales dollar that can be used to pay other expenses and meet the firm's profit objectives. Ideally, businesses would like to see gross profit margins equal to or higher than those of other firms in their industry. A declining gross profit margin may indicate the firm is under some competitive price pressure.

Net Profit Margin

The net profit margin equals net income divided by sales. For 2015, Worthy had a net profit margin of

$$\frac{\text{Net income}}{\text{Sales}} = \frac{\$91.9 \text{ million}}{\$675.0 \text{ million}} = 13.6\%$$

The net profit margin is the percentage of each sales dollar the firm earns in profit or keeps after all expenses have been paid. Companies generally want to see rising, or at least stable, net profit margins.

Return on Assets (ROA)

A third profitability ratio, return on assets, measures the firm's efficiency in generating sales and profits from the total amount invested in the company. For 2015, Worthy's ROA is calculated as follows:

$$\frac{\text{Sales}}{\text{Average assets}} \times \frac{\text{Net income}}{\text{Sales}} = \frac{\text{Net income}}{\text{Average assets}}$$

$$\frac{\$675.0 \text{ million}}{\$595.0 \text{ million}} \times \frac{\$91.9 \text{ million}}{\$675.0 \text{ million}} = 1.13 \times 13.6\% = 15.4\%$$

The ROA ratio actually consists of two components. The first component, *asset turnover,* is the amount of sales generated for each dollar invested. The second component is *net profit margin*. Data for total assets are found on the firm's balance sheet.

Assume Worthy began 2015 with $560 million in assets and ended the year with $630 million in assets. Its average assets for the year would be $595 million. As in the other profitability ratios, Worthy's ROA should be compared with other firms in the industry and with its own previous performance to be meaningful.

Inventory Turnover

Inventory turnover typically is categorized as an activity ratio, because it evaluates the effectiveness of the firm's resource use. Specifically, it measures the number of times a firm "turns" its inventory each year. The ratio can help answer the question of whether the firm has the appropriate level of inventory. Inventory turnover equals sales divided by average inventory. From the income statement, we see Worthy Composites began 2015 with $158 million in inventory and ended the year with

$180 million in inventory. Therefore, the firm's average inventory was $169 million. The firm's inventory turnover ratio equals:

$$\frac{\text{Sales}}{\text{Average inventory}} = \frac{\$675.0 \text{ million}}{\$169.0 \text{ million}} = 3.99$$

For 2015, Worthy Composites turned its inventory almost four times a year. While a faster inventory turn is usually a sign of greater efficiency, to be really meaningful, the inventory turnover ratio must be compared with historical data and appropriate peer firm averages. Different organizations can have very different inventory turnover ratios, depending on the types of products they sell. For instance, a supermarket might turn its inventory every three weeks for an annual rate of roughly 17 times per year. By contrast, a large furniture retailer is likely to average only about two turns per year. Again, the determination of a "good" or "inadequate" inventory turnover rate depends on typical rates in the industry and the firm's performance in previous years.

Accounts Receivable Turnover

Another activity ratio that may be of interest to marketers is accounts receivable turnover. This ratio measures the number of times per year a company turns its receivables. Dividing accounts receivable turnover into 365 gives us the average age of the company's receivables.

Companies make sales on the basis of either cash or credit. Credit sales allow the buyer to obtain a product now and pay for it at a specified later date. In essence, the seller is providing credit to the buyer. Credit sales are common in B2B transactions. It should be noted that sales to buyers using credit cards like MasterCard and Visa are counted as cash sales, because the issuer of the credit card, rather than the seller, is providing credit to the buyer. Consequently, most B2C sales are counted as cash sales.

Receivables are uncollected credit sales. Measuring accounts receivable turnover and the average age of receivables are important for firms in which credit sales make up a high proportion of total sales. Accounts receivable turnover is defined as follows:

$$\text{Accounts receivable turnover} = \frac{\text{Credit sales}}{\text{Average accounts receivable}}$$

Assume all of Worthy Composites' sales are credit sales. Also, assume the firm began 2015 with $50 million in receivables and ended the year with $60 million in receivables (both numbers can be found on the balance sheet). Therefore, it had an average of $55 million in receivables. The firm's receivables turnover and average age equal:

$$\frac{\$675.0 \text{ million}}{\$55.0 \text{ million}} = 12.3 \text{ times}$$

$$\frac{365}{12.3} = 29.7 \text{ days}$$

Worthy turned its receivables slightly more than 12 times per year. The average age of its receivables was slightly less than 30 days. Because Worthy expects its customers to pay outstanding invoices within 30 days, these numbers appear appropriate. As with other ratios, however, receivables turnover and average age of receivables should also be compared with peer firms and historical data.

MARKUPS AND MARKDOWNS

The importance of pricing decisions was discussed earlier. This section expands on the prior comments by introducing two important pricing concepts: markups and markdowns. They can help establish selling prices and evaluate various pricing strategies, and they are closely tied to a firm's income statement.

Markups

The amount a marketer adds to a product's cost to set the final selling price is the markup. The amount of the markup typically results from two marketing decisions:

1. The services performed by the marketer. Other things being equal, retailers who offer more services charge larger markups to cover their costs.

2. The inventory turnover rate. Other things being equal, retailers with a higher turnover rate can cover their costs and earn a profit while charging a smaller markup.

A marketer's markup exerts an important influence on its image among present and potential customers. In addition, the markup affects the retailer's ability to attract shoppers. An excessive markup may drive away customers; an inadequate markup may fail to generate sufficient income to cover costs and return a profit.

Markups are typically stated as percentages of either the selling prices or the costs of the products. The formulas for calculating markups are as follows:

$$\text{Markup percentage of selling price} = \frac{\text{Amount added to cost (markup)}}{\text{Selling price}}$$

$$\text{Markup percentage on cost} = \frac{\text{Amount added to cost (markup)}}{\text{Cost}}$$

Consider a product with an invoice of 60 cents and a selling price of $1. The total markup (selling price less cost) is 40 cents. The two markup percentages are calculated as follows:

$$\text{Markup percentage on selling price} = \frac{\$0.40}{\$1.00} = 40\%$$

$$\text{Markup percentage on cost} = \frac{\$0.40}{\$0.60} = 66.7\%$$

To determine the selling price knowing only the cost and markup percentage on selling price, a marketer applies the following formula:

$$\text{Price} = \frac{\text{Cost in dollars}}{(100\% - \text{Markup percentage on selling price})}$$

In the previous example, to determine the correct selling price of $1, the marketer would calculate as follows:

$$\text{Price} = \frac{\$0.60}{(100\% - 40\%)} = \$1.00$$

Similarly, you can convert the markup percentage from a specific item based on the selling price to one based on cost, and the reverse, using the following formulas:

$$\text{Markup percentage on selling price} = \frac{\text{Markup percentage on cost}}{(100\% + \text{Markup percentage on cost})}$$

$$\text{Markup percentage on cost} = \frac{\text{Markup percentage on selling price}}{(100\% - \text{Markup percentage on selling price})}$$

Again, data from the previous example give the following conversions:

$$\text{Markup percentage on selling price} = \frac{66.7\%}{(100\% + 66.7\%)} = 40\%$$

$$\text{Markup percentage on cost} = \frac{40\%}{(100\% - 40\%)} = 66.7\%$$

Marketers determine markups based partly on their judgments of the amounts consumers will pay for a given product. When buyers refuse to pay a product's stated price, however, or when improvements in other products or fashion changes reduce the appeal of the current merchandise, a producer or retailer must take a markdown.

Markdowns

A markdown is a price reduction a firm makes on an item. Reasons for markdowns include sales promotions featuring price reductions or a decision that the initial price was too high. Unlike markups, markdowns cannot be determined from the income statement, because the price reduction takes place before the sale occurs. The markdown percentage equals dollar markdowns divided by sales. For example, a retailer may decide to reduce the price of an item by $10, from $50 to $40, and sells 1,000 units. The markdown percentage equals:

$$\frac{(1{,}000 \times \$10)}{(1{,}000 \times \$40)} = \frac{\$10{,}000}{\$40{,}000} = 25\%$$

GLOSSARY

80/20 principle Generally accepted rule that 80 percent of a product's revenues come from 20 percent of its customers.

accessory equipment Capital items such as desktop computers and printers that typically cost less and last for shorter periods than installations.

administered marketing system VMS that achieves channel coordination when a dominant channel member exercises its power.

adoption process Stages consumers go through in learning about a new product, trying it, and deciding whether to purchase it again.

advertising Paid, nonpersonal communication through various media about a business firm, not-for-profit organization, product, or idea by a sponsor identified in a message intended to inform or persuade members of a particular audience.

advertising campaign Series of different but related ads that use a single theme and appear in different media within a specified time period.

affinity marketing Marketing effort sponsored by an organization that solicits responses from individuals who share common interests and activities.

AIDA concept Steps through which an individual reaches a purchase decision: attention, interest, desire, and action.

AIO statements Items on lifestyle surveys that describe various activities, interests, and respondents' opinions.

allowance Specified deduction from list price, including a trade-in or promotional allowance.

antitrust Laws designed to prevent restraints on trade such as business monopolies.

app Short for *application*, a free or paid software download that links users to a wide range of goods and services, media and text content, social media platforms, search engines, and the like.

application service providers (ASPs) Outside companies that specialize in providing both the computers and the application support for managing information systems of business clients.

approach Salesperson's initial contact with a prospective customer.

atmospherics Combination of physical characteristics and amenities that contribute to a store's image.

attitudes Person's enduring favorable or unfavorable evaluations, emotions, or action tendencies toward some object or idea.

average total cost Cost calculated by dividing the sum of the variable and fixed costs by the number of units produced.

backward integration Process through which a manufacturer attempts to gain greater control over inputs in its production process, such as raw materials.

banner ad Strip message placed in high-visibility areas of frequently visited websites.

basing-point pricing System used in some industries during the early 20th century in which the buyer paid the factory price plus freight charges from the basing-point city nearest the buyer.

benchmarking Method of measuring quality by comparing performance against industry leaders.

blog Short for *Web log*—an online journal for an individual or organization.

blogging site A platform where a host or writer posts information or opinions on various topics and followers may respond.

bonus pack Specially packaged item that gives the purchaser a larger quantity at the regular price.

bookmarking site A platform that gives users a place to save, organize, and manage links to websites and other Internet resources.

bot (shopbot) Software program that allows online shoppers to compare prices of a particular product offered by several online retailers.

bottom line Reference to overall company profitability.

brand Name, term, sign, symbol, design, or some combination that identifies the products of one firm while differentiating them from those of the competition.

brand equity Added value that a respected, well-known brand name gives to a product in the marketplace.

brand extension Strategy of attaching a popular brand name to a new product in an unrelated product category.

brand insistence Consumer refusal of alternatives and extensive search for desired merchandise.

brand licensing Practice that expands a firm's exposure in the marketplace.

brand manager Marketer responsible for a single brand.

brand mark Symbol or pictorial design that distinguishes a product.

brand name Part of a brand, consisting of letters, numbers, or words, that can be spoken and that identifies and distinguishes a firm's offerings from those of its competitors.

brand preference Consumer choice of a product on the basis of a previous experience.

brand recognition Consumer awareness and identification of a brand.

breakeven analysis Pricing technique used to determine the number of products that must be sold at a specified price to generate enough revenue to cover total cost.

broker Agent wholesaling intermediary that does not take title to or possession of goods in the course of its primary function, which is to bring together buyers and sellers.

bundle pricing Offering two or more complementary products and selling them for a single price.

business cycle Pattern of stages in the level of economic activity: prosperity, recession, depression, and recovery.

business plan Formal document that outlines what a company's objectives are, how they will be met, how the business will obtain financing, and how much money the company expects to earn.

business products Goods and services purchased for use either directly or indirectly in the production of other goods and services for resale.

business services Intangible products firms buy to facilitate their production and operating processes.

business-to-business (B2B) e-marketing Use of the Internet for business transactions between organizations.

business-to-business (B2B) marketing Organizational sales and purchases of goods and services to support production of other products, to facilitate daily company operations, or for resale.

business-to-business (B2B) product Product that contributes directly or indirectly to the output of other products for resale; also called industrial or organizational product.

business-to-consumer (B2C) e-marketing Selling directly to consumers over the Internet.

business-to-consumer (B2C) product Product destined for use by ultimate consumers.

buyer Person who has the formal authority to select a supplier and to implement the procedures for securing a good or service.

buyer partnership Relationship in which a firm purchases goods or services from one or more providers.

buyer's market A market in which there are more goods and services than people willing to buy them.

buying center Participants in an organizational buying action.

buzz marketing Marketing that gathers volunteers to try products and then relies on them to talk about their experiences with their friends and colleagues.

C

cannibalization Loss of sales of an existing product due to competition from a new product in the same line.

captive brand National brand sold exclusively by a retail chain.

cash discount Price reduction offered to a consumer, business user, or marketing intermediary in return for prompt payment of a bill.

category advisor (category captain) Trade industry vendor who develops a comprehensive procurement plan for a retail buyer.

category killer Store offering huge selections and low prices in single product lines.

category management Product management system in which a category manager—with profit and loss responsibility—oversees a product line.

cause marketing Identification and marketing of a social issue, cause, or idea to selected target markets.

Central American Free Trade Agreement-DR (CAFTA-DR) Trade agreement among the United States, Central American nations, and the Dominican Republic.

channel Medium through which a message is delivered.

channel captain Dominant and controlling member of a marketing channel.

channel conflicts Conflicts between manufacturers, wholesalers, and retailers.

click-through rate Percentage of people presented with a banner ad who click on it.

closed sales territory Exclusive geographic selling region of a distributor.

closing Stage of the personal selling process in which the salesperson asks the customer to make a purchase decision.

cluster sample Probability sample in which researchers select a sample of subgroups (or clusters) from which they draw respondents; each cluster reflects the diversity of the whole population sampled.

cobranding Cooperative arrangement in which two or more businesses team up to closely link their names on a single product.

cognitive dissonance Imbalance among knowledge, beliefs, and attitudes that occurs after an action or decision, such as a purchase.

cohort effect Tendency of members of a generation to be influenced and bound together by events occurring during their key formative years—roughly ages 17 to 22.

cold calling Contacting a prospect without a prior appointment.

collaborative planning, forecasting, and replenishment (CPFaR) Planning and forecasting approach based on collaboration between buyers and sellers.

comarketing Cooperative arrangement in which two or more businesses jointly market each other's products.

commercial market Individuals and firms that acquire products to support, directly or indirectly, production of other goods and services.

commission Incentive compensation directly related to the sales or profits achieved by a salesperson.

commission merchant Agent wholesaling intermediary that takes possession of goods shipped to a central market for sale, acts as the producer's agent, and collects an agreed-upon fee at the time of the sale.

common carriers Businesses that provide transportation services as for-hire carriers to the general public.

common market Extension of a customs union by seeking to reconcile all government regulations affecting trade.

comparative advertising Advertising strategy that emphasizes messages with direct or indirect promotional comparisons between competing brands.

competitive bidding Inviting potential suppliers to quote prices on proposed purchases or contracts.

competitive environment Interactive process that occurs in the marketplace among marketers of directly competitive products, marketers of products that can be substituted for one another, and marketers competing for the consumer's purchasing power.

competitive pricing strategy Pricing strategy designed to deemphasize price as a competitive variable by pricing a good or service at the general level of comparable offerings.

competitive strategy Methods through which a firm deals with its competitive environment.

component parts and materials Finished business products of one producer that become part of the final products of another producer.

concentrated (niche) marketing Focusing marketing efforts on satisfying a single market segment.

concept testing Method for subjecting a product idea to additional study before actual development by involving consumers through focus groups, surveys, in-store polling, and similar strategies.

consolidated metropolitan statistical area (CMSA) Urban area that includes two or more PMSAs.

consultative selling Meeting customer needs by listening to them, understanding their problems, paying attention to details, and following through after the sale.

consumer behavior Process through which buyers make purchase decisions.

consumer innovator Someone who purchases a new product almost as soon as the product reaches the market.

consumer orientation Business philosophy incorporating the marketing concept that emphasizes first determining unmet consumer needs and then designing a system for satisfying them.

consumer products Products bought by ultimate consumers for personal use.

consumer rights List of legitimate consumer expectations suggested by President John F. Kennedy.

consumerism Social force within the environment that aids and protects the consumer by exerting legal, moral, and economic pressures on business and government.

containerization Process of combining several unitized loads into a single, well-protected load for shipment.

content marketing Creating and distributing relevant and targeted material to attract and engage an audience, with the goal of driving them to a desired action.

contest Sales promotion technique that requires entrants to complete a task, such as solving a puzzle or answering questions on a quiz, for a chance to win a prize.

contract carriers For-hire transporters that do not offer their services to the general public.

contractual marketing system VMS that coordinates channel activities through formal agreements among participants.

controlled experiment Scientific investigation in which a researcher manipulates a test group (or groups) and compares the results with those of a control group that did not receive the experimental controls or manipulations.

convenience products Goods and services consumers want to purchase frequently, immediately, and with minimal effort.

convenience retailer Store that appeals to customers by having an accessible location, long hours, rapid checkout, and adequate parking.

convenience sample Nonprobability sample selected from among readily available respondents.

conversion rate Percentage of visitors to a website who make a purchase.

cookies Techniques for collecting information about online website visitors in which small text files are automatically downloaded to a user's computer to gather such data as length of visit and the site visited next.

cooperative advertising Strategy in which a retailer shares advertising costs with a manufacturer or wholesaler.

core based statistical area (CBSA) Collective term for metropolitan and micropolitan statistical areas.

core region Region from which most major brands get 40 to 80 percent of their sales.

corporate marketing system VMS in which a single owner operates the entire marketing channel.

corporate website Site designed to increase a firm's visibility, promote its offerings and provide information to interested parties.

cost per response (click-through) Direct marketing technique that relates the cost of an ad to the number of people who click it.

cost per thousand impressions Measurement technique that relates the cost of an ad to every thousand people who view it.

cost-plus pricing Practice of adding a percentage of specified dollar amount—or markup—to the base cost of a product to cover unassigned costs and to provide a profit.

countertrade Form of exporting whereby goods and services are bartered rather than sold for cash.

coupon Sales promotion technique that offers a discount on the purchase price of goods or services.

creative selling Personal selling in which salespeople use well-planned strategies to seek new customers by proposing innovative solutions to customers' needs.

cross-promotion Promotional technique in which marketing partners share the cost of a promotional campaign that meets their mutual needs.

cross-selling Selling multiple, often unrelated, goods and services to the same customer based on knowledge of that customer's needs.

culture Values, beliefs, preferences, and tastes handed down from one generation to the next.

cumulative quantity discount Price discount determined by amounts of purchases over stated time periods.

customary prices Traditional prices that customers expect to pay for certain goods and services.

customer churn Turnover in a company's customer base.

customer relationship management (CRM) Combination of strategies and tools that drives relationship programs, reorienting the entire organization to a concentrated focus on satisfying customers.

customer satisfaction Extent to which customers are satisfied with their purchases.

customer win-back Process of rejuvenating lost relationships with customers.

customer-based segmentation Dividing a business-to-business market into homogeneous groups based on buyers' product specifications.

customs union Establishment of a free-trade area plus a uniform tariff for trade with nonmember unions.

D

data mining Process of searching through customer databases to detect patterns that guide marketing decision making.

database marketing Use of software to analyze marketing information, identifying and targeting messages toward specific groups of potential customers.

decider Person who chooses a good or service, although another person may have the formal authority to complete the sale.

decline stage Final stage of the product lifecycle, in which a decline in total industry sales occurs.

decoding Receiver's interpretation of a message.

Delphi technique Qualitative sales forecasting method that gathers and redistributes several rounds of anonymous forecasts until the participants reach a consensus.

demand Schedule of the amounts of a firm's product that consumers will purchase at different prices during a specified time period.

demarketing Process of reducing consumer demand for a good or service to a level that the firm can supply.

demographic segmentation Division of an overall market into homogeneous groups based on variables such as gender, age, income, occupation, education, sexual orientation, household size, and stage in the family lifecycle; also called *socioeconomic segmentation*.

demonstration Stage in the personal selling process in which the customer has the opportunity to try out or otherwise see how a good or service works before purchase.

department store Large store that handles a variety of merchandise, including clothing, household goods, appliances, and furniture.

derived demand Demand for a resource that results from demand for the goods and services produced by that resource.

differentiated marketing Strategy that focuses on producing several products and pricing, promoting, and distributing them with different marketing mixes designed to satisfy smaller segments.

diffusion process Process by which new goods or services are accepted in the marketplace.

direct channel Marketing channel that moves goods directly from a producer to the business purchaser or ultimate user.

direct mail Communications in the form of sales letters, postcards, brochures, catalogs, and the like conveying messages directly from the marketer to the customer.

direct marketing Direct communications, other than personal sales contacts, between buyer and seller, designed to generate sales, information requests, or store or website visits.

direct sales results test Method for measuring promotional effectiveness based on the specific impact on sales revenues for each dollar of promotional spending.

direct selling Strategy designed to establish direct sales contact between producer and final user.

discount house Store that charges low prices but may not offer services such as credit.

discretionary income Money available to spend after buying necessities such as food, clothing, and housing.

distribution Movement of goods and services from producers to customers.

downstream management Controlling part of the supply chain that involves finished product storage, outbound logistics, marketing and sales, and customer service.

drop shipper Limited-function merchant wholesaler that accepts orders from customers and forwards those orders to producers, which then ship directly to the customers who placed the orders.

dual distribution Network that moves products to a firm's target market through more than one marketing channel.

dumping Controversial practice of selling a product in a foreign market at a price lower than what it receives in the producer's domestic market.

E

e-business Conducting online transactions with customers by collecting and analyzing business information, carrying out the exchanges, and maintaining online relationships with customers.

e-marketing Strategic process of creating, distributing, promoting, and pricing goods and services to a target market over the Internet or through digital tools.

e-procurement Use of the Internet by organizations to solicit bids and purchase goods and services from suppliers.

economic environment Factors that influence consumer buying power and marketing strategies, including stage of the business cycle, inflation and deflation, unemployment, income, and resource availability.

elasticity Measure of responsiveness of purchasers and suppliers to a change in price.

electronic bulletin board Internet forum that allows users to post and read messages on a specific topic.

electronic data interchange (EDI) Computer-to-computer exchanges of invoices, orders, and other business documents.

electronic shopping cart File that holds items the online shopper has chosen to buy.

electronic signatures Electronic identification that allows legal contracts such as home mortgages and insurance policies to be executed online.

electronic storefront Company website that sells products to customers.

embargo Complete ban on the import of specified products.

emergency goods and services Products bought in response to unexpected and urgent needs.

employee satisfaction Employee's level of satisfaction in his or her company and the extent to which that loyalty—or lack thereof—is communicated to external customers.

encoding Translating a message into understandable terms.

encryption The process of encoding data for security purposes.

end-use application segmentation Segmenting a business-to-business market based on how industrial purchasers will use the product.

engagement Amount of time users spend on sites.

Engel's laws Three observations about the impact of household income on consumer spending behavior: as household income increases, a smaller percentage of expenditures goes for food; the percentage spent on housing, household operations, and clothing remains constant; and the percentage spent on other items (such as recreation and education) increases.

enterprise resource planning (ERP) system Software system that consolidates data from among a firm's various business units.

environmental management Attainment of organizational objectives by predicting and influencing the competitive, political–legal, economic, technological, and social–cultural environments.

environmental scanning Process of collecting information about the external marketing environment to identify and interpret potential trends.

ethics Moral standards of behavior expected by a society.

European Union (EU) Customs union that is moving in the direction of an economic union by adopting a common currency, removing trade restrictions, and permitting free flow of goods and workers throughout the member nations.

evaluative criteria Features a consumer considers in choosing among alternatives.

event marketing Marketing of sporting, cultural, and charitable activities to selected target markets.

everyday low pricing (EDLP) Pricing strategy of continuously offering low prices rather than relying on such short-term price cuts as cents-off coupons, rebates, and special sales.

evoked set Number of alternatives a consumer actually considers in making a purchase decision.

exchange control Method used to regulate international trade among importing organizations by controlling access to foreign currencies.

exchange functions Buying and selling.

exchange process Activity in which two or more parties give something of value to each other to satisfy perceived needs.

exchange rate Price of one nation's currency in terms of another country's currency.

exclusive distribution Distribution of a product through a single wholesaler or retailer in a specific geographic region.

expectancy theory Theory that motivation depends on an individual's expectations of his or her ability to perform a job and how that performance relates to attaining a desired reward.

exploratory research Process of discussing a marketing problem with informed sources both within and outside the firm and examining information from secondary sources.

exponential smoothing Quantitative forecasting technique that assigns weights to historical sales data, giving the greatest weight to the most recent data.

exporting Marketing domestically produced goods and services in foreign countries.

external customers People or organizations that buy or use a firm's goods or services.

F

fair-trade laws Statutes enacted in most states that once permitted manufacturers to stipulate a minimum retail price for their product.

family brand Single brand name that identifies several related products.

family lifecycle Process of family formation and dissolution.

feedback Receiver's response to a message.

field selling Sales presentations made at prospective customers' locations on a face-to-face basis.

firewall Electronic barrier between a company's internal network and the Internet that limits access into and out of the network.

first mover strategy Theory advocating that the company first to offer a product in a marketplace will be the long-term market winner.

fixed cost Cost that remains stable at any production level within a certain range (such as lease payments or insurance costs).

fixed-sum-per-unit method Method of promotional budgeting in which a predetermined amount is allocated to each sales or production unit.

FOB origin-freight allowed (freight absorbed) Price quotation system that allows the buyer to deduct shipping expenses from the cost of purchases.

FOB (free on board) plant (FOB origin) Price quotation that does not include shipping charges.

focus group A small group of individuals brought together to discuss a specific topic.

follow-up Postsale activities that often determine whether an individual who has made a recent purchase will become a repeat customer.

foreign licensing Agreement that grants foreign marketers the right to distribute a firm's merchandise or to use its trademark, patent, or process in a specified geographic area.

forward integration Process through which a firm attempts to control downstream distribution.

franchise Contractual arrangement in which a wholesaler or retailer agrees to meet the operating requirements of a manufacturer or other franchiser.

free-trade area Region in which participating nations agree to the free trade of goods among themselves, abolishing tariffs and trade restrictions.

Free Trade Area of the Americas (FTAA) Proposed free-trade area stretching the length of the entire Western Hemisphere and designed to extend free trade benefits to additional nations in North, Central, and South America.

frequency marketing Frequent-buyer or -user marketing programs that reward customers with cash, rebates, merchandise, or other premiums.

friendship, commerce, and navigation (FCN) treaties International agreements that deal with many aspects of commercial relations among nations.

full-cost pricing Pricing method that uses all relevant variable costs in setting a product's price and allocates those fixed costs not directly attributed to the production of the priced item.

full-service research supplier Marketing research organization that offers all aspects of the marketing research process.

G

gatekeeper Person who controls the information that all buying center members will review.

General Agreement on Tariffs and Trade (GATT) International trade accord that has helped reduce world tariffs.

general merchandise retailer Store that carries a wide variety of product lines, stocking all of them in some depth.

generic products Products characterized by plain labels, no advertising, and the absence of brand names.

geographic information systems (GISs) Software packages that assemble, store, manipulate, and display data by their location.

geographic segmentation Division of an overall market into homogeneous groups based on their locations.

global marketing strategy Standardized marketing mix with minimal modifications that a firm uses in all of its domestic and foreign markets.

global sourcing Purchasing goods and services from suppliers worldwide.

goods Tangible products customers can see, hear, smell, taste, or touch.

goods–services continuum Spectrum along which goods and services fall according to their attributes, from pure good to pure service.

grassroots marketing Efforts that connect directly with existing and potential customers through nonmainstream channels.

gray goods Products manufactured abroad under license from a U.S. firm and then sold in the U.S. market in competition with that firm's own domestic output.

green marketing Production, promotion, and reclamation of environmentally sensitive products.

gross domestic product (GDP) Sum of all goods and services produced by a nation in a year.

growth stage Second stage of the product lifecycle that begins when a firm starts to realize substantial profits from its investment in a product.

guerrilla marketing Unconventional, innovative, and low-cost marketing techniques designed to get consumers' attention in unusual ways.

H

high-involvement purchase decisions Purchases with high levels of potential social or economic consequences.

homeshoring Hiring workers to do jobs from their homes.

hypermarket Giant one-stop shopping facility offering wide selections of grocery items and general merchandise at discount prices, typically filling up 200,000 or more square feet of selling space.

hypothesis Tentative explanation for a specific event.

I

import quotas Trade restrictions limiting the number of units of certain goods that can enter a country for resale.

importing Purchasing foreign goods and services.

impulse goods and services Products purchased on the spur of the moment.

inbound telemarketing Sales method in which prospects call a seller to obtain information, make reservations, and purchase goods and services.

incremental-cost pricing Pricing method that attempts to use only costs directly attributable to a specific output in setting prices.

indirect evaluation Method for measuring promotional effectiveness by concentrating on quantifiable indicators of effectiveness such as recall and readership.

individual brand Single brand that uniquely identifies a product.

industrial distributor Channel intermediary that takes title to goods it handles and then distributes these goods to retailers, other distributors, or business or B2B customers; also called a *wholesaler*.

inelastic demand Demand that, throughout an industry, will not change significantly due to a price change.

inflation Rising prices caused by some combination of excess consumer demand and increases in the costs of one or more factors of production.

influencers Individuals with the capability of affecting the opinions or actions of others. Typically, technical staff such as engineers who affect the buying decision by supplying information to guide evaluation of alternatives or by setting buying specifications.

informative advertising Promotion that seeks to develop initial demand for a good, service, organization, person, place, idea, or cause.

infrastructure A nation's basic system of transportation networks, communications systems, and energy facilities.

inside selling Selling by phone, mail, and electronic commerce.

installations Major capital investments in the B2B market.

institutional advertising Promotion of a concept, an idea, a philosophy, or the goodwill of an industry, company, organization, person, geographic location, or government agency.

integrated marketing communications (IMC) Coordination of all promotional activities to produce a unified, customer-focused promotional message.

intensive distribution Distribution of a product through all available channels.

interactive advertising Two-way promotional messages transmitted through communication channels that induce message recipients to participate actively in the promotional effort.

interactive marketing Buyer–seller communications in which the customer controls the amount and type of information received from a marketer through such channels as the Internet and virtual reality kiosks.

interactive television Television service package that includes a return path for viewers to interact with programs or commercials by clicking their remote controls.

intermodal operations Combination of transport modes, such as rail and highway carriers (piggyback), air and highway carriers (birdyback), and water and air carriers (fishyback), to improve customer service and achieve cost advantages.

internal customers Employees or departments within an organization that depend on the work of another employee or department.

internal marketing Managerial actions that help all members of the organization understand, accept, and fulfill their respective roles in implementing a marketing strategy.

internal partnership Relationship involving customers within an organization.

interpretative research Observational research method developed by social anthropologists in which customers are observed in their natural setting and their behavior is interpreted based on an understanding of social and cultural characteristics; also known as *ethnography*, or "going native."

introductory stage First stage of the product lifecycle, in which a firm works to stimulate sales of a new-market entry.

ISO 9001:2008 Standards developed by the International Organization for Standardization in Switzerland to ensure consistent quality management and quality assurance for goods and services throughout the European Union (EU).

ISO (International Organization for Standardization) certification Internationally recognized standards that ensure a company's goods, services, and operations meet established quality levels and its operations minimize harm to the environment.

J

joint demand Demand for a product that depends on the demand for another product used in combination with it.

jury of executive opinion Qualitative sales forecasting method that assesses the sales expectations of various executives.

just-in-time (JIT)/JIT II Inventory practices that seek to boost efficiency by cutting inventories to absolute minimum levels. With JIT II, suppliers' representatives work at the customer's facility.

L

label Branding component that carries an item's brand name or symbol, the name and address of the manufacturer or distributor, information about the product, and recommended uses.

lateral partnership Strategic relationship that extends to external entities but involves no direct buyer–seller interactions.

leader pricing Variant of loss-leader pricing in which marketers offer prices slightly above cost to avoid violating minimum-markup regulations and earn a minimal return on promotional sales.

learning Knowledge or skill acquired as a result of experience, which changes consumer behavior.

lifetime value of a customer Revenues and intangible benefits such as referrals and customer feedback a customer brings to the seller over an average lifetime of the relationship, less the amount the company must spend to acquire, market to, and service the customer.

limited-line store Retailer that offers a large assortment within a single product line or within a few related product lines.

limited-service research supplier Marketing research firm that specializes in a limited number of research activities such as conducting field interviews or performing data processing.

line extension Development of individual offerings that appeal to different market segments while remaining closely related to the existing product line.

list price Established price normally quoted to potential buyers.

logistics Process of coordinating the flow of information, goods, and services among members of the distribution channel.

loss leader Product offered to consumers at less than cost to attract them to stores in the hope that they will buy other merchandise at regular prices.

low-involvement purchase decisions Routine purchases that pose little risk to the consumer.

M

mail-order wholesaler Limited-function merchant wholesaler that distributes catalogs instead of sending sales personnel to contact customers.

mall intercepts Interviews conducted inside retail shopping centers.

manufacturer's brand Brand name owned by a manufacturer or other producer.

manufacturers' representative Agent wholesaling intermediary that represents manufacturers of related but noncompeting products and receives a commission on each sale.

marginal analysis Method of analyzing the relationship between costs, sales price, and increased sales volume.

marginal cost Change in total cost that results from producing an additional unit of output.

markdown Amount by which a retailer reduces the original selling price of a product.

market Group of people with sufficient purchasing power, authority, and willingness to buy.

market development strategy Strategy that concentrates on finding new markets for existing products.

market penetration strategy Strategy that seeks to increase sales of existing products in existing markets.

market-plus pricing Intentionally setting a relatively high price compared with the prices of competing products; also known as *skimming pricing*.

market price Price a consumer or marketing intermediary actually pays for a product after subtracting any discounts, allowances, or rebates from the list price.

market segmentation Division of the total market into smaller, relatively homogeneous groups.

market-share objective Volume-related pricing objective with the goal of controlling a portion of the market for a firm's product.

marketing An organizational function and set of processes for creating, communicating, and delivering value to customers and for managing customer relationships in ways that benefit the organization and its stakeholders.

marketing (distribution) channel System of marketing institutions that enhances the physical flow of goods and services, along with ownership title, from producer to consumer or business user.

marketing communications Messages that deal with buyer–seller relationships.

marketing concept Companywide consumer orientation with the objective of achieving long-run success.

marketing decision support system (MDSS) Marketing information system component that links a decision maker with relevant databases and analysis tools.

marketing ethics Marketers' standards of conduct and moral values.

marketing information system (MIS) Planned, computer-based system designed to provide managers with a continuous flow of information relevant to their specific decisions and areas of responsibility.

marketing intermediary (middleman) Wholesaler or retailer that operates between producers and consumers or business users.

marketing mix Blending of the four strategy elements—product, distribution, promotion, and pricing—to fit the needs and preferences of a specific target market.

marketing myopia Management's failure to recognize the scope of its business.

marketing plan Detailed description of the resources and actions needed to achieve stated marketing objectives.

marketing planning Implementing planning activities devoted to achieving marketing objectives.

marketing public relations (MPR) Focused public relations activities that directly support marketing goals.

marketing research Process of collecting and using information for marketing decision making.

marketing strategy Overall, company-wide program for selecting a particular target market and then satisfying consumers in that market through the marketing mix.

marketing website Site whose main purpose is to increase purchases by visitors.

markup Amount a retailer adds to the cost of a product to determine its selling price.

mass merchandiser Store that stocks a wider line of goods than a department store, usually without the same depth of assortment within each line.

materials handling system Set of activities that move production inputs and other goods within factories, warehouses, and transportation terminals.

maturity stage Third stage of the product lifecycle, in which industry sales level out.

media research Advertising research that assesses how well a particular medium delivers an advertiser's message, where and when to place the advertisement, and the size of the audience.

media scheduling Setting the timing and sequence for a series of advertisements.

meeting competition method Method of promotional budgeting that simply matches competitors' outlays.

merchandisers Trade sector buyers who secure needed products at the best possible prices.

merchant wholesaler Independently-owned wholesaling intermediary that takes title to the goods it handles; also known as an industrial distributor in the business goods market.

message Communication of information, advice, or a request by the sender to the receiver.

message research Advertising research that tests consumer reactions to an advertisement's creative message.

metropolitan statistical area (MSA) Freestanding urban area with a population in the urban center of at least 50,000 and a total MSA population of 100,000 or more.

microblog A blog posting that contains only a few words (such as on Twitter).

micromarketing Targeting potential customers at very narrow, basic levels such as by zip code, specific occupation, or lifestyle—possibly even individuals themselves.

micropolitan statistical area Area with at least one town of 10,000 to 49,999 people with proportionally few of its residents commuting to outside the area.

minimum advertised pricing (MAP) Fees paid to retailers who agree not to advertise products below set prices.

mission Essential purpose that differentiates one company from others.

missionary selling Indirect selling method in which salespeople promote goodwill for the firm by educating customers and providing technical or operational assistance.

mobile marketing Marketing messages transmitted via wireless technology.

modified breakeven analysis Pricing technique used to evaluate consumer demand by comparing the number of products that must be sold at a variety of prices to cover total cost with estimates of expected sales at the various prices.

modified rebuy Situation in which a purchaser is willing to reevaluate available options for repurchasing a good or service.

monopolistic competition Market structure involving a heterogeneous product and product differentiation among competing suppliers, allowing the marketer some degree of control over prices.

monopoly Market structure in which a single seller dominates trade in a good or service for which buyers can find no close substitutes.

motive Inner state that directs a person toward the goal of satisfying a need.

MRO items Business supplies that include maintenance items, repair items, and operating supplies.

multidomestic marketing strategy Application of market segmentation to foreign markets by tailoring the firm's marketing mix to match specific target markets in each nation.

multiple sourcing Purchasing from several vendors.

N

national account selling Promotional effort in which a dedicated sales team is assigned to a firm's major customers to provide sales and service.

national accounts organization Promotional effort in which a dedicated sales team is assigned to a firm's major customers to provide sales and service needs.

nearshoring Moving jobs to vendors in countries close to the business's home country.

need Imbalance between a consumer's actual and desired states.

network marketing Personal selling that relies on lists of family members and friends of a salesperson, who organizes gatherings of potential customers for an in-home presentation of selected products.

new-task buying First-time or unique purchase situation that requires considerable effort by decision makers.

noise Any stimulus that distracts a receiver from receiving a message.

noncumulative quantity discount Price reduction granted on a one-time-only basis.

nonmarketing public relations Organizational messages about general management issues.

nonpersonal selling Promotion that includes advertising, product placement, sales promotion, direct marketing, public relations, and guerrilla marketing—all conducted without being face-to-face with the buyer.

nonprobability sample Sample that involves personal judgment somewhere in the selection process.

North American Free Trade Agreement (NAFTA) Accord removing trade barriers among Canada, Mexico, and the United States.

North American Industry Classification System (NAICS) Classification used by NAFTA countries to categorize the business marketplace into detailed market segments.

O

objection Expression of sales resistance by the prospect.

odd pricing Pricing policy based on the belief that a price ending with an odd number just under a round number is more appealing, for instance, $9.97 rather than $10.

offshoring Movement of high-wage jobs from one country to lower-cost overseas locations.

oligopoly Market structure in which relatively few sellers compete and where high start-up costs form barriers to keep out new competitors.

online forum A platform where users post messages and hold conversations on specified topics.

opening price point An opening price below that of the competition, usually on a high-quality private-label item.

opinion leaders Trendsetters who purchase new products before others in a group and then influence others in their purchases.

order processing Selling, mostly at the wholesale and retail levels, that involves identifying customer needs, pointing them out to customers, and completing orders.

organization marketing Marketing by mutual-benefit organizations, service organizations, and government organizations intended to persuade others to accept their goals, receive their services, or contribute to them in some way.

outbound telemarketing Sales method in which sales personnel place phone calls to prospects and try to conclude the sale over the phone.

outsourcing Using outside vendors to provide goods and services formerly produced in-house.

over-the-counter selling Personal selling conducted in retail and some wholesale locations in which customers come to the seller's place of business.

P

partnership Affiliation of two or more companies that help each other achieve common goals.

penetration pricing strategy Pricing strategy involving the use of a relatively low entry price compared with competitive offerings, based on the theory that this initial low price will help secure market acceptance.

percentage-of-sales method Method of promotional budgeting in which a dollar amount is based on a percentage of past or projected sales.

perception Meaning that a person attributes to incoming stimuli gathered through the five senses.

perceptual screens The mental filtering processes though which all inputs must pass.

person marketing Marketing efforts designed to cultivate the attention, interest, and preferences of a target market toward a person (perhaps a political candidate or celebrity).

personal selling Interpersonal influence process involving a seller's promotional presentation conducted on a person-to-person basis with the buyer.

persuasive advertising Promotion that attempts to increase demand for an existing good, service, organization, person, place, idea, or cause.

phishing High-tech scam that uses authentic-looking email or pop-up messages to get unsuspecting victims to reveal personal information.

physical distribution Broad range of activities aimed at efficient movement of finished goods from the end of the production line to the consumer.

place marketing Marketing efforts to attract people and organizations to a particular geographic area.

planned shopping center Group of retail stores planned, coordinated, and marketed as a unit.

planning Process of anticipating future events and conditions and of determining the best way to achieve organizational objectives.

podcast Online audio or video file that can be downloaded to other digital devices.

point-of-purchase (POP) advertising Display or other promotion placed near the site of the actual buying decision.

political–legal environment Component of the marketing environment consisting of laws and their interpretations that require firms to operate under competitive conditions and to protect consumer rights.

political risk assessment (PRA) Units within a firm that evaluate the political risks of the marketplaces in which they operate as well as proposed new marketplaces.

pop-up ad Separate window that pops up with an advertising message.

population (universe) Total group that researchers want to study.

Porter's Five Forces Model developed by strategy expert Michael Porter that identifies five competitive forces that influence planning strategies.

positioning Placing a product at a certain point or location within a market in the minds of prospective buyers.

positioning map Tool that helps marketers place products in a market by graphically illustrating consumers' perceptions of competing products within an industry.

postage-stamp pricing System for handling transportation costs under which all buyers are quoted the same price, including transportation expenses; also known as *uniform-delivered price.*

posttesting Research that assesses advertising effectiveness after it has appeared in a print or broadcast medium.

precall planning Use of information collected during the prospecting and qualifying stages of the sales process and during previous contacts with the prospect to tailor the approach and presentation to match the customer's needs.

premium Item given free or at a reduced cost with purchases of other products.

preroll video ad Brief marketing message that appears before expected video content.

presentation Personal selling function of describing a product's major features and relating them to a customer's problems or needs.

pretesting Research that evaluates an ad during its development stage.

price Exchange value of a good or service.

price flexibility Pricing policy permitting variable prices for goods and services.

pricing policy General guideline that reflects marketing objectives and influences specific pricing decisions.

primary data Information collected for a specific investigation.

primary metropolitan statistical area (PMSA) Urbanized county or set of counties with social and economic ties to nearby areas.

private brand Brand offered by a wholesaler or retailer.

private carriers Transporters that provide service solely for internally generated freight.

probability sample Sample that gives every member of the population a chance of being selected.

product Bundle of physical, service, and symbolic attributes designed to satisfy a customer's wants and needs.

product advertising Nonpersonal selling of a particular good or service.

product development Introduction of new products into identifiable or established markets.

product diversification strategy Developing entirely new products for new markets.

product liability Responsibility of manufacturers and marketers for injuries and damages caused by their products.

product lifecycle Progression of a product through introduction, growth, maturity, and decline stages.

product line Series of related products offered by one company.

product-line pricing Practice of setting a limited number of prices for a selection of merchandise and marketing different product lines at each of these price levels.

product manager Marketer responsible for an individual product or product line; also called a brand manager.

product mix Assortment of product lines and individual product offerings a company sells.

product placement Form of promotion in which a marketer pays a motion picture or television program owner a fee to display a product prominently in the film or show.

product positioning Consumers' perceptions of a product's attributes, uses, quality, and advantages and disadvantages relative to competing brands.

production orientation Business philosophy stressing efficiency in producing a quality product, with the attitude toward marketing that "a good product will sell itself."

product-related segmentation Division of a population into homogeneous groups based on their relationships to a product.

profit center Any part of an organization to which revenue and controllable costs can be assigned.

Profit Impact of Market Strategies (PIMS) project Research that discovered a strong positive relationship between a firm's market share and product quality and its return on investment.

profit maximization Point at which the additional revenue gained by increasing the price of a product equals the increase in total costs.

promotion Communication link between buyers and sellers; the function of informing, persuading, and influencing a consumer's purchase decision.

promotional allowance Promotional incentive in which the manufacturer agrees to pay the reseller a certain amount to cover the costs of special promotional displays or extensive advertising.

promotional mix Subset of the marketing mix in which marketers attempt to achieve the optimal blending of the elements of personal and nonpersonal selling to achieve promotional objectives.

promotional pricing Pricing policy in which a lower-than-normal price is used as a temporary ingredient in a firm's marketing strategy.

prospecting Personal selling function of identifying potential customers.

protective tariffs Taxes designed to raise the retail price of an imported product to match or exceed that of a similar domestic product.

psychographic segmentation Division of a population into groups having similar attitudes, values, and lifestyles.

psychological pricing Pricing policy based on the belief that certain prices or price ranges make a good or service more appealing than others to buyers.

public relations Firm's communications and relationships with its various publics.

publicity Nonpersonal stimulation of demand for a good, service, place, idea, person, or organization by unpaid placement of significant news regarding the product in a print or broadcast medium.

puffery Exaggerated claims of a product's superiority, or the use of subjective or vague statements that may not be literally true.

pure competition Market structure characterized by homogeneous products in which there are so many buyers and sellers that none has a significant influence on price.

push money Cash reward paid to retail salespeople for every unit of a product they sell.

Q

QR code Short for "quick response," a two-dimensional bar code that can be read by some mobile phones with cameras.

qualifying Determining a prospect's needs, income, and purchase authority as a potential customer.

qualitative forecasting Use of subjective techniques to forecast sales, such as the jury of executive opinion, Delphi technique, sales force composite, and surveys of buyer intentions.

quantitative forecasting Use of statistical forecasting techniques such as trend analysis and exponential smoothing.

quantity discount Price reduction granted for a large-volume purchase.

quick-response merchandising Just-in-time strategy that reduces the time a retailer must hold merchandise in inventory, resulting in substantial cost savings.

quota sample Nonprobability sample divided to maintain the proportion of certain characteristics among different segments or groups seen in the population as a whole.

R

rack jobber Full-function merchant wholesaler that markets specialized lines of merchandise to retail stores.

radio frequency identification (RFID) Technology that uses a tiny chip with identification information that can be read by a scanner using radio waves from a distance.

raw materials Natural resources such as farm products, coal, copper, or lumber that become part of a final product.

rebate Refund of a portion of the purchase price, usually granted by the product's manufacturer.

reciprocity Buying from suppliers who are also customers.

reference groups People or institutions whose opinions are valued and to whom a person looks for guidance in his or her own behavior, values, and conduct, such as a spouse, family, friends, or celebrities.

refund Cash given back to consumers who send in proof of purchase for one or more products.

related party trade Trade by U.S. companies with their subsidiaries overseas as well as trade by U.S. subsidiaries of foreign-owned firms with their parent companies.

relationship marketing Development, growth, and maintenance of long-term, cost-effective relationships with individual customers, suppliers, employees, and other partners for mutual benefit.

relationship selling Regular contacts between sales representatives and customers over an extended period to establish a sustained buyer–seller relationship.

remanufacturing Efforts to restore older products to like-new condition.

reminder advertising Advertising that reinforces previous promotional activity by keeping the name of a good, service, organization, person, place, idea, or cause before the public.

repositioning Changing the position of a product within the minds of prospective buyers relative to the positions of competing products.

research design Master plan for conducting marketing research.

resellers Marketing intermediaries that operate in the trade sector.

retail advertising Advertising by stores that sell goods or services directly to the consuming public.

retail convergence Situation in which similar merchandise is available from multiple retail outlets, resulting in the blurring of distinctions between types of retailers and merchandise offered.

retail cooperative Group of retailers that establish a shared wholesaling operation to help them compete with chains.

retailing Activities involved in selling merchandise to ultimate consumers.

return on investment (ROI) The rate of revenues received for every dollar spent on an expense.

revenue tariffs Taxes designed to raise funds for the importing government.

reverse channel Channel designed to return goods to their producers.

Robinson-Patman Act Federal legislation prohibiting price discrimination not based on a cost differential; also prohibits selling at an unreasonably low price to eliminate competition.

salary Fixed compensation payment made periodically to an employee.

sales analysis In-depth evaluation of a firm's sales.

sales force composite Qualitative sales forecasting method based on the combined sales estimates of the firm's salespeople.

sales forecast Estimate of a firm's revenue for a specified future period.

sales incentives Programs that reward salespeople for superior performance.

sales orientation Belief that consumers will resist purchasing nonessential goods and services, with the attitude toward marketing

that only creative advertising and personal selling can overcome consumers' resistance and persuade them to buy.

sales promotion Marketing activities other than personal selling, advertising, guerrilla marketing, and public relations that stimulate consumer purchasing and dealer effectiveness.

sales quota Level of expected sales for a territory, product, customer, or salesperson against which actual results are compared.

sampling Free distribution of a product in an attempt to obtain future sales; process of selecting survey respondents or research participants.

scrambled merchandising Retailing practice of combining dissimilar product lines to boost sales volume.

search marketing Paying search engines, such as Google, a fee to make sure the company's listing appears toward the top of the search results.

second mover strategy Theory that advocates observing closely the innovations of first movers and then improving on them to gain advantage in the marketplace.

secondary data Previously published information.

Secure Sockets Layer (SSL) Technology that secures a website by encrypting information and providing authentication.

selective distribution Distribution of a product through a limited number of channels.

self-concept Person's multifaceted picture of himself or herself.

seller partnership Relationship involving long-term exchanges of goods or services in return for cash or other valuable consideration.

seller's market A market in which there are more buyers for fewer goods and services.

selling agent Agent wholesaling intermediary for the entire marketing program of a firm's product line.

sender Source of the message communicated to the receiver.

service encounter Point at which the customer and service provider interact.

service quality Expected and perceived quality of a service offering.

services Intangible tasks that satisfy the needs of consumer and business users.

shaping The process of applying a series of rewards and reinforcements to permit more complex behavior to evolve.

shopping products Products consumers purchase after comparing competing offerings.

simple random sample Basic type of probability sample in which every individual in the relevant universe has an equal opportunity of being selected.

skimming pricing strategy Pricing strategy involving the use of a high price relative to competitive offerings.

social–cultural environment Component of the marketing environment consisting of the relationship between the marketer, society, and culture.

social marketing The use of online social media as a communications channel for marketing messages.

social media Different forms of electronic communication through which users can create online communities to exchange information, ideas, messages, and other content such as videos or music.

social media analytics Tools that help marketers trace, measure, and interpret data related to social media marketing initiatives.

social media marketing (SMM) The use of social media portals to create a positive influence on consumers or business customers toward an organization's brand, products, public images, or website.

social media marketing (SMM) plan A formal document that identifies and describes goals and strategies, targeted audience, budget, and implementation methods as well as tactics for monitoring, measuring, and managing the SMM effort.

social media monitoring The process of tracking, measuring, and evaluating a firm's social media marketing initiatives.

social media platform A type of software or technology that allows users to build, integrate, or facilitate a community, interaction among users, and user-generated content.

social media tool Software (such as an app or blog) that enables users to communicate with each other online.

social networking site A website that provides virtual communities through which people can share information, post opinions, and increase their circle of online friends.

social news site A platform where users can post news items to links to outside articles, then vote on which postings get the most prominent display.

social responsibility Marketing philosophies, policies, procedures, and actions that have the enhancement of society's welfare as a primary objective.

sole sourcing Purchasing a firm's entire stock of an item from just one vendor.

spam Popular name for junk email.

span of control Number of representatives who report to first-level sales managers.

specialty advertising Sales promotion technique that places the advertiser's name, address, and advertising message on useful articles that are then distributed to target consumers.

specialty products Products with unique characteristics that cause buyers to prize those particular brands.

specialty retailer Store that combines carefully defined product lines, services, and reputation to persuade shoppers to spend considerable shopping effort there.

split runs Methods of testing alternate ads by dividing a cable TV audience or a publication's subscribers in two, using two different ads, and then evaluating the relative effectiveness of each.

sponsorship Relationship in which an organization provides funds or in-kind resources to an event or activity in exchange for a direct association with that event or activity.

spreadsheet analysis Grid that organizes numerical information in a standardized, easily understood format.

staples Convenience goods and services consumers constantly replenish to maintain a ready inventory.

step out Pricing practice in which one firm raises prices and then waits to see if others follow suit.

stock-keeping unit (SKU) Offering within a product line such as a specific size of liquid detergent.

straight rebuy Recurring purchase decision in which a customer repurchases a good or service that has performed satisfactorily in the past.

strategic alliance Partnership in which two or more companies combine resources and capital to create competitive advantages in a new market.

strategic business units (SBUs) Key business units within diversified firms.

strategic planning Process of determining an organization's primary objectives and adopting courses of action that will achieve these objectives.

strategic window Limited periods when key requirements of a market and a firm's particular competencies best fit together.

stratified sample Probability sample constructed to represent randomly selected subsamples of different groups within the total sample; each subgroup is relatively homogeneous for a certain characteristic.

subcontracting Contractual agreements that assign the production of goods or services to local or smaller firms.

subcultures Groups with their own distinct modes of behavior.

subliminal perception The subconscious receipt of incoming information.

suboptimization Condition that results when individual operations achieve their objectives but interfere with progress toward broader organizational goals.

subsidies Government financial support of a private industry.

supercenter Large store, usually smaller than a hypermarket, that combines groceries with discount store merchandise.

supplies Regular expenses a firm incurs in its daily operations.

supply Schedule of the amounts of a good or service that firms will offer for sale at different prices during a specified time period.

supply chain Complete sequence of suppliers and activities that contribute to the creation and delivery of merchandise.

supply chain management Control of the activities of purchasing, processing, and delivery through which raw materials are transformed into products and made available to final consumers.

survey of buyer intentions Qualitative sales forecasting method that samples opinions among groups of present and potential customers concerning their purchasing plans.

sustainable products Products that can be produced, used, and disposed of with minimal impact on the environment.

sweepstakes Sales promotion technique in which prize winners are selected by chance.

SWOT analysis Review that helps planners compare internal organizational strengths and weaknesses with external opportunities and threats.

syndicated service Organization that provides standardized data on a periodic basis to its subscribers.

systems integration Centralization of the procurement function within an internal division or as a service of an external supplier.

T

tactical planning Planning that guides the implementation of activities specified in the strategic plan.

target market Specific group of people a firm believes is most likely to buy its goods and services.

target-return objective Short-run or long-run pricing objectives of achieving a specified return on either sales or investment.

tariff Tax levied against imported goods.

task-objective method Development of a promotional budget based on evaluation of the firm's promotional objectives.

team selling Selling situation in which several sales associates or other members of the organization are employed to help the lead sales representative reach all those who influence the purchase decision.

technological environment Application to marketing of knowledge based on discoveries in science, inventions, and innovations.

telemarketing Promotional presentation involving the use of the telephone on an outbound basis by salespeople or on an inbound basis by customers who initiate calls to obtain information and place orders.

test marketing Marketing research technique that involves introducing a new product in a specific area and then measuring its degree of success.

third-party (contract) logistics firm Company that specializes in handling logistics activities for other firms.

time-based competition Strategy of developing and distributing goods and services more quickly than competitors.

total quality management (TQM) Continuous effort to improve products and work processes with the goal of achieving customer satisfaction and world-class performance.

trade allowance Financial incentive offered to wholesalers and retailers that purchase or promote specific products.

trade discount Payment to a channel member or buyer for performing marketing functions; also known as a *functional discount*.

trade dress Visual components that contribute to the overall look of a brand.

trade-in Credit allowance given for a used item when a customer purchases a new item.

trade industries Retailers or wholesalers that purchase products for resale to others.

trade promotion Sales promotion that appeals to marketing intermediaries rather than to consumers.

trade show Product exhibition organized by industry trade associations to showcase goods and services.

trademark Brand for which the owner claims exclusive legal protection.

transaction-based marketing Buyer and seller exchanges characterized by limited communications and little or no ongoing relationships between the parties.

transfer price Cost assessed when a product is moved from one profit center in a firm to another.

trend analysis Quantitative sales forecasting method that estimates future sales through statistical analyses of historical sales patterns.

truck wholesaler (truck jobber) Limited-function merchant wholesaler that markets perishable food items.

tying agreement Arrangement that requires a marketing intermediary to carry items other than those they want to sell.

undifferentiated marketing Strategy that focuses on producing a single product and marketing it to all customers; also called *mass marketing*.

unemployment Proportion of people in the economy actively seeking work that do not have jobs.

unfair-trade laws State laws requiring sellers to maintain minimum prices for comparable merchandise.

uniform-delivered pricing Pricing system for handling transportation costs under which all buyers are quoted the same price, including transportation expenses. Sometimes known as *postage-stamp pricing*.

unit pricing Pricing policy in which prices are stated in terms of a recognized unit of measurement or a standard numerical count.

Universal Product Code (UPC) Numerical bar code system used to record product and price information.

unsought products Products marketed to consumers who may not yet recognize a need for them.

upstream management Controlling part of the supply chain that involves raw materials, inbound logistics, and warehouse and storage facilities.

user Individual or group that actually uses a business good or service.

utility Want-satisfying power of a good or service.

VALS Segmentation system that divides consumers into eight psychographic categories: innovators, thinkers, achievers, experiencers, believers, strivers, makers, and survivors.

value analysis Systematic study of the components of a purchase to determine the most cost-effective approach.

value pricing Pricing strategy that emphasizes benefits derived from a product in comparison to the price and quality levels of competing offerings.

variable cost Cost that changes with the level of production (such as labor and raw materials costs).

vendor analysis Assessment of supplier performance such as price, back orders, timely delivery, and attention to special requests.

vendor-managed inventory (VMI) Inventory management system in which the seller—in an existing agreement with a buyer—determines how much of a product is needed.

venture team Group of associates from different areas of an organization who work together in developing new products.

vertical marketing system (VMS) Planned channel system designed to improve distribution efficiency and cost-effectiveness by integrating various functions throughout the distribution chain.

Video Game Generation A cohort whose preferences and behaviors were being shaped at the same time as video games.

viral marketing Efforts that allow satisfied customers to spread the word about products to other consumers.

virtual sales team Network of strategic partners, suppliers, and others who recommend a firm's goods or services.

vishing Scam that collects personal information through voice response systems; stands for *voice phishing*.

VoIP (Voice over Internet Protocol) A phone connection through a personal computer with any type of broadband Internet connection.

Web services Platform-independent information exchange systems that use the Internet to allow interaction between the firms.

Web-to-store shoppers Consumers who use the Internet as a tool when shopping at brick-and-mortar retailers.

wheel of retailing Hypothesis that each new type of retailer gains a competitive foothold by offering lower prices than current suppliers charge, the result of reducing or eliminating services.

wholesaler Channel intermediary that takes title to goods it handles and then distributes those goods to retailers, other distributors, or business or B2B customers.

wholesaling intermediary Comprehensive term that describes wholesalers as well as agents and brokers.

widgets Tiny interactive applications that Internet users can copy and add to their own pages to play music, video, or slide shows.

wiki Web page anyone can edit.

World Trade Organization (WTO) Organization that replaces GATT, overseeing GATT agreements, making binding decisions in mediating disputes, and reducing trade barriers.

yield management Pricing strategy that allows marketers to vary prices based on such factors as demand, even though the cost of providing those goods or services remains the same.

zone pricing Pricing system for handling transportation costs under which the market is divided into geographic regions and a different price is set in each region.

NAME & COMPANY INDEX

SUBJECT INDEX